SAINT THOMAS AQUINAS

COMMENTARY ON THE LETTERS OF SAINT PAUL TO THE CORINTHIANS

BIBLICAL COMMENTARIES

Volume 38
Latin/English Edition of the Works of St. Thomas Aquinas

AQUINAS INSTITUTE | EMMAUS ACADEMIC
GREEN BAY, WI | STEUBENVILLE, OH

This printing was funded in part by donations made in memory of Marcus Berquist and Rose Johanna Trumbull.

Published with the ecclesiastical approval of
The Most Reverend Paul D. Etienne, DD, STL
Bishop of Cheyenne
Given on August 27, 2012

Printed in the United States of America

Second Printing 2021

PUBLISHER'S CATALOGING-IN-PUBLICATION DATA

Aquinas, St. Thomas.
    Commentary on the Letters of Saint Paul to the Corinthians / Saint Thomas Aquinas.
    p. 648 cm.
    ISBN 978-1-62340-001-9

1. Bible. N.T. Corinthians, 1st -- Commentaries -- Early works to 1800.   2. Bible. N.T. Corinthians, 2nd --
    Commentaries -- Early works to 1800.   I. Title.   II. Series

BS2675.T4612 2012
227′.2′07--dc23   2012945234

Notes on the Text

Scripture

The text of Sacred Scripture presented at the beginning of each lecture is given in Latin, English, and Greek. Since St. Thomas appears to be familiar with more than one translation, quotes from memory, and often enough paraphrases, it has proven difficult to reconstruct the version of scripture with which St. Thomas was working. However, the closest available version of Scripture to St. Thomas's text was found to be the Clementine Vulgate of 1598, and this version of the Vulgate is the one found at the beginning of each lecture. The choice of an English version of Scripture to parallel to the Vulgate was therefore the Douay-Rheims. Both of these versions have been slightly modified to fit the text of St. Thomas. The Greek text is from the Nestle-Aland, Novum Testamentum Graece, 27th Revised Edition, edited by Barbara Aland, Kurt Aland, Johannes Karavidopoulos, Carlo M. Martini, and Bruce M. Metzger in cooperation with the Institute for New Testament Textual Research, Münster/Westphalia, © 1993 Deutsche Bibelgesellschaft, Stuttgart. Used with permission. The numbering of Scripture in the lecture headings and the English translation of the commentary is taken from the Nestle-Aland 27th Revised Edition and the RSV, while the numbering St. Thomas uses in the Latin text has been kept intact.

Latin Text of St. Thomas

The Latin texts of the commentaries on First and Second Corinthians are based on the Corpus Thomisticum texts of the Fundación Tomás de Aquino <www.corpusthomisticum.org>. These texts are based on the Marietti 1953 edition, prepared by Fr. Raffaele Cai OP, transcribed by Fr. Roberto Busa SJ, and revised by Dr. Enrique Alarcón and other editors and collaborators of this bilingual edition. © 2012 Fundación Tomás de Aquino, Pamplona. Used with permission.

We do not have the text of St. Thomas on First Corinthians from Chapter 7, Lecture 2, through the end of Chapter 10. This portion has traditionally been replaced by a commentary by Peter of Tarentaise. This present edition has kept the text of Peter of Tarentaise, and provides a translation of it so as to be able to present a commentary on the whole epistle in some form. The portions by Peter of Tarentaise are noted in the page headings.

English Translation of St. Thomas

The majority of the English translation of the commentaries on First and Second Corinthians was prepared by Fr. Fabian Richard Larcher. Paragraphs 987-1046 were translated by Daniel Keating. The translation of the commentary of Peter of Tarentaise on First Corinthians was prepared by Beth Mortensen.

The Aquinas Institute requests your assistance in the continued perfection of these texts.
If you discover any errors, please send a note to us by e-mail: admin@theaquinasinstitute.org.

DEDICATED WITH LOVE TO
OUR LADY OF MT. CARMEL

Contents

Commentary on the First Letter of Saint Paul to the Corinthians

Commentary on the Second Letter of Saint Paul to the Corinthians

COMMENTARY ON THE FIRST LETTER
OF SAINT PAUL TO THE CORINTHIANS

Commentary on the First Letter of Saint Paul to the Corinthians

Prologue

Wisdom 6:22

Quid est autem sapientia, et quemadmodum facta sit, referam, et non abscondam a vobis sacramenta Dei: sed ab initio nativitatis investigabo, et ponam in lucem scientiam illius, et non praeteribo veritatem.	τί δέ ἐστιν σοφία καὶ πῶς ἐγένετο, ἀπαγγελῶ καὶ οὐκ ἀποκρύψω ὑμῖν μυστήρια, ἀλλὰ ἀπ᾽ ἀρχῆς γενέσεως ἐξιχνιάσω καὶ θήσω εἰς τὸ ἐμφανὲς τὴν γνῶσιν αὐτῆς καὶ οὐ μὴ παροδεύσω τὴν ἀλήθειαν.	Now what wisdom is, and what was her origin, I will declare: and I will not hide from you the sacraments of God, but will seek her out from the beginning of her birth, and bring the knowledge of her to light, and will not pass over the truth.

---

1. Sacramenti nomen dupliciter accipi consuevit. Nam quandoque sacramentum dicitur quodcumque secretum, et praecipue de rebus sacris; quandoque sacramentum dicitur sacrae rei signum, ita quod et eius imaginem gerat, et causa existat, secundum quod nos dicimus septem sacramenta Ecclesiae, scilicet baptismus, confirmatio, Eucharistia, poenitentia, extrema unctio, ordo et matrimonium. In qua quidem significatione sacramenti etiam prima significatio continetur; nam in his Ecclesiae sacramentis, divina virtus secretius operatur salutem, ut Augustinus dicit.

2. Haec igitur *sacramenta Dei* praelatus, seu doctor Ecclesiae, fidelibus Christi non debet abscondere sed manifestare, propter tria.

Primo quidem, quia hoc pertinet ad honorem Dei, secundum illud Tob. XII, 7: *sacramentum regis abscondere bonum est, opera autem Dei revelare et confiteri honorificum est.*

Secundo, quia hoc pertinet ad salutem hominum, qui per horum ignorantiam in desperationem labi possent, sicut de quibusdam dicitur Sap. II, 22 quod *nescierunt sacramenta Dei, nec speraverunt mercedem iustitiae*, quia per sacramenta homines purificantur, ut sint praeparati ad recipiendum mercedem iustitiae.

Tertio quia hoc pertinet ad debitum officium praelati vel doctoris, secundum illud Eph. III, 8: *mihi omnium sanctorum minimo data est gratia haec, illuminare omnes quae sit dispensatio sacramenti absconditi a saeculis in Deo.*

1. The word 'sacrament' can be taken in two senses: sometimes it means something secret, particularly in regard to sacred things; and sometimes it means the sign of a sacred thing, in the sense of being its image and cause. It is in this second sense that we speak of the seven sacraments: baptism, confirmation, Eucharist, penance, extreme unction, orders, and matrimony. Furthermore, the first sense is then included in this second sense, for a divine power is secretly at work in these sacraments of the Church, as Augustine says.

2. Consequently, these *sacraments of God* should not be concealed but laid bare to Christ's faithful by their teachers and prelates for three reasons.

First, because this redounds to God's honor: *it is good to hide the secret of the king, but honorable to reveal and confess the works of the Lord* (Tob 12:7).

Second, because this is needed for the salvation of men, who could lapse into despair from not knowing them, for Wisdom says that *some men did not know the secret purposes of God, nor hope for the wages of holiness* (Wis 2:22), because men are purified by the sacraments and prepared for receiving the wages of holiness.

Third, because this is a duty of teachers and prelates as pointed out by the Apostle: *to me, though I am the very least of the saints, this grace was given, to make all men see what is the plan of the mystery hidden for ages in God* (Eph 3:8).

Sic ergo praedicta verba demonstrant nobis materiam huius epistolae, in qua Apostolus agit de sacramentis Ecclesiae.

Cum enim in epistola ad Romanos gratiam Dei commendasset, quae in sacramentis Ecclesiae operatur: hic, scilicet in prima epistola ad Corinthios, de ipsis Ecclesiae sacramentis agit; in secunda vero de ministris sacramentorum.

Videamus ergo primo textum.

Thus the above text discloses to us the subject matter of this epistle, in which the Apostle discusses the sacraments of the Church.

For since in the epistle to the Romans he had discussed God's grace, which works in the seven sacraments, here in the first epistle to the Corinthians he discusses the sacraments themselves and in the second epistle to the Corinthians the ministers of the sacraments.

Let us turn, therefore, to the text.

CHAPTER 1

Lecture 1

1:1Paulus vocatus apostolus Jesu Christi per voluntatem Dei, et Sosthenes frater, [n. 3]

1:2Ecclesiae Dei, quae est Corinthi, sanctificatis in Christo Jesu, vocatis sanctis, cum omnibus qui invocant nomen Domini nostri Jesu Christi, in omni loco ipsorum et nostro. [n. 7]

1:3Gratia vobis, et pax a Deo Patre nostro, et Domino Jesu Christo. [n. 9]

1:4Gratias ago Deo meo semper pro vobis in gratia Dei, quae data est vobis in Christo Jesu: [n. 11]

1:5quod in omnibus divites facti estis in illo, in omni verbo, et in omni scientia. [n. 13]

1:6Sicut testimonium Christi confirmatum est in vobis: [n. 14]

1:7ita ut nihil vobis desit in ulla gratia, exspectantibus revelationem Domini nostri Jesu Christi, [n. 15]

1:8qui et confirmabit vos usque in finem sine crimine, in die adventus Domini nostri Jesu Christi. [n. 17]

1:9Fidelis Deus: per quem vocati estis in societatem Filii ejus Jesu Christi Domini nostri. [n. 18]

1:1Παῦλος κλητὸς ἀπόστολος Χριστοῦ Ἰησοῦ διὰ θελήματος θεοῦ, καὶ Σωσθένης ὁ ἀδελφός,

1:2τῇ ἐκκλησίᾳ τοῦ θεοῦ τῇ οὔσῃ ἐν Κορίνθῳ, ἡγιασμένοις ἐν Χριστῷ Ἰησοῦ, κλητοῖς ἁγίοις, σὺν πᾶσιν τοῖς ἐπικαλουμένοις τὸ ὄνομα τοῦ κυρίου ἡμῶν Ἰησοῦ Χριστοῦ ἐν παντὶ τόπῳ, αὐτῶν καὶ ἡμῶν:

1:3χάρις ὑμῖν καὶ εἰρήνη ἀπὸ θεοῦ πατρὸς ἡμῶν καὶ κυρίου Ἰησοῦ Χριστοῦ.

1:4Εὐχαριστῶ τῷ θεῷ μου πάντοτε περὶ ὑμῶν ἐπὶ τῇ χάριτι τοῦ θεοῦ τῇ δοθείσῃ ὑμῖν ἐν Χριστῷ Ἰησοῦ,

1:5ὅτι ἐν παντὶ ἐπλουτίσθητε ἐν αὐτῷ, ἐν παντὶ λόγῳ καὶ πάσῃ γνώσει,

1:6καθὼς τὸ μαρτύριον τοῦ Χριστοῦ ἐβεβαιώθη ἐν ὑμῖν,

1:7ὥστε ὑμᾶς μὴ ὑστερεῖσθαι ἐν μηδενὶ χαρίσματι, ἀπεκδεχομένους τὴν ἀποκάλυψιν τοῦ κυρίου ἡμῶν Ἰησοῦ Χριστοῦ:

1:8ὃς καὶ βεβαιώσει ὑμᾶς ἕως τέλους ἀνεγκλήτους ἐν τῇ ἡμέρᾳ τοῦ κυρίου ἡμῶν Ἰησοῦ [Χριστοῦ].

1:9πιστὸς ὁ θεὸς δι' οὗ ἐκλήθητε εἰς κοινωνίαν τοῦ υἱοῦ αὐτοῦ Ἰησοῦ Χριστοῦ τοῦ κυρίου ἡμῶν.

1:1Paul, called to be an apostle of Jesus Christ by the will of God, and Sosthenes a brother, [n. 3]

1:2To the church of God that is at Corinth, to them who are sanctified in Christ Jesus, called to be saints, with all who invoke the name of our Lord Jesus Christ in every place of theirs and ours. [n. 7]

1:3Grace to you and peace, from God our Father and from the Lord Jesus Christ. [n. 9]

1:4I give thanks to my God always for you, for the grace of God that is given you in Christ Jesus: [n. 11]

1:5That in all things you are made rich in him, in all utterance and in all knowledge; [n. 13]

1:6As the testimony of Christ was confirmed in you, [n. 14]

1:7So that nothing is wanting to you in any grace, waiting for the manifestation of our Lord Jesus Christ. [n. 15]

1:8Who also will confirm you unto the end without crime, in the day of the coming of our Lord Jesus Christ. [n. 17]

1:9God is faithful: by whom you are called unto the fellowship of his Son, Jesus Christ our Lord. [n. 18]

---

3. Dividitur ergo haec epistola in partes duas.
In prima parte ponit epistolarem salutationem;
in secunda prosequitur suam intentionem, ibi *gratias ago Deo meo.*

4. Circa primum tria facit.
Primo ponit personas salutantes;
secundo, personas salutatas *ecclesiae Dei*, etc.;
tertio bona salutifera optat, ibi *gratia vobis et pax.*

4. Circa primum duo facit.
Primo ponit personam principalem quam describit ex nomine, dicens *Paulus*, de quo quidem nomine satis dictum est in epistola ad Romanos. Hic autem sufficit dicere quod hoc nomen praemittit in signum humilitatis;

3. This epistle is divided into two parts:
in the first he sends his greeting;
and in the other his message, at *I give thanks to my God.*

4. As to the first he does three things:
first, he mentions the persons who send the greeting;
second, the persons greeted, at *to the church of God*;
third, he wishes them well, at *grace to you and peace.*

4. As to the first he does two things.
As to the first he mentions the principal person first and describes him from his name, *Paul*. Enough had been said about this name in the epistle to the Romans. Suffice it to say here that this name is mentioned as a token of humility,

nam Paulus idem est quod modicus, quod ad humilitatem pertinet. I Reg. XV, 17: *cum esses parvulus in oculis tuis, caput in tribubus Israel factus es.* Matth. XI, 25: *abscondisti haec a sapientibus et prudentibus, et revelasti ea parvulis.*

5. Consequenter describit eam a dignitate.

Et primo ponit modum adipiscendae dignitatis, cum dicit **vocatus,** secundum illud Hebr. V, 4: *Nemo sumit sibi honorem, sed qui vocatur a Deo tamquam Aaron.*

Secundo ponit ipsam dignitatem, dicens **apostolus Iesu Christi,** quae quidem est prima dignitas in Ecclesia, et interpretatur missus, quia fuerunt missi a Deo, ut vice eius fungerentur in terris. Unde dicitur Lc. c. VI, 13, *quod elegit duodecim, quos et apostolos nominavit,* et infra XII, 28: **Deus posuit in Ecclesia quosdam, primum quidem apostolos,** etc.

Tertio ponit originem sive causam huius dignitatis, cum dicit **per voluntatem Dei.** Quod est intelligendum de voluntate beneplaciti, ex qua perficiuntur illi qui multipliciter praesunt Ecclesiis. Eccli. X, 4: *in manibus Dei potestas terrae, et utilem rectorem in tempore suscitabit super illam.*

Et de praedicta voluntate sub figura nobis dicitur, Iob XXXVII, 12, quod *lustrant cuncta per circuitum quocumque voluntas gubernantis perduxerit.*

Dimittit autem Deus aliquos praefici propter subditorum peccata, secundum illud Iob XXXIV, 30: *regnare facit hominem hypocritam propter peccata populi.* Talis autem rector non dicitur esse secundum voluntatem Dei, sed secundum eius indignationem, secundum illud Osee XIII, 11: *dabo tibi regem in furore meo, et auferam in indignatione mea.*

6. Secundo ponit personam adiunctam, cum dicit **et Sosthenes frater,** quem sibi salutando adiungit, quia ad Apostolum detulerat contentiones et alios Corinthiorum defectus, ne hoc videretur ex odio fecisse; et ideo nominat eum fratrem, ut ostendat quod ex zelo caritatis hoc fecerat. Prov. IX, 8: *argue sapientem, et diliget te.*

7. Deinde ponit personas salutatas, cum dicit **ecclesiae Dei quae est Corinthi.**

Et, primo, ponit principales personas, quas describit tripliciter. Primo quidem ex loco, cum dicit **ecclesiae Dei quae est Corinthi,** id est, fidelibus Christi Corinthi congregatis. Ps. XXXIV, 18: *Confitebor tibi in Ecclesia magna.* Secundo ex munere gratiae, cum dicit **sanctificatis in Christo Iesu,** id est, in fide, passione et sacramento Christi Iesu. Infra VI, 11: **Sed abluti estis, sed sanctificati estis.** Hebr. ult.: *Iesus ut sanctificaret per suum sanguinem populum, extra portam passus est.* Tertio ponit originem gratiae, cum dicit **vocatis sanctis;**

for 'Paul' means a small amount, which pertains to humility: *though you are little in your own eyes, are you not the head of the tribes of Israel?* (1 Sam 15:17); *you have hidden these things from the wise and understanding and revealed them to babes* (Matt 11:25).

5. Then he describes himself from his dignity.

First, he mentions how a dignity should be obtained when he says, **called,** since it is stated in Hebrews: *one does not take the honor upon himself, but is called by God, as Aaron was* (Heb 5:4).

Second, he mentions his dignity, saying, **an apostle of Jesus Christ.** This, of course, is the highest dignity in the Church and means 'sent,' because they were sent by God to act in his name on earth; hence it says in Luke: *he chose from them twelve, whom he named apostles* (Luke 6:13), and below: **and God indeed has set some in the Church; first apostles** (1 Cor 12:28).

Third, he indicates the source and cause of this dignity when he says, **by the will of God.** This refers to the will of his good pleasure, which chooses those who rule the Church in one way or another: *the government of the earth is in the hands of the Lord, and over it he will raise up the right man for the time* (Sir 10:4).

And concerning the aforesaid will it is told us under a figure that *they go round about, whithersoever the will of him who governs them shall lead them* (Job 37:12).

But when God sets someone in authority an account of the sins of the subjects: *he makes a man that is a hypocrite to reign for the sins of the people* (Job 34:30), such a ruler is not according to God's will but according to his indignation: *I have given you kings in my anger, and I have taken them away in my wrath* (Hos 13:10).

6. Second, he mentions the other person who sends the greeting when he says, **and Sosthenes a brother,** whom he mentions along with himself, because he was the one who had reported to the Apostle the quarrels and other failings current among the Corinthians. He calls him brother, to show that he had done this not out of hatred but out of the zeal of charity: *reprove a wise man and he will love you* (Prov 9:8).

7. Then he mentions the persons he is greeting, saying, **to the church of God that is at Corinth.**

First, he mentions the chief persons, whom he describes in three ways: first, from their region when he says, **to the church of God that is at Corinth,** i.e., Christ's faithful assembled at Corinth: *I will give thanks to you in a great Church* (Ps 35:18). Second, from their gift of grace when he says: **to them who are sanctified in Christ Jesus,** i.e., in the faith, passion and sacraments of Christ Jesus: **but you are washed: but you are sanctified** (1 Cor 6:11); *Jesus also suffered outside the gate in order to sanctify the people* (Heb 13:12). Third, he mentions the source of grace when

quia scilicet ad sanctitatem per gratiam vocationis pervenerunt. Rom. VIII, 30: *quos praedestinavit, hos et vocavit.* I Petr. II, 9: *de tenebris vos vocavit in admirabile lumen suum.*

8. Secundo ponit personas secundarias, fideles scilicet, quae non erant in ipsa civitate sed habitabant in dioecesi civitatis vel districtu. Unde subdit vobis, inquam, qui estis Corinthi scribo, *cum omnibus qui invocant nomen Domini nostri Iesu Christi,* scilicet per veram fidei confessionem. Ioel. c. II, 32: *omnis qui invocaverit nomen Domini salvus erit.* Et hoc *in omni loco ipsorum,* id est eorum iurisdictioni subiecto, *et nostro,* quia per hoc quod subiiciebantur episcopo civitatis, non eximebantur a potestate Apostoli, quinimo magis erant ipsi Apostolo subiecti, quam his quibus ipse eos subiecerat. Ps. CII, 22: *in omni loco dominationis eius, benedic, anima mea, Domino.*

9. Ultimo autem in salutatione ponit bona salutifera quae eis optat, quorum primum est *gratia,* per quam iustificamur a peccatis, Rom. III, 24: *iustificati gratis per gratiam ipsius*; ultimum autem est *pax,* quae perficitur in felicitate aeterna. Ps. CXLVII, 14: *qui posuit fines tuos pacem.* Is. XXXII, 18: *sedebit populus meus in pulchritudine pacis.*

Per haec autem duo, omnia alia includit. Unde dicit *gratia et pax.*

Causam eorum ostendit, subdens *a Deo Patre nostro,* secundum illud Iac. I, 17: *omne datum optimum et omne donum perfectum desursum est, descendens a Patre luminum.*

Addit autem *et Domino Iesu Christo, per quem,* ut dicitur II Petr. I, 4, *maxima et pretiosa promissa donavit nobis Deus.* Io. I, v. 17: *gratia et veritas per Iesum Christum facta est.*

10. Quod autem dicit *a Deo Patre nostro.* Potest intelligi de tota Trinitate, a qua creati sumus et in filios adoptati. Additur autem *et Domino Iesu Christo,* non quia sit persona alia vel hypostasis praeter tres personas, sed propter aliam naturam.

Vel quod dicitur *Deo Patre nostro,* per quamdam appropriationem accipitur pro persona Patris, sicut Io. XX, 17: *ascendo ad Patrem meum, Deum meum et Deum vestrum.* In hoc autem quod subdit *et Domino Iesu Christo,* manifestatur persona Filii. Tacetur autem de Spiritu Sancto, quia est nexus Patris et Filii, et intellectus ex ambobus, vel quia est donum utriusque, intelligitur in donis, de quibus dicit *gratia* et *pax,* quae per Spiritum Sanctum dantur. Infra XII, v. 11: *Haec omnia operatur unus atque idem Spiritus.*

11. Deinde cum dicit *gratias ago Deo meo,* incipit epistolarem tractatum.

Et primo gratias agit de bonis eorum, ut correctionem suorum defectuum tolerabilius ferant;

he says, *called to be saints,* because they arrived at sanctity through the grace of being called: *those whom he predestined he also called* (Rom 8:30); *he called you out of darkness into his marvelous light* (1 Pet 2:9).

8. Then he mentions the other persons, namely the faithful who were not in that city but lived in the diocese of the city or in the environs; hence he says, *with all who invoke the name of our Lord Jesus Christ* by confessing the true faith: *all who call upon the name of the Lord shall be delivered* (Joel 2:32). And this *in every place of theirs,* i.e., subject to their jurisdiction; *and ours,* because their subjection to the bishop of the city did not exempt them from the Apostle's power; rather they were more subject to the Apostle than to those whom he had subjected them: *in all places of his dominion, bless the Lord, O my soul!* (Ps 103:22).

9. Finally, he mentions in this greeting the salutary gifts he wishes them. The first of these is *grace,* by which we are set free of sin: *they are justified by his grace as a gift* (Rom 3:24) and the last is *peace,* which is brought to perfection in eternal happiness: *he makes peace in your borders* (Ps 147:14); *my people will abide in a peaceful habitation* (Isa 32:18).

But these two include all other gifts; hence he says: *grace to you and peace.*

The one who causes them is mentioned when he says: *from God our Father: every good endowment and every perfect gift is from above, coming down from the Father of lights* (Jas 1:17).

He adds, *and from the Lord Jesus Christ, by whom he has granted to us his precious and very great promises* (2 Pet 1:4); *grace and truth came through Jesus Christ* (John 1:17).

10. The phrase, *from God our Father,* can be understood of the whole Trinity, by whom we have been created and adopted as sons; but *the Lord Jesus Christ* is added, not as though he were a person over and above the three persons, but on account of his other nature.

Or *God our Father* is taken for the person of the Father, as in John: *I ascend to my Father and your Father, to my God and your God* (John 20:17), whereas *the Lord Jesus Christ* is added to indicate the person of the Son. The Holy Spirit is not mentioned, because he is the nexus of the Father and Son, and is understood when the other two persons are mentioned, or because he is the gift of both, he is understood in the gifts, *grace* and *peace,* which are granted by the Holy Spirit: *but all these things one and the same Spirit work*s (1 Cor 12:11).

11. Then when he says, *I give thanks to my God,* he begins his message.

First, he gives thanks for their blessings, so that they will more easily bear the correction of their faults;

secundo ponit eorum instructionem, ibi *obsecro vos autem, fratres*.

12. Circa primum duo facit.

Primo gratias agit de bonis quae iam acceperant;

secundo de bonis quae in futurum expectabant, ibi *expectantibus revelationem*.

12. Circa primum duo facit.

Primo ponit gratiarum actionem, cum dicit **gratias ago Deo meo**, qui scilicet etsi sit Deus omnium per creationem et gubernationem, tamen est eius et cuiuslibet iusti per fidem et devotionem. Ps. CXVII, 28: *Deus meus es tu, et confitebor tibi*.

Ostendit etiam quando gratias agit, cum dicit *semper*, quia haec gratiarum actio ex caritatis affectu procedit, qui in eius corde assiduus erat. Prov. XVII, 17: *omni tempore diligit qui amicus est*. Et quamvis omni tempore eos diligeret, et pro eorum bonis gratias ageret actualiter, tamen etiam pro eis gratias agebat omnibus horis quas habebat orationi deputatas.

Ostendit etiam pro quibus gratias agit, cum dicit **pro vobis**, de quorum scilicet bonis propter caritatis unionem gaudebat, sicut de suis. III Io. v. 4: *maiorem horum non habeo gratiam, quam ut audiam filios meos in veritate ambulare*.

13. Secundo ostendit materiam gratiarum actionis, et primo in generali, cum dicit **in gratia Dei**, id est, per gratiam Dei, **quae data est vobis in Christo Iesu**, id est per Christum Iesum. Io. I, 16: *de plenitudine eius omnes nos accepimus gratiam pro gratia*.

Secundo in speciali, ubi primo ostendit gratiae abundantiam cum dicit **quia in omnibus**, scilicet quae pertinent ad salutem, **divites**, id est abundantes, **facti estis in illo**, id est per Christum, secundum illud II Cor. VIII, 9: *propter vos egenus factus est, ut illius inopia divites essetis*.

Et exponit in quibus sint divites facti, cum dicit **in omni verbo**, vel quia omnibus generibus linguarum loquebantur, vel quia in verbo doctrinae abundabant. Verbum autem non proferretur ordinate, nisi ex scientia procederet, et ideo subdit **in omni scientia**, id est, intelligentia omnium Scripturarum, et universaliter omnium quae pertinent ad salutem. Sap. X, 10: *dedit illi scientiam sanctorum*.

Hoc autem quod dicit Apostolus referendum est ad eos qui erant in Ecclesia perfectiores, in quibus etiam alii minores has divitias possidebant, sicut Augustinus dicit super Ioannem: *si amas unitatem cui haeres, habes quicquid in illa alter habet: tolle invidiam, et tuum est quod alius habet; quos enim cupiditas et invidia separat, caritas iungit*.

14. Secundo ostendit rectitudinem, dicens **sicut testimonium Christi confirmatum est in vobis**; non esset rectum verbum doctrinae, neque recta scientia,

second, he begins to instruct them, at **now I beseech you, brethren** (1 Cor 1:10).

12. As to the first he does two things.

First, he gives thanks for the blessings they have already received;

second, for those they expected in the future, at **waiting for the manifestation**.

12. As to the first he does two things.

He mentions his thanks when he says, **I give thanks to my God**, who in addition to being the God of all things by creation and governance, is his and every just man's God through faith and devotion: *you are my God, and I will give thanks to you* (Ps 118:28).

He also mentions this when he gives thanks; hence he says, **always**, because this thanks came from the ardor of charity, which was continually alive in his heart: *a friend loves at all times* (Prov 17:17). But although he loved them at all times and continually gave thanks for their blessings, he gave thanks for them especially at all the hours he set aside for prayer.

He also mentions those for whom he gives thanks when he says, **for you**, in whose blessings he rejoiced as in his own because of the union of charity: *no greater joy can I have than this, to hear that my children follow the truth* (3 John 1:4).

13. Then he indicates the blessings for which he gives thanks. First, in general, when he says: **for the grace of God**, i.e., by the grace of God, **that is given you in Christ Jesus**, i.e., by Christ Jesus: *of his fullness we have all received grace for grace* (John 1:16).

Second, in detail: first, when he mentions the abundance of their grace, saying: **that in all things**, namely, which pertain to salvation, **you are made rich**, i.e., made to overflow **in him**, i.e., through Christ: *for your sake he became poor, so that by his poverty you become rich* (2 Cor 8:9).

He explains in what matters they became rich when he says, **in all utterance**, either because they spoke in all manner of tongues or because they abounded in the utterance of doctrine. But because the word was not uttered properly, unless it proceeded from knowledge, he adds, **and in all knowledge**, i.e., the understanding of all Scriptures and, in general, of all things pertaining to salvation: *he gave them a knowledge of holy things* (Wis 10:10).

What the Apostle says here refers to those in the Church who were more perfect and includes even lesser personages who possessed these riches, as Augustine says: *if you love the unity of which you are a member, you have whatever the others have in it. Remove envy and the possessions of others are yours, for love unites those whom greed and envy would separate*.

14. Second, he shows their correctness when he says, **as the testimony of Christ was confirmed in you**. For the utterance of doctrine would not be correct or knowledge

si a testimonio Christi discordaret, vel si etiam Christi testimonium non firmiter per fidem cordibus inhaereret; quia, ut dicitur Iac. I, 6: *qui haesitat similis est fluctui maris, qui a vento movetur et circumfertur.*

Testimonium autem Christi dicit, vel quia de ipso prophetae praenuntiaverunt, secundum illud Act. X, 43: *huic omnes prophetae testimonium perhibent*; vel quia ipse Christus testimonium perhibuit, secundum illud Io. c. VIII, 14: *si ego testimonium perhibeo de meipso, verum est testimonium meum*; vel etiam quia Apostolus in sua praedicatione Christo testimonium dedit. Act. XXII, 18: *non recipient testimonium tuum de me.*

15. Tertio tangit gratiae perfectionem, cum dicit *ita ut nihil vobis desit in ulla gratia*, quia scilicet in diversis personis omnes gratias gratis datas habebant. Ad divinam enim providentiam pertinet, ut absque defectu necessaria largiatur. Ps. XXXIII, 10: *nihil deest timentibus eum*; et iterum: *inquirentes autem Dominum non minuentur omni bono.*

16. Deinde ponit bona in futurum expectanda. Et circa hoc tria facit.

Primo ponit futuri boni expectationem, dicens *vobis*, inquam, non solum habentibus gratiam in praesenti, sed etiam *expectantibus*, in futurum, *revelationem Domini nostri Iesu Christi*, qua scilicet sanctis suis revelabitur, non solum per gloriam humanitatis, secundum illud Is. XXXIII, 17: *regem in decore suo videbunt*, sed etiam per gloriam divinitatis, secundum illud Is. XL, 5: *revelabitur gloria Domini*; quae quidem revelatio homines beatos facit. I Io. III, 2: *cum autem apparuerit, similes ei erimus: et videbimus eum sicuti est.* Et in hoc vita aeterna consistit, secundum illud Io. XVII, 3: *haec est vita aeterna, ut cognoscant te solum verum Deum, et quem misisti Iesum Christum.*

Sicut autem illi quibus Christus revelatur, sunt beati in re, ita illi qui hoc expectant, sunt beati in spe. Is. XXX, 18: *beati omnes qui expectant eum.* Et ideo de ipsa expectatione gratias agit.

17. Secundo ostendit quod haec expectatio non est vana ex auxilio divinae gratiae. Unde subdit: *qui*, scilicet Christus, qui spem dedit vobis huiusmodi revelationis, etiam *confirmabit vos* in gratia accepta. I Petr. ult.: *modicum passos ipse perficiet, confirmabit solidabitque.* Et hoc *usque in finem*, scilicet vitae vestrae. Matth. c. X, 22: *qui perseveraverit usque in finem, hic salvus erit.* Non autem ut sitis sine peccato: quia, *si dixerimus quoniam peccatum non habemus, ipsi nosmetipsos seducimus, et veritas in nobis non est*, ut dicitur I Io. I, 8, sed ut sitis *sine crimine*, id est, sine peccato mortali. I Tim. III, 10: *ministrent nullum crimen habentes.* Et hoc, inquam, erit *in die adventus Domini nostri Iesu Christi*, quia scilicet qui sine crimine invenitur in die mortis, sine crimine perveniet ad diem iudicii, secundum illud Eccle. XI, 3: *si ceciderit lignum ad Austrum, sive ad Aquilonem, in quocumque*

correct, if it disagreed with the testimony of Christ or if Christ's testimony did not have a firm hold on their hearts by faith, because, as it is said: *he who wavers is like a wave of the sea that is driven and tossed by the wind* (Jas 1:6).

He says: in testimony to Christ, either because the prophets have spoken of him; *to him all the prophets give testimony* (Acts 10:43) or because Christ himself gave testimony: *although I give testimony of myself, my testimony is true* (John 8:14) or even because the Apostle in his own preaching gave testimony to Christ: *they will not receive your testimony concerning me* (Acts 22:18).

15. Third, he touches on the perfection of grace when he says, *so that nothing is wanting to you in any grace*, namely, because various persons among them enjoyed all the Charismatic graces. For it befits divine providence to bestow the necessities of life without stint: *those who fear him have no want* (Ps 34:9) and again *those who seek the Lord lack no good thing* (Ps 34:10).

16. Then he mentions the blessings to be expected in the future. In regard to this he does three things.

First, he mentions their expectation of a future blessing when he says, *to you*, who not only have grace at present but are *waiting for the* future *manifestation of our Lord Jesus Christ*, namely because he will be manifested to his saints not only in the glory of his humanity: *your eyes will see the king in his beauty* (Isa 33:17), but also in the glory of his divinity: *the glory of the Lord shall be revealed* (Isa 40:5). This is the revelation that makes men happy: *when he appears we shall be like him, for we shall see him as he is* (1 John 3:2), and in which eternal life consists: *this is eternal life, that they know you, the only true God, and Jesus Christ whom you have sent* (John 17:3).

Now just as those to whom Christ is revealed are happy in reality, so those who await this are happy in hope: *blessed are all they who wait for him* (Isa 30:18). This is why he gives thanks for their expectations.

17. Second, he shows that this expectation is not vain because of the help of God's grace: hence he adds, *who*, i.e., Christ, who gave them the hope of such a manifestation, *also will confirm you* in the grace received: *after you have suffered a little while, he will restore, establish and strengthen you* (1 Pet 5:10) *unto the end* of your life: *he who endures to the end will be saved* (Matt 10:22). Not that you will be without sin, because *if we say we have no sin, we deceive ourselves and the truth is not in us* (1 John 1:8), but that you may be *without crime*, i.e., without mortal sin: *if they prove themselves blameless let them minister* (1 Tim 3:10). This, I say, will be *in the day of the coming of our Lord Jesus Christ*, because a person found without crime on the day of death will arrive at the day of judgment without crime: *if a tree falls to the south or to the north, in the place where*

loco ceciderit, ibi erit. Nisi autem sine crimine nunc inveniatur, frustra illam revelationem expectaret.

18. Tertio rationem suae promissionis assignat, dicens quod Deus vos confirmabit, quod debetis sperare, quia **Deus est fidelis** (Deut. XXXII, 4: *Deus fidelis et absque ulla iniquitate*), **per quem vocati estis in societatem Filii eius Iesu Christi Domini nostri**, ut scilicet habeatis societatem ad Christum, et in praesenti per similitudinem gratiae, secundum illud I Io. I, 7: *si in luce ambulamus, sicut et ipse in luce est, societatem habemus cum eo ad invicem*, et in futuro per participationem gloriae, Rom. VIII, 17: *si compatimur, ut et simul glorificemur*.

Non autem videretur esse fidelis Deus, si nos vocaret ad societatem Filii et nobis denegaret, quantum in ipso est, ea, per quae pervenire ad eum possemus. Unde Iosue I, v. 5 dicit: *non te deseram, neque derelinquam*.

the tree falls, there it will lie (Eccl 11:3). For unless he is found without crime now, he awaits that revelation in vain.

18. Third, he assigns the reason for his promise, saying that God will strengthen you, because **God is faithful**: *God is faithful and without iniquity* (Deut 32:4). **By whom you are called unto the fellowship of his Son, Jesus Christ our Lord**, i.e., to have fellowship with Christ, both in the present life through the likeness of grace: *if we walk in the light, as he is in the light, we have fellowship with one another* (1 John 1:7) and in the future by sharing in his glory: *provided we suffer with him in order that we may also be glorified with him* (Rom 8:17).

But God would not seem to be faithful, if he called us to the fellowship of his Son and then denied us on his part the things by which we could attain to him. Hence Joshua says: *I will not fail you or forsake you* (Josh 1:5).

Lecture 2

¹:¹⁰Obsecro autem vos fratres per nomen Domini nostri Jesu Christi: ut idipsum dicatis omnes, et non sint in vobis schismata: sitis autem perfecti in eodem sensu, et in eadem sententia. [n. 19]

¹:¹¹Significatum est enim mihi de vobis fratres mei ab iis, qui sunt Chloës, quia contentiones sunt inter vos. [n. 24]

¹:¹²Hoc autem dico, quod unusquisque vestrum dicit: Ego quidem sum Pauli: ego autem Apollo: ego vero Cephae: ego autem Christi.

¹:¹³Divisus est Christus? numquid Paulus crucifixus est pro vobis? aut in nomine Pauli baptizati estis? [n. 26]

¹:¹⁴Gratias ago Deo, quod neminem vestrum baptizavi, nisi Crispum et Caium: [n. 35]

¹:¹⁵ne quis dicat quod in nomine meo baptizati estis.

¹:¹⁶Baptizavi autem et Stephanae domum: ceterum nescio si quem alium baptizaverim. [n. 37]

¹:¹⁷Non enim misit me Christus baptizare, sed evangelizare: [n. 38] non in sapientia verbi, ut non evacuetur crux Christi. [n. 40]

¹:¹⁰Παρακαλῶ δὲ ὑμᾶς, ἀδελφοί, διὰ τοῦ ὀνόματος τοῦ κυρίου ἡμῶν Ἰησοῦ Χριστοῦ, ἵνα τὸ αὐτὸ λέγητε πάντες, καὶ μὴ ᾖ ἐν ὑμῖν σχίσματα, ᾖτε δὲ κατηρτισμένοι ἐν τῷ αὐτῷ νοῒ καὶ ἐν τῇ αὐτῇ γνώμῃ.

¹:¹¹ἐδηλώθη γάρ μοι περὶ ὑμῶν, ἀδελφοί μου, ὑπὸ τῶν Χλόης ὅτι ἔριδες ἐν ὑμῖν εἰσιν.

¹:¹²λέγω δὲ τοῦτο, ὅτι ἕκαστος ὑμῶν λέγει, Ἐγὼ μέν εἰμι Παύλου, Ἐγὼ δὲ Ἀπολλῶ, Ἐγὼ δὲ Κηφᾶ, Ἐγὼ δὲ Χριστοῦ.

¹:¹³μεμέρισται ὁ Χριστός; μὴ Παῦλος ἐσταυρώθη ὑπὲρ ὑμῶν, ἢ εἰς τὸ ὄνομα Παύλου ἐβαπτίσθητε;

¹:¹⁴εὐχαριστῶ [τῷ θεῷ] ὅτι οὐδένα ὑμῶν ἐβάπτισα εἰ μὴ Κρίσπον καὶ Γάϊον,

¹:¹⁵ἵνα μή τις εἴπῃ ὅτι εἰς τὸ ἐμὸν ὄνομα ἐβαπτίσθητε.

¹:¹⁶ἐβάπτισα δὲ καὶ τὸν Στεφανᾶ οἶκον· λοιπὸν οὐκ οἶδα εἴ τινα ἄλλον ἐβάπτισα.

¹:¹⁷οὐ γὰρ ἀπέστειλέν με Χριστὸς βαπτίζειν ἀλλὰ εὐαγγελίζεσθαι, οὐκ ἐν σοφίᾳ λόγου, ἵνα μὴ κενωθῇ ὁ σταυρὸς τοῦ Χριστοῦ.

¹:¹⁰Now I beseech you, brethren, by the name of our Lord Jesus Christ, that you all speak the same thing and that there be no schisms among you: but that you be perfect in the same mind and in the same judgment. [n. 19]

¹:¹¹For it has been signified unto me, my brethren, of you, by them that are of the house of Chloe, that there are contentions among you. [n. 24]

¹:¹²Now this I say, that every one of you says: I indeed am of Paul; and I am of Apollo; and I of Cephas; and I of Christ.

¹:¹³Is Christ divided? Was Paul then crucified for you? Or were you baptized in the name of Paul? [n. 26]

¹:¹⁴I give God thanks, that I baptized none of you but Crispus and Caius: [n. 35]

¹:¹⁵Lest any should say that you were baptized in my name.

¹:¹⁶And I baptized also the household of Stephanus. Beyond that, I know not whether I baptized any other. [n. 37]

¹:¹⁷For Christ sent me not to baptize, but to preach the Gospel: [n. 38] not in wisdom of speech, lest the cross of Christ should be made void. [n. 40]

---

19. Praemissa salutatione et gratiarum actione, hic incipit eos instruere.

Et primo ponitur instructio de his quae ad omnes communiter pertinent, scilicet de his quae pertinent ad ecclesiastica sacramenta.

Secundo instruit eos de his quae ad quosdam pertinebant, XVI cap. *de collectis autem quae fiunt in sanctos*, et cetera.

In sacramentis autem tria sunt consideranda. Primo quidem ipsum sacramentum, sicut baptismus; secundo id quod est res significata et contenta, scilicet gratia; tertio id quod est res significata et non contenta, scilicet gloria resurrectionis.

Primo ergo agit de ipsis sacramentis;

secundo de ipsis gratiis, XII cap. *de spiritualibus autem nolo vos*, etc.,

19. After the greeting, the Apostle begins to instruct them.

First, he instructs them about things pertaining to all generally, namely, about the sacraments.

Second, he instructs them about things pertaining to some of them, at *now concerning the collections that are made for the saints* (1 Cor 16:1).

In the sacraments, three things should be considered: first, the sacrament itself, as baptism; second, the reality signified and contained, namely, grace: third, the reality signified but not contained, namely, the glory of the resurrection.

First, therefore, he discusses the sacraments themselves; second, the graces, at *now concerning spiritual things* (1 Cor 12:1);

tertio, de gloria resurrectionis, infra XV *notum autem vobis facio*.

Circa primum tria facit.

Primo determinat ea quae pertinent ad sacramentum baptismi;

secundo ea quae pertinent ad sacramentum matrimonii, V cap., ibi *omnino auditur inter vos*, etc.;

tertio ea quae pertinent ad sacramentum Eucharistiae, VIII cap., ibi *de his autem quae idolis sacrificantur*.

20. Dominus autem, Matth. ult., discipulis praeceptum dedit de doctrina simul et baptismo, dicens *euntes docete omnes gentes, baptizantes*, et cetera. Et ideo Apostolus in prima parte simul cum baptismo agit de doctrina.

Est autem sciendum quod inter Corinthios fideles erat quaedam dissensio propter baptistas et doctores; illi enim qui erant instructi contemnebant alios, quasi qui meliorem doctrinam acceperint, et meliorem baptismum.

21. Unde circa primum duo facit.

Primo removet contentionem;

secundo contentionis causam quae erat in hoc, quod gloriabantur de quibusdam, et alios Christi ministros contemnebant, infra III capite *et ego, fratres, non potui vobis loqui*.

Circa primum tria facit.

Primo proponit admonitionem;

secundo admonitionis necessitatem ostendit, ibi *significatum est enim mihi*, etc.;

tertio rationem admonitionis assignat, ibi *divisus est Christus?* et cetera.

22. Circa primum duo consideranda sunt.

Primum quidem quod eos inducit ad admonitionem servandam. Uno modo per propriam humilitatem, cum dicit *obsecro autem vos*, et cetera. Prov. XVIII, 23: *cum obsecrationibus loquitur pauper*. Alio modo per fraternam caritatem, cum dicit *fratres*, quia scilicet ex affectu fraternae caritatis hoc dicebat. Prov. XVIII, 19: *frater qui iuvatur a fratre, quasi civitas firma*. Tertio per reverentiam Christi, cum dicit *per nomen Domini nostri Iesu Christi*, quod est ab omnibus honorandum, et cui oportet omnes esse subiectos. Phil. II, 10: *in nomine Iesu omne genu flectatur*.

23. Secundo considerandum est quod inducit eos ad tria.

Primo quidem ad concordiam, cum dicit *ut idipsum dicatis omnes*, id est, omnes eamdem fidem confiteamini, et eamdem sententiam proferatis de his quae sunt communiter agenda. Rom. XV, 6: *ut unanimes uno ore honorificetis Deum*.

third, the glory of the resurrection, at *now I make known unto you* (1 Cor 15:1).

In regard to the first he does three things.

First he determines what pertains to baptism;

second, what pertains to the sacrament of matrimony, at *it is absolutely heard* (1 Cor 5:1);

third, what pertains to the sacrament of the Eucharist, at *now concerning those things that are sacrificed* (1 Cor 8:1).

20. In the first part the Apostle deals with doctrine along with baptism; thus he follows the example of the Lord, who gave the disciples the injunction to teach and to baptize in one command: *go therefore and make disciples of all nations, baptizing them* (Matt 28:19).

Now it should be noted that there was dissension among the Corinthian believers, because those who had been instructed assumed that they had received the better teaching and a better baptism and began to look down on the others.

21. Hence the Apostle does two things.

First, he ends the strife;

second, he attacks the cause of the strife, namely, that they glory in some of Christ's ministers and look down on the other ones, at *and I, brethren, could not speak to you* (1 Cor 3:1).

As to the first he does three things.

First, he gives a friendly warning;

second, he shows the need for the warning, at *for it has been signified unto me*;

third, the reason for the warning, at *is Christ divided*.

22. In regard to the first, two things should be considered.

First, he uses humble language as one way of inducing them to heed his warning; hence he says, *now I beseech you*: the poor will speak with supplications (Prov 18:23); the second way is by brotherly love when he says, *brethren*, because this warning came from the warmth of his fraternal charity: *a brother helped by a brother is like a strong city* (Prov 18:19). The third way is by appealing to their reverence for Christ when he says: *by the name of our Lord Jesus Christ*, who should be honored by all and to whom all should be subject: *in the name of Jesus every knee should bend* (Phil 2:10).

23. The second thing to be considered is that he urges them to three things.

First, to concord when he says, *that you all speak the same thing*, i.e., that all confess the same faith and hold the same opinion in matters that must be done in common: *that together you may with one voice glorify the God and Father of our Lord Jesus Christ* (Rom 15:6).

Secundo prohibet vitium contrarium virtuti, cum dicit *et non sint in vobis schismata*, quia unitas ecclesiastica dividi non debet, in cuius signum milites de tunica inconsutili, Io. XIX, 24 dixerunt: *non scindamus eam, sed sortiamur de ea cuius sit*. Sunt autem proprie schismata, quando, vel propter diversam fidei confessionem, vel propter diversas sententias de agendis, homines unius collegii in diversas separantur partes. Is. XXII, v. 9: *scissuras civitatis David videbitis, quia multiplicatae sunt*.

Tertio inducit eos ad id per quod possunt schismata vitare, scilicet ad perfectionem. Est enim divisionis causa, dum unusquisque partiale bonum quaerit, praetermisso perfecto bono, quod est bonum totius. Et ideo dicit *sitis autem perfecti in eodem sensu*, scilicet quo iudicatur de agendis, *et in eadem scientia*, qua iudicatur de cognoscendis, quasi dicat: per haec perfecti esse poteritis, si in unitate persistatis. Col. III, 14: *super omnia caritatem habete, quod est vinculum perfectionis*. Matth. V, 48: *estote perfecti sicut Pater vester caelestis perfectus est*.

24. Deinde, cum dicit *significatum est mihi*, ostendit necessitatem praedictae admonitionis, quia scilicet contentionis vitio laborabant, quasi dicat: ideo necesse est vos ad hoc inducere, quia *significatum est mihi, fratres mei, ab his qui sunt Cloes*, id est, in quadam villa Corinthiorum iurisdictioni subiecta, vel Cloes potest esse nomen matronae, in cuius domo erant multi fideles congregati, *quia contentiones sunt inter vos*, contra id quod dicitur Prov. XX, 3: *honor est homini qui separat se a contentionibus*.

Et modum contentionis exponit, subdens *hoc autem dico*, id est, contentionem nomino, *quod unusquisque vestrum* nominat se ab eo a quo est baptizatus et instructus, et *dicit: ego quidem sum Pauli*, quia erat a Paulo baptizatus et instructus; alius *ego autem Apollo*, qui scilicet Corinthiis praedicaverat, ut habetur Act. XIX, 1; alius *ego vero Cephae*, scilicet Petri, cui dictum est Io. I, v. 42: *tu vocaberis Cephas, quod interpretatur Petrus*. Quod quidem ideo dicebant, quod putabant a meliori baptista meliorem baptismum dari, quasi virtus baptistae in baptizatis operaretur. Et de hoc pseudoapostoli gloriabantur, secundum illud Ps. XLVIII, 12: *vocaverunt nomina sua in terris suis*. Alius autem dicit *ego autem sum Christi*, qui solus benedixit, quia solius Christi virtus operatur in baptismo Christi. Io. I, 33: *super quem videris Spiritum descendere et manere, ipse est qui baptizat*. Et ideo baptizati a solo Christo denominantur Christiani, non autem a Paulo Paulini. Is. IV, 1: *tantummodo invocetur nomen tuum super nos*.

25. Ad huius autem erroris vitationem, dicuntur Graeci hac forma in baptizando uti *baptizetur servus*

Second, he forbids a vice contrary to virtue when he says: *and that there be no schisms among you*, because ecclesial unity must not be fragmented. As a sign of this unity the soldiers said of the coat without a seam: *let us not cut it, but let us cast lots for it, whose it shall be* (John 19:24). Properly speaking, there are schisms when the members of one group separate into various factions according to their various beliefs or according to their various opinions about conduct: *you shall see the breaches of the city of David* (Isa 22:9).

Third, he urges them to seek perfection, which is the good of the whole. For the cause of division is, while each one seeks a partial good, the perfect good is overlooked, which is the good of the whole. Therefore, he says, *but that you be perfect in the same mind*, which judges about conduct, *and in the same judgment*, which judges about belief. As if to say: these things will enable you to be perfect, if you continue in unity: *over all these things have charity, which is the bond of perfection* (Col 3:14); *be perfect as your heavenly Father is perfect* (Matt 5:48).

24. Then when he says, *it has been signified unto me*, he shows why it was necessary to warn them, namely, because they were burdened with the vice of contention. As if to say: it is necessary to induce you to this, *for it has been signified unto me, my brethren, of you, by them who are of the house of Chloe*, i.e., from a certain villa subject to the jurisdiction of the Corinthians. Or Chloe might be the name of a matron in whose home many believers assembled: *that there are contentions among you*, contrary to what is said in Proverbs: *it is an honor for a man to separate himself from quarrels* (Prov 20:24).

Then he specifies the nature of the contention when he says, *now this I say*, i.e., the contention consists in this, *that every one of you* gives himself a name derived from the person by whom he was baptized and instructed, and *says: I indeed am of Paul*, because he had been baptized and instructed by Paul; another says: *I am of Apollo*, who had preached to the Corinthians (Acts 19); still another says: *and I of Cephas*, i.e., Peter, to whom it had been said: *you shall be called Cephas, which is interpreted Peter* (John 1:42). Now they made these statements because they thought that they received a better baptism from a better baptizer, as though the virtue of the minister had an influence on the one baptized. Finally, others say: *and I of Christ*, who alone gives grace, because the grace of Christ alone works in Christ's baptism: *he upon whom you shall see the Spirit descending and remaining upon him, he it is who baptizes with the Holy Spirit* (John 1:33). Accordingly, the baptized are called Christians from Christ alone and not Paulians from Paul: *only let us be called by your name* (Isa 4:1).

25. In order to avoid this error the Greeks are said to have used the following formula in baptism: *let Christ's*

Christi Nicolaus in nomine Patris, et Filii, et Spiritus Sancti, ut detur intelligi quod homo non baptizat interius, sed baptizatur a Christo. Quia tamen etiam homo baptizat ministerio, ut membrum et minister Christi, ideo Ecclesia utitur hac forma in baptizando: *ego te baptizo in nomine Patris, et Filii, et Spiritus Sancti*, quod quidem est expressius secundum formam a Christo traditam, qui dixit discipulis: *docete omnes gentes, baptizantes eos in nomine Patris, et Filii, et Spiritus Sancti*, etc., ubi ipsos apostolos dicit baptizantes, secundum quem modum sacramenti minister dicit: *ego te baptizo*.

26. Deinde cum dicit **divisus est Christus?** etc., ponit rationem praedictae admonitionis, quare inter eos scissurae et contentiones esse non debebant, et

primo ex parte baptismi;

secundo ex parte doctrinae, ibi **non in sapientia verbi**, et cetera.

Circa primum tria facit.

Primo ponit inconveniens quod ex praedicta contentione sequitur;

secundo manifestat quare illud inconveniens sequatur, ibi **numquid Paulus crucifixus est**, etc.;

tertio excludit quamdam falsam suspicionem, ibi **gratias ago Deo meo**, et cetera.

27. Dicit ergo primo: dixi quod unusquisque vestrum dicit **ego sum Pauli, ego Apollo**, et ex hoc sequitur quod Christus est divisus. Nec refert utrum interrogative vel remissive legatur.

28. Hoc autem potest intelligi, uno modo, quasi diceret: per hoc quod inter vos contenditur, Christus est divisus a vobis, qui non nisi in pace habitat, secundum illud Ps. LXXV, 3: *in pace factus est locus eius.* Is. LIX, 2: *iniquitates vestrae diviserunt inter vos et Deum vestrum.*

Sed melius aliter hoc potest intelligi, ut sit sensus: per hoc quod creditis baptismum esse meliorem, qui a meliori baptista datur, sequitur quod Christus, qui principaliter et interius baptizat, sit divisus, id est, differens in sua virtute et effectu, secundum differentiam ministrorum: quod patet esse falsum per id quod dicitur Eph. IV, 5: *unus Dominus, una fides, unum baptisma.*

Sed adhuc melius hoc intelligitur quod Apostolus dicit: ex hoc quod ea quae sunt propria Christi aliis attribuitis, quodammodo Christum dividitis, plures christos facientes, contra id quod dicitur Matth. XXIII, 10: *magister vester unus est Christus.* Is. XLV, v. 22: *convertimini ad me, et salvi eritis, omnes fines terrae, quia ego Dominus, et non est alius.*

29. Est autem sciendum quod Christus in sacramento baptismi duplicem habet virtutem sibi propriam. Unam quidem divinam, qua simul cum Patre et Spiritu Sancto interius mundat a peccato, et hoc nulli creaturae potuit communicari.

servant, Nicholas, be baptized in the name of the Father and of the Son and of the Holy Spirit, to show that a man is not baptized interiorly, unless he is baptized by Christ. But because a man also baptizes, as a minister and member of Christ, the Church uses this formula in baptizing: *I baptize you in the name of the Father and of the Son and of the Holy Spirit*, which is more in keeping with the formula given by Christ, who said to the disciples: *teach all nations, baptizing them in the name of the Father and of the Son and of the Holy Spirit* (Matt 28:19), where he also calls the apostles baptizers. It is according to this command that the minister says: *I baptize you.*

26. Then when he says, **is Christ divided**, he gives the reason for this warning that there should be no schisms and contentions among them:

first, on the part of baptism:

second, on the part of doctrine, at **not in wisdom of speech** (1 Cor 1:17).

As to the first he does three things.

First, he mentions the mistake which follows from their contention;

second, why that mistake follows, at **was Paul then crucified**;

third, he dismisses a false surmise, at **I give God thanks**.

27. He says, therefore: I have said that everyone of you says, **I indeed am of Paul; and I am of Apollo**; from which it follows that Christ is divided. Nor does it matter whether this is read interrogatively or remissively.

28. This can be understood in one way as though he were saying: inasmuch as there is contention among you, Christ is divided from you, because he dwells only in peace: *his place is in peace* (Ps 76:3); *your iniquities have made a separation between you and your God* (Isa 59:2).

But it is better understood of him as saying: inasmuch as you believe that a baptism performed by a better minister is better, it follows that Christ, who principally and interiorly baptizes, is divided, i.e., differs in his power and effect, depending on the differing ministers. But this is false, because it is said: *one Lord, one faith, one baptism* (Eph 4:5).

An even better interpretation is to understand the Apostles as saying that inasmuch as you attribute to others the things that are exclusively Christ's, you divide Christ by forming many christs, which is contrary to what is stated in Matthew: *one is your master, Christ* (Matt 23:10); *turn to me and be saved, all the ends of the earth! For I am God and there is no other* (Isa 45:22).

29. For it should be noted that there are two powers proper to Christ in the sacrament of baptism: one is the divine power, by which he and the Father and the Holy Spirit cleanse from sin interiorly. This cannot be communicated to any creature.

Alia autem est propria virtus secundum humanam naturam, quae est potestas excellentiae in sacramentis, et consistit in quatuor. Quorum unum est, quod ipse sacramenta instituit; secundum est quod potuit effectum sacramentorum sine sacramento conferre; tertium est quod meritum passionis eius operatur in baptismo et aliis sacramentis; quartum est quod ad invocationem nominis eius sacramenta conferuntur. Hanc autem potestatem excellentiae, et maxime quantum ad ultimum, conferre potuit ministris baptismi, ut scilicet eorum nominibus consecraretur baptismus, sed noluit, ne schisma ex hoc in Ecclesia fieret, dum tot reputarentur baptismi, quot essent baptistae.

Et hoc est quod, secundum expositionem Augustini, Ioannes Baptista de Christo nescisse fatetur, utrum scilicet hanc potestatem sibi retineret.

30. Deinde, cum dicit **numquid Paulus**, etc., ostendit praedictum inconveniens sequi ex eorum errore quod diversum baptisma esse aestimabant secundum differentiam baptistarum; hoc enim esset, si a baptistis baptismus efficaciam haberet, quod quidem solius est Christi.

31. Hoc autem ostendit dupliciter.

Primo quidem ex parte passionis Christi, in cuius virtute baptismus operatur, secundum illud Rom. VI, 3: *1uicumque baptizati sumus in Christo Iesu, in morte ipsius baptizati sumus.* Et ideo dicit **numquid Paulus crucifixus est pro vobis?** Quasi dicat: numquid passio Pauli causa est nostrae salutis, ut secundum ipsum baptismus habeat virtutem salvandi? Quasi dicat: non. Hoc enim proprium est Christo, ut sua passione et morte nostram salutem operatus fuerit. Io. XI, 50: *expedit ut unus homo moriatur pro populo, et non tota gens pereat.* II Cor. c. V, 14: *unus pro omnibus mortuus est.*

32. Sed contra videtur esse quod Apostolus dicit Col. I, 24: *gaudeo in passionibus meis pro vobis, et adimpleo ea quae desunt passionum Christi in carne mea pro corpore eius, quod est Ecclesia.*

Sed dicendum quod passio Christi fuit nobis salutifera non solum per modum exempli, secundum illud I Petr. II, 21: *Christus passus est pro nobis, vobis relinquens exemplum, ut sequamini vestigia eius,* sed etiam per modum meriti, et per modum efficaciae, inquantum eius sanguine redempti et iustificati sumus, secundum illud Hebr. ultimo: *ut sanctificaret per suum sanguinem populum, extra portam passus est.* Sed passio aliorum nobis est salutifera solum per modum exempli, secundum illud II Cor. I, 6: *sive tribulamur, pro vestra exhortatione et salute.*

33. Secundo ostendit idem ex virtute nominis Christi, qui in baptismo invocatur. Unde subdit **aut in nomine Pauli baptizati estis?** Quasi dicat: non. Ut enim dicitur Act. IV, 12, *non est aliud nomen datum hominibus, per*

The other is the power proper to his human nature, which is the power of excellence in the sacraments and consists of four things: one is that he instituted the sacraments; the second is that he can produce the effect of the sacraments without the sacraments; the third is that the merit of his passion works in baptism and the other sacraments; the fourth is that the sacraments are conferred by calling on his name. Now he could have shared this power of excellence with his ministers and particularly the fourth, namely, that baptism be consecrated in their names, but he reserved it for himself; otherwise schism would arise in the Church, for people would suppose that there are as many baptisms as baptizers.

According to Augustine this is why John the Baptist confessed that he did not know whether Christ would keep this power for himself.

30. Then when he says, **was Paul then crucified**, he shows that their mistake follows from their error of supposing that there are diverse baptisms, depending on the different baptizers; for this would be so, if baptism derived its power form the baptizers and not from Christ alone.

31. He shows this in two ways.

First, on the part of Christ's passion, in virtue of which baptism works, as it says in Romans: *know you not that all who are baptized in Christ Jesus are baptized in his death?* (Rom 6:3). Accordingly, he says, **was Paul then crucified for you?** As if to say: were Paul's sufferings the cause of our salvation, so that baptism depends on him for its saving power? As if to say: certainly not. For Christ alone is the one by whose sufferings and death our salvation is wrought: *it is expedient for you that one man should die for the people, and that the whole nation not perish* (John 11:50); *one has died for all* (2 Cor 5:14).

32. On the other hand, the Apostle seems to say the opposite in Colossians: *I rejoice in my sufferings for your sake, and in my flesh I complete what is lacking in Christ's afflictions for the sake of his body, the Church* (Col 1:24).

I answer that Christ's sufferings benefited us not only by their example: *Christ also suffered for us, leaving you an example that you should follow in his steps* (1 Pet 2:21), but also by their merit and efficacy, inasmuch as we have been redeemed and sanctified by his blood: *so Jesus also suffered outside the gate in order to sanctify the people through his own blood* (Heb 13:12). But the sufferings of others benefit us only as an example: *if we are afflicted, it is for your comfort and salvation* (2 Cor 1:6).

33. Second, he shows the same thing from the power of Christ's name invoked in baptism; hence he adds, **or were you baptized in the name of Paul?** As if to say: no. For as it is said: *there is no other name under heaven given to men, whereby we must be saved* (Acts 4:12). Hence, too, Isaiah

quod oporteat nos salvos fieri. Unde et Is. XXVI, 8 dicitur: *nomen tuum et memoriale tuum in desiderio animae.*

34. Sed videtur quod in nomine Christi homines non baptizentur. Dicit enim Matth. ult.: *docete omnes gentes, baptizantes eos in nomine Patris, et Filii, et Spiritus Sancti.*

Dicendum est autem quod in primitiva Ecclesia, quia nomen Christi multum erat odiosum, ut venerabile redderetur, apostoli in nomine Christi baptizabant ex speciali ordinatione Spiritus Sancti. Unde dicitur Act. c. VIII, 12, quod *in nomine Christi baptizati sunt viri et mulieres.* Et tamen, ut Ambrosius dicit *in nomine Christi tota Trinitas intelligitur.* Christus enim interpretatur unctus, in quo intelligitur non solum ille qui ungitur, qui est Filius Dei, sed etiam ipsa unctio, quae est Spiritus Sanctus, et ipse ungens, qui est Pater, secundum Ps. XLIV, 8: *unxit te Deus, Deus tuus, oleo laetitiae prae consortibus tuis.*

Nunc autem quia nomen Christi iam est *magnum in gentibus ab ortu solis usque ad occasum,* ut dicitur Mal. I, 11, Ecclesia utitur forma prius instituta a Christo, baptizans *in nomine Patris, et Filii, et Spiritus Sancti.* Et tamen quicumque in hac forma baptizantur, in nomine eius, qui est vere Filius Dei, baptizantur, secundum illud I Io. c. ult.: *ut simus in vero Filio eius, Iesu Christo.* Baptizantur etiam omnes fideles in nomine Christi, id est, fide et confessione nominis Christi, secundum illud Ioel. c. II, 32: *omnis quicumque invocaverit nomen Domini, salvus erit.* Unde baptizati a Christo Christiani nominantur, quia, ut dicitur Gal. III, 27: *quotquot in Christo baptizati estis, Christum induistis.*

Sic ergo, si solius Christi passio, si solius Christi nomen virtutem confert baptismo ad salvandum, verum est proprium esse Christo, ut ex eo baptismus habeat sanctificandi virtutem. Unde qui hoc aliis attribuit, dividit Christum in plures.

35. Deinde, cum dicit **gratias ago Deo meo**, excludit quamdam suspicionem.

Quia ibi dixerat: **numquid enim Paulus crucifixus est pro vobis?** Posset aliquis credere quod et si non auctoritate, ministerio tamen plures baptizaverit.

Et circa hoc tria facit.

Primo gratias agit de hoc quod paucos baptizavit;

secundo, quibusdam paucis nominatis, quosdam alios addit, ibi **baptizavi autem**;

tertio assignat rationem quare non multos baptizaverit, ibi **non enim misit me Deus**.

36. Dicit ergo primo **gratias ago Deo meo, quod neminem vestrum baptizavi, nisi Crispum**, de quo Act. XVIII, 8: *Crispus archisynagogus credidit Domino cum omni domo sua,* **et Caium**, ad quem scribitur tertia canonica Ioannis.

says: *your name and your remembrance are the desire of the soul* (Isa 26:8).

34. But it seems that men are not baptized in Christ's name, for it is commanded in Matthew: *teach all nations; baptizing them in the name of the Father and of the Son and of the Holy Spirit* (Matt 28:19).

The answer is that in the early Church, because Christ's name was much hated, the apostles were inspired by the Holy Spirit to baptize in the name of Christ. Whence it is said: *in the name of Christ they were baptized, both men and women* (Acts 8:12). Yet, as Ambrose says, *the whole Trinity is understood in the name of Christ.* For 'Christ' means anointed, which implies not only the Son who is anointed, but the anointing itself, which is the Holy Spirit, and the one who anoints, namely, the Father as a psalm says: *God, your God, has anointed you with the oil of gladness above your fellows* (Ps 45:8).

But now that Christ's name is *great among the gentiles from the rising of the sun to its setting* (Mal 1:11), the Church uses the formula first instituted by Christ, baptizing *in the name of the Father and of the Son and of the Holy Spirit.* Nevertheless, everyone baptized in this form is baptized in the name of him who is truly Son of God: *that we may be in his true Son, Jesus Christ* (1 John 5:30). Furthermore, all faithful are baptized in the name of Christ, that is, in faith and by confession of the name of Christ: *everyone who shall call upon the name of the Lord, shall be saved* (Joel 2:32); hence they are called Christians, for *as many of you as have been baptized in Christ alone, have put on Christ* (Gal 3:27).

Therefore, if the sufferings of Christ alone, if the name of Christ alone, confers the power to be saved on the baptized, then it is from Christ alone that baptism has the power to sanctify. Consequently, anyone who attributes this to others divides Christ into many parts.

35. Then when he says, **I give God thanks**, he dismisses a false surmise.

For since he had said, **was Paul then crucified for you**, someone might suppose that though he had not baptized in his own name, he did baptize many people as a minister.

In regard to this he does three things.

First, he gives thanks for having baptized only a few;

second, after naming the few, he adds certain others, at **and I baptized also**;

third, he gives the reason why he did not baptize many, at **for Christ sent me not to baptize** (1 Cor 1:17).

36. He says, therefore: **I give God thanks, that I baptized none of you but Crispus**, of whom it is said: *Crispus, the ruler of the synagogue believed in the Lord with all his house* (Acts 18:8), **and Caius**, to whom John's third epistle is written.

Et quia gratiarum actio locum non habet, nisi in beneficiis perceptis, consequenter Apostolus ostendit qualiter de hoc gratias agat, cum subdit *ne quis dicat quod in nomine meo baptizati estis*. Est enim optabile sanctis viris, ne ex bonis quae ipsi faciunt, alii sumant occasionem erroris sui, sive peccati.

Et quia Corinthii in eum errorem devenerant, ut se a suis baptistis nominarent, dicentes *ego sum Pauli* et *Apollo*, ac si in eorum nominibus essent baptizati, ideo gratias agit de hoc quod de suo ministerio talis error consecutus non fuerit. Et ideo signanter dicit se baptizasse illos qui ab hoc errore immunes erant.

37. Deinde, cum dicit *baptizavi autem*, etc., ponit quosdam alios a se baptizatos, ne in eius verbis aliquid veritatis minus appareret. Unde dicit *baptizavi et domum*, id est familiam, *Stephanae*, scilicet cuiusdam matronae.

Et quia circa particularia facta memoria hominum labilis est, subdit *caeterum nescio*, id est in memoria non habeo, *si quem alium baptizaverim*, in propria persona.

38. Deinde, cum dicit *non enim misit*, etc., assignat rationem quare paucos baptizaverit, dicens *non enim misit me Deus baptizare, sed evangelizare*.

39. Contra quod videtur esse quod dicitur Matth. ult.: *euntes docete omnes gentes, baptizantes eos in nomine Patris, et Filii, et Spiritus Sancti*.

Sed dicendum est quod Christus apostolos misit ad utrumque, ita tamen quod ipsi per seipsos praedicarent, secundum quod ipsi dicebant Act. VI, 2: *non est aequum relinquere nos verbum Dei, et ministrare mensis*.

Baptizarent autem per inferiores ministros, et hoc ideo quia in baptismo nihil operatur industria vel virtus baptizantis: nam indifferens est utrum per maiorem vel minorem ministrum detur baptismus, sed in praedicatione Evangelii multum operatur sapientia et virtus praedicantis, et ideo praedicationis officium per seipsos apostoli tamquam maiores ministri exercebant, sicut et de ipso Christo dicitur Io. IV, 2 quod ipse non baptizabat, sed discipuli eius, qui tamen de seipso dicit Lc. IV, 43: *quia et aliis civitatibus oportet me evangelizare regnum Dei, quia ideo missus sum*. Is. LXI, 1: *ad annuntiandum mansuetis misit me*.

But because thanksgiving has no place except for blessings received, the Apostle shows why he gives thanks in this case when he continues: *lest any should say that you were baptized in my name*. For holy men desire that their good deeds not be taken as an occasion of error or sin by others.

And because the Corinthians had fallen into the error of naming themselves from the baptizer and saying, *I indeed am of Paul* and *Apollo*, he thanked God that such an error had not been occasioned by his ministry. That is why he was careful to say that he had baptized those who were immune from this error.

37. Then when he says, *and I baptized also*, he mentions the others he had baptized, lest anything less than the truth appear in his words; hence he adds, *I baptized also the household*, i.e., family estate, *of Stephanus*, namely, of his wife.

Then because man's memory is unreliable in regard to particular facts, he adds: *beyond that, I know not*, i.e., do not recall, *whether I baptized any other*, in person.

38. Then when he says, *for Christ sent me not*, he gives the reason why he baptized so few, saying, *for Christ sent me not to baptize, but to preach the Gospel*.

39. But this seems to be in opposition to the Lord's command: *teach all nations; baptizing them in the name of the Father, and of the Son, and of the Holy Spirit* (Matt 28:19).

The answer is that Christ sent the apostles to do both, but in such a way that they preached in person, as they said in Acts: *it is not right that we should give up preaching the word of God to serve tables* (Acts 6:2).

But they baptized through their ministers, and they did this because the diligence or virtue of the baptizer contributes nothing in baptism, for it is indifferent whether baptism be given by a greater or lesser personage. But in the preaching of the Gospel the wisdom and virtue of the preacher contributes a great deal; consequently, the apostles, being better qualified, exercised the office of preaching in person. In the same way it is said of Christ that he himself did not baptize but his disciples did (John 4:2); of him it is said: *I must preach the good news of the kingdom of God to the other cities also, for I was sent for that purpose* (Luke 4:43); *the Lord has anointed me to bring good tidings to the afflicted* (Isa 61:1).

Lecture 3

1:17Non enim misit me Christus baptizare, sed evangelizare: [n. 38] non in sapientia verbi, ut non evacuetur crux Christi. [n. 40]

1:18Verbum enim crucis pereuntibus quidem stultitia est: iis autem qui salvi fiunt, id est nobis, Dei virtus est. [n. 46]

1:19Scriptum est enim: *perdam sapientiam sapientium, et prudentiam prudentium reprobabo.* [n. 48]

1:20Ubi sapiens? ubi scriba? ubi conquisitor hujus saeculi? Nonne stultam fecit Deus sapientiam hujus mundi? [n. 51]

1:21Nam quia in Dei sapientia non cognovit mundus per sapientiam Deum: placuit Deo per stultitiam praedicationis salvos facere credentes. [n. 55]

1:22Quoniam et Judaei signa petunt, et Graeci sapientiam quaerunt: [n. 56]

1:23nos autem praedicamus Christum crucifixum: Judaeis quidem scandalum, gentibus autem stultitiam, [n. 58]

1:24ipsis autem vocatis Judaeis, atque Graecis Christum Dei virtutem, et Dei sapientia: [n. 59]

1:25quia quod stultum est Dei, sapientius est hominibus: et quod infirmum est Dei, fortius est hominibus. [n. 62]

1:17οὐ γὰρ ἀπέστειλέν με Χριστὸς βαπτίζειν ἀλλὰ εὐαγγελίζεσθαι, οὐκ ἐν σοφίᾳ λόγου, ἵνα μὴ κενωθῇ ὁ σταυρὸς τοῦ Χριστοῦ.

1:18Ὁ λόγος γὰρ ὁ τοῦ σταυροῦ τοῖς μὲν ἀπολλυμένοις μωρία ἐστίν, τοῖς δὲ σῳζομένοις ἡμῖν δύναμις θεοῦ ἐστιν.

1:19γέγραπται γάρ, Ἀπολῶ τὴν σοφίαν τῶν σοφῶν, καὶ τὴν σύνεσιν τῶν συνετῶν ἀθετήσω.

1:20ποῦ σοφός; ποῦ γραμματεύς; ποῦ συζητητὴς τοῦ αἰῶνος τούτου; οὐχὶ ἐμώρανεν ὁ θεὸς τὴν σοφίαν τοῦ κόσμου;

1:21ἐπειδὴ γὰρ ἐν τῇ σοφίᾳ τοῦ θεοῦ οὐκ ἔγνω ὁ κόσμος διὰ τῆς σοφίας τὸν θεόν, εὐδόκησεν ὁ θεὸς διὰ τῆς μωρίας τοῦ κηρύγματος σῶσαι τοὺς πιστεύοντας.

1:22ἐπειδὴ καὶ Ἰουδαῖοι σημεῖα αἰτοῦσιν καὶ Ἕλληνες σοφίαν ζητοῦσιν,

1:23ἡμεῖς δὲ κηρύσσομεν Χριστὸν ἐσταυρωμένον, Ἰουδαίοις μὲν σκάνδαλον ἔθνεσιν δὲ μωρίαν,

1:24αὐτοῖς δὲ τοῖς κλητοῖς, Ἰουδαίοις τε καὶ Ἕλλησιν, Χριστὸν θεοῦ δύναμιν καὶ θεοῦ σοφίαν·

1:25ὅτι τὸ μωρὸν τοῦ θεοῦ σοφώτερον τῶν ἀνθρώπων ἐστίν, καὶ τὸ ἀσθενὲς τοῦ θεοῦ ἰσχυρότερον τῶν ἀνθρώπων.

1:17For Christ sent me not to baptize, but to preach the Gospel: [n. 38] not in wisdom of speech, lest the cross of Christ should be made void. [n. 40]

1:18For the word of the cross, to them indeed who perish, is foolishness: but to them who are saved, that is, to us, it is the power of God. [n. 46]

1:19For it is written: *I will destroy the wisdom of the wise: and the prudence of the prudent I will reject.* [n. 48]

1:20Where is the wise? Where is the scribe? Where is the disputer of this world? Has not God made foolish the wisdom of this world? [n. 51]

1:21For, seeing that in the wisdom of God, the world, by wisdom, knew not God, it pleased God, by the foolishness of our preaching, to save them who believe. [n. 55]

1:22For the Jews require signs: and the Greeks seek after wisdom. [n. 56]

1:23But we preach Christ crucified: unto the Jews indeed a stumblingblock, and unto the gentiles foolishness: [n. 58]

1:24But unto them who are called, both Jews and Greeks, Christ, the power of God and the wisdom of God. [n. 59]

1:25For the foolishness of God is wiser than men: and the weakness of God is stronger than men. [n. 62]

---

40. Postquam Apostolus improbavit Corinthiorum contentionem, ratione sumpta ex parte baptismi, hic excludit eorum contentionem, ratione sumpta ex parte doctrinae. Quidam enim eorum gloriabantur de doctrina pseudo-Apostolorum, qui ornatis verbis et humanae sapientiae rationibus veritatem fidei corrumpebant. Et ideo Apostolus

primo ostendit hunc modum convenientem non esse doctrinae fidei;

secundo ostendit hoc modo docendi se usum apud eos non fuisse, II cap., ibi *et ego, cum venissem ad* et cetera.

Circa primum duo facit.

Primo proponit quod intendit;

40. After condemning their strife with a reason based on baptism, the Apostle disapproves of it again with a reason based on doctrine. For some of the Corinthians gloried in the doctrine of false apostles, who corrupt the truth of the faith with elegant words and reasons born of human wisdom.

First, therefore, the Apostle says that this method is not suited for teaching the faith;

second, he shows that he did not employ this method of teaching, when he was among them, at *and I, brethren, when I came* (1 Cor 2:1).

As to the first he does two things.

First, he states his proposition;

secundo manifestat propositum, ibi **ut non evacuetur**.

41. Dicit ergo primo: dixi quod misit me Christus evangelizare, non tamen ita quod ego *in sapientia verbi* evangelizem, id est, in sapientia mundana, quae verbosos facit, inquantum per eam multis vanis rationibus homines utuntur. Eccle. VI, 11: *ubi verba sunt plurima, multam in disputando habentia vanitatem.* Prov. XIV, 23: *ubi verba sunt plurima, ibi frequenter egestas.* Vel sapientiam verbi nominat rhetoricam, quae docet ornate loqui, ex quo alliciuntur interdum homines ad assentiendum erroribus et falsitatibus. Unde Rom. XVI, 18: *per dulces sermones seducunt corda innocentium.* Et de meretrice dicitur Prov. II, 16, in figura haereticae doctrinae: *ut eruaris a muliere aliena et extranea, quae mollit sermones suos.*

42. Sed contra dicitur Is. XXXIII, 19: *populum impudentem non videbis,* scilicet in Catholica Ecclesia, *et populum alti sermonis, ita ut non possis intelligere disertitudinem linguae eius, in quo nulla est sapientia.*

Sed quia in Graeco ponitur *logos,* quod rationem et sermonem significat, posset convenientius intelligi sapientia verbi, id est humanae rationis, quia illa quae sunt fidei, humanam rationem excedunt, secundum illud Eccli. III, 25: *plurima supra sensum hominis ostensa sunt tibi.*

43. Sed contra hoc videtur esse quod multi doctores Ecclesiae in doctrina fidei sapientia et rationibus humanis et ornatu verborum sunt usi.

Dicit enim Hieronymus in epistola ad magnum oratorem urbis Romae, quod omnes doctores fidei in ornatu philosophiae doctrinis atque scientiis suos referserunt libros, ut nescias quid in illis primum admirari debeas, eruditionem saeculi, an scientiam Scripturarum. Et Augustinus dicit in quarto *de Doctrina Christiana: sunt viri ecclesiastici qui divina eloquia non solum sapienter, sed etiam suaviter tractaverunt.*

Dicendum est ergo quod aliud est docere in sapientia verbi quocumque modo intelligatur, et aliud uti sapientia verbi in docendo. Ille in sapientia verbi docet qui sapientiam verbi accipit pro principali radice suae doctrinae, ita scilicet quod ea solum approbet, quae verbi sapientiam continent: reprobet autem ea quae sapientiam verbi non habent, et hoc fidei est corruptivum. Utitur autem sapientia verbi, qui suppositis verae fidei fundamentis, si qua vera in doctrinis philosophorum inveniat, in obsequium fidei assumit. Unde Augustinus dicit in secundo *de Doctrina Christiana,* quod *si qua philosophi dixerunt fidei nostrae accommoda, non solum formidanda non sunt, sed ab eis tamquam ab iniustis possessoribus in usum nostrum vindicanda.* Et in IV *de Doctrina Christiana* dicit: *cum posita sit in medio facultas eloquii, quae ad persuadendum seu prava seu recta valent pluribus, cur*

second, he explains it, at **lest the cross of Christ**.

41. He says, therefore: I have stated that Christ sent me to preach the Gospel, but not to preach it **in wisdom of speech**, i.e., the worldly wisdom which makes men verbose, inasmuch as it inclines them to employ many vain reasons: *the more words, the more vanity* (Eccl 6:11); *mere talk tends only to want* (Prov 14:23). Or by eloquent wisdom he means rhetoric, which teaches elegant speech by which men are sometimes drawn to assent to error and falsity: *by fair and flattering words they deceive the hearts of the simple-minded* (Rom 16:18); and under the figure of a harlot, which stands for heretical doctrine, it is said: *you will be saved from the adventures with her smooth words* (Prov 2:16).

42. But on the other hand it is said: *you will see not more the insolent people,* namely, in the Catholic Church, *the people of an obscure speech which you cannot comprehend* (Isa 33:19).

But because the Greek version has *logos,* which signifies reason and speech, it might be more fitting to interpret eloquent wisdom of human reason, because the things of faith transcend human reason: *matters too great for human understanding have been shown you* (Sir 3:25).

43. But the fact that many teachers in the Church have used human reason and human wisdom as well as elegant words would seem to be contrary to this.

For Jerome says in a letter to a great Roman orator, that all the teachers of the faith have crammed their books with an elegant portion of philosophical doctrines and sciences, so that one is at a loss whether to admire their worldly learning more or their knowledge of the Scriptures. And Augustine in the book *On Christian Doctrine* says: *there are churchmen who have treated of divine matters not only with wisdom but with elegance.*

The answer is that it is one thing to teach in eloquent wisdom, however you take it, and another to use it to teach eloquent wisdom in teaching. A person teaches in eloquent wisdom, when he takes the eloquent wisdom, as the main source of his doctrine, so that he admits only those things which contain eloquent wisdom and rejects the others which do not have eloquent wisdom: and this is destructive of the faith. But one uses eloquent wisdom, when he builds on the foundations of the true faith, so that if he finds any truths in the teachings of the philosophers, he employs them in the service of the faith. Hence Augustine says in the book *On Christian Doctrine* that *if philosophers have uttered things suited to our faith, they should not be feared but taken from them as from an unjust possessor for our use.* Again, in the same book he says: *since the faculty of eloquent speech which has great power to win a person over to what is*

non bonorum studio comparetur ut militet veritati, si eam mali in usum iniquitatis et erroris usurpant.

44. Deinde, cum dicit ***ut non evacuetur crux Christi***, probat quod dixerat, et

primo quidem ex parte materiae,

secundo ex parte ipsorum docentium, ibi ***videte enim vocationem vestram***, et cetera.

45. Circa primum tria facit.

Primo ostendit modum docendi qui est in sapientia verbi, non esse congruum fidei Christianae;

secundo probat quod supposuerat, ibi ***verbum enim crucis***;

tertio probationem manifestat, ibi ***quoniam Iudaei signa petunt***.

45. Circa primum considerandum est, quod etiam in philosophicis doctrinis non est idem modus conveniens cuilibet doctrinae. Unde sermones secundum materiam sunt accipiendi, ut dicitur in primo *Ethicorum*. Tunc autem maxime modus aliquis docendi est materiae incongruus, quando per talem modum destruitur id quod est principale in materia illa, puta si quis in rebus intellectualibus velit metaphoricis demonstrationibus uti, quae non transcendunt res imaginatas, ad quas non oportet intelligentem adduci, ut Boetius ostendit in libro *de Trinitate*.

Principale autem in doctrina fidei Christianae est salus per crucem Christi facta. Unde, cap. II, 2, dicit ***non iudicavi me scire aliquid inter vos, nisi Iesum Christum et hunc crucifixum***. Qui autem principaliter innititur in docendo sapientiam verbi, quantum in se est, evacuat crucem Christi. Ergo docere in sapientia verbi non est modus conveniens fidei Christianae. Hoc est ergo quod dicit ***ut non evacuetur crux Christi***, id est, ne si in sapientia verbi praedicare voluero, tollatur fides de virtute crucis Christi. Gal. V, 11: *ergo evacuatum est scandalum crucis*. Ps. CXXXVI, v. 7: *qui dicunt, exinanite usque ad fundamentum in ea*.

46. Deinde, cum dicit ***verbum crucis***, etc., probat quod per doctrinam, quae est in sapientia verbi, crux Christi evacuetur.

Et circa hoc duo facit

primo inducit probationem;

secundo assignat causam dictorum, ibi ***scriptum est enim***, et cetera.

47. Dicit ergo primo: ideo dixi quod si per sapientiam verbi doctrina fidei proponeretur, evacuaretur crux Christi, ***verbum enim crucis***, id est annuntiatio crucis Christi, ***stultitia est***, id est stultum aliquid videtur, ***pereuntibus quidem***, id est, infidelibus qui se secundum mundum existimant sapientes, eo quod praedicatio crucis Christi aliquid continet, quod secundum humanam sapientiam impossibile videtur, puta quod Deus

base or to what is right, why not use it to fight for the truth, if evil men misuse it for sin and error?

44. Then when he says, ***lest the cross of Christ should be made void***, he proves his statement.

First, on the part of the matter;

second, of those who teach, at ***for see your vocation*** (1 Cor 1:26).

45. In regard to the first he does three things.

First, he shows that the method of teaching by eloquent wisdom is not suited to the Christian faith;

second, he proves something he had presupposed, at ***for the word of the cross***;

third, he clarifies the proof, at ***for the Jews require signs***.

45. As to the first point it should be noted that even in philosophical doctrines the same method does not suit every doctrine; hence the forms of speech must fit the material, as it says in *Ethics* I. Now a particular method of teaching is unsuited to the subject matter, when that method destroys the chief element in the subject matter; for example, in purely intelligible matters to employ metaphorical proofs, which do not go beyond the imagination and leave the hearer stranded in images, as Boethius says in the book *On the Trinity*.

But the chief element in the doctrines of the Christian faith is salvation effected by the cross of Christ; hence he says: ***for I judged not myself to know anything among you, but Jesus Christ: and him crucified*** (1 Cor 2:2). On the other hand, a person who depends chiefly on eloquent wisdom when he teaches, to that extent makes the cross of Christ void. Therefore, to teach in eloquent wisdom is not suited to the Christian faith. Consequently, he says, ***lest the cross of Christ should be made void***, i.e., lest in trying to preach in eloquent wisdom, faith in the power of Christ's cross be made void: *then is the stumbling block of the cross made void* (Gal 5:11); *remember how they said: rase it, all the way to its foundation* (Ps 137:7).

46. Then when he says, ***for the word of the cross***, he proves that the cross of Christ is made void by the method of teaching which consists in wisdom of speech.

As to the first he does two things.

First he gives the proof:

second, he gives the reason for his statements, at ***for it is written***.

47. He says, therefore: the reason I have said that the cross of Christ is made void, if the teachings of the faith are presented in eloquent wisdom is that ***for the word of the cross***, i.e., the announcing of Christ's cross ***is foolishness***, i.e., it appears foolish, ***to them indeed who perish***, i.e., to unbelievers, who consider themselves wise according to the world, for the preaching of the cross of Christ contains something which to worldly wisdom seems impossible;

moriatur, quod Omnipotens violentorum manibus su-biiciatur. Continet etiam quaedam quae prudentiae huius mundi contraria videntur, puta quod aliquis non refugiat confusiones, cum possit, et aliqua huiusmodi. Et ideo Paulo huiusmodi annuntianti dixit Festus, ut legitur Act. XXVI, 24: *insanis, Paule, multae litterae ad insaniam te adducunt.* Et ipse Paulus dicit infra IV, 10: **Nos stulti propter Christum.**

Et ne credatur revera verbum crucis stultitiam con-tinere, subdit **his autem qui salvi fiunt, id est nobis,** scilicet Christi fidelibus qui ab eo salvamur, secundum illud Matth. c. I, 21: *ipse enim salvum faciet populum suum a peccatis eorum,* **virtus Dei est,** quia ipsi in cruce Christi mortem Dei cognoscunt, qua diabolum vicit et mundum. Apoc. V, 5: *ecce vicit leo de tribu Iuda.* Item virtutem quam in seipsis experiuntur, dum simul cum Christo vitiis et concupiscentiis moriuntur, secundum il-lud Gal. V, 24: *qui Christi sunt, carnem suam crucifixerunt cum vitiis et concupiscentiis.* Unde in Ps. CIX, 2 dicitur *virgam virtutis tuae emittit Dominus ex Sion.* Lc. VI, 19: *virtus de illo exibat et sanabat omnes.*

48. Deinde cum dicit **scriptum est enim,** ostendit praedictorum causam, et ponit

primo quare verbum crucis sit hominibus stultitia;

secundo ostendit quare ista stultitia sit virtus Dei his, qui salvantur, ibi **nam quia in Dei sapientia,** et cetera.

Circa primum duo facit.

Primo inducit auctoritatem praenuntiantem quod quaeritur;

secundo ostendit hoc esse impletum, ibi **ubi sapiens?**

49. Circa primum considerandum quod id quod est in se bonum, non potest alicui stultum videri, nisi propter defectum sapientiae. Haec est ergo causa quare verbum crucis quod est salutiferum credentibus, quibu-sdam videtur stultitia, quia sunt ipsi sapientia privati. Et hoc est quod dicit **scriptum est enim: perdam sapien-tiam sapientium, et prudentiam prudentium reproba-bo.**

Potest autem hoc sumi ex duobus locis. Nam in Abdia dicitur: *perdam sapientiam de Idumaea, et prudentiam de Monte Esau.* Expressius autem habetur Is. XXIX, v. 14: *peribit sapientia a sapientibus, et intellectus prudentium eius abscondetur.*

Differunt autem sapientia et prudentia. Nam sa-pientia est cognitio divinarum rerum; unde pertinet ad contemplationem, Iob XXVIII, v. 28: *timor Dei ipsa est sapientia*; prudentia vero proprie est cognitio re-rum humanarum, unde dicitur Prov. X, 23: *sapientia est viro prudentia,* quia scilicet scientia humanarum rerum

for example, that God should die or that the all-powerful should suffer at the hands of violent men. Furthermore, that a person not avoid shame when he can, and other things of this sort, are matters which seem contrary to the prudence of this world. Consequently, when Paul was preaching such things, Festus said: *Paul, you are beside yourself: much learning makes you mad* (Acts 26:24). And Paul himself says: **we are fools for Christ's sake** (1 Cor 4:10).

And lest someone believe that in fact, the word of the cross does contain foolishness, he adds, **but to them who are saved, that is, to us,** namely, Christ's faithful who are saved by him: *he will save his people from their sins* (Matt 1:21), **it is the power of God,** because they recognize in the cross of Christ God's power, by which he overcame the devil and the world: *the lion of the tribe of Judah, has conquered* (Rev 5:5), as well as the power they experience in themselves, when together with Christ they die to their vices and concupis-cences, as it says in Galatians: *those who belong to Christ Jesus have crucified the flesh with its passions and desires* (Gal 5:24). Hence it is said: *the Lord sends forth from Zion your mighty scepter* (Ps 110:10); *strength went out of him and healed all* (Luke 6:19).

48. Then when he says, **for it is written,** he states the reason for the above:

first, he tells why the word of the cross is foolishness to men;

second, why this foolishness is the power of God to them who are saved, at **for, seeing that in the wisdom of God.**

As to the first he does two things.

First, he adduces a text which foretells what is asked;

second, he shows that it has been fulfilled, at **where is the wise.**

49. It should be noted in regard to the first point that anything good in itself cannot appear foolish to anyone, un-less there is a lack of wisdom. This, therefore, is the reason why the word of the cross, which is salutary for believers, seems foolish to others, namely, because they are devoid of wisdom; and this is what he says: **for it is written: I will destroy the wisdom of the wise: and the prudence of the prudent I will reject.**

This can be taken from two places: for it is written in Obadiah: *will I not destroy the wisdom out of Edom, and prudence out of Mount Esau?* (Obad 1:8); but it is more ex-plicit in Isaiah: *the wisdom of their wise men shall perish, and the discernment of the prudent shall be hid* (Isa 29:14).

Now wisdom and prudence are different: for wisdom is knowledge of divine things; hence it pertains to con-templation; *the fear of the Lord is wisdom* (Job 28:28). Pru-dence, however, is, properly speaking, knowledge of hu-man things; hence it is said: *wisdom is prudence to a man* (Prov 10:23), namely, because knowledge of human affairs

prudentia dicitur. Unde et Philosophus VI *Ethicorum* dicit quod prudentia est recta ratio agibilium, et sic prudentia ad rationem pertinet.

50. Est autem considerandum quod homines quantumcumque mali non totaliter donis Dei privantur, nec in eis dona Dei reprobantur, sed in eis reprobatur et perditur quod ex eorum malitia procedit. Et ideo non dicit simpliciter *perdam sapientiam*, quia omnis sapientia a Domino Deo est, ut dicitur Is. XXIX, 14 ss., sed *perdam sapientiam sapientium*, id est, quam sapientes huius mundi adinvenerunt sibi contra veram sapientiam Dei, quia, ut dicitur Iac. III, 15, *non est ista sapientia desursum descendens, sed terrena, animalis, diabolica.* Similiter non dicit *reprobabo prudentiam*, nam veram prudentiam sapientia Dei docet, sed dicit *prudentiam prudentium*, id est, quam illi qui se prudentes aestimant in rebus mundanis prudentiam reputant ut scilicet bonis huius mundi inhaereant. Vel quia, ut dicitur Rom. VIII, v. 6, *prudentia carnis mors est.*

Et sic propter defectum sapientiae reputant impossibile Deum hominem fieri, mortem pati secundum humanam naturam; propter defectum autem prudentiae reputant inconveniens fuisse quod homo sustineret crucem, confusione contempta, ut dicitur Hebr. XII, 2.

51. Deinde cum dicit *ubi sapiens*, etc., ostendit esse impletum quod de reprobatione humanae sapientiae et prudentiae fuerat probatum. Et

primo ponit medium sub interrogatione;

secundo conclusionem infert, ibi *nonne stultam Deus fecit sapientiam huius mundi*, et cetera.

52. Dicit ergo primo *ubi sapiens?* Quasi diceret: non invenitur in congregatione fidelium qui salvatur. Per sapientem intelligit illum qui secretas naturae causas scrutatur. Is. XIX, 11: *quomodo dicetis Pharaoni: filius sapientium ego?* Et hoc refertur ad gentiles, qui huius mundi sapientiae studebant. *Ubi Scriba?* Id est peritus in lege, et hoc refertur ad Iudaeos; quasi diceret: non est in coetu fidelium. Io. VII, 48: *numquid ex principibus aliquis credidit in eum? Ubi inquisitor huius saeculi?* Qui scilicet per prudentiam exquirit quae sit convenientia vitae humanae in rebus huius saeculi; quasi dicat: non invenitur inter fideles, et hoc refertur ad utrosque, scilicet Iudaeos et gentiles. Baruch c. III, 23: *filii Agar, qui exquisierunt prudentiam quae de terra est.*

Videtur autem Apostolus hanc interrogationem sumere ab eo, quod dicitur Is. XXXIII, v. 18: *ubi est litteratus?* Pro quo ponit *sapientem. Ubi est verba legis ponderans?* Pro quo ponit *scribam. Ubi est doctor parvulorum?* Pro quo ponit *inquisitorem huius saeculi*, quia parvuli maxime solent instrui de his, quae pertinent ad disciplinam moralis vitae.

is called wisdom. Hence, the Philosopher also says in *Ethics* VI that prudence is the right understanding of things to be done; and so prudence pertains to reason.

50. Yet it should be noted that men, however evil, are not altogether deprived of God's gifts; neither are God's gifts in them destroyed. Consequently, he does not say absolutely, *I will destroy the wisdom*, because *all wisdom is from the Lord God* (Sir 1:1), but **I will destroy the wisdom of the wise**, i.e., which the wise of this world have invented for themselves against the true wisdom of God, because as it is said: *this is not wisdom, descending from above; but earthly, sensual, devilish* (Jas 3:15). Similarly, he does not say, *I will reject prudence*, for God's wisdom teaches true prudence, **but the prudence of the prudent**, i.e., which is regarded as prudent by those who esteem themselves prudent in worldly affairs, so that they cling to the goods of this world, or because *the prudence of the flesh is death* (Rom 8:6).

Consequently, because of their lack of wisdom they suppose that it is impossible for God to become man and suffer death in his human nature; but due to a lack of prudence they consider it unbecoming for a man to endure the cross, despising the shame (Heb 12:2).

51. Then when he says, **where is the wise man**, he shows that the prophecy about the destruction of human wisdom and prudence has been fulfilled.

First, he presents the proving reason in the form of a question;

second, he draws the conclusion, at **has not God made foolish the wisdom of this world**.

52. He says, therefore: **where is the wise?** As if to say: he is not found among the faithful who are saved. By the wise he understands one who searches for the secret causes of nature: *how will you say to Pharaoh: I am the son of the wise?* (Isa 19:11). This refers to the gentiles, who pursue the wisdom of this world. **Where is the scribe**, i.e., the skilled in the law: and this is referred to the Jews. As if to say: not among the believers. *Has any one of the rulers believed in him?* (John 7:48) **Where is the disputer of this world**, who through prudence examines what is suitable to human life in the affairs of this world. As if to say: he is not found among the believers. This refers to both Jews and gentiles: *the sons of Hagar, who seek for understanding on the earth* (Bar 3:23).

The Apostle seems to have based this question on Isaiah: *where is the learned?* (Isa 3:18), for which he substitutes **the wise**; *where is the one who ponders the words of the law?* for which he substitutes **scribe**. *Where is the teacher of little ones?* for which he substitutes **the disputer of this world**, because it is mainly little ones who are customarily instructed in matters pertaining to the moral life.

53. Deinde cum dicit *nonne stultam fecit*, etc., infert conclusionem sub interrogatione, quasi dicat: cum illi qui sapientes mundi reputantur a via salutis defecerint, *nonne Deus sapientiam huius mundi fecit stultam?* Id est, demonstravit esse stultam, dum illi qui hac sapientia pollebant tam stulti inventi sunt ut viam salutis non acciperent. Ier. X, 14 et LI, 17: *stultus factus est omnis homo a scientia sua.* Is. XLVII, 10: *sapientia tua et scientia tua haec decepit te.*

54. Potest autem et aliter intelligi quod dictum est, ac si diceret: *Perdam sapientiam sapientium et prudentiam prudentium reprobabo*, id est eligam eam in primis meis praedicatoribus, secundum illud Prov. XXX, 1: *visio quam locutus est vir cum quo est Deus*; et infra: *stultissimus sum virorum, et sapientia hominum non est mecum.* **Ubi sapiens?** Quasi dicat: inter praedicatores fidei non invenitur. Matth. XI, 25: *abscondisti haec a sapientibus et prudentibus, et revelasti ea parvulis.* **Nonne Deus stultam fecit**, id est demonstravit, **sapientiam huius mundi?** Faciendo quod ipsis impossibile reputabatur, scilicet dictum esse hominem mortuum resurgere, et alia huiusmodi.

55. Deinde cum dicit *nam quia in Dei sapientia*, etc., assignat rationem quare per praedicationis stultitiam salventur fideles. Et hoc est quod dictum est, quod *verbum crucis pereuntibus quidem stultitia est*, virtus vero salvationis credentibus; *nam placuit Deo per stultitiam praedicationis*, id est per praedicationem, quam humana sapientia stultam reputat, *salvos facere credentes*; et hoc ideo, quia mundus, id est mundani, non cognoverunt Deum per sapientiam ex rebus mundi acceptam, et hoc in Dei sapientia.

Divina enim sapientia faciens mundum, sua iudicia in rebus mundi instruit, secundum illud Eccli. I, 10: *effudit illam super omnia opera sua*; ita quod ipsae creaturae, per sapientiam Dei factae, se habent ad Dei sapientiam, cuius iudicia gerunt, sicut verba hominis ad sapientiam eius quam significant. Et sicut discipulus pervenit ad cognoscendum magistri sapientiam per verba quae ab ipso audit, ita homo poterat ad cognoscendum Dei sapientiam per creaturas ab ipso factas inspiciendo pervenire, secundum illud Rom. c. I, 20: *invisibilia Dei per ea quae facta sunt, intellecta conspiciuntur.*

Sed homo propter sui cordis vanitatem a rectitudine divinae cognitionis deviavit. Unde dicitur Io. I, 10: *in mundo erat, et mundus per ipsum factus est, et mundus eum non cognovit.* Et ideo Deus per quaedam alia ad sui cognitionem salutiferam fideles adduxit, quae in ipsis rationibus creaturarum non inveniuntur, propter quod a mundanis hominibus, qui solas humanarum rerum considerant rationes, reputantur stulta. Et huiusmodi sunt fidei documenta. Et est simile, sicut si aliquis magister considerans sensum suum ab auditoribus non

53. Then when he says, **has not God made foolish**, he draws the conclusion contained in the question. As if to say: since those who are considered the wise of this world have failed in the way of salvation, **has not God made foolish the wisdom of this world**, i.e., proved it foolish, inasmuch as those versed in this wisdom have been found so foolish that they have not discovered the road to salvation: *every man is stupid and without knowledge* (Jer 51:17); *your wisdom and your knowledge have led you astray* (Isa 47:10).

54. Another way to interpret this is as if he were saying: **I will destroy the wisdom of the wise: and the prudence of the prudent I will reject**, i.e., I will strike it first from my preachers: *surely I am too stupid to be a man* (Prov 30:1). *I have not the understanding of a man.* **Where is the wise?** As if to say: he is not found among the preachers: *you have hid these things from the wise and prudent, and revealed them to little ones* (Matt 11:25). **Has not God made**, i.e., proved, **foolish the wisdom of this world** by achieving what it considered impossible, namely, that a dead man rise, and other things of this sort?

55. Then when he says, **for, seeing that in the wisdom of God, the world, by wisdom, knew not God**, he states the reason why the faithful are saved by the foolishness of preaching. He had already stated that **the word of the cross, to them indeed who perish, is foolishness**, but **the power of God** to those believing of salvation; **it pleased God, by the foolishness of our preaching**, i.e., by the preaching which human wisdom considers foolish, **to save them who believe**; and this because the world, i.e., worldly men, knew not God by wisdom taken from things of the world; and this in the wisdom of God.

For divine wisdom, when making the world, left indications of itself in the things of the world, as it says in Sirach: *he poured wisdom out upon all his works* (Sir 1:10), so that the creatures made by God's wisdom are related to God's wisdom, whose signposts they are, as a man's words are related to his wisdom, which they signify. And just as a disciple reaches an understanding of the teacher's wisdom by the words he hears from him, so man can reach an understanding of God's wisdom by examining the creatures he made: *his invisible nature has been clearly perceived in the things that have been made* (Rom 1:20).

But on account of the vanity of his heart man wandered from the right path of divine knowledge; hence it is said: *he was in the world, and the world was made through him, yet the world knew him not* (John 1:10). Consequently, God brought believers to a saving knowledge of himself by other things, which are not found in the natures of creatures; on which account worldly men, who derive their notions solely from human things, considered them foolish: things such as the articles of faith. It is like a teacher who recognizes that his meaning was not understood from the words

accipi, per verba quae protulit, studet aliis verbis uti, per quae possit manifestare quae habet in corde.

56. Deinde cum dicit *quoniam et Iudaei*, etc., manifestat probationem praemissorum, et

primo quantum ad id, quod dixerat: *verbum crucis pereuntibus stultitia est.*

Secundo quantum ad id quod dixerat: *his qui salvi fiunt, virtus Dei est ipsis autem vocatis*, etc.

Circa primum duo facit.

Primo ponit pereuntium differens studium et intentionem;

secundo ex hoc rationem assignat eius quod dixerat, ibi *nos autem praedicamus Christum.*

57. Pereuntium autem, id est infidelium, quidam erant Iudaei, quidam gentiles. Dicit ergo: dictum est quod verbum crucis pereuntibus est stultitia, et hoc ideo quoniam *Iudaei signa petunt.* Erant enim Iudaei consueti divinitus instrui, secundum illud Deut. c. VIII, 5: *erudivit eum et docuit.* Quae quidem doctrina cum esset a Deo per multa mirabilia manifestata, secundum illud Ps. LXXVII, 12: *fecit mirabilia in terra Aegypti*, et ideo ab afferentibus quamcumque doctrinam signa quaerebant, secundum illud Matth. c. XII, 38: *Magister, volumus a te signum aliquod videre.* Et in Ps. LXXIII, 9 dicitur: *signa nostra non vidimus.*

Sed *Graeci sapientiam quaerunt*, utpote in studio sapientiae exercitati, sapientiam dico quae per rationes rerum mundanarum accipitur, de qua dicitur Ier. IX, 23: *non glorietur sapiens in sapientia.* Per Graecos autem omnes gentiles dat intelligere qui a Graecis mundanam sapientiam acceperunt. Quaerebant igitur sapientiam, volentes omnem doctrinam eis propositam secundum regulam humanae sapientiae iudicare.

58. Deinde concludit quare verbum crucis sit eis stultitia, dicens *nos autem praedicamus Christum crucifixum*, secundum illud infra cap. XI, 26: *Mortem Domini annuntiabitis donec veniat. Iudaeis scandalum*, quia scilicet desiderabant virtutem miracula facientem et videbant infirmitatem crucem patientem; nam, ut dicitur II Cor. ultimo: *crucifixus est ex infirmitate. gentibus autem stultitiam*, quia contra rationem humanae sapientiae videtur quod Deus moriatur et quod homo iustus et sapiens se voluntarie turpissimae morti exponat.

59. Deinde, cum dicit *ipsis autem vocatis*, manifestat quod dixerat: *his autem qui salvi fiunt, virtus Dei est.* Et

primo manifestat hoc;

secundo rationem assignat; ibi *quia quod stultum*, et cetera.

60. Dicit ergo primo: dictum est quod *praedicamus Christum crucifixum, Iudaeis scandalum et gentibus stultitiam*, sed praedicamus *Christum Dei virtutem et Dei sapientiam ipsis vocatis Iudaeis et Graecis*, id est

he employed, and then tried to use other words to indicate what he meant.

56. Then when he says, *for the Jews*, he explains his proof:

first in regard to the statement that *the word of the cross, to them indeed who perish, is foolishness*;

second, in regard to the statement that *to them who are saved, it is the power of God unto them who are called.*

As to the first he does two things.

First, he mentions the differing interests of those who perish;

second, from this he assigns the reason for what he had said, at *but we preach Christ crucified.*

57. Among those who perish, i.e., unbelievers, some were Jews and some gentiles. He says, therefore: I have said that the word of the cross is foolish to them who perish, and this because *the Jews require signs*, for the Jews were used to being instructed in a divine manner: *he led him about and taught him* (Deut 32:10), in the sense that God's teachings were accompanied by many marvels: *in the sight of their fathers he wrought marvels in the land of Egypt* (Ps 78:12). Consequently, they require signs from everyone asserting a doctrine: *Master, we would see a sign from you* (Matt 12:38); *we have not seen our signs* (Ps 74:9).

But *the Greeks seek after wisdom*, being interested in the pursuit of wisdom: the wisdom, I say, which is founded on the reasons of worldly things and of which it is said: *let not the wise man glory in his wisdom* (Jer 9:23). By the Greeks are understood all the gentiles who received worldly wisdom from the Greeks. When they sought wisdom, therefore, they wished to judge every doctrine proposed to them according to the rule of human wisdom.

58. Then he concludes why the word of the cross is foolishness to them, saying: *but we preach Christ crucified*, as below: *you shall show the death of the Lord, until he comes* (1 Cor 11:26), *unto the Jews indeed a stumbling block* because they desired strength working miracles and saw weakness suffering, for *he was crucified through weakness* (2 Cor 13:4). *Unto the gentiles foolishness*, because it seemed against the nature of human reason that God should die and that a just and wise man should voluntarily expose himself to a very shameful death.

59. Then when he says, *but unto them who are called*, he explains what he meant when he said, *to them who are saved it is the power of God.*

First, he manifests this;

second, he assigns the reason, at *for the foolishness of God.*

60. He says, therefore: it has been stated that *we preach Christ crucified: unto the Jews a stumbling block, and unto the gentiles foolishness*; but we preach *Christ, the power of God and the wisdom of God: unto them who are called,*

his qui ex Iudaeis et gentibus ad fidem Christi vocati sunt, qui in cruce Christi recognoscunt Dei virtutem, per quam et daemones superantur et peccata remittuntur et homines salvantur. Ps. XX, 14: *exaltare, Domine, in virtute tua.*

Et hoc dicit contra scandalum Iudaeorum, qui de infirmitate Christi scandalizabantur et recognoscunt in cruce Dei sapientiam, inquantum per crucem convenientissimo modo humanum genus liberat. Sap. IX, 19: *per sapientiam sanati sunt quicumque placuerunt tibi a principio.*

61. Dicitur autem Dei virtus et Dei sapientia per quamdam appropriationem. Virtus quidem, inquantum per eum Pater omnia operatur, Io. I, 3: *omnia per ipsum facta sunt,* sapientia vero, inquantum ipsum Verbum, quod est Filius, nihil est aliud quam sapientia genita vel concepta. Eccli. c. XXIV, 5: *ego ex ore Altissimi prodii primogenita ante omnem creaturam.*

Non autem sic est intelligendum, quod Deus Pater sit fortis et sapiens virtute aut sapientia genita, quia, ut Augustinus probat VI *de Trinitate,* sequeretur, quod Pater haberet esse a Filio, quia hoc est Deo esse, quod fortem et sapientem esse.

62. Deinde cum dicit **quia quod stultum est Dei,** assignat rationem eius quod dixerat, dicens quomodo id, quod est infirmum et stultum possit esse virtus vel sapientia Dei, quia **quod stultum est Dei sapientius est hominibus,** quasi dicat: iam aliquod divinum videtur esse stultum, non quia deficiat a sapientia, sed quia superexcedit sapientiam humanam. Homines enim quidam consueverunt stultum reputare quod eorum sensum excedit. Eccli. III, 25: *plurima super sensum hominis ostensa sunt tibi.* **Et quod infirmum est Dei, fortius est hominibus,** quia scilicet non dicitur aliquid infirmum in Deo per defectum virtutis, sed per excessum humanae virtutis, sicut etiam dicitur invisibilis, inquantum excedit sensum humanum. Sap. XII, 17: *virtutem ostendis tu qui non crederis esse in virtute consummatus.*

Quamvis hoc possit referri ad incarnationis mysterium: quia id quod reputatur stultum et infirmum in Deo ex parte naturae assumptae, transcendit omnem sapientiam et virtutem. Ex. XV, 11: *quis similis tui in fortibus, Domine?*

both Jews and Greeks, i.e., to those Jews and gentiles who were called to faith in Christ. They recognize the power of God in Christ's cross, by which devils are overcome, sins forgiven and men saved: *be exalted, O Lord, in your strength!* (Ps 21:13).

He says this against the Jews, who made a stumbling block of Christ's weakness. They also recognize in it the wisdom of God, inasmuch as he delivered the human race in a most becoming manner by the cross: *men were taught what pleases you, and were saved by wisdom* (Wis 9:13).

61. He is called the power of God and all the wisdom of God by appropriation: the power, because the Father does all things through him: *all things were made through him* (John 1:3); the wisdom, because the Word, which is the Son, is nothing less than begotten or conceived wisdom: *I came forth from the mouth of the Most High* (Sir 24:5).

But it is not to be understood as though God the Father is powerful and wise by begotten power of wisdom, for, as Augustine proves in *On the Trinity,* it would follow that the Father would have being from the Son, because for God to be wise and to be powerful are his very essence.

62. Then when he says, **for the foolishness of God,** he assigns the reason for what he had said and tells how something weak and foolish could be the power and wisdom of God, **for the foolishness of God is wiser than men.** As if to say: something divine seems to be foolish, not because it lacks wisdom but because it transcends human wisdom. For men are wont to regard as foolish anything beyond their understanding: *matters too great for human understanding have been shown you* (Sir 3:23). **And the weakness of God is stronger than men,** because something in God is not called weak on account of a lack of strength but because it exceeds human power, just as he is called invisible, inasmuch as he transcends human sight: *you show your strength when men doubt the completeness of your power* (Wis 12:17).

However, this could refer to the mystery of the incarnation, because that which is regarded as foolish and weak in God on the part of the nature he assumed transcends all wisdom and power: *who is like to you among the strong, O Lord?* (Ex 15:11)

Lecture 4

1:26Videte enim vocationem vestram, fratres, quia non multi sapientes secundum carnem, non multi potentes, non multi nobiles: [n. 63]

1:27sed quae stulta sunt mundi elegit Deus, ut confundat sapientes: et infirma mundi elegit Deus, ut confundat fortia: [n. 65]

1:28et ignobilia mundi, et contemptibilia elegit Deus, et ea quae non sunt, ut ea quae sunt destrueret: [n. 67]

1:29ut non glorietur omnis caro in conspectu ejus. [n. 68]

1:30Ex ipso autem vos estis in Christo Jesu, qui factus est nobis sapientia a Deo, et justitia, et sanctificatio, et redemptio: [n. 69]

1:31ut quemadmodum scriptum est: *qui gloriatur, in Domino glorietur.* [n. 72]

1:26Βλέπετε γὰρ τὴν κλῆσιν ὑμῶν, ἀδελφοί, ὅτι οὐ πολλοὶ σοφοὶ κατὰ σάρκα, οὐ πολλοὶ δυνατοί, οὐ πολλοὶ εὐγενεῖς·

1:27ἀλλὰ τὰ μωρὰ τοῦ κόσμου ἐξελέξατο ὁ θεὸς ἵνα καταισχύνῃ τοὺς σοφούς, καὶ τὰ ἀσθενῆ τοῦ κόσμου ἐξελέξατο ὁ θεὸς ἵνα καταισχύνῃ τὰ ἰσχυρά,

1:28καὶ τὰ ἀγενῆ τοῦ κόσμου καὶ τὰ ἐξουθενημένα ἐξελέξατο ὁ θεός, τὰ μὴ ὄντα, ἵνα τὰ ὄντα καταργήσῃ,

1:29ὅπως μὴ καυχήσηται πᾶσα σὰρξ ἐνώπιον τοῦ θεοῦ.

1:30ἐξ αὐτοῦ δὲ ὑμεῖς ἐστε ἐν Χριστῷ Ἰησοῦ, ὃς ἐγενήθη σοφία ἡμῖν ἀπὸ θεοῦ, δικαιοσύνη τε καὶ ἁγιασμὸς καὶ ἀπολύτρωσις,

1:31ἵνα καθὼς γέγραπται, Ὁ καυχώμενος ἐν κυρίῳ καυχάσθω.

1:26For see your vocation, brethren, that there are not many wise according to the flesh, not many mighty, not many noble. [n. 63]

1:27But the foolish things of the world, God has chosen, that he may confound the wise: and the weak things of the world, God has chosen, that he may confound the strong. [n. 65]

1:28And the base things of the world, and the things that are contemptible, God has chosen, and things that are not, that he might bring to naught things that are: [n. 67]

1:29That no flesh should glory in his sight. [n. 68]

1:30But of him are you in Christ Jesus, who of God is made unto us wisdom and justice and sanctification and redemption: [n. 69]

1:31That, as it is written: *he who glories may glory in the Lord.* [n. 72]

---

63. Supra ostendit Apostolus quod modus docendi, qui est in sapientia verbi, non convenit doctrinae Christianae, ratione materiae quae est ipsa crux Christi, hic ostendit quod praedictus docendi modus non convenit doctrinae Christianae, ratione doctorum, secundum illud Prov. XXVI, 7: *in derisum est in ore stulti parabola*; et Eccli. c. XX, 22: *ex ore fatui reprobabitur parabola.* Quia igitur primi doctores fidei non fuerunt sapientes sapientia carnali, non erat eis conveniens ut in sapientia verbi docerent.

Circa hoc ergo duo facit.

Primo ostendit quomodo primi doctores fidei non fuerunt sapientes sapientia carnali et in rebus humanis defectum patiebantur;

secundo ostendit quomodo talis defectus est in eis per Christum suppletus, ibi *ex ipso autem vos estis.*

Circa primum tria facit.

Primo excludit a fidei primis doctoribus excellentiam saecularem;

secundo astruit eorum subiectionem quantum ad saeculum, ibi *sed quae stulta sunt mundi*;

tertio rationem assignat, ibi *ut non glorietur.*

64. Dicit ergo primo: dictum est *quod stultum est Dei, sapientius est hominibus*, et hoc considerare

63. After showing that the method of teaching according to eloquent wisdom does not suit Christian doctrine by reason of its subject matter, the cross of Christ, the Apostle now shows that the same method is not suitable for Christian teaching by reason of the teachers: *a parable is unseemly in the mouth of fools* (Prov 26:7); *a parable out of a fool's mouth shall be rejected* (Sir 20:22). Therefore, because the first teachers of the faith were not wise in carnal wisdom, it was not suitable for them to teach according to eloquent wisdom.

In regard to this he does two things.

First, he shows how the first teachers of the faith were not versed in carnal wisdom and suffered from a defect in human affairs;

second, how this defect was made up for them by Christ, at *but of him are you.*

As to the first he does three things.

First, he excludes worldly excellence from the first teachers of the faith;

second, he adds to their subjection in regard to the world, at *but the foolish things of the world*;

third, he assigns the reason, at *that no flesh should glory.*

64. He says, therefore: it has been stated that *the foolishness of God is wiser than men* (1 Cor 1:25), and you can

potestis in ipsa vestra conversione. *Videte enim*, id est diligenter considerate, *vocationem vestram*, quomodo scilicet vocati estis: non enim per vos ipsos accessistis, sed ab eo vocati estis. Rom. VIII, v. 30: *quos praedestinavit, hos et vocavit.* I Petr. II, 9: *de tenebris vos vocavit in admirabile lumen suum.*

Inducit autem eos ut considerent modum suae vocationis, quantum ad eos per quos vocati sunt, sicut Is. LI, 2 dicitur: *attendite ad Abraham patrem vestrum, et ad Saram quae genuit vos.*

A quibus vocationis ministris primo excludit sapientiam, cum dicit *quia non multi*, eorum per quos vocati estis, *sapientes secundum carnem*, id est in carnali sapientia et terrena. Iac. III, 15: *non est ista sapientia desursum descendens, sed terrena, animalis, diabolica.* Baruch III, 23: *filii Agar exquisierunt sapientiam, quae de terra est.* Dicit *non multi*, quia aliqui pauci erant etiam in sapientia mundana instructi, sicut ipse, et ut Barnabas, vel Moyses in Veteri Testamento, de quo dicitur Act. VII, 22, quod *eruditus erat Moyses in omni sapientia Aegyptiorum.*

Secundo excludit saecularem potentiam, cum dicit *non multi potentes*, scilicet secundum saeculum. Unde et Io. VII, 48 dicitur: *numquid aliquis ex principibus credidit in eum?* Et Bar. III, 16 dicitur: *ubi sunt principes gentium? Exterminati sunt, et ad inferos descenderunt.*

Tertio excludit excellentiam generis, cum dicit *non multi nobiles*. Et aliqui inter eos nobiles fuerunt, sicut ipse Paulus, qui in civitate Romana se natum dicit, Act. XXII, 25, et Rom. ult. de quibusdam dicit *qui sunt nobiles in apostolis.*

65. Deinde, cum dicit *sed quae stulta sunt*, etc., ponit e converso eorum abiectionem quantum ad mundum, et primo defectum contrarium sapientiae, cum dicit *quae stulta sunt mundi*, id est, eos qui secundum mundum stulti videbantur, *elegit Deus* ad praedicationis officium, scilicet piscatores illiteratos, secundum illud Act. IV, 13: *comperto quod homines essent sine litteris et idiotae, admirabantur.* Is. XXXIII, 18: *ubi est litteratus, ubi verba legis ponderans?* Et hoc *ut confundat sapientes*, id est eos qui de sapientia mundi confidunt, dum ipsi non cognoverunt quae sunt simplicibus revelata. Matth. XI, 25: *abscondisti haec a sapientibus et prudentibus, et revelasti ea parvulis.* Is. XIX, 12: *ubi sunt nunc sapientes tui? Annuntient tibi.*

66. Secundo ponit defectum contrarium potentiae, dicens *et infirma mundi*, id est homines impotentes secundum mundum, puta rusticos et plebeios, *elegit Deus* ad praedicationis officium. In cuius figura dicitur III Reg. XX, 14: *ego tradens eos in manu tua per pedissequos principum provinciarum*; et Prov. IX, 3 dicitur quod sapientia *misit ancillas ut vocarent ad arcem.* In utrisque autem primorum praedicatorum infirmitas designatur.

consider this in your own life; *for see*, i.e., consider carefully, *your vocation, brethren*, i.e., how you were called: for you did not approach him by yourselves but you were called by him: *whom he predestined he also called* (Rom 8:30); *he called you out of the darkness into his marvelous light* (1 Pet 2:9).

But he urges them to ponder the manner of their calling by considering the ones by whom they were called, as Isaiah says: *look unto Abraham your father, and to Sarah that bore you* (Isa 51:2).

From these ministers of our calling he first of all excludes wisdom when he says: *that there are not many*, of those by whom you were called, *wise according to the flesh*, i.e., in carnal and earthly wisdom: *for this is not wisdom descending from above: but earthly, sensual, devilish* (Jas 3:15); *the children of Hagar also, who search after the wisdom that is of the earth* (Bar 3:23). He says, *not many*, because some few had been instructed even in worldly wisdom, as he himself and Barnabas, or in the Old Testament Moses, of whom Acts says that *he had been instructed in all the wisdom of the Egyptians* (Acts 7:22).

Second, he excludes worldly power when he says, *not many mighty*, namely, according to the world; hence it is said: *has any one of the rulers believed in him?* (John 7:48) *Where are the princes of nations? They are cut off and are gone down into hell* (Bar 3:16, 19).

Third, he excludes lofty birth when he says, *not many noble*. Yet some of them were noble, as Paul himself, who said that he had been born in a Roman city (Acts 22:25), and others referred to in Romans: *they are men of notes among the apostles* (Rom 16:7).

65. Then when he says, *but the foolish things*, he shows that they were lowly according to worldly standards. First, he shows that they lacked wisdom when he says, *the foolish things of the world*, i.e., those whom the world would consider foolish, *God has chosen* for the offices of preaching, namely, ignorant fisherman: *understanding that they were illiterate and ignorant men, they wondered* (Acts 4:13); *where is the learned? Where is he who ponders the words of the law?* (Isa 33:18). And this *that he may confound the wise*, i.e., those who trusted in the wisdom of the world, whereas they themselves did not know the truths revealed to the simple: *you had hidden these things from the wise and understanding and revealed them to babes* (Matt 11:25); *where then are your wise men? Let them tell you what the Lord of hosts has purposed* (Isa 19:12).

66. Second, he shows that they lacked power, saying, *and the weak things of the world*, i.e., men with no power in the world, such as peasants and plebeians, *God has chosen* for the office of preaching: *I will deliver them into your hand by the servants of the governors of the districts* (1 Kgs 20:13); and in Proverbs it says that *wisdom has sent out her maids to call from the highest places in the town* (Prov 9:3). Weakness is designated by both of these

Et hoc ideo *ut confundat fortia*, id est potentes huius mundi. Is. II, 17: *incurvabitur omnis sublimitas hominum, et humiliabitur altitudo virorum.*

67. Tertio ponit defectum contrarium nobilitati, in quo possunt tria considerari.

Primo quidem claritas generis, quam ipsum nomen nobilitatis designat. Et contra hoc dicit *et ignobilia mundi*, id est qui secundum mundum sunt ignobiles. Infra IV, 10: *vos nobiles, nos autem ignobiles.*

Secundo, circa nobilitatem considerantur honor et reverentia quae talibus exhibentur, et contra hoc dicit *et contemptibilia*, id est homines contemptibiles in hoc mundo *elegit Deus* ad praedicationis officium, secundum illud Ps. LXXVIII, 4: *facti sumus opprobrium vicinis nostris, et his qui in circuitu nostro sunt.*

Tertio, in nobilitate consideratur magna opinio quam homines de eis habent. Et contra hoc dicit *et ea quae non sunt*, id est quae non videntur esse in saeculo, elegit Deus ad praedicationis officium. Iob XXX, 2: *quorum virtus manuum erat mihi pro nihilo, et vita ipsa putabantur indigni.* Et hoc ideo *ut destrueret ea quae sunt*, id est eos qui in hoc mundo aliquid esse videntur. Is. XXIII, v. 9: *Dominus exercituum cogitavit hoc, ut detraheret superbiam omnis gloriae, et ad ignominiam deduceret universos inclytos terrae.*

68. Deinde assignat causam dictorum dicens: ideo non elegit in saeculo excellentes sed abiectos, *ut non glorietur omnis caro*, etc., id est ut nullus pro quacumque carnis excellentia glorietur per comparationem ad Dominum. Ier. IX, 23: *non glorietur sapiens in sapientia sua, et non glorietur fortis in fortitudine sua et non glorietur dives in divitiis suis.*

Ex hoc enim quod Deus mundum suae fidei subiecit, non per sublimes in mundo, sive in saeculo, sed per abiectos, non potest gloriari homo quod per aliquam carnalem excellentiam salvatus sit mundus. Videretur autem non esse a Deo excellentia mundana, si Deus ea non uteretur ad suum obsequium. Et ideo in principio quidem paucos, postremo vero plures saeculariter excellentes Deus elegit ad praedicationis officium. Unde in Glossa dicitur, quod *nisi fideliter praecederet piscator, non humiliter sequeretur orator.* Et etiam ad gloriam Dei pertinet, dum per abiectos sublimes in saeculo ad se trahit.

69. Deinde cum dicit *ex ipso autem vos estis*, ne praedicatores fidei tamquam non excellentes, sed abiecti in saeculo contemnerentur, ostendit quomodo Deus praedictum defectum in eis supplet. Et circa hoc tria facit.

70. Primo ostendit cui sit attribuenda salus mundi, quae praedicatorum ministerio facta est, dicens: dictum est quod vocati estis non per excellentes sed per

shortcomings in the first preachers; and this *that he may confound the strong*, i.e., the powerful of this world: *the haughtiness of man shall be humbled, and the pride of men shall be brought low* (Isa 2:17).

67. Third, he mentions a defect of nobility, about which three things can be considered.

First, a certain splendor of rank, which is implied in the word nobility. And against this he says, *and the base things of the world*, i.e., the things that are ignoble according to the world: *you are honorable, but we without honor* (1 Cor 4:10).

Second, about the nobility he considers the honor and reverence which is due to such people, and opposed to these he says, *and the things that are contemptible*, i.e., men looked down upon by the world, *God has chosen* for the office of preaching: *we have become a taunt to our neighbors, mocked and derided by those round about us* (Ps 79:4).

Third, the grand opinion men have of the nobility. Opposed to this he says, *and things that are not*, i.e., men who seem to be nothing in the world: *the strength of whose hands was to me as nothing, and they were thought unworthy of life itself* (Job 30:2), has God chosen for the office of preaching. This he did *that he might bring to naught things that are*, i.e., those who seem to be something in this world: *the Lord of hosts had purposed it, to defile the pride of all glory, to dishonor all the honored of the earth* (Isa 23:9).

68. Then he reveals the cause of all this, saying: he has not chosen the great but the lowly, *that no flesh should glory in his sight*, i.e., that no one may glory in his own worldly greatness as compared with the Lord: *let not the wise man glory in the wisdom, let not the mighty man glory in his might, and let not the rich man glory in his riches* (Jer 9:23).

For inasmuch as God did not subject the world to his faith by employing the great ones of the world but the lowly ones, man cannot boast that the world was saved by employing worldly greatness. However, since it might appear that worldly greatness did not originate from God, if he never employed it for his purposes, God employed a few and later a great number of the worldly great for the office of preaching. Hence a Gloss says that *if the faithful fisherman had not come first, the humble orator could not have come later.* Furthermore, it pertains to God's glory to draw the great of the world by means of the lowly.

69. Then when he says, *but of him are you*, he prevents the preachers of the faith, since they were not the worldly great but the lowly, from being regarded as contemptible, by showing how God supplied for their defects. In regard to this he does three things.

70. First, he indicates who deserves the honor for the world's salvation, which was procured by the ministry of preaching. He says: you have been called not by the great of

abiectos in saeculo, ex quo patet quod vestra conversio non est homini attribuenda sed Deo. Et hoc est quod dicit *ex ipso autem*, id est ex virtute Dei, vocati *estis in Christo Iesu*, id est ei iuncti et incorporati per gratiam. Eph. II, v. 10: *ipsius enim factura sumus, creati in Christo Iesu in operibus bonis.*

71. Deinde ostendit quomodo Deus praedictos defectus in praedicatoribus suis supplet per Christum. Et primo quantum ad defectum sapientiae, cum dicit *qui*, scilicet Christus, *factus est nobis* praedicantibus fidem, et, per nos, omnibus fidelibus, *sapientia*, quia ei inhaerendo, qui est Dei sapientia, et participando ipsum per gratiam, sapientes facti sumus. Et hoc a Deo, qui nobis Christum dedit et nos ad ipsum traxit, secundum illud Io. VI, 44: *nemo potest venire ad me, nisi Pater, qui me misit, traxerit eum.* Deut. c. IV, 6: *haec est vestra sapientia et intellectus coram populis.*

Secundo quantum ad defectum potentiae, dicit *et iustitia*, quae propter sui fortitudinem thoraci comparatur Sap. V, 19: *induet pro thorace iustitiam.* Dicitur autem Christus nobis factus iustitia, inquantum per eius fidem iustificamur, secundum illud Rom. III, v. 22: *iustitia autem Dei per fidem Christi Iesu.*

Tertio quantum ad defectum nobilitatis subdit *et sanctificatio, et redemptio*. Sanctificamur enim per Christum, inquantum per eum Deo coniungimur, in quo consistit vera nobilitas, secundum illud I Reg. II, 30: *1uicumque honorificaverit me, glorificabo eum, qui autem contemnunt me, erunt ignobiles.* Unde dicitur Hebr. ult.: *Iesus ut sanctificaret per suum sanguinem populum, extra portam passus est.* Factus est autem nobis *redemptio*, inquantum per ipsum redempti sumus de servitute peccati, in quo vere ignobilitas consistit. Unde in Ps. XXX, 6 dicitur: *redemisti me, Deus veritatis.*

72. Tertio assignat dictorum causam, cum dicit *ut quemadmodum scriptum est*: Ier. IX, 23 s., *qui autem gloriatur, in Domino glorietur*; ubi nostra littera habet: *in hoc glorietur scire et nosse me.*

Dicit enim: si salus hominis non provenit ex aliqua excellentia humana, sed ex sola virtute divina, non debetur homini gloria, sed Deo, secundum illud Ps. CXIII, 1: *non nobis, Domine, non nobis, sed nomini tuo da gloriam.* Eccli. ult.: *danti mihi sapientiam, dabo gloriam.*

this world but by the lowly; consequently, your conversion should not be attributed to men but to God. In other words, *but of him are you*, i.e., by God's power you are called *in Christ Jesus*, i.e., joined to him by grace: *we are his workmanship, created in Christ Jesus for good works* (Eph 2:10).

71. Then he shows how God supplies for the deficiencies of his preachers by means of Christ: first, as to their lack of wisdom when he says, *who*, namely, Christ, *is made unto us*, who preach the faith, and by us unto all the faithful, *wisdom*, because by adhering to him who is the wisdom of God and by partaking of him through grace, we have been made wise; and this is our God, who gave Christ to us and few us to him, as it says in John: *no man can come to me, except the Father who has sent me draw him* (John 6:44); *this is your wisdom and understanding in the sight of nations* (Deut 4:6).

Second, as to their lack of power he says, *and justice*, which is called a breastplate because of its strength: *he will put on righteousness as a breastplate* (Wis 5:19). Now Christ is said to have been made righteousness for us, inasmuch as we are made righteous by faith, as it says in Romans: *the righteousness of God through faith in Jesus Christ for all who believe* (Rom 3:22).

Third, as to their lack of nobility he says, *and sanctification and redemption*, for we are sanctified by Christ, inasmuch as it is through him that we are joined to God, in whom true nobility is found: *those who honor me I will honor, and those who despise me shall be lightly esteemed* (1 Sam 2:30). Hence it is said: *Jesus suffered outside the gate in order to sanctify the people through his own blood* (Heb 13:12). But he has been made our *redemption*, inasmuch as we have been redeemed by him from the slavery of sin, in which true baseness consists; hence it is said: *you have redeemed me O Lord, faithful God* (Ps 31:6).

72. Third, he assigns the cause of the above when he says, *that, as it is written: he who glories may glory in the Lord*, where our version has: *in this let him glory, that he understands and knows me* (Jer 9:24).

For he is saying: if man's salvation does not spring from any human greatness but solely from God's power, the glory belongs not to man but to God, as it says in a Psalm: *not to us, O Lord, not to us; but to your name give glory* (Ps 115:1); *to him who gives me wisdom will I give glory* (Sir 51:23).

CHAPTER 2

Lecture 1

2:1Et ego, cum venissem ad vos, fratres, veni non in sublimitate sermonis, aut sapientiae, annuntians vobis testimonium Christi. [n. 73.]

2:2Non enim judicavi me scire aliquid inter vos, nisi Jesum Christum, et hunc crucifixum. [n. 75]

2:3Et ego in infirmitate, et timore, et tremore multo fui apud vos: [n. 76]

2:4et sermo meus, et praedicatio mea non in persuasibilibus humanae sapientiae verbis, sed in ostensione Spiritus et virtutis: [n. 77]

2:5ut fides vestra non sit in sapientia hominum, sed in virtute Dei. [n. 79]

2:6Sapientiam autem loquimur inter perfectos: sapientiam vero non hujus saeculi, neque principum hujus saeculi, qui destruuntur: [n. 80]

2:7sed loquimur Dei sapientiam in mysterio, quae abscondita est, quam praedestinavit Deus ante saecula in gloriam nostram, [n. 85]

2:1Κἀγὼ ἐλθὼν πρὸς ὑμᾶς, ἀδελφοί, ἦλθον οὐ καθ' ὑπεροχὴν λόγου ἢ σοφίας καταγγέλλων ὑμῖν τὸ μυστήριον τοῦ θεοῦ.

2:2οὐ γὰρ ἔκρινά τι εἰδέναι ἐν ὑμῖν εἰ μὴ Ἰησοῦν Χριστὸν καὶ τοῦτον ἐσταυρωμένον.

2:3κἀγὼ ἐν ἀσθενείᾳ καὶ ἐν φόβῳ καὶ ἐν τρόμῳ πολλῷ ἐγενόμην πρὸς ὑμᾶς,

2:4καὶ ὁ λόγος μου καὶ τὸ κήρυγμά μου οὐκ ἐν πειθοῖ[ς] σοφίας [λόγοις] ἀλλ' ἐν ἀποδείξει πνεύματος καὶ δυνάμεως,

2:5ἵνα ἡ πίστις ὑμῶν μὴ ᾖ ἐν σοφίᾳ ἀνθρώπων ἀλλ' ἐν δυνάμει θεοῦ.

2:6Σοφίαν δὲ λαλοῦμεν ἐν τοῖς τελείοις, σοφίαν δὲ οὐ τοῦ αἰῶνος τούτου οὐδὲ τῶν ἀρχόντων τοῦ αἰῶνος τούτου τῶν καταργουμένων:

2:7ἀλλὰ λαλοῦμεν θεοῦ σοφίαν ἐν μυστηρίῳ, τὴν ἀποκεκρυμμένην, ἣν προώρισεν ὁ θεὸς πρὸ τῶν αἰώνων εἰς δόξαν ἡμῶν:

2:1And I, brethren, when I came to you, came not in loftiness of speech or of wisdom, declaring unto you the testimony of Christ. [n. 73.]

2:2For I judged not myself to know anything among you, but Jesus Christ: and him crucified. [n. 75]

2:3And I was with you in weakness and in fear and in much trembling. [n. 76]

2:4And my speech and my preaching was not in the persuasive words of human wisdom. but in showing of the Spirit and power: [n. 77]

2:5That your faith might not stand on the wisdom of men, but on the power of God. [n. 79]

2:6Yet we speak wisdom among the perfect: although not the wisdom of this world, neither of the princes of this world that come to naught. [n. 80]

2:7But we speak the wisdom of God in a mystery, a wisdom which is hidden, which God ordained before the world, unto our glory: [n. 85]

---

73. Postquam Apostolus ostendit quis sit conveniens modus doctrinae Christianae, hic ostendit se illum modum observasse.

Et circa hoc tria facit:

primo ostendit se non fuisse usum apud eos aliqua excellentia saeculari;

secundo ostendit apud quos excellentia spirituali utatur, ibi *sapientiam autem loquimur inter perfectos*, etc.,

tertio rationem assignat, ibi *quae etiam loquimur*, et cetera.

Circa primum tria facit.

Primo dicit quod non ostendit apud eos excellentiam saecularis sapientiae;

secundo quod non praetendit excellentiam potentiae saecularis, ibi *et ego in infirmitate*;

tertio non praetendit excellentiam eloquentiae, ibi *et sermo meus*.

73. After indicating the suitable way to present Christian doctrine, the Apostle now shows that he observed it.

In regard to this he does three things:

first, he shows that he did not make use of worldly greatness with them;

second, he shows in which cases he employs spiritual excellence, at *yet we speak wisdom among the perfect*;

third, he indicates the reason, at *which things also we speak* (1 Cor 2:13).

As to the first he does three things.

First, he states that he did not manifest the loftiness of worldly wisdom among them;

second, that he does not pretend to have the excellence of worldly power, at *and I was with you in weakness*;

third, that he does not pretend to lofty eloquence, at *and my speech*.

Circa primum duo facit.

Primo proponit quod intendit;

secundo rationem assignat, ibi *non enim iudicavi.*

74. Dicit ergo primo: quia dictum est quod Christus misit me evangelizare non in sapientia verbi, et quod non sunt multi sapientes, ***et ego, fratres***, quamvis sapientiam saecularem habeam, secundum illud II Cor. XI, 6: *et si imperitus sermone, sed non scientia*, **cum venissem ad vos**, convertendos ad Christum, ut habetur Act. XVIII, 1, *veni annuntians vobis testimonium Christi*, secundum illud Act. IV, 33: *virtute magna reddebant apostoli testimonium resurrectionis Domini nostri Iesu Christi*, et hoc ***non in sublimitate sermonis aut sapientiae.***

Attenditur autem sublimitas sapientiae in consideratione aliquorum sublimium et elevatorum supra rationem et sensum hominum. Eccli. XXIV, 7: *ego in altissimis habitavi.* Sublimitas autem sermonis potest referri vel ad verba significantia sapientiae conceptiones, secundum illud Eccle. ult.: *verba sapientium quasi stimuli, et quasi clavi in altum defixi*, vel ad modum ratiocinandi per aliquas subtiles vias. Nam in Graeco habetur logos, quod et verbum et rationem significat, ut Hieronymus dicit. Hoc autem dicit Apostolus, quia fidem Christi per huiusmodi sublimitates sermonis aut sapientiae confirmare nolebat. I Reg. II, 3: *nolite multiplicare sublimia.*

75. Deinde huius rationem assignat, dicens ***non enim iudicavi me scire aliquid, nisi Christum Iesum***. Non enim ad hoc opus erat ut sapientiam ostentaret sed ut demonstraret virtutem, secundum illud II Cor. IV, 5: *non enim praedicamus nosmetipsos, sed Iesum Christum.* Et ideo solum utebatur his quae ad demonstrandam virtutem Christi pertinebant, existimans se ac si nihil sciret quam Iesum Christum. Ier. IX, 24: *in hoc glorietur qui gloriatur, scire et nosse me.*

In Christo autem Iesu, ut dicitur Col. II, 3, sunt *omnes thesauri sapientiae et scientiae* Dei *absconditi*, et quantum ad plenitudinem deitatis et quantum ad plenitudinem sapientiae et gratiae, et etiam quantum ad profundas incarnationis rationes, quae tamen Apostolus eis non annuntiavit sed solum ea quae erant manifestiora et inferiora in Christo Iesu. Et ideo subdit **et hunc crucifixum**, quasi dicat: sic vobis me exhibui ac si nihil aliud scirem quam crucem Christi. Unde Gal. ult. dicit: *mihi absit gloriari, nisi in cruce Domini nostri Iesu Christi.*

Quia igitur per sapientiam verbi evacuatur crux Christi, ut dictum est ideo ipse Apostolus non venerat in sublimitate sermonis aut sapientiae.

76. Deinde cum dicit **et ego in infirmitate**, etc., ostendit quod non praetenderit apud eos potentiam, sed potius contrarium et foris et intus.

As to the first he does two things.

First, he states his purpose;

second, the reason, at **for I judged not**.

74. He says, therefore: I have said that Christ sent me to preach the Gospel not in eloquent wisdom and that there are not many wise, ***and I, brethren***, although I possess worldly wisdom: *even if I am unskilled in speaking, I am not in knowledge* (2 Cor 11:6), **when I came to you** to convert you to Christ: *teaching the word of God among them* (Acts 18:11); *with great power the apostles gave their testimony to the resurrection of the Lord Jesus* (Acts 4:33); and this ***not in loftiness of speech or of wisdom***.

Now lofty wisdom consists in considering sublime and exalted matters that transcend man's reason and understanding: *I dwelt in the highest places* (Sir 24:7). But lofty words can refer to the words signifying the thoughts of wisdom: *the words of the wise are as goads and as nails deeply fastened in* (Eccl 12:11) or to its method of reasoning by subtle paths; for the Greek version has *logos*, which signifies both speech and reason, as Jerome says. The Apostle says this, because he did not wish to support the teaching of Christ with the lofty speech of wisdom: *talk no more so very proudly* (1 Sam 2:3).

75. Then he discloses the reason for this, saying: ***for I judged not myself to know anything among you, but Jesus Christ***. For this work there was no need to make a display of wisdom but to show his power: *we preach not ourselves but Jesus Christ* (2 Cor 4:5). Consequently, he employed only those things which proved Christ's power, and regarded himself as knowing nothing but Jesus Christ: *let him who glories glory in this, that he understands and knows me* (Jer 9:24).

But in Christ Jesus, as it says in Colossians, *are hid all the treasures of wisdom and knowledge* (Col 2:3), both by reason of the fullness of his godhead and the fullness of his wisdom and grace and by reason of knowing the profound reasons of the incarnation. Yet the Apostle did not declare these things to them but only those that were more obvious and lowly in Christ Jesus; therefore, he adds: **and him crucified**. As if to say: I have presented myself to you, as though I know nothing but the cross of Christ; hence he says in Galatians: *far be it from me to glory except in the cross of our Lord Jesus Christ* (Gal 6:14).

Therefore, since the cross of Christ is made void by the wisdom of speech, as has been stated, the Apostle came not in loftiness of speech or of wisdom.

76. Then when he says, ***and I was with you in weakness***, he shows that he did not pretend to have any power when he was among them, but on the contrary, weakness within and without.

Unde quantum ad id quod foris est dicit *et ego fui apud vos in infirmitate*, id est tribulationes apud vos patiens. Gal. IV, 11: *scitis quia per infirmitatem carnis evangelizavi vobis iampridem.* Ps. XV, 4: *multiplicatae sunt infirmitates eorum.*

Quantum vero ad id quod intus est, dicit *et timore*, scilicet de malis imminentibus, *et tremore*, inquantum scilicet timor interior redundat ad corpus. II Cor. VII, 5: *foris pugnae, intus timores.*

77. Deinde cum dicit *et sermo meus*, ostendit quod non praetenderit apud eos excellentiam eloquentiae: et circa hoc tria facit.

Primo excludit indebitum modum praedicandi, dicens *et sermo meus*, quo scilicet privatim et singulariter aliquos instruebam, Eph. IV, v. 29: *omnis sermo malus ex ore vestro non procedat, sed si quis bonus est ad aedificationem fidei*; *et praedicatio mea*, qua scilicet publice docebam, *non fuit in verbis persuasibilibus humanae sapientiae*, id est per rhetoricam, quae componit ad persuadendum. Ut scilicet supra dixit quod non fuit intentionis quod sua praedicatio niteretur philosophicis rationibus, ita nunc dicit non fuisse suae intentionis niti rhetoricis persuasionibus. Is. c. XXXIII, 19: *populum impudentem non videbis, populum alti sermonis, ita ut non possis intelligere disertitudinem linguae eius, in quo nulla est sapientia.*

78. Secundo ostendit debitum modum quo usus fuit in praedicando, dicens: sermo meus fuit *in ostensione Spiritus et virtutis*, quod quidem potest intelligi dupliciter. Uno modo quantum ad hoc quod credentibus praedicationi eius dabatur Spiritus Sanctus, secundum illud Act. X, 44: *adhuc loquente Petro verba haec, cecidit Spiritus Sanctus super omnes qui audiebant verbum.* Similiter etiam suam praedicationem confirmabat, faciendo virtutes, id est miracula, secundum illud Marc. c. ultimo: *sermonem confirmante sequentibus signis.* Unde Gal. III, 5: *qui tribuit vobis Spiritum, et operatur in vobis.*

Alio modo potest intelligi quantum ad hoc quod ipse per Spiritum loquebatur, quod sublimitas et affluentia doctrinae ostendit. II Reg. c. XXIII, 2: *Spiritus Domini locutus est per me.* Et II Cor. IV, 13: *habentes eumdem Spiritum fidei credimus, propter quod et loquimur.* Confirmat etiam suam praedicationem, ostendendo in sua conversatione multa opera virtuosa. I Thess. II, 10: *vos enim testes estis, et Deus, quam sancte et iuste sine querela vobis qui credidistis, affuimus.*

79. Tertio assignat rationem dictorum, dicens *ut fides vestra non sit in sapientia hominum*, id est non innitatur sapientiae humanae, quae plerumque decipit homines, secundum illud Is. XLVII, 10: *sapientia tua et scientia tua haec decepit te.* **Sed in virtute Dei**, ut scilicet virtuti divinae fides innitatur, et sic non possit deficere. Rom. I, 16: *non erubesco Evangelium, virtus enim Dei est in salutem omni credenti.*

Hence in regard to what is without he says, *and I was with you in weakness*, i.e., I suffered tribulations among you: *you know how through infirmity of the flesh I preached the Gospel to you heretofore* (Gal 4:13); *those who choose another god multiply their sorrows* (Ps 16:4).

As to what is within he says, *and in fear*, namely, of threatening evils, *and in much trembling*, namely, inasmuch as inward fear flows over to the body: *combats without, fears within* (2 Cor 7:5).

77. Then when he says, *and my speech*, he shows that he made no pretence at loftiness of speech among them. In regard to this he does three things.

First, he disavows any unbecoming method of preaching when he says, *and my speech*, whenever I instructed anyone separately and in private: *let no evil talk come out of your mouths, but only such as is good for edifying* (Eph 4:29), *and my preaching*, whenever I spoke in public, *was not in the persuasive words of human wisdom*, i.e., rhetoric, which forms phrases to persuade. Hence, just as he had said earlier that it was not his intention to make his preaching rest on philosophical reasoning, so now he says that it was not his intention to make it rest on persuasions of rhetoric: *you will see no more the insolent people, the people of an obscure speech which you cannot comprehend* (Isa 33:19).

78. Second, he discloses the correct method, which he employed in preaching, when he says: but my speech was *in showing of the Spirit and power*. This can be interpreted in two ways: in one way that the Holy Spirit was given to those who believed his preaching in the sense of Acts: *while Peter was yet speaking these words, the Holy Spirit fell on all of them who heard the word* (Acts 10:44). Similarly, he also confirmed his preaching by showing power, i.e., by working miracles: *confirming the word with signs that followed* (Mark 16:20); *he gives to you the Spirit, and works miracles among you* (Gal 3:5).

In another way it can be taken to mean that the Spirit spoke through him: *the Spirit of the Lord speaks by me* (2 Sam 23:2); *since we have the same Spirit of faith, we too believe* (2 Cor 4:13). He also confirms his preaching by showing forth many powerful works in his manner of life: *you are witnesses, and God also, how holy and righteous and blameless was our behavior to you believers* (1 Thess 2:10).

79. Third, he assigns the reason for this when he says, *that your faith might not stand on the wisdom of men*, i.e., not rest on human wisdom which frequently deceives men: *your wisdom and your knowledge led you astray* (Isa 47:10), *but on the power of God*, i.e., that faith might rest on divine power and so not fall: *I am not ashamed of the Gospel: it is the power of God for salvation to everyone who has faith* (Rom 1:16).

80. Deinde cum dicit *sapientiam loquimur*, etc., ostendit apud quos excellentia spiritualis sapientiae utatur. Et

primo proponit quod intendit;

secundo manifestat propositum, ibi *sapientiam vero*.

81. Dicit ergo: apud vos solum Christum crucifixum praedicavi, *sapientiam autem*, id est profundam doctrinam, *loquimur inter perfectos*.

Dicuntur autem aliqui perfecti dupliciter: uno modo, secundum intellectum; alio modo secundum voluntatem. Haec enim inter potentias animae sunt propria hominis, et ideo secundum eas oportet hominis perfectionem considerari. Dicuntur autem perfecti intellectu illi, quorum mens elevata est super omnia carnalia et sensibilia, qui spiritualia et intelligibilia capere possunt, de quibus dicitur Hebr. c. V, 14: *perfectorum est solidus cibus, eorum qui per consuetudinem exercitatos habent sensus ad discretionem mali et boni.* Perfecti autem secundum voluntatem sunt, quorum voluntas super omnia temporalia elevata soli Deo inhaeret et eius praeceptis. Unde Matth. V, 48, praepositis dilectionis mandatis, subditur: *estote perfecti sicut et Pater vester caelestis perfectus est.*

Quia igitur doctrina fidei ad hoc ordinatur, ut fides per dilectionem operetur, ut habetur Gal. V, 6, necesse est eum qui in doctrina fidei instruitur, non solum secundum intellectum bene disponi ad capiendum et credendum sed etiam secundum voluntatem et affectum bene disponi ad diligendum et operandum.

82. Deinde cum dicit *sapientiam vero*, etc., exponit qualis sit sapientia de qua mentionem fecit. Et

primo ponit expositionem;

secundo rationem expositionis confirmat, ibi *quam nemo principum*, et cetera.

Circa primum duo facit.

Primo exponit qualis sit ista sapientia per comparationem ad infideles;

secundo, per comparationem ad fideles, ibi *sed loquimur Dei sapientiam*, et cetera.

83. Dicit ergo primo: dictum est quod sapientiam loquimur inter perfectos. *Sapientiam* vero dico, *non huius saeculi*, id est de rebus saecularibus, vel quae est per rationes humanas; *neque* eam *principum huius saeculi*.

84. Et sic separat eam a sapientia mundana, et quantum ad modum et materiam inquirendi, et quantum ad auctores, qui sunt principes huius saeculi; quod potest intelligi de triplici genere principum, secundum triplicem sapientiam humanam.

Primo possunt dici principes huius saeculi reges et potentes saeculares, secundum illud Ps. II, 2: *principes convenerunt in unum adversus Dominum et adversus Christum eius.* A quibus principibus venit sapientia humanarum legum, per quas res huius mundi in vita

80. Then when he says, *we speak wisdom*, he shows with whom he uses the loftiness of spiritual wisdom:

first, he states what he intends;

second, he clarifies it, at *although not the wisdom*.

81. He says, therefore: among you I have only preached Christ crucified, *yet we speak wisdom*, i.e., profound doctrine, *among the perfect*.

Now men are said to be perfect in two ways: first, in regard to the intellect; second, in regard to will. For among all the powers of the soul these are peculiar to man. Consequently, man's perfection must be reckoned in terms of these powers. But the perfect in intellect are those whose mind has been raised above all carnal and sense-perceptible things and can grasp spiritual and intelligible things. Of such it is said: *solid food is for the perfect, for those who have their faculties trained by practice to distinguish good from evil* (Heb 5:14). The perfect in will, on the other hand, are those whose will, being raised above all temporal things, clings to God alone and to his commands. Hence after setting forth the commandments of love Christ added: *be perfect as your heavenly Father is perfect* (Matt 5:48).

Consequently, since the teachings of the faith are aimed at making faith work through love (Gal 5:6), it is necessary that a person instructed in the teachings of the faith not only be well-disposed in intellect for accepting and believing the truth, but also well-disposed in will for loving and doing good works.

82. Then when he says, *although not the wisdom*, he explains what sort of wisdom he means.

First, he gives the explanation;

second, he supports the explanation with a reason, at *which none of the princes* (1 Cor 2:8).

As to the first he does two things.

First, he explains the nature of that wisdom in relation to unbelievers;

second, in relation to believers, at *but we speak the wisdom of God*.

83. He says, therefore: I have said that we speak wisdom among the perfect, *although not the wisdom of this world*, i.e., of worldly things, or the wisdom which rests on human reasons, *neither* that *of the princes of this world*.

84. Thus he separates it from worldly wisdom both as to the method and to the subject of inquiry and to the authors, who are the rulers of this world. This can be understood of three classes of rulers, corresponding to the three types of human wisdom.

First, rulers and worldly potentates can be called the rulers of this age in the sense of a Psalm: *the kings of the earth set themselves, and the rules take counsel together, against the Lord and his anointed* (Ps 2:2). From these rulers came the wisdom of human laws, by which the affairs of

humana dispensantur. Secundo possunt dici principes daemones. Io. XIV, 30: *venit princeps mundi huius, et in me non habet quicquam,* et cetera. Et ab his principibus venit sapientia culturae daemonum, scilicet necromantia, et magicae artes, et huiusmodi. Tertio possunt intelligi principes huius saeculi philosophi, qui quasi principes se exhibuerunt hominibus in docendo, de quibus dicitur Is. XIX, v. 11: *stulti principes Thaneos, sapientes consiliarii Pharaonis.* Et ab his principibus processit tota humana philosophia.

Horum autem principum homines destruuntur per mortem et per amissionem potestatis et auctoritatis: daemones vero non per mortem, sed per amissionem potestatis et auctoritatis, secundum illud Io. XII, 31: *nunc princeps huius mundi eicietur foras*; de hominibus autem dicitur Bar. III, 16: *ubi sunt principes gentium?* Et postea subdit: *exterminati sunt et ad Inferos descenderunt.* Sicut ipsi non sunt stabiles, ita et eorum sapientia non potest esse firma: et ideo non ei innitendum est.

85. Deinde cum dicit ***sed loquimur***, etc., exponit qualis sit sapientia per comparationem ad fideles.

Et primo describit eam quantum ad materiam vel auctoritatem, cum dicit ***sed loquimur Dei sapientiam***, id est quae est Deus et a Deo. Quamvis enim omnis sapientia a Deo sit, ut dicitur Eccli. I, 1, tamen speciali quodam modo haec sapientia, quae est de Deo, est etiam a Deo per revelationem, secundum illud Sap. IX, 17: *sensum autem tuum quis sciet, nisi tu dederis sapientiam et miseris Spiritum tuum de altissimis?*

86. Secundo ostendit qualitatem eius, dicens ***in mysterio, quae abscondita est***; haec enim sapientia abscondita est ab hominibus, inquantum hominis intellectum excedit, secundum illud Eccli. III, 25: *plurima supra sensum hominis ostensa sunt tibi.* Unde dicitur Iob c. XXVIII, 21: *abscondita est ab oculis omnium viventium.*

Et quia modus docendi et doctrinae debet esse conveniens, ideo dicitur quod loquitur eam ***in mysterio***, id est in aliquo occulto, vel verbo vel signo. Infra XIV, 2: ***Spiritus loquitur mysteria.***

87. Tertio ostendit fructum huius sapientiae, dicens ***quam Deus praedestinavit***, id est praeparavit, ***in gloriam nostram***, id est praedicatorum fidei, quibus ex praedicatione tam altae sapientiae gloria magna debetur, et apud Deum, et apud homines. Prov. III, 35: *gloriam sapientes possidebunt.*

Et quod dicit ***in gloriam nostram***, exponendum est omnium fidelium, quorum gloria haec est ut in plena luce cognoscant ea quae nunc in mysterio praedicantur, secundum illud Io. c. XVII, 3: *haec est vita aeterna ut cognoscant te solum Deum verum, et quem misisti Iesum Christum.*

this world are conducted in human life. Second, the devils can be called the rulers: *the ruler of this world is coming. He has no power over me* (John 14:30). From these rulers come the wisdom of honoring devils, namely, necromancy, magical arts and the like. Third, philosophers can be called the rulers of this world, insofar as they put themselves forward as rulers of men in teaching. Of these it is said: *the princes of Zoan are utterly foolish; the wise counselors of Pharaoh give stupid counsel* (Isa 19:11). From these rulers all human philosophy has come.

Now the first of these three types of rulers are destroyed by death and the loss of power and authority; the second, i.e., the devils, are destroyed not by death but by the loss of power and authority as in John: *now shall the ruler of this world be cast out* (John 12:31); of the third group Baruch asks: *where are the rulers of the nations?* (Bar 3:16), and then answers: *they have vanished and gone down to Hades* (Bar 3:19). Consequently, just as none of them lasts, so their wisdom cannot be solid. Therefore, it should not be relied on.

85. Then when he says, ***but we speak***, he explains this wisdom as related to believers.

First, he describes it as to its subject manner and authority when he says, ***but we speak the wisdom of God***, i.e., which is God and from God. For although all wisdom is from God (Sir 1:1), this wisdom, which is about God, is from God in a special way, namely, by revelation: *who has learned your counsel, unless you have given wisdom and sent your Holy Spirit from on high?* (Wis 9:17).

86. Second, he indicates one of its characteristics, saying, ***in a mystery, a wisdom which is hidden***, for this wisdom had been hidden from men, inasmuch as it transcends man's intellect: *many things are shown to you above the understanding of men* (Sir 3:25); hence it is said: *it is hid from the eyes of all living* (Job 28:21).

And because the method of teaching should suit the doctrine, he says that he speaks it ***in a mystery***, i.e., in occult words or signs: ***by the Spirit he speaks mysteries*** (1 Cor 14:2).

87. Third, he discloses the fruit of this wisdom, saying, ***which God ordained***, i.e., prepared, ***unto our glory***, i.e., of the preachers of the faith, who deserve great glory before God and men for preaching such a lofty wisdom: *the wise who possess glory* (Prov 3:35).

The phrase, ***unto our glory***, can refer to all the faithful whose glory it is that they shall know in the full light the things now preached in a mystery: *this is eternal life, that they know you, the only true God, and Jesus Christ whom you have sent* (John 17:3).

Lecture 2

2:8quam nemo principum hujus saeculi cognovit: si enim cognovissent, numquam Dominum gloriae crucifixissent. [n. 88]

2:9Sed sicut scriptum est: *quod oculus non vidit, nec auris audivit*, nec in cor hominis ascendit, quae praeparavit Deus iis qui diligunt illum: [n. 96]

2:10nobis autem revelavit Deus per Spiritum suum: Spiritus enim omnia scrutatur, etiam profunda Dei. [n. 99]

2:11Quis enim hominum scit quae sunt hominis, nisi spiritus hominis, qui in ipso est? ita et quae Dei sunt, nemo cognovit, nisi Spiritus Dei. [n. 103]

2:12Nos autem non spiritum hujus mundi accepimus, sed Spiritum qui ex Deo est, ut sciamus quae a Deo donata sunt nobis: [n. 106]

2:8ἣν οὐδεὶς τῶν ἀρχόντων τοῦ αἰῶνος τούτου ἔγνωκεν, εἰ γὰρ ἔγνωσαν, οὐκ ἂν τὸν κύριον τῆς δόξης ἐσταύρωσαν.

2:9ἀλλὰ καθὼς γέγραπται, Ἃ ὀφθαλμὸς οὐκ εἶδεν καὶ οὖς οὐκ ἤκουσεν καὶ ἐπὶ καρδίαν ἀνθρώπου οὐκ ἀνέβη, ἃ ἡτοίμασεν ὁ θεὸς τοῖς ἀγαπῶσιν αὐτόν.

2:10ἡμῖν δὲ ἀπεκάλυψεν ὁ θεὸς διὰ τοῦ πνεύματος· τὸ γὰρ πνεῦμα πάντα ἐραυνᾷ, καὶ τὰ βάθη τοῦ θεοῦ.

2:11τίς γὰρ οἶδεν ἀνθρώπων τὰ τοῦ ἀνθρώπου εἰ μὴ τὸ πνεῦμα τοῦ ἀνθρώπου τὸ ἐν αὐτῷ; οὕτως καὶ τὰ τοῦ θεοῦ οὐδεὶς ἔγνωκεν εἰ μὴ τὸ πνεῦμα τοῦ θεοῦ.

2:12ἡμεῖς δὲ οὐ τὸ πνεῦμα τοῦ κόσμου ἐλάβομεν ἀλλὰ τὸ πνεῦμα τὸ ἐκ τοῦ θεοῦ, ἵνα εἰδῶμεν τὰ ὑπὸ τοῦ θεοῦ χαρισθέντα ἡμῖν·

2:8Which none of the princes of this world knew. For if they had known it, they would never have crucified the Lord of glory. [n. 88]

2:9But, as it is written: *that eye has not seen, nor ear heard*: neither has it entered into the heart of man, what things God has prepared for those who love him. [n. 96]

2:10But to us God has revealed them by his Spirit. For the Spirit searches all things, even the deep things of God. [n. 99]

2:11For what man knows the things of a man, except the spirit of a man which is in him? So the things also that are of God, no one knows, except the Spirit of God. [n. 103]

2:12Now, we have not received the spirit of this world, but the Spirit that is of God: that we may know the things that are given us from God. [n. 106]

---

88. Posita expositione de sapientia quam Apostolus loquitur inter perfectos, hic rationem assignat expositionis praedictae, et

primo quantum ad hoc, quod eam descripserat per comparationem ad infideles;

secundo, quantum ad hoc quod eam descripserat per comparationem ad fideles, ibi **nobis autem revelavit Deus**.

Circa primum duo facit.

Primo proponit quod intendit;

secundo probat propositum, ibi **si enim cognovissent**.

89. Dicit ergo primo: dictum est quod sapientia quam loquimur non est principum huius saeculi, haec enim sapientia est, **quam nemo principum huius saeculi cognovit**, quod verum est, de quibuscumque principibus intelligatur. Saeculares enim principes hanc sapientiam non cognoverunt, quia excedit rationem humani regiminis. Iob XII, 24: *qui immutat cor principum populi terrae, et decipit eos, ut frustra incedant per invium*. Philosophi etiam eam non cognoverunt, quia excedit rationem humanam. Unde dicitur Bar. c. III, 23: *exquisitores prudentiae et scientiae viam sapientiae nescierunt*. daemones etiam eam non cognoscunt, quia excedit omnem creatam sapientiam. Unde dicitur Iob XXVIII, 21: *volucres*

88. Having explained the wisdom he speaks among the perfect, the Apostle now gives the reason behind the explanation:

first, insofar as he described it in relation to unbelievers;

second, in relation to believers, at **but to us God has revealed**.

As to the first he does two things.

First, he states his proposition;

second, he proves it, at **for if they had known it**.

89. He says, therefore: I have said that the wisdom we speak is not the wisdom of the rulers of this world; for this is the wisdom **which none of the princes of this world knew**. This is true regardless of which class of rulers be considered; for worldly rulers did not know this wisdom, because it surpasses the rules of human government: *he takes away understanding from the chiefs of the people of the earth, and makes them wander in a pathless waste* (Job 12:24). Philosophers, too, have not known it, because it transcends human reason; hence it is said: *the searchers for understanding on the earth have not learned the way to wisdom* (Bar 3:23). Finally, the devils have not known it, because it surpasses all created wisdom; hence it is said: *it is hid from the eyes of all living, and the fowls of the air know it not. Destruction*

caeli quoque latent. Perditio et mors dixerunt: auribus nostris audivimus famam eius.

90. Deinde cum dicit *si enim cognovissent*, etc., probat quod dixerat, et

primo quidem probat per signum quod non cognoverunt principes Dei sapientiam, secundum quod est in se abscondita.

Secundo probat per auctoritatem, quod non cognoverunt eam, secundum quod praeparata est in gloriam nostram, ibi *sicut scriptum est.*

91. Dicit ergo primo: recte dico, quod principes huius saeculi Dei sapientiam non cognoverunt, *si enim cognovissent* Dei sapientiam, cognovissent utique Christum esse Deum, qui in hac sapientia continetur, quo cognito, *numquam crucifixissent Deum gloriae*, id est, ipsum Christum Dominum dantem gloriam suis, secundum illud Ps. XXIII, v. 10: *Dominus virtutum ipse est rex gloriae*; et Hebr. II, 10: *qui multos filios in gloriam adduxerat.*

Cum enim creaturae rationali sit naturaliter appetibilis gloria, non potest in voluntatem humanam cadere, quod auctorem gloriae interimat.

Quod autem principes crucifixerunt Iesum Christum, certum est, si intelligatur de principibus qui potestatem habent inter homines. Dicitur enim in Ps. II, 2: *astiterunt reges terrae, et principes convenerunt in unum adversus Dominum, et adversus Christum eius*, quod Act. IV, 27 exponitur de Herode et Pilato, et principibus Iudaeorum qui consenserunt in mortem Christi. Sed etiam daemones operati sunt in mortem Christi, persuadendo, secundum illud Io. XIII, 2: *cum diabolus iam misisset in cor ut eum traderet*, et cetera. Sed et pharisaei, et scribae in lege periti, qui studium sapientiae dabant, operati sunt ad mortem Christi instigando et approbando.

92. Sed circa hoc duplex oritur dubitatio, quarum prima est de hoc quod dicit Deum gloriae crucifixum. Non enim divinitas Christi aliquid pati potuit, secundum quam dicitur Christus Dominus gloriae.

Sed dicendum quod Christus est una persona et hypostasis in utraque natura consistens, divina scilicet et humana. Unde potest utriusque naturae nomine designari, et quocumque nomine significetur, potest praedicari de eo id quod est utriusque naturae, quia utrique non supponitur nisi una hypostasis. Et per hunc modum possumus dicere quod homo creavit stellas, et quod Dominus gloriae est crucifixus, et tamen non creavit stellas secundum quod homo, sed secundum quod Deus, nec est crucifixus secundum quod est Deus, sed inquantum homo.

Unde ex hoc verbo destruitur error Nestorii, qui dixerat unam naturam esse in Christo, Dei et hominis, quia secundum hoc nullo modo posset verificari quod Dominus gloriae sit crucifixus.

and death have said: with our ears we have heard the fame thereof (Job 28:21).

90. Then when he says, *for if they had known*, he proves what he had said:

first, he proves it by a sign which indicates that the rulers did not know God's wisdom, insofar as it is hidden in him;

second, he proves on scriptural authority that they did not know it as prepared for our glory, at *as it is written*.

91. He says, therefore: I am correct in saying that the rulers of this world did not understand God's wisdom; *for if they had known it*, they would certainly have known that Christ is God, who is contained in this wisdom, and knowing it, *they would never have crucified the Lord of glory*, i.e., Christ the Lord, who gives glory to his own: *the Lord of hosts, he is the king of glory* (Ps 24:10) and *he brought many sons into glory* (Heb 2:10).

For since the rational creature by nature desires glory, it cannot occur to the human will to destroy the author of glory.

That the rulers crucified Jesus Christ is certain, if by rulers is meant those in power among men, for it it said: *the kings of the earth set themselves, and the rulers take counsel together, against the Lord and his anointed* (Ps 2:2). In Acts this is referred to Herod and Pilate and the Jewish leaders, who consented to Christ's death (Acts 4:27). But the devils also had a part in Christ's death by persuading, for John says: *the devil, having now put into the heart of Judas Iscariot to betray him* (John 13:2). Furthermore, the pharisees and scribes versed in the law and students of wisdom, procured Christ's death by instigating and approving.

92. Two difficulties arise here: the first concerns the statement that the God of glory was crucified. For Christ's godhead, according to which Christ is called the Lord of glory, cannot suffer anything.

The answer is that Christ is one person subsisting in two natures, the human and the divine. Hence he can be described by names drawn from either nature; furthermore, no matter what the name by which he is designated, it can be predicated of him, because there is but one person underlying both natures. Consequently, we can say that the man created the stars and that the Lord of glory was crucified; however, it was not as man that he created the stars, but as God; nor was it as God that he was crucified, but as man.

Hence this phrase refutes Nestorius' error asserting that there is one nature, composed of God and man, in Christ; because if Nestorius were correct, it would not be true to say that Lord of glory was crucified.

93. Secunda dubitatio est de hoc quod videtur supponere, quod principes Iudaeorum vel daemones non cognoverunt Christum esse Deum. Et quidem, quantum ad principes Iudaeorum, videtur hoc astrui per hoc quod dicit Petrus, Act. III, 17: *Scio quia per ignorantiam hoc feceritis, sicut et principes vestri.*

Videtur autem esse contrarium quod dicitur Matth. XXI, 38: *Agricolae videntes Filium, dixerunt intra se: hic est haeres, venite, occidamus eum*; quod exponens Chrysostomus dicit: *Manifeste Dominus probat his verbis Iudaeorum principes non per ignorantiam, sed per invidiam Dei Filium crucifixisse.*

Solvitur in Glossa quod *sciebant*, principes Iudaeorum, *eum esse qui promissus erat in lege, non tamen mysterium eius quod Filius Dei erat, neque sciebant sacramentum incarnationis et redemptionis.*

Sed contra hoc esse videtur quod Chrysostomus dicit quod *cognoverunt eum esse Filium Dei.*

Dicendum est ergo quod principes Iudaeorum pro certo sciebant eum esse Christum promissum in lege, quod populus ignorabat. Ipsum autem esse verum Filium Dei non pro certo sciebant, sed aliqualiter coniecturabant; sed haec coniecturalis cognitio obscurabatur in eis ex invidia et ex cupiditate propriae gloriae, quam per excellentiam Christi minui videbant.

94. Similiter etiam videtur esse de daemonibus dubitatio.

Dicitur enim Mc. I, 23 ss. et Lc. IV, 34, quod daemonium clamavit, dicens: *scio quod sis sanctus Dei.* Et ne hoc praesumptioni daemonum ascribatur, qui se iactabant scire quod nesciebant, eorum notitia quam habebant de Christo per ipsos Evangelistas asseritur. In Marco quidem sic scribitur: *Non sinebat ea loqui,* scilicet daemonia, *quoniam sciebant eum Christum esse.* Et Lucas dicit: *Increpans non sinebat ea loqui quia sciebant eum esse Christum.*

Et ad hoc respondetur in libro de quaestionibus Novi et Veteris Testamenti, quod daemonia sciebant ipsum esse, qui per legem fuit repromissus, quia omnia signa videbant in eo quae dixerunt prophetae, mysterium autem divinitatis eius ignorabant.

95. Sed contra hoc videtur esse quod Athanasius dicit, quod daemonia dicebant Christum esse sanctum Dei, quasi singulariter sanctum: ipse enim naturaliter est sanctus cuius participatione omnes alii sancti vocantur.

Dicendum est autem quod, sicut Chrysostomus dicit, non habebant adventus Dei firmam et certam notitiam, sed quasdam coniecturas. Unde Augustinus dicit in IX *de Civitate Dei* quod innotuit daemonibus, *non per id quod est vita aeterna, sed per quaedam temporalia sua virtute effecta.*

93. The second difficulty is that he seems to suppose that the Jewish rulers or the devils did not know that Christ was God. Indeed, as far as the Jewish rulers were concerned, this seems to be supported by Peter's statement in Acts: *I know that you did it in ignorance, as did also your rulers* (Acts 3:17).

This in turn seems to be contrary to what it says in Matthew: *but when the tenants saw the son, they said to themselves, this is the heir; come, let us kill him and have his inheritance* (Matt 21:38). Furthermore, in explaining this Chrysostom says: *by these words the Lord proves clearly that the Jewish rulers killed the Son of God not through ignorance but through envy.*

This difficulty is answered in a Gloss, which states that the Jewish rulers *knew* that *he was the one promised in the law, although they did not know his mystery, that he was the Son of God or the sacrament of the incarnation and redemption.*

But this seems to be contradicted by Chrysostom's own statement that *they knew he was the Son of God.*

Therefore, the answer is that the Jewish rulers knew for certain that he was the Christ promised in the law, although the people did not know; yet they did not know for certain but somehow conjectured that he was the true Son of God. However, this conjectural knowledge was obscured in them by envy and from a desire for their own glory, which they saw was being diminished by Christ's excellence.

94. There seems to be difficulty also about devils.

For it says in Mark and Luke that the devil cried out: *I know you are the holy one of God* (Mark 1:23; Luke 4:34). But lest this be ascribed to the devils' boasting to know what they did not know, the knowledge they had of Christ is asserted by the Evangelists. For Mark says: *and he did not permit the demons to speak, because they knew him* (Mark 1:34), and Luke says: *but he rebuked them, and would not allow them to speak, because they knew that he was the Christ* (Luke 4:41).

This is answered in the book of questions of the New and Old Testament: that the devils knew he was the one promised by the law, because they saw in him all the signs foretold by the prophets; nevertheless, they did not know the mystery of his divinity.

95. But opposed to this is Athanasius' statement that devils called Christ the holy one of God, as being uniquely holy, for he is naturally holy, by participation in whom, all others are called holy.

Consequently, it must be said with Chrysostom that they did not have firm and sure knowledge of God's coming, but on conjectures; hence Augustine says in *The City of God* that he was recognized by the devils *not by that which is eternal life, but by certain temporal things effected by his power.*

96. Deinde cum dicit *sed sicut scriptum est*, probat per auctoritatem quod principes huius saeculi Dei sapientiam non cognoverunt, quantum ad hoc quod praedestinata est in gloriam fidelium, dicens: *sed sicut scriptum est* Is. LXIV, 4, ubi littera nostra habet: *oculus non vidit, Deus, absque te, quae praeparasti his qui diligunt te.*

Ostenditur autem illa gloria visionis aperte ab hominibus ignorari dupliciter. Primo quidem quod non subiacet humanis sensibus, a quibus omnis humana cognitio initium sumit. Et ponit duos sensus. Primo visionis quae deservit inventioni, cum dicit *quod oculus non vidit*, Iob XXVIII, 7: *semitam eius ignoravit avis, nec intuitus est eam oculus vulturis.* Et hoc ideo, quia non est aliquid coloratum et visibile. Secundo ponit sensum auditus, qui deservit disciplinae, dicens *nec auris audivit*, scilicet ipsam gloriam, quia non est sonus aut vox sensibilis. Io. V, v. 37: *neque speciem eius vidistis, neque vocem eius audistis.*

97. Deinde excludit notitiam eius intellectualem, cum dicit *neque in cor hominis ascendit.* Quod quidem potest intelligi: uno modo ut ascendere in cor hominis dicatur quidquid quocumque modo cognoscitur ab homine, secundum illud Ier. II, v. 50: *Ierusalem ascendat super cor vestrum*: et sic oporteat, quod cor hominis accipiatur pro corde hominis carnalis, secundum illud quod dicitur infra III, 3: *cum sint inter vos zelus et contentio, nonne carnales estis, et secundum hominem ambulatis?*

Est ergo sensus quod illa gloria non solum sensu non percipitur, sed nec corde hominis carnalis, secundum illud Io. XIV, 17: *quem mundus non potest accipere, quia non videt eum, nec scit eum.*

98. Alio modo potest exponi secundum quod proprie dicitur in cor hominis ascendere id quod ab inferiori pervenit ad hominis intellectum, puta a sensibilibus, de quibus prius fecerat mentionem.

Res enim sunt in intellectu secundum modum eius; res igitur inferiores sunt in intellectu altiori modo quam in seipsis. Et ideo quando ab intellectu capiuntur, quodammodo in cor ascendunt. Unde dicitur Is. LXV, 17: *non erunt in memoria priora, nec ascendent super cor.* Illa vero quae sunt in intellectu superiora, altiori modo sunt in seipsis quam in intellectu. Et ideo quando ab intellectu capiuntur, quodammodo descendunt. Iac. I, v. 17: *omne donum perfectum desursum est descendens a Patre luminum.*

Quia igitur illius gloriae notitia non accipitur a sensibilibus, sed ex revelatione divina, ideo signanter dicit *nec in cor hominis ascendit*, sed descendit, id scilicet quod *praeparavit Deus*, id est, praedestinavit, *diligentibus se*, quia essentiale praemium aeternae gloriae caritati debetur, secundum illud Io. c. XIV, 21: *si quis diligit me diligetur a Patre meo, et ego diligam eum et manifestabo*

96. Then when he says, *but, as it is written*, he proves by Scripture that the rulers of this world did not know God's wisdom as to what it prepared for the glory of believers, saying, *but, as it is written*, where our version has: *the eye has not seen, O God, besides you, what things you have prepared for those who wait for you* (Isa 64:4).

That this glorious vision is unknown to man is shown in two ways: first, because it is not within the range of the human senses, from which all human knowledge begins. And he mentions two senses: first, vision, which is employed when a person finds things out for himself: hence he says: *that eye has not seen*: *the bird has not known the path, neither has the eye of the vulture beheld it* (Job 28:7). The eye is of no use, because the object of inquiry is not something colored and visible. Second, he mentions the sense of hearing, which is employed when a person learns from someone else; hence he says: *nor ear heard* that glory, because it is not a sound or an audible world: *his voice you have never heard, his form you have never seen* (John 5:37).

97. Then he excludes intellectual discovery of this glory when he says: *neither has it entered into the heart of man*. In one sense, whatever is known by men in any manner whatsoever is said to enter into the heart of man: *let Jerusalem come into your mind* (Jer 51:50). In this way, the heart of man refers to the heart of a carnal man in the sense of his statement below: *while there is among you envying and contention, are you not carnal and walk according to man?* (1 Cor 3:3).

The meaning, therefore, is that such glory is not only not known by the senses, but not even by the heart, of a carnal man: *even the Spirit of truth, whom the world cannot receive, because it neither sees him nor knows him* (John 14:17).

98. In another sense, something is said to ascend into the heart of man, when from a lower state, for example, from existing in sense perceptible things, it reaches man's understanding.

For things exist in the understanding according to its mode; therefore, lower things exist in the intellect in a higher state than they exist in themselves. Consequently, when they are grasped by the intellect, they ascend into the heart of man. *The former things shall not be in remembrance, and they shall not come upon the heart* (Isa 65:17). But things which are more excellent than the intellect exist in a higher state in themselves than in the intellect; therefore, when they are grasped by the intellect they somehow descend: *every perfect gift is from above, descending from the Father of lights* (Jas 1:17).

Therefore, since the knowledge of that glory is not obtained from sense perceptible things but by divine revelation, he says quite significantly: *neither has it entered into the heart of man*, but it comes down, namely, that which *God has prepared*, i.e., predestined, *for those who love him*, because the essential reward of eternal glory is due to charity: *if anyone loves me, he will be loved by my*

ei meipsum, in quo perfectio aeternae gloriae consistit; et Iob XXXVI, 33: *annuntiat de ea*, id est de luce gloriae, *amico suo quod possessio eius sit*. Caeterae autem virtutes accipiunt efficaciam merendi vitam aeternam, inquantum informantur caritate.

99. Deinde cum dicit *nobis autem*, etc., probat praedictam expositionem de sapientia divina per comparationem ad fideles. Et

primo proponit quod intendit;

secundo probat propositum, ibi *Spiritus enim*.

100. Dicit ergo primo: dictum est quod sapientiam Dei nemo principum huius saeculi cognovit, *nobis autem Deus revelavit per Spiritum suum*, quem scilicet nobis misit, secundum illud Io. XIV, 26: *Paracletus autem Spiritus Sanctus, quem mittet Pater in nomine meo, ille vos docebit omnia*, Iob c. XXXII, 8: *inspiratio Omnipotentis dat intelligentiam*.

Quia enim Spiritus Sanctus est Spiritus veritatis, utpote a Filio procedens, qui est veritas Patris, his quibus mittitur inspirat veritatem, sicut et Filius a Patre missus notificat Patrem, secundum illud Matth. XI, 27: *nemo novit Patrem nisi Filius, et cui voluerit Filius revelare*.

101. Deinde cum dicit *Spiritus enim*, probat quod dixerat, scilicet quod per Spiritum Sanctum sit sapientia fidelibus revelata. Et

primo ostendit quod Spiritus Sanctus ad hoc sit efficax;

secundo probat quod hoc in discipulis Christi fecerat, ibi *nos autem*.

Circa primum duo facit.

Primo proponit quod intendit;

secundo manifestat propositum, ibi *quis enim scit hominum*, et cetera.

102. Dicit ergo primo: dictum est quod per Spiritum Sanctum revelavit nobis Deus suam sapientiam, et hoc fieri potuit: *Spiritus enim* Sanctus *omnia scrutatur*. Quod non est sic intelligendum, quasi inquirendo quomodo fiant, sed quia perfecte et etiam intima quarumlibet rerum novit, sicut homo quod aliquando diligenter scrutatur. Unde dicitur Sap. VII, 22 s. quod *Spiritus intelligentiae Sanctus est, omnia prospiciens, et qui capiat omnes spiritus intelligibiles, mundos, subtiles*, et non solum res creatas, sed *etiam profunda Dei* perfecte cognoscit. Dicuntur autem profunda ea quae in ipso latent, et non ea quae de ipso per creaturas cognoscuntur, quae quasi superficie tenus videntur esse, secundum illud Sap. XIII, 5: *a magnitudine speciei et creaturae cognoscibiliter poterit Creator eorum videri*.

103. Deinde, cum dicit *quis enim scit hominum*, probat quod dixerat de Spiritu Dei per similitudinem humani spiritus, dicens *quis enim scit hominum ea quae sunt hominis*, id est, ea quae latent in corde, *nisi spiritus*

Father; and I will love him and will manifest myself to him (John 14:21), for it is in this that the perfection of eternal glory consists; and Job says: *he shows his friend concerning it*, i.e., concerning the light of glory, *that it is his possession* (Job 36:33). The other virtues, however, play a role in meriting eternal life, insofar as they are enlivened by charity.

99. Then when he says, *but to us*, he proves the above explanation of divine wisdom in relation to the faithful:

first, he states his proposition;

second, he proves it, at *for the Spirit searches*.

100. He says, therefore: I have stated that none of the rulers of this world knew God's wisdom, *but to us God has revealed them by his Spirit*, whom he sent to us: *but the Counselor, the Holy Spirit, whom the Father will send in my name, he will teach you all things* (John 14:26); *the breath of the Almighty gives me understanding* (Job 33:4).

For since the Holy Spirit is the Spirit of truth, inasmuch as he proceeds from the Son, who is the truth of the Father, he is sent to those to whom he breathes the truth, as Matthew says: *no one knows the Father except the Son and anyone to whom the Son chooses to reveal him* (Matt 11:27).

101. Then when he says, *for the Spirit searches*, he proves what he had said, namely, that wisdom has been revealed to believers by the Holy Spirit.

First, he shows that the Holy Spirit effects this;

second, he proves that he effected this in Christ's disciples, at *now, we have not received*.

As to the first he does two things.

First, he states his proposition;

second, he proves it, at *for what man knows*.

102. He says, therefore: I have stated that God reveals his wisdom through the Holy Spirit. This was possible, *for the* Holy *Spirit searches all things*, not as though he learns them by searching them out, but because he knows fully even the most intimate details of all things. Hence, it is stated in Wisdom that *the wisdom of understanding is holy, overseeing all things, containing all spirits, intelligible, pure, subtle* (Wis 7:2), and knowing not only created things perfectly but *even the deep things of God*. The deep things are those which are hidden in him and not those which are known about him through creatures, which are, as it were, on the surface, as Wisdom says: *for from the greatness and beauty of created things comes a corresponding perception of their Creator* (Wis 13:5).

103. Then when he says, *for what man knows*, he proves what he had said of the Spirit of God by a comparison with man's spirit, saying, *for what man knows the things of a man*, i.e., which are hidden in his heart, *except the*

hominis, qui in eo est, id est, intellectus? Et ideo quae interius latent, videri non possunt.

Signanter autem dicit **quis hominum**, ne ab horum cognitione etiam Deus videatur excludi; dicitur enim Ier. XVII, 9: *pravum est cor hominis, et quis cognoscet illud? Ego Deus probans corda et scrutans renes*, quia scilicet secretorum cordis solus Deus est cognitor.

104. Manifesta autem est ratio quare homo ea quae in corde alterius latent scire non potest, quia cognitio hominis a sensu accipitur, et ideo ea quae sunt in corde alterius, homo cognoscere non potest, nisi quatenus per signa sensibilia manifestantur, secundum illud I Reg. XVI, 7: *homo videt quae foris patent, Deus autem intuetur cor.*

Sed nec angelus bonus, nec malus ea quae in corde hominis latent scire potest, nisi inquantum per aliquos effectus manifestantur, cuius ratio accipi potest ex ipso verbo Apostoli, qui dicit ea ratione spiritum hominis cognoscere quae in corde hominis latent quia in ipso homine est; angelus autem, neque bonus neque malus, illabitur menti humanae, ut in ipso corde hominis sit et intrinsecus operetur, sed hoc solius Dei proprium est. Unde solus Deus est conscius secretorum cordis hominis, secundum illud Iob XVI, 20: *ecce in caelo testis meus, et in excelsis conscius meus.*

105. Secundo similitudinem adaptat ad Spiritum Dei, dicens **ita et quae Dei sunt**, id est, quae in ipso Deo latent, **nemo cognoscit, nisi Spiritus Dei**, secundum illud Iob c. XXXVI, 26: *ecce Deus magnus vincens scientiam nostram.*

Sed sicut ea quae sunt in corde unius hominis alteri manifestantur per sensibilia signa, ita ea quae sunt Dei possunt esse nota homini per sensibiles effectus, secundum illud Sap. XIII, 5: *a magnitudine speciei et creaturae*, et cetera. Sed Spiritus Sanctus, qui est in ipso Deo, utpote Patri et Filio consubstantialis, secreta divinitatis per seipsum videt, secundum illud Sap. VII, 22: *est enim in illa*, scilicet Dei sapientia, *et Spiritus intelligentiae* Sanctus, omnem habens virtutem, omnia prospiciens.

106. Deinde, cum dicit **nos autem**, etc., ostendit quomodo cognitio Spiritus Sancti percipiatur, dicens: licet nullus hominum per se possit scire quae sunt Dei, **nos autem**, Spiritu Sancto scilicet repleti, **non accepimus spiritum huius mundi, sed Spiritum qui a Deo est**.

Nomine autem spiritus vis quaedam vitalis et cognitiva et motiva intelligitur. Spiritus ergo huius mundi potest dici sapientia huius mundi, et amor mundi, quo impellitur homo ad agendum ea quae mundi sunt; hunc autem Spiritum Sancti apostoli non receperunt, mundum abiicientes et contemnentes, sed receperunt Spiritum Sanctum, quo corda eorum illuminata sunt et

spirit of a man which is in him, i.e., the intellect? Hence the things which lie within cannot be seen.

But he says significantly, **what man**, lest he seem to exclude God as knowing them. For it is said: *the heart of man is deceitful above all things, and desperately corrupt; who can understand it? I the Lord search the mind and try the heart* (Jer 17:9), because God alone knows what lies in another's heart.

104. The reason man cannot know what lies in another's heart is obvious, because man's knowledge begins with the senses. Consequently, a man cannot know the things in another's heart, unless they are manifested by certain sense perceptible signs: *man looks on the outward appearance, but the Lord looks on the heart* (1 Sam 16:7).

Furthermore, not even a good or an evil angel can know the things which lie in a man's heart, unless they are manifested by special effects. The reason can be taken from the Apostle's statement that man's spirit knows what lies in man's heart, because it is in him. But no angel, good or evil, can enter the human mind to exist in a man's heart or work from within it. God alone can do this; hence, he alone is aware of the secrets of a man's heart: *my witness is in heaven and he who vouches for me is on high* (Job 16:20).

105. Then he adapts this comparison to the Spirit of God, saying, **so the things also that are of God**, i.e., the hidden things of God, **no one knows, except the Spirit of God**: *behold, God is great, and we know him not* (Job 36:26).

But just as the things in one man's heart are made known to another by sense perceptible signs, so the things of God can be made known to man by sensible effects: *from the greatness and beauty of created things comes a corresponding perception of their Creator* (Wis 13:5). However, the Holy Spirit who is in God himself, being consubstantial with the Father and the Son, sees the secrets of the godhead by himself, *for in her*, i.e., in God's wisdom, *is the Spirit of understanding*, holy, having all power, overseeing all things (Wis 7:22).

106. Then when he says, **now, we have not received**, he shows how knowledge of the Holy Spirit is obtained, saying, **now, we**, filled with the Holy Spirit, **have not received the spirit of this world, but the Spirit that is of God**.

By the word spirit is understood a definite vital power, both cognitive and dynamic. Therefore, the spirit of this world can mean the wisdom of this world and the love of this world, by which a man is impelled to do the things of this world. This is not the spirit received by the holy apostles, who rejected and despised the world; rather, they receive the Holy Spirit, by whom their hearts were enlightened

inflammata ad amorem Dei, secundum illud Io. XIV, 26: *Paracletus autem Spiritus Sanctus, quem mittet Pater in nomine meo*, etc., et Num. XIV, 24: *servum meum Caleb, qui plenus est alio spiritu, et secutus est me, introducam in terram hanc.*

Spiritus autem huius mundi errare facit, secundum illud Is. XIX, 3: *dirumpetur spiritus Aegypti in visceribus eius, et consilium eius praecipitabo.* Ex divino autem Spiritu eius consecuti sumus, **ut sciamus quae a Deo data sunt nobis**, ut sciamus de rebus divinis quantum unicuique Deus donavit: quia, sicut dicitur Eph. IV, 7, *unicuique data est gratia secundum mensuram donationis Christi.*

107. Vel potest intelligi Spiritum Dei donatum sanctis, ut dona spiritualia cognoscant, quae, non habentes, eumdem Spiritum ignorant, secundum illud Apoc. II, 17: *vincenti dabo manna absconditum, quod nemo scit, nisi qui accipit.*

Ex hoc autem accipi potest, quod sicut *nemo novit Patrem nisi Filius, et cui voluerit Filius revelare*, ut dicitur Matth. XI, 27: ita nemo novit quae sunt Dei Patris et Filii, nisi Spiritus Sanctus et qui ipsum acceperunt: et hoc ideo, quia sicut Filius consubstantialis est Patri, ita Spiritus Sanctus Patri et Filio.

and inflamed with the love of God: *the Counselor, the Holy Spirit, whom the Father will send in my name, he will teach you all things* (John 14:26); *but my servant Caleb, because he has a different spirit and has followed me fully, I will bring into the land into which he went* (Num 14:24).

But the spirit of this world can err as Isaiah attests: *the spirit of the Egyptians within them will be emptied out, and I will confound their plans* (Isa 19:3). However, we received his divine Spirit, **that we may know the things that are given us from God**, i.e., that we may know to what extent God has given divine things to each of us: *grace was given to each of us according to the measure of Christ's gift* (Eph 4:7).

107. Or gifts, which are unknown to those not possessing the same Spirit, for *to him who conquers I will give some of the hidden manna, which no one knows except him who receives it* (Rev 2:17).

From this it can be gathered that just as *no one knows the Father but the Son and he to whom it has pleased the Son to reveal him*, so no one knows the things of the Father and of the Son but the Holy Spirit and he who has received him (Matt 11:27). This is so, because just as the Son is consubstantial with the Father, so the Holy Spirit with the Father and Son.

Lecture 3

2:13quae et loquimur non in doctis humanae sapientiae verbis, sed in doctrina Spiritus, spiritualibus spiritualia comparantes. [n. 109]

2:14 Animalis autem homo non percipit ea quae sunt Spiritus Dei: stultitia enim est illi, et non potest intelligere: quia spiritualiter examinatur. [n. 110]

2:15 Spiritualis autem judicat omnia: et ipse a nemine judicatur. [n. 116]

2:16 Quis enim cognovit sensum Domini, qui instruat eum? nos autem sensum Christi habemus. [n. 119]

2:13ἃ καὶ λαλοῦμεν οὐκ ἐν διδακτοῖς ἀνθρωπίνης σοφίας λόγοις ἀλλ' ἐν διδακτοῖς πνεύματος, πνευματικοῖς πνευματικὰ συγκρίνοντες.

2:14ψυχικὸς δὲ ἄνθρωπος οὐ δέχεται τὰ τοῦ πνεύματος τοῦ θεοῦ, μωρία γὰρ αὐτῷ ἐστιν, καὶ οὐ δύναται γνῶναι, ὅτι πνευματικῶς ἀνακρίνεται·

2:15ὁ δὲ πνευματικὸς ἀνακρίνει [τὰ] πάντα, αὐτὸς δὲ ὑπ' οὐδενὸς ἀνακρίνεται.

2:16τίς γὰρ ἔγνω νοῦν κυρίου, ὃς συμβιβάσει αὐτόν; ἡμεῖς δὲ νοῦν Χριστοῦ ἔχομεν.

2:13 Which things also we speak: not in the learned words of human wisdom, but in the doctrine of the Spirit, comparing spiritual things with spiritual. [n. 109]

2:14 But the sensual man perceives not these things that are of the Spirit of God. For it is foolishness to him: and he cannot understand, because it is spiritually examined. [n. 110]

2:15 But the spiritual man judges all things: and he himself is judged of no man. [n. 116]

2:16 For who has known the mind of the Lord, that he may instruct him? But we have the mind of Christ. [n. 119]

---

108. Dixerat supra Apostolus *sapientiam loquimur inter perfectos*. Postquam ergo manifestavit qualis sit haec sapientia, quia mundanis hominibus incognita, cognita autem sanctis, hic manifestat qua ratione hanc sapientiam sancti inter perfectos loquuntur. Et

primo proponit quod intendit;

secundo assignat rationem, ibi *animalis autem homo*, et cetera.

109. Circa primum, primo proponit revelatorum manifestationem, dicens: dictum est quod Spiritum Dei accepimus, ut sciamus quae a Deo donata sunt nobis, *quae* scilicet nobis per Spiritum revelata sunt, *loquimur*. Sunt enim eis revelata ad utilitatem. Unde et Act. II, 4: *repleti sunt omnes Spiritu Sancto, et coeperunt loqui*.

Secundo tangit modum enarrandi, excludens modum inconvenientem, dicens *non in doctis humanae sapientiae verbis*, id est, non nitimur ad probandam nostram doctrinam per verba composita ex humana sapientia, sive quantum ad ornatum verborum, sive quantum ad subtilitatem rationum. Is. XXXIII, v. 19: *populum alti sermonis non videbis*. Astruit enim modum convenientem, cum dicit *sed in doctrina Spiritus*, id est, prout Spiritus Sanctus nos loquentes interius docet, et auditorum corda ad capiendum illustrat. Io. XVI, 13: *cum venerit ille Spiritus veritatis, docebit vos omnem veritatem*.

Tertio determinat auditores, dicens *spiritualibus spiritualia comparantes*, quasi dicat: recta comparatione spiritualia documenta tradimus spiritualibus viris, quibus sunt convenientia. II Tim. II, 2: *haec commenda fidelibus viris, qui idonei erunt et alios docere*. Eosdem autem

108. Above, the Apostle had said, *we speak wisdom among the perfect* (1 Cor 2:6). Therefore, after indicating that it is a mark of this wisdom not to be known by worldly men, but to be known by the saints, he now discloses the way in which the saints speak this wisdom among the perfect.

First, he states his proposition;

second, he gives the reason, at *but the sensual man*.

109. As to the first he shows that the things revealed are now manifest, saying: I have said that we have received the Spirit of God, that we may know the things given us by God; *which things*, namely, revealed by the Spirit, *we speak*, for they were to them for a purpose. Hence it says in Acts: *they were all filled with the Holy Spirit and began to speak* (Acts 2:4).

Second, he touches on the method they employed, and excludes an unsuitable method, saying: *not in the learned words of human wisdom*, i.e., we do not try to prove our doctrine with words drawn from human wisdom, for we depend neither on elegance of speech nor subtlety of reasoning: *the people of profound speech you shall not see* (Isa 33:19). But he indicates the suitable method, when he says, *but in the doctrine of the Spirit*, i.e., accordingly as the Holy Spirit teaches us inwardly and enlightens the hearts of our hearers to understand: *when he shall come, the Spirit of truth, he will teach you all truth* (John 16:13).

Third, he describes the hearers, saying, *comparing spiritual things with spiritual*. As if to say: it is a proper arrangement for us to deliver spiritual teachings to spiritual men to whom they are suited: *commend the same to faithful men, who shall be fit to teach others also* (2 Tim 2:2). Here he

hic nominat spirituales, quos supra perfectos, quia per Spiritum Sanctum homines perficiuntur in virtute, secundum illud Ps. XXXII, 6: *spiritu oris eius omnis virtus eorum.*

110. Deinde, cum dicit **animalis**, etc., assignat rationem dictorum, et

primo ostendit quare spiritualia non sunt tradenda animalibus hominibus;

secundo quare sunt tradenda spiritualibus, ibi **spiritualis**, et cetera.

Circa primum duo facit.

Primo ponit rationem;

secundo manifestat eam, ibi **stultitia enim**, et cetera.

111. Ratio ergo talis est: nulli sunt tradenda documenta quae capere non potest, sed homines animales non possunt capere spiritualia documenta; ergo non sunt eis tradenda. Hoc est ergo quod dicit **animalis homo**, et cetera. Et ideo recta ratione non possunt tradi eis.

112. Ubi primo considerandum est quis homo dicatur animalis. Est ergo considerandum quod anima est forma corporis. Unde propriae animae intelliguntur illae vires quae sunt actus corporalium organorum, scilicet vires sensitivae. Dicuntur ergo homines animales qui huiusmodi vires sequuntur, inter quas est vis apprehensiva, et appetitiva, et ideo potest dici homo dupliciter animalis. Uno modo quantum ad vim apprehensivam, et hic dicitur animalis sensu, qui, sicut dicitur in Glossa, de Deo iuxta corporum phantasiam vel legis litteram, vel rationem philosophicam iudicat, quae secundum vires sensitivas accipiuntur.

Alio modo dicitur quis animalis quantum ad vim appetitivam, qui scilicet afficitur solum ad ea quae sunt secundum appetitum sensitivum, et talis dicitur animalis vita, qui, sicut dicitur in Glossa, sequitur dissolutam lasciviam animae suae, quam intra naturalis ordinis metas spiritus rector non continet. Unde dicitur in canonica Iudae v. 19: *hi sunt qui segregant semetipsos, animales Spiritum non habentes.*

113. Secundo autem videndum quare tales non possunt percipere **ea quae sunt Spiritus Dei**: quod quidem manifestum est, et quantum ad animalem sensum, et quantum ad animalem vitam. Ea enim de quibus Spiritus Sanctus illustrat mentem, sunt supra sensum et rationem humanam, secundum illud Eccli. III, 25: *plura supra sensum hominis ostensa sunt tibi*, et ideo ab eo capi non possunt, qui soli cognitioni sensitivae innititur. Spiritus etiam Sanctus accendit affectum ad diligendum spiritualia bona, sensibilibus bonis contemptis, et ideo ille qui est animalis vitae, non potest capere huiusmodi spiritualia bona, quia Philosophus dicit in IV *Ethic.* quod qualis unusquisque est, talis finis videtur ei. Prov. XVIII, 2: *non*

calls the same men spiritual, whom above he called perfect, because men are made perfect in virtue by the Holy Spirit: *all their virtue by the spirit of his mouth* (Ps 32:6).

110. Then when he says, **but the sensual man**, he assigns the reason for the above:

first, he shows why spiritual things must not be entrusted to sensual men;

second, why they should be entrusted to spiritual men, at **but the spiritual man**.

As to the first he does two things.

First, he gives the reason;

second, he explains it, at **for it is foolishness to him**.

111. The reasoning is this: no one should be taught what he cannot grasp. But sensual men cannot grasp spiritual things. Therefore, they should not be taught to them. This, therefore, lies behind his statement that **the sensual man perceives not these things that are of the Spirit of God**. Therefore, there is good reason why they cannot be entrusted to him.

112. Here should be noted the sort of man called sensual. Recall, therefore, that the soul is the body's substantial form. Hence, those soul powers which are associated with bodily organs, namely, the sense-powers, are proper to the soul. Consequently, those men are called sensual who follow the lead of such powers, among which are the powers of perception and appetition. Hence, men are called sensual in two ways: first, on the basis of the perceptive power, where a man is called sensual in perception, because he judges about God in terms of bodily images or the letter of the law or philosophical reasons, all of which are interpreted in accordance with the sense-powers.

Second, on the basis of the appetitive power, which is attracted only to things that appeal to the sense appetite. In this case a man is called sensual in his manner of life, because he follows the dissolute wantonness of his soul, which his ruling spirit does not confine within the bounds of the natural order. Hence it is said: *it is these that set up divisions, worldly people, devoid of the Spirit* (Jude 1:19).

113. Second, we should note why such men cannot perceive **these things that are of the Spirit of God**, whether they are sensual in perception or in their manner of life. For the things about which the Holy Spirit enlightens the mind transcend sense and human reason, as Sirach attests: *matters too great for human understanding have been shown you* (Sir 3:23). Consequently, they cannot be grasped by a person who relies solely on sense perception. Again, the Holy Spirit inflames the affections to love spiritual goods and despise sensible goods. Hence, a person whose manner of life is sensual cannot grasp spiritual goods of this sort, because the Philosopher says in *Ethics* IV that as a person is, so his end appears to him: *a fool takes no*

recipit stultus verba prudentiae, nisi ei dixeris quae versantur in corde eius. Eccli. XXII, 9: *cum dormiente loquitur, qui narrat sapientiam stulto.*

114. Deinde, cum dicit **stultitia enim**, etc., manifestat quod dixerat per signum; cum enim aliquis aliqua sapienter dicta reprobat quasi stulta, signum est quod ea non capiat. Quia igitur animalis homo ea quae sunt Spiritus Dei reputat stulta, ex hoc manifestatur quod ea non capit. Et hoc est quod dicit **stultitia enim est illi**, scilicet animali. Iudicat enim esse stulta quae secundum Spiritum Dei aguntur. Eccle. X, 3: *in via stultus ambulans, cum ipse sit insipiens, omnes stultos aestimat.*

Quod autem homini animali quae secundum Spiritum sunt videantur stulta, non procedit ex rectitudine sensus: sicut sapientes aliqua iudicant esse stulta quae stultis videntur sapientia propter defectum intellectus; quia homo sensui deditus non potest intelligere ea quae supra sensum sunt, et homo carnalibus affectus non intelligit esse bonum, nisi quod est delectabile secundum carnem.

Et hoc est quod sequitur **et non potest intelligere**, Ps. LXXXI, 5: *nescierunt neque intellexerunt, in tenebris ambulant.*

115. Quare autem non possit intelligere, ostendit subdens **quia spiritualiter examinatur**, id est, spiritualium examinatio fit spiritualiter. Numquam enim inferior potest examinare et iudicare ea quae sunt superioris, sicut sensus non potest examinare ea quae sunt intellectus. Et similiter, neque sensus, neque ratio humana potest iudicare ea quae sunt Spiritus Dei. Et ita relinquitur quod huiusmodi solo Spiritu Sancto examinantur, secundum illud Ps. XVII, 31: *eloquia Domini igne examinata*, probata scilicet a Spiritu Sancto.

Quia ergo animalis homo caret Spiritu Sancto, non potest spiritualia examinare, et per consequens nec ea intelligere.

116. Deinde, cum dicit **spiritualis autem iudicat omnia**, etc., assignat rationem quare spiritualibus spiritualia tradantur, et

primo ponit rationem;

secundo manifestat causam, ibi **quis enim novit**.

117. Assignat autem talem rationem: illi tradenda sunt spiritualia qui potest iudicare, secundum illud Iob XII, 11: *auris verba diiudicat*; sed spiritualis est huiusmodi, ergo ei spiritualia sunt tradenda. Et hoc est quod dicit **spiritualis autem diiudicat omnia, et ipse a nemine iudicatur**.

Ubi primo videndum est quis homo dicatur spiritualis. Est autem notandum quod spiritus nominare consuevimus substantias incorporeas; quia igitur aliqua pars animae est quae non est alicuius organi corporei actus,

pleasure in understanding, but only in expressing his opinion (Prov 18:2); *do not speak in the hearing of a fool, for he will despise the wisdom of your words* (Sir 23:9).

114. Then when he says, **for it is foolishness**, he supports what he had said with a sign: for when a person rejects wise statements as foolish, it is a sign that he does not understand them. Consequently, since the sensual man regards things of the Spirit of God as foolish, it is obvious that he does not understand them. This is what he says, namely, **for it is foolishness to him**, i.e., to the sensual man, for he judges things inspired by the Holy Spirit to be foolish: *even when the fool walks on the road, he lacks sense, and he esteems everyone a fool* (Eccl 10:3).

Now although wise men regard as foolish certain things that appear wise to a fool, because the former are sound in judgment, the sensual man's estimation that things according to the Spirit are foolish does not proceed from sound judgment but from a lack of understanding, because a man given to sense cannot understand things that transcend sense, and a man attracted by carnal things does not realize that there are other goods besides those which please the senses.

That is why he continues: **and he cannot understand**: *they have neither knowledge nor understanding, they walk about in darkness* (Ps 82:5).

115. But why he cannot understand is shown when he says, **because it is spiritually examined**, i.e., spiritual things are examined in a spiritual way. For the lower can never examine and judge things that pertain to the higher, just as the sense cannot examine things that are strictly intellectual. Similarly, neither the senses nor human reason can judge things of the Spirit of God. The consequence is that things of this sort are examined by the Holy Spirit alone: *the words of the Lord are examined by fire* (Ps 18:30), i.e., proved by the Holy Spirit.

Therefore, because the sensual man lacks the Holy Spirit, he cannot examine spiritual things and, consequently, cannot understand them.

116. Then when he says, **but the spiritual man**, he gives the reason why spiritual things are imparted to spiritual men.

First, he gives the reason;

second, he clarifies it, at **for who has known**.

117. The reason given is this: spiritual things should be entrusted to one who can discern: *the ear discerns with words* (Job 12:11); but the spiritual man is such. Therefore, spiritual things should be entrusted to him. And this is what he says: **but the spiritual man judges all things: and he himself is judged of no man**.

Here it should be noted what sort of man is called spiritual. Recall, therefore, that we usually call incorporeal substances, spirits. Consequently, because there is a definite part of the soul not associated with any bodily organ,

scilicet pars intellectiva comprehendens intellectum et voluntatem, huiusmodi pars animae spiritus hominis dicitur, quae tamen a Spiritu Dei et illuminatur secundum intellectum, et inflammatur secundum affectum et voluntatem.

Dupliciter ergo dicitur homo spiritualis. Uno modo ex parte intellectus, Spiritu Dei illustrante. Et secundum hoc in Glossa dicitur quod homo spiritualis est, qui, Spiritui Dei subiectus, certissime ac fideliter spiritualia cognoscit. Alio modo ex parte voluntatis, Spiritu Dei inflammante: et hoc modo dicitur in Glossa quod spiritualis vita est, qua Spiritum Dei habens rectorem animam regit, id est animales vires. Gal. ult.: *vos qui spirituales estis, instruite huiusmodi*, etc.

118. Secundo considerandum est quare spiritualis diiudicat omnia, et ipse a nemine iudicatur.

Ubi notandum est quod in omnibus ille qui recte se habet, rectum iudicium habet circa singula. Ille autem qui in se rectitudinis defectum patitur, deficit etiam in iudicando: vigilans enim recte iudicat et se vigilare et alium dormire; sed dormiens non habet rectum iudicium de se, nec de vigilante. Unde non sunt res tales quales videntur dormienti, sed quales videntur vigilanti. Et eadem ratio est de sano et infirmo circa iudicium saporum, et de debili et forti circa iudicium ponderum, et virtuoso et vitioso circa agibilia. Unde et Philosophus dicit in V *Ethicorum* quod virtuosus est regula et mensura omnium humanorum, quia scilicet in rebus humanis talia sunt singularia, qualia virtuosus iudicat ea esse. Et secundum hunc modum Apostolus hic dicit quod **spiritualis iudicat omnia**, quia scilicet homo habens intellectum illustratum et affectum ordinatum per Spiritum Sanctum, de singulis quae pertinent ad salutem, rectum iudicium habet.

Ille autem qui non est spiritualis habet etiam intellectum obscuratum et affectum inordinatum circa spiritualia bona, et ideo ab homine non spirituali, spiritualis homo iudicari non potest, sicut nec vigilans a dormiente.

Quantum ergo ad primum horum dicitur Sap. III, 8 quod *iudicabunt iusti nationes*. Quantum ad secundum dicitur infra IV, 3: **mihi pro minimo est, ut a vobis iudicer, aut ab humano die**.

119. Deinde cum dicit **quis enim novit**, etc., manifestat rationem inductam. Et

primo inducit auctoritatem;

secundo adaptat ad propositum, ibi **nos autem**, et cetera.

120. Est autem considerandum quod ad hoc quod aliquis possit de aliquo homine iudicare, duo requiruntur.

namely, the intellectual part, which includes both intellect and will, that part of the soul is called the man's spirit. Now in this part of the soul the Spirit of God enlightens the intellect and enkindles the affections and will.

Hence, man is called spiritual in two ways: first, on the part of the intellect enlightened by the Spirit of God. In this way man is called spiritual, because, being subjected to the Spirit of God, he knows spiritual things with the greatest certitude and fidelity. Second, on the part of the will enkindled by the Spirit of God. As it says in the Gloss, in this way a life is called spiritual because, having the Spirit of God as its guide, it rules the soul, i.e., the sensual powers: *you who are spiritual should restore him in a spirit of gentleness* (Gal 6:1).

118. Second, we should note why a spiritual man judges all things and is himself not judged by any man.

The explanation is this: in all matters a person who is sound has a sound judgment regarding individual cases; whereas a person who is unsound in any way fails in his judgements. Thus, a person who is awake makes the sound judgment that he is awake and that someone else is sleeping, but one who is sleeping has no sound judgment about himself or a person who is awake. Hence things are not as they appear to be to a person asleep, but as they appear to be to a person awake. The same holds for a healthy man's judgment of savors and that of a sick man; or a strong man's judgment of the weight of an object and that of a weak man's, and for a virtuous man's judgment of morals and that of a vicious man. Hence the Philosopher says in the *Ethics* V that the virtuous man is the rule and standard of all human acts, because in all human affairs particular acts are such as a virtuous man judges them to be. It is in this vein that the Apostle says here that **the spiritual man judges all things**, namely, because a man with an intellect enlightened by the Holy Spirit and set in good order by him has a sound judgment about the particulars which pertain to salvation.

But a person who is not spiritual has his intellect darkened and his will disarranged, as far as spiritual goods are concerned. Consequently, the spiritual man cannot be judged by a man who is not spiritual any more than a man who is awake by one who is asleep.

Therefore, as to the first group it is said that *the just shall judge all nations* (Wis 3:8), and below the Apostle, speaking about the second group says: **but to me it is a very small thing to be judged by you or by man's day** (1 Cor 4:3).

119. Then when he says, **for who has known**, he supports the reason he gave:

first, he adduces an authority;

second, he applies it to his proposition, at **but we have the mind**.

120. Here it should be noted that if a person is to judge another, two things are required: first, that the judge know

Primo ut iudicans cognoscat ea quae sunt iudicati, quia, ut dicitur I *Ethic.*: *unusquisque bene iudicat quae cognoscit, et horum est optimus iudex.* Ex quo patet quod sensum, id est sapientiam Dei omnia iudicantem, nullus possit diiudicare. Ideo dicit **quis enim novit sensum Domini?** Quasi dicat: nullus: quia sapientia Dei excedit omnem cupiditatem hominis. Eccli. I, 3: *sapientiam Dei praecedentem omnia quis investigavit?* Sap. IX, 17: *sensum autem tuum quis scire poterit, nisi tu dederis sapientiam?*

Secundo requiritur quod iudicans sit superior iudicato. Unde dominus habet iudicium de servo, magister de discipulo. Ex quo etiam patet quod nullus potest sensum Dei iudicare. Propter quod sequitur **aut quis instruxit eum?** Quasi dicat: nullus. Non enim habet scientiam ab aliquo acceptam, sed potius fontem omnis scientiae. Iob XXVI, 3: *cui dedisti consilium? Forsitan ei qui non habet sapientiam?*

Videntur autem verba haec assumpta ex eo quod dicitur Is. XL, 13: *quis adiuvit Spiritum Domini, aut quis consiliarius eius fuit* et ostendit illi? Cum quo iniit consilium et instruxit eum?

121. Deinde adaptat quod dixerat ad propositum, dicens **nos autem**, scilicet spirituales viri, **sensum Christi habemus**, idest, recipimus in nobis sapientiam Christi ad iudicandum. Eccli. XVII, 6: *creavit illis scientiam spiritus, sensu adimplevit corda illorum.* Lc. ult. dicitur quod *aperuit illis sensum, ut intelligerent Scripturas*, et ita, quia sensus Christi diiudicari non potest, conveniens est quod spiritualis, qui sensum Christi habet, a nemine iudicetur.

the things which pertain to the one being judged, because it says in *Ethics* I: *each one judges well the things he knows and of such things he is the best judge.* From this it follows that no one can judge the mind, i.e., the wisdom of God which judges all things; hence he says, **for who has known the mind of the Lord.** As if to say: no one, because God's wisdom transcends all human ability: *who has searched out the wisdom of God that goes before all things?* (Sir 1:3); *who has learned your counsel, unless you have given wisdom?* (Wis 9:17).

Second, it is necessary that the one judging be superior to the one being judged. Hence the lord has judgment over a slave, and the teacher over a student. From this it is clear that no one can judge the mind of God; hence he continues, **that he may instruct him?** As if to say: no one. For God's knowledge is not obtained from just anyone, but he is the source of all knowledge: *how you have counseled him who has no wisdom* (Job 26:3).

It seems that these words of the Apostle were taken from Isaiah: *who has helped the Spirit of the Lord? Or who has been his counselor* (Isa 40:13) and taught him? With whom has he consulted and who has instructed him?

121. Then he applies this to his proposition, saying, **but we**, i.e., spiritual men, **have the mind of Christ**, i.e., receive within ourselves the wisdom of Christ to enable us to judge: *he created in them the science of the spirit: he filled their heart with wisdom* (Sir 17:6); *he opened their understanding, that they might understand the Scriptures* (Luke 24:25). Consequently, because the mind of Christ cannot be judged, it is fitting that the spiritual man, who has the mind of Christ, be judged of no man.

CHAPTER 3

Lecture 1

3:1Et ego, fratres, non potui vobis loqui quasi spiritualibus, sed quasi carnalibus. Tamquam parvulis in Christo, [n. 122]

3:2lac vobis potum dedi, non escam: nondum enim poteratis: sed nec nunc quidem potestis: [n. 125]

3:3adhuc enim carnales estis. Cum enim sit inter vos zelus, et contentio: nonne carnales estis, et secundum hominem ambulatis? [n. 128]

3:4Cum enim quis dicat: ego quidem sum Pauli; alius autem: ego Apollo: nonne homines estis? [n. 131]

3:5Quid igitur est Apollo? quid vero Paulus? ministri ejus, cui credidistis, ut unicuique sicut Dominus dedit. [n. 133]

3:6Ego plantavi, Apollo rigavit: sed Deus incrementum dedit. [n. 136]

3:7Itaque neque qui plantat est aliquid, neque qui rigat: sed qui incrementum dat, Deus. [n. 137]

3:8Qui autem plantat, et qui rigat, unum sunt. [n. 138] Unusquisque autem propriam mercedem accipiet, secundum suum laborem. [n. 139]

3:1Κἀγώ, ἀδελφοί, οὐκ ἠδυνήθην λαλῆσαι ὑμῖν ὡς πνευματικοῖς ἀλλ' ὡς σαρκίνοις, ὡς νηπίοις ἐν Χριστῷ.

3:2γάλα ὑμᾶς ἐπότισα, οὐ βρῶμα, οὔπω γὰρ ἐδύνασθε. ἀλλ' οὐδὲ ἔτι νῦν δύνασθε,

3:3ἔτι γὰρ σαρκικοί ἐστε. ὅπου γὰρ ἐν ὑμῖν ζῆλος καὶ ἔρις, οὐχὶ σαρκικοί ἐστε καὶ κατὰ ἄνθρωπον περιπατεῖτε;

3:4ὅταν γὰρ λέγῃ τις, Ἐγὼ μέν εἰμι Παύλου, ἕτερος δέ, Ἐγὼ Ἀπολλῶ, οὐκ ἄνθρωποί ἐστε;

3:5τί οὖν ἐστιν Ἀπολλῶς; τί δέ ἐστιν Παῦλος; διάκονοι δι' ὧν ἐπιστεύσατε, καὶ ἑκάστῳ ὡς ὁ κύριος ἔδωκεν.

3:6ἐγὼ ἐφύτευσα, Ἀπολλῶς ἐπότισεν, ἀλλὰ ὁ θεὸς ηὔξανεν·

3:7ὥστε οὔτε ὁ φυτεύων ἐστίν τι οὔτε ὁ ποτίζων, ἀλλ' ὁ αὐξάνων θεός.

3:8ὁ φυτεύων δὲ καὶ ὁ ποτίζων ἕν εἰσιν, ἕκαστος δὲ τὸν ἴδιον μισθὸν λήμψεται κατὰ τὸν ἴδιον κόπον.

3:1And I, brethren, could not speak to you as unto spiritual, but as unto carnal. As unto little ones in Christ. [n. 122]

3:2I gave you milk to drink, not meat: for you were not able as yet. But neither indeed are you now able: [n. 125]

3:3For you are yet carnal. For, while there is among you envying and contention, are you not carnal and walk according to man? [n. 128]

3:4For while one says: I indeed am of Paul: and another: I am of Apollo: are you not men? [n. 131]

3:5What then is Apollo and what is Paul? The ministers of him whom you have believed: and to every one as the Lord has given. [n. 133]

3:6I have planted, Apollo watered: but God gave the increase. [n. 136]

3:7Therefore, neither he who plants is anything, nor he who waters: but God who gives the increase. [n. 137]

3:8Now he who plants and he who waters, are one. [n. 138] And every man shall receive his own reward, according to his own labor. [n. 139]

---

122. Supra Apostolus ostenderat contentionem et divisionem Corinthiorum, qui propter ministros Christi, a quibus baptizati et docti erant, ad invicem disceptabant; hic incipit eorum iudicium quod habebant de ministris improbare, ex quo iudicio contentiones in eis procedebant.

Et circa hoc duo facit.

Primo improbat eorum iudicium quantum ad hoc quod quibusdam ministrorum, de quibus gloriabantur, plus attribuebant quam deberent;

secundo, quantum ad hoc quod alios Christi ministros contemnebant, IV cap., ibi *sic nos existimet homo*.

123. Circa primum duo facit.

Primo ostendit detrimentum quod patiebantur propter contentiones ex perverso iudicio provenientes;

122. Above the Apostle disclosed the strife and division among the Corinthians, who disputed among themselves about the particular ministers of Christ who had baptized and instructed them. Here he begins to attack their judgment of these ministers as the root of their strife.

In regard to this he does two things.

First, he attacks their judgment, insofar as they attributed more than they should to those ministers in whom they boast;

second, insofar as they looked down on the other ministers of Christ, at *let a man so account of us* (1 Cor 4:1).

123. In regard to the first he does two things.

First, he shows the loss they suffered from the strifes arising from the perverse judgment;

secundo improbat eorum perversum iudicium, ibi **quid igitur est Apollo?**

Circa primum duo facit.

Primo ponit detrimentum quod hactenus passi erant propter eorum defectum;

secundo ostendit quod adhuc idem patiuntur, ibi **sed nec nunc quidem**.

123. Circa primum tria facit.

Primo ponit detrimentum quod hactenus passi erant propter eorum defectum. Dixerat enim supra quod apostoli quidem spiritualia documenta spiritualibus tradebant, quae animales homines percipere non poterant: quod eis adaptat, dicens **et ego, fratres**, qui scilicet inter alios apostolos spiritualibus spiritualia loquor, **non potui**, scilicet convenienter, **vobis loqui quasi spiritualibus**, ut scilicet traderem vobis spiritualia documenta, **sed quasi carnalibus**, scilicet locutus sum vobis. Eosdem enim carnales dicit quos supra animales, quibus oportet tradi ea quae sunt infirmitati eorum accommoda. Is. XXVIII, 9: *quem docebit scientiam, et quem intelligere faciet auditum? Ablactatos a lacte, avulsos ab uberibus*, id est, carnali conversatione et sensu.

124. Secundo adhibet similitudinem, dicens **tamquam parvulis in Christo**, id est, parum adhuc introductis in perfectam doctrinam fidei, quae spiritualibus debetur. Hebr. c. V, 13: *omnis qui lactis est particeps, expers est sermonis iustitiae; parvulus enim est: perfectorum autem est solidus cibus*.

125. Tertio rationem assignat, ne credatur ex invidia eis spiritualem doctrinam subtraxisse, contra quod dicitur Sap. VII, 13: *quam sine fictione didici, et sine invidia communico*. Unde subditur **nondum enim poteratis**, quasi dicat: non subtraxi vobis escam propter meam invidiam, sed propter vestram impotentiam, quia verba spiritualia **nondum** bene **poteratis** capere, secundum illud Io. XVI, v. 12: *adhuc multa habeo vobis dicere, sed non potestis portare modo*.

126. Deinde, cum dicit **sed nec nunc quidem potestis**, ostendit quod adhuc idem detrimentum patiuntur.

Et primo quidem ponit impotentiam cui adhuc subiacebant, dicens **sed nec nunc quidem potestis**, quasi dicat: quod a principio perfectam doctrinam capere non poteratis, non mirum fuit, quia hoc nescire vestrae novitati competebat, secundum illud I Petr. c. II, 2: *sicut modo geniti infantes lac concupiscite*. Sed hoc videtur esse culpabile, quod post tantum tempus in quo proficere debuistis, eamdem impotentiam retinetis, secundum illud Hebr. V, 12: *cum deberetis magistri esse propter tempus, rursus indigetis doceri, quae sunt elementa sermonum Dei*.

127. Secundo assignat praedictae impotentiae rationem, dicens **adhuc enim carnales estis**, scilicet vita

second, he attacks their perverse judgment, at **what then is Apollo**.

As to the first he does two things.

First, he mentions the loss they have suffered till now on account of this fault;

second, he shows that they are still suffering from it, at **but neither indeed are you now able**.

123. In regard to the first he does three things.

First, he mentions the loss they have suffered till now from this fault. For above he had said that the apostles delivered spiritual things to spiritual men, teachings which sensual men were not able to apprehend. Now he applies this to them saying, **and I, brethren**, who along with all the other apostles speak spiritual things to spiritual men, **could not speak to you as unto spiritual men**, i.e., deliver spiritual teachings to you, **but as unto carnal** I have spoken to you. Here he calls the carnal the same ones he first called sensual, to whom must be delivered things suited to their weakness: *whom will he teach knowledge, and to whom will he explain the message? Those who are weaned from the milk, those taken from the breast* (Isa 28:9), i.e., from a carnal understanding and way of life.

124. Second, he employs a simile, saying, **as unto little ones in Christ**, i.e., barely introduced to the perfect teachings of the faith which is given to spiritual men: *everyone who lives on milk is unskilled in the word of righteousness, for he is a child; but the perfect live on solid food* (Heb 5:13).

125. Third, he gives the reason, lest they suppose that he withholds spiritual teaching from them through envy, which would be opposed to Wisdom: *which I learned without guile and impart without envy* (Wis 7:13). That is why he adds, **for you were not able as yet**. As if to say: it was not through envy that I kept spiritual things from you, but on account of your incapacity, **for you were not able as yet** to grasp well spiritual words: *I have yet many things to say to you; but you cannot bear them now* (John 16:12).

126. Then when he says, **but neither indeed are you now able**, he shows that even now they are suffering the same loss.

First, he shows the incapacity under which they are still laboring when he says, **but neither indeed are you now able**. As if to say: it was not strange that in the beginning you were unable to grasp a fuller teaching, because this was expected of your newness: *as newborn babes, desire the rational milk without guile* (1 Pet 2:2). But it seems sinful that in spite of the time during which you could have made progress, you still show the same incapacity: *for though by this time you ought to be teachers, you need someone to teach you again the first principles of God's word* (Heb 5:12).

127. Second, he gives the reason why they are still unable, saying, **for you are yet carnal** in life and mind. That

et sensu. Et ideo ea quae sunt Spiritus capere non potestis, sed sapitis ea quae sunt carnis, secundum illud Rom. VIII, 5: *qui secundum carnem sunt, quae carnis sunt sapiunt.*

128. Tertio ponit rationem probationis inductae, dicens, *cum enim inter vos sit zelus et contentio, nonne carnales estis, et secundum hominem ambulatis?*

Ubi considerandum est quod recte coniungit **zelum et contentionem**, quia zelus, id est invidia, est contentionis materia. Invidus enim tristatur de bono alterius, quod ille nititur promovere, et ex hoc sequitur contentio. Unde Iac. III, 16: *ubi zelus et contentio, ibi inconstantia et omne opus pravum.* Et similiter e converso caritas, per quam quis diligit bonum alterius, est materia pacis.

129. Secundo considerandum est quod **zelus et contentio** non habent locum nisi in carnalibus hominibus, quia ipsi circa bona corporalia afficiuntur, quae simul a pluribus integre possideri non possunt. Et ideo, propter hoc quod aliquis aliquod bonum corporale possidet, alius impeditur a plena possessione illius, et ex hoc sequitur invidia, et per consequens contentio. Sed spiritualia bona, quibus spirituales afficiuntur, simul a pluribus possideri possunt, et ideo bonum unius non est alterius impedimentum, et propter hoc in talibus nec invidia, nec contentio locum habet. Unde Sap. VII, 13: *sine invidia communico.*

130. Tertio considerandum est quare homines carnales dicit **secundum hominem ambulare**, cum tamen homo ex spiritu et carne componatur, quia naturae humanae consonum est, ut spiritus cognitionem a sensibus carnis accipiat. Unde consequenter affectus rationis humanae secundum ea quae sunt carnis movetur, nisi spiritus hominis per Spiritum Dei supra hominem elevetur. Unde dicitur Eccli. XXXIV, 6: *sicut parturientis, cor tuum phantasias patitur, nisi ab altissimo fuerit emissa visitatio.*

Est ergo sensus **secundum hominem**, id est, secundum naturam humanam sibi a Dei Spiritu derelictam, sicut et in Ps. IV, 3 dicitur: *filii hominum, usquequo gravi corde, ut quid diligitis vanitatem et quaeritis mendacium?*

131. Quarto manifestat probationem inductam, dicens *cum enim quis*, id est, aliquis vestrum, *dicat: ego quidem sum Pauli*, quia a Paulo baptizatus et doctus, *alius autem: ego Apollo* (genitivi casus), per quod denotatur in vobis esse **zelus et contentio**, *nonne homines estis*, scilicet carnales et non spirituales, utpote zelum et contentionem habentes pro rebus humanis? Qualis enim homo est, talibus rebus afficitur et per affectum inhaeret, secundum illud Osee IX, 10: *facti sunt abominabiles, sicut ea quae dilexerunt.*

is the reason why you cannot grasp the things of the Spirit, but have a taste for the things of the flesh: *they who are of the flesh mind the things of the flesh* (Rom 8:5).

128. Third, he gives the reason behind the proof, saying, *for, while there is among you envying and contention, are you not carnal and walk according to man?*

Here it should be noted that he was right in joining **envying** with **contention**, because envying, i.e., jealousy, is the food of contention, for a jealous person is grieved at another's good, which the latter tries to improve and from this arises strife. Hence James says: *where envying and contention exist, there will be disorder and every vile practice* (Jas 3:16). On the other hand, charity through which a person loves another's good is the source of peace.

129. Second, it should be noted that **envying and contention** occur only among carnal persons because, being attracted to material goods which cannot each be possessed by many persons at the same time, whenever one person owns a material good, another person is prevented from fully possessing it. From this follows jealousy and later contention. But spiritual goods, by which spiritual persons are attracted can be possessed by several persons at the same time; consequently, one's good is not another's loss. For this reason neither jealousy nor contention finds a place among them: *which I impart without envy* (Wis 7:13).

130. Third, it should be noted that carnal men are said to **walk according to man**, even though man is composed of spirit and flesh. For it is consonant with human nature to obtain knowledge of the spirit from the senses of the flesh; consequently, the affections of human reason are moved by the things of the flesh, unless man's spirit is raised above man by the Spirit of God, for *the heart fancies as a woman in travail, unless it be a vision sent forth by the Most High* (Sir 34:6).

Therefore, the sense is this, *according to man*, i.e., according to human nature left to itself by the Spirit of God, as in a psalm: *O men, how long shall my honor suffer shame? How long will you love vain words and seek after lies?* (Ps 4:3).

131. Fourth, he clarifies the proof, saying, *for while one says: I indeed am of Paul*, because I have been baptized and instructed by Paul, *and another: I am of Apollo*, which shows that there is **envying and contention** among you, *are you not men*, i.e., carnal and not spiritual, indulging in jealousy and strife for human things? For as a man is, so is he affected by corresponding things and desires them: *they became detestable as the thing they loved* (Hos 9:10).

132. Deinde, cum dicit *quid igitur est Apollo?* Improbat eorum iudicium, quantum ad hoc quod plus ministris attribuebant quam deberent. Et

primo ostendit veritatem;

secundo excludit errorem, ibi *nemo vos seducat*;

tertio infert conclusionem intentam, ibi *itaque nemo glorietur in hominibus*.

Circa primum duo facit.

Primo ostendit conditionem ministrorum;

secundo agit de eorum mercede, ibi *unusquisque propriam mercedem*.

Circa primum tria facit.

Primo ponit ministrorum conditionem;

secundo ponit similitudinem, ibi *ego plantavi, Apollo rigavit*;

tertio ostendit intentum, ibi *itaque neque qui plantat*.

133. Circa conditionem autem ministrorum duo tangit. Primo quod non sunt Domini, sed ministri, dicens: vos de Paulo et Apollo gloriamini, igitur quaero a vobis: *quid est Apollo, et quid Paulus?* Id est, cuius dignitatis vel potestatis, ut digne de eis gloriari possitis? Et respondet: *ministri eius*, scilicet Dei sunt. Quasi dicat: quod agunt in baptismo et in doctrina, non principaliter agunt sicut Domini, sed sicut ministri eius, secundum illud Is. LXI, 6: *ministri Dei, dicetur vobis*.

Posset autem alicui videri magnum esse, ministrum Dei esse, et gloriandum esse in hominibus de ministeriis Dei. Et vere esset, si sine hominibus non pateret accessus ad Deum, sicut illi qui solent gloriari de ministris regis, sine quibus non patet aditus ad regem. Sed hoc hic locum non habet, quia fideles Christi per fidem habent accessum ad Deum, secundum illud Rom. V, 2: *per quem accessum habemus* ad Deum *per fidem et gratiam istam, in qua stamus, et gloriamur in spe gloriae filiorum Dei*. Ideo signanter addit *cui credidistis*, quasi dicat: per fidem iam estis coniuncti Deo, non hominibus. Unde supra II, 5 dictum est: *ut fides vestra non sit in sapientia hominum, sed in virtute Dei*. Et ideo primo de Deo est vobis gaudendum, quam de hominibus.

134. Contingit autem quod ministri hominum, vel Dominorum, vel artificum primo habeant a seipsis aliquam dignitatem, vel virtutem, ex qua idonei ad ministerium fiunt, sed hoc non est de ministris Dei. Et ideo, secundo, ostendit quod tota dignitas et virtus ministrorum est a Deo, dicens *et unicuique sicut Deus divisit*, quasi dicat: in tantum aliquis, et unusquisque nostrum habet de virtute ministrandi, inquantum ei Deus dedit, unde nec sic nobis est gloriandum. II Cor. c. III, 5 s.: *sufficientia nostra a Deo, qui idoneos nos fecit ministros novi testamenti*.

132. Then when he says, *what then is Apollo*, he spurns their judgment, insofar as they attributed more to their ministers than they deserved.

First, he discloses the truth;

second, he excludes their error, at *let no man deceive* (1 Cor 3:18);

third, he draws the conclusion he intended, at *let no man therefore glory in men* (1 Cor 3:21).

As to the first he does two things.

First, he shows the condition of the ministers.

second, he speaks about their reward, at *every man shall receive his own reward* (1 Cor 3:8).

As to the first he does three things.

First, he describes the status of the ministers;

second, he proposes a simile, at *I have planted, Apollo watered*;

third, he explains his intent, at *therefore, neither he who plants*.

133. Touching on the status of the ministers, he mentions two things: first, that they are not masters, but ministers, saying: you boast of Paul and Apollo. So I ask you: *what then is Apollo and what is Paul*, i.e., what is their dignity and power, if you are to be reasonable in boasting of them? And he answers: *the ministers of him*, namely, of God. As if to say: what they do when baptizing and instructing, they do not do as masters but as God's ministers: *men shall speak of you as the ministers of our God* (Isa 61:6).

But someone might consider it great to be a minister of God and suppose that one should boast of men who are ministers of God. This would be true, if God could not be approached without men, as happens when men glory in the king's ministers, without whom the king cannot be approached. But this is not applicable here, because Christ's faithful have access to God by faith, as it says in Romans: *through him we have obtained access to this grace in which we stand, and we rejoice in our hope of sharing the glory of God* (Rom 5:2). Therefore, he is careful to say, *whom you believed*. As if to say: by faith you have now been joined to God and not to men. That is why he said above: *that your faith might not stand on the wisdom of men, but on the power of God* (1 Cor 2:5). Therefore you should take joy first in God and not in men.

134. But it sometimes happens that ministers of men have some dignity or skill that makes them fit to be ministers. This is not true of God's ministers. Therefore, he shows that the worthiness and power of God's ministers is entirely from God, saying, *and to everyone as the Lord has given*. As if to say: each one of us has as much power in ministering as the Lord has granted to him; consequently, there is no reason for boasting in us for ourselves: *our sufficiency is from God, who has qualified us to be ministers of a new covenant* (2 Cor 3:5).

135. Deinde, cum dicit *ego plantavi*, ponit similitudinem ministrorum ex similitudine agricolarum, ubi duplex differentia operationum intelligitur. Una, operationis unius ministri ad operationem alterius. Et quantum ad hoc dicit *ego plantavi*, id est, in praedicatione ad modum plantantis me habui, quia scilicet primo vobis praedicavi fidem, Is. LI, v. 16: *posui verba mea in ore tuo, ut plantes caelos*; *Apollo rigavit*, id est, ad modum rigantis se habuit, qui aquam plantis exhibet ad hoc ut nutriantur et crescant. Et similiter legitur Act. XVIII, 1 s. quod, cum Paulus multos Corinthiorum convertisset, supervenit Apollo, qui multum contulit his qui crediderunt, publice ostendens per Scripturam esse Iesum Christum. Eccli. c. XXIV, 42 dicitur: *rigabo hortum meum plantationum*.

136. Secunda differentia est operationis ministrorum, qui exterius operantur plantando et rigando, ad operationem Dei, qui interius operatur. Unde subdit *sed Deus incrementum dedit*, interius scilicet operando. II Cor. IX, 10: *augebit incrementa frugum iustitiae vestrae*. Sic etiam in rebus corporalibus plantantes et rigantes exterius operantur, sed Deus operatur interius per operationem naturae ad incrementa plantarum.

137. Deinde cum dicit *itaque neque qui plantat, neque qui rigat*, etc., infert ex praemissis duas conclusiones, quarum prima infertur secundum comparationem ministrorum ad Deum, dicens: ex quo Paulus plantavit, et Apollo rigavit, non sunt nisi ministri Dei, et non habent aliquid nisi a Deo, et non operantur nisi exterius, Deo interius operante. *Itaque neque qui plantat est aliquid*, scilicet principaliter et magnum de quo sit gloriandum, *neque qui rigat, sed qui incrementum dat, Deus*.

Ipse enim per se est aliquid principale et magnum, de quo est gloriandum. Actio enim non attribuitur instrumento, cui comparatur minister, sed principali agenti. Unde Is. XL, v. 17 dicitur: *omnes gentes quasi non sint, sic sunt coram eo*.

138. Secundam conclusionem infert pertinentem ad comparationem ministrorum ad invicem, dicens *qui plantat autem, et qui rigat*, cum sint ministri Dei, et nihil nisi a Deo habentes, et solum exterius operantes, *unum sunt*, ex conditione naturae et ministerii ratione: quare scilicet non potest unus alteri praeferri, nisi secundum donum Dei, et ita quantum in seipsis est, unum sunt.

Et quia, consequenter, in intentione ministrandi Deo unum sunt per concordiam voluntatis, ideo stultum est de his qui unum sunt, dissentire. Ps. CXXXII, 1: *ecce quam bonum et quam iucundum habitare fratres in unum*. Rom. XII, 5: *multi unum corpus sumus in Christo*.

135. Then when he says, *I have planted*, he stresses a similarity between ministers and husbandmen, where two differences in their activities should be noted: one is the difference between the activity of one minister and that of another. In regard to this he says, *I have planted*, i.e., in preaching to you I was like a planter, because I was the first one to preach the faith to you: *I have put my words in your mouth, that you might plant the heavens* (Isa 51:16); *Apollo watered*, i.e., he acted as a person who waters plants to nourish them and make them grow. In the same way we read in Acts that after Paul had converted many Corinthians (Acts 19:1), Apollo came on the scene and contributed many things to the believers, showing publicly by the Scriptures that Jesus is Christ, and fulfilling what is said in Sirach: *I will water my orchard* (Sir 24:31).

136. The second difference is found in the work of ministers, who by planting and watering cooperate outwardly with the work of God who works inwardly, hence he adds, *but God gave the increase*: *he will increase the harvest of your righteousness* (2 Cor 9:10). So, too, in material things, planters and waterers work from without, but God works from within by the activity of nature to make plants grow.

137. Then when he says, *therefore, neither he who plants*, he draws two conclusions from these premises. The first of these is based on the minister's dependence on God: inasmuch as Paul planted and Apollo watered, they were but ministers of God, having nothing but what they received from God; and they worked only from without, God working within. *Therefore, neither he who plants is anything*, namely, is important and great, from which he would need to be glorified; *but God who gives the increase*.

For God is independent and great by himself: for an action is not attributed to the instrument, which a minister is, but to the principal cause. Hence it is said: *all nations are as nothing before him* (Isa 40:17).

138. The second conclusion is based on a comparison between the various ministers, *he who plants and he who waters*, since both are God's ministers, having nothing but what they receive from God and working only from without, *are one*. Since the only ground for preferring one over another is some divine gift he has received, they are equal, so far as what they have of themselves is concerned.

Furthermore, since their intention is to be God's ministers, they are one in the harmony of their wills; consequently, it is foolish to have dissensions about persons who are one: *behold, how good and how pleasant it is for brethren to dwell in unity* (Ps 111:1); *we, though many, are one body in Christ* (Rom 12:5).

Lecture 2

³:⁸Qui autem plantat, et qui rigat, unum sunt. [n. 138] Unusquisque autem propriam mercedem accipiet, secundum suum laborem. [n. 139]

³:⁹Dei enim sumus adjutores: Dei agricultura estis, Dei aedificatio estis. [n. 144]

³:¹⁰Secundum gratiam Dei, quae data est mihi, ut sapiens architectus fundamentum posui: alius autem superaedificat. Unusquisque autem videat quomodo superaedificet. [n. 147]

³:¹¹Fundamentum enim aliud nemo potest ponere praeter id quod positum est, quod est Christus Jesus. [n. 151]

³:¹²Si quis autem superaedificat super fundamentum hoc, aurum, argentum, lapides pretiosos, ligna, foenum, stipulam, [n. 153]

³:¹³uniuscujusque opus manifestum erit: dies enim Domini declarabit, quia in igne revelabitur: et uniuscujusque opus quale sit, ignis probabit. [n. 162]

³:¹⁴Si cujus opus manserit quod superaedificavit, mercedem accipiet. [n. 166]

³:¹⁵Si cujus opus arserit, detrimentum patietur: ipse autem salvus erit, sic tamen quasi per ignem. [n. 168]

³:⁸ὁ φυτεύων δὲ καὶ ὁ ποτίζων ἕν εἰσιν, ἕκαστος δὲ τὸν ἴδιον μισθὸν λήμψεται κατὰ τὸν ἴδιον κόπον.

³:⁹θεοῦ γάρ ἐσμεν συνεργοί· θεοῦ γεώργιον, θεοῦ οἰκοδομή ἐστε.

³:¹⁰Κατὰ τὴν χάριν τοῦ θεοῦ τὴν δοθεῖσάν μοι ὡς σοφὸς ἀρχιτέκτων θεμέλιον ἔθηκα, ἄλλος δὲ ἐποικοδομεῖ. ἕκαστος δὲ βλεπέτω πῶς ἐποικοδομεῖ·

³:¹¹θεμέλιον γὰρ ἄλλον οὐδεὶς δύναται θεῖναι παρὰ τὸν κείμενον, ὅς ἐστιν Ἰησοῦς Χριστός.

³:¹²εἰ δέ τις ἐποικοδομεῖ ἐπὶ τὸν θεμέλιον χρυσόν, ἄργυρον, λίθους τιμίους, ξύλα, χόρτον, καλάμην,

³:¹³ἑκάστου τὸ ἔργον φανερὸν γενήσεται, ἡ γὰρ ἡμέρα δηλώσει· ὅτι ἐν πυρὶ ἀποκαλύπτεται, καὶ ἑκάστου τὸ ἔργον ὁποῖόν ἐστιν τὸ πῦρ [αὐτὸ] δοκιμάσει.

³:¹⁴εἴ τινος τὸ ἔργον μενεῖ ὃ ἐποικοδόμησεν, μισθὸν λήμψεται·

³:¹⁵εἴ τινος τὸ ἔργον κατακαήσεται, ζημιωθήσεται, αὐτὸς δὲ σωθήσεται, οὕτως δὲ ὡς διὰ πυρός.

³:⁸Now he who plants and he who waters, are one. [n. 138] And every man shall receive his own reward, according to his own labor. [n. 139]

³:⁹For we are God's fellow workers. You are God's husbandry: you are God's building. [n. 144]

³:¹⁰According to the grace of God that is given to me, as a wise architect, I have laid the foundation: and another builds thereon. But let every man take heed how he builds thereupon. [n. 147]

³:¹¹For another foundation no man can lay, but that which is laid: which is Christ Jesus. [n. 151]

³:¹²Now, if any man builds upon this foundation, gold, silver, precious stones, wood, hay, stubble: [n. 153]

³:¹³Every man's work shall be manifest. For the day of the Lord shall declare it, because it shall be revealed in fire. And the fire shall try every man's work, of what sort it is. [n. 162]

³:¹⁴If any man's work abides, which he has built thereupon, he shall receive a reward. [n. 166]

³:¹⁵If any man's work burns, he shall suffer loss: but he himself shall be saved, yet so as by fire. [n. 168]

---

139. Supra Apostolus ostendit qualis sit conditio ministrorum, hic agit de remuneratione eorum. Et

primo ponit de mercede bonorum ministrorum;

secundo agit de punitione malorum, ibi **nescitis quia templum Dei estis**, et cetera.

Circa primum tria facit.

Primo promittit ministris mercedem propriam;

secundo assignat rationem, ibi **Dei enim sumus**;

tertio agit de diversitate mercedis, ibi **secundum gratiam Dei**.

140. Dicit ergo primo: dictum est, quod **neque qui plantat est aliquid, neque qui rigat**, non tamen inutiliter plantat vel rigat, sed **unusquisque suam propriam mercedem accipiet, secundum suum laborem**. Quamvis enim qui incrementum dat, sit Deus, et ipse solus interius operetur, exterius tamen laborantibus mercedem

139. After describing the status of God's ministers, the Apostle now discusses their reward.

First, he discusses the reward of good ministers;

second, the punishment of evil ones, at **know you not that you are the temple of God** (1 Cor 3:16).

In regard to the first he does three things.

First, he mentions the reward reserved for ministers;

second, he assigns the reason, at **for we are God's fellow workers**;

third, the variety of rewards, at **according to the grace of God**.

140. He says, therefore: I have said that **neither he who plants is anything, nor he who waters** (1 Cor 3:7); nevertheless, he does not plant or water in vain, but **every man shall receive his own reward, according to his own labor**. For although God alone gives the increase and he alone works from within, he gives a reward to those who labor

tribuit, secundum illud Ier. XXXI, 16: *quiescat vox tua a ploratu, et oculi tui a lacrymis; quia merces est operi tuo.* Quae quidem merces est ipse Deus, secundum illud Gen. XV, 1: *ego protector tuus sum, et merces tua multa nimis.* Pro qua mercede laborantes mercenarii laudantur, secundum illud Lc. XV, 17: *quanti mercenarii in domo patris mei abundant panibus?* Alioquin si pro alia mercede in opere Dei aliquis laboret, laudandus non est, secundum illud Io. X, 12: *mercenarius autem, cuius non sunt oves propriae, videt lupum venientem, et fugit.*

141. Haec autem merces et communis est omnibus, et propria singulorum: communis quidem, quia idem est quod omnes videbunt, et quo omnes fruentur, scilicet Deus, secundum illud Iob XXII, 26: *super Omnipotentem deliciis afflues, et levabis ad Deum faciem tuam;* Is. XXVIII, 5: *in illa die erit Dominus exercituum corona gloriae et sertum exultationis populo suo.* Et ideo Matth. c. XX, 9 s. omnibus laborantibus in vinea datur unus denarius.

Propria vero merces erit singulorum: quia unus alio clarius videbit, et plenius fruetur secundum determinatam sibi mensuram. Unde et Dan. XII, 3 illi qui docti sunt, comparantur splendori firmamenti, qui ad iustitiam erudiunt plurimos quasi stellae. Hinc est quod Io. XIV, 2 dicitur: *in domo Patris mei mansiones multae sunt,* propter quod etiam hic dicitur **unusquisque propriam mercedem accipiet**.

142. Ostendit autem secundum quid attendatur mensura propriae mercedis, cum subdit **secundum suum laborem**. Unde et in Ps. CXXVII, 2 dicitur: *labores manuum tuarum, quia manducabis, beatus es et bene tibi erit.*

Non tamen propter hoc designatur aequalitas secundum quantitatem laboris ad mercedem, quia, ut dicitur II Cor. IV, 17: *quod in praesenti est momentaneum et leve tribulationis nostrae, supra modum in sublimitate aeternum gloriae pondus operabitur in nobis.* Sed aequalitatem designat proportionis, ut scilicet ubi est potior labor, ibi sit potior merces.

143. Potest autem intelligi labor esse potior tripliciter. Primo quidem secundum formam caritatis, cui respondet merces essentialis praemii, scilicet fruitionis et visionis divinae. Unde dicitur Io. XIV, 21: *qui diligit me, diligetur a Patre meo, et ego diligam eum, et manifestabo ei meipsum.* Unde qui ex maiori caritate laborat, licet minorem laborem Patiatur, plus de praemio essentiali accipiet.

Secundo ex specie operis; sicut enim in rebus humanis ille magis praemiatur qui in digniori opere laborat, sicut architector quam artifex manualis, licet minus laboret corporaliter: ita etiam in rebus divinis ille qui in nobiliori opere occupatur, maius praemium accipiet quantum ad aliquam praerogativam praemii

outwardly: *let your voice cease from weeping, and your eyes from tears: for there is a reward for your work* (Jer 31:16); this reward is God himself: *I am your protector and your reward exceedingly great* (Gen 15:1). It is for this reward that the laborers are praised: *how many hired servants in my father's house abound with bread!* (Luke 15:17). On the other hand, if he works for any other reward, he is not worthy of praise: *but the hireling, whose own the sheep are not, sees the wolf coming and leaves the sheep* (John 10:12).

141. But this reward is both common to all and peculiar to each: it is common, because what they all see and enjoy is the same God: *then shall you abound in delights in the Almighty, and you shall lift up your face to God* (Job 22:26); *in that day the Lord of hosts shall be a crown of glory, and a garland of joy to the residue of his people* (Isa 28:5). This is why all the laborers in the vineyard receive one penny (Matt 20:9ff).

But the reward will be peculiar to each, because one sees more clearly and enjoys more fully than another according to the measure established for all eternity. Whence they who are learned, are compared to the splendor of the firmament, who unto justice instruct many as though stars. This is why it says in John: *in my Father's house there are many mansions* (John 14:2). For the same reason he says here: *every man shall receive his own reward*.

142. But he indicates the basis for the various rewards when he adds, **according to his own labor**: *you shall eat the labors of you hands; blessed are you and it shall be well with you* (Ps 128:2).

But this does not mean an equal amount of reward for a corresponding amount of labor, because as it is said: *for that which is at present momentary and light of our tribulations, works for us above measure exceedingly an eternal weight of glory* (2 Cor 4:17); rather, it means a proportional equality, so that where the labor is greater the reward is greater.

143. Now there are three ways in which the labor can be considered greater: first, by reason of charity, to which the essential aspect of the reward corresponds, i.e., the enjoyment and sight of God; hence it says in John: *he who loves me will be loved of my Father; and I will love him and will manifest myself to him* (John 14:21). Consequently, one who labors with greater love, even though he endures less difficulties, will receive more of the essential reward.

Second, by reason of the type of work: for just as in human enterprises a person gets a higher wage for a higher type of work, as the architect gets more than the manual laborer, although he does less bodily work, so too in divine matters; a person occupied in a nobler work will receive a greater reward consisting in some special prerogative of the accidental reward, even though he might perhaps

accidentalis, licet forte minus corporaliter laboret. Unde aureola datur doctoribus, virginibus et martyribus.

Tertio ex quantitate laboris, quod quidem contingit dupliciter. Nam quandoque maior labor maiorem mercedem meretur, praecipue quantum ad remissionem poenae, puta quod diutius ieiunat vel longius peregrinatur, et etiam quantum ad gaudium quod percipiet de maiori labore. Unde Sap. X, 17 dicitur: *reddidit, Deus scilicet, iustis mercedem laborum suorum.* Quandoque vero est maior labor ex defectu voluntatis. In his enim quae propria voluntate facimus, minorem laborem sentimus. Et talis magnitudo laboris non augebit, sed minuet mercedem. Unde dicitur Is. XL, 31: *assument pennas ut aquilae, current et non laborabunt, volabunt et non deficient;* et ibi praemittitur: *deficient pueri et laborabunt.*

144. Deinde, cum dicit **Dei enim sumus**, assignat rationem eius quod dixerat. Et

primo ponit rationem;

secundo adhibet similitudinem, ibi **Dei agricultura estis.**

145. Dicit ergo primo: recte quilibet nostrum mercedem accipiet, **Dei enim sumus adiutores**, scilicet secundum nostros labores.

Contra quod videtur esse quod dicitur Iob c. XXVI, 2: *cuius adiutor es, numquid imbecillis?* Et Is. XL, 13: *quis adiuvit Spiritum Domini?*

Dicendum est autem, quod dupliciter aliquis alium adiuvat. Uno modo augendo eius virtutem, et sic nullus potest esse Dei adiutor. Unde et post praemissa verba Iob subditur: *et sustentas brachium eius qui non est fortis.* Alio modo obsequendo operationi alterius, sicut si minister dicatur Domini adiutor, in quantum exequitur opus eius aut ministerium artificis, et hoc modo ministri Dei sunt eius adiutores, secundum illud II Cor. VI, 1: *adiuvantes autem exhortamur.*

Sicut ergo ministri hominum exequentes eorum opera, mercedem ab eis accipiunt secundum suum laborem, ita et minister Dei.

146. Secundo adhibet similitudinem simplicis operis, scilicet agriculturae et aedificationis. Populus quidem fidelis ager est a Deo cultus, in quantum per operationem divinam fructum boni operis Deo acceptum producit, secundum illud Rom. VII, 4: *sitis alterius qui ex mortuis resurrexit, ut fructificetis Deo,* et Io. XV, 1 dicitur: *Pater meus agricola est.*

Et hoc est quod primo dicitur **Dei agricultura estis**, id est, quasi ager a Deo cultus, et fructum ferens eius opere, et populus fidelis est quasi domus a Deo aedificata, inquantum scilicet Deus in eis habitat, secundum illud Eph. II, 22: *et vos coaedificamini in habitaculum Dei.*

Et ideo secundo dicitur **Dei aedificatio estis**, id est aedificium a Deo constructum, secundum illud Ps. CXXVI, 1: *nisi Dominus aedificaverit domum, et*

have done less bodily labor; hence a special crown is given to teachers, to virgins and to martyrs.

Third, by reason of the amount of labor, which happens in two ways: for sometimes a greater labor deserves a greater reward, especially in regard to lightening punishment; as when a person fasts longer or undertakes a longer pilgrimage: and even in regard to the joy he will experience for the greater labor: *he renders to the just the wages of their labors* (Wis 10:17). But sometimes there is greater labor because of a lack of will; for in things we do of our own will, we experience less labor. In this case the amount of labor will not increase but lessen the reward; hence Isaiah says: *they shall take wings as eagles: they shall run and not be weary; they shall walk and not faint* (Isa 40:31); but prior to this he said: *youths shall faint and labor* (Isa 1:30).

144. Then when he says, **for we are God's**, he assigns the reason for what he had said.

First, he gives the reason;

second, he applies a simile, at **you are God's husbandry.**

145. He says, therefore: it is only right that each of us shall receive a reward, **for we are God's fellow workers**, namely, by their labors.

But he seems to be contradicted by Job: *whose helper are you? Is it of him who is weak?* (Job 26:2); *who has helped the Spirit of the Lord?* (Is 40:13).

The answer is that one helps another in two ways: in one way by increasing his strength. In this way no one can be God's helper; hence after the above Job continues, *and do you hold up the arm of him that has no strength?* The other way is by serving in another's work, as when a minister is called a master's helper or an artisan's helper, inasmuch as he does some work for him. In this way God's ministers are his coadjutors: *and we helping do exhort you* (2 Cor 6:1).

Therefore, just as men's ministers receive a reward from them according to their labor, so, too, God's minister.

146. Second, he makes use of a simile referring to simple works, namely, agriculture and building. For the faithful are a field cultivated by God, inasmuch as through God's action they produce the fruit of good works acceptable to God: *that you may belong to another, who is risen again from the dead, that we may bring forth fruit to God* (Rom 7:4); and in John it says: *my Father is the husbandman* (John 15:1).

And this is what he says first: **you are God's husbandry**, i.e., like a field cultivated by God and bearing his fruit. The faithful are also like a house built by God, inasmuch as God lives in them: *you also are built together into a habitation of God in the Spirit* (Eph 2:22).

Therefore, he continues: **you are God's building**, i.e., an edifice constructed by God: *unless the Lord build the house, they labor in vain who build it* (Ps 127:1). In these ways,

cetera. Sic igitur ministri Dei sunt adiutores, inquantum laborant in agricultura et aedificatione fidelis populi.

147. Deinde, cum dicit *secundum gratiam Dei*, etc., agit de diversitate mercedis, et quia merces distinguitur secundum distinctionem laboris, ut dictum est, ideo

primo agit de diversitate laboris;

secundo de diversitate mercedis, ibi *si quis superaedificat*.

148. Circa primum duo facit.

Primo ponit distinctionem laborum;

secundo subiungit admonitionem, ibi *unusquisque autem videat*, et cetera.

148. Circa primum duo facit. Primo, relicta similitudine agriculturae quam supra prosecutus fuerat, sub similitudine aedificationis suum proprium laborem describit, dicens *secundum gratiam Dei quae data est mihi, ut sapiens architectus fundamentum posui*.

Ubi considerandum est quod architectus dicitur principalis artifex, et maxime aedificii, ad quem pertinet comprehendere summam dispositionem totius operis, quae perficitur per operationem manualium artificum. Et ideo dicitur sapiens in aedificio, quia simpliciter sapiens est qui summam causam cognoscit, scilicet Deum, et alios secundum Deum ordinat. Ita sapiens in aedificio dicitur qui principalem causam aedificii, scilicet finem, considerat, et ordinat inferioribus artificibus quid sit propter finem agendum.

Manifestum est autem quod tota structura aedificii ex fundamento dependet, et ideo ad sapientem architectum pertinet idoneum fundamentum collocare. Ipse autem Paulus fundamentum spiritualis aedificii collocavit Corinthiis, unde supra dixit: *ego plantavi*. Sicut enim se habet fundamentum in aedificio, sic plantatio in plantis.

Per utrumque enim significatur spiritualiter prima praedicatio fidei. Unde et ipse dicit Rom. XV, 20: *sic autem praedicavi Evangelium, non ubi nominatus est Christus, ne super alienum fundamentum aedificarem*, et ideo se comparat sapienti architecto.

Hoc autem non suae virtuti attribuit, sed gratiae Dei. Et hoc est quod dicit *secundum gratiam Dei quae data est mihi*, qui scilicet me aptum et idoneum ad hoc ministerium fecit. Infra XV, 10: *abundantius omnibus laboravi, non autem ego, sed gratia Dei mecum*.

149. Secundo describit laborem aliorum, dicens *alius autem*, id est, quicumque inter vos laborat, *superaedificat*, fundamento a me posito.

Quod quidem potest ad duo referri. Uno quidem modo inquantum aliquis superaedificat fidei in seipso fundatae profectum caritatis et bonorum operum. I Petr. II, 5: *et ipsi tamquam lapides vivi superaedificamini*. Alio modo ad doctrinam, per quam quis

then, God's ministers are coadjutors, inasmuch as they labor in cultivating and guiding the faithful.

147. Then when he says, *according to the grace of God*, he discusses the varieties of reward; and because rewards are distinguished according to the varieties of labor.

First he deals with the varieties of labor;

second with the diverse reward, at *now, if any man builds upon*.

148. In regard to the first he does two things.

First, he distinguishes the varieties of labor;

second, he sounds a warning, at *but let every man take heed*.

148. In regard to the first he does two things: first, abandoning the simile based on agriculture, he describes his own labor under the likeness of a building, saying, *according to the grace of God that is given to me, as a wise architect, I have laid the foundation*.

Here it should be noted that an architect, especially of a building, is called the chief artisan, inasmuch as it is his duty to comprehend the entire arrangement of the whole work, which is brought to completion by the activities of the manual laborers. Consequently, he is called wise in building, because he who is wise, simply speaking, considers the highest cause, namely God, and orders all other things according to God. Thus, he who is called wise in building considers the principal cause of the building, i.e., its end, and arranges what is to be done by the subordinate artisans to realize the end.

Now it is obvious that the entire structure of a building depends on the foundation; consequently, it pertains to a wise architect to lay a solid foundation. But Paul himself laid the foundation of the spiritual edifice for the Corinthians; hence he said above, *I have planted* (1 Cor 3:6), for planting is related to plants as the foundations to buildings,

because both signify expressly the first preaching of the faith: *I have preached this Gospel, not where Christ was named, lest I should build upon another man's foundation* (Rom 15:20). This is why he compares himself to a wise architect.

But he attributes this not to his own power but to God's grace; which is what he says, *according to the grace of God that is given to me*, who made me fit and worthy for this ministry: *I have labored more abundantly than all they. Yet not I, but the grace of God with me* (1 Cor 15:10).

149. Second, he describes others' labors, saying, *and another*, i.e., whoever labors among you, *builds thereon* the foundation laid by me.

This can be done in two ways: in one way so that each person builds on the faith produced in him by growing in charity and good works: *be you also as living stone built up* (1 Pet 2:5). In another way by doctrine, whereby one explains more clearly the faith produced in others: *to build*

fundatam fidem in aliis perfectius manifestat. Unde Ier. I, 10 dicitur: *ut aedifices et plantes.* Et secundum hoc idem significat haec superaedificatio, quod supra rigatio.

150. Deinde, cum dicit *unusquisque autem*, etc., subiungit monitionem, dicens: dictum est quod ad alios pertinet superaedificare, *unusquisque autem videat*, id est, diligenter attendat, *quomodo superaedificet*, id est, qualem doctrinam fidei fundatam in aliis superaddat, vel qualia opera fidei in se fundatae habeat. Prov. IV, 25: *oculi tui videant recta, et palpebrae tuae praecedant gressus tuos.*

151. Secundo respondet tacite quaestioni, quare scilicet admoneat alios de superaedificatione et non de fundatione, vel potius assignat rationem quare dixerit quod ad alios pertinet superaedificare, dicens *fundamentum aliud nemo potest ponere, praeter id quod positum est*, scilicet a me, *quod est Iesus Christus*, qui habitat in cordibus vestris per fidem, ut dicitur Eph. III, 17. Et de fundamento dicitur Is. XXVIII, 16: *ecce ego mittam in fundamentis Sion lapidem angularem, probatum, pretiosum*, id est, *in fundamento fundatum.*

152. Sed contra videtur esse quod dicitur Apoc. XXI, 14: *murus civitatis habens fundamenta duodecim, et in ipsis duodecim nomina apostolorum.* Non ergo solus Christus est fundamentum.

Dicendum est autem, quod duplex est fundamentum. Unum quidem quod per se habet soliditatem, sicut rupes aliqua supra quam aedificium construitur, et huic fundamento Christus comparatur. Ipse enim est petra de qua dicitur Matth. VII, 25: *fundata enim erat supra firmam petram.* Aliud est fundamentum, quod habet soliditatem non ex se, sed ex alio solido subiecto, sicut lapides qui primo supponuntur petrae solidae. Et hoc modo dicuntur apostoli esse fundamentum Ecclesiae, quia ipsi primo superaedificati sunt Christo per fidem et caritatem. Unde dicitur Eph. II, 20: *superaedificati supra fundamentum apostolorum.*

153. Deinde cum dicit *si quis superaedificat*, etc., agit de mercedis differentia quantum ad hoc, quod quidam eam accipiunt sine detrimento, quidam cum detrimento.

Et circa hoc tria facit.

Primo docet quod diversitas operationum manifestatur ex retributione;

secundo ostendit quando manifestatur, ibi *dies enim Domini*;

tertio ostendit quomodo manifestatur, ibi *si cuius opus*, et cetera.

154. Circa primum considerandum est quod Apostolus intendens ostendere diversitatem superaedificationis, sex ponit, videlicet tria contra tria. Ex una quidem parte *aurum*, *argentum*, et *lapides pretiosos*; et ex alia parte *lignum*, *foenum* et *stipulam*, quorum tria,

and to plant (Jer 1:10). In this interpretation the building up signifies the same thing as watering signified.

150. Then when he says, **but let every man take heed**, he gives a warning, saying: I have said that it pertains to others to build on the foundation: **but let every man take heed**, i.e., pay careful attention to **how he builds thereupon**, i.e., what sort of doctrine he adds to the faith already existing in others or what sort of works to the faith existing in himself: *let your eyes look straight on, and let your eyelids go before your steps* (Prov 4:25).

151. Second, he answers a tacit question: why he warns them about the superstructure and not the foundations; or rather, he states the reason why he said that the task of others is to build on the foundation. He says: **for another foundation no man can lay, but that which is laid: which is Christ Jesus**, who dwells in your heart by faith: of the foundation it is said (Isa 28:16): *behold, I will lay a stone in the foundations of Zion, a tried stone, a corner stone, a precious stone, founded in the foundation.*

152. On the other hand it seems that Christ is not the sole foundation, because: *the wall of the city had twelve foundations, and in them the twelve names of the twelve apostles* (Rev 21:14).

The answer is that there are two kinds of foundations: one is solid of itself, such as the rock on which the building is constructed. This is the foundation to which Christ is compared; for he is the rock mentioned in Matthew: *for it was founded on a rock* (Matt 7:25). The other is the foundation, which is not solid of itself but rests on a solid object, as the stones placed on solid rock. This is the way the apostles are called the foundation of the Church, because they were the first to be built on Christ by faith and charity: *built on the foundation of the apostles* (Eph 2:20).

153. Then when he says, **now, if any man builds**, he discusses the variety of rewards accordingly as some receive a wage without any loss and some with a loss.

In regard to the first he does three things.

First, he teaches that a variety of works is revealed by the wages;

second, when this is revealed, at **for the day of the Lord**;

third, how it is revealed, at **if any man's work abides**.

154. As to the first it should be noted that the Apostle, in order to point out the varieties of superstructures, mentions six things, i.e., three against three: on the one hand, **gold, silver** and **precious stones**; on the other hand, **wood, hay** and **stubble**. The first three have a striking brilliance,

scilicet aurum, argentum, et lapides pretiosi habent quamdam inclytam claritatem simul et inconsumptibilitatem et pretiositatem. Alia vero tria obscura sunt, et facile ab igne consumuntur, et vilia sunt. Unde per **aurum, argentum** et **lapides pretiosos** intelligitur aliquid praeclarum et stabile; per **lignum** vero, **foenum** et **stipulam** aliquid materiale et transitorium.

Dictum est autem supra quod superaedificatio potest intelligi, et quantum ad opera quae unusquisque superaedificat fidei fundamento, et quantum ad doctrinam quam aliquis doctor vel praedicator superaedificat in fundamento fidei ab Apostolis fundatae. Unde ista diversitas quam hic Apostolus tangit, ad utramque superaedificationem referri potest.

155. Quidam ergo referentes haec ad superaedificationem operum, dixerunt quod per **aurum**, et **argentum**, et **lapides pretiosos** intelliguntur bona, quae quis fidei superaddit. Sed per lignum, foenum, et stipulam debent intelligi peccata mortalia quae quis facit post fidem susceptam. Sed ista expositio penitus stare non potest.

Primo quidem quia peccata mortalia sunt opera mortua, secundum illud Hebr. IX, 14: *mundabit conscientias nostras ab operibus mortuis.* In hoc autem aedificio nihil aedificatur nisi vivum, secundum illud I Petr. II, v. 5: *et ipsi tamquam lapides vivi superaedificamini.* Unde qui cum fide habet peccata mortalia, non superaedificat, sed magis destruit vel violat, contra quem dicitur infra: *si quis templum Dei violaverit, disperdet illum Deus.*

Secundo, quia peccata mortalia magis comparantur ferro, vel plumbo, vel lapidi, tum propter gravitatem, tum quia etiam non renovantur per ignem, sed semper in eo manent in quo sunt: peccata vero venialia comparantur **ligno, foeno** et **stipulae**, tum propter levitatem, tum etiam quia ab eis aliquis de facili expurgatur per ignem.

Tertio, quia secundum hanc expositionem videtur sequi, quod ille qui moritur in peccato mortali, dummodo fidem retineat, finaliter salutem consequatur, licet primo aliquas poenas sustineat. Sic enim sequitur: ***si cuius opus arserit, detrimentum patietur, ipse autem salvus erit, sic tamen quasi per ignem.*** Quod quidem contrariatur manifeste sententiae Apostoli qua dicitur infra VI, 9 s.: ***neque fornicarii, neque idolis servientes***, etc. ***regnum Dei possidebunt***; et Gal. V, 21: *qui talia agunt, regnum Dei non possidebunt.* Non est autem alicui salus nisi in regno Dei. Nam qui ab eo excluduntur, mittuntur in ignem aeternum, ut dicitur Matth. XXV, 41.

Quarto quia fides non potest dici fundamentum, nisi quia per eam Christus habitat in nobis, cum supra dictum sit quod fundamentum est ipse Christus Iesus. Non enim habitat Christus in nobis per fidem informem, alioquin habitaret in daemonibus, de quibus scriptum est Iac. II, 19: *et daemones credunt et contremiscunt.* Unde quod dicitur Eph. III, 17, *habitare Christum per*

as well as being indestructible and precious; but the other three are, easily consumed by fire and worthless. Hence by **gold**, **silver** and **precious stones** are understood something brilliant and lasting; but by **wood**, **hay** and **stubble** something material and transitory.

Now he stated above that the superstructure can refer either to the works everyone builds on the foundation of faith or to the doctrine which a teacher or preacher builds on the foundation of faith laid by an apostle. Hence, the variety the Apostle mentions here can refer to both superstructures.

155. Therefore, some, referring this to the superstructure of works, have said the **gold**, **silver** and **precious stones** mean the good works a person adds to his faith; but wood, hay, and stubble mean the mortal sins a person commits after receiving the faith. However, this interpretation cannot stand.

First, because mortal sins are dead works: *he will cleanse our consciences from dead works* (Heb 9:14), whereas only living works are built onto this building: *be you also as living stone built up* (1 Pet 2:5). Consequently, those who have mortal sins along with faith do not build up, but rather destroy or profane. Against such persons he says: **but if any man violates the temple of God, him shall God destroy** (1 Cor 3:17).

Second, because mortal sins are better compared to iron or lead or stone, since they are heavy and not destroyed by fire but always remain in the thing in which they exist; whereas venial sins are compared to **wood**, **hay**, and **stubble**, because they are light and easily cleansed from a person by fire.

Third, because it seems to follow from this interpretation that a person who dies in mortal sin, as long as he keeps the faith, will finally attain to salvation after undergoing punishment. For he continues: ***if any man's work burns, he shall suffer loss: but he himself shall be saved, yet so as by fire***, which is obviously contrary to the Apostle's statement below: ***neither fornicators, nor idolaters, nor adulterers . . . shall posses the kingdom of God*** (1 Cor 6:9–10), and to the Galatians: *those who do such things shall not possess the kingdom of God* (Gal 5:21). But one possesses salvation only in the kingdom of God; for everyone excluded from it is sent into eternal fire (Matt 25:41).

Fourth, because faith can be called a foundation, only because by it Christ dwells in us, since it was stated that the foundation is Christ Jesus himself. For Christ does not dwell in us by unformed faith; otherwise he would dwell in the devils, of whom James says: *the devils believe and tremble* (Jas 2:19). Hence Ephesians says: *that Christ by faith may dwell in your hearts* (Eph 3:17). This should

fidem in cordibus nostris, oportet intelligi de fide per caritatem formata, cum scriptum sit I Io. IV, 16: *qui manet in caritate in Deo manet, et Deus in eo.* Haec est fides quae per dilectionem operatur, ut dicitur infra XIII, 4: *caritas non agit perperam.* Unde manifestum est quod illi qui operantur peccata mortalia, non habent fidem formatam, et ita non habent fundamentum.

Oportet ergo intelligere quod tam ille qui superaedificat fundamento *aurum, argentum, lapides pretiosos,* quam etiam ille qui superaedificat *lignum, foenum, stipulam,* vitet peccata mortalia.

156. Ad horum ergo distinctionem intelligendum est, quod actus humani ex obiectis speciem habent.

Duplex est autem obiectum humani actus, scilicet res spiritualis et res corporalis, quae quidem obiecta differunt tripliciter. Primo quidem quantum ad hoc quod res spirituales sunt perpetuae, res autem corporales sunt transitoriae. Unde II Cor. IV, 18: *quae videntur, temporalia sunt; quae autem non videntur, aeterna.* Secundo, quantum ad hoc quod res spirituales in seipsis claritatem habent, secundum illud Sap. VI, 13: *clara est et quae numquam marcescit sapientia.* Res corporales obscuritatem habent ex materia. Unde dicitur Sap. II, 5: *umbrae transitus est tempus nostrum.* Tertio, quantum ad hoc quod res spirituales sunt pretiosiores et nobiliores rebus corporalibus; unde Prov. III, 15 dicitur de sapientia: *pretiosior est cunctis opibus*; et Sap. VII, 9: *omne aurum in comparationem illius, arena est exigua, et tamquam lutum aestimabitur argentum in conspectu illius.*

Et ideo opera quibus homo innititur rebus spiritualibus et divinis comparantur *auro, argento* et *lapidi pretioso,* quae sunt solida, clara et pretiosa. Ita tamen quod per *aurum* designentur ea quibus homo tendit in ipsum Deum per contemplationem et amorem; unde dicitur Cant. V, 11: *caput eius aurum optimum.* Caput enim Christi est Deus, ut dicitur I Cor. XI, 3. De quo auro dicitur Apoc. III, 18: *suadeo tibi emere a me aurum ignitum,* id est sapientiam cum caritate. Per *argentum* significantur actus, quibus homo adhaeret spiritualibus credendis, et amandis, et contemplandis; unde in Glossa refertur argentum ad dilectionem proximi, propter quod et in Psalmo LXVII, 14 pennae columbae describuntur deargentatae, cuius superior pars, id est, posteriora describuntur esse in pallore auri. Sed per *lapides pretiosos* designantur opera diversarum virtutum, quibus anima humana ornatur; unde dicitur Eccli. l, 10: *quasi vas auri solidum ornatum omni lapide pretioso.* Vel etiam mandata legis Dei, secundum illud Ps. CXVIII, 127: *dilexi mandata tua super aurum et topazion.*

Opera vero humana quibus homo intendit rebus corporalibus procurandis, comparantur stipulae, quae vilia sunt, namque fulgent et facile comburuntur; habent tamen quosdam gradus, prout quaedam sunt aliis

be understood of faith informed by charity, since 1 John says: *he who abides in love abides in God and God in him* (1 John 4:16). This is the faith that works through love, as it says below: **charity deals not perversely** (1 Cor 13:4). Consequently, it is obvious that persons who commit mortal sins do not have formed faith, and so do not have the foundation.

Therefore, it is necessary to suppose that the person who builds upon the foundation **gold, silver** and **precious stones,** as well as one who builds upon it **wood, hay, stubble,** avoids mortal sin.

156. Therefore to understand the difference between these two sets of things, it should be noted that human acts are characterized by their objects.

But there are two objects of a human act: a spiritual thing and a bodily thing. Now these objects differ in three ways: first, spiritual things last forever, but bodily things pass away; hence it is said: *the things that are seen are transient, but the things that are unseen are eternal* (2 Cor 4:18). Second, spiritual things are brilliant in themselves: *wisdom is glorious and never fades away* (Wis 6:13), but bodily things on account of their matter are dingy: *our time is as the passing of a shadow* (Wis 2:5). Third, spiritual are more precious and nobler than bodily things: *wisdom is more precious than all riches* (Prov 3:15); *all gold in comparison of her, is as a little sand: and silver in comparison to her shall be counted as clay* (Wis 7:9).

Therefore, the works that engage a person in spiritual and divine things are compared to **gold, silver** and **precious stones,** which are firm, bright, and precious. By **gold** are signified those by which a man tends to God himself by contemplation and love. Hence it is said: *his head is as the finest gold* (Song 5:11); for the head of Christ is God, and the gold is that mentioned in Revelation: *therefore I counsel you to buy from me gold tried by fire* (Rev 3:18), i.e., wisdom with charity. By **silver** are signified those acts by which a man clings to spiritual things to believe, love, and contemplate them; hence in a Gloss the silver is referred to as love of neighbor, and in a psalm the wings of a dove are described as covered with silver and its pinions with green gold (Ps 68:13). But **precious stones** signify the works of the various virtues with which the soul is adorned; hence it says in Sirach: *like a vessel of hammered gold adorned with all kinds of precious stones* (Sir 50:9), or they signify the commandments of God's law: *therefore I love your commandments above gold, above fine gold* (Ps 119:127).

But the human acts by which a person aims at acquiring bodily things are compared to tinder, which is worthless; for although it has a sheen, it burns easily. Yet there are various kinds, some of which are stronger than others

stabiliora, quaedam vero facilius consumptibilia; nam ipsi homines inter creaturas carnales et digniores sunt, et per successionem conservantur. Unde comparantur **lignis**, secundum illud Iudic. IX, 8: *ierunt ligna sylvarum ut eligerent super se regem.* Caro autem hominis facilius corrumpitur per infirmitatem et mortem; unde comparatur **foeno**, secundum illud Is. XL, 6: *omnis caro foenum.* Ea vero quae pertinent ad gloriam huius mundi facillime transeunt, unde **stipulae** comparantur; unde in Ps. LXXXII, 14 sequitur: *pone illos ut rotam et ut stipulam ante faciem venti.*

157. Sic ergo superaedificare **aurum**, et **argentum** et **lapides pretiosos**, est superaedificare fidei fundamento ea quae pertinent ad contemplationem sapientiae divinorum, et amorem Dei, et devotionem sanctorum, et obsequium proximorum, et ad exercitium virtutum.

Superaedificare vero **lignum**, **foenum** et **stipulam**, est superaddere fidei fundamento ea quae pertinent ad dispositionem humanarum rerum, et ad curam carnis, et ad exteriorem gloriam.

158. Sciendum tamen quod contingit aliquem hominem id intendere tripliciter. Uno modo ita quod in his finem constituat; et cum hoc sit peccatum mortale, per hoc homo non superaedificat sed, everso fundamento, aliud fundamentum collocat. Nam finis est fundamentum in rebus appetibilibus quae quaeruntur propter finem.

Alio modo aliquis intendit uti praedictis rebus totaliter ordinans eas in Dei gloriam; et quia opera specificantur ex fine intento, hoc iam non erit aedificare **lignum**, **foenum** et **stipulam**, sed **aurum**, **argentum** et **lapides pretiosos**.

Tertio modo aliquis licet in his finem non constituat, nec vellet propter ista contra Deum facere, afficitur tamen istis magis quam deberet, ita quod per haec retardatur ab his quae Dei sunt, quod est peccare venialiter: et hoc proprie est superaedificare **lignum, foenum, stipulam**, non quia ipsa superaedificentur proprie loquendo, sed quia opera ad temporalium curam pertinentia habent venialia adiuncta propter vehementiorem affectum ad ipsa, quae quidem affectio, secundum quod magis et minus inhaeret, **ligno, foeno** et **stipulae** comparatur. Et dupliciter potest distingui. Uno modo secundum permanentiam rerum spiritualium, ut prius dictum est, alio modo secundum vehementiam adhaesionis.

159. Sciendum tamen quod et illi qui spiritualibus rebus intendunt, non omnino possunt absolvi a cura rerum temporalium, nec etiam qui in caritate rebus temporalibus intendunt, sunt omnino a rebus spiritualibus vacui, sed studio diversificantur. Nam quidam studium vitae suae ordinant ad spiritualia, temporalibus vero non intendunt, nisi inquantum requirit necessitas corporalis vitae. Quidam vero studium vitae suae applicant ad

are some are more easily burned. For among bodily creatures men are the more noble and conserved by succession; hence they are compared to **wood**: *the trees once went forth to anoint a king over them* (Judg 9:8). But man's flesh is easily destroyed by sickness and death; hence he is compared to **hay**: *all flesh is hay* (Isa 49:6). Again, the things which contribute to the glory of this world quickly pass away; hence they are compared to **stubble**: *O my God, make them like a tumbleweed, like stubble before the wind* (Ps 83:13).

157. And so when one builds thereon **gold** and **silver** and **precious stones**, he builds upon the foundation of faith those things which pertain to contemplating the wisdom of divine matters, to loving God, to performing devout exercises, to helping his neighbor and performing virtuous works.

But to build upon it **wood, hay**, and **stubble** is to erect on the foundation of faith things which pertain to arranging human affairs, to caring for the flesh and for outward glory.

158. However, it should be noted that there are three possible attitudes, when a person intends these latter things: first, he might make them an end. Since this would be a mortal sin, a person with such an attitude would not be building upon the foundation by laying another foundation: for the end is the foundation for the desirable things sought for its sake.

Second, a person might tend toward these things, directing them entirely to the glory of God; and because they are qualified by the end one intends, a person with such an attitude will not be building **wood**, **hay**, and **stubble** on the foundation but **gold**, **silver**, and **precious stones**.

Third, a person could have the attitude that although he is not making these things an end or would act contrary to God for their sake, nevertheless he is drawn toward them more than he ought, so that he is kept back from the things of God by them; which is to sin venially. And this is what is meant by building **wood**, **hay**, and **stubble** on the foundation; not because they are, properly speaking, erected on the foundation, but because acts of caring about temporal things have venial sins attached to them due to a stronger attachment to them. This attachment is compared to **wood, hay** or **stubble**, depending on how strong it is.

159. Yet is should be kept in mind that those who tend after spiritual things cannot be altogether freed from caring for temporal things, any more than those who tend after temporal things from a duty of charity are altogether free from tending toward spiritual things. The difference is one of emphasis: for some emphasize spiritual things and make no provision for temporal things, except as the needs of bodily life require; others place the emphasis in their lives

temporalia procuranda, utuntur tamen spiritualibus rebus ad directionem vitae suae. Primi igitur superaedificant *aurum*, *argentum* et *lapides pretiosos*; secundi vero superaedificant *foenum*, *lignum* et *stipulam*.

Ex quo patet, quod illi qui superaedificant aurum, argentum et lapides pretiosos, habent aliquid de peccatis venialibus, sed non in quantitate notabili, propter hoc quod modicum attingunt de cura temporalium rerum. Illi etiam qui superaedificant lignum, foenum, stipulam, habent aliquid stabile, pretiosum et praeclarum, sed in minori quantitate, scilicet inquantum diriguntur per bona spiritualia.

160. Potest autem et haec diversitas referri ad superaedificationem doctrinae. Nam illi qui fidei ab apostolis fundatae per suam doctrinam superaedificant solidam veritatem et claram, sive manifestam, et ad ornamentum Ecclesiae pertinentem, superaedificant *aurum, argentum, lapides pretiosos*. Unde Prov. X, 20: *argentum electum labia iusti.* Illi vero qui fidei ab apostolis fundatae superaddunt in doctrina sua aliqua inutilia, et quae non sunt manifesta, nec veritatis ratione firmantur, sed sunt vana et inania, superaedificant *lignum, foenum, stipulam*. Unde dicitur Ier. XXIII, 28: *qui habet somnium, narret somnium, et qui habet sermonem meum, loquatur sermonem meum vere. Quid paleis ad triticum?* Qui vero falsitatem doceret, non superaedificaret, sed magis subverteret fundamentum.

161. Dicit ergo *si quis superaedificat*, vel operando, vel docendo, *super fundamentum hoc*, id est, super fidem formatam in corde, vel super fidem fundatam ab apostolis et praedicatam, *aurum, argentum* aut *lapides pretiosos*, id est spiritualia opera vel praeclaram doctrinam, vel *lignum, foenum, stipulam*, id est corporalia opera, vel frivolam doctrinam, *uniuscuiusque opus manifestum erit*, scilicet in divino iudicio, *quale sit*. Non enim latet per humanam ignorantiam. Nam quidam videntur superaedificare *aurum, argentum, lapidem pretiosum*, qui tamen superaedificant *lignum, foenum, stipulam*, in rebus spiritualibus corporalia meditantes, puta lucrum vel favorem humanum; quidam vero videntur superaedificare *lignum, foenum, stipulam*, qui tamen aedificant *aurum, argentum* et *lapidem pretiosum*, quia in administratione temporalium nihil nisi spiritualia cogitant. Unde et Sophon. I, 12 dicitur: *Scrutabor Ierusalem in lucernis*, et Lc. XII, v. 2: *nihil opertum quod non reveletur.*

162. Deinde, cum dicit *dies enim Domini*, ostendit quando haec manifestatur.

Et primo ponit tempus manifestationis, cum dicit *dies enim Domini declarabit*. Circa quod sciendum est quod tunc dicitur esse tempus et dies alicuius rei, quando est in optimo statu et maximo sui posse. Unde Ecle. III, 1 dicitur: *omnia tempus habent*. Quando ergo homo suam voluntatem implet, etiam contra Deum,

on procuring temporal things, but use spiritual things to direct their life. The first group, therefore, builds *gold, silver*, and *precious stones*; but the second *hay*, *wood*, and *stubble* on the foundation.

From this it is clear that the former have some venials but not a notable amount, because they are only slightly concerned with the care of temporal things; but the latter have something stable, precious and brilliant, but only a small amount, namely, to the extent that they are directed by spiritual considerations.

160. They can also be differentiated on the basis of doctrine. For some, by teaching sound, true, and clear doctrine, erect *gold, silver*, and *precious stones* upon the foundation of faith laid by the apostles; hence it says in Proverbs: *the tongue of the righteous is choice silver* (Prov 10:20). On the other hand, those who add to the faith laid down by the apostles doctrines that are useless, unclear or not supported by true reasons, but vain and empty, erect *wood*, *hay*, and *stubble*, hence it is said: *let the prophet who has a dream tell the dream, but let him who has my word speak my word faithfully. What has straw in common with wheat? Says the Lord* (Jer 23:28). Finally those who teach falsehood do not build on the foundation but subvert it.

161. He says, therefore: *if any man builds* by his works or teachings *upon this foundation*, i.e., upon the formed faith in his heart or upon the faith founded and taught by the apostles, *gold, silver*, or *precious stones*, i.e., spiritual works or sound, clear teachings, or *wood, hay, stubble*, i.e., corporal works or silly teachings, *every man's work shall be manifest*, i.e., in the divine judgment, it will be manifest *what sort it is*: for man's ignorance of it will not keep it hidden forever. For some appear to be erecting *gold, silver*, and *precious stones*, who are nevertheless erecting *wood, hay*, and *stubble* by looking for temporal benefits, such as profit or human favor, from spiritual things. Others, however, seem to be erecting *wood, hay*, and *stubble*, but are really erecting *gold, silver*, and *precious stones*, because in administering temporal things they have their eye on spiritual things alone. Hence it is said: *I will search Jerusalem with lamps* (Zeph 1:12) and in Luke: *nothing is covered up that will not be revealed* (Luke 12:2).

162. Then when he says, *for the day for the Lord*, he shows when these things will be disclosed.

And first he specifies the time of manifestation, when he says, *the day of the Lord shall declare it*. Here it should be noted that the time and day of a thing is said to be present when it exists in its best state and in the fullness of its power. This is the sense in which *all things have their season* (Eccl 3:1). Therefore, when a man is fulfilling his will even

tunc est dies hominis. Unde dicitur Ier. XVII, 16: *diem hominis non desideravi, tu scis.* Dies vero Domini dicitur quando voluntas Domini completur de hominibus, qui per eius iustitiam vel praemiabuntur vel damnabuntur, secundum illud Ps. LXXIV, 3: *cum accepero tempus, ego iustitias iudicabo.*

Unde secundum triplex Dei iudicium tripliciter potest intelligi dies Domini.

163. Erit nempe quoddam iudicium generale omnium, secundum illud Matth. XII, v. 41: *viri Ninivitae surgent in iudicio.* Et secundum hoc dies Domini dicitur novissimus dies iudicii, de quo II Thess. II, 2: *non terreamini quasi instet dies Domini.* Et secundum hoc intelligitur **dies Domini declarabit**, quia in die iudicii manifestabitur differentia humanorum meritorum. Rom. II, 16: *in die quando iudicabit Dominus occulta hominum.*

Aliud autem est particulare iudicium quod fit de unoquoque in morte ipsius, de quo habetur Lc. XVI, 23: *mortuus est dives, et sepultus est in inferno, mortuus est autem mendicus, et portatus est ab angelis in sinum Abrahae.* Et secundum hoc dies Domini potest intelligi dies mortis, secundum illud I Thess. V, 2: *dies Domini sicut fur in nocte veniet.* Sic ergo **dies Domini declarabit**, quia in morte uniuscuiusque eius merita patent. Unde dicitur Prov. XI, 7: *mortuo homine impio, nulla erit ultra spes*; et eiusdem XIV, v. 32: *sperat autem iustus in morte sua.*

Tertium autem est iudicium in hac vita, inquantum Deus per tribulationes huius vitae interdum homines probat. Unde dicitur infra XI, 32: **cum iudicamur, a Domino corripimur, ut non cum hoc mundo damnemur.** Et secundum hoc dicitur **dies Domini**, dies temporalis tribulationis, de quo dicitur Sophon. I, 14: *vox diei Domini amara, tribulabitur ibi fortis.* **Dies** ergo **Domini declarabit**, quia in tempore tribulationis affectus hominis probatur. Eccli. XXVII, 6: *vasa figuli probat fornax, et homines iustos tentatio tribulationis.*

164. Secundo ostendit per quod fiet ista declaratio, quia per ignem, unde sequitur **quia in igne revelabitur**, scilicet **dies Domini**.

Nam dies iudicii revelabitur in igne, qui praecedet faciem iudicis, exurens faciem mundi, et involvens reprobos, et iustos purgans: de quo dicitur in Ps. XCVI, 3: *ignis ante ipsum praecedet, et inflammabit in circuitu inimicos eius.* Dies autem Domini, qui est dies mortis, revelabitur in igne Purgatorii, per quem purgabitur si quid in elementis invenietur purgandum, de quo potest intelligi quod dicitur Iob XXIII, 10: *probabit me quasi aurum quod per ignem transit.* Dies vero qui est dies tribulationis divino iudicio permissae, revelabitur in igne tribulationis, de quo dicitur Eccli. II, 5: *in igne probatur*

contrary to God, it is man's day. Hence it is said: *you know that I have not desired the day of man* (Jer 17:16). But it is the day of the Lord, when his will is accomplished in regard to men, who are rewarded or punished according to his justice: *at the set time which I appoint I will judge with equity* (Ps 73:2).

Hence the day of the Lord can be taken in three senses, depending on the three times the Lord will judge.

163. For there will be a general judgment of all man, as it says in Matthew: *the men of Nineveh will arise at the judgment* (Matt 12:41). In this sense the day of the Lord will be the last day—judgment day—alluded to in 2 Thessalonians: *be not terrified as if the day of the Lord were at hand* (2 Thess 2:2). This is the interpretation of the statement that **the day of the Lord shall declare it**, because on the day of judgment the differences among men's merits will be disclosed: *on that day when God judges the secrets of men by Jesus Christ* (Rom 2:16).

Another is the particular judgment, which takes place for each person at his death. Luke says of this judgment: *the rich man died and was buried in hell; and the poor man also died and was carried to Abraham's bosom* (Luke 16:22). In this sense the day of the Lord refers to the day of death, as in 1 Thessalonians: *the day of the Lord will come like a thief in the night* (1 Thess 5:2). **The day of the Lord shall declare it**, because every man's merits will be plain at his death. Hence it says in Proverbs: *when the wicked dies, his hope perishes* (Prov 11:7) and in Proverbs: *the righteous man has hope when he dies* (Prov 14:32).

The third judgment takes place in this life, inasmuch as God sometimes proves a man by the tribulations of this life; hence it says below: **but while we are judged, we are chastised by the Lord, that we be not condemned with this world** (1 Cor 11:32). In this sense, temporal tribulations are called **the day of the Lord**: *the sound of the day of the Lord is bitter, the mighty man cries aloud there* (Zeph 1:14). Therefore, **the day of the Lord shall declare**, because during the time of tribulation a man's affections are tested: *the kiln tests the potter's vessels; so the trial of affliction just men* (Sir 27:5).

164. Second, he shows the means by which it will be disclosed, namely, by fire; hence he continues: **because it shall be revealed in fire**, namely, **the day of the Lord**.

For the day of judgment will be revealed in the fire which will precede the face of the judge, burning the face of the world, enveloping the wicked and cleansing the just. A psalm says of this: *fire goes before him, and burns up his adversaries round about* (Ps 96:3). But the day of the Lord which occurs at death will be revealed in the fire of purgatory, by which the elect will be cleansed, if any require cleansing: Job can be interpreted as referring to this fire: *when he has tried me, I shall come forth as gold* (Job 23:10). Finally, the day of the Lord, which is the day of tribulation permitted by God's judgment, will be revealed in the fire of

aurum et argentum, homines vero acceptabiles in camino tribulationis.

165. Tertio ponit effectum manifestationis, cum subdit *et uniuscuiusque opus quale sit, ignis probabit*, quia scilicet per quemlibet ignium praedictorum probantur merita hominis vel demerita: unde in Ps. XVI, 3 dicitur: *igne me examinasti, et non est inventa in me iniquitas.*

In his tribus quae hic Apostolus ponit, primum est conclusio duorum sequentium. Si enim dies Domini revelatur in igne, et ignis probat quale sit uniuscuiusque opus, consequens est quod dies Domini declaret differentiam operum humanorum.

166. Deinde cum dicit *si cuius opus*, ostendit modum praedictae manifestationis.

Et primo quantum ad bona opera, cum dicit *si cuius*, id est, alicuius *opus, quod* ipse *superaedificavit, manserit*, scilicet in igne, ille, scilicet qui superaedificavit, *mercedem accipiet*. Ier. XXXI, 16: *est merces operi tuo.* Et Is. XL, 10: *ecce merces eius cum eo.*

167. Dicitur autem aliquod opus in igne permanere illaesum dupliciter. Uno modo ex parte ipsius operantis, quia scilicet ille qui hoc facit opus, scilicet bonae doctrinae, vel quodcumque bonorum operum, propter huiusmodi opus non punitur, inquantum scilicet nec torquebitur igne Purgatorii, nec igne qui praecedit faciem iudicis, nec etiam aestuat igne tribulationis. Qui enim non immoderate temporalia dilexit, consequens est quod non nimis doleat de eorum amissione. Dolor enim causatur ex amore rei quae amittitur. Unde superfluus amor superfluum generat dolorem.

Alio modo potest intelligi ex parte ipsius operis: quolibet enim praedictorum iudiciorum superveniente homini, permanet et opus bonae doctrinae, vel quodcumque aliud bonum opus. Nam igne tribulationis superveniente, non cessat homo neque a vera doctrina, neque a bono opere virtutis; utrumque autem horum permanet homini quantum ad meritum et in igne Purgatorii et in igne qui praecedit faciem iudicis.

168. Secundo ostendit diem quantum ad mala opera, dicens *si cuius*, id est, alicuius, *opus arserit*, scilicet per aliquem ignium praedictorum, *detrimentum patietur*, scilicet qui hoc operatus est, non tamen usque ad damnationem. Unde subdit: *ipse autem salvus erit*, scilicet salute aeterna, secundum illud Is. XLV, 17: *salvatus est Israel in Domino salute aeterna. Sic tamen quasi per ignem*, quem scilicet prius sustinuit, vel in hac vita, vel in fine huius vitae, vel in fine mundi. Unde dicitur in Ps. LXV, 12: *transivimus per ignem et aquam, et eduxisti nos in refrigerium.* Et Is. XLIII, 2 s.: *cum transieris per ignem, non combureris, et flamma non comburet te, quia ego Dominus Deus Salvator tuus.*

tribulation: *for gold is tested in the fire, and acceptable men in the furnace of humiliation* (Sir 2:5).

165. Third, he mentions the effect of the disclosure when he says, *and the fire shall try every man's work, of what sort it is*, namely, because each of these fires will prove a man's merits or demerits: *if you test me, you will find no wickedness in me* (Ps 17:3).

In these three events mentioned by the Apostle, the first is the conclusion of the two which follow: for if the day of the Lord will be revealed in fire, and if the fire tests the quality of a man's work, the consequence is that the day of the Lord will disclose the differences among men's works.

166. Then when he says, *if any man's work abides*, he indicates the manner in which the above disclosures will be made.

First, in regard to good works when he says, *if any man's work, which he has built thereupon, abides* the fire, *he*, i.e., the one who erected it, *shall receive a reward*: *there is a reward for your work* (Jer 31:16); *behold, his reward is with him* (Isa 40:10).

167. One's work is said to abide unharmed by the fire in two ways: in one way on the part of the worker, because the one performing the work, say of good teachings or any good work, is not punished for such works by the fire of purgatory or by the fire which goes before the face of the judge or even by the fire of tribulation. For a person who has not loved temporal things immoderately is not excessively saddened at their loss, because sadness is caused by one's love of a thing which is lost; hence superfluous love produces sorrow.

In another way on the part of the work itself: for no matter which of the above fires tests a man, the work of good teachings abides as does any other good work. For when the fire of tribulation comes, a man does not depart from his good teachings or from any good work of virtue; rather, each of these abides as to its merit both in the fire of purgatory and in the fire which goes before the face of the judge.

168. Second, he shows the same thing in regard to evil works, saying, *if any man's work burns* because of any of the above fires, *he shall suffer loss* for doing them, but not to the point of damnation; hence he adds, *but he himself shall be saved* with eternal salvation: *Israel is saved by the Lord with everlasting salvation* (Isa 45:17), *yet so as by fire*, which he previously endured either in this life or at the end of the world; hence it is said: *we went through fire and through water; yet you have brought us forth to a spacious place* (Ps 66:12); *when you walk through fire you shall not be burned, and the flame shall not consume you, for I am the Lord, your Savior* (Isa 43:2).

169. Dicitur autem opus alicuius ardere dupliciter. Uno modo ex parte operantis, inquantum scilicet aliquis affligitur igne tribulationis propter immoderatum affectum quo superflue terrena diligit, et punitur igne Purgatorii, vel igne qui praecedet faciem iudicis propter peccata venialia, quae circa curam temporalium commisit, sive etiam per frivola et vana quae docuit.

Alio modo ardet opus in igne ex parte ipsius operis, quia scilicet tribulatione superveniente, homo non potest vacare nec doctrinae vanae, nec terrenis operibus, secundum illud Ps. CXLV, 4: *in illa die peribunt omnes cogitationes eorum.* Nec etiam igne purgatorii vel praecedente faciem iudicis remanebit ei aliquid praedictorum vel ad remedium vel ad meritum. Et similiter dupliciter patitur detrimentum, vel inquantum ipse punitur, vel inquantum perdit id quod fecit, et quantum ad hoc dicitur Eccli. XIV, 20 s.: *omne opus corruptibile in fine deficiet, et qui operatur illud ibit cum illo, et omne opus electum in fine iustificabitur, et qui operatur illud honorificabitur in illo.*

Quorum primum pertinet ad eum qui superaedificat **lignum**, **foenum** et **stipulam**, quod est opus in igne ardens; secundum autem pertinet ad eum qui superaedificat **aurum**, **argentum** et **lapides pretiosos**, quod est opus manens in igne absque detrimento.

169. Now a man's work is said to burn in two ways: in one way on the part of the worker, inasmuch as he is afflicted by the fire of tribulation on account of the immoderate attachment he has to earthly things and by the fire of purgatory or by the fire which goes before the face of the judge on account of venial sins, which he committed by caring for temporal things or even by the frivolous and vain things he taught.

In another way a work burns in the fire on the part of the work itself, because when tribulation comes, a person cannot find time for foolish teaching or worldly works: *on that day all his plans perish* (Ps 146:4). Furthermore, the fire of purgatory or the fire which goes before the face of the judge will not leave any of these things to act as a remedy or as merit. Similarly, he suffers a loss in two ways: either because he is punished or because he loses what he accomplished. On this point it is said: *every product decays and ceases to exist, and the man who made it will pass away with it. And every excellent work shall be justified; and the worker thereof shall be honored therein* (Sir 14:19).

The first of these refers to the person who erects **wood**, **hay**, and **stubble**, which is the work that burns in the fire; but the second refers to the person who erects **gold**, **silver**, and **precious stones**, which is the work that abides in the fire without any loss.

Lecture 3

3:16Nescitis quia templum Dei estis, et Spiritus Dei habitat in vobis? [n. 170]

3:17Si quis autem templum Dei violaverit, disperdet illum Deus. Templum enim Dei sanctum est, quod estis vos. [n. 174]

3:18Nemo se seducat: si quis videtur inter vos sapiens esse in hoc saeculo, stultus fiat ut sit sapiens. [n. 176]

3:19Sapientia enim hujus mundi, stultitia est apud Deum. Scriptum est enim: *comprehendam sapientes in astutia eorum.* [n. 179]

3:20Et iterum: *Dominus novit cogitationes* sapientium *quoniam vanae sunt.* [n. 180]

3:21Nemo itaque glorietur in hominibus. Omnia enim vestra sunt, [n. 181]

3:22sive Paulus, sive Apollo, sive Cephas, sive mundus, sive vita, sive mors, sive praesentia, sive futura: omnia enim vestra sunt: [n. 182]

3:23vos autem Christi: Christus autem Dei. [n. 183]

3:16οὐκ οἴδατε ὅτι ναὸς θεοῦ ἐστε καὶ τὸ πνεῦμα τοῦ θεοῦ οἰκεῖ ἐν ὑμῖν;

3:17εἴ τις τὸν ναὸν τοῦ θεοῦ φθείρει, φθερεῖ τοῦτον ὁ θεός· ὁ γὰρ ναὸς τοῦ θεοῦ ἅγιός ἐστιν, οἵτινές ἐστε ὑμεῖς.

3:18Μηδεὶς ἑαυτὸν ἐξαπατάτω· εἴ τις δοκεῖ σοφὸς εἶναι ἐν ὑμῖν ἐν τῷ αἰῶνι τούτῳ, μωρὸς γενέσθω, ἵνα γένηται σοφός.

3:19ἡ γὰρ σοφία τοῦ κόσμου τούτου μωρία παρὰ τῷ θεῷ ἐστιν· γέγραπται γάρ, Ὁ δρασσόμενος τοὺς σοφοὺς ἐν τῇ πανουργίᾳ αὐτῶν·

3:20καὶ πάλιν, Κύριος γινώσκει τοὺς διαλογισμοὺς τῶν σοφῶν ὅτι εἰσὶν μάταιοι.

3:21ὥστε μηδεὶς καυχάσθω ἐν ἀνθρώποις· πάντα γὰρ ὑμῶν ἐστιν,

3:22εἴτε Παῦλος εἴτε Ἀπολλῶς εἴτε Κηφᾶς εἴτε κόσμος εἴτε ζωὴ εἴτε θάνατος εἴτε ἐνεστῶτα εἴτε μέλλοντα, πάντα ὑμῶν,

3:23ὑμεῖς δὲ Χριστοῦ, Χριστὸς δὲ θεοῦ.

3:16Know you not that you are the temple of God and that the Spirit of God dwells in you? [n. 170]

3:17But if any man violates the temple of God, him shall God destroy. For the temple of God is holy, which you are. [n. 174]

3:18Let no man deceive himself. If any man among you seems to be wise in this world, let him become a fool, that he may be wise. [n. 176]

3:19For the wisdom of this world is foolishness with God. For it is written: *I will catch the wise in their own craftiness.* [n. 179]

3:20And again: *the Lord knows the thoughts* of the wise, *that they are vain.* [n. 180]

3:21Let no one therefore glory in men. For all things are yours, [n. 181]

3:22Whether it be Paul or Apollo or Cephas, or the world, or life, or death, or things present, or things to come. For all are yours. [n. 182]

3:23And you are Christ's. And Christ is God's. [n. 183]

---

170. Supra ostendit Apostolus, quae sit merces bene laborantium, hic agit de poena male laborantium sive destruentium.

Et circa hoc duo facit.

Primo demonstrat poenam;

secundo excludit errorem contrarium, ibi *nemo vos seducat*.

Ostendit autem poenam operantium ad destructionem, prosequens similitudinem aedificii spiritualis, et circa hoc tria facit.

Primo ostendit dignitatem spiritualis aedificii;

secundo determinat poenam destruentium, ibi *si quis*;

tertio assignat rationem poenae, ibi *templum enim Dei*, et cetera.

171. Dicit ergo primo: dictum est quod ille qui superaedificat, mercedem salutis accipiet, vel sine detrimento vel cum detrimento; sed ut possitis agnoscere, quae sit poena male in vobis laborantium, oportet vos vestram dignitatem agnoscere; quam primo ponit, dicens: an vos *nescitis quia*, vos fideles Christi, *estis templum Dei*? Eph. c. II, 21 s.: *in quo omnis aedificatio constructa crescit*

170. Having indicated the reward in store for those who labor well, the Apostle now deals with the punishment in store for those who do evil or destructive works.

In regard to this he does two things.

First, he indicates the punishment;

second, he dismisses a contrary error, at *let no man deceive*.

He indicates the punishment in store for those who work unto destruction by continuing with the metaphor of the spiritual building. In regard to his he does three things.

First, he shows the dignity of the spiritual edifice;

second, he mentions the punishment in store for those who destroy it, at *but if any man*;

third, he assigns the reason for the punishment, at *for the temple of God*.

171. He says, therefore: I have said that everyone who builds on the foundation will receive the reward of salvation without a loss or with a loss. But if you are to understand the punishment in store for those who labor evilly among you, you must recognize your dignity, which he indicates when he says, *know you not that you*, Christ's faithful, *are the temple of God*? *In whom the whole structure is*

in templum sanctum in Domino, in quo et vos coaedificamini in habitaculum Dei.

172. Secundo probat quod fideles sint templum Dei.

Est enim de ratione templi quod sit habitaculum Dei, secundum illud Ps. X, 5: *Deus in templo sancto suo.* Unde omne illud in quo Deus habitat, potest dici templum. Habitat autem Deus principaliter in seipso, quia ipse solus se comprehendit. Unde et ipse Deus templum Dei dicitur Apoc. XXI, 22: *Dominus Deus omnipotens templum illius est.* Habitat etiam Deus in domo sacrata per spiritualem cultum, qui in ea sibi exhibetur; et ideo domus sacrata dicitur templum, secundum illud Ps. V, 8: *adorabo ad templum sanctum tuum,* et cetera. Habitat etiam Deus in hominibus per fidem, quae per dilectionem operatur, secundum illud Eph. III, 17: *habitare Christum per fidem in cordibus vestris.*

Unde et ad probandum quod fideles sint templum Dei, subiungit quod inhabitantur a Deo, cum dicit **et Spiritus Dei habitat in vobis.** Et Rom. VIII, 11 dictum est: *Spiritus, qui suscitavit Iesum Christum habitabit in vobis.* Ez. XXXVI, 27: *Spiritum meum ponam in medio vestri.*

Ex quo patet quod Spiritus sanctus est Deus, per cuius inhabitationem fideles dicuntur templum Dei. Sola enim inhabitatio Dei templum Dei facit, ut dictum est.

173. Est autem considerandum quod Deus est in omnibus creaturis, in quibus est per essentiam, potentiam et praesentiam, implens omnia bonitatibus suis, secundum illud Ier. XXIII, 24: *caelum et terram ego impleo.* Sed spiritualiter dicitur Deus inhabitare tamquam in familiari domo in sanctis, quorum mens capax est Dei per cognitionem et amorem, etiam si ipsi in actu non cognoscant et diligant, dummodo habeant per gratiam habitum fidei et caritatis, sicut patet de pueris baptizatis. Et cognitio sine dilectione non sufficit ad inhabitationem Dei, secundum illud I Io. IV, 16: *qui manet in caritate, in Deo manet, et Deus in eo.* Inde est quod multi cognoscunt Deum, vel per naturalem cognitionem, vel per fidem informem, quos tamen non inhabitat Spiritus Dei.

174. Deinde cum dicit **si quis autem templum,** etc., subiungit poenam male operantium secundum convenientiam praedictorum, dicens **si quis autem,** et cetera.

Violatur autem **templum Dei** dupliciter. Uno modo per falsam doctrinam, quae non superaedificatur fundamento, sed magis subruit fundamentum et destruit aedificium. Unde dicitur Ez. XIII, 19 de falsis prophetis: *violabant me ac populum meum propter pugillum hordei et fragmentum panis.* Alio modo violat aliquis templum Dei per peccatum mortale, per quod aliquis vel seipsum corrumpit vel alium, opere vel exemplo. Unde dicitur

joined together and grows into a holy temple in the Lord; in whom you also are built into it for a dwelling place of God in the Spirit (Eph 2:21).

172. Second, he proves that the faithful are God's temple.

For it is the mark of a temple to be God's dwelling place: *the Lord is in his holy temple* (Ps 11:4); hence everything in which God dwells can be called a temple. Now God dwells chiefly in himself, because he alone comprehends himself; hence God himself is called a temple: *its temple is the Lord God* (Rev 21:22). God also dwells in a building consecrated by the special worship offered him in it; therefore, a holy building is called a temple: *I will worship at the holy temple in your fear* (Ps 5:8). Furthermore, he dwells in men by faith, which works through love: *that Christ may dwell by faith in your hearts* (Eph 3:17).

Hence to prove that the faithful are God's temple, he adds that they are dwelt in by God when he says, **and that the Spirit of God dwells in you,** as in Romans when he said: *the Spirit who raised Jesus Christ dwells in you* (Rom 8:11); *I will put my Spirit within you* (Ez 36:27).

This shows that the Spirit is God, by whose indwelling the faithful are called God's temple, for only God's indwelling makes a thing God's dwelling, as has been said.

173. But it should be noted that God exists in all creatures. He exists in them by his essence, power, and presence, filling all things with his goodness: *do I not fill heaven and earth?* (Jer 23:24). But God is said to dwell spiritually as in a family in the saints, whose mind is capable of God by knowledge and love, even though they may not be actually thinking of him or loving him, provided that by grace they possess the habit of faith and charity, as is the case with baptized infants. However, knowledge without love does not suffice for God's indwelling: *he who abides in love abides in God and God in him* (1 John 4:16). That is why many persons know God either by natural knowledge or by unformed faith, yet God's Spirit does not dwell in them.

174. Then when he says, **but if any man,** he mentions the punishment in store for those who do evil works, saying, **but if any man violates the temple of God, him shall God destroy.**

Now the **temple of God** is violated in two ways: in one way, by false teaching, which does not build on the foundation, but rather uproots it and destroys the edifice; hence, Ezekiel says of false prophets: *you have profaned me among my people for handfuls of barley and for pieces of bread* (Ezek 13:19). In another way a person violates the temple of God by mortal sin, through which he destroys himself or someone else by his works or example; hence it is said:

Malac. II, 11: *contaminavit Iudas sanctificationem Domini quam dilexit.*

Sic autem dignum est, ut disperdatur ille a Deo per damnationem aeternam qui violat spirituale templum Dei, vel qualitercumque polluit. Unde dicitur Malac. II, 12: *disperdet Dominus virum qui fecerit hoc, magistrum et discipulum.* Et in Ps. XI, 4: *disperdet Dominus universa labia dolosa,* et cetera.

175. Deinde cum dicit **templum Dei**, etc., assignat rationem eius quod dixerat de sanctitate templi.

Qui enim aliquam rem sacram violat, sacrilegium committit, unde dignum est ut disperdatur. ***Templum enim Dei sanctum est quod estis vos***, sicut supra dictum est, et in Ps. LXIV, 5 dicitur: *sanctum est templum tuum, mirabile in aequitate*; et alibi *domum tuam, Domine, decet sanctitudo.* Et quidem in materiali templo est quaedam sacramentalis Sanctitas, prout templum divino cultui dedicatur, sed in fidelibus Christi est sanctitas gratiae, quam consecuti sunt per baptismum, secundum illud infra IV, 11: ***abluti estis, sanctificati estis.***

176. Deinde cum dicit **nemo vos seducat**, excludit errorem contrarium. Et

primo monet fideles ut sibi caveant a seductione errorum;

secundo docet modum cavendi, ibi **si quis inter vos**;

tertio assignat rationem, ibi ***sapientia enim huius mundi***, et cetera.

177. Circa primum sciendum quod quidam dixerunt quod Deus neque punit, neque remunerat hominum facta; ex quorum persona dicitur Sophon. I, 12: *qui dicunt in cordibus suis: non faciet bene Dominus, et non faciet male.* Et Thren. III, 37 s.: *quis est iste qui dixit, ut fieret, Domino non iubente? Ex ore Altissimi non egredietur bonum neque malum.* Ad hunc ergo errorem excludendum dicit **nemo vos seducat**, asserens scilicet quod ille qui templum Dei violat, non disperdatur a Deo, sicut Eph. V, 6 dicitur: *nemo vos seducat inanibus verbis, propter hoc enim venit ira Dei in filios diffidentiae.*

178. Deinde cum dicit **si quis inter vos**, etc., docet modum cavendi huiusmodi seductionem.

Ubi sciendum est quod quidam dixerunt Deum non punire peccata hominum, innitentes rationibus humanae sapientiae, puta quod Deus non cognoscat singularia, quae fiunt hic, ex quorum persona dicitur Iob XXII, v. 14: *circa cardines caeli perambulat, nec nostra considerat.* Ad hoc ergo vitandum dicit **si quis inter vos videtur esse sapiens in hoc saeculo**, id est, sapientia saeculari, quae in eo quod contrariatur veritati fidei, non est sapientia, licet videatur esse, ***stultus fiat***, abiiciendo istam sapientiam apparentem, ***ut sit sapiens***, scilicet secundum sapientiam divinam, quae est vera sapientia.

Judah has profaned the sanctuary of the Lord, which he loves (Mal 2:11).

Therefore, any person who violates a spiritual temple of God or profanes it in any way deserves to be destroyed by God through eternal damnation; hence Malachi continues: *may the Lord cut off from the tents of Jacob and the man who does this, both the master and the disciple* (Mal 2:12), and in a psalm: *may the Lord cut off all flattering lips, the tongue that makes great boasts* (Ps 12:3).

175. Then when he says, ***for the temple***, he gives the reason for what he had said about the holiness of the temple.

For a person who profanes a sacred thing commits a sacrilege; hence he deserves to be destroyed. ***For the temple of God is holy, which you are***, as he stated earlier and as stated in a psalm: *holy is your temple, wonderful in justice* (Ps 65:4), and again: *holiness befits your house, O Lord* (Ps 93:5). In a material temple, however, is a certain sacramental holiness, inasmuch as the temple is dedicated to divine worship; but in Christ's faithful is the holiness of grace, which they acquired by baptism: ***you are washed, you are sanctified*** (1 Cor 6:11).

176. Then when he says, ***let no man deceive***, he excludes an opposite error.

First, he warns the faithful to be careful not to be deceived by error;

second, he teaches how to be careful, at ***if any man among you***;

third, he assigns the reason, at ***for the wisdom of this world***.

177. In regard to the first it should be noted that some people say that God neither rewards nor punishes men's deeds: *they say in their hearts: the Lord will not do good, nor will he do ill* (Zeph 1:12); *who has commanded and it came to pass, unless the Lord has ordained it? Is it not from the mouth of the Most High that good and evil come?* (Lam 3:37). To exclude this error he says, ***let no man deceive himself*** with the assertion that a person who violates the temple of God will not be destroyed: *let no man deceive you with empty words, for it is because of these things that the wrath of God comes upon the sons of disobedience* (Eph 5:6).

178. Then when he says, ***if any man***, he shows how to avoid being deceived in this way.

Here it should be noted that some, appealing to the reasons of human wisdom, have declared that God does not punish men's sins on the ground that God does not know the particular things that happen here: *and you say: thick clouds enwrap him, so that he does not see* (Job 22:14). Therefore, to avoid this he says: ***if any man among you seems to be wise in this world***, i.e., has worldly wisdom, which in those points that are contrary to the faith is not wisdom, even though it appears to be, ***let him become a fool*** by eschewing that seeming wisdom, ***that he may be wise***, namely, according to divine wisdom, which is the true wisdom.

Et hoc etiam observandum est non solum in his in quibus saecularis sapientia contrariatur veritati fidei, sed etiam in omnibus in quibus contrariatur honestati morum. Unde Prov. XXX, 1 dicitur: *Deo secum morante confortatus est*, et cetera.

179. Deinde cum dicit *sapientia huius mundi*, etc., assignat rationem eius quod dixerat.

Et primo ponit rationem. Videbatur enim ineptam monitionem fecisse, ut aliquis fieret stultus, et vere inepta esset si stultitia illa, de qua loquebatur, esset per abnegationem verae sapientiae, sed non est ita. *Sapientia enim huius mundi stultitia est apud Deum*.

Dicitur autem sapientia huius mundi, quae principaliter mundo innititur. Nam illa, quae per res huius mundi ad Deum attingit, non est sapientia mundi, sed sapientia Dei, secundum illud Rom. I, 19 s.: *Deus enim illis revelavit. Invisibilia enim ipsius a creatura mundi per ea quae facta sunt, intellecta conspiciuntur.* Sapientia ergo mundi, quae sic rebus intendit, ut ad divinam veritatem non pertingat, *stultitia est apud Deum*, id est, stultitia reputatur secundum divinum iudicium. Is. XIX, 11: *stulti principes Thaneos, sapientes consiliarii Pharaonis dederunt consilium insipiens*.

180. Secundo probat quod dixerat per duas auctoritates, quarum prima scribitur Iob V, 13. Unde dicit *scriptum est: comprehendam sapientes in astutia eorum*. Comprehendit autem sapientes Dominus in astutia eorum, quia per hoc ipsum quod astute cogitant contra Deum, impedit Deus eorum conatum, et implet suum propositum; sicut per malitiam fratrum Ioseph volentium impedire eius principatum, impletum est per divinam ordinationem, quod Ioseph in Aegypto venditus principaretur. Unde et ante praemissa verba dicit Iob: *qui dissipat cogitationes eorum*, scilicet malignorum, *ne possint implere manus eorum, quod coeperant*; quia, ut dicitur Prov. XXI, 30, *non est sapientia, non est scientia, non est consilium contra Dominum*.

Secunda auctoritas sumitur ex Ps., unde dicit *et iterum* scriptum est: *'Dominus novit cogitationes sapientium'*, id est, secundum sapientiam mundi, *'quoniam vanae sunt'*; quia scilicet non pertingunt ad finem cognitionis humanae, quae est cognitio veritatis divinae. Unde dicitur Sap. XIII, v. 1: *vani sunt homines, in quibus non subest sapientia Dei*.

181. Deinde cum dicit *itaque nemo glorietur in hominibus*, infert conclusionem principaliter intentam, scilicet quod non debeant gloriari de ministris Dei.

Et primo concludit propositum ex praedictis dicens *itaque*, ex quo ministri nihil sunt, sed laborant pro mercede, *nemo glorietur in hominibus*; sicut et in Ps. CXLV, 2 s. dicitur: *nolite confidere in principibus, neque in filiis hominum, in quibus non est salus*. Et

And this must be observed not only in those matters in which worldly wisdom is contrary to the truth of faith, but also in all matters in which it is contrary to genuine morality; hence: *he is a shield to those who take refuge in him* (Prov 30:5).

179. Then when he says, *for the wisdom*, he assigns the reason for what he had said.

For it seems to be inept to advise a person to become foolish, as, indeed, it would be if the foolishness were the denial of true wisdom. But that is not the case, *for the wisdom of this world is foolishness with God*.

But that is called the wisdom of this world that rests mainly on this world, whereas the wisdom that attains to God through the things of this world is not the wisdom of the world but the wisdom of God: *for what can be known about God is plain to them, because God has shown it to them. His invisible nature has been clearly perceived in the things that have been made* (Rom 1:19). Therefore, the wisdom of this world, which considers the things of this world in such a way that it does not reach divine truth *is foolishness with God*, i.e., in God's judgment it is folly: *the princes of Zoan are utterly foolish; the wise counselors of Pharaoh give stupid counsel* (Isa 19:11).

180. Second, he proves what he had said by citing two authorities: the first of these is from Job (Job 5:13); hence he says: *it is written: I will catch the wise in their own craftiness*. Now the Lord catches the wise in their own craftiness because when they lay crafty plans contrary to God, he frustrates them and fulfills his own plan. Thus, by the malice of Joseph's brothers attempting to prevent his ascendancy, it came to pass by divine providence that Joseph, after being sold, became a ruler in Egypt. Hence just before the words quoted, Job says: *he frustrates the devices of the crafty, so that their hands achieve no success*; because, as it says in Proverbs: *no wisdom, no understanding, no counsel, can avail against the Lord* (Prov 21:30).

The second authority is taken from a psalm (Ps 94:11); hence he says: *and again* it is written: *the Lord knows the thoughts of the wise*, i.e., according to the wisdom of the world, *that they are in vain*, namely, because they do not reach unto the goal of human knowledge, which is the knowledge of divine truth. Hence, *all men who are ignorant of God are foolish* (Wis 13:1).

181. Then when he says, *let no one therefore glory*, he draws his main conclusion, namely, that they should not glory in God's ministers.

First, he draws the conclusion, saying: since ministers are nothing but persons laboring for a reward, *let no one therefore glory in men*, as it says in a psalm: *put not your trust in princes, in a son of man, in whom there is no help*

Ier. XVII, 5: *maledictus vir qui confidit in homine*, et cetera.

182. Secundo rationem assignat ex dignitate fidelium Christi, assignans ordinem fidelium in rebus.

Et primo ponit ordinem rerum ad fideles Christi, dicens *omnia vestra sunt*, quasi dicat: sicut homo non gloriatur de rebus sibi subiectis, ita et vos gloriari non debetis de rebus huius mundi, quae omnia sunt vobis data a Deo, secundum illud Ps. VIII, 8: *omnia subiecisti sub pedibus eius*.

Exponit autem, quae *omnia*, inter quae primo ponit ministros Christi, qui sunt divinitus ordinati ad ministerium fidelium, secundum illud II Cor. IV, 5: *nos autem servos vestros per Iesum*. Et hoc est, quod dicit *sive Paulus*, qui plantavit, *sive Apollo*, qui rigavit, *sive Cephas*, id est, Petrus, qui est universalis pastor ovium Christi, ut dicitur Io. ult. Post haec ponit res exteriores, cum dicit *sive mundus*, qui est continentia omnium creaturarum, qui quidem est fidelium Christi, eo quod homo per res huius mundi iuvatur, vel quantum ad necessitatem corporalem, vel quantum ad cognitionem Dei, secundum illud Sap. XIII, 5: *a magnitudine speciei et creaturae*, et cetera.

183. Consequenter ponit ea quae pertinent ad ipsam hominis dispositionem, dicens *sive vita, sive mors*, quia scilicet fidelibus Christi et vita est utilis in qua merentur, et mors per quam ad praemia perveniunt, secundum illud Rom. XIV, 8: *sive vivimus, sive morimur*, et cetera. Et Phil. I, 21: *mihi vivere Christus est, et mori lucrum*.

Ad haec autem duo reducuntur omnia bona vel mala huius mundi, quia per bona conservatur vita, per mala pervenitur ad mortem.

Ultimo ponit quae pertinent ad statum hominis praesentem vel futurum, dicens *sive praesentia*, id est, res huius vitae, quibus iuvamur ad merendum; *sive futura*, quae nobis reservantur ad praemium. *Non enim habemus hic civitatem permanentem, sed futuram inquirimus*, ut dicitur Hebr. ult. *Omnia*, inquit, *vestra sunt*, id est, vestrae utilitati deservientia, secundum illud Rom. VIII, 28: *diligentibus Deum omnia cooperantur in bonum*.

184. Sic ergo primus ordo est rerum Christi ad fideles; secundus vero fidelium Christi ad Christum, quos ponit subdens *vos autem Christi* estis, quia scilicet sua morte vos redemit. Rom. XIV, 8: *sive vivimus, sive morimur, Domini sumus*. Tertius ordo est Christi, secundum quod homo ad Deum; ideo addit *Christus autem*, secundum quod homo, *Dei est*. Unde eum Deum et Dominum in Ps. VII, 2 nominat, dicens: *Domine Deus meus, in te speravi*, ut nomine Dei tota Trinitas intelligatur.

Quia ergo nullus debet gloriari de eo quod infra ipsum est, sed de eo quod est supra ipsum, ideo non debent fideles Christi gloriari de ministris, sed magis ministri

(Ps 146:3); *cursed is the man who trusts in man and makes flesh his arm* (Jer 17:5).

182. Second, he assigns a reason based on the dignity of Christ's faithful.

First, he mentions the relationship between things and Christ's faithful, saying, *for all things are yours*. As if to say: just as a man does not glory in things subject to himself, so neither should you glory in the things of the world, all of which have been given to you by God: *you have put all things under his feet* (Ps 8:8).

Then he specifies what he means by *all things*; and first he mentions Christ's ministers, who are appointed by God in minister to the faithful: *with ourselves as your servants for Jesus' sake* (2 Cor 4:5), which is what he says: *whether it be Paul*, who planted, *or Apollo*, who watered, *or Cephas*, i.e., Peter, who is the universal shepherd of Christ's sheep (John 21). After these he mentions external things when he says, *or the world*, which contains all creatures and belongs to Christ's faithful, inasmuch as a person is helped by the things of this world to fulfill his bodily needs and to attain to a knowledge of God: *from the greatness and beauty of created things comes a corresponding perception of their Creator* (Wis 13:5).

183. Then he lists things which pertain to the very disposition of man, saying, *or life, or death*, because life is useful to Christ's faithful as the time for meriting; and so is death, by which they reach their reward: *whether we live or die, we are the Lord's* (Rom 14:8); and *for me to live is Christ and to die is gain* (Phil 1:21).

Indeed, all good and evil in this world are reduced to these two, because by good things life is preserved and by evil things death is reached.

Finally, he lists the things which pertain to man's present or future state, saying: *or things present*, i.e., things of this life by which we are aided in meriting, *or things to come*, i.e., things reserved for us as a reward: *we have not here a lasting city, but we seek one that is to come* (Heb 13:14). *All are yours*, i.e., serve your advantage: *in everything God works for good with those who love him* (Rom 8:28).

184. Thus, the first relationship is that of Christ to the faithful, but the second is that of Christ's faithful to Christ. He mentions this when he says: *and you are Christ's*, because he redeemed us by his death: *whether we live it whether we die, we are the Lord's* (Rom 14:8). The third relationship is that of Christ as man to God; hence he adds: *and Christ* as man *is God's*. Hence he is called God and Lord: *O Lord my God, in you I take refuge* (Ps 7:1), where the whole Trinity is understood by the name, God.

Therefore, because no one should glory in anything below him but in what is above him, the faithful of Christ should not glory in his ministers, but rather the ministers

de ipsis. II Cor. VII, 4: *multa mihi fiducia est apud vos, multa mihi gloriatio pro vobis.* Sed fideles Christi debent gloriari de Christo, secundum illud Gal. ult.: *mihi absit gloriari, nisi in cruce Domini nostri Iesu Christi,* sicut Christus de Patre, secundum illud Sap. II, 16: *gloriatur se Patrem habere Deum.*

in them: *I have great confidence in you; I have great pride in you* (2 Cor 7:4). But Christ's faithful should glory in Christ: *far be it from me to glory except in the cross of our Lord Jesus Christ* (Gal 6:14), as Christ glories in the Father: *he boasts that God is his father* (Wis 2:16).

CHAPTER 4

Lecture 1

4:1Sic nos existimet homo ut ministros Christi, et dispensatores mysteriorum Dei. [n. 185]

4:2Hic jam quaeritur inter dispensatores ut fidelis quis inveniatur. [n. 189]

4:3Mihi autem pro minimo est ut a vobis judicer, aut ab humano die: [n. 190] sed neque meipsum judico. [n. 192]

4:4Nihil enim mihi conscius sum, sed non in hoc justificatus sum: qui autem judicat me, Dominus est. [n. 190]

4:5Itaque nolite ante tempus judicare, quoadusque veniat Dominus: qui et illuminabit abscondita tenebrarum, et manifestabit consilia cordium: et tunc laus erit unicuique a Deo. [n. 194]

4:1Οὕτως ἡμᾶς λογιζέσθω ἄνθρωπος ὡς ὑπηρέτας Χριστοῦ καὶ οἰκονόμους μυστηρίων θεοῦ.

4:2ὧδε λοιπὸν ζητεῖται ἐν τοῖς οἰκονόμοις ἵνα πιστός τις εὑρεθῇ.

4:3ἐμοὶ δὲ εἰς ἐλάχιστόν ἐστιν ἵνα ὑφ' ὑμῶν ἀνακριθῶ ἢ ὑπὸ ἀνθρωπίνης ἡμέρας: ἀλλ' οὐδὲ ἐμαυτὸν ἀνακρίνω:

4:4οὐδὲν γὰρ ἐμαυτῷ σύνοιδα, ἀλλ' οὐκ ἐν τούτῳ δεδικαίωμαι, ὁ δὲ ἀνακρίνων με κύριός ἐστιν.

4:5ὥστε μὴ πρὸ καιροῦ τι κρίνετε, ἕως ἂν ἔλθῃ ὁ κύριος, ὃς καὶ φωτίσει τὰ κρυπτὰ τοῦ σκότους καὶ φανερώσει τὰς βουλὰς τῶν καρδιῶν: καὶ τότε ὁ ἔπαινος γενήσεται ἑκάστῳ ἀπὸ τοῦ θεοῦ.

4:1Let a man so account of us as of the ministers of Christ and the dispensers of the mysteries of God. [n. 185]

4:2Here now it is required among the dispensers that a man be found faithful. [n. 189]

4:3But to me it is a very small thing to be judged by you or by man's day. [n. 190] But neither do I judge my own self. [n. 192]

4:4For I am not conscious to myself of anything. Yet I am not hereby justified: but he who judges me is the Lord. [n. 190]

4:5Therefore, judge not before the time: until the Lord comes, who both will bring to light the hidden things of darkness and will make manifest the counsels of the hearts. And then shall every man have praise from God. [n. 194]

---

185. Superius redarguit Apostolus Corinthios de hoc, quod de quibusdam ministris gloriabantur, hic autem arguit eos quod alios ministros contemnebant.

Et circa hoc duo facit.

Primo arguit eorum culpam;

secundo instat ad eorum correctionem, ibi *non ut confundam vos.*

Circa primum duo facit.

Primo arguit eorum temeritatem, qua male de ministris iudicabant;

secundo arguit eorum elationem, qua Christi ministros contemnebant, ibi *hoc autem, fratres.*

Circa primum duo facit.

Primo ostendit, quid sit de ministris Christi firmiter sentiendum;

secundo quod non sit de eis temere iudicandum, ibi *hic iam quaeritur inter dispensatores.*

186. Dicit ergo primo: dixi quod nullus vestrum debet gloriari de hominibus, tamen quilibet vestrum debet cognoscere auctoritatem officii nostri, ad quod pertinet quod sumus mediatores inter Christum cui servimus, ad quos pertinet quod dicit *sic nos existimet homo ut ministros Christi*, Is. LXI, v. 6: *sacerdotes Dei vocabimini*

185. Having rebuked the Corinthians for glorying in certain ministers, the Apostle now attacks them for looking down on other ministers.

In regard to this he does two things.

First, he censures their guilt;

second, he concentrates on correcting them, at *I do not write these things* (1 Cor 4:14).

In regard to the first he does two things.

First, he censures their rashness in judging ill of ministers;

second, their arrogance in looking down on ministers of Christ, at *but these things, brethren* (1 Cor 4:6).

In regard to the first he does two things.

First, he shows what should be assuredly felt about Christ's ministers;

second, that they should not be judged rashly, at *here now it is required.*

186. First, therefore, he says: I have said that none of you should glory in men; nevertheless, each of you should recognize the authority of our office, which is that we are mediators between Christ whom we serve—he refers to this when he says, *let a man so account of us as of the ministers of Christ*; *men shall speak of you as the ministers of our*

ministri Dei nostri, dicetur vobis, et inter membra eius, quae sunt fideles Ecclesiae, quibus dona Christi dispensant, ad quos pertinet quod subditur **et dispensatores mysteriorum Dei**, id est, secretorum eius, quae quidem sunt spiritualia eius documenta, secundum illud infra XIV, 2: **Spiritus est, qui loquitur mysteria**; vel etiam ecclesiastica sacramenta, in quibus divina virtus secretius operatur salutem. Unde et in forma consecrationis Eucharistiae dicitur: *mysterium fidei*.

187. Pertinet ergo ad officium praelatorum Ecclesiae, quod in gubernatione subditorum soli Christo servire desiderent, cuius amore oves eius pascunt, secundum illud Io. ult.: *si diligis me, pasce oves meas*. Pertinet etiam ad eos, ut divina populo dispensent, secundum illud infra IX, 17: **dispensatio mihi credita est**, et secundum hoc sunt mediatores inter Christum et populum, secundum illud Deut. V, 5: *ego sequester fui, et medius illo tempore inter Deum et vos*.

Haec autem aestimatio de praelatis Ecclesiae necessaria est ad salutem fidelium; nisi enim eos recognoscerent ministros Christi, non eis obedirent, tamquam Christo, secundum illud Gal. IV, 14: *sicut angelum Dei excepistis me, sicut Iesum Christum*. Rursum, si eos non cognoscerent dispensatores, recusarent ab eis dona recipere, contra illud quod idem Apostolus dicit II Cor. II, 10: *quod donavi, si quid donavi, propter vos in persona Christi donavi*.

188. Deinde cum dicit **hic iam quaeritur inter dispensatores**, ostendit circa ministros Christi, temere iudicari non debere.

Et circa hoc tria facit.

Primo, ponit quoddam per quod iudicare satagunt de fidelitate ministrorum;

secundo, ostendit de hoc iudicio se non curare, sed Deo reservare, ibi **mihi autem pro minimo est**;

tertio, concludit prohibitionem temerarii iudicii, ibi **itaque nolite**.

189. Circa primum considerandum est, quod ministrorum et dispensatorum Christi, quidam sunt fideles, quidam infideles. Infideles dispensatores sunt, qui in dispensandis divinis ministeriis non intendunt utilitatem populi, et honorem Christi, et utilitatem membrorum eius, secundum illud Lc. XVI, v. 11: *in iniquo mammona fideles non fuistis*. Fideles autem, qui in omnibus intendunt honorem Dei, et utilitatem membrorum eius, secundum illud Lc. XII, 42: *quis, putas, est fidelis servus et prudens, quem constituit Dominus super familiam suam?* Qui autem sunt fideles divino iudicio manifestabuntur in futuro.

Sed Corinthii temere volebant discutere, qui dispensatores essent fideles vel infideles. Et hoc est quod dicit **hic**, hoc est, inter vos, **iam**, id est, praesenti tempore,

God (Isa 61:6)—and his members who are the faithful of the Church, to whom we dispense Christ's gifts. He refers to this when he says, **and the dispensers of the mysteries of God**, i.e., of his secrets. These are his spiritual teachings: **by the Spirit he speaks mysteries** (1 Cor 14:2) or the sacraments of the Church, in which divine power secretly works salvation; hence in the formula for consecrating the Eucharist it is said: *the mystery of faith*.

187. Therefore, in governing their subjects the prelates of the Church should seek to serve Christ alone, for love of whom they feed his sheep: *if you love me, feed my sheep* (John 21:17). Furthermore, they should dispense the things of God to the people: **a dispensation is committed to me** (1 Cor 9:17). It is in this way that they are mediators between Christ and the people: *I stood between the Lord and you at that time* (Deut 5:5).

This view of the Church's prelates is necessary for the salvation of the faithful, for unless they recognize them as Christ's ministers, they will not obey them as Christ: *you received me as an angel of God, as Christ Jesus* (Gal 4:14). Again, if they do not regard them as stewards, they would refuse to receive gifts from them, contrary to what the Apostle says: *what I have forgiven, if I have forgiven anything, has been for your sake in the presence of Christ* (2 Cor 2:10).

188. Then when he says, **here now it is required**, he shows that they should not judge rashly in matters concerning Christ's ministers.

In regard to this he does three things.

First, he mentions the standard by which to judge the faithfulness of ministers;

second, he shows that he is not concerned about this judgment but leaves it to God, at **but to me it is a very small thing**;

third he concludes his prohibition against rash judgment, at **therefore, judge not**.

189. In regard to the first it should be noted that some are faithful ministers and dispensers of Christ, and some unfaithful. The unfaithful ministers do not seek the people's welfare and Christ's honor, when they dispense the divine mysteries: *you have not been faithful in the unrighteous mammon* (Luke 16:11). But the faithful ones seek the honor of God and the welfare of his members in all things: *who then is the faithful and wise steward, whom his master will set over his household?* (Luke 12:42). Who the faithful ministers are will be disclosed in the divine judgment to come.

But the Corinthians rashly desired to discuss which dispensers were faithful and which unfaithful. And this is what he says: **here now**, i.e., in the present time, **it is required**, i.e.,

quaeritur, id est, discutitur, *ut quis*, id est aliquis, *inter dispensatores fidelis inveniatur*. Iudicabant enim plures esse infideles, vix aliquem virum putantes esse fidelem, secundum illud Prov. XX, 6: *multi viri misericordes vocantur, virum autem fidelem quis inveniet?*

190. Deinde cum dicit **mihi autem pro minimo est**, ostendit se hoc iudicium reputare nihil, et circa hoc tria facit.

Primo ponit, quod non curat circa hoc ab aliis iudicari, dicens **mihi autem**, qui sum minimus inter dispensatores, **pro minimo est**, id est, minima bona reputo, **ut a vobis iudicer**, scilicet esse fidelis, vel infidelis.

Et ne putarent ab apostolo haec dici in eorum contemptum, ac si eorum iudicium despiceret, quasi vilium personarum, subiungit **aut ab humano** intellectu, qui est **dies** hominis, secundum illud Io. XI, 9: *qui ambulat in die, non offendit, quia lucem huius mundi videt*. Vel ad litteram **aut ab humano die**, id est, ab intellectu in hoc tempore iudicantibus, quasi dicat: vestrum, vel quorumcumque hominum iudicium parum curo. Ier. XVII, 16: *diem hominis non desideravi, tu scis*.

191. Est autem sciendum, quod de iudicio hominum dupliciter debet curari. Uno modo, quantum ad alios, qui ex eorum bono, vel aedificantur, vel scandalizantur, et sic sancti non pro minimo, sed pro magno habent ab hominibus iudicari, cum Dominus dicat Matth. V, 16: *videant opera vestra bona, et glorificent Patrem vestrum, qui in caelis est*.

Alio modo quantum ad seipsos, et sic non curant multum, quia nec gloriam humanam concupiscunt, secundum illud I Thess. II, 6: *neque gloriam ab hominibus quaerentes, neque aliquid a vobis, neque ab aliis*. Neque opprobrium hominis timent, secundum illud Is. LI, 7: *nolite timere opprobrium hominum, et blasphemias eorum ne timeatis*. Unde Apostolus signanter dicit **mihi autem**, etc., id est, quantum ad me pertinet, non autem id pro nullo est, sed **pro minimo**, quia bona temporalia, inter quae bona fama computatur, non sunt nulla bona, sed minima, ut Augustinus dicit in libro *de Libero arbitrio*. Unde et Sap. VII, 9: *omne aurum in comparatione illius arena est exigua*.

192. Secundo ostendit, quod neque seipsum iudicare praesumit, dicens **sed neque meipsum iudico**.

Videtur autem hoc esse contra id quod infra XI, 31 dicitur: **si nosmetipsos diiudicaremus, non utique iudicaremur**. Debet ergo quilibet iudicare seipsum.

Sed sciendum est, quod iudicio discussionis, de quo Apostolus hic loquitur, quilibet debet iudicare seipsum, secundum illud Ps. LXXVI, 7: *exercitabar et scopebam spiritum meum*, et similiter iudicio condemnationis et reprehensionis in manifestis malis, secundum illud Iob XIII, 15: *arguam coram eo vias meas*; sed iudicio

it is being discussed, **among the dispensers that a man be found faithful**. For they judged that many were unfaithful, supposing that scarcely anyone was faithful: *many a man proclaims his own loyalty, but a faithful man who can find?* (Prov 20:6).

190. Then when he says, **but to me it is a very small thing**, he shows that he has no regard for this judgment.

First, he asserts that he is not concerned about the judgment of others on this point, saying, **but to me**, who am the least of the dispensers, **it is a very small thing**, i.e., I regard it a trivial good, **to be judged by you** as faithful or unfaithful.

But lest they suppose that he says these things out of contempt, as though he scorned their opinion as coming from worthless persons, he adds, **or by man's** intellect, which is the **day** of man: *if a man walks in the day he stumbles not, because he sees the light of this world* (John 11:9). Or, **by man's day**, i.e., by the intellect of persons judging in this time. As if to say: I am little concerned about your judgment or any man's: *I have not desired the day of man, you know* (Jer 17:16).

191. It should be noted, however, that one should have regard for men's judgment in two ways: first, in regard to others who are edified or scandalized by what is heard. For this reason the saints did not regard it a small thing but very important to be judged by men, since the Lord said: *that they may see your good works and give glory to your Father, who is in heaven* (Matt 5:16).

Second, in regard to themselves, and then they do not care much, because they neither desire human glory: *nor sought we the glory of men, neither of you nor of others* (1 Thess 2:6), nor fear men's reproaches: *Fear not the reproach of men, and be not afraid of their blasphemies* (Isa 51:7). Hence the Apostle says significantly, **but to me**, i.e., as far as it pertains to me. Nor does he regard it as nothing, but as **a very small thing**, because temporal things, among which a good reputation finds a place, are not null goods but very small ones, as Augustine says in the book *On Free Will*. Hence it is also stated in Wisdom: *all gold in comparison of her is as a little sand* (Wis 7:9).

192. Second, he shows that he does not even presume to judge himself, saying, **but neither do I judge my own self**.

But this seems to conflict with a later statement: **but if we would judge ourselves, we should not be judged** (1 Cor 11:31). Therefore, everyone should judge himself.

However, it should be noted that everyone should judge himself with the judgment of self-examination, about which the Apostle speak here, according to a psalm: *I meditate and search my spirit* (Ps 77:6), as well as with the judgment of condemnation and reproach in the face of obvious evils: *I will reprove my ways in his sight* (Job 13:15). But with

absolutionis non debet aliquis praesumere se iudicare ut innocentem; unde dicitur Iob IX, 20: *si iustificare me voluero, os meum condemnabit me; si innocentem considero, pravum me comprobabit.*

Cuius rationem assignat, dicens **nihil mihi conscius sum**, id est, non habeo alicuius peccati mortalis conscientiam, secundum illud Iob XXVII, 6: *neque reprehendit me cor meum in omni vita mea.* **Sed non in hoc iustificatus sum**, id est, non sufficit ad hoc, quod me iustum pronunciem, quia possunt aliqua peccata in me latere, quae ignoro, secundum illud Ps.: *delicta quis intelligit?* Et Iob c. IX, 21 dicitur: *et si simplex fuero, hoc ipsum ignorabit anima mea.*

193. Tertio concludit cui hoc iudicium reservetur, dicens **qui autem iudicat me Dominus est**, id est, ad solum Deum pertinet iudicare utrum sim fidelis minister an non; hoc enim pertinet ad intentionem cordis, quam solus Deus ponderare potest, secundum illud Prov. XVI, 2: *spirituum ponderator est Dominus.* Et Ier. XVII, 9: *pravum est cor hominis et inscrutabile, quis cognoscet illud? Ego Dominus probans renes et scrutans corda.*

194. Deinde cum dicit **itaque nolite**, etc., concludit prohibitionem temerarii iudicii, et circa hoc tria facit.

Primo prohibet praevenire divinum iudicium, dicens: itaque exemplo meo qui neque meipsum iudico, neque ab aliis iudicari curo, sed iudicium meum Deo reservo, **nolite ante tempus iudicare**, quia, ut dicitur Eccle. c. VIII, 6, *omni negotio tempus est et opportunitas.* **Quoadusque veniat Dominus**, scilicet ad iudicandum, secundum illud Is. III, v. 14: *Dominus ad iudicium veniet cum senatoribus populi sui.* Unde et Dominus dixit Matth. VII, 1: *nolite iudicare.* Sed hoc intelligendum est de occultis; de manifestis autem iudicare commissum est a Deo hominibus, secundum illud Deut. I, 16: *audite illos, et quod iustum est iudicate.*

195. Sunt enim aliqua manifesta non solum per evidentiam facti, sicut notoria, sed et propter confessionem, aut testium probationem. Occulta vero Deus suo reservat iudicio. Sunt autem occulta nobis, quae latent in corde, vel etiam in abscondito fiunt, et de his dicitur in Ps. IV, 5: *quae dicitis in cordibus vestris, et in cubilibus vestris compungimini.* Unde homo quidem de his est temerarius iudex, sicut iudex delegatus, qui excedit formam mandati iudicii de causa non sibi commissa.

Est ergo temerarium iudicium, quando aliquis de dubiis iudicat. Perversum autem, quando falsum iudicium profert. Et quamvis non sit iudicandum circa personas, puta ut aliquis iudicet malum hominem, qui bonus est, tamen multo gravius est, ut iudicium pervertatur de rebus ipsis, puta si quis diceret virginitatem esse malam, et

the judgment of absolution a person should not presume to judge himself innocent: *though I am innocent, my own mouth would condemn me; though I am blameless, he would prove me perverse* (Job 9:20).

He assigns the reason for this when he says, **I am not conscious to myself of anything**, i.e., I am not aware of any mortal sin: *my heart does not reproach me for any of my days* (Job 27:6); **yet I am not hereby justified**, i.e., that does not suffice for pronouncing myself just, because certains sins can be hiding in me, which I do not know: *who can discern his sins?* (Ps 19:12) *I am blameless; I do not regard myself* (Job 9:21).

193. Third, he concludes to the one to whom this judgment should be reserved, saying, **but he who judges me is the Lord**, i.e., it is God's exclusive province to judge whether I am a faithful minister or not, because this pertains to the heart's intention, which God alone can weigh: *the Lord weighs the spirit* (Prov 16:2); *the heart is deceitful above all things, and desperately corrupt; who can understand it? I the Lord search the mind and try the heart* (Jer 17:9).

194. The when he says, **therefore, judge not**, he concludes the prohibition against rash judgment. In regard to this he does three things.

First, he forbids them to anticipate God's judgment, saying: therefore, in keeping with my example, who neither judge myself nor care about being judged by others, but reserve my judgment to God, **judge not before the time**, because *every matter has its time* (Eccl 8:6), **until the Lord comes** to judge: *the Lord enters into judgment with the elders and princes of his people* (Isa 3:14). Hence the Lord himself said: *do not judge* (Matt 7:1). However, this must be understood of hidden things, because God has commissioned men to judge manifest things: *hear them, and judge what is just* (Deut 1:16).

195. For some things are manifested not only by the evidence of the fact, being notorious, but also by confession or by the proved testimony of witnesses. But God reserves hidden things for his own judgment. But things which lie in our heart or are done in secret are hidden to ourselves. Of these it is said: *the things you say in your hearts, be sorry for them upon your beds* (Ps 4:5). Hence a man is as rash in judging about these matters as a delegated judge, who exceeds his mandate by judging matter not committed to him.

Consequently, a judgment is rash when a person judges about doubtful matters; but it is perverse when he pronounces a false judgment. Now although judgment should not be made concerning persons, as when a person judges as evil a man who is good, nevertheless it is more grievous, when it is a perverse judgment about things themselves,

fornicationem bonam. Contra quod dicitur Is. V, 20: *vae qui dicitis bonum malum, et malum bonum.*

196. Secundo describit perfectionem futuri divini iudicii, dicens *qui*, scilicet Dominus ad iudicandum veniens, *illuminabit abscondita tenebrarum*, id est faciet esse lucida et manifesta ea quae occulte in tenebris facta sunt. *Et manifestabit consilia cordium*, id est omnia cordis occulta, secundum illud Iob XII, 22: *qui revelat occulta de tenebris, et producit in lucem umbram mortis.* Et Sophon. I, 12: *scrutabor Ierusalem in lucernis.* Quod quidem est intelligendum tam de bonis, quam de malis, quae non sunt per poenitentiam tecta, secundum illud Ps. XXXI, v. 1: *beati quorum remissae sunt iniquitates, et quorum tecta sunt peccata.*

197. Tertio ponit fructum, quem boni reportabunt de divino iudicio, dicens *et tunc laus erit unicuique*, scilicet bonorum *a Deo.* Quae quidem laus vera erit, quia Deus nec decipi, nec decipere potest. Rom. II, 29: *cuius laus non ex hominibus, sed ex Deo est.* II Cor. X, 18: *non enim qui seipsum commendat ille probatus est, sed quem Deus commendat.*

as when a person says that virginity is evil and fornication good, against which Isaiah says: *woe to you that call good evil and evil good* (Isa 5:20).

196. Second, he describes the completeness of the divine judgment to come, saying: *who*, namely the Lord coming to judgment, *will bring to light the hidden things of darkness*, i.e., will make clear and obvious the things done secretly in darkness; *and will make manifest the counsels of the hearts*, i.e., all the secrets of the heart: *he reveals deep things out of darkness, and brings up to light the shadow of death* (Job 12:22); *I will search Jerusalem with lamps* (Zeph 1:12). This, of course, refers both to good things and to evil things that have been committed and covered over by penance, according to a psalm: *blessed is he whose transgressions is forgiven, whose sin is covered* (Ps 32:1).

197. Third, he mentions the fruit which good men will obtain from the divine judgment, saying, *and then shall every man have praise from God*, i.e., every man that is good. This commendation will be true, because God can neither deceive nor be deceived: *his praise is not from men but from God* (Rom 2:29); *it is not the man who commends himself that is accepted, but the man whom the Lord commends* (2 Cor 10:18).

Lecture 2

4:6Haec autem, fratres, transfiguravi in me et Apollo, propter vos: ut in nobis discatis, ne supra quam scriptum est, unus adversus alterum infletur pro alio. [n. 198]

4:7Quis enim te discernit? quid autem habes quod non accepisti? si autem accepisti, quid gloriaris quasi non acceperis? [n. 200]

4:8Jam saturati estis, jam divites facti estis: sine nobis regnatis: et utinam regnetis, ut et nos vobiscum regnemus. [n. 203]

4:9Puto enim quod Deus nos Apostolos novissimos ostendit, tamquam morti destinatos: quia spectaculum facti sumus mundo, et angelis, et hominibus. [n. 208]

4:10Nos stulti propter Christum, vos autem prudentes in Christo: nos infirmi, vos autem fortes: vos nobiles, nos autem ignobiles. [n. 211]

4:11Usque in hanc horam et esurimus, et sitimus, et nudi sumus, et colaphis caedimur, et instabiles sumus, [n. 214]

4:12et laboramus operantes manibus nostris: maledicimur, et benedicimus: persecutionem patimur, et sustinemus: [n. 217]

4:13blasphemamur, et obsecramus: tamquam purgamenta hujus mundi facti sumus, omnium peripsema usque adhuc.

4:6Ταῦτα δέ, ἀδελφοί, μετεσχημάτισα εἰς ἐμαυτὸν καὶ Ἀπολλῶν δι' ὑμᾶς, ἵνα ἐν ἡμῖν μάθητε τὸ Μὴ ὑπὲρ ἃ γέγραπται, ἵνα μὴ εἷς ὑπὲρ τοῦ ἑνὸς φυσιοῦσθε κατὰ τοῦ ἑτέρου.

4:7τίς γάρ σε διακρίνει; τί δὲ ἔχεις ὃ οὐκ ἔλαβες; εἰ δὲ καὶ ἔλαβες, τί καυχᾶσαι ὡς μὴ λαβών;

4:8ἤδη κεκορεσμένοι ἐστέ: ἤδη ἐπλουτήσατε: χωρὶς ἡμῶν ἐβασιλεύσατε: καὶ ὄφελόν γε ἐβασιλεύσατε, ἵνα καὶ ἡμεῖς ὑμῖν συμβασιλεύσωμεν.

4:9δοκῶ γάρ, ὁ θεὸς ἡμᾶς τοὺς ἀποστόλους ἐσχάτους ἀπέδειξεν ὡς ἐπιθανατίους, ὅτι θέατρον ἐγενήθημεν τῷ κόσμῳ καὶ ἀγγέλοις καὶ ἀνθρώποις.

4:10ἡμεῖς μωροὶ διὰ Χριστόν, ὑμεῖς δὲ φρόνιμοι ἐν Χριστῷ: ἡμεῖς ἀσθενεῖς, ὑμεῖς δὲ ἰσχυροί: ὑμεῖς ἔνδοξοι, ἡμεῖς δὲ ἄτιμοι.

4:11ἄχρι τῆς ἄρτι ὥρας καὶ πεινῶμεν καὶ διψῶμεν καὶ γυμνιτεύομεν καὶ κολαφιζόμεθα καὶ ἀστατοῦμεν

4:12καὶ κοπιῶμεν ἐργαζόμενοι ταῖς ἰδίαις χερσίν: λοιδορούμενοι εὐλογοῦμεν, διωκόμενοι ἀνεχόμεθα,

4:13δυσφημούμενοι παρακαλοῦμεν: ὡς περικαθάρματα τοῦ κόσμου ἐγενήθημεν, πάντων περίψημα, ἕως ἄρτι.

4:6But these things, brethren, I have in a figure transferred to myself and to Apollo, for your sakes: that in us you may learn that one be not puffed up against the other for another, above that which is written. [n. 198]

4:7For who distinguishes you? Or what do you have that you have not received, and if you have received, why do you glory, as if you had not received it? [n. 200]

4:8You are now full: you are now become rich: you reign without us; and I would that you did reign, that we also might reign with you. [n. 203]

4:9For I think that God has set forth us apostles, the last, as it were men appointed to death. We are made a spectacle to the world and to angels and to men. [n. 208]

4:10We are fools for Christ's sake, but you are wise in Christ: we are weak, but you are strong: you are honorable, but we without honor. [n. 211]

4:11Even unto this hour we both hunger and thirst and are naked and are buffeted and have no fixed abode. [n. 214]

4:12And we labor, working with our own hands. We are reviled: and we bless. We are persecuted: and we suffer it. [n. 217]

4:13We are blasphemed: and we entreat. We are made as the refuse of this world, the offscouring of all, even until now.

---

198. Postquam Apostolus reprehendit in Corinthiis temeritatem, qua ministros Christi iudicabant, hic arguit eorum elationem, qua ministros Christi contemnebant.

Et circa hoc tria facit.
Primo proponit quod intendit;
secundo rationem assignat, ibi *quis enim te discernit?*
Tertio eorum contemptum ironice loquens irridet, ibi *iam saturati estis*.

199. Circa primum considerandum est, quod Apostolus supra volens reprimere contentiones Corinthiorum, quas habebant ratione ministrorum, usus fuerat

198. After berating the Corinthians for the rashness with which they judged Christ's ministers, the Apostle now censures the self-satisfaction with which they scorned Christ's ministers.

In regard to his he does three things.
First, he states his proposition;
second, he assigns a reason, at *for who distinguishes you*;
third, he belittles their contemptuous attitude, at *you are now full*.

199. In regard to the first it should be noted that above when the Apostle tried to repress the rivalry about ministers among the Corinthians, he had used the names of

nominibus bonorum ministrorum Christi, sicut supra I, 12 dixit: *unusquisque vestrum dicit: ego quidem sum Pauli, ego autem Apollo, ego vero Cephae*; et supra III, 22 ubi dixit: *sive Paulus, sive Apollo, sive Cephas*, et tamen non gloriabantur de bonis ministris Christi, nec propter eos dissidebant, sed propter pseudo-Apostolos, quos nominare noluit, ne videretur ex odio, vel invidia contra eos loqui; sed loco eorum posuerat nomen suum et aliorum bonorum praedicatorum, et hoc est quod dicit *haec autem, fratres*, scilicet quae dixi de ministris, de quibus gloriamini, et pro quibus contenditis, *transfiguravi* id est, figuraliter loquens, transtuli, *in me et Apollo*. Dicit enim Prov. I, 6: *animadvertent parabolam et interpretationem verba sapientium et aenigmata eorum*. Et hoc *propter vos*, id est, vestram utilitatem, II Cor. IV, 15: *omnia propter vos*; *ut in vobis discatis, ne unus vestrum infletur*, id est, superbiat, *adversus alium* proximum suum, *pro alio*, scilicet pro quocumque ministro Christi, *ne supra quam scriptum est*, id est, ultra formam vobis in praemissis descriptam. Dicitur enim Sap. IV, v. 19: *disrumpens illos inflatos sine voce*.

200. Deinde cum dicit *quis enim te discernit?* Assignat rationem quare unus non debeat contra alium inflari.

Et primo ponit rationem, dicens *quis enim te discernit?* Quod potest intelligi dupliciter: uno modo sic: quis enim te discernit a massa perditorum? Tu teipsum discernere non potes: unde non habes in te unde contra alium superbias. Et de hac discretione dicitur in Ps. XLII, 1: *iudica me, Deus, et discerne causam meam de gente non sancta*. Alio modo potest intelligi *quis te discernit*, scilicet superiorem faciens proximo tuo? Hoc quod tu facere non potes, unde contra eum superbire non debes. Et de hac discretione dicitur Eccli. XXXIII, 11: *in multitudine disciplinae Domini separavit eos, et immutavit vias illorum*. Sed inter homines, inquantum sunt fideles Christi, non est discretio, quia, ut dicitur Rom. XII, 5, *multi unum corpus sumus in Christo*. Et dicit Petrus: *nihil discernit inter nos et illos, fide purificans corda eorum*.

201. Secundo excludit quamdam rationem.

Posset enim aliquis discerni a bonis vel a malis, melior eis existens, propter bona quae habet, puta fidem, sapientiam, et huiusmodi. Sed hoc excludit Apostolus, dicens *quid autem habes, quod non accepisti?* Quasi dicat: nihil. Omnia enim bona sunt a Deo, secundum illud Ps. CIII, 28: *aperiente te manum tuam, omnia implebuntur bonitate*; et Par. XXIX, 14: *tua sunt omnia, et quae de manu tua accepimus, dedimus tibi*.

Et ex hoc concludit propositum, dicens *si autem accepisti, quid gloriaris, quasi non acceperis?* Ille igitur gloriatur quasi non accipiens, qui de seipso gloriatur, et non de Deo, sicut de quibusdam dicitur in Ps. XLVIII, v. 7:

good ministers of Christ, as when he said, *every one of you says: I indeed am of Paul; and I am of Apollo; and I of Cephas* (1 Cor 1:12), and again: *whether it be Paul or Apollo or Cephas* (1 Cor 3:22). But in fact they were not glorying in Christ's good ministers or disagreeing over them but over the false apostles, whom he chose not to name, lest it seem that he was speaking against them from hatred or envy. Rather he had employed his own name and the names of other good preachers. And that is what he is saying now: *but these things, brethren*, namely, what I have said about the ministers in whom you glory and for whom you compete, *I have in a figure transferred*, i.e., speaking figuratively, I have transferred *to myself and to Apollo*. For it says in Proverbs: *to understand a proverb and a figure, the words of the wise and their riddles* (Prov 1:6), and this for your benefit: *all things are for your sakes* (2 Cor 4:15); *that in us you may learn that one be not puffed up*, i.e., with pride, *against the other*, your neighbor, *for another*, i.e., for any of Christ's ministers, *above that which is written*, i.e., beyond the form described in the foregoing; for it is written: *he will dash them puffed up and speechless to the ground* (Wis 4:19).

200. Then he assigns the reason why one should not be puffed up against another, at *for who distinguishes you*.

First, he lays down the reason, saying, *for who distinguishes you?* This can be interpreted in two ways: in one way so that it means: who distinguished you from the mass of the damned? You cannot distinguish yourself; hence you have nothing in you as a ground for exalting yourself. Of this distinction it is said: *judge me, O God, and distinguish my cause from an ungodly people* (Ps 43:1). It can be understood in another way: *who distinguishes you* to make you superior to your neighbor? This is something you cannot do; hence you should not exalt yourself above him. Of this exaltation Sirach says: *in the fullness of his knowledge God distinguished them and appointed their different ways* (Sir 33:11). But there is no distinction among men, insofar as they are Christ's faithful, because *we, though many, are one body in Christ* (Rom 12:5); *God put no difference between us and them, purifying their hearts by faith* (Acts 15:9).

201. Then he dismisses an apparent reason.

For someone could be distinguished from good or from evil men, because he is better than they on account of the blessings he has, such as faith, wisdom and the like. But the Apostle excludes this, saying, *what do you have that you have not received*. As if to say: nothing; for all blessings come from God: *when you open your hand, they are filled with good things* (Ps 104: 28); *all things come from you, and of your own have we given you* (1 Chr 29:14).

From this he draws his conclusion, saying, *and if you have received, why do you glory, as if you had not received it?* Accordingly, a person boasts as though he did not receive, when he boasts in himself and not in God, as those

qui confidunt in virtute sua, et in multitudine divitiarum suarum gloriantur.

202. Et ad hoc pertinet prima species superbiae, qua scilicet aliquis superbiendo, quod habet, dicit a seipso habere, iuxta illud Ps. XI, 5: *labia nostra a nobis sunt, quis noster Dominus est?* Ille autem gloriatur quasi accipiens, qui omnia Deo adscribens, gloriatur de ipso, sicut supra dictum est: *qui gloriatur, in Domino glorietur.* Sic autem gloriari non est superbire, sed humiliari sub Deo, cui homo dat gloriam, secundum illud Eccli. ult.: *danti mihi sapientiam, dabo gloriam.*

203. Deinde, cum dicit *iam saturati estis*, irridet eorum superbiam, qui apostolos Christi contemnebant. Et
primo in generali,
secundo in speciali, ibi *nos stulti sumus*, et cetera.
Circa primum duo facit.
Primo irridet in eis quod de se nimis praesumebant;

secundo deridet in eis, quod apostolos contemnebant, ibi *puto enim quod Deus*, et cetera.
Circa primum duo facit.
Primo irridet eos de praesumptione, qua sibi attribuebant quod non habebant;

secundo irridet eos de hoc, quod sibi singulariter attribuebant, quod singulariter non habebant, ibi *sine nobis regnatis.*

204. Attribuebant autem sibi abundantiam bonorum, quorum quaedam sunt interiora; et quantum ad hoc dicit *iam saturati estis*, id est, vobis videtur quod saturati estis, id est, abundanter refecti spirituali dulcedine, de qua dicitur in Ps. XVI, 15: *satiabor dum manifestabitur gloria tua.* Poterat autem eis secundum veritatem dici, quod iam saturati estis, non plenitudine, sed fastidio, secundum illud Prov. XXVII, 7: *anima satiata calcabit favum.* Quaedam vero sunt bona exteriora, et quantum ad hoc dicit *iam divites facti estis*, sicut vobis videtur, scilicet divitiis spiritualibus, de quibus dicitur Is. c. XXXIII, 6: *divitiae salutis sapientia et scientia.* Simile est, quod dicitur Apoc. III, v. 17: *dicis, quia dives sum, et locuples valde, et nullius egeo.*

205. Sed contra hoc videtur illud quod supra dixit in principio, dicens quia *in omnibus divites facti estis in illo, in omni verbo, et in omni scientia*, etc.

Sed dicendum est, quod supra dixit quantum ad bonos, qui inter eos erant; hic autem dicit quantum ad praesumptuosos, qui superbiebant de eo quod non habebant.

Potest et aliter distingui satietas et divitiae, ut saturitas referatur ad usum gratiae, quo quis spiritualibus fruitur; divitiae autem ad ipsos habitus gratiarum.

mentioned in a psalm: *men who trust in their wealth and boast of the abundance of their riches* (Ps 49:6).

202. This is the way the first form of pride expresses itself, namely, when a person, taking pride in what he has, says that he has it of himself, as a psalm: *with our tongue we will prevail, our lips are with us; who is our master?* (Ps 12:4) But a person boasts as one receiving, when he glories in himself by ascribing everything to God, as was said above: *he who glories may glory in the Lord* (1 Cor 1:31). To boast in this way is not pride but humility under God, to whom a man gives glory: *to him who gives me wisdom I will give glory* (Sir 51:17).

203. Then when he says, *you are now full*, he mocks the pride of those who looked down on Christ's apostles:
first, in general;
then specifically, at *we are fools*.
As to the first he does two things.
First, he ridicules them for presuming too much on themselves;
second, for looking down on the apostles, at *for I think that God*.
In regard to the first he does two things.
First, he mocks them for presuming to attribute to themselves what they did not have;
second, for attributing to themselves an abundance of good things, some of which are internal, at *you reign without us*.

204. In regard to these he says, already you are filled, i.e., it seems to you that *you are now full*, i.e., you seem to yourselves to be full, that is, completely sated with spiritual delights, about which it is said: *I shall be satisfied, when your glory shall appear* (Ps 17:15). But it could have been true to say to them, already you are filled, not with fullness but with nausea: *he who is sated loathes honey* (Prov 27:7). But some goods were external. In regard to these he says, *you are now become rich*, as it seems to you, with spiritual riches, about which Isaiah says: *riches of salvation, wisdom and knowledge* (Isa 33:6). This is similar to Revelation: *you say, I am rich, I have prospered, and I need nothing* (Rev 3:17).

205. But this seems to conflict with his earlier statement: *in all things you are made rich in him, in all utterance and in all knowledge* (1 Cor 1:5).

The answer is that the earlier statement referred to the good men among them; but there he is speaking about the presumptuous ones, who took pride in what they did not have.

Or a distinction can be made between fullness and riches, so that the former refers to using grace to enjoy spiritual things, whereas riches would refer to the very possession of grace.

206. Secundo cum dicit *sine nobis regnatis*, irridet eos, quod sibi singulariter attribuebant quod non habebant.

Unde dicit *sine nobis regnatis*, id est, ita vobis videtur, quod regnum ad vos pertineat, non ad nos. Sic enim erant decepti a pseudo-Apostolis, ut crederent se solos habere fidei veritatem, quae in regno Dei consistit, Apostolum autem et sequaces eius errare. Contra quos dicitur Is. V, 8: *numquid habitabitis vos soli in medio terrae?*

Et ne videatur Apostolus ex invidia hoc dicere, subiungit *utinam regnetis*. Optat enim ut veram fidem habeant, secundum illud Act. XXVI, 29: *opto omnes qui audiunt, tales fieri, qualis et ego sum, exceptis vinculis his.*

Et ut eis exempla humilitatis praebeat, subiungit *ut et nos regnemus vobiscum*, quasi dicat: si aliquam excellentiam habetis, non dedignamur vos sequi, sicut vos dedignamini sequi nos, contra illud quod dicitur Gal. IV, v. 18: *quod bonum est, aemulamini in bono semper.*

207. Et est advertendum, quod Apostolus hic quatuor species superbiae tangit, quarum prima est, quando aliquis reputat se non habere a Deo quod habet, quam tangit dicens *quid gloriaris quasi non acceperis?* Et hoc etiam potest reduci ad secundam speciem qua aliquis existimat propriis meritis accepisse. Tertia species est, qua quis iactat se habere quod non habet, et quantum ad hoc dicit *iam saturati estis, iam divites facti estis.* Quarta species, quando aliquis, despectis caeteris, singulariter vult videri, et quantum ad hoc pertinet quod dicit *sine nobis regnatis.*

208. Deinde, cum dicit *puto quod Deus*, etc., irridet eos de hoc quod apostolos Christi contemnebant, et

primo irrisorie ponit contemptum;

secundo causam contemptus, ibi *quia spectaculum facti sumus.*

209. Dicit ergo primo: prius dixi, quod *sine nobis regnatis, puto enim*, id est, vos putare videmini, *quod Deus nos apostolos ostendit novissimos*, cum tamen infra c. XII, 28 dicatur, quod *Deus in Ecclesia posuit primum apostolos.* Sic enim impletur quod dicitur Matth. XX, 16: *erunt primi novissimi, et novissimi primi.*

Et ponit exemplum: *tamquam morti destinatos.* Illi enim, qui sunt condemnati ad mortem, novissimi habentur inter homines, utpote quos indignum sit vivere, et tales apostoli reputantur a mundanis hominibus, secundum illud Ps. XLIII, 22: *aestimati sumus sicut oves occisionis.*

210. Deinde, cum dicit *quia spectaculum*, assignat causam contemptus.

206. Second, when he says, *you reign without us*, he makes sport of them for attributing to themselves individually things they did not possess individually.

Hence he says, *you reign without us*, i.e., you seem to think that the kingdom belongs to you and not to us. For they had been deceived by the false apostles to such an extent as to suppose that they alone possessed the truths of faith, which consists in the kingdom of God, and that the Apostle and his followers were in error. Against these it is said: *do you alone live in the middle of the earth?* (Isa 5:8).

And lest it seem that the Apostle says this out of envy, he continues: *and I would that you did reign.* Thus he wishes them to have the true faith: *I wish that not only you but also all who hear me this day might become such as I am except for these chains* (Acts 26:29).

And to offer them an example of humility he adds, *that we also might reign with you*, as if to say: if you have anything worthwhile, I am not too proud to follow you, as you disdain to follow us, contrary to what he advises in Galatians: *be zealous for what is good in a good thing always* (Gal 4:18).

207. It should be noted that the Apostle here touches on four kinds of pride. The first is when a person considers that what he has was not received from God. He touches on this form when he says: *if you have received it, why do you glory, as if you had not received it?* Which can also pertain to the second form in which a person thinks that he has received by his own merits. The third form is when a person boasts that he has something he really does not have. In regard to this he says, *you are now full: you are now become rich.* The fourth is when a person, looking down on others, wishes to seem unique. In regard to this he says, *you reign without us.*

208. Then when he says, *for I think that God*, he taunts them for looking down on Christ's apostles.

First, he describes the contempt ironically;

second, the cause of the contempt, at *we are made a spectacle.*

209. He says, therefore: I have just said that *you reign without us. For I think*, i.e., you seem to think, *that God has set forth us apostles, the last*, whereas it says below: *God indeed has set some in the church; first apostles* (1 Cor 12:28). In this way is fulfilled what is stated in Matthew: *the first shall be last, and the last first* (Matt 20:26).

Then he gives an example, *as it were men appointed to death*; for those condemned to death are reckoned last by men, as though not worthy to live. That is what the apostles were considered to be by worldly men: *we are accounted as sheep for the slaughter* (Ps 44:22).

210. Then when he says, *we are made a spectacle*, he indicates the cause of the contempt.

Circa quod considerandum est, quod quando aliqui sunt condemnati ad mortem, convocantur homines ad eorum occisionem, quasi ad spectaculum, et hoc maxime fiebat circa eos, qui damnabantur ad bestias. Quia apostoli erant quasi morti destinati, subiungit **quia spectaculum facti sumus mundo**, quasi totus mundus concurrat ad spectandum nostram occisionem, secundum illud Ps. XLIII, v. 14: *posuisti nos opprobrium vicinis nostris.*

Exponit autem quid nomine mundi intelligat, cum subdit **et angelis, et hominibus**, scilicet bonis et malis. Concurrebant enim ad eorum spectaculum boni angeli ad confortandum, mali autem ad impugnandum; boni homines ad compatiendum, et exemplum patientiae sumendum, mali homines ad persequendum, et irridendum.

211. Deinde cum dicit **nos stulti**, etc., irridet eos in speciali, quod apostolos contemnebant.

Et circa hoc duo facit.

Primo ponit contemptum;

secundo causam contemptus, ibi **usque in hanc horam**, et cetera.

212. Circa primum irridet eorum contemptum quantum ad hoc, quod sibi excellentiam, apostolis defectum attribuebant.

Et primo quantum ad perfectionem intellectus. Et quantum ad hoc dicit **nos stulti sumus propter Christum**, id est stulti reputamur, quia crucem Christi praedicamus, supra I, 18: **verbum crucis pereuntibus stultitia est**, et etiam quia propter Christum opprobria et contentiones sustinemus, secundum illud Sap. V, 4: *nos insensati vitam illorum aestimabamus insaniam.* Item, ut legitur Act. c. XXVI, 24, Festus dixit Paulo: *insanis, Paule, multae te litterae ad insaniam adducunt.* **Vos**, secundum vestram reputationem, estis **prudentes in Christo**, quia scilicet nec crucem eius publice confiteri audetis, nec persecutionem pro eo sustinetis. Prov. XXVI, 16: *sapientior sibi videtur piger septem viris sequentibus sententias.*

213. Secundo quantum ad potestatem actionis, cum dicit **nos infirmi**, reputamur scilicet in exterioribus, propter afflictiones quas sustinemus. II Cor. XII, 9: *libenter gloriabor in infirmitatibus meis.* **Vos autem**, scilicet secundum vestram reputationem, estis **fortes**, scilicet in rebus corporalibus, quia secure vivitis sine tribulatione. Is. V, 22: *vae qui potentes estis ad bibendum vinum, et viri fortes ad miscendam ebrietatem.* **Vos nobiles**, scilicet estis, secundum vestram aestimationem, id est, honore digni, qui exterius contumelias non patimini. Is. XIX, 11: *filius sapientium, ego filius regum antiquorum.* **Nos autem ignobiles** sumus, secundum vestram et aliorum reputationem, quia contemptibiles habemur. Supra I, 27: **quae contemptibilia sunt mundi et ignobilia elegit Deus**. Et

In regard to this it should be noted that when people were condemned to death, men were summoned to the execution as to a spectacle, especially when they were condemned to be thrown to wild animals. Now because the apostles had been, as it were, appointed for death, he adds, *we are made a spectacle to the world*, as though the whole world had assembled to witness their slaughter: *you have made us the taunt of our neighbors* (Ps 44:13).

Then he explains what he meant by the word world, when he continues, *to angels and to men*, namely, good and evil. For good angels came to the spectacle to comfort, but evil angels to assail; and good men came to sympathize and to witness an example of patience, but evil men to persecute and ridicule.

211. Then when he says, *we are fools*, he derides them in particular for scorning the apostles.

As to this he does two things.

First, he mentions the contempt;

second, the cause, at *even unto this hour*.

212. In regard to the first he taunts them for attributing greatness to themselves and shortcomings to the apostles.

First, in regard to perfect understanding; hence he says, *we are fools for Christ's sake*, i.e., we are accounted fools, because we preach the cross of Christ: *the word of the cross, to them indeed that perish, is foolishness* (1 Cor 1:18), and also because we suffer reproach and opposition for the sake of Christ, in keeping with Wisdom: *we fools! We thought that his life was madness and that his end was without honor* (Wis 5:4), and as exemplified in Acts: *Festus said with a loud voice: Paul, you are mad; your great learning is turning you mad* (Acts 26:24). *But you* in your opinion *are wise in Christ*, namely, because you neither dare to confess his cross publicly nor suffer persecution for him: *the sluggard is wiser in his own eyes than seven men who can answer discreetly* (Prov 26:16).

213. Second, in regard to power to act when he says, *we are weak*, namely, in externals on account of the afflictions we endure: *I will all the more boast of my weaknesses* (2 Cor 12:9); *but you* in your opinion *are strong*, namely, in material things, because you live in security without harassment: *woe to you who are heroes at drinking wine, and valiant men in mixing strong drink* (Isa 5:22). *You are honorable*, i.e., in your own eyes you are worthy of honor, because you do not suffer public shame: *I am a son of the wise, a son of ancient kings* (Isa 19:11), *but we without honor*, according to your opinion and that of others, because we are considered contemptible: *the base things of the world, and the things that are contemptible, God has chosen* (1 Cor 1:28). And yet the truth is the exact opposite,

tamen secundum rei veritatem est e converso. Soli enim contemptibiles illi sunt, qui Deum contemnunt, secundum illud I Reg. c. II, 30: *qui autem contemnunt me, erunt ignobiles.*

214. Deinde, cum dicit **usque in hanc horam**, etc., assignat causam contemptus. Et

primo ponit pro causa defectum bonorum temporalium;

secundo mala quae in eis intelligebantur, ibi **maledicimur et benedicimus**;

tertio concludit intentum, ibi **tamquam purgamenta**.

215. Circa primum duo facit. Primo ponit defectum quem patiebantur in rebus necessariis.

Unde quantum ad ea, quae pertinent ad victum, dicit **usque in hanc horam**, id est, continue a conversione nostra usque in praesens tempus, **esurimus et sitimus**. II Cor. XI, 27: *in fame et siti.* Quantum vero ad vestitum, subdit **et nudi sumus**, id est, propter vestimentorum inopiam, quia etiam interdum expoliabantur. Iob XXIV, 7: *nudos dimittunt homines vestimenta tollentes, quibus non est operimentum in frigore.*

Sed contra est quod dicitur in Ps. XXXVI, v. 25: *non vidi iustum derelictum, nec semen eius quaerens panem.*

Sed dicendum est, quod ita patiebantur Apostoli, quod non derelinquebantur, quia divina providentia moderabatur in eis et abundantiam et inopiam, quantum eis expediebat ad virtutis exercitium. Unde et Apostolus Phil. IV, 11 ss.: *ubique et in omnibus institutus sum, et saturari, et esurire, et abundare, et penuriam pati; omnia possum in eo, qui me confortat.*

216. Secundo ponit defectum eorum, quae pertinent ad bene esse humanae vitae, quorum primum est reverentia ab hominibus exhibita, contra quod dicit **et colaphis caedimur**, quod quidem fit magis ad opprobrium, quam ad poenam. Unde de Christo legimus Matth. XXVI, 67 quod *expuerunt in faciem suam, et colaphis eum caeciderunt.*

Secundo requiritur quies in loco, contra quod dicitur **et instabiles sumus**, tum quia expellebantur a persecutoribus de loco in locum, secundum illud Matth. X, 23: *si vos persecuti fuerint in una civitate, fugite in aliam*, tum etiam quia pro executione sui officii discurrebant ubique, secundum illud Io. c. XV, 16: *posui vos ut eatis.*

Tertio requiritur ministrantium auxilium, contra quod dicitur **et laboramus operantes manibus nostris**, tum quia aliquando nullus dabat eis unde possent sustentari; tum etiam, quia labore manuum suarum victum acquirebant vel ad vitandum fidelium gravamen, vel ad repellendum pseudo-apostolos, qui propter quaestum praedicabant, ut habetur II Cor. XII, 16 ss.; tum etiam, ut darent otiosis laborandi exemplum, ut habetur

for only those who scorn God are worthy of scorn: *those who despise me shall be lightly esteemed* (1 Sam 2:30).

214. Then when he says, **even unto this hour**, he discloses the cause of this scorn.

First, he assigns the lack of temporal goods as the cause;

second, the evils they suffered, at **we are reviled: and we bless**;

third, he reaches his conclusion, at **we are made as the refuse**.

215. As to the first he mentions the privations they suffered in necessary things.

Hence in regard to food and drink he says: **even unto this hour we both hunger and thirst**, namely, without interruption from the time of our conversion to the present moment: *in hunger and thirst* (2 Cor 11:17). As to clothing he says, **and are naked**, i.e., because of our need for clothing, since we are sometimes despoiled: *they lie all night naked, without clothing, and have no covering in the cold* (Job 24:7).

But this seems to conflict with a psalm: *I have not seen the righteous forsaken or his children begging bread* (Ps 37:25).

The answer is that although the apostles suffered, they were not abandoned, because divine providence set limits to their abundance and their needs according to what was suitable for exercising virtue. Hence the Apostle says in Philippians: *I have learned the secret of facing plenty and hunger, abundance and want. I can do all things in him who strengthens me* (Phil 4:12).

216. Second, he mentions their lack of things pertaining to the better aspects of human life, the first of which is respect from others. But they received the opposite: **and are buffeted**, which aims more at shame than punishment; hence we read of Christ that *they spat in his face and slapped him* (Matt 26:67).

The second is peace and quiet. Here again they endured the opposite: **and have no fixed abode**, both because they were expelled from place to place by their persecutors: *if they persecute you in one city, flee to another* (Matt 10:23), and because they went everywhere to perform their office: *I have appointed you that you should go* (John 15:16).

The third is help from servants. But they experienced the opposite: **and we labor, working with our own hands**, both because they often received nothing from anyone to support them and because they earned their living by the work of their own hands either to avoid being a burden to the faithful or to rebuff false apostles who preached for money, and also because they wanted to give the idle an example of work (2 Thess 3:9); hence Paul says: *these hands*

II Thess. III, 9. Unde dicit Paulus Act. XX, v. 34: *ad ea quae mihi opus erant, et his qui mecum sunt, ministraverunt manus istae.*

217. Deinde, cum dicit **maledicimur**, etc., ponit mala quae apostoli patiebantur. Et primo in verbis, cum dicit **maledicimur**, id est, male de nobis dicunt homines, vel ad detrahendum, vel ad contumelias inferendum, vel etiam mala imprecando. Ier. XV, v. 10: *Omnes maledicunt mihi.* **Et benedicimus**, id est, reddimus bonum pro malo, secundum illud I Petr. III, 9: *non reddentes maledictum pro maledicto, sed e contrario benedicentes.*

Secundo in factis, et quantum ad hoc dicit **persecutionem patimur**, non solum quantum ad hoc, quod fugamur de loco ad locum, quod proprie persecutio dicitur, sed quantum ad hoc quod multipliciter tribulamur, secundum illud Ps. CXVIII, 157: *multi qui persequuntur me, et tribulant me.* **Et sustinemus**, in Christo scilicet omnia patienter. Eccli. I, 29: *usque ad tempus sustinebit patiens.*

Tertio tangit causam utriusque, cum dicit **blasphemamur**, id est, blasphemia imponuntur nobis, dum dicimur magi vel malefici, et reputamur Dei inimici, secundum illud Io. c. XVI, 2: *venit hora, ut omnis qui interficit vos, arbitretur obsequium se praestare Deo*; et Rom. III, 8: *sicut blasphemamur, et sicut aiunt quidam nos dicere, faciamus mala, ut veniant bona.* Tamen, **obsecramus** Deum pro his qui nos persequuntur et blasphemant, secundum illud Matth. V, 44: *orate pro persequentibus et calumniantibus vos.*

218. Deinde cum dicit **tamquam purgamenta**, etc., concludit ex omnibus praemissis eorum contemptum, dicens: et propter omnia praedicta **facti sumus tamquam purgamenta huius mundi**, id est, reputati sumus et a Iudaeis et a gentilibus, ut per nos mundus inquinetur: et propter nostram occisionem mundus purgetur, et tamquam simus **peripsema omnium**. Dicitur peripsema quodcumque purgamentum, puta vel pomi, vel ferri, vel cuiuscumque alterius rei. Et hoc, **usque adhuc**, quia scilicet continue hoc patimur. Sed quandoque deficiet, secundum illud Sap. V, 3, ubi ex ore impiorum dicitur: *hi sunt, quos aliquando habuimus in derisum, et in similitudinem improperii.* Et postea subditur: *quomodo ergo computati sunt inter filios Dei?*

ministered to my necessities, and to those who were with me (Acts 20:34).

217. Then when he says, **we are reviled**, we bless, he mentions the evils when the apostles endured: first, in words when he says, **we are reviled**, i.e., men speak evil of us either to detract us or to insult us to even to curse us: *all curse me* (Jer 15:10), **and we bless**, i.e., return good for evil: *do not return evil for evil, but on the contrary, bless* (1 Pet 3:9).

Second, in deeds; hence he says, **we are persecuted**, not only because we are chased from place to place, which is persecution in the strict sense, but also because we are harassed in many ways: *many are my persecutors and my adversaries* (Ps 119:157), **and we suffer it**, namely, in Christ: *a patient man will endure until the right moment* (Sir 1:23).

Third, he touches on the cause of each when he says: **we are blasphemed**, i.e., blasphemies are put against us, and we are called sorcerers, evil-doers and enemies of God: *the hour comes what whosoever kills you, will think that he does a service to God* (John 16:2); *why not do evil that good may come?—as some people slanderously charge us with saying.* (Rom 3:8); **and we entreat** God for those who persecute and slander us: *love your enemies and pray for those who persecute you* (Matt 5:44).

218. Then when he says, **we are made as the refuse**, he sums up their contempt, saying: on account of the foregoing, **we are made as the refuse of the world**, i.e., both Jews and gentiles think that the world is befouled by us and that it would be cleansed by our slaughter, **the offscouring of all**. Offscouring is the filth scraped from fruit or iron or any other things. He says, **even until now**, because they suffer these things without interruption. But it will stop sometime according to Wisdom, where from the mouth of the impious it is said: *this is the man whom we once held in derision and made a byword of reproach* (Wis 5:4), and then continues: *why has he been numbered among the songs of God?* (Wis 5:5)

Lecture 3

4:14Non ut confundam vos, haec scribo, sed ut filios meos carissimos moneo. [n. 219]

4:15Nam si decem millia paedagogorum habeatis in Christo, sed non multos patres. Nam in Christo Jesu per Evangelium ego vos genui. [n. 221]

4:16Rogo ergo vos, imitatores mei estote, sicut et ego Christi. [n. 223]

4:17Ideo misi ad vos Timotheum, qui est filius meus carissimus, et fidelis in Domino: qui vos commonefaciet vias meas, quae sunt in Christo Jesu, sicut ubique in omni ecclesia doceo. [n. 224]

4:18Tamquam non venturus sim ad vos, sic inflati sunt quidam. [n. 225]

4:19Veniam autem ad vos cito, si Dominus voluerit: et cognoscam non sermonem eorum qui inflati sunt, sed virtutem. [n. 226]

4:20Non enim in sermone est regnum Dei, sed in virtute.

4:21Quid vultis? in virga veniam ad vos, an in caritate, et spiritu mansuetudinis? [n. 227]

4:14Οὐκ ἐντρέπων ὑμᾶς γράφω ταῦτα, ἀλλ' ὡς τέκνα μου ἀγαπητὰ νουθετῶ[ν]:

4:15ἐὰν γὰρ μυρίους παιδαγωγοὺς ἔχητε ἐν Χριστῷ, ἀλλ' οὐ πολλοὺς πατέρας, ἐν γὰρ Χριστῷ Ἰησοῦ διὰ τοῦ εὐαγγελίου ἐγὼ ὑμᾶς ἐγέννησα.

4:16παρακαλῶ οὖν ὑμᾶς, μιμηταί μου γίνεσθε.

4:17διὰ τοῦτο ἔπεμψα ὑμῖν Τιμόθεον, ὅς ἐστίν μου τέκνον ἀγαπητὸν καὶ πιστὸν ἐν κυρίῳ, ὃς ὑμᾶς ἀναμνήσει τὰς ὁδούς μου τὰς ἐν Χριστῷ [Ἰησοῦ], καθὼς πανταχοῦ ἐν πάσῃ ἐκκλησίᾳ διδάσκω.

4:18ὡς μὴ ἐρχομένου δέ μου πρὸς ὑμᾶς ἐφυσιώθησάν τινες:

4:19ἐλεύσομαι δὲ ταχέως πρὸς ὑμᾶς, ἐὰν ὁ κύριος θελήσῃ, καὶ γνώσομαι οὐ τὸν λόγον τῶν πεφυσιωμένων ἀλλὰ τὴν δύναμιν,

4:20οὐ γὰρ ἐν λόγῳ ἡ βασιλεία τοῦ θεοῦ ἀλλ' ἐν δυνάμει.

4:21τί θέλετε; ἐν ῥάβδῳ ἔλθω πρὸς ὑμᾶς, ἢ ἐν ἀγάπῃ πνεύματί τε πραΰτητος;

4:14I do not write these things to confound you: but I admonish you as my dearest children. [n. 219]

4:15For if you have ten thousand instructors in Christ, yet not many fathers. For in Christ Jesus, by the Gospel, I have begotten you. [n. 221]

4:16Wherefore, I beseech you, be followers of me as I also am of Christ. [n. 223]

4:17For this cause have I sent to you Timothy, who is my dearest son and faithful in the Lord. Who will put you in mind of my ways, which are in Christ Jesus: as I teach everywhere in every church. [n. 224]

4:18As if I would not come to you, so some are puffed up. [n. 225]

4:19But I will come to you shortly, if the Lord wills: and will know, not the speech of them that are puffed up, but the power. [n. 226]

4:20For the kingdom of God is not in speech, but in power.

4:21What do you want? Shall I come to you with a rod? Or in charity and in the spirit of meekness? [n. 227]

---

219. Postquam, Apostolus reprehendit Corinthios de hoc quod Apostolos temere iudicabant, et praesumptuose contemnebant, hic instat ad eorum correctionem, et
primo admonitionis verbo;
secundo, exemplo, ibi *rogo ergo vos, fratres*, etc.;
tertio, correctionis flagello, ibi *tamquam non venturus sim*, et cetera.

220. Circa primum tria facit. Primo ponit admonitionis modum, dicens *haec*, scilicet quae in serie epistolae hucusque vobis dixi, *scribo non ut confundam vos*, scilicet mala confusione, quae in desperationem mittit, quamvis velim vos confundi confusione, quae peccatum vitat, secundum illud Eccli. IV, 25: *est confusio adducens peccatum, et est confusio adducens gratiam et gloriam*. Sed praedicta *moneo* vos, *ut filios*. Eccle. VII, 25: *filii tibi sunt? Erudi illos, et cura illos a pueritia eorum*.

221. Secundo ostendit debitum admonendi modum, dicens *nam si decem millia paedagogorum habeatis in Christo, sed non multos patres*.

219. After censuring the Corinthians for rashly judging the apostles and presumptuously despising them, the Apostle now applies himself to correcting them.
First, by oral advice;
second, by examples, at *wherefore, I beseech you*;
third, with the rod of correction, at *as if I would not come to you*.

220. In regard to the first he does three things: first, he tells how he means to admonish them, saying, *I do not write these things*, which I have said so far in the epistle, *to confound you* in an evil way, which leads to despair, although I would like you to be bewildered with the sort of confusion that avoids sin: *there is a confusion that brings sin, and there is a confusion that brings glory and grace* (Sir 4:25). But to *admonish you* with the above advice *as my dearest children*: *do you have children? Discipline them and make them obedient from their youth* (Sir 7:25).

221. Second, he shows the correct way to admonish, saying, *for if you have ten thousand instructors in Christ, yet not many fathers*.

83

Ubi considerandum est quod Pater est qui primo generat: paedagogus autem est qui iam natum nutrit et erudit. Gal. III, 24: *lex paedagogus noster fuit in Christo.* Dicit ergo Apostolus se patrem eorum in Christo, quia eis primo Evangelium praedicavit.

222. Unde, assignans rationem eius quod dixerat, subdit *nam in Christo Iesu per Evangelium vos genui.* Est autem generatio processus ad vitam, homo autem vivit in Christo per fidem. Gal. II, 20: *quod autem nunc vivo in carne, in fide vivo Filii Dei.* Fides autem, ut dicitur Rom. X, 17, est ex auditu, auditus autem per verbum. Unde verbum Dei est semen, quo Apostolus eos genuit in Christo. Unde Iac. I, 18: *voluntarie nos genuit verbo veritatis.*

Alios autem dicit paedagogos, quia postquam fidem receperant, eos adiuvarunt: ut intelligatur esse eadem comparatio, quantum ad praedicationem Evangelii, paedagogi ad patrem, quae supra III, 6 ss. posita est, rigatoris ad plantatorem, et superaedificatoris ad fundatorem.

223. Deinde, cum dicit *rogo ergo vos, fratres*, instat ad corrigendum eos suo exemplo.

Et primo hortatur eos ad imitandum suum exemplum, dicens: ergo ex quo estis filii, cum bonorum filiorum sit imitari patres, *rogo vos, imitatores mei estote*, scilicet ut non temere iudicetis, sicut nec ego, quia neque meipsum iudicare praesumo, et de vobis humilia sentiatis, et de aliis maiora. Unde non sine causa tali modo loquendi usus est: *nos infirmi, vos fortes.* II Thess. c. III, 9: *ut formam nosmetipsos daremus vobis ad imitandum.*

Advertendum est autem quod eosdem, quos supra filios nominavit, nunc nominat fratres. Dixerat autem suos filios in Christo, quia eos non sibi, sed Christo genuerat, et quia ipse genitus erat a Christo, ex consequenti eos habebat ut fratres et filios. Intantum ergo debebant eum imitari ut patrem, inquantum et ipse Christum imitabatur, qui est omnium principalis pater.

Et per hoc subtrahitur subditis occasio de adhaerendo malis exemplis praelatorum. Unde in hoc subditi solum praelatos imitari debent, in quo ipsi Christum imitantur, qui est infallibilis regula veritatis; unde seipsum apostolis in exemplum posuit. Io. XIII, 15: *exemplum dedi vobis, ut quemadmodum ego feci*, et cetera. Quod quidem exemplum Paulus sequebatur, secundum illud Iob XXIII, 11: *vestigia eius secutus est pes meus, viam eius custodivi, et non declinavi ab ea.*

224. Secundo removet excusationem ignorantiae, dicens *ideo misi ad vos Timotheum, qui est filius meus charissimus et fidelis in Domino*, secundum illud Phil. II, v. 20, de Timotheo loquens: *neminem habeo ita unanimem, qui sincera affectione pro vobis sollicitus sit. Qui vos commonefaciat vias meas*, id est, qui vos doceat

Here it should be noted that a father is one who begets, but a guide nurses and trains the child: *the law was our custodian until Christ came* (Gal 3:24). Therefore, the Apostle calls himself their father in Christ, because he was the first to preach the Gospel to them.

222. Hence he assigns the reason for this when he continues, *for in Christ Jesus, by the Gospel, I have begotten you*. But begetting is a process leading to life; and man lives in Christ by faith: *in the flesh I live now by faith in the Son of God* (Gal 2:20). Faith, however, comes by hearing; and hearing by word (Rom 10:17). Hence the word of God is the seed by which the Apostle begot them in Christ: *by his own will he has begotten us by the word of truth* (Jas 1:18).

But he calls others instructors, because they helped them after receiving the faith. In this way we are given to understand that as far as the preaching of the Gospel is concerned, there is the same relationship between instructor and father as that of waterer and planter and that of builder and superstructure to layer of foundation.

223. Then when he says, *wherefore, I beseech you*, he starts to correct them with his own example.

First, he urges them to follow his example, saying: then, since you are my children and good children should imitate their fathers, *I beseech you, be followers of me*, so as not to judge rashly (just as I don't, because I do not ever presume to judge myself) but to think humbly of yourselves and highly of others. Hence it wasn't by chance that he had said earlier: *we are weak, but you are strong, but that we might give ourselves a pattern unto you to imitate us* (2 Thess 3:4).

Note that here he is calling the same persons brothers, whom he had just called his children. However, he had called them his children in Christ, because he had begotten them not for himself but for Christ; and because he himself had been begotten in Christ, he could regard them as his brothers and his children. Consequently, they should have imitated him as a father to the same degree as he imitated Christ, who is the main father of all.

This, therefore, removes from subjects an excuse for following the evil examples of their prelates; they should rather imitate their prelates only to the degree that they imitate Christ, who is the infallible standard of truth. Hence he gave himself as an example to the apostles when he said: *I have given you an example, that as I have done so you also do* (John 13:15). Paul, of course, followed this example: *my foot has followed his steps, I have kept his way, and have not declined from it* (Job 23:11).

224. Second, he removes the excuse of ignorance, saying, *for this cause have I sent to you Timothy, who is my dearest son and faithful in the Lord*, which agrees with what he said of Timothy in Philippians: *I have no one like him, who will be genuinely anxious for your welfare* (Phil 2:20). *Who will put you in mind of my ways*, i.e., he will teach

meos processus, id est, omnia opera, et moneat vos ad ea sequendum, secundum illud Ier. c. VI, 16: *interrogate de semitis antiquis, quae sit via bona, et ambulate in ea.* **Quae** quidem viae **sunt in Christo**, et ideo non debetis dedignari eas sequi, secundum illud Ps. XXIV, 4: *vias tuas, Domine, demonstra mihi.* Et non videatur vobis hoc onerosum, quia hoc communiter omnibus impono. Unde subdit **sicut ubique in ecclesia doceo**. Col. I, 5 s.: *audistis veritatis Evangelium, quod pervenit ad vos, sicut et in universo mundo.*

Vel hoc quod dicit **vias meas**, referendum est ad opera, quod vero dicit **sicut et ubique**, ad documenta. Ad hoc enim missus erat Timotheus, ut induceret eos ad imitanda opera, et tenenda Apostoli documenta.

225. Deinde, cum dicit **tamquam non venturus sim ad vos**, comminatur eis correctionis flagellum.

Et primo ostendit eos esse dignos correctionis flagello, dicens **tamquam non venturus sim ad vos, inflati sunt quidam**, scilicet vestrum, quasi non timentes per me de sua superbia convinci, et tamen digni sunt flagellis: nam humiles solis verbis corriguntur, superbi flagellis indigent, secundum illud Iob c. XL, 7: *respice cunctos superbos, et confunde eos.*

226. Secundo praenuntiat eis suum adventum quo veniet ad iudicandum, ubi primo praenuntiat adventum, dicens **veniam autem cito ad vos**. Et quia dicitur Prov. XVI, v. 9: *cor hominis disponit viam suam, sed Domini est dirigere gressus eius*, ideo subdit **si Dominus voluerit**. Iac. IV, 15: *si Dominus voluerit, et si vixerimus, faciemus hoc aut illud.*

Secundo praenuntiat eis suam iudiciariam cognitionem, cum dicit **et cognoscam**, scilicet ordine iudiciario, secundum illud Iob c. XXIX, 16: *causam, quam nesciebam, diligentissime investigabam.* **Non sermonem eorum, qui inflati sunt, sed virtutem**, quasi dicat: non propter haec ex mea examinatione approbabuntur, qui abundant in verbis, sed si abundarent in virtute; quia, ut dicitur Prov. XIV, 23, *ubi verba sunt plurima, ibi frequenter egestas.*

Tertio rationem assignat, dicens **non enim in sermone est regnum Dei, sed in virtute**, id est, non ideo aliqui pertinent ad regnum Dei, qui abundant in sermone, secundum illud Matth. VII, 21: *non omnis qui dicit mihi: Domine, Domine, intrabit in regnum caelorum, sed qui facit voluntatem Patris mei.*

227. Ultimo comminatur eis correctionem, reservans tamen correctionem arbitrio eorum, dicens **quid vultis? In virga**, scilicet disciplinae, **veniam ad vos**, scilicet castigandos, **an in caritate**, id est, ostensione amoris, **et in spiritu mansuetudinis** ut scilicet nihil durius vobiscum agam? Hoc enim pendet ex vobis; nam si vos in via stultitiae permanetis, oportet me ad vos cum virga venire, secundum illud Prov. XXII, 15: *stultitia colligata*

you my procedures, i.e., all that is to be done and advise you to follow them: *ask for the old paths, which is the good way, and walk on it* (Jer 6:16), **which** ways **are in Christ Jesus**. Hence you should not disdain to follow them: *show me your ways, O Lord* (Ps 25:4); or consider them a burden, because this is what I generally lay upon all; hence he says: **as I teach everywhere in every church**. *You have heard the word of the truth of the Gospel, which is come unto you, as also it is in the whole world* (Col 1:5).

Or **my ways** can refer to good works, **as I teach everywhere**, to doctrines. For Timothy had been sent to induce them to imitate the works and abide by the doctrines of the Apostle.

225. Then when he says, **as if I would not come**, he threatens them with the rod of correction.

First, he shows that they deserve the rod of correction, saying, **as if I would not come to you, so some are puffed up**, as though not fearing to be convicted of pride by me; and yet they deserved the rod, because the humble are corrected by words alone, but the proud need stripes: *look on all that are proud, and confound them and crush the wicked in their place* (Job 40:7).

226. Second, he tells them of his visit, when he will come to judge them. First, he foretells his coming when he says, **but I will come to you shortly**. But because in says in Proverbs: *the heart of man disposes his way, but the Lord must direct his steps* (Prov 16:9), he adds, **if the Lord wills**: *if the Lord will and if we shall live, we will do this or that* (Jas 4:5).

Second, he tells them that he will make a searching judgment when he says, **and will know**, namely, by a judicial process: *the cause which I knew not, I searched out diligently* (Job 29:16); **not the speech of them that are puffed up, but the power**, as if to say: because they who abound in words will not be approved by my examination, but rather they who abounded in virtue: *mere talk tends only to want* (Prov 14:23).

Third, he assigns the reason, saying, **the kingdom of God is not in speech, but in power**, i.e., therefore, some who abound in speech do not attain to the kingdom of God: *not everyone that says to me, Lord, Lord, shall enter the kingdom of heaven, but he who does the will of my Father* (Matt 7:21).

227. Finally, he threatens to chastise them, but leaves the choice to them, saying: **what do you want? Shall I come to you with a rod**, namely, of discipline, **or in charity**, i.e., with a display of love, **and in the spirit of meekness?** As if to say: it depends on you whether or not I shall deal more harshly with you. For if you persist in the foolish way, I must come to you with the rod, as Proverbs says: *folly is bound up in the heart of a child, and the rod of correction shall drive*

est in corde pueri, et virga disciplinae fugabit eam. Si vero vos correxeritis, ostendam vobis caritatem et mansuetudinem, Gal. ult.: *vos qui spirituales estis, instruite huiusmodi in spiritu lenitatis.* Hoc autem non dicit quin si in virga veniens, non cum caritate veniret, cum scriptum sit Prov. c. XIII, 24: *qui parcit virgae, odit filium suum: qui autem diligit illum, instanter erudit,* sed quia ille qui castigatur virga, non sentit interdum dulcedinem caritatis, sicut illi quos blande consolatur.

it away (Prov 22:15). But if you amend your lives, I will act charitably and meekly: *you who are spiritual, instruct such a one in a spirit of meekness* (Gal 6:1). However, this does not mean that if he came with the rod, he would not come in charity, since it says in Proverbs: *he who spares the rod hates his son; but he who loves him corrects him betimes* (Prov 13:24), but because a person chastened with the rod fails at times to sense the gentleness of charity, as those who are encouraged gently.

CHAPTER 5

Lecture 1

5:1 Omnino auditur inter vos fornicatio, et talis fornicatio, qualis nec inter gentes, ita ut uxorem patris sui aliquis habeat. [n. 228]

5:2 Et vos inflati estis: et non magis luctum habuistis ut tollatur de medio vestrum qui hoc opus fecit. [n. 231]

5:3 Ego quidem absens corpore, praesens autem spiritu, jam judicavi ut praesens eum, qui sic operatus est, [n. 233]

5:4in nomine Domini nostri Jesu Christi, congregatis vobis et meo spiritu, cum virtute Domini nostri Jesu, [n. 235]

5:5tradere hujusmodi Satanae in interitum carnis, ut spiritus salvus sit in die Domini nostri Jesu Christi. [n. 236]

5:1Ὅλως ἀκούεται ἐν ὑμῖν πορνεία, καὶ τοιαύτη πορνεία ἥτις οὐδὲ ἐν τοῖς ἔθνεσιν, ὥστε γυναῖκά τινα τοῦ πατρὸς ἔχειν.

5:2καὶ ὑμεῖς πεφυσιωμένοι ἐστέ, καὶ οὐχὶ μᾶλλον ἐπενθήσατε, ἵνα ἀρθῇ ἐκ μέσου ὑμῶν ὁ τὸ ἔργον τοῦτο πράξας;

5:3ἐγὼ μὲν γάρ, ἀπὼν τῷ σώματι παρὼν δὲ τῷ πνεύματι, ἤδη κέκρικα ὡς παρὼν τὸν οὕτως τοῦτο κατεργασάμενον

5:4ἐν τῷ ὀνόματι τοῦ κυρίου [ἡμῶν] Ἰησοῦ, συναχθέντων ὑμῶν καὶ τοῦ ἐμοῦ πνεύματος σὺν τῇ δυνάμει τοῦ κυρίου ἡμῶν Ἰησοῦ,

5:5παραδοῦναι τὸν τοιοῦτον τῷ Σατανᾷ εἰς ὄλεθρον τῆς σαρκός, ἵνα τὸ πνεῦμα σωθῇ ἐν τῇ ἡμέρᾳ τοῦ κυρίου.

5:1 It is absolutely heard that there is fornication among you and such fornication as the like is not among the heathens: that one should have his father's wife. [n. 228]

5:2 And you are puffed up and have not rather mourned: that he might be taken away from among you that has done this thing. [n. 231]

5:3I indeed, absent in body but present in spirit, have already judged, as though I were present, him that has so done, [n. 233]

5:4 In the name of our Lord Jesus Christ, you being gathered together and my spirit, with the power of our Lord Jesus: [n. 235]

5:5 To deliver such a one to Satan for the destruction of the flesh, that the spirit may be saved in the day of our Lord Jesus Christ. [n. 236]

---

228. Postquam Apostolus prosecutus est ea, quae pertinent ad baptismi sacramentum, hic incipit prosequi ea quae pertinent ad matrimonium. Et

primo arguit peccatum contrarium matrimonio, scilicet fornicationem;

secundo agit de ipso matrimonio, c. VII, ibi *de quibus autem scripsistis*, et cetera.

229. Circa primum duo facit.

Primo ponit culpam;

secundo redarguit eam, ibi *non est bona gloriatio*, et cetera.

Circa primum duo facit.

Primo ponit culpam cuiusdam fornicarii;

secundo culpam aliorum, qui peccatum fornicarii tolerabant, ibi *et vos inflati estis*, et cetera.

229. Circa primum, primo ponit tria, quae pertinent ad culpae gravitatem.

Primo namque ostendit peccatum esse notorium, dicens: non sine causa quaesivi, an velitis quod in virga veniam ad vos. Est enim in vobis aliquid dignum virga disciplinae, quia *fornicatio auditur inter vos omnino*, secundum publicam formam; contra quod dicitur Eph. V, 3: *fornicatio autem nec nominetur in vobis*;

228. After discussing matters which pertain to the sacrament of baptism, the Apostle begins to consider matters which pertain to matrimony.

First, he attacks a sin contrary to matrimony, namely, fornication;

second, he discusses matrimony itself, at *now concerning the things* (1 Cor 7:1).

229. In regard to the first he does two things.

First, he mentions the crime;

second, he censures it, at *your glorying is not good* (1 Cor 5:6).

As to the first he does two things.

First, he mentions the crime of a certain fornicator;

second, the crime of those who condoned this sin, at *and you are puffed up*.

229. In regard to the first he mentions three things which pertain to the gravity of the crime.

First, he shows that the sin is notorious, saying: it was not without reason that I asked whether you wish me to come to you with the rod. For there is one among you deserving the rod of discipline, *because it is absolutely heard*, i.e., publicly known, *that there is fornication among you*, against which it is said: *fornication must not even be named*

Is. III, 9: *peccatum suum quasi Sodoma praedicaverunt, nec absconderunt.*

230. Secundo aggravat peccatum ex comparatione, cum dicit *et talis fornicatio, qualis nec inter gentes* licita reputatur vel invenitur. Apud gentiles enim simplex fornicatio non reputabatur peccatum. Unde apostoli Act. XV, 20, ad hunc errorem excludendum, gentilibus ad fidem conversis imposuerant, quod abstineant se a fornicatione.

Erat tamen quaedam fornicationis species, quae et apud gentiles illicita habebatur. Et ideo dicit *ita ut uxorem patris aliquis habeat*, sicut dicitur Gen. XLIX, 4: *effusus es sicut aqua, non crescas, quia ascendisti cubile patris tui, et maculasti stratum eius.* Hoc autem erat horribile etiam apud gentiles, utpote contrarium naturali rationi existens. Per naturalem enim reverentiam filii ad parentes secundum omnem statum et legem pater et mater a matrimonio excluditur. Ut sic etiam possit intelligi, quod habetur Gen. II, 24: *propter hoc relinquet homo patrem et matrem*, scilicet in contractu matrimonii, *et adhaerebit uxori suae*. Sicut autem ibi subditur: *vir et mulier erunt duo in carne una.* Et ideo uxor patris repellitur a matrimonio: sicut persona patris vel matris, secundum illud Lev. XVIII, 8: *turpitudinem uxoris patris tui ne discooperias, turpitudo enim patris tui est.*

231. Deinde, cum dicit *vos inflati estis*, ponit culpam eorum qui hoc peccatum tolerabant. Et

primo reprehendit eorum tolerantiam;

secundo supplet quod illi negligebant ibi *ego quidem*, et cetera.

232. Circa primum notat in eis tria vitia.

Primo superbiam, cum dicit *et vos inflati estis*, scilicet vento superbiae, reputantes vos innocentes ex comparatione peccatoris, sicut, Lc. XVIII, 11, Pharisaeus dicebat: *non sum sicut caeteri hominum, velut etiam hic publicanus.* Sap. IV, 19: *disrumpam illos inflatos sine voce.*

Secundo tangit eorum iniustitiam, cum dicit *et non magis luctum habuistis*, scilicet patiendo causam peccatoris, sicut Ier. IX, 1 dicitur: *quis dabit capiti meo aquam, et oculis meis fontem lacrymarum, ut plorem die ac nocte interfectos filiae populi mei? Vera enim iustitia*, ut dicit Gregorius, *compassionem habet, non dedignationem.*

Tertio tangit eorum iudicii negligentiam *ut tollatur de medio vestrum qui hoc opus fecit*. Talis enim compassio viri iusti ad peccatorem vulnerat et liberat, secundum illud Prov. XXIII, 14: *tu virga percutis eum, et animam eius de inferno liberabis.* Per hoc etiam alii corriguntur, secundum illud Prov. c. XIX, 25: *pestilente flagellato, stultus sapientior erit.* Unde Eccle. VIII, 11: *quia non profertur cito contra malos sententia, absque ullo timore filii hominum perpetrant mala.* Debet autem ad

among you (Eph 5:3); *they proclaim their sin like Sodom, they do not hide it* (Isa 3:9).

230. Second, he amplifies the sin by a comparison when he says, *and such fornication as the like is not among the heathens*. For example, fornication was not considered a sin among the pagans; hence to rid them of this error the apostles (Acts 15:29) imposed on pagans converted to the faith the obligation to abstain from fornication.

Yet it was a form of fornication regarded as unlawful even among pagans; hence he says, *that one should have his father's wife*: unstable as water, you shall not have preeminence because you went up to your father's bed and defiled his couch (Gen 49:4). This was monstrous even among the pagans, being contrary to natural reason. For the laws of every civilization dictated that the natural reverence owed to parents prevents sons and daughters from marrying their father or mother. This is even implied in Genesis: *wherefore a man shall leave father and mother* (in contracting matrimony) *and shall cleave to his wife* (Gen 2:24). Furthermore, since it goes on to say that *the man and woman will be two in one flesh*, the wife of the father is excluded from marrying; just as the person of the father or mother: *you shall not uncover the nakedness of your father's wife; for it is the nakedness of the father* (Lev 18:8).

231. Then when he says, *you are puffed up*, he mentions the guilt of those who condoned this sin.

First, he condemns them for condoning it;

second, he supplies what they failed to supply, at *I indeed, absent in body*.

232. In regard to the first he detects three vices.

First, pride, when he says, *and you are puffed up*, namely, with the wind of pride, for considering yourselves innocent as compared with the sinner, just as the Pharisee who said: *I am not as the rest of men, or even as this tax collector* (Luke 18:11); *he will dash them puffed up and speechless to the ground* (Wis 4:19).

Second, he touches on their injustice, when he says, *and have not rather mourned*, namely, by suffering for the benefit of the sinner: *O that my head were waters, and my eyes a fountain of tears, that I might weep day and night for the slain of the daughters of my people!* (Jer 9:1) For true justice, as Gregory says in *On the Gospel*, homily 34, *shows compassion, not disdain.*

Third, he touches on their failure to judge: *that he might be taken away from among you that has done this thing*. For such compassion on the part of a just man bruises the sinner to deliver him: *if you beat him with the rod, you will save his life from Sheol* (Prov 23:14). This also helps to correct others: *the wicked man being scourged, the fool shall be wiser* (Prov 19:25). *Because sentence against an evil deed is not executed speedily, the heart of the sons of men is fully set to do evil* (Eccl 8:11). Indeed, if others are to be corrected,

correctionem aliorum interdum peccator separari, ubi de contagione timetur, secundum illud Prov. XXII, 10: *eiice derisorem, et exibit cum eo iurgium, cessabuntque causae et contumeliae.*

233. Deinde, cum dicit *ego quidem absens corpore,* etc., supplet eorum negligentiam, sententiam proferens contra peccatorem.

Et circa hoc tria facit.

Primo ponit auctoritatem iudicantis;

secundo modum iudicandi, ibi *congregatis vobis,* etc.;

tertio sententiam iudicis, ibi *tradere huiusmodi,* et cetera.

234. Circa primum duo facit. Primo ponit auctoritatem ministri, scilicet sui ipsius. Videbatur autem contra iudiciarium ordinem, ut condemnaret absentem, secundum illud Act. XXV, 16: *non est consuetudo Romanis condemnare aliquem, priusquam is qui accusatur, praesentes habeat accusatores;* sed hoc Apostolus excusat, dicens *ego quidem absens corpore, praesens autem spiritu,* id est, affectu et sollicitudine mentis, secundum illud Col. II, 5: *et si corpore absens sum, sed spiritu vobiscum sum, gaudens et videns ordinem vestrum.* Vel *praesens spiritu,* quia per spiritum cognoscebat ea quae apud ipsos agebantur, ac si praesens esset, sicut et Eliseus dixit IV Reg. V, 26: *nonne cor meum in praesenti erat, quando reversus est homo de cursu suo?* Et quia sum spiritu praesens, *iam iudicavi,* id est, sententiam condemnationis ordinavi in eum, qui sic operatus est.

Secundo ponit auctoritatem principalis domini, dicens *in nomine Domini nostri Iesu Christi,* id est, vice et auctoritate, seu cum virtute et invocatione nominis eius, secundum illud Col. III, 17: *omne quodcumque facitis verbo aut opere, in nomine Domini nostri Iesu Christi facite.*

235. Deinde, cum dicit *congregatis vobis in unum,* ostendit modum iudicandi, ubi tria tangit: primo fidelium congregationem, cum dicit *congregatis vobis.* Ea enim, quae gravia sunt, multorum concordi deliberatione punienda sunt. Unde et antiquitus iudices sedebant in portis, ubi populus congregabatur, secundum illud Deut. XVI, 18: *iudices constitues in omnibus portis tuis.* Unde dicitur in Ps. CX, 1: *in consilio iustorum et congregatione magna opera Domini.* Et Matth. XVIII, 20: *ubi sunt duo vel tres congregati in nomine meo, ibi sum in medio.*

Secundo adhibet suum assensum, cum dicit *et meo spiritu,* id est, mea voluntate et auctoritate, secundum illud quod dixerat: *praesens autem spiritu.*

Tertio adhibet auctoritatem principalis Domini, scilicet Christi, dicens *cum virtute Domini nostri Iesu Christi,* ex qua iudicium Ecclesiae habet robur firmitatis,

the sinner must sometimes be cast out, when there is fear of his conduct spreading: *drive out the scoffer, and strife will go out, and quarreling and abuse will cease* (Prov 22:10).

233. Then when he says, **I indeed, absent in body**, he supplies for their failure by pronouncing sentence against the sinner.

In regard to this he does three things.

First, he shows the authority of the judge;

second, the method of judging, at **you being gathered**;

third, the sentence of the judge, at **to deliver such a one**

234. As to the first he does two things: first, he shows the authority of the minister, i.e., himself. Here he seems to act contrary to proper judicial procedure by condemning an absent person, for *it was not the custom of the Romans to give up anyone, before the accused met the accusers face to face* (Acts 25:16). But the Apostle justifies this, saying, **I indeed, absent in body but present in spirit**, i.e., with love and concern: *for though I am absent in body, yet I am with you in spirit, rejoicing to see your good order and the firmness of your faith in Christ* (Col 2:5). Or, **present in spirit**, because by the spirit he knew what was taking place among them as if he were there, as Elisha also says: *did I not got with you in spirit when the man turned from his chariot to meet you?* (2 Kgs 5:26) Because I am present in spirit, I **have already judged**, i.e., I have passed a sentence of condemnation on the one who has acted in this manner.

Second, he mentions the authority of the principal lord, saying, **in the name of our Lord Jesus Christ**, i.e., in his place and by his authority, or with the power and invocation of his name: *whatever you do in word or in deed, do all in the name of our Lord Jesus Christ* (Col 3:17).

235. Then when he says, **you being gathered together**, he shows the manner of judging, and touches on three things: first, the assembling of the congregation when he says, **you being gathered together**. For serious offenses should be punished according to the considered agreement of many persons; hence in old times judges sat on the gates where the people were gathered together: *you shall appoint judges in all your gates* (Deut 16:18); *in the company of the upright, in the congregation* (Ps 111:1); *where two or three are gathered in my name, there am I in the midst of them* (Matt 18:20).

Second, he indicates his assent when he says, **and my spirit**, i.e., with my will and authority, according to what he had said, **present in spirit**.

Third, he presents the authority of the principal lord, namely, Jesus Christ, saying, **with the power of our Lord Jesus**, the power which gives strength and validity to the

secundum illud Matth. XVIII, 18: *quodcumque ligaveris super terram, erit ligatum et in caelis.*

236. Deinde, cum dicit *tradere huiusmodi*, etc., ponit condemnationis sententiam, circa quam tria ponit. Primo poenam, cum dicit *tradere huiusmodi Satanae* supple: iudicavi. Quod potest dupliciter intelligi.

Primo quod, sicut dicitur Matth. X, 8, Dominus dedit apostolis potestatem spirituum immundorum, ut eiicerent eos, et per eamdem potestatem poterant imperare spiritibus immundis, ut vexarent corporaliter quos hac poena iudicabant dignos. Mandavit ergo Apostolus Corinthiis in eius auctoritate tradere praedictum fornicarium Satanae corporaliter vexandum.

Unde ponit, secundo, huius sententiae effectum, cum dicit *in interitum carnis*, id est, ad vexationem carnis et afflictionem in qua peccavit, secundum illud Sap. XI, 17: *per quae peccat quis, per haec et torquetur.*

Tertio ponit fructum, cum dicit *ut spiritus salvus sit in die Domini nostri Iesu Christi*, id est, ut salutem consequatur in die mortis, vel in die iudicii, sicut supra tertio expositum est et sic impletur quod ibi subditur: *ipse autem salvus erit, sic tamen quasi per ignem*, poenae scilicet temporalis.

Non enim Apostolus Satanae tradidit peccatorem, ut eius potestati perpetuo subiaceret, sed ut carnis vexatione ad poenitentiam convertatur, secundum illud Is. XXVIII, 19: *sola vexatio intellectum dat auditui.* Est autem haec sententia Apostoli, quam Dominus servavit Iob II, 6, ubi Satanae dixit: *ecce in manu tua est*, scilicet caro eius, *verumtamen animam illius serva*, scilicet illaesam.

237. Alio modo intelligi potest quod dicitur tradere huiusmodi Satanae, scilicet per excommunicationis sententiam, per quam aliquis separatur a communione fidelium, et a participatione sacramentorum, et privatur Ecclesiae suffragiis, quibus homo munitur contra impugnationem Satanae, propter quod de Ecclesia dicitur Cant. IV, 9: *terribilis ut castrorum acies ordinata*, scilicet daemonibus.

Quod autem subditur *in interitum carnis*, intelligitur, ut scilicet ab Ecclesia separatus, et tentationibus Satanae expositus liberius ruat in peccatum, secundum illud Apoc. ult.: *qui in sordibus est, sordescat adhuc.* Vocat autem peccata mortalia *carnis interitum*, quia, ut dicitur Gal. ult., *qui seminat in carne, de carne et metet corruptionem.* Subdit autem *ut spiritus salvus sit*, ut scilicet peccatorum turpitudinem cognoscens confundatur et poeniteat, et sic sanetur, secundum illud Ier. XXXI, 19: *confusus sum et erubui, quoniam sustinui opprobrium adolescentiae meae.*

Potest etiam intelligi, ut Spiritus eius, scilicet Ecclesiae, id est Spiritus Sanctus Ecclesiae salvus sit fidelibus

judgment of the Church: *whatever you bind on earth shall be bound also in heaven* (Matt 18:18).

236. Then when he says, *to deliver such a one*, he delivers the sentence of condemnation, in regard to which he does three things. First, he assigns the punishment when he says, *to deliver such a one to Satan.* This can be understood in two ways.

First, that just as the Lord gave the apostles power over unclean spirits to cast them out (Matt 10:8), so by the same power they could command the unclean spirits to torment in the body those whom they judged deserved it. Accordingly, the Apostle commanded the Corinthians on his own authority to deliver this fornicator to Satan to be tortured.

Hence, second, he discloses the effect of this sentence when he says: *for the destruction of the flesh*, i.e., for the torment and affliction of the flesh in which he sinned: *one is punished by the very things by which he sins* (Wis 11:16).

Third, he mentions its fruit when he says, *that the spirit may be saved in the day of our Lord Jesus Christ*, i.e., that he may be saved on the day of death or on the day of judgment, as was explained above: *but he himself shall be saved, yet so as by fire* (1 Cor 3:15), i.e., of temporal punishment.

For the Apostle did not deliver the sinner over to Satan's power forever, but until the time when he would be converted to repentance by bodily torment: *vexation alone shall make you understand what you hear* (Isa 28:19). This sentence of the Apostle corresponds to what the Lord observed, when he said to Satan: *behold he is in your hand* (namely, his flesh), *but yet keep his life unharmed* (Job 2:6).

237. To deliver this man to Satan can also be understood as referring to the sentence of excommunicating by which a person is cut off from the community of believers and from partaking of the sacraments and is deprived of the blessings of the Church, by which a man is defended against the attacks of Satan. Hence it is said of the Church: *terrible as an army set in array* (Song 6:10), i.e., to the devils.

For the destruction of the flesh would mean that, being cut off from the Church and exposed to the temptations of the devil, he might more easily fall into sin: *let the filthy still be filthy* (Rev 22:11). Hence he calls mortal sins *the destruction of the flesh*, because *he who sows to his own flesh will from the flesh reap corruption* (Gal 6:8). But he adds, *that the spirit may be saved*, i.e., that the sinner, recognizing his vileness, may repent and thus be healed: *I was ashamed, and I was confounded, because I bore the disgrace of my youth* (Jer 31:19).

This can also mean that his Spirit, namely, the Church's Holy Spirit, may be saved for the faithful in the day of

in diem iudicii, ne scilicet perdant eum per contagium peccatoris, quia, ut dicitur Sap. I, 5. *Spiritus Sanctus disciplinae effugiet fictum*, et cetera.

judgment, i.e., that they not destroy it by contact with the sinner: *for a holy and disciplined spirit will flee from deceit and will rise and depart from foolish thoughts* (Wis 1:5).

Lecture 2

^{5:6}Non est bona gloriatio vestra. Nescitis quia modicum fermentum totam massam corrumpit? [n. 238]

^{5:7}Expurgate vetus fermentum, ut sitis nova conspersio, sicut estis azymi. Etenim pascha nostrum immolatus est Christus. [n. 242]

^{5:8}Itaque epulemur: non in fermento veteri, neque in fermento malitiae et nequitiae: sed in azymis sinceritatis et veritatis. [n. 247]

^{5:6}Οὐ καλὸν τὸ καύχημα ὑμῶν. οὐκ οἴδατε ὅτι μικρὰ ζύμη ὅλον τὸ φύραμα ζυμοῖ;

^{5:7}ἐκκαθάρατε τὴν παλαιὰν ζύμην, ἵνα ἦτε νέον φύραμα, καθώς ἐστε ἄζυμοι. καὶ γὰρ τὸ πάσχα ἡμῶν ἐτύθη Χριστός·

^{5:8}ὥστε ἑορτάζωμεν, μὴ ἐν ζύμῃ παλαιᾷ μηδὲ ἐν ζύμῃ κακίας καὶ πονηρίας, ἀλλ' ἐν ἀζύμοις εἰλικρινείας καὶ ἀληθείας.

^{5:6}Your glorying is not good. Know you not that a little leaven corrupts the whole lump? [n. 238]

^{5:7}Purge out the old leaven, that you may be a new paste, as you are unleavened. For our pasch is Christ sacrificed. [n. 242]

^{5:8}Therefore, let us feast, not with the old leaven, nor with the leaven of malice and wickedness: but with the unleavened bread of sincerity and truth. [n. 247]

---

238. Supra Apostolus memoravit duplicem culpam, scilicet Corinthii fornicatoris, et aliorum qui eius peccatum tolerabant, hic utramque culpam redarguit.

Primo culpam tolerantium eius peccatum;

secundo culpam fornicatoris, ibi *corpus autem non fornicationi*, et cetera.

Circa primum duo facit.

Primo redarguit in Corinthiis negligentiam iudicii;

secundo redarguit in eis quaedam alia vitia circa iudicium, VI cap. *audet aliquis*, et cetera.

Circa primum duo facit.

Primo redarguit eos qui fornicatorem a se non separaverunt;

secundo reprobat falsum intellectum quem ex verbis suis conceperant, ibi *scripsi vobis in epistola*, et cetera.

Circa primum duo facit.

Primo reprehendit quod fecerant;

secundo ostendit quid faciendum sit, ibi *expurgate vetus fermentum*, et cetera.

239. Circa primum duo facit. Primo reprehendit culpam praeteritam quantum ad suam radicem. Dixerat enim supra quod ex inflatione sequitur in eis incompassio, et ex incompassione correctionis negligentia. Arguit ergo primo Corinthiorum elationem, dicens *non est bona gloriatio vestra*, qua scilicet defectibus aliorum gloriamini, quasi vos sitis innocentes.

Debet enim unusquisque in Domino gloriari de bonis sibi divinitus datis, non de aliis, secundum illud Gal. VI, 4: *opus autem suum unusquisque probet, et sic in semetipso gloriam habebit, et non in alio*. Praecipue autem malum est de malis aliorum gloriari. Dicitur enim in Ps. LI, 3: *quid gloriaris in malitia?*

240. Secundo assignat rationem eius quod dixerat, dicens *an nescitis quod modicum fermentum totam massam corrumpit?* Quasi dicat: hoc ignorare non potestis.

238. After reminding the Corinthians of two crimes, namely, that of the fornicator and that of those who condoned the sin, the Apostle now censures both crimes.

First, the crime of condoning his sin;

second, the sin of the fornication, at *but the body is not for fornication* (1 Cor 6:13).

As to the first he does two things.

First, he rebukes the Corinthians for failing to pass judgment;

second, for other vices concerning judgment, at *dare any of you* (1 Cor 6:1).

In regard to the first he does two things.

First, he blames them for not casting out the fornicator;

second, he corrects the false understanding they took from his words, at *I wrote to you* (1 Cor 5:9).

As to the first he does two things.

First, he reprehends what they had done;

second, he shows what should be done, at *purge out the old leaven*.

239. First, he reprehends their past crime as to its root; for he had said above that as a result of being puffed up they lack compassion, from which followed their failure to set others straight by correcting them. First of all, therefore, he censures them for being puffed up, saying, *your glorying is not good*, because you boast of the defects of others, as though you were without faults.

For everyone should boast of the blessings given him by God and not of others: *let each one test his own work, and then his reason to boast will be in himself alone and not in his neighbor* (Gal 6:4). And it is especially evil to glory in the failures of others: *why do you boast of mischief?* (Ps 51:3).

240. Second, he gives the reason for what he had said, saying, *know you not that a little leaven corrupts the whole lump?* As if to say: certainly you cannot be unaware of this.

Est autem sciendum quod in fermento duo possunt considerari. Primo sapor quem tribuit pani, et secundum hoc per fermentum significatur sapientia Dei, per quam omnia quae sunt hominis sapida redduntur, et secundum hoc dicitur Matth. XIII, 33: *simile est regnum caelorum fermento, quod acceptum mulier abscondit in farinae satis tribus, donec fermentatum est totum.*

Secundo, in fermento potest considerari corruptio, et secundum hoc per fermentum potest intelligi uno modo peccatum, quia scilicet per unum hominis peccatum omnia opera eius corrupta redduntur, puta per peccatum simulationis, quod comparatur fermento. Lc. XII, 1: *attendite a fermento Pharisaeorum, quod est hypocrisis.* Alio modo per fermentum potest intelligi homo peccator, et ad hoc inducitur haec similitudo.

241. Sicut enim per modicum fermentum tota massa pastae corrumpitur, ita per unum peccatorem tota societas inquinatur. Unde Eccli. XI, 34: *ab una scintilla augetur ignis, et ab uno doloso augetur sanguis.* Et hoc quidem contingit, dum per peccatum unius alii provocantur aliqualiter ad peccandum. Vel etiam dum peccanti consentiunt, saltem non corrigendo, dum possunt corrigere, secundum illud Rom. I, 32: *digni sunt morte, non solum qui faciunt ea, sed etiam qui consentiunt facientibus.* Et ideo Corinthiis non erat gloriandum de peccato unius, sed magis cavendum, ne peccato unius omnes inquinarentur ex eius consortio, secundum illud Cant. II, 2: *sicut lilium inter spinas, sic amica mea inter filias*, ubi dicit Glossa: *non fuit bonus, qui malos tolerare non potuit.*

242. Deinde, cum dicit **expurgate vetus fermentum**, ostendit quid de caetero sit faciendum. Et

    primo ponit documentum;

    secundo rationem assignat, ibi **pascha nostrum**, et cetera.

243. Dicit ergo primo **quia modicum fermentum totam massam corrumpit**, ideo **expurgate vetus fermentum**, id est, expurgate vos, abiiciendo a vobis vetus fermentum, id est fornicarium, qui peccando rediit in vetustatem corruptionis antiquae, secundum illud Baruch III, 11: *inveterasti in terra aliena, coinquinatus es cum mortuis.* Quod quidem dicit, quia per separationem unius peccatoris tota societas expurgatur. Unde et, egresso Iuda, Dominus dixit Io. XIII, 31: *nunc clarificatus est Filius hominis.*

Potest etiam per vetus fermentum intelligi antiquus error, secundum illud Is. XXVI, 3: *vetus error abiit*, vel etiam corruptio originalis peccati, secundum illud Rom. VI, 6: *vetus homo noster simul crucifixus est*, vel etiam quodcumque peccatum actuale, secundum illud Col. III, 9: *expoliantes vos veterem hominem cum actibus suis*: horum enim admonitione homo expurgatur.

244. Ponit autem consequenter purgationis effectum, dicens **ut sitis nova conspersio**. Dicitur autem

It should be noted that there are two factors to consider in leaven: the first is the taste it gives to bread. In this way leaven signifies the wisdom of God, through which everything human is rendered tasteful: *the kingdom of heaven is like leaven which a woman took and hid in three measures of meal, till it was all leavened* (Matt 13:33).

The second factor is corruption. Then in one way leaven can signify sin, because by one sin all of a man's works are corrupted; for example, by the sin of hypocrisy which is compared to leaven: *beware of the leaven of the Pharisees, which is hypocrisy* (Luke 12:1). In another way a sinful man himself can be signified by leaven.

241. And this is precisely the point of his metaphor, for just as the entire lump of dough is corrupted by a little leaven, so by one sinner a whole group can be defiled: *from one spark comes a great fire and from one deceitful man much blood* (Sir 11:34). This happens when by the sin of one person others are prompted to sin or even when they consent to his sin, by not at least correcting him when they can: *they are worthy of death not only who do these things but also who consent to those what do them* (Rom 1:32). Consequently, the Corinthians should not have boasted of another's sin but rather taken steps to prevent others from being defiled by associating with him: *as a lily among brambles, so is my love among maidens* (Song 2:2), on which a Gloss says: *he was not a good man, who could not endure evil men.*

242. Then when he says, **purge out the old leaven**, he shows what should be done in the future.

    First, he presents the teaching;

    second, he assigns reason, at **for our pasch**.

243. He says, therefore, first, **that a little leaven corrupts the whole lump**, therefore **purge out the old leaven**, i.e., purge yourselves by casting out from your midst the old leaven, i.e., the fornicator who returned to the old state of former corruption by sinning: *you are growing old in a foreign country, you are defiled with the dead* (Bar 3:10). And this is what he says, because by cutting off one sinner the whole group is purged; hence when Judas left the Lord said: *now is the Son of man glorified* (John 13:31).

By the old leaven can also be understood the old error: *the old error is passed away* (Isa 26:3), or even the corruption of original sin: *our old man is crucified with him* (Rom 6:6), or even any actual sin: *seeing that you have put off the old nature with its practices* (Col 3:9), for a man is purged by removing them.

244. Second, he mentions the effect of this cleansing, saying, **that you may be a new paste**. Here paste

conspersio commixtio aquae et farinae novae, antequam admisceatur fermentum. Remoto ergo fermento a fidelibus, id est peccatore, vel peccato, remanent sicut nova conspersio, id est, in puritate suae novitatis, secundum illud Ps. CII, 5: *renovabitur ut aquilae iuventus tua*; Eph. IV, v. 23: *renovamini spiritu mentis vestrae*.

Deinde ponit modum debitum expurgationis cum dicit *sicut estis azymi*, id est, sine fermento peccati. Dicitur enim ab *a*, quod est sine, et *zyma*, quod est fermentum. Unde Dominus Matth. XVI, 6 dicit discipulis *cavete a fermento Pharisaeorum et Sadducaeorum*.

245. Deinde, cum dicit *etenim pascha nostrum*, assignat rationem eius quod dixerat, scilicet quare fideles debent esse azymi, quae quidem ratio sumitur ex mysterio passionis Christi. Unde

primo proponit ipsum mysterium;

secundo concludit propositum, ibi *itaque epulemur*, et cetera.

246. Circa primum considerandum est quod inter caetera sacramenta legalia celeberrimum erat agnus paschalis, qui, ut praecipitur Ex. XII, 1 ss., immolabatur ab universa multitudine filiorum Israel in memoriam illius beneficii, quo angelus percutiens primogenita Aegypti pertransivit domos Iudaeorum, quorum fores linitae essent sanguine agni. Unde nomen Paschae sumitur, secundum quod ibi dicitur *est enim phase, id est, transitus Domini*, et ultimo virtute huius beneficii transivit populus Mare Rubrum, ut dicitur Ex. XIV, 15 ss.

Ille enim agnus figura fuit Christi innocentis, de quo dicitur Io. I, 29: *ecce Agnus Dei*. Sicut ergo ille agnus figuralis immolabatur a filiis Israel, ut populus Dei liberaretur ab angelo percutiente, et ut transirent Mare Rubrum, liberati de servitute Aegypti, ita Christus est occisus a filiis Israel, per cuius sanguinem populus Dei liberatur a diaboli impugnatione et servitute peccati per baptismum quasi per Mare Rubrum. Ille autem agnus figuralis pascha Iudaeorum dicebatur, quia in signum transitus immolabatur. Unde dicitur Matth. XXVI, 17: *ubi vis paremus tibi comedere pascha?* Id est, agnum paschalem.

Dicit ergo Apostolus: ideo debetis esse azymi, *etenim*, id est, quia, sicut figurale pascha veteris populi est agnus immolatus, ita *pascha nostrum*, id est, novi populi, *est Christus immolatus*, cuius etiam immolationi convenit nomen paschae, tum significatione linguae Hebreae, quod significat transitum, Ex. XII, 11: *est enim phase, id est, transitus*, tum significatione linguae Graecae, prout nomen paschae significat passionem. Christus enim per passionem, qua fuit immolatus, transivit ex hoc mundo ad Patrem, ut dicitur Io. XIII, 1.

247. Deinde, cum dicit *itaque epulemur*, concludit propositum.

means a mixture of water and new flour, before leaven is mixed with it. Therefore, once the leaven, i.e., the sinner or sin, is removed from the faithful, they become as it were a new paste, renewed in purity: *your youth is renewed like the eagle's* (Ps 103:5); *be renewed in the spirit of your minds* (Eph 4:23).

Third, he mentions the form purging should take when he says, *as you are unleavened*, i.e., without the leaven of sin. In this sense the Lord says: *beware of the leaven of the Pharisees and Sadducees* (Matt 16:6).

245. Then when he says, *for our pasch is Christ sacrificed*, he assigns the reason for what he had said, namely, why the faithful should be unleavened; and this reason is taken from the mystery of Christ's passion.

First, therefore, he mentions the mystery;

second, he concludes to his point, at *therefore, let us feast*.

246. As to the first it should be noted that the most excellent sacrament of the old law was the paschal lamb which, as was commanded in Exodus 11, was sacrificed by the whole multitude of the children of Israel in commemoration of the event in which the angel striking the first born in Egypt passed by the homes of the Jews, whose posts were smeared with the blood of a lamb. The word pasch is derived from this event: *it is the Lord's Passover* (Exod 12:11). It was in virtue of the blessing that the people passed over the Red Sea (Exod 24:15ff).

But this lamb was a figure of the innocent Christ, of whom it is said: *behold the Lamb of God* (John 1:36). Therefore, just as that lamb was slain by the children of Israel in order that God's people be delivered from the avenging angel and after being freed from the slavery under the Egyptians, pass over the Red Sea, so Christ was slain by the children of Israel, in order that God's people be delivered from the attacks of the devil by his blood and from the slavery of sin by baptism, as though by the Red Sea. Now that lamb was called the pasch of the Jews, because it was immolated as a sign of the passing; hence the disciples ask: *where do you wish us to prepare for you to eat the pasch?* (Matt 26:17), i.e., the paschal lamb.

Therefore, the Apostle says: you ought to be unleavened, *for*, i.e., because as the pasch of the old people was the sacrificed lamb, so *our pasch*, i.e., of the new people, *is Christ sacrificed*. His immolation deserves the name 'pasch' both by reason of what the word means in Hebrew, namely, 'passage': *it is the Lord's Passover* (Exod 12:11), and what it means in Greek, namely, 'passion': for Christ passed from this world to the Father by means of the passion, in which he was sacrificed (John 13:1).

247. Then when he says, *therefore, let us feast*, he reaches his conclusion.

Ad cuius evidentiam considerandum est, quod, sicut legitur Ex. XII, 8, agnus paschalis post immolationem manducabatur cum azymis panibus. Sicut ergo agnus figuralis fuit figura nostri paschae immolati, ita figuralis observantia paschalis debet conformari observantiae novi paschae. Ergo quia Christus immolatus est pascha nostrum, *itaque epulemur*, scilicet manducantes Christum, non solum sacramentaliter, secundum illud Io. VI, v. 54: *nisi manducaveritis carnem Filii hominis, et biberitis eius sanguinem, non habebitis vitam in vobis*, sed spiritualiter fruendo sapientia eius, secundum illud Eccli. XXIV, v. 29: *qui edunt me, adhuc esurient, et qui bibunt me, adhuc sitient*, et sic cum gaudio spirituali, secundum illud Ps. XLI, 5: *in voce exultationis et confessionis, sonus epulantis.*

248. Deinde determinat modum epulandi secundum conformitatem veritatis ad figuram, dicens *non in fermento veteri, neque in fermento malitiae, et nequitiae.* Mandabatur enim Ex. XII, 15, quod omne fermentum non inveniretur in domibus manducantium agnum paschalem. Fermentum autem habet et vetustatem et corruptionem.

Unde per remotionem fermenti, primo quidem potest intelligi amotio observantiae praeceptorum veteris legis, quae per passionem Christi est mortificata, secundum illud Lev. c. XXVI, 10: *vetera, novis supervenientibus, proiicietis.* Secundo, per remotionem fermenti potest intelligi remotio corruptionis peccati, sicut supra dictum est, quod *modicum fermentum totam corrumpit massam.* Et quantum ad hoc subdit *neque in fermento malitiae et nequitiae*, ut malitia referatur ad perversitatem operis, secundum illud Iac. I, v. 21: *abiicientes omnem immunditiam et abundantiam malitiae.* Per nequitiam vero intelligitur fraudulenta machinatio. Prov. XXVI, v. 25: *quando sumpserit vocem suam, non credideris ei, quoniam septem nequitiae sunt in corde eius.*

Vel secundum Glossam cum dicit *non in fermento veteri*, removet vetustatem peccati in communi. Quod autem subdit *neque in fermento malitiae et nequitiae*, explicat peccatum per partes; ut malitia dicatur peccatum quod committitur in seipsum, nequitia peccatum quod committitur in alium.

249. Excluso ergo modo indebito epulandi, determinat modum convenientem, subdens *sed in azymis sinceritatis et veritatis*, id est, sinceritate et veritate, quae significantur per azyma.

Ponitur autem sinceritas contra corruptionem peccati, quod significavit, cum dixit *non in fermento malitiae et nequitiae.* Nam sincerum dicitur quod est sine corruptione. Unde II Cor. II, 17 dicitur: *non sumus sicut plurimi adulterantes verbum Dei, sed ex sinceritate in Christo loquimur.* Veritas vero ponitur contra figuras veteris legis, sicut Io. I, v. 17 dicitur *veritas et gratia per Iesum Christum facta est*, quia scilicet verum pascha cum

To understand this it should be noted that the paschal lamb, after being sacrificed, was eaten with unleavened bread. Therefore, just as the paschal lamb was a figure of our sacrificed pasch, so the observance of the new pasch should conform to the old paschal observances. Accordingly, because the sacrificed Christ is our pasch, *therefore, let us feast* the festival by eating Christ not only sacramentally: *unless you eat the flesh of the Son of man and drink his blood, you have no life in you* (John 6:54), but also spiritually by relishing his wisdom: *those who eat me will hunger for more, and those who drink me will thirst for more* (Sir 24:21), and doing so with spiritual joy: *with glad shouts and songs of thanksgiving; a multitude keeping festival* (Ps 42:4).

248. Then he describes the way to feast by conforming the truth to the figure, saying, *not with the old leaven, nor with the leaven of malice and wickedness.* For it was commanded in Exodus 12 that no leaven be found in the homes of those eating the paschal lamb. But leaven involves oldness and corruption.

Hence the removal of leaven could mean the removal of the obligation to observe the precepts of the old law, which was made dead by the passion of Christ: *the new coming on, you shall cast away the old* (Lev 26:10). Second, the removal of leaven could mean the removal of the corruption of sin, as we said above, namely, *that a little leaven corrupts the whole lump.* In this sense, therefore, he says, *nor with the leaven of malice and wickedness*, where malice would refer to perverse actions: *casting away all uncleanness and abundance of malice* (Jas 1:21), and evil would refer to crafty mischief: *when he speaks graciously, believe him not, for there are seven mischiefs in his heart* (Prov 26:25).

Or, according to a Gloss, when he says, *not with the old leaven*, he refers to sin in general, but in adding, *nor with the leaven of malice and wickedness*, he becomes more precise, because malice refers to sin committed against oneself, and evil a sin against someone else.

249. Therefore, having set aside the improper way to feast, he describes the proper way when he continues, *but with the unleavened bread of sincerity and truth*, i.e., in sincerity and truth which are signified by unleavened bread.

Here sincerity is set in opposition to the corruption of sin, which he signified when he said, *nor with the leaven of malice and wickedness*: for sincere means without corruption: *we do not adulterate the word of God but with sincerity in Christ we speak* (2 Cor 2:17). But truth is set in opposition to the figures of the old law: *truth and grace came by Jesus Christ* (John 1:17), namely, because we should celebrate the true pasch in truth and not in figures. Hence according

veritate et non cum figuris celebrare debemus. Unde secundum Glossam per sinceritatem intelligitur innocentia a vitiis, seu novitas vitae: per veritatem autem iustitia bonorum operum, vel rectitudo, quae fraudem excludit.

to a Gloss, by sincerity is understood innocence from vices or newness of life; by truth the righteousness of good works or directness which excludes deception.

Lecture 3

^{5:9}Scripsi in epistola: Ne commisceamini fornicariis: [n. 250]

^{5:10}non utique fornicariis hujus mundi, aut avaris, aut rapacibus, aut idolis servientibus: alioquin debueratis de hoc mundo exiisse. [n. 252]

^{5:11}Nunc autem scripsi vobis non commisceri: si is qui frater nominatur, est fornicator, aut avarus, aut idolis serviens, aut maledicus, aut ebriosus, aut rapax, cum ejusmodi nec cibum sumere. [n. 255]

^{5:12}Quid enim mihi de iis qui foris sunt, judicare? nonne de iis qui intus sunt, vos judicatis? [n. 259]

^{5:13}nam eos qui foris sunt, Deus judicabit. Auferte malum ex vobis ipsis. [n. 261]

^{5:9}Ἔγραψα ὑμῖν ἐν τῇ ἐπιστολῇ μὴ συναναμίγνυσθαι πόρνοις,

^{5:10}οὐ πάντως τοῖς πόρνοις τοῦ κόσμου τούτου ἢ τοῖς πλεονέκταις καὶ ἅρπαξιν ἢ εἰδωλολάτραις, ἐπεὶ ὠφείλετε ἄρα ἐκ τοῦ κόσμου ἐξελθεῖν.

^{5:11}νῦν δὲ ἔγραψα ὑμῖν μὴ συναναμίγνυσθαι ἐάν τις ἀδελφὸς ὀνομαζόμενος ᾖ πόρνος ἢ πλεονέκτης ἢ εἰδωλολάτρης ἢ λοίδορος ἢ μέθυσος ἢ ἅρπαξ, τῷ τοιούτῳ μηδὲ συνεσθίειν.

^{5:12}τί γάρ μοι τοὺς ἔξω κρίνειν; οὐχὶ τοὺς ἔσω ὑμεῖς κρίνετε;

^{5:13}τοὺς δὲ ἔξω ὁ θεὸς κρινεῖ. ἐξάρατε τὸν πονηρὸν ἐξ ὑμῶν αὐτῶν.

^{5:9}I wrote to you in an epistle not to keep company with fornicators. [n. 250]

^{5:10}I do not mean with the fornicators of this world or with the covetous or the extortioners or the servers of idols: otherwise you would need to go out of this world. [n. 252]

^{5:11}But now I have written to you, not to keep company, if any man that is named a brother be a fornicator or covetous or a server of idols or a reviler or a drunkard or an extortioner: with such a one, not so much as to eat. [n. 255]

^{5:12}For what is it to me to judge them that are without? Do you not judge them that are within? [n. 259]

^{5:13}For them that are without, God will judge. Put away the evil one from among yourselves. [n. 261]

---

250. Induxerat supra Apostolus Corinthios ad hoc, quod a seipsis peccatorem separarent, quod quidem praetermiserant propter falsum intellectum cuiusdam verbi, quod continebatur in epistola quadam, quam eis prius miserat. Et ideo pravum sensum, quem ex verbis conceperant, nunc excludit.

Unde circa hoc tria facit.

Primo resumit verbum prioris epistolae;

secundo excludit falsum intellectum, ibi: **non utique fornicariis**;

tertio exponit verum intellectum, ibi: **nunc autem scripsi vobis**.

251. Dicit ergo primo: dixi **vobis in epistola** quadam alia, quae in canone non habetur, **ne commisceamini fornicariis**, id est, non habeatis cum eis societatem, vel communionem, secundum illud Prov. I, 15: *fili mi, ne ambules cum eis, prohibe pedem tuum a semitis eorum*; Eccli. IX, 6: *non des fornicariis animam tuam in ullo*.

252. Deinde, cum dicit **non utique fornicariis**, excludit falsum intellectum praedicti verbi. Et

primo proponit quod intendit;

secundo concludit propositum, ibi **alioquin debueratis**, et cetera.

253. Circa primum considerandum est, quod in praedicto verbo apostoli dupliciter falsum intellectum conceperant Corinthii. Primo quantum ad hoc, quod intelligebant illud esse dictum de fornicariis infidelibus. Sed illud excludit apostolus, dicens **non utique** intendo

250. Above the Apostle had advised the Corinthians to remove a sinner from their midst. But they postponed doing this, because they gave a false interpretation to something he had written in a previous epistle. And therefore he now excludes the incorrect sense, which they had devised from his words.

Hence, he does three things.

First, he repeats what he had said in the previous epistle;

second, he corrects the false interpretation, at **I mean not with the fornicators**;

third, he gives the true interpretation, at **but now I have written to you**.

251. First, therefore, he says: I said **to you in an epistle**, which is not in the canon, **not to keep company with fornicators**, i.e., not have any fellowship or communion with them: *my son, walk not with them, restrain your feet from their paths* (Prov 1:15); *give not your soul to harlots in any point* (Sir 9:6).

252. Then when he says, **I do not mean**, he corrects the false interpretation of the above words.

First, he states what he does mean;

second, he draws a conclusion, at **otherwise you would need**.

253. In regard to the first it should be noted that the Corinthians had given two false interpretations to his statement. First, they supposed that he was referring to fornicators who are unbelievers. He corrects this when he says: **I do not mean** that you shall avoid communicating **with the**

dicere quod non commisceamini *fornicariis huius mundi*. Vocat autem infideles nomine mundi, secundum quod dicitur Io. I, 10: *mundus eum non cognovit*; supra c. I, 21: **non cognovit mundus per sapientiam Deum.**

Secundo conceperant falsum intellectum quantum ad hoc, quod putabant prohibuisse Apostolum solum de fornicariis, non autem de aliis peccatoribus. Et ideo ad hoc excludendum subdit *aut avaris*, qui scilicet iniuste detinent aliena. Eph. V, 5: *avaritia, quae est idolorum servitus, non habet haereditatem in regno Christi et Dei. Aut rapacibus*, qui scilicet violenter diripiunt aliena. Infra eodem: **neque rapaces regnum Dei possidebunt. Aut idolis servientibus**, contra quos dicitur Sap. XIV, 27: *nefandorum enim idolorum cultura omnis malitiae causa est, initium et finis.* Et est sensus: non solum vobis prohibui societatem fornicatorum, sed etiam omnium aliorum peccatorum.

Et est advertendum, quod per fornicationem quis peccat contra seipsum, per avaritiam autem et rapacitatem contra proximum, per idolorum autem culturam contra Deum; et in his, quae ponit, omne peccati genus intelligitur.

254. Deinde cum dicit *alioquin*, etc., assignat rationem propositi, dicens *alioquin*, si scilicet sit intelligendum verbum praedictum de fornicariis huius mundi, *debueratis de hoc mundo exisse*, quia scilicet totus mundus talibus plenus est. Unde non possetis tales fornicarios vitare, nisi de hoc mundo exeundo. Dicitur enim I Io. V, 19: *totus mundus in maligno positus est.*

Vel aliter: debueratis de hoc mundo exisse, quasi dicat: a tempore conversionis vestrae debueratis ab infidelibus mundi separari. Unde non oportet vos super hoc moneri; dicitur enim Io. XV, 16: *ego elegi vos de mundo.*

Vel aliter: debueratis de hoc mundo exisse, scilicet per mortem. Melius est enim hominibus mori, quam peccatoribus in peccatis consentire. Unde dicitur infra IX, 15: **melius est enim mihi mori, quam ut gloriam meam quis evacuet.**

255. Deinde, cum dicit **nunc autem scripsi vobis**, exponit eis verum intellectum et

primo proponit quod intendit;

secundo rationem assignat, ibi: **quid enim mihi est?**;

Tertio infert conclusionem intentam, ibi **auferte malum**, et cetera.

256. Dicit ergo primo: **nunc autem** sic expono, quod olim **scripsi vobis: non commisceamini**, scilicet fornicariis et aliis peccatoribus. **Si is qui**, inter vos, **frater nominatur**, eo modo quo Dominus dicit, Matth. c. XXIII, 8: *omnes vos fratres estis.* Non tamen dicit: si is qui frater est, sed: *si is, qui frater nominatur*, quia per peccatum mortale aliquis a caritate recedit, quae est spiritualis fraternitatis causa. Unde Hebr. ult. dicitur *caritas fraternitatis maneat*

fornicators of this world. He refers to unbelievers by the name 'world': *the world has not know him* (John 1:21); **the world, by wisdom, knew not God** (1 Cor 1:21).

Second, they falsely supposed that the Apostle's prohibition referred only to fornicators and not to other sinners. To correct this he now adds, **or with the covetous**, who unjustly retain what belongs to others: *no one who is covetous (which is serving of idols) has any inheritance in the kingdom of Christ and of God* (Eph 5:5), **or extortioners**, who violently plunder the property of others; *nor extortioners shall possess the kingdom of God* (1 Cor 6:10); **or the servers of idols**, against whom it is written: *the worship of abominable idols is the cause, and the beginning and the end of all evil* (Wis 14:27). Consequently, the Apostle is prohibiting fellowship not only with fornicators but with all other sinners.

It should be noted that by fornication a person sins against himself; by greed and robbery against his neighbor, and by the worship of idols he sins against God. Consequently, in mentioning these he includes every type of sin.

254. Then when he says, **otherwise**, he gives the reason for this clarification, saying, **otherwise**, i.e., if he had meant the fornicators of this world, **you would need to go out of the world**, for the whole world is filled with them; hence you could not avoid them except by going out of this world: *the whole world is in the power of the evil one* (1 John 5:19).

Or, you would need to go out of the world, could mean: since you should have been separated from the sinners of this world from the time of your conversion, there is no need to advise you further about this: *I chose you out of the world* (John 15:19).

Or again: you would need to go out of the world, i.e., by dying, for it is better for man to die than consent to sinners in sin; hence it says below: **for it is good for me to die rather than that any man should make my glory void** (1 Cor 9:15).

255. Then when he says, **but now I have written to you**, he presents the true interpretation.

First, he states his intention;

second, he assigns a reason, at **for what is it to me**;

third, he draws the intended conclusion, at **put away the evil one**.

256. First, therefore, he says: **but now** I shall explain what **I have written to you** earlier, **not to keep company** with fornicators and other sinners, **if any man**, among you, **is named a brother** in the sense in which the Lord speaks: *you are all brothers* (Matt 23:8). The Apostle does not say if any man is a brother, but if any man is called a brother, because by mortal sin a man departs from charity, which is the cause of spiritual brotherhood. Hence: *let brotherly*

in vobis. Nominatur ergo frater propter fidei veritatem, non autem est vere frater, propter caritatis defectum, qui est ex peccato. Unde subditur ***aut fornicator, aut avarus, aut idolis serviens, aut maledicus, aut rapax, aut ebriosus, cum huiusmodi nec cibum sumere***, scilicet debetis, secundum illud Io. II Canon.: *si quis venit ad vos, et hanc doctrinam non affert, nolite eum recipere in domo vestra, nec ave dixeritis ei*; quasi dicat: per hoc quod dixi non debere vos misceri peccatoribus, intellexi de fidelibus qui nominantur fratres, et sunt inter vos.

257. Non autem per hoc intelligendum est, sicut dicit Augustinus in libro *Contra Parmenianum*, et habetur in Glossa hic, quod aliquis extraordinario iudicio debeat a communione aliorum separari, quia frequenter posset errare, sed potius hoc debet fieri secundum ordinem Ecclesiae, quando aliquis a communione repellitur, ut convictus, vel sponte confessus. Et ideo signanter dicit *si is qui nominatur*, ut eam nominationem intelligamus, quae fit per sententiam Ecclesiae ordine iudiciario contra aliquem prolatam. Illi autem qui sic a communione pelluntur, sunt vitandi quantum ad mensam, sicut hic dicitur, et quantum ad salutationem, ut dicitur in praedicta auctoritate Ioannis, et ulterius quantum ad sacram communionem. Unde in versu dicitur: *os, orare, vale, communio, mensa negatur*, scilicet excommunicato.

258. Sed notandum quod Apostolus supra non numeravit nisi peccata mortalia, in signum, quod pro solo peccato mortali debet aliquis excommunicari. Et de aliis quidem quae ponit manifestum est; sed de ebrietate potest esse dubium, quae non semper videtur esse peccatum mortale. Dicit enim Augustinus in sermone de purgatorio, quod ebrietas, nisi sit frequens, non est peccatum mortale. Quod credo ideo esse, quia ebrietas ex suo genere est peccatum mortale. Quod enim aliquis propter delectationem vini velit perdere usum rationis, exponens se periculo multa alia peccata perpetrandi, videtur esse contrarius caritati. Contingit tamen per accidens ebrietatem non esse peccatum mortale propter ignorantiam vini fortitudinis, vel debilitatis proprii capitis, quae tamen excusatio tollitur per frequentem experientiam: et ideo Apostolus signanter non dicit ebrius sed *ebriosus*.

Addit autem duo peccata his quae supra posuerat, scilicet ***ebriosum*** et ***maledicum***. Refertur autem ebrietas ad genus peccati quod committitur contra seipsum, sub quo continetur non solum luxuria, sed etiam gula; maledicus autem refertur ad genus peccati quod committitur contra proximum, cui nocet aliquis non solum facto, sed etiam verbo, mala imprecando, vel male diffamando: quod pertinet ad detractionem, vel mala in faciem dicendo: quod pertinet ad contumeliam, et hoc totum pertinet ad rationem maledici, ut supra dictum est.

love continue (Heb 13:1). Therefore a man is called a brother on account of the true faith, even though he is not really a brother, if he lacks charity as a result of sin. Hence he adds, ***be a fornicator or covetous or a server of idols or a reviler or a drunkard or an extortioner: with such a one, not so much as to eat***. *If any one comes to you and does not bring this doctrine, do not receive him into the house or give him any greeting* (2 John 1:10). In other words: when I said that you should not keep company with sinners, I meant with believers who are called brothers and live among you.

257. However, by this it should not be understood, as Augustine says in *Contra Parmenianum*, and as it says here in the Gloss, that someone by an extraordinary judgment should be separated from communion with others, because often one can be mistaken, but rather this ought to be done according to the order of the Church, when someone is expelled from communion as convicted or freely confessed. And this he says clearly, ***if any man that is named***, so that we understand that designation which is made through the sentence of the Church by a judicial order against someone brought forward. But those who are expelled from communion are to be shunned as to the table, as it says here, and as to greeting, as it says in what is preached by the authority of John, and further, as to sacred communion. Hence it is said in verse: *the mouth, to pray, farewell communion, the table is denied*, that is, he is excommunicated.

258. It should be noted that the Apostle mentions only mortal sins to show that a man should not be excommunicated except for mortal sin. However, there seems to be some question about one of these sins, namely, drunkenness, which does not always seem to be a mortal sin. For Augustine says in a sermon on purgatory that drunkenness, unless it is frequent, is not a mortal sin. I believe the reason for this is that drunkenness is a mortal sin in general. For it seems to be contrary to charity that for the pleasure of wine a man is willing to lose the use of reason and expose himself to the danger of committing many other sins. Yet it might happen that drunkenness is not a mortal sin, because the strength of the wine or one's own physical weakness were not known. However, this excuse loses its validity, when drunkenness is frequent. Hence it is significant that the Apostle does not say a drinker but ***a drunkard***.

It is noteworthy that to the list given earlier he added two sins, namely, the ***reviler*** and the ***drunkard***. Drunkenness is among the class of sins committed against oneself, which includes not only lust but gluttony as well. Reviling is among the sins committed against one's neighbor, whom a man can harm not only by deed but also by word, by calling down evil upon him or by defaming him, which pertains to detraction, or by speaking evil to his face, which pertains to contumely. All this is included under the notion of reviler, as has been stated.

259. Deinde, cum dicit *quid enim mihi est*, etc., assignat rationem eius quod dixerat. Et circa hoc tria facit. Primo assignat rationem, dicens: dixi hoc esse intelligendum de fratribus, et non de infidelibus. *Quid enim mihi est*, id est, quid ad me pertinet, *iudicare*, id est, sententiam condemnationis ferre, *de his qui foris sunt?* Id est, de infidelibus, qui sunt omnino extra Ecclesiam? Praelati enim Ecclesiarum accipiunt spiritualem potestatem super eos tantum, qui se fidei subdiderunt, secundum illud II Cor. X, 6: *in promptu habentes ulcisci omnem inobedientiam, cum impleta fuerit vestra obedientia.* Indirecte tamen praelati Ecclesiarum habent potestatem super eos qui foris sunt, inquantum propter eorum culpam prohibent fideles, ne illis communicent.

260. Secundo adhibet similitudinem, dicens *nonne de his qui intus sunt vos iudicatis?* Quasi dicat: eadem auctoritate vos iudicatis, qua et ego. Unde nec vos non iudicatis nisi de vestris, ita et ego. Dicitur Eccli. X, 1: *iudex sapiens iudicabit populum suum.*

261. Tertio respondet tacitae dubitationi. Posset enim videri, quod infideles essent meliores, qui propter peccata praedicta non condemnantur; sed hoc excludit, dicens: ideo nihil mihi de his qui foris sunt iudicare, *nam eos qui foris sunt*, id est, infideles, *iudicabit Deus*, scilicet iudicio condemnationis, non examinationis; quia, ut Gregorius dicit in *Moralibus*, infideles damnabuntur sine iudicio discussionis et examinationis. Et quantum ad hoc dicitur Io. III, 18: *qui non credit, iam iudicatus est*, id est, manifestam in se habet causam condemnationis, et hoc gravius reservatur Dei iudicio, secundum illud Hebr. X, 31: *horrendum est incidere in manus Dei viventis.*

262. Deinde, cum dicit *auferte malum*, etc., infert conclusionem principaliter intentam, dicens: ex quo hoc quod dixi *non commisceamini fornicariis*, intelligendum est de fidelibus, non de his qui foris sunt. Ergo *auferte malum*, scilicet hominem, *ex vobis ipsis*, id est, de vestra societate eiicite, secundum illud Deut. XIII, 5: *auferes malum de medio tui.*

263. Est ergo considerandum ex praemissis Apostoli verbis, quod non prohibemur communicare infidelibus, qui numquam fidem receperunt propter eorum poenam. Est tamen hoc cavendum aliquibus, scilicet infirmis, propter eorum cautelam, ne seducantur. Illi vero qui sunt firmi in fide, possunt eis licite communicare, et dare operam conversioni eorum, ut dicitur infra X, 27: *si quis infidelium vocat vos ad caenam et vultis ire, omne quod appositum fuerit manducate.*

Infidelibus autem qui aliquando fideles fuerunt, vel sacramentum fidei receperunt, sicut haereticis et apostatantibus a fide, subtrahitur omnino communio fidelium, et hoc in eorum poenam, sicut et caeteris peccatoribus qui adhuc subduntur potestati Ecclesiae.

259. Then when he says, *for what is it to me*, he gives the reason for what he had said. In regard to this he does three things: first, he gives the reason, saying: I have said that this is to be understood of brothers and not unbelievers, *for what is it to me*, i.e., what business is it of mine *to judge*, i.e., pass a sentence of condemnation *on them that are without*, i.e., on unbelievers who are completely outside the Church? For the hierarchy has spiritual power over those alone who have submitted to the faith: *being ready to punish every disobedience, when your obedience is complete* (2 Cor 10:6). Indirectly, however, the hierarchy has power over those who are without, inasmuch as it forbids believers to deal with them on account of their guilt.

260. Second, he uses a simile, saying, *do you not judge them that are within?* As if to say: you judge with the same authority as I; hence just as you do not judge anyone but your own, so I also: *a wise judge shall judge his people* (Sir 10:1).

261. Third, he settles a doubt. For some one might conclude that unbelievers are better for not being condemned for the above mentioned sins. But he rejects this when he says that it is not his business to judge those that are without, *for them that are without*, i.e., unbelievers, *God will judge*, namely, with the judgment of condemnation, not examination; because as Gregory says in *Morals*, unbelievers will be condemned without discussion and investigation. This is in line with what is said in John: *he who does not believe has already been judged* (John 3:18), i.e., has within himself an obvious cause for condemnation, and this more serious case is reserved for the judgment of God: *it is a fearful thing to fall into the hands of the living God* (Heb 10:31).

262. Then when he says, *put away the evil one*, he draws the main conclusion saying: since my command that you not *keep company with fornicators* must be understood as referring to believers and not to those who are outside, *put away the evil one*, i.e., this man, *from among yourselves*, i.e., expel him from your company: *you shall purge the evil from the midst of you* (Deut 13:5).

263. These words of the Apostle do not mean that we are forbidden to associate with unbelievers who have never received the faith, for the sake of their punishment. Yet the weak are cautioned to avoid them, lest they be drawn away. But those strong in the faith can lawfully associate with them and try to convert them, as it says below: *if any of them that believes not, invites you, and you are willing to go: eat of any thing that is set before you* (1 Cor 10:27).

But unbelievers who once were believers, or received the sacrament of faith, as heretics or apostates from the faith, are excluded from all contact with believers. This is a punishment for them, as it is for other sinners still subject to the power of the Church.

CHAPTER 6

Lecture 1

6:1Audet aliquis vestrum habens negotium adversus alterum, judicari apud iniquos, et non apud sanctos? [n. 264]

6:2an nescitis quoniam sancti de hoc mundo judicabunt? et si in vobis judicabitur mundus, indigni estis qui de minimis judicetis? [n. 268]

6:3Nescitis quoniam angelos judicabimus? quanto magis saecularia? [n. 271]

6:4Saecularia igitur judicia si habueritis: contemptibiles, qui sunt in Ecclesia, illos constituite ad judicandum. [n. 273]

6:5Ad verecundiam vestram dico. Sic non est inter vos sapiens quisquam, qui possit judicare inter fratrem suum? [n. 275]

6:6Sed frater cum fratre judicio contendit: et hoc apud infideles?

6:1Τολμᾷ τις ὑμῶν πρᾶγμα ἔχων πρὸς τὸν ἕτερον κρίνεσθαι ἐπὶ τῶν ἀδίκων, καὶ οὐχὶ ἐπὶ τῶν ἁγίων;

6:2ἢ οὐκ οἴδατε ὅτι οἱ ἅγιοι τὸν κόσμον κρινοῦσιν; καὶ εἰ ἐν ὑμῖν κρίνεται ὁ κόσμος, ἀνάξιοί ἐστε κριτηρίων ἐλαχίστων;

6:3οὐκ οἴδατε ὅτι ἀγγέλους κρινοῦμεν, μήτι γε βιωτικά;

6:4βιωτικὰ μὲν οὖν κριτήρια ἐὰν ἔχητε, τοὺς ἐξουθενημένους ἐν τῇ ἐκκλησίᾳ τούτους καθίζετε;

6:5πρὸς ἐντροπὴν ὑμῖν λέγω. οὕτως οὐκ ἔνι ἐν ὑμῖν οὐδεὶς σοφὸς ὃς δυνήσεται διακρῖναι ἀνὰ μέσον τοῦ ἀδελφοῦ αὐτοῦ;

6:6ἀλλὰ ἀδελφὸς μετὰ ἀδελφοῦ κρίνεται, καὶ τοῦτο ἐπὶ ἀπίστων;

6:1Dare any of you, having a matter against another, go to be judged before the unjust: and not before the saints? [n. 264]

6:2Know you not that the saints shall judge this world? And if the world shall be judged by you, are you unworthy to judge the smallest matters? [n. 268]

6:3Know you not that we shall judge angels? How much more things of this world? [n. 271]

6:4If therefore you have judgments of things pertaining to this world, set them to judge who are the most despised in the Church. [n. 273]

6:5I speak to your shame. Is it so that there is not among you any one wise man that is able to judge between his brethren? [n. 275]

6:6But brother goes to law with brother: and that before unbelievers?

---

264. Supra Apostolus reprehenderat Corinthios de negligentia iudicii, hic reprehendit in eis quaedam alia peccata circa iudicia. Et

primo quantum ad iudices eorum coram quibus litigabant;

secundo quantum ad ipsa iudicia, ibi *iam quidem omnino*.

Circa primum tria facit.

Primo arguit eos de inordinatione;

secundo rationem reprehensionis assignat, ibi *an nescitis*;

tertio remedium adhibet, ibi *saecularia igitur iudicia*.

265. Dicit ergo primo: ita negligitis in iudicando vestros, sed tamen praesumptuosi estis subire infidelium iudicia, et hoc est quod dicit *audet*, id est, praesumit, *aliquis vestrum habens negotium*, scilicet saeculare, *adversus alium, iudicari apud iniquos*, id est, subire iudicium infidelium, *et non apud sanctos*, id est, apud fideles, qui sunt sacramentis fidei sanctificati.

264. After rebuking the Corinthians for failing to judge, the Apostle now rebukes them for other failings in matters of judgment.

First, in regard to the judges before whom they present their grievances;

second, in regard to the grievances themselves, at *already indeed* (1 Cor 6:7).

In regard to the first he does three things.

First, he charges them with unbecoming conduct;

second, he gives the reason for this charge, at *know you not that the saints*;

third, he applies a remedy, at *if therefore you have judgments*.

265. First, therefore, he says: you fail to judge yourselves but allow yourselves to be judged by the unrighteous. Hence he says: *dare* i.e., i.e., presume, *any of you, having a matter*, i.e., secular business, *against another, go to be judged before the unjust*, i.e., submit to the decision of an unbeliever, *and not before the saints*, i.e., before believers, who have been sanctified by the sacraments of faith?

266. Hoc enim est inordinatum multipliciter. Primo quidem, quia per hoc derogatur auctoritati fidelium; secundo, quia derogatur dignitati fidelium quantum ad hoc quod infidelium iudicia subeunt; tertio quia per hoc datur occasio infidelibus iudicibus contemnendi fideles, quos dissentire vident; quarto, quia per hoc datur occasio infidelibus iudicibus calumniandi et opprimendi fideles, quos odio habent propter fidem et ritus diversitatem. Et ideo dicitur Deut. I, v. 15 s.: *tuli de tribubus vestris viros sapientes et nobiles, praecepique eis, dicens: audite illos, et quod iustum est iudicate.* Et eod. XVII, 15: *non poteris alterius gentis facere regem, qui non sit frater tuus.*

267. Sed videtur esse contra id quod dicitur I Petr. II, 13: *subditi estote omni humanae creaturae propter Deum, sive regi tamquam praecellenti, sive ducibus tamquam ab eo missis*: pertinet enim ad auctoritatem principis iudicare de subditis. Est ergo contra ius divinum prohibere quod eius iudicio non stetur, si sit infidelis.

Sed dicendum quod Apostolus non prohibet, quin fideles, sub infidelibus principibus constituti, eorum iudicio compareant, si vocentur, hoc enim esset contra subiectionem, quae debetur principibus; sed prohibet quod fideles non eligant voluntarie infidelium iudicium.

268. Deinde cum dicit **an nescitis**, etc., assignat rationem contra id, quod illi faciebant, sumptam ex hoc, quod derogabant auctoritati sanctorum. Et

primo quantum ad auctoritatem quam habent super res mundanas;

secundo quantum ad auctoritatem quam habent ad res supermundanas, id est, super angelos, ibi **an nescitis, quoniam angelos iudicabimus?**

269. Dicit ergo primo: inordinatum est iudicium apud infideles, quia fideles habent auctoritatem iudicandi, **an nescitis, quia sancti de hoc mundo iudicabunt**, id est, de hominibus mundanis huius mundi?

Quod quidem impletur tripliciter. Primo quidem secundum comparationem, scilicet secundum quod non solum boni iudicabunt malos, et sancti mundanos; sed etiam secundum quod boni iudicabuntur a melioribus, et mali iudicabunt peiores, secundum illud Matth. c. XII, 41: *viri Ninivitae surgent in iudicio cum generatione ista, et condemnabunt eam.*

Secundo iudicabunt approbando sententiam iudicis, scilicet Christi, et hoc erit proprie iustorum, secundum illud Ps.: *laetabitur iustus cum viderit vindictam.* Unde Sap. III, 8 dicitur: *iudicabunt sancti nationes.*

Tertio modo per sententiae prolationem. Et hoc erit apostolorum et similium, qui contemptis rebus mundi, solis spiritualibus inhaeserunt. **Spiritualis enim iudicat omnia**, ut dictum est supra II, 15. Unde et Matth. c. XIX, 28 dicitur: *vos qui secuti estis me,*

266. This is unbecoming in a number of ways. First, because it detracts from the full power of believers; second, it insults the dignity of believers to take their lawsuits to unbelievers; third, it gives unbelieving judges occasion for looking down on believers, whom they see at odds among themselves; fourth, it gives the same judges occasion for calumniating and oppressing believers, whom they hate on account of their faith and rites which differ from their own. Hence it says: *I took the heads of your tribes, wise and experienced men, and set them as heads over you. And I charged them: hear the cases between your brethren, and judge righteously* (Deut 1:15). Again: *you may not put a foreigner over you, who is not your brother* (Deut 17:15).

267. But this seems contrary to what is commanded by Peter: *be subject for the Lord's sake to every human institution, whether it be to the emperor as supreme, or to governors sent by him* (1 Pet 2:13); for it pertains to the prince's authority to judge his subjects. Therefore, it is against the divine law to forbid one's conforming to the decision of a judge, who is an unbeliever.

The answer is that the Apostle is not forbidding believers who are under the jurisdiction of unbelieving princes to accept their judgment, if they are summoned; for this would be contrary to the loyalty owed to princes, but he is forbidding believers voluntarily to prefer being judged by unbelievers.

268. Then when he says, **know you not**, he gives a reason against this policy, inasmuch as it detracts from the full power of the saints.

First, in regard to the power they have over worldly affairs;

second, in regard to the power they have over otherworldly things, i.e., over angels, at **know you not that we shall judge angels**.

269. First, therefore, he says: it is unbecoming to take your lawsuits to unbelievers, because believers have authority to judge, **know you not that the saints shall judge this world**, i.e., the worldly men of this world?

They do this in three ways: first, comparatively, i.e., not only in the sense that good men will judge evil men, and saints the worldly, but also that the good will be judged by the better and the evil by the worse, according to Matthew: *the men of Nineveh will arise at the judgment with this generation and condemn it* (Matt 12:41).

Second, they will judge by approving the sentence of the judge, i.e., Christ; and this will be reserved to the just: *the just man will rejoice when he sees the vengeance* (Ps 58:10); *the saints shall judge nations* (Wis 3:8).

In a third way by passing sentence, and this will be done by the apostles and those like them who held worldly things in contempt and clung only to spiritual things, for as was said above: *the spiritual man judges all things* (1 Cor 2:15). Hence it is said: *you who have followed me will sit on twelve*

sedebitis super sedes, iudicantes duodecim tribus Israel. Et in Ps. CXLIX, 6 s. dicitur: *gladii ancipites in manibus eorum, ad faciendam vindictam in nationibus.*

Intelligitur autem ista prolatio sententiae non vocalis, sed spiritualis, inquantum per superiores sanctos inferiores vel etiam peccatores spirituali quadam illuminatione illuminabuntur, quales poenae, et qualia praemia eis debeantur: sicut etiam nunc homines illuminantur ab angelis, vel etiam inferiores angeli a superioribus.

270. Secundo ex hoc, quod dictum est, argumentatur ad propositum, dicens *et si in vobis*, id est, per vos, *iudicabitur mundus*, id est, mundani homines, numquid *indigni estis, qui iudicetis de minimis*, scilicet de negotiis saecularibus, Lc. XVI, 10: *qui in modico iniquus est, et in maiori iniquus erit.*

271. Deinde cum dicit *nescitis*, etc., argumentatur ad idem ex auctoritate sanctorum super angelos.

Et primo ponit eam, dicens *an nescitis, quoniam* nos, scilicet fideles Christi, *iudicabimus angelos?* Quod quidem potest intelligi de malis angelis, qui condemnabuntur a sanctis, quorum virtute sunt victi. Unde Dominus, Lc. X, 19, dicit: *ecce dedi vobis potestatem calcandi super serpentes, et super omnem virtutem inimici.* Et in Ps. XC, 13: *super aspidem et basiliscum ambulabis.*

Potest etiam hoc intelligi de bonis angelis, quorum plurimi in comparatione quadam invenientur Paulo et similibus sibi inferiores. Unde signanter non dicit: *iudicabitis*, sed *iudicabimus*. Quamvis etiam dici possit, quod ex consequenti, si sancti iudicabunt homines bonos et malos, erit iudicium de bonis angelis, quorum accidentale praemium augetur ex praemio sanctorum per angelos illuminatorum, et etiam de malis angelis, quorum poena augetur ex poena hominum per eos seductorum.

272. Secundo argumentatur ad propositum, dicens *quanto magis saecularia*, scilicet iudicia, idonei erimus iudicare: qui enim est idoneus ad maiora, multo magis est idoneus ad minora. Unde et Dominus, cui commiserat quinque talenta, postmodum commisit unum, ut habetur Matth. XXV, 28.

273. Deinde cum dicit *saecularia igitur iudicia*, adhibet remedium contra culpam eorum. Et

primo ponit remedium;

secundo exponit, ibi *ad verecundiam vestram dico.*

274. Dicit ergo primo: ergo ex quo *sancti de hoc mundo iudicabunt*, si habueritis inter vos saecularia iudicia, quae tamen habere non debetis, illos qui *sunt contemptibiles in Ecclesia* constituite ad iudicandum, potius scilicet quam iudicemini apud infideles. Unde et in Ps. CXL, 5 dicitur: *corripiet me iustus in misericordia, et increpabit me, oleum autem peccatoris non impinguet*

thrones judging the twelve tribes of Israel (Matt 19:28), and: *two edged swords in their hands to wreak vengeance on the nations* (Ps 149:4).

This passing of sentence will not be vocal but spiritual, inasmuch as lesser saints or even sinners will be enlightened with a spiritual light by the higher saints to understand what sort of punishments or rewards are owed to them; just as even now men are enlightened by angels, or even lesser angels by higher ones.

270. Second, from what has been stated he argues to his proposition, saying: *and if the world*, i.e., worldly men, *shall be judged by you, are you unworthy to judge the smallest matters*, i.e., worldly business? *He who is dishonest in a very little, is dishonest also in much* (Luke 16:10).

271. Then when he says, *know you not that we shall judge angels*, he argues to the same conclusion, from the authority of the saints over angels.

And first he lays down the argument, saying, *know you not that we*, namely, the faithful of Christ, *shall judge angels?* This can be understood of bad angels, who will be condemned by the saints, by whose virtue they were overcome. Hence the Lord says: *I have given you power to tread upon serpents and scorpions, and all the power of the enemy* (Luke 10:19). And in a psalm: *the young lion and the serpent you will trample under foot* (Ps 91:3).

It can also be understood of good angels, most of whom in some way will be found inferior to Paul and others like him. Hence, it is significant that he does not say *you shall judge* but *we shall judge*. Although it might also be said, as a consequence, that if saints will judge good and evil men, there will be a judgment of good angels, whose accidental reward is increased by the reward of saints enlightened by angels and a judgment of evil angels, whose punishment is increased by the punishment of men led astray by them.

272. Second, he argues to the proposition, saying: *how much more things of this world*, namely, judgments, will we be fit to judge. For one capable of greater things is even more capable of lesser. Hence to the person entrusted with five talents the Lord later entrusted one (Matt 25:28).

273. Then when he says, *if therefore you have judgments*, he applies the remedy for their fault.

First he mentions the remedy;

second, he explains, at *I speak to your shame.*

274. First, therefore, he says: therefore, since *the saints shall judge this world*, if you should have secular trials among you, which, nevertheless you should not have, those *most despised in the Church* should be appointed to judge, rather than be judged by unbelievers. *Let a good man strike or rebuke me in kindness, but let the oil of the wicked never*

caput meum. Et Eccle. IX, 4 dicitur: *melius est canis vivus leone mortuo.*

275. Deinde cum dicit **ad verecundiam vestram dico**, exponit quo sensu praedicta dixit.

Posset enim aliquis credere, quod ad litteram essent eligendi contemptibiliores ad iudicandum; sed hoc excludit, dicens **ad verecundiam vestram dico**. Quasi dicat: non hoc dixi ut ita fiat, sed ut vos faciam verecundari, illa scilicet confusione, quae adducit gratiam et gloriam, ut dicitur Eccli. IV, 25. **Contemptibiles** enim *in Ecclesia* essent eligendi ad iudicandum, si non invenirentur inter vos sapientes, quod esset vobis verecundum. Unde subdit *sic non est inter vos sapiens quisquam, qui possit iudicare inter fratrem et fratrem, sed frater cum fratre in iudicio contendit, et hoc apud infideles?* Potius autem quam hoc faceretis, deberetis constituere **contemptibiles, qui sunt in Ecclesia**, ad iudicandum et supplendum defectum sapientum, qui tamen non est apud vos, secundum illud quod supra primo, dixerat: *divites facti estis in illo, in omni verbo et in omni scientia.*

276. Vel aliter ab illo loco *saecularia*, et cetera. Dixerat enim, quod sancti idonei sunt ad iudicandum saecularia, et ideo vult ostendere per quos iudicia saecularia debeant exerceri, scilicet per **contemptibiles qui sunt in Ecclesia**. Vocat autem **contemptibiles** illos, qui sunt sapientes in rebus mundanis, per comparationem ad illos, qui sunt sapientes in rebus divinis, quibus est reverentia exhibenda, qui in rebus temporalibus non occupantur, ut solis spiritualibus vacent. Et hoc est quod subditur **ad verecundiam vestram dico**; secundum aliam litteram: **ad reverentiam vestram**. Unde et apostoli dixerunt Act. c. VI, 2: *non est aequum relinquere nos verbum Dei, et ministrare mensis.*

Postmodum autem redit ad id quod supra reprehenderat, scilicet quod Corinthii sub infidelibus iudicibus litigabant, dicens *sic non est inter vos sapiens quisquam*, scilicet in rebus temporalibus, quem supra contemptibilem dixit.

Unde alia non mutantur a prima expositione, quae tamen videtur esse magis litteralis.

anoint my head (Ps 141:5); and it says: *a living dog is better than a dead lion* (Eccl 9:4).

275. Then when he says, **I speak to your shame**, he explains in what sense he meant the foregoing.

For someone could believe that literally the least esteemed were to be chosen judges. But he excludes this, saying, **I speak to your shame**. As if to say: I did not say this as though it were to be done, but I said it to shame you, namely, with that confusion which brings grace and glory (Sir 4:25): for **the most despised in the Church** should be chosen for judging, if no wise men were to be found among you, which would be shameful for you. That is why he continues, **is it so that there is not among you any one wise man that is able to judge between his brethren? But brother goes to law with brother: and that before unbelievers?** Rather than do this, you should appoint **the most despised in the Church** to judge and to supply for the lack of wisdom, which, of course, is not wanting to you, as I said above: **in all things you are made rich in him, in all utterance and in all knowledge** (1 Cor 1:5).

276. Or in another way from **if therefore you have**: for he had said that the saints are worthy to judge worldly matters; consequently, he wants to show by whom worldly judgments should be passed, namely, by **the most despised in the Church**. By **most despised** he means those who are wise in worldly matter as opposed to those wise in divine matters and are not occupied with temporal things, in order to devote themselves strictly to spiritual things. And this is what is added to: **I speak to your shame**. Hence the apostles said: *it is not right that we should give up preaching the word of God to serve tables* (Acts 6:2).

After that he returns to what he had censured earlier, namely, that the Corinthians took their lawsuits to unbelieving judges, saying, **is it so that there is not among you any one wise man**, namely in temporal affairs, which he called contemptible earlier.

Hence the other things are not changed from the first explanation, which seems to be more literal.

Lecture 2

6:7Jam quidem omnino delictum est in vobis, quod judicia habetis inter vos. Quare non magis injuriam accipitis? quare non magis fraudem patimini? [n. 277]

6:8Sed vos injuriam facitis, et fraudatis: et hoc fratribus. [n. 281]

6:9An nescitis quia iniqui regnum Dei non possidebunt? Nolite errare: neque fornicarii, neque idolis servientes, neque adulteri, neque molles, neque masculorum concubitores, [n. 282]

6:10neque fures, neque avari, neque ebriosi, neque maledici, neque rapaces regnum Dei possidebunt.

6:11Et haec quidam fuistis: sed abluti estis, sed sanctificati estis, sed justificati estis in nomine Domini nostri Jesu Christi, et in Spiritu Dei nostri. [n. 286]

6:12Omnia mihi licent, sed non omnia expediunt: omnia mihi licent, sed ego sub nullis redigar potestate. [n. 290]

6:13Esca ventri, et venter escis: Deus autem et hunc et has destruet: [n. 295] corpus autem non fornicationi, sed Domino: et Dominus corpori. [n. 297]

6:7ἤδη μὲν [οὖν] ὅλως ἥττημα ὑμῖν ἐστιν ὅτι κρίματα ἔχετε μεθ' ἑαυτῶν· διὰ τί οὐχὶ μᾶλλον ἀδικεῖσθε; διὰ τί οὐχὶ μᾶλλον ἀποστερεῖσθε;

6:8ἀλλὰ ὑμεῖς ἀδικεῖτε καὶ ἀποστερεῖτε, καὶ τοῦτο ἀδελφούς.

6:9ἢ οὐκ οἴδατε ὅτι ἄδικοι θεοῦ βασιλείαν οὐ κληρονομήσουσιν; μὴ πλανᾶσθε· οὔτε πόρνοι οὔτε εἰδωλολάτραι οὔτε μοιχοὶ οὔτε μαλακοὶ οὔτε ἀρσενοκοῖται

6:10οὔτε κλέπται οὔτε πλεονέκται, οὐ μέθυσοι, οὐ λοίδοροι, οὐχ ἅρπαγες βασιλείαν θεοῦ κληρονομήσουσιν.

6:11καὶ ταῦτά τινες ἦτε· ἀλλὰ ἀπελούσασθε, ἀλλὰ ἡγιάσθητε, ἀλλὰ ἐδικαιώθητε ἐν τῷ ὀνόματι τοῦ κυρίου Ἰησοῦ Χριστοῦ καὶ ἐν τῷ πνεύματι τοῦ θεοῦ ἡμῶν.

6:12Πάντα μοι ἔξεστιν, ἀλλ' οὐ πάντα συμφέρει. πάντα μοι ἔξεστιν, ἀλλ' οὐκ ἐγὼ ἐξουσιασθήσομαι ὑπό τινος.

6:13τὰ βρώματα τῇ κοιλίᾳ, καὶ ἡ κοιλία τοῖς βρώμασιν· ὁ δὲ θεὸς καὶ ταύτην καὶ ταῦτα καταργήσει. τὸ δὲ σῶμα οὐ τῇ πορνείᾳ ἀλλὰ τῷ κυρίῳ, καὶ ὁ κύριος τῷ σώματι·

6:7Already indeed there is plainly a fault among you, that you have lawsuits one with another. Why do you not rather take wrong? Why do you not rather suffer yourselves to be defrauded? [n. 277]

6:8But you do wrong and defraud: and that to your brethren. [n. 281]

6:9Know you not that the unjust shall not possess the kingdom of God? Do not err: neither fornicators nor idolaters nor adulterers: nor the effeminate nor those who lie with men [n. 282]

6:10Nor thieves nor the covetous nor drunkards nor revilers nor extortioners shall possess the kingdom of God.

6:11And such some of you were. But you are washed: but you are sanctified: but you are justified: in the name of our Lord Jesus Christ and the Spirit of our God. [n. 286]

6:12All things are lawful for me: but all things are not expedient. All things are lawful for me: but I will not be brought under the power of any. [n. 290]

6:13Meat for the belly and the belly for the meats: but God shall destroy both it and them. [n. 295] But the body is not for fornication, but for the Lord: and the Lord for the body. [n. 297]

---

277. Postquam Apostolus reprehendit Corinthios de hoc quod coram infidelibus iudicibus litigabant, hic reprehendit eos quantum ad ipsa iudicia. Et

circa hoc duo facit.

Primo ponit in quo peccabant circa iudicia;

secundo manifestat quod dixerat, ibi **an nescitis**, et cetera.

Circa primum duo facit.

Primo reprehendit in eis circa iudicia id quod est licitum, sed non expediens;

secundo id quod est penitus illicitum, ibi **sed et vos**, et cetera.

Circa primum duo facit:

primo ponit reprehensionem;

277. After rebuking the Corinthians for bringing their lawsuits before unbelieving judges, the Apostle now rebukes them for the judgments themselves.

In regard to this he does two things.

First, he states how they sinned in regard to judgments;

second, he clarifies what he had said, at **know you not that the unjust**.

In regard to the first he does two things:

first, he rebukes them in something lawful in regard to judgment, but not expedient;

second, in what is utterly unlawful, at **but you do wrong**.

In regard to the first he does two things.

first, he rebukes them;

secundo removet excusationem, ibi *quare non magis*, et cetera.

278. Dicit ergo primo: dictum est, quod frater cum fratre in iudicio contendit, quod non solum malum est quod apud infideles contenditis, sed *iam quidem*, post conversionem vestram, *omnino delictum est in vobis*, id est, ad delictum vobis reputatur, *quod iudicia habetis inter vos*, inter quos scilicet debet esse pax: quia, ut dicitur II Tim. II, 24, *servum Domini non oportet litigare, sed mansuetum esse ad omnes*.

279. Apparet autem ex hoc, ut dicit hic Glossa Augustini, quod *peccatum est iudicium habere contra aliquem*, sed hoc videtur esse falsum: quia si peccatum est iudicium habere, videtur sequi quod etiam peccatum sit iudices constituere, cum hoc sit occasionem dare iudicium habentibus, cum tamen dicatur Deut. I, 16: *audite illos, et quod iustum est iudicate*, et postea subditur, *quia Dei iudicium est*.

Solvitur enim in Glossa quod infirmis permittitur in iudicio sua repetere, non autem perfectis: quibus licet sua repetere, sed non in iudicio.

Est autem sciendum hic, quod aliquid est perfectis illicitum, aliquid autem omnibus. Perfecti quidem proprium non habent, secundum illud Matth. XIX, 21: *si vis perfectus esse, vade et vende omnia quae habes, et da pauperibus, et veni, sequere me*; et ideo non licet eis in iudicio repetere quasi propria, cum eis non liceat habere proprium, licet tamen eis in iudicio repetere ea quae sunt communia. Non enim hoc faciendo peccant, sed magis merentur.

Est enim opus caritatis defendere vel recuperare res pauperum, secundum illud Ps. LXXXI, 4: *eripite pauperem, et egenum de manu peccatoris liberate*.

Sed iudicium adversus aliquem est illicitum omnibus quantum ad tria. Primo quidem quantum ad causam ex qua aliquis iudicium habet, puta ex cupiditate et avaritia. Unde, Lc. XII, 13, cum quidam de turba Domino dixisset: *dic fratri meo ut dividat mecum haereditatem*, Dominus dixit: *quis me constituit iudicem ad dividendum inter vos*? Postea subdit: *videte et cavete ab omni avaritia*.

Secundo quantum ad modum iudicii, quia scilicet cum contentione et detrimento pacis iudicium prosequuntur; ut enim dicitur Iac. c. III, 16, *ubi zelus et contentio, ibi inconstantia et omne opus pravum*. Et hoc videtur Apostolus in eis reprehendere, ut patet ex hoc quod supra dixit: *frater cum fratre in iudicio contendit*.

Tertio ex perversitate iudicii, puta cum aliquis iniuste et fraudulenter in iudicio procedit, secundum illud Is. X, 2: *ut opprimerent pauperem, et vim facerent causae humilium populi mei*. Et hoc etiam Apostolus in eis

second, he rejects an excuse, at *why do you not rather take wrong*.

278. First, therefore, he says: it has been stated that brother contends with brother in judgment. It is not only bad that you contend before unbelievers, but *already indeed*, after your conversion, *there is plainly a fault among you*, i.e., it is regarded as a failing, *that you have lawsuits one with another*, between whom there should be peace, because *the Lord's servant must not be quarrelsome but kindly to everyone* (2 Tim 2:24).

279. It appears from this, as a Gloss of Augustine says, *that it is a sin to have a lawsuit against anyone*; but this seems to be false. For if it is a sin to have a lawsuit, it seems to follow that it is also a sin to appoint judges, since this is tantamount to giving an occasion to those having lawsuits, whereas it is said: *hear the cases between your brethren and judge righteously* (Deut 1:16).

For it is answered in a Gloss that the weak are permitted to seek their rights in a lawsuit, but not the perfect, who can lawfully seek their rights but not in a lawsuit.

But it should be noted that one thing is lawful for the perfect and another thing for all others. The perfect, indeed, do not have anything they can call their own: *if you would be perfect, go see what you possess and you will have treasure in heaven; and come, follow me* (Matt 19:21). Consequently, it is not lawful for them to seek in a lawsuit anything that can be considered their own, since it is not lawful for them to possess anything as their own, although they may seek common property in a lawsuit. For they do not sin in doing this, but rather they merit.

For it is a work of charity to defend or recover the property of the poor, as it says in a psalm: *rescue the weak and the needy, deliver them from the hand of the wicked* (Ps 82:4).

But a lawsuit against anyone is unlawful for four reasons. First, as to its cause on account of which one brings a lawsuit, say from covetousness and greed. Hence, when someone had said to the Lord: *bid my brother divide the inheritance with me*, the Lord said: *who made me judge or divider over you*; then he added: *take heed and beware of covetousness* (Luke 12:13ff.).

Second, in regard to the way a lawsuit is conducted, because it is conducted with strife and harm to peace: for as it is said: *where jealousy and selfish ambition exist, there will be disorder and every vile practice* (Jas 3:16). And this is what the Apostle seems to rebuke them for, as is clear from what he had said above: *but brother goes to law with brother* (1 Cor 6:6).

Third, on account of the perversity of the judgment, say when someone proceeds unjustly and fraudulently in a lawsuit, as it is said: *you turn aside the needy from justice and rob the poor of my people of their right* (Isa 10:2). This, too,

reprehendit, ut patet per id quod subdit: *sed vos iniuriam facitis*.

Quarto propter scandalum quod sequitur. Unde et Dominus mandat, Matth. V, 40: *qui vult tecum in iudicio contendere, et tunicam tuam tollere, dimitte ei et pallium.*

Ex caritate vero, sua in iudicio repetere licitum est. Unde Gregorius dicit in *Moralibus*: *cum curam rerum nobis necessitas imponit, quidam dum ea repetunt, solummodo sunt tolerandi: quidam vero servata caritate sunt prohibendi, scilicet ne rapientes non sua, semetipsos perdant.*

280. Deinde cum dicit *quare non magis*, etc., tollit excusationem.

Possent enim dicere: necessitas nos inducit ad iudicia habenda, ut scilicet resistamus iniuriis et fraudibus aliorum; sed hoc excludit, subdens, quantum ad primum, *quare non magis iniuriam*, scilicet manifestam, *accipitis*, scilicet patienter sustinendo, secundum illud quod Dominus dicit, Matth. V, 39: *si quis te percusserit in maxillam, praebe ei et alteram.*

Quantum vero ad secundum subdit *quare non magis fraudem patimini*, id est, dolosam seductionem, secundum illud Matth. V, 41: *si quis te angariaverit mille passus, vade cum illo et alia duo.* Sed, sicut Augustinus dicit in libro *de Sermone Domini in monte*, haec praecepta Domini non sunt semper observanda in executione operis, sed semper sunt habenda in praeparatione animi, ut scilicet simus parati hoc facere vel sustinere potius, quam aliquid agere contra caritatem fraternam.

281. Deinde cum dicit *sed vos*, etc., reprehendit in eis id quod est omnino illicitum.

Et primo arguit in eis manifestam iniustitiam, cum dicit *sed vos iniuriam facitis*, scilicet manifeste loquendo contra iustitiam aliorum, vel in iudicio, vel extra iudicium. Eccli. IX, 17: *non placeat tibi iniuria iniustorum.* Secundo dolosam deceptionem, cum subdit *et fraudatis*, Prov. XII, 5: *consilia impiorum fraudulenta.* Tertio aggravat utrumque, cum subdit *et hoc fratribus*, id est, fidelibus, ad quos debemus bonum maxime operari, secundum illud Gal. ult.: *dum tempus habemus, operemur bonum ad omnes; maxime autem ad domesticos fidei.* Et ideo contra quosdam dicitur Ier. IX, 4: *omnis frater supplantans, supplantabit, et omnis amicus fraudulenter incedet.*

282. Deinde, cum dicit *an nescitis*, etc., manifestat quod dixerat. Et

primo, quantum ad id quod est omnino illicitum;

secundo, quantum ad id quod est licitum, sed non expediens, ibi *omnia mihi licent*.

Circa primum duo facit.

Primo movet quaestionem;

secundo determinat eam, ibi *nolite errare*, et cetera.

the Apostle reprehends in them, as he shows from what he adds, *but you do wrong and defraud*.

Fourth, on account of the scandal which follows. Hence the Lord commands: *if anyone would sue you and take your coat, let him have your cloak as well* (Matt 5:40).

But out of charity it is lawful to seek your own in a lawsuit. Hence Gregory in *Morals*: *when necessity forces us to have charge of things, some are merely to be tolerated, when they demand things, but others to be forestalled, as long as charity is preserved, from snatching what is not theirs and thus destroying themselves.*

280. Then when he says, *why do you not rather take wrong*, he takes away their excuse.

For they could say a necessity forces us to have lawsuits in order to resist harm and dishonesty from other men. But he rejects this, as to the first, saying: *why do you not rather take wrong* by enduring it with patience, as the Lord says: *if anyone strikes you on the right cheek, turn to him the other also* (Matt 5:31).

As to the second he says, *why do you not rather suffer yourselves to be defrauded*, i.e., suffer the crafty wheedling, for it says: *if anyone forces you to go one mile, go with him another two miles* (Matt 5:41). But, as Augustine says in *The Lord's Sermon on the Mount*, these precepts of the Lord are not always to be observed in the performance of a work, but we should be prepared to obey them, so that we would be always prepared to do this or endure that, rather than do anything against fraternal charity.

281. Then when he says, *but you do wrong*, he rebukes them for something altogether illicit.

First, he accuses them of obvious injustice, when he says: *but you do wrong*, namely, by speaking openly against the justice of others either in court or outside: *do not delight in what pleases the unjust* (Sir 9:12). Second, for crafty deception when he says: *and defraud*: *the counsels of the wicked are treacherous* (Prov 12:5). Third, he adds to the weight of both, when he adds, *and that to your own brethren*, i.e., believers to whom you should do good: *as we have opportunity, let us do good to all men, but especially to those who are of the household of the faith* (Gal 6:10). Therefore, it is said against some: *every brother is a supplanter, and every neighbor goes about as a slanderer* (Jer 9:4).

282. Then when he says, *know you not*, he clarifies what he had said.

First, as to what is altogether unlawful;

second as to what is unlawful but not expedient, at *all things are lawful for me*.

In regard to the first he does two things.

First, he presents a question;

second, he answers it, at *do not err*.

283. Dicit ergo primo: dixi quod vos iniuriam facitis, et defraudatis, quod est iniquitatem committere, sed *an nescitis quod iniqui regnum Dei non possidebunt?* Quasi dicat: videmini haec nescire, dum ab iniquitate non receditis, cum tamen in Ps. VI, 9 et Matth. VII, 23 dicatur: *discedite a me, omnes qui operamini iniquitatem.*

284. Deinde, cum dicit *nolite errare*, etc., determinat veritatem. Et

primo ostendit periculum quod imminet iniquis;

secundo ostendit quomodo ipsi hoc periculum evaserunt, ut timeant iterum in ipsum incidere, ibi *et hoc quidem aliquando fuistis*, et cetera.

285. Dicit ergo primo: *nolite errare*, quod signanter dicit, quia circa impunitatem peccatorum aliqui multipliciter errabant, secundum illud Sap. II, 21: *et cogitaverunt, et erraverunt.* Quidam enim philosophi erraverunt credentes Deum non habere curam rerum humanarum, secundum illud Soph. I, 12: *non faciet Dominus bene, et non faciet Dominus male.* Quidam vero credentes solam fidem sufficientem esse ad salutem, secundum illud Io. XI, 26: *qui credit in me, non morietur in aeternum.* Quidam vero credentes per sola Christi sacramenta salvari, propter id quod dicitur Mc. ult.: *qui crediderit et baptizatus fuerit, salvus erit*, et Io. c. VI, 55: *qui manducat meam carnem, et bibit meum sanguinem, habet vitam aeternam.* Quidam vero propter sola opera misericordiae se impune peccare arbitrantur, propter illud quod dicitur Lc. XI, 41: *date eleemosynam, et ecce omnia munda sunt vobis.*

Nec intelligunt quod haec omnia sine caritate non prosunt, secundum illud quod dicitur infra XIII, 2 s.: *si habuero omnem fidem, et distribuero in cibos pauperum omnes facultates meas, caritatem autem non habuero, nihil mihi prodest.* Et ideo subdit quod peccata contraria caritati a regno Dei excludunt, in quod sola caritas introducit, dicens *neque fornicarii, neque idolis servientes, neque adulteri* (de quibus dicitur Hebr. ult.: *fornicatores et adulteros iudicabit Deus*), *neque molles*, id est, mares muliebria patientes, *neque masculorum concubitores*, quantum ad agentes in illo vitio, de quibus dicitur Gen. XIII, 13: *homines Sodomitae pessimi erant et peccatores coram Domino nimis*, *neque avari, neque fures* (de quibus dicitur Zach. V, 3: *omnis fur, sicut scriptum est, iudicabitur*), *neque ebriosi, neque maledici, neque rapaces regnum Dei possidebunt.* Dicitur enim Is. XXXV, 8: *Via Sancta vocabitur, non transibit per eam pollutus.* Et Apoc. XXI, 27: *non intrabit in illam aliquid coinquinatum, faciens abominationem.*

Et est advertendum quod hic enumerat eadem vitia quae in praecedenti capitulo posuerat. Addit autem quaedam in genere luxuriae, scilicet adulterium et vitium contra naturam, in genere autem iniustitiae, furtum.

283. First, therefore, he says: I have stated that you do wrong and defraud, which is to commit sin, *know you not that the unjust shall not possess the kingdom of God?* As if to say: you seem not to know this, as long as you do not give up your sin; whereas it it says in a psalm: *depart from me all you workers of evil* (Psalm 6:8).

284. Then when he says, *do not err*, he determines the truth.

First he shows the impious their danger;

second he shows how they were snatched from this peril and feared falling into it again, at *and such some of you were*.

285. First, therefore, he says: *do not err*, which is said with a purpose, because some have been deceived frequently about sinning with impunity: *thus they reasoned, but they were led astray* (Wis 2:21). For certain philosophers erred in believing that God does not have charge of human affairs: *the Lord will not do good, nor will he do ill* (Zeph 1:12). But others, believing that faith alone is sufficient for salvation: *whoever lives and believes in me shall never die* (John 11:26); others believing that they will be saved just by Christ's sacraments, on account of which it says in Mark: *he who believes and is baptized will be saved* (Mark 16:16), and in John: *he who eats my flesh and drinks my blood will have eternal life* (John 6:55). Still others suppose that they can sin with impunity on account of the works of mercy they perform, inasmuch as it says in Luke: *give for alms those things which are within you; and behold, everything is clean for you* (Luke 11:40).

But they do not understand that all these things are of no benefit without charity, for it says below: *if I should have all faith . . . and if I should distribute all my goods to feed the poor . . . and have not charity, it profits me nothing* (1 Cor 13:2–3). Therefore, he continues: sins contrary to charity exclude one from the kingdom of God, which charity alone permits one to enter, saying, *neither fornicators nor idolaters nor adulterers*, concerning whom it is said: *God will judge fornicators and adulterers* (Heb 13:4); *nor the effeminate*, i.e., males suffering in a womanly manner, *nor those who lie with men*, of which it is said: *the men of Sodom were wicked, great sinners against the Lord* (Gen 13:13); *nor theives nor the covetous*: *everyone that steals shall be cut off henceforth* (Zech 5:3); *nor drunkards nor revilers nor extortioners shall possess the kingdom of God.* For it says in Isaiah: *and a highway shall be there, and it shall be called the Holy Way; the unclean shall not pass over it* (Isa 35:8); and in Revelation: *but nothing unclean shall enter it, nor anyone who practices abominations* (Rev 21:27).

It should be noted that the vices mentioned here are the same as those mentioned in the previous chapter. But he added some in the category of lust, namely, adultery, and sins against nature, and thievery in the category of injustice.

286. Deinde, cum dicit *et haec quidem*, etc., ostendit quomodo praedictum periculum evaserunt.

Et primo commemorat statum praeteritum, dicens *et quidem aliquando fuistis*, scilicet fornicarii et idolis servientes, etc., et ideo specialiter haec vitia commemorat, quia in eis abundaverunt, secundum illud Eph. V, 8: *eratis enim aliquando tenebrae, nunc autem lux in Domino.*

287. Secundo ostendit quomodo ab his intus fuerunt liberati, dicens *sed abluti estis*, scilicet virtute sanguinis Christi in baptismo, secundum illud Apoc. I, 5: *lavit nos a peccatis nostris in sanguine suo. Sed sanctificati estis* virtute sanguinis Christi per gratiam consecrati, secundum illud Hebr. ult.: *Iesus ut sanctificaret per suum sanguinem populum, extra portam passus est. Sed iustificati estis*, ad statum iustitiae et virtutis, secundum illud Rom. VIII, 30: *quos vocavit, hos et iustificavit.*

288. Subditur autem horum beneficiorum causa. Et primo ex parte humanitatis, Christi, cum dicit *in nomine Domini nostri Iesu Christi*, id est, in fide et invocatione nominis Christi, secundum illud Act. IV, 12: *non est aliud nomen datum sub caelo hominibus, in quo oporteat nos salvos fieri.* Secundo ex parte divinitatis, cum subdit *et in Spiritu Dei nostri*, secundum illud Ez. XXXVII, v. 5: *ecce ego mittam in vos Spiritum, et vivetis.* Quia igitur tam potenti virtute liberati estis, ad eadem redire non debetis.

289. Deinde, cum dicit *omnia mihi licent*, etc., manifestat id quod dixerat de prohibitione iudicii, ostendens quo sensu id reprehenderit, quia scilicet non reprehendit illud quasi omnino illicitum, sed quasi non expediens et nocivum.

Et circa hoc duo facit.

Primo proponit quod intendit;

secundo rationem assignat, ibi *esca ventri*, et cetera.

290. Circa primum duo facit.

Primo proponit quod reprehenderat esse licitum, sed non expediens, dicens *omnia mihi licent*. Dicuntur autem illa licita quae homo facere non prohibetur; est autem duplex prohibitio, una coactionis, alia praecepti, et secundum hoc quidam intellexerunt illa licere a quibus non prohibetur aliqua necessitate cogente; et ideo, quia arbitrium hominis naturaliter liberum est a coactione, intellexerunt Apostolum eo sensu dicere: *omnia mihi licent*, quia scilicet libero arbitrio hominis subiacent, sive sint bona, sive sint mala, secundum illud Eccli. XV, 18: *ante hominem bonum et malum, vita et mors, quodcumque voluerit, dabitur ei.*

Sed hic modus loquendi alienus est a Scriptura Sacra, in qua dicitur non licere ea quae divina lege prohibentur, secundum illud Matth. XIV, 4: *non licet tibi habere uxorem fratris tui.* Et ideo quod hic Apostolus dicit *omnia*

286. Then when he says, *and such some of you were*, he shows how they escaped from the above-mentioned danger.

First, he reminds them of their past state, saying, *and such some of you were*, namely, fornicators and idolaters, etc. He makes particular mention of these vices, because they abounded in them, as it is said: *for once you were darkness, but now you are light in the Lord* (Eph 5:8).

287. Second, he shows how they were freed of them inwardly, saying, *but you are washed* by the power of Christ's blood in baptism: *he freed us from our sins in his blood* (Rev 1:5). *But you are sanctified* by the power of Christ's blood and consecrated in grace, as it is said: *so Jesus also suffered outside the gate, in order to sanctify the people through his own blood* (Heb 3:12). *But you are justified*, i.e., raised to the state of justice, according to Romans: *those whom he called he also justified* (Rom 8:30).

288. Then he mentions the cause of these blessings: first, on the part of the humanity of Christ when he says: *in the name of our Lord Jesus Christ*, i.e., in believing and calling on that name: *there is no other name under heaven given among men by which they must be saved* (Acts 4:12). Second, on the part of the divinity when he adds, *and the Spirit of our God*: *behold, I shall cause breath to enter you and you shall live* (Ezek 37:3). Therefore, since you have been freed by such great power, you should not return to the same former ways.

289. Then when he says, *all things are lawful for me*, he clarifies what he had said about forbidding lawsuits, and shows in what sense he rejects them, namely, he does not reject them as altogether unlawful, but as not expedient and as harmful.

In regard to this he does two things.

First, he states his proposition;

second, he assigns a reason, at *meat for the belly*.

290. As to the first he does two things.

First, he states that what he rejects is lawful but not expedient, saying, *all things are lawful for me*. Now those things are lawful which a man is not forbidden to do. But prohibitions are of two kinds: one is by force and the other by precept. According to this, some have understood that something is lawful from which they are not prohibited by any necessitating force; because man's decision is naturally free of force, they understand the Apostle to mean it in that sense when he said: *all things are lawful for me*, namely, that all things are subject to man's free choice, be they good or evil, according to what is said in Sirach: *before a man is life and death, good and evil, that which he chooses will be given to him* (Sir 15:17).

But this way of speaking is alien to Sacred Scripture, in which it says that things forbidden by the divine law are not lawful: *it is not lawful for you to have your brother's wife* (Matt 14:4). Consequently, what the Apostle says here, *all*

mihi licent, non potest absolute intelligi, sed ut sit accomoda distributio sub hoc sensu: omnia mihi licent, quae scilicet divina lege non prohibentur.

291. Et potest hoc ad tria referri, primo quidem ad id quod dixerat de iudiciis, quia scilicet unicuique licet omnia sua iudicio repetere, cum non sit lege divina prohibitum. Alio modo potest referri ad id quod infra VIII, 8 dicturus est de indifferenti usu ciborum, ut sit sensus: licitum est mihi omnes cibos comedere, secundum illud Tit. I, v. 15: *omnia munda mundis*. Tertio potest referri ad id quod dicturus est infra IX, 4 ss., de sumptibus accipiendis, ut sit sensus: **omnia mihi licent**, scilicet accipere ad necessitatem vitae, sicut coapostolis meis.

292. Subdit autem **sed non omnia expediunt**. Dicitur autem illud expedire, quod est sine impedimento finem consequendi. Contingit autem quod aliquid non totaliter excludit finem, sed impedimentum aliquod affert, sicut matrimonium non excludit hominem a regno Dei, impedimentum tamen affert, quia scilicet, ut infra VII, 34 dicit **quae sub viro est mulier, cogitat quomodo placeat viro**. Unde, Matth. XIX, 10, discipuli dicunt: *si ita est causa hominis cum uxore sua, non expedit nubere*. Sic ergo fornicari nec licet, nec expedit, quia totaliter excludit finem, qui est vita aeterna; matrimonium autem est licitum, sed non expediens.

Secundum igitur hunc modum, sua in iudicio repetere, indifferenter omnibus cibis uti, sumptus accipere ab his quibus praedicatur, est quidem licitum, quia non est contra iustitiam, nec aliqua prohibetur lege; non tamen est expediens, vel quia impeditur pax ad proximum, vel infirmis scandalum aliquod generatur, vel aliqua maledicendi occasio praebetur; unde Eccli. XXXVII, 31: *non omnia omnibus expediunt*.

293. Alio modo potest intelligi non absolute, sed sub conditione, ut sit sensus: dixi quod **neque fornicarii**, etc., **regnum Dei possidebunt**, et ideo non licent, quia finem excludunt; sed si omnia licerent mihi, **non omnia expediunt**, quia per ea praestatur impedimentum vitae humanae. Unde in persona impiorum dicitur Sap. V, 7: *lassati sumus in via iniquitatis et perditionis, et ambulavimus vias difficiles*.

294. Secundo ostendit esse nocivum id quod supra reprehendit, dicens **omnia mihi licent**, ut supra expositum est, **sed** tamen **ego sub nullius redigar potestate**, scilicet hominis. Ille enim qui utitur eo quod non expedit, sive licitum, sive illicitum, quodammodo redigitur sub potestate rei alicuius, vel hominis. Rei quidem, quia qui nimis rem aliquam amat, quodammodo servus illius rei efficitur, secundum illud Rom. ult.: *huiusmodi non Christo Domino serviunt, sed suo ventri*. Hominis autem, quia dum aliquis facit quod non expedit, quodammodo subiicitur iudicio aliorum, et specialiter ille qui sua in

things are lawful for me, must not be understood absolutely but in this sense: all things are lawful for me which are not forbidden by the divine law.

291. This can be referred to three things: first, to what he had said about lawsuits, namely, that it is lawful for anyone to obtain his property through lawsuits, since it is not forbidden by divine law. Second, it can be referred to what he will say below about indiscriminate use of food (1 Cor 8:8), so that the sense would be: it is lawful for me to eat all foods: *to the clean all things are clean* (Titus 1:15). Third, it can be referred to what he will say below about taking food and drink (1 Cor 9:4), so that the sense is this: *all things are lawful for me*, namely, to take what is necessary for life, just as it is for my co-apostles.

292. But he adds, **but all things are not expedient**. That is said to be expedient, which is without a hindrance to attaining an end. Now it happens that something does not entirely exclude the end, but it offers some hindrance, as marriage does not exclude a person from the kingdom of God, but it offers a hindrance, namely, because as it says below: *she who is married thinks on the things of the world: how she may please her husband* (1 Cor 7:34). Hence, *if the case of a man with his wife be so, it is not expedient to marry* (Matt 19:10). So fornication is neither lawful nor expedient, because it totally excludes one from the end, which is eternal life; but marriage is lawful but not expedient.

Therefore, according to this mode, to get back one's own in a lawsuit or to use all foods without distinction or to take one's food from those to whom he preaches are all lawful, because they are not against justice or forbidden by any law; yet it is not expedient, either because peace towards one's neighbor is endangered, or scandal of the weak is produced, or an occasion for reviling is offered: *not everything is good for everyone* (Sir 37:28).

293. In another way it can be understood not absolutely but conditionally, so that the sense is this: I have said that **neither fornicators nor idolaters . . . shall possess the kingdom of God**. Therefore they are not lawful, because they exclude the end; but if all things were licit for me, **all things are not expedient**, because they pose a hindrance to eternal life. Hence in the person of the wicked: *we took our fill of the power of lawlessness and destruction, and we journeyed through trackless deserts* (Wis 5:7).

294. Second, he shows that what he rejected above is harmful, saying, **all things are lawful for me: but I will not be brought under the power of any**, namely, man. For one who uses something not expedient, whether it be lawful or unlawful, is somehow put under the power of that man or thing. Of a thing, indeed, because one who loves a thing too much is made its slave, as it is said: *such persons do not serve the Lord Jesus Christ, but their own appetites* (Rom 16:18). But of a man, because as long as one does something not expedient, he is in thrall to the judgment of others; and particularly one who tries to get back his own in a lawsuit is

iudicio repetit, subiicitur potestati iudicis. Infra X, 29: *ut quid enim libertas mea iudicatur ab aliena conscientia?*

295. Deinde, cum dicit *esca ventri*, etc., assignat rationem eius quod dixerat.

Et primo quare omnia licent, dicens *esca ventri*, scilicet debetur, ut scilicet in ventre decocta in nutrimentum totius corporis cedat. *Et venter escis*, scilicet recipiendis et decoquendis deservit. Quia igitur ex Dei ordinatione venter est sollicitus ad escas recipiendas, et escae ad hoc deputatae sunt, quod in ventre ponantur, secundum illud Gen. I, v. 29 s.: *ecce dedi vobis omnem escam et cunctis animantibus, ut habeant ad vescendum*, non est illicitum quod homo res suas repetat, vel praedicator stipendia accipiat propter necessitatem escarum, vel ut etiam homo omnibus escis utatur.

296. Secundo ibi *Deus autem*, etc., assignat rationem quare omnia non expediunt. Non enim expedit, quod homo patiatur aliquod detrimentum in eo quod numquam corrumpitur, scilicet in regno caelesti, propter id quod corrumpitur; et hoc accidit de esca et de ventre. Cessabit enim post hanc vitam escarum usus et ventris, quia corpora resurgentium conservabuntur absque cibo, Deo id faciente. Et hoc est quod dicit *Deus autem destruet*, id est, cessare faciet, *hunc*, scilicet ventrem, non quidem quantum ad essentiam, sed quantum ad effectum, quem nunc habet; *et has*, scilicet escas, quantum pertinent ad usum hominis, quia in resurrectione homines erunt sicut angeli in caelo, ut dicitur Matth. XXII, 30.

under the power of the judge: *why is my liberty judged by another man's conscience?* (1 Cor 10:29)

295. Then when he says, *meat for the belly*, he assigns a reason for what he has said.

First, why all things are lawful, saying, *meat for the belly*, in order, namely, that after the stomach has done its work, it may nourish the entire body; *and the belly for the meats*, i.e., it serves to receive food and work on it. Therefore, since by God's ordinance the stomach is desirous of receiving food, and food was made to be put in the stomach: *behold, I have given you every plant yielding seed and every tree with seed in its fruit; you shall have them for food* (Gen 1:29), it is not unlawful for a man to get property back, or a preacher to get wages for necessary food, or even that a man eat all foods without distinction.

296. Second, when he says, *but God shall destroy both*, he gives the reason why all things are not expedient. For it is not expedient that a person suffer a loss in that which is never corrupted, namely, the heavenly kingdom, for the sake of something corrupted; and this happens in regard to food and stomach. After this life the use of good and of the stomach will cease, because the bodies of those who rise will be conserved without food by God's power. And that is what he says: *but God shall destroy*, i.e., will make cease *both it*, namely, the stomach, not as to its essence but as to its effect which it has now, *and them*, namely, foods, so far as they pertain to man's use, because in the resurrection men will be as the angels in heaven (Matt 22:30).

Lecture 3

6:13 Esca ventri, et venter escis: Deus autem et hunc et has destruet: [n. 295] corpus autem non fornicationi, sed Domino: et Dominus corpori. [n. 297]

6:14 Deus vero et Dominum suscitavit: et nos suscitabit per virtutem suam. [n. 300]

6:15 Nescitis quoniam corpora vestra membra sunt Christi? Tollens ergo membra Christi, faciam membra meretricis? Absit. [n. 302]

6:16 An nescitis quoniam qui adhaeret meretrici, unum corpus efficitur? *Erunt* enim (inquit) *duo in carne una*. [n. 304]

6:17 Qui autem adhaeret Domino, unus spiritus est. [n. 305]

6:18 Fugite fornicationem. Omne peccatum, quodcumque fecerit homo, extra corpus est: qui autem fornicatur, in corpus suum peccat. [n. 306]

6:19 An nescitis quoniam membra vestra, templum sunt Spiritus Sancti, qui in vobis est, quem habetis a Deo, [n. 309] et non estis vestri? [n. 310]

6:20 Empti enim estis pretio magno. Glorificate, et portate Deum in corpore vestro.

6:13τὰ βρώματα τῇ κοιλίᾳ, καὶ ἡ κοιλία τοῖς βρώμασιν· ὁ δὲ θεὸς καὶ ταύτην καὶ ταῦτα καταργήσει. τὸ δὲ σῶμα οὐ τῇ πορνείᾳ ἀλλὰ τῷ κυρίῳ, καὶ ὁ κύριος τῷ σώματι·

6:14ὁ δὲ θεὸς καὶ τὸν κύριον ἤγειρεν καὶ ἡμᾶς ἐξεγερεῖ διὰ τῆς δυνάμεως αὐτοῦ.

6:15οὐκ οἴδατε ὅτι τὰ σώματα ὑμῶν μέλη Χριστοῦ ἐστιν; ἄρας οὖν τὰ μέλη τοῦ Χριστοῦ ποιήσω πόρνης μέλη; μὴ γένοιτο.

6:16[ἢ] οὐκ οἴδατε ὅτι ὁ κολλώμενος τῇ πόρνῃ ἓν σῶμά ἐστιν; Ἔσονται γάρ, φησίν, οἱ δύο εἰς σάρκα μίαν.

6:17ὁ δὲ κολλώμενος τῷ κυρίῳ ἓν πνεῦμά ἐστιν.

6:18φεύγετε τὴν πορνείαν· πᾶν ἁμάρτημα ὃ ἐὰν ποιήσῃ ἄνθρωπος ἐκτὸς τοῦ σώματός ἐστιν, ὁ δὲ πορνεύων εἰς τὸ ἴδιον σῶμα ἁμαρτάνει.

6:19ἢ οὐκ οἴδατε ὅτι τὸ σῶμα ὑμῶν ναὸς τοῦ ἐν ὑμῖν ἁγίου πνεύματός ἐστιν, οὗ ἔχετε ἀπὸ θεοῦ, καὶ οὐκ ἐστὲ ἑαυτῶν;

6:20ἠγοράσθητε γὰρ τιμῆς· δοξάσατε δὴ τὸν θεὸν ἐν τῷ σώματι ὑμῶν.

6:13 Meat for the belly and the belly for the meats: but God shall destroy both it and them. [n. 295] But the body is not for fornication, but for the Lord: and the Lord for the body. [n. 297]

6:14 Now God has raised up the Lord and will raise us up also by his power. [n. 300]

6:15 Know you not that your bodies are the members of Christ? Shall I then take the members of Christ and make them the members of a harlot? Never! [n. 302]

6:16 Or know you not that he who is joined to a harlot is made one body? For *they shall be*, he says, *two in one flesh*. [n. 304]

6:17 But he who is joined to the Lord is one spirit. [n. 305]

6:18 Flee fornication. Every sin that a man does is without the body: but he who commits fornication sins against his own body. [n. 306]

6:19 Or know you not that your members are the temple of the Holy Spirit, who is in you, whom you have from God: [n. 309] and you are not your own? [n. 310]

6:20 For you are bought with a great price. Glorify and bear God in your body.

---

297. Supra Apostolus tripliciter reprehendit Corinthios circa iudicia, nunc autem redit ad reprehendendum peccatum fornicarii, cuius supra V, 1 mentionem fecerat, et in cuius iudicio Corinthii negligentes erant; improbat autem fornicationem quatuor rationibus, quarum

prima sumitur ex divina ordinatione;

secunda ex unione ad Christum, ibi *an nescitis quoniam corpora*, etc.;

tertia ex corporis inquinatione, ibi *fugite fornicationem*;

quarta ex gratiae dignitate, ibi *an nescitis*, et cetera.

298. Circa primum duo facit.

Primo ponit divinam ordinationem;

secundo ordinationis finem, ibi *Deus enim*, et cetera.

297. After rebuking the Corinthians about lawsuits, the Apostle now returns to reprehending the sin of fornication, which he mentioned above (1 Cor 5:11) and in the judgment of which the Corinthians had been negligent. He condemns fornication for four reasons:

the first of which is taken from God's ordinance;

second, from one's union with Christ, at *know you not that your bodies*;

third, from bodily defilement, at *flee fornication*;

fourth, from the dignity of grace, at *or know you not that your members*.

298. In regard to the first he does two things.

First, he presents God's ordinance;

second, the end of the ordinance, at *now God has raised*.

298. Circa primum considerandum est quod aliqui argumentum suae lasciviae sumunt ex ordinatione Dei. Qui enim fornicantur, utuntur suo corpore ad usum a Deo institutum. Sed hoc excludit, dicens quod esca est ordinata ad ventrem, et venter ad escas, ***corpus autem*** hominis ***non fornicationi***, id est, non est ordinatum ad fornicandum, ***sed Domino***, id est, ad hoc est ordinatum, ut sit Domini nostri Iesu Christi, ***et Dominus corpori***, id est, Dominus Iesus Christus ad hoc datus est hominibus, ut humana corpora suae gloriae conformet, secundum illud Phil. III, 21: *reformabit corpus humilitatis nostrae, configuratum corpori claritatis suae.*

299. Sed contra hoc videtur esse quod sicut venter ordinatus est a Deo ad usum ciborum; ita quaedam membra humani corporis sunt ordinata a Deo ad usum generationis, quibus fornicatio exercetur.

Sed attendenda est differentia quantum ad duo. Primo quidem quod Apostolus supra locutus est de uno corporis membro, scilicet de ventre, hic autem loquitur de toto corpore, quod sicut non est ordinatum ad fornicandum, ita nec ad escas sumendum; sed potius usus escarum est propter corpus, corpus autem propter animam, a qua percipit vitam secundum eius conditionem. Et quia omnia ordinantur in Deum sicut in finem, ideo corpus debet esse subiectum Domino et ei dedicatum.

Et quia supra locutus est de usu escarum in communi absque inordinatione, fornicatio autem est usus inordinatus ex membro fornicatoris. Unde nec ipsa membra sunt propter fornicationem, sed propter usum generationis ordinata ratione, cui omnia membra corporis deservire debent, sicut etiam venter non propter crapulam et ebrietatem, sed propter convenientem usum ciborum.

300. Deinde, cum dicit ***Deus vero***, etc., ponit finem ordinationis praedictae.

Et primo ponit quid Deus circa Dominum fecerit, dicens ***Deus vero et Dominum***, scilicet Dominum Iesum Christum, *suscitavit* a mortuis, a quo ipse Christus petit in Ps. XL, v. 11: *tu autem, Domine, miserere mei, et resuscita me.* Deus autem est et Pater, et Filius, et Spiritus Sanctus, unde et ipse Christus, qui est Filius Dei, se suscitavit, et sua virtute resurrexit, secundum illud Ps. III, 6: *ego dormivi, et soporatus sum, et exsurrexi, quia Dominus suscepit me*; et II Cor. ult.: *si crucifixus est ex infirmitate, sed vivit ex virtute Dei.*

Secundo ponit quid circa nos facturus sit, dicens quod ***nos suscitabit Deus per virtutem suam***, per quam scilicet Christum suscitavit, secundum illud Rom. VIII, 11: *qui suscitavit Iesum Christum a mortuis, vivificabit et mortalia corpora vestra.*

301. Et est advertendum, quod supra de escis et ventre loquens, quae pertinent ad usum animalis vitae, dixit

298. In regard to the first it should be noted that some take their argument for lascivious conduct from God's ordinance. For those who fornicate use their body for a use established by God. But he excludes this, saying that food is ordained to the stomach and the stomach to food, ***but the body is not for fornication, but for the Lord***, i.e., it had been ordained to this, namely, that it be for the Lord Jesus Christ ***and the Lord for the body***, i.e., Jesus Christ was given to man in order that human bodies be conformed to his glory: *he will change our lowly body to be like his glorious body* (Phil 3:21).

299. But against this seems to be the fact that just as the stomach is ordained to the use of food, so certain members of the human body are ordained by God to be used for generation, i.e., the members by which fornication is performed.

But attention must be paid to the difference between the two. First, the Apostle spoke above about one member of the body, namely, the stomach, but here he is speaking about the entire body, which is not ordained to fornication any more than it is ordained to eating food; rather, food is used for the benefit of the body and the body exists for the sake of the soul, from which it receives life according to its condition. And because all things are ordered to God as to an end, the body should be subjected to the Lord and dedicated to him.

And because he spoke above about the eating of food in general terms without disorder, but fornication is a disordered use of the member used in fornication. Hence, the members exist not for fornication, but for generation ordained by reason, which the members of the body should serve, just as even the stomach is not for gluttony and drunkenness, but for the proper use of food.

300. Then when he says, ***now God has raised up***, he indicates the end of the above-mentioned ordination.

First, he indicates what God had done in regard to the Lord, saying, ***now God has raised up the Lord***, namely, the Lord Jesus Christ, from the dead, from whom Christ himself petitions in a psalm: *do you, O Lord, be gracious to me and raise me up* (Ps 41:10). But God is the Father and the Son and the Holy Spirit; hence Christ himself, who is the Son of God, also raised himself and arose by his own power: *I will lie down and sleep; I wake again, for the Lord sustains me* (Ps 3:5), and: *he was crucified in weakness, but lives by the power of God* (2 Cor 13:4).

Second, he indicates what he will do in regard to us saying, ***and will raise us up also by his power***, by which he also raised up Christ, as it is said: *he who raised Christ Jesus from the dead will give life to your mortal bodies* (Rom 8:11).

301. It should be noted that when speaking above about food and stomach, which pertain to the use of animal life,

eas a Deo destruendas; nunc autem loquens de corpore et Domino, facit mentionem de resurrectione, quia scilicet animali vita cessante natura corporis in melius reformabitur. Unde patet quod non est utendum corpore ad fornicationem, quae impedit futuram incorruptionem, secundum illud Gal. ult.: *qui seminat in carne, de carne et metet corruptionem.*

302. Deinde, cum dicit ***nescitis,*** etc., ponit secundam rationem, quae sumitur ex affinitate humani corporis ad Christum, quae talis est: membra hominis fornicantis sunt membra meretricis; sed membra hominis sunt membra Christi; ergo per fornicationem fiunt membra Christi membra meretricis, quod est inconveniens.

Circa quod quatuor facit. Primo ponit maiorem, dicens ***an nescitis quoniam corpora vestra sunt membra Christi?*** Quasi dicat: hoc non debetis nescire, quia quicumque estis regenerati in Christo, membra Christi estis effecti, secundum illud infra XII, 27: ***vos estis corpus Christi, et membra de membro.*** Et hoc non solum quantum ad animas quae ab eo iustificantur, sed etiam quantum ad corpora quae ab eo resuscitabuntur, ut dictum est.

303. Secundo ponit conclusionem, dicens ***tollens ergo membra Christi,*** id est, iuste subtrahens servitio Christi, cui debent deputari (secundum illud Rom. VI, 13: *exhibeatis membra vestra, arma iustitiae, Deo*), ***faciam,*** scilicet eadem, ***membra meretricis*** esse fornicando? ***Absit***: hoc enim est horrendum sacrilegium. Unde dicitur Mal. II, v. 11: *contaminavit Iudas sanctificationem Domini quam dilexit, et habuit filiam dei alieni.*

304. Tertio ponit minorem, dicens ***an nescitis quia qui adhaeret meretrici,*** scilicet fornicando, ***unum corpus efficitur?*** Scilicet per immundam commixtionem.

Et ad hoc probandum, inducit auctoritatem Genesis, dicens: ***inquit,*** enim Scriptura, scilicet Gen. II, 24: ***erunt duo,*** scilicet vir et mulier, ***in carne una,*** id est, per mixtionem carnalem una caro efficiuntur, et sic membra unius fiunt membra alterius. Sunt enim haec verba Adae de viro et uxore loquentis, quae Apostolus hic etiam ad fornicationem refert, quia secundum speciem naturae non differunt utriusque actus.

Est autem intelligendum, quod, sicut dicit Philosophus in libro *de Generatione animalium,* in masculo est principium activum generationis, in foemina est passivum. Et sicut in planta, cuius vita principaliter ordinatur ad generationem, semper est unum corpus, in quo utrumque principium unitur; ita in animalibus quae ordinantur ad altiores actus vitae, non semper est unum corpus habens haec duo principia, sed ex duobus fit unum in actu generationis. Quod quidem non est

he said that they would be destroyed by God; but now, speaking of the body and of the Lord, he makes mention of the resurrection, because when animal life ceases, the nature of the body will be transformed into something better. Hence it is clear that the body should not be used for fornication, which impedes future incorruption according to Galatians: *he who sows to his own flesh will from the flesh reap corruption* (Gal 6:8).

302. Then when he says, ***know you not that your bodies,*** he presents a second reason, which is taken from the human body's affinity to Christ, namely: the fornicating man's members are the prostitute's members, but a man's members are Christ's members. Therefore, by fornicating, Christ's members become the prostitute's members, which is unbecoming.

In regard to this he does four things: first, he presents the major, saying, ***know you not that your bodies are the members of Christ?*** As if to say: you should not be unaware of this, because all of you reborn in Christ have become members of Christ, as it says below: ***now you are the body of Christ and members of member*** (1 Cor 12:27), and this not only as to souls justified by him but also as to bodies, which will be raised up by him, as has been stated.

303. Second, he presents the conclusion, saying, ***shall I then take the members of Christ,*** i.e., remove them from the service of Christ to whom they should be dedicated, as it says in Romans: *yield your members to God as instruments of righteousness* (Rom 6:13), ***and make them the members of a harlot*** by fornicating? ***Never!*** For this is a horrible sacrilege. Hence it says: *Judah has profaned the sanctuary of the Lord which he loves and has married the daughter of a foreign god* (Mal 2:11).

304. Third he presents the minor premise, saying, ***or know you not that he who is joined to a harlot,*** namely, by fornicating, ***is made one body?*** Namely, by an unclean union.

To prove this he appeals to the authority of Genesis, saying, ***he says,*** namely in Genesis, ***they shall be . . . two*** (Gen 2:24), namely man and woman, ***in one flesh,*** i.e., by the carnal union they are made one flesh, and so the members of one become the other's members. For these are Adam's words about husband and wife, which the Apostle here relates to fornication, because there is no specific difference between the two acts.

But it should be noted that, as the Philosopher says in the book, *On the Generation of Animals,* the active principle of generation is in the male, and the passive in the female. And just as in a plant whose life is ordained chiefly to generation, there is always one body in which both principles are united, so in animals, which are ordained to higher acts of life, there is not always one body with these two principles, but one is made from two in the act of generation. In the case of humans, it is not only the man's body, because

tantum viri, quia, sicut infra cap. VII, 4 dicitur, *vir non habet potestatem sui corporis, sed mulier.*

305. Quarto probat minorem, dicens *qui autem adhaeret Domino*, etc., scilicet per fidem et caritatem, *est unus spiritus* cum illo, quia scilicet unitur ei unitate spirituali, non corporali. Unde et Rom. VIII, 9 dicitur: *si quis Spiritum Christi non habet, hic non est eius;* et Io. XVII, 21 s.: *ut sint unum in nobis, sicut nos unum sumus*, scilicet per connexionem Spiritus: et quia corpus deservit spiritui, consequens est ut etiam corpora nostra, membra eius sint, cui per Spiritum unimur, non quidem carnali coniunctione, sed spirituali.

Potest autem ex praemissis duabus rationibus una ratio conflari, ut scilicet quia corpus nostrum non est deputatum fornicationi, sed Domino, hoc scilicet modo quod membra nostra sunt membra Christi, ut postmodum exponit, non faciamus ea membra meretricis fornicando.

306. Deinde, cum dicit *fugite fornicationem*, etc., ponit tertiam rationem, quae sumitur ex corporis inquinatione.

Primo ponit conclusionem intentam, dicens *fugite fornicationem*. Ubi notandum quod caetera vitia vincuntur resistendo, quia quanto magis homo particularia considerat et tractat, tanto minus in eis invenit unde delectetur, sed magis anxietur: sed vitium fornicationis non vincitur resistendo, quia quanto magis ibi homo cogitat particulare, magis incenditur; sed vincitur fugiendo, id est, totaliter vitando cogitationes immundas, et quaslibet occasiones, ut dicitur Zach. II, 6: *fugite de terra Aquilonis, dicit Dominus.*

307. Secundo assignat rationem, dicens *omne peccatum* aliud *quodcumque fecerit homo*, et cetera. Ad cuius evidentiam sciendum quod quaedam peccata non consummantur in carnali delectatione, sed in sola spirituali, ideo spiritualia vitia dicuntur, sicut superbia, avaritia, acedia; fornicatio autem completur maxime in carnali delectatione, et secundum hoc posset intelligi quod hic dicitur *omne peccatum quodcumque fecerit homo, extra corpus est*, quia scilicet completur praeter sui corporis delectationem. *Qui autem fornicatur, in corpus suum peccat*, quia scilicet eius peccatum in carne consummatur.

308. Sed huic expositioni contrarium videtur esse, quod etiam peccatum gulae consummatur in delectatione corporis.

Ad quod posset dici quod peccatum gulae sub luxuria continetur, inquantum ad ipsam ordinatur, secundum illud Eph. V, 18: *nolite inebriari vino, in quo est luxuria.*

Sed melius potest dici, quod Apostolus non dicit *qui fornicatur* corpore suo peccat, quod congrueret primae expositioni; sed *peccat in corpus suum*, id est, contra

as it says below: *the husband also has not power of his own body: but the wife* (1 Cor 7:14).

305. Second he proves the minor premise, saying, *but he who is joined to the Lord*, namely, by faith and charity, *is one spirit* with him, namely, because he is united to him in a spiritual, not a bodily, unity. Hence it says: *anyone who does not have the Spirit of Christ does not belong to him* (Rom 8:9), and: *that they may be one in us, as we are one* (John 17:21), namely by a connection of the Spirit. And because the body serves the spirit, it follows that our bodies too are members of him to whom we are united by the Spirit, not of course, by a bodily but by a spiritual union.

From the two reasons given above one reason can be formed, namely, that because our body is not destined for fornication but for the Lord in such a way that our members are Christ's members, as he explains later, we should not make them members of a prostitute by fornicating.

306. Then when he says, *flee fornication*, he presents a third reason, which is taken from the body's contamination.

First, he presents the conclusion, saying, *flee fornication*. Here it should be noted that other vices are overcome by resisting, because the more a man considers and deals with particulars, the less will he find in them anything in which to take delight, but more to be cautious about. But the vice of fornication is not overcome by resisting, because the more a man considers the particular case the more is he inflamed; but it is overcome by fleeing, i.e., by avoiding entirely all unclean thoughts and all occasions whatsoever, for it is said: *flee from the land of the north* (Zech 2:6).

307. Second he assigns the reason, saying: *every* other *sin a man commits is outside the body.* To understand this is should be noted that some sins do not end in carnal delight, but only in spiritual, and are then called spiritual sins; for example, pride, greed and spiritual apathy. But fornication is entirely completed in carnal delight. According to this it could be understood what is said here: *every sin that a man does is without the body*, namely, because it is completed outside the pleasure of the body. *But he who commits fornication sins against his own body*, namely, because the sin is completed in the flesh.

308. But the fact that the sin of gluttony is terminated in bodily pleasure seems to be contrary to the above explanation.

A possible answer might be that the sin of gluttony is contained under lust, inasmuch as it is ordained to it, as it is said: *and do not get drunk with wine, for that is debauchery* (Eph 5:8).

But it is better to say that the Apostle is not saying that *he who commits fornication* sins with his own body, which would agree with the first explanation, but he *sins against*

corpus suum, corrumpendo et inquinando illud praeter usum rationis. Unde et Apoc. III, 4: *habes pauca nomina in Sardis, qui non inquinaverunt vestimenta sua*, id est, corpus; et Apoc. XIX, 4: *hi sunt qui cum mulieribus non sunt coinquinati.*

Vel aliter secundum Augustinum, hic in Glossa, qui fornicatur, in corpus suum peccat, quia anima eius totaliter carni in illo actu subiicitur, ita quod non possit aliud ibi cogitare. Unde in Ps. XXXI, 9 dicitur: *nolite fieri sicut equus et mulus, quibus non est intellectus.*

Vel aliter: in corpus suum peccat, id est, contra uxorem suam, quae dicitur corpus viri, contra quam non ita directe sunt alia peccata, sicut viri fornicatio. Unde et I Thess. c. IV, 4 dicitur: *ut sciat unusquisque vestrum possidere vas suum in sanctificatione*, id est, uxorem suam.

Vel secundum Augustinum potest intelligi de fornicatione spirituali, per quam anima adhaeret per amorem mundo, et recedit a Deo, secundum illud Ps. LXXII, 27: *perdes omnes qui fornicantur abs te.* Est ergo sensus ***qui fornicatur***, recedens a Deo propter amorem mundi, ***in corpus suum peccat***, id est, per corporalem concupiscentiam. Omne autem aliud peccatum, puta quod homo committit ex oblivione, vel ex ignorantia, seu negligentia, ***est extra corpus***, id est, corporalem concupiscentiam.

309. Deinde, cum dicit ***an nescitis***, etc., ponit quartam rationem, quae sumitur ex dignitate gratiae, quae quidem ex duobus consurgit, scilicet ex gratia Spiritus Sancti, et ex redemptione sanguinis Christi.

Circa hoc igitur tria facit. Primo proponit dignitatem corporis nostri, quam habet ex gratia Spiritus Sancti, dicens ***an nescitis***, quasi dicat, ignorare non debetis, ***quoniam membra vestra***, scilicet corporalia, ***templum sunt Spiritus Sancti?*** Sicut supra III, 16 dictum est: ***nescitis quia templum Dei estis.***

Et huius rationem assignat subdens ***qui in vobis est.*** Dicitur autem templum, domus Dei; quia igitur Spiritus Sanctus Deus est, conveniens est, quod in quocumque est Spiritus Sanctus, templum Dei dicatur. Est autem Spiritus Sanctus principaliter quidem in cordibus hominum, in quibus caritas Dei diffunditur per Spiritum Sanctum, ut dicitur Rom. V, 5. Sed secundario etiam est in membris corporalibus, inquantum exequuntur opera caritatis. Unde in Ps. LXXXIII, 3 dicitur: *cor meum et caro mea exultaverunt in Deum vivum.*

Et ne hanc dignitatem sibi ascriberent, subdit ***quem habetis a Deo***, non ex vobis. Unde Ioel. II, 28: *effundam de Spiritu meo super omnem carnem*; et Act. V, 23: *Spiritum suum dedit obedientibus sibi.*

his own body by corrupting and contaminating it beyond the bounds of reason. Hence: *you still have a few names in Sardis, people who have not soiled their garments* (Rev 3:4), and: *it is these who have not defiled themselves with women* (Rev 14:14).

Or in another way according to Augustine: whoever fornicates sins against his own body, because his soul is totally subjected to the flesh in that act, so that it cannot at that time think of anything else. *Be not like a horse or a mule, without understanding* (Ps 32:9).

Or in another way: he sins against his own body, i.e., against his wife, who is called the husband's body, against whom other sins are not as directly opposed as the husband's fornication. Hence it is said: *that each one of you know how to take a wife for himself in holiness and honor* (1 Thess 4:4).

Or again according to Augustine, it can be understood of spiritual fornication through which the soul clings through love to the world and recedes from God: *those who are far from you shall perish* (Ps 73:27). The sense, therefore, is that ***he who commits fornication*** and recedes from God for love of the world ***sins against his own body***, i.e., by bodily desire. But every other sin, for example, which one commits from forgetfulness or ignorance or negligence, ***is without the body***, i.e., outside of bodily desire.

309. Then when he says, ***or know you not that your members***, he presents the fourth reason, which is taken from the dignity of grace, which arises from two sources, namely, from the grace of the Holy Spirit and from the redemption of Christ's blood.

In regard to this he does three things: first, he declares the dignity of our body, which it has from the grace of the Holy Spirit, saying, ***or know you not***, as though you should not be unaware of it, ***that your members***, namely, bodily, ***are the temple of the Holy Ghost***, just as he said above: ***know you not that you are the temple of God*** (1 Cor 3:16).

Then he assigns a reason for this, saying, ***who is in you.*** God's house is called a temple. Therefore, because the Holy Spirit is God, it is correct to say that anyone in whom the Holy Spirit exists is called a temple of God. But the Holy Spirit is chiefly in the heart of men, in whom the love of God is poured out by the Holy Spirit (Rom 5:5). But secondarily, he is also in the bodily members, inasmuch as they perform acts of charity. Hence it is said: *my heart and my flesh sing for joy to the living God* (Ps 84:2).

But lest they ascribe this dignity to themselves, he adds, ***whom you have from God*** and not from yourselves. Hence: *I will pour out my Spirit on all flesh* (Joel 2:28); and: *the Holy Spirit, whom God has given to all that obey him* (Acts 5:32).

310. Secundo ponit dignitatem, quam habent corpora nostra ex redemptione sanguinis Christi, dicens *et non estis vestri* sed Iesu Christi, secundum illud Rom. XIV, 8: *sive vivimus, sive morimur, Domini sumus*; II Cor. V, 15: *qui vivit, iam non sibi vivat.*

Rationem huius assignat, dicens *empti estis pretio magno*, et ideo servi estis eius, qui vos redemit de servitute peccati. Unde infra VII, 22 dicitur: *qui liber vocatus est, servus est Christi; pretio enim empti estis*; et in Ps. XXX, 6: *redemisti me, Domine Deus veritatis.*

Dicitur autem pretium redemptionis magnum, quia non est corruptibile, sed aeternam habens virtutem, cum sit sanguis ipsius Dei aeterni. Unde I Petr. I, 18 s.: *redempti estis de vana vestra conversatione, non corruptibilibus auro vel argento, sed sanguine agni immaculati et incontaminati, Iesu Christi.*

311. Tertio infert conclusionem intentam, dicens *glorificate ergo et portate Deum in corpore vestro*. Quia enim membra vestra sunt templum Dei, in corpore vestro nihil debet apparere, nisi quod ad gloriam Dei pertinet, et hoc est glorificare Deum in corpore vestro, quia in Ps. XXVIII, 9 dicitur: *in templo eius omnes dicent gloriam.* Ex. ult. dicitur: *operuit nubes tabernaculum testimonii, et gloria Domini implevit illud.* Quia vero non estis vestri, sed estis servi Dei, debet corpus vestrum portare Deum, sicut equus vel aliud animal portat Dominum suum. Unde in Ps. LXXII, 23 dicitur: *ut iumentum factus sum apud te.* Portat autem corpus nostrum Dominum, inquantum divino ministerio deputatur. Sic ergo homo debet vitare, ne in corpus suum peccet fornicando, quod est contra gloriam Dei, et contra ministerium quod corpus nostrum debet Deo.

310. Second, he mentions the dignity our bodies have from the redemption of Christ, saying, **and you are not your own** but Jesus Christ's: *whether we live or whether we die, we are the Lord's* (Rom 14:8); *those who live no longer live for themselves* (2 Cor 5:15).

He assigns the reason for this when he says, **you are bought with a great price**; therefore, you are slaves of him who has redeemed you from the slavery of sin; hence it says below, **he who is called, being free, is the slave of Christ** (1 Cor 7:22); and: *you have redeemed me, O Lord, God of truth* (Ps 31:5).

The price of redemption is called great, because it is not corruptible, but has everlasting power, since it is the blood of the everlasting God. Hence: *you know that you were ransomed from the futile ways inherited from your fathers, not with perishable things, such as silver and gold, but with the precious blood of Christ* (1 Pet 1:18).

311. Third, he draws the intended conclusion, saying, **glorify and bear God in you body**. For since your members are a temple of God, nothing should appear in your body except what pertains to God's glory: and this is to glorify God in your body, because it is said: *in his temple all cry: glory* (Ps 29:9); and again, *then the cloud covered the tent of meeting and the glory of the Lord filled the tabernacle* (Exod 40:34). Furthermore, because you are not your own, but you are slaves of God, you should carry God as a horse or other animal carries it lord. Hence it is said: *I was like a beast towards you* (Ps 73:23). Our body carries the Lord, inasmuch as it is deputed to a divine ministry. Thus, therefore, a man should avoid sinning against his own body by fornicating, which is against the glory of God and against the ministry our body owes to God.

CHAPTER 7

Lecture 1

7:1De quibus autem scripsistis mihi: bonum est homini mulierem non tangere: [n. 312]

7:2propter fornicationem autem unusquisque suam uxorem habeat, et unaquaeque suum virum habeat. [n. 315]

7:3Uxori vir debitum reddat: similiter autem et uxor viro. [n. 320]

7:4Mulier sui corporis potestatem non habet, sed vir. Similiter autem et vir sui corporis potestatem non habet, sed mulier. [n. 322]

7:5Nolite fraudare invicem, nisi forte ex consensu ad tempus, ut vacetis orationi: et iterum revertimini in idipsum, ne tentet vos Satanas propter incontinentiam vestram. [n. 325]

7:6Hoc autem dico secundum indulgentiam, non secundum imperium. [n. 326]

7:7Volo enim omnes vos esse sicut meipsum: sed unusquisque proprium donum habet ex Deo: alius quidem sic, alius vero sic. [n. 330]

7:8Dico autem non nuptis, et viduis: bonum est illis si sic permaneant, sicut et ego. [n. 334]

7:9Quod si non se continent, nubant. Melius est enim nubere, quam uri.

7:1Περὶ δὲ ὧν ἐγράψατε, καλὸν ἀνθρώπῳ γυναικὸς μὴ ἅπτεσθαι:

7:2διὰ δὲ τὰς πορνείας ἕκαστος τὴν ἑαυτοῦ γυναῖκα ἐχέτω, καὶ ἑκάστη τὸν ἴδιον ἄνδρα ἐχέτω.

7:3τῇ γυναικὶ ὁ ἀνὴρ τὴν ὀφειλὴν ἀποδιδότω, ὁμοίως δὲ καὶ ἡ γυνὴ τῷ ἀνδρί.

7:4ἡ γυνὴ τοῦ ἰδίου σώματος οὐκ ἐξουσιάζει ἀλλὰ ὁ ἀνήρ: ὁμοίως δὲ καὶ ὁ ἀνὴρ τοῦ ἰδίου σώματος οὐκ ἐξουσιάζει ἀλλὰ ἡ γυνή.

7:5μὴ ἀποστερεῖτε ἀλλήλους, εἰ μήτι ἂν ἐκ συμφώνου πρὸς καιρὸν ἵνα σχολάσητε τῇ προσευχῇ καὶ πάλιν ἐπὶ τὸ αὐτὸ ἦτε, ἵνα μὴ πειράζῃ ὑμᾶς ὁ Σατανᾶς διὰ τὴν ἀκρασίαν ὑμῶν.

7:6τοῦτο δὲ λέγω κατὰ συγγνώμην, οὐ κατ' ἐπιταγήν.

7:7θέλω δὲ πάντας ἀνθρώπους εἶναι ὡς καὶ ἐμαυτόν: ἀλλὰ ἕκαστος ἴδιον ἔχει χάρισμα ἐκ θεοῦ, ὁ μὲν οὕτως, ὁ δὲ οὕτως.

7:8Λέγω δὲ τοῖς ἀγάμοις καὶ ταῖς χήραις, καλὸν αὐτοῖς ἐὰν μείνωσιν ὡς κἀγώ:

7:9εἰ δὲ οὐκ ἐγκρατεύονται γαμησάτωσαν, κρεῖττον γάρ ἐστιν γαμῆσαι ἢ πυροῦσθαι.

7:1Now concerning the things whereof you wrote to me: it is good for a man not to touch a woman. [n. 312]

7:2But for fear of fornication, let every man have his own wife: and let every woman have her own husband. [n. 315]

7:3Let the husband render the debt to his wife: and the wife also in like manner to the husband. [n. 320]

7:4The wife has not power of her own body: but the husband. And in like manner the husband also has not power of his own body: but the wife. [n. 322]

7:5Do not defraud one another, except, perhaps, by consent, for a time, that you may give yourselves to prayer: and return together again, lest Satan tempt you for your incontinency. [n. 325]

7:6But I speak this by indulgence, not by commandment. [n. 326]

7:7For I would that all were even as myself. But every one has his proper gift from God: one after this manner, and another after that. [n. 330]

7:8But I say to the unmarried and to the widows: it is good for them if they so continue, even as I. [n. 334]

7:9But if they do not contain themselves, let them marry. For it is better to marry than to be burnt.

---

312. Postquam Apostolus reprehendit fornicarium et sustinentes eum, hic accedit ad tractandum de matrimonio.

Et circa hoc tria facit.

Primo determinat de coniugatis et matrimonio iunctis;

secundo, de virginibus, ibi *de virginibus autem*, etc.;

tertio, de viduis, ibi *mulier alligata est*, etc.

Circa primum duo facit.

312. After rebuking the fornicator and those who upheld him, the Apostle now begins to treat of marriage.

In regard to this he does three things.

First, he discusses those joined in matrimony;

second, virgins, at *now, concerning virgins* (1 Cor 7:25);

third, widows, at *a woman is bound by the law* (1 Cor 7:39).

In regard to the first he does two things.

Primo instruit eos qui non sunt matrimonio iuncti, utrum scilicet debeant matrimonium contrahere;

secundo manifestat quod dixerat, ibi *hoc autem dico*, et cetera.

Circa primum duo facit.

Primo manifestat quid circa hoc sit per se bonum;

secundo, quid necessarium, ibi *propter fornicationem autem*, et cetera.

313. Circa primum considerandum quod in detestationem fornicationis, contra quam locutus iam fuerat, aliqui non habentes zelum Dei secundum scientiam, intantum procedebant, quod etiam matrimonium condemnabant, secundum illud I Tim. IV, 2 s.: *in hypocrisi loquentium mendacium, prohibentium nubere.* Et quia hoc durum Corinthiis videbatur fidelibus, super hoc Apostolo scripserunt, eius sententiam requirentes, et ideo Apostolus eis respondet: ita reprehendi ea quae facitis. *De quibus autem scripsistis mihi*, respondeo, quantum ad matrimonium, *bonum est homini mulierem non tangere*.

314. Circa quod notandum quod mulier data est viro ad adiutorium generationis: et in hoc differt vis generativa a nutritiva, quia vis nutritiva deservit homini ad conservationem individui; unde bonum est homini nutrimento uti, quia per hoc eius vita conservatur; generativa autem non deservit homini ad conservationem individui, sed ad conservationem speciei. Unde non potest dici quod *bonum est homini*, ad suum individuum, *mulierem tangere*, primo quidem quantum ad animam, quia, ut Augustinus dicit in *Soliloquiis, nihil sic deiicit animam ab arce virtutis suae, sicut contactus ille corporum, sine quo uxor haberi non potest*; et ideo Ex. XIX, 15 dicitur populo accepturo legem Dei: *estote parati in diem tertium, et ne appropinquetis uxoribus vestris.* I Reg. XXI, 4 dixit Abimelech ad David: *si mundi sunt pueri, maxime a mulieribus, manducent panem sanctum.*

Secundo quantum ad corpus, quod vir subiicit per matrimonium potestati uxoris, se ex libero servum constituens. Servitus autem haec prae omnibus aliis est amara. Unde et Eccle. VII, 27 dicitur: *inveni amariorem morte mulierem.*

Tertio quantum ad res exteriores, quarum occupatione necesse est hominem implicari, qui habet uxorem et filios nutriendos, cum tamen dicatur II Tim. II, 4: *nemo militans Deo implicat se negotiis saecularibus, ut ei placeat cui se probavit.*

315. Deinde cum dicit *propter fornicationem*, etc., ostendit quid circa hoc sit necessarium.

Primo quantum ad contractum matrimonii;

secundo quantum ad actum matrimonii iam contracti, ibi *uxori vir debitum*, et cetera.

First, he instructs those not joined in matrimony whether to contract matrimony;

second, he clarifies what he had said, at *but I speak this by indulgence*.

In regard to the first he does two things.

First, he shows what is essentially good in this matter;

second, what is necessary, at *but for fear of fornication*.

313. In regard to the first it should be noted that in their dislike for fornication, against which he had just spoken, some, whose zeal for God was not accompanied by wisdom, arrived at a point where they even condemned marriage. Hence it is said: *through the hypocrisy of liars who forbid marriage* (1 Tim 4:2ff). Because this seemed harsh to the Corinthian believers, they wrote to the Apostle about it. Therefore, the Apostle answered: I have disapproved of things you do. *Now concerning the things whereof you wrote to me*, I answer in regard to matrimony: *it is good for a man not to touch a woman*.

314. In this matter it should be noted that the woman was given to man as a help in generation, and the generative power differs from the nutritive power in the fact that the latter serves man in preserving him as an individual. Hence, it is good for man to take nourishment, because his life is preserved by it. But the generative power does not serve man as a help in preserving him as an individual, but to preserve the species. Hence, it cannot be said that *it is good for a man*, as his own individual, *to touch a woman*; first, in regard to the soul, because as Augustine says in the *Soliloquies: nothing so casts a man down from the citadel of his power as that contact of bodies without which a wife cannot be had.* Consequently, it is said to the people about to receive the law: *be ready by the third day; do not go near a woman* (Exod 19:15); and: *I have no common bread at hand, but there is holy bread; if only the young men have kept themselves from women* (1 Sam 21:4).

Second, as to the body, the fact that a man subjects himself to a woman by marriage and makes himself a slave out of a freedman. This is the most bitter of all servitudes. Hence it is said: *I found more bitter than death the woman whose heart is snares and nets* (Eccl 7:26).

Third, as to external things with which a man must occupy himself, when he has a wife and children to be fed; whereas it is said: *no soldier on service gets entangled in civilian pursuits, since his aim is to satisfy the one who enlisted him* (2 Tim 2:4).

315. Then when he says, *but for fear of fornication*, he shows what is necessary in this matter.

First, as to contracting marriage;

second, as to the use of the matrimony once contracted, at *let the husband render the debt*.

316. Circa primum considerandum est, quod actus generativae virtutis ordinatur ad conservationem speciei per generationem filiorum, et quia mulier data est viro in adiutorium generationis, prima necessitas tangendi mulierem est propter procreationem filiorum. Unde Gen. I, 27 s. dicitur: *masculum et foeminam creavit eos, et benedixit eis Deus, et ait: crescite et multiplicamini, et replete terram.* Sed haec necessitas fuit circa institutionem humani generis, quamdiu oportuit multiplicari populum Dei per successionem carnis.

Sed Apostolus, considerans humanum genus iam multiplicatum et populum Dei iam esse augmentatum, non propagatione carnis, sed generatione quae est ex aqua et Spiritu Sancto, ut dicitur Io. III, 5, praetermisit hanc necessitatem, qua scilicet primitus institutum fuerat matrimonium in officium naturae, et proponit secundam necessitatem secundum quam institutum est in remedium culpae. Quia enim carnalis concupiscentia adhuc post baptismum in fidelibus remanet, licet non Dominetur, instigat homines maxime ad actus venereos propter vehementiam delectationis. Et quia maioris virtutis est totaliter hanc concupiscentiam superare, quam possit hominibus convenire, secundum illud Matth. XIX, v. 11: *non omnes capiunt verbum hoc*, necessarium est quod in parte concupiscentiae cedatur, et in parte superetur; quod quidem fit dum actus generationis ratione ordinatur, et non totaliter homo concupiscentia ducitur, sed magis concupiscentia subditur rationi.

317. Habet autem hoc ratio naturalis, quod homo utatur generationis actu, secundum quod convenit generationi et educationi filiorum. Hoc autem in brutis animalibus invenitur, quod in quibuscumque speciebus animalium sola foemina non sufficit ad educationem prolis, masculus simul nutrit prolem cum foemina; et ad hoc exigitur, quod masculus cognoscat propriam prolem. Et ideo in omnibus talibus animalibus, ut patet in columbis, turturibus et huiusmodi, naturaliter indita est sollicitudo de educatione prolis. Et propter hoc in huiusmodi non sunt vagi et indifferentes concubitus, ex quibus sequeretur incertitudo prolis; sed masculus determinatus determinatae foeminae coniungitur, non indifferenter quaelibet cuilibet, sicut accidit in canibus et aliis huiusmodi animalibus, in quibus sola foemina nutrit prolem.

Maxime autem in specie humana masculus requiritur ad prolis educationem, quae non solum attenditur secundum corporis nutrimentum, sed magis secundum nutrimentum animae, secundum illud Hebr. XII, 9: *patres quidem carnis nostrae habuimus eruditores et reverebamur eos*; et ideo ratio naturalis dictat quod in specie humana non sint vagi et incerti concubitus, quales sunt concubitus fornicarii, sed sint determinati viri ad

316. In regard to the first it should be noted that the act of the generative power is ordained to the conservation of the species by the generation of offspring. And because the woman was given to the man as a helper in generation, the first need for touching a woman is for the procreation of children. Hence it is said: *male and female he created them. And God blessed them, and God said to them: be fruitful and multiply, and fill the earth* (Gen 1:27). But this need was directed to the formation of the human race, as long as there was need for the people of God to be multiplied by succession according to the flesh.

But the Apostle, considering that the human race had now multiplied and that the people of God were now increased not by fleshly propagation but by the generation which is from water the Holy Spirit (John 3:5), he passed over this necessity whereby marriage had been originally instituted as a function of nature, and proposed a second necessity according to which it was instituted as a remedy for sin. For since carnal desire remains alive in believers even after baptism, although it does not rule, it impels men especially toward venereal acts on account of the vehemence of their pleasure. And because it requires greater virtue to conquer this desire entirely than can belong to men, according to Matthew: *not all men can receive this saying* (Matt 19:11), it is necessary that this desire be in part yielded to and in part mastered. This, indeed, happens when the act of generation is ordained by reason and man is not totally mastered by the desire, but the desire is rather subjected to reason.

317. Natural reason teaches that man use the act of generation according as it is suitable for generation and education of children. But in brute animals it is found that in certain species the female alone is not sufficient for the training of the offspring, but the male takes care of the offspring with the female. For this it is required that the male recognize its offspring. Therefore, in all such animals, as doves, pigeons and the like, solicitude for the training of offspring is inspired by nature. Wherefore, in such animals coition is not random and indiscriminate, but a definite male is joined to a definite female, not one to another promiscuously, as happens in dogs and such animals, in which the female alone takes care of the offspring.

But above all in the human species, the male is required for the education of the offspring, which are attended to not only regarding bodily nourishment, but to a greater degree regarding the nourishment of the soul, as it says in Hebrews: *we have had earthly fathers to discipline us and we respected them* (Heb 12:9). And consequently, natural reason dictates that in the human species coition is not random and uncertain, but is by a definite man to a definite

determinatam foeminam, quae quidem determinatio fit per legem matrimonii.

318. Sic igitur triplex bonum habet matrimonium, primum quidem quod est in officium naturae, prout scilicet ordinatur ad generationem et educationem prolis, et hoc bonum est bonum prolis.

Secundum bonum habet prout est in remedium concupiscentiae, quae scilicet coarctatur ad determinatam personam, et hoc bonum dicitur fides, quam scilicet vir servat uxori suae, non accedens ad aliam, et similiter uxor viro.

Tertium bonum habet, prout in fide contrahitur Christi, quod quidem bonum dicitur sacramentum, inquantum significat coniunctionem Christi et Ecclesiae, secundum illud Eph. V, 32: *sacramentum hoc magnum est, ego autem dico in Christo, et Ecclesia.*

319. Hoc est ergo quod dicit: dictum est quod **bonum est homini mulierem non tangere**, sed quia ad hoc bonum non sunt omnes homines idonei, **unusquisque vir, propter fornicationem**, scilicet vitandam, **suam uxorem habeat**, id est, sibi determinatam, ut tollantur vagi et incerti concubitus, quod pertinet ad fornicationem. Unde et Prov. V, 18: *laetare cum muliere adolescentiae tuae*, et postea subditur: *quare seduceris, fili mi, ab aliena?*

320. Deinde cum dicit **uxori vir debitum reddat**, etc., agit de usu matrimonii contracti. Et

primo agit de debito reddendo;

secundo de debiti intermissione, ibi **nolite fraudare**, et cetera.

321. Circa primum duo facit.

Primo proponit quod intendit, dicens: dictum est quod vir habeat uxorem, et uxor virum; habendi autem haec est ratio, ut **vir reddat debitum uxori**, scilicet de suo corpore per carnalem commixtionem, **similiter autem et uxor viro**, quia quantum ad hoc ad paria iudicantur. Unde mulier non est formata de pedibus viri tamquam ancilla, nec de capite tamquam domina, sed de latere tamquam socia, ut legitur Gen. II, 21. Unde et mutuo debent sibi debitum reddere, secundum illud Rom. XIII, 7: *reddite omnibus debita*.

322. Secundo assignat debiti rationem, dicens **mulier non habet potestatem sui corporis**, scilicet ad actum generationis, ut scilicet possit proprio arbitrio vel continere, scilicet vel alteri se tradere; **sed vir**, scilicet habet potestatem sui corporis, quantum scilicet ad usum carnalis copulae, et ideo uxor debet viro proprii corporis officium offerre. **Similiter autem et vir sui corporis potestatem non habet, sed mulier**, et cetera. Unde et ipse debet sui corporis officium offerre uxori, legitimo impedimento cessante. Unde et Gen. c. II, 24 dicitur: *adhaerebit uxori suae, et erunt duo in carne una*.

female, who in fact made the arrangement through the law of matrimony.

318. Thus, therefore, matrimony has three goods. The first is that it is a function of nature in the sense that it is ordered to the production and education of offspring; and this good is the good of offspring.

The second good is that it is a remedy for desire, which is restricted to a definite person; and this good is called fidelity, which a man preserves toward his wife, by not going to another woman, and similarly the wife toward the husband.

The third good, insofar as the marriage is contracted in the faith of Christ, is called the sacrament, inasmuch as it signifies the union of Christ and the Church, as it is said: *this mystery is a profound one, and I am saying that it refers to Christ and the Church* (Eph 5:32).

319. This therefore is what he says: it has been stated that, **it is good for a man not to touch a woman**. But because all men are not equipped for this good, **for fear of fornication**, which must be shunned, **let every man have his own wife**, that is, determined by himself, so as to avoid uncertain and promiscuous concubinage, which pertains to fornication: *rejoice in the wife of your youth* (Prov 5:18); *why should you be infatuated, my son, with a loose woman?* (Prov 5:20)

320. Then when he says, **let the husband render**, he deals with the use of the marriage contract.

First, about rendering the conjugal debt;

second, about postponing the debt, at **do not defraud one another**.

321. In regard to the first he does two things.

First, he states his proposition, saying: it has been stated that a man should have a wife and a wife her husband. The reason for the 'having' is that **the husband render the debt to his wife**, namely, with his own body through carnal union, **and the wife also in like manner to the husband**, because in this matter they are judged equal. Hence the woman was not formed from the feet of the man as a servant, nor from the head as lording it over her husband, but from the side as a companion (Gen 2:21). Hence, they must pay the debt to one another: *pay all of them their dues* (Rom 13:7).

322. Second, he assigns the reason for the debt saying, **the wife has not power of her own body**, namely, in regard to the act of generation as though she could by her own choice be continent or give herself to someone else; **but the husband**, that is, has power over her body as to the use of carnal union. Therefore the wife must offer the husband the use of her body. **And in like manner the husband also has not power of his own body: but the wife**. Hence he must offer the use of his body to the wife, when any lawful impediment ceases. Hence it is said: *therefore a man leaves his father and his mother and cleaves to his wife, and they become one flesh* (Gen 2:24).

323. Deinde cum dicit *nolite fraudare invicem*, etc., agit de intermissione debiti reddendi. Et primo ostendit qualiter intermitti debeat actus coniugalis.

Circa quod docet unum esse cavendum, ne scilicet hoc per fraudem fiat, dicens *nolite fraudare invicem*, ut scilicet velit vir continere, invita uxore, aut etiam e converso. Quod Apostolus fraudem nominat, quia unus subtrahit alteri quod ei debetur, quod ad fraudem pertinet, non minus in actu matrimonii, quam in aliis rebus. Unde et Prov. c. XII, 27 dicitur: *non inveniet fraudulentus lucrum*, quia scilicet ille, qui tali fraude continentiam Deo offert, non lucratur meritum vitae aeternae. Sicut enim dicit Augustinus non vult Deus tale lucrum tali damno compensari, ut dum unus coniugum continet, altero invito, ille incidat in damnabiles corruptelas.

324. Tria autem docet observanda in tali intermissione: quorum primum est ut fiat ex communi consensu. Unde dicit *nisi forte ex consensu*. Unde dicitur Eccli. XXV, 1 s.: *in tribus beneplacitum est spiritui meo, quae sunt probata coram Deo et hominibus: concordia fratrum, et amor proximorum, vir et mulier bene sibi consentientes.* Secundum est, ut sit ad certum tempus. Unde subdit *nisi forte ad tempus*, secundum illud Eccle. c. III, 5: *tempus amplexandi, et tempus longe fieri ab amplexibus.* Tertium est, ut hoc fiat propter debitum finem, scilicet causa spiritualium actuum, ad quos continentia reddit magis aptos. Unde subdit *ut vacetis orationi*, secundum illud Ioel. II, 14: *sacrificium et libamen Domino Deo nostro*, et postea subdit: *egrediatur sponsus de cubili suo, et sponsa de thalamo suo.*

325. Secundo agit de reiteratione coniugalis actus; et primo ponit documentum, dicens *iterum revertimini in idipsum*, ut scilicet vobis invicem debitum reddatis, finito tempore orationis. Unde et III Reg. VIII, 66 dicitur, quod celebratis dedicationis solemniis, *profecti sunt in tabernacula sua laetantes.*

Secundo assignat rationem documenti. Non enim hoc dicit, quasi sit necessarium ad salutem, sed ad periculum vitandum. Unde subdit *ne tentet vos Satanas*, id est, ne sua tentatione vos prosternat; sicut etiam dicitur I Thess. III, 5: *ne forte vos tentaverit is qui tentat, et inanis sit labor noster.* Tentatio autem Satanae non est fortibus timenda, de quibus dicitur I Io. II, 14: *scribo vobis, iuvenes, quoniam fortes estis, et verbum Dei manet in vobis, et vicistis malignum.* Est autem timenda debilibus, unde subdit *propter incontinentiam vestram*, id est, propter pronitatem ad incontinentiam, ex quo contingit, quod diabolus hominem tentando prosternit, et provocatur ad tentandum, secundum illud I Petr. ult.: *circuit quaerens quem devoret.*

326. Deinde cum dicit *hoc autem dico*, etc., manifestat quo sensu praedicta sunt accipienda, et

323. Then when he says, ***do not defraud one another***, he deals with postponing the debt to be rendered. First, he shows how the conjugal act should be postponed.

In regard to this he teaches that one thing must be avoided, saying, ***do not defraud one another***, as, for example, the husband might wish to abstain when the wife is unwilling, or even conversely. The Apostle calls this fraud, because one is taking away what belongs to another—and this pertains to fraud no less in marriage than in other affairs (Prov 12:27): *the fraudulent man will not catch his prey*, namely, because one who offers God his continence accompanied by that fraud does not gain merit for eternal life. For as Augustine says, God does not want such gain compensated with such harm, so that while one of the spouses is continent against the will of the other, the former falls into dangerous temptations.

324. Three things must be observed in such postponement. The first is that it be done with mutual consent. Hence he says, ***except, perhaps, by consent***. Hence it is said: *my soul takes pleasure in three things, and they are beautiful in the sight of the Lord and of men; agreement between brothers, friendship between neighbors, and a wife and a husband who live in harmony* (Sir 25:1). The second is that it be for a definite time. Hence he says, except perhaps ***for a time***: *a time to embrace, and a time to refrain from embracing* (Eccl 3:5). The third is that it be done for a suitable purpose, that is, for the sake of spiritual acts, for which continence renders one more suitable. Hence he adds, ***that you may give yourselves to prayer***: *a cereal offering and a drink offering for the Lord, your God* (Joel 2:14), and later he adds, *let the bridegroom leave his room, and the bride her chamber* (Joel 2:16).

325. Then he deals with the resumption of the conjugal act. First he presents the teaching, saying, ***and return together again***, that is, in order that you may render to each other the debt, now that the time of prayer is finished. Hence it is said that after celebrating the dedication of the feast: *they went to their homes joyful and glad of heart* (1 Kgs 8:66).

Second he assigns a reason for the teaching. For he does not say this as though it were necessary for salvation, but to avoid danger. Hence he adds, ***lest Satan tempt you***, that is, lest he subvert you with his temptation: *for fear that somehow the tempter had tempted you and that our labor would be in vain* (1 Thess 3:5). Satan's temptation should not be feared by the strong, about whom it is said: *I write to you, young men, because you are strong, and the word of God abides in you, and you have overcome the evil one* (1 John 2:14). But he should be feared by the weak. Hence he says, through lack of self-control, that is, ***for your incontinency***, as a result of which the devil overcomes man by tempting, and he is inclined to tempt: *the devil prowls around like a roaring lion, seeking some one to devour* (1 Pet 5:8).

326. Then when he says, ***but I speak this***, he tells in what sense the above doctrine should be taken.

primo facit quod dictum est;

secundo, rationem assignat, ibi **volo autem**, etc.;

tertio, exponit quod dixerat, ibi **dico autem**, et cetera.

327. Dicit ergo primo: dixi, quod unusquisque suam uxorem habeat, et unaquaeque mulier virum suum, et iterum quod post continentiam determinati temporis, iterum revertamini in idipsum. **Hoc autem dico secundum indulgentiam**, id est, parcens infirmitati vestrae, **non secundum imperium**, quasi scilicet vobis necessarium ad salutem. Subditis enim sunt quaedam eorum infirmitati indulgenda, et non ad bona imperio cogendi. Unde contra quosdam praelatos dicitur Ez. XXXIV, 4 s.: *cum austeritate imperabatis eis, et cum potentia, et dispersi sunt greges mei.*

328. Sed videtur Apostolus inconvenienter loqui; indulgentia enim non est nisi de peccato. Per hoc ergo quod Apostolus, secundum indulgentiam se dicit matrimonium concessisse, videtur exprimere quod matrimonium sit peccatum.

Sed ad hoc potest responderi dupliciter. Uno modo ut indulgentia sumatur hic pro permissione. Est autem duplex permissio: una quidem de minus malo, sicut dicitur Matth. c. XIX, 8, quod *Moyses permisit Iudaeis dare libellum repudii propter duritiam cordis eorum*, scilicet ad vitandum uxoricidium, ad quod erant proni. Talis enim permissio non fit in Novo Testamento propter sui perfectionem, secundum illud Hebr. VI, 1: *ad perfectum feramur.* Alia autem est permissio de minus bono, cum scilicet homo praecepto non cogitur ad maius bonum; et hoc modo Apostolus hic indulget, id est, permittit matrimonium, quod est minus bonum quam virginitas, quae non praecipitur, quae est maius bonum.

Alio modo potest accipi indulgentia prout respicit culpam, secundum illud Is. XXVI, 15: *indulsisti, Domine, indulsisti genti.* Et secundum hoc indulgentia refertur ad actum coniugalem secundum quod habet annexam culpam venialem, tamen propter bona matrimonii sine quibus esset mortalis.

329. Unde considerandum est quod actus coniugalis quandoque quidem est meritorius, et absque omni culpa mortali vel veniali, puta cum ordinatur ad bonum prolis procreandae et educandae ad cultum Dei: sic enim est actus religionis; vel cum fit causa reddendi debitum: sic enim est actus iustitiae. Omnis autem actus virtutis est meritorius, si sit cum caritate. Quandoque vero est cum culpa veniali, scilicet cum quis ad actum matrimonialem ex concupiscentia excitatur, quae tamen infra limites matrimonii sistit, ut scilicet cum sola uxore sit contentus. Quandoque vero est culpa mortalis, puta cum concupiscentia fertur extra limites matrimonii, scilicet cum

First, he does what has been said;

second, he assigns a reason, at **for I would that all**;

third, he explains what he had said, at **but I say to the unmarried**.

327. First, therefore, he says: I have said that each one should have his own wife and each woman her own husband; furthermore, after practicing continence for a time, they should return once more to each other. **But I speak this by indulgence**, that is, to spare your weakness, **not by commandment**, namely as though necessary for your salvation. For certain things must be conceded to subjects on account of their weakness, and they should not be compelled by commanding what is good. Hence it is said against some prelates: *with force and harshness you have ruled them, so they were scattered* (Ezek 24:4).

328. But the Apostle seems to be speaking in an unsuitable manner, for concessions are concerned only with sin. Therefore, by the fact that the Apostle says he is speaking by way of concession, he seems to express that marriage is a sin.

But this can be answered in two ways. In one way so that the concession is taken for permission. But there are two kinds of permission: one is concerned with a lesser evil: *for your hardness of heart Moses allowed you to divorce your wives* (Matt 19:8), that is, to avoid the murder of one's wife, to which they were prone. Such a permission is not found in the New Testament on account of its perfection: *let us go on to perfection* (Heb 6:1). Another permission is about the lesser good, namely, when a man is not compelled by precept to a greater good. This is the sense in which the Apostle makes a concession here, that is, permits matrimony, which is a lesser good than virginity, which is not commanded and is a greater good.

In another way, concession can be taken as regarding guilt: *but you have increased the nation, O Lord, you have increased the nation* (Isa 26:15). In this sense, concession refers to the conjugal act, accordingly as it has venial guilt attached to it along with the good of matrimony, without which it would be mortal.

329. Hence it should be noted that the conjugal act is sometimes meritorious and without any mortal or venial sin, as when it is directed to the good of procreation and education of a child for the worship of God; for then it is an act of religion; or when it is performed for the sake of rendering the debt, it is an act of justice. But every virtuous act is meritorious, if it is performed with charity. But sometimes it is accompanied with venial sin, namely, when one is excited to the matrimonial act by concupiscence, which nevertheless stays within the limits of the marriage, namely, that he is content with his wife only. But sometimes it is performed with mortal sin, as when concupiscence is carried

aliquis accedit ad uxorem, aeque libenter vel libentius ad aliam accessurus.

Primo ergo modo actus matrimonii non requirit indulgentiam; secundo modo habet indulgentiam inquantum aliquis consentiens concupiscentiae in uxorem, non fit reus peccati mortalis; tertio modo omnino indulgentiam non habet.

330. Deinde cum dicit *volo autem* etc., assignat rationem eius quod dixerat, et

primo quare non loquatur secundum imperium;

secundo quare loquatur secundum indulgentiam, ibi *sed unusquisque*, et cetera.

331. Circa primum considerandum est quod nullus sapiens praecipit illud cuius contrarium magis vult fieri. Ideo Apostolus non praecipit quod homines matrimonium contrahant, vel matrimonio contracto utantur, quia magis vult quod homines contineant. Et hoc est quod dicit *volo autem omnes*, homines, *esse sicut meipsum*, ut scilicet contineant, sicut ego contineo. Et similiter dicit Act. XXVI, 29: *opto apud Deum omnes qui audiunt, fieri tales qualis ego sum.*

332. Sed contra hoc videtur esse, quia si omnes homines continerent, sicut Apostolus continebat, cessasset generatio, et sic non fuisset impletus numerus electorum, quod erat contra dispositionem divinam.

Dicunt quidam quod Apostolo revelatum erat, quod si omnes homines salvarentur in continentia viventes, sicut ipse vivebat, sufficiebat ad implendum numerum electorum. Sed hoc nulla auctoritate fulcitur; et ideo potest dici, quod Apostolus volebat omnes esse continentes, quia scilicet volebat hoc de singulis, non tamen volebat quod omnes simul continerent.

Vel potest dici, et melius, quod volebat omnes homines esse continentes voluntate antecedente, sicut ipse dicit I Tim. II, 4, quod *Deus vult omnes homines salvos fieri*, non autem voluntate consequente, qua Deus vult quosdam salvare, scilicet praedestinatos, et quosdam damnare, scilicet reprobatos, secundum illud Mal. I, 2 s.: *Iacob dilexi, Esau autem odio habui.* Est autem voluntas antecedens de eo, quod absolute consideratum est melius, sicut omnes homines esse salvos, vel continentes: voluntas autem consequens est de eo, quod est melius, consideratis circumstantiis personarum et negotiorum, et secundum hoc Deus vult quosdam damnare, et Apostolus quosdam matrimonio iungi.

333. Deinde cum dicit *sed unusquisque*, assignat rationem quare secundum indulgentiam matrimonium permiserit, quia scilicet non quilibet tantae virtutis donum accepit a Deo, ut scilicet possit totaliter continere, sicut et Dominus dixit Matth. XIX, 11: *non omnes capiunt verbum hoc, sed qui capere potest, capiat.* Et hoc est quod dicit: vellem quidem omnes esse continentes, *sed*

beyond the limits of the marriage; for example, when the husband approaches the wife with the idea that he would just as gladly or more gladly approach another woman.

In the first way, therefore, the act of marriage requires no concession; in the second way it obtains a concession, inasmuch as someone consenting to concupiscence toward the wife is not guilty of mortal sin; in the third way there is absolutely no concession.

330. Then when it says, *for I would that all*, he assigns the reason for what he has said.

First, why he does not speak as commanding;

second, why he speaks according to a concession, at *but every one has his proper gift*.

331. In regard to the first it should be noted that no wise man commands that whose opposite he would rather have done. Therefore, the Apostle does not command that men contract marriage or make use of a marriage already contracted, because he wishes rather that men be continent. And this is what he says: *for I would that all* men *were even as myself*, that is, continent as I am. He says likewise: *I would to God that not only you but also all who hear me this day might become such as I am* (Acts 26:29).

332. But there seems to be something against this, because if all men practiced continence, as the Apostle did, generation would cease and, as a result, the number of the elect would never be fulfilled, and this is against God's arrangement.

Some say that it had been revealed to the Apostle that if all men were saved practicing continence, as he practiced it, it would suffice to fill up the number of the elect. But this rests on no authority; consequently, it can be said that the Apostle wished all men to be continent, because he wished this for certain individuals, but he did not wish that all would be continent at the same time.

Or it can be said, and this is better, that he wished all men to be continent in his antecedent will: *God desires all men to be saved* (1 Tim 2:4), but not by his consequent will, by which God wills to save certain persons, namely the predestined and to damn others, namely, the reprobate: *I have loved Jacob, but I have hated Esau* (Mal 1:2ff). Now the antecedent will is concerned with that which considered absolutely is better, as all men to be saved or continent; but the consequent will is concerned with that which is better considering circumstances of persons and events, and according to this, God wills to damn some and the Apostle wishes some to be united in marriage.

333. Then when he says, *but every one*, he tells the reason why he permitted marriage as a concession, namely, because each one has not received from God so much virtue as to enable him to practice total continence, as the Lord himself said: *not all men can receive this saying. He who is able to receive this, let him receive it* (Matt 19:11f). And this is what he says: I should wish that all were continent, *but*

unusquisque proprium, id est, secundum certam mensuram, **habet donum ex Deo, alius quidem sic**, puta ut in virginitate Deo serviat, **alius vero sic**, id est, ut Deo serviat in matrimonio, secundum illud Matth. XXV, v. 15: *uni dedit quinque talenta, alii vero duo, alii vero unum, unicuique secundum propriam virtutem.* Et Sap. VIII, 21: *scivi quoniam aliter non possum esse continens, nisi Deus det, et hoc ipsum erat sapientiae scire cuius esset hoc donum.*

334. Deinde cum dicit **dico autem**, etc., exponit quod obscure dixerat.

Et primo quantum ad hoc quod dixerat: **Volo omnes homines esse sicut meipsum**, quia scilicet hoc est absolute melius. Unde dicit **dico autem**, scilicet exponendo, **non nuptis**, id est, virginibus, **et viduis: bonum est illis si sic permanserint**, scilicet continentes, **sicut ego**, secundum illud Sap. c. IV, 1: *quam pulchra est casta generatio cum claritate.*

335. Secundo quantum ad hoc quod dixerat: **sed unusquisque**, etc., quasi dicat: quia non quilibet hoc donum accepit a Deo ut contineat. Unde dicit **quod si non continent**, id est, si donum continendi non acceperunt, **nubant**, id est, matrimonio iungantur, secundum illud I Tim. V, 14: *volo iuvenes nubere.*

Et assignat rationem, subdens **melius est enim nubere, quam uri**, id est, concupiscentia superari. Concupiscentia enim est calor quidam noxius; qui ergo concupiscentia impugnatur, calescit quidem, sed non uritur, nisi humorem gratiae perdat a concupiscentia superatus. Unde Iob XXXI, 12 dicitur: *ignis est usque ad consummationem devorans, et universa eradicans germina.*

Est autem hic attendendum quod Apostolus utitur abusiva comparatione; nam nubere bonum est, licet minus, uri autem est malum. Melius est ergo, id est magis tolerandum, quod homo minus bonum habeat, quam quod incurrat incontinentiae malum; et hoc est quod supra dixit **propter fornicationem**, scilicet vitandam, **unusquisque suam uxorem habeat**, etc., et postmodum: **ne tentet vos Satanas propter incontinentiam vestram.**

every one has his proper gift from God, that is, in a definite measure, **one after this manner**, for example, to serve God in virginity, **and another after that**, say, to serve God in marriage. Hence it is said: *to one he gave five talents, to another two, to another one, each according to his ability* (Matt 25:15). And: *but I perceived that I would not possess wisdom unless God gave her to me—and it was a mark of insight to know whose gift she was* (Wis 8:21).

334. Then when he says, **but I say to the unmarried**, he explains what he had said obscurely.

First, as to his statement, **I would that all were even as myself**, namely, because this is absolutely better. Hence he says, **to the unmarried**, that is, virgins, **and to the widows: it is good for them if they so continue** to be continent, **even as I**, for it is said: *blessed is the chaste generation with glory* (Wis 4:1).

335. Second, as to his statement, **but every one has his proper gift**; as if to say: not everyone has received from God the gift of continence. Hence he says, **if they do not contain themselves**, that is, if they have not yet received this gift, **let them marry**, that is, be joined in matrimony: *I would have younger widows marry* (1 Tim 5:14).

Then he gives the reason, saying, **it is better to marry than to be burnt**, that is, be overcome by concupiscence. For concupiscence is a harmful heat; therefore one assailed by concupiscence is warmed but not burned, unless he is overcome by concupiscence and destroys the water of grace. Hence it is said: *a fire which consumes unto Abaddon, and it would burn to the root all my increase* (Job 31:8).

It should be noted that the Apostle uses a helpful comparison here, for it is good to marry, although it is a lesser good. But to be burned is an evil. Therefore it is better, that is, more tolerable, that a man should have the lesser good than incur the evil of incontinence. And this is what he said above: **for fear of fornication**, which must be shuned, **let every man have his own wife: and let every woman have her own husband**; and later: **lest Satan tempt you for your incontinency**.

Lecture 2

^{7:10}Iis autem qui matrimonio juncti sunt, praecipio non ego, sed Dominus, uxorem a viro non discedere: [n. 336]

^{7:11}quod si discesserit, manere innuptam, aut viro suo reconciliari. Et vir uxorem non dimittat. [n. 338]

^{7:12}Nam ceteris ego dico, non Dominus. Si quis frater uxorem habet infidelem, et haec consentit habitare cum illo, non dimittat illam. [n. 341]

^{7:13}Et si qua mulier fidelis habet virum infidelem, et hic consentit habitare cum illa, non dimittat virum:

^{7:14}sanctificatus est enim vir infidelis per mulierem fidelem, et sanctificata est mulier infidelis per virum fidelem: alioquin filii vestri immundi essent, nunc autem sancti sunt. [n. 344]

---

^{7:10}τοῖς δὲ γεγαμηκόσιν παραγγέλλω, οὐκ ἐγὼ ἀλλὰ ὁ κύριος, γυναῖκα ἀπὸ ἀνδρὸς μὴ χωρισθῆναι

^{7:11}ἐὰν δὲ καὶ χωρισθῇ, μενέτω ἄγαμος ἢ τῷ ἀνδρὶ καταλλαγήτω καὶ ἄνδρα γυναῖκα μὴ ἀφιέναι.

^{7:12}Τοῖς δὲ λοιποῖς λέγω ἐγώ, οὐχ ὁ κύριος· εἴ τις ἀδελφὸς γυναῖκα ἔχει ἄπιστον, καὶ αὕτη συνευδοκεῖ οἰκεῖν μετ' αὐτοῦ, μὴ ἀφιέτω αὐτήν·

^{7:13}καὶ γυνὴ εἴ τις ἔχει ἄνδρα ἄπιστον, καὶ οὗτος συνευδοκεῖ οἰκεῖν μετ' αὐτῆς, μὴ ἀφιέτω τὸν ἄνδρα.

^{7:14}ἡγίασται γὰρ ὁ ἀνὴρ ὁ ἄπιστος ἐν τῇ γυναικί, καὶ ἡγίασται ἡ γυνὴ ἡ ἄπιστος ἐν τῷ ἀδελφῷ· ἐπεὶ ἄρα τὰ τέκνα ὑμῶν ἀκάθαρτά ἐστιν, νῦν δὲ ἅγιά ἐστιν.

---

^{7:10}But to them who are married, not I, but the Lord, commands that the wife depart not from her husband. [n. 336]

^{7:11}And if she departs, that she remain unmarried or be reconciled to her husband. And let not the husband put away his wife. [n. 338]

^{7:12}For to the rest I speak, not the Lord. If any brother has a wife who believes not and she consents to dwell with him: let him not put her away. [n. 341]

^{7:13}And if any woman has a husband who believes not and he consents to dwell with her: let her not put away her husband.

^{7:14}For the unbelieving husband is sanctified by the believing wife: and the unbelieving wife is sanctified by the believing husband. Otherwise your children should be unclean: but now they are holy. [n. 344]

---

336. Supra Apostolus posuit documenta de contractu matrimonii, hic instruit eos qui iam matrimonium contraxerunt de matrimonio non dissolvendo: et

primo docet eos qui sunt in matrimonio iuncti, ut in matrimonio maneant;

secundo ponit utilem doctrinam quantum ad omnes status vel conditiones hominum, ibi *unumquemque sicut vocavit Deus*, et cetera.

Circa primum duo facit:

primo agit de indissolubilitate matrimonii quantum ad eos qui sunt unius cultus;

secundo quantum ad eos qui sunt in dispari cultu, ibi *nam caeteris ego dico*, et cetera.

Circa primum duo facit:

primo ponit praeceptum de indissolubilitate matrimonii;

secundo docet quid sit servandum quando matrimonium quodammodo separatur, ibi *quod si discesserit*, et cetera.

337. Dicit ergo primo: dixi non nuptis, id est, virginibus et viduis, quod melius est eis si sic permanserint, *his autem qui matrimonio sunt iuncti* non patet eadem conditio: his enim *praecipio non ego*, scilicet indicta mihi auctoritate, *sed Dominus*, hoc praecepit.

336. After presenting teachings about the contract of marriage, the Apostle now instructs those who have already contracted marriage, that they must not dissolve the marriage.

First, he teaches those already joined in marriage to continue in it;

second, he gives them a useful teaching as to all the states or conditions of men, at *as God has called everyone: so let him walk* (1 Cor 7:17).

In regard to the first he does two things.

First, he deals with the indissolubility of marriage, as it applies to those who are of one worship;

second, when there is disparity of cult, at *for to the rest I speak*.

In regard to the first he does two things.

First, he lays down a precept about the indissolubility of marriage;

second, he teaches what should be done when the marriage is broken by separation, at *and if she departs*.

337. First, therefore, he says: I have said to the unmarried, i.e., virgins and widows, that it is better for them to remain as they are; *but to them who are married*, the same condition does not prevail. For to them I give the charge, *not I*, by the authority entrusted to me, *but the Lord* commands this.

Dicens Matth. XIX, 6: *quos Deus coniunxit, homo non separet*. Praecipio, inquam, **uxorem a viro non discedere**, et subintelligendum est, excepta causa fornicationis, quam Christus excepit, et hic tacetur, quia notissima est. Hanc solam excepit Dominus, caeteras omnes molestias iubet pro fide coniugii fortiter sustineri. Matth. XIX, 9: *quicumque dimiserit uxorem suam et aliam duxerit, excepta causa fornicationis, moechatur*.

Hoc autem quod dicitur hic, secundum Glossam Augustini, intelligitur de coniunctis matrimonialiter, quorum uterque fidelis est.

338. *Quod si discesserit*, scilicet propter causam fornicationis, **praecipio**, inquam, **manere innuptam**, vivente marito, quia si solvitur matrimonium quoad thorum, non tamen quoad vinculum, **aut viro suo reconciliari**, scilicet si vir non continet. Et similiter **vir uxorem non dimittat**, nisi ob causam fornicationis. Similis forma in viro et in muliere servatur. Unde supplendum est quod de uxore praemisit, scilicet quod si omnino dimiserit, non ducat aliam, vel reconcilietur uxori.

339. Sed contrarium videtur dicere Ambrosius super hunc locum. Unde dicit: *ideo non subdit de viro sicut de muliere, quia licet viro aliam ducere, quia inferior non omnino hac lege utitur qua et superior*.

Sed Magister dicit a falsariis esse appositum, et ideo nullatenus est tenendum.

340. Notandum est hic quod septem sunt casus in quibus vir non potest ob causam fornicationis uxorem dimittere. Primus casus quando ipsemet eam prostituit; secundus quando ipse cum alia fornicatus fuerit; tertius quando ipse ei occasionem fornicandi dedit, ut quia non vult reddere debitum; quartus quando ipsa credens probabiliter virum mortuum, alteri nupsit; quintus quando violenter ab aliquo oppressa fuit; sextus quando sub specie viri sui ab altero cognita fuit; septimus quando fuit a viro post adulterium manifeste deprehensum, nihilominus retenta.

341. Deinde cum dicit **nam caeteris dico**, etc., agit de inseparabilitate matrimonii personarum disparis cultus, cum alter est fidelis, alter non.

Ubi primo dicit quod fidelis non dimittat infidelem volentem sine contumelia Creatoris cohabitare;

secundo quod si non vult, fidelis non tenetur eum sequi, sed potest alteri nubere, ibi **quod si infidelis discedit**, etc.;

tertio quod nisi infidelis prior recedat, fidelis debet patienter commanere, ibi **unde enim mulier**, et cetera.

What God has joined together, let no man put asunder (Matt. 19:6). I command, I say, **that the wife depart not from her husband**, except on account of fornication, an exception which Christ made and is not mentioned here, because it is well known. The Lord made this the sole exception; all other troubles he commands to be patiently endured for the faith of the marriage: *whoever divorces his wife, except for unchastity, and marries another, commits adultery* (Matt 19:9).

According to a Gloss of Augustine, what is said here is understood of the union of matrimony when both are faithful.

338. *But if she departs*, namely, on account of fornication, **that she remain unmarried**, as long as the husband is alive, because although the marriage is dissolved as to bed and board, not as to bond. ***Or be reconciled to her husband***, namely, if the husband is not continent. ***And let not the husband put away his wife***, except on account of fornication. A similar form is kept in regard to the man and to the woman. Hence it is necessary to supply what was said about the wife, namely, that if he dismissed her completely, he should not get another, but be reconciled to his wife.

339. But Ambrose, commenting here, seems to say something contrary to this. He says: *he does not say the same things for the man as for the woman, because it is lawful for the husband to marry another woman, for the inferior does not use this law as fully as the superior*.

But the Master says that this was added by a falsifier and should not be maintained at all.

340. It should be noted here that there are seven cases when a husband cannot dismiss his wife on account of fornication. The first is when he himself prostituted her; the second, when he commits fornication with another woman; the third is when he gave her the occasion of fornication, as when he is unwilling to render the debt; the fourth is when she has probable certitude that her husband is dead and she married another; the fifth is when she has been violently oppressed by him; the sixth is when she was known by another who seemed to be her husband; the seventh is when she has been manifestly caught in adultery, but is retained by her husband.

341. Then when he says, **for to the rest I speak**, he treats of the inseparability of marriage between persons of disparate cult, when one is a believer.

First, he says that the believer should not dismiss an unbelieving spouse, who is willing to continue living together without insulting the Creator;

second, that if the unbeliever does not wish to live together, the believer is not bound to follow, but can marry another, at **but if the unbeliever departs** (1 Cor 7:15);

third, that unless the unbeliever leaves first, the believer should patiently remain together, at **for how do you know** (1 Cor 7:16).

In prima,

primo ponit admonitionem;

secundo admonitionis rationem, ibi *sanctificatus est enim*, et cetera.

In prima,

primo loquitur generaliter tam viris quam foeminis;

secundo specialiter viris, ibi *si quis frater*, etc.;

tertio specialiter foeminis, ibi *et si qua mulier*, et cetera.

342. Dicit ergo *nam caeteris*, id est, ubi non uterque fidelis est, sed alter fidelis, alter infidelis, *dico ego*, consulendo non praecipiendo, *non Dominus* dixit hoc proprio ore. Ac si dicat: et hoc dico ex Deo, licet ipse non dicat hoc ore proprio. Dico, inquam, hoc: *si quis frater*, fidelis, conversus scilicet ad fidem in coniugio. Intelligitur enim hoc de his qui in infidelitate contraxerunt, non de his qui in dispari cultu; tunc enim nullum esset matrimonium, sed essent separandi, sicut fecit Esdras Esdrae X, T. *Si quis*, inquam, *habet* talem *uxorem infidelem, et haec consentit habitare cum illo*, sine contumelia scilicet Creatoris, *non dimittat illam*; consilium est, non praeceptum, ut qui contrarium agit, non sit transgressor, secundum Glossam.

343. Deinde cum dicit *et si qua mulier*, hic loquitur specialiter foeminis, ubi primo supponit fidem in aliquo, cum dicit *et si qua mulier*; secundo infidelitatem in altero, cum addit *virum infidelem*; tertio infidelis voluntatem cohabitandi, ibi *et hic consentit*; quarto consulit fideli commanere illi, ibi *non dimittat*.

Dicit ergo: et similiter *si qua mulier fidelis habet virum infidelem, et consentit habitare cum illa* sine contumelia Creatoris; nam si nollet cohabitare sine contumelia nominis Christi, debet fidelis eum dimittere, quia *contumelia Creatoris solvit matrimonium*, secundum Glossam, et potest fidelis contrahere. Si, inquam, ita est, *non dimittat virum*: consilium est, non praeceptum; licet enim infidelem fideli dimittere, sed tunc non expediebat.

344. Deinde cum dicit *sanctificatus est vir*, posita admonitione, hic ponit admonitionis rationem, ubi allegat exemplum; secundo periculum, ibi *alioquin*, etc.; tertio fructum, ibi *nunc autem sancti*, et cetera.

345. In prima primo exemplificat de viro infideli, secundo de muliere, ibi: *et sanctificata est mulier*, et cetera.

Dicit ergo, *sanctificatus est*, quasi dicat: fidelis infidelem volentem cohabitare non dimittat; hoc ideo dico, *sanctificatus est enim*, et cetera.

Hoc dupliciter legitur. Primo modo sic: *sanctificatus est enim vir infidelis*, aliquando, *per mulierem fidelem*;

In regard to the first:

first, he gives an admonition;

second, the reason for the admonition, at *for the unbelieving husband*.

In regard to the first:

first, he speaks in general to men and women;

second, in particular to the men, at *if any brother has a wife*;

third, in particular to the women, at *and if any woman has a husband*.

342. He says therefore, *for to the rest*, i.e., where both are not believers, but one is a believer and the other an unbeliever, *I speak*, by way of counsel and not of command, *not the Lord*. As if to say: I say this from the Lord, although he does not say it with his own lips. This is what I say: *if any brother*, a believer, is converted to the faith while married. For this is understood of those who married as unbelievers, not of those who are in disparity of cult; for then there was no marriage, and they would have to be separated as Ezra did in Ezra 10. *If a brother*, I say, *has a wife who believes not and she consents to dwell with him* without insulting the Creator, *let him not put her away*. It is a counsel not a precept, so that if one does the contrary, he is not a transgressor, according to a Gloss.

343. Then when he says, *and if any woman*, he speaks in particular to women, where he first of all supposes faith in someone; second, unbelief in this other when he says, *has a husband who believes not*; third, the unbeliever is willing to live together, when he says, *and he consents to dwell with her*; fourth, he advises the believer to remain with him when he says, *let her not put away her husband*.

He says, therefore: and likewise, *if any woman has a husband who believes not and he consents to dwell with her* without insulting the Creator; for if he were unwilling to live with her without insulting the name of Christ, the believer should divorce him, because *insulting the Creator dissolves a marriage*, as a Gloss says, and she may marry again. If, I say, that is the case, *let her not put away her husband*. It is a counsel, not a precept; for it is lawful for the unbeliever to divorce the believer, but then it was not expedient.

344. Then when he says, *for the unbelieving husband*, he gives the reason for the admonition just given. First, he proposes an example; second, the danger, at *otherwise your children*; third, the fruit, at *but now they are holy*.

345. In regard to the first he does two things: first, he gives the example of an unbelieving husband; second, of an unbelieving wife, at *and the unbelieving wife*.

He says, therefore, *the unbelieving husband is sanctified by the believing wife*; as if to say: the wife who believes should not divorce the unbelieving spouse willing to live with her, because he *is sanctified by the believing wife*.

This is read in two ways. In the first way thus: *the unbelieving husband is* sometimes *sanctified by the believing*

id est, aliquando contingit quod unus per alium convertitur ad fidem, et sic sanctificatur; et hoc iam forte contigerat, sicut Sisinnius per Theodoram Romae tempore Clementis conversus est. Et similiter *sanctificata est mulier infidelis per virum fidelem*, scilicet per ipsius admonitionem et doctrinam.

Alio modo legitur sic: ita fidelis infidelem non dimittat, *sanctificatus est enim vir*, etc., id est, nullam immunditiam contrahit fidelis ex cohabitatione vel ex commixtione cum infideli, sed servat veram pudicitiam, secundum Augustinum.

346. Deinde cum dicit *alioquin filii*, etc., hoc legitur dupliciter: uno modo de filiis nascituris; alio modo de iam natis.

Primo modo sic: *alioquin*, scilicet si disceditis, et vos aliis copulatis, *filii vestri*, qui de hac copula nascerentur, *immundi essent*, scilicet spurii, quia non de legitimo matrimonio. *Nunc autem*, si permanetis, *sancti sunt*, id est, mundi, quia de legitimis coniugiis nati.

Secundo modo legitur sic: *alioquin*, scilicet si disceditis, *filii vestri*, iam nati, *immundi essent*, id est, in infidelitate remanerent, sequentes scilicet maiorem partem quae tunc erat infidelium; *nunc autem*, si permanetis, *sancti sunt*, id est, Christiani fiunt.

347. Deinde cum dicit *sanctificatus est vir infidelis per mulierem fidelem*.

Thema in festo Beatae Caeciliae quae convertit virum suum ad fidem.

Inter omnia quae regunt hominem in via salutis praecipuum est sequi societatem sanctorum. Hoc ostendit Psalmista verbo, cum dicit: *cum sancto sanctus eris*, etc.; hoc ostendit Caecilia facto, secundum quod hic dicitur: *sanctificatus est vir*, etc.; in quibus verbis tria commendant ipsam, scilicet natura, gratia et doctrina.

Natura humana quae notatur in muliere: gratia, quae notatur in viri sanctificatione, ut sibi sit nobilis per naturam, Deo humilis per fidem, proximo utilis per doctrinam. Doctrina enim redditur commendabilior consideranti actum, obiectum, et oppositum.

Actus est sanctificare, obiectum est vir, oppositum est infidelitas. Infidelitas est culpa tenacior: virilitas sexus robustior: sanctificare actus difficilior. Et tamen cum esset mulier, per doctrinam suam convertit incredulum, emollivit robustum, mundavit immundum, et sic sanctificavit infidelem virum.

Multae vero sunt proprietates mulieris commendabiles, quae huic conveniunt, ut sint tres proprietates quoad actum cordis, tres quoad actum oris, et tres quoad actum operis.

wife, i.e., it sometimes happens that one is converted to the faith by the other. And this has probably happened already, as Sisinnius was converted to the faith in Rome by Theodora during the reign of Clement. Likewise, *the unbelieving wife is sanctified by the believing husband*, namely, by his admonition and doctrine.

In another way it can be read thus: so the believer should not divorce the unbeliever, *for the unbelieving husband is sanctified by the believing wife*, i.e., the believer does not contract uncleanness by cohabiting with or uniting with the unbelieving spouse, but preserves true modesty, according to Augustine.

346. Then when he says, *otherwise your children*, this is read in two ways: first, of children to be born; second, of children already born.

In the first way it is read thus: *otherwise*, if you depart and you both have relations with others, *your children*, who would be born of this union, *should be unclean*, i.e., spurious, because not born of a lawful union. *But now*, if you endure, *they are holy*, i.e., clean, because they are born of a lawful union.

In the second way it is read thus: *otherwise*, namely, if you separate, *your children* already born *should be unclean*, i.e., would remain in unbelief, following the majority, which would be unbelievers; *but now*, if you remain together, *they are holy*, i.e., become Christians.

347. Then when he says *the husband who is not a believer is sanctified by a believing wife*,

One recalls the theme of the feast of Blessed Cecilia, who converted her husband to the faith.

Among everything that directs man in the way of salvation the greatest is entering fellowship with the saints. The psalmist shows this by his words, when he says: *with the holy you will be holy*; Cecilia shows this by her deeds, as is here said: *the husband is sanctified*, in which words three things commend her, namely nature, grace and teaching.

Human nature, which is observed in the woman: grace, which is observed in the sanctification of her husband, so that she is honorable in herself by nature, humble toward God by faith, useful to her neighbor by teaching. For the teaching is rendered particularly praiseworthy to one who considers its act, its object, and its opposite.

The act is sanctification, its object is the man, its opposite is unbelief. Unbelief is a particularly obstinate fault: the manly sex particularly resistant to change: to sanctify a particularly difficult act. Yet though she was a woman, by her teaching she converted the unbeliever, softened the firm, cleansed the unclean, and thus sanctified the unbelieving husband.

Many indeed are the commendable properties of woman that she possesses: three properties as to the act of her heart, three as to the act of the mouth, and three as to the work she does.

Tres primae sunt: sapientia ex parte rationalis, Prov. XIV, 1: *sapiens mulier aedificat sibi domum*, munditia ex parte concupiscibilis, Eccli. XL, 19: *aedificatio civitatis confirmabit nomen, et super eam mulier immaculata computabitur*, constantia ex parte irascibilis, Ruth III, 11: *scit omnis populus te esse mulierem virtutis*, etc.;

tres secundae sunt: modestia contra multiloquium, Eccli. XXVI, 18: *mulier sensata et tacita non est immutatio animae eruditae*: veritas contra mendacium, Iudith VIII, 28: *omnia quae locuta es vera sunt*, discretio contra stultiloquium, I Reg. XXV, 3: *erat mulier prudentissima et speciosissima*; Iudith c. XI, 19: *non est talis mulier super terram in aspectu, et in pulchritudine et in sensu verborum.*

Tres ultimae sunt: sanctimonia in facto, Iudith VIII, 29: *ora pro populo, quia mulier sancta es*, verecundia in signo, Eccli. XXVI, v. 19: *gratia super gratiam mulier sancta et pudorata*, gratia in conversando, Prov. XI, 16: *mulier gratiosa inveniet gloriam.*

Propter eminentiam horum dicitur de Beata Virgine Maria: *benedicta tu in mulieribus.*

The first three are: wisdom in regard to the rational part: *a wise woman builds a house for herself* (Prov 14:1); purity in regard to the concupisible: *the building of a city will confirm her name, and upon it she will be reckoned an immaculate woman* (Sir 40:19); constancy in regard to the irascible: *all people know you to be a woman of virtue* (Ruth 3:11).

The second three are: modesty against over-speaking: *an intelligent and silent woman is not a change for a learned soul* (Sir 26:18); truth against lying: *all that she has said is true* (Jdt 8:38); discretion against foolish talk: *she was a most wise and most beautiful woman*(1 Kgs 25:3); *there is no other such woman on earth in appearance, beauty, and in wisdom of words* (Jdt 11:19).

The last three are: sanctity in deed: *pray for the people, since you are a holy woman* (Jdt 8:29); modesty in signs: *a holy and modest woman is grace upon grace* (Sir 26:19); gracefulness in conversing: *a gracious woman will find glory* (Prov 11:16).

By reason of her eminence in these properties it is said of the Blessed Virgin Mary: *blessed are you among women.*

Lecture 3

7:15Quod si infidelis discedit, discedat: non enim servituti subjectus est frater, aut soror in hujusmodi: in pace autem vocavit nos Deus. [n. 348]

7:16Unde enim scis mulier, si virum salvum facies? aut unde scis vir, si mulierem salvam facies? [n. 350]

7:17Nisi unicuique sicut divisit Dominus, unumquemque sicut vocavit Deus, ita ambulet, et sicut in omnibus ecclesiis doceo. [n. 352]

7:18Circumcisus aliquis vocatus est? non adducat praeputium. In praeputio aliquis vocatus est? non circumcidatur. [n. 353]

7:19Circumcisio nihil est, et praeputium nihil est: sed observatio mandatorum Dei. [n. 355]

7:20Unusquisque in qua vocatione vocatus est, in ea permaneat. [n. 356]

7:15εἰ δὲ ὁ ἄπιστος χωρίζεται, χωριζέσθω· οὐ δεδούλωται ὁ ἀδελφὸς ἢ ἡ ἀδελφὴ ἐν τοῖς τοιούτοις· ἐν δὲ εἰρήνῃ κέκληκεν ὑμᾶς ὁ θεός.

7:16τί γὰρ οἶδας, γύναι, εἰ τὸν ἄνδρα σώσεις; ἢ τί οἶδας, ἄνερ, εἰ τὴν γυναῖκα σώσεις;

7:17Εἰ μὴ ἑκάστῳ ὡς ἐμέρισεν ὁ κύριος, ἕκαστον ὡς κέκληκεν ὁ θεός, οὕτως περιπατείτω· καὶ οὕτως ἐν ταῖς ἐκκλησίαις πάσαις διατάσσομαι.

7:18περιτετμημένος τις ἐκλήθη; μὴ ἐπισπάσθω. ἐν ἀκροβυστίᾳ κέκληταί τις; μὴ περιτεμνέσθω.

7:19ἡ περιτομὴ οὐδέν ἐστιν, καὶ ἡ ἀκροβυστία οὐδέν ἐστιν, ἀλλὰ τήρησις ἐντολῶν θεοῦ.

7:20ἕκαστος ἐν τῇ κλήσει ᾗ ἐκλήθη ἐν ταύτῃ μενέτω.

7:15But if the unbeliever departs, let him depart. For a brother or sister is not under servitude in such cases. But God has called us in peace. [n. 348]

7:16For how do you know, O wife, whether you shall save your husband? Or how do you know, O man, whether you shall save your wife? [n. 350]

7:17But as the Lord has distributed to every one, as God has called every one: so let him walk. And so in all churches I teach. [n. 352]

7:18Is any man called, being circumcised? Let him not procure uncircumcision. Is any man called in uncircumcision? Let him not be circumcised. [n. 353]

7:19Circumcision is nothing and uncircumcision is nothing: but the observance of the commandments of God. [n. 355]

7:20Let every man abide in the same calling in which he was called. [n. 356]

---

348. Superius ostendit quod fidelis non debet dimittere infidelem cohabitare volentem, hic autem dicit quod si non vult cohabitare, non tenetur fidelis eum sequi, sed potest alteri nubere; ubi primo ponitur ipsa concessio; secundo concessionis ratio duplex: prima est libertas, ibi *non est enim servituti*, etc.; secunda est pacis tranquillitas, ibi *in pace autem*, et cetera.

349. Dicit ergo: *quod si infidelis*, vel mulier, *discedit*, a fideli, odio fidei, *discedat*, et potest fidelis qui dimittitur contrahere; primum enim matrimonium dissolubile erat, quia numquam fuit ratum. *Non enim servituti*, scilicet coniugali, *subiectus est frater aut soror*, fidelis, id est, non cogitur sequi infidelem odio fidei discedentem, sicut dicit Glossa Io. VIII, 36: *si filius vos liberaverit, vere liberi eritis*. *In pace autem*, quasi dicat: ideo discedat fidelis, quia *in pace vocavit nos Deus*, id est, ideo non debemus litigare cum eo qui odio fidei discedit.

Vel sic, quamvis ita sit quod fidelis non est subiectus servituti, nihilominus tamen non debet occasionem

348. Above he showed that the believer should not send away an unbelieving spouse who desires to continue living together; here he says that if he does not want to live together, the believer is not bound to follow him, but can marry another: first he sets forth the concession itself; second the twofold reason for the concession: the first is freedom, when he says *for a brother or sister is not under servitude*; the second the tranquillity of peace, when he says *God has called us in peace*.

349. He says, therefore: *but if an unbeliever*, or wife, *departs*, from the believer, out of hatred for the faith, *let her depart*, and the believer who is left can marry; for the first marriage was dissoluble, since it was never ratified. *For a brother or sister is not under servitude*, namely conjugal servitude; that is, a believer is not bound to follow the unbeliever who departs out of hatred for the faith, as the Gloss says on John 8:36, *if the son has set you free, you will be truly free*. *But God has called us in peace*, as though to say, the believer may depart because *God has called us in peace*, i.e., therefore we should not quarrel with him who departs out of hatred for the faith.

Or in this way: although the believer is not subject to servitude, still he should not give an occasion for discord

discordiae et dissidii praebere, sed pacem servare. *In pace autem vocavit nos Deus. Non est* enim *Deus dissensionis, sed pacis*, infra XIV, 33.

350. Deinde cum dicit *unde enim scis, mulier*, etc., hic dicit quod si infidelis non discedat, fidelis debet patienter commanere. Ad quod allegat

primo spem alienae conversionis;

secundo permanentiam in statu propriae vocationis, ibi *unumquemque sicut vocavit Deus*, etc.;

tertio exemplum in ritu conversationis, ibi *circumcisus aliquis*, etc.;

quarto exemplum in statu conditionis, ibi *servus vocatus es*, et cetera.

In prima, primo innuit quod mulier fidelis commanendo, virum ad fidem potest convertere; secundo quod similiter vir fidelis mulierem infidelem potest salvare, ibi *aut unde scis hoc, vir*, etc.; tertio quod ideo debent patienter commanere, ibi *nisi unicuique*, et cetera.

351. Dicit ergo *unde enim scis*, quasi dicat: vere debet manere fidelis cum infideli, quia *unde scis*, id est, scire potes, o tu mulier fidelis, *si virum* infidelem *salvum facies?* Eum scilicet commonendo et convertendo ad fidem; quasi dicat, hoc potest contingere. Ambrosius: hoc ideo dicit, quia forsan potest credere qui horret nomen Christi. *Aut unde scis*, id est, scire potes, o tu *vir* fidelis, *si mulierem* infidelem *salvam facies*, eam ad fidem convertendo? Quia hoc sperare debes.

Nisi unicuique, hoc dupliciter legitur; uno modo sic: unde scis hoc, *nisi* ita habeas te, supple ad tuum comparem, *sicut Dominus divisit unicuique?* Scilicet viro praeesse, et mulieri subesse. Secundo modo sic: unde scis hoc, *nisi*, supple, patienter expectes fieri, *sicut divisit Dominus unicuique?* Id est, ordinavit de unoquoque quando credat et quando salvetur. Ergo tu debes expectare et commanere. Rom. XII, 3: *unicuique sicut divisit Dominus*.

352. Deinde cum dicit *unumquemque sicut vocavit*, etc., hic ostendit quod fidelis debet manere cum infideli coniuge, allegans permanentiam in statu propriae vocationis. Primo ergo allegat divinam vocationem; secundo suam auctoritatem, ibi *sicut in omnibus ecclesiis*, et cetera.

Dicit ergo, *unumquemque*, quasi dicat: et quomodo scis hoc, o vir et mulier, nisi quilibet *ambulet* perseveranter *ita sicut Deus vocavit unumquemque*, id est, in eo statu in quo Deus vocavit unumquemque, non autem quomodo sint. Quasi dicat: et hoc ita praedico in ecclesia vestra, *sicut in omnibus ecclesiis*. Turpis enim est pars quae suo toto non convenit.

and disagreement, but preserve peace. *God has called us in peace: for God is not the God of dissension, but of peace* (1 Cor 14:33).

350. Then when he says, *how do you know, O wife*, he says that if the unbeliever does not depart, the believer should patiently remain together. To this end he alleges:

first, the hope of the other's conversion;

second, the continuance in the state of one's own vocation, at *let each remain as God called him*;

third, an example in ritual behavior, at *is any man called*;

fourth, an example in legal condition, at *were you called* (1 Cor 7:21).

In the first statement, he first suggests that a believing woman by remaining can convert her husband to the faith; second, that likewise a believing man can save an unbelieving wife, at *or how do you know, O man*; third, that therefore they should patiently remain together, at *but as the Lord has distributed*.

351. He therefore says *how do you know*, as though to say: truly a believing wife should remain with an unbelieving husband, since *how do you know*, i.e., how can you know, *O* believing *wife, whether you shall save your husband* who does not believe? That is, by recalling and converting him to the faith, as though to say: this can happen. Ambrose: he therefore says this, because perhaps he who shudders at the name of Christ can come to believe. Or *how do you know*, i.e., can you know, *O you believing man, whether you shall save your wife*, who does not believe, by converting her to the faith. For you should hope for this.

But as the Lord has distributed, can be understood in two ways; in one way as follows: *how do you know* this, unless you stand to your partner *as the Lord has distributed for every one*? i.e., that the man be superior, and the woman subject. It can also be understood in a second way: *how do you know* this except patiently awaiting that to happen, *as the Lord has distributed for every one*? i.e., he has ordained regarding each one when he believes and when he is saved. Therefore you ought to await it and remain with him. *As the Lord has appointed for each* (Rom 12:3).

352. Then he says, *as God has called every one: so let him walk*, he shows that the believer should remain with the unbelieving spouse, alleging continuance in the state of his own calling. First he alleges the divine calling; second his own authority, at *and so in all churches I teach*.

Therefore he says, *every one*, as though to say: and how do you know this, O man and woman, unless each one *walk* perseveringly *as God has called every one*, i.e., in that state in which God called each one, but not as they are. As though to say: and I preach this in your church, *and so in all churches*. For a part that does not agree to its whole is shameful.

Est ergo sua ratio talis: unusquisque debet manere in eo statu in quem Deus vocavit; ergo si vocavit aliquos in coniugium, debent manere in ipso. Haymo: *si habeas uxorem, maneas cum ea, et si non habeas, ducere non concupiscas.*

353. Deinde cum dicit *circumcisus aliquis*, etc., hic ponit exemplum: ubi

primo ponit ipsum exemplum;

secundo exempli rationem, ibi *circumcisio enim nihil est*;

tertio regulam generalem, ibi *unusquisque in qua vocatione*.

354. Ponit autem exemplum in ritu vivendi, primo Iudaeorum, secundo gentilium, ibi *in praeputio aliquis vocatus est*, et cetera.

Dicit ergo *circumcisus*, etc., quasi dicat: unusquisque ambulet in eo statu in quo vocatus est; verbi gratia *circumcisus quis vocatus est*, id est in ritu Iudaico? *Non adducat*, id est, non cogatur adducere, *praeputium*, id est, ritum gentilium. *In praeputio*, id est, in ritu gentili, *quis vocatus est? Non circumcidatur*, id est non cogatur ad ritus Iudaicos. Augustinus: servat ubique Apostolus construere ecclesias, sive Iudaeorum, sive gentilium; numquam enim aufert consuetudinem, quae servata non impedit salutem; ergo si coniugium non impediat, debent vocati in coniugio commanere.

355. Deinde cum dicit *circumcisio enim nihil est*, hic subdit rationem exempli, quae talis est: ritus non impediens salutem, non debet mutari propter vocationem ad fidem, sed ritus tam Iudaicus quam gentilis est huiusmodi, ergo et cetera. A simili ergo arguit in matrimonio.

Primo ergo tangit quod est ad salutem indifferens; secundo quod est necessarium et expediens, ibi *sed observatio mandatorum*, et cetera.

Dicit igitur *circumcisio nihil est*, id est nihil prodest, *et praeputium nihil est*, id est nihil prodest vel obest; quasi dicat: talis vel talis ritus vivendi nihil proficit ad salutem. Gal. ult.: *in Christo Iesu nec circumcisio aliquid valet, nec praeputium, sed nova creatura.* Ambr.: *ad salutem nec prodest nec obest Iudaicus aut gentilis ritus.* *Sed observatio mandatorum Dei*, aliquid prodest. Sap. VI, 19: *custoditio legum, consummatio est incorruptionis.*

356. Deinde cum dicit *unusquisque in qua vocatione*, etc., hic concludit regulam generalem, dicens *unusquisque*, etc., quasi dicat: ita gentilis non inducatur ad circumcisionem, nec econverso; sed potius unusquisque in qua conditione vocatus est, *in ea*, scilicet conditione vocationi non repugnante, *in ea permaneat*, et *in qua*, non *a qua*. In Glossa Augustini: *hoc enim ad eas consuetudines vitae retulit, quae nihil obsunt fidei bonisque*

So his reasoning is as follows: each one should remain in that state unto which God called him; therefore if he called some to marriage, they should remain in it. Haymo: *if you have a wife, remain with her, and if you do not have a wife, do not desire to marry one.*

353. Then when he says *is any man called*, he gives an example.

He first gives the example itself;

second, the explanation of the example, at *circumcision is nothing*;

third, the general rule, at *let every man abide*.

354. He gives in an example in the ceremonies of life, first of the Jews, then of the Gentiles, at *is any man called in circumcision*.

Therefore he says *circumcised*, as though to say, let each one walk in that state in which he was called, for example, *is any man called, being circumcised*, i.e., in the Jewish rite? Let him not take, i.e., not be forced to take, *uncircumcision*, i.e., the rite of the Gentiles. *Is any man called in uncircumcision*, i.e., in the rite of the Gentiles? *Let him not be circumcised*, i.e., not be forced to the Jewish rites. Augustine: the Apostle upholds the upbuilding of the churches, both the Jewish and the gentile; for he never takes away a custom, the keeping of which is no obstacle to salvation; therefore if marriage is not an obstacle, those called should remain in marriage.

355. Then when he says, *circumcision is nothing*, he adds an explanation of the example, which is as follows: a rite that is not an obstacle to salvation, should not be changed on account of the vocation to faith, but both the Jewish and the gentile is of this sort, therefore etc. He argues in the case of marriage from this similar case.

First he touches on that which is indifferent in regard to salvation, second on that which is necessary and expedient, at *but the observance of the commandments*.

Therefore he says *circumcision is nothing*, i.e., brings no gain, *and uncircumcision is nothing*, i.e., brings neither gain nor loss, as though to say: this or that rite of living contributes nothing to salvation: *in Christ Jesus neither circumcision is of any value, nor uncircumcision, but a new creature* (Gal 6:15). Ambrose says: *the Jewish or the gentile rite neither contributes to nor hinders salvation.* **But the observance of the commandments of God** brings gain. *The keeping of the laws is the consummation of incorruption* (Wis 6:19).

356. Then when he says, *let every man abide in the same calling in which he was called*, he deduces the general rule, saying *let every man abide* as though to say: thus let not the gentile be led to circumcision, nor conversely, but rather in that condition in which each one was called, *in the same*, namely a condition that is not opposed to the vocation, *abide in the same*. And he says *in which*, not *from which*. In Augustine's Gloss: *for this bears on those ways of*

moribus; sicut enim coniux, sic et latro ad fidem vocatur. Sed ille in coniugio manet, non a coniugio revocatur. Iste vero a latrocinio revocatur, et in latrocinio non manet. Non enim necesse est ut coniuges desinant esse coniuges propter Christi fidem, sicut necesse est ut latrones desinant esse latrones.

357. Hic quaeritur super illud **uxorem a viro non discedere**, quare solam causam fornicationis Dominus excipit, caeteras vero omnes molestias iubet fortiter sustineri.

Contra Lev. XIII, 26 praecipit lex leprosum extra castra eiicere; ergo pro lepra debet uxor a viro discedere.

Respondeo: licet possit ob lepram discedere a cohabitatione, non tamen a thoro, quin aliquando teneatur reddere debitum, prope eam manendo.

358. Item **aut viro suo reconciliari**.

Contra, Deut. XXIV, 4 dicitur, quod semel repudiata non potest amplius reconciliari.

Respondeo: illud habebat locum in repudio legali, istud vero in divortio evangelico. Lex enim erat severitatis, sed Evangelium pietatis.

359. Item super illud: **vir uxorem non dimittat**, Glossa notabilis: *non subdit de viro sicut de muliere, quia licet viro aliam ducere.*

Contra Augustinus dicit quod similis forma debet servari in viro et muliere.

Respondeo: illud primum in libris Ambrosii a falsariis creditur additum. Vel dicendum quod illud Ambrosii intelligitur in repudio, hoc autem in divortio; nam in repudio legali licebat viro contrahere, non uxori, quia licebat antiquitus uni viro habere plures uxores, non econverso, quia per repudium illud solvebatur matrimonium, non autem per divortium.

360. Item **nam caeteris ego dico, non Dominus**.

Contra Matth. IX: *qui vos audit, me audit.*

Respondeo. Non Dominus dicit ore proprio, sed inspirando.

361. Item super illud **si quis frater habet uxorem**, Glossa: *coniux fidelis licite potest dimittere infidelem.*

Contra, Catholica non potest dimittere haereticum.

Glossa loquitur de infideli qui caret sacramento fidei, non solum habitu.

362. Item ibidem Glossa: *non est reputandum matrimonium quod extra decretum Dei factum est.*

life, that are in no measure contrary to faith or to good morals; for as a married person, so also a thief is called to the faith. But the former remains in marriage, is not called from marriage, while the latter is called from thievery, and does not remain in thievery. For it is not necessary for spouses to cease to be spouses for the sake of the faith of Christ, as it is necessary for thieves to cease to be thieves.

357. Here it is asked in reference to the command that **the wife not depart from her husband** (1 Cor 7:10), why the Lord made an exception only on account of fornication, but commands all other troubles to be courageously endured.

Against this, the law commands one to cast a leper outside of the camp (Lev 13:36); therefore for leprosy a woman should depart from her husband.

I respond: although she can depart from living together on account of leprosy, she cannot depart from his bed, but is sometimes bound to render the debt, remaining near him.

358. Again **or be reconciled to her husband** (1 Cor 1:11).

Against this, it is said that a wife once repudiated cannot be again reconciled (Deut 24:4).

I respond: that applies to legal repudiation, while the other applies to evangelical divorce. For the law contained severity, but the Gospel piety.

359. Again, in reference to **let not the husband put away his wife** (1 Cor 7:11), a notable Gloss says: *he does not add it about the husband as about the wife, because it is permitted to the husband to marry another.*

Against this Augustine says that the same form should be kept in the case of man and wife.

I respond: that first gloss is believed to have been added by forgers to the books of Ambrose. Or it should be said that that saying of Ambrose is understood in the case of repudiation, while this is understood in the case of divorce; for in legal divorce it was permitted for the man to marry, but not for the wife, because in ancient times one man was allowed to have many wives, but not conversely – for the marriage was dissolved by that repudiation, but not by divorce.

360. Again **for to the rest I speak, not the Lord** (1 Cor 7:12).

Against this: *he who hears you, hears me* (Luke 10:16).

I respond, the Lord does not speak with his own mouth, but by inspiring.

361. Again, on **if any brother has a wife** (1 Cor 7:12), the Gloss says: *a believing spouse can licitly send away an unbelieving spouse.*

Against this, a Catholic cannot send away a heretic.

The Gloss speaks about the unbeliever who lacks the sacrament of faith, not only the habit.

362. Again, the Gloss on the same passage: *marriage done outside of God's decree is not to be regarded as marriage.*

Contra: ergo matrimonium contractum causa volup-
tatis non est matrimonium.

Respondeo. Extra decretum Dei matrimonium contrahi dicitur, quando contrahitur inter personas lege
prohibitas.

363. Item *si qua mulier habet virum infidelem*, et
cetera.

Contra: ergo Iudaea conversa non debet dimittere virum Iudaeum, cohabitare volentem.

Respondeo. Secus est hodie quam tempore primiti-
vae Ecclesiae, quia tunc erat spes conversionis, nunc autem potius est spes subversionis propter obstinationem
infidelium.

364. Item super illud *quod si infidelis, discedat*,
Glossa: *recte dimittitur mulier si dicat viro. Non ero mulier tua, nisi de latrocinio divitias mihi augeas.*

Contra Matth. XIX, 9 excipitur sola causa fornicationis.

Respondeo. Tunc debet dimitti, ne scandalum, ad
tempus exortum, sit in perpetuum.

365. Item super illud *non est enim servituti subiectus*, Glossa: *contumelia creatoris solvit ius matrimonii in
eo qui relinquitur.*

Contra: matrimonium semper est inter duos; ergo in
utroque solvitur vel in nullo.

Respondeo. Matrimonium solvitur in utroque, sed
impedimentum ex matrimonio resultans, manet in di-
scedente solum.

366. Item *circumcisio nihil est*.

Contra *circumcisio quidem prodest, si legem observes.*

Respondeo. Ante Christum proderat, sed post non
prodest.

367. Item super illud *unusquisque in qua vocatione*, Glossa: *ad salutem nihil prodest vel obest Iudaicus vel
gentilis ritus.*

Contra, Gal. V, 2: *si circumcidimini, Christus vobis
nihil prodest.*

Responsio. Glossa loquitur de ritu conversandi inter
homines, non de ritu Deum colendi.

Against this: therefore marriage contracted for the sake
of pleasure is not marriage.

I respond: marriage is said to be contracted outside
God's decree, when it is contracted between persons prohibited by the law.

363. Again, *if any woman has a husband who believes
not* (1 Cor 7:13).

Against this: therefore a Jewish woman who converts
should not send away a Jewish husband, who wants to continue living together.

I respond, it is different today than it was in the time of
the early Church, because then there was hope of conversion, but now there is rather hope of ruin on account of the
obstinancy of the unbelievers.

364. Again, on the text *but if the unbeliever departs*,
the Gloss says: *a woman is rightly sent away if she says to her
husband: I will not be your wife unless you gain wealth for
me by robbery.*

Against this, an exception is made only in the case of
fornication (Matt 19:9).

I respond, she should be sent away then, lest the scandal
that has arisen temporarily become permanent.

365. Again, on the text *for a brother or sister is not under servitude*, the Gloss says: *insulting the Creator releases
from the marital duty for him who is left behind.*

Against this: marriage is always between two persons;
therefore it is either dissolved in both or in neither one.

I respond, the marriage is dissolved in both, but the impediment resulting from marriage remains only in the one
who departs.

366. Again, *circumcision is nothing*.

Against this, *circumcision is indeed of value, if you keep
the law.*

I respond, it was of value before Christ, but it is not of
value after him.

367. Again, on the text *let every man abide in the same
calling*, the Gloss says: *the Jewish or the gentile rite neither
contributes to nor hinders salvation.*

Against this stands: *if you are circumcised, Christ will be
of no value to you* (Gal 5:2).

The response to this is that the Gloss speaks about the
rite of living as regards relationships among men, not about
the rite of worshiping God.

Lecture 4

7:21Servus vocatus es? non sit tibi curae: sed et si potes fieri liber, magis utere. [n. 368]	7:21δοῦλος ἐκλήθης; μή σοι μελέτω: ἀλλ' εἰ καὶ δύνασαι ἐλεύθερος γενέσθαι, μᾶλλον χρῆσαι.	7:21Were you called, being a slave? Care not for it: but if you can become made free, rather use it. [n. 368]
7:22Qui enim in Domino vocatus est servus, libertus est Domini: similiter qui liber vocatus est, servus est Christi. [n. 370]	7:22ὁ γὰρ ἐν κυρίῳ κληθεὶς δοῦλος ἀπελεύθερος κυρίου ἐστίν: ὁμοίως ὁ ἐλεύθερος κληθεὶς δοῦλός ἐστιν Χριστοῦ.	7:22For he who is called in the Lord, being a slave, is the freedman of the Lord. Likewise he who is called, being free, is the slave of Christ. [n. 370]
7:23Pretio empti estis: nolite fieri servi hominum.	7:23τιμῆς ἠγοράσθητε: μὴ γίνεσθε δοῦλοι ἀνθρώπων.	7:23You are bought with a price: do not become the slaves of men.
7:24Unusquisque in quo vocatus est, fratres, in hoc permaneat apud Deum. [n. 374]	7:24ἕκαστος ἐν ᾧ ἐκλήθη, ἀδελφοί, ἐν τούτῳ μενέτω παρὰ θεῷ.	7:24Brethren, let every man, wherein he was called, therein abide with God. [n. 374]

368. Superius ostendit quod si infidelis coniux non discedat, fidelis debet patienter commanere. Primo ad hoc allegando spem conversionis infidelis; secundo permanentiam in statu propriae vocationis; tertio exemplum in ritu conversationis, hic; quarto allegat exemplum in statu conditionis. Ubi

primo ipsum exemplum ponit;

secundo rationem exempli subdit, ibi *qui enim in Domino*, etc.;

tertio ex hoc regulam generalem concludit, ibi *unusquisque ergo*, et cetera.

In prima primo proponit in aliquo statum servilem; secundo supponit libertatis possibilitatem, ibi *sed et si potes*, etc.; tertio horum praeeminentiam ad salutem, ibi *magis utere*.

369. Dicit ergo *servus*, etc., quasi dicat: unusquisque in qua vocatione vocatus est, in ea permaneat, verbi gratia, *servus vocatus es?* Ad fidem scilicet Christi, *non sit tibi curae*, ut scilicet velis servitutem effugere. Unde Onesimum servum Philemonis, qui ad eum confugerat, cum precibus remittit ad Dominum, ut patet in epistola ad Philemonem; *sed*, potius, *si potes fieri liber*, maneas in servitute, quia causa est humilitatis. Et sicut ait Ambrosius: *quanto quis despectior est in hoc saeculo propter Dominum, tanto magis exaltabitur in futuro*. Gregorius: *quanto quis Deo pretiosior est, tanto propter eum utilior*. Boetius: *cum omnis fortuna timenda sit, magis tamen prospera quam adversa*.

370. Deinde cum dicit *qui enim in Domino vocatus est*, etc., hic subdit rationem exempli. Et primo ponit rationem exempli ex parte servorum; secundo ex parte liberorum, ibi *similiter qui liber est*, et cetera.

Et est ratio talis in generali: servitus et libertas sunt in Domino ad salutem, sed solum debemus esse solliciti

368. Above he showed that if an unbelieving spouse does not depart, the believer should patiently remain. To show this he adduced first the hope of the conversion of the unbeliever, second the continuance in the state of one's own vocation, third an example in the rite of living; here, fourth, he adduces an example in legal condition.

First he gives the example itself;

second he adds the explanation of the example, at *for he who is called in the Lord*;

third, he deduces the general rule from this, at brethren, *let every man*.

And first he supposes in someone the servile state; second he supposes the possibility of liberty, at *but if you can*; third which of these is more beneficial for salvation, at *rather, use it*.

369. He says therefore, *were you called, being as slave?* as though to say: each one should remain in that vocation in which he was called, for example, *were you called* i.e., to faith in Christ *being a slave? Care not for it* as wanting to flee servitude. Hence Onesimus, Philemon's slave, who had fled to him, he sent back to his master with prayers, as one sees in the epistle to Philemon; *but if you can become free*, remain rather in servitude, since it is a cause of humility. And as Ambrose says: *the more someone is despised in this age on account of the Lord, the more he will be exalted in the future age*. Gregory says: *the more someone is precious to God, the more useful on his account*. Boethius says: *though all fortune is to be feared, still good fortune more than adverse fortune*.

370. Then when he says, *for he who is called in the Lord*, he adds an explanation of the example. And first he gives the explanation of the example on the part of slaves, then on the part of free men, at *likewise he who is called*.

And the reason in general is as follows: servitude and liberty in the Lord are conducive to salvation, but we should only be solicitous about things pertaining to salvation,

de pertinentibus ad salutem, ergo pro indifferenti debet esse nobis servitus et libertas.

Dicit ergo *qui enim in Domino*, quasi dicat: et vere non debes curare, *enim*, pro *quia*, *qui in Domino*, id est in fide Domini, *vocatus est servus*, servitute corporali, *libertus est Domini*; quia scilicet a Domino manumissus liber est libertate spirituali. Est autem libertus a servitute liberatus, et talis a servitute peccati a Domino est liberatus; ideo Domini libertus. Io. VIII, 36: *si Filius vos liberaverit, vere liberi eritis*.

371. Deinde cum dicit *similiter qui liber vocatus est*, etc., hic ponit rationem ex parte liberorum.

Ubi primo tangit in liberis cum servis pro Christo debitam servitutem; secundo servitutis rationem, ibi *pretio empti*; tertio servitutis obligationem, ibi *nolite*, et cetera.

Dicit ergo: *similiter et qui liber vocatus est*, libertate corporali, *servus est Christi*, servitute spirituali, Rom. I, 1: *Paulus servus Christi Iesu*, etc., quia sive servus, sive liber, omnes tamen servi. Et hoc iustum est, quia *pretio empti estis*. Hoc dicitur, quia pretio inaestimabili sanguine Christi. I Petr. I, 18: *non corruptibilibus auro vel argento redempti estis de vestra vana conversatione, et cetera*. Et quia tanto *pretio empti estis, nolite fieri servi hominum*, postponendo servitium Dei et vos humanis superstitionibus occupando, hoc enim faciebant isti. Supra I, 12: *ego sum Pauli, ego autem Apollo*.

372. *Unusquisque ergo*, et circumcisus et praeputiatus, servus et liber, *in quo*, statu, *vocatus est frater*, id est fidelis, *in hoc permaneat apud Deum*, scilicet observando divina mandata. *Qui enim perseveraverit usque in finem, hic salvus erit*, Matth. XXIV, v. 13. Ergo si coniugatus vocatus est ad fidem, maneat coniugatus, servando fidem.

therefore servitude or liberty should be a matter of indifference to us.

He says therefore *for he who is called in the Lord*, as though to say: and truly you should not care, *for*—standing for *because*—*he who is called in the Lord*, i.e., in the faith of the Lord, *being a slave*, by bodily slavery, *is the freedman of the Lord*; because, namely, he has been liberated by the Lord from servitude to sin, and therefore is a freedman of the Lord: *if the Son shall set you free, you shall be truly free* (John 8:36).

371. Then when he says *likewise he who is called, being free*, he gives an explanation on the part of freemen.

Here he first takes up the servitude due to Christ of both freemen and slaves, second the explanation of this servitude, at *you are bought with a price*, third the obligation of this servitude, at *do not become the slaves*.

He says, therefore: *likewise he who is called, being free*, with bodily freedom, *is the slave of Christ*, with spiritual servitude: *Paul, a slave of Christ Jesus* (Rom 1:1), since whether a slave or free, all are slaves. And this is just, since *you are bought with a price*. This is said on account of the inestimable price of the blood of Christ: *you were not redeemed with corruptible things, as gold or silver, from your vain ways of life* (1 Pet 1:18). And since *you are bought with so great a price, do not become the slaves of men* by considering service to God as secondary and occupying yourselves with human superstitions, as these persons indeed were doing. *I indeed am of Paul; and I am of Apollo* (1 Cor 1:12)

372. Faithful *brethren, let every man*, both the circumcised and the uncircumcised, slave and free, *wherein he was called*, i.e., in whatever state, *therein abide with God*, namely by keeping the divine commandments. *For he who perseveres unto the end shall be saved* (Matt 24:13). Therefore if a married man is called to the faith, he should remain married, keeping faith.

Lecture 5

7:25De virginibus autem praeceptum Domini non habeo: consilium autem do, tamquam misericordiam consecutus a Domino, ut sim fidelis. [n. 373]

7:26Existimo ergo hoc bonum esse propter instantem necessitatem, quoniam bonum est homini sic esse. [n. 375]

7:27Alligatus es uxori? noli quaerere solutionem. Solutus es ab uxore? noli quaerere uxorem. [n. 376]

7:28Si autem acceperis uxorem, non peccasti. Et si nupserit virgo, non peccavit: tribulationem tamen carnis habebunt hujusmodi. Ego autem vobis parco. [n. 377]

7:25Περὶ δὲ τῶν παρθένων ἐπιταγὴν κυρίου οὐκ ἔχω, γνώμην δὲ δίδωμι ὡς ἠλεημένος ὑπὸ κυρίου πιστὸς εἶναι.

7:26Νομίζω οὖν τοῦτο καλὸν ὑπάρχειν διὰ τὴν ἐνεστῶσαν ἀνάγκην, ὅτι καλὸν ἀνθρώπῳ τὸ οὕτως εἶναι.

7:27δέδεσαι γυναικί; μὴ ζήτει λύσιν: λέλυσαι ἀπὸ γυναικός; μὴ ζήτει γυναῖκα.

7:28ἐὰν δὲ καὶ γαμήσῃς, οὐχ ἥμαρτες: καὶ ἐὰν γήμῃ ἡ παρθένος, οὐχ ἥμαρτεν. θλῖψιν δὲ τῇ σαρκὶ ἕξουσιν οἱ τοιοῦτοι, ἐγὼ δὲ ὑμῶν φείδομαι.

7:25Now, concerning virgins, I have no commandment of the Lord: but I give counsel, as having obtained mercy of the Lord, to be faithful. [n. 373]

7:26I think therefore that this is good on account of the pressing necessity: because it is good for a man to be so. [n. 375]

7:27Are you bound to a wife? Seek not to be loosed. Are you loosed from a wife? Seek not a wife. [n. 376]

7:28But if you take a wife, you have not sinned. And if a virgin marries, she has not sinned: nevertheless, such shall have tribulation of the flesh. But I spare you. [n. 377]

---

373. A principio huius cap. egit de matrimonio, hic incipit pars secunda, in qua agit de virginitate. Ubi

primo agit de virginibus;

secundo de virginum custodibus, ibi *si quis autem turpem se videri existimat*, et cetera.

In prima,

primo ponit virginibus permanendi in virginitate consilium;

secundo nubentibus dat bene vivendi modum, ibi *hoc itaque dico, fratres*, et cetera.

Tertio ostendit quod magis expedit servare continentiae propositum, ibi *volo autem vos sine sollicitudine esse*, et cetera.

In prima parte virginitatem consulit et laudat;

secundo matrimonium iam contractum concedit et approbat, ibi *alligatus es uxori*, etc.;

tertio matrimonium contrahendum defendit, et a peccato excusat, ibi *si autem acceperis uxorem*, et cetera.

In prima dicit duo de virginitate.

Primo quod non est servanda ex praecepto;

secundo quod est servanda ex consilio, ibi *consilium autem do*. Ubi ponit duplicem rationem quare istud consilium est servandum. Prima est consiliarii auctoritas; secunda rei consultae dignitas, ibi *existimo enim hoc bonum*.

374. Dicit ergo *de virginibus*, etc., quasi dicat: de coniugatis non separandis praeceptum Dei est, *de virginibus autem praeceptum Domini non habeo*; ut scilicet

373. At the beginning of this chapter he treated of marriage; here begins the second part, in which he treats of virginity.

He first treats of virgins;

second of the guardians of virgins, at *if any man thinks that he seems dishonored* (1 Cor 7:36).

And in the first considerations,

he first gives virgins the counsel of remaining in virginity.

Second, he indicates to those who marry the mode of living well, at *this therefore I say, brethren* (1 Cor 7:29);

Third, he shows that it is more expedient to hold to a resolution to be continent, at *I would have you be without solicitude* (1 Cor 7:32).

In the first part he counsels and praises virginity;

In the second part he allows as a concession, and approves marriage already contracted, at *are you bound to a wife*.

In the third part he defends contracting marriage and excuses it from sin, at *if you take a wife*.

In the first part he says two things about virginity.

First he says that one is not obliged by a precept to preserve it.

Second he says that it is a matter of counsel to preserve it, at *but I give counsel*. There he gives a twofold reason why this counsel should be kept. The first reason is the authority of the one giving the counsel, the second is the dignity of the thing counseled, at *I think therefore that this is good*.

374. Therefore he says, *concerning virgins*, as though to say, that spouses should not separate is a precept of God, *but concerning virgins, I have no commandment of the Lord*,

contineant, vel ut nubant. Quod enim de hoc dixit Dominus, Matth. XIX, 12, dixit consulendo: *qui potest*, inquit, *capere, capiat*. Virginitas autem, secundum Augustinum *res est non praecepta, suaderi potest, imperari non potest*. **Consilium autem do**, scilicet de continendo, consilium mihi a Spiritu Sancto inspiratum. Tob. IV, 19: *consilium semper a sapiente perquire*. Consilium, inquam, do, et hoc **tamquam consecutus a Domino misericordiam**, id est, apostolatum mihi misericorditer concessum. Consecutus, inquam, ad hoc **ut sim fidelis**, in dispensatione mihi credita. Unde credendum est mihi in consiliis. Lc. c. XII, 42: *quis putas est fidelis servus?* Haymo: *quia ei mandatum fuit ut esset fidelis consiliator, non debuit consilium indigentibus abscondere*. Et est argumentum quod est acquiescendum consilio praelati.

375. Deinde cum dicit **existimo ergo**, etc., hic tangitur dignitas eius quod consulitur. Et haec duplex: una quia expediens bonum; secunda, quia honestum, ibi **quoniam bonum est**, et cetera.

Dicit ergo **existimo**, etc., quasi dicat: quia fidelis consiliarius sum, **existimo ergo hoc bonum esse**, scilicet manere in virginitate, et hoc **propter instantem necessitatem**, coniugium scilicet vitandum, quia multae necessitates instant. Unde dicuntur esse in mola, Lc. XVII, 31. Unde vulgariter dicitur quod *matrimonium habet magnum os*.

Existimo, inquam, et vere, quia **bonum est homini sic esse**, scilicet in virginitate. Bonum scilicet honestum propter puritatem, delectabile propter libertatem, utile propter mercedem, quia ei debetur aureola et fructus centesimus, Lc. VIII. Augustinus in Glossa: *supergreditur virginitas conditionem humanae naturae, per quam homines angelis assimilantur. Maior tamen victoria virginum quam angelorum. Angeli enim sine carne vivunt, virgines autem in carne triumphant.*

376. Deinde cum dicit **alligatus es uxori**, etc., hic matrimonium contractum concedit et approbat. Ubi primo dicit quod coniugatus non debet quaerere divortium; secundo consulit quod solutus non quaerat coniugium, ibi **solutus es ab uxore**, et cetera.

Dicit ergo **alligatus**, etc.; quasi dicat: licet continere sit bonum, tamen **alligatus es uxori? Noli quaerere solutionem**, maxime si bona est. Eccli. VII, 21: *noli discedere a muliere sensata*. Et dicit **alligatus**, quasi duplici vinculo ligatus, scilicet consensu per matrimonium initiatum, et copula carnali per matrimonium consummatum. Si enim tantum uno vinculo, scilicet solo consensu ligatus esset, posset quaerere solutionem, scilicet intrando religionem.

namely that they remain in continence or that they marry. For concerning this the Lord spoke by way of counsel: *he who can accept this, let him accept it* (Matt 19:12). Now virginity, according to Augustine, *is not something prescribed; it can be recommended, but cannot be commanded*. **I give counsel**, in regard, namely, to remaining continent, a counsel inspired in me by the Holy Spirit: *always seek counsel of a wise man* (Tob 4:19). **I give counsel**, he says, and this **as having obtained mercy of the Lord**, i.e., as the apostolate was granted to me by mercy. Obtained, he says, unto this: **to be faithful**, in the dispensation entrusted to me. Hence credence should be given me in the matter of counsels: *who, do you think, is the faithful servant?* (Luke 12:42) Haymo: *because he was commanded to be a faithful counselor, it would not have been right for him to hide counsel from those who needed it*. And this is an argument for acceding to the counsel of a prelate.

375. Then when I says, **I think therefore**, he takes up the dignity of that which is counseled. And this is twofold: it has dignity in one way as expediting what is good; it has dignity in another way because it is honorable, at **that it is good**.

He says therefore, **I think**, as though to say: since I am a faithful counseler, **I therefore think that this is good**, namely to remain in virginity, and this **on account of the pressing necessity**, namely of avoiding marriage, since many necessities are pressing; hence they are said to be as a millstone (Luke 17:31). Hence the folk-saying that *marriage has a big mouth*.

I think, he says, and truly, that **it is good for a man to be so**, namely in virginity. An honorable good, namely, by reason of purity, pleasurable by reason of liberty, useful by reason of the reward, since to it is due the aureole and the hundredfold fruit (Luke 8). Augustine in the Gloss: *virginity, by which men are like unto angels, surpasses the condition of human nature. Yet the victory of virgins is greater than that of angels. For angels live without flesh, whereas virgins triumph in the flesh.*

376. Then when he says, **are you bound to a wife**, he allows as a concession, and approves marriage already contracted. Here he first says that a married man should not seek divorce; second, he gives counsel that one free of marriage should not seek to be married, at **are you loosed from a wife**.

He says, therefore, **are you bound to a wife?** As though to say: granted that remaining continent is good, **are you bound to a wife? Seek not to be loosed**, especially if she is good: *depart not from a wise wife* (Sir 7:21). And he says **bound**, as bound with a twofold bond, namely bound with the consent through the marriage initiated, and with the fleshly bond through the marriage consummated. For if there were only one bond, namely if he were bound only by consent, he could seek to be loosed, namely by entering religious life.

Solutus es ab uxore? Noli quaerere uxorem, si potes continere, quia, sicut dicunt apostoli Matth. XIX, 10, *si ita est causa hominis cum uxore, non expedit nubere*.

377. Deinde cum dicit ***si autem acceperis***, etc., hic excusat matrimonium contrahendum a peccato. Ubi primo ostendit quod matrimonium potest contrahi sine peccato; secundo quod levius est esse sine coniugio, ibi ***tribulationem tamen***, et cetera. In prima, primo proponit veritatem de non virgine; secundo de virgine, ibi ***et si nupserit***, et cetera.

Dicit ergo: si autem solutus es, noli quaerere uxorem. ***Si autem acceperis uxorem***, scilicet bono fine, non ad expletionem libidinis, ***non peccasti***. Hic autem est argumentum evidens contra haereticos qui contemnunt matrimonium, de quibus I Tim. IV, 3: *prohibentes nubere*.

Et similiter ***si nupserit virgo***, non virgo Deo dicata, quia, secundum Hieronymum, *voventibus virginitatem non solum nubere, sed etiam velle nubere peccatum est*, ***non peccavit***, scilicet nubendo, alioquin peccasset Beata Virgo, cum desponsata esset Ioseph. ***Tribulationem tamen carnis habebunt huiusmodi***, scilicet coniugati, id est, afflictionem pro rebus necessariis procurandis et sibi et filiis suis et aliis. Unde levius est esse sine coniugio.

Ego autem vobis parco, quasi dicat: consulo evitare coniugium, quod tamen concedo, parcendo infirmitati vestrae. Vel sic: ***ego autem vobis parco***, in hoc quod consulo cavere tribulationes carnis.

378. Notandum est hic quod sancta virginitas magnum bonum est propter multa.

Primo, quia carnis munditiam servat, Apoc. c. XIV, 4: *hi sunt qui cum mulieribus non sunt coinquinati, virgines enim sunt*: sicut bonum est sal quia conservat carnem a corruptione.

Secundo, quia animam decorat et ornat. Unde frequenter in Scriptura iungitur virgo pulchra, Sap. IV, 1: *o quam pulchra est casta generatio cum claritate*; Cant. IV, 7: *tota pulchra es, amica mea*.

Tertio, quia angelis caeli assimilatur, sicut hic dicit Glossa, et Matth. XXII, 30: *in resurrectione neque nubent, neque nubentur, sed erunt sicut angeli Dei*. Hieronymus: *in carne praeter carnem vivere*, et cetera.

Quarto, quia Christo desponsat, II Cor. c. XI, 2: *despondi enim vos uni viro virginem castam exhibere Christo*.

Quinto, quia iungit et approximat Deo, Ps. XLIV, 15: *adducentur regi virgines post eam*; Ier. III, 4: *dux virginitatis meae tu es*.

Sexto, quia caeteris statibus praeponderat, Eccli. XXVI, 20: *non est digna ponderatio animae*

Are you loosed from a wife? Seek not a wife, if you can be continent, for, as the apostles say: *if the case of a man with his wife be so, it is not expedient to marry* (Matt 19:10).

377. Then when he says, ***but if you take a wife***, he excuses from sin the one contracting marriage. Here he shows first that marriage can be contracted without sin, and second that it is easier to be without marriage, at ***nevertheless, such shall have tribulation***. In the first part, he first proposes the truth about the one who is not a virgin; second about the virgin, at ***and if a virgin marries***.

He says, therefore: if you are free, do not seek a wife. ***But if you take a wife***, namely for a good purpose, not for the satisfaction of lust, ***you have not sinned***. This is an evident argument against the heretics who despise marriage, about which it is said: *forbidding marriage* (1 Tim 4:30.

And similarly ***if a virgin marries***—not a virgin dedicated to God, since, according to Jerome: *it is a sin for those who vow virginity not only to marry, but also to want to marry*—***she has not sinned***, namely by marrying; if it were otherwise the Blessed Virgin would have sinned when she was betrothed to Joseph. ***Nevertheless such***, i.e., married persons, ***shall have tribulation of the flesh***, i.e., affliction with procuring the things necessary for themselves and their children and others. Hence it is easier to be without marriage.

But I spare you, as though to say: I counsel you to avoid marriage, yet I allow it as a concession, sparing your weakness. Or thus: ***but I spare you***, in counseling you to avoid the tribulations of the flesh

378. It should here be noted that holy virginity is a great good on account of many things.

First, because it preserves cleanness of the flesh: *these are they who have not defiled themselves with women, for they are virgins* (Rev 14:4), as salt is good because it preserves flesh from corruption.

Second, because it decorates and adorns the soul. Hence in Scripture virgin is frequently joined to beautiful: *how beautiful is the chaste generation with glory* (Wis 4:1); *you are all beautiful, my love* (Song 4:7).

Third, because it is like unto the angels of heaven, as the Gloss says here, and in Matthew: *in the resurrection they shall neither marry nor be given in marriage, but shall be like the angels of God* (Matt 22:30); and Jerome says: *to live in the flesh apart from the flesh*.

Fourth, because it betroths one to Christ: *I betrothed you to one husband, to present you as a chaste virgin to Christ* (2 Cor 11:2).

Fifth, because it unites to and draws close to God: *after her shall virgins be brought to the king* (Ps 45:14); *you are the guide of my virginity* (Jer 3:4).

Sixth, because it exceeds the other states in value: *no price is worthy of the continent soul* (Sir 26:20); and below:

continentis; infra: ***qui matrimonio iungit virginem bene facit, qui non iungit melius facit.***

Septimo, quia odorem bonae famae spirat. Lucae dicitur: *et nomen Virginis Maria*; Cant. II, 2: *sicut lilium inter spinas, sic amica mea inter filias Ierusalem.*

Octavo, quia ad nuptias aeternas invitat, Matth. XXV, 10: *quae paratae erant intraverunt cum eo ad nuptias.*

Sed, heu, quia ad conservandum difficilis, ideo Eccli. XLII, 9: *filia patris abscondita est*, et cetera. Et hoc quia diabolus suggerit contrarium. Corruptio inclinat ad actum, pulchritudo allicit ad consensum.

he who gives his virgin in marriage does well: and he who does not give her does better (1 Cor 7:38).

Seventh, because it breathes the odor of a good reputation. In Luke it is said: *and the virgin's name was Mary* (Luke 1:27); *as the lily among thorns, so is my love among the daughters of Jerusalem* (Song 2:2).

Eighth, because it invites one to the eternal wedding feast: *those who were ready went in with him to the wedding feast* (Matt 25:10).

But, alas, since it is difficult to preserve: *a daughter is a father's hidden vigil* (Sir 42:9). And this is because the devil suggests the contrary. Corruption inclines one to an action, beauty entices one to consent to it.

Lecture 6

7:29Hoc itaque dico, fratres: tempus breve est: reliquum est, ut et qui habent uxores, tamquam non habentes sint: [n. 379]	7:29τοῦτο δέ φημι, ἀδελφοί, ὁ καιρὸς συνεσταλμένος ἐστίν· τὸ λοιπὸν ἵνα καὶ οἱ ἔχοντες γυναῖκας ὡς μὴ ἔχοντες ὦσιν,	7:29This therefore I say, brethren: the time is short. It remains that they also who have wives be as if they had none: [n. 379]
7:30et qui flent, tamquam non flentes: et qui gaudent, tamquam non gaudentes: et qui emunt, tamquam non possidentes: [n. 381]	7:30καὶ οἱ κλαίοντες ὡς μὴ κλαίοντες, καὶ οἱ χαίροντες ὡς μὴ χαίροντες, καὶ οἱ ἀγοράζοντες ὡς μὴ κατέχοντες,	7:30And they that weep, as though they wept not: and they that rejoice, as if they rejoiced not: and they that buy as if they possessed not: [n. 381]
7:31et qui utuntur hoc mundo, tamquam non utantur: praeterit enim figura hujus mundi. [n. 383]	7:31καὶ οἱ χρώμενοι τὸν κόσμον ὡς μὴ καταχρώμενοι· παράγει γὰρ τὸ σχῆμα τοῦ κόσμου τούτου.	7:31And they that use this world, as if they used it not. For the form of this world passes away. [n. 383]

379. Haec est secunda pars, ubi nubentibus sive nuptis ostendit bene vivendi modum, docens

primo qualiter utantur uxoribus;

secundo qualiter fortunae casibus sive eventibus, ibi *et qui flent*, etc.;

tertio qualiter mundi rebus sive possessionibus, ibi *et qui emunt*, etc.;

quarto subdit rationem in his admonitionibus, ibi *praeterit enim figura*.

380. In prima implicat tria, scilicet auctoritatem consiliarii, *hoc itaque dico*, etc.; necessitatem consulendi *tempus breve est*, etc.; formam consilii *reliquum est*, et cetera.

Dicit ergo *hoc itaque*, quasi dicat: quia non est peccatum nubere, *hoc itaque dico, fratres*, si coniugii *tempus breve est*, quo scilicet non generatione carnali propagandus est populus Dei, sed regeneratione spirituali colligendus, secundum Glossam; et quia tempus breve est, *reliquum est*, id est hoc solum restat agendum, *ut qui habent uxores, sint tamquam non habentes*, studendo servitio Dei, non autem operi carnali, debitum scilicet exigendo. Unde dicitur *sint tamquam non habentes*, non dicit: tamquam non habenti, sicut erant antiqui Patres; propter quod dicit Augustinus quod *caelibatus Ioannis non praefertur coniugio Abrahae*; sed hodie faciunt e converso, quia qui non habent sunt tamquam habentes.

Est autem notandum quod tamquam non habens uxorem est qui vel uxori debitum reddit nec exigit, vel propter infirmitatem uxorem ducit, dolens quod sine ea esse nequit, vel pari affectu continentiam custodit, vel causa generandae prolis ad cultum Dei uxorem propriam cognoscit.

381. *Et qui flent*, pro casibus coniugii vel pro aliqua tristitia saeculi, sint *tamquam non flentes*, consolati scilicet spe appropinquantis boni futuri. Prov. XII, 21: *non*

379. This is the second part, where he shows those who marry or who are married how to live well, teaching

first, how they should treat their wives;

second, how they should treat the accidents and occurrences of fortune, at *and they that weep*;

third, how they should treat things or possessions, at *and they that buy*;

fourth, he adds an explanation to these admonitions, at *for the form*.

380. In the first part he includes three things, namely the authority of the one giving counsel, at *this therefore I say*; the necessity of giving counsel, at *the time is short*; and the form of the counsel, at *it remains*.

He says therefore *this therefore I say*, as though to say: since it is not a sin to marry, *this therefore I say, brethren*, if *the time* of marriage *is short*, namely, the time in which the people of God is not to be propagated by fleshly generation, but brought together by spiritual regeneration, according to the Gloss; and because the time is brief, *it remains*, i.e., the only thing that remains to be done, is *that they also who have wives be as if they had none*, devoting themselves to the service of God, not to a fleshly work, by demanding the marital debt. Hence it is said *be as if they had none*; he does not say: have wives as if they had none, as was the case with the Fathers of old, on account of which Augustine says that *the celibacy of John is not better than the marriage of Abraham*; but today they act differently, since those who do not have wives live as though they had them.

It should be noted, however, that one who lives as though not having a wife is one who either neither demands nor renders the debt to his wife, or on account of weakness takes a wife, sorrowing that he cannot be without her, or with equal affection guards continence, or knows his own wife for the sake of begetting offspring for the worship of God.

381. *And they that weep*, by reason of the fortunes of conjugal life or for some worldly sorrow, be *as if they wept not*, consoled by the hope of the approaching future good.

contristabit iustum quidquid ei acciderit. **Et qui gaudent**, pro aliqua prosperitate saeculi, **tamquam non gaudentes**, sed tamquam in timore existentes imminentis mali periculi. Eccli. XI, v. 27: *in die bonorum ne immemor sis malorum.*

382. Deinde, cum dicit **et qui emunt**, hic ostendit qualiter utantur mundi rebus sive possessionibus. Et primo qualiter uti debeant acquirendis; secundo qualiter acquisitis, ibi **et qui utuntur**, et cetera.

Dicit ergo **qui emunt, tamquam non possidentes**, id est, post haec terrena non sedentes, scilicet supple, non apponendo cor rebus perituris. Ps. LXI, 11: *divitiae si affluant, nolite cor apponere.* Ez. VII, 12: *qui emit, non laetetur: et qui vendit, non lugeat.* Et, ut universaliter colligam, **qui utuntur hoc mundo**, id est, rebus mundanis; non dico fruuntur ut mali qui de eis malum faciunt finem, qui dicunt, Sap. II, 6: *fruamur bonis quae sunt*, id est, praesentibus; sed qui utuntur eis ad finem debitum referendo, sint **tamquam non utantur**, id est, non adhaereant eis nimia delectatione. I Tim. VI, 8: *habentes alimenta et quibus tegamur, his contenti simus.*

Praeter actum ergo coniugalem ponit quatuor differentias actuum circa sollicitudinem mundanorum, scilicet flere, gaudere, emere, uti. Duo primi pertinent ad affectum, duo alii ad effectum. Ex humana vero sollicitudine generatur duplex effectus, scilicet emendi respectu habendorum, et utendi respectu habitorum; et secundum hoc ponit Apostolus consilium temperantiae in his quatuor actibus.

383. Deinde, cum dicit **praeterit enim figura**, etc., hic subdit rationem praedictarum admonitionum, quae talis est: transitoria sunt reputanda quasi non sint, sed talia sunt mundana peritura, ergo quasi non sint sunt reputanda. Et hoc est quod dicit, quod ideo mundana quasi non sint aestimanda sunt, quia **praeterit figura**, id est, exterior pulchritudo, vel quod est ibi fragile conveniens statui fragilitatis. Transibunt enim qualitates mortales, et remanebunt immortales. Ideo transibit mundus et concupiscentia eius.

Omnia notanda: quia **figura**, non substantia **mundi**, non paradisi, **praeterit**, non sistit.

384. Hic quaeritur super illud: **si potest fieri liber**, Glossa: *quanto quis propter Deum despectior est in hoc saeculo, tanto magis exaltabitur in futuro.*

Contra, ergo magis exaltabitur bonus subditus, quam bonus praelatus.

Respondeo. Glossa intelligenda est caeteris paribus.

Whatever happens to a righteous man, it will not make him sad (Prov 12:21). **And they that rejoice**, by reason of some worldly prosperity, **as if they rejoiced not**, but rather as fearing the danger of imminent evil. *In prosperous days do not be unmindful of evil days* (Sir 11:27).

382. Then, when he says **they that buy**, he shows how they should use worldly things or possessions. And first how they should acquire them; second how to use the goods they have acquired, at **they that use**.

He says therefore, **they that buy, as if they possessed not**, that is, not relying upon these earthly goods, namely, not setting one's heart on things that are to perish: *if riches increase, set not your heart on them* (Ps 41:11); *do not let the buyer rejoice, nor the seller mourn* (Ezek 7:12) And, to sum it up universally, **they that use this world**, i.e., worldly things—I do not speak of those who enjoy them, as evil persons who turn them to an evil end, who say: *let us enjoy the good things that exist* (Wis 2:6) that is, present goods, but of those who use them, referring them to a due end—**let them be as if they used it not**, that is, let them not cling to worldly things with excessive delight. *Having food and clothing, with these let us be content* (1 Tim 6:8).

Therefore beyond the marital act he lays down four different acts in regard to the cares of the world, namely to weep, to rejoice, to buy, and to use. The first two pertain to affection, the second two to the effect of affection. Indeed from human care arises two effects, namely buying things one desires to have, and using things one has. The Apostle accordingly counsels temperance in these four acts.

383. Then, when he says **for the form of this world**, he adds an explanation of the aforesaid admonitions, which is as follows: transitory things should be regarded as though non-existent, but since worldly things that are to pass away are transitory, they should be regarded as though non-existent. And this is what he says, that worldly things should be valued as though non-existent, because **the form passes away**, i.e., the exterior beauty, or that which is impermanent and fitting for the statue of impermanence. For mortal qualities shall pass away and immortal qualities shall remain. Therefore the world and its concupiscence shall pass away.

All to be noted is: that it is the **form**, not the substance, **of this world**, and not of paradise, which **passes**, i.e., does not stand.

384. Here a question is raised about the text: **if you can become free** (1 Cor 7:21), where the Gloss says: *the more someone is despised in this age on account of God, the more he will be exalted in the future age.*

Against this, it seems that on this account a good subordinate will be exalted more than a good superior.

I respond that the Gloss should be understand on the supposition of other things being equal.

385. Item super illud: *unusquisque, in quo vocatus est*.

Glossa: *contra, ergo qui vocatus est in statu saeculari, non debet intrare religionem.*

Respondeo. Apostolus loquitur de statibus promoventibus ad salutem, non de impedientibus.

386. Item, super illud: *existimo hoc bonum esse*, Glossa: *maior est victoria virginum, quam angelorum.*

Contra, ergo maior corona; ergo homines erunt maiores angelis, non solum aequales.

Respondeo. Maior extensive, id est, multiplicative, quia habent aureolam non solum auream.

387. Item super illud: *bonum est homini sic esse*, Glossa: *in virginitate.*

Contra Gen. I, 28: *crescite et multiplicamini*; virginitas autem contraria est huic praecepto.

Respondeo. Illud praeceptum non est perpetuum, sed datum usque ad tempus sufficientis multiplicationis humani generis.

388. Item super illud: *qui habent uxores*, Glossa: *beatiora coniugia iudicanda sunt quae prole concepta, pari consensu continentiam servare potuerunt.*

Contra, unumquodque tanto beatius est, quanto magis convenit fini suo: finis autem coniugii est generatio prolis.

Respondeo. Expone: *coniugia*, id est, *coniuges*. Vel dicendum est quod ille non est ultimus finis coniugii, sed adimpletio numeri electorum, qui citius impleretur, si omnes continerent.

389. Item super illud: *praeterit figura huius mundi*, Glossa: *in iudicio mundanorum ignium flagratione huius mundi peribit non substantia, sed figura.*

Contra II Petr. III, 10: *per quem caeli magno impetu transient.*

Respondeo. Ille transitus et illa solutio accidentalis est, non substantialis, id est, secundum qualitatem, non secundum substantiam.

385. Again, on the text: *let every man, wherein he was called, therein abide* (1 Cor 7:24).

The Gloss says: *against this, therefore, he who was called in a worldly state should not enter religious life.*

I respond that the Apostle is speaking about states that lead one toward salvation, not about states that hinder one.

386. Again, on the text, *I think therefore that this is good* (1 Cor 7:26), the Gloss says: *the victory of virgins is greater than that of angels.*

Against this: therefore the crown would be greater, and therefore men would be be greater than angels, not merely equal to them.

I respond, it is greater extensively, that is, numerically, because they have an aureola, and not only a golden crown.

387. Again, on the text: *it is good for a man to be so* (1 Cor 7:26), the Gloss says: *in virginity.*

Against this: it is said, *increase and multiply* (Gen 1:28), yet virginity is contrary to this precept.

I respond that precept is not everlasting, but was given up till the time when the human race had sufficiently increased.

388. Again, on the text: *they also who have wives*, the Gloss says: *marriages are to be considered more blessed when, after having conceived offspring, they have been able to preserve continence by mutual consent.*

Against this: each thing is more blessed to the degree that it more closely attains its end, and the end of marriage is the procreation of offspring.

I respond: explain *marriages* as meaning *married persons*. Or it should be said that the final end of marriage is not the procreation of offspring, but the filling up of the number of the elect, which would be filled up more quickly if all were continent.

389. Again, on the text: *the form of this world*, the Gloss says: *in the judgment, not the substance but rather the form of this world shall perish in the blaze of worldly fire.*

Against this: *through it the heavens shall pass away with great violence* (1 Pet 3:10).

I respond that passing away and dissolution are accidental, not substantial; that is, they are according to quality, not according to substance.

Lecture 7

7:32Volo autem vos sine sollicitudine esse. Qui sine uxore est, sollicitus est quae Domini sunt, quomodo placeat Deo. [n. 390]

7:33Qui autem cum uxore est, sollicitus est quae sunt mundi, quomodo placeat uxori, [n. 393]

7:34et divisus est. Et mulier innupta, et virgo, cogitat quae Domini sunt, ut sit sancta corpore, et spiritu. Quae autem nupta est, cogitat quae sunt mundi, quomodo placeat viro. [n. 394]

7:35Porro hoc ad utilitatem vestram dico: non ut laqueum vobis injiciam, sed ad id, quod honestum est, et quod facultatem praebeat sine impedimento Dominum obsecrandi. [n. 397]

7:32θέλω δὲ ὑμᾶς ἀμερίμνους εἶναι. ὁ ἄγαμος μεριμνᾷ τὰ τοῦ κυρίου, πῶς ἀρέσῃ τῷ κυρίῳ:

7:33ὁ δὲ γαμήσας μεριμνᾷ τὰ τοῦ κόσμου, πῶς ἀρέσῃ τῇ γυναικί,

7:34καὶ μεμέρισται. καὶ ἡ γυνὴ ἡ ἄγαμος καὶ ἡ παρθένος μεριμνᾷ τὰ τοῦ κυρίου, ἵνα ᾖ ἁγία καὶ τῷ σώματι καὶ τῷ πνεύματι: ἡ δὲ γαμήσασα μεριμνᾷ τὰ τοῦ κόσμου, πῶς ἀρέσῃ τῷ ἀνδρί.

7:35τοῦτο δὲ πρὸς τὸ ὑμῶν αὐτῶν σύμφορον λέγω, οὐχ ἵνα βρόχον ὑμῖν ἐπιβάλω, ἀλλὰ πρὸς τὸ εὔσχημον καὶ εὐπάρεδρον τῷ κυρίῳ ἀπερισπάστως.

7:32But I would have you be without solicitude. he who is without a wife is solicitous for the things that belong to the Lord: how he may please God. [n. 390]

7:33But he who is with a wife is solicitous for the things of the world: how he may please his wife. [n. 393]

7:34And he is divided. And the unmarried woman and the virgin thinks on the things of the Lord: that she may be holy both in body and in spirit. But she who is married thinks on the things of the world: how she may please her husband. [n. 394]

7:35And this I speak for your profit, not to cast a snare upon you, but for that which is noble and which may give you power to attend upon the Lord, without impediment. [n. 397]

---

390. Superius dedit primo virginibus consilium continendi, secundo nubentibus documentum bene vivendi, hic tertio ostendit quod magis expedit tempus continendi. Et hoc ostendit,

primo ratione maioris tranquillitatis;

secundo ratione maioris sanctitatis, ibi *et mulier innupta*, etc.;

tertio ratione maioris utilitatis, ibi *porro hoc ad utilitatem vestram*, et cetera.

391. Prima ratio talis est: tranquillitas in amore solius Dei praeferenda est sollicitudini mundanorum; sed continentes habent tranquillitatem, coniugati sollicitudinem mundi: ergo status continentium praeferendus est statui coniugatorum.

Primo ergo dehortatur sollicitudinem mundi; secundo subdit quod continentes non sunt solliciti nisi in his quae sunt Dei, ibi *quoniam qui sine uxore*, etc.; tertio ostendit quod coniugatos oportet esse sollicitos in his quae sunt mundi, ibi *qui autem cum uxore*, et cetera.

392. Dicit ergo *volo autem*, quasi dicat: si nubitis, praedicta facere consulo; sed magis *volo vos esse sine sollicitudine* rei uxoriae. Phil. IV, 6: *nihil solliciti sitis.*

Nota quod dehortatur nos Scriptura a sollicitudine triplici: scilicet circa mulierem, ut hic *volo vos sine sollicitudine esse*, circa ventrem, Matth. VI, 25: *ne solliciti*

390. Above he first gave virgins the counsel to remain continent; second, he gave married persons instruction on living well; third, he shows here that at this time it is more advantageous to remain continent.

First, by reason of greater tranquility;

second, by reason of greater holiness, at *the unmarried woman*;

third, by reason of greater utility, at *and this I speak for your profit*.

391. The first reason is as follows: tranquility in the love of God alone is preferable to solicitude for worldly things; but persons living continence have tranquility, while married persons have worldly solicitude; therefore the state of persons living continence is preferable to the state of married persons.

First, therefore, he advises against worldly solicitude, then adds that persons living continence are solicitous only for the things of God, at *he who is without a wife*; third he shows that married persons must be solicitous for the things of the world, at *he who is with a wife*.

392. He says therefore *but I would have you*, as though to say: if you marry, I advise you to do the aforesaid, but even more I would have you be without solicitude of marital affairs: *be solicitous about nothing* (Phil 4:6).

Note that Scripture advises us against three kinds of solicitude: namely, as regarding a woman, as here: *I would have you be without solicitude*; as regarding the stomach: *be not solicitous for your life, what you shall eat* (Matt 6:25);

sitis animae vestrae, etc., circa bursam, Prov. XI, 7: *expectatio sollicitorum peribit.*

Et recte hoc volo, quia **qui sine uxore est, sollicitus est quae Domini sunt**, ut complaceat ei. Non enim habet excusationem illorum qui dicunt Lc. XIV, 20: *uxorem duxi, et non possum venire.* **Sollicitus**, inquam, scilicet **quomodo placeat Deo**, interiori scilicet pulchritudine sua. Felix cuius votum est uxorem fugere, cuius sollicitudo est Domino servire, cuius intentio est Deo placere.

393. Deinde, cum dicit **qui autem cum uxore est**, etc., hic ostendit quomodo coniugatos oportet esse sollicitos in his quae sunt mundi, ubi implicantur quatuor gravia. Primo vinculum coniugale, ibi **qui cum uxore est**, studium mundiale, ibi **sollicitus est**, subiectio uxoris, ibi **quomodo placeat**, operis divisio, ibi **et divisus est**.

Dicit ergo **qui autem cum uxore est**, scilicet in matrimonio, **sollicitus est quae sunt mundi**, id est, de regimine familiae et huiusmodi. Unde Iacob, acceptis uxoribus, ait Gen. XXX, 30: *iustum est ut aliquando provideam domui meae*, id est, sollicitus sim quomodo placeam uxori. Et hoc fine potest se licite ornare. Nam, secundum Glossam, *magna amaritudo in domo est uxor tristis.* Et talis **divisus est** non natura, sed actu, scilicet divisione officii, non intentionis principalis; unde Glossa *partim servit Deo, partim mundo.*

394. Deinde, cum dicit **et mulier innupta**, etc., hic ponitur secunda ratio probans quod magis expedit servare propositum continentiae quam nubere, ratione maioris sanctitatis. Et est ratio sua talis: continens studet sanctitati et divinitati et amori Dei, nupta vero mundo: ergo illa praeferenda est isti.

Primo ergo tangit studium innuptae, quia cogitat totaliter placere Deo;

secundo studium nuptae, quia cogitat partim placere mundo, ibi **quae autem nupta est.**

395. In prima implicat tria, scilicet continentium statum, cogitatum et fructum; statum honestum, quia **innupta et virgo**; cogitatum rectum, quia **cogitat quae Domini sunt**; multiplicatum fructum, quia **ut sit sancta**, et cetera.

Dicit ergo: et similiter **mulier innupta**, id est vidua, **et virgo cogitat**, id est, maiorem habet facultatem cogitandi, **quae Domini sunt**, id est, spiritualia et aeterna. Cogitat, inquam, **ut sit sancta**, magis quam nupta. Multae enim nuptae sunt sanctae. Augustinus, *de Bono coniugali: ampliorem non nuptarum et in corpore et in spiritu sanctificationem intelligi voluit, non tamen nuptas omnino sanctificatione privavit.* **Sancta**, inquam,

and as regarding money: *the expectation of the solicitous shall perish* (Prov 11:7).

And rightly I wish this, since **he who is without a wife, is solicitous for the things of the Lord**, to please him. For he does not have the excuse of those who say: *I have taken a wife and cannot come* (Luke 14:20). Solicitous, I mean, for **how he may please God**, namely with his inner beauty. Happy the man who vows to avoid taking a wife, whose solicitude is to serve the Lord, whose intention is to please God.

393. Then, when he says **he who is with a wife**, he shows how spouses must be solicitous for the things of the world, wherein four important things are included. First, the marital bond, at **he who is with a wife**; the marital devotion, at **is solicitous**; the subjection to his wife, at **how he may please**; the division of work, at **and he is divided**.

He says, therefore, **he who is with a wife**, namely in marriage, **is solicitous for the things of the world**, that is, for governing the family and other such things. Hence Jacob, having taken wives, said: *it is just that I should also sometime provide for my house* (Gen 30:30), that is, that I may be solicitous how I may please my wife. And to this end one can licitly adorn oneself. For, according to the Gloss, *a sad wife is a great bitterness in the home.* And such a person **is divided**, not in nature, but in activity, that is, by the division of service, not of principal intention: hence the Gloss says: *he partly serves God and partly serves the world.*

394. Then, when he says **and the unmarried woman**, he gives the second reason proving that it is better to hold to a resolution of continence than to marry, by reason of greater holiness. And his reasoning is as follows: the continent woman pursues holiness and divinity and love of God, while the married woman pursues the world; therefore the former is preferable to the latter.

Therefore, he first mentions what the unmarried woman pursues, that she thinks completely about how to please God;

second, what the married woman pursues, that she thinks partly about how to please the world, at **but she who is married**.

395. In the first part he includes three elements, namely the state, the thought, and the fruit of continent persons; the state is noble, at **the unmarried woman and the virgin**; the thought is right, at **thinks on the things of the Lord**; the fruit is many, at **that she may be holy**.

He says therefore: and similarly **the unmarried woman**, i.e., the widow, **and the virgin thinks**, i.e., has a greater ability to think, **on the things of the Lord**, i.e., spiritual and eternal things. Thinks, that is, so **that she may be holy**, more than the married woman. For many married women are holy. Augustine, in *On the Good of Marriage*: he wished a fuller sanctification of the unmarried both in body and in spirit to be understood, yet did not deprive

corpore, id est, corporalibus actionibus, *et spiritu*, id est, spiritualibus actionibus. Vel *sancta corpore*, contra vitia carnalia, *et spiritu*, contra spiritualia.

396. Deinde, cum dicit *quae autem nupta est*, hic tangit sollicitudinem nuptarum, ubi implicat tria. Primo coniugium; secundo sollicitudinem, ibi *cogitat quae*, etc.; tertio coniugii studium, ibi *quo modo placeat*, et cetera.

Dicit ergo: *quae autem nupta est cogitat quae mundi sunt*, scilicet de cura filiorum, de regimine domus, et huiusmodi. Unde parentes monuerunt Saram honorare socrum, diligere maritum, gubernare domum, etc., Tob. X, 30. Cogitat, inquam, *quomodo placeat viro*, unde hoc fine ornantes se non peccant: verumtamen magis debent studere ei placere ornatu morum quam vestimentorum. I Tim. II, 9: *mulieres in habitu ornato ornantes se, non in tortis crinibus, auro*, et cetera.

397. Deinde, cum dicit *porro hoc ad utilitatem*, etc., hic allegat tertiam rationem, scilicet maiorem utilitatem.

Et est ratio talis: illud quod est utilius, magis expedit; sed continere est utilius quam nubere, ergo magis expedit eligere continentiam quam nuptias.

Primo ergo ostendit quod utile est continere; secundo quod honestum est, ibi *sed id quod est honestum*, etc.; tertio quod facile, ibi *et quod facultatem*, et cetera.

398. Dicit ergo *porro*, etc., quasi dicat: consulo non nubere, *porro hoc ad utilitatem vestram*, maiorem scilicet, *dico*, ut expeditius Deo serviatis, quia sic mortificatur caro quae est inimica spiritus. Augustinus *de Verbis Domini*: *sicut inimicus occisus non facit tibi iniuriam, sic caro mortificata non turbat animam*. Dico, inquam, non *ut laqueum*, fornicationis scilicet, incontinentibus *vobis iniiciam*, aliquid difficile super hoc faciendo; imo potius laqueus poneretur, si consuleret nubere, quia de muliere dicitur Eccle. VII, 27, quod *laqueus venatorum est*, sed potius intendens inducere omnes *ad id quod honestum est*, scilicet ad sanctitatem corporis et animae: non quia coniugalis status non sit honestus, sed quia minus honestus. Augustinus, *de Bono viduali*: *non matrimonium turpe esse monstravit, sed quod honestius erat generalis honesti nomine commendavit, et monens ad illud quod facultatem praebeat alicui observandi se in Domino*, id est, ad servitium Domini, et hoc sine impedimento quod est in coniugio. II Cor. XI, 2: *despondi vos uni viro virginem castam exhibere Christo*.

Vere eligendus est status continentiae, ubi maius commodum, quia *hoc ad utilitatem*, ubi minus periculum, quia *non ut laqueum*, maior honestas, quia *id quod*

married women of all sanctification. *Holy*, that is to say, *both in body*, i.e., bodily actions, *and in spirit*, i.e., spiritual actions. Or *holy both in body*, against fleshly vices, *and in spirit*, against spiritual vices.

396. Then, when he says *but she who is married*, he mentions the solicitude of married women, wherein he includes three things. First, the marriage; second the solicitude, at *thinks on the things*; third what marriage pursues, at *how she may please*.

He says, therefore: *she who is married thinks on the things of the world*, that is on the care of children, the ruling of the household, and things of this sort. Hence Sarah's parents admonished her to honor her father-in-law, to love her husband, to govern her household, etc. (Tob 10:30). She thinks, I say, *how she may please her husband*, hence those who adorn themselves for this purpose do not sin; nevertheless they should be more zealous to please him with the adornment of good character than of clothing: *women in honorable apparel, adorning themselves not with braided hair or gold* (1 Tim 2:9).

397. Then, when he says, *and this I speak for your profit*, he lays down the third reason, namely greater utility.

And the reasoning is as follows: that which is more useful, is more advantageous; but being continent is more useful than marrying is; therefore it is more advantageous to choose continence than marriage.

He shows first, therefore, that it is useful to be continent, second that it is noble, at *that which is noble*, third that it is easy, at *and which may give you power*.

398. He says therefore *and this I speak*; as though to say, I do not advise you to marry, *and this I speak for your profit*, i.e., greater profit, that you may more expeditiously serve God, since thus is the flesh, the enemy of the spirit, mortified. Augustine in *On the Words of the Lord*: *as an enemy once killed does not injure you, so mortified flesh does not trouble the soul*. I say this, again, *not to cast a snare*, of fornication, that is *upon you* as incontinent persons, counseling something difficult in this matter: indeed he would rather be laying a snare if he counseled marriage, since it is said of woman that she is *a hunter's snare* (Eccl 7:27); but intending, rather, to lead all to *that which is noble*, namely to holiness of body and soul, not that the married state is not noble, but that it is less noble. Augustine, in *On the Good of Widowhood*: *he did not show marriage to be base, but commended what was more honorable with the name of honorable as such, advising that which would offer one power to heed himself in the Lord*, i.e., unto the service of the Lord, and this without the impediment that marriage presented by marriage. *I betrothed you to one husband, to present you as a chaste virgin to Christ* (2 Cor 11:2).

Truly the state of continence is worthy of choice, where there is greater gain, since, *this I speak for your profit*; where there is less danger, since I say this *not to cast a snare*; greater honor, since it *is honorable*; freer power to serve

honestum, liberior facultas serviendi Deo, quia *facultatem praebet*, et cetera.

399. Notandum est hic quod multiplex sollicitudo est bona.

Prima praelationis, sicut nauta sollicitus est de regimine navis, pater de filiis. Rom. XII, v. 8: *qui praeest in sollicitudine.*

Secunda praedicationis, sicut paedagogus sollicitus est de puero, doctor de discipulis. I Thess. II, 2: *fiduciam habuimus loqui ad vos verbum Dei in multa sollicitudine.*

Tertia dilectionis, sicut amicus verus sollicitus est de conservatione amoris. Eph. IV, 3: *solliciti servare unitatem spiritus in vinculo pacis*, et cetera.

Quarta compassionis, sicut vir misericors sollicitus est de egenis et afflictis. II Tim. I, v. 17: *cum venisset Romam, sollicite me quaesivit et invenit.*

Quinta devotionis, sicut servus sollicitus est de placendo Domino, religiosus Deo. Mich. VI, 8: *indicabo tibi, o homo, quid sit bonum*, et post: *sollicite ambulare cum Deo tuo.*

Sexta circumspectionis, sicut speculator est de castro custodiendo. Deut. IV, 15: *custodite animas vestras sollicite.* Corpus enim cum organis, anima cum potentiis quoddam castrum est.

Septima actionis, sicut agricola sollicitus est de opere perficiendo. Lc. X, 41: *Martha, Martha, sollicita es.* II Tim. II, 15: *sollicite cura teipsum probabilem exhibere Deo.*

Octava provisionis, sicut dispensator de domo, mercator de computo, pauper de pane quaerendo. Rom. XII, 11: *sollicitudine non pigri.*

God, since it ***may give you power to attend upon the Lord, without impediment***.

399. It should here be noted that many kinds of solicitude are good.

First the solicitude of someone in command, as a sailor is solicitous for the government of the ship, or a father for his children: *he who rules, with solicitude* (Rom 12:8).

Second, of preaching, as a tutor is solicitous for the child, or a teacher for his disciples: *we had confidence to speak to you the word of God in great solicitude* (1 Thess 2:2).

Third, of love, as a true friend is solicitous for the preservation of love: *solicitous to keep the unity of the spirit in the bond of peace* (Eph 4:3).

Fourth, of compassion, as a merciful man is solicitous for the needy and afflicted: *when he came to Rome, he solicitously sought me and found me* (2 Tim 1:17).

Fourth, of devotion, as a servant is solicitous to please his master, or a religious to please God: *I will show you, O man, what is good . . . to walk solicitous with your God* (Mic 6:8).

Sixth, of caution, as a watchman is solicitous to guard the camp: *solicitously guard your souls* (Deut 4:15). For the body with its organs, and the soul with its powers is a kind of camp.

Seventh, of action, as a farmer is solicitous to complete his work: *Martha, Martha, you are solicitous* (Luke 10:41); *solicitously take care to present yourselves to God as one approved* (2 Tim 2:15).

Eighth, of provision, as a steward is solicitous for the household, or a merchant in reckoning, or a poor man in seeking bread: *in solicitude, not slothful* (Rom 12:11).

Lecture 8

7:36 Si quis autem turpem se videri existimat super virgine sua, quod sit superadulta, et ita oportet fieri: quod vult faciat: non peccat, si nubat. [n. 400]

7:37 Nam qui statuit in corde suo firmus, non habens necessitatem, potestatem autem habens suae voluntatis, et hoc judicavit in corde suo, servare virginem suam, bene facit. [n. 403]

7:38 Igitur et qui matrimonio jungit virginem suam, bene facit: et qui non jungit, melius facit. [n. 404]

7:39 Mulier alligata est legi quanto tempore vir ejus vivit, quod si dormierit vir ejus, liberata est: cui vult nubat, tantum in Domino. [n. 405]

7:40 Beatior autem erit si sic permanserit secundum meum consilium: puto autem quod et ego Spiritum Dei habeam. [n. 408]

7:36Εἰ δέ τις ἀσχημονεῖν ἐπὶ τὴν παρθένον αὐτοῦ νομίζει ἐὰν ᾖ ὑπέρακμος, καὶ οὕτως ὀφείλει γίνεσθαι, ὃ θέλει ποιείτω: οὐχ ἁμαρτάνει: γαμείτωσαν.

7:37ὃς δὲ ἕστηκεν ἐν τῇ καρδίᾳ αὐτοῦ ἑδραῖος, μὴ ἔχων ἀνάγκην, ἐξουσίαν δὲ ἔχει περὶ τοῦ ἰδίου θελήματος, καὶ τοῦτο κέκρικεν ἐν τῇ ἰδίᾳ καρδίᾳ, τηρεῖν τὴν ἑαυτοῦ παρθένον, καλῶς ποιήσει:

7:38ὥστε καὶ ὁ γαμίζων τὴν ἑαυτοῦ παρθένον καλῶς ποιεῖ, καὶ ὁ μὴ γαμίζων κρεῖσσον ποιήσει.

7:39Γυνὴ δέδεται ἐφ' ὅσον χρόνον ζῇ ὁ ἀνὴρ αὐτῆς: ἐὰν δὲ κοιμηθῇ ὁ ἀνήρ, ἐλευθέρα ἐστὶν ᾧ θέλει γαμηθῆναι, μόνον ἐν κυρίῳ.

7:40μακαριωτέρα δέ ἐστιν ἐὰν οὕτως μείνῃ, κατὰ τὴν ἐμὴν γνώμην, δοκῶ δὲ κἀγὼ πνεῦμα θεοῦ ἔχειν.

7:36 But if any man thinks that he seems dishonored with regard to his virgin, because she is above the age, and it must so be: let him do what she wills. He does not sin if she marries. [n. 400]

7:37 For he who has determined, being steadfast in his heart, having no necessity, but having power of her own will: and has judged this in his heart, to keep his virgin, does well. [n. 403]

7:38 Therefore both he who gives his virgin in marriage does well: and he who does not give her does better. [n. 404]

7:39A woman is bound by the law as long as her husband lives: but if her husband has fallen asleep, she is at liberty. Let her marry to whom she wills: only in the Lord. [n. 405]

7:40 But more blessed shall she be, if she so remain, according to my counsel. And I think that I also have the Spirit of God. [n. 408]

---

400. Superius egit de virginibus hic agit de virginum custodibus, ostendens

primo quod licet eis virgines suas coniugio copulare;

secundo quod non similiter nuptis licet, nisi post mortem viri, contrahere, ibi *mulier alligata est*, et cetera.

401. In prima, primo ostendit quod custos potest dare virginem suam in coniugio;

secundo quod non peccat hoc faciendo, ibi *nec peccat, si nubat*, etc.;

tertio quod etiam bene facit servando, ibi *nam qui statuit*, etc.;

quarto quod licet utrumque sit bonum, tamen hoc est melius illo, ibi *igitur et qui matrimonio*, et cetera.

401. In prima, primo supponit in virgine aetatem nubilem; secundo voluntatem nubendi, ibi *et ita oportuit fieri*, etc.; tertio dat nubendi licentiam, ibi *quod vult faciat*, et cetera.

Dicit ergo *si quis autem*, etc., quasi dicat: esse sine coniugio, honestius est et expeditus, sed tamen *si quis turpem se videri existimat* apud iudicium hominum *super virgine sua*, timens ne corrumpatur, eo *quod sit*

400. Above he treated of virgins. Here he treats about the guardians of virgins, showing,

first, that they are permitted to give their virgins in marriage;

second, that this is not similarly permitted to married persons to contract marriage, except after the death of the husband, at *a woman is bound*.

401. In the first part, he first shows that a guardian can give his virgin in marriage;

second, that he does not sin by doing this, at *he does not sin if she marries*;

third, that he also does well by keeping her as a virgin, at *for he who has determined*;

fourth, that although both are good, the former is better than the latter, at *therefore both he who gives his virgin in marriage*.

401. In the first part, he first supposes the virgin to be of marriageable age; second, that she has the will to marry, at *and it must be so*; third, that he gives permission to marry, at *let him do what she wills*.

He says therefore, *but if any man*, as though to say, it is more honorable and advantageous to be without marriage, but still *if any man thinks that he seems dishonored* according to the judgment of men *with regard to his virgin*,

superadulta, id est, ultra pubertatem et iam in nubilibus annis, *et ita oportet fieri* ut nubat, quia non vult continere, *quod vult*, virgo, *faciat, custos*. Eccli. VII, 27: *trade filiam tuam, et grande opus fecisti, et homini sensato da illam.*

402. Nec *peccat* custos, *si nubat* virgo: hoc ideo dicit, secundum Glossam, ne, *etsi virgo non peccet, custos videatur peccare*. Augustinus, *de Bono viduitatis: quae se non continet, nubat; quae non coepit, deliberet; quae egressa est, perseveret; nulla adversario detur occasio, sed falsa retrahatur oblatio.*

403. Deinde, cum dicit **nam qui statuit**, etc., hic ostendit quod custos virginis bene facit eam in statu virginali servando, ubi implicatur quadruplex conditio ad hoc expediens. Prima quod custos firmus sit in proposito eam virginem custodiendi; secunda quod non timeat de casu virginali, ibi **non habens necessitatem**, etc., tertia quod cognoscat in virgine propositum continendi, ibi **potestatem autem habens**, etc., quarta quod hoc faciat ex deliberatione, ibi **et hoc iudicavit**.

Dicit ergo **nam qui statuit**, etc., quasi dicat: ideo autem dico quod non peccat qui tradit virginem, nam de alio, qui servat eam, patet quod bene faciat. **Nam qui statuit in corde servare virginem suam, firmus** in proposito suo, non curans sobolem, vel aliud huiusmodi, **non habens necessitatem** tradendi eam, cum virgo velit continere, **potestatem autem habens**, secundum alumnae continentiam, **voluntatis suae** perficiendae. **Et hoc iudicavit in corde suo**, id est, ex iudicio rationis, non ex levitate mentis discernit esse bonum. I Tim. V, 21: *sine praeiudicio nihil facias*. Iudicavit, inquam, **servare virginem suam**. Ambrosius, super hunc locum: *non ingerens ei fomitem nuptiarum*. Eccli. c. VII, 26: *filiae tibi sunt? Serva corpus illarum*. Qui facit, inquam, sic **bene facit**.

404. Deinde, cum dicit **igitur et qui matrimonio**, etc., hic ostendit quod licet utrumque sit bonum, tamen virginitas est melior matrimonio. Ubi primo approbat statum coniugalem: secundo praeponit statum virginalem, ibi **qui non iungit**, et cetera.

Dicit ergo **igitur et qui**, etc., quasi dicat: quia oportet fieri ut diximus, **igitur et qui matrimonio iungit virginem, bene facit**, quia licitum est quod facit; **et qui non iungit**, cum virgo acquiescat continere, **melius facit**. Glossa: *melius facit qui apud Deum meritum suum collocat, et a sollicitudine liberat eam. Melius est enim quod licet et expedit, quam quod licet et non expedit. Hic enim bene utitur malo, ibi vero bene utitur bono. Bene utitur quis bono, continentiam dedicans Deo; male utitur quis bono, continentiam dedicans idolo. Male utitur quis malo, concupiscentiam relaxans adulterio; bene utitur malo, concupiscentiam restringens connubio. Bonum est*

fearing lest she be seduced, **because she is above the age**, that is, beyond puberty and already of marriageable years, **and it must be so** that she marry, because she does not want to be continent, **what she**, the virgin, **wills, let him**, the guardian, **do**.

402. Nor does the guardian **sin, if the virgin marries**; he says this, according to the Gloss, lest, *even if the virgin does not sin, the guardian might seem to sin*. Augustine says in *On the Good of Widowhood: she who is not continent, let her marry; she who has not begun, let her deliberate; she who has set out, let her persevere; let no opportunity be given to the adversary, but let a false offering be withdrawn.*

403. Then, when he says **for he who has determined**, he shows that the guard of a virgin does well by keeping her in a virginal state, where he mentions a fourfold condition advantageous for this. First, that the guardian be firm in the resolution to keep her as a virgin, second that he does not fear regarding the virgin's own case, at **having no necessity**, third that he recognizes in the virgin the resolve of being continent, at **but having power**, fourth that he does this after deliberation, at **and has judged this**.

He says therefore, **for he who has determined**, as though to say: I say that he does not sin who gives his virgin, because in the other case, of a man who keeps her, it is evident that he does well. **For he who has determined, in his heart to keep his virgin, being steadfast** in his resolve, not being worried about offspring or anything of this kind, **having no necessity** of giving her, since the virgin wills to be continent, **but having power**, according to the continence of the ward, of fulfilling **her own will**, and **has judged this in his heart**, i.e., has discerned this by the judgment of reason, not by fickleness of mind: *without prejudice, doing nothing from partiality* (1 Tim 5:21). Has judged this, **to keep his virgin**. Ambrose says on this passage: *nor forcing on her the kindling of marriage. Do you have daughters? Care for their bodies* (Sir 7:26). He, finally, who does this, thus **does well**.

404. Then, when he says **therefore both he who gives his virgin**, he shows that although both are good, still virginity is better than marriage. Here he first approves the marital state; second, he gives preference to the virginal state, at **he who does not give his virgin**.

He says, then, **therefore both he**, as though to say: since it must happen as we said, **therefore both he who gives his virgin in marriage** does well, since what he does is licit, and **he who does not give her**, when the virgin agrees to be continent, **does better**. The Gloss says: *he does better who places his merit before God, and frees her from solicitude. For that which is licit and advantageous is better than that which is licit but not advantageous. In the latter case one uses well an evil, in the former case one uses well a good. One uses well a good who dedicates continence to God, one uses badly a good, who dedicates continence to an idol. One uses badly an evil, relieving concupiscence by adultery, one uses well an evil, restraining concupiscence by marriage. Conjugal*

pudicitia coniugalis, sed melius est continentia virginalis vel vidualis, secundum Glossam.

405. Deinde cum dicit *mulier alligata est legi*, etc., hic ostendit quod non similiter coniugata, nisi viro mortuo, potest contrahere. Ubi primo ostendit quod coniugata non potest nubere, viro vivente; secundo quod, viro mortuo, potest alii nubere, ibi *quod si dormierit*, etc.; tertio quod melius est illi continere, ibi *beatior autem erit*, etc.; quarto quod debet consilio eius credere, ibi *puto autem quod et ego*, et cetera.

406. Dicit ergo *mulier alligata est*, etc.; quasi dicat: qui non iungit virginem suam, melius facit. Et vere melius, quia *mulier alligata est*, et cetera. Vel sic: virgo quocumque tempore potest nubere, sed uxorata non, quia *mulier alligata est legi*, ita ut non possit nubere alteri *quanto tempore vir eius vivit*. Rom. VII, 2: *quae autem sub viro est mulier, vivente viro est alligata legi viri.*

407. Deinde, cum dicit *quod si dormierit*, somno mortis. De qua dormitione Io. c. XI, 11: *lazarus amicus noster dormit*. *Vir eius*, et cetera. Augustinus: *non dicit primus, secundus, vel tertius, vel quartus, vel quousque licet. Nec nobis diffiniendum est quod non diffinit Apostolus. Unde nec ullas nuptias debeo damnare, nec eis verecundiam numerositatis afferre.*

Si dormierit, inquam, *liberata est* a lege viri, unde permittitur ei nubere. Hic patet quod resurgenti non tenetur copulari.

Sed *cui vult nubat*. Invitae enim nuptiae solent habere malos proventus; ideo dicitur Gen. XXIV, 57: *vocemus puellam, et quaeramus voluntatem eius*. Nubat, inquam, *tantum in Domino*, id est, viro suae religionis; nam in dispari cultu prohibitum est in lege matrimonium. Deut. VII, 3.

Per hanc licentiam Apostoli revocatae sunt omnes poenae et infamiae, quae secundum leges infligebantur olim mulieri secundo nubenti infra tempus luctus, scilicet intra annum.

Ergo in nuptiis exigitur personarum legitimitas, unde dicitur *liberata est*, consensus libertas, unde addit *cui vult nubat*, cultus paritas, unde subdit *tantum in Domino*.

408. Deinde, cum dicit *beatior autem erit*, etc., hic ostendit quod melius est illi continere quam nubere, dicens: quamvis liceat ei nubere, tamen *beatior erit, si sic permanserit*, scilicet innupta. Et hoc est consilium meum super eodem datum: habebit enim fructum sexagesimum qui debetur viduis, Matth. XIII. Augustinus:

chastity is good, but virginal or widowed continence is better, according to the Gloss.

405. Then when he says, *a woman is bound to the law*, he shows that a married woman cannot similarly contract marriage, unless her husband has died. Here he first shows that a married woman cannot marry while her husband is alive; second that if her husband has died, she can marry another, at *but if her husband has fallen asleep*; third that it is better for her to be continent, at *but more blessed shall she be*; fourth that she should trust his advice, at *and I think that I also have*.

406. He says, therefore, *a woman is bound*, as though to say: he who does not give his virgin, does better. And truly better, because *a woman is bound*. Or he can be understood in this way: a virgin can marry at any time, but a married *woman is bound to the law*, so that she cannot marry another man *as long as her husband lives*. A woman who has a husband, is bound to the law while her husband is alive (Rom 7:2).

407. Then, when he says, *but if her husband has fallen asleep*, in the sleep of death, about which sleep we read in John: *Lazarus our friend has fallen asleep* (John 11:11). Augustine remarks: *he does not say the first, second, third, or fourth, or how often it is licit. Nor should we determine what the Apostle has not determined. Hence I should neither condemn any marriages nor pronounce them shameful by reason of their number.*

If her husband has fallen asleep, I say, *she is at liberty* from the law of her husband, hence she is permitted to marry. Here it is evident that she is not bound to join herself to a previous husband who rises again.

But *let her marry whom she wills*. Unwilling marriages usually have bad outcomes: therefore it is said in Genesis: *let us call the maid, and ask her what she wills* (Gen 24:57). Let her marry, again, *only in the Lord*, that is, with a husband of her religion, for disparity of cult is prohibited by the law of marriage (Deut 7:3).

By this permission of the Apostle all the punishments and infamies are revoked that were formerly inflicted on a woman who entered a second marriage within the period of mourning, namely within a year.

Therefore in marriage is required legitimacy of persons, hence it is said *she is at liberty*, freedom of consent, hence he adds *let her marry to whom she wills*, parity of cult, hence he adds *only in the Lord*.

408. Then, when he says *but more blessed shall she be*, he shows that it is better for her to be continent than to marry, saying: although she is permitted to marry, *more blessed shall she be, if she so remain*, namely unmarried. And this is my counsel that I have given on the same matter: for she will have the sixty-fold fruit that is due to widows

satis ostendit beatam esse post mortem viri, et secundo nubentem, sed beatior est non nubens.

409. Deinde, cum dicit **puto autem quod et ego**, etc., hic ultimo ostendit quod debent consilio eius credere, quia, inspirante Spiritu Sancto, hoc consulit. Et hoc est quod dicit **puto autem**, etc., quasi dicat: faciendum est secundum consilium meum, quia **puto quod et ego**, sicut caeteri apostoli, **Spiritum Dei habeam**. Rom. VIII, 23: *sed et nosipsi primitias Spiritus habentes, et cetera.*

Hoc ergo consilium debet impleri et propter fructum sequentem, quia **beatior erit**, et propter consulentis auctoritatem, quia **secundum consilium meum**, et propter Spiritum Dei inspirantem, quia **puto**, et cetera.

410. Hic quaeritur super illo verbo **volo vos sine sollicitudine esse**.

Contra Rom. XII, 11: *sollicitudine non pigri.*

Responsio. Ibi loquitur de sollicitudine spirituali, hic de temporali.

411. Item super illo **divisus est**.

Contra Osee X, 2: *divisum est cor eorum, nunc interibunt.*

Responsio. Ibi loquitur de divisione intentionis principalis, hic de divisione actionis.

412. Item Glossa ibid.: *partim servit Deo, partim mundo.*

Contra Matth. VI, 24: *nemo potest duobus Dominis servire.*

Responsio. Verum est ita quod aequaliter serviat utrique in eo quod duo, id est contrarii, sunt.

413. Item super illud: **mulier innupta cogitat quae Domini sunt**, Glossa: *non cogitat ne damnetur a Deo.*

Contra: damnari potest, ut patet in parabola de fatuis virginibus.

Responsio. Non cogitat hoc solum, sed cum hoc etiam ne offendat sponsum.

414. Item super illud: **ut sit sancta corpore et spiritu**, Glossa: *non potest fieri ut non sit sanctum corpus quo utitur sanctificator Spiritus.*

Contra: Spiritus Sanctus usus est lingua Caiphae non sancta, Io. XI, 49 s.

Responsio. Utebatur ea ut Spiritus, non ut sanctificator.

415. Item: **sed ad id quod honestum est**. Contra: ergo matrimonium turpe.

(Matt 13). Augustine: *he clearly showed that one who marries a second husband after the death of a first is blessed, but more blessed is one who does not marry.*

409. Then, when he says **and I think that I also**, he shows finally that they should trust his counsel because he makes this counsel under the inspiration of the Holy Spirit. And so he says **and I think that I also**, as though to say, one should act according to my counsel, because **I think that I also**, like the rest of the apostles, **have the Spirit of God**. *But we ourselves, having the Spirit as first fruits* (Rom 8:23).

Therefore this counsel should be followed both on account of the subsequent fruit, since **more blessed shall she be**, and on account of the authority of the one giving the counsel, since **according to my counsel**, and on account of the Spirit of God that inspires it, since **I think that I also have the Spirit of God**.

410. Here a question is asked about the saying **I would have you to be without solicitude** (1 Cor 7:32).

Against this: *in solicitude, not slothful* (Rom 12:11).

I respond that there spiritual solicitude is meant, but here temporal solicitude.

411. Again, on the text **he is divided** (1 Cor 7:34).

Against this: *their heart is divided, now they shall perish* (Hos 10:2).

I respond that there the division of principal intention is meant, but here the division of action.

412. Again the Gloss on the same passage says: *he partly serves God, partly the world.*

Against this: *no one can serve two masters* (Matt 6:24).

I respond that this is true with respect to equally serving two inasmuch as they are two, that is, inasmuch as they are contrary.

413. Again, on the passage: **the unmarried woman . . . thinks on the things of the Lord** (1 Cor 7:34), the Gloss says: *she does not think about avoiding damnation by God.*

Against this: she can be damned, as is evident in the parable of the foolish virgins.

I respond that she does not think on this alone, but together with this thinks about avoiding offending her spouse.

414. Again on the passage: **that she may be holy both in body and spirit** (1 Cor 7:34), the Gloss says: *it cannot happen that it is not a holy body which the sanctifying Spirit uses.*

Against this: the Holy Spirit used the tongue of Caiphas, which was not holy (John 11:49 ff).

I respond that the Spirit used it, but not as sanctifying.

415. Again, on the text: **but for that which is noble** (1 Cor 7:35). Against this: therefore matrimony would be base.

Responsio. Secundum Glossam *positivum posuit pro comparativo.*

416. Item super illud: **qui non iungit, melius facit**, Glossa: *hic*, scilicet in coniugio, *bene utitur homo malo.*

Contra: cuius usus bonus est, ipsum quoque bonum est.

Responsio. Illud intelligitur de usu rei per se, scilicet ad quem ordinata est, non per accidens, scilicet ad quem ex prudentia utentis ordinatur.

417. Item Glossa ibid.: *melius est bene uti bono, quam bene uti malo.*

Contra: hoc difficilius illo.

Responsio. Loquitur hic de malo vitii, non supplicii.

418. Item super illo verbo in Glossa, *duae permissae.*

Contra: ergo duae nuptiae non sunt a Deo.

Responsio. Non ex eo quod duae, nisi ex consequenti.

419. Item **si dormierit vir**; quid dicendum est, si resuscitatur?

Responsio. Requiritur consensus novus ad hoc quod sit matrimonium.

420. Item super illud **puto quod Spiritum Dei habeam**.

Contra, Rom. VIII, 38: *certus sum quod neque mors, neque vita, et cetera.*

Responsio. Secundum Glossam non dicit hoc dubitando, sed quasi increpando.

I respond that according to the Gloss, *the author used the positive form to stand for the comparative.*

416. Again, on the passage: **he who does not give her, does better**, the Gloss says, *here*, namely in marriage, *a man makes good use of an evil.*

On the contrary, that of which the use is good, is itself good.

I respond: that is understood about the *per se* use of a thing, i.e., for that to which it is ordered, not about the accidental use of it, namely for that to which it is ordered by the prudence of the one using it.

417. Again the Gloss on the same passage: *it is better to make good use of a good thing, than to make good use of an evil thing.*

On the contrary: the latter is more difficult than the former.

Response: here the evil of vice is meant, not of punishment.

418. Again, on that saying in the Gloss: *two are permitted.*

On the contrary: therefore second marriages are not from God.

Response: not inasmuch as they are second, except as a logical consequence.

419. Again, **if her husband has fallen asleep**, what should be said, if he reawakens?

I respond that renewed consent is required in order for there to be marriage.

420. Again, on the text **I think that I also have the Spirit of God**.

Against this: *I am sure that neither death, nor life . . . shall be able to separate us from the love of God* (Rom 8:38).

I respond that according to the Gloss he says this not by way of doubt, but as it were by way of rebuke.

CHAPTER 8

Lecture 1

8:1De iis autem quae idolis sacrificantur, scimus quia omnes scientiam habemus. Scientia inflat, caritas vero aedificat. [n. 421]

8:2Si quis autem se existimat scire aliquid, nondum cognovit quemadmodum oporteat eum scire. [n. 424]

8:3Si quis autem diligit Deum, hic cognitus est ab eo. [n. 426]

8:4De escis autem quae idolis immolantur, scimus quia nihil est idolum in mundo, et quod nullus est Deus, nisi unus. [n. 428]

8:5Nam etsi sunt qui dicantur dii sive in caelo, sive in terra (siquidem sunt dii multi, et Domini multi): [n. 430]

8:6nobis tamen unus est Deus, Pater, ex quo omnia, et nos in illum: et unus Dominus Jesus Christus, per quem omnia, et nos per ipsum.

8:7Sed non in omnibus est scientia. Quidam autem cum conscientia usque nunc idoli, quasi idolothytum manducant: et conscientia ipsorum cum sit infirma, polluitur. [n. 431]

8:8Esca autem nos non commendat Deo. Neque enim si manducaverimus, abundabimus: neque si non manducaverimus, deficiemus. [n. 432]

8:1Περὶ δὲ τῶν εἰδωλοθύτων, οἴδαμεν ὅτι πάντες γνῶσιν ἔχομεν. ἡ γνῶσις φυσιοῖ, ἡ δὲ ἀγάπη οἰκοδομεῖ.

8:2εἴ τις δοκεῖ ἐγνωκέναι τι, οὔπω ἔγνω καθὼς δεῖ γνῶναι:

8:3εἰ δέ τις ἀγαπᾷ τὸν θεόν, οὗτος ἔγνωσται ὑπ' αὐτοῦ.

8:4Περὶ τῆς βρώσεως οὖν τῶν εἰδωλοθύτων οἴδαμεν ὅτι οὐδὲν εἴδωλον ἐν κόσμῳ, καὶ ὅτι οὐδεὶς θεὸς εἰ μὴ εἷς.

8:5καὶ γὰρ εἴπερ εἰσὶν λεγόμενοι θεοὶ εἴτε ἐν οὐρανῷ εἴτε ἐπὶ γῆς, ὥσπερ εἰσὶν θεοὶ πολλοὶ καὶ κύριοι πολλοί,

8:6ἀλλ' ἡμῖν εἷς θεὸς ὁ πατήρ, ἐξ οὗ τὰ πάντα καὶ ἡμεῖς εἰς αὐτόν, καὶ εἷς κύριος Ἰησοῦς Χριστός, δι' οὗ τὰ πάντα καὶ ἡμεῖς δι' αὐτοῦ.

8:7Ἀλλ' οὐκ ἐν πᾶσιν ἡ γνῶσις: τινὲς δὲ τῇ συνηθείᾳ ἕως ἄρτι τοῦ εἰδώλου ὡς εἰδωλόθυτον ἐσθίουσιν, καὶ ἡ συνείδησις αὐτῶν ἀσθενὴς οὖσα μολύνεται.

8:8βρῶμα δὲ ἡμᾶς οὐ παραστήσει τῷ θεῷ: οὔτε ἐὰν μὴ φάγωμεν ὑστερούμεθα, οὔτε ἐὰν φάγωμεν περισσεύομεν.

8:1Now concerning those things that are sacrificed to idols: we know we all have knowledge. Knowledge puffs up: but charity edifies. [n. 421]

8:2And if any man thinks that he knows any thing, he has not yet known as he ought to know. [n. 424]

8:3But if any man loves God, the same is known by him. [n. 426]

8:4But as for the meats that are sacrificed to idols, we know that an idol is nothing in the world and that there is no God but one. [n. 428]

8:5For although there are those that are called gods, either in heaven or on earth (for there are many gods and many lords): [n. 430]

8:6Yet to us there is but one God, the Father, from whom are all things, and we unto him: and one Lord Jesus Christ, through whom are all things, and we through him.

8:7But there is not knowledge in every one. For some, being hitherto with conscience of the idol, eat as a thing sacrificed to an idol: and their conscience, being weak, is defiled. [n. 431]

8:8But meat does not commend us to God. For neither, if we eat, shall we have the more: nor, if we eat not, shall we have the less. [n. 432]

---

421. Excluso errore circa correctionem criminum, cap. V et VI; item circa virginitatem et matrimonium, cap. VII, hic excludit errorem circa esum et abstinentiam ciborum, cap. isto, IX et X, loquens de his quae idolis immolabantur, a quibus, quamvis in se licitis, abstinere monet,

primo allegando eis scandalum infirmorum, cap. isto;

421. Having excluded an error regarding the correction of sins in chapters five and six, and again regarding virginity and marriage in chapter seven, here he excludes an error regarding consumption of and abstinence from food in this chapter and in chapters nine and ten, speaking about those foods which were offered to idols, from which, although in themselves licit, he advises one to abstain.

First, he does this by laying before them the scandal to the weak, in this chapter;

secundo exemplum sui, qui propter alios absti-net a receptione sumptuum licitorum, cap. IX;

tertio exemplum poenae Iudaeorum post tanta bene-ficia Dei in deserto prostratorum, cap. X.

Ergo propter scandalum proximi, exemplo Apostoli, non propter timorem supplicii debemus abstinere a cibis aliquando licitis. In

primo ostendit quod in se licita est comestio idolo-thitorum;

secundo monet nihilominus abstinere propter scan-dalum fratrum infirmorum, ibi *videte ne forte*, et cetera.

In prima,
primo proponit quod maiores eorum habent scien-tiam de idolothitis;

secundo ostendit qualem scientiam habent de eis, ibi *de escis autem quae idolis immolantur*, etc.;

tertio quod quidam infirmi hac scientia carent, ibi *sed non in omnibus est scientia*, etc.;

quarto quod alii coram eis idolothita edere non de-bent, ibi *esca autem nos non commendat Deo*.

In prima,
primo dicit, quod de idolothitis scientiam habent;

secundo quod eam sine caritate inutiliter habent, ibi *scientia autem inflat*, etc.;

tertio ostendit a quibus habeatur haec scientia insuf-ficienter, ibi *si quis autem existimat*;

quarto a quibus sufficienter, ibi *si quis autem diligit*, et cetera.

422. Dicit ergo *de his autem*, etc., quasi dicat: de praedictis quaesivistis a me, scilicet de pertinentibus ad matrimonium: de aliis autem, ut de immolatis idolo, non fuit necesse quaerere; quia omnes scitis super hoc verita-tem. Et hoc est quod dicit *de his autem quae idolis sacri-ficantur*, an liceat edere vel non, scimus ego et vos, quod liceat ea comedere secundum illud ad Tit. I, 15: *omnia munda mundis*. *Scimus quia omnes scientiam habemus*, ego scilicet et vos perfecti inter alios, id est, scientiam de Creatore et creaturis; et ideo minus excusabiles si male facimus.

423. Deinde cum dicit *scientia autem inflat*, etc., hic ostendit quomodo sine caritate scientiam inutiliter habent, quasi dicat: habetis quidem scientiam, sed non valet vobis, quia inde superbitis contra ignaros; scientia autem si sola est, inflat. Eccle. I, 18: *in multa sapientia, multa est indignatio*. Act. c. XXVI, 24: *multae litterae te*

second, the example of himself, who for the sake of oth-ers abstains from licit reimbursement from others, in chap-ter nine;

third, the example of the punishment of the Jews brought low in the desert after so great benefits of God, in chapter ten.

Therefore we should sometimes abstain from licit foods on account of scandal to neighbors, and the example of the Apostle, not account of fear of punishment.

First he shows that the eating of food offered to idols is in itself licit.

Second, he nonetheless advises abstinence from these foods on account of the scandal thereby occasioned to weak brethren, at *take heed lest perhaps* (1 Cor 8:9).

In the first part,
he first lays down that the greater men among them have knowledge concerning things offered to idols;

second, he shows what kind of knowledge they have concerning them, at *but as for the meats which are offered to idols*;

third, that certain weak persons lack this knowledge, at *but there is not knowledge in everyone*;

fourth, that the others should not eat foods offered to idols in their presence, at *but meat does not commend us to God*.

In the first part,
he first says that they have knowledge concerning things offered to idols;

second, that having this knowledge is useless for them without charity, at *knowledge puffs up*;

third he shows who has this knowledge in an insuffi-cient manner, at *if any man thinks*;

fourth who has this knowledge sufficiently, at *but if anyone loves*.

422. He says, therefore, *concerning those things*, as though to say, about the aforesaid matters you asked of me, namely about those things pertaining to marriage; but about the others, as about things offered to an idol, it was not necessary to ask, since you all know the truth concern-ing this matter. And so he says, *concerning those things that are sacrificed to idols*, whether it is licit to eat them or not, you and I both know that it is licit to eat them: *all things are clean to the clean* (Tit 1:15). *We know that we all have knowledge*, namely I and you who are perfect in comparison with others, have knowledge that is about the Creator and creatures, and therefore we are less excusable if we do evil.

423. Then when he says, *knowledge puffs up*, he shows how without charity having knowledge is useless to them, as though to say: you have knowledge, but it does not profit you, because you pride yourselves in it over the ignorant, and knowledge, if it is alone, puffs up. *In much wisdom there is much indignation* (Eccle 1:18). *Much learning is driving*

faciunt insanire. Haec enim fuit plaga Aegyptiorum, id est, sapientium huius mundi, *vesicae turgentes*, Ex. IX, 9. **Caritas vero aedificat** infirmos, quae quod eis obesse potest, dimittit, quia non quaerit quae sua sunt.

Unde addenda est scientiae caritas. Augustinus: *addite ergo scientiae caritatem, et utilis erit scientia.* Per se quidem est inutilis, ex caritate vero utilis. Philosophus: *scire aut nihil, aut parum prodest ad virtutem.*

424. Deinde cum dicit **si quis autem existimat**, etc., hic ostendit a quibus haec scientia habetur insufficienter, quia ab illis, qui ea utuntur in nocumentum proximi. Et est sua ratio talis: quicumque habet scientiam et non modum utendi ea, habet scientiam insufficienter; sed qui habet scientiam sine caritate est huiusmodi: ergo qui habet scientiam sine caritate, habet insufficienter scientiam.

Primo ergo supponit scientiam sine caritate; secundo ostendit insufficientiam talis scientiae, ibi **nondum cognovit**, etc.; tertio rationem insufficientiae, ibi **quemadmodum oporteat**, et cetera.

Dicit ergo **si quis autem**, etc., quasi dicat: habetis scientiam, sed non sufficientem, quia si quis vestrum **existimat se scire**, habens scientiam sine caritate, aliquid scit, scilicet quod liceat comedere idolothita. **Nondum tamen cognovit**, quia non se cognoscere facto ostendit, **quomodo oporteat eum scire**, id est, qualiter debeat uti scientia, quia in aedificationem, non in nocumentum aliorum.

425. Scire autem contingit dupliciter, scilicet habere scientiam et uti scientia: sicut videre, habere visum, et uti visu.

Glossa Bernardi: hic non approbat Apostolus multa scientem, si modum sciendi nescierit. Modus enim sciendi est, ut scias quo ordine, quo studio, quo fine scire quaeque oporteat: quo ordine, ut id prius quod maturius ad salutem; quo studio, ut id ardentius quod efficacius est ad amorem; quo fine, ut non ad inanem gloriam vel curiositatem velle aliquid, sed ad aedificationem tui et proximi.

Sunt namque qui scire volunt eo fine tantum, ut sciant, et curiositas est; quidam ut sciantur, et vanitas est; quidam ut scientiam vendant, et turpis quaestus est; quidam ut aedificentur, et prudentia est; quidam ut aedificent, et caritas est.

426. Deinde cum dicit **si quis autem diligit**, etc., hic ostendit a quibus haec scientia habetur sufficienter, quia ab illis qui utuntur ea ex caritate. Primo ergo supponit scientiam cum caritate; secundo ostendit sufficientiam talis scientiae, ibi **hic cognitus est**.

you mad (Acts 26:24). For this the plague of the Egyptians, i.e., of the wisemen of this world, was swelling blains (Exod 9:9). **But charity edifies** the weak, as it renounces the things that can hurt them, because it does not seek its own.

Hence charity must be added to knowledge. Augustine says: *add therefore charity to knowledge, and knowledge will be useful.* Of itself it is useless, but due to charity it is useful. The Philosopher says: *knowing is of little or no value for virtue.*

424. Then when he says, **if any man thinks**, he shows who have knowledge in an insufficient manner—by those who use it in a manner harmful to their neighbor. And his reasoning is as follows: whoever has knowledge and not the measure to use it, has knowledge in an insufficient manner, but he who has knowledge without charity is such, therefore he who has knowledge without charity, has knowledge in an insufficient manner.

He supposes first, therefore, knowledge without charity; second he shows the insufficiency of such knowledge, at **he has not yet known**; third the reason for the insufficiency, at **as he ought**.

He says, therefore, **if any man**, as though to say: you have knowledge, but not sufficient, because if any of you **thinks that he knows**, having knowledge without charity, he knows something, namely that it is licit to eat food offered to idols. **He has not yet known**, since he does not show by deed that he knows, **as he ought to know**, i.e., how he ought to use his knowledge—in a manner that builds up, rather than harming others.

425. Now there are two ways of knowing: having knowledge, and making use of knowledge, just as there are two ways of seeing: to have sight, and to make use of sight.

Bernard's Gloss says: here the Apostle does not approve of one who knows many things, if he does not know the measure of knowing. The measure of knowing is that you know in what order, with what eagerness, and with what end you ought to know anything: in what order, that what leads more speedily to salvation comes first; with what eagerness, that you have more ardor for that which is more efficacious for love; with what end, that you not want to know anything for vain glory or curiosity, but for the building up of yourself and your neighbor.

There are namely those who want to know for that end, that they may know, and this is curiosity; some that they may be known, and this is vanity; some that they may sell knowledge, and this is shameful profit; some that they may be built up, and this is prudence; some that they may build others up, and this is charity.

426. Then when he says, **but if any man loves**, he shows who has this knowledge in a sufficient manner: those who use it out of charity. First, therefore, he supposes knowledge with charity; second he shows the sufficiency of such knowledge, at **the same is known**.

Dicit ergo *si quis*, etc., quasi dicat: ille perfecte non scit qui nescit quemadmodum oporteat eum scire. *Si quis autem diligit Deum*, et ita cum scientia habet caritatem, *hic cognitus*, id est approbatus, *est ab eo*. Novit enim Dominus qui sunt eius, II Tim. c. II, 19. Unde talis vere scit Deo approbante, quia bene utitur scientia propter caritatem annexam.

427. Notandum est hic, quod ad hoc quod aliquis sciat quemadmodum oporteat scire, novem sunt necessaria.

Primo humiliter sine inflatione. Phil. IV, v. 12: *scio humiliari*. Ps. CXXX, 2: *si non humiliter sentiebam*.

Secundo sobrie sine praesumptione. Supra c. II, 2: *non iudicavi me scire*. Rom. XII, v. 3: *non plus sapere quam oportet*.

Tertio certitudinaliter sine haesitatione. II Tim. I, 12: *scio cui credidi, et certus sum*.

Quarto veraciter et sine errore. II Tim. III, v. 7: *semper discentes, et numquam ad scientiam veritatis pervenientes*.

Quinto simpliciter sine deceptione. I Tim. c. VI, 20: *oppositiones falsi nominis scientiae*.

Sexto salubriter cum caritate et dilectione. Infra XIII, 2: *si habuero omnem scientiam, caritatem autem non habuero*.

Septimo utiliter cum proximorum aedificatione. Infra XII, 8: *alii datur sermo scientiae in eodem spiritu*.

Octavo liberaliter cum gratuita communicatione. Sap. VI, 24: *ponam in lucem sapientiam eius*.

Nono efficaciter cum bona operatione. Iac. IV, 17: *scienti enim bonum, et non facienti, peccatum est illi*.

Primum, scilicet humilitas scientiae, arguit sapientes superbos, sobrietas curiosos, certitudo dubiosos, veritas haereticos, simplicitas advocatos, salubritas magnos, utilitas iniquos, liberalitas avaros, efficacia otiosos.

428. Deinde cum dicit *de escis autem quae idolis*, etc., hic ostendit qualem scientiam habent de idolothitis, ostendens

primo quod sciunt idolum nihil esse;

secundo quod sciunt omnia a Deo esse, ibi *nam etsi sunt qui dicantur dii*.

429. In prima, primo dicit idolum nihil esse; secundo iuxta hoc ad declarationem ostendit Deum non nisi unum esse, ibi *et quod nullus Deus*, et cetera.

Dicit ergo *de escis autem*, etc., quasi dicat: praedictis modis non valet scientia, sed tamen, *de escis quae immolantur idolis, scimus*, scientia vera scilicet, quod in se

He says, therefore, *if any man*, as though to say: he does not know perfectly who does not know as he ought to know. *But if any man loves God*, and thus with knowledge has charity, *the same is known*, i.e., approved, *by him. For the Lord knows those who are his* (2 Tim 2:19). Hence such a one truly knows with God's approval, because he knows to use his knowledge out of the charity connected with it.

427. It should be noted here that in order for someone to know as he ought to know, nine things are necessary.

First, to know humbly, without being puffed up: *I know how to be humbled* (Phil 4:12); *if I was not humbly minded* (Ps 131:1).

Second, to know soberly, without presumption: *I judged myself not to know* (1 Cor 2:2); *do not be more wise than you ought* (Rom 12:3).

Third, to know with assurance, without hesitation: *I know whom I have believed, and I am certain* (2 Tim 1:12).

Fourth, to know truthfully and without error: *always learning, and never attaining to the knowledge of the truth* (2 Tim 3:7).

Fifth, to know in simplicity, without deception: *oppositions of what is falsely called knowledge* (1 Tim 6:20).

Sixth, to know wholesomely, without charity and love: *if I have all knowledge, but have not charity* (1 Cor 13:2).

Seventh, to know usefully, so as to build up one's neighbor: *to another is given the word of knowledge, according to the same Spirit* (1 Cor 12:8).

Eighth, to know liberally, so as to communicate freely: *I will bring the knowledge of her to light* (Wis 6:24).

Ninth, to know efficaciously, with good activity: *to one who knows what is good, but does not do it, to him it is sin* (Jas 4:17).

The first, namely the humility of knowledge, convicts the proud wisemen, sobriety the curious, assurance the doubtful, truthfulness the heretics, simplicity the advocates, wholesomeness the great, usefulness the wicked, liberality the avarice, efficacity the idle.

428. Then when you says, *but as for the meats that are sacrificed to idols*, he shows what kind of knowledge they have about things offered to idols, showing

first, that they know an idol is nothing;

second, that they know all things are from God, at *for although there are those that are called gods*.

429. In the first part, he first says that an idol is nothing; second, in accordance with this, he proceeds to declare and show clearly that there is only one God, at *and that there is no God but one*.

He says, therefore, *but as for meats*, as though to say: in the aforesaid modes science is not of value, but yet, *as for meats that are sacrificed to idols*, we know, namely with

sunt licitae, nec propter idolum sunt immundae; et hoc quia *idolum nihil est in mundo*.

Hoc tripliciter exponitur. Primo modo sic: *idolum nihil est in mundo*, id est, inter creaturas mundi quantum ad formam idoli; licet enim materia idoli sit aliquid, scilicet aurum, vel argentum, vel huiusmodi, tamen nil est forma, scilicet quae creditur ibi esse ab idololatris, qui credunt idolum esse Deum. Is. XLI, 24: *ecce vos estis ex nihilo, et opus vestrum ex eo quod non est*.

Secundo modo sic: *idolum nihil est*, scilicet persona subsistens ex simulacro et spiritu praesidente. Ex istis enim duobus nihil fit, sicut ab idololatris putatur. Ier. X, 14: *confusus est omnis artifex in sculptili, quia falsum est quod conflavit, et non est spiritus in eo*.

Tertio modo sic: *idolum nihil est in mundo*, id est, nullius rei quae sit in mundo habens similitudinem. Est enim differentia inter idolum et simulacrum, quia simulacrum dicitur quod fit ad similitudinem rei alicuius naturalis: idolum autem ad nullius rei est similitudinem, ut si corpori humano addatur caput equinum. Is. XL, 18: *cui similem fecistis Deum*, et cetera.

Et *scimus* etiam *quod nullus Deus nisi unus*. Deut. VI, 4: *audi Israel, Dominus Deus tuus, Deus unus est*.

430. Deinde cum dicit *nam etsi sunt qui*, etc., hic ostendit quod sciunt omnia a Deo esse, non a diis nuncupativis vel adoptivis, ut sunt idola, vel sancti, sed ab uno summo. Primo ergo dicit, quomodo potest intelligi deorum pluralitas, scilicet per adoptionem vel nuncupationem; secundo quomodo est divinitatis unitas, scilicet per essentiam, ibi *nobis tantum unus Deus*, et cetera. Ubi primo tangit unitatem in Patre; secundo in Filio, ibi *et unus Dominus*, et cetera. In prima tangit tria, scilicet essentiam, quia unus Deus; personam, quia Fater; potentiam, ex quo omnia; clementiam, quia *et nos in illo*; similiter ista tangit in Filio.

Dicit ergo *nam etsi sunt*, etc., quasi dicat: et vere non est nisi unus Deus, *nam etsi sunt qui dicantur dii*, vere participatione divinitatis, ut sancti, Ps. LXXXI, 6: *ego dixi, dii estis*, *sive in caelo*, ut sancti comprehensores, *sive in terra*, ut sancti viatores; *siquidem sunt dii multi* vere participatione divinitatis, ut sancti et iusti Domini apostoli et praelati, *nobis tamen*, et cetera.

Alio modo legitur sic *nam etsi sunt qui dicuntur dii* a gentibus, scilicet falsa nuncupatione, *sive in caelo*, ut sol et luna, *sive in terra*, ut Mercurius et Diana. *Siquidem sunt dii multi*, sola scilicet nuncupatione secundum gentiles. Ps. XCV, 5: *dii gentium daemonia*. *Et*

true knowledge, that they are licit in themselves, nor are they unclean on account of the idol, and this, because *an idol is nothing in the world*.

This may be explained in three ways. The first way is: *an idol is nothing in the world*, i.e., among the creatures of the world with respect to the form of an idol; for although the material of an idol is something, namely gold or silver or something similar, its form is nothing, namely what idoloters believe to be there, who believe an idol to be God: *behold you are of nothing, and your work is of that which is not* (Isa 41:24).

The second way of explaining it is: *an idol is nothing*, namely a person consisting of a likeness and a governing spirit. For of those two things nothing comes to be, as idolators think it does: *every craftsman is brought to confusion by his graven image, because what he has forged is false, and there is no spirit in it* (Jer 10:14).

The third way of explaining it is: *an idol is nothing in the world*, i.e., having a likeness to no thing that is in the world. For the difference between an idol and an image is that an image names that which is made to the likeness of some natural thing, whereas an idol is a likeness of no thing, as if a horse's head were added to a human body: *to whom have you likened God* (Isa 40:18).

And *we know* also *that there is no God but one*: *hear Israel, the Lord your God, God is one* (Deut 6:4).

430. Then when he says, *for although there are those*, he shows that they know all things are from God, not from those called gods either by adoption, as idols are, or called gods as the saints are, but from one supreme God. He therefore first says how the plurality of gods can be understood, namely by adoption or naming; second of what sort the unity of the divinity is, namely a unity in essence, at *to us there is but one God*. Here he first mentions unity in the Father, then in the Son, at *and one Lord*. In the first part he touches on three things, namely essence, in saying one God; person, in saying Father; power, in saying from whom are all things; clemency, in saying *and we unto him*; similarly he touches on those in the Son.

He says therefore, *for although there are those*, as though to say: and truly there is only one God, *for although there are those that are called gods*, truly by participation of divinity, as the saints: *I said, you are gods* (Ps 82:6), whether in heaven, as the saints who have reached the final goal, or on earth, as saints still journeying on the way, as indeed there are many gods truly by participation of divinity, as the holy and righteous apostles and prelates of the Lord, *yet to us there is but one God*.

One may read it in another way as follows: *for although there are those that are called gods* by the gentiles, namely by a false naming, *either in heaven*, as the sun and the moon, *or on earth*, as Mercury and Diana. *For there are many gods*, only according to the name of the gentiles:

domini multi, qui aliis praesunt, **nobis tamen** tantum **unus est Deus** essentialiter, scilicet **Pater, ex quo omnia** secundum naturam et per paternam auctoritatem, Rom. c. XI, 36: *ex quo omnia, et nos in illo per gratiam*. Act. XVII, 28: *in ipso vivimus, movemur et sumus*. **Et unus** cum Patre Deus **Dominus Iesus Christus**. Io. X, 30: *ego et Pater unum sumus*. **Per quem omnia**, scilicet facta sunt secundum naturam, Io. I, 3: *omnia per ipsum facta sunt*. **Et nos per illum**, scilicet sumus in Deo per gratiam. Rom. I, v. 5: *pcer quem accepi gratiam, et cetera*. Ergo unus est altissimus Creator omnium omnipotens.

Ex his elicitur talis ratio: non est nisi unus Deus qui fecit omnia, sed multa sunt idola, ergo non sunt Deus qui fecit omnia, nec creduntur aliquid, ergo nihil.

431. *Sed non in omnibus est scientia*. Habito quod maiores illorum habent scientiam de idolothitis, hic ostendit quod minores hac scientia carent.

Ubi primo ostendit quod in quibusdam defuit praedicta de idolothitis scientia; secundo quod propter hoc, esu scilicet idolothitorum, polluitur eorum conscientia. Ubi primo tangit pollutae conscientiae rationem; secundo ipsam pollutionem, ibi **et conscientia ipsorum**, et cetera.

Dicit ergo **sed non in omnibus**, etc., quasi dicat: hoc scimus nos, scilicet quod **idolum nihil est, sed non in omnibus**, ut in infirmis, **est scientia** haec. Et vere non est in omnibus: **quidam tamen**, et cetera.

Vel sic: nos scimus quod **idolum nihil est in mundo, quidam enim cum conscientia idoli**, quia scilicet putant idolum aliquid divinum esse, **usque nunc**, id est, post conversionem, sicut ante **manducant idolothitum**, id est, de sanctificatis idolis, et hoc non quasi cibum simpliciter, sed **quasi idolothitum**, scilicet ad reverentiam idoli, et **conscientia illorum, cum sit infirma, polluitur**, per illos scilicet qui habent rectam scientiam, sed non cum caritate, per quos in hunc errorem infirmi inducuntur. Deut. XXVII, 19: *maledictus qui errare facit caecum in itinere*.

Hic innuit quod non cibus, sed conscientia polluitur per peccatum, comedendo ad exemplum malorum.

432. Deinde cum dicit **esca autem non commendat**, etc.; hic, quarto, ostendit quod coram eis idolothita comedere non debent. Ubi primo ostendit quod huiusmodi comestio nihil prodest apud Deum; secundo probat quod non praestat aliquod bonum augmentum, ibi **neque enim si non manducaveritis**.

Dicit ergo **esca autem**, etc., quasi dicat: illis nocet vestra comestio, vobis autem non prodest. **Esca enim nos**

---

the Gods of the nations are demons (Ps 96:5). **And many lords**, who rule over others, **yet to us there is but one God** in essence, namely **the Father, from whom are all things** according to nature and by fatherly authority: *from whom are all things, and we in him* (Rom 31:36) by grace; and *in him we live and move and exist* (Acts 17:28). **And one** with God the Father **Lord Jesus Christ**: *I and the Father are one* (John 10:30), **through whom are all things**, namely made according to nature: *all things were made through him* (John 1:3), **and we through him**, namely we are in God through grace: *through whom I received grace* (Rom 1:5). Therefore there is one highest, all-powerful Creator of all things.

From these things the following argument may be drawn: there can only be one God who made all things, but there are many idols; therefore, they are not the God who made all things, nor are they believed to be anything, therefore they are nothing.

431. But there is not knowledge in everyone. Given that the greater men among them have knowledge of foods sacrificed to idols, here he shows that lesser men are free from this knowledge.

And there he first shows that in certain people this knowledge of the food of idols was absent; second, that because of this eating of the foods of idols, their conscience is defiled. Then he first deals with the reason for the defiled conscience; and second with the defilement itself, at **and their conscience**.

Therefore he says, **but there is not knowledge**, as if he were saying: we know this, **that an idol is nothing**, but this **knowledge is not in everyone**. And indeed, it is not in everyone: **for some, being hitherto with conscience of an idol, eat as a thing sacrificed to an idol**.

Or it can be taken like this: **we know that an idol is nothing in the world**, for **some, being with conscience of the idol**, namely, because they think idols to be something divine, **hitherto**, that is, after their conversion, just as before **they eat** things **sacrificed to an idol**, that is, of things consecrated for idols, and this not as food simply, but **as a thing sacrificed to an idol**, namely for honoring an idol, and, **their conscience, being weak, is defiled**, by those very ones who have right knowledge without charity, by whom the weak are led into this error: *cursed be he who makes the blind to wander out of his way* (Deut 27:18).

Here he agrees that not food but conscience is defiled by sin, when someone eats after the example of the wicked.

432. Then when he says, **but meat does not commend us**, here he fourth shows that in the presence of those people they should not eat food sacrificed to idols. Then he shows first that food like this does nothing to benefit one before God; and second, he proves that it does not bring about any good increase, at **nor, if we eat not**.

Therefore he says **but meat**, as if he were saying, your food harms those people, but it does not benefit you. For

non commendat Deo, sed recta fides in edendo. Nam nec Esau esu lenticulae iustificatus est, nec Elias esu carnium pollutus est. Rom. XIV, 17: *non est regnum Dei esca et potus.* Hebr. ult.: *bonum est gratia stabilire cor, non escis.*

Deinde cum dicit ***neque enim si non manducaverimus***, etc., hic probat quod proposuit, et est sua ratio talis: non comedere idolothitum non diminuit bonum, comedere non auget, ergo talis esca sumpta vel non sumpta nihil prodest apud Deum. Et hoc est quod dicit ***neque enim si non manducaverimus, deficiemus***, id est, minus ab eo habebimus, ***neque si manducaverimus, abundabimus*** in virtutibus, quia esca ventri, non menti proficit, et ita cum non sit de veritate vitae, iustitiae et doctrinae, dimittenda est propter scandalum.

meat does not commend us to God, but upright faith when eating. For neither was Esau justified by eating lentils, nor was Elijah defiled by eating meat: *for the kingdom of God is not meat and drink* (Rom 14:17); *for it is best that the heart be established with grace, not with meats* (Heb 13:9).

Next when he says, ***nor if we eat not***, he proves what he had proposed, and his reasoning is as follows: not to eat the food sacrificed to idols does not diminish one's good; to eat does not increase it, therefore, such meat consumed or not consumed benefits nothing before God. And this is why he says ***nor if we eat not, shall we have the less***, that is, we will have less by it, ***neither if we eat, shall we have the more*** in virtue, for meat profits the stomach, not the mind; and thus since it is not concerning the truth of life, justice and doctrine, it is to be set aside because of scandal.

Lecture 2

8:9Videte autem ne forte haec licentia vestra offendiculum fiat infirmis. [n. 433]

8:10Si enim quis viderit eum, qui habet scientiam, in idolio recumbentem: nonne conscientia ejus, cum sit infirma, aedificabitur ad manducandum idolothyta? [n. 435]

8:11Et peribit infirmus in tua scientia, frater, propter quem Christus mortuus est? [n. 436]

8:12Sic autem peccantes in fratres, et percutientes conscientiam eorum infirmam, in Christum peccatis. [n. 438]

8:13Quapropter si esca scandalizat fratrem meum, non manducabo carnem in aeternum, ne fratrem meum scandalizem. [n. 439]

8:9βλέπετε δὲ μή πως ἡ ἐξουσία ὑμῶν αὕτη πρόσκομμα γένηται τοῖς ἀσθενέσιν.

8:10ἐὰν γάρ τις ἴδῃ σὲ τὸν ἔχοντα γνῶσιν ἐν εἰδωλείῳ κατακείμενον, οὐχὶ ἡ συνείδησις αὐτοῦ ἀσθενοῦς ὄντος οἰκοδομηθήσεται εἰς τὸ τὰ εἰδωλόθυτα ἐσθίειν;

8:11ἀπόλλυται γὰρ ὁ ἀσθενῶν ἐν τῇ σῇ γνώσει, ὁ ἀδελφὸς δι' ὃν Χριστὸς ἀπέθανεν.

8:12οὕτως δὲ ἁμαρτάνοντες εἰς τοὺς ἀδελφοὺς καὶ τύπτοντες αὐτῶν τὴν συνείδησιν ἀσθενοῦσαν εἰς Χριστὸν ἁμαρτάνετε.

8:13διόπερ εἰ βρῶμα σκανδαλίζει τὸν ἀδελφόν μου, οὐ μὴ φάγω κρέα εἰς τὸν αἰῶνα, ἵνα μὴ τὸν ἀδελφόν μου σκανδαλίσω.

8:9But take heed lest perhaps this your liberty become a stumbling block to the weak. [n. 433]

8:10For if a man sees him that has knowledge sit at meat in the idol's temple, shall not his conscience, being weak, be emboldened to eat those things that are sacrificed to idols? [n. 435]

8:11And through your knowledge shall the weak brother perish, for whom Christ has died? [n. 436]

8:12Now when you sin thus against the brethren and wound their weak conscience, you sin against Christ. [n. 438]

8:13Wherefore, if meat scandalizes my brother, I will never eat flesh, lest I should scandalize my brother. [n. 439]

---

433. Haec est secunda pars huius capituli; superius enim ostendit quod in se licita est comestio idolothitorum, hic monet abstinere ab ea propter scandalum infirmorum. Ubi

primo monet ne offendant fratres sua comestione;

secundo quod potest offendere, ibi *si enim quis viderit*, etc.;

tertio ostendit malum quod inde potest accidere, ibi *et peribit infirmus*, etc.;

quarto praebet se in exemplum abstinentium, ibi *quapropter si esca scandalizat*, et cetera.

434. Dicit ergo: videte, quia quantum ad nos nihil prodest vel obest esca ipsa, sed tamen *videte ne forte haec licentia vestra*, qua scitis licere vobis comedere de idolothitis, *offendiculum fiat infirmis* in fide, qui nondum sciunt idolum nihil esse. Lev. XIX, 14: *coram caeco non pones offendiculum*.

435. Deinde cum dicit *si quis viderit*, etc., hic ostendit quomodo possunt offendere, quia comedendo idolothitum coram infirmis: ubi implicantur quatuor concurrentia ad scandalum. Primo maiorum scientia; secundo comestio idolothiti publica, ibi *in idolio recumbentem*, tertio occasio scandali accepti, ibi *nonne conscientia eius?*

Dicit ergo *si enim quis*, etc.; quasi dicat: et vere potest esse offendiculum, *si enim quis infirmus viderit eum qui habet scientiam, recumbentem in idolio*, id est, in

433. This is the second part of this chapter; for above he shows that, in itself, eating food sacrificed to idols is permitted; here he warns to abstain from it because of scandalizing the weak.

First he warns the brothers lest they offend by their eating;

second why it can offend, at *for if a man sees*;

third, he shows the evil that can occur from this, at *and through your knowledge*;

fourth, he presents himself as an example of those abstaining, at *wherefore if meat scandalizes*.

434. He says, therefore: see that as concerns us, this meat neither helps nor harms, but nevertheless *take heed lest perhaps this your liberty*, which we know permits you to eat of the food of idols, *become a stumbling block to the weak* in faith, who do not yet know that idols are nothing: *you shall not place a stumbling block before the blind* (Lev 19:14).

435. Next, when he says *if a man should see*, here he shows how it can offend by eating the food of idols in the presence of the weak: and four concurrent things are involved in scandal. The first is the knowledge of the greater ones; the second is the public eating of the food sacrificed to idols, at *sit at meat in the idol's temple*; the third is the occasion of scandal taken up, at *shall not his conscience?*

Therefore he says, *for if man*, as if to say: and indeed it can be a stumbling block, *for if a man, being weak, sees him that has knowledge sit at meat in the temple of an idol*,

praesentia idoli, *nonne conscientia eius cum sit infirma*, per te, *aedificabitur*, id est, per factum tuum, *ad manducandum idolothita*, id est, sacrificata in reverentiam idoli? Quasi dicat: sic videns enim quis fratrem peritum in idolio sacrificata comedere, incipit ipse edere non illa conscientia qua ille, scilicet peritiae causa, sed id putat esse numen in cuius reverentia hoc fiat.

436. Deinde cum dicit *et peribit infirmus*, hic ostendit malum quod inde potest accidere, et hoc duplex:

primo scandalum proximi;

secundo offensam proximi, ibi *sic autem peccantes*, et cetera.

437. In prima implicantur tria, peccantis conditio, quia infirmus; peccandi occasio, quia in tua conscientia; peccati exaggeratio, quia propter quem Christus mortuus est.

Dicit ergo: et ita *peribit infirmus*, in fide idest, *in tua scientia, frater*, id est, occasione accepta a tua scientia, quia te sapientem videt comedere, putans quod sub idoli veneratione comedas, *propter quem* salvandum *Christus mortuus est*, et ita graviter peccas. Rom. XIV, 15: *noli cibo perdere illum pro quo mortuus est Christus.*

438. *Sic autem peccantes in fratres*, peccato scandali, *et percutientes conscientiam eorum infirmam*, gladio mali exempli, Amos IX, 1: *percute cardinem*, id est conscientiam, *et commovebuntur superliminaria*, id est, intellectus et affectus; *in Christo peccatis*, cuius membra sunt.

Non ait in Christum, secundum Glossam, quia in Christum peccare, est Christum negare, id est, peccare in fide. In Christo peccare est in his quae Christi sunt peccare, scilicet in moribus; sicut ille qui in lege est, dicitur in lege peccare: qui autem in lege non est, dicitur peccare in legem.

439. Deinde cum dicit *quapropter si esca*, etc., hic ultimo proponit se in exemplum abstinentiae, ubi primo implicat scandalum; secundo ex hoc explicat abstinentiae propositum, ibi *non manducabo*, etc.; tertio praevenit dubium, ibi *ne fratrem meum*, et cetera.

Dicit ergo: *quapropter*, ne scilicet peccem in Christum, *si esca scandalizat fratrem meum, non manducabo carnem* aliquam, non solum idolothita, *in aeternum*: si ergo propter scandalum fratrum abstinendum est quasi a necessariis vitae, multo magis a superfluis. Et hoc, non ideo quod esca in se mala sit, sed *ne scandalizem fratrem meum. Nam qui scandalizaverit unum de pusillis istis, expedit ei ut suspendatur in collo eius mola asinaria*, etc., Matth. XVIII, 6. Rom. XIV, v. 20: *omnia munda mundis, sed malum est homini qui per offendiculum manducat.*

that is, in the presence of an idol, *shall not his conscience, being weak, be emboldened* by you, that is, by your deed, *to eat those things that are sacrificed to idols*, that is, sacrificed to honor idols? As if to say, for thus seeing his more experienced brother eating food sacrificed to idols, he too will begin to eat, not with that consciousness that the experienced man has, namely by reason of his expertise, but he thinks it happens in honor of a deity.

436. Next, when he says, *and through your knowledge*, he shows the evil that can arise from this, and here two things must be distinguished:

first, the scandal of the neighbor;

second, the offense of the neighbor, at *now when you sin thus*.

437. In the first, three things are implied: the condition of the one sinning, because it is weak; the occasion of sin, because it is in your conscience; and the exacerbation of the sin, since Christ died on account of him.

Therefore he says, and thus *shall the weak perish*, in faith, that is, *through your knowledge, brother*, that is, having taken the occasion from your knowledge, for he sees you, the wise man, eat, and he thinks that you eat out of veneration of an idol—him *for whom*, that is, for whose salvation, *Christ has died*, and so you sin gravely: *do not destroy with your meat him for whom Christ died* (Rom 14:15).

438. *Now when you sin thus against the brethren*, in the sin of scandal, *and wound their weak conscience*, with the sword of bad example: *strike the hinges*, that is, the conscience, *and let the lintels be shook* (Amos 9:1), that is, the intellect and the affections; *you sin against Christ*, whose members they are.

According to a Gloss, he does not say unto Christ, because to sin unto Christ is to deny Christ, that is, to sin against faith. To sin against Christ is to sin against those who are of Christ, namely in morals; just as the man who is under the law is said to sin against the law; but who is not under the law is said to sin unto the law.

439. Then when he says *wherefore if meat*, here he finally sets himself forth as an example of abstinence, where he first gives the implications of scandal; second, he explains from that the reason for abstinence, at *I will never eat*; and third, he anticipates questions, at *lest I should scandalize*.

Therefore he says, *wherefore*, lest namely I should sin against Christ, *if meat scandalizes my brother, I will never eat* any *flesh*, not only food sacrificed to idols: if therefore something like a necessity of life is to be abstained from on account of scandal of the brethren, how much more from unnecessary things. And this, not because meat is bad in itself, but *lest I should scandalize my brother. For whoever scandalizes one of these little ones, it would be better for him if a millstone were hung around his neck* (Matt 18:6). *All things are clean to the clean, but it is evil for that man who eats to offend* (Rom 14:20).

440. Hic quaeritur super illud *scientia inflat*, Glossa: *scientia per se inutilis est.*

Contra, scientia per se bona est, ergo et utilis.

Responsio. Inutilis est ad salutem, utilis tamen ad multa alia.

441. Item *caritas aedificat*. Contra: sicut scientia inflat, non per causam, sed per occasionem, sic et caritas.

Responsio. Non est simile, quia scientia habenti se manifestat, sed non sic caritas, quia nemo certus est de caritate.

442. Item super illud *idolum nihil est*, Glossa: *naturam Deus formavit, sed stultitia hominum formam dedit.*

Contra: omne esse est a Deo, ergo omnis forma.

Responsio. Glossa loquitur de forma putativa in natura, non de vera.

443. Item ibidem Glossa: *forma hominis in idolo non est facta per Verbum.*

Contra Io. I, 3: *omnia per ipsum facta sunt.*

Responsio: quamvis forma hominis in illo sit facta per Verbum, non tamen in idolo, id est, ad colendum.

444. Item ibidem Glossa: *idolum nihil est, quia nullius rei quae sit in mundo similitudinem habet.*

Contra: non potest artifex cogitare vel formare nisi qualia vidit.

Responsio. Non habet similitudinem in toto, sed in partibus.

445. Item super illud *nullus Deus nisi unus*, Glossa: *hoc dicit ne putetur esse Deus in idolo.*

Contra: Deus, licet sit unus, tamen est ubique.

Responsio. In idolo est per potentiam, non per praesentiam vel unionem, ut putabant gentiles.

446. Item ibidem Glossa: *pars Trinitatis non potest esse quicumque unus in tribus.*

Contra: cuiuslibet numeri pars est unitas.

Responsio. Trinitas non est numerus simpliciter, sed numerus personarum.

447. Item super illud *et si sunt qui dicuntur dii*, Glossa: *participatione divinitatis.*

Contra: divinitas est imparticipabilis.

Responsio. Participatio haec per causam est, non per essentiam.

448. Item ibid. Glossa quaeritur utrum angeli vocandi sint dii.

440. Here it is asked concerning the fact that *knowledge puffs up* (1 Cor 8:1), where the Gloss has: *knowledge is useless by itself.*

Against this: knowledge is good in itself; therefore it is also useful.

Response: it is useless for salvation, but useful for many other things.

441. Likewise, *charity edifies* (1 Cor 8:1). Against this: just as knowledge puffs up, not as a cause, but as an occasion, so also does charity.

Response: it is not similar, for knowledge manifests itself to the someone who has it, but not so charity, for no one is certain of charity.

442. Likewise, concerning *an idol is nothing* (1 Cor 8:4), the Gloss says: *God formed nature, but the stupidity of man gave it form.*

Against this: every being is from God, and therefore, every form.

Response: the Gloss speaks of the putative form in nature, not of the true one.

443. Likewise, the Gloss says in the same place: *the form of man in an idol was not made by the Word.*

Against this: *all things were made by him* (John 1:3).

Answer: although man's form was made in him by the Word, it was not made in an idol, that is, for worshiping.

444. Likewise, the Gloss says in the same place: *an idol is nothing, for it has the likeness of no thing that is in the world.*

Against this: a craftsman cannot think or form except such as he sees.

Response: it does not have a likeness in everything, but only in part.

445. Likewise regarding *there is no God but one*, the Gloss says: he says this lest it be believed that God is in an idol.

Against this: God, although he is one, nevertheless is everywhere.

Response: he is in an idol by power, not by presence or union, as the gentiles believe.

446. Likewise, the Gloss says in the same place: *a part of the Trinity cannot be every one in three whatsoever.*

Against this: unity is a part of any number.

Response: Trinity is not simply a number, but a number of persons.

447. Likewise, regarding *although there are those that are called gods* (1 Cor 8:5), the Gloss says: *by participation of the divinity.*

Against this: divinity is not participable.

Response: this participation is by its cause, not by its essence.

448. Likewise, the Gloss says in the same place that it is asked whether the angels should be called gods.

Responsio. Quamvis participent divinitatem, tamen, secundum Glossam, non sunt dicendi dii propter periculum adorationis.

449. Item super illud *nobis tamen unus Pater*, Glossa: *Trinitas est nobis unus Pater, non tamen ille qui tertia in Trinitate persona alius.*

Contra: idem et diversum dividunt ens.

Respondeo, quod quamvis idem et diversum dividant ens creatum, non tamen increatum, quia ibi est identitas in essentia cum diversitate in personis.

450. Item *non in omnibus est scientia*. Contra, supra eodem: omnes scientiam habemus.

Responsio. Illud non intelligitur universaliter, sed de maioribus.

451. Item super illud *esca non commendat nos Deo*, dicit Glossa *sumpta vel non sumpta*. Contra: ergo abstinentia nihil meretur.

Responsio. Non virtus escae, sed virtus abstinentiae prodest.

452. Item *si esca scandalizat*, et cetera.

Contra: ergo pro scandalo fratris a pane et vino abstinendum est in perpetuum.

Responsio: non est simile de necessariis et superfluis; vel loquitur hic de scandalo activo, non passivo. Vel perfectionis est hoc, non necessitatis.

453. Notandum est hic super illud: *unus Deus*, quod Deus potest accipi multipliciter, scilicet falsa nuncupatione, et sic idola dicuntur dii. Ps. XCV, 5: *omnes dii gentium daemonia*, Ier. X, 11: *dii qui caelum et terram non fecerunt, pereant de terra.*

Vera adoptione, et sic sancti dicuntur dii. Ps. LXXXI, 6: *ego dixi: dii estis, et filii excelsi omnes, vos autem sicut*, et cetera.

Mundana praelatione, et sic praelati dicuntur dii. Ex. XXII, 28: *diis non detrahes.* Io. c. X, 35: *si illos dixit deos, ad quos*, et cetera.

Essentiae proprietate, et sic Trinitas dicitur Deus. Deut. VI, 4: *audi, Israel, Dominus Deus tuus unus est.*

454. Item notandum quod Christus unus sine pari multipliciter dicitur. Primo unus Deus propter naturam divinitatis; unde sic nullus est Deus nisi unus.

Secundo unus Creator propter infinitatem potestatis. Eccli. I, 8: *unus est altissimus Creator omnium.*

Tertio unus homo propter singularem eminentiam sanctitatis. Ps. XIII, 1: *non est qui faciat bonum*, et cetera. Io. XI, 50: *expedit ut unus moriatur homo.*

Response: although they participate in divinity, nevertheless, according to the Gloss, the are not to be called gods because of the danger of adoration.

449. Likewise, concerning *yet to us there is but one . . . Father* (1 Cor 8:6), the Gloss says: *the Trinity is to us one Father, yet not he who is a third distinct person in the Trinity.*

Against this: same and different divide being.

I respond that although same and different divide created being, they do not divide uncreated being, since there is there identity in essence together with diversity in persons.

450. Likewise, *there is not knowledge in everyone* (1 Cor 8:7). Against this, in the preceding passage: we all have knowledge.

Response: that is not understood universally, but about the greater men.

451. Likewise, on the saying that *meat does not commend us to God* (1 Cor 8:8), the Gloss says *taken or not taken*. Against this: therefore abstinence is of no merit.

Response: not the virtue of meat, but the virtue of abstinence is profitable.

452. Likewise *if meat scandalizes my brother, I will never eat flesh*.

Against this: therefore on account of scandal to a brother one should abstain from bread and wine forever.

Response: the case of necessary things is not the same as the case of superfluous things; or he speaks here about active, not passive scandal; or this abstinence is a matter of perfection, not of necessity.

453. It should be noted on the passage, *one God*, that God can be taken in many ways, namely: by false naming, and in this way idols are called gods: *all the gods of the nations are demons* (Ps 96:5); *the gods that did not make heaven and earth, let them perrish from the earth* (Jer 10:11).

Or by true adoption, and in this way the saints are called gods: *I said: you are gods, and sons of the Most High* (Ps 82:6).

Or by ruling in this world, and in this way rulers are called gods: *you shall not speak ill of the gods* (Exod 22:28); *if he called them gods* (John 10:35).

Or by property of essence, and in this way the Trinity is called God: *hear, O Israel, the Lord your God is one* (Deut 6:4).

454. Likewise it should be noted that Christ being one without equal is said in many ways. First, one God on account of the nature of divinity; hence in this way there is no God but one.

Second, one Creator on account of infinity of power: *there is one most high Creator of all things* (Sir 1:8).

Third, one man on account of the singular eminence of holiness: *there is no one who does good* (Ps 14:1); *it is expedient that one man die* (John 11:50).

Quarto unus Dominus propter gubernationem praelationis. Eph. IV, 5: *unus Dominus, una fides*, et cetera. Et hoc modo unus Dominus Iesus Christus.

Quinto unus magister propter infusionem cognitionis. Matth. XXIII, 10: *non vocemini magistri, quia magister vester unus est Christus.*

Sexto unus Pater propter productionem universitatis. Matth. XXIII, 9: *unus est enim Pater vester qui in caelis est.*

Septimo unus pastor propter generalem refectionem populi fidelis. Io. X, 16: *fiet unum ovile et unus pastor.*

Octavo una hostia propter singulare pretium nostrae redemptionis. Hebr. X, 14: *una enim oblatione consummavit in aeternum sanctificatos.*

Fourth, one Lord on account of governance as a superior: *one Lord, one faith* (Eph 4:5). And in this way there is one Lord Jesus Christ.

Fifth, one teacher on account of infusion of knowledge: *do not be called teachers, for one is your teacher, Christ* (Matt 23:10).

Sixth, one Father on account of producing the universe: *one is your Father, who is in heaven* (Matt 23:9).

Seventh, one shepherd on account of his universal refreshment of the people of faith: *there shall be one flock and one shepherd* (John 10:16).

Eighth, one victim on account of the singular price of our redemption: *for by one oblation he has perfected forever those who are sanctified* (Heb 10:14).

CHAPTER 9

Lecture 1

9:1Non sum liber? non sum apostolus? nonne Christum Jesum Dominum nostrum vidi? nonne opus meum vos estis in Domino? [n. 455]

9:2Et si aliis non sum apostolus, sed tamen vobis sum: nam signaculum apostolatus mei vos estis in Domino. [n. 457]

9:3Mea defensio apud eos qui me interrogant, haec est:

9:4Numquid non habemus potestatem manducandi et bibendi? [n. 458]

9:5numquid non habemus potestatem mulierem sororem circumducendi sicut et ceteri apostoli, et fratres Domini, et Cephas? [n. 460]

9:6aut ego solus, et Barnabas, non habemus potestatem hoc operandi? [n. 461]

9:7Quis militat suis stipendiis umquam? quis plantat vineam, et de fructu ejus non edit? quis pascit gregem, et de lacte gregis non manducat? [n. 462]

9:8Numquid secundum hominem haec dico? an et lex haec non dicit? [n. 464]

9:9Scriptum est enim in lege Moysi: *non alligabis os bovi trituranti.* Numquid de bobus cura est Deo? [n. 466]

9:10an propter nos utique hoc dicit? Nam propter nos scripta sunt: quoniam debet in spe qui arat, arare: et qui triturat, in spe fructus percipiendi.

9:1Οὐκ εἰμὶ ἐλεύθερος; οὐκ εἰμὶ ἀπόστολος; οὐχὶ Ἰησοῦν τὸν κύριον ἡμῶν ἑόρακα; οὐ τὸ ἔργον μου ὑμεῖς ἐστε ἐν κυρίῳ;

9:2εἰ ἄλλοις οὐκ εἰμὶ ἀπόστολος, ἀλλά γε ὑμῖν εἰμι: ἡ γὰρ σφραγίς μου τῆς ἀποστολῆς ὑμεῖς ἐστε ἐν κυρίῳ.

9:3Ἡ ἐμὴ ἀπολογία τοῖς ἐμὲ ἀνακρίνουσίν ἐστιν αὕτη.

9:4μὴ οὐκ ἔχομεν ἐξουσίαν φαγεῖν καὶ πεῖν;

9:5μὴ οὐκ ἔχομεν ἐξουσίαν ἀδελφὴν γυναῖκα περιάγειν, ὡς καὶ οἱ λοιποὶ ἀπόστολοι καὶ οἱ ἀδελφοὶ τοῦ κυρίου καὶ Κηφᾶς;

9:6ἢ μόνος ἐγὼ καὶ Βαρναβᾶς οὐκ ἔχομεν ἐξουσίαν μὴ ἐργάζεσθαι;

9:7τίς στρατεύεται ἰδίοις ὀψωνίοις ποτέ; τίς φυτεύει ἀμπελῶνα καὶ τὸν καρπὸν αὐτοῦ οὐκ ἐσθίει; ἢ τίς ποιμαίνει ποίμνην καὶ ἐκ τοῦ γάλακτος τῆς ποίμνης οὐκ ἐσθίει;

9:8Μὴ κατὰ ἄνθρωπον ταῦτα λαλῶ, ἢ καὶ ὁ νόμος ταῦτα οὐ λέγει;

9:9ἐν γὰρ τῷ Μωϋσέως νόμῳ γέγραπται, Οὐ κημώσεις βοῦν ἀλοῶντα. μὴ τῶν βοῶν μέλει τῷ θεῷ;

9:10ἢ δι' ἡμᾶς πάντως λέγει; δι' ἡμᾶς γὰρ ἐγράφη, ὅτι ὀφείλει ἐπ' ἐλπίδι ὁ ἀροτριῶν ἀροτριᾶν, καὶ ὁ ἀλοῶν ἐπ' ἐλπίδι τοῦ μετέχειν.

9:1Am I not I free? Am not I an apostle? Have not I seen Christ Jesus our Lord? Are not you my work in the Lord? [n. 455]

9:2And if unto others I am not an apostle, but yet to you I am. For you are the seal of my apostleship in the Lord. [n. 457]

9:3My defense with them that examine me is this.

9:4Have not we power to eat and to drink? [n. 458]

9:5Have we not power to carry about a woman, a sister, as well as the rest of the apostles and the brethren of the Lord and Cephas? [n. 460]

9:6Or I only and Barnabas, have not we power to do this? [n. 461]

9:7Who serves as a soldier, at any time, at his own expense? Who plants a vineyard and eats not of the fruit thereof? Who feeds the flock and eats not of the milk of the flock? [n. 462]

9:8Do I speak these things according to man? Or does not the law also say these things? [n. 464]

9:9For it is written in the law of Moses: *you shall not muzzle the mouth of the ox that treads out the corn.* Does God take care for oxen? [n. 466]

9:10Or does he say this indeed for our sakes? For these things are written for our sakes: so that he who ploughs, should plough in hope and he who threshes, in hope to receive fruit.

---

455. Superius monuit cavere ab edendo idolothita coram infirmis, propter scandalum fratrum infirmorum, hic proponit se in exemplum, quia propter alios abstinet se a sibi licitis, scilicet ab acceptione sumptuum, ubi

455. Above he advised avoiding eating food offered to idols in the presence of the weak, on account of the scandal caused to weak brethren; here he gives himself as an example, because for the sake of other persons he abstains from things licit in themselves, namely from accepting means of living.

primo proponit multipliciter, quia licitum est sumptus accipere;

secundo quod nihilominus non vult accipere, ibi *ego autem nullo horum usus sum*, et cetera.

In prima parte, quod licitum sit sumptus accipere, probat tripliciter.

Primo per auctoritatem;

secundo per rationem, ibi *si nos vobis spiritualia seminavimus*, etc.;

tertio per exemplorum similitudinem, ibi *nescitis quod hi qui*, et cetera.

In prima, primo probat per auctoritatem apostolicae dignitatis;

secundo per auctoritatem humanae consuetudinis, ibi *quis militat suis stipendiis*, etc.;

tertio per auctoritatem divinae legis, ibi *numquid secundum hominem*, et cetera.

In prima primo probat quod sit apostolus generaliter;

secundo quod sit apostolus eorum specialiter, ibi *et si aliis non sum apostolus*;

tertio quod potest accipere sumptus licite, ibi *numquid non habemus*, et cetera.

456. In prima, primo quaerit an habeat libertatem accipiendi sumptus; secundo an sit apostolus, ibi *non sum apostolus*, etc.; tertio probat duplici ratione quod sit liber, et apostolus, ibi *nonne Dominum Iesum Christum*, et cetera.

Dicit ergo *non sum liber?* etc., quasi dicat: abstinete ab hoc licito, scilicet ab esu idolothitorum, quia ego etiam abstineo a stipendiis, cum tamen habeam libertatem accipiendi. Numquid enim *non sum apostolus?* Immo vere sum apostolus. Gal. II, 8: *qui operatus est Petro in apostolatum circumcisionis, operatus est et mihi inter gentes.*

Est ergo ratio sua talis: omnis apostolus ratione sui apostolatus habet libertatem accipiendi sumptus; sed ego sum apostolus: utrumque probat postea; ergo, et cetera.

Deinde cum dicit *nonne Dominum Iesum Christum*, etc., hic probat duplici ratione quod sit apostolus, primo per causam, secundo per effectum, ibi *nonne opus meum*, et cetera. Prima ratio sumitur ex parte Christi mittentis; secunda ex parte Corinthiorum quibus mittitur.

Prima ratio talis est: ego vidi Dominum qui me misit ad praedicandum, ergo sum apostolus. Et hoc est quod dicit *nonne*, etc.; quasi dicat: vere sum apostolus, *nonne Dominum Iesum Christum vidi?* Hoc dicit propter pseudoapostolos, qui dicebant ipsum non esse apostolum, quia non fuerat in societate Domini sicut caeteri apostoli. Ipse autem vidit eum iam immortalem, secundum Glossam, vel in via, Act. III, 9, vel in templo,

He first shows in many ways that it is licit to accept means of living;

second, that he nonetheless does not wish to accept them, at *but I have used none of these things* (1 Cor 9:15).

In the first part, he proves in three ways that it is licit to accept means of living:

first, by authority;

second, by reason, at *if we have sown unto you spiritual things* (1 Cor 9:11);

third, by the example of a like case, at *know you not that they who work* (1 Cor 9:13).

In the first part, he first proves it by the authority of the apostolic dignity;

second by the authority of human custom, at *who serves as a solder at his own expense*;

third by the authority of the divine law, at *do I speak these things*.

In the first part, he first proves that he is an apostle in general;

second that he is specially their apostle, at *if unto others I am not an apostle*;

third that he can licitly accept means of living, at *have we not*.

456. In the first part, he first asks whether he has freedom of accepting means of living; second whether he is an apostle, at *am I not an apostle*; third he proves with two reasons that he is free and an apostle, at *have I not seen Jesus Christ our Lord*.

He says, therefore, *am I not free?* As though to say: abstain from this licit thing, namely from eating foods offering to idols, because I too abstain from wages, although I have the freedom to accept them. For *am I not an apostle?* Indeed I am truly an apostle: *he who worked in Peter for the apostleship of the circumcision, worked in me also among the gentiles* (Gal 2:8).

His reasoning is therefore as follows: every apostle by reason of his apostolate has freedom of accepting means of living; but I am an apostle – each of these he proves afterwards – therefore, etc.

Then, when he says *have I not seen Jesus Christ our Lord*, he proves with two reasons that he is an apostle. First through the cause, second through the effect, at *are not you my work*. The first reason is taken on the part of Christ who sent him, the second on the part of the Corinthians to whom he was sent.

The first reason is this: I have seen the Lord who sent me to preach, therefore I am an apostle. And this is what he means in saying *have I not*, as though to say: truly I am an apostle; *have I not seen Jesus Christ our Lord?* He says this on account of the pseudoapostles, who say that he is not an apostle, because he was not in the Lord's company as the rest of the apostles were. But he saw him as an immortal, according to the Gloss, either on the way (Acts 3:9), or

Act. XXII, 19. Unde, Act. IX, 27, *Barnabas apprehensum illum duxit ad apostolos, et narravit quomodo in via vidisset Dominum*. Infra, XV, 8: *novissime omnium tamquam abortivo visus est et mihi.*

Nonne opus meum, et cetera. Ecce secunda ratio talis: vos estis conversi ad fidem per me missum ad hoc; ergo sum apostolus; *nonne opus meum vos estis*, o Corinthii? Sicut templum architecti, supra III, 10: *ut sapiens architectus fundamentum posui*. Item ut filius opus genitoris, supra IV, 15: *in Christo Iesu per Evangelium vos genui*. *Opus*, inquam, *meum*, et hoc *in Domino*, id est, Domino cooperante. Vel in Domino, id est ad gloriam Domini, quasi dicat: sic estis.

457. Deinde cum dicit *et si aliis apostolus*, etc., hic probat quod est apostolus eorum specialiter. Ubi primo proponit quod est apostolus eorum specialiter; secundo probat hoc per effectum, ibi *nam sigillum apostolatus*, etc.; tertio ostendit quod per effectum illum defendit se esse apostolum, ibi *mea defensio ad eos*, et cetera.

Dicit ergo *et si*, etc., quasi dicat: vere opus meum estis, quia *et si aliis*, scilicet Iudaeis quorum legem evacuo, *non sum*, id est non videor esse, *apostolus, sed tamen vobis sum*, qui per me conversi estis specialiter. Rom. XI, 13: *quamdiu gentium sum apostolus, ministerium meum honorificabo*. Et vere vobis sum apostolus, nam *vos estis sigillum apostolatus mei*, id est forma et sigillum, quia apostolatus meus impressus est in vobis, sicut forma sigilli in cera. Glossa: *in vobis apparet quod sum apostolus dum habetis per me quod etiam per alios apostolos*. I Cor. IX, 2: *signa apostolatus mei facta sunt super vos*. *Vos estis*, inquam, *in Domino*, id est Domino principali auctore.

Et vere ita est, quia *mea defensio ad eos qui me interrogant*, utrum scilicet sim apostolus, scilicet hoc estis vos; per vos enim ostendo me esse apostolum.

458. Deinde cum dicit *numquid non habemus*, etc., hic ostendit quod potest accipere sumptus licenter. Ubi

    primo quaerit an habeat hanc potestatem generaliter;

    secundo quantum ad personas determinatas specialiter, ibi *numquid non habemus potestatem*, etc.;

    tertio an ipse et Barnabas sint hac potestate privati singulariter, ibi *an ego solus*, et cetera.

459. Dicit ergo *numquid*, etc., quasi dicat: nam cum sim apostolus, *numquid non habemus*, ego et mei, *potestatem manducandi et bibendi* nostra, id est, vivendi stipendiis nostris? Augustinus: *permisit Dominus, non iussit apostolis accipere necessaria a subditis.*

460. *Numquid non habemus potestatem mulierem sororem*, scilicet fide, *circumducendi nobiscum*, propter sumptus ministrandos? Ambrosius in Glossa: *mulieres*

in the temple (Acts 22:19). Hence: *Barnabas took him and brought him to the apostles, and told them how he had seen the Lord on the way* (Acts 9:27) *And last of all, he was seen also by me, as by one born out of due time* (1 Cor 15:8).

Are not you my work in the Lord? See the second reason, which is this: you were converted to the faith by me, who were sent to you; therefore I am an apostle; *are not you my work*, O Corinthians? As a temple is the work of an architect: *as a wise architect, I have laid the foundation* (1 Cor 3:10). Again, as a son is the work of him who begets him: *for in Christ Jesus, by the Gospel, I have begotten you* (1 Cor 4:15). Again, *my work*, and this *in the Lord*, i.e., as fellow worker with the Lord. Or in the Lord, i.e., for the glory of the Lord, as though to say: thus you are.

457. Then, when he says *and if unto others I am not an apostle*, he proves that he is especially an apostle to them. Here he first states that he is especially an apostle to them; second he proves this by the effect, at *for you are the seal of my apostleship*; third he shows that he makes a defense of himself as an apostle by that effect, at *my defense with them*.

He says, therefore, *and if*, as though to say: truly you are my work, because even *if unto others*, namely to the Jews whose law I empty out, *I am not*, i.e., do not seem to be, *an apostle, but yet to you I am*; to you, that is, who were especially converted by me: *as long as I am the apostle of the gentiles, I will honor my ministry* (Rom 11:13). And truly I am to you an apostle, for *you are the seal of my apostleship*, i.e., the form and the seal, since my apostleship is impressed in you, as the form of a seal in wax. A Gloss says: *in you is seen that I am an apostle, when you have from me what you also have from the other apostles*. And *the signs of my apostleship have been wrought on you* (2 Cor 12:12). *You are*, indeed, *in the Lord*, i.e., with the Lord as principal author.

And truly it is so, *that my defense with them that examine me*, namely about whether I am an apostle, is you yourselves, for by you I show that I am an apostle.

458. Then, when he says *have we not power*, he shows that he can licitly accept means of living.

He first asks whether he has this power in general;

second, with regard to determinate persons in particular, at *have we not power*;

third, whether he and Barnabas in particular are deprived of this power, at *or I only*.

459. He says, therefore, *have we not*, as though to say, since I am an apostle, *have we not*, I and mine, *the power to eat and to drink* our things, i.e., of living from our wages. Augustine says: *the Lord permitted, not commanded, the apostles to accept the things necessary for them from those placed in their charge.*

460. *Have we not the power to carry about a woman, a sister*, namely in faith, for the sake of ministering to us the means of living? Ambrose says in a Gloss: *women*

desiderio doctrinae Dominicae et virtutum cupidae, apostolos sequebantur, et ministrabant eis sumptus, et servitia. Et similiter Christum secutae sunt, Lc. VIII, 2 s. et XXIII, v. 27, **sicut caeteri apostoli**, ut habetur Act. VI, 1, **et sicut fratres**, id est, cognati, **Domini**, qui maiores sunt. Gal. II, 9: *Iacobus et Ioannes, qui videbantur columnae esse*, etc., **et Cephas**, qui maximus est inter apostolos, unde Cephas interpretatur caput. Ambrosius: *non hos reprehendit Apostolus, sed eorum more sibi probat licere*; idcirco autem, ut ait Augustinus; *Dominus mulieres ministraturas sequi voluit, ostendens quid debetur a plebibus Evangelistis.* Vel ideo etiam ne viderentur alienae a salute.

461. Aut numquid **ego solus et Barnabas** (isti enim fuerunt coniuncti ad praedicandum gentibus, Act. XIII, 2: *segregate mihi Barnabam et Paulum in opus ad quod assumpsi eos*), **non habemus**, secundum opinionem vestram, **potestatem hoc operandi?** Scilicet mulieres circumducendi, et sumptus accipiendi, quasi dicat: imo habemus sicut alii, sed omnes alii licite accipiunt, ergo et nobis licet.

462. Deinde cum dicit **quis militat suis stipendiis**, etc., hic secundo probat quod licet accipere sumptus per auctoritatem humanae consuetudinis: et primo in statu militis; secundo agricolae, ibi: **quis plantat vineam**, etc.; tertio pastoris, ibi: **quis pascit gregem**, et cetera.

Militi comparatur praelatus propter subsidium, agricolae propter verbum, pastori propter exemplum. Debet enim subditos defendere suffragio, plantare verbo, pascere exemplo. Primum respicit extra Ecclesiam existentes, secundum Ecclesiam intrantes, tertium in Ecclesia commorantes.

Dicit ergo, **quis militat**, quasi dicat: utique habemus potestatem accipiendi sumptus, et merito **quis militat suis stipendiis?** Quasi dicat: unquam nullus, dabantur enim militibus stipendia de republica. Unde Ioannes dicit: *contenti estote stipendiis vestris.* Sic praedicatores et praelati accipere possunt sumptus a subditis. I Tim. I, 18: *ut milites in illis militiam bonam.* **Quis** enim **plantat vineam, et de fructu eius non edit?** Vinea Domini est Ecclesia. Is. V, 7: *vinea Domini sabaoth, domus Israel est.* Apostoli enim fuerunt plantatores huius vineae. Supra XIV, 6: **ego plantavi, Apollo rigavit. Quis etiam pascit gregem, et de lacte eius non manducat?** Quasi dicat: nullus. Grex Domini sunt fideles Ecclesiae. Ez. XXIV, v. 31: *vos greges pascuae meae.* Huius gregis pastores sunt praelati et praedicatores. Unde primo praelato dictum est: *pasce oves meas*, Io. XXI, 17. Tales possunt pasci de lacte gregis, quia possunt accipere sumptus a subditis.

Si ergo defendimus, plantamus et pascimus more boni militis, boni agricolae, boni pastoris, licet nobis

moved by desire for the teaching of the Lord and eager for virtue followed the apostles and ministered to them means of living and services. And similarly they followed Christ (Luke 8:2 ff.; 23:27); **as well as the rest of the apostles**, as we see elsewhere (Acts 6:1), **and the brethren**, that is, the relatives, **of the Lord**, who are greater men: *Jacob and John, who seemed to be pillars* (Gal 2:9), **and Cephas**, who is the greatest of the apostles, wherefore Cephas means head. Ambrose says: *the Apostle does not reprehend these persons, but proves that their customs are permitted to him*; and on that account, as Augustine says: *the Lord willed ministering women to follow him, showing what is due evangelists from the people.* Or also lest they seem strangers to salvation.

461. Or **only I and Barnabas**—for they were united in preaching to the gentiles: *separate for me Barnabas and Paul for the work for which I have taken them* (Acts 13:2)—**have not**, in your opinion, **power to do this?** Namely, of taking about women, and accepting means of living, as though to say: indeed we have it as the other do; but all the others accept licitly, so therefore it is licit for us too.

462. Then, when he says **who serves as a soldier at his own expense**, he proves that it is licit to accept means of living by the authority of human custom: first, as regards a soldier; second, as regards a farmer, at **who plants a vineyard**; third, as regards a shepherd, at **who feeds the flock**.

A prelate is compared to a soldier by reason of protection, to a farmer by reason of the word, to a shepherd by reason of example. For he should defend his subjects by his intercession, plant them by his word, feed them by his example. The first regards those outside the Church, the second those entering the Church, the third those remaining in the Church.

He says, therfore, **who serves as a soldier**, as though to say: we have indeed power of accepting means of living, and rightly, for **who serves as a solider at his own expense?** As though to say: no one, ever, for stipends from the republic were given soldiers. Hence John the Baptists says: *be content with your stipends* (Luke 3:14). Thus preachers and prelates can accept means of living from their subjects: *that you wage in them a good war* (1 Tim 1:18). **For who plants a vineyard and eats not of the fruit thereof?** The Lord's vineyard is the Church: *the vineyard of the Lord of hosts is the house of Israel* (Isa 5:7). For the apostles were planters of this vineyard: **I planted, Apollos watered** (1 Cor 3:6). **Who feeds the flock and eats not of the milk?** As though to say: no one. The Lord's flock is the Church's faithful: *you are the flocks of my pasture* (Ezek 24:31). The shepherds of this flock are prelates and preachers. Hence it is first said to a prelate: *feed my sheep* (John 21:17). Such can be fed by the milk of the flock, because they can accept means of living from their subjects.

Therefore if we defend, plant, and feed in the manner of a good soldier, a good farmer, a good shepherd, we are

sumptus accipere. Sed quia hodie multi sunt qui stipendia accipiunt, et non militant, edunt fructum vineae, et non plantant, lac comedunt, et gregem non pascunt. Ez. XXXIV, 3: *lac comedebatis, gregem autem meum non pascebatis.*

463. Notandum super illud **nonne Dominum Iesum vidi?** Quod multiplicem Domini legimus visionem. Unam corporalem, quae praeteriit, de qua Bar. IV, 38: *post haec in terris visus est, et cum hominibus conversatus est.* Secundam spiritualem, quae praesens est. Ps. XLV, 11: *vacate et videte, quoniam ego sum Deus*, et cetera. Tertiam aeternalem, quae futura est, de qua Io. XVII, 24: *volo ut ubi ego sum, et illi sint mecum, ut videant claritatem meam.* Iob XIX, 26: *in carne mea videbo Deum.* Quartam momentaneam, quae etiam futura est, de qua Lc. XXI, 27: *tunc videbunt Filium hominis venientem in nube cum potestate magna.*

Prima fuit in mundo, secunda in animo, tertia in caelo erit, quarta erit in iudicio.

Prima visio dat exemplum vivendi; secunda adiutorium proficiendi; tertia desiderium perveniendi; quarta odium peccandi.

Prima dat exemplum vivendi tripliciter, quia visus est pauper et pannosus, ut refrenetur cupiditas divitiarum. Ps. LXVIII, 30: *ego sum pauper et dolens*, etc., et, v. 33: *videant pauperes, et laetentur.* Sic viderunt pastores, Lc. II, 16. Vilis et abiectus, ut refrenetur ambitio honorum. Is. LIII, 2: *vidimus eum, et non erat aspectus, et desideravimus eum virum despectum.* Ideo dicitur Matth. XI, 29: *discite a me, quia mitis et humilis sum.* Afflictus et passus, ut refrenetur concupiscentia voluptatum. Thren. I, v. 12: *o vos omnes, qui transitis per viam, videte*, et cetera.

Secunda visio dat adiutorium proficiendi tripliciter, quia dat robur poenitentibus, culpas et poenas ostendendo, sicut sol atomos. Dan. V, 5: *vidit Balthassar manum scribentis.* Iob XLII, 5: *Nunc oculus meus videte*, et cetera. Spem certantibus, mercedem manifestando, sicut Dominus operanti. Act. VII, v. 55: *ecce video caelos*, et cetera. Laetitiam contemplantibus, praegustationes offerendo, sicut tabernarius modicum vini. Ps. XXXIII, v. 9: *gustate et videte, quoniam suavis est Dominus.* Gen. XXXII, 30: *vidi Dominum facie ad faciem*, sicut Paulus hic.

Tertia visio aeternalis dat desiderium perveniendi propter tria, videlicet propter veram iucunditatem. Is. ult.: *videbitis, et gaudebit cor vestrum*, quia dulce lumen et delectabile, et cetera. Hoc significatum est Io. XX, 20: *gavisi sunt discipuli, viso Domino.* Propter iucunditatis multiplicitatem, sive pluralitatem. Is. LX, 5: *tunc videbis et afflues*, etc.; quippe quia videbimus eum sicuti est, et ipse erit omnia in omnibus. Erit enim rationi plenitudo

allowed to accept means of living. But because today there are many who accept stipends, and do not fight, who eat the fruit of the vine, and do not plant, who drink milk, and do not feed the flock, it is said: *you ate the milk, but my flock you did not feed* (Ezek 34:3).

463. It should be noted on the saying **have I not seen Christ Jesus our Lord?**, that we understand many kinds of vision of the Lord. One is a bodily vision, which passes away, about which it is said: *afterwards he was seen upon earth, and conversed with men* (Bar 4:38). In a second way as a spiritual vision, which is dealt with at present: *be still and see that I am God* (Ps 46:10). In a third way as an eternal vision, which is to come, about which we read: *I will that where I am, they also may be with me, that they may see my glory* (John 17:24); *in my flesh I shall see God* (Job 19:26). In a fourth way as a momentary vision that is also future, about which it is said: *then they shall see the Son of man coming on a cloud with great power* (Luke 21:27).

The first was in the world, the second in the soul, the third shall be in heaven, the fourth shall be in the judgment.

The first vision gives the example of living; the second, help of progressing; the third, desire of attaining; the fourth, hatred of sinning.

The first gives the example of living in three ways, because he seemed poor and tattered, so that the lust for riches might be curbed. *I am poor and sorrowful* (Ps 69:29); *let the poor see and rejoice* (Ps 69:29). And it was in this way that the shepherds saw him (Luke 2:16). He seemed common and lowly, so that the ambition for honors might be curbed: *we saw him, and there was no comeliness, and we desired him a man despised* (Isa 53:2). Hence it is said: *learn from me, for I am meek and humble* (Matt 11:29). He seemed afflicted and suffering, so that the concupiscence of sensual pleasures might be curbed: *O see, all you who pass by the way* (Lam 1:12).

The second vision gives help of progressing in three ways, for it gives strength to the penitent, by displaying faults and punishments, just as the sun displays atoms: *Balthasar saw the hand of the one writing* (Dan 5:5). *Now my eye sees you* (Job 42:5). It gives hope to the struggling, by showing the reward, like a master shows to his worker: *behold, I see the heavens* (Acts 7:55). It gives joy to those who contemplate, by offering a foretaste, like a bartender offers a taste of wine: *taste and see how sweet the Lord is* (Ps 34:8). *I saw the Lord face to face* (Gen 32:30), like Paul here.

The third vision, the eternal one, gives the desire of attaining because of three things, namely, because of true delight. Isaiah, further: *you will see, and your heart will rejoice* (Isa 66:14), because the light is sweet and delightful. This is the meaning of the passage: *the disciples rejoiced to see the Lord* (John 20:20). Because of the multiplication or plurality of delightfulness. *Then you will see and abound* (Isa 60:5), naturally because we will see him as he is, and he will be all

lucis, voluntati multitudo pacis, memoriae continuatio aeternitatis. Propter puritatis aeternitatem. Apoc. ult.: *servi eius servient illi, et videbunt faciem eius, et regnabunt in saecula saeculorum.* Ps.: *adimplebis me laetitia,* et cetera.

Quarta visio dat odium sive terrorem peccandi propter tria, videlicet propter furtum propalandum coram iudice vidente. Mal. III, v. 2: *ecce veniet, et quis stabit ad videndum eum? Ipse enim quasi ignis conflans,* et cetera. Propter malefactorum severam ultionem. Latro enim videns socium suum suspendi, plus timet furari. Ier. VII, 12: *ite ad locum meum in Sylo, et videte quod fecerim ibi.* Sylo interpretatur avulsa. Apoc. I, 13: *vidi similem filio hominis,* et infra v. 16: ***ex ore eius, quasi gladius ex utraque parte acutus exibat,*** et cetera. Propter visam bonorum praemiationem; videns enim clericus alium praebendari, quia bonus, cavet a malo. Ps. CVI, 42: *videbunt iusti, et laetabuntur, et omnis iniquitas oppilabit os suum.*

464. Deinde cum dicit **numquid secundum hominem**, etc., hic probat tertio, quod licet sumptus accipere per auctoritatem divinae legis. Ubi primo proponit, quod lex haec dicit; secundo verbum legis ponit, ibi **scriptum est enim**, etc.; tertio qualiter intelligendum sit, ostendit ibi **numquid de bobus cura est**, et cetera.

465. Dicit ergo **numquid**, etc., quasi dicat: probavi ratione humanae consuetudinis, quod licet nobis sumptus accipere; sed **numquid secundum hominem**, id est, secundum humanam consuetudinem vel similitudinem tantum, **dico hoc? An non lex** Moysi divinitus promulgata **hoc dicit?** Quasi dicat: immo dicit. **Scriptum est enim in lege Moysi**, Deut. XXV, 4, et habetur idem I Tim. c. V, 18: **non alligabis os bovi trituranti**, ut possit vivere de labore suo, id est, non prohibebis praedicatorem vivere de Evangelio. Triturare enim est separare granum a paleis, quod facit praedicator abstrahendo animas a terrenis, discernendo virtutes a vitiis, separando utilia a vanis. Ier. XV, 19: *si separaveris pretiosum a vili, quasi os meum eris.*

466. Deinde cum dicit **numquid de bobus**, etc., hic ostendit qualiter dicta auctoritas intelligenda sit. Et primo, quod intelligenda sit litteraliter de bobus; secundo quod non tantum litteraliter de bobus, sed spiritualiter de praedicatoribus, ibi **an propter nos**, etc.; tertio replicat, quod licet accipere sumptus, ibi **nam propter nos utique scripta**, et cetera.

Dicit ergo **numquid**, etc.; quasi dicat: haec auctoritas de bobus spiritualibus, id est praedicatoribus, intelligitur. **Numquid enim de bobus** materialibus **cura est Deo**, ut de eis lege praecipiat? **An propter nos hoc utique**

in all. For there will be the fullness of light for our reason, the multitude of peace for the will, the continuation of eternity for the memory. On account of eternity of purity. *His servants will serve him, and they will see his face, and they will reign forever* (Rev 22:3–5). And in the psalms: *you will fill me with gladness.*

The fourth vision gives hatred or terror of sinning because of three things, namely, because of hidden crimes being displayed before the watching judge: *behold he shall come, and who shall stand to see him? For he is like a refining fire* (Mal 3:2). Because of the severe retribution of evil deeds. For the thief, seeing his partner strung up, fears to steal anymore. *Go to my place in Silo, and see what I have done there* (Jer 7:12). Silo is interpreted as 'ripped away.' *I saw a figure like a son of man* (Rev 1:13), *and out of his mouth came a sharp, two-edged sword* (Rev 1:16). Because of the rewarding of the good being seen; for a clergyman who sees another receive a prebend because he is good, is wary of evil. *The just shall see, and rejoice, and all iniquity shall stop up their mouth* (Ps 107:42).

464. Next, when he says **do I speak these things according to man**, here he proves the third, that it is allowed to accept expenses by the authority of divine law. There he first proposes that it is because the law says these things; second, he sets forth the word of the law, at **for it is written**; third, he shows how it is to be understood, at **does God take care for oxen**.

465. Therefore he says **do I speak**, as though to say, I have proved by reason of human custom, that we are permitted to receive our expenses; but **according to man**, that is, according to human custom or likeness alone, **do I speak these things? Or does not** the divinely promulgated **law** of Moses **also say these things?** As though he were saying, it says the contrary. **For it is written in the law of Moses**, namely, in both Deuteronomy and 1 Timothy: **you shall not muzzle the ox that treads out the corn** (Deut 25:4; 1 Tim 5:18), so that it can live from its own labor, that is, you shall not prevent a preacher from living by the Gospel. For to tread out the corn is to separate the grain from the chaff, which the preacher does by drawing souls away from earthly things, by distinguishing virtues from vices, by separating useful things from vain ones: *if you will separate the precious from the vile, you shall be as my mouth* (Jer 15:19).

466. Next when he says **does God take care for oxen**, here he shows how the authorities cited are to be understood. And first, that concerning the oxen it is to be understood literally; second, that non only literally about the oxen, but spiritually about preachers, at **or does he say this**; third, he reiterates that it is permitted to accept the means of living, at **for these things are written for our sakes**.

Therefore he says, **does God**, as if he were saying, this authority is understood concerning spiritual oxen, that is, preachers. **Does God take care for** material **oxen**, such that he makes commands concerning them in the law? **Or does**

dicit? Quasi dicat: hoc utique propter nos dicit. ***Nam propter nos scripta sunt haec*** et similia. Rom. XV, 4: *quaecumque scripta sunt, ad nostram doctrinam scripta sunt.* ***Propter nos***, inquam; idcirco, ***quoniam*** praedicator, qui corda aperit ad fidem, ***debet arare in spe*** stipendiorum temporalium, non tamen propter spem hanc. Debet enim primum quaerere regnum Dei. ***Et qui triturat***, id est bonos a malis, quasi grana a paleis, discernit praedicando, scilicet ad mores, debet hoc facere ***in spe fructus percipiendi***. II Tim. II, 6: *laborantem agricolam oportet primum de fructibus percipere.* Eccli. VI, v. 19: *is qui arat et qui seminat accedit ad illam, et sustinet bonos fructus illius.*

he say this indeed for our sakes? As though he were saying: he does indeed say this for our sake. ***For these things are written for our sakes***, and other things like this: *whatever things were written, were written for our instruction* (Rom 15:4). ***For our sakes***, I say; on that account ***so that*** the preacher, who opens hearts to the faith, ***should plow in hope*** of temporal pay, but not for the sake of this hope. For he must first seek the kingdom of God. ***And he who threshes***, that is, the good from the bad, like wheat from chaff, discerns by preaching, namely, for morals, he should do this ***in the hope to receive fruit***: *the farmer who labors must partake of the fruits first* (2 Tim 2:6). *He who plows and sows comes to her, and receives of her good fruits* (Sir 6:19).

Lecture 2

9:11Si nos vobis spiritualia semina-vimus, magnum est si nos carnalia vestra metamus? [n. 467]

9:12Si alii potestatis vestrae partici-pes sunt, quare non potius nos? Sed non usi sumus hac potestate: sed omnia sustinemus, ne quod offen-diculum demus Evangelio Christi. [n. 469]

9:13Nescitis quoniam qui in sacrario operantur quae de sacrario sunt, edunt: et qui altari deserviunt, cum altari participant? [n. 471]

9:14Ita et Dominus ordinavit iis qui Evangelium annuntiant, de Evange-lio vivere.

9:11εἰ ἡμεῖς ὑμῖν τὰ πνευματικὰ ἐσπείραμεν, μέγα εἰ ἡμεῖς ὑμῶν τὰ σαρκικὰ θερίσομεν;

9:12εἰ ἄλλοι τῆς ὑμῶν ἐξουσίας μετέ-χουσιν, οὐ μᾶλλον ἡμεῖς; Ἀλλ' οὐκ ἐχρησάμεθα τῇ ἐξουσίᾳ ταύτῃ, ἀλλὰ πάντα στέγομεν ἵνα μή τινα ἐγκοπὴν δῶμεν τῷ εὐαγγελίῳ τοῦ Χριστοῦ.

9:13οὐκ οἴδατε ὅτι οἱ τὰ ἱερὰ ἐργαζό-μενοι [τὰ] ἐκ τοῦ ἱεροῦ ἐσθίουσιν, οἱ τῷ θυσιαστηρίῳ παρεδρεύοντες τῷ θυσιαστηρίῳ συμμερίζονται;

9:14οὕτως καὶ ὁ κύριος διέταξεν τοῖς τὸ εὐαγγέλιον καταγγέλλουσιν ἐκ τοῦ εὐαγγελίου ζῆν.

9:11If we have sown unto you spiri-tual things, is it a great matter if we reap your carnal things? [n. 467]

9:12If others are partakers of this power over you, why not we more? Nevertheless, we have not used this power: but we bear all things, lest we should give any hindrance to the Gospel of Christ. [n. 469]

9:13Know you not that they who work in the holy place eat the things that are of the holy place; and they that serve the altar partake with the altar? [n. 471]

9:14So also the Lord ordained that they who preach the Gospel should live by the Gospel.

---

467. Superius probavit per auctoritatem, quod licet accipere sumptus, hic probat idem per rationem. Et

primo probat hoc ex eorum obligatione;

secundo ex pseudo-apostolorum accipientium ab eis comparatione, ibi *si alii potestatis vestrae*, etc.;

tertio dicit, quod nihilominus noluit uti hac potesta-te, ibi *sed non usi sumus*, et cetera.

468. Prima ratio talis est: maius est dare spiritualia quam accipere temporalia; ergo si Apostolus dat spiri-tualia, licet ei accipere temporalia.

Primo ergo explicat beneficium impensum; secundo explicat stipendium exhibendum, ibi *magnum est si nos*, et cetera.

Dicit ergo *si nos*, etc., quasi dicat: vere habemus pote-statem accipiendi sumptus a vobis; *si enim nos semina-vimus vobis spiritualia*, fidem scilicet et sacramenta spi-ritum alentia, a Spiritu Sancto ministrata, *magnum est si nos metamus*, ad sustentationem nostram, *carnalia?* Id est, ad carnis sustentationem concessa. Quasi dicat: non est magnum. Rom. XV, 27: *si spiritualium eorum parti-cipes facti sunt gentiles, debent in carnalibus ministrare.*

469. Deinde cum dicit *si autem alii*, et cetera. Ecce secunda ratio ad idem talis: veri apostoli licentius parti-cipant bona subditorum, quam pseudo, sed pseudo-apo-stoli participant, ergo multo plus veri apostoli participare

467. Above he proved by authority that it is permitted to accept the means of living, and here he proves the same thing by reason.

First he proves this from their duty;

second, from comparing what pseudo-apostles received from them, at *if others are partakers of this power over you*;

third, he says that nevertheless he has not wished to use this power, at *nevertheless, we have not used this power*.

468. The first argument goes as follows: it is greater to give spiritual things than to receive temporal things; there-fore, if the Apostle gives spiritual things, he is permitted to receive temporal things.

Therefore, first, he explains the benefit doled out; secon, he explains the payment furnished, at *is it a great matter if we*.

Therefore he says, *if we*, as though to say: we certainly have the power of receiving our expenses from you; for *if we have sown unto you spiritual things*, namely, the faith and the sacraments nourishing the spirit, administered by the Holy Spirit, *is it a great matter if we reap your car-nal things* for our sustenance? That is, those permitted for the sustenance of the flesh. As though he were saying: it is not a great matter. *For if the gentiles have been made partak-ers in their spiritual things, they should administer to them in carnal things* (Rom 15:27).

469. Next, when he says *if others*. Here the second argu-ment for the same thing goes as follows: true apostles may partake more freely of the goods of their subjects than false apostles, but false apostles do partake of them, therefore,

debent. Primo ergo ponit antecedens; secundo consequens, ibi *quare non potius nos*, et cetera.

Dicit ergo *si autem alii*, scilicet pseudo, quos non exprimit ex nomine, ne confundantur, vocat eos alios quasi a consortio alienos Ecclesiae. Omnes enim Catholici unum sunt. Io. XVII, 11: *Ut sint unum*, et cetera. *Si*, inquam, *alii potestatis vestrae participes sunt*, id est, tam potenter utuntur bonis vestris, *quare non potius nos* apostoli, qui causa salutis vestrae laboramus? Eccli. XII, 5: *da bono, et ne receperis peccatorem*.

470. Deinde cum dicit *sed non usi sumus*, hic ostendit, quod noluit uti hac potestate. Ubi dicit primo se sumptus non accepisse; secundo dicit se nihilominus indiguisse, ibi *sed omnia sustinemus*, etc.; tertio rationem utriusque assignat, ibi *ne quod offendiculum*, et cetera.

Dicit ergo *sed non*, etc., quasi dicat: ecce patet quod licet nobis sumptus accipere, *sed* tamen *usi non sumus hac potestate*. Supra VI, 12: *omnia mihi licent, sed non omnia expediunt*. *Non sumus*, inquam, *usi*, non quia non indigeamus; *sed omnia sustinemus*, quia et si penuriam patiamur, tamen patienter sustinemus. II Cor. XI, 9: *cum essem apud vos et egerem, nulli onerosus fui*.

Et hoc feci ideo, *ne quod offendiculum demus Evangelio Christi*. Hoc autem posset accidere, vel quia pseudo-apostolis daret exemplum accipiendi; vel quia Corinthii avari erant et scandalizarentur si ab eis acciperet, vel forte putarent se emisse licentiam peccandi et diminueretur in Apostolo auctoritas arguendi, et his modis daret offendiculum Evangelio Christi. Prov. XV, 19: *via iustorum absque offendiculo*.

471. Deinde cum dicit *nescitis quoniam qui in sacrario*, et cetera. Probavit quod licet sumptus accipere, primo per auctoritatem, secundo per rationem; tertio idem probat hic per exemplorum multitudinem. Ubi primo inducit similitudinem eorum qui templa reparant: secundo, eorum qui templo ministrant, ibi *et qui altari deserviunt*, etc.; tertio adaptat similitudinem his, qui praedicant, ibi *et Dominus ordinavit his*, et cetera.

Quasi dicat: et vere licet mihi sumptus accipere: *nescitis quoniam qui in sacrario*, id est, templo Iudaeorum vel gentilium, *operantur*, ut artifices, *quae de sacrario sunt, edunt?* Sustentabantur enim artifices de denariis qui in gazophylacio templi offerebantur, ut patet tempore Ioas IV Reg. XII, 4 ss. *Et qui altari* templi Ierosolymitani, vel etiam ipsi templo, ut sacerdotes, *deserviunt*, id est, devote serviunt: una enim de duodecim abusionibus

much more should true apostles partake of them. Therefore first he sets forth the premises; second, the conclusion, at *why not we more*.

Therefore he says *if others*, that is, false ones, whom he does not mention by name, lest they be confused; he calls them others as though strangers to the community of the Church. For all Catholics are one: *that they may be one* (John 17:11). He says, *if others are partakers of this power over you*, that is, they take advantage of your goods so arrogantly, *why not we* apostles *more*, who labor for the sake of your salvation? *Give to the good man and do not receive the sinner* (Sir 12:5).

470. Next when he says *nevertheless, we have not used*, here he shows that he does not wish to use this power. He says first that he has not accepted the means of living; second he says that he nevertheless was needful, at *but we bear all things*; third he assigns the reason for both, at *lest we should give any hindrance*.

Therefore he says, *nevertheless, we have not*, as though to say: look, it is clear that we are allowed to accept our expenses, but *nevertheless, we have not used this power*. As above: *all things are lawful to me: but all things are not expedient* (1 Cor 6:12). He says, *we have not used*, not because we have no need; *but we bear all things*, because if we also suffer want; nevertheless we endure it patiently. *When I was present with you, and was needful, I made myself burdensome to no man* (2 Cor 11:9).

And so I have done this, *lest we should give a hindrance to the Gospel of Christ*. But this could have happened, either because he might have given the example of receiving expenses to the false apostles; or because the Corinthians were greedy and were scandalized if he accepted means from them, or perhaps they thought they had bought the permission to sin and the authority of admonishing was diminished in the Apostle, and in these ways he might have hampered the Gospel of Christ. *The way of the just is without offense* (Prov 15:19).

471. Next he says *know you not that they who work in the holy place*. He has proved that it is permitted to accept living expenses, first by authority, second by reason, and third he proves the same thing here by a multitude of examples. Now he first brings forth the similar case of those who repair temples; second, of those who minister in the temple, at *and they that serve the altar*; third, he adapts the similarity to these, the ones who preach at *also the Lord ordained that they*.

As though he were saying: I am also allowed to accept the means of living: *know you not that they who work*, as craftsmen, *in the holy place*, that is, the temple of the Jews, or gentiles, *eat the things that are of the holy place?* For they were allowing silversmiths of the coins that were being offered in the treasury of the temple, as is clear at the time of Joas (2 Kings 12:4ff). *And they that serve*, that is, serve faithfully—for one of the twelve crimes that cry out to

est irreverentia coram altari; *cum altari participant?* Quia partem habent de his, quae offeruntur in altari, ut patet per totum Leviticum, et maxime VI et VII cap., et sicut fit hic. *Ita et Dominus ordinavit*, id est rationabiliter disposuit, *his qui Evangelium annuntiant, de Evangelio vivere.* Hoc ordinavit, dicens Matth. X, 10 et Lc. X, v. 7: *dignus est enim operarius mercede sua.*

472. Notandum est hic, quod Apostolus nominibus multorum officiorum, praedicatorem hic designat, quia vocat eum primo militem propter officium, Ecclesiam contra adversarios defendendo. II Cor. X, 4: *arma militiae nostrae*, et cetera. II Tim. II, 3: *labora sicut bonus miles Christi.*

Secundo vinitorem, propter officium palmites superfluos, id est malos, resecandi. Os. II, v. 15: *dabo ei vinitores eius ex eodem loco.* Sed heu Cant. I, 5 dicitur *vineam meam non custodivi.*

Tertio pastorem, propter officium subditos bono exemplo pascendi. I Petr. V, 2: *pascite qui in vobis est gregem.* Sed heu, quia hodie impletur illud Zach. XI, 17: *O pastor et idolum derelinquens gregem*, et cetera.

Quarto bovem, propter officium maturitatis in omnibus procedendi. Prov. XIV, 4: *ubi non sunt boves, praesepe vacuum est.* Iob I, v. 14: *boves arabant, et asinae pascebantur iuxta eos*, et cetera.

Quinto aratorem, propter officium corda ad fidem et poenitentiam aperiendi. Os. X, v. 11: *arabit Iudas, confringet sibi sulcos Iacob*, et cetera.

Sexto trituratorem, propter officium malos a bonis discernendi. Is. XLI, 15: *ego posui te quasi plaustrum triturans novum, habens rostra ferrantia, et triturabis montes*, et cetera.

Septimo seminatorem, propter officium frequenter et utiliter praedicandi. Lc. VIII, 5: *exiit qui seminat seminare semen suum.* Ps. CXXV, 6: *euntes ibant*, et cetera.

Octavo templi architectum, propter officium Ecclesiam construendi et reparandi. Supra III, 10: *ut sapiens architectus fundamentum posui*, et cetera.

Nono altaris ministrum, propter officium Deo devotum impendendi. Supra IV, 1: *sic nos existimet homo*, et cetera.

473. Quaeritur hic super illud *non sum liber*, Glossa: *ipse enim apostolica dignitate potestatem habens non operari manibus, sed de Evangelio vivere.*

heaven is irreverence before the altar—*the altar* of the temple in Jerusalem, or even for this very temple, as priests do; *partake with the altar?* For they have a part of those things, which are offered on the altar, as is clear in the whole book of Leviticus, and especially in chapters six and seven, and in the same way it happens here. *So also the Lord ordained*, that is, reasonably arranged, *that they who preach the Gospel should live by the Gospel.* He ordained this, saying, *the laborer is worthy of his hire* (Matt 10:10; Luke 10:7).

472. This should be noted, that the Apostle here refers to the preacher with the names of many offices, for he calls him first soldier because of his duty of defending the Church against foes. *For the weapons of our warfare* (2 Cor 10:4). *Labor as good soldiers of Christ* (2 Tim 2:3).

Second, he calls him a vineyard worker, because of the duty of pruning the excess branches, which are the wicked. *I will give her vine-dressers out of the same place* (Hos 2:15). But alas it is said: *my vineyard I have not kept* (Song 1:5).

Third, he calls him pastor, because of the duty of feeding those committed to him by his good example. *Feed the flock of God which is among you* (1 Pet 5:2). But alas, for today what is said in Zechariah is fulfilled: *O shepherd, and idol, that forsakes his flock* (Zech 11:17).

Fourth, he calls him an ox, on account of the duty of advancing in ripeness of all things. *Where there are no oxen, the corncrib is empty* (Prov 14:4). *The oxen were plowing, and the donkeys feeding beside them* (Job 1:14).

Fifth, he calls him a plow, on account of the duty of opening hearts to the faith and to repentance. *Judah will plow, Jacob will break up the furrows for himself* (Hos 10:11).

Sixth, he calls him a thresher, because of the duty of discerning the bad from the good. *I placed you like a new threshing cart, having an iron beak, and you will thresh the mountains* (Isa 41:15).

Seventh, he calls him a sower, because of his duty of preaching frequently and effectively. *The sower went out to sow his seed* (Luke 8:5). *Going, they went and wept, casting their seed* (Ps 126:6).

Eighth, he calls him an architect of the temple, because of his duty of building and repairing the Church. As he says above, *as a wise architect, I have laid a foundation* (1 Cor 3:10).

Ninth, he calls him a minister of the altar, because of the office of dedicating one's devotion to God. As said above, *let a man so account of us as of the ministers of Christ* (1 Cor 4:1).

473. Here it should be asked concerning the Gloss on *am I not free* (1 Cor 9:1): *for he, possessing this power by his apostolic dignity, does not do manual labor, but lives by the Gospel.*

Contra: ergo qui praedicant, non habentes apostolicam dignitatem, non possunt sine opere manuum de Evangelio vivere.

Responsio. Glossa loquitur de potestate qua potest invitos ad hoc cogere, non de spontanea, qua potest a voluntarie dantibus petere et accipere.

474. Item ex dicta Glossa videtur quod praelati non teneantur manibus operari.

Contra Gen. III, 19: *in sudore vultus tui vesceris pane tuo*. Ipsi non sunt exempti ab hac maledictione; ergo, et caetera.

Responsio. Tenentur ad laborem spiritualem, non corporalem, tamen bene facerent si occuparent se in honestis antequam vacarent.

475. Item super illud: *nonne opus meum?* Glossa: *perfectum*. Contra: ipsi erant imperfecti.

Responsio. Opus perfectum dicebantur, quia eis Apostolus praedicaverat, vel quia eos perfecte docuerat quantum in se erat.

476. Item super illud: *numquid non habemus potestatem manducandi?*

Contra Matth. X, 8: *gratis accepistis, gratis date*.

Responsio. *Gratis*, id est, sine pretio, sed non sine stipendio.

477. Item super illud: *quis pascit gregem*, Glossa: *ex Evangelio viventes, panem gratuitum manducabant*.

Contra, subditi tenebantur dare.

Responsio. Gratuitas erat ex parte recipientium, quia humiliter, non potestative recipiebant, licet debitus ex parte dantium.

478. Item: *numquid de bobus cura est Deo?* Quasi dicat: non. Contra Sap. c. VI, 8: *cura est illi de omnibus*.

Respondeo. Ibi loquitur de cura generali, scilicet providentiae; hic de speciali, scilicet disciplinae.

479. Item *debet in spe qui arat arare*. Contra: spes non est de visibilibus, sed aeternis.

Responsio. Spes accipitur aequivoce.

480. Item *in spe fructus percipiendi*. Contra: *non debet poni lucerna* praedicationis *sub modio* rei temporalis.

Respondeo. Praedicare in spe rei temporalis, non est ponere lucernam sub modio, sed praedicare propter spem.

481. Item *si nos vobis seminaverimus spiritualia*, et cetera. Contra Gal. VI, 6: *quae seminaverit homo, haec et metet*; ergo qui seminat spiritualia, debet metere spiritualia, non carnalia, et cetera.

Against this: therefore, those who preach but do not possess the dignity of apostles cannot live by the Gospel without the work of their hands.

Answer: the Gloss is speaking of the power by which one can compel the reluctant to this, not about voluntary giving, by which he can ask and receive from those giving willingly.

474. Again, from the Gloss mentioned, it seems that prelates are not bound to work with their hands.

Against this: *by the sweat of your brow you will earn your bread* (Gen 3:19). They are not exempt from this curse, therefore, etc.

Answer: they are bound to spiritual labor, not physical, but even so they would do well if they busied themselves in honest work sooner than allowing themselves to be idle.

475. Again, concerning *are you not my work?*, the Gloss has: *perfect*. Against this: they were imperfect.

Answer: they were called a perfect work, because the Apostle had preached to them, or because he had taught them perfectly as he was in himself.

476. Again, concerning *have not we power to eat?* (1 Cor 9:5).

Against this: *freely you have received, freely give* (Matt 10:8).

Answer: *freely* means without price, but not without the means of living.

477. Again, concerning *who feeds the flock* (1 Cor 9:7), the Gloss has: *living by the Gospel, they were eating free bread*.

Against this: subjects are bound to give.

Answer: it was free on the part of the one receiving, because they were receiving it humbly, not officiously, although it was due on the part of the ones giving.

478. Again: *does God take care for oxen?* As though he said, no. Against this: *he has care of all* (Wis 6:8).

Answer: there it is speaking of general care, which is the care of providence; here it is about special care, which is the care of instruction.

479. Again, *he who plows should plow in hope* (1 Cor 9:10). Against this: hope is not concerning visible things, but eternal.

Answer: hope is taken equivocally.

480. Again, *in hope to receive fruit* (1 Cor 9:10). Against: *the lamp* of preaching *should not be placed under the bushel-basket* of temporal things.

Answer: to preach in the hope of temporal goods is not to place one's lamp under a bushel-basket, but to preach on account of that hope would be.

481. Again, *if we have sown unto you spiritual things*. Against this: *whatever a man has sown, these things shall he reap* (Gal 6:6); therefore, whoever sows spiritual things, should reap spiritual things, not carnal things, etc.

Respondeo. Ibi loquitur de messione mercedis, hic de messione stipendii.

Answer: there it is speaking about the harvest of heavenly rewards, here about the reaping of payment.

Lecture 3

^{9:15}Ego autem nullo horum usus sum. Non autem scripsi haec ut ita fiant in me: bonum est enim mihi magis mori, quam ut gloriam meam quis evacuet. [n. 482]

^{9:16}Nam si evangelizavero, non est mihi gloria: necessitas enim mihi incumbit: vae enim mihi est, si non evangelizavero. [n. 486]

^{9:17}Si enim volens hoc ago, mercedem habeo: si autem invitus, dispensatio mihi credita est.

^{9:18}Quae est ergo merces mea? ut Evangelium praedicans, sine sumptu ponam Evangelium, ut non abutar potestate mea in Evangelio. [n. 488]

^{9:15}ἐγὼ δὲ οὐ κέχρημαι οὐδενὶ τούτων. οὐκ ἔγραψα δὲ ταῦτα ἵνα οὕτως γένηται ἐν ἐμοί, καλὸν γάρ μοι μᾶλλον ἀποθανεῖν ἤ τὸ καύχημά μου οὐδεὶς κενώσει.

^{9:16}ἐὰν γὰρ εὐαγγελίζωμαι, οὐκ ἔστιν μοι καύχημα· ἀνάγκη γάρ μοι ἐπίκειται· οὐαὶ γάρ μοί ἐστιν ἐὰν μὴ εὐαγγελίσωμαι.

^{9:17}εἰ γὰρ ἑκὼν τοῦτο πράσσω, μισθὸν ἔχω· εἰ δὲ ἄκων, οἰκονομίαν πεπίστευμαι.

^{9:18}τίς οὖν μού ἐστιν ὁ μισθός; ἵνα εὐαγγελιζόμενος ἀδάπανον θήσω τὸ εὐαγγέλιον, εἰς τὸ μὴ καταχρήσασθαι τῇ ἐξουσίᾳ μου ἐν τῷ εὐαγγελίῳ.

^{9:15}But I have used none of these things. Neither have I written these things, that they should be so done unto me: for it is good for me to die rather than that any man should make my glory void. [n. 482]

^{9:16}For if I preach the Gospel, it is no glory to me: for a necessity lies upon me. For woe is unto me if I preach not the Gospel. [n. 486]

^{9:17}For if I do this thing willingly, I have a reward: but if against my will, a dispensation is committed to me.

^{9:18}What is my reward then? That preaching the Gospel, I may deliver the Gospel without charge, that I abuse not my power in the Gospel. [n. 488]

---

482. Superius multipliciter probavit, quod sibi licet accipere sumptus, hic ostendit, quod nihilominus non vult accipere, sed abstinere tribus rationibus.

Primo propter intentionem praemii;

secundo propter dilectionem Evangelii, ibi *nam cum liber essem ex omnibus*, etc.;

tertio propter expeditionem cursus sui, ibi *nescitis quod hi, qui in stadio currunt*.

In prima, primo dicit quare non vult accipere, scilicet ne gloria sua evacuetur;

secundo ostendit, quod accipiendo evacuaretur, ibi *nam si evangelizavero, non est mihi gloria*, etc.;

tertio quod non accipiendo conservabitur, ibi *quae est ergo merces mea*, et cetera.

483. In prima, primo ostendit quod potestate accipiendi uti noluit; secundo quod uti non intendit, ibi *non autem scripsi hoc, ut*, et cetera.

Dicit ergo *ego autem*, etc., quasi dicat: tot modis constat, quod licet mihi sumptus accipere, sed tamen ego nulla horum auctoritate, ratione, exemplo, ad accipiendum usus sum. Ipse enim vel ab aliis ecclesiis accipiebat, ut II Cor. XI, 8: *alias ecclesias spoliavi*, etc., vel manibus operabatur, Act. XX, v. 34.

Non autem, etc., quasi dicat: *non sum usus*, sed nec uti volo. *Non enim scripsi haec*, scilicet quod licet mihi

482. Above he proved in many ways that he is allowed to accept the means of living, here he shows that nevertheless he does not wish to accept it, but to abstain for three reasons.

First, because of the aim of recompense;

second, because of his love of the Gospel, at *for whereas I was free to all* (1 Cor 9:19);

third, because of the running of his race, at *know you not that they that run in the race* (1 Cor 9:24).

In the first, he says first that he does not wish to accept, namely so that his glory will not be made void;

second, he shows that by accepting it might be made void, at *for if I preach the Gospel, it is no glory to me*;

third, that he will not be preserved by accepting means, at *what is my reward then?*

483. In the first, he shows first that he has not wished to make use of his power of receiving means of living; second that he does not intend to make use of it, at *neither have I written these things*.

Therefore he says, *but I*, as though he were saying: it is clear in so many ways that I am permitted to receive my living expenses, but nevertheless, I have used not one of these arguments by authority, by reason, or by example, in order to accept them. For either he was receiving his means from other churches, as is said: *I have taken wages from other churches* (2 Cor 11:8) or he was working by his own hands (Acts 20:34).

Neither have I, as though he said: *I have used none of these things*, nor do I wish to use. *For neither have I written*

accipere, *ut ita fiat in me*, sicut scripsi, id est, ut ego accipiam, quia non quaero datum, sed fructum.

484. Deinde cum dicit *bonum est enim mihi*, etc., hic ostendit quare hoc fecit, scilicet ne gloria sua evacuetur. Ubi primo multiplicat afflictionem corporalem; secundo supponit ei gloriae diminutionem, ibi *quam ut gloriam*, et cetera.

Dicit ergo *bonum est*, etc., quasi diceret: non accipiam, nam si acciperem, gloriam meam evacuarem, quod nullatenus facerem. *Bonum est enim mihi mori*, non solum sumptuum egestate affligi, magis *quam ut gloriam meam*, quam habeo de gratuita sinceritate praedicationis, de praemio supererogationis, abstinendo a licitis, *quis evacuet*, ab aliquo importune accipiendo, vel propter sumptus evangelicos.

Multi tamen moderni doctores gloriam istam evacuant, vel propter intentionem sumptuum, vel propter favorem humanum, dicente Iob XII, 19: *ducit sacerdotes inglorios et optimates supplantat.*

485. Notandum est hic, quod gloria amittitur septempliciter propter septem vitia.

Nam gloria gulosorum evacuatur. Unde hic dicitur: *bonum est enim mihi magis*, et cetera.

Gloria luxuriosorum maculatur. Eccli. c. XLVII, 21 s.: *inclinasti faemora tua mulieribus, dedisti maculam in gloria tua.*

Gloria superborum captivatur. I Mach. c. II, 9: *vasa gloriae eius captiva ducta sunt.*

Gloria iracundorum intermittitur. Ps. XII, v. 5: *si reddidi retribuentibus mihi mala*, etc., et post: *persequatur inimicus animam meam*, etc., et post: *et gloriam meam in pulverem deducat.*

Gloria invidorum excluditur. Rom. III, 27: *ubi est gloriatio tua?*

Gloria avarorum annihilatur. Ps.: *ne timueris dum dives factus erit homo*, et cetera.

Gloria accidiosorum culpatur. I Mach. IX, v. 10: *moriamur in virtute propter fratres nostros, et non inferamus crimen gloriae nostrae.* Eccli. XXXIII, 44: *praecellens esto in operibus tuis, et ne dederis maculam in gloria tua.*

Ergo per gulam evacuatur gloria sobrietatis: per luxuriam maculatur gloria castitatis: per superbiam captivatur gloria humilitatis: per iracundiam intermittitur gloria mansuetudinis: per invidiam excluditur gloria caritatis: per avaritiam annihilatur gloria liberalitatis: per accidiam culpatur gloria strenuitatis.

De istis dicitur Osee IV, 7: *gloriam eorum in ignominiam commutabo.*

---

these things, namely, that it is permissible for me to accept means, *that they should be so done unto me*, as I have written—that is, that I should receive—since I do not seek gifts, but fruit.

484. Next when he says *for it is good to me*, here he shows why he did this, namely, so that his glory would not be made void. There he first lists his bodily afflictions; second, he supposes the diminution of his glory at *rather than that any man*.

Therefore he says, *it is good*, as though he were saying: I do not accept living expenses, for if I did accept them, I might make my glory void, which I would never do for any reason. *It is good for me to die*, not only afflicted with need for bodily sustenance, *rather than that any man should make my glory*, which I have from the free sincerity of my preaching, from the prize of supererogation, by abstaining from what is permitted; *should make my glory void* because of accepting what is grudgingly given, or because of the living expenses of evangelizers.

But many modern teachers make void this glory, either out of the design of making a good living, or on account of human favor, as in the saying: *he leads away priests without glory and overthrows nobles* (Job 12:19).

485. Here it should be noted that glory is lost in seven ways, because of seven vices.

First, the glory of the gluttonous is made void. Wherefore it is said here: *for it is good for me to die rather*;

The glory of the lustful is stained: *you have bowed your thighs to women, you gave stain to your glory* (Sir 47:21–22).

The glory of the proud is taken prisoner: *the vessels of her glory are carried off as captives* (1 Macc 2:9).

The glory of the wrathful is interrupted: *if I have rendered back to them who have repaid me evils . . . let the enemy pursue my soul . . . and bring down my glory in the dust* (Ps 7:5ff).

The glory of the envious is prevented: *where is your boasting?* (Rom 3:27)

The glory of the greedy is brought to nothing: *do not fear when a man has become rich* (Ps 49:16).

The glory of the slothful is condemned: *let us die bravely for our brothers, and let us not bring a blot upon our glory* (1 Macc 9:10). *Be excellent in all your works, and do not cast a stain upon your glory* (Sir 33:44).

Therefore, by gluttony the glory of sobriety is made void: by lust the glory of chastity is stained: by pride the glory of humility is taken captive: by wrathfulness the glory of meekness is interrupted: by envy the glory of charity is prevented: by greed the glory of generosity is destroyed: by slothfulness the glory of activity is turned to blame.

Concerning these things it is said: *I will change their glory into shame* (Hos 4:7).

De primo exemplum in Esau, Gen. XXV, v. 29, in Holoferne, Iudith XIII, 1; de secundo in Salomone, III Reg. II, 13; de tertio in Lucifero, Is. XIV, 12; de quarto in Achitophel, II Reg. XVI, 20; de quinto in Cain, Gen. IV, v. 3; de sexto in Giezi, IV Reg. V, 20; de septimo in exploratoribus, Num. XIII et XIV.

486. *Nam et si evangelizavero*, et cetera. Hic ostendit quod accipiendo sumptus evacuaretur gloria eius, quia non supererogaret. Et est sua ratio talis: gloria quae est praemium supererogationis, non debetur operibus necessitatis, ad quae tenemur ex praecepto; sed evangelizare tenebatur ex praecepto, ergo ex hoc non habebat gloriam supererogationis, sed potius ex hoc, quod non accipiebat sumptus.

Primo ergo tangit gloriae evacuationem; secundo evacuationis rationem, ibi *necessitas enim mihi est*, etc.; tertio rationis declarationem, ibi *vae enim mihi est*, etc.; quarto recte evangelizantium mercedem, ibi *si volens hoc ago*, et cetera.

Dicit ergo *nam si evangelizavero*, etc., quasi diceret: vere evacuaretur gloria mea, *nam si evangelizavero*, ita quod sumptus accipiam, *non est mihi gloria*, id est, supererogationis praemium; *necessitas enim mihi incumbit*, Act. XXII, 21: *vade, quoniam ad nationes longe mittam te*. Et vere necessitas *vae enim mihi est*, id est poena transgressionis in me manet, *si non evangelizavero*, Is. VI, 5: *vae mihi, quia tacui*.

487. Aliter legitur secundum Glossam. Et hoc dupliciter. Primo modo sic *nam si*, etc., quasi dicat: utique evacuaretur gloria mea caelestis, scilicet si ideo praedicarem, ut sumptus acciperem. *Nam si evangelizavero* tantum, ita quod non ex dilectione Dei et proximi hoc faciam, nec libera voluntate, *non est mihi gloria* apud Deum; *necessitas enim* praecepti, quod non audeo omittere, *mihi incumbit*; unde si solo timore servili praedico, *vae enim*, id est, aeterna damnatio, *mihi est si non evangelizavero*, sicut mihi iniunctum est. *Si autem volens*, et cetera. Quasi dicat: si necessitate hoc facio, non est mihi gloria, *si autem volens hoc ago*, id est, si voluntatem adiungo necessitati, *mercedem* aeternam *habeo*; ideo Ps. LIII, 8 dicit: *voluntarie sacrificabo tibi, et confitebor*, et cetera. *Si autem invitus*, id est, solo praecepto coactus evangelizo, *dispensatio mihi credita est*, sicut servo, ut scilicet dispensem ad aliorum utilitatem, non meam; quasi dicat, aliis proficio, non mihi. Intelligit enim hoc de dispensatione servili, non filiali; secundum Glossam Augustini, *nemo invitus bene facit, etsi bonum est, quod facit*. Infra XIII, 3: *si caritatem non habuero, factus sum velut aes sonans*, et cetera.

We see an example of the first in Esau (Gen 25:29) and in Holofernes (Jdt 13:1); of the second, in Solomon (1 Kgs 2:13); of the third in Lucifer (Isa 14: 12); of the fourth in Achitophel (2 Sam 16:21); of the fifth in Cain, (Gen 4:3); of the sixth in Giezi, (2 Kgs 5:20); of the seventh in the scouts (Num 13, 14).

486. *For if I preach the Gospel*. Here he shows that by accepting living expenses his glory might be made void, for he does not strive supererogatively. And his reason is as follows: the glory that is the prize of supererogation is not owed to the works of necessity, to which we are bound by divine command; but he was bound to preach the Gospel by divine command, therefore, from this fact he would not have the glory of supererogation, but rather from the fact that he did not accept the means of living.

Therefore, he first deals with the voiding of glory; second with the reason for this voiding, at *for a necessity lies upon me*; third, the declaration of this reason, at *for woe is unto me*; fourth, the reward for those who preach the Gospel rightly, at *if I do this thing willingly*.

Therefore he says *for if I preach the Gospel*, as though he had said: truly my glory would be voided, *for if I preach the Gospel*, such that I receive my living expenses, *it is no glory to me*, that is, the prize of supererogation; *for a necessity lies upon me*: go, for I will send you to the gentiles far away (Acts 22:21). And necessity indeed, *for woe is unto me*, that is, the punishment for transgressions remains for me, *if I preach not the Gospel*: woe is unto me because I have kept silent (Isa 6:5)

487. It can be read otherwise according to the Gloss. And this in two ways. In the first way, as if he were saying by *for if I preach the Gospel, it is not glory to me*: my heavenly glory would certainly be made void if I were preaching for the sake of receiving a living. *For if I preach the Gospel* alone, such that I do it not out of love of God and my neighbor, nor by free will, *it is no glory to me* before God; *for a necessity* of divine command *lies upon me*, which I dare not fail; wherefore if I preach out of servile fear alone, *woe*, that is eternal damnation, *is unto me if I preach not the Gospel*, as was enjoined upon me. *But if I do this thing willingly*, as though he were saying: if I do this out of necessity, it is no glory to me, but *if I do this thing willingly*, that is, if I join my own will to the necessity, *I have* an eternal *reward*; therefore it is said: *I will freely sacrifice to you, and will confess* (Psalm 54:8). *But if against my will*, that is, if I preach the Gospel only compelled by divine precept, *a dispensation is committed to me*, like a slave, so that I dispense matters for the convenience of others, not myself; as though he said: I profit others, not myself. For he understands this as a servile dispensing, not a filial dispensing; according to the Gloss of Augustine: *no one does well unwillingly, even if it is good what he does*. And below: *if I have not charity, I am become as sounding brass* (1 Cor 13:1).

Secundo modo legitur sic: *nam si evangelizavero* pro sumptibus accipiendis, *non est mihi gloria* de supererogatione in praedicando. Peto enim contra me (Matth. X, 8: *gratis accepistis, gratis date*); *necessitas enim* vitae sustentandae *mihi incumbit*; quia pro necessitate vitae praedico. *Vae enim mihi est*, id est, famis cruciatio, *si non evangelizavero. Si autem volens*, id est, si non pro victus necessitate, sed pro caritate, *hoc ago, mercedem* aeternam *habeo: si autem invitus*, id est, pro necessitate coactus, *dispensatio mihi credita est* sicut servo, et cetera.

488. Deinde cum dicit *quae est ergo merces mea*, etc., hic ostendit, quod non capiendo sumptus, gloria eius conservatur. Ubi primo quaerit, secundo solvit, ibi *ut Evangelium praedicans*, et cetera.

Dicit ergo *quae est merces mea*, id est, quid faciendo mercedem accipiam? Quia hoc est meritum mercedis, *ut* scilicet *ego praedicans Evangelium sine sumptu, ponam*, id est stabiliam, *Evangelium*, Is. XXVIII, 25: *ponet triticum per ordinem*, et cetera. Hoc autem faciebat, secundum Glossam, ne Evangelium venale putaretur. *Sine sumptu*, inquam, et hoc *ut non abutar potestate mea*, id est, mihi commissa in Evangelio praedicando, quod esset si acciperem indistincte, quia perderem auctoritatem libere arguendi: quia, Eccli. XX, 31, *xenia et dona excaecant oculos iudicum, et quasi mutus in ore avertet correptionem*.

Ecclesiastica ergo utilitas implicatur in hac solutione, scilicet confirmatio boni, quia *ut Evangelium praedicans*, et declinatio mali, quia *ne abutar potestate*.

489. Et notandum, quod quatuor tetigit differentias eorum, qui tenentur praedicare.

Quidam enim tenentur, sed non evangelizant, hi merentur poenam.

Quidam tenentur et evangelizant, sed coacti, hi non merentur mercedem, sed vitant poenam.

Quidam tenentur et evangelizant voluntarie, sed accipiunt sumptus, et hi merentur mercedem, et vitant poenam, sed non habent supererogationis gloriam.

Quidam tenentur et evangelizant voluntarie, nec accipiunt sumptus, et hi mercedem merentur, et vitant poenam, et habent supererogationis gloriam.

Primum statum tangit, ibi *vae mihi est*, etc.; secundum ibi *nam si invitus*, etc.; tertium ibi *si autem volens*, etc.; quartum, ibi *quae est ergo merces*, et cetera.

In the second way, it can be read thus: *for if I preach the Gospel* for the sake of receiving living expenses, *it is no glory to me* of supererogation in preaching. For I seek against myself —*freely you have received, freely give* (Matt 10:8)— for the *necessity* of sustaining my *life lies upon me*; since I preach for the sake of the necessities of life. *For woe is unto me*, that is, the torture of starving, *if I preach not the Gospel*. But *if I do this thing willingly*, that is if not out of the necessity of provisions, but out of charity, *I have* an eternal *reward*: *but if against my will*, that is, compelled by my necessity, *a dispensation is committed to me*, just as to a slave.

488. Next when he says *what is my reward then*, here he shows that by not taking living expenses, his glory is preserved. Wherefore first he asks, and second he resolves it, at *that preaching the Gospel*.

Therefore he says *what is my reward*, that is, by doing what, will I receive a reward? For this is the merit of a reward, namely, *that* I, *preaching the Gospel without charge*, that is, I may establish the Gospel: *he will put wheat in order* (Isa 28:25). But he was doing this, according to the Gloss, so that the Gospel would not be thought to be for sale. *Without charge*, he says, and this *that I abuse not my power*, that is, committed to me in preaching the Gospel, which it would be if I accepted payment indiscriminately, for I would lose the authority to admonish freely: since *presents and gifts blind the eyes of the judges, and he will turn away from censuring as though mute in his mouth* (Sir 20:31).

Therefore, the welfare of the Church is involved in this solution, namely, strengthening of the good, since I am as one *preaching the Gospel*, and turning away from evil, since *I abuse not my power*.

489. And it should be noted that he has touched on four distinguishing characteristics of those who are bound to preach.

For some people are bound, but if they do not preach the Gospel, they deserve punishment.

Some people are bound to preach the Gospel as well, but since they are compelled, these do not merit a reward, but they do avoid punishment.

Certain people are also bound to preach the Gospel willingly, but they receive a living, and these merit a reward, and they avoid punishment, but they don't have the glory of supererogation.

Some people also preach the Gospel willingly, and accept no living expenses, and these merit a reward, and avoid punishment, and have the glory of supererogation.

He refers to the first state at *woe is unto me*; the second at *for if against my will*; the third at but *if . . . willingly*; the fourth, at *what is my reward then?*

Lecture 4

9:19Nam cum liber essem ex omnibus, omnium me servum feci, ut plures lucrifacerem. [n. 490]

9:20Et factus sum Judaeis tamquam Judaeus, ut Judaeos lucrarer: iis qui sub lege sunt, quasi sub lege essem (cum ipse non essem sub lege) ut eos qui sub lege erant, lucrifacerem: [n. 492]

9:21iis qui sine lege erant, tamquam sine lege essem (cum sine lege Dei non essem: sed in lege essem Christi) ut lucrifacerem eos qui sine lege erant. [n. 494]

9:22Factus sum infirmis infirmus, ut infirmos lucrifacerem. Omnibus omnia factus sum, ut omnes facerem salvos. [n. 496]

9:23Omnia autem facio propter Evangelium: ut particeps ejus efficiar. [n. 497]

9:19Ἐλεύθερος γὰρ ὢν ἐκ πάντων πᾶσιν ἐμαυτὸν ἐδούλωσα, ἵνα τοὺς πλείονας κερδήσω:

9:20καὶ ἐγενόμην τοῖς Ἰουδαίοις ὡς Ἰουδαῖος, ἵνα Ἰουδαίους κερδήσω: τοῖς ὑπὸ νόμον ὡς ὑπὸ νόμον, μὴ ὢν αὐτὸς ὑπὸ νόμον, ἵνα τοὺς ὑπὸ νόμον κερδήσω:

9:21τοῖς ἀνόμοις ὡς ἄνομος, μὴ ὢν ἄνομος θεοῦ ἀλλ' ἔννομος Χριστοῦ, ἵνα κερδάνω τοὺς ἀνόμους:

9:22ἐγενόμην τοῖς ἀσθενέσιν ἀσθενής, ἵνα τοὺς ἀσθενεῖς κερδήσω: τοῖς πᾶσιν γέγονα πάντα, ἵνα πάντως τινὰς σώσω.

9:23πάντα δὲ ποιῶ διὰ τὸ εὐαγγέλιον, ἵνα συγκοινωνὸς αὐτοῦ γένωμαι.

9:19For whereas I was free as to all, I made myself the servant of all, that I might gain the more. [n. 490]

9:20And I became to the Jews a Jew, that I might gain the Jews: to them that are under the law, as if I were under the law (whereas I myself was not under the law), that I might gain them that were under the law. [n. 492]

9:21To them that were without the law, as if I were without the law (whereas I was not without the law of God, but was in the law of Christ), that I might gain them that were without the law. [n. 494]

9:22To the weak I became weak, that I might gain the weak. I became all things to all men, that I might save all. [n. 496]

9:23And I do all things for the Gospel's sake, that I may be made a partaker thereof. [n. 497]

---

490. Superius ostendit, quod non vult sumptus accipere, et hoc propter intentionem praemii, hic ostendit, quod idem fecit propter amorem Evangelii. Ubi primo dicit, quod omnium se servum fecit; secundo quod omnibus se contemperare studuit, ibi *et factus sum Iudaeis*, etc.; tertio subdit causam quare hoc fecit, ibi *omnia autem facio propter Evangelium*, et cetera.

491. In prima implicat triplicem conditionem commendabilem in servitio: quae sunt generalitas, liberalitas, utilitas. Servit ergo gratis sive liberaliter, ibi *cum essem liber*, etc., generaliter, ibi *omnium me*, etc., utiliter, ibi *ut plures lucrifacerem*, et cetera.

Dicit ergo *nam cum essem*, etc., quasi dicat: sine sumptu ponam Evangelium, nam et maius feci, scilicet quod *cum liber essem ex omnibus*, etc., id est, nullius meritis obnoxius, *omnium me servum feci*, omnibus me contemperando per vilitatem, et quasi debitorem constituendo, II Cor. IV, 5: *nos autem servos vestros per Iesum*. Et hoc *ut plures lucrifacerem*, id est, lucrum meae praedicationis et servitutis facerem. Quaerebat enim non res, sed animas. II Cor. XII, v. 14: *non quaero vestra, sed vos*.

Si enim commendabile est servire in temporalibus propter lucrum temporale, quanto plus in spiritualibus propter lucrum spirituale?

490. He shows above that he does not wish to accept living expenses, and this because of his intention of a prize; here he shows that he did the same out of love of the Gospel. For first he says that he has made himself servant of all; second, that he has striven to temper himself to all men, at and *I became to the Jews*; third, he submits the reason why he did it, at *and I do all things for the Gospel's sake*.

491. In the first he develops three commendable aspects to slavery: which are commonality, liberality, and usefulness. Therefore, he serves freely or generously, at *whereas I was free*; to all in common, at *I made myself the servant of all*; usefully, at *that I might gain the more*.

Therefore he says, *for whereas I was*, as though he said: without charge I set forth the Gospel, for I have also done a greater thing, which is that although *I was free as to all*, that is, deserving of nothing in merits, *I made myself the servant of all*, bringing myself to the level of all by lowliness, and by establishing myself like a debtor: *ourselves your servants through Jesus* (2 Cor 4:5). And this so *that I might gain the more*; that is, I would make my gain of preaching and servitude. For he was not asking for things, but for souls. *I do not seek your belongings, but yourselves* (2 Cor 12:14).

For if it is commendable to serve in temporal things, for the sake of temporal gain, how much more is it to serve in spiritual things, for the sake of spiritual gain?

492. Deinde, cum dicit *et factus sum Iudaeis*, etc., hic ostendit, quod omnibus se contemperare studuit. Et

primo dicit quod contemperavit se nondum conversis;

secundo quod etiam iam conversis, ibi *factus sum infirmis*, etc.;

tertio quod generaliter universis, ibi *omnibus omnia factus sum*, etc.

in prima

primo dicit, quod contemperavit se Iudaeis;

secundo quod Samaritanis, ibi *et his qui sub lege*, etc.;

tertio quod gentilibus, ibi *his qui sine lege erant*, et cetera.

493. In prima, primo tangit contemperationem; secundo contemperationis rationem, ibi *ut Iudaeos*, et cetera.

Dicit ergo: *et factus sum Iudaeis tamquam Iudaeus*, scilicet aliqua legalia servando, sicut in discretione ciborum, in circumcisione Timothei Act. XVI, 3, in purificatione legali Act. XXI, 24.

Potest autem hoc intelligi dupliciter. Uno modo, secundum Hieronymum, *factus sum Iudaeis tamquam Iudaeus*, per simulationis dispensationem. Simulabat enim se servare legalia aliqua, quae tamen non servabat. Alio modo, secundum Augustinum, *factus sum Iudaeus*, et cetera. Vere enim condescendebat eis in observatione aliquorum legalium propter piam compassionem; et hoc fecit, ut Iudaeos lucraretur Christo, id est, eos ad fidem Christi converteret.

494. Deinde, cum dicit *et his qui sub lege sunt*, etc., hic dicit quod contemperabat se Samaritanis.

Ubi notantur tria de ipso. Primo eius sagacitas in hoc quod se contemperabat; secundo eius libertas in hoc quod sub lege non erat; tertio eius utilitas in hoc quod lucrifaciebat.

Dicit ergo: sum etiam *his qui sub lege* Moysi *sunt*, id est Samaritanis, qui non sunt Iudaei sed Assyrii, qui fuerunt adducti ad inhabitandum terram Israel, IV Reg. XVII, v. 24 ss. Isti etiam erant sub lege Moysi, quia tantum quinque libros Moysi recipiebant. His ergo *factus sum quasi sub lege essem*, approbando scilicet legem, et ex ea docendo Christum, *cum tamen ipse sub lege non essem*, secundum litteralem observantiam, vel serviliter, quia *iusto non est lex posita*, I Tim. I, 9. Et hoc ideo feci *ut eos, qui sub lege erant*, scilicet ipsos Samaritanos, *lucrifacerem*, eos ad fidem Christi convertendo.

492. Next, when he says *and I became to the Jews*, here he shows that he strove to make himself of the same stuff as everyone else.

First he says that he mingled himself with those not yet converted;

second, with those also who had converted, at *to the weak I became weak*;

third, commonly to all the world, at *I became all things to all men*.

As to the first,

he says first that he made himself one with Jews;

second, with Samaritans, at and *to them that are under the law*;

third, with the Gentiles, at *to them that were without the law*.

493. In the first, he first deals with the fact of becoming one of them; second, the reason for becoming one of them, at *so that I might gain the Jews*.

Therefore he says, *and I became to the Jews, a Jew*, that is by observing certain legalities, like in the separation of foods, and in the circumcision of Timothy (Acts 16:3), in the purification called for by the law (Acts 21:24).

But this can be understood two ways. In one way, according to Jerome, *I became to the Jews a Jew*, by the dispensation of pretense. For he was pretending to observe certain legalities, which, however, he was not observing. In another way, according to Augustine, *I became a Jew*. For he truly condescended to them in his observation of certain legalities because of his faithful compassion; and he did this so that he might gain the Jews for Christ, that is, to convert them to the faith of Christ.

494. Next, when he says, and *to them that are under the law*, here he says that he made himself one of the Samaritans.

Three things are noted about this. First, his shrewdness in the fact that he made himself one of them; second, his freedom in the fact that he was not under the law; and third, his usefulness in the fact that it was paying off.

Therefore he says: I am even *to them that are under the law* of Moses, that is, Samaritans, who are not Jews but Assyrians, who were brought back to inhabit the land of Israel (2 Kgs 17:24). Those people were also under the law of Moses, for they received only the five books of Moses. Therefore to them, *I became . . . as if I were under the law*, namely by endorsing the law, and from it teaching Christ, *whereas I myself was not under the law*, according to the observance of the letter, or in a servile way, because *the law is not made for the just man* (1 Tim 1:9). And therefore I did this *so that them that were under the law*, namely, those Samaritans, *I might gain*, by converting them to the faith of Christ.

495. Deinde, cum dicit *his qui sine lege erant*, etc., hic dicit quod contemperavit se gentilibus.

Ubi primo tangit suam conformitatem; secundo suae fidei veritatem, ibi *cum tamen sine lege*, etc.; tertio suae intentionis rectitudinem, ibi *ut lucrifacerem*, et cetera.

Et hoc est: *et factus sum his qui sine lege erant*, id est gentibus, Rom. II, 14: *cum enim gentes, quae legem non habent, tamquam sine lege essem*, id est, assentiendo rationibus eorum, et bonis positionibus philosophorum, ut patet Act. XVII; *Cum tamen sine lege non essem*. Rom. VII, 25: *mente servio legi Dei. Sed in lege essem*, non Iudaica, sed *Christi*, qui est Deus, non autem Moyses. De qua Gal. VI, 2: *alter alterius onera portate, et sic adimplebitis*, et cetera. Et hoc ideo feci *ut lucrifacerem eos qui sine lege erant*, gentiles ad fidem convertendo. O felix zelator. Gregorius: *nullum tale sacrificium quale zelus animarum*.

496. Deinde, cum dicit *factus sum infirmis*, etc., hic ostendit quod se contemperavit iam conversis. Ubi primo ponit modum bonum, secundo finem debitum, ibi *ut infirmos*.

Dicit ergo *factus sum etiam infirmis*, in fide, *infirmus*, a licitis abstinendo. II Cor. c. XI, 29: *quis infirmatur, et ego non infirmor?* Sic facit bonus medicus, qui comedit cibum infirmi, ut eum provocet ad comedendum, et sic sanet. Et hoc feci *ut infirmos lucrifacerem*, eos in fide roborando.

Et breviter *omnibus omnia factus sum*, quasi essem omnium sectarum. Ideo dicitur infra X, 33: *sicut et ego per omnia omnibus placeo*. Et hoc *ut omnes facerem salvos*. In vestimento poderis quod habebat Aaron, totus orbis terrarum erat descriptus, Sap. c. XVIII, 24. Et, IV Reg. IV, 34, Eliseus contraxit se ad modum pueri, et sic suscitavit illum.

Et quia, secundum Boetium, *omnis alteritas discors, similitudo vero appetenda est*; ideo viri spirituales, salva vitae et religionis suae observantia, omnibus se debent conformare.

497. Deinde, cum dicit *omnia facio propter Evangelium*, superius ostendit quod omnibus se contemperare studuit; hic subdit rationem quare hoc facit, et hanc duplicem: unam ex parte Evangelii, scilicet ut cursum liberum habeat; aliam ex parte sui, scilicet ut promissum praemium obtineat, ibi *ut particeps*, et cetera.

Et hoc est quod dicit *omnia autem facio propter Evangelium*, sine impedimento praedicandum, *ut particeps eius*, id est, promissionum, quae in eo continentur, *efficiar*. Matth. V, 19: *qui fecerit et docuerit, hic magnus vocabitur in regno caelorum*.

495. Next, when he says *to them that were without the law*, here he is saying that he made himself one of the gentiles.

First he deals with his own conformity; second, the truth of his faith, at *whereas I was not without the law*; third, the uprightness of his intention, at *that I might gain*.

And this is: *and I became . . . to them that are without the law*, that is, the gentiles: *the gentiles who have not the law* (Rom 2:14), *as if I were without the law*, that is, by agreeing with their arguments, and the good positions of their philosophers, as is clear in Acts 17; *whereas I was not without the law*: *I serve the law of God with my mind* (Rom 7:25). But I *was in the law*, not the Jewish one, but *the law of Christ*, who is God, but not Moses. Concerning this, it is said: *carry each other's burdens, and so you shall fulfill the law of Christ* (Gal 6:2). And this therefore I did so *that I might gain them who were without the law*, by converting gentiles to the faith. O happy zealous lover. Gregory says: *there is no sacrifice as great as zeal for souls*.

496. Next, when he says *to the weak I became weak*, he shows that he made himself one of those already converted. There he sets forth first the good way; second, the due end, at *that I might gain the weak*.

Therefore he says *to the weak* in faith *I also became weak* by abstaining from things that were allowed. *Who is weak and I am not weak?* (2 Cor 11:29) In this way works a good doctor, who eats the food of the sick, so that he can provoke them to eat, and so heal them. And I did this so *that I might gain the weak*, by strengthening them in faith.

And in sum, *I became all things to all men*, as though I were of all groups. Therefore it is said below: *as I also in all things please all men* (1 Cor 10:33). And this, *that I might save all*. In the priestly robe that Aaron had, the whole world was pictured, (Wis 18:24). And Eliseus shrunk himself down to the size of a child, so that he could bring him back to life (2 Kgs 4:34).

And because, according to Boethius, *every difference is discordant*, indeed likeness must be sought; therefore, spiritual men, except for those observing a religious rule of life, should conform themselves to all others.

497. Next, when he says *I do all things for the Gospel's sake*, he shows that he has striven to make himself one with all men; here he puts forth his reason why he did it, and this is two-fold: one on the part of the Gospel, so that it would have a free course; and the other on his own part, so that he might obtain the promised prize, at *that I may be made a partaker*.

And this is what he says at *I do all things for the Gospel's sake*, without impediment to his preaching, *that I may be made a partaker thereof*, that is, of the promises that are contained in it: *he who shall do and teach, he shall be called great in the kingdom of heaven* (Matt 5:19).

Lecture 5

9:24Nescitis quod ii qui in stadio currunt, omnes quidem currunt, sed unus accipit bravium? Sic currite ut comprehendatis. [n. 498]

9:25Omnis autem qui in agone contendit, ab omnibus se abstinet, et illi quidem ut corruptibilem coronam accipiant: nos autem incorruptam. [n. 501]

9:26Ego igitur sic curro, non quasi in incertum: sic pugno, non quasi aërem verberans: [n. 502]

9:27sed castigo corpus meum, et in servitutem redigo: ne forte cum aliis praedicaverim, ipse reprobus efficiar. [n. 505]

9:24Οὐκ οἴδατε ὅτι οἱ ἐν σταδίῳ τρέχοντες πάντες μὲν τρέχουσιν, εἷς δὲ λαμβάνει τὸ βραβεῖον; οὕτως τρέχετε ἵνα καταλάβητε.

9:25πᾶς δὲ ὁ ἀγωνιζόμενος πάντα ἐγκρατεύεται, ἐκεῖνοι μὲν οὖν ἵνα φθαρτὸν στέφανον λάβωσιν, ἡμεῖς δὲ ἄφθαρτον.

9:26ἐγὼ τοίνυν οὕτως τρέχω ὡς οὐκ ἀδήλως, οὕτως πυκτεύω ὡς οὐκ ἀέρα δέρων·

9:27ἀλλὰ ὑπωπιάζω μου τὸ σῶμα καὶ δουλαγωγῶ, μή πως ἄλλοις κηρύξας αὐτὸς ἀδόκιμος γένωμαι.

9:24Know you not that they that run in the race, all run indeed, but one receives the prize. So run that you may obtain. [n. 498]

9:25And every one that strives for the mastery refrains himself from all things. And these indeed that they may receive a corruptible crown: but we an incorruptible one. [n. 501]

9:26I therefore so run, not as at an uncertainty: I so fight, not as one beating the air. [n. 502]

9:27But I chastise my body and bring it into subjection: lest perhaps, when I have preached to others, I myself should become a castaway. [n. 505]

---

498. Superius ostendit quod proposuit a sumptibus abstinere, primo propter intentionem praemii, secundo propter amorem Evangelii, hic, tertio, propter expeditionem cursus et agonis sui.

Primo quidem ostendit quod oportet in stadio expedite currere;

secundo quod similiter oportet in agone expedite certare, ibi **omnis enim qui in agone**, etc.;

tertio quod ipse facit utrumque, ibi **ego igitur sic curro**, et cetera.

499. In prima, primo ponit exemplum expedite currentium; secundo monet eos ad similiter currendum, ibi **sic currite**, et cetera. In prima, primo tangit currendi exercitium; secundo convenientiam currentium, ibi **omnes quidem currunt**, etc.; tertio differentiam pervenientium, ibi **sed unus accipit bravium**, et cetera.

In primo notatur conditio viatorum; in secundo multitudo vocatorum; in tertio paucitas electorum. Matth. XX, 16: *multi sunt vocati, pauci vero electi*.

Conditionem vero viatorum describit a tribus. A certitudine, cum quaerit **nescitis**; a brevitate, cum addit **in stadio**; a labore, cum subdit **currunt**.

500. Dicit ergo **nescitis**. Quod tripliciter continuatur. Primo modo sic quasi dicat: recte abstineo a sumptibus sumendis, ut particeps efficiar. Nam si non abstinerem a contrariis Evangelio, non essem eius particeps. **Nescitis** enim **quod hi**, et cetera.

498. Above he showed that he planned to abstain from living expenses, first because of his intention of the prize, second because of his love of the Gospel, and here, third, because of the facilitating of his race and his struggle.

First then he shows that one must run in the race unencumbered;

second, that in a similar way one must compete unencumbered in the contest, at **and every one that strives for the mastery**;

third, that he himself is doing both, at **I therefore so run**.

499. In the first point, he first sets forth the example of runners unencumbered; second, he advises them to run like that, at **so run**. In the first part, he refers first to the training for running; second, to what the runners all share, at **all run indeed**; third, to what distinguishes those who win, at **but one receives the prize**.

In the first example, the condition of wayfarers is described; in the second, the great number of those who are called; in the third example, the small number of those chosen. *Many are called but few are chosen* (Matt 20:16).

Now he describes the condition of wayfarers by three things. By certitude, where he asks, **know you not**; by briefness, when he adds, **in the race**; and by labor, where he includes, **they run**.

500. Therefore, he says **know you not**, which is continued in three ways. First, as if he said it this way: correctly do I abstain from consuming my means of living, so that I might be made a partaker. For if I did not abstain from things contrary to the Gospel, I would not be a partaker. For **know you not, that they that run in the race, all run indeed, but one receives the prize**.

Vel sic: ***nescitis quod*** hoc facio, ut particeps Evangelii efficiar? Et utique possum esse particeps. Nam non sic est de Evangelii praemio, vel de cursus bravio; quia hic unus accipit bravium, ibi vero omnes accipere possunt.

Tertio modo sic: ***nescitis***, quasi diceret: ideo autem sic curro, quia licet multi currentes sint, pauci tamen sunt pervenientes. Nescitis enim ***quod hi qui in stadio currunt, omnes quidem currunt***, in labore pares sunt, ***sed unus tantum accipit bravium***, id est, praemium cursus? Stadium enim est spatium in quo pedites currunt, quod Hercules dicitur statuisse. Perficiunt autem stadium 125 passus. Et dicitur stadium a stando, quia Hercules tot passus currebat et postea stabat et respirabat; in fine huius spatii ponebatur aliquid quod erat praemium cursus, ut equus et pannus purpureus, et hoc dicitur bravium. Et licet in hoc stadio omnes currerent, unus tamen solus accipiebat bravium, scilicet qui citius perveniebat. Sic in cursu spirituali unus tantum, scilicet perseverans, accipit bravium. Quia qui perseveraverit usque in finem, hic salvus erit.

Deinde, cum dicit ***sic currite***, etc., monet eos ad currendum. Ubi implicat tria: actum strenuum ***currite***, modum debitum ***sic***, finem optimum ***ut comprehendatis***.

Dicit ergo ***sic***, etc., quasi diceret: quia unus accipit bravium, ***sic currite***, per viam veritatis perseverantes, ***ut comprehendatis*** bravium vitae aeternae. Hebr. XII, 1: *per patientiam curramus ad propositum nobis certamen.*

501. Deinde, cum dicit ***omnis autem qui in agone***, etc., ostendit quod in agone oportet expedite certare.

Ubi primo tangit agonizantium pugnam; secundo pugnandi formam firmam, ibi ***ab omnibus se abstinet***, etc.; tertio sic pugnantium mercedem debitam, ibi ***et illi quidem ut corruptibilem***, et cetera.

Primum est necessitatis, scilicet pugnare; secundum virtutis, scilicet abstinere; tertium felicitatis, scilicet coronam accipere.

Dicit ergo ***omnis qui in agone***, etc., quasi diceret: vere sic agendum est, quod patet exemplo: quia ***omnis qui in agone contendit, ab omnibus*** impedientibus ***se abstinet***. Unde et nudi agonizabant in palaestra.

Attende, ut Augustinus ait, quod *de rebus non laudandis multae trahuntur similitudines.*

Deinde, cum dicit ***et illi quidem ut corruptibilem***, etc., tangit pugnantium mercedem, et primo pugnantium materialiter; secundo pugnantium spiritualiter, ibi ***nos autem incorruptam***, et cetera.

Or as follows: ***know you not*** that I do this, so that I might be made a partaker of the Gospel? And yes, I can be a partaker. For the prize of the Gospel is not like the award for the race, because in the latter only one receives the award, but in the former all can receive it.

In a third way, as follows: ***know you not***, as though he were saying: but for this reason I run like this, because although there may be many runners, still few are winners. For ***know you not that they that run in the race, all run indeed***, they are the same in labor, ***but one receives the prize***, that is, for the race? For the stadium is large where the runners run, because Hercules is said to have stood there. But they complete the race in 125 paces. And it is called a stadium from standing, for Hercules ran so many steps and afterward he was standing and resting; at the boundary of this area something was placed that was the prize for the race, like a horse or a purple cloth, and this is called the award. And although in this race many ran, only one received the award, namely, the one who accomplished it the fastest. In the same way, in the spiritual race, only one, namely, the one who perseveres, receives the award. For whoever perseveres until the end, he is the one who will be saved.

Next, when he says, ***so run***, he advises them about the running. There three things are involved: a strenuous act: ***run***; the due manner: ***so***; and the best end: ***that you may obtain***.

Therefore he says, ***so***, as though he were saying: because one receives the prize, ***so run***, remaining in the way of truth, ***that you may obtain*** the prize of eternal life. *Let us run by patience to the fight proposed to us* (Heb 12:1).

501. Next, when he says ***but everyone who strives for the mastery***, he shows that in the contest one has to contend unencumbered.

There he first deals with the fight of those competing; second, the firm form of the fighting, at ***refrains himself from all things***; third, the due reward for those fighting, at ***and these indeed that they may receive***.

The first thing is of necessity, namely, to fight; the second thing of virtue, namely, to abstain; the third thing is of happiness, namely, to receive the crown.

Therefore he says ***everyone who strives***, as if he were saying: truly, it must be done this way, which is clear from this example: for ***everyone who strives for the mastery refrains himself from all things*** that hamper him. For this reason they also competed naked in the gymnasiums.

Be careful, as Augustine says, because *many comparisons are drawn from things that are not praiseworthy.*

Next, when he says ***and these indeed that they may receive a corruptible crown***, he refers to the reward for those fighting; and first those fighting materially; second, those fighting spiritually, at ***but we an incorruptible one***.

Dicit ergo *et illi quidem* abstinent, *ut corruptibilem coronam accipiant*, quod modicum est. *Nos autem* abstinere debemus, ut accipiamus *incorruptam*, scilicet coronam vitae, de qua Iac. I, 12: *beatus vir qui suffert tentationem, quoniam cum probatus fuerit*, et cetera.

502. Deinde, cum dicit *ego igitur sic curro*, etc., ponit exemplum utriusque, scilicet currendi et pugnandi. Ubi
primo tangit cursum suum in profectu boni;

secundo pugnam suam in victoria mali, ibi *sic pugno*, etc.;

tertio rationem utriusque facti, ibi *sed castigo*, et cetera.

503. Dicit ergo *ego igitur* etc., quasi dicat: quia talis corona servatur, igitur *ego sic curro*, bonum operando, *non quasi in incertum*, id est, ut sim incertus de praemio. In incertum enim currit qui talia facit, ut de quibusdam sperare, ex aliis vero possit desperare.

Omnia instruunt ad bonum: et persona apostolica, quae notatur ibi *ego*, et forma implicita, quae notatur ibi *sic*, et actio strenua, quae notatur ibi *curro*, et merces sperata, quae notatur ibi *non quasi in incertum*. Phil. II, 16: *non in vacuum cucurri, nec in vacuum laboravi.*

504. *Sic pugno* contra hostes, decertando contra malum, *non quasi aerem verberans*, id est, non verbis tantum, sed factis. *Non enim in sermone est regnum Dei, sed in virtute*, supra IV, 20. Vel *non quasi aerem verberans*, id est, non inaniter me fatigando, adversarium non laedendo.

Sic erit perfectus homo, si sic se habeat, ut sit intentus in confessione, Is. XXXVIII, 15: *recogitabo tibi omnes annos meos in amaritudine animae meae*, devotus in oratione, Matth. VI, 9: *sic ergo orabitis: Pater noster, qui es in caelis*, etc., efficax in praedicatione, Iac. II, 12: *sic loquimini, et sic facite.*

Haec tria pertinent ad actum oris recti, ita tamen quod confessio dirigitur Deo et proximo, oratio soli Deo, praedicatio soli proximo.

Fortis in pugnando. Unde *sic pugno*, et cetera. Apoc. III, 5: *qui vicerit, sic vestietur veste alba.* Patiens in sustinendo. Iudith VIII, 23: *sic Isaac, sic Iacob, sic Moyses, et omnes qui placuerunt Deo, per multas tribulationes transierunt fideles.* Cautus in servando. Ios. c. II, 16: *ad montana conscendite, ne forte occurrant vobis revertentes*, et cetera. *Et sic ibitis viam vestram.*

Primum propter malum culpae, scilicet pugna; secundum contra malum poenae, scilicet patientia; tertium contra malum tentationis, scilicet cautela.

Therefore he says and *these indeed* refrain *that they may receive a corruptible crown*, which is a little thing. But we should refrain so that we receive *an incorruptible one*, namely, the crown of life, of which St. James speaks: *blessed is the man who endures temptation, for when he has been proved* (Jas 1:12).

502. Next, when he says *I therefore so run*, he sets the example of both, namely of running and fighting.

He first deals with his race in the accomplishment of good;

second his fight in the victory over evil, at *I so fight*;

third, the reason of both deeds at *but I chastise*.

503. Therefore he says *I therefore*, as though saying: because such a crown is saved, *I therefore so run*, by doing good, *not as at an uncertainty*, that is, so that I am unsure of the prize. For someone runs at an uncertainty who does things such that he can hope about certain things, but despair of others.

All things instruct to the good: both apostolic persons, who he refers to with that *I*; and implied forms, which he notes with that *so*; and strenuous action, which he refers to at *run*; and hoped-for rewards, which he refers to with *not as though at an incertainty*. *I did not run in vain, nor in vain did I labor* (Phil 2:16).

504. *I so fight* against enemies, struggling to the finish against evil, *not as one beating the air*, that is, not only by words, but by deeds: *for the kingdom of God is not in speech but in power* (1 Cor 4:20). Or *not as one beating the air*, that is, not by foolishly wearing myself out, while not injuring the adversary.

The perfect man will be like this, if he behaves so that he is directed in his confession: *I will recount to you all my years in the bitterness of my soul* (Isa 38:15), devout in praying: *pray then, like this: our Father, who art in heaven* (Matt 6:9), and effective in preaching: *so speak, and so do* (Jas 2:12).

These three things pertain to the act of an upright mouth, so that the confession is directed to God and one's neighbor, prayer to God alone, preaching to one's neighbor alone.

Strong in fighting. Hence, *I so fight*: *whoever has overcome, shall be dressed so in white garments* (Rev 3:5). Patient in enduring: *thus Isaac, thus Jacob, thus Moses, and all who pleased God, passed through many tribulations, faithful* (Jdt 8:23). Careful in guarding: *go up to the mountains, lest by chance they happen upon you when they return . . . and so you will go on your way* (Josh 2:16).

The first one is because of the evil of guilt, namely, the fight; the second, against the evil of punishment, namely, patience; the third, against the evil of temptation, namely, watchfulness.

Benignus in condonando. Matth. XVIII, 14: *sic non est voluntas ante Patrem*, et cetera. Inutilem se reputando. Lc. XVII, 10: *sic et vos cum feceritis omnia quae praecepta*, et cetera. Sollicitus, se discutiendo. Infra XI, 28: **probet autem se homo, et sic de pane illo edat**, et cetera.

Primum reprobat malitiam proximi; secundum probat bonitatem Dei; tertium dubietatem status proprii.

Humilis in obsequendo. Matth. III, 15: *sic decet nos implere omnem iustitiam*. Agilis in proficiendo. Unde hic v. 24: **sic currite**, id est, proficite in bono, **ut comprehendatis**. Constans in perseverando. Unde hic v. 24: **sic currite**. Phil. IV, 1: *sic state in Domino, charissimi*. Famosus in conversando. Supra IV, 1: **sic nos existimet homo**, et cetera.

Primum respicit incipientes; secundum proficientes; tertium perseverantes; quartum perfectos.

505. Deinde, cum dicit **sed castigo corpus meum**, etc., tangit rationem praedictorum utriusque. Ubi primo tangit austeritatem vitae; secundo commendationem doctrinae, ibi **ne forte**, etc.; tertio rationem concordiae utriusque, ibi **ipse reprobus**, et cetera.

Ergo implet facto, quod docet verbo, ne se damnet ore proprio. Et hoc est quod dicit **sed castigo corpus meum**, per declinationem mali, motus carnis illicitos reprimendo. **Castigo** ergo, non occido, **corpus meum**, non tantum alienum. Rom. XII, 1: *exhibeatis corpora vestra hostiam viventem, sanctam, Deo placentem, rationabile obsequium vestrum*. **Et in servitutem redigo** per operationem boni, corpus scilicet spiritui servire cogendo et sensualitatem rationi subiiciendo, sicut de Beato Martino legitur: *carnem spiritui servire cogebat*. Et hoc facio, **ne forte, cum aliis praedicaverim**, et cetera. Augustinus: *suo timore nos terruit Apostolus; quid enim faciet agnus, ubi aries timet et tremit?* **Ipse reprobus**, id est, a Deo reprobatus, **efficiar**, quod turpe esset. Rom. II, 21: *qui praedicas non furandum, furaris*. De huiusmodi posset vere dici illud Iob IV, 3: *ecce docuisti plurimos*, etc.: *nunc autem venit super te plaga, et defecisti*.

506. Hic quaeritur, ibi **melius est mihi mori**, et cetera. Contra: gloria non evacuatur nisi per peccatum; ergo accipere esset ei peccatum, non ergo licitum.

Respondeo. Gloria essentialis per hoc non evacuaretur, sed gloria accidentalis est de hoc opere supererogationis.

507. Item **si evangelizavero, non est mihi gloria**. Contra: evangelizanti et sumptus accipienti debetur et aurea et aureola.

Kind in forgiving: *so it is not the will of your Father* (Matt 8:14). Considering oneself useless: *so also you, when you have done all that is commanded* (Luke 17:10). Anxious in pleading one's own case: *but let a man prove himself: and so let him eat of that bread* (1 Cor 11:28).

The first counteracts the malice of one's neighbor; the second shows the goodness of God; the third shows the uncertainty about one's own state.

Humble in yielding: *thus it befits us to fulfill every justice* (Matt 3:15). Nimble in advancing: hence here he says, **so run**, that is, advance in the good, **that you may obtain**. Steadfast in persevering: hence here he says: **so run**: so remain in the Lord, beloved (Phil 4:1). Renowned in conduct, as said above: **let a man so account of us as of the ministers of Christ** (1 Cor 4:1).

The first regards beginners; the second, the proficient; the third, those persevering; the fourth, the perfect.

505. Next, when he says **but I chastise my body**, he refers to the reason for both of the aforementioned things. For he first refers to the austerity of life; second, to the entrusting of doctrine, at **lest perhaps**; and third, to the reason for harmony between both, at **I myself should become a castaway**.

Therefore, he fulfills by deed what he teaches in words, lest he condemn himself by his own mouth. And this is what he says **but I chastise my own body**, by the refusal of evil, when he rejects the illicit movements of the flesh. Therefore, **I chastise**, not kill, **my body**, not only something outside me. *May you present your bodies as a living sacrifice, holy, pleasing to God, your reasonable service* (Rom 12:1). **And bring it into subjection** by the working of good, namely by compelling the body to serve the spirit and by subjecting my sensuality to reason, just as is written of Blessed Martin: *he compelled his flesh to serve his spirit*. And I do this, **lest perhaps, when I have preached to others**—Augustine says: *the Apostle has frightened us by his fear; for what will the lamb do, where the ram fears and trembles?*—**I myself should become a castaway**, that is, cast off by God, which would be a shameful thing. *You who preach against stealing, you steal* (Rom 2:21). Regarding this kind of thing, it could indeed be said what is said to Job: *behold, you have taught many . . . but now the scourge is come upon you, and you are failing* (Job 4:3–5).

506. Here it is asked, at **it is good for me to die rather** (1 Cor 9:15). Against this: glory is not made void by anything but sin; therefore, to accept living expenses would be for him a sin, and therefore not permitted.

Answer: glory in its essence is not made void by this, but incidental glory comes from this work of supererogation.

507. Again, **if I preach the Gospel, it is no glory to me** (1 Cor 9:16). Against this: to someone preaching the Gospel and receiving a living, both a golden crown and a halo are due.

Sed Glossa exponit: *quando evangelizatur ex necessitate timoris, vel ex cupiditate mercedis temporalis.*

508. Item super illud **dispensatio mihi credita est**, Glossa: *non debemus evangelizare, ut manducemus.*

Contra: ergo praedicatores quaestuarii peccant mortaliter, quia faciunt quod non debent.

Respondeo. Si propter quaestum principaliter faciunt, peccant: sed si propter fructum spiritualem inde provenientem, bene faciunt,

509. item ibidem Glossa: *propter regnum Dei debemus operari omnia non solum, sed cum regno Dei mercedem temporalem meditari.*

Contra: ergo qui vadunt ad Ecclesiam pro distributionibus, peccant.

Respondeo. Verum est, si solum vel principaliter propter hoc vadant.

510. Item super hoc **ut non abutar potestate**, Glossa: *quod esset, si acciperet, quod probavit supra eodem quod ei licet accipere.*

Respondeo. Intelligendum est si acciperetur indiscrete et inordinate et immoderate.

511. Item **omnium servum me feci**. Contra supra VII, 23: **nolite servi effici hominum**.

Respondeo. Hic loquitur de servitute caritatis, scilicet in bono, ibi de servitute iniquitatis, scilicet in malo.

512. Item **factus sum Iudaeis Iudaeus**, Glossa: *in cibis accipiendis, vel non accipiendis.*

Contra Glossa: *iniuste ergo reprehendit Petrum de discretione ciborum*, Gal. II, 11. Immo bene, quia Petrus discernebat cum scandalo gentium, scilicet in locis gentilium, Paulus autem non.

513. Item ibidem Glossa: *propter scandalum Iudaeorum circumcidit Timotheum*, Act. XVI, 3.

Contra: veritas doctrinae vitae et iustitiae non debet dimitti propter scandalum.

Respondeo. Usque ad divulgationem Evangelii non erat de veritate doctrinae sive vitae, ne homines circumciderentur, sed ne spem ponerent in circumcisione.

514. Item **ut omnes facerem salvos**. Contra, sciebat non omnes salvandos.

Respondeo. Volebat omnes in particulari, id est, quemlibet per se, non omnes simul.

515. Item super illud **omnes quidem currunt**, Glossa: *in spirituali agone, quotquot quidem currunt, si*

But the Gloss expounds: *when the Gospel is preached out of fearful necessity, or out of greed for temporal rewards.*

508. Again, concerning **a dispensation is committed to me** (1 Cor 9:17), the Gloss says: *we must not preach the Gospel so that we may eat.*

Against this: therefore mercenary preachers sin mortally, for they do what they should not.

Answer: if they do it chiefly for the sake of profit, they sin: but if for the sake of the spiritual fruit it produces, they do well.

509. Again, the Gloss says in the same place: *we should work all things not only for the sake of the kingdom of God, but we should constantly ponder the temporal reward with the kingdom of God.*

Against this: therefore, those who go to the Church for the distributions, sin.

I answer that this is true, if they go there only or chiefly for that.

510. Again, concerning **that I abuse not my power** (1 Cor 9:18), the Gloss has: *which would be the case, if he received a living, because he has proved above that it would be permissible for him to receive it.*

I answer that it has to be understood as if he received a living indiscretely, and inordinately, and immoderately.

511. Again, **I made myself the servant of all** (1 Cor 9:19). Against this, what is said above: **be not made the slaves of men** (1 Cor 7:23).

I answer that here he speaks of the servitude of charity, namely, in a good man; that verse refers to the servitude of iniquity, namely in a bad man.

512. Again, **I became to the Jews, a Jew** (1 Cor 9:20), the Gloss has: *in accepting food or not accepting.*

Against this the Gloss has: *therefore he unjustly reprimanded Peter for being selective about food*, namely, in his letter to the Galatians (Gal 2:11). On the contrary, he did well, for Peter was setting himself apart to the scandal of the gentiles, namely, while in a gentile region, but not Paul.

513. Again, the Gloss in the same place says: *on account of the scandal of the Jews, he circumcised Timothy*, as mentioned in Acts (Acts 16: 3).

Against this: the truth of the doctrine of life and of justice should not be set aside for the sake of scandal.

I answer that up until the spread of the Gospel there was nothing about the truth of teaching or of life that went against men being circumcised, but rather against their placing their hope in circumcision.

514. Again, **that I might save all** (1 Cor 9:22). Against this: he knew that not all would be saved.

I answer that he was wanting to save all as individuals, that is, each one in himself, not all together.

515. Again, concerning **all indeed run**, the Gloss has: *in the spiritual contest, however many run, if they run*

spiritualiter currunt, accipiunt; et qui prior venerit, expectat, ut coronetur cum posteriori.

Contra, unusquisque in morte coronatur.

Respondeo. Hoc intelligitur de gloria corporis, non animae.

516. Item super illud *ne forte cum praedicaverim*, Glossa: *suo timore nos terret Apostolus.*

Contra, I Io. IV, 18: *perfecta caritas foras mittit timorem.*

Verum est timorem poenae, sed non timorem separationis sive offensae.

spiritually, they receive; and whoever has come first, he waits to be crowned with those behind.

Against this: each one is crowned in death.

I answer that this is to be understood as to the glory of the body, not the soul.

516. Again, concerning *lest perhaps, when I have preached*, the Gloss says: *the Apostle terrifies us by his own fear.*

Against this: *perfect charity casts out fear* (1 John 4:18).

The fear of punishment is something real, but not the fear of separation or of offense.

CHAPTER 10

Lecture 1

10:1Nolo enim vos ignorare fratres, quoniam patres nostri omnes sub nube fuerunt, et omnes mare transierunt, [n. 517]

10:2et omnes in Moyse baptizati sunt in nube, et in mari:

10:3et omnes eamdem escam spiritalem manducaverunt, [n. 519]

10:4et omnes eumdem potum spiritalem biberunt (bibebant autem de spiritali, consequente eos, petra: petra autem erat Christus):

10:5sed non in pluribus eorum beneplacitum est Deo: nam prostrati sunt in deserto. [n. 521]

10:1Οὐ θέλω γὰρ ὑμᾶς ἀγνοεῖν, ἀδελφοί, ὅτι οἱ πατέρες ἡμῶν πάντες ὑπὸ τὴν νεφέλην ἦσαν καὶ πάντες διὰ τῆς θαλάσσης διῆλθον,

10:2καὶ πάντες εἰς τὸν Μωϋσῆν ἐβαπτίσθησαν ἐν τῇ νεφέλῃ καὶ ἐν τῇ θαλάσσῃ,

10:3καὶ πάντες τὸ αὐτὸ πνευματικὸν βρῶμα ἔφαγον,

10:4καὶ πάντες τὸ αὐτὸ πνευματικὸν ἔπιον πόμα: ἔπινον γὰρ ἐκ πνευματικῆς ἀκολουθούσης πέτρας: ἡ πέτρα δὲ ἦν ὁ Χριστός.

10:5ἀλλ' οὐκ ἐν τοῖς πλείοσιν αὐτῶν εὐδόκησεν ὁ θεός, κατεστρώθησαν γὰρ ἐν τῇ ἐρήμῳ.

10:1For I would not have you ignorant, brethren, that our fathers were all under the cloud: and all passed through the sea. [n. 517]

10:2And all in Moses were baptized, in the cloud and in the sea:

10:3And all did eat the same spiritual food: [n. 519]

10:4And all drank the same spiritual drink (and they drank of the spiritual rock that followed them: and the rock was Christ).

10:5But with most of them God was not well pleased: for they were overthrown in the desert. [n. 521]

---

517. Superius monuit abstinere ab idolothitis, primo propter vitandum scandalum fratrum infirmorum, cap. VIII, secundo propter exemplum suum, qui abstinet propter alios ab acceptione sumptuum, c. IX, hic, tertio, monet ad idem ex consideratione poenae Iudaeorum in deserto idola venerantium, ubi, exemplo poenae istorum,

primo monet abstinere a perpetratione peccatorum similium;

secundo specialiter a comestione idolis immolatorum, ibi **propter quod, charissimi, fugite ab idolorum cultura**, et cetera.

In prima,

primo ostendit quod antiquitus Iudaeis contigit;

secundo propter quod, quia non propter se tantum, sed propter nos corrigendos ita evenit **haec autem in figura facta sunt nostri**, etc.;

tertio, ut exemplo eorum caveant, concludit, ibi **itaque qui se existimat stare**, et cetera.

Ergo poena timenda, causa memoranda, cautela adhibenda.

In prima,

primo ponit beneficia gratiae eis impensa existentibus in Aegypto;

secundo praestita in deserto, ibi **et omnes eamdem escam**, etc.;

517. Above he warned them to abstain from the food of idols, first in order to avoid the scandal of weaker brothers (chapter eight); second, because of his own example, who refrains from accepting living expenses for the sake of others (chapter nine). Here, by a third argument he warns them about the same thing from the consideration of the punishment of the Jews who venerated idols in the desert, where, by the example of their punishment,

he firsts warns them to refrain from committing similar sins;

second, he particularly warns against eating food sacrificed to idols, where he says, **wherefore, my dearly beloved, flee from the service of idols** (1 Cor 10:14).

In the first part,

he first shows what befell the Jews in ancient times;

second, the reason why, since it happened that way not only for them, but for our correction: **these things were done in a figure of us** (1 Cor 10:6);

third, so that they would be careful of the example of those people, he concludes at **wherefore, he who thinks that he stands** (1 Cor 10:12).

Therefore, the punishment should be feared, the reason remembered, and caution applied.

In the first part,

he first lists the benefits of grace allotted to them while living in Egypt;

second, he lists the even better things given to them in the desert, at **and all did eat the same**;

tertio flagella propter ingratitudinem inflicta, ibi **sed non in pluribus**, et cetera.

518. In prima tangit tria beneficia. Primum, in protectione nubis; secundum, in transitu Maris Rubri, ibi **et omnes mare transierunt**, etc.; tertium, in purgatione baptismatis, ibi **et omnes in Moyse**, et cetera.

Dicit ergo **nolo vos**, etc., quasi dicat: sic agendum est, sicuti monui. Non enim sufficiunt sacramenta Ecclesiae suscepta vobis postea peccantibus, sicut nec Iudaeis Dei beneficia, quin postea punirentur.

Nolo enim vos ignorare, et cetera. Hoc dupliciter legitur. Uno modo de bonis et malis communiter; alio modo de malis specialiter.

Primo modo sic: **nolo vos ignorare, fratres, quoniam patres nostri**, institutores fidei nostrae, **omnes**, tam boni quam mali, **sub nube** protegente **fuerunt**. Ex. XIII, 21: *Dominus praecedebat eos ad ostendendum viam per diem in columna nubis*, et cetera. Vel **sub nube**, id est, sub figura et umbra. Hebr. X, 1: *umbram habens lex futurorum*, et cetera. **Et omnes Mare** Rubrum, submersis hostibus, **transierunt**, non de una ripa ad ripam oppositam, sed ad eamdem, unde transierunt quemdam sinum maris. **Et omnes in Moyse**, id est, in ducatu Moysi, **baptizati sunt in nube et in mari**, id est, per visa signa illa purgati ab ignorantia; vel a vitiis per fidem, scilicet submersis Aegyptiis. Ex. XIV, 31: *timuit populus Dominum, et crediderunt Domino et servo suo Moysi*. Vel **baptizati sunt**, id est, signum baptismi receperunt. Nam baptismus constat ex aqua et spiritu. Io. III, 5: *nisi quis renatus fuerit ex aqua et Spiritu*. Nubes autem symbolum erat Spiritus, mare vero aquae, ut dicit Damascenus.

519. Deinde, cum dicit **et omnes eamdem escam spiritualem**, etc., post beneficia exhibita Israel de Aegypto exeunti, hic tangit beneficia exhibita in deserto. Et primo beneficium mannae; secundo beneficium aquae, ibi **et omnes eumdem potum**, etc.; tertio potus originem mirabilem, ibi **bibebant autem**, etc.; quarto, originis significationem, ibi **petra autem**, et cetera.

Dicit ergo **et omnes eamdem escam spiritualem manducaverunt**, manna scilicet de caelo. Vocat autem eam spiritualem, cum esset corporalis, quia miraculose fuit data; de hoc habetur Sap. XVI, 20: *panem de caelo praestitisti eis*. **Et omnes eumdem potum spiritualem**, scilicet aquam de petra. Num. c. XX, 8: *loquimini ad petram, et ipsa dabit vobis aquam. Percussit petram, et fluxerunt aquae*. **Bibebant autem de petra spirituali**, quae dicitur spiritualis propter effectum miraculosum, propter futuri signum.

third, he lists the scourges inflicted because of their ingratitude at **but with most of them, God was not well pleased**.

518. In the first section he refers to three benefits. First, the protection of the cloud; second; the crossing of the Red Sea, at **and all passed through the sea**; third, the purification of baptism, at **and all in Moses were baptized**.

Therefore he says **I would not have you**, as though saying: you should act as I have warned you. For the receiving the sacraments of the Church does not suffice for you when you sin afterwards, just as neither did the benefits of God keep the Jews from being punished afterward.

For I would not have you ignorant. This can be read two ways. In one way, about the good and the bad together; in another way, about the bad in particular.

The first way goes as follows: **I would not have you ignorant, brethren, that our fathers**, the founders of our faith, **were all**, both good and bad, **under the** protecting **cloud**. *The Lord went ahead of them to show the way by day in a column of cloud* (Exod 13:21). Or else, under the cloud could mean under figure and shadow. *The law having the shadow of future things* (Heb 10:1). **And**, once their enemies had drowned, **all passed through the** Red **Sea**, not from one shore to the other, but to the same one from which they crossed a certain bay of the sea. **And all in Moses**, that is, under the leadership of Moses, **were baptized in the cloud and in the sea**, that is, they were purged of ignorance by having seen those signs; or, they were purged of vices by faith, namely, in the drowning of the Egyptians. *The people of the Lord feared, and they believed in the Lord and his servant Moses* (Exod 14:31). Or, they **were baptized**, that is, they received the sign of baptism. For baptism depends upon water and the spirit: *unless someone has been reborn from water and the Spirit* (John 3:5). However, the cloud is the symbol of the Spirit, but the sea is the symbol of water, as Damascene says.

519. Next, when he says **and all did eat the same spiritual food**; after the benefits shown to Israel when leaving Egypt, here he traces the benefits shown in the desert. And first, the benefit of manna; second, the benefit of water, at **and all drank the same**; third, the drink's miraculous origin, at **and they drank**; fourth, the signification of this origin, at **and the rock**.

He says therefore, **and all did eat the same spiritual food**, namely, manna from heaven. But he calls it spiritual, although it was bodily, because it was miraculously given; and this is found in Wisdom: *you have given them bread from heaven* (Wis 16:20). **And all drank the same spiritual drink**, namely, water from the rock. *Speak to the rock and it will give you water. He struck the rock, and waters flowed out* (Num 20:8). **And they drank of the spiritual rock**, which is called spiritual because of the miraculous effect, for the sake of a sign of the future.

Petra *consequente eos*. Dupliciter intelligitur *consequente*, id est, satisfaciente voluntati eorum. Ps. LXXVII, 29: *desiderium eorum attulit eis*. Aquae enim ubique sequebantur eos. Is. XLVIII, 21: *aquam de petra produxit eis*, et cetera. Vel *consequente eos*, id est veritatem sequentem significante. *Petra autem erat Christus*, non per substantiam, sed per significationem. Matth. XXI, 42: *hic est lapis quem reprobaverunt*, et cetera.

520. Alio modo legitur de bonis breviter sic *nolo vos ignorare, fratres, quoniam patres nostri*, institutores fidei nostrae, omnes boni spiritualiter. Unde dicit: *patres nostri*, non illorum, *sub nube fuerunt*, sicut prius, *et omnes eamdem escam manducaverunt spiritualem*, id est, Corpus Christi in signo spiritualiter intellecto. Unde eamdem escam spiritalem manducaverunt, idem scilicet quod nos, sed aliam escam corporalem quam nos; et hoc quantum ad maiores in Christum credentes. Manducabant Christum spiritualiter, secundum illud: *crede, et manducasti*. *Et omnes eumdem potum biberunt*, scilicet Christi Sanguinem, in signo. Sic loquitur de signo et potu spirituali per fidem, non de corporali. *Bibebant autem de spirituali*, etc., sicut prius. Appetendus cibus et potus, quia sufficiens; unde dicit *omnes manducaverunt*, indeficiens, quia eumdem; utilis, quia potus et cibus spiritualis: quod notatur in ipso nomine spiritualis, et cetera.

521. Deinde, cum dicit *sed non in pluribus*, etc., post beneficia tangit flagella. Et primo offensam, secundo poenam, ibi *nam prostrati sunt*.

Dicit ergo *sed non in pluribus*, etc., quasi dicat: his omnibus beneficiis usi sunt Iudaei, *sed non in pluribus eorum beneplacitum est Deo*: in illis scilicet qui Deum offenderunt, sed tantum in duobus, scilicet Caleph et Iosue, quibus solis concessum est terram promissionis obtinere, Num. XIV, 24. Mal. I, 10: *non est mihi voluntas in vobis*.

The rock *that followed them*. There are two ways to understand *followed*, that is, satisfied their desire: *he gave to them their desire* (Ps 78:29). *He brought forth water out of a rock for them* (Isa 48:21). Or *that followed them*, that is, which signified the following truth. *And the rock was Christ*, not by his substance, but by signification: *here is the stone which the builders rejected* (Matt 21:42).

520. In another way it can be read as concerning the good, in a nutshell like this: *I would not have you ignorant, brethren, that our fathers*, the founders of our faith, were all spiritually good men. For which reason he says, *our fathers*, not theirs, *were under the cloud*, (the same interpretation as before), *and all did eat the same spiritual food*, that is, the Body of Christ spiritually understood as a sign. For which reason, they ate the same spiritual food, that is, the same as we eat, but a different bodily food than we eat; and this, meaning the ancestors who believed in Christ. They ate Christ spiritually, according to this: *believe and eat*. *And all drank the same spiritual drink*, namely the Blood of Christ, in a sign. Thus he speaks about a sign and a drink that through faith were spiritual, not bodily. *And they drank of the spiritual rock* (the same reading as before). This is the food and drink to seek, because it is sufficient: wherefore he says *all did eat*; unfailing, because they ate the same thing; useful, because it was spiritual food and drink: which is noted in the very word spiritual.

521. Next, when he says *but with most of them*, after the benefits he deals with the scourges. And first the offense; second, the punishment, at *for they were overthrown*.

Therefore he says *but with most of them*, as though saying: the Jews enjoyed all these benefits, *but with most of them God was not well pleased*: namely, the ones who offended God; and to only two men, Caleb and Joshua, was it granted to reach the promised land (Num 14:24). *I have no desire for you* (Mal 1:10).

Lecture 2

10:6Haec autem in figura facta sunt nostri, ut non simus concupiscentes malorum, sicut et illi concupierunt. [n. 522]

10:7Neque idololatrae efficiamini, sicut quidam ex ipsis: quemadmodum scriptum est: *sedit populus manducare, et bibere, et surrexerunt ludere.* [n. 524]

10:8Neque fornicemur, sicut quidam ex ipsis fornicati sunt, et ceciderunt una die viginti tria millia. [n. 526]

10:9Neque tentemus Christum, sicut quidam eorum tentaverunt, et a serpentibus perierunt. [n. 527]

10:10Neque murmuraveritis, sicut quidam eorum murmuraverunt, et perierunt ab exterminatore. [n. 528]

10:11Haec autem omnia in figura contingebant illis: scripta sunt autem ad correptionem nostram, in quos fines saeculorum devenerunt. [n. 530]

10:6ταῦτα δὲ τύποι ἡμῶν ἐγενήθησαν, εἰς τὸ μὴ εἶναι ἡμᾶς ἐπιθυμητὰς κακῶν, καθὼς κἀκεῖνοι ἐπεθύμησαν.

10:7μηδὲ εἰδωλολάτραι γίνεσθε, καθώς τινες αὐτῶν: ὥσπερ γέγραπται, Ἐκάθισεν ὁ λαὸς φαγεῖν καὶ πεῖν, καὶ ἀνέστησαν παίζειν.

10:8μηδὲ πορνεύωμεν, καθώς τινες αὐτῶν ἐπόρνευσαν, καὶ ἔπεσαν μιᾷ ἡμέρᾳ εἴκοσι τρεῖς χιλιάδες.

10:9μηδὲ ἐκπειράζωμεν τὸν Χριστόν, καθώς τινες αὐτῶν ἐπείρασαν, καὶ ὑπὸ τῶν ὄφεων ἀπώλλυντο.

10:10μηδὲ γογγύζετε, καθάπερ τινὲς αὐτῶν ἐγόγγυσαν, καὶ ἀπώλοντο ὑπὸ τοῦ ὀλοθρευτοῦ.

10:11ταῦτα δὲ τυπικῶς συνέβαινεν ἐκείνοις, ἐγράφη δὲ πρὸς νουθεσίαν ἡμῶν, εἰς οὓς τὰ τέλη τῶν αἰώνων κατήντηκεν.

10:6Now these things were done in a figure of us, that we should not covet evil things, as they also coveted. [n. 522]

10:7Neither become idolaters, as some of them, as it is written: *the people sat down to eat and drink and rose up to play.* [n. 524]

10:8Neither let us commit fornication, as some of them that committed fornication: and there fell in one day three and twenty thousand. [n. 526]

10:9Neither let us tempt Christ, as some of them tempted and perished by the serpents. [n. 527]

10:10Neither murmur, as some of them murmured and were destroyed by the destroyer. [n. 528]

10:11Now all these things happened to them in figure: and they are written for our correction, upon whom the ends of the world are come. [n. 530]

---

522. Superius ostendit quid antiquis Iudaeis contigit; hic ostendit quod non propter se tantum, sed propter nos corrigendos ita evenit. Ubi

primo ostendit quod propter nos corrigendos a peccato praedicta facta sunt;

secundo quod propter hoc etiam scripta sunt, ibi *haec autem omnia in figura*, et cetera.

In prima ostendit quod ideo facta sunt, ut cohibeamur a peccato, et

primo a peccato cordis;

secundo a peccato operis, ibi *neque idololatrae efficiamini*, etc.;

tertio a peccato oris, ibi *neque murmuraveritis sicut quidam*, et cetera.

523. In prima, primo deterret per poenam; secundo ex hoc dehortatur culpam, ibi *ut non simus concupiscentes*, etc.; tertio malos reducit ad memoriam, ibi *sicut et illi concupierunt*, et cetera.

Dicit ergo *haec autem in figura facta sunt nostri*, non ficta, sed vere facta. *In figura*, inquam, ideo scilicet nos considerantes illorum supplicia, *non simus concupiscentes malorum, sicut et illi concupierunt*, de quibus Ps. CV, 14: *concupierunt concupiscentiam in deserto*. Num. XI, 4 dicitur quod vulgus promiscuum flagravit desiderio carnium.

522. Above he showed what befell the ancient Jews; here he shows that it was not for them alone, but for our correction that it happened this way.

He first shows that the things mentioned happened for our correction from sin;

second, that because of this also these were written, at *now all these things happened to them*.

In the first part, he shows that these things happened for this, that we might be held back from sin:

first from the sin of the heart;

second from the sin of action, at *neither become idolaters*;

third, from the sin of the mouth, at *neither murmur, as some of them*.

523. In the first section, he begins by deterring through punishment; second, from this he urges against guilt, at *that we should not covet*; third he recalls the evildoers to memory, at *as they also coveted*.

Therefore he says *now these things were done in a figure of us*, not invented, but truly done. *In a figure*, I say, so *that we*, considering their sufferings, *should not covet evil things, as they also coveted*, about which it is said: *they coveted their desire in the desert* (Ps 106:14). It is also said that the common people were inflamed by the desire for flesh (Num 9:4).

Et notandum quod sicut in bonis longe melius est quod figuratur quam ipsa figura, ut regnum caelorum quam terra promissionis, ita in malis longe peius est quod figuratur, quam figura significans. Secundum autem Augustinum, illa supplicia quae sustinuerunt, figura Gehennae fuerunt, quae omni poena maior est. Haec autem pertinent ad sapientes inter Corinthios, qui desiderio carnes comedebant in idolio, et scandalizabant infirmos. Unde similes erant Iudaeis carnes desiderantibus in deserto, unde digni erant etiam simili poena.

524. Deinde, cum dicit *neque idololatrae*, etc., dehortatur peccatum operis, ubi tangit tria peccata. Primo idolatriae; secundo fornicationis, ibi *neque fornicemur*, etc.; tertio divinae tentationis, ibi *neque tentemus*, et cetera.

525. In prima, primo dissuadet idololatriae vitium; secundo deterret per exemplum, ibi *sicut quidam ex ipsis*, etc.; tertio explicat exemplum implicitum, ibi *quemadmodum scriptum est*, et cetera.

Dicit ergo *neque idololatrae efficiamini* idolothitis vescendo in venerationem idoli, vel scandalum infirmorum, *sicut quidam* illorum, supple idololatrae, fuerunt, Ex. XXXII, v. 4 et Ps. CV, 19: *et fecerunt vitulum in Horeb, et adoraverunt sculptile*, *quemadmodum scriptum est*. Ex. XXXII, 6: *sedit populus*, id est, quidam de populo, *manducare et bibere* coram idolo, quibus similes sunt qui comedunt idolothita, idola venerando, *et surrexerunt ludere*, id est, ludos facere, sicut choreas et huiusmodi, in venerationem idoli. Vel *surrexerunt ludere*, id est, idolum adorare, quod est simile ludo puerorum, qui faciunt imagines luteas.

526. Deinde, cum dicit *neque fornicemur*, etc., tangit peccatum fornicationis, ubi primo dissuadet tale peccatum; secundo deterret per exemplum culpae, ibi *sicut quidam*, etc.; tertio poenae, ibi *et ceciderunt una die*.

Dicit ergo *neque fornicemur*, ut quidam ex vobis, supra V, 1: *omnino auditur fornicatio inter vos, sicut quidam ex ipsis fornicati sunt*, cum Madianitis scilicet, Num. XXV, v. 1 ss., *et ideo ceciderunt una die viginti tria*, immo viginti quatuor *millia*, sed maior numerus non excludit minorem, unde non dicitur hic cum praecisione, vel forte vitium scriptorum est.

527. Deinde, cum dicit *neque tentemus Christum*, etc., tangit peccatum divinae tentationis, quod dissuadet, primo, verbo, secundo, exemplo, ibi *sicut quidam*, etc., tertio, supplicio, ibi *et a serpentibus*, et cetera.

Dicit ergo *neque tentemus Christum*, diffidendo de eius potentia, sicut illi qui in vobis desperant de

And it should be noted that just as in good things what is represented is a far better thing than the figure itself, like the kingdom of heaven is compared with the promised land; so also in bad things, the thing that is represented is far worse than the signifying figure. And according to Augustine, those punishments which they suffered were a figure of Gehenna, which is a greater punishment than anything. But here it has to do with the more knowledgeable ones among the Corinthians, who, out of desire, were eating meats in the temple of an idol, and they were giving scandal to the weaker ones. Wherefore, they were like Jews desiring meat in the desert, for which reason they were deserving of a similar punishment.

524. Next, when he says, *neither become idolaters*, he urges against sin of action, where he deals with three sins. The first is idolatry; the second, fornication, at *neither let us commit fornication*; the third, of divine temptation, at *neither let us tempt*.

525. In the first, he first advises against the vice of idolatry; second, he turns them away by an example, at *as some of them*; third he explains what is implied in the example, at *as it is written*.

Therefore he says, *neither become idolaters*, gorging on the food of idols in honor of idols, or a scandal to the weak, *as some*, i.e., idolaters, were to those people: *and they made a calf in Horeb, and they adored a carved thing* (Exod 32:4; Ps 106:19). *As it is written: the people sat down*, that is, certain of the people, *to eat and drink* before the idol, like those who eat the food of idols in veneration of idols, *and rose up to play*, that is to have games, like dances and things of that nature, in veneration of this idol. But they *rose up to play*, that is, to adore the idol, which is like the play of children, who make pretend things out of mud.

526. Next, when he says, *neither let us commit fornication*, he touches on the sin of fornication, where first he urges them to avoid such a sin; second, he deters them by the example of guilt, at *as some*; third, by the example of their punishment, at *and there fell in one day*.

Therefore he says *neither let us commit fornication*, as certain among you do—as seen above: *it is absolutely heard that there is fornication among you* (1 Cor 5:1)—*as some of them committed fornication* with the Midianites, that is (Num 25:1ff), *and there fell in one day three and twenty*, or rather four and twenty *thousand*; but a greater number does not exclude a smaller one, which is why it is not said here with precision, or perhaps there is a defect in the writings.

527. Next, when he says *neither let us tempt Christ*, he refers to the sin of testing God, which he urges against first, in word; second, in example, at *as some of them*; third, by punishment, at *and perished by the serpents*.

Therefore he says *neither let us tempt Christ*, by distrusting his power, like those among you who disbelieve in

resurrectione, *sicut quidam eorum tentaverunt* Deum vel Christum in Moyse, dicentes: *numquid poterit parare mensam in deserto? Et* ideo *a serpentibus perierunt*, donec scilicet serpens aeneus erectus est, ad cuius aspectum sanabantur. De hoc habetur Num. XXI, 8 s., et Deut. VI, 16: *non tentabis Dominum Deum tuum.*

528. Deinde, cum dicit *neque murmuraveritis*, etc., post peccatum cordis et operis dehortatur peccatum oris. Ubi primo dissuadet murmurationis vitium; secundo adducit quosdam in exemplum, et primo culpae, ibi *sicut quidam*, etc.; secundo poenae, ibi *et perierunt a serpentibus*.

Dicit ergo *neque murmuraveritis* contra me, vel minores contra maiores. Sap. I, 11: *custodite vos a murmuratione. Sicut quidam eorum murmuraverunt* contra Moysen. Num. c. XVI, 41: *murmuravit omnis congregatio filiorum Israel contra Moysen, et* ideo *perierunt ab exterminatore*, ab angelo scilicet, qui extra terminos terrae eos percussit. Bar. c. III, 19: *exterminati sunt, et ad Inferos descenderunt.*

529. Notandum super illud: *in Moyse baptizati sunt*, quod Damascenus in libro, IV cap. *de Baptismo* distinguit novem genera baptismatum, accipiendo baptismata large. Primum est aqua diluvii, de quo habetur Gen. VI, 11 ss.; secundum Mare Rubrum, de quo Ex. XIV, 15; tertium aqua expiationis, de qua Num. XIX, 20 s.; quartum Baptismus Ioannis, de quo Matthaei III, 6; quintum baptismus de quo Christus baptizatus fuit, Lc. III, 21; sextum baptismus Spiritus Sancti super discipulos, Act. I, 5: *vos autem baptizabimini Spiritu Sancto*; septimum baptismus poenitentiae et contritionis, de quo Eccli. XXIV, 30: *qui baptizatur a mortuo*, etc.; octavum baptismus sanguinis, de quo Lc. XII, 50: *baptismo habeo baptizari, et quomodo coarctor, usque dum perficiatur*; nonum baptismus aquae et Spiritus, de quo Io. III, 5: *nisi quis renatus fuerit ex aqua et Spiritu Sancto.* Matth. ult.: *baptizantes eos in nomine Patris et Filii et Spiritus Sancti.*

530. Deinde cum dicit *haec autem omnia in figura*, etc., habito quod propter nos praedicta facta sunt, hic ostendit, quod propter nos etiam scripta sunt. Et primo quod in significatione, secundo quod in correctione, ibi *scripta sunt autem*, et cetera. Dicit ergo: *haec autem*, etc.; quasi dicat: ista contigerunt illis, et hoc non tantum propter sua peccata, non autem pro se, sed *omnia in figura*, nostri scilicet, *contingebant illis*: erat enim tunc tempus figurarum.

531. Deinde cum dicit *scripta sunt autem ad correptionem*, tangit quod scripta sunt ad correctionem nostram. Ubi implicantur tria incitantia ad correctionem nostram. Primo antiquorum exempla, quae notantur in Scripturis; secundo exemplorum causa, quae est correctio nostra; tertio, aetas novissima, quae est finis saeculorum.

the resurrection, *as some of them tempted* God or Christ in Moses by saying: *how could he ever lay a table in the desert? And* thus they *perished by the serpents*, until the brass serpent was raised up, at the sight of which they were healed (Num 21:8ff). *Do not test the Lord your God* (Deut 6:16).

528. Next, when he says, *neither murmur*, after the sin of the heart and of action, he deters them from the sin of the mouth. There he first dissuades them from the vice of murmuring; second he brings in certain people as an example, first of guilt, at *as some of them*; second, of punishment, at *and were destroyed by the destroyer*.

Therefore he says *neither murmur* against me, or inferiors against superiors. *Keep yourselves from murmuring* (Wis 1:11). *As some of them murmured* against Moses. All the congregation of the sons of Israel murmured against Moses, and thus they *were destroyed by the destroyer*, namely by an angel, who struck them outside the borders of the land. *They were cut down, and have gone down into hell* (Bar 3:19).

529. It should be noted about the fact that they *were baptized in Moses* (1 Cor 10:2), that John Damascene in *On Baptism*, Book Four, distinguishes nine kinds of baptism, taking baptism in the broad sense. First is the water of the flood, concerning which we read in Genesis (Gen 6:11ff); second, the Red Sea (Exod 14:15); the third is the water of expiation (Num 19:20ff); fourth the baptism of John (Matt 3:6); fifth, the baptism with which Christ was baptized (Luke 3:21); sixth, the baptism of the Holy Spirit upon the disciples: *but you will be baptized in the Holy Spirit* (Acts 1:5); seventh, the baptism of repentence and contrition: *he who washes after touching the dead* (Sir 34:30); eighth, the baptism of blood: *I have a baptism that I shall be baptised with, and how I am distressed until it shall be accomplished* (Luke 12:50); the ninth is the baptism of water and the Spirit: *unless someone is reborn of water and the Holy Spirit* (John 3:5); *baptizing them in the name of the Father and of the Son and of the Holy Spirit* (Matt 28:19).

530. Next he says *now all these things happened to them in figure*, and having held that the events mentioned were done for our sake, he here shows that for our sake also they were written. And first, what it is in signification; second, what it is in correction, at *and they were written*. Therefore he says: *now all these things*, as though saying: those things happened to them, and not only on account of their sins, and not for themselves, but *all these things happened to them in figure*, of us that is: for that was the time of figures.

531. Next when he says *and they are written for our correction*, he mentions that they were written for our correction. There he develops three things working toward our correction. The first is the examples of the ancients, which are noted in the Scriptures; the second is the reason for their examples, which is our correction; the third is the last age, which is the end of the world.

198

Dicit ergo *scripta sunt autem ad correptionem nostram*, quia *quaecumque scripta sunt, ad nostram doctrinam scripta sunt*, Rom. XV, 4. Nos, dico, *in quos fines saeculorum devenerunt*, id est, sexta aetas, quae est ultima aetas laborantium. I Io. II, 18: *filioli mei, novissima hora est*. Quia ergo in ultima saeculi aetate sumus, tot exemplis priorum corrigi debemus. Vel *in quos fines saeculorum devenerunt*, id est, in quibus per fidem et amorem Christi finita est saecularitas, quia Phil. III, 20 dicitur: *conversatio nostra in caelis est*. Unde temporalia non promittuntur tempore gratiae, sicut tempore legis. Unde nec in pactum deducuntur, sed adiiciuntur. Matth. VI, 33: *primum quaerite regnum Dei*, et cetera. Sed antiquitus erant in pactum. Is. I, 19: *si volueritis, et audieritis*, et cetera.

Ecce ergo exempla certa, quia *scripta sunt*; utilia, quia *ad correctionem nostram*; durabilia, quia *in quos fines*, et cetera.

Therefore he says *and they were written for our correction*, because *whatever things were written, were written for our instruction* (Rom 15:4). We, I say, *upon whom the ends of the world are come*, that is, the sixth age, which is the last age of those laboring (I John 2:18). *My little children, it is the last hour*. Because, therefore, we are in the last age of the world, we should be corrected by so many examples of those who went before. Or *upon whom the ends of the world are come*, that is, in whom by the faith and love of Christ, there is an end to secularity, for it is said: *our conversation is in heaven*. For which reason temporal things are not promised in the time of grace, like in the time of the Law. Wherefore neither are people marrying or given in marriage: *seek first the kingdom of God* (Matt 6:33). But our ancestors were marrying. *If you are willing and will hear* (Isa 1:19).

Thus here we have sure examples, which *are written*; useful ones, because they are *for our correction*; and lasting ones, because *upon whom the ends of the world are come*.

Lecture 3

10:12Itaque qui se existimat stare, videat ne cadat. [n. 532]

10:13Tentatio vos non apprehendat nisi humana: fidelis autem Deus est, qui non patietur vos tentari supra id quod potestis, sed faciet etiam cum tentatione proventum ut possitis sustinere. [n. 534]

10:12ὥστε ὁ δοκῶν ἑστάναι βλεπέτω μὴ πέσῃ.

10:13πειρασμὸς ὑμᾶς οὐκ εἴληφεν εἰ μὴ ἀνθρώπινος· πιστὸς δὲ ὁ θεός, ὃς οὐκ ἐάσει ὑμᾶς πειρασθῆναι ὑπὲρ ὃ δύνασθε, ἀλλὰ ποιήσει σὺν τῷ πειρασμῷ καὶ τὴν ἔκβασιν τοῦ δύνασθαι ὑπενεγκεῖν.

10:12Wherefore, he who thinks that he stands, let him take heed lest he fall. [n. 532]

10:13Let no temptation take hold on you, except such as is human. And God is faithful, who will not suffer you to be tempted above that which you are able: but with the temptation will also make the success, so that you may be able to bear it. [n. 534]

---

532. Habita primo Iudaeorum punitione, secundo punitionis ratione, hic tertio concludit, quod exemplo eorum debent a malo cavere; ubi

primo monet, ut caveant casum;

secundo cavendi docet modum, ibi *vos non apprehendat*, etc.;

tertio promittit firmum adiutorium, ibi *fidelis autem Deus est*, et cetera.

533. In primo implicat quatuor sollicitantia sapientem, scilicet multitudinem cadentium, cum dicit *itaque*, incertitudinem stantium, cum subdit *qui se existimat stare*, etc., necessitatem cautelae, cum addit *videat*, facilitatem ruinae, cum dicit *ne cadat*.

Dicit ergo *itaque*, etc., quasi dicat: illi et si beneficiis Dei usi sunt, nihilominus propter peccata perierunt. *Itaque* ex eorum consideratione, *qui existimat*, aliqua coniecturatione, *se stare*, id est quod sit in gratia et caritate, *videat*, diligenti attentione, *ne cadat*, peccando, vel alios faciendo peccare. Is. XIV, 12: *quomodo cecidisti, Lucifer?* Ps. XC, 7: *cadent a latere tuo mille*, et cetera. Ideo Eph. V, 15: *videte quomodo caute ambuletis*.

534. Deinde cum dicit *tentatio vos non apprehendat*, etc., docet modum cavendi causam, scilicet cavendo tentationem. Ubi primo docet aliquam tentationem fugiendam; secundo aliquam sustinendam, ibi *nisi humana*. Primo notificat, quia pulsat ut introeat: unde dicitur *tentatio*; secundo quia impugnat, ut praevaleat; unde subditur *non vos apprehendat*.

Dicit ergo *tentatio*, etc., quasi diceret: ne cadatis, *tentatio*, scilicet peccati, *non vos apprehendat*, trahendo in consensum peccati, *nisi humana*.

Hoc dupliciter exponitur. Uno modo de tentatione interiori mala, et tunc est permissio; quasi dicat: nulla peccati dilectio *vos apprehendat*, nisi forte de malis, sine qua vita humana non ducitur. Non enim est homo, qui

532. Having established first the punishment of the Jews, and second the reason for the punishment, here he concludes third, that by their example they should be careful about evil.

He first warns that they be careful of falling;

second, he teaches them how to be careful at *let no temptation take hold on you*;

third, he promises firm help at *and God is faithful*.

533. In the first, he lays out four things troubling the wise, namely, the great number of those falling, when he says, *wherefore*; the uncertainty of those standing, when he adds, *he who thinks that he stands*; the necessity of caution, when he adds, *let him take heed*; and the ease with which ruin comes, when he says, *lest he fall*.

Therefore he says, *wherefore*, as if saying: even those who have enjoyed the benefits of God, nevertheless have perished for their sins. *Wherefore*, from consideration of them, *he who thinks* by some conjecture *that he stands*, which is to say, that he is in grace and charity, *let him take heed*, by diligent attention, *lest he fall* by sinning or by making others sin. *How did you fall, Lucifer?* (Isa 14:12) *A thousand fall at your side* (Ps 91:7). *Thus see how you walk carefully* (Eph 5:15).

534. Next when he says *let no temptation take hold on you*, he teaches the manner of being wary, namely, by being careful of temptation. There he first teaches which temptation to flee; second, which one to endure, at *except such as is human*. First he makes known, for it knocks that it may enter: for this reason *temptation* is said; second because it attacks so that it might prevail; wherefore it is added, let it not *take hold on you*.

Therefore he says *temptation*, as though he had said: lest you fall, *let no temptation*, namely of sin, *take hold on you*, drawing you into consenting to sin, *except such as is human*.

This is explained in two ways. One way concerns an interior evil temptation, and then there is the consent; as though he said: *let no* love of sin *take hold on you*, except perhaps concerning those evils without which human life

semper faciat bonum et non peccet, III Reg. VIII, 46 et II Paralip. VI, 36.

Alio modo exponitur de tentatione exterioris boni. Et tunc est exhortatio, sic: **tentatio vos non apprehendat, nisi humana**, scilicet tribulationum praesentium propter Christum tolerantia. Augustinus: *propter Christum pati humana tentatio est.* Tob. XII, v. 13: *quia acceptus eras Deo, necesse fuit, ut tentatio probaret te.*

535. Deinde cum dicit **fidelis Deus**, ostendit paratum adiutorium in tentatione. Ubi commendat Deum adiutorem, quia dat nobis resistendi potentiam, quod notatur ibi **sed faciet cum tentatione**, etc.; perseverantiam, quod notatur ibi **ut possitis sustinere**, vere fidelis Deus, qui dat potentiam, ne vincamur, gratiam ut mereamur, constantiam ut vincamus.

Dicit ergo **fidelis** etc., quasi diceret: vos ad hoc hortor et moneo, quod potestis: *fidelis Dominus in omnibus verbis suis,* **qui non patietur vos tentari supra id, quod potestis**: quod utique posset diabolus, si permitteretur, quia *non est potestas super terram, quae ei comparetur,* Iob XLI, 24.

Et Is. XL, 29: *dat lasso virtutem.* Ideo Iac. I, 2: *omne gaudium existimate, fratres, cum in varias tentationes incideritis.* Augustinus: *qui dat diabolo tentandi licentiam, ipse dat tentatis misericordiam.* **Proventum**, inquam, **ita ut possitis sustinere**, ne deficiatis in lucta, sed vincatis: quod fit per humilitatem, ut dicit Augustinus. Illi enim non crepant in fornace, qui non habent ventum superbiae.

536. Notandum est super illud **qui se existimat stare**, etc., quod ad casum impellunt nos primo debilitas virium, sicut cadunt pueri, decrepiti, infirmi, Is. XL, 30: *in infirmitate cadent,* quod contingit per tepiditatem bene operandi et instabilitatem.

Secundo onus peccatorum sicut cadunt asini sub onere nimio, Ps. XXXV, 13: *ceciderunt qui operantur iniquitatem,* quod contingit per negligentiam poenitendi: quia peccatum, quod per poenitentiam, et cetera.

Tertio multitudo trahentium, sicut arbor vel domus multis trahentibus deorsum cadit, supra: **neque fornicemur**, etc., quod contingit per impulsum hostium.

Quarto lubricitas viarum, sicut incauti cadunt in lubrico, Eccli. XXVIII, 30: *attende ne forte labaris in lingua, et cadas, et in conspectu,* etc., quod contingit per incautam custodiam sensuum.

Quinto varietas offendiculorum, sicut avis capta in medio laqueorum, Prov. XIX, 8: *hi in curribus,* et cetera.

cannot be lived. For there is no man who always does good and does not sin (1 Kgs 8; 2 Chr 6:36).

In another way it can be explained about the temptation of an exterior good. And then there is an exhortation, as follows: **let no temptation take hold on you, except such as is human**, namely, tolerance of present tribulations for Christ's sake. Augustine says: *human temptation is to be suffered for Christ's sake: because you had been accepted by God, it was necessary that temptation should test you* (Tob 12:13).

535. Next when he says **God is faithful**, he shows the ready help in temptation. He commends God as help, because he gives us the power to resist, which is noted at **but with the tempation will also make the success**; he also gives us perseverance, which is noted at **so that you may be able to bear it**; truly faithful is God, who gives us power so that we may not be vanquished, grace so that we may merit, constancy so that we may conquer.

Therefore he says **faithful**, as though he were saying: I urge you and I advise you for this, what you are able to do: *the Lord is faithful in all his words,* **who will not suffer you to be tempted above that which you are able**: because the devil certainly could, if he were permitted, *because there is no power upon the earth that compares to him* (Job 41:24).

And *he gives strength to the weary* (Isa 40:29). Therefore *consider it all joy, brothers, when you meet with various temptations* (Jas 1:2). Augustine says: *he who gives the devil permission to tempt, is the very one who gives mercy to the tempted.* **The success**, I say, **so that you might be able to bear it**, so that you may not sink in grief, but rather you may overcome: which is done by humility, as Augustine says. For they do not crackle in the furnace who do not have the wind of pride.

536. It should be noted concerning **he who thinks that he stands**, that we are impelled to fall first by the feebleness of our strength, in the way that children, the aged, and the weak fall: *they will fall in their weakness* (Isa 40:30), which happens by instability and a lukewarmness for acting well.

Second, by the burden of sins, in the way that donkeys fall under burdens too heavy: *those who work iniquity have fallen* (Ps 36:12), which happens by neglecting repentance: because sin, which by penance, etc.

Third, by the great number of people pulling us down, in the way that a tree or a house falls by many people pulling on it, as said above: **neither let us commit fornication**, which happens by the incitement of the enemy.

Fourth, by the slipperiness of the path, in the way that the careless fall on a slippery floor: *take heed lest perhaps you slip with your tongue, and fall and in the sight of your enemies* (Sir 28:30), which happens by careless guarding of the senses.

Fifth, by different kinds of stumbling blocks, in the way that a bird is caught in the middle of many snares: *some trust*

Prov. XXIV, 16: *septies in die cadit iustus*, quod contingit per corruptionem creaturarum.

Sexto ignorantia agendorum, sicut caeci cadunt de facili, Matth. XV, 14: *si caecus caeco ducatum praestet*, etc., quod contingit per negligentiam addiscendi necessaria.

Septimo exempla cadentium, sicut angeli ad exemplum Luciferi, Ps. XC, 7: *cadent a latere tuo mille*, et cetera. Prov. XXV, 26: *fons turbatus pede et vena corrupta iustus cadens coram impio*, quod contingit per imitationem malorum.

Octavo ponderositas corporum, corpus enim quod corrumpitur aggravat animam, sicut lapis in collo natantis, Iob XIV, 18: *mons cadens defluit*, quod contingit per carnis fomentum superfluum.

in chariots (Ps 20:7). *The just man falls seven times a day* (Prov 24:16), which happens by the corruption of creation.

Sixth, by the ignorance of what should be done, in the way that the blind fall easily: *if the blind lead the blind* (Matt 15:14), which happens by neglecting to learn the necessary things.

Seventh, by the example of others falling, in the way that the angels fell after the example of Lucifer: *a thousand fall at your side* (Ps 91:7). *A just man falling down before the wicked is a fountain stirred up by the foot, and a ruined spring* (Prov 25:26), which happens by the imitation of the wicked.

Eighth, the weightiness of bodies, for the body that is corrupted drags down the soul, in the way that a stone around the neck of someone swimming does: *a mountain falling melts away* (Job 14:18), which happens by excess tinder in the flesh.

Lecture 4

^{10:14}Propter quod, carissimi mihi, fugite ab idolorum cultura: [n. 537]

^{10:15}ut prudentibus loquor, vos ipsi judicate quod dico. [n. 539]

^{10:16}Calix benedictionis, cui benedicimus, nonne communicatio Sanguinis Christi est? et panis quem frangimus, nonne participatio Corporis Domini est? [n. 541]

^{10:17}Quoniam unus panis, unum corpus multi sumus, omnes qui de uno pane participamus. [n. 542]

^{10:14}Διόπερ, ἀγαπητοί μου, φεύγετε ἀπὸ τῆς εἰδωλολατρίας.

^{10:15}ὡς φρονίμοις λέγω: κρίνατε ὑμεῖς ὅ φημι.

^{10:16}τὸ ποτήριον τῆς εὐλογίας ὃ εὐλογοῦμεν, οὐχὶ κοινωνία ἐστὶν τοῦ αἵματος τοῦ Χριστοῦ; τὸν ἄρτον ὃν κλῶμεν, οὐχὶ κοινωνία τοῦ σώματος τοῦ Χριστοῦ ἐστιν;

^{10:17}ὅτι εἷς ἄρτος, ἓν σῶμα οἱ πολλοί ἐσμεν, οἱ γὰρ πάντες ἐκ τοῦ ἑνὸς ἄρτου μετέχομεν.

^{10:14}Wherefore, my dearly beloved, flee from the service of idols. [n. 537]

^{10:15}I speak as to the prudent: you yourselves judge what I say. [n. 539]

^{10:16}The chalice of benediction which we bless, is it not the communion of the Blood of Christ? And the bread which we break, is it not the partaking of the Body of the Lord? [n. 541]

^{10:17}For we, being many, are one bread, one body: all that partake of one bread. [n. 542]

---

537. Superius ex consideratione Iudaeorum poenae monuit abstinere a perpetratione peccatorum similium, hic specialiter monet cavere a comestione idolis immolatorum. Ubi

primo ponit commonitionem cavendi ab idolothitis;

secundo subdit causam commonitionis, ibi *quid ergo dico*, etc.;

tertio docet modum cavendi a dictis, ibi *omne quod in macello venit, manducate*, et cetera.

In prima cavere ab idolothitorum comestione monet,

primo ex timore poenae consimilis;

secundo ex communione sancti altaris, ibi *ut prudentibus loquor*, etc.;

tertio ex similitudine sacrificii legalis, ibi *videte Israel secundum carnem*, et cetera.

538. In prima, ut eius obediant dictis, primo arguit inferendo, cum dicit *propter quod*; secundo allicit blandiendo, cum subdit *charissimi mei*; tertio instruit exhortando, cum addit *fugite*, et cetera.

Dicit ergo *propter quod*, etc., quasi diceret: quia sacramenta sola non salvant, et qui cadit punitur, et auxilium Dei non deest, *propter quod, charissimi mei, fugite ab idolorum cultura*, id est, ab omni idoli veneratione. Glossa: *ideo hos Apostolus hortatur fugere ab idololatriae superstitione, vel ne sapientes comedant idolothita cum offendiculo infirmorum quibus idololatrare viderentur; vel ne ipsi infirmi idolatrae sint, edendo in idoli veneratione.* **Fugite** ergo *ab idolorum cultura*, vel putativa, quo ad esum sapientium; vel vera quo ad esum infirmorum.

537. Above, by the consideration of the punishment of the Jews, he warned them to refrain from committing similar sins; here he warns them especially to be careful about eating the foods sacrificed to idols.

He first sets forth the admonition to beware of the food of idols;

second, he offers the reason for this admonition at *what then? Do I say* (1 Cor 10:19);

third, he teaches the way of being careful from what has been said, at *whatever is sold in the market, eat* (1 Cor 10:25).

In the first part, he warns to beware of eating the food of idols,

first, out of fear of a comparable punishment;

second, by the sharing of the holy altar, at *I speak as to the prudent*;

third, from a comparison to the sacrifice of the law, at *behold Israel according to the flesh* (1 Cor 10:18).

538. In the first part, so that they will obey his commands, first he argues by inference when he says *wherefore*; second, he wins them over by sweet words, when he calls them *my dearly beloved*; third he instructs by exhorting, when he adds, *flee*.

Therefore he says *wherefore*, as though he were saying: because the sacraments alone do not save, and whoever falls is punished, and the help of God is not lacking, *wherefore, my dearly beloved, flee from the service of idols*, that is from all honoring of an idol. The Gloss says: *therefore the Apostle urges them to fly from the superstition of idolatry, whether lest wise men should eat the food of idols as a stumbling block for the weak to whom they seemed to be worshiping idols; or lest those very weak ones should be idol-worshippers, by eating in honor of idols.* Therefore, *flee from the service of idols*, whether apparent, as when the wise eat; or actual, as when the weak eat.

539. Deinde cum dicit *ut prudentibus loquor*, etc., monet cavere ab idolothitorum comestione ex communione sacramenti altaris. Ubi

primo quod dicturus est supponit eorum iudicio;

secundo ostendit quid est illud, scilicet quod per communionem Eucharistiae efficimur unum cum Christo, ibi *calix benedictionis*, etc.;

tertio probat, quod ita est, quod omnes sumus unum in corpore eius mystico, ibi *quoniam unus panis*, et cetera.

540. Dicit ergo *ut prudentibus*, etc.; quasi dicat: ut fugiatis *loquor* vobis *ut prudentibus*. Vel sic *loquor* vobis altum quid, scilicet quod sequitur *ut prudentibus*. Vel sic: *loquor* infirmis, scilicet qui sunt inter vos, ut supra locutus sum prudentibus. Et ideo, *vos ipsi*, maiores, *iudicate quod dico* Iob XXXI, 13: *si contempsi subire iudicium cum servo meo*.

541. *Iudicate*, inquam, hoc quod sequitur *calix benedictionis*, id est, potus calicis, per quem participantes benedicuntur, Lc. XXII, 20: *similiter et calicem postquam caenavit, dicens: hic calix*, et cetera. *Cui benedicimus*, id est, quod nos fideles exaltamus credendo et gratias agendo; vel *cui benedicimus*, id est, quem nos sacerdotes consecramus; *nonne communicatio Sanguinis Christi est?* Faciens nos unum cum ipso, secundum illud Augustini: *nec tu me mutabis in te, sicut cibum carnis tuae, sed tu mutaberis in me*.

Est ergo sua ratio talis: sicut participans calicem Domini fit unum cum eo, sic participans calicem daemoniorum fit unum cum eis; sed daemonum unitas est maxime fugienda, ergo et participatio idolothitorum in eorum veneratione. Et ideo fugite ab idolorum cultura.

Et panis quem frangimus, id est, sumptio panis fracti in altari, *nonne participatio Corporis Domini est?* Faciens nos unum cum Christo: quia sub specie panis sumitur Corpus Christi.

542. Deinde cum dicit *quoniam unus panis*, etc., ostendit, quod omnes sumus unum in corpore eius mystico. Ubi proponit primo unitatem, secundo subdit unitatis rationem, ibi *omnes qui de uno*, et cetera. In primo tangit duplicem unitatem: primam incorporationis, qua in Christum transformamur, cum dicit *unus panis*, et cetera. Aliam vitae et sensus, quam a Christo capite accipimus, cum addit *et unum corpus*, et cetera.

Dicit ergo *quoniam unus*, etc., quasi dicat: per hoc patet, quod unum sumus cum Christo, *quoniam unus panis*, unione fidei, spei et caritatis, et *unum corpus multi sumus*, per subministrationem operum caritatis. Corpus scilicet illius capitis, qui est Christus. *Multi*, dico, scilicet omnes, *qui de uno pane*, id est Corporis Christi, et de uno calice, id est Sanguine, *participamus*, digna

539. Next when he says *I speak as to the prudent*, he warns them to be wary of eating the food of idols because of the sharing of the sacrament of the altar.

He first guesses what will be said by their own judgment;

second, he shows what this is, namely, that by sharing the Eucharist, we are made one with Christ at *the chalice of benediction*;

third, he proves that this is the way it is, that we all are one in his mystical body, at *for we, being many, are one bread*.

540. Therefore he says *as to the prudent*, as though saying: *I speak* to you *as to the prudent*. Or like this: *I speak* to you something from above, namely, what comes after, *as to the prudent*. Or like this: *I speak* to those among you who are weak, as I have spoken above *to the prudent*. And thus, *you yourselves*, greater ones, *judge what I say*: *if I have scorned to go to judgment with my servant* (Job 31:13).

541. *Judge*, he says, what follows *the chalice of benediction*, that is, the drink in the chalice, by which those partaking are blessed: *in the same way he took the chalice also after he had eaten, saying: this is the chalice* (Luke 22:20). *Which we bless*, that is, which we the faithful exalt by believing and giving thanks; or *which we bless*, that is, which we priests consecrate; *is it not the communion of the Blood of Christ?* Making us one with him, according to Augustine: *nor do you change me into you, like the food of your flesh, but rather you are changed into me*.

Here, therefore is his reason: just as someone partaking in the chalice of the Lord is made one with him, so also someone partaking in the chalice of demons becomes one with them; but union with demons is most greatly to be fled from, therefore also partaking of the food of idols in veneration of them. And thus, fly from the worship of idols.

And the bread which we break, that is, the receiving of the bread broken on the altar, *is it not a participation of the Body of the Lord?* Making us one with Christ: because under the species of bread the Body of Christ is received.

542. Next when he says *for we, being many, are one bread*, he shows that we all are one in his mystical body. There he first sets forth unity; second, he gives the reason for the unity, at *all that partake of one*. In the first, he deals with unity in two ways: the first is unity of incorporation, by which we are transformed into Christ, when he says *one bread*. The second is unity of life and sense, which we have received from Christ our head, where he adds, *one body*.

He says therefore *for we are one bread*, as though saying: by this it is clear, that we are one with Christ, *for we are one bread*, by the union of faith, hope, and charity, and *we being many, are one body*, by our working under him the works of charity. Namely, the body of this head, which is Christ. I say *many*, that is, all, who *of one bread*, that is the Body of Christ, and of one chalice, that is his Blood,

participatione, scilicet spirituali, non tantum sacramentali. Augustinus: *accipite, quia unus panis et unum corpus Ecclesia Christi dicitur, pro eo quod sicut unus panis ex multis granis, et unum corpus ex multis membris componitur, sic Ecclesia Christi ex multis fidelibus caritate copulatis connectitur.* De ista unitate infra cap. XII dicitur.

543. Hic quaeritur super illo **omnes in Moyse baptizati**. Glossa: *per visa illa legalia purgati.*

Contra, legalia non iustificabant.

Respondeo. Iustificabant dispositive a remotis, non causative, quia per modum signi, non causae.

544. Item super illud **petra autem erat Christus**, Glossa: *non petra dedit aquas, sed Christus.*

Contra Num. XX, 8: *loquimini ad petram, et ipsa dabit vobis aquas.*

Respondeo. Petra dabat originaliter, non effective.

545. Item super illud **omnes eamdem escam**, Glossa: *si quis manducaverit ex hoc pane, non morietur in aeternum, scilicet qui manducat corde, non qui premit ore.*

Contra: ergo non oportet sacramentaliter manducare.

Respondeo. Non qui premit ore, solum scilicet.

546. Item super illud **eumdem potum spiritualem**, Glossa: *idem est effectus in illis sacramentis, sed non tantum quantum in nostris.*

Contra, sacramenta vetera non efficiebant quod figurabant.

Respondeo. Idem est effectus, sed aliter: nam illorum per modum signi: nostrorum per modum causae.

547. Item super illud **haec autem in figura facta sunt**, Glossa: *omnes poenae minores sunt Gehenna.*

Contra, carentia visionis Dei maior est, quam Gehenna, secundum Chrysostomum.

Respondeo. Loquitur de poenis temporalibus.

548. Item super illud **qui stat, videat ne cadat**, Glossa: *non quod sit aliquis sine casu.*

Contra, multi sunt sine mortali.

Respondeo. Duplex est casus, unus a Domino per mortale, alter in Domino per veniale.

549. Item super illud **fidelis Deus**, Glossa: *qui dat tentandi diabolo licentiam, dat tentatis misericordiam.*

Contra, quod fit de licentia, licite fit. Ergo licet diabolo tentare.

partake, by a worthy participation, namely, a spiritual one, not only a sacramental one. Augustine says: *receive, for the Church of Christ is called one bread and one body, for the fact that just as one bread is composed of many grains of wheat, and one body of many members, so the Church of Christ is constructed of many believers bound together by charity.* This unity is discussed below in chapter twelve.

543. Here it is asked about **all in Moses were baptized** (1 Cor 10:2). The Gloss has: *purified by having seen those things of the law.*

Against this: matters of the law did not justify.

I answer that they did not justify causatively, but dispositively, by what they removed, for they worked in the mode of a sign, not a cause.

544. Again, about **and the rock was Christ** (1 Cor 10:4), the Gloss says: *the rock did not give water, rather Christ did.*

Against this: *speak to the rock, and it will give you water* (Num 20:8).

I answer that the rock was giving as the source, not as the cause.

545. Again, about **all did eat the same spiritual food** (1 Cor 10:3), the Gloss says: *if someone ate of this bread, he will not die forever, namely, whoever eats with his heart, not who stuffs his mouth.*

Against this: then it is not necessary to eat sacramentally.

I answer that it means not who only stuffs his mouth.

546. Again regarding **the same spiritual drink** (1 Cor 10:4), the Gloss has: *the effect is the same in those sacraments, but not as great as in ours.*

Against this: the old sacraments did not effect what they represented.

I answer that the effect is the same, but with a difference: for theirs was by the mode of a sign: ours by the mode of a cause.

547. Again concerning **but these things were done in a figure** (1 Cor 10:6), the Gloss says: *all punishments are less than Gehenna.*

Against this: lacking the vision of God is a greater suffering than Gehenna, according to John Chrysostom.

I answer that he speaks of temporal sufferings.

548. Again, about **let him take heed lest he fall** (1 Cor 10:12), the Gloss says: *but there is no one who doesn't fall.*

Against this: many are without mortal sins.

I answer that there are two kinds of falls, one is falling away from the Lord by mortal sin, the other is falling in the Lord by venial sin.

549. Again, about **God is faithful** (1 Cor 10:13), the Gloss says: *the one who gives permission to the devil to tempt, gives mercy to the tempted.*

Against this: what happens by permission, happens licitly. Therefore the devil tempts licitly.

Respondeo. Licentia accipitur hic pro permissione, non pro concessione.

550. Item *vos ipsi iudicate*. Contra, non est inferiorum iudicare de factis superiorum.

Respondeo. Non debent iudicare iudicio superordinationis, sed licet iudicio discretionis.

551. Item super illud *benedicimus*, Glossa: *nos sacerdotes*.

Contra: quod minus est a maiori benedicitur.

Respondeo. In sacramento altaris benedictio sacerdotis fertur super terminum a quo, id est, super panem, non super terminum ad quem, id est, Corpus Christi.

552. Item *panis, quem frangimus*, et cetera. Contra: iam tunc non est ibi panis.

Respondeo. Ponitur significatum pro signo, id est, panis pro specie panis.

553. Item super illud *nonne participatio*, etc., Glossa: *per partes manducatur in sacramento, et manet integer in caelo*.

Contra: Christus sub sacramento est impartibilis.

Respondeo. Manducatur per partes sacramenti, non sui.

554. Item ibidem Glossa: *in illo sacramento Corpus suum et Sanguinem commendavit, quod est, fecit nos ipsos*.

Contra: non fecit nos Corpus Christi verum.

Respondeo. Quod id est cuius significatum, unde relatio est simplex.

I answer that permission is taken here for permitting, not conceding.

550. Again, *you yourselves judge*. Against this: inferiors shouldn't judge of things above them.

I answer that they shouldn't judge by a judgment of superordination, but they are allowed a judgment of discretion.

551. Again, about *which we bless*, the Gloss has: *we priests*.

Against this: what is lower is blessed by the greater.

I answer that in the sacrament of the altar, the blessing of the priest is directed toward the starting point, that is, the bread, not the ending point, that is, the Body of Christ.

552. Again, *the bread which we break*. Against this: at that time there is no longer bread there.

I answer that the thing signified is put in place of the sign, that is, the bread for the species of bread.

553. Again about *is not the partaking*, the Gloss has: *in the sacrament it is eaten in pieces, but it remains whole in heaven*.

Against this: Christ under the form of the sacrament cannot be divided into pieces.

I answer that the pieces of the sacrament are eaten, not pieces of him.

554. Again, the Gloss has in the same place: *in that sacrament he entrusted his Body and Blood, which means, he made us into them*.

Against this: he did not really make us the Body of Christ.

I answer that it is the signifying of it, for which reason, the relation is simple.

Lecture 5

¹⁰:¹⁸Videte Israël secundum carnem: nonne qui edunt hostias, participes sunt altaris? [n. 555]

¹⁰:¹⁹Quid ergo? dico quod idolis immolatum sit aliquid? aut quod idolum, sit aliquid? [n. 556]

¹⁰:²⁰Sed quae immolant gentes, daemoniis immolant, et non Deo. Nolo autem vos socios fieri daemoniorum:

¹⁰:²¹non potestis calicem Domini bibere, et calicem daemoniorum; non potestis mensae Domini participes esse, et mensae daemoniorum. [n. 558]

¹⁰:²²An aemulamur Dominum? numquid fortiores illo sumus? [n. 559]

¹⁰:²³Omnia mihi licent, sed non omnia expediunt. Omnia mihi licent, sed non omnia aedificat. [n. 561]

¹⁰:²⁴Nemo quod suum est quaerat, sed quod alterius.

¹⁰:¹⁸βλέπετε τὸνἸσραὴλ κατὰ σάρκα: οὐχ οἱ ἐσθίοντες τὰς θυσίας κοινωνοὶ τοῦ θυσιαστηρίου εἰσίν;

¹⁰:¹⁹τί οὖν φημι; ὅτι εἰδωλόθυτόν τί ἐστιν; ἢ ὅτι εἴδωλόν τί ἐστιν;

¹⁰:²⁰ἀλλ' ὅτι ἃ θύουσιν, δαιμονίοις καὶ οὐ θεῷ [θύουσιν], οὐ θέλω δὲ ὑμᾶς κοινωνοὺς τῶν δαιμονίων γίνεσθαι.

¹⁰:²¹οὐ δύνασθε ποτήριον κυρίου πίνειν καὶ ποτήριον δαιμονίων: οὐ δύνασθε τραπέζης κυρίου μετέχειν καὶ τραπέζης δαιμονίων.

¹⁰:²²ἢ παραζηλοῦμεν τὸν κύριον; μὴ ἰσχυρότεροι αὐτοῦ ἐσμεν;

¹⁰:²³Πάντα ἔξεστιν, ἀλλ' οὐ πάντα συμφέρει. πάντα ἔξεστιν, ἀλλ' οὐ πάντα οἰκοδομεῖ.

¹⁰:²⁴μηδεὶς τὸ ἑαυτοῦ ζητείτω ἀλλὰ τὸ τοῦ ἑτέρου.

¹⁰:¹⁸Behold Israel according to the flesh. Are not they that eat of the sacrifices partakers of the altar? [n. 555]

¹⁰:¹⁹What then? Do I say that what is offered in sacrifice to idols is anything? Or that the idol is anything? [n. 556]

¹⁰:²⁰But the things which the heathens sacrifice, they sacrifice to devils and not to God. And I do not want you to be made partakers with devils.

¹⁰:²¹You cannot drink the chalice of the Lord and the chalice of devils: you cannot be partakers of the table of the Lord and of the table of devils. [n. 558]

¹⁰:²²Do we provoke the Lord to jealousy? Are we stronger than he? [n. 559]

¹⁰:²³All things are lawful for me: but all things are not expedient. All things are lawful for me: but all things do not edify. [n. 561]

¹⁰:²⁴Let no man seek his own, but that which is another's.

---

555. Superius monuit abstinere a comestione idolothitorum, primo ex timore poenae consimilis, secundo ex communione altaris; hic tertio monet ad idem ex similitudine sacrificii legalis. Ubi primo excitat attentionem; secundo ostendit propositum, ibi **nonne qui edunt hostias**.

Dicit ergo **videte**. Hoc dupliciter legitur. Uno modo de sacrificiis Iudaeorum, alio modo de ritu gentilium. Primo modo hoc, quod dico **Israel**, est accusativi casus, alio modo vocativi. Primo modo sic, quasi dicat: multi unum corpus sumus, qui de uno pane, et de uno calice participamus. Et hoc patet per hanc similitudinem **videte Israel secundum carnem**, supple ambulantem, id est carnalibus sacrificiis deservientem. Hoc dicit ad differentiam Israel secundum spiritum. De utroque Rom. II, 28: *non enim qui in manifesto Iudaeus*, et cetera. **Nonne qui edunt hostias**, legales, **participes sunt altaris**, legalis? Sicut qui edunt Carnem Christi et Sanguinem, participes sunt corporis eius.

Secundo modo legitur sic: **videte**, o **Israel**, o vos qui estis Israel, spiritualis videntis, scilicet Deum; **videte**,

555. Above he warned them to refrain from eating the food of idols, first out of fear of a like punishment, second, by the sharing of the altar; here he advises the same thing in a third way, by the likeness to a sacrifice of the law. Here he first catches their attention; second he shows his aim, at **are not they that eat of the sacrifices**.

Therefore he says **behold**. This can be read in two ways. In the first, it is about the sacrifices of the Jews; in the other, it is about the rites of the gentiles. In the first way, so that **Israel** is in the accusative case; in the second way, it is in the vocative. Thus in the first reading, it is as if he says: we, being many, are one body, who partake of one bread and one chalice. And this is clear by that comparison, **behold Israel according to the flesh**; namely, walking according to the flesh, that is, serving carnal sacrifices. He says this to differentiate Israel according to the spirit. About both it is said: *for he is not a Jew who is one outwardly* (Rom 2:28). Are not they that eat of the sacrifices—the sacrifices of the law—partakers of the altar—the altar of the law? Just as the ones who eat the Flesh of Christ and his Blood, are partakers of his body.

The second way is read like this: **behold**, O **Israel**, O you who are of the spiritual Israel, because you see

inquam, ea quae sunt **secundum carnem**, id est, in ido-lolatriae ritu carnali. **Nonne qui edunt hostias**, idolis scilicet immolatas, **participes sunt altaris**, daemonum et idolorum? Quasi dicat: sic. Est ergo sua ratio talis: qui edunt hostias oblatas altari, participes sunt altaris. A si-mili qui edunt hostias immolatas idolis, participes sunt idolorum sive daemoniorum.

556. Deinde cum dicit **quid ergo dico**, etc., superius posuit monitionem cavendi ab idolothitorum comestio-ne, hic ponit causam admonitionis. Ponit autem qua-tuor causas quare debent ab idolothitis abstinere: primo propter vitandam daemonis societatem, secundo prop-ter vitandam sacrae communionis exclusionem, ibi **quia non potestis calicem Domini bibere**, etc., tertio propter vitandam Dei indignationem, ibi **an aemulamur Domi-num**, etc., quarto propter fratrum laesionem, ibi **omnia mihi licent**, et cetera.

557. In prima, primo ostendit per hoc, quod non di-cit hoc, eo quod alicuius virtutis reputet idolum, vel ido-lothitum; secundo, quod potius ideo, quia daemonibus est immolatum, ibi **sed quae immolant**, etc.; tertio, quod non vult eos esse socios daemonum, ibi **nolo autem vos socios**, et cetera.

Dicit ergo: **quid ergo?** Quasi dicat: moneo cavere ab idolothitis. Quid ergo dico? Id est, quid dicere videor hoc monendo? Numquid hoc, supple quod illud, **quod idolis est immolatum, sit aliquid**, vel alicuius virtutis, ut noceat, **aut quod idolum sit aliquid** veneratione di-gnum? Quasi dicat: non. Ps. CXXXIV, 17: *neque enim est spiritus in ore ipsorum*. **Sed** hoc potius dico quod **quae immolant gentes**, idolo, **daemoni immolant, et non Deo**. Ps. XCV, 5: *omnes dii gentium daemonia*. Deut. XXXII, 17: *immolaverunt daemonibus, et non Deo*.

Deinde cum dicit **nolo autem vos fieri**, etc., ostendit, quod non vult eos fieri socios daemonum, quod fieret si communicarent mensae idolorum. Et hoc est, quod dicit **nolo autem vos**, qui fideles estis, **socios fieri dae-monum**, edendo scilicet de his, quae idolis immolantur. II Cor. VI, 14 s.: *quae societas lucis ad tenebras, aut quae conventio Christi ad Belial?*

558. Deinde cum dicit **non potestis calicem**, et cete-ra. Ecce secunda ratio quare abstinendum est ab idolo-thitis, quae est talis: omne quod excludit a communione Corporis et Sanguinis Christi, vitandum est: comestio idolothitorum est huiusmodi; ergo vitanda est. Primo ergo ostendit, quod huiusmodi comestio excludit a com-munione Sanguinis Christi; secundo, quod et a commu-nione Corporis Christi, ibi **non potestis mensae Domini participes**, et cetera.

God; **behold**, I say, those things that are **according to the flesh**, that is, in the carnal rituals of idolatry. Are not they that eat of the sacrifice—that is, sacrificed to idols—partak-ers of the altar—the altar of demons and idols? As though he said: yes. Therefore his argument is as follows: those who eat sacrifices poured out on the altar, are partakers of the altar. By the same token, whoever eats sacrifices sacrificed to idols, is a partaker of idols and demons.

556. Next he says **what then? Do I say**; above, he set forth the warning to be wary of eating food of idols, and here he gives the reason for the admonition. But he gives four reasons why they should abstain from the food of idols; first in order to avoid the company of demons; sec-ond, in order to avoid being excluded from the sacred com-munion, at **you cannot drink the chalice of the Lord**; third, in order to avoid offending God at **do we provoke the Lord to jealousy**; fourth, in order to avoid injuring our brother, at **all things are lawful for me**.

557. In the first reason, he first shows by this, that he does not say this from the fact that he considers an idol to have any power, or the food of idols; second, that rather because it is sacrificed to demons, at **but the things which the heathens sacrifice**; third, that he does not wish them to be partners with demons, at **but I do not want you to be partakers**.

Then he says, **what then?** as though saying: I warn you to stay away from food of idols. **What then do I say?** That is, what do I seem to say by this warning? Surely not this, **that what is offered in sacrifice to idols is anything**, or has any power, that it may harm, **or that the idol is anything** worthy of veneration? As though he said: no. *For neither is there any breath in their mouths* (Ps 135:16). But rather I say this, that **the things which the heathens sacrifice** to an idol, **they sacrifice to devils and not to God**. *All the gods of the gentiles are demons* (Ps 96:4). *They have sacrificed to demons, and not to God* (Deut 32:17).

Next when he says, **I do not want you to be made**, he shows that he does not want them to become the coworkers of demons, which would happen if they shared the table of idols. And this is why he says **I do not want you**, who are members of the faithful, **to be made partakers with dev-ils**, by eating of those things which were sacrificed to idols: *what society does light have with darkness, or what agree-ment can there be between Christ and Belial?* (2 Cor 6:14).

558. Next when he says **you cannot drink the chalice**. Here is the second reason for abstaining from the food of idols, which is this: everything that shuts one off from the communion of the Body and Blood of Christ, must be avoided: eating the food of idols is one of these things; therefore it must be avoided. Therefore, first he shows that eating this kind of thing shuts one off from the communion of the Blood of Christ; second, it also shuts one off from the communion of the Body of Christ, at **you cannot be partakers of the table of the Lord**.

Dicit ergo *non potestis*, etc., quasi dicat: *nolo vos fieri socios daemoniorum*. Hoc autem ideo dicit quia *non potestis calicem Domini bibere*, potu spirituali, non sacramentali tantum, Ps. CXV, 13: *calicem salutaris accipiam*, *et calicem daemoniorum*, simul: et hoc quoad sacramentum Sanguinis. *Non potestis mensae Domini participes esse*, quoad sacramentum corporis, *et mensae daemoniorum*. Matth. VI, 24: *nemo potest duobus Dominis servire*.

Ecce ergo calix fructuosus, quia ad bibendum spiritualiter pretiosus, quia Domini specialiter purus et mundus, quia non datur immundis utiliter. Similiter potest dici de mensa.

559. Deinde cum dicit *an aemulamur Dominum*, etc., ecce tertia ratio, talis: omne illud quod provocat iram Dei, vitandum est; comestio idolothitorum est huiusmodi, ergo vitanda est. Primo ergo ostendit, quod Deus provocatur ex tali comestione; secundo, quod stultum est eum provocare, ibi *numquid fortiores illo*, et cetera.

Dicit ergo *an aemulamur*, id est, ad iram provocare volumus *Dominum*, comedendo idolothita? Vel sic *an aemulamur Dominum*, id est, invidemus ei, ut quasi in contemptum eius hoc faciamus? Deut. XXXII, v. 16: *provocaverunt eum in diis*. *Numquid*, quasi dicat: non debemus eum provocare. *Numquid illo fortiores sumus?* Quasi dicat: non. Iob IX, 19: *si fortitudo quaeritur, robustissimus est*. Fatuum est enim provocare fortiorem se.

560. Notandum super illud *nolo autem vos socios fieri*, quod est societas bona et mala, et utraque quadruplex.

Est ergo societas bona, prima personarum divinarum, de qua I Io. I, 3: *ut societatem habeamus cum Deo, et societas nostra sit cum patre et cum Filio eius Iesu Christo*. Et hoc exigit summa iucunditas, quia nullius rei sine socio iucunda est possessio. Secunda angelorum sanctorum, de qua Tob. V, 27: *credo enim, quod angelus Dei bonus comitetur ei*, et hoc exigit hominis dignitas. Hieronymus: *magna est dignitas animarum*, et cetera. Tertia virorum iustorum, de qua Gal. c. II, 9: *Iacobus et Ioannes dextras dederunt mihi et Barnabae societatis*, et hoc exigit nostra utilitas. Eccle. IV, 9: *melius est duos*, et cetera. Quarta beatorum, de qua Apoc. I, 9: *ego Ioannes socius vester et frater in tribulatione et regno*, et hoc exigit communis felicitas; quia si socii sumus passionis, erimus et consolationis, II Cor. I, 7.

Societas mala similiter quadruplex: prima a parte malorum, de qua Is. I, 23: *principes tui infideles socii*

He says therefore, *you cannot*, as though saying: *I do not want you to be made partakers with devils*. But he says this because *you cannot drink the chalice of the Lord*, with a spiritual drink, not only a sacramental one: *I will take the chalice of salvation* (Ps 116:13), *and the chalice of devils* at the same time: and this has to do with the sacrament of the Blood. *You cannot be partakers of the table of the Lord*—and this has to do with the sacrament of the Bod—*and the table of devils*: no one can serve two masters (Matt 6:24).

Here is the fruitful chalice, because it is precious for drinking spiritually, because it is the Lord's; it is especially pure and clean, because it is not given effectively to the unclean. The same thing is said of the table.

559. Next when he says *do we provoke the Lord to jealousy*, here is the third reason, thus: everything that provokes the wrath of God must be avoided; eating the food of idols is one of these things; therefore it must be avoided. Therefore he shows that God is provoked by that kind of eating; second, that it is stupid to provoke him, at *are we stronger than he?*

He says therefore *do we provoke*, that is, do we wish to provoke *the Lord* to anger, by eating the food of idols? Or like this: *do we provoke the Lord to jealousy*, that is, do we envy him, that almost in contempt of him we do this? *They provoked him by their gods* (Deut 32:16). *Are we stronger*, as though to say: we should not provoke him. *Are we stronger than he?* As though to say: no. *If you look for strength, he is the strongest* (Job 9:19). For it is foolish to provoke someone stronger than oneself.

560. It should be noted concerning *I do not want you to be made partakers*, that there is good and bad association, and either one is of four kinds.

The first good association, therefore, is the one we have with the divine persons, of which it is said: *that we may have fellowship with God, and our fellowship may be with the father and his Son Jesus Christ* (1 John 1:3). And this requires the greatest delightfulness, because the possession of no thing is delightful without someone to share it. The second is the association of the holy angels, of which it is written: *for I believe that a good angel of God accompanies him* (Tob 5:27), and this requires the dignity of man. Jerome says: *great is the dignity of our souls*. The third is the association of just men, of which it is said: *James and John gave to me and Barnabas their right hands in fellowship* (Gal 2:9), and this depends on our worth: *it is better that two should be together* (Eccl 4:9). The fourth is the association of the blessed, about which is written: *I John, your brother and your partner in tribulation, and in the kingdom* (Rev 1:9), and this requires shared happiness; for if we are sharers of the suffering, we will be sharers of the consolation as well (2 Cor 1:7).

There are likewise four kinds of bad association: the first, by association with evil men, about which is written:

furum. Haec est societas Herodis et Pilati in crucifixione Christi. Secunda hypocritarum, de qua Iob XXX, 29: *frater fui draconum et socius struthionum,* quae alas habere videtur et volare non potest. Haec est societas vulpis et lupi. Tertia daemonum, de qua Iob XVIII, 15: *habitent in tabernacula eius socii eius, qui non est.* Haec societas catti et muris, carnificis et bovis. Quarta damnatorum, de qua II Cor. c. VI, 14: *quae societas lucis ad tenebras?* Haec est societas incarceratorum in igne.

561. Deinde cum dicit **omnia mihi licent**, etc., ponitur quarta ratio talis: omne illud quod laedit proximorum salutem vitandum est; sed comestio idolothitorum est huiusmodi, ergo vitanda. Primo ostendit, quod talis comestio comedenti non proficit; secundo, quod alterum laedit, ibi **omnia mihi licent**, et cetera.

Dicit ergo **omnia mihi**, etc., quasi dicat: si illos peccare dicam, qui comedunt idolothita, non tamen dico cibos in se illicitos, quia **omnia** quae ad escam pertinent, **mihi licent**. Vel: et si **omnia mihi licent, sed non omnia expediunt**, id est, adiuvant me in cursu meo. Simile supra VI, 12. **Omnia mihi licent**, id est, et si omnia mihi licerent **sed non omnia aedificant** proximos, sed ea, quae caritatis sunt, supra VIII, 1: **scientia inflat, caritas aedificat**. Et quia non omnia aedificant, **nemo quod suum est quaerat tantum**, caritas enim non **quae sua sunt quaerit**, infra XIII, 5, **sed quod alterius**, id est, quod alteri proficit. Sed heu. Phil. II, 21 dicitur: *omnes quae sunt sua quaerunt.* Audiendus est ergo Apostolus, qui et docet verum, et monet bonum. Docet verum duplex, scilicet expedientiae sibi, quia **omnia licent, sed non expediunt**, et aedificationis aliis, quia **omnia licent, sed non omnia aedificant**. Monet bonum duplex, scilicet expedientiae sibi **nemo quod suum est quaerat**, et aedificationis aliis **sed quod alterius**.

your leaders are faithless, the partners of thieves (Isa 1:23). This is the partaking that Herod and Pilate had in the crucifixion of Christ. The second is the association of hypocrites, about which is written: *I was brother of dragons and the companion of ostriches* (Job 30:29), which seem to have wings but cannot fly. This is the companionship of the fox and the wolf. The third is the association of demons, of which it is written: *let the companions of him who is no longer, live in his tent* (Job 18:15). This is the companionship of cat and mouse, butcher and cow. The fourth is the society of the damned, about which is written: *what fellowship has light with darkness?* (2 Cor 6:14). This is the companionship of those imprisoned in fire.

561. Next when he says **all things are lawful for me**, he sets forth the fourth reason thus: everything that injures the salvation of my neighbor must be avoided; but eating the food of idols is that sort of thing, and therefore to be avoided. First he shows that this kind of eating does not profit the one eating; second, that it injures others at **all things are lawful for me**.

Therefore he says **all things are lawful for me**, as though he said: if I say that those people sin who eat the foods of idols, nevertheless I do not call the food illicit in itself, because **all things** that have to do with food **are lawful for me**. Or: **all things are lawful for me, but all things are not expedient**, that is, helpful to me in my race. The same thing is said above at (1 Cor 6:12). **All things are lawful for me**, that is, even if all things were lawful for me, **but all things do not edify** my neighbors, except those things which are of charity, as was said above: **knowledge puffs up but charity edifies** (1 Cor 8:1). And because not all things edify, **let no man seek** only **his own**— for as said below, charity **seeks not her own** (1 Cor 13:5)—**but that which is another's**, that is, what profits the other. But alas it is said: *all seek the things that are their own* (Phil 2:21). Therefore the Apostle must be heeded, who both teaches the truth and advises the good. He teaches a double truth, namely one's own expedience, because **all things are lawful . . . but all are not are expedient**, and the edification of others, because **all things are lawful . . . but all do not edify**. He advises a twofold good, namely, one's own expedience, **let no man seek what is his own**, and the edification of others, **but that which is another's**.

Lecture 6

10:25Omne quod in macello venit, manducate, nihil interrogantes propter conscientiam. [n. 562]

10:26Domini est terra, et plenitudo ejus.

10:27Si quis vocat vos infidelium, et vultis ire: omne quod vobis apponitur, manducate, nihil interrogantes propter conscientiam. [n. 564]

10:28Si quis autem dixerit: Hoc immolatum est idolis: nolite manducare propter illum qui indicavit, et propter conscientiam: [n. 565]

10:29conscientiam autem dico non tuam, sed alterius. Ut quid enim libertas mea judicatur ab aliena conscientia? [n. 567]

10:30Si ego cum gratia participo, quid blasphemor pro eo quod gratias ago? [n. 568]

10:25Πᾶν τὸ ἐν μακέλλῳ πωλούμενον ἐσθίετε μηδὲν ἀνακρίνοντες διὰ τὴν συνείδησιν,

10:26τοῦ κυρίου γὰρ ἡ γῆ καὶ τὸ πλήρωμα αὐτῆς.

10:27εἴ τις καλεῖ ὑμᾶς τῶν ἀπίστων καὶ θέλετε πορεύεσθαι, πᾶν τὸ παρατιθέμενον ὑμῖν ἐσθίετε μηδὲν ἀνακρίνοντες διὰ τὴν συνείδησιν.

10:28ἐὰν δέ τις ὑμῖν εἴπῃ, Τοῦτο ἱερόθυτόν ἐστιν, μὴ ἐσθίετε δι' ἐκεῖνον τὸν μηνύσαντα καὶ τὴν συνείδησιν

10:29συνείδησιν δὲ λέγω οὐχὶ τὴν ἑαυτοῦ ἀλλὰ τὴν τοῦ ἑτέρου. ἱνατί γὰρ ἡ ἐλευθερία μου κρίνεται ὑπὸ ἄλλης συνειδήσεως;

10:30εἰ ἐγὼ χάριτι μετέχω, τί βλασφημοῦμαι ὑπὲρ οὗ ἐγὼ εὐχαριστῶ;

10:25Whatever is sold in the markets, eat: asking no question for conscience's sake. [n. 562]

10:26The earth is the Lord's and the fullness thereof.

10:27If any of the unbelievers invites you, and you are willing to go: eat of any thing that is set before you, asking no question for conscience's sake. [n. 564]

10:28But if any man says: this has been sacrificed to idols: do not eat of it, for the sake of him that told it and for conscience's sake. [n. 565]

10:29Conscience, I say, not your own, but the other's. For why is my liberty judged by another man's conscience? [n. 567]

10:30If I partake with thanksgiving, why am I spoken ill of for that for which I give thanks? [n. 568]

---

562. Superius monuit cavere ab idolothitis, et posuit rationem quadruplicem suae monitionis: hic tertio docet modum cavendi a praedictis, ostendendo quomodo liceat edere, et quomodo non.

Primo ergo ostendit an liceat edere;

secundo quando non licet, *si quis autem dixerit*, etc.;

tertio quid in utrisque debent attendere, ibi *sive ergo manducatis*, et cetera.

In prima primo ponit duos casus in quibus licet idolothita comedere. Primus, quando comedit per se; secundus, quando cum aliis, ibi *si quis autem infidelium*, et cetera.

Vel primus, quando nescit idolis immolatum; secundus, quando non in proximi scandalum. In primo casu primo tangit comedendi licentiam, secundo comedendi praestat cautelam, ibi *nihil interrogantes*, et cetera.

563. Dicit ergo *omne quod in macello venit*, id est venditur, etc.; quasi dicat: quia licet edere, sed non expedit aliquando, ideo sic edite. *Omne quod in macello venit*, id est, venditur, *manducate*, si vultis. *Omnis enim creatura Dei bona, et nihil reiiciendum*, et cetera. I Tim. IV, 4. Vos, dico, *nihil interrogantes*, scilicet an sit idolis immolatum, vel non, et hoc *propter conscientiam*, astantis infirmi. *Domini est terra*, et cetera. Quasi dicat: hoc secure potestis facere, quia *Domini est terra, et plenitudo eius*, id est, omnia quibus terra impletur.

562. Above he warned them to beware eating the food of idols, and he has given four reasons for his admonition: here he teaches, third, the way to beware the abovementioned things, by showing how one is allowed to eat, and how not.

First therefore he shows whether it is licit to eat;

second, when it is not licit, at *but if any man says*;

third, what to attend to in either case at *therefore, whether you eat* (1 Cor 10:31).

In the first part he sets forth two cases in which it is permitted to eat the food of idols. The first, when someone eats for himself; second, when he is with others at *but if any of the unbelievers*.

Or the first case, when someone does not know that it was sacrificed to idols; the second case, when it does not scandalize one's neighbor. In the first case, he first refers to the permission to eat; second, he favors caution in eating at *asking no question*.

563. Therefore he says *whatever is sold in the market*, that is, everything that is sold; as though saying: because it is licit to eat, but sometimes not expedient, therefore eat like this. *Whatever is sold in the market*, that is, everything that is sold, *eat*, if you wish. *For every creature of God is good, and nothing is to be rejected* (1 Tim 4:4). You, I say, *asking no questions*, namely, whether it was sacrificed to an idol, or not, and this *for conscience's sake*, of assisting the weak. *The earth is the Lord's.* As though saying: you can do this securely, because *the earth is the Lord's and the*

Ps. XLIX, 10: *quoniam meae sunt omnes ferae*. Ambrosius hoc in loco: *non potest esse immundum, quod Domini est; sed omnes carnes sunt Domini, ergo de se mundae sunt et licitae*.

564. Deinde cum dicit **si quis autem vocat**, etc., ostendit quando licet comedere idolothita cum aliis, quando, si dantur in convivio, et ignoratur ab infirmis, quod sint idolis immolata. Ubi implicantur quatuor expedientia cuilibet convivae, scilicet ne sit impudens, se ingerendo, quod notatur ibi **si quis vocat vos**, quod non sit offendens in respuendo, quod notatur ibi **et vultis ire**, quod non sit onerosus in petendo, quod notatur ibi **omne quod vobis apponitur**, quod non sit indiscretus in loquendo, ibi **nihil interrogantes**.

Dicit ergo **si quis infidelium**, id est, gentilium. Nam cum Iudaeis comedere prohibitum est, XXVIII, qu. 1, c. *omnes*, ubi sic dicitur: *omnes deinceps, sive clerici, sive laici, Iudaeorum convivia vitent, nec eos ad convivium quisquam recipiat, quia cum Iudaei apud Christianos cibis communibus non utantur, indignum atque sacrilegum est eorum cibos a Christianis sumi*.

Si quis ergo **infidelium**, id est gentilium, **vocat vos** ad coenam, **et vultis ire**, id est placet vobis invitatio, **omne** comestibile **quod vobis apponitur, manducate**. Concessio est, non iussio. Lc. X, 8: *manducate quae vobis apponuntur*. Vos dico, **nihil interrogantes**, an sit immolatum idolis, vel non. Et hoc **propter conscientiam** infirmorum.

565. Deinde cum dicit **si quis autem dixerit**, etc., ostendit quando non licet comedere. Ubi assignat triplicem causam quare non licet comedere.

Primo propter alterius conscientiam;

secundo propter damnationem propriam, ibi **ut quid enim libertas mea**, etc.;

tertio propter imperitorum blasphemiam, ibi **si cum gratia participo**, et cetera.

566. Prima ratio talis est: nihil faciendum est scienter, quod laedat conscientiam eius qui facit, sed comestio idolothiti est huiusmodi; ergo nihil tale est faciendum. Primo ergo proponit idolothiti cognitionem; secundo dissuadet eius comestionem, ibi **nolite manducare**, etc.; tertio subdit huius rationem, ibi **propter illum qui indicavit**.

Dicit ergo **si quis autem dixerit**, etiam non interrogatus, **hoc est immolatum idolis, nolite manducare**; et hoc **propter illum, qui indicavit**, hoc esse immolatum idolis, ne scilicet credat te manducare sub veneratione idoli, non quod cibus de se sit immundus. Rom. XIV, 14: *scio et confido in Domino, quod nihil commune est per ipsum, nisi illi, qui existimat aliquid commune esse*. Sed

fullness thereof, that is all things with which the earth is filled. *For the wild beasts are all mine* (Ps 50:10). Ambrose says about this text: *what is the Lord's cannot be unclean; but all meats are the Lord's, therefore they are clean in themselves and licit*.

564. Next when he says **if any of the unbelievers invite you**, he shows when it is permitted to eat the food of idols with others, if it is served at a banquet, and it is unknown by the weaker ones that it had been sacrificed to an idol. Here four expediencies of this banquet are implied: namely, it should not be shameless, by crashing the dinner party, which is noted by **if any of the unbelievers invite you**; that you would not offend them by refusing, which is referred to at **and you are willing to go**; that you would not be burdensome by asking, which is noted at **any thing that is set before you**; and you should not be indiscreet in speaking, at **asking no questions**.

Therefore he says, **if any of the unbelievers**, that is, the gentiles. For with Jews it is forbidden to eat, (28, q. 1, c.) where it is said thus: *from now on, all, whether clergy, or laymen, must avoid the banquets of the Jews, nor may anyone receive them at his own dinner party, for since Jews do not enjoy sharing food with Christians, it is unfitting and a sacrilege for their food to be consumed by Christians*.

If therefore, **any of the unbelievers**, that is, gentiles, **invites you** to dinner, **and you are willing to go**, that is, this invitation pleases you, **eat** everything edible that is set before you. It is a concession, not a command. *Eat the things that are served to you* (Luke 10:8). I tell you, **asking no questions** about whether it was sacrificed to idols or not. And this for **conscience's sake**, namely, the conscience of the weak.

565. Next when he says **but if any man says**, he shows when it is not licit to eat. There he assigns three reasons why it is not licit to eat.

The first is because of the conscience of another.

second, because of one's own damnation, at **for why is my liberty**;

third, on account of the blasphemy of the inexperienced, at **if I partake with thanksgiving**.

566. The first reason goes as follows: nothing should be done knowingly which injures the conscience of him who does it, but eating the food of idols is this kind of thing; therefore nothing of the kind is to be done. First, therefore, he suggests investigating the food of idols; second, he recommends not eating it, at **do not eat**; third, he gives the reason for this, at **for the sake of him that told it**.

Therefore he says **but if any man says**, even when you have not asked, **this has been sacrificed to idols: do not eat**; and this **for the sake of him that told it** to you that it had been sacrificed to idols, lest he should believe that you are eating it out of veneration for the idol, not because the food is unclean in itself: *I know and I am confident in the Lord, that nothing is common in itself, except to someone*

etiam *propter conscientiam* aliorum infirmorum. *Conscientiam autem non tuam*, quae firma est, *sed alterius*, scilicet infirmi, II Cor. c. VI, 3: *nemini dantes ullam offensionem.*

567. Deinde cum dicit *ut quid enim libertas mea*, et cetera. Ecce iam secunda ratio, quae est talis: quod facit ad iudicium damnationis propriae vitandum est: sed comestio idolothiti cum scandalo proximi est huiusmodi; ergo talis comestio vitanda est. Et hoc est, quod dicit *ut quid*, etc., quasi dicat: nolite manducare propter conscientiam infirmi, *ut quid enim libertas mea*, id est, quod liberum mihi est, *iudicatur ab aliena conscientia?* Id est, mihi fit damnabile propter conscientiam alienam ratione scandali. Quasi dicat: si comedo cum alterius scandalo, sic ago ut reddam me damnabilem. Matth. XVIII, 6: *qui scandalizaverit unum de pusillis istis, expedit ei ut suspendatur mola asinaria*, et cetera. Ut quid ergo sic ago? Quasi dicat, male ago.

568. Deinde cum dicit *si ego cum gratia participo*, et cetera. Ecce ratio tertia talis: cavendus est casus in blasphemiam et vituperium aliorum; sed comedendo idolothitum, cum scandalo comedo sic; ergo, et cetera. Ubi primo tangit modum edendi debitum, secundo nihilominus blasphemiam insipientium, ibi *quid blasphemor*.

Dicit ergo *si ego cum gratia*, id est cum gratiarum actione, *participo*, id est, comedo. Sic enim semper sumendus est cibus, Io. VI, v. 11: *gratias agens benedixit et fregit. Quid blasphemor?* Ab imperitis dicentibus idololatrare. *Blasphemor*, inquam, *pro eo, quod gratias ago*, id est, quod gratias agendo participo. Rom. XIV, 16: *non ergo blasphemetur bonum nomen vestrum.*

who considers it to be common (Rom 14:14). But also *for conscience's sake*, namely, the conscience of other weaker ones. *Conscience, I say, not your own*, which is firm, *but the other's*, that is, the weaker man's: *giving offense to no one* (2 Cor 6:3).

567. Next he says *for why is my liberty*. Here we are at the second reason, which is this: whatever he does to the judgment of his own damnation must be avoided: but eating the food of idols when it scandalizes one's neighbor is this kind of thing; therefore, eating these things must be avoided. And this is because he says *why*, as though saying: do not eat for the sake of the weaker man's conscience, *for why is my liberty*, that is, that which is free to me, *judged* by a stranger's conscience? That is, it becomes damnable for me by reason of the scandal on account of the conscience of another. As though saying: if I eat with scandal to another, I act so as to render myself damnable: *whoever scandalizes one of these little ones, it would be better for him if a millstone were hung about his neck* (Matt 18:6). So why would I act this way? As though to say: I act wickedly.

568. Next he says *if I partake with thanksgiving*. Here is the third reason: one has to be careful of falling under the revilement and disparagement of others; but by eating the food of idols, I do eat with scandal; therefore, etc. Here he first touches on the due way of eating; second, foolish backbiting as well, at *why am I spoken ill of*.

Therefore he says, *if I partake*, that is, I eat, *with thanksgiving*, that is, with gratitude. For in this way food is always to be received: *giving thanks he blessed it and broke it* (John 6:11). *Why am I spoken ill of* by ignorant people saying I worship idols? *I am spoken ill of*, I say, *for that for which I give thanks*, that is, because I partake while giving thanks: *then let not our good be spoken ill of* (Rom 14:16).

Lecture 7

10:31Sive ergo manducatis, sive bibitis, sive aliud quid facitis: omnia in gloriam Dei facite. [n. 569]

10:32Sine offensione estote Judaeis, et gentibus, et Ecclesiae Dei: [n. 571]

10:33sicut et ego per omnia omnibus placeo, non quaerens quod mihi utile est, sed quod multis: ut salvi fiant. [n. 573]

10:31εἴτε οὖν ἐσθίετε εἴτε πίνετε εἴτε τι ποιεῖτε, πάντα εἰς δόξαν θεοῦ ποιεῖτε.

10:32ἀπρόσκοποι καὶ Ἰουδαίοις γίνεσθε καὶ Ἕλλησιν καὶ τῇ ἐκκλησίᾳ τοῦ θεοῦ,

10:33καθὼς κἀγὼ πάντα πᾶσιν ἀρέσκω, μὴ ζητῶν τὸ ἐμαυτοῦ σύμφορον ἀλλὰ τὸ τῶν πολλῶν, ἵνα σωθῶσιν.

10:31Therefore, whether you eat or drink, or whatever else you do, do all to the glory of God. [n. 569]

10:32Be without offense to the Jews, and to the gentiles, and to the Church of God: [n. 571]

10:33As I also in all things please all men, not seeking that which is profitable to myself but to many: that they may be saved. [n. 573]

---

569. Habito quando licet de idolothitis comedere et quando non, hic ostendit, quin in utroque debent intendere.

Primo respectu Dei, quia debent quaerere eius gloriam;

secundo quid respectu proximi, quia debent cavere eius offensam, ibi *sine offensione estote*, et cetera.

570. In prima, primo inducit actum multiplicem; secundo persuadet actuum intentionem debitam, ibi *omnia in gloria Dei*, et cetera.

Dicit ergo *sive ergo*, etc., quasi dicat: quia haec mala contingunt, *ergo sive manducatis, sive bibitis*, quae sunt opera necessitatis, *vel aliud quid facitis, omnia in gloriam Dei facite*, et cum invocatione Creatoris, ea intentione, ut Deus laudetur et glorificetur. Matth. V, 16: *sic luceat lux vestra coram hominibus*, et cetera. Col. III, 17: *omne quodcumque facitis in verbo aut opere, omnia in gloriam Dei facite*.

Augustinus in Ps. XXXIV, concione II, in fine: *haec si recte fiunt, laudes Dei sunt. Non ergo solum vox tua sonet laudes Dei, sed etiam opera tua concordent cum voce tua. Cum enim Deus laudatur de bono opere, Deum laudas, et cum blasphematur Deus de malo opere tuo, Deum blasphemas.*

571. Deinde cum dicit *sine offensione estote*, etc., monet ut caveant ab offensa aliorum, et persuadet hoc primo, verbo, secundo, exemplo, ibi *sicut et ego per omnia*, et cetera.

Ubi ponit se in exemplum, primo pacificae conversationis; secundo fructuosae operationis, ibi *non quaerens quod mihi utile*, etc.; tertio rectae intentionis, ibi *ut salvi fiant*.

Felix cuius conversatio amabilis, operatio utilis, intentio salubris.

572. Dicit ergo *sine offensione*, etc., quasi dicat: ut omnia in gloriam Dei fiant, *sine offensione estote Iudaeis*, qui non adorant idola, et ideo in tali comestione scandalizantur, *et gentibus*, qui adorant idola, et ideo

569. Having shown when it is permitted to eat the food sacrificed to idols and when it is not, here he shows that they should not try to do both.

First with respect to God, because they should seek his glory;

second, with respect to one's neighbor, because they should be careful of offending him, at *be without offense*.

570. Under the first point, he first brings forth the many aspects of the act; second, he urges the due intention of actions, at *do all things to the glory of God*.

Therefore he says, *therefore, whether*, as though he said: since these bad things can happen, *therefore, whether you eat or drink*, which are works of necessity, *or whatever else you do, do all to the glory of God*, and with the invocation of the Creator, by this intention, that God be praised and glorified. *So let your light shine among men* (Matt 5:16). *Whatever you do in word or work, do all for the glory of God* (Col 3:17).

Augustine in his commentary on Psalm 34, sermon two, at the end, says: *if these things be done rightly, they are praises of God. Therefore, do not only let your voice sound the praises of God, but also let your works harmonize with your voice. For when God is praised by a good work, you praise God, and when God is blasphemed by your evil work, you blaspheme God.*

571. Next when he says, *be without offense*, he warns them to be careful of offending others, and convinces them of this first by word, second by example, at *as I also in all things*.

Here he sets himself forth as example, first, by making peace by his companionship; second, by his fruitful work, at *not seeking that which is profitable to myself*; and third, by his right intention, at *that they may be saved*.

Happy the man whose companionship is delightful, whose work is useful, and whose intention is saving.

572. He says therefore, *without offense*, as though he said: so that all things may be for the glory of God, *be without offense to the Jews*, who do not worship idols, and therefore are scandalized by eating these things, *and to the*

per huiusmodi comestionem in errore confirmantur, *et Ecclesiae Dei*, quantum ad infirmos in fide, qui inde offenduntur. Iudaei sunt sub lege, sed non sunt sub fide; gentes nec sub lege, nec in fide; Ecclesia Dei et sub lege et in fide. Rom. XII, 18: *si fieri potest, quod ex vobis est, cum omnibus hominibus pacem habentes.*

573. *Sicut et ego per omnia omnibus placeo*, tamquam conversus sine scandalo. *Ego*, inquam, *non quaerens quod mihi utile est* tantum, *sed quod multis*. Ecce optimus modus placendi omnibus, si omnium utilitas, non privatum commodum procuretur. *Caritas*, inquam, *non quaerit quae sua sunt* (1 Cor 13:5). *Quod est utile*, inquam, *multis*, et non hoc ad aliquod commodum temporale, sed ad hoc *ut salvi fiant*. Phil. ult.: *non quaero datum, sed fructum.*

574. Notandum, quod multa sunt quae merito placere faciunt hominibus. Primum prudentia in consiliis, sicut advocatus clienti, dispensator principi placet. Gen. XLI, 37: *placuit Pharaoni consilium, et omnibus servis eius.* Eccli. XX, 29: *vir prudens placebit magnatis.*

Secundum, munditia in factis, sicut coniux coniugi, instrumentum utenti placet. I Reg. II, 26: *puer autem Samuel crescebat et proficiebat, placens tam Deo, quam hominibus.* Non sic filii Heli.

Tertium, pietas in suffragiis, sicut medicus infirmanti, baculus seni placet. Unde de sepultura Abner dicitur II Reg. III, 36: *placuerunt eis omnia, quae fecit David*, et cetera.

Quartum, sapientia in verbis, sicut lumen viatori, viror visui placet. Ios. XXII, 33: *placuit sermo cunctis audientibus.* Eccli. XX, 29: *sapiens in verbis producet seipsum, et homo prudens placebit magnatis.*

Quintum, clementia in responsis, sicut sapor gustui, melodia auri placet. II Par. X, 7: *si placueris populo huic, et lenieris eos verbis clementibus, servient tibi omni tempore.*

Sextum, fortitudo in bellis, sicut pugil conductori, miles principi placet. I Reg. XVIII, v. 22: *dixerunt servi Saul ad David: ecce places regi, et omnes servi eius diligunt te.*

Septimum, largitas in beneficiis, sicut pluvia terrae arenti, sicut fons sitienti placet. I Mac. XIV, 4 de Simone: *quaesivit bona gentis suae, et placuit illis potestas eius.*

575. Hic quaeritur super illud *nolo vos esse socios daemoniorum*. Glossa: *ad hoc genus pertinent quae fiunt in quibusdam rebus suspendendis, vel alligandis.*

gentiles, who worship idols, and therefore would be confirmed in their error by eating this kind of thing, *and to the Church of God*, as to those weak in faith, who are offended by this. Jews are under the law, but not under the faith; gentiles are not under the law or in the faith; the Church of God is both under the law and in the faith. *If it can be done, as much as is in you, have peace with all men* (Rom 12:18).

573. *As I also in all things please all men*, changing, so to speak, without scandal. *I*, he says, *not seeking that which is profitable to myself* alone, *but to many*. Here is the best way of pleasing everyone: if the profit of all, and not one's private convenience is procured. *Charity*, I says, *seeks not her own* (1 Cor 13:5). *That which is profitable*, I say, *to many*, and not this for some temporal convenience, but in order *that they may be saved*. I do not seek a gift, but fruit (Phil 4:17).

574. It should be noted that there are many things which they do deservedly to please men. The first is by prudence in counsels, as an attorney pleases his client, or a steward pleases his employer. *This advice pleased Pharaoh, and all his servants.* (Gen 41:37). *The prudent man shall please the great ones* (Sir 20:29).

Second, by cleanness in deeds, as a husband pleases his wife, or an instrument pleases the one using it. *But the boy Samuel grew and advanced, pleasing God as well as men* (1 Sam 2:26). Unlike the sons of Eli.

Third, faithfulness in giving one's support, as a doctor pleases his patient, or a walking stick pleases an elderly person. Hence it is said at the tomb of Abner: *and all the things that David did pleased them* (2 Sam 3:36).

Fourth, wisdom in words, as a light pleases a wayfarer, or green lands please the sight. *His words pleased all those who heard* (Josh 22:33). *The wise man shall advance by his words, and the prudent man shall please the great ones* (Sir 20:29).

Fifth, clemency in answering, as flavor pleases the taste-buds, or a melody pleases the ear. *You have so pleased this nation, and calmed them with clement words, they will serve you for all time* (2 Chr 10:7).

Sixth, courage in battles, as the boxer pleases his manager, or a soldier pleases his commander: *the servants of Saul said to David: behold, you please the king, and all his servants love you* (1 Sam 18:22).

Seventh, generosity in giving things, as the rain pleases dry earth, or as a spring pleases the thirsty. As is said of Simon: *he sought the goods of his people, and his power pleased them* (1 Macc 14:4).

575. Here it is asked about *I do not want you to be made partakers with devils* (1 Cor 10:20). The Gloss says: *what is done with certain things that are hung up or tied on relates to this kind of thing.*

Contra, ergo suspensio herbarum ad collum, vel chartularum, quae fieri solet, ad idololatriam pertinet.

Responsio. Aut herbae habent a natura vim naturalem ad effectum illum, aut non. In primo casu non pertinet ad idololatriam, sed in secundo.

Similiter cedulae, aut continent solum verba sacra, et ex hoc creduntur habere vim, aut non. In primo casu non pertinet ad idololatriam, sed in secundo.

576. Item super illud **omnia mihi licent**, Glossa: *potestate liberi arbitrii, et doctrina legis naturalis.*

Contra, secundum legem naturalem multa sunt illicita.

Respondeo. Hic loquitur de cibis specialiter.

577. Item ibidem Glossa: *praecepto Domini illa prohibentur.*

Respondeo. Illa praecepta ad tempus fuerunt, et revocata sunt.

578. Item **nihil interrogantes**. Contra, Tob. II, 21: *videte ne forte furtivus sit.*

Respondeo. Non est simile, quia cibum furtivum non est licitum in se comedere, sed idolo immolatum licet edere, nisi propter scandalum alterius.

579. Item **omnia in gloriam Dei facite**. Contra: ergo nullus actus est indifferens.

Respondeo. Relatio haec in gloriam Dei intelligitur, vel in actu, vel in aptitudine referendi, quae non est solum in bonis, sed etiam in indifferentibus.

580. Item **Domini est terra et plenitudo**. Contra, eadem ratio fuit sub lege. Ergo si omnia sunt modo munda, quia Domini sunt, et tunc fuerunt.

Respondeo. Reputatione legis immunda dicta sunt, sed non sui natura.

581. Item **sicut ego per omnia omnibus placeo**. Contra Gal. I, 10: *si hominibus placerem, Christi servus non essem.*

Item, quomodo placebat persecutoribus suis.

Respondeo ad primum: placere volebat hominibus propter Deum, non propter se.

Ad argumentum secundum intelligitur hoc, non de omnibus generaliter, sed de ecclesiasticis viris, secundum Glossam.

Against this: hanging herbs around the neck, or small pieces of paper, which commonly happens, relates to idolatry.

Answer: either herbs have a natural power from their nature to this effect, or else they do not. In the first case, it does not relate to idolatry, but in the second case it does.

Likewise, *cedulae* (official slips of paper) either contain only sacred words, and are believed to have power only from that, or else not. In the first case, they do not pertain to idolatry, but in the second, they do.

576. Again, concerning **all things are lawful for me** (1 Cor 10:23), the Gloss says: *by the power of free will and the teaching of natural law.*

Against this: according to natural law, many things are not allowed.

I answer that here he is speaking specifically of food.

577. Again, the Gloss says in the same place: *by the command of the Lord those things are prohibited.*

I answer that those commands were made for that time, and they have been repealed.

578. Again, **asking no question** (1 Cor 10:27). Against this: *watch out lest perhaps it is stolen: restore it to its owners, for it is not lawful for us either to eat or to touch anything that comes by theft* (Tob 2:21).

I answer that this is not the same, since it is not permitted in itself to eat stolen food, but it is permitted to eat the food sacrificed to idols, except on account of the scandal of another.

579. Again, **do all to the glory of God**. Against this: therefore, no act is indifferent.

I answer that something is understood to be referred to the glory of God either actually or in its aptitude for being so related, and this does not only happen among good things, but also among indifferent ones.

580. Again, **the earth is the Lord's and the fullness thereof** (1 Cor 10:26). Against this: the same reason existed under the law. Therefore if all things are now clean, because they are the Lord's, then they were at that time too.

I answer that they are called unclean according to the law, but not by their nature.

581. Again, **as I also in all things please all men**. Against this: *if I pleased men, I would not be the servant of Christ* (Gal 1:10).

Again, how did he please his persecutors?

I answer to the first objection: he wanted to please men for the sake of God, not for their sakes.

To the second objection, this is understood not of all men generally, but of the men of the Church, according to the Gloss.

CHAPTER 11

Lecture 1

11:1Imitatores mei estote, sicut et ego Christi. [n. 582]

11:2Laudo autem vos fratres quod per omnia mei memores estis: et sicut tradidi vobis, praecepta mea tenetis. [n. 584]

11:3Volo autem vos scire quod omnis viri caput, Christus est: caput autem mulieris, vir: caput vero Christi, Deus. [n. 586]

11:1μιμηταί μου γίνεσθε, καθὼς κἀγὼ Χριστοῦ.

11:2Ἐπαινῶ δὲ ὑμᾶς ὅτι πάντα μου μέμνησθε καὶ καθὼς παρέδωκα ὑμῖν τὰς παραδόσεις κατέχετε.

11:3θέλω δὲ ὑμᾶς εἰδέναι ὅτι παντὸς ἀνδρὸς ἡ κεφαλὴ ὁ Χριστός ἐστιν, κεφαλὴ δὲ γυναικὸς ὁ ἀνήρ, κεφαλὴ δὲ τοῦ Χριστοῦ ὁ θεός.

11:1Be followers of me, as I also am of Christ. [n. 582]

11:2Now I praise you, brethren, that in all things you are mindful of me and keep my ordinances as I have delivered them to you. [n. 584]

11:3But I would have you know that the head of every man is Christ: and the head of the woman is the man: and the head of Christ is God. [n. 586]

---

582. Supra Apostolus removit a fidelibus id quod est contrarium Eucharistiae sacramento, scilicet participationem mensae idolorum, nunc autem instruit fideles de ipso Eucharistiae sacramento. Et

primo praemittit quamdam admonitionem generalem;

secundo accedit ad propositum, ibi *volo autem vos scire*, et cetera.

Circa primum duo facit.

Primo proponit admonitionem;

secundo significat quomodo Corinthii ad praedictam admonitionem se habebant, ibi *laudo autem vos, fratres*, et cetera.

583. Circa primum considerandum est, quod ita se habet naturalis ordo rerum, quod ea quae sunt inferiora in entibus imitantur ea quae sunt superiora secundum suum posse. Unde etiam naturale agens tamquam superius assimilat sibi patiens.

Primordiale autem principium totius processionis rerum est Filius Dei, secundum illud Io. I, 3: *omnia per ipsum facta sunt*. Et ipse ideo est primordiale exemplar, quod omnes creaturae imitantur tamquam veram et perfectam Imaginem Patris. Unde dicitur Col. I, 15: *qui est Imago Dei invisibilis primogenitus omnis creaturae, quia in ipso condita sunt universa*. Speciali tamen quodam modo exemplar est spiritualium gratiarum, quibus spirituales creaturae illustrantur, secundum illud quod in Ps. CIX, 3 dicitur ad Filium: *in splendoribus sanctorum ex utero ante Luciferum genui te*, quia scilicet genitus est ante omnem creaturam per gratiam lucentem, habens exemplariter in se splendores omnium sanctorum.

Hoc autem exemplar Dei prius erat a nobis valde remotum, secundum illud Eccle. II, v. 12: *quid est homo, ut sequi possit Regem factorem suum?* Et ideo homo

582. Having eliminated from the believers a practice contrary to the sacrament of the Eucharist, namely, partaking of food offered to idols, the Apostle now instructs them about the sacrament of the Eucharist itself.

First, he gives a general admonition;

second, he develops his proposition, at *but I would have you know*.

In regard to the first he does two things.

First, he presents the admonition;

second, he signifies how the Corinthians regarded that admonition, at *now I praise you, brethren*.

583. In regard to the first it should be noted that the natural order of things is so arranged, that lower beings imitate higher beings, as far as it is possible. Hence even a natural agent, being superior, makes the thing it acts on similar to itself.

Now the primordial principle of the production of things is the Son of God: *all things were made through him* (John 1:3). He is, therefore, the primordial exemplar, which all creatures imitate as the true and perfect Image of the Father. Hence it is said: *he is the Image of the invisible God, the firstborn of every creature, for in him all things were created* (Col 1:15). But in a special way he is the exemplar of spiritual graces, with which spiritual creatures are endowed, as is said to the Son: *in the splendors of the saints before the morning star I begot you* (Ps 110:3), namely, because he was begotten before every creature through resplendent grace, having in himself as exemplar the splendors of all the saints.

But this exemplar of God has been very remote from us at first, as it is said: *what is man that he could follow the King, his maker?* (Eccl 2:12). And therefore he willed to

fieri voluit, ut hominibus humanum exemplar praeberet. Unde Augustinus dicit *de Agone Christiano: qua perversitate non careat, qui dicta et facta illius hominis intueri diligit et sectatur, in quo se nobis ad exemplum vitae praebuit Filius Dei?*

Et sicut divinitatis eius exemplar primo quidem imitantur angeli, secundario vero reliquae creaturae, ut Dionysius dicit X cap. *Angelicae hierarchiae,* ita humanitatis exemplar principaliter quidem imitandum proponitur praelatis Ecclesiae tamquam superioribus. Unde et Dominus apostolis dicit Io. c. XIII, 15: *exemplum dedi vobis, ut quemadmodum ego feci, ita et vos faciatis.* Secundario vero ipsi praelati informati exemplo Christi, proponuntur exemplar vitae subditis, secundum illud I Petr. ult.: *forma facti gregis ex animo;* et II Thess. III, 9: *ut nosmetipsos formam daremus vobis ad imitandum nos.*

Et ideo Apostolus signanter dicit: dixi **ut sine offensione** omnibus sitis, et hoc quidem facere poteritis, si hoc quod dico servetis. **Imitatores mei estote, sicut et ego Christi**, scilicet sum imitator. Imitabatur enim eum primo quidem in mentis devotione. Gal. c. II, 20: *vivo ego, iam non ego, vivit vero in me Christus.* Secundo in subditorum sollicitudine. Unde dicebat Phil. II, 17: *si immolor supra sacrificium et obsequium fidei vestrae, gaudeo et congratulor omnibus vobis,* sicut et Christus obtulit semetipsum pro nobis, ut dicitur Eph. V, 2. Tertio quantum ad passionis tolerantiam. II Cor. IV, 10: *semper mortificationem Iesu in corpore circumferentes.* Et Gal. ult.: *ego stigmata Domini Iesu in corpore meo porto.*

Est autem notandum, quod non simpliciter dicit, **imitatores mei estote**, sed addit **sicut et ego Christi**, quia scilicet subditi praelatos suos imitari non debent in omnibus, sed in quibus illi Christum imitantur, qui est indeficiens sanctitatis exemplar.

584. Deinde, cum dicit **laudo autem vos, fratres,** ostendit qualiter Corinthii se habebant ad admonitionem praedictam.

Circa quod considerandum est, quod subditi suos praelatos sequuntur dupliciter, scilicet quantum ad facta et dicta. Quantum quidem ad facta, dum subditi praelatorum exempla imitantur, unde dicitur Iac. V, 10: *exemplum accipite, fratres mei, prophetarum, qui locuti sunt in nomine Domini.* Quantum vero ad dicta, dum eorum praeceptis obediunt. Prov. IV, 4: *custodi praecepta mea et vives.*

In his autem Corinthii deficiebant, et maxime quantum ad maiorem multitudinem, et ideo Apostolus, alloquens eos, dicit **laudo autem vos, fratres,** quasi dicat: super hoc laudandos vos praebere debetis, sed non facitis, **quod per omnia memores estis,** quasi ad imitandum mea exempla. Non enim possumus illorum exempla imitari, quorum memoriam non habemus. Unde dicitur

become man, that he might offer humans a human exemplar. Hence Augustine says in *The Christian Combat: this perversity he does not lack who loves to inspect and imitate that man's words and actions, in which the Son of God offered himself to us as an example of living.*

Just as angels were first to imitate the exemplar of his divinity, but secondarily the other creatures, as Dionysius says in *The Angelic Hierarchy,* so the exemplar of humanity is chiefly proposed to be imitated by the prelates of the Church, as being higher. Hence the Lord says: *I have given you an example that as I have done, so do you* (John 13:15). Second, however, the prelates informed by the example of Christ are proposed to their subjects as exemplars of living: *being examples to the flock* (1 Pet 5:3); *to give you in our conduct an example to imitate* (2 Thess 3:9).

Therefore, the Apostle expressly says: I have said that you should **be without offense** (1 Cor 10:32) to anyone. And this, of course, you can do, if you take note of what I say: **be followers of me, as I also am of Christ**, i.e., an imitator. For he imitated him, first, in devotion of mind: *I live, now not I, but Christ lives in me* (Gal 2:20). Second, in anxiety for his subjects: *even if I am to be poured as a libation upon the sacrificial offering of your faith, I am glad and rejoice with you all* (Phil 2:17); Jesus Christ also offered himself for us (Eph 5:2). Third, as to tolerating suffering: *always carrying in the body the death of Jesus* (2 Cor 4:10); *I bear on my body the marks of Jesus* (Gal 6:17).

But it must be noted that he does not merely say, **be followers of me**, but he adds, **as I also am of Christ**, namely, because subjects ought not imitate their prelates in everything but in those things in which they imitate Christ, who is the unfailing exemplar of holiness.

584. Then when he says, **now I praise you, brethren**, he shows how the Corinthians were acting in regard to the above admonition.

In regard to this it should be observed that subjects follow their prelates in two ways: namely, as to their deeds and words. In regard to deeds, when they imitate the example of their prelates; hence it is said: *as an example take the prophets who spoke in the name of the Lord* (Jas 5:10). In regard to deeds, when they obey their precepts: *keep my commandments and live* (Prov 4:4).

But the Corinthians failed in these things and especially the greater majority; consequently, the Apostle addressed them thus: **now I praise you, brethren.** As if to say: you should offer yourselves to be praised on this point, but you do not, **that in all things you are mindful of me**, so as to imitate my example. For we cannot imitate examples of ones we do not remember. Hence it is said: *remember your*

Hebr. c. XIII, 7: *mementote praepositorum vestrorum, quorum intuentes exitum conversationis, imitamini fidem.*

Quantum vero ad dicta, subdit *et sicut tradidi vobis, praecepta mea tenetis*, quasi dicat: eodem tenore observatis, quo ego tradidi; hoc enim dicit, quia ab observantia praeceptorum eius recesserant. Io. XV, 20: *si sermonem meum servaverunt, et vestrum servabunt.*

585. Sed videtur hic modus loquendi non esse conveniens veritati Sacrae Scripturae, quae nihil patitur falsitatis, secundum illud Prov. VIII, 8: *iusti sunt omnes sermones mei, et non est in eis pravum quid, neque perversum.*

Sed dicendum, quod ironica locutio est una de locutionibus figurativis, in quibus veritas non attenditur secundum sensum quem verba faciunt, sed secundum id quod loquens exprimere intendit per simile, vel contrarium, vel quocumque alio modo. Et ideo in ironica locutione veritas attenditur secundum contrarium eius quod verba sonant, sicut in metaphorica, secundum simile.

586. Deinde cum dicit *volo autem vos scire, fratres*, etc., accedit ad propositum, instruens scilicet fideles de Eucharistiae sacramento.

Et circa hoc tria facit.

Primo redarguit eorum errores circa ritum huius sacramenti;

secundo ostendit huius sacramenti dignitatem, ibi *ego enim accepi a Domino*, etc.;

tertio docet convenientem ritum, ibi *itaque, fratres mei.*

Circa primum tria facit.

Primo redarguit eorum errorem, quo scilicet errabant in habitu, quia scilicet mulieres ad sacra mysteria conveniebant capite non velato;

secundo arguit errorem in conventu, quia scilicet dum convenirent ad sacra mysteria contentionibus vacabant, ibi *haec autem praecipio non laudans*, etc.;

tertio quantum ad certum cibum, quia scilicet pransi ad sacra mysteria sumenda accedebant, ibi: *convenientibus autem vobis*, et cetera.

Circa primum duo facit.

Primo praemittit quoddam documentum, ex quo sumitur ratio subsequentis monitionis;

secundo ponit monitionem, ibi *omnis autem vir orans*, et cetera.

587. Circa primum ponit triplicem comparationem, quarum prima est Dei ad hominem, dicens: dixi quod praecepta mea tenetis per contrarium; sed ut appareat vos irrationabiliter agere, *volo vos scire*, tamquam rem necessariam, secundum illud Is. c. V, 13: *captivus ductus est populus meus, quia non habuit scientiam*, *quod omnis viri caput Christus est*, quod quidem dicitur secundum

leaders; consider the outcome of their life and imitate their faith (Heb 13:7).

As to words he adds, *and keep my ordinances as I have delivered them to you*. As if to say: you observe them in the same tenor as I delivered them to you: for he says this because they had departed from observing the commandments: *if they keep my word, they will also keep yours* (John 15:20).

585. But this seems to be a manner of speaking not suited to the truth of the Sacred Scripture, which contains no falsity, as it is said: *all the words of my mouth are righteous; and there is nothing twisted or crooked in them* (Prov 8:8).

The answer is that irony is one of the figures of speech, in which one does not pay attention to the sense which the words make in order to get the truth, but what the speaker intends to express by a similar or contrary or other way. Therefore, in irony the truth is really the contrary of what the words indicate, as in a metaphor the truth consists in a similarity.

586. Then when he says, *but I would have you know*, he proceeds to his intention of instructing believers in the sacrament of the Eucharist.

In regard to this he does three things.

First, he reproves their errors regarding the rite of this sacrament;

second, he shows the dignity of this sacrament, at *for I have received of the Lord* (1 Cor 11:23);

third, he teaches the correct rite, at *therefore, whosoever shall eat* (1 Cor 11:27).

In regard to the first he does three things.

first, he refutes their error, by which they erred in clothing, namely, because the women gathered for the sacred mysteries with heads uncovered;

second, he corrects them in their gathering, because, when they came together for the sacred mysteries, they indulged in quarrels, at *now this I ordain* (1 Cor 11:17);

third, as to food, because they approach to take the sacred mysteries after they had just eaten, at *when you come together* (1 Cor 11:20).

In regard to the first he does two things.

First, he lays down a teaching from which is drawn the reason for the next admonition;

second, he gives an admonition, at *every man praying* (1 Cor 11:4).

587. In regard to the first he mentions three comparisons, the first of which is of God to man, saying: I have said you hold my precepts, by irony, but in order that you may see how unreasonably you act, *I would have you know* as something necessary: *my people went into exile for want of knowledge* (Isa 5:13), *that the head of every man is Christ.*

similitudinem capitis naturalis, in quo quatuor considerantur.

Primo quidem perfectio, quia cum caetera membra unum solum sensum habeant, scilicet tactum, in capite vigent omnes sensus; et similiter in aliis viris inveniuntur singulae gratiae, secundum illud quod dicitur infra XII, 8: *alii datur per spiritum sermo sapientiae, alii sermo scientiae*, etc.; sed in homine Christo est plenitudo omnium gratiarum. Non enim ad mensuram dat ei Deus Spiritum, ut dicitur Io. III, 34.

Secundo in capite invenitur sublimitas, quia ut, scilicet in homine, est superius omnibus membris, ita etiam Christus supereminet non solum omnibus hominibus, sed et omnibus angelis, secundum illud ad Ephesios I, 20 s.: *constituens illum ad dexteram suam in caelestibus, super omnem principatum et potestatem*, et infra: *et ipsum dedit caput super omnem Ecclesiam*.

Tertio in capite invenitur influentia, quia scilicet quodam modo influit caeteris membris sensum et motum, ita a capite Christo in caetera membra Ecclesiae motus et sensus spiritualis derivatur, secundum illud Col. II, v. 19: *non tenens caput, ex quo totum corpus per nexum et coniunctiones subministratum et constructum crescit in augmentum Dei*.

Quarto in capite invenitur conformitas naturae ad caetera membra, et similiter in Christo ad alios homines, secundum illud Phil. II, v. 7: *in similitudinem hominum factus et habitu inventus, ut homo*.

588. Secundam comparationem ponit hominis ad hominem, cum dicit *caput autem mulieris vir*. Quod etiam secundum praedicta quatuor verificatur. Nam primo quidem vir est perfectior muliere, non solum quantum ad corpus, quia, ut Philosophus dicit in libro *de Generatione animalium*, foemina est masculus occasionatus, sed etiam quantum ad animae vigorem, secundum illud Eccle. VII, 29: *virum ex mille reperi unum, mulierem ex omnibus non inveni*.

Secundo, quia vir naturaliter supereminet foeminae, secundum illud Eph. V, 22 s.: *mulieres viris suis subiectae sint sicut Domino, quoniam vir caput est mulieris*.

Tertio, quia vir influit gubernando mulierem, secundum illud Gen. III, 16: *sub viri potestate eris, et ipse dominabitur tui*.

Quarto vir et foemina conformes sunt in natura, secundum illud Gen. II, 18: *faciamus ei adiutorium simile sibi*.

589. Tertiam comparationem ponit Dei ad Dominum, cum dicit *caput vero Christi, Deus*.

Est autem considerandum, quod hoc nomen *Christus* significat personam praedictam ratione humanae naturae: et sic hoc nomen *Deus* non supponit solum personam Patris, sed totam Trinitatem, a qua in humanitate

This is said according to a likeness of a natural head, in which four things are considered.

First, perfection, because while the other members have but one sense, namely, touch, all the senses flourish in the head; and similarly in other men are found single graces, as it says below: *to one indeed, by the Spirit, is given the word of wisdom: and to another, the word of knowledge* (1 Cor 12:8), but in Christ alone is found the fullness of all graces. For it is not by measure that God gives him the Spirit (John 3:34).

Second, in the head is found sublimity, because as in a man it is superior to all the members, so Christ is super-eminent not only over all men but also all angels: *he made him sit at his right hand in the heavenly places far above all power and dominion* (Eph 1:20), and below: *Christ is the head of the Church* (Eph 1:22).

Third, in the head is found outflowing power, namely, because in some way it imparts sensation and movement to the other members; so from Christ is derived movement and sense to the other members of the Church: *not holding fast to the head from whom the whole body, nourished and knit together, grows with a growth that is from God* (Col 2:19).

Fourth, in the head is found a conformity of nature to the other members; likewise in Christ relative to other men: *taking the form of a servant, being born in the likeness of man* (Phil 2:7).

588. The second comparison he presents is of man to man, when he says, *the head of the woman is the man*. This is verified according to the four comparisons mentioned above. For, first of all, man is more perfect than woman not only in regard to the body, because, as the Philosopher says in the book *On Generation of Animals*, the female is an occasioned male, but also in regard to the soul's vigor: *one man among a thousand I found, but a woman among all these I have not found* (Eccl 7:29).

Second, because man is naturally superior to the female: *wives, be subject to your husband as to the Lord. For the husband is the head of the wife* (Eph 5:22).

Third, because the man exerts an influence by governing the wife: *your desire will be for your husband, and he shall rule over you* (Gen 3:16).

Fourth, the man and the woman are alike in nature: *I will make him a helper like to him* (Gen 2:18).

589. The third comparison he makes is of God to the Lord, when he says, *the head of Christ is God*.

Here it should be noted that this name, *Christ*, signifies the person mentioned by reason of his human nature: and so this name, *God*, does not refer only to the person of the Father but the whole Trinity, from which as from the more

Christi, sicut a perfectiori, omnia bona derivantur, et cui humanitas Christi subiicitur.

Alio modo potest intelligi, secundum quod hoc nomen **Christus** supponit dictam personam ratione divinae naturae: et sic hoc nomen **Deus** supponit solum personam Patris, quae dicitur caput Filii, non quidem secundum maiorem perfectionem, vel secundum aliquam suppositionem, sed solum originem et secundum conformitatem naturae, sicut in Ps. II, 7 dicitur: *Dominus dixit ad me: Filius meus es tu, ego hodie genui te.*

590. Possunt tamen haec mystice accipi, prout in anima est quoddam spirituale coniugium.

Nam sensualitas foeminae comparatur, ratio vero viro, per quem sensualitas regi debet. Unde et caput eius dicitur. Vel potius ratio inferior, quae inhaeret temporalibus disponendis, mulieri comparatur; viro autem ratio superior, quae vacat contemplationi aeternorum, quae caput inferioris dicitur: quia secundum rationes aeternas sunt temporalia disponenda, secundum illud Ex. XXV, 40: *inspice et fac secundum exemplar quod tibi in monte monstratum est.* Dicitur autem caput viri Christus, quia sola ratio secundum superiorem sui partem Deo inhaeret.

perfect all goods in the humanity of Christ are derived and to which the humanity of Christ is subjected.

It can be understood in another way, so that this name, **Christ**, stands for that person by reason of his divine nature; then this name, **God**, stands only for the person of the Father, who is called the head of the Son not by reason of a greater perfection or by reason of any supposition, but only according to origin and conformity of nature; as it is said: *the Lord said to me: you are my Son; today I have begotten you* (Ps 2:7).

590. But these can be taken mystically, inasmuch as there is in the soul a certain spiritual union.

For sensibility is compared to the female, but reason to the man, by whom sensibility ought to be ruled. Hence he is called her head. Or: the lower reason, which is interested in disposing of and arranging temporal things, is compared to the women. To the man is compared the higher reason, which occupies itself with contemplating eternal things and is called the head of the lower reason, because temporal things should be disposed according to eternal reasons: *make it according to the pattern I showed you on the mountain* (Exod 25:9). But Christ is called the head of the man, because reason alone according to its superior part belongs to God.

Lecture 2

^{11:4}Omnis vir orans, aut prophetans velato capite, deturpat caput suum. [n. 591]

^{11:5}Omnis autem mulier orans, aut prophetans non velato capite, deturpat caput suum: unum enim est ac si decalvetur. [n. 596]

^{11:6}Nam si non velatur mulier, tondeatur. Si vero turpe est mulieri tonderi, aut decalvari, velet caput suum. [n. 597]

^{11:7}Vir quidem non debet velare caput suum: quoniam imago et gloria Dei est, mulier autem gloria viri est. [n. 602]

^{11:4}πᾶς ἀνὴρ προσευχόμενος ἢ προφητεύων κατὰ κεφαλῆς ἔχων καταισχύνει τὴν κεφαλὴν αὐτοῦ:

^{11:5}πᾶσα δὲ γυνὴ προσευχομένη ἢ προφητεύουσα ἀκατακαλύπτῳ τῇ κεφαλῇ καταισχύνει τὴν κεφαλὴν αὐτῆς: ἓν γάρ ἐστιν καὶ τὸ αὐτὸ τῇ ἐξυρημένῃ.

^{11:6}εἰ γὰρ οὐ κατακαλύπτεται γυνή, καὶ κειράσθω: εἰ δὲ αἰσχρὸν γυναικὶ τὸ κείρασθαι ἢ ξυρᾶσθαι, κατακαλυπτέσθω.

^{11:7}ἀνὴρ μὲν γὰρ οὐκ ὀφείλει κατακαλύπτεσθαι τὴν κεφαλήν, εἰκὼν καὶ δόξα θεοῦ ὑπάρχων: ἡ γυνὴ δὲ δόξα ἀνδρός ἐστιν.

^{11:4}Every man praying or prophesying with his head covered disgraces his head. [n. 591]

^{11:5}But every woman praying or prophesying with her head not covered disgraces her head: for it is all one as if she were shaven. [n. 596]

^{11:6}For if a woman is not covered, let her be shorn. But if it is a shame to a woman to be shorn or made bald, let her cover her head. [n. 597]

^{11:7}The man indeed ought not to cover his head: because he is the image and glory of God. But the woman is the glory of the man. [n. 602]

---

591. Praemisso documento subiungit admonitionem, cuius ratio sumitur ex documento praedicto.

Et circa hoc duo facit.

Primo ponit admonitionem ex parte viri;

secundo ex parte mulieris, ibi *omnis autem mulier*, et cetera.

592. Dicit ergo primo: dictum est quod caput mulieris est vir, *omnis autem vir orans aut prophetans velato capite, deturpat caput suum*. Circa quod considerandum est, quod quilibet homo iudici assistens, suam conditionem vel dignitatem debet profiteri, et praecipue assistens Deo, qui est omnium iudex; et ideo, qui Deo assistunt, ordinatissime et convenientissime se gerere debent, secundum illud Eccle. IV, 17: *custodi pedem tuum ingrediens domum Dei*.

Dupliciter autem homo Deo assistit. Uno modo humana in Deum referens, quod quidem fit orando, secundum illud Eccli. XXXIX, v. 6 s.: *in conspectu Altissimi deprecabitur, aperiet os suum in oratione, et pro delictis suis deprecabitur*. Alio modo divina ad homines deferens, quod quidem fit prophetando, secundum illud Ioel. II, 28: *effundam Spiritum meum super omnem carnem, et prophetabunt filii vestri*. Unde signanter Apostolus dicit *vir orans et prophetans*. His enim duobus modis vir Deo tamquam iudici, vel Domino assistit.

Dicitur autem prophetans dupliciter. Uno modo inquantum homo aliis annuntiat, quae ei divinitus revelantur, secundum illud Lc. I, v. 67 s.: *Zacharias pater eius impletus est Spiritu Sancto, et prophetavit, dicens: benedictus Dominus Deus Israel*, et cetera. Alio modo dicitur homo prophetans, inquantum profert ea quae sunt aliis revelata; unde illi qui in ecclesia dicunt prophetias, vel

591. Having set forth the doctrine, he adds the admonition, the reason for which is taken from the doctrine mentioned.

In regard to this he does two things.

First, he gives the admonition on the man's part;

second, on the woman's, at *but every woman*.

592. First, therefore, he says: it has been stated that the head of the woman is the man, *every man praying or prophesying with his head covered disgraces his head*. In regard to this it should be noted that any man assisting a judge should display a condition or dignity, and especially assisting God, who is judge of all. Therefore, those who assist God should conduct themselves in the best behaved and suitable way: *guard your steps, when you go to the house of God* (Eccl 5:1).

Now man assists God in two ways: in one way by relating human things to God, and that is done by praying: *he will make supplication before the Most High; he will open his mouth in prayer, and make supplication for his sins* (Sir 39:5); in another way by bringing things down from God to men, and that is done by prophesying: *I will pour out my Spirit on all flesh, and your sons and your daughters shall prophesy* (Joel 2:28). Hence the Apostle is careful to say, *man praying or prophesying*. For in these two ways man assists God as judge, or he assists the Lord.

He is said to prophesy in two ways: in one way, inasmuch as man announces to others what has been divinely revealed to him: *and his father Zechariah was filled with the Holy Spirit and prophesied, saying: blessed be the Lord, the God of Israel* (Luke 1:67). A man prophesies in another way, inasmuch as he utters things which have been revealed to others; hence, those who read the prophecies or other

alias Sacras Scripturas legunt, dicuntur prophetantes. Et sic accipitur infra XIV, 4: *qui prophetat, Ecclesiam aedificat*; et ita etiam hic accipitur.

Pertinet autem ad dignitatem viri (ut infra patebit) carere velamine capitis, et ideo dicit quod *omnis vir orans, aut prophetans velato capite, deturpat caput suum*, id est, rem inconvenientem sibi agit.

Sicut enim in corpore pulchritudo dicitur ex debita proportione membrorum in convenienti claritate vel colore, ita in actibus humanis dicitur pulchritudo ex debita proportione verborum vel factorum, in quibus lumen rationis resplendet. Unde et per oppositum turpitudo intelligitur, quando contra rationem aliquid agitur, et non observatur debita proportio in verbis et factis. Unde supra VII, 36 dictum est: *si quis turpem se videri existimat, super virgine sua, quod sit superadulta*.

593. Sed contra hoc obiicitur: nam multi velato capite in Ecclesia orant absque omni turpitudine secretius orare volentes.

Dicendum est autem, quod duplex est oratio. Una privata, quam scilicet quis Deo offert in propria persona; alia publica, quam quis offert Deo in persona totius Ecclesiae, ut patet in orationibus, quae in ecclesia per sacerdotes dicuntur, et de talibus orationibus Apostolus hic intelligit.

594. Item obiicitur de hoc quod dicit Glossa, quod prophetans dicitur *Scripturas reserans*, et secundum hoc ille qui praedicat, prophetat. Episcopi autem praedicant capite tecto mitra.

Sed dicendum est, quod ille qui praedicat vel docet in scholis, ex propria persona loquitur. Unde et Apostolus, Rom. II, 16, nominat Evangelium suum, scilicet propter industriam qua utebatur in praedicatione Evangelii; sed ille, qui Sacram Scripturam in ecclesia recitat, puta legendo lectionem, vel epistolam, vel Evangelium, ex persona totius Ecclesiae loquitur. Et de tali prophetante intelligitur, quod hic Apostolus dicit.

595. Sed tunc remanet obiectio de his, qui cantant Psalmos in choro capite tecto.

Sed dicendum, quod Psalmi non cantantur, quasi ab uno singulariter se Deo praesentante, sed quasi a tota multitudine.

596. Deinde cum dicit *omnis autem mulier*, etc., ponit admonitionem quantum ad mulieres, dicens *omnis autem mulier orans, aut prophetans*, ut supra, *non velato capite*, quod repugnat propter conditionem eius, *deturpat caput suum*, id est, rem inconvenientem facit circa sui capitis detectionem.

Sed contra hoc obiicitur, quia Apostolus dicit I Tim. II, 12: *docere in ecclesia mulieres non permitto*. Quomodo ergo competit mulieri, ut oret, aut prophetet publica oratione, aut doctrina?

Sacred Scriptures are said to be prophesying. It is taken in this sense below: *he who prophesies, edifies the Church* (1 Cor 14:4); it is also taken in that sense here.

But it pertains to man's dignity (as will be clear below) not to wear a covering on his head; consequently, he says that *every man praying or prophesying with his head covered disgraces his head*, i.e., does something unbecoming a man.

For as in a body, beauty depends on due proportion of the members, on proper light and color, so in human acts beauty depends on due proportion of words or deeds, in which the light of reason shines forth. Hence in an opposite way ugliness is present when something is done against reason and due proportion is not observed in words and deeds. Hence it was said above: *if any man thinks that he seems dishonored with regard to his virgin, because she is above the age* (1 Cor 7:36).

593. The following objection is raised: for many with heads covered pray in church without any disgrace, as they wish to pray more secretly.

The answer is that prayer is twofold: one is private and is offered to God in one's own person; the other is public and is offered to God in the person of the entire Church, as is clear from the prayers said in the church by priests. It is these latter prayers that the Apostle has in mind here.

594. There is also an objection against a Gloss which states that prophesying is called *unlocking the Scriptures*. According to this, anyone who preaches prophesies. But bishops preach with their head covered with a miter.

The answer is that one who preaches or teaches in the schools speaks from his own person. Hence even the Apostle (Rom 2:16) calls the Gospel his own, namely, on account of the energy he used in preaching it. But one who recites Sacred Scripture in the church, for example, by reading a lesson or an epistle or a Gospel, speaks from the person of the whole Church. This is the kind of prophesying that the Apostle understands here.

595. Then there is an objection about those who chant psalms in choir with their head covered.

The answer is that psalms are not chanted as by one singly presenting himself to God, but as by the whole multitude.

596. Then when he says, *but every woman*, he gives an admonition as it applies to women, saying, *but every woman praying or prophesying with her head not covered*, which is unbecoming, considering her condition, *disgraces her head*, i.e., does something unsuitable in regard to covering her hair.

But against this is the Apostle's statement: *I permit no woman to teach in church* (1 Tim 2:12). How, then, does it befit a woman to pray or prophesy in public prayer or in doctrine?

Sed dicendum est, hoc intelligendum esse de orationibus ac lectionibus, quas mulieres in suis collegiis proferunt.

597. Deinde cum dicit *unum est enim*, etc., probat admonitionem praedictam. Et

primo inducit probationem,

secundo probationis iudicium auditoribus committit, ibi *vos ipsi iudicate*, et cetera.

598. Circa primum duo facit.

Primo inducit probationem,

secundo excludit obiectionem, ibi *verumtamen neque vir*, et cetera.

Circa primum ponit triplicem probationem, quarum prima sumitur per comparationem ad humanam naturam;

secunda per comparationem ad Deum, ibi *vir quidem non debet*, etc.;

tertia per comparationem ad angelos, cum dicit *et propter angelos*.

598. Circa primum considerandum est, quod natura, quae caeteris animalibus providit auxilia sufficientia vitae, hominibus praebuit ea imperfecta, ut per rationem, arte, usu, manu sibi ea perficerent, sicut tauris dedit cornua ad defensionem, homines autem arma defensionis sibi praeparant manuali artificio rationis. Et inde est, quod ars imitatur naturam, et perficit ea quae natura facere non potest. Sic igitur ad tegumentum capitis natura homini dedit capillos. Sed quia hoc tegumentum insufficiens est, per artem praeparat homo sibi aliud velamen.

Eadem igitur ratio est de velamine naturali capillorum, et de velamine artificiali. Naturale autem est mulieri, quod comam nutriat. Habet enim ad hoc dispositionem naturalem, et ulterius inclinatio quaedam inest mulieribus ad comam nutriendam. In pluribus enim hoc accidit, quod mulieres magis student ad nutriendam comam, quam viri. Videtur ergo conditioni mulierum conveniens esse, quod magis utantur artificiali velamine capitis, quam viri.

599. Circa hoc ergo tria facit. Primo ponit convenientiam velaminis naturalis et artificialis, dicens: dictum est mulier non velans caput, deturpat caput suum, *unum est enim*, scilicet unius rationis, privari scilicet velamine artificiali, *ac si decalvetur*, id est, ac si privetur naturali velamine capillorum, quod in poenam quibusdam praedicitur Is. III, 17: *decalvabit Dominus verticem filiarum Sion, et crinem earum nudabit.*

600. Secundo ducit ad inconveniens, dicens *nam et si non velatur mulier, tondeatur*, quasi dicat: si abiicit velamen artificiale, abiiciat pari ratione etiam naturale, quod est inconveniens.

The answer is that this must understood of prayers and readings which women say in their own groups.

597. Then when he says, *for it is all one as if*, he proves the above admonition.

First, he induces a proof;

second, he submits judgment of the proof to his hearers, at *you yourselves judge* (1 Cor 11:13).

598. In regard to the first he does two things.

First, he induces a proof;

second, he excludes an objection, at *but yet neither is the man* (1 Cor 11:11).

In regard to the first he presents three proofs: the first is taken by a comparison to human nature;

the second by a comparison to God, at *the man indeed ought not*;

the third by a comparison to angels, at *because of the angels* (1 Cor 11:10).

598. In regard to the first it should be noted that nature, which provides the other animals with aids sufficient for life, offers them to man imperfectly, so that through reason, art and use, man with his hands provides those things for himself; as it gave bulls horns for defense, whereas men prepare for themselves arms for defense by reason's direction of the hands. Hence it is that art imitates nature and produces things which nature cannot make. Thus, for the covering of the head, nature gave man hair. But because this covering is not sufficient, man through art prepares for himself another covering.

The same explanation is true in regard to the natural covering and the artificial. But it is natural for a woman to have long hair. For she has a natural disposition to this, and further a definite inclination is present in women to take care of their hair. For this is true in the majority of cases that women take more pains with their hair than men. Therefore, it seems to be a condition suitable to women that they use an artificial covering for the head more than men.

599. In regard to this he does three things: first, he mentions the suitability of a natural and artificial covering, saying: it has been stated that a woman not covering her head dishonors her head, *for it is all one*, namely, the same thing to be deprived of an artificial covering, *as if she were shaven*, i.e., as if she were deprived of the natural covering of hair, which is predicted as punishment for certain people: *the Lord will smite with a scab the heads of the daughters of Zion and the Lord will lay bare their secret parts* (Isa 3:17).

600. Second, he leads to something unacceptable, saying, *for if a woman is not covered, let her be shorn*. As if to say: if she throws aside the artificial covering, let her for the same reason cast aside the natural covering; which is unacceptable.

Sed contra hoc videtur esse, quod sanctimoniales tondentur.

Ad quod dupliciter potest responderi: primo quidem, quia ex hoc ipso quod votum viduitatis vel virginitatis assumunt, Christo desponsante, promoventur in dignitatem virilem, utpote liberatae a subiectione virorum, et immediate Christo coniunctae.

Secundo quia assumunt poenitentiae lamentum, religionem intrantes. Est autem consuetudo viris, quod tempore luctus comam nutriant, quasi hoc sit suae conditioni conveniens: mulieres autem e contrario tempore luctus comam deponunt. Unde dicitur Ier. c. VII, 29: *capillum tuum tonde, et proiice, et sume indirectum planctum.*

601. Tertio concludit propositum dicens **si vero turpe**, id est indecens, **est mulieri tonderi aut decalvari**, id est, privari naturali velamine, arte, vel natura, **velet caput suum**, utens scilicet velamine artificiali.

602. Deinde cum dicit **vir quidem**, etc., ponit secundam probationem, quae accipitur per comparationem ad Deum. Et

primo inducit ad probationem,

secundo probat quod supposuerat, ibi **non enim est vir**, et cetera.

Circa primum duo facit.

Primo ponit rationem eius quod est ex parte viri,

secundo illud quod est ex parte mulieris, ibi **mulier autem**, et cetera.

603. Dicit ergo primo: dictum est quod turpe est mulieri tonderi, sicut et non velari; viro autem non est turpe, cuius ratio est haec **vir quidem non debet velare caput suum, quia est imago et gloria Dei.**

604. Per hoc autem quod dicit **est imago Dei**, excluditur quorumdam error, dicentium quod homo solum est ad imaginem Dei, non autem est imago, cuius contrarium hic Apostolus dicit. Dicebant autem, quod solus Filius est imago, secundum illud Col. c. I, 15: *qui est Imago invisibilis Dei.*

Est ergo dicendum, quod homo **imago Dei** dicitur et ad imaginem. Est enim imago imperfecta: Filius autem dicitur Imago, non ad imaginem, quia est Imago perfecta.

Ad cuius evidentiam considerandum est, quod de ratione imaginis in communi duo sunt. Primo quidem similitudo, non in quibuscumque, sed vel in ipsa specie rei, sicut homo filius assimilatur patri suo. Vel in aliquo quod sit signum speciei, sicut figura in rebus corporalibus. Unde qui figuram equi describunt, dicuntur imaginem eius depingere. Et hoc est, quod dicit Hilarius in libro *de Synodis*, quod imago est species indifferens. Secundo requiritur origo. Non enim duorum hominum, qui sunt similes specie, unus imago alterius dicitur, nisi

But against this seems to be the fact that nuns are shaved.

To this there are two answers: first, because from the very fact that they take a vow of virginity or widowhood with Christ as their spouse, they are promoted to the dignity of men, being freed from subjection to men and joined to Christ himself.

Second, because they assume a garb of penance, when they enter religion. Now it is custom for men that in time of sorrow they take care of their hair, but for women, on the contrary, to cut their hair. Hence it is said: *cut off your hair and cast it away, raise a lamentation on the bare heights* (Jer 7:21).

601. Third, he concludes his proposition, saying, **but if it is a shame**, i.e., unbecoming, **to be shorn or made bald**, i.e., be deprived of her natural covering by art or by nature, **let her cover her head**, using an artificial covering.

602. Then when he says, **the man indeed**, he presents the second proof, which is taken from a comparison to God.

First, he induces to the proof;

second, he proves what he had supposed, at **for the man is not of the woman** (1 Cor 11:8).

In regard to the first he does two things.

First, he lays down the reason for that which is on man's part;

second, on the woman's part, at **but the woman is the glory**.

603. First, therefore, he says: it has been stated that it is disgraceful for a woman to be shorn, just as it is for her not to be veiled; **the man indeed ought not to cover his head: because he is the image and glory of God.**

604. In saying that **he is the image . . . of God**, the error is excluded of those who say that man is only made to the image of God, but is not the image; the opposite of which the Apostle says here. For they said that the Son alone is the image: *he is the Image of the invisible God* (Col 1:15).

Therefore, one must say that man is said to be **the image . . . of God** and to his image. For he is an imperfect image, but the Son is said to be the 'Image' but not 'to the image', because he is the perfect Image.

To clarify this it should be noted that two things are generally involved in the notion of an image. First, a likeness, not in just any way, but in the very species of a thing, as a human son is similar to this father. Or in something which is a sign of the species, as the shape, in bodily things. Hence one who draws the shape of a horse is said to depict his image. And this is what Hilary says in the book, *On Synods*, that an image is an indifferent species. Second, origin is required. For one of two men who are similar in species is not the image of the other, unless he sprang from him,

225

ex eo oriatur, sicut filius a patre. Nam imago dicitur ab exemplari. Tertio ad rationem perfectae imaginis requiritur aequalitas.

Quia igitur homo similatur Deo secundum memoriam, intelligentiam et voluntatem mentis, quod pertinet ad speciem intellectualis naturae, et hoc habet a Deo, dicitur esse Dei imago; quia tamen deest aequalitas, est Dei imago imperfecta. Et ideo dicitur ad imaginem, secundum illud Gen. I, 26: *faciamus hominem ad imaginem et similitudinem nostram.* Sed Filius, qui est aequalis Patri, est Imago perfecta, non autem ad imaginem.

605. Considerandum est etiam, quod gloria Dei dupliciter dicitur. Uno modo qua Deus in se gloriosus est, et sic homo non est gloria Dei, sed potius Deus est gloria hominis, secundum illud Ps. III, 4: *tu, Domine, susceptor meus es et gloria mea.* Alio modo dicitur gloria Dei claritas eius ab eo derivata, secundum illud Ex. ult.: *gloria Domini implevit illud.*

Et hoc modo hic dicitur, quod vir **est gloria Dei**, inquantum claritas Dei immediate super virum refulget, secundum illud Ps. IV, 7: *signatum est super nos lumen vultus tui, Domine.*

606. Deinde cum dicit **mulier autem**, etc., ponit id quod est ex parte mulieris, dicens **mulier autem est gloria viri**, etc., quia claritas mulieris derivatur a viro, secundum illud Gen. II, 23: *haec vocabitur virago, quoniam de viro sumpta est.*

607. Sed contra hoc obiicitur, quia imago Dei attenditur in homine secundum spiritum, in quo non est differentia maris et foeminae, ut dicitur Col. III, 11. Non ergo magis debet dici, quod vir dicitur imago Dei, quam mulier.

Dicendum est autem, quod vir dicitur hic specialiter imago Dei secundum quaedam exteriora, scilicet quia vir est principium totius sui generis, sicut Deus est principium totius universi, et quia de latere Christi dormientis in cruce fluxerunt sacramenta sanguinis et aquae, a quibus fabricata est Ecclesia. Potest etiam quantum ad interiora dici, quod vir specialius dicitur imago Dei secundum mentem, inquantum in eo ratio magis viget.

Sed melius dicendum est quod Apostolus signanter loquitur. Nam de viro dixit, quod vir imago et gloria Dei est: de muliere autem non dixit, quod esset imago et gloria viri, sed solum quod est gloria viri, ut detur intelligi quod esse imaginem Dei, commune est viro et mulieri: esse autem gloriam Dei immediate proprium est viri.

608. Restat autem considerandum, propter quid vir non debeat velare caput, sed mulier.

Quod quidem dupliciter accipi potest. Primo quidem quia velamen, quod capiti superponitur, designat potestatem alterius super caput existentis ordine naturae: et

as a son from the father. Third, the notion of a perfect image requires equality.

Therefore, because man is similar to God in memory, intelligence and will, which pertain to the species of an intellectual nature and he has this from God, he is said to be God's image; but because equality is lacking, he is an imperfect image of God. For this reason he is said to be to the image: *let us make man to our image and likeness* (Gen 1:26). But the Son, who is equal to the Father, is the perfect Image and not to the image.

605. It should also be noted that the glory of God is spoken of in two ways: in one way the glory by which God is glorious in himself; this is not how man is God's glory, but rather God is man's glory: *but you, O Lord, are a shield about me, my glory* (Ps 3:3). In another way the glory of God is his splendor derived from him: *the glory of the Lord filled the tabernacle* (Exod 40:34).

This is the way it says here that man is the **glory of God**, inasmuch as God's splendor shines on man: *the light of your countenance has been signed upon us, O Lord* (Ps 4:6).

606. Then when he says, **but the woman**, he presents that which is on the part of the woman, saying, **but the woman is the glory of the man**, because: *she shall be called woman, because she was taken out of man* (Gen 2:23).

607. Some object that because the image of God in man is regarded with respect to the spirit, in which there is no difference between male and female (Gal 3:28). Therefore, there is no more reason why man is called the image of God than a woman is.

The answer is that man is here called the image of God in a special way, namely, because man is the principle of his entire race, as God is the principle of the entire universe and because from the side of Christ dying on the cross flowed the sacraments of blood and water, from which the Church has been organized. Furthermore, in regard to what is within, man is more especially called the image of God, inasmuch as reason is more vigorous in him.

But it is better to say that the Apostle speaks clearly here. For he said of man that he is the image and glory of God; but he did not say of the woman that she is the image and glory of man, but only that she is the glory of the man. This gives us to understand that it is common to man and woman to be the image of God; but it is immediately characteristic of man to be the glory of God.

608. We must consider why man should not veil his head, but the woman.

This can be taken in two ways: first, because a veil put on the head designates the power of another over the head of a person existing in the order of nature. Therefore, the

ideo vir sub Deo existens, non debet velamen habere, super caput, ut ostendat se immediate Deo subesse, mulier autem debet velamen habere, ut ostendat se praeter Deum alteri naturaliter subesse. Unde cessat obiectio de servo et subdito: quia haec subiectio non est naturalis.

Secundo ad ostendendum, quod gloria Dei non est occultanda, sed revelanda: gloria autem hominis est occultanda; unde in Ps. CXIII, v. 9 s. dicitur: *non nobis, Domine, non nobis, sed nomini tuo da gloriam.*

man existing under God should not have a covering over his head to show that he is immediately subject to God; but the woman should wear a covering to show that besides God she is naturally subject to another. Hence a stop is put to the objection about servant and subject, because this subjection is not natural.

Second, to show that the glory of God should not be concealed but revealed; but man's glory is to be concealed. Hence it is said: *not to us, O Lord, not to us, but to thy name give the glory* (Ps 115:1).

Lecture 3

11:8Non enim vir ex muliere est, sed mulier ex viro. [n. 609]

11:9Etenim non est creatus vir propter mulierem, sed mulier propter virum. [n. 611]

11:10Ideo debet mulier potestatem habere supra caput propter angelos. [n. 612]

11:11Verumtamen neque vir sine muliere: neque mulier sine viro in Domino. [n. 615]

11:12Nam sicut mulier de viro, ita et vir per mulierem: omnia autem ex Deo. [n. 616]

11:13Vos ipsi judicate: decet mulierem non velatam orare Deum? [n. 618]

11:14Nec ipsa natura docet vos, quod vir quidem si comam nutriat, ignominia est illi:

11:15mulier vero si comam nutriat, gloria est illi: quoniam capilli pro velamine ei dati sunt.

11:16Si quis autem videtur contentiosus esse: nos talem consuetudinem non habemus, neque Ecclesia Dei. [n. 620]

11:8οὐ γάρ ἐστιν ἀνὴρ ἐκ γυναικός, ἀλλὰ γυνὴ ἐξ ἀνδρός:

11:9καὶ γὰρ οὐκ ἐκτίσθη ἀνὴρ διὰ τὴν γυναῖκα, ἀλλὰ γυνὴ διὰ τὸν ἄνδρα.

11:10διὰ τοῦτο ὀφείλει ἡ γυνὴ ἐξουσίαν ἔχειν ἐπὶ τῆς κεφαλῆς διὰ τοὺς ἀγγέλους.

11:11πλὴν οὔτε γυνὴ χωρὶς ἀνδρὸς οὔτε ἀνὴρ χωρὶς γυναικὸς ἐν κυρίῳ:

11:12ὥσπερ γὰρ ἡ γυνὴ ἐκ τοῦ ἀνδρός, οὕτως καὶ ὁ ἀνὴρ διὰ τῆς γυναικός: τὰ δὲ πάντα ἐκ τοῦ θεοῦ.

11:13ἐν ὑμῖν αὐτοῖς κρίνατε: πρέπον ἐστὶν γυναῖκα ἀκατακάλυπτον τῷ θεῷ προσεύχεσθαι;

11:14οὐδὲ ἡ φύσις αὐτὴ διδάσκει ὑμᾶς ὅτι ἀνὴρ μὲν ἐὰν κομᾷ ἀτιμία αὐτῷ ἐστιν,

11:15γυνὴ δὲ ἐὰν κομᾷ δόξα αὐτῇ ἐστιν; ὅτι ἡ κόμη ἀντὶ περιβολαίου δέδοται [αὐτῇ].

11:16Εἰ δέ τις δοκεῖ φιλόνεικος εἶναι, ἡμεῖς τοιαύτην συνήθειαν οὐκ ἔχομεν, οὐδὲ αἱ ἐκκλησίαι τοῦ θεοῦ.

11:8For the man is not of the woman: but the woman of the man. [n. 609]

11:9For the man was not created for the woman: but the woman for the man. [n. 611]

11:10Therefore, the woman ought to have power over her head, because of the angels. [n. 612]

11:11But yet neither is the man without the woman, nor the woman without the man, in the Lord. [n. 615]

11:12For as the woman is of the man, so also is the man through the woman: but all things of God. [n. 616]

11:13You yourselves judge. Does it become a woman to pray unto God uncovered? [n. 618]

11:14Does not even nature itself teach you that a man indeed, if he nourishes his hair, it is a shame unto him?

11:15But if a woman nourishes her hair, it is a glory to her; for her hair is given to her for a covering.

11:16But if any man seems to be contentious, we have no such custom, nor the Church of God. [n. 620]

---

609. Praemiserat Apostolus quod mulier est gloria viri, quod hic probare intendit.

Et circa hoc tria facit.

Primo ponit probationem;

secundo assignat rationem eius quod dixerat, ibi *etenim non est creatus*, etc.;

tertio infert conclusionem intentam, ibi *ideo debet*, et cetera.

610. Circa primum considerandum, quod, sicut supra dictum est, mulier dicitur gloria viri per quamdam derivationem, et ideo, ad hoc probandum, subdit *non enim*, prima scilicet rerum conditione, *vir est ex muliere*, scilicet formatus, *sed mulier ex viro*. Dicitur enim Gen. II, 22, quod *aedificavit Dominus Deus costam, quam tulerat de Adam in mulierem*. De viro autem dicitur *formavit Dominus Deus hominem de limo terrae*.

611. Deinde cum dicit *etenim*, etc., assignat rationem eius quod dixerat.

Ad cuius evidentiam considerandus est talis ordo perfecti et imperfecti, quod imperfectum in uno et

609. Having stated that the woman is the glory of man, the Apostle now prepares to prove it.

In regard to this he does three things.

First, he presents the proof;

second, he assigns a reason for what he had said, at *for the man was not created for the woman*;

third, he draws the conclusion intended, at *therefore the woman ought*.

610. In regard to the first it should be noted that, as was stated above, the woman is called the glory of man through something derived. Consequently, to prove this he says: *for the man* in the original condition of things *is not of the woman*, namely, formed out of the woman, *but the woman of the man*. For it is said: *and the rib from with the Lord God had taken from the man he made into a woman* (Gen 2:22). About man it is said that *the Lord formed man of dust from the ground* (Gen 2:7).

611. Then when he says, *for the man was not created*, he assigns the reason for what he had said.

To understand this it should be noted that the order of the perfect and of the imperfect is such that in one and the

eodem subiecto prius est tempore, quam perfectum. Prius enim aliquis homo est puer, quam vir; simpliciter tamen perfectum est prius imperfecto, tempore et natura. Nam puer producitur ex viro.

Haec igitur est ratio quare mulier producta est ex viro, quia perfectior est muliere, quod ex hoc probat Apostolus, quia finis est perfectior eo quod est ad finem: vir autem est finis mulieris. Et hoc est quod dicit **etenim non est creatus vir propter mulierem, sed mulier propter virum**, in adiutorium scilicet generationis: sicut patiens est propter agens, et materia propter formam. Unde dicitur Gen. II, 18: *non est bonum hominem esse solum, faciamus ei adiutorium simile sibi.*

612. Deinde cum dicit **ideo debet**, etc., infert conclusionem intentam, dicens *ideo*, scilicet quia vir est imago et gloria Dei, mulier autem est gloria viri, **mulier debet habere velamen super caput suum**, quando scilicet Deo assistit orando, vel prophetando, ut per hoc ostendatur, quod non immediate subest Deo, sed subiicitur etiam viro sub Deo; hoc enim significat velamen, quod capiti superponitur. Unde alia littera habet, quod **mulier debet habere potestatem super caput suum**, et idem est sensus: nam velamen est signum potestatis, secundum quod in Ps. LXV, 12 dicitur: *imposuisti homines super capita nostra.*

613. Deinde cum dicit **et propter angelos**, etc., assignat tertiam rationem, quae sumitur ex parte angelorum, dicens et etiam **mulier debet habere velamen super caput suum propter angelos**. Quod quidem dupliciter intelligi potest. Uno modo de ipsis angelis caelestibus, qui conventus fidelium visitare creduntur, praecipue quando sacra mysteria celebrantur. Et ideo tunc tam mulieres, quam viri ad reverentiam eorum honeste et ordinate se debent habere, secundum illud Ps. CXXXVII, 1: *in conspectu angelorum psallam tibi.*

Alio modo potest intelligi, secundum quod angeli dicuntur sacerdotes, inquantum divina populo annuntiant, secundum illud Mal. II, v. 7: *labia sacerdotis custodiunt scientiam, et legem requirent ex ore eius, quia angelus Domini exercituum est.*

Debet ergo mulier velamen habere semper in Ecclesia propter angelos, id est, propter sacerdotes, duplici ratione. Primo quidem propter eorum reverentiam, ad quam pertinet quod mulieres coram eis honeste se habeant. Unde dicitur Eccli. VII, 33: *honora Deum ex tota anima tua, et sacerdotes illius.* Secundo propter eorum cautelam, ne scilicet ex conspectu mulierum non velatarum ad concupiscentiam provocentur. Unde dicitur Eccli. c. IX, 5: *virginem ne aspicias, ne forte scandalizeris in decore illius.*

614. Augustinus autem aliter exponit praedicta. Ostendit enim quod tam mulier quam vir est ad

same subject the imperfect precedes the perfect in the order of time. For one is a boy, before he is a man. Absolutely speaking, however, the perfect precedes the imperfect in the order of time and of nature. For a boy is produced from the man.

This, therefore, is the reason why the woman was produced from the man, because he is more perfect than the woman, which the Apostle proves from the fact that the end is more perfect than that which is for the end; but man is the woman's end. And this is what he says: **for the man was not created for the woman: but the woman for the man**, as a helper, namely, in reproduction, as the patient is for the sake of the agent and matter for the sake of form: *it is not good for man to be alone: let us make him a helper like unto him* (Gen 2:18).

612. Then when he says, **therefore, the woman**, he draws the intended conclusion, saying: that is why, namely, because man is the image and glory of God, but woman the glory of man, **the woman ought to have a covering over her head**, when she places herself before God by praying or prophesying. In this way it is shown that she is not immediately under God, but is also subjected to man under God. For the veil put on the head signifies this. Hence another translation has it that **the woman ought to have power over her head**, but the sense is the same. For a veil is a sign of power, as it is said: *you let men ride over our heads* (Ps 66:4).

613. Then when he says, **because of the angels**, he gives a third reason, which is taken on the part of the angels, saying, **the woman ought to have a covering over her head, because of the angels**. This can be understood in two ways: in one way about the heavenly angels who are believed to visit congregations of the faithful, especially when the sacred mysteries are celebrated. And therefore at that time women as well as men ought to present themselves honorably and ordinately as reverence to them: *before the angels I sing your praise* (Ps 138:1).

In another way it can be understood in the sense that priests are called angels, inasmuch as they proclaim divine things to the people: *for the lips of a priest should guard knowledge, and men should seek instruction from his mouth; for he is the angel of the Lord of hosts* (Mal 2:7).

Therefore, the woman should always have a covering over her head because of the angels, i.e., the priests, for two reasons: first, as reverence toward them, to which it pertains that women should behave honorably before them. Hence it is said: *with all your might love your maker and do not forsake his priests* (Sir 7:30). Second, for their safety, lest the sight of a woman not veiled excite their concupiscence. Hence it is said: *do not look intently at a virgin, lest you stumble and incur penalties for her* (Sir 9:5).

614. Augustine explains the above in another way. For he shows that both man and woman are made to the image

imaginem Dei, per hoc quod dicitur Eph. IV, 23 s.: *reno-vamini spiritu mentis vestrae, et induite novum hominem, qui renovatur in agnitione Dei secundum imaginem eius qui creavit eum*, ubi non est masculus et foemina. Et sic patet, quod imago Dei attenditur in homine secundum spiritum, in quo non est differentia masculi et foeminae; et ideo mulier est imago Dei sicut et vir. Expresse enim dicitur Gen. I, 27, quod *creavit Deus hominem ad ima-ginem suam, masculum et foeminam creavit eos*: et ideo Augustinus dicit hoc esse intelligendum in spirituali co-niugio, quod est in anima nostra, in qua (sicut supra dic-tum est) sensualitas, vel etiam inferior ratio se habet per modum mulieris, ratio autem superior per modum viri, in qua attenditur imago Dei. Et secundum hoc mulier est ex viro et propter virum, quia administratio rerum temporalium, vel sensibilium, cui intendit inferior ratio vel etiam sensualitas, debet deduci ex contemplatione aeternorum, quae pertinent ad superiorem rationem, et ad eam ordinari.

Et ideo mulier dicitur habere velamen, vel potesta-tem super caput suum, ad significandum quod circa temporalia dispensanda debet homo cohibitionem qua-mdam et refraenationem habere, ne ultra modum homo progrediatur in eis diligendis. Quae quidem cohibitio circa amorem Dei adhiberi non debet, cum praecep-tum sit Deut. VI, 5: *diliges Dominum Deum tuum ex toto corde tuo*. Nam circa desiderium finis non appo-nitur mensura, quam necesse est apponi circa ea quae sunt ad finem. Medicus enim sanitatem inducit quanto perfectiorem potest, non tamen dat medicinam quanto maiorem potest, sed secundum determinatam mensu-ram. Sic vir non debet habere velamen super caput. Et hoc debet propter angelos sanctos: quia, sicut in Glossa dicitur *grata est sanctis angelis sacrata et pia significatio*. Unde et Augustinus dicit *de Civit. Dei*, quod Daemones alliciuntur quibusdam sensibilibus rebus, non sicut ani-malia cibis, sed sicut spiritus signis.

615. Deinde cum dicit **verumtamen neque vir**, etc., excludit dubitationem quae posset ex dictis oriri. Quia enim dixerat, quod vir est gloria Dei, mulier autem est gloria viri, posset aliquis credere, vel quod mulier non esset ex Deo, vel quod non haberet potestatem in gratia.

Unde primo hoc excludit, dicens: licet mulier sit glo-ria viri, qui est gloria Dei, **verumtamen neque vir est in Domino**, id est, a Domino productus, **sine muliere, ne-que mulier sine viro**; utrumque enim Deus fecit, secun-dum illud Gen. I, 27: *masculum et foeminam creavit eos*.

Vel aliter: **neque vir est sine muliere in Domino**, scilicet in gratia Domini nostri Iesu Christi, **neque mulier sine viro**, quia uterque per gratiam Dei salva-tur, secundum illud Gal. III, 27: *quicumque in Christo baptizati estis, Christum induistis*. Et postea subdit: *non*

of God, according to what is said: *be renewed in the spir-it of your minds and put on the new man created after the likeness of God according to the image of him who created him* (Eph 4:23), where considered according to the spirit, in which there is no difference between male and female; consequently, the woman is the image of God, just as the male. For it is expressly stated that *God created man to his own image, male and female he created them* (Gen 1:27). Therefore, Augustine says that this must be understood in a spiritual union, which is in our soul, in which the sen-sibility or even the lower reason has itself after the manner of the woman, but the superior reason after the manner of the man, in whom the image of God is considered to be. And according to this the woman is from the man and for the sake of the man, because the administration of tempo-ral or sensible things, in which the lower reason or even the sensibility is adept, ought to be deduced from the contem-plation of eternal things, which pertain to the higher reason and is ordained to it.

Therefore, the woman is said to have a veil or power over her own head, in order to signify that in regard to dispens-ing temporal things man should apply a certain restraint, lest he transgress the limits in loving them. This restraint should not be applied to the love of God, since it is com-manded: *you shall love the Lord your God with your whole heart* (Deut 6:5). For no limit is placed in regard to lov-ing the end, although one is placed in regard to the means to the end. For a doctor produces as much health as he can, but he does not give as much medicine as he can, but in a definite amount. Thus a man should not have a cover-ing on his head. And this on account of the angels, because, as is said in a Gloss: *sacred and pious signification is pleasing to the holy angels*. Hence Augustine also says in *The City of God*, that the demons are attracted by certain sensible things, not as animals to food but as spirits to signs.

615. Then when he says, **but yet neither is the man**, he excludes a doubt which could arise from these statements. For because he had said that man is God's glory and the woman man's glory, someone might believe either that the woman was not from God or that she should not have pow-er in grace.

Hence he excludes the first, saying: although the woman is the glory of man, who is the glory of God, **but yet nei-ther is the man . . . in the Lord**, i.e., produced by the Lord, **without the woman, nor the woman without the man**; for God made both of them: *male and female he created them* (Gen 1:27).

Or in another way: **neither is the man without the woman . . . in the Lord**, namely, in the grace of our Lord Je-sus Christ, **nor the woman without the man**, because both are saved by God's grace: *for as many of you as were bap-tized have put on Christ* (Gal 3:27), and then he adds: *there*

est masculus, neque foemina, scilicet differens in gratia Christi.

616. Secundo assignat rationem, dicens: ***nam sicut*** in prima rerum institutione ***mulier*** est ***de viro*** formata, ***ita et*** in subsequentibus generationibus, ***vir per mulierem*** productus est, secundum illud Iob XIV, 1: *homo natus de muliere*.

Nam prima productio hominis fuit sine viro et muliere, quando Deus *formavit hominem de limo terrae*, ut dicitur Gen. Secunda autem fuit de viro sine muliere, quando formavit Evam de costa viri, ut ibidem legitur. Tertia autem est ex viro et muliere, sicut Abel natus est ex Adam et Eva, ut legitur Gen. IV, 2. Quarta autem est ex muliere sine viro, ut Christus ex virgine, secundum illud Gal. IV, 4: *misit Deus Filium suum factum ex muliere*.

617. Tertio ostendit rationem esse convenientem, dicens ***omnia autem ex Deo***, quia scilicet et hoc ipsum, quod mulier primo fuit ex viro, et hoc quod postmodum vir est ex muliere, est ex operatione divina. Unde ad Deum pertinent tam vir, quam mulier. Unde dicitur Rom. XL, 36: *ex ipso, et per ipsum, et in ipso sunt omnia*.

618. Deinde cum dicit ***vos ipsi iudicate***, etc., committit iudicium eius quod dixerat auditoribus.

Et circa hoc duo facit.

Primo committit iudicium rationalibus auditoribus;

secundo comprimit protervos auditores, ibi ***si quis autem videtur***, et cetera.

619. Circa primum quatuor facit. Primo committit auditoribus iudicium eius quod dixerat, more eius qui confidit se sufficienter probasse, dicens ***vos ipsi iudicate***, et cetera. Pertinet enim ad bonum auditorem iudicare de auditis. Unde dicitur Iob VI, 29: *loquentes id quod iustum est iudicate*. Et XII, 11: *nonne auris verba diiudicat?*

Secundo proponit sub quaestione id de quo debet esse iudicium, dicens ***decet mulierem non velatam orare Deum***. Hoc prohibetur I Petr. III, 3, ubi dicitur: *quarum sit non exterius capillatura*.

Tertio ostendit unde debeant sumere suum iudicium, quia ab ipsa natura, et hoc est quod dicit ***nec ipsa natura docet vos***. Et vocat hic naturam ipsam inclinationem naturalem, quae est mulieribus ad nutriendum comam, quae est naturale velamen, non autem viris. Quae quidem inclinatio naturalis esse ostenditur, quia in pluribus invenitur. Oportet autem ab ipsa natura doceri, quia est Dei opus: sicut in pictura instruitur aliquis artificio pictoris. Et ideo contra quosdam dicitur Is. XXIV, 5: *transgressi sunt leges, mutaverunt ius, dissipaverunt foedus sempiternum*, id est, ius naturale.

Quarto autem a natura sumit rationem; et primo ponit id quod est ex parte viri, dicens ***quod vir quidem, si comam nutriat***, more mulieris, ***ignominia est illi***, id

is neither male nor female, namely, differing in the grace of Christ.

616. Second, he assigns the reason, saying: ***for as*** in the first condition of things, ***the woman is of the man***, formed from the man, ***so also*** in subsequent generations ***the man*** was produced ***through the woman***, as Job says: *man born of a woman* (Job 14:1).

For the first production of man took place without man or woman, when God *formed man from the dust of the earth* (Gen 2:7). The second was from man without the woman, when he formed Eve from Adam's rib, as it says in the same place. But the third is from man and woman, as Abel was born from Adam and Eve (Gen 4:2). But the fourth was from the woman without the man, as Christ from the virgin: *God sent forth his Son born of woman* (Gal 4:4).

617. Third, he shows that the reason is apt, saying, ***but all things of God***, namely, because even the fact that the woman was first from the man, and afterwards man is from the woman, is the result of God's action. Hence both man and woman pertain to God. Hence it is said: *for from him and through him and in him are all things* (Rom 11:36).

618. Then when he says, ***you yourselves judge***, he submits to his hearers' judgment the things he had said.

In regard to this he does two things.

First, he submits the judgment to his rational hearers;

second, he subdues the impudent ones, at ***but if any man seem***.

619. In regard to the first he does four things: first, he submits to his hearers to judge what he had said, after the manner of one who is confident that he has sufficiently proved his point, saying: ***you yourselves judge***. For it pertains to a good hearer to judge what is heard. Hence it is said: *judge, speaking what is just* (Job 6:29) and: *does not the ear judge words?* (Job 12:11).

Second, he proposes in the form of a question that about which they should judge, saying, ***does it become a woman to pray unto God uncovered?*** This is forbidden where it is said: *let not yours be the outward adorning with braiding of hair* (1 Pet 3:3).

Third, he shows whence they should derive their judgment, namely, from nature itself; and this is what he says, ***does not even nature itself teach you***. By 'nature' he means the 'natural inclination' in women to take care of their hair, which is a natural covering, but not in men. This inclination is shown to be natural, because it is found in the majority. But it is taught by nature, because it is a work of God; just as in a picture one is instructed about the skill of the artist. Therefore, Isaiah says against certain people: *they have transgressed the law, violated the statutes, broken the everlasting covenant* (Isa 24:5), i.e., the natural law.

Fourth, he takes a reason from nature: first, he presents that which is on the part of the man, saying, ***that a man indeed, if he nourishes his hair*** like a woman, ***it is a shame***

est, ad ignominiam ei reputatur apud plures homines, quia per hoc videtur muliebris esse. Et ideo Ez. XLIV, 20 dicitur: *sacerdotes comam non nutriant*. Nec est instantia de quibusdam, qui in veteri lege comam nutriebant, quia hoc erat signum, quod tunc erat positum in lectione Veteris Testamenti, ut dicitur II Cor. III, 14.

Secundo ponit id quod est ex parte mulieris, dicens **mulier et si comam nutriat, gloria est illi**, quia videtur ad ornatum eius pertinere. Unde dicitur Cant. VII, 5: *comae capitis eius sicut purpura regis*.

Et assignat consequenter rationem, cum dicit **quoniam capilli dati sunt ei**, scilicet mulieri, **pro velamine**; et ideo eadem ratio est de capillis nutriendis, et de velamine artificiali apponendo. Cant. IV, 1: *capilli tui sicut grex caprarum*, et cetera.

620. Deinde cum dicit **si quis autem videtur**, etc., comprimit protervos auditores, dicens **si quis autem videtur contentiosus esse**, ut scilicet rationibus praedictis non acquiescat, sed confidentia clamoris veritatem impugnet, quod pertinet ad contentionem, ut Ambrosius dicit, contra id quod dicitur Iob c. VI, 29: *respondete, obsecro, absque contentione*; et Prov. XX, 3: *honor est ei, qui separat se a contentionibus*.

Hoc sufficiat ad comprimendum talem, quod nos Iudaei in Christum credentes **talem consuetudinem non habemus**, scilicet quod mulieres orent non velato capite, **neque** etiam tota **ecclesia Dei** per gentes diffusa.

Unde si nulla esset ratio, hoc solum deberet sufficere, ne aliquis ageret contra communem Ecclesiae consuetudinem. Dicitur enim in Ps. LXVII, 7: *qui habitare facit unius moris in domo*. Unde Augustinus dicit in *Epistola ad Casulanum* quod *omnibus, in quibus nihil certi diffinit Sacra Scriptura, mos populi Dei, atque instituta maiorum pro lege habenda sunt*.

unto him, i.e., the majority of men regard this as degrading, because it makes the man seem feminine. Therefore, it is said: *they shall not let their locks grow long* (Ezek 44:20). It is no argument that some in the old law grew long hair, because this was a sign presented in the reading of the Old Testament (2 Cor 3:14).

Second, he presents that which is on the part of the woman, saying, **but if a woman nourishes her hair, it is a glory to her**, because it seems to pertain to her adornment. Hence it is said: *your flowing locks are like purple* (Song 7:5).

Then he assigns the reason when he says, **for her hair is given to her for a covering**. Consequently, the same reason applies to growing long hair and to wearing an artificial covering: *your hair is like a flock of goats* (Song 4:1).

620. Then when he says, **if any man**, he silences the impudent hearers, saying, **if any man seems to be contentious** and does not acquiesce in the above reason but would attack the truth with confident clamoring, which pertains to contentiousness, as Ambrose says, contrary to Job: *respond, I pray, without contentiousness* (Job 6:29); *it is an honor for a man to keep aloof from strife* (Prov 20:3).

Let this suffice, then, to silence them, that we Jews believing in Christ **have no such custom**, namely, of women praying with their heads uncovering, **nor** even **the** whole **Church of God** dispersed among the gentiles.

Hence if there were no reason, this alone should suffice, that no one should act against the common custom of the Church: *he makes those of one outlook to dwell in their house* (Ps 68:7). Hence Augustine says: *in all cases in which Sacred Scripture has defined nothing definite, the customs of the people of God and the edicts of superiors must be regarded as the law*.

Lecture 4

11:17 Hoc autem praecipio: non laudans quod non in melius, sed in deterius convenitis. [n. 621]

11:18 Primum quidem convenientibus vobis in ecclesiam, audio scissuras esse inter vos, et ex parte credo. [n. 623]

11:19 Nam oportet et haereses esse, ut et qui probati sunt, manifesti fiant in vobis. [n. 626]

11:20 Convenientibus ergo vobis in unum, jam non est Dominicam coenam manducare. [n. 629]

11:21 Unusquisque enim suam coenam praesumit ad manducandum, et alius quidem esurit, alius autem ebrius est. [n. 633]

11:22 Numquid domos non habetis ad manducandum, et bibendum? aut ecclesiam Dei contemnitis, et confunditis eos qui non habent? Quid dicam vobis? laudo vos? in hoc non laudo. [n. 636]

11:17Τοῦτο δὲ παραγγέλλων οὐκ ἐπαινῶ ὅτι οὐκ εἰς τὸ κρεῖσσον ἀλλὰ εἰς τὸ ἧσσον συνέρχεσθε.

11:18πρῶτον μὲν γὰρ συνερχομένων ὑμῶν ἐν ἐκκλησίᾳ ἀκούω σχίσματα ἐν ὑμῖν ὑπάρχειν, καὶ μέρος τι πιστεύω.

11:19δεῖ γὰρ καὶ αἱρέσεις ἐν ὑμῖν εἶναι, ἵνα [καὶ] οἱ δόκιμοι φανεροὶ γένωνται ἐν ὑμῖν.

11:20Συνερχομένων οὖν ὑμῶν ἐπὶ τὸ αὐτὸ οὐκ ἔστιν κυριακὸν δεῖπνον φαγεῖν,

11:21ἕκαστος γὰρ τὸ ἴδιον δεῖπνον προλαμβάνει ἐν τῷ φαγεῖν, καὶ ὃς μὲν πεινᾷ, ὃς δὲ μεθύει.

11:22μὴ γὰρ οἰκίας οὐκ ἔχετε εἰς τὸ ἐσθίειν καὶ πίνειν; ἢ τῆς ἐκκλησίας τοῦ θεοῦ καταφρονεῖτε, καὶ καταισχύνετε τοὺς μὴ ἔχοντας; τί εἴπω ὑμῖν; ἐπαινέσω ὑμᾶς; ἐν τούτῳ οὐκ ἐπαινῶ.

11:17 Now this I ordain: not praising you, that you come together, not for the better, but for the worse. [n. 621]

11:18 For first of all I hear that when you come together in the church, there are schisms among you. And in part I believe it. [n. 623]

11:19 For there must be also heresies: that they also, who are approved may be made manifest among you. [n. 626]

11:20 When you come together therefore into one place, it is not now to eat the Lord's supper. [n. 629]

11:21 For every one takes before his own supper to eat. And one indeed is hungry and another is drunk. [n. 633]

11:22 What, have you no houses to eat and to drink in? Or do you despise the church of God and put them to shame that have not? What shall I say to you? Do I praise you? In this I praise you not. [n. 636]

---

621. Postquam Apostolus redarguit Corinthios de eorum errore in habitu, quia scilicet mulieres ad sacra mysteria conveniebant capite non velato consequenter arguit eorum errorem de scissuris in conventu, quia scilicet dum convenirent ad sacra mysteria, contentionibus vacabant. Et

primo tangit eorum defectum in generali;

secundo in speciali, ibi **primum quidem**, et cetera.

622. Dicit ergo primo **hoc autem**, quod dictum est supra quod mulieres velatae sint in Ecclesiis, **praecipio**, ut sic tripliciter eos induceret ad huiusmodi observantiam. Primo quidem ratione, secundo consuetudine, tertio praecepto: quod solum sine aliis necessitatem induceret. Prov. IV, 4: *custodi praecepta mea, et vives.* Et Eccle. IV, v. 12 dicitur: *funiculus triplex difficile rumpitur.* Non **laudans**, sed magis vituperans, **quod convenitis**, in ecclesiam, **non in melius**, sicut deberet esse, **sed in deterius**, ex culpa vestra.

Omnia enim animalia gregalia, puta columbae, grues, oves, naturali instinctu in unum conveniunt, ut sit eis corporaliter melius. Unde et homo cum sit animal gregale vel sociale, ut Philosophus probat, I Lib. *Politic.,* secundum rationem agere debet, ut multi in unum conveniant propter aliquod melius, sicut in rebus saecularibus multi in unitatem civitatis conveniunt, ut sit eis

621. After reproaching the Corinthians for their error in covering, namely, because the women came to the sacred mysteries with their head uncovered, the Apostle then argues against their error about factions in the assembly, because while they gathered for the sacred mysteries, they spent their time in contentions.

First, he touches on their shortcoming in general;

second, in particular, at **for first of all**.

622. First, therefore, he says, **now this**, which was stated above, namely, that women should be veiled in church, **I ordain**, in order that he might thus induce them to this observance in three ways. First, indeed, by reason; second, by custom; third, by command, which should persuade them without the other two: *keep my commandments and you shall live* (Prov 4:4); *a three-ply cord is not quickly broken* (Eccl 4:12) **Not praising you**, but rather censuring you, **that you come together** into the church **not for the better**, as it should be, **but for the worse** through your fault.

For all gregarious animals, for example, doves, cranes, cows, each form one group by natural instinct, in order that things be better for them in a bodily way. Hence man, too, being a gregarious or social animal, as the Philosopher proves in *Politics* I, should act according to reason, so that many form one group for their betterment, just as in secular affairs many come together to form the unity of a city; so

melius saeculariter, scilicet propter securitatem et sufficientiam vitae. Et ideo fideles in unum convenire debent propter aliquod melius spirituale, secundum illud Ps. ci, 23: *in conveniendo populos in unum, et reges ut serviant Domino*. Et alibi: *in consilio iustorum et congregatione, magna opera Domini*. Sed isti in deterius conveniebant propter culpas quas committebant dum convenirent. Is. I, 13: *iniqui sunt caetus vestri*. Eccli. XXI, 10: *stupa collecta synagoga peccantium*.

623. Deinde cum dicit *primum quidem*, etc., ponit in speciali quomodo in deterius convenirent.

Et primo ponit iudicium culpae, dicens *primum quidem*, inter caetera scilicet quod in deterius convenitis, *convenientibus vobis in ecclesia, audio scissuras esse inter vos*, scilicet per contentiones quas exercebant. Quod quidem Ecclesiae non convenit, quae in unitate constituitur, secundum illud Eph. c. IV, 4: *unum corpus et unus spiritus, sicut vocati estis in una spe vocationis vestrae*. Hoc autem praedicitur Is. XXII, 9: *scissuras civitatis David videbitis, quia multiplicatae sunt*.

624. Dicit autem Glossa, quod *dicendo, **primum**, ostendit quod primum malum est dissensio, unde cetera oriuntur. Ubi enim est dissensio, nihil rectum est.*

Sed contra videtur esse, quod dicitur Eccli. c. X, 15: *initium omnis peccati superbia*; et I Tim. ult.: *radix omnium malorum cupiditas*.

Dicendum est autem, quod hae auctoritates loquuntur quantum ad peccata personalia singularium hominum, quorum primum est superbia ex parte aversionis, et cupiditas ex parte conversionis. Sed Glossa hic loquitur de peccatis multitudinis; inter quae primum est dissensio, per quam solvitur rigor disciplinae. Unde dicitur Iac. III, 16: *ubi est zelus et contentio, ibi inconstantia et omne opus pravum*.

625. Secundo ponit credulitatem auditorum, cum dicit *et ex parte credo*, id est, quantum ad aliquos vestrum, qui erant ad contentionem proni, secundum illud quod dixerat supra I cap., v. 11 ss.: *contentiones sunt inter vos. Hoc autem dico, quod unusquisque vestrum dicit: ego quidem sum Pauli, ego Apollo, ego vero Cephae*. Alii vero non erant contentiosi, ex quorum persona ibi subditur *ego autem Christi*. Unde et Cant. c. II, 2 dicitur: *sicut lilium inter spinas, sic amica mea inter filias*, id est, boni inter malos.

626. Tertio assignat rationem suae credulitatis, dicens *nam oportet*, non solum quascumque scissuras, sed etiam *haereses esse*.

Ubi duo consideranda sunt. Primo quid sit haeresis, secundo quomodo oportet haereses esse.

627. Circa primum sciendum, quod, sicut Hieronymus dicit super epistolam ad Galatas, haeresis Graece ab electione dicitur: quia scilicet eam sibi unusquisque eligat disciplinam, quam putat esse meliorem: ex quo duo

that it is better for them in a worldly way, namely, because of the security and sufficiency of life. Therefore, believers should come together into a unity for some better spiritual things: *when people gather together and kings, to worship the Lord* (Ps 102:22); *in the counsel and congregation of the just the works of the Lord are great* (Ps 111:1). But they came together for the worse on account of the sins they committed, when they assembled: *I cannot endure iniquity and solemn assembly* (Isa 1:13); *an assembly of the wicked is like two gathered together* (Sir 21:9).

623. Then when he says, *for first of all*, he mentions in detail how they assemble for the worse.

First, he presents a judgment of guilt, saying, *for first of all*, among others, namely, that you come together for the worse, *I hear that when you come together in the church, there are schisms among you*, namely, through contentions, which they practiced. This by no means is suited to the Church, which is established in unity: *there is one body and one spirit, just as you were called to one hope that belongs to your call* (Eph 4:4). But his was predicted: *you saw that the breaches of the city of David were many* (Isa 22:9).

624. But a Gloss says: *by saying, **first of all**, he shows that the first evil is dissension, from which all the rest arise. For where there is dissension, nothing is right.*

But this seems to be opposed by the following statements: *the beginning of every sin is pride* (Sir 9:15) and *the love of money is the root of all evils* (1 Tim 6:10).

But it must be said that these authorities speak in regard to personal sins of individual men, the first of which is pride on the part of aversion and greed for money on the part of conversion. But the Gloss here speaks about the sins of the multitude, among which the first is dissension, by which the reign of discipline is weakened. Hence it is said: *where jealousy and contention exist, there will be disorder and every vile practice* (Jas 3:16).

625. Second, he presents the credulity of his hearers when he says, *and in part I believe it*, i.e., as to some of you who were prone to contention, according to what was said above: *there are contentions among you. Now this I say, that every one of you says: I indeed am of Paul; and I am of Apollo; and I of Cephas* (1 Cor 1:11–12). But others were not contentious, who said, *and I of Christ* (1 Cor 1:12). Hence it is said: *as a lily among brambles, so is my love among maidens* (Song 2:2), i.e., good among the evil.

626. Third, he assigns the reason for their credulity, saying, *for there must be* not only factions among you but *also heresies*.

Two things must be considered here: first, what heresy is; second, how it is necessary that there be heresies.

627. In regard to the first it should be known that, as Jerome comments on the epistle to the Galatians, the Greek word, *heresy*, means 'election' or 'choice', namely, because each one selects for himself that discipline which he

accipi possunt. Primo quidem quod de ratione haeresis est, quod aliquis privatam disciplinam sequatur, quasi per electionem propriam: non autem disciplinam publicam, quae divinitus traditur.

Secundo quod huic disciplinae aliquis pertinaciter inhaereat. Nam electio firmam importat inhaesionem: et ideo haereticus dicitur, qui spernens disciplinam fidei, quae divinitus traditur, pertinaciter proprium errorem sectatur.

Pertinet autem aliquid ad disciplinam fidei dupliciter. Uno modo directe, sicut articuli fidei, qui per se credendi proponuntur. Unde error circa hos secundum se facit haereticum, si pertinacia adsit. Non possunt autem a tali errore propter simplicitatem aliquam excusari, praecipue quantum ad ea, de quibus Ecclesia solemnizat, et quae communiter versantur in ore fidelium, sicut mysterium Trinitatis, nativitatis Christi, et alia huiusmodi.

Quaedam vero indirecte pertinent ad fidei disciplinam, inquantum scilicet ipsa non proponuntur, ut propter se credenda, sed ex negatione eorum sequitur aliquid contrarium fidei: sicut si negetur Isaac fuisse filium Abrahae, sequitur aliquid contrarium fidei, scilicet Sacram Scripturam continere aliquid falsi.

Ex talibus autem non iudicatur aliquis haereticus, nisi adeo pertinaciter perseveret, quod ab errore non recedat, etiam viso quid ex hoc sequatur. Sic igitur pertinacia qua aliquis contemnit in his quae sunt fidei directe vel indirecte subire iudicium Ecclesiae, facit hominem haereticum. Talis autem pertinacia procedit ex radice superbiae, qua aliquis praefert sensum suum toti Ecclesiae. Unde Apostolus dicit I ad Tim. VI, 3 s.: *si quis aliter docet, et non acquiescit sanis sermonibus Domini nostri Iesu Christi, et ei quae secundum pietatem est doctrinae, superbus est, nihil sciens, sed languens circa quaestiones et pugnas verborum.*

628. Secundo considerandum est, quomodo oporteat haereses esse. Si enim opportunum est haereticos esse, videtur quod sint commendabiles, et non sint extirpandi.

Sed dicendum est quod dupliciter de aliquo dicitur quod oportet illud esse. Uno modo ex intentione illius, qui hoc agit, puta si dicamus quod oportet iudicia esse: quia scilicet iudices, iudicia exercentes, intendunt iustitiam et pacem in rebus humanis constituere. Alio modo ex intentione Dei, qui etiam mala ordinat in bonum, sicut persecutionem tyrannorum ordinavit in gloriam martyrum. Unde Augustinus dicit in *Enchiridion*, quod *Deus est adeo bonus, quod nullo modo permitteret fieri aliquod malum, nisi esset adeo potens quod de quolibet malo posset elicere bonum.* Et secundum hoc dicitur Matth. XVIII, 7: *necesse est, ut veniant scandala,*

considers to be better. From this two things can be taken: first, that it is of the very nature of heresy that a person follow his own private discipline, as though by his own choice, but not the public discipline handed down by God.

Second, that he obstinately cling to this discipline. For choice implies firm adherence; and therefore the heretic is one who scorns the discipline of the faith handed down by God and obstinately follows his own error.

Now something pertains to the discipline of the faith in two ways: in one way directly, as the articles of faith, which are proposed to be believed of themselves. Hence an error in regard to them makes one a heretic, if obstinacy is present. But a person cannot be excused from such an error on account of some simplicity especially in regard to those about which the Church made a solemn proclamation and which are generally spoken about by the faithful, such as the mystery of the Trinity, the birth of Christ, and so on.

But other things pertain to the discipline of the faith indirectly, namely, inasmuch as they are not proposed as something to be believed of themselves, but from their denial something contrary to the faith follows; for example, if it is denied that Isaac was the son of Abraham, something contrary to the faith follows, namely, that Sacred Scripture contains something false.

From such things one is not judged heretical, unless he continues in his opinion so obstinately, that he would not depart from his error, even though he sees what follows from his position. Therefore, the obstinacy with which someone spurns the judgment of the Church in matters pertaining to the faith directly or indirectly makes a man a heretic. Such obstinacy proceeds from pride, whereby a person prefers his own feelings to the entire Church. Hence the Apostle says: *if anyone teaches otherwise and does not agree with the sound words of our Lord Jesus Christ and the teaching which accords with godliness, he is puffed up with conceit, he knows nothing; he has a morbid craving for controversy and for disputes about words* (1 Tim 6:3ff).

628. Second, it must be considered how it is suitable that heresies exist. For if it is suitable for heretics to be, it seems that they are commendable and should not be stamped out.

But it should be noted that there are two ways in which something is described as suitable to be. In one way from the intention of the one who does this; for example, if we should say that judgments ought to be, because judges make judgments intending to establish justice and peace in human affairs. In another way from the intention of God who ordains evil things to good, who directs the persecutions of tyrants to the glory of the martyrs. Hence Augustine says in *Enchiridion*, that *God is so good that he would not permit evil in any way, unless he were powerful enough that from each evil he can draw some good.* And according to this it is said: *woe to the world for temptations to sin. For*

verumtamen vae homini illi per quem scandalum venit. Et secundum hoc hic dicit Apostolus, quod **oportet haereses esse**, ex eo quod Deus malitiam haereticorum ordinavit in bonum fidelium.

Et hoc dicit primo quidem ad maiorem declarationem veritatis. Unde dicit Augustinus *de Civit. Dei*, Lib. XVI in Glossa: *ab adversario mota quaestio, discendi existit occasio: multa quippe ad fidem Catholicam pertinentia, dum haereticorum callida inquietudine excogitantur, ut adversus eos defendi possint, et considerantur diligentius, et intelliguntur clarius, et praedicantur instantius.* Unde et Prov. XXVII, v. 17: *ferrum ferro acuitur, et homo exacuit faciem amici sui.* Secundo ad manifestandam infirmitatem fidei in his qui recte credunt. Et hoc est quod hic subdit Apostolus **ut et qui probati**, id est, approbati sunt a Deo, **manifesti fiant in vobis**, id est, inter vos. Sap. III, 6: *tamquam aurum in fornace probavit illos.*

629. Deinde cum dicit **convenientibus ergo vobis**, etc., redarguit eos de tertio delicto, quia scilicet peccabant in modo et ordine sumendi corpus Christi. Et potest totum quod sequitur, dupliciter exponi. Secundum autem primam expositionem redarguuntur de hoc quod corpus Christi pransi accipiebant.

Circa hoc ergo quatuor facit.

Primo ponit detrimentum quod incurrebant;

secundo ponit culpam, ibi **unusquisque enim**, etc.;

tertio inquirit de causa culpae, ibi **numquid domos**, etc.;

quarto concludit eorum vituperationem, ibi **quid dicam vobis**, et cetera.

630. Dicit ergo, primo, ita: **convenientibus vobis, scissurae sunt inter vos**, ergo **convenientibus vobis in unum**, corpore, non animo, **iam** ad hoc advenistis, quod **non est**, id est, non licet vel non competit vobis, **Dominicam coenam manducare**, id est sumere Eucharistiae sacramentum, quod Dominus in coena discipulis dedit. *Hoc enim sacramentum*, ut Augustinus dicit *Super Ioannem*, est *sacramentum unitatis et caritatis.* Et ideo non competit dissentientibus. Cant. c. V, 1: *comedite, amici, et bibite, et inebriamini, charissimi.*

631. Vel melius potest referri ad ea quae sequuntur, ut sit sensus: non solum **convenientibus vobis** scissurae sunt inter vos, sed convenit vobis convenientibus **iam**, id est in praesenti hoc determinatum habetis, quod **non est**, id est non licet vobis, **Dominicam coenam manducare**, ad quam pransi acceditis. Quia enim Dominus discipulis suis post coenam hoc sacramentum tradidit, ut legitur Matth. XXVI, 26, volebant etiam Corinthii post communem coenam sumere corpus Christi.

Sed Dominus hoc rationabiliter fecit propter tria. Primo quidem, quia ordine congruo figura praecedit veritatem. Agnus autem paschalis erat figura, sive

it is necessary that temptations come, but woe to that man from whom temptations come (Matt 18:7). And according to this the Apostle says, **there must be also heresies**, inasmuch as God has ordained the malice of heretics to the good of the faithful.

He says this, first, for the clearer declaration of truth. Hence Augustine says in *The City of God*: *a question raised by an adversary is an occasion for learning; indeed, many things pertaining to the Catholic faith, when they are devised by the clever energy of heretics, in order that they may be defended against them, are considered more carefully and understood more clearly and preached with more emphasis.* Hence it is said: *iron sharpens iron; and one man sharpens another* (Prov 27:17). Second, to reveal the weakness of faith in those who believe rightly. And this is what the Apostle says, **that they also, who are approved**, i.e., approved by God, **may be made manifest among you**: *like gold in the furnace he tried them* (Wis 3:6).

629. Then when he says, **when you come together therefore**, he accuses them of a third fault, namely, that they sinned in the way and order in which they took the body of Christ. All that follows can be explained in two ways. According to the first explanation they are accused of taking the body of Christ just after eating.

In regard to this he does four things.

First, he mentions the harm they incur;

second, he mentions the fault, at **for every one takes**;

third, he looks for the cause of the fault, at **what, have you no houses**;

fourth, he concludes his rebuke, **what shall I say to you**.

630. He says, therefore, first, **when you come together**, **there are schims among you**, therefore, **you come together therefore into one**, in body, not in mind, **now** you have come to this which **is not**, i.e., not lawful or is not becoming for you, **to eat the Lord's supper**, i.e., receive the sacrament of the Eucharist, which the Lord gave his disciples at supper. *For this sacrament*, says Augustine in *On John*, *is the sacrament of unity and love.* Therefore, it is not suited to dissenters; *eat, O friends and drink; drink deeply, O lovers* (Song 5:2).

631. Or better: it can be referred to what follows, so that the sense is: not only are there disputes among you when **you come together**, but it has **now** become your custom to do what **is not** lawful for you, namely, **to eat the Lord's supper**, which you approach right after eating. For because the Lord gave this sacrament to his disciples after supper (Matt 26:26), the Corinthians also wanted to take the body of Christ after a common meal.

But the Lord did this for three reasons: first, because the figure precedes the truth in proper order. But the paschal lamb was a figure or shadow of this sacrament. Accordingly,

umbra huius sacramenti. Et ideo post coenam agni pa-schalis, Christus hoc sacramentum dedit. Dicitur enim Coloss. II, 17 de omnibus legalibus, quod *sunt umbra futurorum, corpus autem Christi*. Secundo ut ex hoc sa-cramento statim ad passionem transiret, cuius hoc sa-cramentum est memoriale. Et ideo dixit discipulis *sur-gite, eamus hinc*, scilicet ad passionem. Tertio ut arctius imprimeretur hoc sacramentum cordibus discipulorum, quibus ipsum tradidit in ultimo suo recessu.

Sed in reverentiam tanti sacramenti postmodum Ec-clesia instituit, quod non nisi a ieiunis sumatur, a quo excipiuntur infirmi, qui in necessitate, quae legem non habet, possunt non ieiuni sumere corpus Christi.

632. Quia vero aqua non solvit ieiunium, aestimave-runt quidam, quod post potum aquae posset aliquis su-mere hoc sacramentum, praesertim quia, ut dicunt, aqua non nutrit, sicut nec aliquod aliud simplex elementum.

Quamvis autem aqua secundum se non nutriat, et ob hoc non solvat ieiunium Ecclesiae, secundum quod dicuntur aliqui ieiunantes, nutrit tamen aliis admixta, et ideo solvit ieiunium naturae. Et secundum hoc dicuntur aliqui ieiuni, qui scilicet eadem die nihil sumpserunt, nec cibi, nec potus. Et quia reliquiae cibi, quae in ore re-manent, sumuntur per modum salivae, hoc non impe-dit aliquos esse ieiunos. Similiter et non impedit aliquos esse ieiunos, si tota nocte nihil dormierint, vel si etiam non sint plene digesti, dummodo eadem die omnino cibi vel potus nihil sumpserint.

Unde quia principium diei est sumendum secundum usum Ecclesiae a media nocte, ideo quicumque post me-diam noctem aliquid sumpserit quantumcumque modi-cum cibi vel potus, non potest eadem die sumere hoc sacramentum.

633. Deinde, cum dicit *unusquisque enim*, etc., ponit culpam, et

primo secundum quod peccabant in Deum;

secundo prout peccabant in proximum, ibi *et alius quidem*, et cetera.

634. Dicit ergo primo: ideo dico quod non licet *vobis Dominicam coenam manducare*, quia *unusquisque* ve-strum *praesumit*, id est ante sumit, *suam coenam*, scili-cet ciborum communium, *ad manducandum*. Quilibet enim eorum portabat ad ecclesiam fercula praeparata, et comedebat quilibet seorsum antequam sumeret sacra mysteria. Os. IV, v. 18: *separatum est convivium eorum, nunc interibunt*. Eccli. XI, 19 dicitur in persona parci: *inveni requiem mihi, et comedebam de bonis meis solus*.

635. Deinde, cum dicit *et alius quidem*, etc., arguit culpam eorum, inquantum erat contra proximum.

Divites enim laute comedebant in ecclesia, et bi-bebant usque ad ebrietatem, pauperibus autem nihil

after the supper of the paschal lamb, Christ gave this sacra-ment. For it is said about all practices of the law: *these are only a shadow of what is to come; but the substance belongs to Christ* (Col 2:17). Second, in order that from this sacrament he might pass immediately to his passion, of which this sac-rament is the memorial. Therefore, he said to the disciples: *arise, let us go from here* (John 14:31), namely, to his pas-sion. Third, in order that this sacrament be impressed more sharply on the hearts of the disciples, to whom he gave it in his last quiet retreat.

But out of reverence for this great sacrament the Church later established that it can be taken only by those fasting; from which the sick were excepted, who in necessity, which knows no law, could take the body of Christ without fast-ing.

632. But because water does not break the fast, some supposed that after a drink of water they could take this sacrament, especially because, as they say, water is not nourishment any more than any other element.

But although water by itself is not nourishment and, therefore, does not break the Eucharistic fast in the sense that some are said to fast, nevertheless when it is mixed with other things, it does nourish. And in this sense some are said to be fasting who on the same day take neither food nor drink. And because the pieces of food remaining in the mouth are consumed after the manner of saliva, this does not prevent one from being fasting. Likewise, the fast is not broken, if a person does not sleep at all during the night, or even if the food is not fully digested, provided that on one and the same day he took absolutely no food or drink.

Hence because the beginning of a day is reckoned from midnight according to the custom of the Church, then whoever partakes of food or drink, no matter how little, after midnight, cannot receive this sacrament on that day.

633. Then when he says, *for every one*, he mentions the fault:

first, insofar as they sinned against God;

second, insofar as they sinned against their neighbor, at *and one indeed is hungry*.

634. He says, therefore, first: the reason I say that it is not lawful for you *to eat the Lord's supper* is that *every one takes before his own supper to eat*, namely, of com-mon food. For each one carried to the church a tray of food already prepared, and each one ate by himself, before he took the sacred mysteries: *they banquet separately; now they shall perish* (Hos 9:9); and in the person of the frugal, it is said: *I have found rest, and I ate of my own goods alone* (Sir 11:19).

635. Then when he says, *and one indeed is hungry*, he accuses them of the sin against the neighbor.

For the wealthy ate lavishly in church and imbibed un-til they were drunk; they gave nothing to the poor, who

dabant, ita quod remanebant esurientes. Et hoc est quod dicitur *et alius quidem esurit*, scilicet pauper, qui non habebat unde sibi praepararet, *alter autem ebrius est*, scilicet dives, qui superflue comedebat et bibebat, contra id quod dicitur Nehem. c. VIII, 10: *comedite pinguia, et bibite mulsum, et mittite partes eis, qui non praeparaverunt sibi*. Iob XXXI, 17: *si comedi buccellam meam solus, et non comedit pupillus ex ea*.

636. Deinde, cum dicit *numquid domos*, etc., inquirit de causa huius culpae.

Et primo excludit causam per quam poterant excusari. Non enim est licitum domum Dei, quae est deputata sacris usibus, communibus usibus applicare. Unde et Dominus Io. II, 16 eiiciens ementes et vendentes de templo, dixit *domus mea domus orationis vocabitur, vos autem fecistis eam domum negotiationis*. Et Augustinus dicit in *Regula*: *in oratorio nemo aliquid faciat, nisi ad quod factum est, unde et nomen accepit*. Tamen propter necessitatem, quando scilicet aliquis aliam domum non inveniret, licite posset ecclesia uti ad manducandum, vel ad alios huiusmodi licitos usus.

Hanc ergo excusationem excludit Apostolus, dicens *numquid non habetis domos*, scilicet proprias, *ad manducandum et bibendum?* Ut propter hoc excusemini, si in Ecclesia convivia celebretis, quae debetis in propriis domibus facere. Unde et Lc. V, 29 dicitur quod levi fecit Christo convivium magnum in domo sua.

637. Secundo, cum dicit *aut ecclesiam Dei*, etc., asserit causam quae eos inexcusabiles reddit, quarum prima est contemptus Ecclesiae Dei. Et hanc ponit dicens *aut ecclesiam Dei contemnitis?* Et ideo in Ecclesia praesumitis coenam vestram ad manducandum.

Et potest hic sumi *ecclesia* tam pro congregatione fidelium, quam pro domo sacra, quae non est contemnenda, secundum illud Ps. XCII, 5: *domum tuam decet sanctitudo*; et Ier. VII, 11: *numquid spelunca latronum facta est domus ista, in qua invocatum est nomen meum in oculis vestris?* Isti autem utrumque contemnebant, dum, praesente conventu fidelium, in loco sacro convivia celebrabant.

Secundo ponit contemptum proximorum in hoc quod subditur *et confunditis eos qui non habent*. In hoc enim pauperes erubescebant, quod ipsi esuriebant in conspectu totius multitudinis, aliis laute comedentibus et bibentibus. Dicitur autem Prov. XVII, 5: *qui despicit pauperem, exprobrat factori eius*. Et Eccli. IV, 2: *animam esurientem ne despexeris*.

638. Deinde, cum dicit *quid dicam*, etc., concludit eorum vituperationem, dicens: *quid dicam vobis* ex consideratione praedictorum? Numquid *laudo vos?* Et respondet: et si in aliis factis laudo vos, *in hoc* tamen facto *non laudo*.

remained hungry. And this is what he says, *and one indeed is hungry*, namely, the poor man, who did not have the means to prepare anything, *and another is drunk*, namely, the rich, who overate and over-drank, which is contrary to what is said: *go your way, eat the fat and drink sweet wine and send portions to him for whom nothing is prepared* (Neh 8:10); and: *I have eaten my morsel alone, and the fatherless has not eaten of it* (Job 31:17).

636. Then when he says, *what, have you no houses*, he looks into the cause of this sin.

First, he excludes a reason, by which they could be excused. For it is not lawful to apply to profane uses the house of God, which is set aside for sacred uses. Hence the Lord, when driving the buyers and sellers from the temple, said: *my house is a house of prayer, but you have made it a den of thieves* (Matt 21:13). And Augustine says in his *Rule*: *in the oratory let no one do anything except for what it was built and from which it gets its name*. Yet in case of necessity, namely, when one can find no other house, he may lawfully use the church for eating, or for other such lawful uses.

But the Apostle rejects this excuse, saying, *what, have you no houses*, namely, your own, *to eat and to drink in?* Then you would have an excuse, if you celebrated banquets in the church, which you ought to do in your own homes. Hence it is said that Levi made Christ a great feast in his house (Luke 5:29).

637. Second, when he says, *or do you despise*, he asserts the cause which makes them inexcusable, the first of which is contempt for the church of God. And he states this, saying, *or do you despise the Church of God*. Is that why you presume to eat your supper in the church?

Here *church* can be taken for either the congregation of believers of the sacred house, which is not to be despised: *holiness befits your house* (Ps 93:5), and: *has this house, which is called by my name, become a den of robbers in your eyes?* (Jer 7:11). But they despise both, when in the presence of the congregation of believers, they hold feasts in a holy place.

Second, he mentions their contempt of neighbor when he says: *and put them to sham that have not?* For the poor were humiliated, inasmuch as they were hungry in the presence of the entire group, while others were eating and drinking lavishly. But it is said: *he who mocks the poor insults his maker* (Prov 17:7) and: *do not grieve the one who is hungry* (Sir 4:2).

638. Then when he says, *what shall I say to you*, he concludes his reprimand, saying, *what shall I say to you* in the light of the above? *Do I praise you?* And he answers: although I praise you for other things, *in this I praise you not*.

Et est advertendum quod supra dum de habitu mulierum loqueretur, saltem ironice laudavit eos, dicens: **laudo vos quod per omnia mei**, et cetera. Hic vero nec ironice vult eos laudare, quia in gravioribus delictis nullo modo sunt peccatores palpandi. Unde et in Ps. IX, 3 dicitur: *quoniam laudatur peccator in desideriis animae suae, et iniquus benedicitur. Exacerbavit Dominum peccator.* Et Is. III, 12: *popule meus, qui beatum te dicunt, ipsi te decipiunt.*

639. Secundum aliam vero expositionem arguuntur de alia culpa.

In primitiva enim Ecclesia fideles panem et vinum offerebant, quae consecrabantur in sanguinem et corpus Christi, quibus iam consecratis, divites, qui multa obtulerant, eadem sibi repetebant, et sic ipsi abundanter sumebant, pauperibus nihil sumentibus, qui nihil obtulerant.

De hac ergo culpa Apostolus eos hic reprehendit, dicens **convenientibus enim vobis in unum, iam non est**, id est, non contigit inter vos, **Dominicam coenam manducare**. Coena enim Domini est communis toti familiae; unusquisque autem vestrum sumit eam, non quasi communem, sed quasi propriam, dum sibi vult vindicare quod Deo obtulit; et hoc est quod subdit **unusquisque praesumit**, id est, praesumptuose attentat, **ad manducandum coenam**, scilicet Domini, id est panem et vinum consecratum, quasi suam, id est, quasi propriam vindicans, scilicet ea quae consecrata sunt Domino in suos usus. **Et** ita sequitur quod **alius**, scilicet pauper qui nihil obtulit, **esurit**, nihil scilicet sumens de consecratis, **alius autem**, scilicet dives qui multa obtulit, **ebrius est**; ad litteram, propter hoc quod nimium sumpsit de vino consecrato quod scilicet quasi proprium repoposcit.

640. Sed videtur hoc esse impossibile, quod de vino consecrato aliquis inebrietur, vel etiam nutriatur de pane, quoniam post consecrationem sub speciebus panis et vini nihil remanet, nisi substantia corporis Christi et sanguinis, quae non possunt converti in corpus hominis, ad hoc quod ex eis nutriatur, aut inebrietur.

641. Dicunt ergo quidam, quod hoc non fit per aliquam conversionem, sed per solam immutationem sensuum hominis ab accidentibus panis et vini, quae remanent post consecrationem. Consueverunt enim homines ex solo ciborum odore confortari, et ex multo odore vini stupefieri et quasi inebriari.

Sed confortatio vel stupefactio, quae provenit ex sola immutatione sensuum, parvo tempore durat, cum tamen post consecrationem panis aut vini, si vinum in magna quantitate sumeretur aut panis, diu sustentaretur homo propter panem aut stupefieret propter vinum. Et praeterea manifestum est quod panis consecratus in aliam substantiam converti potest, ex hoc quod per putrefactionem resolvitur in pulveres, aut per combustionem in cineres.

It should be noted that above when he spoke about women's apparel, he praised them at least ironically, saying, *I praise you . . . that in all things you are mindful of me* (1 Cor 11:2). But here he does not want to praise them even ironically, because in more serious matters sinners must in no way be handled gently. Hence it is said: *for the sinner is praised in the desires of his soul and the wicked man is blessed* (Ps 10:3). *And the sinner renounces the Lord*; and: *my people, those who called you happy, misled you* (Isa 3:12).

639. According to another explanation, they are reprimanded for a different fault.

For in the early Church the faithful offered bread and wine, which were consecrated into the body and blood of Christ. After the consecration the rich, who had offered much, wanted the same amount returned; and so they took an abundant share, while the poor, who had offered nothing, received nothing.

Therefore, it is for this fault that the Apostle reprimands them, saying, **when you come together therefore into one place, it is not now to eat the Lord's supper**. For the Lord's supper is common to the whole family; but each of you takes it not as common but as his own, while he tries to justify himself, because he offered it to God. And this is what he adds, **every one takes**, i.e., presumptuously attempts **to eat**, namely of the Lord, i.e., consecrated bread and wine, as his own, i.e., taking them as though they were his own, namely, the things consecrated to the Lord, for their use. **And** so it follows that **one**, namely, the poor person who offered nothing **is hungry**, but **another**, namely, the rich man who offered much **is drunk**; literally, because he took too much of the consecrated wine, which he demanded as his own.

640. But it seems to be impossible for one to get drunk from consecrated wine or even be nourished by the bread, because after consecration nothing remains under the appearance of bread and wine except the substance of Christ's body and blood, which cannot be changed into man's body, so as to nourish him or make him drunk.

641. Therefore, some say that this does not come to pass by any conversion, but by the sole change of a man's senses by the accidents of bread and wine, which remain after consecration. For men were wont to be strengthened by the mere order of food and be stupefied and, as it were, made drunk from the strong odor of wine.

But strengthening or stupefaction, which come solely from a change of the senses, lasts a short time, while, nevertheless, after the consecration of the bread and wine, if the wine or bread were taken in large quantities, a man would be sustained for a long time on account of the bread or stupefied on account of the wine. Besides, it is clear that the consecrated bread can be changed into another substance, since it is changed into dust by putrefaction or into ashes by burning.

Unde nulla ratio est, quare negetur posse nutrire, cum ad nutriendum nihil aliud requiratur, quam quod cibus convertatur in substantiam nutriti.

642. Quidam ergo posuerunt, quod panis aut vinum consecratum possunt converti in aliud, et sic nutrire, quia remanet ibi substantia panis aut vini cum substantia corporis Christi et sanguinis.

Sed hoc repugnat verbis Scripturae. Non enim verum esset quod Dominus dicit Matth. c. XXVI, 26: *hoc est enim corpus meum*, quia hoc demonstratum, est panis, sed potius esset dicendum *hic*, id est, in hoc loco, *est corpus meum*. Et praeterea corpus Christi non incipit esse in hoc sacramento per loci mutationem, quia iam desineret esse in caelo. Unde relinquitur quod ibi incipiat esse per conversionem alterius, scilicet panis, in ipsum; unde non potest esse quod remaneat substantia panis.

Et ideo alii dixerunt quod remanet ibi forma substantialis panis, ad quam pertinet operatio rei: et ideo nutrit, sicut et panis nutriret.

Sed hoc non potest esse, quia nutrire est converti in substantiam nutriti, quod non competit nutrimento ratione formae, cuius est agere, sed magis ratione materiae, cuius est pati. Unde si esset ibi forma substantialis, panis nutrire non posset.

643. Alii vero dixerunt quod aer circumstans convertitur vel in substantiam nutriti, vel in quodcumque aliud huiusmodi; sed hoc non posset fieri absque multa condensatione aeris, quae sensui latere non posset.

Et ideo alii dixerunt quod divina virtute ad hoc quod sacramentum non deprehendatur in huiusmodi conversionibus, redit substantia panis et vini.

Sed hoc videtur esse impossibile, quia, cum substantia panis conversa sit in corpus Christi, non videtur quod possit substantia panis redire, nisi e converso corpus Christi converteretur in panem.

Et praeterea si substantia panis redit, aut hoc est manentibus accidentibus panis: et sic simul erit ibi substantia panis et substantia corporis Christi, quod supra improbatum est; nam tamdiu est ibi substantia corporis Christi, quamdiu species remanent. Aut redit speciebus non manentibus, quod etiam est impossibile, quia sic esset substantia panis absque propriis accidentibus, nisi forte intelligatur quod Deus in termino conversionis causaret ibi quamdam materiam quae sit subiectum huius conversionis. Sed melius est ut dicatur quod sicut virtute consecrationis miraculose confertur speciebus panis et vini, ut subsistant sine subiecto ad modum substantiae, ita etiam eis miraculose confertur ex consequenti quod agant et patiantur quidquid agere aut pati posset substantia panis aut vini, si adesset. Et hac ratione

Hence there is no reason to deny that they can nourish, since nourishment requires no more than that the food be changed into the substance of the one fed.

642. Therefore, others assert that the bread or consecrated wine can be converted into something else and so can nourish, because the substance of bread or wine remain there with the substance of the body and blood of Christ.

But this conflicts with the words of Scripture. For what the Lord says would not be true, namely, *this is my body* (Matt 26:26), because this thing pointed to is bread; he should rather have said: *here*, i.e., in this place, *is my body*. Besides, the body of Christ does not begin to be in this sacrament by local motion, because he would then cease to be in heaven. Hence, what is left is that he begins to be there by the conversion of something else, i.e., of the bread, into himself; hence, it cannot be that the substance of bread remains.

Therefore, others say that there remains the bread's substantial form, from which springs a thing's activity; consequently, it nourishes, just as bread itself nourishes.

But this cannot be, because to nourish is to be converted into the substance of the nourished. But his does not belong to any nutriment by reason of the form, whose function is to act, but rather by reason of the matter, whose function is to be acted upon. Hence, if the substantial form were there, it would be unable to nourish.

643. But others say that the surrounding air is converted either into the substance of the one nourished or into anything else of the sort. But this could not happen without much condensation of air, which would not fail to be detected by a sense.

Therefore, others say that by divine power the substance of bread and wine return, in order that the sacrament not be detected in these changes.

But this seems to be impossible, because, since the substance of bread was converted into the body of Christ, it does not seem that the substance of bread could return, unless the body of Christ were converted into bread.

Besides, if the substance of bread returns, this occurs either with the accidents of bread remaining, and then there will simultaneously be the substance of bread and the substance of Christ's body, which was disproved above: for the substance of Christ's body is there as long as the species remain. Or it returns with the species not remaining, which is also impossible, because then the substance of bread would be there without its own accidents; unless, perhaps, it is understood that God at the end of the conversion would cause to be there a certain matter which would be the subject of this conversion. But it is better to say that just as in virtue of the consecration, it is miraculously given to the appearance of bread and wine to subsist without a subject and to subsist after the manner of a substance, so also it is miraculously given as a consequence that they act or be acted upon in the

species illae panis et vini possunt nutrire et inebriare, sicut si esset ibi substantia panis et vini.

Caetera non mutantur a prima expositione.

same way as the substance of bread and wine would, if they were present. And for this reason those species of bread and wine can nourish and inebriate, just as if the substance of bread and wine were there.

As for the rest there are no changes from the first explanation.

Lecture 5

^{11:23}Ego enim accepi a Domino quod et tradidi vobis, quoniam Dominus Jesus in qua nocte tradebatur, accepit panem, [n. 644]

^{11:24}et gratias agens fregit, et dixit: *accipite, et manducate: hoc est corpus meum, quod pro vobis tradetur: hoc facite in meam commemorationem.* [n. 649]

^{11:23}Ἐγὼ γὰρ παρέλαβον ἀπὸ τοῦ κυρίου, ὃ καὶ παρέδωκα ὑμῖν, ὅτι ὁ κύριος Ἰησοῦς ἐν τῇ νυκτὶ ᾗ παρεδίδετο ἔλαβεν ἄρτον

^{11:24}καὶ εὐχαριστήσας ἔκλασεν καὶ εἶπεν, Τοῦτό μού ἐστιν τὸ σῶμα τὸ ὑπὲρ ὑμῶν· τοῦτο ποιεῖτε εἰς τὴν ἐμὴν ἀνάμνησιν.

^{11:23}For I have received of the Lord that which also I delivered unto you, that the Lord Jesus, the same night in which he was betrayed, took bread, [n. 644]

^{11:24}And giving thanks, broke and said: *take, and eat: this is my body, which shall be delivered for you. Do this for the commemoration of me.* [n. 649]

---

644. Postquam Apostolus redarguit Corinthiorum inordinationes, quas committebant conveniendo ad Eucharistiae sacramentum sumendum, hic agit de ipso sacramento. Et

primo agit de dignitate huius sacramenti;

secundo inducit fideles ad reverenter sumendum, ibi *itaque quicumque manducaverit* et cetera.

Circa primum duo facit.

Primo commendat auctoritatem doctrinae quam daturus est;

secundo ponit doctrinam de dignitate huius sacramenti, ibi *quoniam Dominus noster*, et cetera.

645. Circa primum duo facit. Primo commendat auctoritatem doctrinae ex parte auctoris, qui est Christus, dicens: dixi quod iam non est vobis Dominicam coenam manducare, sacramentum Eucharistiae Dominicam coenam vocans, *ego enim accepi a Domino*, scilicet Christo, qui est auctor huius doctrinae, non ab aliquo puro homine. Gal. c. I, 1: *Paulus apostolus non ab hominibus, neque per hominem, sed per Iesum Christum.* Hebr. II, 3: *quae cum initium accepisset enarrari per Dominum*, et cetera.

Secundo commendat auctoritatem doctrinae ex parte ministri, qui est ipse Paulus, cum subdit *quod et tradidi vobis*. Is. XXI, 10: *quae audivi a Domino exercituum Deo Israel, annuntiavi vobis.* Sap. VII, 13: *quam sine fictione didici, et sine invidia communico.*

646. Deinde cum dicit *quoniam Dominus Iesus*, commendat dignitatem huius sacramenti, tradens institutionem ipsius. Et

primo ponit institutionem;

secundo tempus institutionis, cum dicit *in qua nocte tradebatur*, et cetera.

Tertio modum instituendi, ibi *accepit panem*, et cetera.

647. Institutor autem sacramenti est ipse Christus. Unde dicit *quoniam Dominus noster Iesus Christus*, et cetera. Dictum est enim supra cum de baptismo ageretur, quod Christus in sacramentis habet excellentiae

644. After rebuking the Corinthians for their unbecoming behavior, when they came together to take the Eucharist, the Apostle now deals with the sacrament itself.

First, he discusses the dignity of this sacrament;

second, he urges the faithful to receive it reverently, at *therefore, whosoever shall eat* (1 Cor 11:27).

In regard to the first he does two things.

First, he commends the authority of the doctrine he is about to deliver;

second, he presents the doctrine about the dignity of this sacrament, at *that the Lord Jesus*.

645. In regard to the first he does two things. First, he commends the authority of the doctrine on the part of the author, who is Christ, saying: I have said that it is no longer of interest to eat the Lord's supper, calling the sacrament of the Eucharist the Lord's supper, *for I have received of the Lord*, namely, Christ, who is the author of this doctrine and not any mere man: *Paul, an apostle—not from men nor through men but through Jesus Christ* (Gal 1:1); *it was declared at first by the Lord* (Heb 2:3).

Second, he commends the authority of the doctrine on the part of the minister, who is Paul himself, when he adds, *that which also I delivered unto you*: what I have heard from the Lord of hosts, the God of Israel, I announce to you (Isa 21:10); I learned without guile and I impart without envy (Wis 7:13).

646. Then when he says, *that the Lord Jesus*, he commends the dignity of this sacrament, describing its institution.

First, he mentions the institution;

second, the time of the institution, at *the same night*;

third, the manner of instituting, at *took bread*.

647. The one who institutes this sacrament is Christ. Hence he says, *that the Lord Jesus*, for it was stated above, when the sacrament of baptism was discussed, that Christ has in the sacraments the excellence of power, to which

potestatem, ad quam quatuor pertinent. Primo quidem quod virtus et meritum eius operetur in sacramentis; secundo quod in nomine eius sanctificetur sacramentum; tertio quod effectum sacramenti sine sacramento praebere potest; quarto institutio novi sacramenti.

Specialiter tamen congruebat ut hoc sacramentum ipse in sua persona institueret, in quo corpus et sanguis eius communicatur. Unde et ipse dicit Io. VI, 52: *panis quem ego dabo vobis, caro mea est pro mundi vita.*

648. Deinde cum dicit **qua nocte tradebatur**, describit tempus institutionis huius sacramenti, quod quidem congruum fuit, primo quidem quantum ad qualitatem temporis. Fuit enim in nocte. Per virtutem enim huius sacramenti anima illuminatur. Unde I Reg. XIV, 27 dicitur quod Ionathas *intinxit virgam in favum mellis, et convertit manum suam ad os suum, et illuminati sunt oculi eius*; propter quod et in Ps. CXXXVIII, v. 11 dicitur: *nox illuminatio mea in deliciis meis.*

Secundo quantum ad negotium quod in illo tempore gerebatur, quia scilicet quando tradebatur ad passionem, per quam transivit ad Patrem, hoc sacramentum, quod est memoriale passionis, instituit. Unde dicitur Eccli. XXIX, 33: *transi, hospes, et orna mensam, et quae in manu habes, ciba caeteros.*

649. Deinde cum dicit **accepit panem**, etc., ostendit modum institutionis. Et

primo ponit ea quae fecit et dixit Christus instituendo hoc sacramentum;

secundo exponit, ibi **quotiescumque enim**, et cetera.

Circa primum duo facit.

Primo agit de institutione sacramenti huius quantum ad corpus Christi;

secundo quantum ad eius sanguinem, ibi **similiter et calicem**, et cetera.

650. Circa primum ante expositionem litterae, oportet primo considerare necessitatem institutionis huius sacramenti.

Est autem sciendum quod sacramenta instituta sunt propter necessitatem vitae spiritualis. Et quia corporalia sunt quaedam similitudines spiritualium, oportet sacramenta proportionari eis quae sunt necessaria ad vitam corporalem. In qua primo invenitur generatio, cui proportionatur baptismus, per quem regeneratur aliquis in vitam spiritualem.

Secundo ad vitam corporalem requiritur augmentum, per quod aliquis perducitur ad quantitatem et virtutem perfectam: et huic proportionatur sacramentum confirmationis, in quo Spiritus Sanctus datur ad robur.

Tertio ad vitam corporalem requiritur alimentum, per quod corpus hominis sustentatur, et similiter vita

pertain four things: first, that his virtue and merit operate in the sacraments; second, that the sacraments are sanctified in his name; third, that he can produce the effect of a sacrament without the sacrament; fourth, the institution of a new sacrament.

Yet it was especially suitable that he institute in his own person this sacrament, in which his body and blood are communicated. Hence he himself says: *the bread that I shall give is my flesh for the life of the world* (John 6:52).

648. Then when he says, **the same night in which he was betrayed**, he describes the time of the institution of this sacrament. It was fitting to do this: first, as to the quality of the time. For it was night. For the soul is enlightened by virtue of this sacrament. Hence is it said that Jonathon *put forth the tip of his staff and dipped it in the honeycomb and put his hand to his mouth, and his eyes became bright* (1 Sam 14:27); on which account it is said: *the night is as bright as the day* (Ps 139:12).

Second, as to the negotiations carried on at that time, namely, it was when he was delivered over to the passion, by which he passed to the Father that he instituted this sacrament, which is a memorial of the passion: *come here, stranger, and prepare the table, and if you have anything at hand, let me have it to eat* (Sir 29:26).

649. Then when he says, **took bread**, he shows the manner of the institution.

First, he relates what Christ said and did in instituting this sacrament;

second, he explains, at **for as often as you shall eat** (1 Cor 11:26).

In regard to the first he does two things.

First, he deals with the institution of this sacrament as to the body of Christ;

second, as to his blood, at **in like manner also the chalice** (1 Cor 11:25).

650. In regard to the first, before explaining the text one must first consider the need for instituting this sacrament.

So it should be noted that the sacraments were instituted on account of a need in the spiritual life. And because bodily things are likenesses of spiritual things, it is fitting that the sacrament be proportionate to things which are necessary to bodily life, in which generation comes first, to which baptism is proportionate and through which one is reborn into the spiritual life.

Second, for bodily life is required growth, by which one is brought to perfect size and power. To this is proportionate the sacrament of confirmation, in which the Holy Spirit is given for strength.

Third, for the spiritual life is required food, by which man's body is sustained, and likewise the spiritual life is fed

spiritualis per sacramentum Eucharistiae reficitur, secundum illud Ps. XXII, 2: *in loco pascuae ibi me collocavit, super aquam refectionis educavit me.*

651. Est autem notandum quod generans non coniungitur genito secundum substantiam sed solum secundum virtutem, sed cibus coniungitur nutrito secundum substantiam. Unde in sacramento baptismi, quo Christus regenerat ad salutem, non est ipse Christus secundum suam substantiam, sed solum secundum suam virtutem. Sed in sacramento Eucharistiae, quod est spirituale alimentum, Christus est secundum suam substantiam.

652. Continetur autem sub alia specie propter tria. Primo quidem ne esset horribile fidelibus sumentibus hoc sacramentum, si in propria specie carnem hominis ederent, et sanguinem biberent; secundo ne hoc ipsum esset derisibile infidelibus; tertio ut cresceret meritum fidei, quae consistit in hoc quod creduntur ea quae non videntur.

653. Traditur autem hoc sacramentum sub duplici specie propter tria. Primo quidem propter eius perfectionem, quia, cum sit spiritualis refectio, debet habere spiritualem cibum et spiritualem potum. Nam et corporalis refectio non perficitur sine potu et cibo. Unde et supra X, 3 s. dictum est quod *omnes eamdem escam spiritualem manducaverunt, et omnes eumdem potum spiritualem biberunt*; nam et corporalis refectio non perficitur sine cibo et potu.

Secundo propter eius significationem. Est enim memoriale Dominicae passionis, per quam sanguis Christi fuit separatus a corpore; et ideo in hoc sacramento seorsum offertur sanguis a corpore.

Tertio propter huius sacramenti effectum salutarem. Valet enim ad salutem corporis, et ideo offertur corpus: et valet ad salutem animae, et ideo offertur sanguis. Nam *anima in sanguine est*, ut dicitur Gen. IX, 4 ss.

654. Offertur autem specialiter hoc sacramentum sub specie panis et vini. Primo quidem, quia pane et vino communius utuntur homines ad suam refectionem. Et ideo assumuntur in sacramento haec, sicut aqua ad ablutionem in baptismo, et oleum ad unctionem. Secundo propter virtutem huius sacramenti. Nam panis confirmat cor hominis, vinum vero laetificat.

Tertio quia panis, qui ex multis granis fit, et vinum ex multis uvis, significant Ecclesiae unitatem, quae constituitur ex multis fidelibus. Est autem haec Eucharistia specialiter sacramentum unitatis et caritatis, ut dicit Augustinus *Super Ioannem.*

655. His autem visis circa litterae expositionem,

primo considerandum est quid Christus fecerit;
secundo quid dixerit, ibi *et dixit*, et cetera.

by the sacrament of the Eucharist: *he makes me lie down in green pastures. He leads me beside still waters* (Ps 23:2).

651. It should be known that the cause of generation is not joined according to its substance to the one generated, but only according to its power; but food is joined according to its substance to the fed. Hence in the sacrament of baptism, by which Christ regenerates us to salvation, it is not Christ according to his substance but only according to his power. But in the sacrament of this Eucharist, which is spiritual food, Christ is there according to his substance.

652. He is contained under another appearance for three reasons: first, indeed, it would be horrifying for the faithful to receive this sacrament, if they ate the flesh of a man under its ordinary appearance and drank his blood; second, so that it would not be a source of derision to unbelievers; third, in order that the merit of faith grow, which consists in believing something not seen.

653. This sacrament is presented under two species for three reasons: first, indeed, on account of its perfection, because, since it is spiritual refreshment, ought to be spiritual food and spiritual drink. For even bodily refreshment is not complete without food and drink. Hence he also says above: *and did all eat the same spiritual food: and all drank the same spiritual drink* (1 Cor 10:3–4).

Second, on account of its signification. For it is the memorial of the Lord's passion, through which the blood of Christ was separated from his body; that is why in this sacrament the blood is offered separately from the body.

Third, on account of the salutary effect of this sacrament, for it avails for the health of the body, and so the body is offered; and it avails for the health of the soul, and so the blood is offered. *For the soul is in the blood* (Lev 17:11).

654. This sacrament is offered specifically under the appearance of bread and wine: first of all, because men generally use bread and wine for their refreshment. Therefore, these are used in this sacrament, as water in baptism. Second, on account of the power of this sacrament: for bread strengthens the heart of man, but wine gladdens it.

Third, because the bread, which is made up of many grains, and the the wine, which is made from many grapes, signify the unity of the Church, which is made up of many believers. Furthermore, this Eucharist is especially the sacrament of unity and charity, as Augustine says *On John.*

655. Having seen these matters relating to the explanation of the text:

first, what Christ did must be explained;
second, what he said, at *and said.*

656. Tria autem facit. Primum quidem designatur, cum dicit *accepit panem*, per quod duo significari possunt: primo quidem quod ipse voluntarie passionem accepit, cuius hoc sacramentum est memoriale, secundum illud Is. LIII, 7: *oblatus est, quia ipse voluit*. Secundo potest significari quod ipse accepit a Patre potestatem perficiendi hoc sacramentum, secundum illud Matth. c. XI, 27: *omnia tradita sunt mihi a Patre meo*.

Secundum tangit, cum dicit *et gratias agens*. In quo datur nobis exemplum gratias agendi de omnibus quae nobis divinitus dantur, secundum illud I Thess. ult.: *in omnibus gratias agite*.

Tertium tangit, cum dicit *fregit*. Is. LVIII, v. 7: *frange esurienti panem tuum*.

657. Sed videtur hoc esse contrarium usui Ecclesiae, secundum quam prius consecratur corpus Christi, et postea frangitur: hic autem dicitur quod prius fregit, postea protulit verba consecrationis.

Et ideo quidam dixerunt quod Christus consecravit prius verbis aliis, et postea protulit verba quibus nos consecramus. Sed hoc non potest esse, quia sacerdos, dum consecrat, non profert ista verba quasi ex persona sua sed quasi ex persona Christi consecrantis. Unde manifestum est quod eisdem verbis quibus nos consecramus, et Christus consecravit.

Et ideo dicendum est quod hoc quod hic dicitur *et dixit*, non est sumendum consequenter, quasi Christus acceperit panem, et gratias agens fregerit, et postea dixerit verba quae sequuntur, sed concomitanter, quod dum accepit per se panem, gratias agens fregit et dixit. Et ideo cum Matth. XXVI, 26 dicatur quod *Iesus accepit panem, et benedixit, ac fregit*, Apostolus non curavit hic de benedictione facere mentionem, intelligens nihil aliud esse illam benedictionem, quam hoc quod Dominus dixit *hoc est corpus meum*.

658. Deinde cum dicit *et dixit*, ostendit quid Christus dixerit instituendo hoc sacramentum. In verbis autem

primo quidem iniunxit sacramenti usum;
secundo expressit sacramenti veritatem;
tertio docuit mysterium.

659. Usum quidem sacramenti iniunxit, dicens *accipite*. Quasi diceret: non ex potestate vel merito humano competit vobis usus huius sacramenti, sed ex eminenti Dei beneficio. Sap. XVI, 20: *angelorum esca nutrivisti populum tuum, Domine*. Supra IV, 7: *quid habes quod non accepisti?*

Et determinat speciem usus, cum dicit *et manducate*. Io. VI, 54: *nisi manducaveritis carnem Filii hominis*. Iob XXXI, 31: *si non dixerunt viri tabernaculi mei: quis det de carnibus eius, ut saturemur?*

660. Sciendum est tamen quod haec verba non sunt de forma consecrationis.

656. But he does three things: the first is designated when he says, *took bread*. Two things can be signified by this: first, that he voluntarily accepted the passion, of which this sacrament is the memorial: *he was offered up because he willed it* (Isa 53:5). Second, that he received from the Father the power of completing this sacrament: *all things have been handed over to me by my Father* (Matt 11:27).

He touches on the second, when he says, *and giving thanks*. In which is given to us an example of giving thanks for all that is given to us by God: *in all things give thanks* (1 Thess 5:18).

He touches on the third, when he says, *broke*: *share your bread with the hungry* (Isa 58:7).

657. But this seems contrary to the practice of the Church, according to which the body of Christ is first consecrated and then broken, whereas here it is said that he first broke it and then said the words of consecration.

For this reason, some have said that Christ first consecrated with other words and later said the words with which we consecrate. But this cannot be, because the priest, while he is consecrating, does not pronounce those words as from his own person, but as from the person of Christ consecrating. Hence it is clear that Christ consecrated with the same words with which we consecrate.

Therefore, it should be noted that what is said here, *and said*, is not to be taken successively, as though Christ took bread and giving thanks broke it, and later said the words which follow; rather, they are taken concomitantly, namely, that while he took bread, giving thanks he broke it and said. Therefore with Matthew it should be stated that *Jesus took bread and blessed and broke* (Matt 26:26). The Apostle here did not care to mention about the blessing, understanding that the blessing was nothing else than what the Lord said, *this is my body*.

658. Then when he says, *and said*, he shows what Christ said when instituting this sacrament.

First, he enjoined the use of the sacrament;
second, he expressed the truth of the sacrament;
third, he taught the mystery.

659. He enjoined the use of the sacrament, saying, *take*. As if not from any human power or merit is it proper for you to use this sacrament, but from an eminent gift of God: *you gave your people the food of angels* (Wis 16:20); *what do you have that you have not received?* (1 Cor 4:7)

And he determines the kind of use when he says, *and eat*: *unless you eat the flesh of the Son of man* (John 6:54); *if the men of my tent have not said: who will give of his flesh that we may be filled?* (Job 31:31).

660. It should be noted, however, that these words are not from the form of consecration.

Est enim haec differentia inter haec et alia sacramenta, quia alia sacramenta perficiuntur non quidem in consecratione materiae, sed in usu materiae consecratae, sicut in ablutione aquae, aut in unctione olei seu chrismatis. Et hoc ideo, quia in materiis aliorum sacramentorum non est aliqua natura rationalis, quae sit gratiae Sanctificantis susceptiva; et ideo in forma aliorum sacramentorum fit mentio de usu sacramenti, sicut cum dicitur: *ego te baptizo*, vel *confirmo te chrismate salutis*, et cetera. Sed hoc sacramentum perficitur in ipsa consecratione materiae, in qua continetur ipse Christus, qui est finis totius gratiae Sanctificantis.

Et ideo verba quae pertinent ad usum sacramenti, non sunt de substantia formae, sed solum illa quae continent veritatem et continentiam sacramenti, quae consequenter ponit, subdens **hoc est corpus meum**.

661. Circa quae verba tria oportet considerare. Primo quidem de re significata per haec verba, quod scilicet sit ibi corpus Christi; secundo de veritate huius locutionis, tertio utrum haec sit conveniens forma huius sacramenti.

662. Circa primum considerandum est, quod quidam dixerunt corpus Christi non esse in hoc sacramento secundum veritatem, sed solum sicut in signo, sic exponentes quod hic dicitur **hoc est corpus meum**, id est, hoc est signum et figura corporis mei, sicut et supra X, 4 dictum est: **petra autem erat Christus**, id est, figura Christi.

Sed hoc est haereticum, cum expresse Dominus dicat, Io. VI, 56: *caro mea vere est cibus, et sanguis meus vere est potus*.

Unde alii dixerunt quod est ibi vere corpus Christi, sed simul cum substantia panis, quod est impossibile, ut supra ostensum est.

Unde alii dixerunt quod est ibi solum corpus Christi, substantia panis non remanente, quae annihilatur, vel in praeiacentem materiam resolvitur. Sed hoc non potest esse, quia, sicut Augustinus dicit in libro *LXXXIII Quaest.*: *Deus non est auctor tendendi in non esse*. Secundo quia etiam per hanc positionem tollitur hoc quod substantia panis convertatur in corpus Christi, et sic cum corpus Christi non incipiat esse in hoc sacramento per conversionem alterius in ipsum, relinquitur quod incipiat ibi esse per motum localem, quod est impossibile, ut supra dictum est.

Oportet igitur dicere, quod corpus Christi vere sit in hoc sacramento per conversionem panis in ipsum.

663. Considerandum tamen quod haec conversio differt ab omnibus conversionibus quae sunt in natura.

Actio enim naturae praesupponit materiam, et ideo eius actio non se extendit, nisi ad immutandum aliquid secundum formam vel substantialem vel accidentalem. Unde omnis conversio naturalis dicitur esse formalis. Sed Deus qui facit hanc conversionem, est auctor

For there is this difference between this and other sacraments, that the latter are completed not in the consecration of the matter but in the use of consecrated matter, as in the washing with water or in the anointing with oil or chrism. The reason is that in the matter of the other sacraments, it is not some rational nature which is receptive of sanctifying grace; and for this reason, in the form of other sacraments mention is made of the use of the sacrament, as when it is stated: *I baptize you in the name of the Father and of the Son and of the Holy Spirit*. But this sacrament is completed in the very consecration of the matter, in which Christ himself is contained, who is the end of all sanctifying grace.

Therefore, the words which pertain to the use of the sacrament are not of the substance of the form, but only those containing the truth and content of the sacrament, which he mentions last, adding, **this is my body**.

661. In regard to these words three things should be considered: first, the reality signified by these words, namely, that the body of Christ is there; second, the truth of this statement; third, whether this is a suitable form for this sacrament.

662. In regard to the first it should be noted that some have said that the body of Christ is not truly present in this sacrament, but only as in a sign explaining what is said here: **this is my body**, i.e., this is a sign and figure of my body, just as it was said above: **and the rock was Christ** (1 Cor 10:4), i.e., as a figure of Christ.

But this is heretical, since the Lord expressly says: *my flesh is food indeed, and my blood is drink indeed* (John 6:56).

Hence others say that the body of Christ is truly there but along with the substance of bread. This is impossible, as was shown above.

Therefore, others said that only the body of Christ is there, the substance of bread not remaining because it is annihilated or reduced to prejacent matter. But this cannot be, because, as Augustine says in *The Book of Eighty Three Questions*: *God is not the author of tending to non-existence*. Second, because even this position takes away the fact the substance of bread is converted into the body of Christ; and so, since the body of Christ begins to be in this sacrament by the conversion of something else into it, the consequence is that he begins to be there by local motion: but that is impossible, as was shown above.

Therefore, one must say that the body of Christ is truly in this sacrament by the conversion of bread into it.

663. Yet it should be noted that this conversion differs from all conversions that occur in nature.

For the action of nature presupposes matter, and therefore its action does not extend beyond changing something according to its form, either substantial or accidental. Hence every natural conversion is said to be formal. But God, who makes this conversion is the author of form and

materiae et formae, et ideo tota substantia panis, materia non remanente, potest converti in totam substantiam corporis Christi. Et quia materia est individuationis principium, totum hoc individuum signatum, quod est substantia particularis, convertitur in aliam substantiam particularem, propter quod dicitur ista conversio substantialis seu transubstantiatio.

Contingit igitur in hac conversione contrarium eius quod accidit in conversionibus naturalibus, in quibus, manente subiecto, fit transmutatio interdum circa accidentia. Hic autem, transmutata substantia, manent accidentia sine subiecto, virtute divina, quae sicut causa prima sustentat ea sine causa materiali, quae est substantia causata ad hoc quod corpus Christi et sanguis sumatur in specie aliena rationibus supradictis. Et quia ordine quodam accidentia referuntur ad substantiam, ideo dimensiones sine subiecto remanent, et alia accidentia remanent in ipsis dimensionibus, sicut in subiecto.

664. Si autem sub illis dimensionibus nulla substantia remaneat, nisi corpus Christi, dubium potest esse de fractionibus hostiae consecratae, cum corpus Christi glorificatum sit, et per consequens infrangibile. Unde non potest huic fractioni substare, sed nec etiam aliud potest fingi quod subsistat, quia sacramentum veritatis non decet aliqua fictio. Unde nihil sensu percipitur in hoc sacramento, quod non sit ibi secundum veritatem. Sensibilia enim per se sunt qualitates, quae quidem remanent, sicut prius fuerant in hoc sacramento, ut dictum est.

Et ideo alii dixerunt quod est quaedam ibi vero fractio sine subiecto, unde nihil ibi frangitur. Sed nec hoc dici potest, quia cum fractio sit in genere passionis, quae habet debilius esse quam qualitas, non potest esse in hoc sacramento sine subiecto, sicut nec qualitas.

Unde restat dicendum, quod fractio illa fundatur sicut in subiecto in dimensionibus panis et vini remanentibus. Corpus autem Christi non attingitur ab huiusmodi fractione, quia totum remanet sub qualibet parte dimensionum divisarum.

Quod quidem hoc modo considerari potest. Nam corpus Christi est in hoc sacramento ex conversione substantiae panis in ipsum. Non autem fit conversio ratione dimensionum. Nam dimensiones panis remanent, sed solum ratione substantiae. Unde et corpus Christi est ibi ratione suae substantiae, non autem ratione suarum dimensionum, licet dimensiones eius sunt ibi ex consequenti, inquantum non separantur a substantia ipsius. Quantum autem ad naturam substantiae pertinet, tota est sub qualibet parte dimensionum. Unde sicut ante consecrationem tota veritas substantiae et natura panis erat sub qualibet parte dimensionum: ita post

of matter, and therefore the entire substance of bread, the matter not remaining, can be converted into the entire substance of the body of Christ. And because matter is the principle of individuation, this whole signated individual, which is a particular substance, is converted into another particular substance. For this reason it is called a substantial conversion or transubstantiation.

In this conversion, therefore, occurs the contrary of what happens in natural conversions, in which, the subject remaining, a change sometimes occurs affecting the accidents. But here the substance is changed, while the accidents remain intact without a subject. This is done by divine power, which as the first cause sustains them without a material cause, which is the substance caused in order that the body of Christ and the blood be consumed under a different appearance, for the reasons given above. And because accidents are referred to their substance in a definite order, the dimensions remain without a subject and the other accidents remain in those dimensions as in a subject.

664. But if no substance remains under those dimensions except the body of Christ, there could be no doubt about the breaking of the consecrated host, since the body of Christ is glorified and, therefore, unbreakable. Hence he cannot exist under this particle nor can it be pretended that he subsists, because the sacrament of truth is incompatible with any pretense. Hence nothing is perceived by the senses in this sacrament, which is not truly there. For the *per se* sensibles are qualities, which indeed remain as they previously existed, in this sacrament, as we have stated.

Therefore, others have said that a certain breaking without a subject occurs there; hence nothing is broken there. But this cannot be said either, because, since breaking is in the category of 'being acted upon', which is a weaker category than quality, it cannot exist in this sacrament without a subject any more than quality can.

Hence it must be said that the breaking is founded, as on a subject, on the dimensions of bread and wine which remain. But the body of Christ is not affected by such breaking, because the whole body remains under each part of the divided dimensions.

This indeed can be considered in this way. For the body of Christ is in this sacrament from the conversion of the substance of bread into it. But the conversion does not come about by reason of the dimensions. For the dimensions of the bread remain, but only by reason of the substance. Hence, too, the body of Christ is there by reason of its own substance, but not by reason of its own dimensions, although its dimensions are there by way of consequence, inasmuch as they are not separated from his substance. But as far as the nature of the substance is concerned, it is entire under each part of the dimensions. Hence, just before the consecration the whole truth of the substance and nature of bread was under each part of its dimensions, so after the

consecrationem totum corpus Christi est sub qualibet parte panis divisi.

665. Significat autem hostiae consecratae divisio, primo quidem passionem Christi, per quam corpus eius fuit vulneribus fractum, secundum illud Ps. XXI, 17: *foderunt manus meas et pedes meos.*

Secundo distributionem donorum Christi ex ipso progredientium, secundum illud infra XII, 4: **divisiones gratiarum sunt.**

Tertio diversas partes Ecclesiae. Nam eorum qui sunt membra Christi, quidam adhuc in hoc mundo peregrinantur; quidam vivunt in gloria cum Christo, et quantum ad animam et quantum ad corpus; quidam autem expectant finalem resurrectionem in fine mundi, et hoc significat divisio hostiae in tres partes.

666. Secundo considerandum est de veritate huius locutionis. Videtur enim haec locutio esse falsa **hoc est corpus meum.** Conversio enim panis in corpus Christi fit in termino prolationis horum verborum. Tunc enim completur significatio huius locutionis. Formae enim sacramentorum significando efficiunt; et ideo sequitur quod in principio locutionis quando dicitur quod non sit ibi corpus Christi, sed sola substantia panis, quae demonstratur per hoc pronomen **hoc**, quando est demonstrativum substantiae. Idem est ergo, hoc, cum dicitur **hoc est corpus meum**, ac si diceret *substantia panis est corpus meum*, quod manifeste falsum est.

667. Dixerunt ergo quidam, quod sacerdos haec verba materialiter et recitative profert ex persona Christi, et ideo demonstratio huius pronominis non refertur ad praesentem materiam, ut ex hoc locutio falsa reddatur, secundum quod obiectio procedebat.

Sed hoc non potest stare. Primo quidem, quia si haec locutio non applicetur ad praesentem materiam, nihil faciet circa eam, quod est falsum. Dicit enim Augustinus *Super Ioannem*: *accedit verbum ad elementum, et fit sacramentum.* Unde necesse est dicere, quod verba ista formaliter accipiantur, referendo ea ad praesentem materiam. Profert autem ea sacerdos ex persona Christi, a quo virtutem sumpserunt, ad ostendendum quod eamdem efficaciam nunc habent, sicut quando Christus ea protulit. Non enim virtus his verbis collata evanescit, neque temporis diversitate, neque ministrorum varietate.

Secundo, quia eadem difficultas remanet de prima prolatione qua Christus ea protulit.

668. Ideo alii dicunt quod sensus huius est **hoc est corpus meum**, id est hic panis, designat corpus meum, ut **hoc**, designet id quod est in principio locutionis.

consecration the whole body of Christ is under each part of the divided bread.

665. The division of the consecrated host signifies, first of all, the passion of Christ through which his body was broken by wounds: *they have pierced by hands and my feet* (Ps 22:16).

Second, the distribution of the gifts of Christ from his own, as it says below: **there are diversities of graces** (1 Cor 12:4).

Third, the various parts of the Church. For among Christ's members some are still pilgrims in this world, some may be in glory with Christ, both as to the soul and as to the body, but some await the final resurrection at the end of the world, and this is signified by the division of the host into three parts.

666. Second, one should consider the truth of this statement. For the statement, **this is my body**, seems to be false. For the conversion of bread into the body of Christ occurs at the time of the pronouncing of these words. For it is then that the signification of these words is completed. For the forms of the sacrament effect by signifying; therefore, it follows that in the beginning of the statement, when it is stated that the body of Christ is not there but only the substance of the bread, which is pointed out by the pronoun, **this**, when it points out a substance. It is the same, therefore, to say, **this is my body**, as to say: *the substance of bread is my body*, which is obviously false.

667. Therefore, some have said that the priest pronounces these words materially and recitatively from the person of Christ and, therefore, this pronoun's function of pointing out is not referred to the matter present, such that as a result the statement should be rendered false as the objection supposed.

But this cannot stand. First of all, because if this statement is not applied to the material present, it will do nothing in regard to it, which is false. For Augustine *On John* says: *the word comes to the element and the sacrament comes to be.* Hence it is necessary to say that the words are taken formally as referring to the material present. But the priest, in the person of Christ, from whom he has obtained power, says them from the same efficacy now, as when Christ spoke them. For the power conferred on these words does not vanish either by the difference of time or by the variety of ministers.

Second, because the same difficulty remains in regard to the first time these words were spoken, namely, by Christ.

668. Therefore, others say that the sense of these words is, **this is my body**, i.e., this bread designates my body, so that **this** designates that which is present at the beginning of the statement.

Sed hoc etiam esse non potest, quia cum sacramenta efficiant quod figurant, haec verba nihil efficiant, nisi quod significant.

Secundo, quia ex hoc sequeretur, quod per haec verba nihil efficeretur, quam quod corpus Christi esset ibi: sicut sub signo, quod supra improbatum est.

Et ideo alii dicunt quod *hoc*, facit demonstrationem ad intellectum, et demonstrat id quod erit in fine locutionis, scilicet corpus Christi. Sed nec hoc videtur convenienter dici, quia secundum hoc sensus esset *corpus meum est corpus meum*, quod non fit per haec verba, cum hoc ante verba consecrationis fuerit verum.

669. Et ideo aliter dicendum est, quod formae sacramentorum non solum sunt significativae, sed etiam factivae: significando enim efficiunt. In omni autem factione oportet subiici aliquid commune tamquam principium. Commune autem in hac conversione non est aliqua substantia, sed accidentia quae et prius fuerunt, et postea manent; et ideo ex parte subiecti in hac locutione non ponitur nomen, quod significat certam speciem substantiae, sed ponitur pronomen, quod significat substantiam sine determinata specie.

Est ergo sensus *hoc*, id est, contentum sub his accidentibus, *est corpus meum*. Et hoc est quod fit per verba consecrationis. Nam ante consecrationem id quod erat contentum sub his accidentibus non erat corpus Christi, quod tamen fit corpus Christi per consecrationem.

670. Tertio autem oportet considerare quomodo est haec conveniens forma huius sacramenti.

Nam hoc sacramentum, ut dictum est, non consistit in usu materiae, sed in consecratione ipsius. Consecratio autem non fit per hoc, quod materia consecrata solum suscipiat aliquam virtutem spiritualem, sed per hoc quod transubstantiatur secundum esse in corpus Christi; et ideo nullo alio verbo utendum fuit, nisi verbo substantivo, ut dicatur *hoc est corpus meum*. Per hoc enim significatur id quod est finis, quod significando efficitur.

671. Deinde cum dicit *quod pro vobis tradetur*, tangit mysterium huius sacramenti.

Est enim sacramentum repraesentativum divinae passionis, per quam corpus suum tradidit in mortem pro nobis, secundum illud Is. l, 6: *corpus meum dedi percutientibus*; et Eph. V, 2: *tradidit semetipsum pro nobis*.

Et ut ostendat rationem frequentandi hoc mysterium, subiungitur *hoc facite in meam commemorationem*, hoc recolendo scilicet tam magnum beneficium, pro quo vobis me tradidi in morte. Unde et Thren. III, 19 dicitur: *recordare paupertatis meae, absinthii et fellis*. Et

But even this cannot be, because since the sacraments effect what they signify, these words effect nothing except what they signify.

Second, because it would follow from this that nothing would be effected by these words, except that the body of Christ would be there, as under a sign, which was disproved earlier.

Therefore, others say that the *this* points out something to the intellect and indicates that which will be at the end of the utterance, namely, the body of Christ. But neither does this seem to be suitable, because according to this the sense would be: *my body is my body*, which is not brought about by these words. Since this was true before the words of consecration.

669. Therefore, there must be another explanation, namely, that the forms of the sacraments not only signify, but also make: for by signifying they make. But in every instance of making, something common must be subject as a principle. But in this conversion the common factor is not a substance but the accidents, which were present in the beginning and continue to remain. Therefore, on the part of the subject in this statement no noun is used, which signifies a definite species of substance, but a pronoun, which signifies a substance without naming its species.

The sense, therefore, is, *this*, i.e., which is contained under these accidents, *is my body*. And this is what occurs through the words of consecration. For before the consecration that which was contained under these accidents was not the body of Christ, but it is made the body of Christ through consecration.

670. Third, it is important to consider how this is a suitable form for this sacrament.

For this sacrament, as has been said, does not consist in the use of the matter but in its consecration. But the consecration does not occur by the consecrated matter merely receiving some spiritual power, but by the fact that it is transubstantiated according to its being into the body of Christ. Therefore, no other word was to be used except a substantive, so as to say, *this is my body*. For by this is signified that which is at the end, which is effected by signifying.

671. Then when he says, *which shall be delivered for you*, he touches on the mystery of this sacrament.

For this sacrament represents the Lord's passion, through which his body was delivered over to death for us: *I gave my back to the smiters* (Isa 1:6), and: *he gave himself for us* (Eph 5:2).

And to show the reason for making frequent use of this mystery, he adds: *do this for the commemoration of me*, by recalling this to mind, namely, such a great blessing, for which I gave myself in death. Hence it is said: *remember my affliction and my bitterness, the wormwood and the gall*

in Ps. CX, 4: *memoriam fecit mirabilium suorum misericors et miserator Dominus, escam dedit timentibus se.*

(Lam 3:9), and: *he has caused his wonderful works to be remembered; the Lord is gracious and merciful. He provides food for those who fear him* (Ps 111:4).

Lecture 6

^{11:25}Similiter et calicem, postquam coenavit, dicens: *hic calix novum testamentum est in meo sanguine: hoc facite quotiescumque bibetis, in meam commemorationem.* [n. 672]

^{11:26}Quotiescumque enim manducabitis panem hunc, et calicem bibetis, mortem Domini annuntiabitis donec veniat. [n. 686]

^{11:25}ὡσαύτως καὶ τὸ ποτήριον μετὰ τὸ δειπνῆσαι, λέγων, Τοῦτο τὸ ποτήριον ἡ καινὴ διαθήκη ἐστὶν ἐν τῷ ἐμῷ αἵματι· τοῦτο ποιεῖτε, ὁσάκις ἐὰν πίνητε, εἰς τὴν ἐμὴν ἀνάμνησιν.

^{11:26}ὁσάκις γὰρ ἐὰν ἐσθίητε τὸν ἄρτον τοῦτον καὶ τὸ ποτήριον πίνητε, τὸν θάνατον τοῦ κυρίου καταγγέλλετε, ἄχρις οὗ ἔλθῃ.

^{11:25}In like manner also the chalice, after he had supped, saying: *this chalice is the new testament in my blood. Do this, as often as you shall drink, for the commemoration of me.* [n. 672]

^{11:26}For as often as you shall eat this bread and drink the chalice, you shall show the death of the Lord, until he comes. [n. 686]

---

672. Postquam Apostolus posuit institutionem huius sacramenti quantum ad consecrationem corporis, hic ponit institutionem eius quantum ad sanguinis consecrationem. Et

primo ponit ordinem institutionis;

secundo verba, cum dicit *hic calix*, et cetera.

673. Ordo autem attenditur quantum ad duo.

Primo ad concomitantiam utriusque speciei, cum dicit *similiter et calicem.* Utrumque enim est de perfectione huius sacramenti, tum propter perfectionem refectionis, tum propter repraesentationem passionis, tum propter efficientiam salutis animae et corporis, ut supra dictum est.

Sed si prius consecratur in hoc sacramento corpus Christi, et postea sanguis, videtur sequi quod ante consecrationem sanguinis, corpus Christi in hoc sacramento sit exsangue: quod quidam inconveniens reputantes dixerunt, quod duae formae se expectant in efficiendo, ita scilicet quod prima forma consecrationis corporis non consequitur suum effectum, antequam perficiatur forma consecrationis sanguinis; sicut etiam dictum est, quod verba quae proferuntur in consecratione corporis, non consequuntur suum effectum usque ad finem prolationis verborum.

Sed hoc non est simile. Nam significatio verborum quibus consecratur corpus Christi, non completur nisi in termino prolationis eorum. Et quia verba sacramentalia significando efficiunt, ideo non possunt habere effectum ante terminum prolationis. Tunc autem habent plenam significationem, etiam antequam proferantur verba consecrationis sanguinis, et ideo necesse est quod etiam tunc habeant suum effectum. Alioquin sacerdos peccaret statim, post verba consecrationis, proponens hostiam non consecratam populo adorandam, nisi iam esset corpus Christi, quia induceret populum ad idololatriam.

Est ergo dicendum, quod ante consecrationem sanguinis est in hoc sacramento corpus Christi, non sine sanguine.

672. After setting forth the institution of this sacrament as to the consecration of the body, the Apostle now sets forth its institution as to the consecration of the blood.

First, he presents the order of institution;

second, the words, at *this chalice.*

673. The order is considered with respect to two things.

First, the co-presence of both species, when he says, *in like manner also the chalice.* For both are required for the perfection of this sacrament, both for the perfection of nourishment and on account of its representing the passion, and as its effecting the salvation of the soul and of the body, as has been stated above.

But if the body of Christ is consecrated first in this sacrament and the blood later, it seems to follow that before the consecration of the blood, the body of Christ is without blood in the sacrament. Some who considered this unfitting have said that the two forms await each other in effecting, so that, namely, the first form of the consecration of the body does not achieve its effect before the form of consecration of the blood is completed; just as it was said that the words pronounced in consecrating the body do not achieve their effect until the end of the pronunciation of the words.

But this is not similar. For the signification of the words by which the body of Christ is consecrated is not completed except at the end of the pronouncing of the words. And because sacramental words produce their effect by signifying, they cannot have effect before the end of their pronunciation. At that time they have full signification, even before the words of the consecration of the blood are begun. Therefore, it is necessary that even then they have their effect. Otherwise the priest would sin immediately after the words of consecration by showing an unconsecrated host to the people to be adored, unless the body of Christ were already there; because he would be inducing the people to idolatry.

Therefore, it must be said that before the consecration of the blood the body of Christ is in this sacrament not without his blood.

251

674. Sciendum est enim quod in hoc sacramento dupliciter aliquid est. Uno modo ex vi consecrationis, illud scilicet in quod terminatur conversio panis et vini, sicut per formam consecrationis significatur, et sic sub specie panis est corpus Christi.

Alio modo est aliquid in hoc sacramento ex reali concomitantia, sicut divinitas Verbi est in hoc sacramento propter indissolubilem unionem ipsius ad corpus Christi, licet nullo modo substantia panis in divinitatem convertatur. Et similiter est ibi anima, quae coniuncta est realiter ipsi corpori. Si vero in triduo mortis Christi, fuisset corpus Christi ab aliquo apostolorum consecratum, non fuisset ibi anima quae tunc realiter erat a corpore separata.

Et idem dicendum est de sanguine. Nam sub speciebus panis ex vi consecrationis est corpus Christi, in quod substantia panis convertitur. Sanguis autem est ibi ex reali concomitantia, quia tunc realiter sanguis Christi non est ab eius corpore separatus. Et, eadem ratione, sub specie vini est sanguis Christi ex vi consecrationis, corpus autem ex reali concomitantia, ita quod sub utraque specie est totus Christus. Si vero tempore passionis quando sanguis Christi erat ex corpore effusus, fuisset hoc sacramentum ab aliquo apostolorum perfectum, sub panis specie fuisset solum corpus Christi exsangue, sub speciebus autem vini fuisset solus sanguis Christi.

675. Secundo, attenditur ordo per comparationem ad cibos materiales, qui praecesserant, ubi subdit **postquam coenavit**, quod videtur signanter addidisse.

Nam Christus corpus suum tradidit inter coenam. Unde Matth. XXVI, 26 dicitur, quod *coenantibus illis accepit Iesus panem*, et cetera. Sed sanguinem dedit expresse post coenam. Unde et Lc. XXII, 20 dicitur *similiter et calicem postquam coenavit, dicens*, et cetera. Cuius ratio est, quia corpus Christi repraesentat mysterium Incarnationis, quae facta est adhuc legalibus observantiis statum habentibus, inter quas praecipua erat coena agni paschalis. Sed sanguis Christi in sacramento directe repraesentat passionem, per quam est effusus et per quam sunt terminata omnia legalia. Unde Hebr. IX, 12 dicitur, quod *per proprium sanguinem introivit semel in sancta, aeterna redemptione inventa*.

676. Deinde ponit verba, dicens **hic calix**, et cetera. Et

primo demonstrat veritatem huius sacramenti;
secundo iniungit usum, ibi **hoc facite**, et cetera.

677. Quantum ergo ad primum, dicit **hic calix**, et cetera. Quod quidem dupliciter sumi potest. Uno modo metonymice, ut scilicet ponatur continens pro contento, quasi dicat: contentum in hoc calice; quod convenientius

674. For it should be noted that in this sacrament something is present in two ways: in one way in virtue of the consecration, that, namely, into which the conversion of the bread and wine is terminated, as is signified by the form of consecration; and in this way under the appearance of bread the body of Christ is present.

In another way something is present in this sacrament by real concomitance, as the divinity of the Word is present in this sacrament on account of its indissoluble union with the body of Christ, although the substance of bread is in no way converted into the divinity. Likewise, the soul is there, which is really joined to the body. But if at any time during the three days of Christ's death, the body of Christ had been consecrated by any of the apostles, the soul would not have been there, because it was really separated from the body.

The same is true of the blood. For under the appearances of bread in virtue of the consecration is present Christ's body, into which the substance of bread is converted. But the blood is there by real concomitance, because then the blood of Christ is not really separated from the body. And for the same reason under the appearance of wine the blood of Christ is present in virtue of the consecration, but the body by real concomitance, so that the whole Christ is under both species. But if during the time of the passion, when the blood of Christ had been drained from his body, this sacrament had been celebrated by any of the apostles, there would have been under the appearances of bread only the body of Christ without the blood; under the appearances of wine would there have been only the blood of Christ.

675. The second order considered is to the material foods which had preceded when he says, **after he had supped**. This is a significant phrase.

For Christ gave his body during the meal, as it is said: *as they were eating, Jesus took bread* (Matt 26:26). But he gave his blood expressly after the meal, as it is said: *and likewise the cup after supper* (Luke 22:20). The reason for this is that the body of Christ represents the mystery of the Incarnation, which occurred while the observance of the law was still in vogue. Among these observances the most important was the meal of the paschal lamb. But the blood of Christ in the sacrament directly represents the passion, through which it was poured out and through which all observances of the law came to an end; hence it is said: *he went once for all into the holy place, taking not the blood of goats and calves but his own blood, thus securing an eternal redemption* (Heb 9:12).

676. Then he presents the words, saying, **this chalice**.

First, he demonstrates the truth of this sacrament;
second, he enjoins its use, at **do this**.

677. In regard to the first he says, **this chalice**. This can be taken in two ways: in one way as metonymy, where the container is put for the content. As if to say: contained in this cup, which is more fittingly used in the consecration of

ponitur in consecratione vini, quod ratione suae humiditatis indiget aliis terminis contineri, quam in consecratione panis, qui ratione suae siccitatis, propriis terminis continetur.

Alio modo potest accipi metaphorice, ut sit sensus: sicut calix inebriat et perturbat, ita et passio. Unde Matth. XX, 22 dicit: *potestis bibere calicem, quem ego bibiturus sum?* Et Matth. XXVI, 39: *transeat a me calix iste.*

Est ergo sensus *hic calix*, id est, contentum in hoc calice, vel haec mea passio, *est novum testamentum in meo sanguine.*

678. Unde considerandum est, quod *testamentum* dupliciter sumitur in Scripturis.

Uno modo communiter pro quolibet pacto, quod quidem testibus confirmatur, et sic considerandum est, quod Deus dupliciter pactum iniit cum humano genere. Uno modo promittendo bona temporalia et a malis temporalibus liberando: et hoc vocatur Vetus Testamentum, vel pactum. Alio modo promittendo bona spiritualia et a malis oppositis liberando: et hoc vocatur Testamentum Novum. Unde dicitur Ier. XXXI, 31: *feriam domui Israel et domui Iuda foedus novum, non secundum pactum quod pepigi cum patribus vestris, ut educerem eos de terra Aegypti, sed hoc erit pactum: dabo legem meam in visceribus eorum, et ero eis in Deum.*

Est autem considerandum quod apud antiquos erat consuetudo ut alicuius victimae sanguinem funderent ad confirmationem pacti. Unde Gen. XXXI, 54 legitur, quod postquam inierunt enim foedus Laban et Iacob, *immolatis victimis in monte, vocavit fratres suos.* Unde et Ex. XXIV, 8 legitur, quod *Moyses sumptum sanguinem respersit in populum, et ait: hic est sanguis foederis, quod pepigit Dominus vobiscum.* Sicut ergo Vetus Testamentum seu pactum confirmatum est sanguine figurali taurorum, ita Novum Testamentum seu pactum confirmatum est in sanguine Christi, qui per passionem est effusus. Et in hoc calice sacramentum taliter continetur.

679. Alio modo *testamentum* accipitur magis stricte pro dispositione haereditatis percipiendae, quam necesse est secundum leges certo numero testium confirmare. Non autem testamentum sic acceptum confirmatur nisi per mortem, quia, ut Apostolus dicit Hebr. IX, 17, *testamentum in mortuis confirmatum est, alioquin nondum valet, dum vivit qui testatus est.*

Deus autem primo quidem dispositionem fecerat de aeterna haereditate percipienda, sed sub figura temporalium bonorum, quod pertinet ad Vetus Testamentum; sed postmodum fecit Novum Testamentum, expresse promittens haereditatem aeternam, quod quidem confirmatum est per sanguinem mortis Christi. Et ideo Dominus de hoc dicit *hic calix novum testamentum est in meo sanguine*; quasi dicat: per id quod in

the wine, which by reason of its wetness needs to be contained by other boundaries than in the consecration of the bread, which by reason of its dryness is contained within its own boundaries.

In another way it can be taken metaphorically, so that the sense would be: just as the cup intoxicates and confuses, so also the passion. Hence: *are you able to drink the cup I am to drink?* (Matt 20:22); *let this cup pass from me* (Matt 26:39).

The sense, therefore, is this: *this chalice*, i.e., what is contained in this cup, or this my passion, *is the new testament in my blood*.

678. Hence it should be noted that *testament* is taken in two senses in the Scriptures.

In one way for any pact which is confirmed by witnesses; and so it must be supposed that God entered into a pact with the human race in two ways: in one way by promising temporal goods and by freeing from temporal evils; and this is called the Old Testament or pact. In another way by promising spiritual goods and by freeing from opposite evils, and this is called the New Testament. Hence it is said: *I will make a new covenant with the house of Israel, not like the covenant which I made with their fathers, when I took them by the hand to bring them out of the land of Egypt. But this will be the testament: I will put my law within them and I will be their God* (Jer 31:31).

But it should be noted that in antiquity the custom was that they would pour out the blood of some victim to confirm a pact. Hence it is read that after Laban and Jacob made a pact, *victims were sacrificed on the mountain and called his kinsmen* (Gen 31:54). Hence, too, its says that Moses took the blood and threw it upon the people and said: *behold, the blood of the covenant, which the Lord has made with you* (Exod 24:8). Therefore, just as the Old Testament or pact was confirmed by the figural blood of bulls, so the New Testament or pact was confirmed in Christ's blood, which was poured out in the passion. And in the cup the sacrament is so contained.

679. In another way *testament* is taken more strictly for the disposition of an inheritance to be received and which must be confirmed by a certain number of witnesses. Such a covenant, however, is not confirmed except by death, because, as the Apostle says: *for a will takes effect only at death, since it is not in force as long as the one who made it is alive* (Heb 9:17).

God, first of all, made disposition of eternal rewards to be received, but under the figure of temporal goods which pertain to the Old Covenant. But later he made a New Covenant, expressly promising an eternal inheritance, which was confirmed by the blood of Christ's death. And therefore, the Lord says of this: *this chalice is the new testament in my blood*. As if to say: through that which is contained

calice continetur commemoratur novum testamentum per Christi sanguinem confirmatum.

680. Est autem advertendum quod eadem verba quae hic Apostolus ponit, habentur Lc. XXII, 20, nisi quod ibi additur: *qui pro vobis effundetur.* Lucas enim discipulus fuit Pauli et eum in conscriptione Evangelii est secutus. Sed Matth. XXVI, 28 dicitur *hic est enim sanguis meus novi testamenti, qui pro multis effundetur in remissionem peccatorum.* Eadem verba ponuntur in Mc. XIV, v. 24.

Dicunt ergo quidam, quod quaecumque formae horum verborum proferantur, quae sunt scripta in canone sufficere ad consecrationem.

Probabilius autem dici videtur quod illis solis verbis perficitur consecratio, quibus Ecclesia utitur ex traditione apostolorum structa. Evangelistae enim verba Domini recitare intenderunt quantum pertinet ad rationem historiae, non autem secundum quod ordinantur ad consecrationem sacramentorum, quas in occulto habebant in primitiva Ecclesia, propter infideles. Unde Dionysius dicit in ultimo cap. *Ecclesiasticae hierarchiae: perfectivas invocationes non est fas in Scripturis exponere, neque mysticum ipsarum ante factas in ipsis ex Deo virtutes ex occulto in communi adducere.*

681. Sed circa ista verba quibus Ecclesia utitur in consecratione sanguinis, quidam opinantur quod non omnia sint de necessitate formae sed solum quod dicitur *hic est calix sanguinis mei,* non autem residuum quod sequitur: *novi et aeterni testamenti, mysterium fidei, qui pro vobis et pro multis effundetur in remissionem peccatorum.*

Sed hoc non videtur convenienter dici. Nam totum illud quod sequitur est quaedam determinatio praedicati. Unde et ad eiusdem locutionis sententiam seu significationem pertinet. Et quia, ut saepe dictum est, formae sacramentorum significando efficiunt, totum pertinet ad vim effectivam formae.

Nec obstat ratio quam inducunt, quia in consecratione corporis sufficit quod dicitur **hoc est corpus meum**, quia sanguis seorsum consecratus, specialiter repraesentat passionem Christi, per quam eius sanguis separatus est a corpore.

682. Et ideo in consecratione sanguinis oportuit exprimere Christi passionis virtutem, quae attenditur, primo quidem, respectu nostrae culpae quam Christi passio abolet, secundum illud Apoc. I, 5: *lavit nos a peccatis nostris in sanguine suo*, et, quantum ad hoc, dicit *qui pro vobis et pro multis effundetur in remissionem peccatorum.* Effusus est siquidem sanguis in remissionem peccatorum, non solum pro multis, sed etiam pro omnibus, secundum illud I Io. II, 2: *ipse est propitiatio pro peccatis nostris, non pro nostris autem tantum, sed etiam pro totius mundi.* Sed quia quidam se reddunt indignos ad recipiendum talem effectum, quantum ad efficaciam

in the cup is commemorated the new covenant confirmed by the blood of Christ.

680. But it should be noted that the same words the Apostle gives here are found in Luke, except that Luke adds: *which shall be shed for you* (Luke 22:20). For Luke was a disciple of Paul and followed him in writing his Gospel. But it is also said: *this is my blood of the new covenant which is poured out for many for the forgiveness of sins* (Matt 26:28). The same words appear in Mark (Mark 14:24).

Therefore, some say that whichever forms of these words written in the canon are said, they suffice for consecration.

But it seems more probable to say that consecration is accomplished only by those words which the Church structured on the apostles' uses. For the evangelists intended to recite the Lord's words as part of his history, but not as they are ordained to consecration of the sacrament, which they held in secret in the early Church on account of unbelievers. Hence Dionysius says in *Ecclesiastical Hierarchy*: *it is not permitted to explain openly in writing the perfective invocations in the Scriptures or to bring to light their secret meaning.*

681. But in regard to the words the Church uses in the consecration of the blood, some believe that not all are necessary for the form, but only that *this is the cup of my blood* but not *of the new and eternal covenant, a mystery of faith, which will be shed for you and for many unto the remission of sins.*

But it does not seem fitting to say this. For all that follows is a determination of the predicate. Hence, it pertains to the meaning or signification of the same statement; and because, as has often been said, the forms of the sacraments effect by signifying, and totality pertains to the effective power of the sacrament.

Nor is there any merit in the reason they adduce, because in the consecration of the body it is enough to say, **this is my body** (1 Cor 11:24), because the blood separately consecrated especially represents the passion of Christ, through which his blood was separated from the body.

682. Therefore, in the consecration of the blood it was necessary to express the power of Christ's passion, which is looked at, first of all, with respect to our guilt, which the passion of Christ abolishes: *he washed us from our sins in his blood* (Rev 1:5). In regard to this he says, *which will be shed for you and for many unto the remission of sins.* The blood was indeed shed for the remission of sins, not only for many but for all: *he is the expiation for our sins, and not for ourselves only but also for the sins of the whole world* (1 John 2:2). But because some make themselves unworthy to receive such an effect, as far as its efficacy is concerned, it is said to have been shed for many, in which the passion

dicitur esse effusus pro multis, in quibus habet effectum passio Christi. Dicit autem signanter *pro vobis et pro multis*, quia hoc sacramentum valet in remissionem peccatorum sumentibus per modum sacramenti, quod notatur signanter, cum dicitur *pro vobis*, quibus dixerat *accipite*. Valet etiam per modum sacrificii multis non sumentibus, pro quibus offertur; quod significatur cum dicitur: *et pro multis*.

Secundo, virtus eius consideratur per comparationem ad vitam iustitiae, quam facit per fidem, secundum illud Rom. III, 24: *iustificati gratis per gratiam ipsius, per redemptionem quae est in Christo Iesu, quem proposuit propitiationem per fidem in sanguine ipsius*. Et quantum ad hoc, dicit: *mysterium*, id est occultum fidei, quia scilicet fides passionis Christi erat occulta in omnibus sacrificiis Veteris Testamenti, sicut veritas in signo. Hoc autem Ecclesia habet ex traditione apostolorum, cum in canone Scripturae non inveniatur.

Tertio, virtus eius attenditur quantum ad vitam gloriae, in quam per passionem Christi introducitur, secundum illud Hebr. X, 19: *habentes fiduciam in introitum sanctorum in sanguine Christi*. Et quantum ad hoc, dicit: *novi et aeterni testamenti*. Aeterni siquidem, quia est dispositio de haereditate aeterna. Novi autem, ad differentiam Veteris, quia temporalia promittebat. Unde Hebr. IX, 15 dicitur: *ideo novi testamenti mediator est, ut morte intercedente, repromissionem accipiant, qui vocati sunt aeternae haereditatis*.

683. Deinde cum dicit **hoc facite**, etc., iniungit usum huius sacramenti, dicens **hoc facite, quotiescumque sumitis, in meam commemorationem**, scilicet in memoriam meae passionis. Unde et Thr. III, 20 dicit propheta: *memoria memor ero, et tabescet in me anima mea*. Et Is. LXIII, 7: *miserationum Domini recordabor*.

684. Est autem notandum quod in calice principaliter quidem debet poni vinum, rationibus supradictis. Debet autem apponi et aqua. Probabile enim est quod Christus in coena vinum mixtum discipulis dederit, propter consuetudinem terrae illius, in qua, ut temperetur fortitudo vini, ab omnibus vinum bibitur aqua mixtum. Unde et Prov. IX, 5 sapientia dicit: *bibite vinum quod miscui vobis*.

Nihilominus tamen aqua vino mixta significat populum Christianum Christo per passionem coniunctum, secundum illud Apoc. c. XVII, 15: *aquae, populi sunt et gentes*. Et participatio sanguinis Christi a fidelibus pertinet ad usum sacramenti, qui non est de necessitate huius sacramenti.

Sed potest vinum consecrari absque aqua, licet peccet qui sic consecrat, non servans ritum Ecclesiae. Et ideo si sacerdos ante consecrationem vini advertat quod aqua non fuerit apposita calici, debet apponere. Si vero post consecrationem advertat, non debet apponere, sed debet perficere sacramentum. Nihil enim post consecrationem

of Christ has an effect. But he expressly says, *for you and for many*, because this sacrament can produce remission of sin for those who receive it after the manner of a sacrament, which is clearly signified when it is said: *for you*, to whom he had said **take**. Or for those who receive it after the manner of sacrifice for many not receiving, for whom it is offered; which is signified when it is said: *and for many*.

Second, its power is considered with respect to the life of justice it effects through faith: *they are justified by his grace as a gift through the redemption which is in Christ Jesus, whom God put forward as an expiation by his blood to be received by faith* (Rom 3:24). As to this he says: *the mystery*, i.e., the sacrament of faith, namely, because faith in the passion of Christ was hidden in all the sacrifices of the Old Covenant, as the truth in a figure. But the Church has this from the tradition of the apostles, since it is not found in the canon of Scripture.

Third, its power is regarded with respect to the life of glory: *having confidence to enter the sanctuary by the blood of Jesus* (Heb 10:19). As to this he says: *of the new and eternal covenant*. Eternal, indeed, because it is the disposition for the eternal inheritance. New to distinguish from the Old, which promised temporal things. Hence it is said: *therefore, he is the mediator of a new covenant, so that those who are called may receive the promised eternal inheritance, since his death has occurred* (Heb 9:15).

683. Then when he says, **do this**, he enjoins the use of this sacrament, saying, **do this as often as you shall drink, for the commemoration of me**, namely, in memory of my passion. Hence the prophet says: *my soul continually thinks of it and is bowed down within me* (Lam 3:20); *I will recall the mercies of the Lord* (Isa 63:7).

684. But it should be noted that principally wine should be put in the cup. But water should be added. For it is probable that Christ at the meal gave the disciples wine mixed with water on account of a custom of that land, in which the strength of the wine had to tempered, so that all drink their wine mixed with water. Hence Wisdom says: *drink the wine I have mixed for you* (Prov 9:5).

Nevertheless, water mixed with wine signifies the Christian people joined to Christ by passion: *the waters you saw are peoples and nations* (Rev 17:15). And partaking of the blood of Christ by the faithful pertains to the use of the sacrament, although it is not necessary.

But wine can be consecrated without water, although one so consecrating would sin by not observing the rite of the Church. Therefore, if the priest before the consecration of the wine recalls that water was not added to the wine, he should add it. But if he recalls it after the consecration, he should not add it but should complete the sacrament. For

est sanguini Christi miscendum quia talis permixtio non posset esse sine qualicumque corruptione vini consecrati, quod pertinet ad crimen sacrilegii.

685. Dicunt autem quidam quod cum de latere Christi pendentis in cruce fluxerit sanguis et aqua, ut legitur Io. XIX, 34, sicut vinum convertitur in sanguinem, ita aqua in aquam. Sed hoc non competit, quia in illa aqua figuratur ablutio quae est per baptismum.

Et ideo alii dicunt quod, facta conversione vini in sanguinem, aqua remanet in sua substantia, et circuntegitur accidentibus vini. Sed hoc non competit, quia aqua admiscetur vino ante consecrationem, quando non differt ab alio vino. Unde non seorsum manet, sed permiscetur.

Et ideo dicendum est, quod aqua convertitur in vinum et sic totum convertitur in sanguinem Christi. Propter quod mos est modicum de aqua apponere et praecipue si sit vinum debile, quod non potest nisi modicum aquae in seipsum convertere.

686. Deinde cum dicit **quotiescumque**, etc., exponit verba Domini quae dixerat: **hoc facite in meam commemorationem**, dicens **quotiescumque enim manducabitis panem hunc**, et cetera.

Et dicit **panem**, propter species remanentes. Dicit autem **hunc**, propter idem numero corpus significatum et contentum.

Et calicem, scilicet hunc, **bibetis, mortem Domini annuntiabitis**, repraesentando scilicet eam per hoc sacramentum.

Et hoc, **donec veniat**, id est, usque ad ultimum eius adventum, in quo datur intelligi, quod hic ritus Ecclesiae non cessabit usque ad finem mundi, secundum illud Matth. ult.: *ecce ego vobiscum sum usque ad consummationem saeculi*. Et Lc. XXI, 32: *non praeteribit generatio haec*, scilicet Ecclesiae, *donec omnia fiant*.

after the consecration, nothing should be mixed with the blood of Christ, because such a mixing could not take place without some sort of corruption of the consecrated wine, which pertains to the crime of sacrilege.

685. But some say that when from the side of Christ hanging on the cross blood and water flowed (John 19:34), then as wine is converted into blood, so water into water. But this is not suitable, because in that water is figured the washing which is through baptism.

But some say that after the conversion of wine into the blood the water remains as water and is surrounded by the accidents of the wine. But this is awkward, because the water is mixed with the wine before consecration, when it does not differ from other wine. Hence, they do not remain separated but are commingled.

Therefore, it must be said that water is converted into wine and this whole is converted into the blood of Christ. Accordingly, the custom is to add a small amount of water, especially if the wine is weak, which can convert only a slight amount of water into itself.

686. Then when he says, **for as often as**, he explains the Lord's words, which said: **do this . . . for the commemoration of me**, saying, **for as often as you shall eat this bread**.

He says **bread** on account of the appearances that remain. He says **this** on account of the numerically same body signified and contained.

And drink the chalice, you shall show the death of the Lord, namely, by representing it through this sacrament.

And this, **until he comes**, i.e., until his final coming. This gives us to understand that this rite of the Church will not cease until the end of the world: *I am with you always to the end of the world* (Matt 27:20); *this generation*, namely, of the Church, *will not pass away, till all has taken place* (Luke 21:32).

Lecture 7

^{11:27}Itaque quicumque manducaverit panem hunc, vel biberit calicem Domini indigne, reus erit corporis et sanguinis Domini. [n. 687]

^{11:28}Probet autem seipsum homo: et sic de pane illo edat, et de calice bibat. [n. 695]

^{11:29}Qui enim manducat et bibit indigne, judicium sibi manducat et bibit, non dijudicans corpus Domini. [n. 697]

^{11:30}Ideo inter vos multi infirmi et imbecilles, et dormiunt multi. [n. 700]

^{11:31}Quod si nosmetipsos dijudicaremus, non utique judicaremur. [n. 702]

^{11:32}Dum judicamur autem, a Domino corripimur, ut non cum hoc mundo damnemur. [n. 705]

^{11:33}Itaque fratres mei, cum convenitis ad manducandum, invicem exspectate. [n. 706]

^{11:34}Si quis esurit, domi manducet, ut non in judicium conveniatis. Cetera autem, cum venero, disponam. [n. 708]

^{11:27}Ὥστε ὃς ἂν ἐσθίῃ τὸν ἄρτον ἢ πίνῃ τὸ ποτήριον τοῦ κυρίου ἀναξίως, ἔνοχος ἔσται τοῦ σώματος καὶ τοῦ αἵματος τοῦ κυρίου.

^{11:28}δοκιμαζέτω δὲ ἄνθρωπος ἑαυτόν, καὶ οὕτως ἐκ τοῦ ἄρτου ἐσθιέτω καὶ ἐκ τοῦ ποτηρίου πινέτω·

^{11:29}ὁ γὰρ ἐσθίων καὶ πίνων κρίμα ἑαυτῷ ἐσθίει καὶ πίνει μὴ διακρίνων τὸ σῶμα.

^{11:30}διὰ τοῦτο ἐν ὑμῖν πολλοὶ ἀσθενεῖς καὶ ἄρρωστοι καὶ κοιμῶνται ἱκανοί.

^{11:31}εἰ δὲ ἑαυτοὺς διεκρίνομεν, οὐκ ἂν ἐκρινόμεθα·

^{11:32}κρινόμενοι δὲ ὑπὸ [τοῦ] κυρίου παιδευόμεθα, ἵνα μὴ σὺν τῷ κόσμῳ κατακριθῶμεν.

^{11:33}ὥστε, ἀδελφοί μου, συνερχόμενοι εἰς τὸ φαγεῖν ἀλλήλους ἐκδέχεσθε.

^{11:34}εἴ τις πεινᾷ, ἐν οἴκῳ ἐσθιέτω, ἵνα μὴ εἰς κρίμα συνέρχησθε. Τὰ δὲ λοιπὰ ὡς ἂν ἔλθω διατάξομαι.

^{11:27}Therefore, whosoever shall eat this bread, or drink the chalice of the Lord unworthily, shall be guilty of the body and of the blood of the Lord. [n. 687]

^{11:28}But let a man prove himself: and so let him eat of that bread and drink of the chalice. [n. 695]

^{11:29}For he who eats and drinks unworthily eats and drinks judgment to himself, not discerning the body of the Lord. [n. 697]

^{11:30}Therefore, there are many infirm and weak among you: and many sleep. [n. 700]

^{11:31}But if we would judge ourselves, we should not be judged. [n. 702]

^{11:32}But while we are judged, we are chastised by the Lord, that we be not condemned with this world. [n. 705]

^{11:33}Wherefore, my brethren, when you come together to eat, wait for one another. [n. 706]

^{11:34}If any man be hungry, let him eat at home; that you come not together unto judgment. And the rest I will set in order, when I come. [n. 708]

---

687. Postquam Apostolus ostendit dignitatem huius sacramenti hic excitat fideles ad sumendum illud reverenter: et

primo ponit periculum quod imminet indigne sumentibus;

secundo adhibet salutare remedium, ibi **probet autem**, et cetera.

688. Dicit ergo primo **itaque**, ex quo hoc quod sacramentaliter manducatur, est corpus Christi et, quod bibitur, est sanguis Christi, **quicumque manducaverit hunc panem, vel biberit calicem indigne, reus erit corporis et sanguinis Domini.**

In quibus verbis, primo, considerandum est qualiter aliquis indigne manducat et bibit: quod quidem, secundum Glossam contingit tripliciter.

Primo quidem quantum ad celebrationem huius sacramenti, quia scilicet aliquis aliter celebrat sacramentum Eucharistiae, quam a Christo traditum est: puta si offerat in hoc sacramento alium panem quam triticeum, vel alium liquorem, quam vinum de vite. Unde

687. After showing the dignity of this sacrament, the Apostle now rouses the faithful to receive it reverently.

First, he outlines the peril threatening those who receive unworthily;

second, he applies a saving remedy, at **but let a man prove himself.**

688. First, therefore, he says, **therefore**, from the fact that this which is received sacramentally is the body of Christ and what is drunk is the blood of Christ, **whosoever shall eat this bread, or drink the chalice of the Lord unworthily, shall be guilty of the body and of the blood of the Lord.**

In these words must be considered, first, how someone eats or drinks unworthily. According to a Gloss this happens in three ways.

First, as to the celebration of this sacrament, namely, because someone celebrates the sacrament in a manner different from that handed down by Christ; for example, if he offers in this sacrament a bread other than wheaten or some liquid other than wine from the grape of the vine. Hence it

Lev. X, 1 s. dicitur quod Nadab et Abiu, filii Aaron, obtulerunt coram Domino *ignem alienum, quod eis praeceptum non erat: egressusque ignis a Domino, devoravit eos.*

689. Secundo ex hoc quod aliquis non devota mente accedit ad Eucharistiam. Quae quidem indevotio quandoque est veniale: puta cum aliquis, distracta mente ad saecularia negotia, accedit ad hoc sacramentum habitualiter retinens debitam reverentiam ad ipsum; et talis indevotio licet impediat fructum huius sacramenti, qui est spiritualis refectio, non tamen facit reum corporis et sanguinis Domini, sicut hic Apostolus loquitur.

Quaedam vero indevotio est peccatum mortale, quae scilicet est cum contemptu huius sacramenti, prout dicitur Malach. I, 12: *vos polluistis nomen meum in eo quod dicitis: mensa Domini contaminata est, et quod supponitur contemptibile.* Et de tali indevotione loquitur Glossa.

690. Tertio modo dicitur aliquis indignus ex eo quod cum voluntate peccandi mortaliter, accedit ad Eucharistiam. Dicitur enim Levit. XXI, 23: *non accedat ad altare qui maculam habet.*

Intelligitur aliquis maculam peccati habere, quamdiu est in voluntate peccandi, quae tamen tollitur per poenitentiam. Per contritionem quidem, quae tollit voluntatem peccandi, cum proposito confitendi et satisfaciendi, quantum ad remissionem culpae et poenae aeternae; per confessionem autem et satisfactionem quantum ad totalem remissionem poenae et reconciliationem ad membra Ecclesiae.

Et ideo in necessitate quidem, puta quando aliquis copiam confessionis habere non potest, sufficit contritio ad sumptionem huius sacramenti. Regulariter autem debet confessio praecedere cum aliqua satisfactione. Unde in libro *de Eccl. dogmatibus* dicitur: *communicaturus satisfaciat lacrymis et orationibus, et confidens de Domino mundus accedat ad Eucharistiam intrepidus et securus. Sed hoc de illo dico quem capitalia peccata et mortalia non gravant. Namque, quem mortalia crimina post baptismum commissa premunt, hortor prius publica poenitentia satisfacere, et ita sacerdotis iudicio reconciliatum communioni sociari, si non vult ad condemnationem Eucharistiam percipere.*

691. Sed videtur quod peccatores non indigne accedant ad hoc sacramentum. Nam in hoc sacramento sumitur Christus, qui est spiritualis medicus, qui de se dicit Matth. c. IX, 12: *non est opus valentibus medicus, sed male habentibus.*

Sed dicendum quod hoc sacramentum est spirituale nutrimentum, sicut baptismus est spiritualis nativitas. Nascitur autem aliquis ad hoc ut vivat, sed non nutritur nisi iam vivus. Et ideo hoc sacramentum non competit peccatoribus, qui nondum vivunt per gratiam: competit eis tamen baptismus.

is said that Nadab and Abihu, sons of Aaron, offered before the Lord *unholy fire, such as he had not commanded them. And fire came forth from the presence of the Lord and devoured them* (Lev 10:1).

689. Second, from the fact that someone approached the Eucharist with a mind not devout. This lack of devotion is sometimes venial, as when someone with his mind distracted by worldly affairs approaches this sacrament habitually retaining due reverence toward it; and such lack of devotion, although it impedes the fruit of this sacrament, which is spiritual refreshment, does not make one guilty of the body and blood of the Lord, as the Apostle says here.

But a certain lack of devotion is a mortal sin, i.e., when it involves contempt of this sacrament, as it is said: *but you profane it when you say that the Lord's table is polluted and its food may be despised* (Mal 1:12). It is of such lack of devotion that the Gloss speaks.

690. In a third way someone is said to be unworthy, because he approaches the Eucharist with the intention of sinning mortally. For it is said: *he shall not approach the altar, because he has a blemish* (Lev 21:23).

Someone is understood to have a blemish as long as he persists in the intention of sinning, which, however, is taken away through penitence. By contrition, indeed, which takes away the will to sin with the intention of confession and making satisfaction, as to the remission of guilt and eternal punishment; by confession and satisfaction as to the total remission of punishment and reconciliation with the members of the Church.

Therefore, in cases of necessity, as when someone does not have an abundance of confessors, contrition is enough for receiving this sacrament. But as a general rule, confession with some satisfaction should precede. Hence in the book *On Church Dogmas* it says: *one who desires to go to communion should make satisfaction with tears and prayers, and trusting in the Lord approach the Eucharist clean, free from care, and secure. But I say this of the person not burdened with capital and mortal sins. For the one whom mortal sins committed after baptism press down, I advise to make satisfaction with public penance, and so be joined to communion by the judgment of the priest, if he does not wish to receive the condemnation of the Church.*

691. But it seems that sinners do not approach this sacrament unworthily. For in this sacrament Christ is received, and he is the spiritual physician, who says of himself: *those who are well have no need of a physician, but those who are sick* (Matt 9:12).

The answer is that this sacrament is spiritual food, as baptism is spiritual birth. But one is born in order to live, but he is not nourished unless he is already alive. Therefore, this sacrament does not befit sinners who are not yet alive by grace; although baptism befits them.

Et, praeterea, Eucharistia est *sacramentum caritatis et ecclesiasticae unitatis*, ut dicit Augustinus *Super Ioannem*. Cum igitur peccator careat caritate, et sit separatus merito ab Ecclesiae unitate, si accedat ad hoc sacramentum, falsitatem committit, dum significat se habere caritatem, quam non habet.

Quia tamen peccator quandoque habet fidem huius sacramenti, licitum est ei hoc sacramentum inspicere, quod omnino infidelibus denegatur, ut Dionysius dicit III cap. *Ecclesiasticae hierarchiae*.

692. Secundo considerandum est, quomodo ille qui indigne sumit hoc sacramentum, sit reus corporis et sanguinis Domini. Quod quidem in Glossa tripliciter exponitur.

Uno modo materialiter: incurrit enim reatum ex peccato commisso circa corpus et sanguinem Domini, prout in hoc sacramento continetur, quod indigne sumit, et ex hoc eius culpa aggravatur. Tanto est enim eius culpa gravior, quanto maior est contra quem peccatur. Hebr. X, 29: *quanto magis putatis deteriora mereri supplicia eum, qui Filium Dei conculcaverit, et sanguinem testamenti pollutum duxerit?*

693. Secundo exponitur per similitudinem, ut sit sensus **reus erit corporis et sanguinis Domini**, et mortis Domini poenas dabit, hoc est, ac si Christum occiderit, punietur, secundum illud Hebr. VI, 6: *rursum crucifigentes sibimetipsis Filium Dei, et ostentui habentes.*

Sed secundum hoc videtur gravissimum esse peccatum eorum qui indigne sumunt corpus Christi.

Sed dicendum quod peccatum aliquod habet gravitatem dupliciter. Uno modo ex ipsa specie peccati, quae sumitur ex obiecto, et secundum hoc gravius est peccatum quod contra divinitatem committitur, puta infidelitas, blasphemia vel aliquid huiusmodi, quam quod committitur contra humanitatem Christi. Unde et ipse Dominus Matth. XII, 32 dicit, quod *qui dixerit verbum contra filium hominis remittetur ei: qui autem dixerit contra Spiritum Sanctum, non remittetur ei.* Et iterum, gravius est peccatum quod committitur contra humanitatem in propria specie, quam sub specie sacramenti.

Alio modo gravitas peccati attenditur ex parte peccantis. Magis autem peccat qui ex odio aut invidia vel ex quacumque malitia peccat, sicut peccaverunt illi qui Christum crucifixerunt, quam qui peccat ex infirmitate, sicut interdum peccant illi qui indigne sumunt hoc sacramentum. Non ergo per hoc intelligitur quod peccatum indigne sumentium hoc sacramentum, comparetur peccato occidentium Christum secundum aequalitatem sed secundum similitudinem speciei: quia utrumque est circa eumdem Christum.

694. Tertio modo exponitur **reus erit corporis et sanguinis Domini**, id est corpus et sanguis Domini facient eum reum. Ita enim bonum male sumptum nocet, sicut

Furthermore, *the Eucharist is the sacrament of love and ecclesial unity*, as Augustine say *On John*. Since, therefore, the sinner lacks charity and is deservedly separated from the unity of the Church, if he approaches this sacrament, he commits a falsehood, since he is signifying that he has charity, but does not.

Yet because a sinner sometimes has faith in this sacrament, it is lawful for him to look at this sacrament, which is absolutely denied to unbelievers, as Dionysius says in *Ecclesiastical Hierarchy*.

692. Second, it is necessary to consider how one who receives this sacrament unworthily is guilty of the body and blood of the Lord. This is explained in three ways in a Gloss.

In one way materially: for one incurs guilt from a sin committed against the body and blood of Christ, as contained in this sacrament, which he receives unworthily and from this his guilt is increased. For his guilt is increased to the extent that a greater person is offended against: *how much worse punishment do you think will be deserved by the man who has spurned the Son of God and profaned the blood of the covenant?* (Heb 10:29).

693. Second, it is explained by a similitude, so that the sense would be: he **shall be guilty of the body and of the blood of the Lord**, i.e., he will be punished as if he had killed Christ: *they crucify the Son of God on their own account and hold him up to contempt* (Heb 6:6).

But according to this the gravest sin seems to be committed by those who receive the body of Christ unworthily.

The answer is that a sin is grave in two ways: in one way from the sin's species, which is taken from its object; according to this a sin against the godhead, such as unbelief, blasphemy and so on, is graver than one committed against the humanity of Christ. Hence, the Lord himself says: *whoever says a word against the son of man will be forgiven; but whoever speaks against the Holy Spirit will not be forgiven* (Matt 12:32). And again a sin committed against the humanity in its own species is graver than under the sacramental species.

In another way the gravity of sin is considered on the part of the sinner. But one sins more, when he sins from hatred or envy or any other maliciousness, as those sinned who crucified Christ, than one who sins from weakness, as they sometimes sin who receive this sacrament unworthily. It does not follow, therefore, that the sin of receiving this sacrament unworthily should be compared to the sin of killing Christ, as though the sins were equal, but on account of a specific likeness: because each concerns the same Christ.

694. He **shall be guilty of the body and of the blood of the Lord** is explained in a third way, i.e., the body and blood of the Lord will make him guilty. For something good evilly

prodest malum quo quis bene utitur, sicut stimulus Satanae Paulo.

Per haec autem verba excluditur error quorumdam dicentium, quod quam statim hoc sacramentum tangitur a labiis peccatoris, desinit sub eo esse corpus Christi. Contra quod est quod Apostolus dicit: *quicumque manducaverit panem hunc, vel biberit calicem Domini indigne*. Secundum enim praedictam opinionem nullus indignus manducaret vel biberet. Contrariatur autem praedicta opinio veritati huiusmodi sacramenti, secundum quam tamdiu corpus et sanguis Christi manent in sacramento, quamdiu remanent species, in quocumque loco existant.

695. Deinde cum dicit *probet autem*, etc., adhibet remedium contra praedictum periculum. Et

primo ponit remedium;

secundo assignat rationem, ibi *qui enim manducat*, etc.;

tertio rationem manifestat per signum, ibi *ideo inter vos*, et cetera.

696. Dicit ergo primo: quia tantum reatum incurrit qui indigne sumit hoc sacramentum, ideo necesse est ut primo homo seipsum probet, id est, diligenter examinet suam conscientiam, ne sit in eo voluntas peccandi mortaliter, vel aliquod peccatum praeteritum, de quo non sufficienter poenituerit. *Et sic*, post diligentem examinationem securus, *de pane illo edat, et de calice bibat*, quia digne sumentibus non est venenum, sed medicina. Gal. ult.: *opus autem suum probet unusquisque*. II Cor. XIII, 5: *si estis in fide Christi, vos probate*.

697. Deinde cum dicit *quicumque enim manducaverit*, etc., assignat rationem praedicti remedii, dicens: ideo probatio praeexigitur, *qui enim indigne manducat et bibit, iudicium*, id est condemnationem, *sibi manducat et bibit*, sicut dicitur Io. V, 29: *resurget qui male egerunt in resurrectionem iudicii*. *Non diiudicans corpus Domini*, id est ex eo quod non discernit corpus Domini ab aliis, indifferenter ipsum assumens, sicut alios cibos. Lev. XXII, 3: *omnis homo qui accesserit ad ea quae consecrata sunt, in quo est immunditia, peribit coram Domino*.

698. Sed contra videtur esse quod dicitur Io. VI, 58: *qui manducat me, vivit propter me*.

Sed dicendum est, quod duplex est modus manducandi hoc sacramentum, scilicet spiritualis et sacramentalis. Quidam ergo manducant sacramentaliter et spiritualiter, qui scilicet ita sumunt hoc sacramentum, quod etiam rem sacramenti participant, scilicet caritatem, per quam est ecclesiastica unitas. Et de talibus intelligitur verbum Domini inductum: *qui manducat me, vivit propter me*.

Quidam vero manducant sacramentaliter tantum, qui scilicet ita hoc sacramentum percipiunt, quod rem

received hurts one, inasmuch as evil well used profits one, as the sting of Satan profited Paul.

By these words is excluded the error of those who say that as soon as this sacrament is touched by the lips of a sinner, the body of Christ ceases to be under it. Against this is the word of the Apostle: **whosoever shall eat this bread, or drink the chalice of the Lord unworthily**. For according to the above opinion no one unworthy would eat or drink. But this opinion is contrary to the truth of this sacrament, according to which the body and blood of Christ remain in this sacrament, as long as the appearances remain, no matter where they exist.

695. Then when he says, **but let a man prove himself**, he applies a remedy against this peril.

First, he suggests the remedy;

second, he assigns a reason, at **for he who eats**;

third, he clarifies the reason with a sign, at **therefore, there are many**.

696. First, therefore, he says: because one who receives this sacrament unworthily incurs so much guilt, it is necessary that a man first examine himself, i.e., carefully inspect his conscience, lest there exist in it the intention to sin mortally or any past sin for which he has not repented sufficiently. **And so**, secure after a careful examination, **let him eat of that bread and drink of the chalice**, because for those who receive worthily, it is not poison but medicine: *let each one test his own work* (Gal 6:4); *examine yourselves to see whether you are holding to your faith* (2 Cor 13:5).

697. Then when he says, **for he who eats**, he assigns the reason for the above remedy, saying: a previous examination is required, **for he who eats and drinks unworthily eats and drinks judgment**, i.e., condemnation, **to himself**: *those who have done evil will rise to the resurrection of judgment* (John 5:29). **Not discerning the body of the Lord**, i.e., from the fact that he does not distinguish the body of the Lord from other things, receiving him indiscriminately as other foods: *anyone who approaches the holy things while he has an uncleanness, that person shall be cut off from my presence* (Lev 22:3).

698. On the other hand it says in John (6:58): *he who eats me shall live because of me*.

The answer is that there are two ways of receiving this sacrament, namely, spiritually and sacramentally. Therefore, some receive sacramentally and spiritually, namely, those who receive this sacrament in such a way that they also share in the reality of the sacrament, namely, charity through which ecclesial unity exists. To such the Lord's words apply: *he who eats me will live because of me*.

But some receive only sacramentally, namely, those who receive this sacrament in such a way that they do not have

sacramenti, id est, caritatem non habent, et de talibus intelligitur quod hic dicitur: *qui manducat et bibit indigne, iudicium sibi manducat et bibit.*

Est autem praeter duos modos quibus sumitur sacramentum hoc, tertius modus sumendi, quo manducatur per accidens, dum scilicet sumitur non ut sacramentum, quod quidem contingit tripliciter. Uno modo sicut quando aliquis fidelis sumit hostiam consecratam, quam non credit esse consecratam; talis enim habet habitum utendi hoc sacramento, sed non utitur eo actu, ut sacramento. Alio modo sicut quando hostiam consecratam sumit aliquis infidelis, qui nullam fidem habet huius sacramenti; talis enim non habet habitum utendi hoc sacramento, sed solum potentiam. Tertio modo sicut quando hostiam sacratam comedit mus vel quodlibet animal brutum, quod etiam non habet potentiam utendi hoc sacramento.

699. Ex hoc igitur quod spiritualiter sumentes hoc sacramentum acquirunt vitam, alliciuntur quidam ad hoc quod frequenter hoc sacramentum assumant. Ex hoc autem quod indigne sumentes acquirunt sibi iudicium, plures deterrentur, ut rarius sumant: et utrumque commendandum videtur.

Legimus enim Lc. XIX, 6, quod *Zachaeus recepit Christum gaudens in domum suam*, in quo eius caritas commendatur. Legitur etiam eodem, VII, 6, quod centurio dixit Christo: *non sum dignus ut intres sub tectum meum*. In quo commendatur honor et reverentia eius ad Christum.

Quia tamen amor praefertur timori, per se loquendo, commendabilius esse videtur quod aliquis frequentius sumat, quam quod rarius. Quia tamen quod est in se eligibilius, potest esse minus eligibile quantum ad hunc vel illum: considerare quilibet in seipso debet, quem effectum in se habeat frequens susceptio huius sacramenti. Nam si aliquis sentiat se proficere in fervore dilectionis ad Christum et in fortitudine resistendi peccatis, quae plurimum consequuntur homines, debet frequenter sumere. Si vero ex frequenti sumptione sentiat aliquis in se minus reverentiam huius sacramenti, monendus est ut rarius sumat. Unde et in libro *de Ecclesiasticis dogmatibus* dicitur: *quotidie Eucharistiam sumere, nec laudo nec vitupero.*

700. Deinde cum dicit *ideo inter vos*, etc., manifestat praedictam rationem per signum. Et

primo ponit signum;

secundo assignat causam illius signi, ibi *quod si nosmetipsos*, et cetera.

701. Circa primum considerandum est, quod, sicut Augustinus dicit in I *de Civit. Dei*, cap. VIII: *si omne peccatum nunc manifeste Deus plecteret poena, nihil ultimo iudicio reservari putaretur. Rursus, si nullum peccatum nunc puniret, nulla esse divina providentia crederetur.*

the reality of the sacrament, i.e., charity. To these are applied the words spoken here: *he who eats and drinks unworthily eats and drinks judgment to himself*.

Besides these two ways by which the sacrament is taken, there is a third way, by which one eats *per accidens*, namely, when it is taken not as a sacrament. This can happen in three ways: in one way, as when a believer receives the consecrated host, which he does not believe is consecrated: such a one has the habit of receiving this sacrament, but he does not use it actually as a sacrament. In another way, as when an unbeliever receives the consecrated host, but he has no faith about this sacrament: such a person does not have the habit of using this sacrament, but only the potentiality. In a third way, as when a mouse or other brute animal eats the sacred host: such animals do have even the potentiality to use this sacrament.

699. Therefore, from the fact that those who receive this sacrament spiritually acquire life, some are drawn to receive this sacrament frequently. But from the fact that those who receive unworthily acquire judgment upon themselves, many are deterred and rarely receive.

Both seem commendable, for we read: *Zacheaus rejoiced to receive the Lord into his house* (Luke 19:6). In this his charity is commended. We also read that the centurion said to Christ: *I am not worthy that you should enter under my roof* (Luke 7:6). In this case his honor and reverence toward Christ is commended.

But because of themselves love is preferred to fear, it seems more commendable to receive more frequently rather than more rarely. Yet because something more choiceworthy in itself can be less choiceworthy in regard to this or that person, each one should consider in himself which effect the frequent reception of this sacrament would have in him. For if someone feels that it helps him make progress to the fervor of his love of Christ and in his strength to resist sins, he ought to receive frequently. But if someone feels in himself less reverence for his sacrament by receiving it frequently, he should be advised to receive it rarely. Hence, even in the book *On the Dogmas of the Church* it says: *I neither praise nor condemn daily communion.*

700. Then when he says, *therefore, there are many*, he clarifies the reason he gave with a sign.

First, he mentions the sign;

second, he assigns the cause of that sign, at *but if we would judge ourselves*.

701. In regard to the first it should be noted that, as Augustine says in *The City of God*: *if God punished every sin with a penalty now, it would be thought that nothing was left for the final judgment. Again, if he punished no sin now, it would be believed that there is no divine providence.*

In signum ergo futuri iudicii Deus etiam in hoc mundo pro peccato quosdam temporaliter punit, quod maxime observatum videtur in principio legislationis, tam Novae quam Veteris. Legimus enim Ex. c. XXXII, 28, propter peccatum vituli aurei adorati, multa millia hominum perempta. Rursum legitur Act. V, 1–11, propter peccatum mendacii et furti Ananiam et Saphiram interiisse. Unde et propter peccatum huius sacramenti indigne sumpti, aliqui in primitiva Ecclesia puniebantur a Deo infirmitate corporali vel etiam morte.

Unde dicit *ideo*, scilicet in signum futuri iudicii, *inter vos*, multi indigne sumentes corpus Christi, sunt *infirmi* corporaliter. Ps. XV, v. 4: *multiplicatae sunt infirmitates*. *Et imbecilles*, id est longa invaletudine laborantes, *et dormiunt multi*, scilicet morte corporali, secundum quod sumitur dormitio I ad Thess. IV, 12: *nolumus vos ignorare de dormientibus*.

702. Deinde cum dicit *quod si nosmetipsos*, etc., assignat duplicem rationem praedicti signi, quarum

prima sumitur ex parte nostri,

secunda ex parte Dei, ibi *cum iudicamur autem*, et cetera.

703. Ex parte autem nostra causa divinae punitionis est a negligentia, quia in nobis ipsis peccata commissa punire negligimus. Unde dicit *quod si nosmetipsos diiudicaremus*, redarguendo et puniendo peccata nostra, *non utique iudicaremur*, id est, non puniremur a Domino neque postmodum in futuro, neque etiam in praesenti.

704. Sed contra est quod supra IV, 3 dictum est: *sed neque meipsum iudico*, et Rom. XIV, 22 dicitur: *beatus qui non iudicat semetipsum*.

Sed dicendum est quod aliquis potest seipsum iudicare tripliciter: uno modo discutiendo, et sic aliquis debet iudicare seipsum et quantum ad opera praeterita et quantum ad futura, secundum illud Gal. ult.: *opus suum probet unusquisque*.

Alio modo sententialiter seipsum absolvendo, quasi iudicando se innocentem quantum ad praeterita, et secundum hoc nullus debet iudicare seipsum, ut scilicet se innocentem iudicet, secundum illud Iob IX, 20: *si iustificare me voluero, os meum condemnabit me. Si innocentem me ostendero, pravum me comprobabit*.

Tertio modo reprehendendo, ut scilicet faciat aliquid quod ipse iudicat esse malum. Et hoc modo intelligitur quod inductum est: *beatus est qui non iudicat semetipsum in eo quod probat*. Sed quantum ad ea quae iam fecit, debet quilibet se ipsum iudicare, reprehendendo et puniendo pro maleficiis. Unde dicitur Iob XIII, 15: *vias meas in conspectu eius arguam*, et XXIII, 4: *ponam coram eo iudicium, et os meum replebo increpationibus*.

Et de hoc iudicio Augustinus dicit in libro *de Poenitentia*, et inducitur hic in Glossa: *versetur ante oculos*

As a sign of the future judgment, God even in this world punishes certain ones temporarily in this world. This is especially seen in the beginning of the legislation both of the Old and of the New. For we read that on account of the sin of adoring the golden calf many thousands of men fell (Exod 32:28). Again we read that on account of the sin of lying and of theft Ananias and Sapphira were destroyed (Acts 5:1–11). Hence also for the sin of receiving this sacrament unworthily some in the early Church were punished by God with bodily infirmity or even death.

Hence he says, *therefore*, namely, as a sign of the future judgment, *among you* many unworthily receiving the body of Christ are *infirm* bodily: *their sorrows are multiplied* (Ps 16:4); *and weak*, i.e., labor under a long sickness, *and many sleep*, namely, by bodily death. *We will not have you ignorant concerning them that are asleep* (1 Thess 4:12).

702. Then when he says, *but if we would judge*, he assigns two reasons for the above sign:

the first is taken on our part;

the second on God's part, *but while we are judged*.

703. On our part the cause of divine punishment is from negligence, because we neglect to punish ourselves for sins committed. Hence he says *but if we would judge ourselves* truly by rebuking and punishing our sins, *we should not be judged*, i.e., not punished by the Lord either later in the future or even in the present.

704. But on the other hand it says above: *but neither do I judge my own self* (1 Cor 4:3); *blessed is he who does not judge himself* (Rom 14:22).

The answer is that someone can judge himself in three ways: in one way by examination, and in this way one ought to judge himself both as to past works and as to future ones: *let each one prove his own work* (Gal 6:4).

In another way by absolving himself decisionally as though judging himself innocent as to the past; and according to this, no one should judge himself, namely, that he judge himself innocent: *though I am innocent, my own mouth would condemn me; though I am blameless, he would prove me perverse* (Job 9:20).

In a third way by reprehending, namely, that he did something he judges evil. In this way is understood the statement: *blessed is he who does not judge himself for what he approves*. But as to things already done, each one ought to judge himself by blaming and punishing oneself for evil deeds. Hence it is said: *I will defend my ways to his face* (Job 13:15); *I would lay my case before him and fill my mouth with arguments* (Job 23:4).

In the book *On Penance*, Augustine says of this judgment: *let the image of the future judgment play before your*

nostros imago futuri iudicii, et ascendat homo adversum se ante faciem suam, atque constituto in corde iudicio adsit accusans cogitatio, et testis conscientia, et carnifex cor. Inde quidem sanguis animi confitentis per lacrymas profluat, postremo ab ipsa mente talis sententia proferatur, ut se indignum homo iudicet participem corporis et sanguinis Domini.

705. Deinde cum dicit **cum iudicamur autem**, etc., ponit causam quae est ex parte Dei, dicens **cum iudicamur autem, a Domino**, id est in hoc mundo punimur, **corripimur**, id est hoc fit ad correctionem nostram, ut scilicet quilibet propter poenam quam sustinuit a peccato recedat. Unde et Iob V, 17 dicitur: *beatus vir qui corripitur a Domino.* Et Prov. III, 12: *quem diligit Dominus, corripit.* Vel etiam dum per poenam unius, alius peccare desistit, Prov. XIX, 25: *pestilente flagellato stultus sapientior erit,* et hoc ideo, **ut non damnemur**, aeterna damnatione in futuro, **cum hoc mundo**, id est cum hominibus mundanis.

706. Deinde cum dicit **itaque, fratres mei**, etc., reducit eos ad debitam observantiam: et

primo ponitur id quod nunc ordinat,

secundo ponitur promissio de ordinatione futura, ibi **caetera autem**.

707. Circa primum tria facit. Primo ponit ordinationem suam, dicens **itaque, fratres mei**, etc., ne unusquisque coenam suam praesumat ad manducandum, **cum convenitis**, scilicet in ecclesia, **ad manducandum**, scilicet corpus Christi, **invicem expectate**, ut scilicet simul omnes sumatis. Unde Ex. XII, 6 dicitur: *immolabit haedum multitudo filiorum Israel.*

Secundo excludit excusationem, dicens **si quis autem esurit**, etc., et non potest tantum expectare, **domi manducet**, scilicet communes cibos, postmodum Eucharistiam non sumpturus. Eccli. XXXVI, 20: *omnem escam manducabit venter.*

Tertio rationem assignat, dicens **ut non conveniatis**, scilicet ad sumendum corpus Christi, **in iudicium**, id est in vestram condemnationem.

708. Deinde ponitur promissio, cum dicit **caetera**, scilicet quae non sunt tanti periculi, **cum venero**, praesentialiter, **disponam**, qualiter scilicet ea conservare debeatis.

Ex quo patet quod Ecclesia multa habet ex dispositione Apostolorum, quae in Sacra Scriptura non continentur. Eccli. X, 3: *civitates inhabitabuntur,* id est ecclesiae disponentur, *per sensum prudentium,* scilicet apostolorum.

eyes and let a man rise up against himself before his own face, and having made a judgment in his heart, let thought be the accuser and conscience the witness and the heart executioner. Then let the blood of the confessing spirit break out in tears. Finally, from the mind itself let such a sentence issue that the man judges himself unworthy to partake of the body and blood of the Lord.

705. Then when he says, **but when we**, he presents the cause on God's part, saying: **but when we are judged by the Lord**, i.e., punished in this world, **we are chastened**, i.e., this is done for our correction, in order, namely, that each one withdraw from sin on account of the punishment he endured: *happy is the man whom God reproves* (Job 5:17); *whom the Lord loves he chastises* (Prov 3:12), or even when through the punishment of one, another ceases to sin: *strike a scoffer and the simple will learn prudence* (Prov 19:25) and this **in order that we may not be condemned** with eternal damnation in the future, **along with the world**, i.e., with worldly men.

706. Then when he says, **so then**, he leads them back to due observance:

first, he presents what he now ordains;

second, he gives a promise of a future ordination, at **and the rest**.

707. In regard to the first he does three things: first, he makes his ordination, saying: **so then, my brethren**, so that no one will presume to eat his meal, **when you come together**, namely, in the church, **to eat**, namely, the body of Christ, **wait for one another**, so that all may receive at the same time. Hence it is said: *the holy assembly of the congregation of Israel shall kill their lamb* (Exod 12:6).

Second, he excludes an excuse, saying: **if anyone is hungry** and cannot wait, **let him eat at home**, namely, ordinary food, not to receive the Eucharist later: *the stomach will take any food* (Sir 36:18).

Third, he gives the reason saying: **that you come not together**, namely, to receive the body of Christ, **unto judgment**, that is, to be condemned.

708. Then a promise is made when he says: **and the rest**, namely, which are not so perilous, **when I come** very soon, **I will set in order**, namely, how to conserve them.

From this it is clear that the Church has many things arranged by the Apostle that are not contained in Sacred Scripture: *the cities will be inhabited*, i.e., the churches will be set in order *by the sense of prudent men*, namely, of the apostles (Sir 10:3).

CHAPTER 12

Lecture 1

12:1De spiritualibus autem, nolo vos ignorare fratres. [n. 709]

12:2Scitis quoniam cum gentes essetis, ad simulacra muta prout ducebamini euntes. [n. 711]

12:3Ideo notum vobis facio, quod nemo in Spiritu Dei loquens, dicit anathema Jesu. Et nemo potest dicere, Dominus Jesus, nisi in Spiritu Sancto. [n. 715]

12:4Divisiones vero gratiarum sunt, idem autem Spiritus: [n. 720]

12:5et divisiones ministrationum sunt, idem autem Dominus: [n. 722]

12:6et divisiones operationum sunt, idem vero Deus qui operatur omnia in omnibus. [n. 723]

12:1Περὶ δὲ τῶν πνευματικῶν, ἀδελφοί, οὐ θέλω ὑμᾶς ἀγνοεῖν.

12:2Οἴδατε ὅτι ὅτε ἔθνη ἦτε πρὸς τὰ εἴδωλα τὰ ἄφωνα ὡς ἂν ἤγεσθε ἀπαγόμενοι.

12:3διὸ γνωρίζω ὑμῖν ὅτι οὐδεὶς ἐν πνεύματι θεοῦ λαλῶν λέγει, Ἀνάθεμα Ἰησοῦς, καὶ οὐδεὶς δύναται εἰπεῖν, Κύριος Ἰησοῦς, εἰ μὴ ἐν πνεύματι ἁγίῳ.

12:4Διαιρέσεις δὲ χαρισμάτων εἰσίν, τὸ δὲ αὐτὸ πνεῦμα:

12:5καὶ διαιρέσεις διακονιῶν εἰσιν, καὶ ὁ αὐτὸς κύριος:

12:6καὶ διαιρέσεις ἐνεργημάτων εἰσίν, ὁ δὲ αὐτὸς θεός, ὁ ἐνεργῶν τὰ πάντα ἐν πᾶσιν.

12:1Now concerning spiritual things, my brethren, I would not have you ignorant. [n. 709]

12:2You know that when you were heathens, you went to dumb idols, according as you were led. [n. 711]

12:3Wherefore, I give you to understand that no man, speaking by the Spirit of God, says anathema to Jesus. And no man can say the Lord Jesus, but by the Holy Spirit. [n. 715]

12:4Now there are diversities of graces, but the same Spirit. [n. 720]

12:5And there are diversities of ministries, but the same Lord. [n. 722]

12:6And there are diversities of operations, but the same God, who works all in all. [n. 723]

709. Postquam Apostolus prosecutus est de tribus sacramentis, scilicet baptismo, matrimonio et Eucharistia, hic incipit determinare de his quae pertinent ad rem sacramentorum. Est autem duplex res sacramenti: una significata et contenta, scilicet gratia, quae statim cum sacramento confertur; alia significata et non contenta, scilicet gloria resurrectionis, quae in fine expectatur.

Primo ergo agit de donis gratiarum;

secundo de gloria resurrectionis, XV capit., ibi *notum autem vobis facio*, et cetera.

Circa primum agit de gratiis gratis datis;

secundo praefert omnibus his caritatem, quae pertinet ad gratiam gratum facientem, XIII cap., ibi *si linguis hominum*, etc.;

tertio comparat gratias datas ad invicem, XIV cap., ibi *sectamini caritatem*, et cetera.

710. Circa primum duo facit. Primo principaliter exponit quid intendat, dicens: dixi quod *caetera*, quae pertinent ad usum sacramentorum, *cum venero disponam*, sed quaedam statim vobis tradere oportet. Et hoc est quod dicit *de spiritualibus autem*, id est de donis gratiarum quae sunt a Spiritu Sancto, *o fratres, nolo vos ignorare*.

Est enim maximum genus ingratitudinis ignorare beneficia accepta, ut Seneca dicit in libro *de Beneficiis*; et

709. After discussing the three sacraments of baptism, matrimony and the Eucharist, the Apostle begins to talk about things pertaining to the reality signified in the sacraments. But this is twofold: one is signified and contained, namely, grace, which is conferred at once by the sacrament; the other is signified but not contained, namely, the glory of the resurrection, which is expected at the end.

First, therefore, he deals with the gifts of graces;

second, with the glory of the resurrection, at *now I make known unto you* (1 Cor 15:1).

In regard to the first he deals with the charismatic graces;

second, he prefers to all of these charity, which pertains to sanctifying grace, at *if I speak with the tongues of men* (1 Cor 13:1);

third, he compares the charismatic graces to one another, at *follow after charity* (1 Cor 14:1).

710. In regard to the first he does two things: first, he principally explains his intention, saying: I have said that *and the rest*, which pertain to the use of the sacraments, *I will set in order when I come* (1 Cor 11:34). And this is what he says: *now concerning spiritual things*, i.e., the gifts of the graces which come from the Holy Spirit, *I would not have you ignorant, brethren*.

For it is the worst form of ingratitude to be ignorant of benefits received, as Seneca says in the book *On Benefits*.

ideo ut homo non sit Deo ingratus, non debet spirituales gratias ignorare. Supra II, 12: *Spiritum accepimus qui ex Deo est, ut sciamus quae a Deo donata sunt nobis.* Is. V, 13: *propterea captivus ductus est populus meus, quia non habuit scientiam,* scilicet spiritualium.

711. Secundo ibi *scitis, quoniam cum gentes,* etc., prosequitur suam intentionem et

primo ostendit spiritualium gratiarum necessitatem;

secundo ponit gratiarum distributionem, ibi *divisiones vero,* et cetera.

Necessitas autem alicuius rei maxime cognoscitur ex defectu ipsius.

Unde circa primum duo facit.

Primo ponit defectum quem patiebantur ante susceptam gratiam;

secundo concludit gratiae necessitatem, ibi *ideo notum vobis,* et cetera.

712. Dicit ergo primo: *scitis,* quasi experti, *quoniam cum gentes essetis,* id est gentiliter viventes, nondum suscepta gratia per baptismum. Gal. II, 15: *nos enim natura Iudaei, non ex gentibus peccatores.* Eph. c. IV, 17: *gentes ambulant in vanitate sensus sui.* Eratis *euntes* quasi prompta mente et assidua, secundum illud Ier. VIII, 6: *omnes conversi sunt ad cursum suum, quasi equus impetu vadens in proelium;* Prov. I, v. 16: *pedes eorum ad malum currunt.* **Ad simulacra muta,** scilicet adoranda et colenda, secundum illud Ps. CXIII, 5: *os habent et non loquuntur.* Et ponitur specialiter in eis defectus locutionis, quia locutio est proprius effectus cognitionis; unde ostenditur non intelligere simulacra, et per consequens nihil divinitatis habere si sunt muta.

Et hoc **prout ducebamini,** id est sine aliqua resistentia. Ducebantur autem vel allecti ex pulchritudine simulacrorum, unde dicitur in epistola Ier.: *videbitis in Babylonia deos aureos et argenteos, videte ne metus vos capiat in ipsis;* aut etiam ex imperio alicuius principis, sicut legitur Dan. III, 1, quod Nabuchodonosor cogebat homines adorare statuam auream. Et II Mac. VI, 7 dicitur de quibusdam quod *ducebantur cum amara necessitate in die natalis regis ad sacrificia.* Vel etiam instinctu Daemonum, qui ad hoc praecipue anhelant, ut divinus cultus eis exhibeatur, secundum illud Matth. IV, 9: *haec omnia tibi dabo, si cadens adoraveris me.*

Ibant ergo ad idola colenda, prout ducebantur, id est sine aliqua resistentia, sicut de iuvene etiam vecorde dicitur Prov. VII, v. 22: *statim eam sequitur, quasi bos ductus ad victimam.*

Per hoc ergo apparet, quod homo ante susceptam gratiam prompte currit in peccatum sine resistentia.

713. Specialiter autem facit mentionem de peccato idololatriae propter tria. Primo quidem, quia hoc est peccatum gravissimum introducere alium Deum, sicut

Therefore, in order that man not be ungrateful to God, he should not be ignorant of spiritual gifts: *we have received the Spirit which is from God, that we might understand the gifts bestowed on us by God* (1 Cor 2:12); *therefore, my people go into exile for want of knowledge* (Isa 5:13), i.e., of spiritual things.

711. Second, when he says, *you know that when you were heathen,* he follows out his intention:

first, he shows the need for spiritual graces;

second, he presents the distribution of graces, at *now there are diversities.*

Now the need for a thing is best known from its absence.

Hence, in regard to the first he does two things:

first, he manifests the loss they suffered, before they received grace;

second, he concludes to the need for grace, at *wherefore, I give you to understand.*

712. First, therefore, he says: *you know* by experience *that when you were heathen,* i.e., living as heathen without having yet received grace through baptism: *we are Jews by birth and not gentile sinners* (Gal 2:15); *the gentiles living in the futility of their minds* (Eph 4:17). You *went,* as though with a ready and constant mind: *everyone turns to his own course, like a horse plunging into battle* (Jer 8:6); *their feet run to evil* (Prov 1:16). **To dumb idols,** namely, to adore and worship: *they have a mouth but do not speak* (Ps 114:5). Their lack of speech is particularly stressed, because speech is the proper effect of knowledge. Hence it is shown that idols do not understand and, as a consequence, they have nothing divine, if they are mute.

And this, **as you were led,** i.e., without any resistance. For they were led, either attracted by the beauty of the idols; hence it says in one of Jerome's letters: *you will see in Babylon gods of gold and silver; see that fear does not overtake you in them.* Or even by the command of some prince, as it is read that Nebuchadnezzar compelled men to adore a golden statue (Dan 3:1). It is stated that *some were led to the sacrifice with bitter necessity on the king's birthday* (2 Macc 6:7). Or even by the instigation of demons, who aspire in a special way to have divine worship paid to them: *all these things will I give you, if falling down you adore me* (Matt 4:9).

Therefore, they went to cultivate idols according as they were led without resistance, as it is said of the silly youth: *all at once he follows her as an ox is led to the slaughter* (Prov 7:22).

This shows that before receiving grace, man quickly runs into sin without resistance.

713. He makes special mention of the sin of idolatry for three reasons: first, because it is a very grave sin to introduce another God, just as one would sin very gravely

gravissime peccaret contra regem qui alium regem in regnum eius introduceret. Unde dicitur Iob c. XXXI, 26: *si vidi solem cum fulgeret, et lunam incedentem clare, et osculatus sum manum meam*, scilicet quasi cultor solis et lunae, quae est iniquitas maxima et negatio contra Deum Altissimum.

Secundo, quia a peccato idololatriae omnia alia peccata oriebantur, secundum illud Sap. XIV, 27: *nefandorum idolorum cultura omnis malis causa est*.

Tertio, quia hoc peccatum apud gentiles commune erat et non reputabatur, unde in Ps. XCV, 5 dicitur: *omnes dii gentium daemonia*.

714. Est autem considerandum quod quidam dixerunt hominem in peccato mortali existentem sine gratia quadam non posse a peccato, cui subiacet, liberari, quia remissio peccatorum non fit nisi per gratiam, secundum illud Rom. III, 24: *iustificati per gratiam eius*; posse autem se praeservare a peccato mortali, sine gratia, per liberum arbitrium.

Sed haec positio non videtur vera. Primo quidem, quia non potest aliquis se a peccato mortali praeservare, nisi omnia legis praecepta servando, cum nullus mortaliter peccet nisi transgrediendo aliquod legis praeceptum; et ita posset aliquis observare omnia legis praecepta sine gratia, quod est haeresis Pelagiana.

Secundo quia caritatem, per quam Deus diligitur super omnia, nullus potest habere sine gratia, secundum illud Rom. V, 5: *caritas Dei diffusa est in cordibus nostris per Spiritum Sanctum qui datus est nobis*. Non potest autem esse quod homo omnia peccata declinet, nisi Deum super omnia diligat: sicut illud magis contemnitur, quod minus diligitur.

Poterit ergo esse per aliquod tempus, quod ille qui caret gratia, a peccato abstinebit quousque occurrat illud, propter quod Dei praeceptum contemnet, a quo ducitur ad peccandum. Signanter autem Apostolus dicit *prout ducebamini*.

715. Deinde cum dicit *ideo notum vobis facio*, etc., concludit duos effectus gratiae, quorum

primus est quod facit abstinere a peccato;

secundus est quod facit operari bonum et hoc ponit ibi *et nemo potest*, et cetera.

716. Dicit ergo primo: ex quo quando sine gratia eratis, prompte ad peccandum currebatis, *ideo notum vobis facio*, quod si gratiam habuissetis hoc vobis non contigisset, *nemo enim in Spiritu Dei*, etc., id est, per Spiritum Dei, *loquens, dicit: anathema Iesu*, etc., id est blasphemiam contra Iesum secundum illud I Io. IV, 3: *omnis spiritus qui solvit Iesum, ex Deo non est*.

Notandum quod supra posuit gravissimum peccatum, quod est blasphemia, quod per gratiam declinatur, ut de aliis minoribus peccatis intelligatur.

against a king by introducing another king into his kingdom. Hence, it is said: *if I have looked at the sun when it shone, or the moon moving in splendor and my mouth has kissed my hand* (Job 31:26), namely, as a worshipper of the sun and moon, which is the greatest iniquity and denial against God Most High.

Second, because from the sin of idolatry all other sins arise: *for the worship of idols not to be named is the beginning and cause and end of every evil* (Wis 14:27).

Third, because this sin was common among the heathens and was not counted; hence it is said: *all the gods of the heathens are demons* (Ps 96:5).

714. It should be noted that some have said that man existing in mortal sin cannot without grace be freed from the sin he lies under, because the remission of sins is brought about only by grace: *they are justified by his grace* (Rom 3:24); but he can preserve himself from mortal sin without grace, through free will.

But this position does not seem to be true. First, because one cannot preserve himself from mortal sin except by observing all the precepts of the law, since no one sins mortally except by transgressing some precept of the law. And so someone could observe all the precepts without grace, which is the Pelagian heresy.

Second, because no one can without grace have charity, through which God is loved above all things: *God's love has been poured into our hearts through the Holy Spirit which has been given to us* (Rom 5:5). But no one can avoid all sins, unless he loves God above all things: just as that is more despised which is loved less.

Therefore, it could happen that for some time a person who lacks grace will abstain from sin, until he encounters that for which he will despise God's precept, and by which he is led into sin. It is significant that the Apostle says, *as you were led*.

715. Then when he says, *therefore*, he concludes to two effects of grace:

the first is that it makes one abstain from sin;

the second is that it makes one do good works, at *and no man can say*.

716. First, therefore, he says: from the fact that when you were without grace, you ran after sin rapidly, *I give you to understand* that if you had possessed grace, this would not have happened to you, *for no one speaking by the Spirit of God says anathema to Jesus*, i.e., blasphemes Jesus: *every spirit which does not confess Jesus is not of God* (1 John 4:3).

It should be noted that above he said that the gravest sin is blasphemy, which is avoided through grace; hence the other lesser sins are avoided.

Potest autem per hoc quod dicitur **anathema Iesu**, intelligi quodlibet peccatum mortale. Anathema enim separationem significat. Dicitur ab *ana*, quod est sursum, et *thesis*, quod est positio, quasi sursum positum, quia olim res, quae ab usu hominum separabantur, suspendebantur in templis vel in locis publicis. Omne autem peccatum mortale separat a Iesu, secundum illud Is. LIX, 2: *iniquitates vestrae diviserunt inter vos, et Deum vestrum*. Quicumque ergo mortaliter peccat, dicit corde vel ore: anathema, id est, separationem a Iesu. Nemo ergo in Spiritu Dei loquens dicit: anathema Iesu, quia nullus per Spiritum Dei peccat mortaliter, quia, ut dicitur Sap. I, 5: *Spiritus Sanctus disciplinae effugiet fictum*.

717. Sed secundum hoc videtur quod quicumque habet Spiritum Sanctum, non possit peccare mortaliter; quia etiam dicitur I Io. III, 9: *omnis qui natus est ex Deo peccatum non facit, quoniam semen ipsius in eo manet*.

Sed dicendum est quod quantum est ex Spiritu Dei, homo non facit peccatum, sed magis a peccato retrahitur. Potest tamen peccatum facere ex defectu voluntatis humanae, quae Spiritui Sancto resistit, secundum illud Act. VII, 51: *vos autem semper Spiritui Sancto restitistis*. Non enim per Spiritum Sanctum inhabitantem tollitur facultas peccandi a libero arbitrio totaliter in vita praesenti. Et ideo signanter Apostolus non dixit: *nemo Spiritum Dei habens*, sed *nemo in Spiritu Dei loquens*.

718. Deinde cum dicit **et nemo potest**, etc., ponit secundum effectum gratiae, scilicet quod sine ea homo non potest bonum operari. Dicit ergo **et nemo potest dicere**, quod **Iesus est Dominus, nisi in Spiritu Sancto**.

Contra quod videtur esse, quia per Spiritum Sanctum homo introducitur in regnum caelorum, secundum illud Ps. CXLII, 10: *Spiritus tuus bonus deducet me in terram rectam*. Dominus autem dicit Matth. VII, 21: *non omnis qui dicit: Domine, Domine, intrabit in regnum caelorum*. Non omnis ergo qui dicit: **Dominum Iesum**, dicit hoc in Spiritu Sancto.

Dicendum est autem quod dicere aliquid in Spiritu Sancto, potest intelligi dupliciter. Uno modo in Spiritu Sancto movente, sed non habito. Movet enim Spiritus Sanctus corda aliquorum ad loquendum, quos non inhabitat sicut legitur Io. XI, 49 ss., quod Caiphas hoc quod de utilitate mortis Christi praedixerat, a semetipso non dixit, sed per Spiritum prophetiae. Balaam etiam multa vera praedixit motus a Spiritu Sancto, ut legitur Num. c. XXIII et XXIV, licet eum non haberet. Secundum hoc ergo intelligendum est quod nullus potest dicere quodcumque verum, nisi a Spiritu Sancto motus, qui est Spiritus veritatis, de quo dicitur Io. XVI, 13: *cum autem venerit ille Spiritus veritatis, docebit vos omnem veritatem*. Unde et in Glossa Ambrosius, hoc in loco dicit: *omne verum a quocumque dicatur, a Spiritu Sancto est*. Et specialiter in illis quae sunt fidei, quae per specialem revelationem Spiritus Sancti sunt habita, inter quae est

By saying, **anathema to Jesus**, any mortal sin can be understood. For 'anathema' signifies separation. It is derived from *ana*, which means above and *thesis*, which is a placing; as it were, placed above, because in olden times things separated from men's use, were hung up in temples or in public places. But every mortal sin separates from Jesus: *your iniquities have made a separation between you and your God* (Isa 59:2). Therefore, whoever sins mortally says in his heart or with his mouth, anathema, i.e., separation from Jesus. Therefore, no one speaking by the Spirit of God says anathema to Jesus, because no one through the Spirit of God sins mortally because, as it is said: *the Holy Spirit of discipline will flee from deceit* (Wis 1:5).

717. But according to this it seems that whoever had the Holy Spirit cannot sin mortally; further, it is said: *no one born of God commits sin, because God's seed abides in him* (1 John 3:9).

The answer is that as far as the Spirit of God is concerned, man does not commit sin but rather is drawn away from sin. But he can sin through a defect of the human will which resists the Holy Spirit: *you always resist the Holy Spirit* (Acts 7:51). For by the indwelling Holy Spirit the ability to sin is not taken away totally from the free will in this life. Therefore, it is significant that the Apostle did not say: *no one having the Holy Spirit*, but *no one speaking by the Spirit of God*.

718. Then when he says, **and no man**, he mentions the second effect of grace, namely, that without it man cannot perform a good work. He says, therefore: **and no man can say** that **Jesus** is **Lord, except by the Holy Spirit**.

But against this seems to be the fact that by the Holy Spirit man is introduced to the kingdom of heaven: *your good spirit leads me along the right path* (Ps 143:10). The Lord, however, says: *not everyone who says, Lord, Lord, will enter the kingdom of heaven* (Matt 7:21). Therefore, not everyone who says **Lord Jesus**, says it in the Holy Spirit.

The answer is that saying something in the Holy Spirit can be understood in two ways: in one way in the Holy Spirit moving but not possessed. For the Holy Spirit moves the hearts of certain men to speak, although he does not dwell in them, as it is read that in predicting the utility of the Lord's death Caiaphas did not speak from himself but through the Spirit of prophecy (John 11:49). Balaam also predicted many true things, but moved by the Holy Spirit, although he did not possess him (Num 23–24). According to this, therefore, it must be understood that no one can say anything true, unless moved by the Holy Spirit, who is the Spirit of truth, of whom it is said: *when the Spirit of truth comes, he will guide you into all the truth* (John 16:13). Hence Ambrose says in a Gloss: *every truth by whomsoever spoken is from the Holy Spirit*. This applies especially to matters of faith, which are had by a special revelation of the Holy Spirit. Among these is the fact that Jesus is Lord of

quod Iesus sit omnium Dominus, unde Act. II, 36 dicitur: *certissime sciat omnis domus Israel, quia Deus fecit hunc Dominum Iesum quem vos crucifixistis.*

Alio modo loquitur aliquis in Spiritu Sancto movente et habito. Et secundum hoc etiam potest verificari quod hic dicitur, ita tamen quod dicere accipiatur non solum ore, sed etiam corde et opere. Dicitur enim aliquid corde, secundum illud Ps. XIII, 1: *dixit insipiens in corde suo: non est Deus.* Dicitur etiam aliquid opere, inquantum exteriori opere aliquis suum conceptum manifestat. **Nemo**, ergo nisi habendo Spiritum Sanctum, **potest dicere Iesum Dominum**, ita scilicet quod non solum hoc ore confiteatur, sed etiam corde revereatur ipsum ut Dominum et opere obediat ipsi quasi Domino.

719. Sic igitur ex verbis praemissis tria circa gratiam considerare possumus. Primo quod, sine ea, peccatum homo vitare non potest, secundum illud Ps. XCIII, 17: *nisi quia Dominus adiuvit me, paulo minus in inferno habitasset anima mea.*

Secundo quod per eam vitatur peccatum, secundum illud I Io. III, 9: *qui natus est ex Deo, non peccat.*

Tertio quod sine ea non potest homo bonum facere, secundum illud Io. XV, 5: *sine me nihil potestis facere.*

720. Deinde cum dicit **divisiones vero**, etc., incipit distinguere gratis datas, et

primo distinguit eas in generali;

secundo manifestat in speciali, ibi **unicuique autem datur**, et cetera.

721. In his autem quae per gratiam Spiritus Sancti conferuntur, tria oportet considerare. Primo quidem facultatem hominum ad operandum, secundo auctoritatem, tertio executionem utriusque.

Facultas quidem habetur per donum gratiae, puta per prophetiam vel potestatem faciendi miracula, aut per aliquid huiusmodi. Auctoritas autem habetur per aliquod ministerium, puta per apostolatum vel aliquid huiusmodi. Executio autem pertinet ad operationem.

Primo ergo distinguit gratias, secundo ministeria, tertio operationes.

Quantum ergo ad primum ostendit necessitatem gratiae, quae tamen non totaliter advenit omnibus, nisi Christo, cui datus est Spiritus non ad mensuram, ut dicitur Io. III, v. 34; sed quantum ad alios sunt divisiones gratiarum, quia quidam abundant in una, quidam in alia. Sicut enim in corpore naturali caput habet omnes sensus, non autem alia membra, ita in Ecclesia solus Christus habet omnes gratias, quae in aliis membris dividuntur, quod significatur Gen. II, 12, ubi dicitur quod *fluvius*, scilicet gratiarum, *egrediebatur ad irrigandum Paradisum, qui inde dividitur in quatuor capita.* Et Matth. XXV, v. 15 dicitur et quod *uni dedit quinque talenta, alii duo, alii unum.*

them all. Hence it is said: *let all the house of Israel know assuredly that God has made him both Lord and Christ, this Jesus whom you crucified* (Acts 2:36).

In another way someone speaks in the Holy Spirit moving and possessed. And according to this, what is said here can be verified, but in such a way that 'to speak' refers not only to the mouth but also to the heart and the deed. For something is said by the heart: *the fool says in his heart: there is no God* (Ps 14:1). But something is said by deed, inasmuch as someone by an external work manifests his thought. **No man**, therefore, except by having the Holy Spirit **can say the Lord Jesus**, is such a way that he confesses this not only by the mouth but also with the heart reveres him as Lord and in work obeys him as Lord.

719. Therefore, from the foregoing words we can consider three things about grace. First, that without it man cannot avoid sin: *if the Lord had not been my help, my soul soon would have dwelt in hell* (Ps 94:17).

Second, that through it sin is avoided: *no one born of God commits sin* (1 John 3:9).

Third, that without it a man cannot do good: *apart from me you can do nothing* (John 15:9).

720. Then when he says, **there are diversities of graces**, he begins to distinguish the charismatic graces:

first, he distinguishes them in general;

second, he manifests each in particular, at **and the manifestation of the Spirit** (1 Cor 12:7).

721. In things conferred by the grace of the Holy Spirit three things must be considered. First, indeed, men's faculty to work; second, the authority; third, the execution of both.

The faculty is had by the gift of grace; for example, by prophecy or the power to work miracles or by something of that sort. The authority is had through some ministry; for example, by the apostolate or something of that sort. Execution pertains to operation.

First, therefore, he distinguishes the graces; second, the ministries; third, the operations.

In regard to the first, therefore, he shows the need for grace which, nevertheless, does not come in its totality to all, but only to Christ, to whom the Spirit was given without measure (John 3:34). But in regard to others there are divisions of graces, because some abound in one and some in another. For as in a natural body the head has all the senses, while the other members do not; so in the Church Christ alone has all graces, which are divided in the other members. This is signified where it says that *a river*, namely, of graces, *flowed out to water the garden, and there it divided and became four rivers* (Gen 2:12); and it is said that *to one he gave five talents, to another two, and to another one* (Matt 25:15).

Et quamvis dona gratiarum sint diversa, quae a diversis habentur, non tamen procedunt a diversis auctoribus, sicut ponebant gentiles, qui sapientiam attribuebant Minervae, locutionem Mercurio, et sic de aliis. Ad quod excludendum subdit *idem autem Spiritus*, scilicet Sanctus, qui est auctor omnium gratiarum. Eph. IV, 4: *unum corpus, et unus Spiritus*, et, Sap. VII, 22: *est Spiritus unus et multiplex*: unus in substantia, multiplex in gratiis.

722. Deinde ponit distinctiones ministrationum, dicens *et divisiones ministrationum sunt*, id est diversa ministeria et officia requiruntur ad gubernationem Ecclesiae. Praelati enim Ecclesiae ministri dicuntur, supra c. IV, 1: *sic nos existimet homo ut ministros Christi*. Pertinet autem ad decorem et perfectionem Ecclesiae, ut in ea diversa ministeria sint, quae significantur per ordines ministrantium, quod mirabatur regina Saba in domo Salomonis, ut legitur III Reg. X, 5. Omnes tamen uni Domino serviunt. Unde subditur *idem autem Dominus*. Supra VIII, 6: *nobis unus Dominus Iesus Christus, per quem omnia*.

723. Deinde ponit distinctionem operationum, dicens *et divisiones operationum sunt*, quibus aliquis in seipso bonum operatur, sicut per ministrationes ad proximum. Ps. CIII, 23: *exibit homo ad opus suum*, scilicet sibi proprium. Eccli. XXXIII, 11: *immutavit*, id est distinxit, *vias*, id est operationes, *eorum*, quae tamen omnes procedunt ab uno principio. Unde subdit *idem vero Deus, qui operatur omnia*, sicut prima causa creans omnes operationes. Ne tamen aliae causae videantur esse superfluae subdit *in omnibus*, quia in causis secundariis prima causa operatur. Isa. XXVI, 12: *omnia opera nostra operatus es in nobis*.

Et notandum quod Apostolus valde congrue gratias attribuit Spiritui qui est amor, quia ex amore procedit quod aliquid gratis detur ministerii a Domino cui ministratur; operationes Deo sicut primae causae moventi.

Et quod dicit *Spiritus*, potest referri ad personam Spiritus Sancti; quod dicit *Dominus*, ad personam Filii; quod dicit *Deus*, ad personam Patris. Vel haec tria possunt attribui Spiritui Sancto, qui est Dominus Deus.

And although the gifts of graces possessed by diverse persons are diverse, they do not proceed from diverse authors, as the gentiles believed, who attributed wisdom to Minerva, speech to Mercury, and so on for other gifts. To exclude this, he adds: *but the same Spirit*, namely, the Holy Spirit, who is the author of all graces: *one body and one Spirit* (Eph 4:4); *the Spirit is one and manifold* (Wis 7:22): one in substance, manifold in graces.

722. Then he mentions the distinctions of service, saying: *and there are diversities of ministries*, i.e., diverse ministries and offices are required to govern the Church. For the prelates of the Church are called servants: *one should regard us as servants of Christ* (1 Cor 4:1). But it pertains to the beauty and perfection of the Church that in it there be diverse ministries, which are signified by the orders of service, which the queen of Sheba admired in Solomon's house (1 Kgs 3:5). Yet all serve one Lord; hence he adds: *but the same Lord: to us there is but one . . . Lord Jesus Christ, by whom are all things* (1 Cor 8:6).

723. Then he mentions the distinctions of operations, saying: *and there are diversities of operations*, by which one works the good in himself as by services to his neighbor; *man goes forth to his work* (Ps 104:23), namely, proper to himself: *he distinguished them and appointed their different ways*, i.e., operations (Sir 33:11). All of which come from one source. Hence he adds: *but the same God, who works all*, as the first cause creating all actions. But lest the other causes seem to be superfluous, he adds: *all in all*, because the first cause works in secondary causes: *you have worked all our works in us* (Isa 26:12).

It should be noted that the Apostle very fittingly attributes things to the Spirit who is love, because from love proceeds that someone is freely given the ministry from the Lord, to whom he ministers works to God, as to the first movent cause.

And that he says, *Spirit*, can be referred to the person of the Holy Spirit, what he calls *Lord* to the person of the Son, what he calls *God* in the person of the Father; or these three can be attributed to the Holy Spirit, who is the Lord God.

Lecture 2

^{12:7}Unicuique autem datur manifestatio Spiritus ad utilitatem. [n. 724]

^{12:8}Alii quidem per Spiritum datur sermo sapientiae: alii autem sermo scientiae secundum eumdem Spiritum: [n. 727]

^{12:9}alteri fides in eodem Spiritu: alii gratia sanitatum in uno Spiritu:

^{12:10}alii operatio virtutum, alii prophetia, alii discretio spirituum, alii genera linguarum, alii interpretatio sermonum.

^{12:11}Haec autem omnia operantur unus atque idem Spiritus, dividens singulis prout vult. [n. 730]

^{12:7}ἑκάστῳ δὲ δίδοται ἡ φανέρωσις τοῦ πνεύματος πρὸς τὸ συμφέρον.

^{12:8}ᾧ μὲν γὰρ διὰ τοῦ πνεύματος δίδοται λόγος σοφίας, ἄλλῳ δὲ λόγος γνώσεως κατὰ τὸ αὐτὸ πνεῦμα,

^{12:9}ἑτέρῳ πίστις ἐν τῷ αὐτῷ πνεύματι, ἄλλῳ δὲ χαρίσματα ἰαμάτων ἐν τῷ ἑνὶ πνεύματι,

^{12:10}ἄλλῳ δὲ ἐνεργήματα δυνάμεων, ἄλλῳ [δὲ] προφητεία, ἄλλῳ [δὲ] διακρίσεις πνευμάτων, ἑτέρῳ γένη γλωσσῶν, ἄλλῳ δὲ ἑρμηνεία γλωσσῶν·

^{12:11}πάντα δὲ ταῦτα ἐνεργεῖ τὸ ἓν καὶ τὸ αὐτὸ πνεῦμα, διαιροῦν ἰδίᾳ ἑκάστῳ καθὼς βούλεται.

^{12:7}And the manifestation of the Spirit is given to every man unto profit. [n. 724]

^{12:8}To one indeed, by the Spirit, is given the word of wisdom: and to another, the word of knowledge, according to the same Spirit: [n. 727]

^{12:9}To another, faith in the same Spirit: to another, the grace of healing in one Spirit:

^{12:10}To another the working of miracles: to another, prophecy: to another, the discerning of spirits: to another, diverse kinds of tongues: to another, interpretation of speeches.

^{12:11}But all these things, one and the same Spirit works, dividing to every one according as he wills. [n. 730]

---

724. Posita in generali distinctione gratiarum et ministrationum, et operationum, hic manifestat ea quae dixerat in speciali. Et

primo quantum ad divisionem gratiarum;

secundo quantum ad divisionem ministrationum, ibi *et quosdam quidem posuit Deus*, et cetera.

Circa primum duo facit.

Primo ponit distinctionem gratiarum in speciali;

secundo adhibet similitudinem, ibi *sicut enim corpus*, et cetera.

Circa primum tria facit.

Primo ponit conditionem gratiarum gratis datarum;

secundo ponit earum distinctionem, ibi *alii quidem datur*, etc.;

tertio describit earum actionem, ibi *haec autem omnia*, et cetera.

725. Dicit ergo primo: dictum est, quod sunt divisiones gratiarum, *unicuique autem datur*: in quo designatur earum subiectum. Sicut enim nullum membrum est in corpore quod non participet aliquo modo sensum vel motum a capite, ita nullus est in Ecclesia qui non aliquid de gratiis Spiritus sancti participet, secundum illud Matth. XXV, v. 15: *dedit unicuique secundum propriam virtutem* et, Eph. IV, 7: *unicuique nostrum data est gratia*.

Manifestatio Spiritus, in quo designatur officium gratiae gratis datae. Pertinet autem ad gratiam gratum facientem, quod per eam Spiritus Sanctus inhabitet, quod quidem non pertinet ad gratiam gratis datam, sed solum ut per eam Spiritus Sanctus manifestetur, sicut interior motus cordis per vocem. Unde Io. III, 8 dicitur:

724. Having set forth in general the distinction of graces, ministrations and operations, the Apostle here manifests the things he had said in general.

First, as to the division of graces;

second, as to the division of operation, at ***and God indeed has set some in the Church*** (1 Cor 12:28).

In regard to the first he does two things:

first, he presents the distinction of graces in general;

second, he applies a similitude, at ***for as the body*** (1 Cor 12:12).

In regard to the first he does three things:

first, he lays down the condition of charismatic graces;

second, he distinguishes them, at ***to one indeed***;

third, he describes their action, at ***but all these things***.

725. First, therefore, he says: it has been stated that there are divisions of graces, ***given to every man***; in which is designated their subject. For just as there is no member in the body, which does not partake in some way of the sense and motion from the head, so no one is in the Church, who does not participate in some grace of the Spirit: *he gave to each according to his ability* (Matt 25:15); *grace was given to each of us according to the measure of God's gifts* (Eph 4:7).

The manifestation of the Spirit, in which is designated the office of charismatic graces. But it pertains to sanctifying grace that through it the Holy Spirit indwells, which, indeed, does not pertain to charismatic graces, but only that through them the Holy Spirit is manifested, as the interior motion of the heart through the voice. Hence it is said: *you*

271

vocem eius audis, et in Ps. XCVII, 2 dicitur: *notum fecit Dominus salutare suum*.

Manifestatur autem, per huiusmodi gratias, Spiritus Sanctus dupliciter. Uno modo ut inhabitans Ecclesiam et docens et Sanctificans eam, puta cum aliquis peccator, quem non inhabitat Spiritus Sanctus, faciat miracula ad ostendendum, quod fides Ecclesiae quam ipse praedicat, sit vera. Unde dicitur Hebr. II, 4: *contestante Deo signis et prodigiis, et variis Spiritus Sancti distributionibus*.

Alio modo manifestatur per huiusmodi gratias Spiritus Sanctus, ut inhabitans eum cui tales gratiae conceduntur. Unde dicitur Act. VI, 8, quod Stephanus plenus gratia faciebat prodigia et signa multa, quem Spiritu Sancto plenum elegerunt; sic autem non conceduntur huiusmodi gratiae nisi Sanctis.

726. Et ne huiusmodi manifestatio vana videatur, subdit **ad utilitatem**, scilicet communem. In quo designatur finis harum, et hoc vel dum probatur vera doctrina Ecclesiae; et sic fideles confirmantur et infideles convertuntur; vel dum sanctitas alicuius proponitur aliis in exemplum. Unde et infra XIV, v. 12: **ad aedificationem Ecclesiae quaerite ut abundetis**, et supra X, 33: **non quaerens quod mihi utile est, sed quod multis, ut salvi fiant**.

727. Deinde cum dicit **alii quidem**, etc., ponit distinctionem gratiarum, quae quidem, ut dictum est, dantur ad utilitatem communem. Et ideo oportet earum distinctionem accipere secundum quod per unum potest aliorum salus procurari. Quod quidem homo non potest facere interius operando, hoc enim solius Dei est, sed solum exterius persuadendo. Ad quod quidem tria requiruntur. Primo quidem facultas persuadendi; secundo facultas persuasionem confirmandi; tertio persuasionem intelligibiliter proponendi.

Ad facultatem autem persuadendi requiritur quod homo habeat peritiam conclusionum et certitudinem principiorum, circa ea in quibus debemus persuadere. Conclusiones autem in his quae pertinent ad salutem, quaedam sunt principales, scilicet res divinae et ad hoc pertinet sapientia, quae est cognitio divinarum rerum, ut Augustinus dicit, libro XIII *de Trinitate*. Et quantum ad hoc dicitur **alii quidem per Spiritum datur**, scilicet Sanctum, **sermo sapientiae**, ut possit persuadere ea quae ad cognitionem divinorum pertinent. Lc. XXI, 15: *ego dabo vobis os et sapientiam, cui non poterunt resistere et contradicere omnes adversarii vestri*. Supra II, 6: **sapientiam loquimur inter perfectos**.

Secundariae conclusiones sunt quae pertinent ad notitiam creaturarum, quarum cognitio dicitur scientia, secundum Augustinum ibidem. Et quantum ad hoc subdit **alii autem**, scilicet datur, **sermo scientiae, secundum eumdem Spiritum**, ut scilicet per creaturas ea quae sunt Dei, manifestare possit. Huic enim scientiae attribuitur illud *quo pia fides defenditur et roboratur*, non autem

hear his voice (John 3:8); *the Lord has made known his victory* (Ps 98:2).

The Holy Spirit is manifested in two ways by graces of this sort. In one way as dwelling in the Church by teaching and sanctifying it, as when a sinner, in whom the Holy Spirit does not dwell, works miracles to show that the faith of the Church which he professes is true: *while God also bore witness by signs and wonders and various miracles and by gifts of the Holy Spirit* (Heb 2:4).

In another way the Holy Spirit is manifested by such charismatic graces as dwelling in the one to whom such graces are granted. Hence it is said that Stephen, filled with grace, worked prodigies and many signs, whom they chose filled with the Holy Spirit (Acts 6:8). In this way such graces are granted to the saints.

726. And lest such a manifestation seems futile, he adds: **unto profit**, namely, for the common good. In this is designated the end of these gifts, and this either when the true doctrine of the Church is proved or when someone's holiness is proposed as an example. Hence he says below: **seek to abound unto the edifying of the Church** (1 Cor 14:12); and above: **not seeking that which is profitable to myself but to many: that they may be saved** (1 Cor 10:33).

727. Then when he says, **to one is given**, he presents the distinction of graces which, indeed, as has been said, are given for the common good. Therefore, it is required to take the distinction in the sense that by one the salvation of others can be procured. Man, indeed, cannot do this by working within, for this belongs to God, but only by persuading outwardly. For this, three things are required: first, the faculty of persuading; second, the faculty of confirming the persuasion; third, the faculty of proposing the persuasion intelligibly.

For the faculty of persuading it is required that man have skill in conclusions and certitude of principles in regard to those matters in which he ought to persuade. But in matters that pertain to salvation, some conclusions are principal, namely, divine matters; and to this pertains wisdom, which is the knowledge of divine things, as Augustine says in Book 13, *On the Trinity*. In regard to this it is said that **to one indeed, by the Spirit**, namely, the Holy Spirit, **is given the word of wisdom**, so that he can persuade one in things pertaining to the knowledge of divine things: *I will give you a mouth and wisdom, which none of your adversaries will be able to withstand* (Luke 21:15); **we speak wisdom among the perfect** (1 Cor 2:6).

Secondary conclusions are those which pertain to the knowledge of creatures, the knowledge of which is called scientific, according to Augustine. And in regard to this he adds: **and to another** is given **the word of knowledge, according to the same Spirit**, in order, namely, that that might manifest things of God through creatures. To this knowledge is attributed that *by which the holy faith is defended*

quidquid curiositatis in humanis scientiis invenitur, ut Augustinus ibidem dicit. Sap. X, v. 10: *dedit illi scientiam sanctorum.* Is. c. XXXIII, 6: *divitiae salutis sapientia et scientia.*

Est tamen notandum quod sapientia et scientia inter septem dona Spiritus Sancti computantur, sicut habetur Is. XI, 2. Unde Apostolus signanter inter gratias gratis datas non ponit sapientiam et scientiam, sed sermonem sapientiae et scientiae, quae pertinent ad hoc ut homo aliis persuadere valeat per sermonem, ea quae sunt sapientiae et scientiae.

Principia autem doctrinae salutis sunt articuli fidei et ideo quantum ad hoc subditur **alteri**, scilicet datur, **fides in eodem Spiritu**. Non autem hic accipitur pro fidei virtute, quia hoc commune est omnibus membris Christi, secundum illud Hebr. XI, 6: *sine fide impossibile est placere Deo.* Sed accipitur pro sermone fidei, prout scilicet homo potest recte proponere ea quae fidei sunt, vel pro certitudine fidei quam aliquis habet excellenter, secundum illud Matth. XV, 28: *mulier, magna est fides tua.*

728. Ea vero quae pertinent ad salutarem doctrinam non possunt confirmari seu probari ratione, quia rationem humanam excedunt, secundum illud Eccli. III, 25: *plurima supra sensum hominis ostensa sunt tibi.* Confirmantur seu probantur signo divino; unde et Moyses, mittendus ad populum Israel, signum accepit a Deo, per quod confirmaret ea, quae ex parte Dei dicebat, ut patet Ex. IV, 1–9, sicut et signo regio confirmatur quod aliquid sit de mandato regis.

Signum autem Dei sumitur uno quidem modo ab eo quod solus Deus facere potest, sicut sunt miracula, quae Apostolus hic in duo distinguit. Nam primo dicit **alii**, scilicet datur, **gratia sanitatum**, id est per quam alicuius possit sanare infirmitatem, **in uno**, scilicet et eodem, **Spiritu**. Ier. XVII, 14: *sana me, Domine, et sanabor.* Ex his enim persuadetur aliquis, non solum propter magnitudinem facti, sed etiam propter beneficium. Secundo autem dicit **alii datur operatio virtutum**, ex quibus aliquis persuadetur solum propter magnitudinem facti, puta cum mare dividitur, ut legitur Ex. XIV, 21, vel quod sol et luna stetit in caelo, sicut legitur Ios. X, 13. Gal. III, 5: *quis tribuit nobis Spiritum, et operatur virtutes in nobis?*

Alio autem modo accipitur signum divinum ab eo quod solus Deus cognoscere potest. Hoc autem est vel futurum contingens, secundum illud Is. XLI, 23: *annuntiate quae ventura sunt, et sciemus quia dii estis vos.* Et quantum ad hoc dicit **alii**, scilicet datur, **prophetia**, quae est divina revelatio inter eventus immobili veritate denuntians. Ioel. c. II, 28: *effundam de Spiritu meo super omnem carnem, et prophetabunt filii vestri.* Aliud autem est cognitio humani cordis, secundum illud Ier. XVII, 9 s.: *pravum est cor hominis et inscrutabile, quis cognoscet illud? Ego Dominus scrutans corda et probans renes.* Et quantum ad hoc subdit **alii discretio spirituum**,

and strengthened, but not anything curious found in human knowledge, as Augustine says. *He gave him knowledge of holy things* (Wis 10:10); *the riches of salvation are wisdom and knowledge* (Isa 33:6).

Yet it should be noted that wisdom and knowledge are numbered among the seven gifts of the Holy Spirit (Isa 11:2). Hence it is significant that the Apostle places in the charismatic graces not wisdom and knowledge, but the utterance of wisdom and knowledge, which pertain to the ability to persuade other by speech about matters pertaining to wisdom and knowledge.

Now, the principles of the doctrine of salvation are the articles of faith, and in regard to this he adds: **to another** is given **faith in the same Spirit**. It is not taken there for the virtue of faith, because this is common to all members of Christ: *without faith it is impossible to please God* (Heb 11:6). But it is taken for the utterance of faith in the sense that a man is able rightly to propose manners of faith, or for the certainty of faith someone has in an excellent way: *woman, great is your faith* (Matt 15:28).

728. But matters pertaining to the teaching of salvation cannot be confirmed or proved by reason, because they transcend human reason: *matters too great for human wisdom have been shown* (Sir 3:23). They are confirmed or proved by a divine sign; hence Moses, about to be sent to the people of Israel, received a sign from God through which he could confirm what he said on God's part (Exod 4:1–7), just as a royal sign confirms that something is the command of a king.

But God's sign is based in one way on something God alone can do, such as miracles, which the Apostle here distinguishes into two kinds. For he says first: **to another** is given **the grace of healing**, i.e., through which he can heal someone's infirmity, **in one** and the same **Spirit**. *Heal me, O Lord, and I will be healed* (Jer 17:14). For by these, one is persuaded not only on account of the greatness of the deed, but also on account of the benefit. Second, he says: **to another the working of miracles**, by which a person is persuaded solely by the greatness of the deed; for example, when the sea was divided (Exod 14:21), or when the sun and moon stood still in the heavens (Josh 10:13). *Who has given you the Spirit and works marvels among you?* (Gal 3:5)

In another way a divine sign is based on something God alone can know, i.e., the future contingent: *tell us what is to come hereafter, that we may know that you are gods* (Isa 41:23). As to this he says: **to another** is given **prophecy**, which is divine revelation declaring with unchangeable truth among events: *I will pour out my Spirit on all flesh, and your sons and your daughters shall prophesy* (Joel 2:28). Another is knowledge of the human heart: *the heart is deceitful above all things and desperately corrupt; who can understand it? I, the Lord, search the mind and try the heart* (Jer 17:9). In regard to this he says: **to another, the discerning of spirits**, namely, in order that a man be able to discern by what spirit

ut scilicet homo discernere possit, quo spiritu aliquis moveatur ad loquendum vel operandum, puta utrum spiritu caritatis vel spiritu invidiae. I Io. IV, 1: *nolite credere omni spiritui, sed probate spiritus si ex Deo sunt.*

729. Facultas autem persuasionem pronuntiandi consistit in hoc quod homo possit loqui intelligibiliter aliis. Quod quidem impeditur dupliciter. Uno modo per diversitatem idiomatum. Contra quod remedium adhibetur per hoc quod dicit *alii*, scilicet datur, ***genera linguarum***, ut scilicet possit loqui diversis linguis, ut intelligatur ab omnibus, sicut de apostolis legitur Act. II, 4, quod loquebantur variis linguis.

Alio modo per obscuritatem Scripturae inducendae. Contra quod remedium datur per id quod subditur ***alii interpretatio sermonum***, id est difficilium Scripturarum. Dan. V, v. 16: *audivi de te quod possis obscura interpretari.* Gen. XL, 8: *numquid non Dei est interpretatio?*

730. Deinde cum dicit *haec autem omnia*, etc., determinat auctorem praedictarum gratiarum. Circa quod tres errores excludit. Primo quidem gentilium attribuentium diversa dona diversis diis. Contra quod dicit ***haec autem omnia operatur unus atque idem Spiritus***. Eph. IV, 4: *unum corpus et unus Spiritus.*

Secundo errorem eorum qui Deo attribuebant solum universalem providentiam rerum, ponentes quod distinctiones particularium fiunt solum per causas secundas. Contra quod subditur ***dividens singulis prout vult***. Eccli. c. XXXIII, 11: *in multitudine disciplinae Domini separavit eos.*

Tertio excludit errorem eorum qui diversitatem gratiarum attribuebant vel fato, vel humano merito, et non solum voluntati divinae, sicut Macedonii, qui dicebant Spiritum Sanctum esse ministerium Patris et Filii. Et hoc excludit per hoc quod subdit ***prout vult***. Io. III, 8: *Spiritus ubi vult spirat.*

someone is moved to speak or work; for example, whether by the spirit of charity or by the spirit of envy: *do not believe every spirit, but test the spirits to see whether they are of God* (1 John 4:1).

729. But the faculty of speaking persuasively consists in being able to speak intelligibly to others. This can be prevented in two ways: in one way by a diversity of dialects. Against this is applied the remedy signified by what he says: ***to another*** is given ***diverse kinds of tongues***, namely, in order that he be able to speak in diverse languages, so that he will be understood by all, as it says of the apostles that they spoke in various languages (Acts 2:4).

In another way by the obscurity of a Scripture passage to be quoted. Against this is given the remedy he mentions: ***to another, the interpretation of speeches***, i.e., of difficult Scripture passages: *I have heard that you can give interpretations of obscure things* (Dan 5:16); *do no interpretations belong to God?* (Gen 40:8)

730. Then when he says, ***all these things***, he identifies the author of these graces. In regard to this he excludes three errors. The first is that of the gentiles attributing different gifts to different gods. Against this he says: ***all these things, one and the same Spirit works***: *one body and one Spirit* (Eph 4:4).

Second, the error of those who attributed to God only a general providence and assigned the distinctions of particular things to second causes alone. Against this he adds: ***dividing to every one according as he wills***: *in the fullness of his knowledge the Lord separated them* (Sir 33:11).

Third, he excludes the error of those who attributed the diversity among graces to fate, or to human merit, and not solely to the divine will, as the Macedonians, who said that the Holy Spirit is the servant of the Father and of the Son. And he excludes this by saying: ***as he wills***: *the Spirit breathes where he wills* (John 3:8).

Lecture 3

¹²:¹²Sicut enim corpus unum est, et membra habet multa, omnia autem membra corporis cum sint multa, unum tamen corpus sunt: ita et Christus. [n. 731]

¹²:¹³Etenim in uno Spiritu omnes nos in unum corpus baptizati sumus, sive Judaei, sive gentiles, sive servi, sive liberi: et omnes in uno Spiritu potati sumus. [n. 734]

¹²:¹⁴Nam et corpus non est unum membrum, sed multa. [n. 736]

¹²:¹⁵Si dixerit pes: quoniam non sum manus, non sum de corpore: num ideo non est de corpore? [n. 738]

¹²:¹⁶Et si dixerit auris: quoniam non sum oculus, non sum de corpore: num ideo est de corpore? [n. 739]

¹²:¹⁷Si totum corpus oculus: ubi auditus? Si totum auditus: ubi odoratus? [n. 740]

¹²:¹⁸Nunc autem posuit Deus membra, unumquodque eorum in corpore sicut voluit. [n. 742]

¹²:¹⁹Quod si essent omnia unum membrum, ubi corpus? [n. 743]

¹²:²⁰Nunc autem multa quidem membra, unum autem corpus.

¹²:²¹Non potest autem oculus dicere manui: opera tua non indigeo: aut iterum caput pedibus: non estis mihi necessarii. [n. 744]

¹²:²²Sed multo magis quae videntur membra corporis infirmiora esse, necessariora sunt: [n. 746]

¹²:²³et quae putamus ignobiliora membra esse corporis, his honorem abundantiorem circumdamus: et quae inhonesta sunt nostra, abundantiorem honestatem habent. [n. 747]

¹²:²⁴Honesta autem nostra nullius egent: sed Deus temperavit corpus, ei cui deerat, abundantiorem tribuendo honorem, [n. 749]

¹²:¹²Καθάπερ γὰρ τὸ σῶμα ἕν ἐστιν καὶ μέλη πολλὰ ἔχει, πάντα δὲ τὰ μέλη τοῦ σώματος πολλὰ ὄντα ἕν ἐστιν σῶμα, οὕτως καὶ ὁ Χριστός·

¹²:¹³καὶ γὰρ ἐν ἑνὶ πνεύματι ἡμεῖς πάντες εἰς ἓν σῶμα ἐβαπτίσθημεν, εἴτε Ἰουδαῖοι εἴτε Ἕλληνες, εἴτε δοῦλοι εἴτε ἐλεύθεροι, καὶ πάντες ἓν πνεῦμα ἐποτίσθημεν.

¹²:¹⁴καὶ γὰρ τὸ σῶμα οὐκ ἔστιν ἓν μέλος ἀλλὰ πολλά.

¹²:¹⁵ἐὰν εἴπῃ ὁ πούς, Ὅτι οὐκ εἰμὶ χείρ, οὐκ εἰμὶ ἐκ τοῦ σώματος, οὐ παρὰ τοῦτο οὐκ ἔστιν ἐκ τοῦ σώματος·

¹²:¹⁶καὶ ἐὰν εἴπῃ τὸ οὖς, Ὅτι οὐκ εἰμὶ ὀφθαλμός, οὐκ εἰμὶ ἐκ τοῦ σώματος, οὐ παρὰ τοῦτο οὐκ ἔστιν ἐκ τοῦ σώματος·

¹²:¹⁷εἰ ὅλον τὸ σῶμα ὀφθαλμός, ποῦ ἡ ἀκοή; εἰ ὅλον ἀκοή, ποῦ ἡ ὄσφρησις;

¹²:¹⁸νυνὶ δὲ ὁ θεὸς ἔθετο τὰ μέλη, ἓν ἕκαστον αὐτῶν, ἐν τῷ σώματι καθὼς ἠθέλησεν.

¹²:¹⁹εἰ δὲ ἦν τὰ πάντα ἓν μέλος, ποῦ τὸ σῶμα;

¹²:²⁰νῦν δὲ πολλὰ μὲν μέλη, ἓν δὲ σῶμα.

¹²:²¹οὐ δύναται δὲ ὁ ὀφθαλμὸς εἰπεῖν τῇ χειρί, Χρείαν σου οὐκ ἔχω, ἢ πάλιν ἡ κεφαλὴ τοῖς ποσίν, Χρείαν ὑμῶν οὐκ ἔχω·

¹²:²²ἀλλὰ πολλῷ μᾶλλον τὰ δοκοῦντα μέλη τοῦ σώματος ἀσθενέστερα ὑπάρχειν ἀναγκαῖά ἐστιν,

¹²:²³καὶ ἃ δοκοῦμεν ἀτιμότερα εἶναι τοῦ σώματος, τούτοις τιμὴν περισσοτέραν περιτίθεμεν, καὶ τὰ ἀσχήμονα ἡμῶν εὐσχημοσύνην περισσοτέραν ἔχει,

¹²:²⁴τὰ δὲ εὐσχήμονα ἡμῶν οὐ χρείαν ἔχει. ἀλλὰ ὁ θεὸς συνεκέρασεν τὸ σῶμα, τῷ ὑστερουμένῳ περισσοτέραν δοὺς τιμήν,

¹²:¹²For as the body is one and has many members; and all the members of the body, whereas they are many, yet are one body: so also is Christ. [n. 731]

¹²:¹³For in one Spirit were we all baptized into one body, whether Jews or gentiles, whether slaves or free: and in one Spirit we have all been made to drink. [n. 734]

¹²:¹⁴For the body also is not one member, but many. [n. 736]

¹²:¹⁵If the foot should say: because I am not the hand, I am not of the body: is it therefore not of the body? [n. 738]

¹²:¹⁶And if the ear should say: because I am not the eye, I am not of the body: is it therefore not of the body? [n. 739]

¹²:¹⁷If the whole body were the eye, where would be the hearing? If the whole were hearing, where would be the smelling? [n. 740]

¹²:¹⁸But now God has set the members, every one of them, in the body as it has pleased him. [n. 742]

¹²:¹⁹And if they all were one member, where would be the body? [n. 743]

¹²:²⁰But now there are many members indeed, yet one body.

¹²:²¹And the eye cannot say to the hand: I do not need your help. Nor again the head to the feet: I have no need of you. [n. 744]

¹²:²²But much more, those who seem to be the more feeble members of the body are more necessary [n. 746]

¹²:²³And such as we think to be the less honorable members of the body, about these we put more abundant honor: and those that are our uncomely parts have more abundant comeliness. [n. 747]

¹²:²⁴But our comely parts have no need: but God has tempered the body together, giving to that which wanted the more abundant honor. [n. 749]

^{12:25}ut non sit schisma in corpore, sed idipsum pro invicem sollicita sint membra. [n. 750]

^{12:26}Et si quid patitur unum membrum, compatiuntur omnia membra: sive gloriatur unum membrum, congaudent omnia membra. [n. 751]

^{12:27}Vos autem estis corpus Christi, et membra de membro. [n. 753]

^{12:28}Et quosdam quidem posuit Deus in Ecclesia primum apostolos, secundo prophetas, exinde doctores, deinde virtutes, exinde gratias curationum, opitulationes, gubernationes, genera linguarum, interpretationes sermonum. [n. 754]

^{12:29}Numquid omnes apostoli? numquid omnes prophetae? numquid omnes doctores? numquid omnes virtutes? [n. 757]

^{12:30}numquid omnes gratiam habent curationum? numquid omnes linguis loquuntur? numquid omnes interpretantur?

^{12:31}Aemulamini autem charismata meliora. Et adhuc excellentiorem viam vobis demonstro. [n. 758]

---

^{12:25}ἵνα μὴ ᾖ σχίσμα ἐν τῷ σώματι, ἀλλὰ τὸ αὐτὸ ὑπὲρ ἀλλήλων μεριμνῶσιν τὰ μέλη.

^{12:26}καὶ εἴτε πάσχει ἓν μέλος, συμπάσχει πάντα τὰ μέλη: εἴτε δοξάζεται [ἓν] μέλος, συγχαίρει πάντα τὰ μέλη.

^{12:27}Ὑμεῖς δέ ἐστε σῶμα Χριστοῦ καὶ μέλη ἐκ μέρους.

^{12:28}καὶ οὓς μὲν ἔθετο ὁ θεὸς ἐν τῇ ἐκκλησίᾳ πρῶτον ἀποστόλους, δεύτερον προφήτας, τρίτον διδασκάλους, ἔπειτα δυνάμεις, ἔπειτα χαρίσματα ἰαμάτων, ἀντιλήμψεις, κυβερνήσεις, γένη γλωσσῶν.

^{12:29}μὴ πάντες ἀπόστολοι; μὴ πάντες προφῆται; μὴ πάντες διδάσκαλοι; μὴ πάντες δυνάμεις;

^{12:30}μὴ πάντες χαρίσματα ἔχουσιν ἰαμάτων; μὴ πάντες γλώσσαις λαλοῦσιν; μὴ πάντες διερμηνεύουσιν;

^{12:31}ζηλοῦτε δὲ τὰ χαρίσματα τὰ μείζονα. Καὶ ἔτι καθ' ὑπερβολὴν ὁδὸν ὑμῖν δείκνυμι.

---

^{12:25}That there might be no schism in the body: but the members might be mutually careful one for another. [n. 750]

^{12:26}And if one member suffer any thing, all the members suffer with it: or if one member glory, all the members rejoice with it. [n. 751]

^{12:27}Now you are the body of Christ and members of a member. [n. 753]

^{12:28}And God indeed has set some in the Church; first apostles, second prophets, third doctors: after that miracles: then the graces of healings, helps, governments, kinds of tongues, interpretations of speeches. [n. 754]

^{12:29}Are all apostles? Are all prophets? Are all doctors? Are all workers of miracles? [n. 757]

^{12:30}Have all the grace of healing? Do all speak with tongues? Do all interpret?

^{12:31}But be zealous for the better gifts. And I show unto you yet a more excellent way. [n. 758]

---

731. Posita distinctione gratiarum, hic manifestat eam per similitudinem corporis naturalis. Et

primo ponit similitudinem in generali;

secundo exemplificat eam in speciali, ibi ***nam et corpus***, et cetera.

732. Circa primum duo facit.

Primo ponitur similitudo;

secundo similitudinis adaptatio, ibi ***ita et Christus***, et cetera.

732. Circa primum considerandum est, quod, sicut in V *Metaphysicae*, tripliciter dicitur aliquid unum *per se*. Uno modo indivisibilitate, ut unitas et punctum, secundum quem modum unitas excludit totaliter multitudinem, non solum actualem, sed etiam potentialem. Alio modo dicitur unum continuitate, ut linea et superficies, quae quidem unitas excludit multitudinem actualem, sed non potentialem. Tertio modo integritate, quae non excludit multitudinem neque potentialem, neque actualem, sicut domus est una quae constituitur ex diversis lapidibus et lignis.

Et, eodem modo, corpus hominis aut cuiuslibet animalis est unum, quia eius perfectio integratur ex diversis membris, sicut ex diversis animae instrumentis; unde et

731. Having set forth the distinction among graces, the Apostle now explains it by a likeness to a natural body.

First, he presents the likeness in general;

second, in more detail, at ***for the body***.

732. In regard to the first he does two things:

first, the likeness is presented;

second, its adaptation, at ***so also is Christ***.

732. In regard to the first it should be noted that as it says in *Metaphysics* V, there are three ways in which something is said to be 'one' *per se*. In one way by indivisibility, as unity and a point. According to this way unity totally excludes not only actual multitude but potential as well. In another way something is called one by reason of continuity, as a line and a surface. Such unity excludes actual multitude but not potential. In a third way something is one by wholeness, which excludes neither actual nor potential multitude, as a house is one thing composed of various stones and types of wood.

In the same way the body of a man or of any other animal is one, because its perfection is made up of various members as of diverse instruments of the soul; hence the

anima dicitur esse actus corporis organici, id est, ex diversis organis constituti.

Proponit ergo primo Apostolus quod unitas corporis, membrorum multitudinem non excludit, dicens quod *sicut corpus unum est, et multa membra habet*, unde et Rom. XII, v. 4 dicitur *in uno corpore multa membra habemus*. Item proponit quod multitudo membrorum non tollit corporis unitatem, unde subdit *omnia autem membra corporis cum sint multa*, nihilominus *unum corpus sunt*, quod ex omnibus perficitur. Unde et Iob X, 11 dicitur: *pelle et carne vestisti me, ossibus et nervis compegisti me.*

733. Deinde cum dicit *ita et Christus*, etc., ponitur adaptatio similitudinis. Et primo adaptat similitudinem, dicens *ita et Christus*, scilicet est unus, secundum illud, supra c. VIII, 6: *unus Dominus noster Iesus, per quem omnia*. Et tamen multa et diversa habet membra, scilicet omnes fideles, secundum illud Rom. XII, 5: *multi unum corpus sumus in Christo.*

734. Secundo ponitur ratio adaptationis, ubi ponitur duplex ratio distinctionis. Una quidem ratio unitatis est Spiritus Sanctus, secundum illud Eph. IV, 4: *unum corpus et unus Spiritus.*

Sed per virtutem Spiritus Sancti duplex beneficium consequimur. Primo quidem, quia per ipsum regeneramur, secundum illud Io. c. III, 5: *nisi quis renatus fuerit ex aqua et Spiritu Sancto*. Unde dicit *etenim in uno Spiritu*, scilicet per virtutem unius Spiritus Sancti, *omnes nos*, qui sumus membra Christi, *sumus baptizati in unum corpus*, id est in unitatem Ecclesiae, quae est corpus Christi, secundum illud Eph. I, 22: *ipsum dedit caput super omnem Ecclesiam, quae est corpus eius*; et Gal. III, 27: *omnes qui in Christo baptizati estis, Christum induistis.*

Secundo, per Spiritum Sanctum reficimur ad salutem. Unde subdit *et omnes potati sumus in uno Spiritu*, id est per virtutem unius Spiritus Sancti.

Potest autem hic potus intelligi dupliciter. Uno modo de interno refrigerio quod Spiritus Sanctus cordi humano praebet, extinguendo sitim carnalium desideriorum et concupiscentiarum. Unde Eccli. XV, 3: *aqua salutaris sapientiae potavit eum*, et, Io. VII, 38, *flumina de ventre eius fluent aquae vivae*. Alio modo potest intelligi de potu sacramentali, qui per Spiritum sacratur. Supra X, v. 4: *omnes eumdem potum spiritualem biberunt.*

735. Interponitur autem duplex ratio diversitatis. Una ex parte ritus, cum dicit *sive Iudaei, sive gentiles*, etc., alia ex parte conditionis, cum dicit *sive servi, sive liberi*. Nulla enim huiusmodi diversitas impedit unitatem corporis Christi. Unde Gal. III, 28 dicitur: *non est Iudaeus, neque Graecus; non est servus, neque liber; unum enim estis in Christo Iesu.*

soul is said to be the act of an organic body, i.e., one made up of various organs.

The Apostle, therefore, first proposes that the unity of the body does not exclude a multitude of members, saying: *as the body is one and has many members*: *in one body we have many members* (Rom 12:4). Likewise, he proposes that a multitude of members does not take away the unity of the body; hence he adds: *and all the members of the body, whereas they are many*, are one body, which is completed by all. Hence it is said: *you clothed me with skin and flesh and knit me together with bones and sinews* (Job 10:11).

733. Then when he says: *so also is Christ*, the adaptation of the likeness begins. First, he adapts the likeness, saying: *so also is Christ*, namely, he is one, as it says above: *our one Lord Jesus through whom are all things* (1 Cor 8:6). Yet he has many and diverse members, namely, all the faithful: *though many we are one body in Christ* (Rom 12:5).

734. Second, he presents the ground of the adaptation, in which is presented a twofold ground of distinction. One ground of unity is the Holy Spirit: *one body and one Spirit* (Eph 4:4).

But we receive a double benefit by the power of the Holy Spirit. First, indeed, because we are reborn through him: *unless a man is born again of water and the Holy Spirit* (John 3:5), hence he says: *for in one Spirit*, namely, by the power of the one Holy Spirit, *we were all*, who are members of Christ, *baptized into one body*, i.e., into the unity of the Church, which is the body of Christ: *he had made him head over all things for the Church, which is his body* (Eph 1:22); *as many of you as were baptized into Christ have put on Christ* (Gal 3:27).

Second, by the Holy Spirit we are refreshed unto salvation. Hence he adds: *and we have all been made to drink in one Spirit*, i.e., by the power of the one Holy Spirit.

This drink can be understood in two ways: in one way of the inward refreshment which the Holy Spirit offers to the human heart by extinguishing the thirst for carnal desires and concupiscences. Hence: *he will give him the water of salutary wisdom to drink* (Sir 15:3); *out of his heart shall flow rivers of living water* (John 7:38). In another way it can be understood of a sacramental drink, which is consecrated by the Spirit: *all drank the same spiritual drink* (1 Cor 10:4).

735. Then he interposes two aspects of diversity: one is on the part of rites when he says: *Jews or gentiles*; the other is on the part of status, when he says: *slaves or free*. No diversity of this kind impedes the unity of the body of Christ. Hence it is said: *there is neither Jew or Greek, there is neither slave nor free; for you are all one in Christ Jesus* (Gal 3:28).

736. Deinde cum dicit *nam et corpus*, explicat similitudinem in speciali. Et

primo describit conditionem corporis naturalis et membrorum ipsius.

Secundo adaptat ad corpus mysticum Christi, ibi *vos autem estis*, et cetera.

Circa primum duo facit.

Primo describit integritatem corporis naturalis;

secundo habitudinem membrorum ad invicem, ibi *non potest autem oculus dicere*, et cetera.

Circa primum tria facit.

Primo proponit quod intendit;

secundo manifestat exemplificando, ibi *si dixerit pes*, etc.;

tertio probat ducendo ad inconveniens, ibi *si totum corpus oculus*, et cetera.

737. Dicit ergo primo: dictum est quod, omnes nos in unum corpus mysticum baptizati sumus, quod repraesentat similitudo corporis naturalis. Nam corpus naturale hominis non est unum membrum, sed multa. Quia scilicet eius perfectio non salvatur in uno membro, sed integratur ex multis, quae necesse habent deservire diversis potentiis et actibus animae. Unde et Rom. XII, 4 dicitur: *sicut in uno corpore multa membra habemus, omnia autem membra corporis non eumdem actum habent, ita multi unum corpus sumus in Christo.*

738. Deinde cum dicit *si dixerit pes*, etc., manifestat quod dixerat exemplificando in membris quibusdam.

Et primo in membris deservientibus motui: et ponit duo membra: pedem, tamquam ignobilius membrum, eo quod calcat terram et portat totius corporis pondus; manum autem tamquam membrum nobilius, eo quod ipsa est organum organorum. Et hoc est quod dicit *si dixerit pes: non sum de corpore, quoniam non sum manus, non ideo non est de corpore?* Quasi dicat: perfectio corporis non tota consistit in uno membro, quamvis nobiliori sed ad eius perfectionem requiruntur etiam ignobiliora.

Per membra autem deservientia motui, designantur in Ecclesia homines dediti vitae activae, ita quod pedes sunt subditi, de quibus dicitur Ez. I, 7: *pedes eorum pedes recti*; per manus autem figurantur praelati, per quos alii disponuntur, unde et Cant. V, 14 dicitur: *manus illius tornatiles aureae, plenae hyacinthis.* Sunt autem in Ecclesia necessariae non solum manus, id est praelati, sed etiam pedes, id est subditi. Unde Prov. XIV, v. 28 dicitur: *in multitudine populi dignitas regis.*

739. Secundo exemplificat de membris servientibus virtuti apprehensivae, et ponit oculum qui deservit visui et aurem quae deservit auditui. Nam isti duo sensus praecipue deserviunt humanae sapientiae: visus quidem quantum ad inventionem, eo quod plures rerum differentias ostendit; auditus autem quantum ad disciplinam,

736. Then when he says, *for the body*, he explains the likeness in detail.

First, he describes the condition of a natural body and its members;

second, he adapts this to the mystical body of Christ, at *now you are the body of Christ*.

In regard to the first he does two things:

first, he describes the completeness of a natural body;

second, the relations of the members to each other, at *and the eye cannot say to the hand*.

In regard to the first he does three things:

first, he states his intention;

second, he explains with examples, at *if the foot should say*;

third, he proves by leading to something awkward, at *if the whole body were the eye*.

737. First, therefore, he says: it has been stated that all of us have been baptized into one mystical body, which represents a likeness to a natural body. For the natural body of a man is not one member but many, because its perfection is not saved in one member, but is composed of many, which of necessity must serve the various potencies and acts of the soul. Hence it is said: *for as in one body we have many members and all the members do not have the same function, so we, though many are one body in Christ* (Rom 12:4).

738. Then when he says: *if the foot should say*, he clarifies what he had said by using certain members as examples.

First, the members involved in motion, and he mentions two members: the foot as the more ignoble member in that it treads the earth and carries the weight of the entire body; but the hand, is the nobler member, inasmuch as it is the organ of the organs. And this is what he says: *if the foot should say: because I am not the hand, I am not of the body: is it therefore not of the body?* As if to say: the perfection of the body does not consist in one member, although it be more noble, but its perfection requires even the more ignoble ones.

But by the members involved in motion are designated in the Church men given to the active life, in such a way that the feet are subjects. About these it is said: *their legs were straight* (Ezek 1:7); by the hands are denoted prelates, through whom others are disposed; hence it is said: *his hands are rounded gold, filled with hyacinth* (Song 5:14). In the Church not only the hands, i.e., prelates, but also the feet are necessary, i.e., subjects. Hence it is said: *in a multitude of people is the glory of a king* (Prov 14:2).

739. Second, he uses as examples the members or powers which serve knowledge and he mentions the eye, which serves sight, and the ear, which serves hearing. For these two senses are the special servants of human knowledge: sight, indeed, in regard to discovery, because it reveals the many differences among things; hearing, however, in

quae fit per sermonem. Horum tamen sensuum dignior est visus quam auditus, quia et spiritualior est et plura demonstrat, ac per hoc oculus est dignior aure.

Dicit ergo *et si dixerit auris*, quae est ignobilius membrum, ***non sum de corpore, quia non sum oculus***, qui est membrum nobilius, ***non ideo non est de corpore?*** et cetera.

Per membra ergo deservientia virtuti apprehensivae, designantur in Ecclesia illi qui student vitae contemplativae, inter quos sunt, sicut oculi, doctores, qui per seipsos veritatem inspiciunt. Unde dicitur Cant. V, 12: *oculi eius sicut columbae super rivos aquarum, quae resident iuxta fluenta plenissima*. Per aures autem significantur discipuli, qui a magistris veritatem audiendo recipiunt. Unde et Matth. XIII, 19 dicitur: *qui habet aures audiendi, audiat*. Sunt enim in Ecclesia necessarii non solum doctores sed etiam discipuli. Unde et Iob XXIX, 11 dicitur: *auris audiens beatificavit me*.

740. Deinde cum dicit *si totum corpus*, etc., probat ducendo ad inconveniens duplex, quorum primum est subtractio necessariorum a corpore,

secundum est remotio integritatis corporis, ibi ***quod si essent omnia***, et cetera.

741. Circa primum duo facit. Primo ponit inconveniens quod sequitur, dicens *si totum corpus* esset *oculus*, quod est membrum nobilius, *ubi* esset *auditus?* Id est instrumentum audiendi, quasi dicat: si in Ecclesia omnes essent magistri. Unde dicitur Iac. III, 1: *nolite plures magistri fieri, fratres mei*.

Et, iterum: *si totum* corpus esset *auditus*, id est instrumentum audiendi, *ubi* esset *odoratus?* et cetera. Per quem possunt in Ecclesia intelligi illi qui, et si non sint capaces verborum sapientiae, percipiunt tamen quaedam eius indicia a remotis, quasi odorem. Unde et Cant. I, 3 dicitur *in odorem unguentorum tuorum currimus*.

742. Secundo asserit contrariam veritatem, scilicet quod nec auditus corpori debet deesse, dicens ***nunc autem Deus posuit***, id est ordinate disposuit, ***membra*** diversa. Nam et si membrorum distinctio sit opus naturae, hoc tamen agit natura ut instrumentum divinae providentiae. Et ideo primam causam dispositionis membrorum assignans, subdit ***unumquodque eorum in corpore***, quasi dicat: non sic posuit membra diversa, ut unumquodque eorum secundum se separatim existeret, sed ut omnia convenirent in uno corpore. Et ***sicut voluit***; nam prima causa institutionis rerum est voluntas divina, secundum illud Ps. CXIII, 3: *omnia quaecumque voluit fecit*.

Sic autem et in Ecclesia disposuit diversa officia, diversos status secundum suam voluntatem. Unde et

regard to doctrine, which is presented by speech. The more dignified of these senses is sight, because it is more spiritual and reveals more things; as a result the eye is more noble than the ear.

He says, therefore: ***and if the ear***, which is the more ignoble member, ***should say, I am not of the body, because I am not the eye***, which is the more noble member, ***is it therefore not of the body?***

By the members which serve knowledge are designated in the Church those who apply themselves to the contemplative life among whom there are, as eyes, teachers who investigate truth. Hence it is said: *his eyes are like doves beside springs of water, which live near the fullest waters* (Song 5:12). By ears are significant disciples who receive the truth by hearing their masters. Hence it is said: *he who has ears hears to hear, let him hear* (Matt 13:9). In the Church not only teachers but also disciples are necessary. Hence it is said: *when the ear heard, it called me blessed* (Job 29:11).

740. Then when he says, ***if the whole body were the eye***, he proves by leading to two awkward conclusions, the first of which is the removal of necessary things from the body;

the second is the removal of bodily completeness, at ***and if they all were one member***.

741. In regard to the first he does two things: first, he presents the awkward conclusion which follows, saying: ***if the whole body were the eye***, which is a nobler member, ***where would be the hearing?*** i.e., the organ of hearing. As if to say: if all in the Church were masters; hence it is said: *let not many of you become teachers, my brethren* (Jas 3:1).

Again, ***if the whole*** body ***were hearing, where would be the smelling?*** By this can be understood those in the Church who, even though they are not capable of words of wisdom, nevertheless perceive some of its indications from afar, as an odor. Hence it is said: *we run after the odor of your anointing oils* (Song 1:5).

742. Second, he asserts the contrary truth, namely, that neither sight nor hearing should be lacking, saying: ***but now God has set***, i.e., put in order, the various ***members***. For even if the distinction of the members is a work of nature, nevertheless nature did this as an instrument of divine providence. And therefore, he assigns the first cause of the arrangement of the members when he says: ***every one of them, in the body***. As if to say: he did not arrange various members in order that each of them should exist separately by itself, but that all should come together in one body. And ***as it pleased him***; for the first cause of the arrangement of things is the divine will: *great are the works of the Lord* (Ps 111:2).

So, too, in the Church he arranged various offices and diverse states according to his will. Hence it is said:

Eph. I, 11 dicitur: *praedestinati secundum propositum eius qui operatur omnia secundum consilium voluntatis suae.*

743. Deinde cum dicit **quod si esset**, etc., ducit ad aliud inconveniens, quod est defectus integritatis corporis.

Unde primo ponit hoc inconveniens, dicens **quod si essent omnia unum membrum, ubi esset corpus?** Id est ubi esset integritas corporalis? Quasi dicat: non esset. Ita si omnes in Ecclesia unius conditionis et gradus essent, tolleretur perfectio et decor Ecclesiae, quae in Ps. XLIV, 10 describitur *circumamicta varietate.*

Secundo asserit veritatem contrariam, dicens **nunc autem multa quidem sunt membra, sed unum corpus** quod ex omnibus integratur. Sic Ecclesia ex diversis ordinibus constituitur. Unde et Cant. VI, 9 describitur: *terribilis ut castrorum acies ordinata.*

744. Deinde cum dicit **non potest autem oculus**, etc., ponit comparationem membrorum ad invicem. Et

primo quantum ad necessitatem;

secundo quantum ad cultum membris adhibitum, ibi **et quae putamus**, etc.;

tertio quantum ad mutuam sollicitudinem, ibi **sed in ipsum**, et cetera.

Circa primum duo facit.

Primo proponit omnia membra corporis esse necessaria, quamvis quaedam sint ignobilia;

secundo ponit necessitatis comparationem, ibi **sed multo magis**, et cetera.

745. Ostendit autem primo rationem necessitatis membrorum secundum duplicem differentiam.

Primo quidem secundum differentiam membrorum deservientium motui, unde dicit **non potest autem oculus**, qui deservit cognitioni et significat contemplativos, **dicere manui**, quae deservit motui et significat activos **opera tua non indigeo**. Indigent enim contemplativi per opera activorum sustentari. Unde et Lc. X, 39 s. dicitur quod cum Maria secus pedes Domini sederet, audiens verba eius, Martha satagebat circa frequens ministerium.

Secundo ostendit idem secundum differentiam praelatorum, qui significantur per caput, et subditorum, qui significantur per pedes; et hoc est quod subdit **aut iterum caput**, id est praelatus, secundum illud I Reg. XV, 17: *caput in tribubus Israel factus es*, **non potest dicere pedibus**, id est subditis, **non estis mihi necessarii**, quia, ut dicitur Prov. XIV, 28, *in multitudine populi dignitas regis.*

746. Deinde cum dicit **sed multo magis**, etc., comparat diversa membra ad invicem quoad necessitatem eorum, dicens quod membra corporis quae videntur esse infirmiora, sunt magis necessaria, sicut intestina. Ita etiam in Ecclesia sine officio aliquarum abiectarum

according to the purpose of him who accomplishes all things according to the counsel of his will (Eph 1:11).

743. Then when he says, **if they were all one member**, he comes to another awkward conclusion, which is a lack of bodily completeness.

Hence, he first posits this awkwardness, saying: **if they were all one member, where would be the body?** i.e., where would the completeness of the body be? As if to say: it would not be. Thus, if all the Church were of one state and grade, it would destroy the perfection and beauty of the Church, which is described as *adorned with many-colored robes* (Ps 45:14).

Second, he asserts the contrary truth, saying: **but now there are many members indeed, yet one body**, which is made complete by all the parts. Thus, the Church is composed of diverse orders: *terrible as an army with banners* (Song 6:10).

744. Then when he says, **the eye cannot**, he compares the members with one another:

first, as to need;

second, as to the care shown to the members, at **and such as we think**;

third, as to mutual solicitude, at **and if one member suffers**.

In regard to the first he does two things:

first, he states that all the members of the body are necessary, although some are less honorable;

second, he presents a comparison of their need, at **but much more**.

745. First, he shows the reason for needing the members by reason of a two-fold difference.

First, indeed, according to the difference of members involved in movement; hence he says, **the eye**, which serves knowledge and signifies contemplatives **cannot say to the hand**, which serves movement and signifies those in the active life, **I do not need your help**. For the contemplatives need to be sustained by the labors of those in the active life. Hence it is said that while Mary sat at the feet of Jesus listening to his words, Martha was busy with much serving (Luke 10:39).

Second, he shows the same according to the differences of prelates signified by the head, and of subjects signified by the feet; and this is what he adds: **nor again the head**, i.e., the prelates: *you have become the head of the tribes of Israel* (1 Sam 15:17), **to the feet**, i.e., the subjects, **I have no need of you**, because as it is said: *in a multitude of people is the glory of the king* (Prov 14:28).

746. Then when he says, **but much more**, he compares various members to one another in regard to their necessity, saying that the members of the body that seem weaker are more necessary, as the intestine. So, too, in the Church without the functions performed by certain lowly persons,

personarum, puta agricultorum et aliorum huiusmodi, praesens vita transiri non posset; quae tamen posset duci sine aliquibus excellentioribus personis contemplationi et sapientiae deputatis, quae Ecclesiae deserviunt ad hoc quod sit ornatior et melius se habens. Ex hoc enim aliquid dicitur necessarium, quod est utile ad finem. Illa vero quae sunt nobilissima, non se habent in ratione utilium, sed sunt per seipsa appetenda ut fines. Et ideo dicitur Iob XXXI, 39: *si fructus terrae comedi absque pecunia, et animam agricolarum eius afflixi.*

747. Deinde cum dicit *et quae putamus*, etc., comparat membra quantum ad exteriorem cultum. Et

primo ponit diversitatem quae diversis membris adhibetur;

secundo causam diversitatis assignat, ibi **Deus temperavit**, et cetera.

748. Cultus autem exterior membris adhibitus ad duo pertinet scilicet ad honorem, sicut ea quae apponuntur ad ornatum, ut monilia et inaures; et ad honestatem, sicut quae apponuntur ad tegumentum, ut brachae et alia huiusmodi.

Quantum ergo ad primum cultum, dicit primo *et quae putamus esse ignobiliora membra corporis, his circumdamus abundantiorem honorem*, idest maiorem ornatum, sicut auribus alicubi suspenduntur inaures, oculis autem nihil apponitur, et pedibus apponuntur calceamenta depicta et gemmata, secundum illud Cant. VII, 1: *quam pulchri sunt gressus tui in calceamentis, filia principis.* Manus autem nudae habentur. Et, similiter in Ecclesia, imperfectioribus sunt magis consolationes adhibendae, quibus perfectiores non egent. Unde dicitur Is. XL, 11: *in brachio suo congregabit agnos, et in sinu suo levabit, foetas ipse portabit*, et, I Petr. III, 7 dicitur: *viri quasi infirmiori vasculo muliebri impartientes honorem.*

Secundo prosequitur quantum ad cultum honestatis, dicens *et quae inhonesta sunt, abundantiorem honestatem habent*, scilicet per studium humanum. Dicuntur autem membra aliqua inhonesta in sanctis, non propter aliquam peccati turpitudinem, sed propter inobedientiam membrorum genitalium subsecutam ex peccato originali. Vel etiam quia sunt ignobili usui deputata, sicut omnia membra quae deserviunt emissioni superfluitatum, quibus abundantior honestas adhibetur dum studiosius teguntur, quo non indigent membra nobilibus usibus deputata.

Unde subdit **honesta autem nostra nullius egent**, scilicet exterioris honestatis, unde nec faciei velamen apponitur. Et similiter in Ecclesia illi qui sunt in aliquo culpabiles, sunt admonendi et custodiendi, secundum illud Eccli. XLII, 11: *super filiam luxuriosam confirma custodiam.* Et Gal. VI, 1 dicitur: *si praeoccupatus quis*

such as farmers and others of that kind, the present life could not be gone through, which, however, can be led without certain more excellent persons dedicated to contemplation and to wisdom, who serve the Church by making it more ornate and in better condition. For something is called necessary, if it is useful to an end. But the noblest things are not considered useful, but they are of themselves to be sought as ends. Therefore, it is said: *if I have eaten its yield without payment, and caused the death of its owners* (Job 31:39).

747. Then when he says, **and such as we think to be the less honorable members of the body**, he compares the members as far as external adornment is concerned:

first, he mentions the different things applied to different members;

second, he assigns the cause of the difference, at **but God has tempered**.

748. The external adornment applied to members pertains to two things, namely, to honor, as things used for decoration, such as necklaces and ear rings, and to modesty, as something used for clothing, such as trousers and the like.

In regard to the first adornment he says first: **and such as we think to be the less honorable members of the body, about these we put more abundant honor**, i.e., more ornamentation, as ear rings from the ears, but nothing is added to the eyes, while shoes adorned with pictures and precious stones are worn on the feet: *how graceful are your feet in sandals, O queenly maiden* (Song 7:1); the hands are kept bare, however. And likewise in the Church the more imperfect receive more consolations, which the more perfect do not need. Hence it is said: *he will gather the lambs in his arms, he will carry them in his bosom* (Isa 40:11); *husbands, bestow honor on the woman as the weaker sex* (1 Pet 3:7).

Second, he continues with the ornaments of honor saying: **and those that are our uncomely parts have more abundant comeliness**, namely, by human assiduity. Some members are called base in holy things, not on account of any baseness of sin, but on account of the disobedience of the genital parts, as a result of original sin. Or because they are directed to a base use, as the members which serve the emission of superfluities. To these a greater modesty is applied, when they are more carefully covered, which the members designed for nobler uses do not require.

Hence he adds: **our comely parts have no need**, namely, of external covering; hence no veil is used to cover the face. Likewise, in the Church those who are culpable in any matter must be admonished and guarded: *keep strict watch over a headstrong daughter* (Sir 42:11); *if a man is overtaken in any sin, you who are spiritual should instruct him*

fuerit in aliquo delicto vos, qui spirituales estis, huiusmodi instruite in spiritu lenitatis; illi autem qui sunt absque culpa his non egent.

Et est notandum quod triplicem defectum circa membra notavit, scilicet inhonestatis, ignobilitatis et infirmitatis. Quorum primum in membris Ecclesiae pertinet ad culpam; secundum ad conditionem servilem; tertium ad statum imperfectionis.

749. Deinde cum dicit *et Deus temperavit*, etc., ponit causam praedicti cultus, et primo assignat causam efficientem primam.

Licet enim homines taliter se habeant ad cultum membrorum, hoc tamen procedit ex ordinatione divina, unde dicit *sed Deus temperavit corpus, abundantiorem honorem tribuendo ei* membro *cui deerat*. Nam homines hoc faciunt ex quodam divino instinctu, secundum illud Iob XXXIII, 16: *aperit aures virorum et erudiens eos instruit disciplina*.

750. Secundo ponit causam finalem, dicens *ut non sit schisma in corpore*. Quod quidem sequeretur, si defectui membrorum non subveniretur. Hoc autem schisma quantum ad membra corporis mystici manifeste vitatur, dum pax Ecclesiae custoditur per hoc, quod singulis ea quae sunt necessaria attribuuntur. Unde et supra dictum est cap. I, v. 10: *idipsum dicatis omnes, et non sint in vobis schismata*. Sed quantum ad membra corporis naturalis, schisma esset in corpore si debita proportio membrorum tolleretur.

751. Deinde cum dicit *sed in idipsum*, etc., ponit comparationem membrorum ad invicem quantum ad mutuam sollicitudinem.

Et, primo, proponit eam, dicens: non solum praedicta membra operantur ad invicem, sed etiam per se invicem sunt sollicita in idipsum, id est in unitatem corporis conservandi. Et hoc quidem manifeste in corpore naturali apparet. Nam quodlibet membrum naturalem quamdam inclinationem habet ad iuvamentum aliorum membrorum. Unde et naturaliter homo opponit manum ad protegendum alia membra ab ictibus. Et similiter alii fideles, qui sunt membra corporis mystici, pro se invicem sollicitudinem gerunt, secundum illud Eccli. XVII, 12: *unicuique mandavit Deus de proximo suo*, et, Gal. VI, 2: *alter alterius onera portate*.

752. Secundo, specificat hanc sollicitudinem; et primo in malis, in quibus magis est manifestum. Unde dicit *et si quid*, scilicet mali, *patitur unum membrum, compatiuntur omnia membra*. Quod quidem manifestum est in corpore naturali. Nam uno membro languente, totum corpus quasi languescit, et ad locum languoris confluunt spiritus et humores quasi ad subveniendum. Et similiter debet esse in fidelibus Christi, ut unus, malo

in a spirit of gentleness (Gal 6:1); but those who are without guilt do not need this.

It should be noted that he mentioned a triple difficulty in the members, namely, baseness, ignobility and weakness. The first of these refers to guilt in the members of the Church; the second to a servile condition; the third to the state of imperfection.

749. Then when he says, *but God has tempered*, he proposes the cause of the above-mentioned care, and first he assigns the first efficient cause.

For although men do take care of the members in this way, nevertheless it proceeds from the divine plan; hence he says: *God has tempered the body together, giving to that which wanted the more abundant honor*. For men do this in virtue of a certain divine instinct: *then he opens the ears of men and teaching, he instructs them in discipline* (Job 33:16).

750. Second, he proposes the final cause, saying: *that there might be no schism in the body*. Which, of course, would follow, if no help were given to the weaker members. Schism in regard to the members of the mystical body is openly avoided as long as the peace of the Church is maintained by giving to each person whatever is necessary. Hence it was said above: *let all of you agree and let there be no dissensions among you* (1 Cor 1:10). But in regard to the members of the natural body, there would division in body if the due proportion of the members were removed.

751. Then when he says, *but that the members*, he presents a comparison of the members with one another in regard to mutual care.

First, he proposes it, saying: not only do the above-mentioned members work for one another, but they are also of themselves solicitous for one another, i.e., by keeping them within the unity of the body. This is clearly evident in the natural body. For each member has a natural inclination to protect the other members from blows. Similarly, the other believers, who are members of the mystical body, show solicitude for one another: *he gave commandment to each of them concerning his neighbor* (Sir 17:14); *carry one another's burdens* (Gal 6:2).

752. Second, he specifies this solicitude: first, in regard to evil, in which it is more obvious. Hence he says: *if one member suffer*, namely, evil, all suffer together. This is obvious in the natural body. *And if one member suffer anything, all the members suffer with it*, which is manifest in a natural body; for if one member is ailing, spirits and humors flock to the ailing part to help it. And the same should happen among Christ's faithful, so that one suffers

alterius compatiatur, secundum illud Iob XXX, 25: *flebam quondam super eo qui afflictus erat, et anima mea compatiebatur.*

Secundo in bonis, unde subdit *sive gloriatur*, id est, quocumque modo vigoratur, **unum membrum, congaudent omnia membra**. Quod etiam manifestum est in corpore naturali, in quo vigor unius membri in iuvamentum cedit aliis membris. Sic debet etiam esse in membris Ecclesiae, ut unusquisque bonis alterius congaudeat. Phil. II, v. 17: *gaudeo et congratulor omnibus vobis.* Rom. XII, 15: *gaudere cum gaudentibus, et flere cum flentibus.*

753. Deinde cum dicit *vos autem estis*, etc., adaptat similitudinem ad propositum.

Et, primo, quantum ad corporis unitatem, dicens *vos autem*, scilicet qui estis in unitate fidei congregati, *estis corpus Christi*, secundum illud Eph. I, 22 s.: *ipsum dedit caput super omnem Ecclesiam, quae est corpus eius.*

Secundo quantum ad membrorum distinctionem, cum subdit *et estis membra de membro*. Quod potest intelligi tripliciter. Uno modo sic: estis membra dependentia de Christo membro, quod quidem dicitur membrum secundum humanitatem secundum quam, praecipue, dicitur Ecclesiae caput. Nam secundum divinitatem non habet rationem membri aut partis, cum sit commune bonum totius universi. Alio modo sic: vos estis membra dependentia de membro, inquantum per me Christo acquisiti estis, secundum illud, supra IV, 15: *in Christo Iesu per Evangelium ego vos genui.* Tertio modo posset exponi ut designaretur distinctio et series membrorum, ut sit sensus: vos *estis membra de membro*, id est ita distinguimini et ordinamini ad invicem, sicut unum membrum ad aliud.

754. Deinde cum dicit *et quosdam quidem*, etc., prosequitur de distinctione ministrationum.

Circa quod tria facit.

Primo assignat ordinem ministrationum;

secundo manifestat earum distinctionem, ibi **numquid apostoli omnes**, etc.;

tertio ordinat eorum affectionem circa diversas administrationes et gratias, ibi **aemulamini autem**, et cetera.

Circa primum duo facit.

Primo ponit maiores seu principales administrationes;

secundo ministrationes secundarias, ibi **opitulationes**, et cetera.

755. Maiores autem ministri in Ecclesia sunt apostoli ad quorum officium tria pertinent, quorum primum est auctoritas gubernandi fidelem populum, quae proprie pertinet ad officium apostolatus; secundo facultas docendi; tertio potestas miracula faciendi ad confirmationem

along with the misfortune of another: *I used to weep over one who was afflicted, and my soul grieved* (John 30:25).

Second, in good things; hence he adds: **or if one member glory**, i.e., is invigorated in any way, **all the members rejoice with it**. This is also noticeable in the natural body, in which the vigor of one member yields help to the other members. So, too, should it be in the members of the Church, that each should take joy in the welfare of another. *I am glad and rejoice with you all* (Phil 2:17); *rejoice with those that rejoice; weep with those who weep* (Rom 12:15).

753. Then when he says: **now you are**, he adapts the likeness to his proposition.

First, in regard to the unity of the body, saying: **now you**, who are assembled in the unity of faith, **are the body of Christ**: *he made him the head over all things for the Church, which is his body* (Eph 1:22).

Second, as to the distinction of members, when he adds: **And members of a member**. This can be understood in three ways: in one way thus: you are members depending on the member Christ, who is called a member in virtue of his human nature, in virtue of which, especially, he is called the head of the Church. For according to his godhead he does not have the nature of a member or of a part, since he is the common good of the entire universe. In another way thus: you are members depending on a member, inasmuch as it was through me that you were acquired for Christ, as was said above: *in Christ Jesus, by the Gospel, I have begotten you* (1 Cor 4:15). In a third way, it could be explained so that the distinction and series of members is designated, so that the sense is this: you are **members of a member**, i.e., you are distinguished and arranged in such a way to one another, as one member to another.

754. Then when he says: **and God indeed has set**, he discusses the distinction of ministries.

In regard to this he does three things:

first, he assigns the order of ministries;

second, he explains their difference, at **are all apostles**;

third, he tempers their affection for various ministries and graces, at **but be zealous**.

In regard to the first he does two things:

first, he presents the greater or principal ministries;

second, the secondary ministries, at **helps, governments**.

755. The great ministers in the Church are the apostles, to whose office pertain three things, the first of which is the authority to govern the faithful, which properly belongs to the apostolic office; second, the faculty of teaching; third, the power to work miracles to confirm doctrine.

doctrinae. Et de his tribus habetur Lc. IX, 1 s., ubi dicitur: *convocatis Iesus duodecim apostolis, dedit illis virtutem et potestatem super omnia daemonia, et ut languores curarent, et misit illos praedicare regnum Dei.*

In omnibus autem potestatibus seu virtutibus ordinatis, illud quod est principale reservatur supremae potestati; alia vero etiam inferioribus communicantur. Potestas autem faciendi miracula, ordinatur ad doctrinam sicut ad fidem, secundum illud Marc. ult.: *sermonem confirmante sequentibus signis.* Doctrina autem ordinatur ad gubernationem populi sicut ad finem, secundum illud Ier. III, 15: *dabo vobis pastores secundum cor meum, et pascent vos in scientia et doctrina.* Et ideo primus gradus inter ecclesiastica ministeria est apostolorum, quibus specialiter competit Ecclesiae regimen.

Et propter hoc dicit **et Deus posuit**, id est ordinate collocavit, **in Ecclesia, quosdam**, scilicet in determinatis ministeriis, secundum illud Io. XV, 16: *posui vos, ut eatis.* **Primum quidem apostolos**, quorum regimini commisit Ecclesiam, secundum illud Lc. XXII, v. 29: *ego dispono vobis, sicut disposuit mihi Pater meus regnum.* Unde et Apoc. XXI, v. 19 s. super duodecim fundamenta civitatis describuntur duodecim apostolorum nomina. Propter quod et ipsi inter caeteros fideles primatum in Spiritualibus gratiis obtinuerunt, secundum illud Rom. VIII, 23: *nos ipsi primitias Spiritus habentes.*

Et quamvis ad apostolos praecipue pertineat doctrinae officium, quibus dictum est Matth. ult.: *euntes docete omnes gentes*, tamen alii in communionem huius officii assumuntur, quorum quidam per seipsos revelationes a Deo accipiunt, qui dicuntur prophetae; quidam vero de his, quae sunt aliis revelata, populum instruunt, qui dicuntur doctores, unde subdit **secundo prophetas**, qui etiam in Novo Testamento fuerunt. Quod enim dicitur Matth. XI, 13: *lex et prophetae usque ad Ioannem*, intelligitur de prophetis qui futurum Christi adventum praenuntiaverunt. **Tertio doctores**, unde et Act. XIII, 1 dicitur: *erant in Ecclesia quae erat Antiochiae, prophetae et doctores.*

Similiter etiam et gratia miraculorum fuit aliis communicata, quae primitus a Christo data fuit apostolis, unde subdit **deinde virtutes**, qui scilicet miracula faciunt circa ipsa elementa mundi. Gal. III, 5: *operatur virtutes in nobis.* Quantum autem ad miracula quae fiunt in corporibus humanis, subdit **exinde gratias curationum**, secundum illud Lc. IX, 1: *ut languores curarent.*

756. Deinde cum dicit **opitulationes**, etc., ponit minores sive secundarias administrationes, quarum quaedam ordinantur ad regimen Ecclesiae, quod ad apostolatus dignitatem pertinere diximus; quaedam vero ad doctrinam.

Ad regimen Ecclesiae pertinent in generali quaedam opitulationes, id est illi qui opem ferunt maioribus praelatis in universali regimine, sicut archidiaconi episcopis,

Concerning these three it is said: *and he called the twelve together and gave them power and authority over all demons and to cure all diseases, and he sent them out to preach the kingdom of God* (Luke 9:1).

But in all powers or virtues set in order, that which is chief is reserved to the supreme power; others are even communicated to lower powers. But the power to work miracles is ordained to teaching, as to the faith: *the Lord confirmed the message by the signs that attended it* (Mark 16:20). But teaching is directed to governing the people as to an end: *I will give you shepherds after my own heart, who will feed you with knowledge and understanding* (Jer 3:15). Therefore, the first degree among ecclesiastical ministries is that of the apostles, to whom the government of the Church belongs in a special way.

For this reason he says: **and God indeed has set**, i.e., in orderly fashion, **some in the Church**, namely, in definite ministries: *I appointed you that you should go* (John 15:16), **first apostles**, to whose rule he entrusted the Church: *as my Father appointed a kingdom for me, so do I appoint for you* (Luke 22:29). Hence, too, it is said that over the foundations of the city were written the name of the twelve apostles (Rev 21:19). For this reason they obtained among the rest of the faithful a primacy in spiritual graces: *we ourselves who have the first fruits of the Spirit* (Rom 8:23).

Although the office of teaching belongs primarily to the apostles, to whom it was said: *going, teach all nations* (Matt 28:10), yet others are allowed to communicate in this office, some of whom receive revelations of God directly and are called prophets; but others instruct the people in matters revealed to others and are called teachers. Hence he adds, **second prophets**, who even existed in the New Testament. For it is said: *the law and the prophets prophesied until John* (Matt 11:13), which is understood of prophets who foretold the coming of Christ. **Third teachers**; hence it is said: *in the church at Antioch there were prophets and teachers* (Acts 13:1).

Likewise the grace of miracles was communicated to others, although originally it had been given to the apostles; hence he adds: **after that miracles**, who work miracles affecting the elements of the world: *he works miracles among you* (Gal 3:5). But as to miracles done on human bodies, he says: **then the graces of healings**: *he gave them power to heal* (Luke 9:1).

756. Then when he says, **helps**, he mentions the minor or secondary ministries, some of which are directed to the ruling of the Church, which we have said pertains to the apostolic dignity; but others pertain to teaching.

To the rule of the Church pertain in general certain services, i.e., those who help the major prelates in the universal rule of the Church, as archdeacons help bishops: *help these*

secundum illud Phil. IV, 3: *adiuva illas quae mecum laboraverunt in Evangelio cum Clemente et caeteris adiutoribus meis.* In speciali autem ponit gubernationes, sicut sunt parochiales sacerdotes, quibus committitur gubernatio aliquarum particularium plebium. Prov. XI, v. 14: *ubi non est gubernator, corruet populus.*

Ad doctrinam autem pertinet secundario, quod subdit *linguarum genera*, quantum ad illos qui variis linguis loquuntur magnalia, ut dicitur Act. II, 4; nec scilicet propter varietatem idiomatum evangelica doctrina impediretur.

Quantum vero ad amovendum impedimentum doctrinae, quod posset provenire ex obscuritate sermonum, subdit *interpretationes sermonum.* Infra XIV, 13: *qui loquitur lingua, oret ut interpretetur.*

757. Deinde cum dicit *numquid omnes apostoli*, etc., manifestat distinctionem praedictarum ministrationum, dicens *numquid omnes* in Ecclesia sunt *apostoli?* Quasi dicat: non. *Numquid omnes prophetae?* et cetera. Ex quo patet diversitas harum administrationum. Eccli. XXXIII, 11: *in multitudine disciplinae Domini separavit eos.* Et XXXVII, v. 31: *non omnia omnibus expediunt.*

758. Deinde cum dicit *aemulamini autem*, etc., ordinat eorum affectum circa praedicta Spiritualia dona, dicens: cum multa sint dona Spiritus Sancti, ut dictum est, *aemulamini*, id est desiderate, *charismata meliora*, id est gratias potiores, ut scilicet magis desideretis ea quae sunt meliora, puta prophetiam quam donum linguarum, ut infra c. XIII, 1 s. dicetur. I Thess. ult.: *omnia probate, quod bonum est tenete.*

Et ne in praemissis donis eorum affectus quiesceret, subdit *et adhuc excellentiorem viam vobis demonstro*, scilicet caritatem, qua directius in Deum itur. Ps. CXVIII, 32: *viam mandatorum tuorum cucurri.* Is. c. XXX, 21: *haec est via, ambulate in ea.*

women, *for they have labored side by side with me together with Clement and the rest of my fellow workers* (Phil 4:3). In particular he mentions, administrators, such as parish priests, to whom it entrusted the care of certain people: *where there is no guidance a people falls* (Prov 11:14).

To teaching pertains secondarily what he calls **kinds of tongues** as to those who speak marvelous things in various tongues (Acts 2:4), lest the teaching of the Gospel be hindered by the variety of dialects.

In regard to removing hindrances to teaching which could arise from obscure speech he mentions **interpretations of speeches**: *he who speaks by a tongue, let him pray that he may interpret* (1 Cor 14:13).

757. Then when he says, *are all apostles? Are all teachers?* He clarifies the distinction among these ministries, saying, *are all* in the Church *apostles?* As if to say: no! *Are all teachers?* This shows the variety of these ministries: *in the fullness of his knowledge the Lord distinguished them* (Sir 33:11). *All things are not expedient for all* (Sir 37:31).

758. Then when he says, *but be zealous*, he rectifies their affection for the above spiritual gifts, saying: since there are many gifts of the Holy Spirit, *be zealous for* the higher gifts, namely, have a desire, *for the better gifts*, i.e., for the better graces; for example, prophecy than the gift of tongues, as will be said below (1 Cor 13:1); *test everything; hold fast what is good* (1 Thess 5:21).

And in order that their affections may not come to rest in the above-mentioned gifts, he adds: *I will show unto you yet a more excellent way*, namely, the way of charity, by which one goes to God in a more direct way: *I will run in the way of thy commandments* (Ps 119:32); *this is the way, walk in it* (Isa 30:21).

CHAPTER 13

Lecture 1

13:1Si linguis hominum loquar, et angelorum, caritatem autem non habeam, factus sum velut aes sonans, aut cymbalum tinniens. [n. 759]

13:2Et si habuero prophetiam, et noverim mysteria omnia, et omnem scientiam: et si habuero omnem fidem ita ut montes transferam, caritatem autem non habuero, nihil sum. [n. 764]

13:3Et si distribuero in cibos pauperum omnes facultates meas, et si tradidero corpus meum ita ut ardeam, caritatem autem non habuero, nihil mihi prodest. [n. 768]

13:1Ἐὰν ταῖς γλώσσαις τῶν ἀνθρώπων λαλῶ καὶ τῶν ἀγγέλων, ἀγάπην δὲ μὴ ἔχω, γέγονα χαλκὸς ἠχῶν ἢ κύμβαλον ἀλαλάζον.

13:2καὶ ἐὰν ἔχω προφητείαν καὶ εἰδῶ τὰ μυστήρια πάντα καὶ πᾶσαν τὴν γνῶσιν, καὶ ἐὰν ἔχω πᾶσαν τὴν πίστιν ὥστε ὄρη μεθιστάναι, ἀγάπην δὲ μὴ ἔχω, οὐθέν εἰμι.

13:3κἂν ψωμίσω πάντα τὰ ὑπάρχοντά μου, καὶ ἐὰν παραδῶ τὸ σῶμά μου ἵνα καυχήσωμαι, ἀγάπην δὲ μὴ ἔχω, οὐδὲν ὠφελοῦμαι.

13:1If I speak with the tongues of men and of angels, and have not charity, I am become as sounding brass, or a tinkling cymbal. [n. 759]

13:2And if I should have prophecy and should know all mysteries and all knowledge, and if I should have all faith, so that I could remove mountains, and have not charity, I am nothing. [n. 764]

13:3And if I should distribute all my goods to feed the poor, and if I should deliver my body to be burned, and have not charity, it profits me nothing. [n. 768]

---

759. Apostolus gratiarum gratis datarum distinctionem assignavit, et ministrationum in quibus membra Ecclesiae distinguuntur, hic agit de caritate, quae inseparabiliter concomitatur gratiam gratum facientem. Et quia promiserat eis se demonstraturum viam excellentiorem, ostendit praeeminentiam caritatis ad caetera gratuita dona. Et

primo quantum ad necessitatem, quia scilicet sine caritate alia dona gratuita non sufficiunt;

secundo quantum ad utilitatem, quia scilicet per caritatem omnia mala vitantur, et omnia bona aguntur, ibi *caritas patiens est*, etc.;

tertio quantum ad permanentiam, ibi *caritas numquam excidit*, et cetera.

Omnia autem dona gratuita reducere videtur Apostolus ad tria. Nam

primo ostendit quod donum linguarum, quod pertinet ad locutionem, sine caritate non valet;

secundo quod etiam non valent ea quae pertinent ad cognitionem, ibi *et si habuero prophetiam*, etc.;

tertio ostendit idem de his quae pertinent ad operationem, ibi *et si distribuero in cibos pauperum*, et cetera.

760. Erat autem apud Corinthios multum desiderabile donum linguarum, ut infra c. XIV T. patebit; et ideo, ab eo incipiens, dicit: promisi me demonstraturum excellentiorem viam, et hoc primo patet in dono linguarum, quia *si linguis hominum*, scilicet omnium, *loquar*, id est, si habuero donum gratiae, per quod loqui possim linguis omnium hominum; et ad maiorem abundantiam

759. Having assigned the differences among charismatic graces and the ministries in which the members of the Church are distinguished, the Apostle now deals with charity, which is inseparably connected with sanctifying grace. And because he had promised to show them a more excellent way, he shows how charity outranks the others, i.e., the charismatic graces.

First, in regard to its necessity, namely, because without charity the other gifts are not enough;

second, as to their utility, namely, because through charity all evils are avoided and good is performed, at *charity is patient* (1 Cor 13:4);

third, as to its permanence, at *charity never falls away* (1 Cor 13:8).

But all the charismatic gifts seem to be reduced to three by the Apostle:

for, first, he shows that the gift of tongues, which pertains to speech, is of no value without charity;

second, that those which pertain to knowledge are of no value without charity, at *and if I should have prophecy*;

third, he shows the same for the gifts which pertain to works, at *and if I should distribute*.

760. The Corinthians had a great desire for the gift of tongues, as will be shown below (1 Cor 14); therefore, beginning with that he says: I have promised to show you a more excellent way; and this is, first of all, clear in the gift of tongues, because, *if I speak with the tongues of men*, namely, of all, i.e., if I should have the gift through which I could speak in the languages of all men; and for greater abundance he adds: *and of angels, and have not*

subdit *et angelorum: caritatem autem non habeam, factus sum velut aes sonans aut cymbalum tinniens.*

Recta comparatione utitur. Anima enim per caritatem vivit quae vivit Deo, qui est animae vita, secundum illud Deut. XXX, 20: *ipse est vita tua.* Unde et I Io. III, 14 dicitur: *translati sumus de morte ad vitam, quoniam diligimus fratres; qui non diligit manet in morte.*

761. Recte ergo comparat loquelam caritate carentem, sono rei mortuae, scilicet aeris aut cymbali, qui licet clarum sonum reddat, non tamen est vivus sed mortuus. Ita etiam locutio hominis caritate carentis, quantumcumque sit diserta, tamen habetur pro mortua, quia non proficit ad meritum vitae aeternae.

Est autem differentia inter aes sonans et cymbalum tinniens, quia aes, cum sit planum, ex percussione simplicem sonum emittit; cymbalum autem, cum sit concavum, ex una percussione sonum multiplicat, quod pertinet ad tinnitum. Aeri ergo comparantur qui veritatem simpliciter pronuntiant, cymbalo vero qui veritatem multiplicant et pronuntiant, multas rationes et similitudines apponendo, et conclusiones plurimas eliciendo, quae tamen omnia sine caritate habentur ut mortua.

762. Considerandum est autem quae linguae angelorum dicantur. Nam cum lingua sit membrum corporeum et ad eius usum pertineat donum linguarum, quod interdum lingua dicitur, ut patebit infra XVI, neutrum videtur angelis competere qui membra non habent.

Potest ergo dici quod per angelos intelliguntur homines angelorum officium habentes, qui scilicet aliis hominibus divina annuntiant, secundum illud Mal. II, 7: *labia sacerdotis custodiunt scientiam, et legem requirunt ex ore eius, quia angelus Domini exercituum est.* Sub hoc ergo sensu dicitur **si linguis hominum loquar et angelorum**, id est non solum minorum sed etiam maiorum qui alios docent.

Potest etiam intelligi de ipsis incorporeis angelis, prout in Ps. CIII, 4 dicitur: *qui facit angelos suos spiritus.* Et quamvis non habeant linguam corpoream, per similitudinem tamen lingua in eis dici potest vis, qua manifestant aliis quod habent in mente.

763. Est autem sciendum quod in cognitione mentis angelicae aliquid est, de quo superiores angeli non loquuntur inferioribus, neque e converso, scilicet ipsa divina essentia quam omnes immediate vident, Deo se omnibus monstrante, secundum illud Ier. c. XXXI, 34: *non docebit ultra vir proximum suum, et vir fratrem suum, dicens: cognosce Dominum. Omnes enim cognoscent me a minimo usque ad maximum eorum.*

Aliquid autem est in cognitione mentis angelicae, de quo superiores loquuntur inferioribus, sed non econverso. Et huiusmodi sunt divinae providentiae mysteria,

charity, I am become as sounding brass, or a tinkling cymbal.

He uses the right comparison. For the soul lives through charity, which lives through God, who is the life of the soul (Deut 30:20): *he is your life.* Hence, too, it is said: *we know that we have passed out of death into life, because we love the brethren. He who does not love remains in death* (1 John 3:14).

761. Correctly, therefore, does he compare speech without charity to the sound of a dead thing, namely, a brass gong and a cymbal, which, although they produce a clear sound, are not living but dead. So, too, the speech of a man without charity, no matter how erudite, is considered dead, because it does not yield merit for eternal life.

There is a difference between a sounding brass gong and a tinkling cymbal, because brass, since it is flat, gives forth a simple sound, when it is struck; but a cymbal, since it is concave, when it is struck once, multiples the sound, which pertains to clanging. To brass, therefore, are compared those who pronounce the truth simply, but to the cymbal those who multiply the truth and present it by adding many reasons and similitudes and by drawing very many connections: all of which, without charity, are regarded as dead.

762. But it should be noted what is meant by the tongues of angels. For since the tongue is a bodily member and to its use pertains the gift of tongues, which is sometimes called a tongue, as will be clear below (1 Cor 16), it neither seems to belong to angels, who do not have members.

Therefore, it can be said that by angels are understood men with the office of angels, namely, who announce divine things to other men: *the lips of the priest should guard knowledge, and men should seek instruction from his mouth, for he is the angel of the Lord of hosts* (Mal 2:7). Therefore, under this sense, **if I speak with the tongues of men and of angels**, i.e., not only of the lesser but even of the greater who teach others.

It can also be understood of the incorporeal angel, as it is said: *who makes your angels spirits* (Ps 104:4). And although they do no have a bodily tongue, by a likeness the power by which they manifest their thoughts to others can be called a tongue.

763. But it should be known that in the knowledge of the angelic mind is something about which the higher angels do not speak to the lower, or vice versa, namely, the divine essence, which they all see immediately, God showing himself to all: *and no longer shall each man teach his neighbor and each his brother, saying: know the Lord. For all shall know immediately, from the least to the greatest* (Jer 31:34).

But something is in the angelic mind about which the higher angels speak to the lower, but not vice versa. Such are the mysteries of divine providence, of which the higher

quorum plura cognoscunt in ipso Deo superiores, qui clarius eum vident quam inferiores. Unde superiores de huiusmodi inferiores instruunt vel illuminant, quod locutio potest dici.

Aliquid vero est in cognitione mentis angelicae, de quo superiores loquuntur inferioribus et econverso; et huiusmodi sunt occulta cordium quae ex libero arbitrio dependent, quae soli Deo patent, et his quorum sunt, secundum illud supra II, 11: *quae sunt hominis, nemo novit nisi spiritus hominis qui in ipso est*. Quae in notitiam alterius deveniunt, eo cuius sunt manifestante, sive sit inferior, sive superior.

Fit autem huiusmodi manifestatio dum inferior angelus superiori loquitur, non per illuminationem, sed per quemdam significationis modum. Est enim in quolibet angelo aliquid quod naturaliter ab altero angelo cognoscitur. Dum ergo id quod est naturaliter notum, proponitur ut signum eius quod est ignotum, manifestatur occultum. Et talis manifestatio dicitur locutio ad similitudinem hominum, qui occulta cordium manifestant aliis per voces sensibiles, aut per quodcumque aliud corporale exterius apparens. Unde et ea, quae sunt in angelis naturaliter nota, inquantum assumuntur ad manifestationem occultorum, dicuntur signa vel nutus. Potestas autem manifestandi conceptum suum hoc modo metaphorice lingua nominatur.

764. Deinde cum dicit *et si habuero*, etc., ostendit idem de his quae pertinent ad cognitionem.

Est autem attendendum quod supra proposuit quatuor dona gratuita ad cognitionem pertinentia, scilicet sapientiam, scientiam, fidem et prophetiam. Incipit ergo hic a prophetia, dicens *et si habuero prophetiam*, per quam divinitus occulta revelantur, secundum illud II Petr. I, 21: *non enim voluntate humana allata est aliquando prophetia, sed Spiritu Sancto inspirati locuti sunt sancti Dei homines.*

Secundo, quantum ad sapientiam, subdit *et noverim omnia mysteria*, id est occulta divinitatis, quod pertinet ad sapientiam, secundum illud supra II, 7: *loquimur Dei sapientiam in mysterio absconditam.*

Tertio, quantum ad scientiam, dicit *et omnem scientiam*, sive humanitus acquisitam, sicut habuerunt philosophi, sive divinitus infusam, sicut habuerunt eam apostoli. Sap. c. VII, 17: *dedit mihi eorum quae sunt veram scientiam.*

Quarto, quantum ad fidem, subdit *et si habuero omnem fidem, ita ut montes transferam*. Potest autem exponi id quod dicit *omnem fidem*, id est omnium articulorum; sed merito est ut exponatur *omnem*, id est perfectam fidem, propter illud quod subditur *ita ut montes transferam*. Dicitur enim Matth. XVII, 19: *si habueritis fidem sicut granum sinapis, dicetis monti huic: transi hinc, et transibit.* Et quamvis granum sinapis sit

angels know more of these mysteries in God himself, because they see him more clearly than the lower. Hence, the higher angels instruct and enlighten the lower angels about these things and this can be called speech.

But something is in the angelic mind about which the higher speak to the lower, and vice versa. These are the secrets of the heart which depend on free will and are known to God alone and to those with the secret, as it says above: *for what man knows the things of a man, except the spirit of a man which is in him?* (1 Cor 2:11) These reach another's knowledge when the one whose they are reveals them, whether it be a lower or a higher.

A manifestation of this kind happens when a lower angel speaks to a higher, not by enlightening but by some form of signification. For in each angel is something which is naturally known by another angel. Therefore, when that which is naturally known is proposed as a sign of that which is unknown, the occult is manifested. And such a manifestation is called speech after the likeness of men who manifest the secrets of their hearts to others by means of sensible words or through other bodily things outwardly apparent. Hence, even things naturally known in angels, inasmuch as they are employed to manifest secrets, are called signs or nods. But the power of manifesting his own concept in this way is called a tongue metaphorically.

764. Then when he says, *and if I should have prophecy*, he shows the same about things pertaining to knowledge.

But it should be noted that above he proposed four charismatic graces pertaining to knowledge, namely, wisdom, knowledge, faith and prophecy. He begins here with prophecy, saying, *if I should prophecy*, through which secrets are divinely revealed: *no prophecy every came by the impulse of man, but men moved by the Holy Spirit spoke from God* (2 Pet 1:21).

Second, as to wisdom, he adds: *and should know all mysteries*, i.e., the secrets of the divinity which pertains to wisdom, as it says above: *we impart a secret and hidden wisdom of God* (1 Cor 2:7).

Third, as to knowledge as he says: *and all knowledge*, whether humanly acquired as by the philosophers or divinely infused as in the apostles: *it was he who gave me unerring knowledge of what exists* (Wis 7:17).

Fourth, as to faith he adds: *and if I should have all faith, so that I could remove mountains*. It is possible to explain *all faith* as all the articles; but it is useful to explain *all*, i.e., perfect faith on account of what is added: *so that I could remove mountains*. For it is said: *if you have faith as a grain of mustard seed, you will say to this mountain: move hence to yonder place; and it will move* (Matt 17:20). And although a grain of mustard seed is very tiny, it is not

minimum quantitate, non tamen intelligitur parva, sed perfecta fides grano sinapis comparari. Dicitur enim Matth. XXI, v. 21: *si habueritis fidem, et non haesitaveritis, non solum de ficulnea facietis, sed etiam si monti huic dixeritis: tolle et iacta te in mare, fiet.* Fides ergo quae non haesitat, grano sinapis comparatur, quod quanto magis atteritur, tanto magis eius fortitudo sentitur.

765. Obiiciunt autem aliqui quod cum multi Sancti perfectam fidem habuerint, nullus legitur montes transtulisse; quod quidem solvitur per id quod supra XII, 7 dictum est: **unicuique datur manifestatio Spiritus ad utilitatem**. Illo nempe modo, loco et tempore miracula per gratiam Spiritus Sancti fiunt, quo Ecclesiae requiritur utilitas. Fecerunt autem Sancti multo maiora, quam translationem montium, prout erat fidelibus utile, puta suscitando mortuos, dividendo mare et alia huiusmodi opera faciendo. Et hoc etiam fecissent, si necessitas adfuisset.

Potest etiam hoc transferri ad expulsionem daemonum de humanis corporibus, qui montes dicuntur propter superbiam. Ier. XIII, 16: *antequam offendant pedes vestri ad montes caliginosos, ecce ego ad te, mons pestifer, qui corrumpis universam terram.*

Attribuitur autem operatio miraculorum fidei non haesitanti, quia fides innititur omnipotentiae, per quam miracula fiunt.

766. Si, inquam, habuero omnia praedicta ad perfectionem intellectus pertinentia, **caritatem autem non habuero**, per quam perficitur voluntas, **nihil sum**, scilicet secundum esse gratiae, de quo dicitur Eph. II, 10: *ipsius sumus factura, creati in Christo Iesu in operibus bonis.* Unde et contra quemdam dicitur Ez. XXVII, 19: *nihil factus es, et non eris in perpetuum.* Quod quidem fit propter defectum caritatis, per quam homo bene utitur intellectu perfecto. Sine caritate autem eius usus bonus non est. Unde et supra c. VIII, 1 dicitur, quod **scientia inflat, caritas aedificat**.

767. Est autem notandum quod Apostolus hic loquitur de sapientia et scientia, secundum quod pertinent ad dona gratiae gratis datae, quae sine caritate esse possunt. Nam secundum quod computantur inter septem dona Spiritus Sancti, numquam sine caritate habentur. Unde et Sap. I, 4 dicitur: *in malevolam animam non intrabit sapientia.* Et Sap. X, 10 dicitur: *dedit illi scientiam sanctorum.* De prophetia autem et fide manifestum est, quod sine caritate haberi possunt.

Sed notandum est hic quod fides firma, etiam sine caritate, miracula facit. Unde, Matth. VII, 22, dicentibus: *nonne in nomine tuo prophetavimus, et multas virtutes fecimus?* Dicitur: *numquam novi vos.* Spiritus enim Sanctus operatur virtutes etiam per malos, sicut et per eos loquitur veritatem.

considered tiny, but perfect faith is compared to a grain of mustard seed: *if you have faith and never doubt, you will not only do what has been done to the fig tree, but even if you say to this mountain: be taken up and cast into the sea, it will be done* (Matt 21:21). Faith, therefore, which does not doubt is compared to a grain of mustard seed, which, the more it is rubbed, the more its strength is sensed.

765. But some object that although many saints had perfect faith, no one is recorded to have moved mountains. This is solved by what is said above: **the manifestation of the Spirit is given to every man unto profit** (1 Cor 12:7), i.e., in that time, place and manner miracles are worked by the grace of the Holy Spirit as the needs of the Church require. But many saints have done much greater things than moving mountains, according as it was useful to the faith: for example, by raising the dead, dividing the sea and performing other works of this nature. And they would have done this, if it had been necessary.

This can also be referred to the expulsion of demons from human bodies, who are called mountains on account of pride: *before your feet stumble on the twilight mountains, I am against you, O destroying mountain, which destroys the whole earth* (Jer 13:16).

The working of miracles is attributed to faith that does not doubt, because faith rests on omnipotence, through which miracles are performed.

766. If, I say, I had all the above pertaining to the perfection of the intellect, **and have not charity**, through which the intellect is perfected, **I am nothing**, according to the order of grace, about which it is said: *for we are his workmanship, created in Christ Jesus for good works* (Eph 2:10). Hence it is said against someone: *you have come to a dreadful end, and shall be no more forever* (Ezek 27:19). This occurs on account of a lack of charity, through which man uses a perfected intellect well. Without charity, however, its use is not good. Hence it says above: **knowledge puffs up, but charity edifies** (1 Cor 8:1).

767. But it should be noted that the Apostle speaks here about wisdom and knowledge as they pertain to the charismatic gifts, which cannot be without charity. For accordingly as they are numbered among the seven gifts of the Holy Spirit, they are never possessed without charity. Hence it is said: *wisdom will not enter a deceitful soul* (Wis 1:4); *she gave him the knowledge of holy things* (Wis 10:10). As far as prophecy and faith are concerned, it is clear that they cannot be possessed without faith.

But it should be noted here that strong faith, even without charity, can perform miracles. Hence: *did we not prophesy in your name and do many mighty works in your name?* (Matt 7:22). The answer is given: *I know you not.* For the Holy Spirit works wonders even through the wicked, just as he speaks the truth through them.

768. Deinde cum dicit *et si distribuero*, etc., ostendit idem in his quae pertinent ad opera, quae consistunt in hoc quod homo faciat bona, secundum illud Gal. VI, v. 9: *bonum facientes, non deficiamus*; et in hoc quod patienter sustineat mala, secundum illud Ps. XCI, 15 s.: *bene patientes erunt, ut annuntient*.

Inter caetera vero bona opera magis commendantur opera pietatis, secundum illud I Tim. IV, 8: *pietas ad omnia utilis est*. Circa quod opus quatuor conditiones designat. Quarum prima est, quod opus pietatis non totum congregetur in unum, sed dividatur in plures, secundum illud Ps. CXI, 9: *dispersit, dedit pauperibus*. Et hoc designatur cum dicitur *si distribuero*.

Secundo ut opus pietatis fiat ad subveniendum necessitati, non ad serviendum superfluitati, secundum illud Is. LVIII, 7: *frange esurienti panem tuum*, et hoc designatur, cum dicitur *in cibos pauperum*.

Tertio ut opus pietatis exhibeatur indigentibus, secundum illud Lc. XIV, 13: *cum facis convivium, voca pauperes*; et hoc designatur, cum dicitur *pauperum*.

Quarto ad perfectionem pertinet, ut homo omnia bona sua in opera pietatis expendat, secundum illud Matth. XIX, 21: *si vis perfectus esse, vade, vende omnia quae habes, et da pauperibus*; et hoc designatur, cum dicitur *omnes facultates meas*.

769. Inter mala vero quae quis sustinet patienter, potissimum est martyrium. Unde dicitur Matth. V, 10: *beati qui persecutionem patiuntur propter iustitiam*. Quod etiam quadrupliciter commendat.

Primo quidem, quia laudabilius est quod, necessitate imminente, puta propter defensionem fidei, seipsum offerat passioni, quam si deprehensus patiatur. Et ideo dicit *si tradidero*. Sicut et de Christo dicitur Eph. V, 2: *tradidit semetipsum pro nobis*.

Secundo quia gravior est corporis humani iactura, quam rerum, de quo tamen quidam commendantur Hebr. X, 34: *rapinam bonorum vestrorum cum gaudio sustinuistis*. Et ideo dicit *corpus*. Is. l, 6: *dedi corpus meum percutientibus*.

Tertio laudabilius est quod aliquis exponat corpus suum supplicio, quam corpus filii, vel cuiuscumque propinqui, de quo tamen commendatur quaedam mulier II Mac. VII, 20: *supra modum videtur mirabilis et bonorum memoria digna, quae pereuntes septem filios sub unius diei tempore conspiciens, bono animo ferebat*. Et ideo dicit *meum*. Iudicum V, v. 9: *qui propria voluntate obtulistis vos discrimini pro Domino*.

Quarto redditur martyrium laudabilius ex acerbitate poenae, de quo subditur *ita ut ardeam*, sicut Laurentius. Eccli. l, 9: *quasi ignis effulgens et thus ardens in igne*.

770. Si, inquam, praedicta opera tam excellentia fecero, *caritatem autem non habuero*, vel quia simul cum

768. Then when he says: *and if I should distribute*, he shows the same in matters pertaining to works which consists in man's doing good works: *let us not grow weary in well-doing* (Gal 6:9), and in his enduring evils patiently: *for justice will return to the righteous and all the upright in heart will follow it* (Ps 94:15).

Among the rest of the good works more commendation is paid to acts of piety: *piety is of value in every way* (1 Tim 4:8). In regard to this work he designates four conditions: the first is that the work of piety not be entirely gathered into one but divided among many: *he has distributed freely, he has given to the poor* (Ps 112:9). And this is designated when he says, *if I should distribute*.

Second, that the work of piety be performed to relieve a need, not to serve a superfluity: *share your bread with the hungry* (Isa 58:17); and this is designated when he says, *to feed the poor*.

Third, that the work of piety be directed to those in need: *when you give a feast, invite the poor* (Luke 14:13), and this is designated when he says, *the poor*.

Fourth, it pertains to perfection that a man expend all his goods for the works of piety: *if you would be perfect, go, sell what you possess and give to the poor* (Matt 19:21), and this is designated when he says, *all my goods*.

769. But among the evils which one endures patiently the greatest is martyrdom. Hence it is said: *blessed are those who suffer persecution for justice's sake, for theirs is the kingdom of heaven* (Matt 5:10). This he commends in four ways:

first, because it is more praiseworthy, when the need is imminent, for example, for the defense of the faith that one offer himself to suffering, than if he is apprehended and suffers. Therefore, he says, *if I should deliver*. This is what is said of Christ: *he gave himself up for us* (Eph 5:2).

Second, because loss to the human body is graver than loss of things, about which, however, some are commanded: *you joyfully accepted the plundering of your property* (Heb 10:34). Therefore, he says, *body*: *I gave my back to the smiters* (Isa 50:6).

Third, it is more praiseworthy that one expose his body to punishment than the body of his son or some relative. About this a certain woman is commended: *though she saw her seven sons perish on a single day, she bore it with great courage* (2 Macc 7:21). And therefore he says, *my*: *my heart goes out to the commanders of Israel who offered themselves willingly more than the people* (Judg 5:9).

Fourth, martyrdom is rendered praiseworthy from the sharpness of the pain, concerning which he adds: *to be burned*, as Lawrence: *like fire and incense in the censer* (Sir 1:9).

770. If, I say, I should do the works mentioned, *and have not charity*, or because along with these works the will

praedictis operibus adest voluntas peccandi mortaliter, vel quia fiunt propter inanem gloriam, ***nihil mihi prodest***, scilicet quantum ad meritum vitae aeternae, quae solis diligentibus Deum repromittitur, secundum illud Iob XXXVI, 33: *annuntiat de ea amico suo quod possessio eius sit*.

Et notandum quod locutionem, quae est vox animalis, si sit sine caritate, comparat non existenti, opera autem quae fiunt propter fidem, si sint sine caritate, dicit esse infructuosa. Sap. III, 11: *vacua est spes eorum, et labores sine fructu*.

to sin mortally is present, or they are done for vain glory, ***it profits me nothing***, namely, as far as merit of eternal life is concerned, which is promised only to those who love God: *he shows his friend concerning it, that it is his possession* (Job 36:33).

And it should be noted that he compares speech, which is an animal voice, if it is without charity, to the non-existent, but works done for an end, if they are without charity, he calls fruitless: *their hope is vain, their work unprofitable* (Wis 3:11).

Lecture 2

^{13:4}Caritas patiens est, benigna est. [n. 771] Caritas non aemulatur, non agit perperam, non inflatur, [n. 774]

^{13:5}non est ambitiosa, non quaerit quae sua sunt, non irritatur, non cogitat malum, [n. 778]

^{13:6}non gaudet super iniquitate, [n. 782] congaudet autem veritati: [n. 783]

^{13:7}omnia suffert, omnia credit, omnia sperat, omnia sustinet. [n. 785]

^{13:4}Ἡ ἀγάπη μακροθυμεῖ, χρηστεύεται ἡ ἀγάπη, οὐ ζηλοῖ, [ἡ ἀγάπη] οὐ περπερεύεται, οὐ φυσιοῦται,

^{13:5}οὐκ ἀσχημονεῖ, οὐ ζητεῖ τὰ ἑαυτῆς, οὐ παροξύνεται, οὐ λογίζεται τὸ κακόν,

^{13:6}οὐ χαίρει ἐπὶ τῇ ἀδικίᾳ, συγχαίρει δὲ τῇ ἀληθείᾳ:

^{13:7}πάντα στέγει, πάντα πιστεύει, πάντα ἐλπίζει, πάντα ὑπομένει.

^{13:4}Charity is patient, is kind: [n. 771] charity envies not, deals not perversely, is not puffed up, [n. 774]

^{13:5}Is not ambitious, seeks not her own, is not provoked to anger, thinks no evil: [n. 778]

^{13:6}Rejoices not in iniquity, [n. 782] but rejoices with the truth: [n. 783]

^{13:7}Bears all things, believes all things, hopes all things, endures all things. [n. 785]

---

771. Postquam Apostolus ostendit caritatem esse adeo necessariam, quod sine ea nullum spirituale donum sufficiat ad salutem, hic ostendit eam adeo esse utilem et efficacis virtutis, quod per eam cuncta opera virtutis implentur. Et

primo praemittit duo quasi generalia;

secundo subiungit in speciali virtutum opera, quae per caritatem complentur, ibi *caritas non aemulatur*, et cetera.

772. Circa primum duo facit. Nam omnis virtus consistit in hoc quod aliquis in operando bene se habeat in sustinendo mala, vel in operando bona.

Quantum ergo ad tolerantiam malorum, dicit *caritas patiens est*, id est facit patienter tolerari mala. Cum enim homo diligit aliquem propter eius amorem, de facili tolerat quaecumque difficilia; et similiter qui diligit Deum, propter eius amorem patienter tolerat quaecumque adversa. Unde et Cant. VIII, 7 dicitur: *aquae multae non poterunt extinguere caritatem, nec flumina obruent eam*. Iac. I, 4: *patientia opus perfectum habet*.

773. Quantum autem ad operationem bonorum, subdit *benigna est*; benignitas autem dicitur quasi *bona igneitas*, ut scilicet sicut ignis liquefaciendo effluere facit, ita caritas hoc efficit, ut bona quae homo habet, non sibi soli retineat, sed ad alios derivet, secundum illud Prov. V, 16: *deriventur fontes tui foras, et in plateis aquas tuas divide*. Quod quidem caritas facit. Unde I Io. III, 17 dicitur: *qui habuerit substantiam huius mundi, et viderit fratrem suum necesse habere, et clauserit viscera sua ab eo, quomodo caritas Dei manet in eo?* Unde et Eph. IV, 32 dicitur: *estote invicem benigni et misericordes*. Et Sap. I, 6 dicitur: *benignus est spiritus sapientiae*.

774. Deinde cum dicit *caritas non aemulatur*, etc., proponit in speciali virtutum opera, quae caritas efficit, et quia ad virtutem duo pertinent, scilicet abstinere a malo

771. After showing that charity is so necessary that without it no spiritual gifts are sufficient for salvation, the Apostle now shows that it is so useful and of such efficacious strength that through it all virtuous works are completed.

First, he makes two quasi-general statements;

second, he mentions in particular the virtuous works which are completed by charity, at *charity envies not*.

772. In regard to the first he does two things. For every virtue consists in this, that in acting, one is well disposed for enduing evil things, or in accomplishing good things.

Therefore, in regard to enduring evil he says, *charity is patient*, i.e., makes one endure evils patiently. For when a man loves someone on account of the beloved's love, he endures all difficulties with ease; similarly, a person who loves God patiently endures any adversity for love of him. Hence it is said: *many waters cannot quench love, neither can floods drown it* (Song 8:7); *patience has a perfect work* (Jas 1:4).

773. But as to performing good works, he adds: *is kind*; benignity is described as 'a good fire,' so that just as fire by melting metal makes it flow, so charity inclines a person not to keep the good things he has, but makes them flow to others: *let your springs be scattered abroad, and streams of water in the streets* (Prov 5:16), and this is what charity does: hence, it is said: *if anyone has the world's goods and sees a brother in need, yet closes his heart against him, how does God's love abide him?* (1 John 3:17). Hence, it is also said: *be kind and merciful to one another* (Eph 4:32); *wisdom is kindly spirit* (Wis 1:6).

774. Then when he says, *charity envies not*, he mentions in particular the virtuous works which charity produces, and because two things pertain to a virtue, namely,

et facere bonum, secundum illud Ps. XXXIII, v. 15: *declina a malo, et fac bonum*, et Is. c. I, 16 s.: *quiescite agere perverse, discite benefacere*.

Primo ostendit quomodo caritas facit omnia mala vitare; secundo quomodo facit omnia bona efficere, ibi *congaudet autem veritati*, et cetera.

Malum autem efficaciter non potest homo Deo facere, sed solum sibi et proximo, secundum illud Iob XXXV, 6: *si peccaveris, quid ei nocebis?* Et postea subditur: *homini qui similis tui est, nocebit impietas tua*. Primo ergo ostendit quomodo per caritatem vitantur mala, quae sunt contra proximum; secundo quomodo vitantur mala, quibus aliquis deordinatur in seipso, ibi *non inflatur*, et cetera.

775. Malum autem quod est contra proximum, potest esse in affectu et in effectu. In affectu autem praecipue est, cum per invidiam quis dolet de bonis proximi, quod directe contrariatur caritati, ad quam pertinet quod homo diligat proximum sicut seipsum, ut habetur Lev. XIX, 18. Et ideo ad caritatem pertinet, ut sicut homo gaudet de bonis propriis, ita gaudeat de bonis proximi. Ex quo sequitur quod caritas excludat invidiam. Et hoc est quod dicit *caritas non aemulatur*, id est non invidet, quia scilicet facit cavere invidiam. Unde et in Ps. XXXVI, 1 dicitur: *noli aemulari in malignantibus*. Et Prov. c. XXIII, 17: *non aemuletur cor tuum peccatores*.

Quantum ad effectum, subdit *non agit perperam*, id est perverse contra aliquem. Nullus enim iniuste agit contra illum quem diligit sicut seipsum. Is. I, 16: *quiescite agere perverse*.

776. Deinde cum dicit *non inflatur* etc., ostendit quomodo caritas facit vitare mala, quibus aliquis deordinatur in seipso. Et

primo quantum ad passiones,

secundo quantum ad electionem, ibi *non cogitat malum*.

777. Ostendit ergo primo quod caritas repellit inordinatam passionem, quantum ad tria.

Primo quidem quantum ad superbiam, quae est inordinatus appetitus propriae excellentiae. Tunc autem inordinate suam excellentiam quis appetit, quando non sufficit ei contineri in eo gradu, qui sibi est a Deo praestitus. Et ideo dicitur Eccli. X, 14: *initium superbiae hominis, apostatare a Deo*. Quod quidem fit, dum homo non vult contineri sub regula ordinationis divinae. Et hoc repugnat caritati, qua quis super omnia Deum diligit. Col. II, 18 s.: *inflatus sensu carnis suae, et non tenens caput*, et cetera.

Recte autem superbia inflationi comparatur. Nam id quod inflatur, non habet solidam magnitudinem, sed apparentem; ita superbi videntur quidem esse sibi magni, cum tamen vera magnitudine careant, quae non potest esse absque ordine divino. Sap. IV, v. 19: *dirumpet illos inflatos sine voce*.

to refrain from evil and to do good: *depart from evil and do good* (Ps 34:14); *cease to do evil, learn to do good* (Isa 1:16).

First, he shows how charity avoids all evil; second, how it accomplishes the good, at **but rejoices with the truth**.

But man cannot do evil effectively to God, but only to himself and to his neighbor: *if you have sinned, what do you accomplish against him?* (Job 35:6); *your wickedness concerns a man like yourself* (Job 35:8). First, therefore, he shows how charity avoids evils against one's neighbor; second, how evils are avoided by which someone is disarranged in himself, at **is not puffed up**.

775. Evil against one's neighbor can exist in the will or emotions and externally. It exists in the former, especially when a person through envy grieves over his neighbor's good. This is directly contrary to charity which inclines a person to love his neighbor as himself (Lev 19:18). Hence it pertains to charity that just as a person rejoices in his own goods, so he should rejoice in the goods of his neighbor. It follows from this that charity excludes envy. And this is what he says: **charity envies not**. Hence it is said: *do not be envious of wrongdoers* (Ps 37:1); *do not let your heart envy sinners* (Prov 23:17).

As to the outward effect he adds: **deals not perversely**, i.e., perversely, against anyone. For no one deals unjustly against one he loves: *cease to do evil* (Isa 1:16).

776. Then when he says, **is not puffed up**, he shows that charity makes one avoid evils by which one is disarranged in himself.

First, as to passions;

second, as to choice, at **thinks no evil**.

777. Therefore, he first shows that charity drives away inordinate passions in regard to three things.

First, indeed, as to pride, which is a disarranged desire for one's own excellence. One seeks his own excellence in a disarranged manner, when it does not satisfy him to be contained in that station which has been established for him by God. Therefore it is said: *the beginning of man's pride is to depart from the Lord* (Sir 10:12). This happens when a man does not wish to be contained under the rule of God's arrangement. And this is opposed to charity, by which one loves God above all things: *puffed by without reason by this sensuous mind and not holding fast to the head* (Col 2:18).

It is right to compare pride to arrogance. For that which is puffed up does not have solidity but its appearance; so the proud seem to themselves to be great, while they really lack true greatness, which cannot exist without the divine order: *he will dash them speechless to the ground* (Wis 4:19).

778. Est autem principalis superbiae filia, ambitio, per quam aliquis quaerit praeesse; quam etiam caritas excludit, quae potius proximis eligit ministrare, secundum illud Gal. V, 13: *per caritatem spiritus servite invicem.* Et ideo subdit **non est ambitiosa**, id est, facit hominem ambitionem vitare. Eccli. VII, 4: *noli quaerere ab homine ducatum, neque a rege cathedram honoris.*

779. Secundo, ostendit quomodo caritas excludit inordinationem cupiditatis, cum dicit **non quaerit quae sua sunt**, ut intelligatur cum praecisione, id est neglectis bonis aliorum. Nam qui diligit alios sicut seipsum, bona aliorum quaerit sicut et sui ipsius. Unde et supra X, 33 Apostolus dixit **non quaerens quod mihi utile est, sed quod multis, ut salvi fiant.** Contra quod de quibusdam dicitur Phil. II, 21: *omnes quae sua sunt quaerunt, non quae Iesu Christi.*

Potest et aliter intelligi **non quaerit quae sua sunt**, id est, non repetit ea quae sunt sibi ablata, scilicet in iudicio cum scandalo: quia magis amat salutem proximi, quam pecuniam, secundum illud Phil. ult.: *non quaero datum, sed requiro fructum abundantem in iustitia vestra.* Quod tamen qualiter intelligendum sit, supra VI dictum est.

780. Tertio, ostendit quomodo caritas excludat inordinationem irae, dicens **non irritatur**, id est non provocatur ad iram.

Est enim ira inordinatus appetitus vindictae. Ad caritatem autem pertinet magis remittere offensas, quam supra modum aut inordinate vindicare, secundum illud Col. III, v. 13: *donantes vobismetipsis, si quis adversus aliquem habet querelam*; Iac. I, 20: *ira viri iustitiam Dei non operatur.*

781. Deinde cum dicit **non cogitat**, etc., ostendit quomodo per caritatem excluditur inordinatio electionis.

Est autem electio, ut dicitur in III *Ethic. appetitus praeconsiliati.* Tunc ergo homo peccat ex electione et non ex passione, quando ex consilio rationis affectus eius provocatur ad malum.

Caritas ergo primo quidem excludit perversitatem consilii. Et ideo dicit **non cogitat malum**, id est non permittit excogitare quomodo aliquis perficiat malum. Mich. II, 1: *vae qui cogitatis inutile, operamini malum in cubilibus vestris.* Is. I, 16: *auferte malum cogitationum vestrarum ab oculis meis.*

Vel caritas **non cogitat malum**, quia non permittit hominem per varias suspiciones et temeraria iudicia cogitare malum de proximo. Matth. IX, 4: *ut quid cogitatis mala in cordibus vestris?*

782. Secundo, caritas excludit inordinatum affectum malorum, cum dicit **non gaudet super iniquitate.** Ille enim qui ex passione peccat, cum quodam remorsu et dolore peccatum committit; sed ille qui peccat ex electione, gaudet ex hoc ipso quod peccatum committit, secundum illud Prov. II, 14: *qui laetantur cum male*

778. The chief daughter of pride is ambition, through which one seeks to be foremost; which charity also excludes, seeking rather to serve: *through love be servants of one another* (Gal 5:13). Therefore, he adds: **is not ambitious**, i.e., makes a man avoid ambition: *do not seek from the Lord the highest office nor the seat of honor from the king* (Sir 7:4).

779. Second, he shows how charity excludes the disorder of cupidity, when he says: **seeks not her own**. This is understood precisely, i.e., it does not neglect the good of others. For one who loves others as himself seeks the good of others just as his own. Hence the Apostle said above: **not seeking my own advantage, but that of many** (1 Cor 10:10). Against which it is said of some: *they all look after their own interests, not those of Jesus Christ* (Phil 2:21).

It is possible to understand in another way that charity **seeks not her own**, i.e., it does not seek the return of what has been taken from it, namely, in a court case with scandal; because he loves the salvation of his neighbor more than money: *not that I seek the gift; but I seek the fruit which increases to your credit* (Phil 4:17).

780. Third, he shows how charity excludes the disorder of anger, saying: **it is not provoked to anger**, i.e., is not provoked to anger.

For anger is an inordinate desire for revenge. But it pertains to charity rather to forgive offenses than to seek revenge beyond measure: *forbearing one another, if one has a complaint against another* (Col 3:13); *the anger of man does not work the righteousness of God* (Jas 1:20).

781. Then when he says, **thinks no evil**, he shows how by charity disordered choosing is excluded.

Now choice is, as it says in *Ethics* III, *the desire for what has already been thought about and weighed*. Therefore, a man sins from choice and not from passion, when by a plan of his reason his affections are bestirred to evil.

Charity, therefore, first of all, excludes perverse counsel. Therefore, he says: charity **thinks no evil**, i.e., does not permit devising how to complete something evil: *woe to those who devise wickedness and work evil upon their beds* (Mic 2:1); *remove the evil of your doings from before my eyes* (Isa 1:16).

Or charity **thinks no evil**, because it does not permit one to think evil about his neighbor by various suspicions and rash judgments: *why do you think evil in your hearts?* (Matt 9:4).

782. Second, charity excludes an inordinate love for evil; hence he says: **rejoices not in iniquity**. For one who sins from passion commits sin with some remorse and sorrow, but one who sins from choice rejoices in the fact that he commits sin: *you rejoice in doing evil and delight in the perseverance of evil* (Prov 2:14). But charity prevents this,

fecerint, et exultant in rebus pessimis. Hoc autem caritas impedit, inquantum est amor summi boni, cui repugnat omne peccatum.

Vel dicit quod caritas **non gaudet super iniquitate**, scilicet a proximo commissa, quinimo de ea luget, inquantum contrariatur proximorum saluti quam cupit. II Cor. XII, v. 21: *ne iterum cum venero humiliet me Deus apud vos, et lugeam multos ex his, qui ante peccaverunt.*

783. Deinde cum dicit **congaudet autem**, etc., ostendit quomodo caritas facit operari bonum. Et

    primo quantum ad proximum;

    secundo quantum ad Deum, ibi **omnia credit**, et cetera.

784. Quantum ad proximum autem, homo operatur bonum dupliciter. Primo quidem gaudendo de bonis eius. Et quantum ad hoc dicit **congaudet autem veritati**, scilicet proximi, vel vitae, vel doctrinae, vel iustitiae, ex eo quod proximum diligit sicut seipsum. In III Io. v. 3: *gavisus sum valde venientibus fratribus, et testimonium perhibentibus veritati tuae, sicut in caritate ambulas.*

Secundo in hoc quod homo mala proximi sustinet prout decet. Et quantum ad hoc dicit **omnia suffert**, id est absque turbatione sustinet omnes defectus proximorum, vel quaecumque adversa. Rom. XV, 1: *debemus nos firmiores imbecillitates infirmorum sustinere.* Gal. VI, 2: *alter alterius onera portate, et sic adimplebitis legem Christi*, scilicet caritatem.

785. Deinde cum dicit **omnia credit**, ostendit quomodo caritas faciat operari bonum in comparatione ad Deum. Quod quidem fit praecipue per virtutes theologicas, quae habent Deum pro obiecto. Sunt autem praeter caritatem duae virtutes theologicae, ut infra dicitur, scilicet fides et spes.

Quantum ergo ad fidem dicit **omnia credit**, scilicet quae divinitus traduntur. Gen. XV, v. 6: *credidit Abraham Deo, et reputatum est ei ad iustitiam.* Credere vero omnia quae ab homine dicuntur, est levitatis, secundum illud Eccli. XIX, 4: *qui cito credit, levis est corde.*

Quantum autem ad spem, dicit **omnia sperat**, quae scilicet promittuntur a Deo. Eccli. c. II, 9: *qui timetis Deum, sperate in eum.*

Et ne spes frangatur per dilationem, subdit **omnia sustinet**, id est patienter expectat quae promittuntur a Deo quamvis dilata, secundum illud Hab. II, 3: *si moram fecerit, expecta eum*; Ps. XXVI, 14: *confortetur cor tuum, et sustine Dominum.*

inasmuch as it is the love of the supreme good, to whom all sin is obnoxious.

Or he says that charity **rejoices not in iniquity**, namely, committed by a neighbor: in fact it laments over it, inasmuch as it is opposed to our neighbor's salvation, which it desires: *I fear that when I come again my God will humble me before you, and I may have to mourn over many of those who sinned before* (2 Cor 12:21).

783. Then when he says, **but rejoices**, he shows how charity makes one do the good:

    first, as to one's neighbor;

    second, as to God, at **believes all things**.

784. In regard to his neighbor man does the good in two ways: first, by rejoicing in his good. In regard to this he says: **but rejoices with the truth**, namely, of the neighbor or of life or doctrine or justice, inasmuch as he loves his neighbor as himself: *I was exceedingly glad when the brethren came and gave testimony to the truth in you, even as you walk in the truth* (3 John 3).

Second, in the fact that a person endures the evils of his neighbor to the extent that it is fitting. In regard to this he says: **bears all things**, i.e., without disquiet it tolerates all the shortcomings of the neighbor of any adversity whatever: *we who are strong ought to bear with the failings of the weak* (Rom 15:1); *carry one another's burdens and so you will fulfill the law of Christ* (Gal 6:2), namely, charity.

785. Then when he says: **believes all things**, he shows how charity makes one do the good in relation to God. This is done especially through the theological virtues which have God for their object. In addition to charity the other two, as will be said below, are faith and hope.

Therefore, in regard to faith he says: **believes all things**, namely, which are divinely revealed. *Abraham believed God and it was reputed to him as righteousness* (Gen 15:6). But to believe all things said by men is lightmindedness: *one who trusts others to quickly is light-minded* (Sir 19:4).

In regard to hope he says: **hopes all things**, namely, which are promised by God: *you who fear the Lord hope for good things* (Sir 2:9).

And in order that hope not be discouraged by the delay, he adds: **endures all things**, i.e., patiently awaits what God has promised in spite of delay: *if it seem slow, wait for it* (Heb 2:3); *let your heart take courage and wait for the Lord* (Ps 27:14).

Lecture 3

13:8Caritas numquam excidit: sive prophetiae evacuabuntur, sive linguae cessabunt, sive scientia destruetur. [n. 786]

13:9Ex parte enim cognoscimus, et ex parte prophetamus. [n. 792]

13:10Cum autem venerit quod perfectum est, evacuabitur quod ex parte est. [n. 794]

13:11Cum essem parvulus, loquebar ut parvulus, sapiebam ut parvulus, cogitabam ut parvulus. Quando autem factus sum vir, evacuavi quae erant parvuli. [n. 796]

13:8Ἡ ἀγάπη οὐδέποτε πίπτει. εἴτε δὲ προφητεῖαι, καταργηθήσονται: εἴτε γλῶσσαι, παύσονται: εἴτε γνῶσις, καταργηθήσεται.

13:9ἐκ μέρους γὰρ γινώσκομεν καὶ ἐκ μέρους προφητεύομεν:

13:10ὅταν δὲ ἔλθῃ τὸ τέλειον, τὸ ἐκ μέρους καταργηθήσεται.

13:11ὅτε ἤμην νήπιος, ἐλάλουν ὡς νήπιος, ἐφρόνουν ὡς νήπιος, ἐλογιζόμην ὡς νήπιος: ὅτε γέγονα ἀνήρ, κατήργηκα τὰ τοῦ νηπίου.

13:8Charity never falls away: whether prophecies shall be made void or tongues shall cease or knowledge shall be destroyed. [n. 786]

13:9For we know in part: and we prophesy in part. [n. 792]

13:10But when that which is perfect is come, that which is in part shall be done away. [n. 794]

13:11When I was a child, I spoke as a child, I understood as a child, I thought as a child. But, when I became a man, I put away the things of a child. [n. 796]

---

786. Postquam Apostolus ostendit quod caritas excellit alia dona Spiritus Sancti necessitate et fructuositate, hic ostendit excellentiam caritatis ad alia dona quantum ad permanentiam.

Et circa hoc tria facit.

Primo proponit differentiam caritatis ad alia dona Spiritus Sancti, quantum ad permanentiam;

secundo probat quod dixerat, ibi *ex parte enim cognoscimus*, etc.;

tertio infert conclusionem intentam, ibi *nunc autem manent*, et cetera.

Circa primum duo facit.

Primo proponit permanentiam caritatis;

secundo cessationem aliorum donorum, ibi *sive prophetiae*, et cetera.

787. Dicit ergo primo *caritas numquam excidit*. Quod quidem male intelligentes, in errorem ceciderunt, dicentes, quod caritas semel habita, numquam potest amitti, cui videtur consonare quod dicitur I Io. III, v. 9: *omnis qui natus est ex Deo, peccatum non facit, quoniam semen ipsius in eo manet.*

Sed huius dicti primo quidem sententia falsa est. Potest enim aliquis caritatem habens, a caritate excidere per peccatum, secundum illud Apoc. II, 4 s.: *caritatem tuam primam reliquisti. Memor esto itaque unde excideris, et age poenitentiam.* Et hoc ideo est, quia caritas recipitur in anima hominis secundum modum ipsius, ut scilicet possit ea uti, vel non uti. Dum vero ea utitur homo, peccare non potest: quia usus caritatis est dilectio Dei super omnia, et ideo nihil restat propter quod homo Deum offendat. Et per hunc modum intelligitur verbum Ioannis inductum.

Secundo, praedicta sententia non est secundum intentionem Apostoli, quia non loquitur hic de cessatione donorum spiritualium, per peccatum mortale, sed potius

786. After showing that charity excels the other gifts of the Holy Spirit by reason of need and fruitfulness, the Apostle now shows the excellence of charity over the other gifts in regard to permanence.

In regard to this he does three things:

first, he mentions the difference between charity and other gifts of the Holy Spirit as to permanence;

second, he proves what he had said, at *for we know in part*;

third, he draws the intended conclusion, at *and now there remain faith* (1 Cor 13:13).

In regard to the first he does two things:

first, he declares the permanence of charity;

second, the cessation of other gifts, at *whether prophecies*.

787. First, therefore, he says: *charity never falls away*. Some, indeed, have misunderstood this and fallen into error, saying that charity once possessed can never be lost. This opinion seems to be consistent with what is said: *no one born of God commits sin, because his seed remains in him* (1 John 3:9).

But this opinion is false, because someone possessing charity can fall away from it by sin: *you have abandoned the love you had at first. Remember, then, from what you have fallen, and do penance* (Rev 2:4). This is so, because charity is received in a man's soul according to his mode, namely, that he can use it or not. But as long as he uses it, a man cannot sin; because the use of charity is loving God above all things, and nothing remains for the sake of which a man should offend God. And this is the way John's quoted statement is understood.

Second, the quotation cited is not in accord with the Apostle's intention, because he is not speaking here about the cessation of spiritual gifts through mortal sin, but

de cessatione donorum spiritualium, quae pertinent ad hanc vitam per gloriam supervenientem. Unde sensus Apostoli est *caritas numquam excidit*, quia scilicet sicut est in statu viae, ita permanebit in statu patriae et cum augmento, secundum illud Is. XXXI, 9: *dixit Dominus cuius ignis est in Sion*, scilicet in Ecclesia militante *et caminus eius in Ierusalem*, id est in pace caelestis patriae.

788. Deinde cum dicit *sive prophetiae*, etc., proponit cessationem aliorum donorum spiritualium, et specialiter eorum quae praecipua videntur.

Primo quantum ad prophetiam, dicit *sive prophetiae evacuabuntur*, id est cessabunt, quia scilicet in futura gloria prophetia locum non habebit, propter duo. Primo quidem quia prophetia respicit futurum, status autem ille non expectabit aliquid in futurum, sed erit finale complementum omnium eorum quae ante fuerant prophetata. Unde in Ps. XLVII, v. 9 dicitur: *sicut audivimus*, scilicet per prophetas, *ita et vidimus*, praesentialiter, *in civitate Domini virtutum*.

Secundo quia prophetia est cum cognitione figurali et aenigmatica, quae cessabit in patria. Unde dicitur Num. XII, 6: *si quis fuerit inter vos propheta Domini, per somnium aut in visione apparebo ei, vel per somnium loquar ad illum*. Et Osee XII, 10: *in manibus prophetarum assimilatus sum*.

789. Secundo quantum ad donum linguarum, dicit *sive linguae cessabunt*. Quod quidem non est intelligendum quantum ad ipsa membra corporea, quae linguae dicuntur, ut dicitur infra XV, 52: *mortui resurgent incorrupti*, id est, absque diminutione membrorum. Neque autem intelligendum est quantum ad usum linguae corporeae. Est enim futura in patria laus vocalis, secundum illud Ps. CXLIX, 6: *exultationes Dei in gutture eorum*, ut Glossa ibidem exponit.

Est ergo intelligendum quantum ad donum linguarum, quo scilicet aliqui in primitiva Ecclesia linguis variis loquebantur, ut dicitur Act. II, 4. In futura enim gloria, quilibet quamlibet linguam intelliget. Unde non erit necessarium variis linguis loqui. Nam etiam a primordio generis humani, ut dicitur Gen. c. XI, 1: *unus erat sermo, et unum labium omnibus*, quod multo magis erit in ultimo statu, in quo erit unitas consummata.

790. Tertio quantum ad scientiam, subdit: *sive scientia destruetur*. Ex quo quidam accipere voluerunt quod scientia acquisita totaliter perditur cum corpore.

Ad cuius veritatis inquisitionem considerare oportet, quod duplex est vis cognitiva, scilicet vis sensitiva et vis intellectiva. Inter quas est differentia, quia vis sensitiva est actus organi corporalis, et ideo necesse est quod desinat corpore corrupto; vis autem intellectiva non est actus alicuius organi corporei, ut probatur in III *de Anima*, et ideo necesse est quod maneat corpore corrupto. Si ergo aliquid scientiae acquisitae conservetur in parte animae

rather about the cessation of spiritual gifts which pertain to this life through supervening glory. Hence, the sense of the Apostle is that *charity never falls away*, namely, because just as it exists in the state toward heaven, so it will remain in the state of glory and with increase: *says the Lord, whose fire is in Zion* (Isa 31:9), i.e., in the Church Militant, *and whose furnace is in Jerusalem*, i.e., in the peace of the heavenly fatherland.

788. Then when he says, *whether prophecies*, he sets forth the cessation of other spiritual gifts, and especially of those which seem principal.

First as to prophecy he says, *whether prophecies shall be made void*, i.e., will cease, namely, because in future glory prophecy will have no place for two reasons: first, because prophecy regards the future; but that state does not await anything in the future, but will be the final completion of everything previously foretold. Hence it is said: *as we have heard*, namely, through the prophets, *so have we seen in the city of our God* (Ps 48:9).

Second, because prophecy occurs with figurative and enigmatic knowledge, which will cease in heaven: *if there is a prophet among you, I, the Lord, will make myself known to him in a vision, I will speak with him in a dream* (Num 12:6); *it was I who multiplied visions and through the prophets gave parables* (Hos 12:10).

789. Second, as to the gift of tongues he says: *or tongues shall cease*. This is not to be understood of the bodily members called tongues, as it says below: *the dead shall rise again incorruptible* (1 Cor 15:52), i.e., without loss of members. Nor is it to be understood of the use of the bodily tongue. For in heaven there will be vocal praise: *let the high praises of God be in their throats* (Ps 149:6), as a Gloss explains.

Therefore, it must be understood of the gift of tongues, by which some in the early Church spoke in various tongues (Acts 2:4). For in future glory each one will understand each tongue. Hence, it will not be necessary to speak in various tongues. For even from the beginning of the human race, as it is said: *the whole earth had one language and few words* (Gen 11:1), which will be more true in the final state, in which there will be complete unity.

790. Third, as to knowledge he adds: *or knowledge shall be destroyed*. From this some have wanted to suppose that acquired knowledge is totally destroyed with the body.

To investigate the truth it is necessary to consider that the cognitive power is twofold, namely, the sensitive power and the intellective. Between these there is a difference, because the sensitive power is the act of an organic power and therefore ceases to be, when the body dies; but the intellective power is not the act of any bodily organ, as is proved in *On the Soul* III, and therefore, it must remain when the body dies. Therefore, if any acquired knowledge

intellectivae, necesse est quod id permaneat post mortem.

791. Quidam ergo posuerunt quod species intelligibiles non conservantur in intellectu possibili, nisi quamdiu intelligit. Conservantur autem species phantasmatum in potentiis animae sensitivae, puta in memorativa et imaginativa; ita scilicet quod semper intellectus possibilis quando de novo vult intelligere, etiam quae prius intellexit, indiget abstrahere a phantasmatibus per lumen intellectus agentis, et secundum hoc consequens est quod scientia hic acquisita non remaneat post mortem.

Sed haec positio est primo quidem contra rationem. Manifestum est enim quod species intelligibiles in intellectu possibili recipiuntur ad minus dum actu intelligit. Quod autem recipitur in aliquo, est in eo per modum recipientis. Cum ergo substantia intellectus possibilis sit immutabilis et fixa, consequens est, quod species intelligibiles remaneant in eo immobiliter.

Secundo est contra auctoritatem Aristotelis in III *de Anima*, qui dicit quod cum intellectus possibilis est sciens unumquodque, tunc etiam est intelligens in potentia. Et sic patet quod habet species intelligibiles per quas dicitur sciens, et tamen adhuc est in potentia ad intelligendum in actu, et ita species intelligibiles sunt in intellectu possibili, etiam quando non intelligit actu. Unde etiam, ibidem, Philosophus dicit, quod anima intellectiva est locus specierum, quia scilicet in ea conservantur species intelligibiles.

Indiget tamen in hac vita convertere se ad phantasmata, ad hoc quod actu intelligat, non solum ut abstrahat species a phantasmatibus, sed etiam ut species habitas phantasmatibus applicet: cuius signum est quod laeso organo virtutis imaginativae, vel etiam memorativae, non solum impeditur homo ab acquisitione novae scientiae, sed etiam ab usu scientiae prius habitae.

Sic ergo remanet scientia in anima post corporis mortem, quantum ad species intelligibiles, non autem quantum ad inspectionem phantasmatum, quibus anima separata non indigebit, habens esse et operationem absque corporis communione.

Et secundum hoc Apostolus hic dicit, quod scientia destruetur, scilicet secundum conversionem ad phantasmata. Unde et Is. XXIX, v. 14 dicitur: *peribit sapientia a sapientibus, et intellectus prudentium eius abscondetur.*

792. Deinde cum dicit *ex parte enim cognoscimus*, probat quod dixerat: et

primo inducit probationem;

secundo manifestat ea, quae in probatione continentur, ibi *cum essem parvulus*, et cetera.

is preserved in the intellective part of the soul, it must remain after death.

791. Some, therefore, have supposed that the intelligible species are not conserved in the possible intellect except as long as it is understanding. But the species of the phantasms are conserved in the powers of the sensitive soul; for example in the memory or the imagination, in such a way that when the possible intellect wants to think of something anew, even things it previously understood, it always needs to abstract from the phantasms by the light of the active intellect. Therefore, according to this the consequence is that knowledge acquired here does not remain after death.

But this position is, of course, against reason. For it is obvious that the intelligible species in the possible intellect are received at least while it is actually understanding. But whatever is received in something exists in it after the manner of the recipient. Therefore, since the substance of the possible intellect is fixed and unchangeable, the consequence is that the intelligible species remain in it unchangeably.

Second, it is against the authority of Aristotle in *On the Soul* III, who says that when the possible intellect is knowing anything, then also it is understanding in potency. And so it is clear that it has an intelligible species, through which it is said to be knowing, and yet it is still in potency to understanding in act, and so the intelligible species are in the possible intellect, even when it is not actually understanding. Hence the Philosopher says that the intellective soul is the locus of the species, namely, because the intelligible species are conserved in it.

Yet it needs to refer to the phantasms in this life in order actually to understand, not only to abstract species from the phantasms but also to apply the species it has to the phantasms. The sign of this is that if the organ of the imagination or even of the memory is injured, a man is not only prevented from acquiring new knowledge, but also from the use of knowledge previously possessed.

Thus, therefore, knowledge remains in the soul after the death of the body as to the intelligible species, but not as to inspecting phantasms, which the separated soul does not need, since it has existence and activity without union with the body.

And according to this the Apostle says here that knowledge is destroyed, namely, according to referring to phantasms: hence, is is said: *the wisdom of their wise men shall perish* (Isa 29:14).

792. Then when he says: *for we know in part*, he proves what he had said:

first, he presents a proof;

second, he clarifies things contained in the proof, at *when I was a child*.

793. Inducit ergo primo ad probandum propositum talem rationem: adveniente perfecto cessat imperfectum; sed dona alia praeter caritatem habent imperfectionem; ergo cessabunt superveniente perfectione gloriae.

Primo ergo proponit minorem propositionem quo ad imperfectionem scientiae, cum dicit **ex parte enim cognoscimus**, id est imperfecte. Nam pars habet rationem imperfecti. Et hoc praecipue verificatur quantum ad cognitionem Dei, secundum illud Iob XXXVI, v. 26: *ecce Deus magnus vincens scientiam nostram*; et XXVI, 14: *ecce haec ex parte dicta sunt viarum eius.*

Proponit etiam imperfectionem prophetiae, cum subdit **et ex parte** id est imperfecte, **prophetamus**. Est enim prophetia cognitio cum imperfectione, ut dictum est. Tacet autem de dono linguarum, quod est imperfectius his duobus, ut infra XIV, 2 patebit.

794. Secundo ponit maiorem, dicens **cum autem venerit quod perfectum est**, id est, perfectio gloriae, **evacuabitur quod ex parte est**, id est, omnis imperfectio tolletur. De qua perfectione dicitur I Petr. ult.: *modicum passos ipse perficiet.*

795. Sed secundum hoc videtur, quod etiam caritas evacuetur per futuram gloriam, quia ipsa est imperfecta in statu viae per comparationem ad statum patriae.

Dicendum ergo, quod imperfectio dupliciter se habet ad id quod dicitur imperfectum. Quandoque enim est de ratione eius, quandoque vero non, sed accidit ei; sicut imperfectio est de ratione pueri, non autem de ratione hominis, et ideo, adveniente perfecta aetate, cessat quidem pueritia: sed humanitas fit perfecta. Imperfectio est ergo de ratione scientiae, prout hic de Deo habetur, inquantum scilicet cognoscitur ex sensibilibus; et similiter de ratione prophetiae, inquantum est cognitio figuralis et in futurum tendens. Non est autem de ratione caritatis ad quam cognitum bonum diligere pertinet. Et ideo superveniente perfectione gloriae, cessat prophetia et scientia; caritas autem non cessat, sed magis perficitur, quia quanto perfectius cognoscetur Deus, tanto etiam perfectius amabitur.

796. Deinde cum dicit **cum essem parvulus**, etc., manifestat ea quae praemissa sunt. Et

primo manifestat maiorem, scilicet quod veniente perfecto cessat imperfectum;

secundo manifestat minorem, scilicet quod scientia, et prophetia sint imperfecta, ibi **videmus nunc**, et cetera.

797. Ostendit autem primum per similitudinem perfecti et imperfecti, quod invenitur in aetate corporali.

Unde et primo describit imperfectum aetatis corporalis, dicens **cum essem parvulus**, scilicet aetate, **loquebar ut parvulus**, id est prout congruit parvulo, scilicet balbutiendo. Unde propter naturalem defectum locutionis, qui est in parvulis, commendatur Sapientia quod

793. To prove the proposition he presents this proof: when the perfect comes, the imperfect ceases; but gifts other than charity have imperfection. Therefore, they will cease, when the perfection of glory triumphs.

First, therefore, he proposes the minor proposition referring to the imperfection of knowledge, when he says: **for we know in part**, i.e., imperfectly. For a part has the nature of something imperfect. And this is especially true in regard to knowledge of God: *behold, God is great, and we know him not* (Job 36:26); *behold, these are not but the outskirts of his ways* (Job 26:14).

He also proposes the imperfection of prophecy, when he adds: **and we prophesy in part**, i.e., imperfectly. For prophecy is knowledge with imperfection, as has been said. But he is silent about the gift of tongues, which is more imperfect than these two, as will be shown (1 Cor 14:2).

794. Second, he proves the major proposition, saying: **but when that which is perfect is come**, the imperfect will pass away, i.e., every imperfection will be taken away. Of this perfection it is said: *after you have suffered a little while, he will restore and strengthen you* (1 Pet 5:10).

795. But according to this it seems that even charity will pass away through future glory, because it is imperfect in the present life as compared with the life of glory.

The answer is that imperfection is related in two ways to that which is called imperfect. For sometimes it pertains to a thing's very nature and sometimes not, but is accidental to it. For example, imperfection pertains to the very notion of a boy, but not of a man; therefore, when perfect age comes, boyhood ceases, but the human nature becomes perfect. Imperfection, therefore, is of the very notion of knowledge, as we possess it of God here, inasmuch as it is known from sensible things; the same is true of the nature of prophecy, inasmuch as it is a figural knowledge tending into the future. But it is not so in the very notion of charity, to which it pertains to love a known good. Therefore, with the coming of perfect grace prophecy and knowledge cease; but charity does not cease. It is made perfect, because the more perfectly God will be known, the more perfectly will he be loved.

796. Then when he says: **when I was a child**, he clarifies what he had said above:

first, he clarifies the major, namely, with the coming of the perfect the imperfect ceases;

second, he clarifies the minor, namely, that knowledge and prophecy are imperfect, at **we see now** (1 Cor 3:12).

797. He shows the first by a likeness of the perfect and imperfect found in bodily age.

Hence, he first describes the imperfect state of bodily age, saying: **when I was a child**, namely, in age, **I spoke as a child**, i.e., as befitted a child, by babbling. Hence, on account of the natural lack of speech in children, Wisdom is commended *for making the tongues of babes speak clearly*

linguas infantium facit disertas, Sap. X, v. 21; et ut parvulus loquitur, qui vana loquitur. Ps. XI, 3: *vana locuti sunt unusquisque ad proximum suum.*

Quantum vero ad iudicium subdit **sapiebam ut parvulus**, id est, approbabam vel reprobabam aliqua stulte, ut faciunt parvuli, qui quandoque pretiosa contemnunt, et vilia appetunt, ut dicitur Prov. I, 22: *usquequo, parvuli, diligitis infantiam, et stulti ea quae sunt sibi noxia cupient?* Sapiunt ergo ut parvuli, qui, spiritualibus contemptis, terrenis inhaerent; de quibus dicitur Phil. III, v. 19: *gloria in confusione eorum, qui terrena sapiunt.*

Quantum autem ad rationis discursum, dicit **cogitabam ut parvulus**, id est aliqua vana. Unde et in Ps. XCIII, 11 dicitur: *Dominus scit cogitationes hominum, quoniam vanae sunt.*

Et videtur Apostolus ordine praepostero haec tria ponere. Nam locutio praeexigit iudicium sapientiae: iudicium vero praesupponit cogitationes rationis. Et hoc satis congruit imperfectioni puerili, in qua est locutio sine iudicio, et iudicium sine deliberatione.

Potest autem referri, quod dicit **loquebar ut parvulus**, ad donum linguarum; cum dicit **sapiebam ut parvulus**, ad donum prophetiae; quod autem subdit **cogitabam ut parvulus**, ad donum scientiae.

798. Secundo ponit id quod pertinet ad perfectionem aetatis, dicens **quando autem factus sum vir**, id est quando perveni ad perfectam et virilem aetatem, **evacuavi**, id est abieci, **quae erant parvuli**; quia, ut dicitur Is. LXV, 20, *puer centum annorum morietur, et peccator centum annorum maledictus erit.*

Et est attendendum, quod Apostolus hic comparat statum praesentem pueritiae propter imperfectionem; statum autem futurae gloriae propter perfectionem, virili aetati.

(Wis 10:2) and that he child should speak who utters vanities: *everyone utters vanities to his neighbor* (Ps 12:2).

As to judgment he adds: ***I understood as a child***, i.e., I accepted or rejected certain things foolishly, as children do, who sometimes reject precious things and desire base things, as it is said: *how long, O simple ones, will you love being simple* (Prov 1:22). Therefore, they think as children who despise spiritual things and desire those of earth. Of such it is said: *they glory in their shame with their minds set on earthly things* (Phil 3:19).

As to reasoning he says: ***I thought as a child***, i.e., certain vain things: *the Lord knows the thoughts of man, that they are vain* (Ps 94:11).

Now the Apostle seems to place these three in reverse order. For speech precedes the judgment of reason; but judgment presupposes the activity of reason. And this sufficiently befits childish imperfection, in which there is speech without judgment, and judgment without deliberation.

I spoke as a child can be referred to the gift of tongues; ***I understood as a child*** to the gift of prophecy; finally, ***I thought as a child*** to the gift of knowledge.

798. Second, he mentions what pertains to perfect age, saying: ***when I became a man***, i.e., when I reached the perfect and virile age, ***I put away***, i.e., cast off, ***the things of a child***, because, as it is said: *the child shall die a hundred years old, and the sinner a hundred years old shall be accursed* (Isa 65:20).

It should be recognized that the Apostle is here comparing the present to childhood on account of its imperfection; but the state of future glory to the manly state on account of its perfection.

Lecture 4

13:12Videmus nunc per speculum in aenigmate: tunc autem facie ad faciem. Nunc cognosco ex parte: tunc autem cognoscam sicut et cognitus sum. [n. 800]

13:13Nunc autem manent fides, spes, caritas, tria haec: major autem horum est caritas. [n. 805]

13:12βλέπομεν γὰρ ἄρτι δι' ἐσόπτρου ἐν αἰνίγματι, τότε δὲ πρόσωπον πρὸς πρόσωπον: ἄρτι γινώσκω ἐκ μέρους, τότε δὲ ἐπιγνώσομαι καθὼς καὶ ἐπεγνώσθην.

13:13νυνὶ δὲ μένει πίστις, ἐλπίς, ἀγάπη, τὰ τρία ταῦτα: μείζων δὲ τούτων ἡ ἀγάπη.

13:12We see now through a glass in a dark manner: but then face to face. Now I know in part: but then I shall know even as I am known. [n. 800]

13:13And now there remain faith, hope, and charity, these three: but the greatest of these is charity. [n. 805]

---

799. Hic loquitur de visione, quae est cognitio Dei. Unde omnia praecedentia dona evacuanda, sunt intelligenda secundum quod ordinantur ad cognitionem Dei.

Circa hoc duo facit.
Primo enim probat id quod intendit in generali;
secundo in speciali de seipso, ibi **nunc cognosco**, et cetera.

800. Dicit ergo: dixi quod ex parte cognoscimus, quia nunc **videmus per speculum in aenigmate**, sed tunc, scilicet in patria videbimus **facie ad faciem**.

Ubi primo considerandum est, quid sit videre **per speculum in aenigmate**; secundo quid sit videre **facie ad faciem**.

Sciendum est ergo, quod sensibile aliquid potest tripliciter videri, scilicet aut per sui praesentiam in re vidente, sicut ipsa lux, quae praesens est oculo; aut per praesentiam suae similitudinis in sensu immediate derivatam ab ipsa re, sicut albedo quae est in pariete videtur, non existente ipsa albedine praesentialiter in oculo, sed eius similitudine, licet ipsa similitudo non videatur ab eo; aut per praesentiam similitudinis non immediate derivatae ab ipsa re, sed derivatae a similitudine rei in aliquid aliud, sicut cum videtur aliquis homo per speculum. Non enim similitudo hominis immediate est in oculo, sed similitudo hominis resultantis in speculo.

Per hunc ergo modum loquendo de visione Dei, dico quod naturali cognitione solus Deus videt seipsum: quia in Deo idem est sua essentia et suus intellectus. Et ideo sua essentia est praesens suo intellectui. Sed secundo modo forte angeli naturali cognitione Deum vident, inquantum similitudo divinae essentiae relucet immediate in eos. Tertio vero modo cognoscimus nos Deum in vita ista, inquantum invisibilia Dei per creaturas cognoscimus, ut dicitur Rom. I, 20. *Et ita tota creatura est nobis sicut speculum quoddam*: quia ex ordine, et bonitate, et magnitudine, quae in rebus a Deo causata sunt, venimus in cognitionem sapientiae, bonitatis et eminentiae divinae. Et haec cognitio dicitur visio in speculo.

801. Ulterius autem sciendum est, quod huiusmodi similitudo, quae est similitudinis in alio relucentis, est

799. Here he speaks of the vision, which is knowledge of God. Hence, all the preceding gifts must be understood as destined to be eliminated inasmuch as they are directed to knowledge of God.

In regard to this he does two things:
first, he proves what he proposes in general;
second, in detail about himself, at **now I know in part**.

800. He says, therefore: I have said that we know imperfectly, because **we see now through a glass in a dark manner**, but then, namely, in heaven, we shall see **face to face**.

The first consideration concerns what it is to see **through a glass in a dark manner**; the second concerns what it is to see **face to face**.

It should be noted, therefore, that something sensible can be seen in three ways, namely, by its presence in the one seeing, as light itself, which is present in the eye, or by the presence of its likeness in the sense and immediately derived from the thing, as whiteness in a wall is seen, even though the whiteness does not exist in the eye, but its likeness (although the likeness is not seen by the eye); or by the presence of a likeness not immediately derived from the thing itself but from a likeness of the thing in something else, as when a man is seen through a mirror. For the likeness of the man is not immediately in the eye, but the likeness of the man reflected in a mirror.

Therefore, speaking in this way about the vision of God, I say that by natural knowledge God alone sees himself; because in God essence and intellect are the same. Therefore, his essence is present to his intellect. But in a second way the angels perhaps see God by natural knowledge, inasmuch as a likeness of the divine essence immediately shines back on them. But in a third way we know God in this life, inasmuch as we know the invisible things of God through creatures, as it is said: *and so all creation is a mirror for us* (Rom 1:20); because from the order and goodness and multitude which are caused in things by God, we come to a knowledge of his power, goodness and eminence. And this knowledge is called seeing in a mirror.

801. It should be further noted that a likeness of this sort, which is of a likeness gleaming back on someone

duplex: quia aliquando est clara et aperta, sicut illa quae est in speculo; aliquando obscura et occulta, et tunc illa visio dicitur aenigmatica, sicut cum dico: *me mater genuit, et eadem gignitur ex me.* Istud est per simile occultum. Et dicitur de glacie, quae gignitur ex aqua congelata, et aqua gignitur ex glacie resoluta. Sic ergo patet, quod visio per similitudinem similitudinis est in speculo per simile occultum in aenigmate, sed per simile clarum et apertum facit aliam speciem allegoricae visionis.

Inquantum ergo invisibilia Dei per creaturas cognoscimus, dicimur videre per speculum. Inquantum vero illa invisibilia sunt nobis occulta, videmus in aenigmate.

Vel aliter, **videmus nunc per speculum**, id est per rationem nostram, et tunc **per**, designat virtutem tantum. Quasi dicat **videmus per speculum**, id est virtute animae nostrae.

802. Circa secundum vero sciendum est, quod Deus, secundum quod Deus, non habet faciem, et ideo hoc, quod dicit, **facie ad faciem**, metaphorice dicitur. Cum enim videmus aliquid in speculo, non videmus ipsam rem, sed similitudinem eius; sed quando videmus aliquid secundum faciem, tunc videmus ipsam rem sicut est. Ideo nihil aliud vult dicere apostolus, cum dicit: videbimus in patria **facie ad faciem**, quam quod videbimus ipsam Dei essentiam. I Io. III, 2: *videbimus eum sicuti est*, et cetera.

Sed contra est, quia Gen. XXXII, 30 dicitur: *vidi Dominum facie ad faciem*, et cetera. Sed constat, quod tunc non vidit essentiam Dei; ergo videre facie ad faciem, non est videre essentiam Dei.

Responsio. Dicendum est quod illa visio fuit imaginaria; visio autem imaginaria est quidam gradus altior, scilicet videre illud quod apparet: in ipsa imagine in qua apparet et alius gradus infimus scilicet audire tantum verba. Unde Iacob, ut insinuaret excellentiam visionis imaginariae sibi ostensae, dicit *vidi Dominum facie ad faciem*, id est vidi Dominum imaginarie apparentem in sua imagine et non per essentiam suam. Sic enim non fuisset visio imaginaria.

803. Sed tamen quidam dicunt, quod in patria ipsa divina essentia videbitur per similitudinem creatam.

Sed hoc est omnino falsum et impossibile, quia numquam potest aliquid per essentiam cognosci per similitudinem, quae non conveniat cum re illa in specie. Lapis enim non potest cognosci secundum illud quod est, nisi per speciem lapidis, quae est in anima. Nulla enim similitudo ducit in cognitionem essentiae alicuius rei, si differat a re illa secundum speciem, et multo minus si differt secundum genus. Non enim per speciem equi, vel albedinis potest cognosci essentia hominis, et multo minus essentia angeli. Multo ergo minus per aliquam speciem creatam, quaecumque sit illa, potest videri divina

else, is twofold: because sometimes it is clear and open, as that which appears in a mirror, sometimes it is obscure and secret, and then that vision is said to be enigmatic, as when I say: *me a mother begot, and the same is born from me.* That is secret by a simile. And it is said of ice, which is born from frozen water and the water is born from the melted ice. Thus, therefore, it is clear that vision through the likeness of a likeness is in a mirror, by a likeness hidden in an enigma, but a clear and open likeness makes another kind of allegorical vision.

Therefore, inasmuch as we know the invisible things of God through creatures, we are said to see through a mirror. Inasmuch as those invisible things are secrets to us, we see in an enigma.

Or another way, **we see now through a glass**, i.e., by our reason, and then **through** designates the power only. As if to say: **we now see through a glass**, i.e., by a power of our soul.

802. In regard to the second it should be noted that God as God does not have a face, and therefore the expression **face to face** is metaphorical. For when we see something in a mirror, we do not see it, but its likeness; but when we see someone by face, then we see him as he is. Therefore, the Apostle wishes to say nothing else, when he says: in heaven we shall see **face to face**, then that we shall see the very essence of God: *we shall see him as he is* (1 John 3:2).

But opposed to this it is said: *I have seen God face to face and yet my life is preserved* (Gen 32:30). But it is evident that he did not at that time see the essence of God; therefore, to see face to face is not to see the essence of God.

The answer is that that vision was imaginary; but an imaginary vision is of a higher degree, namely, seeing what appears: in the image in which he appears is another lowest grace, namely, only to hear words. Hence Jacob, to indicate the excellence of the imaginary vision showed to him says: *I have seen the Lord face to face*, i.e., I have seen the Lord through my imagination in his own image and not through his essence. For then it would not have been an imaginary vision.

803. But still some say that in heaven the divine essence will be seen through a created likeness.

This, however, is entirely false and impossible, because something can never be known through its essence by a likeness, which does not agree with that thing in species. For a stone cannot be known as it is except through the stone's species, which is in the soul. For no likeness leads to knowledge of a thing's essence, if it differs from that according to species; and much less if they differ in genus. For the essence of a man, much less than the essence of an angel, cannot be known through the species of a horse or of whiteness. Much less, then, can the divine essence be seen through any created species, whatever it be, since any

essentia, cum ab essentia divina plus distet quaecumque species creata in anima, quam species equi, vel albedinis ab essentia angeli. Unde ponere quod Deus videatur solum per similitudinem, seu per quamdam refulgentiam claritatis suae, est ponere divinam essentiam non videri.

Et, praeterea, cum anima sit quaedam similitudo Dei, visio illa non magis esset specularis et aenigmatica, quae est in via, quam visio clara et aperta, quae repromittitur sanctis in gloria, et in qua erit beatitudo nostra. Unde Augustinus dicit hic in Glossa, quod visio Dei, quae est per similitudinem, pertinet ad visionem speculi et aenigmatis.

Sequeretur etiam quod beatitudo hominis ultima esset in alio, quam in ipso Deo, quod est alienum a fide. Naturale etiam hominis desiderium, quod est perveniendi ad primam rerum causam, et cognoscendi ipsam per seipsam, esset inane.

804. Sequitur *nunc cognosco ex parte*, et cetera. Hic, illud quod probavit in generali, probat in speciali de cognitione sui ipsius, dicens *nunc*, id est in praesenti vita, ego Paulus *cognosco ex parte*, id est obscure et imperfecte; *tunc autem*, scilicet in patria, *cognoscam sicut et cognitus sum*, id est: sicut Deus cognovit essentiam meam, ita Deum cognoscam per essentiam; ita quod *sicut*, non importat hic aequalitatem cognitionis, sed similitudinem tantum.

805. Consequenter infert principalem conclusionem cum dicit *nunc autem manent*, et cetera.

Causa autem quare non facit mentionem de omnibus donis, sed de istis tribus tantum est quia haec tria coniungunt Deo, alia autem non coniungunt Deo, nisi mediantibus istis; alia etiam dona sunt quaedam disponentia ad gignendum ista tria in cordibus hominum. Unde et solum ista tria, scilicet fides, spes et caritas, dicuntur virtutes theologicae, quia habent immediate Deum pro obiecto.

806. Sed cum dona sint ad perficiendum vel affectum vel intellectum, et caritas perficiat affectum, fides intellectum: non videtur quod spes sit necessaria, sed superflua.

Ad hoc sciendum, quod amor est quaedam vis unitiva, et omnis amor in unione quadam consistit. Unde et secundum diversas uniones, diversae species amicitiae a Philosopho distinguuntur.

Nos autem habemus duplicem coniunctionem cum Deo. Una est quantum ad bona naturae, quae hic participamus ab ipso; alia quantum ad beatitudinem, inquantum nos hic sumus participes per gratiam supernae felicitatis, secundum quod hic est possibile, speramus etiam ad perfectam consecutionem illius aeternae beatitudinis pervenire et fieri cives caelestis Ierusalem. Et secundum primam communicationem ad Deum, est amicitia naturalis secundum quam unumquodque, secundum quod

created species in the soul is more distant from the divine essence than the species of a horse or whiteness from the essence of an angel. Hence, to suppose that God is seen only by a likeness or through some brilliance of his clarity is to suppose that the divine essence is not seen.

Furthermore, since the soul is a certain likeness of God, that vision would not be more mirror-like or enigmatic, which it is in this life, than clear and open vision, which is promised to the saints in glory and in which will consist our beatitude. Hence Augustine says in a Gloss that a vision of God through a likeness pertains to a vision in a mirror and enigma.

It would also follow that man's final beatitude would be in something other than God; which is alien to the faith. Even man's natural desire, which is to arrive at the first cause of things and of knowing him in himself, would be in vain.

804. He continues: *now I know in part*. Here he proves in particular what he had proved in general about knowledge of himself, saying: *now*, i.e., in the present life, I, Paul, *know in part*, i.e., obscurely and imperfectly, *but then*, namely, in heaven, *I shall know even as I am known*. Just as God knows my essence, so I shall know God through his essence, so that the *as* does not imply equality of knowledge but only similarity.

805. Then he infers the principal conclusion, when he says: *and now there remain*.

But the reason he does not mention all the gifts but only three is that these three join to God; the others do not join to God, except through the mediation of those three; also the other gifts dispose for the birth of those three in the hearts of men. Hence, too, only those three, namely, faith, hope and charity, are called theological virtues, because they have God for their immediate object.

806. But since the gifts exist for perfecting the affections or intellect, and charity perfects the affections, and faith the intellect, it does not seem that hope is necessary but superfluous.

The answer is that love is a unitive force and all love consists in some union. Hence according to the various unions, the various species of friendship are distinguished by the Philosopher.

Now we have a twofold union with God: one refers to the goods of nature, which we partake of here from him; the other refers to beatitude, inasmuch as through grace we partake here of heavenly felicity, as far as it is possible here. We also hope to arrive at the perfect attainment of that eternal beatitude and become citizens of the heavenly Jerusalem. According to the first communication with God there is a natural friendship, according to which each one, inasmuch as he is, seeks and desires as his end God as first

est, Deum ut causam primam et summum bonum appetit et desiderat, ut finem suum. Secundum vero communicationem secundam est amor caritatis, qua solum creatura intellectualis Deum diligit.

Quia vero nihil potest amari nisi sit cognitum, ideo ad amorem caritatis exigitur primo cognitio Dei. Et quia hoc est supra naturam, primo exigitur fides, quae est non apparentium. Secundo ne homo deficiat, vel aberret, exigitur spes, per quam tendat in illum finem, sicut ad se pertinentem. Et de his tribus dicitur Eccli. II, 8: *qui timetis Deum, credite in illum*, quantum ad fidem; *qui timetis Deum, sperate in illum*, quantum ad spem; *qui timetis Deum, diligite eum*, quantum ad caritatem.

Ista ergo tria manent nunc, sed caritas maior est omnibus, propter ea quae dicta sunt supra.

cause and supreme being. According to the second communication there is the love of charity, by which only an intellectual creature loves God.

But because nothing can loved unless it is known, for the love of charity a knowledge of God is first required. And because this is above nature, there is required, first of all, faith which is concerned with things not seen. Second, in order that a man not fail or fall away, hope is required through which he tends to that end as pertaining to himself. Concerning these three it is said: *you who fear the Lord, believe in him*, as to faith; *you who fear the Lord, hope in him*, as to hope; *you who fear the Lord, love him* (Sir 2:8), as to charity.

Therefore, these three remain now, but charity is greater than the others for the reasons indicated above.

CHAPTER 14

Lecture 1

14:1Sectamini caritatem, aemulamini spiritualia: magis autem ut prophetetis. [n. 807]

14:2Qui enim loquitur lingua, non hominibus loquitur, sed Deo: nemo enim audit. Spiritu autem loquitur mysteria. [n. 817]

14:3Nam qui prophetat, hominibus loquitur ad aedificationem, et exhortationem, et consolationem. [n. 818]

14:4Qui loquitur lingua, semetipsum aedificat: qui autem prophetat, Ecclesiam Dei aedificat. [n. 819]

14:1Διώκετε τὴν ἀγάπην, ζηλοῦτε δὲ τὰ πνευματικά, μᾶλλον δὲ ἵνα προφητεύητε.

14:2ὁ γὰρ λαλῶν γλώσσῃ οὐκ ἀνθρώποις λαλεῖ ἀλλὰ θεῷ, οὐδεὶς γὰρ ἀκούει, πνεύματι δὲ λαλεῖ μυστήρια:

14:3ὁ δὲ προφητεύων ἀνθρώποις λαλεῖ οἰκοδομὴν καὶ παράκλησιν καὶ παραμυθίαν.

14:4ὁ λαλῶν γλώσσῃ ἑαυτὸν οἰκοδομεῖ: ὁ δὲ προφητεύων ἐκκλησίαν οἰκοδομεῖ.

14:1Follow after charity, be zealous for spiritual gifts; but rather that you may prophesy. [n. 807]

14:2For he who speaks in a tongue speaks not unto men, but unto God: for no man hears. Yet by the Spirit he speaks mysteries. [n. 817]

14:3But he who prophesies speaks to men unto edification and exhortation and comfort. [n. 818]

14:4He who speaks in a tongue edifies himself: but he who prophesies, edifies the Church. [n. 819]

---

807. Posita excellentia caritatis ad alia dona, hic consequenter apostolus comparat alia dona ad invicem, ostendens excellentiam prophetiae ad donum linguarum.

Et circa hoc duo facit.

Primo ostendit excellentiam prophetiae ad donum linguarum;

secundo quomodo sit utendum dono linguarum, et prophetiae, ibi *quid ergo est, fratres*, et cetera.

808. Circa primum duo facit.

Primo ostendit, quod donum prophetiae est excellentius, quam donum linguarum, rationibus sumptis ex parte infidelium,

secundo ex parte fidelium, ibi *fratres mei*, et cetera.

Prima pars dividitur in duas.

Primo ostendit, quod donum prophetiae est excellentius dono linguarum, quantum ad usum eorum in exhortationibus seu praedicationibus;

secundo quantum ad usum linguarum, qui est in orando. Ad haec enim duo est usus linguae, ibi *et ideo loquitur*, et cetera.

808. Circa primum duo facit. Primo enim praemittit unum, per quod continuat se ad sequentia, et hoc est quod dicit: dictum est, quod caritas omnia dona excellit, si ergo ita est, *sectamini*, scilicet viribus, *caritatem*, quae est dulce et salubre vinculum mentium. I Petr. IV, 8: *ante omnia caritatem*, et cetera. Col. III, 14: *super omnia autem caritatem habete*, et cetera.

807. Having stated that charity excels the other gifts, the Apostle then compares the other gifts to each other, showing the excellence of prophecy over the gift of tongues.

In regard to this he does two things:

first, he shows that prophecy excels the gift of tongues;

second, how the gifts of tongues and prophecy should be used, at *how is it then, brethren?* (1 Cor 14:26).

808. In regard to the first he does two things:

first, he shows that the gift of prophecy is more excellent than the gift of tongues with reasons taken on the part of unbelievers;

second, on the part of believers, at *brethren, do not become children* (1 Cor 14:20).

The first part is divided into two:

first, he shows that the gift of prophecy is more excellent than the gift of tongues as to their use in exhortations or sermons;

second, as to the use of tongues in praying. For the use of the tongue is ordained to these two, at *and therefore he who speaks* (1 Cor 14:13).

808. In regard to the first he does two things: first, he mentions one thing by which he connects the preceding to the following; and this is what he says: it has been stated that charity excels all the gifts; if, therefore, that is so, *follow after charity*, for it is a sweet and healthful bond of minds: *above all, hold unfailing your love for one another* (1 Pet 4:8); *above all these things put on love which is the bond of perfection* (Col 3:4).

809. Secundo subdit illud per quod continuat se ad sequentia. Et hoc est quod dicit *aemulamini*, et cetera. Quasi dicat: licet caritas sit maior omnibus donis, tamen alia non sunt contemnenda. Sed *aemulamini*, *id est ferventer ametis*, *spiritualia dona* Spiritus Sancti. I Petr. III, 13: *quid est, quod vobis noceat, et cetera.*

810. Licet autem aemulatio quandoque sumatur pro ferventi dilectione, quandoque pro invidia, tamen non est aequivocatio; imo unum procedit ab alio; zelari enim et aemulari designat ferventem amorem alicuius rei.

Contingit autem quod res amata ita diligatur ferventer ab aliquo, quod non patitur sibi consortem, sed ipse vult eam solus et singulariter. Et iste est zelus, qui secundum quosdam est amor intensus, non patiens consortium in amato. Hoc tamen contingit in spiritualibus, quae possunt perfectissime a multis participari, sed solum in illis quae non possunt a multis participari. Unde in caritate non est huiusmodi zelus non patiens consortium in amato, sed tantum in corporalibus, in quibus provenit, quod si aliquis habet illud quod ipse zelat, doleat: et ex hoc consurgit aemulatio, quae est invidia. Sicut si ego amo dignitatem seu divitias, doleo quod aliquis habet eas, unde et ei invideo. Et sic patet, quod ex zelo surgit invidia.

Cum ergo dicitur *aemulamini spiritualia*, non intelligitur de invidia, quia spiritualia possunt a multis haberi, sed dicit, *aemulamini*, ut inducat ad ferventer amandum Deum.

811. Et quia inter spiritualia est gradus quidam, quia prophetia excedit donum linguarum, ideo dicit *magis autem, ut prophetetis*, quasi dicat: inter spiritualia magis aemulamini donum prophetiae. I Thess. V, v. 19 s.: *Spiritum nolite extinguere, prophetias nolite spernere.*

812. Ad explanationem autem totius capitis praenotanda sunt tria, scilicet quid sit prophetia, quot modis dicatur in Scriptura sancta prophetia et quid sit loqui linguis.

Circa primum sciendum est, quod propheta dicitur, quasi procul videns, et secundum quosdam dicitur a *for faris*, sed melius dicitur a *pharos*, quod est videre. Unde I Reg. c. IX, 9 dicitur, quod *qui nunc dicitur propheta, olim videns dicebatur*. Unde visio eorum quae sunt procul, sive sint futura contingentia, sive supra rationem nostram, dicitur prophetia. Est igitur prophetia visio seu manifestatio futurorum contingentium, seu intellectum humanum excedentium.

Ad huiusmodi autem visionem quatuor requiruntur. Cum enim cognitio nostra sit per corporalia et per phantasmata a sensibilibus accepta, primo exigitur quod in imaginatione formentur similitudines corporales eorum quae ostenduntur, ut Dionysius dicit quod impossibile

809. Second, he adds that through which he connects himself with what follows. And this is what he says: *be zealous for spiritual gifts*. As if to say: although charity is greater than all gifts, nevertheless the others are not to be despised. *Be zealous for spiritual gifts*, i.e., *fervently love the spiritual gifts* of the Holy Spirit: *now who is there to harm you, if you are zealous for what is right?* (1 Pet 3:13).

810. Although earnest desire is sometimes taken for fervent love and sometimes for envy, it is not equivocation; indeed, one proceeds from the other. For to be zealous and to be earnestly desirous designate a fervent love for something.

It happens, however, that the thing loved is loved so fervently by someone that he does not permit a sharer, but wants it alone and by himself. And this is zeal which, according to some, is intense love not allowing a participation in the one loved. Yet this occurs not in spiritual things, which can be shared most perfectly by others, but only in those which cannot be shared by many. Hence in charity there is not this sort of zeal which does not allow a participation in the one loved, but only in bodily things, in which it comes about that if anyone else has that for which I am zealous, I am sad; and from this arises earnest desire, which is envy. Just as if I love dignity or riches, I grieve if someone else has them; hence I envy him. And so it is clear that from zeal arises envy.

Therefore, when it is said: *be zealous for spiritual gifts*, it is not understood of envy, because spiritual things can be possessed by many; but he says: *be zealous* to induce them to love God fervently.

811. And because among spiritual things there is a gradation, for prophecy exceeds the gift of tongues, he says: *but rather that you may prophesy*. As if to say: among spiritual gifts be more zealous for the gift of prophecy: *do not quench the Spirit; do not despise prophesying* (1 Thess 5:19ff).

812. To explain the entire chapter, three things must be mentioned beforehand, namely, what is prophecy, in how many ways is prophecy mentioned in Scripture, and what it is to speak in tongues.

In regard to the first it should be noted that prophecy is said to be 'seeing from afar', and according to some it is named after 'speaking afar', but it is better to say that it is from *pharos*, which is 'to see'. Hence it is said: *he who is now called a prophet was formerly called a seer* (1 Sam 9:9). Hence the sight of things far off, whether they be future contingents or beyond human reason, is called prophecy. Prophecy, therefore, is the sight or manifestation of future contingents or of things transcending human understanding.

For such a sight four things are required. For since our knowledge is through bodily things and phantasms received from sensible things, it is first required that in the imagination be formed the bodily likeness of things which are shown, as Dionysius says that it is impossible otherwise

est aliter lucere nobis divinum radium, nisi varietate sacrorum velaminum circumvelatum.

Secundum quod exigitur est lumen intellectuale illuminans intellectum ad ea quae supra naturalem cognitionem nostram ostenduntur cognoscenda. Nisi enim ad similitudines sensibiles in imaginatione formatas intelligendas adsit lumen intellectuale, ille cui similitudines huiusmodi ostenduntur, non dicitur propheta, sed potius somniator. Sicut Pharao, qui licet viderit spicas et vaccas, quae erant indicativa futurorum quorumdam, quia tamen non intellexit quod vidit, non dicitur propheta, sed potius ille, scilicet Ioseph, qui interpretatus est. Et similiter est de Nabuchodonosor, qui vidit statuam, et non intellexit, unde nec propheta dicitur, sed Daniel. Et propter hoc dicitur, Dan. X, 1: *intelligentia opus est in visione.*

Tertium quod exigitur, est audacia ad annuntiandum ea quae revelantur. Ad hoc enim Deus revelat, ut aliis denuntientur. Ier. I, 9: *ecce dedi verba mea in ore.*

Quartum est operatio miraculorum, quae sunt ad certitudinem prophetiae. Nisi enim facerent aliqua, quae excedunt operationem naturae, non crederetur eis in his, quae naturalem cognitionem transcendunt.

813. Secundum ergo hos modos prophetiae, dicuntur aliqui diversis modis prophetae. Aliquando enim aliquis dicitur propheta, qui habet omnia ista quatuor, scilicet quod videt imaginarias visiones, et habet intelligentiam de eis, et audacter annuntiat aliis, et operatur miracula, et de hoc dicitur Num. XII, 6: *si quis fuerit inter vos propheta*, et cetera.

Aliquando autem dicitur propheta ille, qui habet solas imaginarias visiones, sed tamen improprie et valde remote.

Aliquando etiam dicitur propheta, qui habet intellectuale lumen ad explanandum etiam visiones imaginarias, sive sibi, sive alteri factas, vel ad exponendum dicta prophetarum, vel Scripturas apostolorum. Et sic dicitur propheta omnis qui discernit doctorum Scripturas, quia eodem spiritu interpretatae sunt quo editae sunt. Et sic Salomon et David possunt dici prophetae, inquantum habuerunt lumen intellectuale, ad clare et subtiliter intuendum; nam visio David intellectualis tantum fuit.

Dicitur etiam propheta aliquis solum ex hoc quod prophetarum dicta denuntiat, seu exponit, seu cantat in ecclesia, et hoc modo dicitur I Reg. XIX, 24 quod Saul erat inter prophetas, id est, inter canentes dicta prophetarum.

Dicitur etiam aliquis propheta ex miraculorum operatione, secundum illud Eccli. c. XLVIII, 14, quod *corpus Elisei mortuum prophetavit*, id est, miraculum fecit.

for the divine ray to shine in us, unless surrounded by the variety of sacred veils.

The second thing required is an intellectual light enlightening the intellect for knowing things shown beyond our natural knowledge. For unless an intellectual light be present for understanding the sensible likenesses formed in the imagination, the one to whom these likenesses are shown in not called a prophet but a dreamer. Thus, Pharaoh, who, although he saw ears of corn and cattle, which indicated future events, did not understand what he saw, is not called a prophet, but rather Joseph, who interpreted it. The same is true of Nebuchadnezzar, who saw a statue but did not understand it; hence, neither is he a prophet, but Daniel. For this reason it is said: *understanding is needed in a vision* (Dan 10:1).

The third thing required is the courage to announce the things revealed. For God reveals in order that it be announced to others: *behold, I have put my words in your mouth* (Jer 1:9).

The fourth thing is the working of miracles, which lend certitude to the prophecy. For unless they did things which exceed the works of nature, they would not be believed in matters that transcend natural knowledge.

813. Therefore, according to these modes of prophecy some are called prophets in various ways. For sometimes one is called a prophet, because he possesses all four, namely, that he sees imaginary visions, and has an understanding of them and he boldly announces to others and he works miracles. Concerning such a one it is said: *if there is a prophet among you, I, the Lord, will appear to him in a dream, or will speak to him by means of a dream* (Num 12:6).

But sometimes one who has solely imaginary visions is called a prophet, but in an improper sense and very remotely so.

Again, one is called a prophet, if he has the intellectual light to explain even imaginary visions made to himself or someone else, or for explaining the sayings of the prophets or the Scriptures of the apostles. In this way a prophet is anyone who discerns the writings of the doctors, because they have been interpreted in the same spirit as they were edited; and so Solomon and David can be called prophets, inasmuch as they had the intellectual light to understand clearly and subtly. For the vision of David was intellectual only.

Someone is even called a prophet merely because he announces the statements of prophets or explains them or sings in the church. This is the way Saul was counted among the prophets, i.e., among those singing the words of the prophets (1 Sam 19:24).

Someone is also called a prophet from working miracles: *the dead body of Elijah prophesied* (Sir 48:14), i.e., worked a miracle.

Quod ergo dicit hic apostolus per totum caput de prophetis, intelligendum est de secundo modo, scilicet quod ille dicitur prophetare, qui per lumen intellectuale divinum, visiones sibi et aliis factas exponit. Et secundum hoc planum erit, quod hic dicitur de prophetis.

814. Circa secundum sciendum est, quod quia in Ecclesia primitiva pauci erant quibus imminebat fidem Christi praedicare per mundum, ideo Dominus, ut commodius et pluribus verbum Dei annuntiarent, dedit eis donum linguarum, quibus omnibus praedicarent. Non quod una lingua loquentes ab omnibus intelligerentur, ut quidam dicunt, sed, ad litteram, quod linguis diversarum gentium, imo omnium loquerentur. Unde dicit apostolus *gratias ago Deo, quod omnium vestrum lingua loquor*. Et Act. II, 4 dicitur: *loquebantur variis linguis*, et cetera. Et hoc donum multi adepti sunt a Deo in Ecclesia primitiva. Corinthii autem, quia curiosi erant, ideo libentius volebant illud donum, quam donum prophetiae.

Quod ergo dicitur hic loqui lingua, vult apostolus intelligi lingua ignota, et non explanata, sicut si lingua Theutonica loquatur quis alicui Gallico, et non exponat, hic loquitur lingua. Vel etiam si loquatur visiones tantum, et non exponat, loquitur lingua. Unde omnis locutio non intellecta, nec explanata, quaecumque sit illa, est proprie loqui lingua.

815. His ergo visis ad expositionem litterae accedamus, quae plana est.

Circa hoc ergo duo facit.

Primo probat, quod donum prophetiae excellentius est dono linguarum;

secundo excludit quamdam obiectionem, ibi *volo autem vos*, et cetera.

816. Quod autem donum prophetiae excedat donum linguarum, probat duabus rationibus, quarum prima sumitur ex comparatione Dei ad Ecclesiam; secunda ratio sumitur ex comparatione hominum ad Ecclesiam.

817. Prima autem ratio talis est: illud per quod facit homo ea non solum quae sunt ad honorem Dei sed etiam ad utilitatem proximorum est melius, quam illud quod fit tantum ad honorem Dei; sed prophetia est non tantum ad honorem Dei sed etiam ad proximi utilitatem, per donum vero linguarum solum illud fit quod est ad honorem Dei; ergo, et cetera.

Huius autem rationis ponit medium, et primo quantum ad hoc quod dicit, quod qui loquitur lingua, honorat tantum Deum. Et hoc est quod dicit *qui loquitur lingua*, scilicet ignota, *non loquitur hominibus*, id est, ad intellectum hominum, *sed Deo*, id est, ad honorem Dei tantum. Vel *Deo*, quia ipse Deus solus intelligit. Sap. I, 10: *auris zeli Dei audit omnia*, et cetera.

Therefore, what the Apostle says through this chapter of the prophets must be understood in the second mode, namely, that one is said to prophesy who through a divine intellectual light explains visions made to him and others. According to this, what is said here about prophets will be plain.

814. In regard to the second it should be noted that because there were few in the early Church assigned to preaching faith of Christ throughout the world, the Lord enabled them to proclaim the word to more people by giving them the gift of tongues, by which they could all preach to all. Not that they spoke in one language and were understood by all, as some say, but that they spoke the languages of different nations and, indeed, of all. Hence the Apostle says: *I thank my God I speak with all your tongues* (1 Cor 14:18), and it is said: *they began to speak in other tongues, as the Spirit gave them utterance* (Acts 2:4). Furthermore, many received this gift from God in the early Church. But the Corinthians, being inquisitive, were more desirous of this gift than the gift of prophecy.

Therefore, when the Apostle mentions here about speaking in a tongue, he means an unknown language not interpreted; as when one might speak German to a Frenchman without an interpreter, he is speaking in a tongue. Hence, all speech not understood not explained, no matter what it is, is properly called speaking in a tongue.

815. Having mentioned these things, let us return to the text, which is clear.

In regard to this he does two things:

first, he proves that the gift of prophecy is greater than the gift of tongues;

second, he excludes an objection, at *and I would have you all to speak* (1 Cor 14:5).

816. That the gift of prophecy is more excellent than the gift of tongues he proves with two reasons: the first is based on the relationship of God with the Church; the second on the relationship of men with the Church.

817. The first reason is this: that through which man does things which are not only for the glory of God but for the benefit of his neighbors is better than that which is done only for the glory of God. But prophecy is not only for the honor of God but also useful to our neighbor, whereas by the gift of tongues something is done solely for the honor of God.

He presents the middle term of this reasoning: first, inasmuch as he says that one who speaks in a tongue only honors God. And this is what he says: *he who speaks in a tongue speaks not unto men*, i.e., not to the human intellect, *but unto God*, i.e., only to the honor of God. Or *unto God*, because God alone understands: *the zealous ear of God hears all things* (Wis 1:10).

Et quod non loquatur homini, subdit *nemo enim audit*, id est intelligit. Sic enim frequenter accipitur, non audire, pro non intelligere. Matth. XIII, 9: *qui habet aures audiendi, audiat.*

Quare autem soli Deo loquatur, subdit quod ipse Deus loquitur. Unde dicit *Spiritus autem Dei loquitur mysteria*, id est occulta. Matth. X, 20: *non enim vos estis, qui loquimini*, et cetera. Supra II, 11: *nemo novit quae sunt Spiritus Dei*, et cetera.

818. Secundo probat id quod dicit, quod prophetia est ad honorem Dei et utilitatem proximorum. Unde dicit *nam qui prophetat*, etc., id est explanat visiones seu Scripturas, *loquitur hominibus*, id est ad intellectum hominum, et hoc *ad aedificationem* incipientium, et ad *exhortationem* proficientium. I Thess. V, 14: *consolamini, pusillanimes*. Tit. II, 15: *loquere et exhortare*, et ad *consolationem* desolatorum.

Vel aedificatio pertinet ad spiritualem affectionem, quia ibi primo incipit aedificium spirituale. Eph. II, 22: *in quo et vos coaedificamini*, et cetera. Exhortatio vero ad inductionem ad bonos actus, quia si affectus est bonus, tunc actus est bonus. Tit. II, 15: *haec loquere et exhortare*. Consolatio vero inducit ad tolerantiam malorum. Rom. XV, 4: *quaecumque scripta sunt, ad nostram doctrinam scripta sunt.*

Ad haec enim tria inducunt praedicantes divinam Scripturam.

819. Secunda ratio talis est: illud quod est utile soli facienti est minus quam illud quod prodest etiam aliis; loqui autem linguis est utile soli ei qui loquitur, prophetare vero aliis prodest; igitur, et cetera.

Huius autem rationis ponit medium, et primo quantum ad primam partem medii, et hoc est quod dicit *qui loquitur lingua, semetipsum*, et cetera. Ps. XXXVIII, 4: *concaluit cor meum intra me*, et cetera. Secundo quantum ad secundam partem, et hoc est quod dicit *qui autem prophetat, Ecclesiam*, id est fideles, *aedificat* instruendo. Eph. II, 20: *superaedificati supra fundamentum apostolorum et prophetarum.*

That he does not speak to man is indicated when he says: *for no man hears*, i.e., understands. For it often happens that not to hear means not to understand: *he who has ears to hear, let him hear* (Matt 13:9).

Why he speaks only to God he indicates, when he says that God himself is speaking; hence he says: *yet by the Spirit he speaks mysteries*, i.e., hidden things: *for it is not you who speak, but the Spirit of your Father* (Matt 10:20); *no one understands the thoughts of God except the Spirit of God* (1 Cor 2:11).

818. Second, he proves his statement that prophecy is for the honor of God and the benefit of our neighbors. Hence he says, *he who prophesies*, i.e., explains visions or Scriptures, *speaks to men*, i.e., to the human intellect *unto edification* of beginners and encouragement of the proficient and the *exhortation* of the desolate. *Comfort the fainthearted* (1 Thess 5:14); *speak and persuade* (Titus 2:15), and for the *comfort* of the desolate.

Or edification pertains to spiritual affection, because one's spiritual edifice first begins there: *in whom you are also built into it* (Eph 2:22). But exhortation pertains to inducement to good acts, because if the will is good, then the act is good: *declare and exhort these things* (Titus 2:15). Consolation on the other hand induces one to tolerate evils: *whatever was written in former days was written for our instruction* (Rom 15:4).

Those who preach the divine Scriptures induce people to these three things.

819. The second reason is this: that which is useful only to the doer is less than that which also profits others. But to speak in tongues is useful only to the speaker, whereas to prophesy benefits others.

He presents the middle term of this reasoning: first, in regard to its first part and he says: *he who speaks in a tongue edifies himself: my heart became hot within me* (Ps 39:3). Second, in regard to the second part he says: *but he who prophecies edifies the church*, i.e., believers, by instructing them: *built upon the foundation of the apostles and prophets* (Eph 2:20).

Lecture 2

14:5Volo autem omnes vos loqui linguis: magis autem prophetare. Nam major est qui prophetat, quam qui loquitur linguis; nisi forte interpretetur ut Ecclesia aedificationem accipiat. [n. 820]

14:6Nunc autem, fratres, si venero ad vos linguis loquens: quid vobis prodero, nisi vobis loquar aut in revelatione, aut in scientia, aut in prophetia, aut in doctrina? [n. 823]

14:7Tamen quae sine anima sunt vocem dantia, sive tibia, sive cithara; nisi distinctionem sonituum dederint, quomodo scietur id quod canitur, aut quod citharizatur? [n. 827]

14:8Etenim si incertam vocem det tuba, quis parabit se ad bellum? [n. 829]

14:9Ita et vos per linguam nisi manifestum sermonem dederitis: quomodo scietur id quod dicitur? eritis enim in aëra loquentes.

14:10Tam multa, ut puta genera linguarum sunt in hoc mundo: et nihil sine voce est. [n. 830]

14:11Si ergo nesciero virtutem vocis, ero ei, cui loquor, barbarus: et qui loquitur, mihi barbarus. [n. 832]

14:12Sic et vos, quoniam aemulatores estis spirituum, ad aedificationem Ecclesiae quaerite ut abundetis. [n. 833]

14:5θέλω δὲ πάντας ὑμᾶς λαλεῖν γλώσσαις, μᾶλλον δὲ ἵνα προφητεύητε· μείζων δὲ ὁ προφητεύων ἢ ὁ λαλῶν γλώσσαις, ἐκτὸς εἰ μὴ διερμηνεύῃ, ἵνα ἡ ἐκκλησία οἰκοδομὴν λάβῃ.

14:6Νῦν δέ, ἀδελφοί, ἐὰν ἔλθω πρὸς ὑμᾶς γλώσσαις λαλῶν, τί ὑμᾶς ὠφελήσω, ἐὰν μὴ ὑμῖν λαλήσω ἢ ἐν ἀποκαλύψει ἢ ἐν γνώσει ἢ ἐν προφητείᾳ ἢ [ἐν] διδαχῇ;

14:7ὅμως τὰ ἄψυχα φωνὴν διδόντα, εἴτε αὐλὸς εἴτε κιθάρα, ἐὰν διαστολὴν τοῖς φθόγγοις μὴ δῷ, πῶς γνωσθήσεται τὸ αὐλούμενον ἢ τὸ κιθαριζόμενον;

14:8καὶ γὰρ ἐὰν ἄδηλον σάλπιγξ φωνὴν δῷ, τίς παρασκευάσεται εἰς πόλεμον;

14:9οὕτως καὶ ὑμεῖς διὰ τῆς γλώσσης ἐὰν μὴ εὔσημον λόγον δῶτε, πῶς γνωσθήσεται τὸ λαλούμενον; ἔσεσθε γὰρ εἰς ἀέρα λαλοῦντες.

14:10τοσαῦτα εἰ τύχοι γένη φωνῶν εἰσιν ἐν κόσμῳ, καὶ οὐδὲν ἄφωνον·

14:11ἐὰν οὖν μὴ εἰδῶ τὴν δύναμιν τῆς φωνῆς, ἔσομαι τῷ λαλοῦντι βάρβαρος καὶ ὁ λαλῶν ἐν ἐμοὶ βάρβαρος.

14:12οὕτως καὶ ὑμεῖς, ἐπεὶ ζηλωταί ἐστε πνευμάτων, πρὸς τὴν οἰκοδομὴν τῆς ἐκκλησίας ζητεῖτε ἵνα περισσεύητε.

14:5And I would have you all to speak with tongues, but more to prophesy. For greater is he who prophesies than he who speaks with tongues: unless perhaps he interprets, that the Church may receive edification. [n. 820]

14:6But now, brethren, if I come to you speaking with tongues, what shall I profit you, unless I speak to you either in revelation or in knowledge or in prophecy or in doctrine? [n. 823]

14:7Even things without life that give sound, whether pipe or harp, except they give a distinction of sounds, how shall it be known what is piped or harped? [n. 827]

14:8For if the trumpet gives an uncertain sound, who shall prepare himself to the battle? [n. 829]

14:9So likewise you, except you utter by the tongue plain speech, how shall it be known what is said? For you shall be speaking into the air.

14:10There are, for example, so many kinds of tongues in this world: and none is without voice. [n. 830]

14:11If then I know not the power of the voice, I shall be to him to whom I speak a barbarian: and he who speaks a barbarian to me. [n. 832]

14:12So you also, forasmuch as you are zealous of spirits, seek to abound unto the edifying of the Church. [n. 833]

---

820. Hic apostolus excludit obiectionem seu falsum intellectum, qui posset esse circa praemissa. Possent enim aliqui credere, quod ex quo apostolus praefert prophetiam dono linguarum, quod donum linguarum esset contemnendum. Unde, ut hoc excludat, dicit *volo autem vos*, et cetera. Ubi

    primo ostendit, quid intenderit insinuare;

    secundo rationem horum assignat, ibi *nam maior*, et cetera.

821. Dicit ergo: licet haec, quae dicta sunt supra, dixerim, non tamen volo vos donum linguarum spernere,

820. Here the Apostle excludes an objection or false understanding, which could occur in respect to the foregoing. For some might believe that since the Apostle prefers prophecy to the gift of tongues, the latter should be scorned. Hence, to exclude this he says: *and I would have you all*, where

    he first shows what he intends to insinuate;

    second, he gives the reason, at *for greater is he*.

821. He says, therefore: although I said the things stated above, I do not wish to spurn the gift of tongues, but *I would*

sed *volo vos omnes loqui linguis*, tamen *magis volo ut prophetetis*. Num. XI, 29: *quis tribuat ut omnis populus*, et cetera.

822. Cuius rationem assignat, cum dicit *nam maior*, etc., quasi dicat: ideo volo ut magis prophetetis, quia *maior est*, et cetera.

Et huius ratio est, quia aliquando aliqui moventur a Spiritu Sancto loqui aliquid mysticum, quod ipsi non intelligunt; unde isti habent donum linguarum. Aliquando autem non solum loquuntur linguis, sed etiam ea, quae dicunt, interpretantur. Et ideo dicit *nisi forte interpretetur*.

Nam donum linguarum cum interpretatione est melius quam prophetia; quia, sicut dictum est, interpretatio cuiuscumque ardui pertinet ad prophetiam. Unde qui loquitur et qui interpretatur propheta est et donum linguarum habet, et interpretatur, ut Ecclesiam Dei aedificet; ideo dicit *ut Ecclesia*, etc., id est non solum intelligat se, sed etiam ut Ecclesia aedificetur. Rom. XIV, 19: *quae aedificationis sunt invicem custodiamus*. Et Rom. XV, v. 2: *unusquisque proximo suo placeat in bonum ad aedificationem*.

823. *Nunc autem, fratres*, et cetera. Hic probat donum prophetiae esse excellentius quam donum linguarum, per exempla, et hoc tripliciter.

Primo per exemplum a seipso sumptum;

secundo per exemplum sumptum a rebus inanimatis, ibi *tamen quae sine anima*, etc.;

tertio per exemplum sumptum ab hominibus diversimode loquentibus, ibi *tam multa*, et cetera.

824. Ex seipso autem argumentatur sic: constat ergo quod ego non minus habeo donum linguarum quam vos; sed si loquerer vobis solum linguis, et non interpretarer, nihil vobis prodessem. Ergo nec vos ab invicem.

Et hoc est quod dicit *nunc autem, fratres, si venero ad vos linguis loquens*. Hoc dupliciter potest intelligi, scilicet vel linguis ignotis, vel, ad litteram, quibuscumque signis non intellectis.

825. *Quid vobis prodero, nisi loquar vobis aut in revelatione*, et cetera.

Ubi notandum quod ista quatuor, scilicet *aut in revelatione*, etc., possunt dupliciter distingui.

Uno modo penes ea de quibus sunt. Et sic sciendum est, quod illustratio mentis ad cognoscendum, est de quatuor, quia vel est de divinis, et haec illustratio pertinet ad donum sapientiae. Divinorum enim, ut supra dictum est II, 11 est revelatio, quia, *quae sunt Dei, nemo*

have you all to speak with tongues, but *more to prophesy*: *would that the Lord's people were prophets* (Num 11:29).

822. He assigns the reason for this when he says: *for greater is he who prophecies*. As if to say: the reason I wish that you would prophesy more is that it is *greater*.

The reason for this is that some are sometimes moved by the Holy Spirit to speak something mystical, which they do not understand. Hence, they have the gift of tongues. But sometimes they not only speak in tongues, but also interpret what they say. Hence he says: *unless perhaps he interprets*.

For the gift of tongues with interpretation is better than prophecy, because as has been said, the interpretation of anything arduous pertains to prophecy. Hence, one who speaks and interprets is a prophet and has the gift of tongues, and he interprets in order to edify the Church. Hence he says, *that the Church may receive edification*, i.e., that he not only understand himself but also edify the Church: *let us pursue what makes for mutual edification* (Rom 14:19); *let each of you please the neighbor for his good to edify him* (Rom 15:2).

823. Then when he says: *now, brethren*, he proves by examples that the gift of prophecy is more excellent than the gift of tongues, and this in three ways:

first, by giving an example taken from himself;

second, by an example taken from inanimate things, at *even things without life*;

third by an example taken from men speaking different language, at *there are, for example*.

824. Using himself as an example he argues this: consequently, it is clear that I do not have the gift of tongues less than you. But if I were to speak to you only in tongues and did not interpret, you would not profit at all. Therefore, neither would you from one another.

And this is what he says: *now brethren, if I come to you speaking with tongues*. This can be understood in two ways, namely, either by an unknown language, or literally, by whatever sign that is not understood.

825. *What shall I profit you, unless I speak to you either in revelation or in knowledge or in prophecy or in doctrine?*

It should be noted that those four things, namely, *revelation, knowledge, prophecy, doctrine*, can be distinguished in two ways:

in one way according to the things they concern. In this way, it should be noted that the illumination of the mind for understanding concerns four things, because it is either about divine things, and this illumination of the mind pertains to the gift of wisdom. For, as was stated

novit, et cetera. Et ideo dicit *in revelatione*, qua scilicet illuminatur mens ad cognoscendum divina.

Vel est de terrenis, et non de quibuscumque, sed de illis tantum, quae sunt ad aedificationem fidei, et hoc pertinet ad donum scientiae, et ideo dicit *in scientia*, non geometriae, nec astrologiae, quia haec non pertinent ad aedificationem fidei, sed in scientia quae est sanctorum. Sap. X, 10: *dedit illi scientiam sanctorum*, et cetera.

Vel est de eventibus futurorum, et hoc pertinet ad donum prophetiae; et ideo dicit *aut in prophetia*. Sap. VIII, 8: *signa et monstra scit antequam fiant, et eventus temporum et saeculorum*.

Notandum autem quod prophetia non accipitur hic communiter, scilicet secundum quod supra dictum est, sed accipitur hic particulariter prout est manifestatio futurorum tantum. Et secundum hoc diffinitur a Cassiodoro: *prophetia est divina inspiratio rerum futura immobili veritate denuntians*. Eccli. XXIV, 46: *adhuc doctrinam quasi prophetiam effundam*, et cetera.

Vel est de agendis moralibus, et hoc pertinet ad doctrinam; et ideo dicit *aut in doctrina*. Rom. XII, 7: *qui docet in doctrina*. Prov. XIII, 15: *doctrina bona dabit gratiam*.

826. Alio modo possunt haec distingui penes diversos modos acquirendi cognitionem.

Et sic sciendum est quod omnis cognitio aut est a supernaturali principio, scilicet Deo, aut naturali, scilicet lumine naturali intellectus nostri.

Si autem a supernaturali principio, scilicet lumine divino infuso, hoc potest esse dupliciter, quia aut infunditur subito cognitio, et sic est revelatio; aut infunditur successive, et sic est prophetia, quam non subito habuerunt prophetae, sed successive et per partes, ut eorum prophetiae ostendunt.

Si vero cognitio acquiratur a naturali principio, hoc est aut per studium proprium, et sic pertinet ad scientiam; aut traditur ab alio, et sic pertinet ad doctrinam.

827. *Tamen quae sine anima*, et cetera. Hic ostendit idem per exempla sumpta ex rebus inanimatis, scilicet per instrumenta quae videntur vocem habere. Et

primo per instrumenta gaudii;

secundo per instrumenta pugnae, ibi *etenim si incertam*, et cetera.

828. Dicit ergo: hoc non solum patet per ea quae supra dicta sunt, sed etiam quantum ad ea, quae sine anima vocem dant, quod loqui linguis non solum non prodest aliis. Et *quae sine anima sunt vocem dantia*.

above, revelation is concerned with divine things, because *the things of God no one knows except the Spirit of God* (1 Cor 2:11). Therefore, he says: *in revelation*, by which the mind is enlightened to know divine things.

Or it is about earthly things, and not just any but only about those which pertain to the building up of faith: and this pertains to the gift of knowledge. Therefore he says: *in knowledge*, not geometry or astronomy, because these do not pertain to the building up of the faith, but in knowledge of holy things: *he gave them knowledge of holy things* (Wis 10:10).

Or it is about future events, and this pertains to the gift of prophecy: hence he says: *or in prophecy*: *she has foreknowledge of signs and wonders and of the outcome of seasons and of times* (Wis 8:8).

It should be noted that prophecy is not taken here as it is generally used and was explained above, but it is taken here in a special sense, as a manifestation of future events only. In this sense it is defined by Cassiodorus: *prophecy is divine inspiration announcing with infallible truth the future of things. I will again pour out teaching like prophecy* (Sir 24:33).

Or is it is about moral acts, and this pertaining to teaching; therefore he says: *or in doctrine*: *he who teaches, in teaching* (Rom 12:7); *good teaching wins favor* (Prov 13:15).

826. They can be distinguished in another way according to the various ways that knowledge is acquired.

And thus it should be known that all knowledge is either from a supernatural source, namely, God, or from a natural, i.e., the natural light of the intellect.

If it is from a supernatural principle, namely, by a divinely infused light, it can happen in two ways: because it is either infused by sudden knowledge, and then it is revelation; or it is infused successively, and then it is prophecy, which the prophets did not have suddenly but successively and by parts, as their prophecies show.

But if the knowledge is acquired by a natural principle, this is either through one's own study and then it pertains to knowledge, or it is presented by someone else, and then it pertains to teaching.

827. *Even things without life that give sound.* Here he shows the same thing with examples taken from inanimate things, namely, instruments which seem to have a voice:

first, with instruments of joy;

second, the instruments of battle, at *for if the trumpet gives an uncertain sound*.

828. He says, therefore: that speaking in tongues does not benefit others is shown not only from what has been said above: but also from *things without life that give sound*.

Contra. Vox est sonus ab ore animalis prolatus, naturalibus instrumentis formatus. Non ergo ea quae sunt sine anima dant vocem.

Dicendum est quod licet vox non sit nisi animalium, tamen potest dici per quamdam similitudinem, scilicet secundum quod quaedam, sicuti instrumenta, habent quamdam consonantiam et melodiam, et ideo de illis facit mentionem, scilicet de cithara, quae dat vocem tactu, et tibia, quae flatu.

Si ergo haec dant vocem sine distinctione, *quomodo scietur*, et cetera. Cum enim homo per instrumenta aliquid intendat exprimere, scilicet aliquos cantus, qui ordinantur vel ad fletum, vel ad gaudium, Is. XXX, 29: *canticum erit vobis sicut vox sanctificatae solemnitatis et laetitia cordis, sicut qui pergit cum tibia, ut intret in montem Domini*, vel etiam ad lasciviam, non poterit diiudicari ad quid canitur tibia, aut ad quid cithara, si sonus sit confusus et indistinctus. Ita si homo loquitur linguis, et non interpretatur, non poterit sciri quid velit dicere.

829. *Etenim si incertam vocem dederit*, et cetera. Hic ostendit idem per exempla inanimatorum, scilicet per instrumenta ad pugnam ordinata.

Et sumitur haec similitudo ex Lib. Num. X, v. 1–10. Ibi enim legitur quod Dominus praecepit Moysi ut faceret duas tubas argenteas, quae essent ad conveniendum populum, ad movendum castra et ad pugnandum. Et pro quolibet istorum habebant certum modum tubandi, quia aliter dabant vocem quando debebant convenire ad Concilium, aliter quando movebant castra, et aliter quando pugnabant. Et ideo arguit apostolus quod sicut *si tuba det incertam vocem*, id est indistinctam, nescitur utrum se debeant parare ad bellum; et ita vos, si loquimini tantum linguis, nisi distinctum sermonem dicatis interpretando, vel exponendo, non poterit quis scire quid loquamini. Per *tubam* potest intelligi *praedicator*. Is. LVIII, 1: *quasi tuba exalta vocem tuam*, et cetera.

Ratio autem quare non potest sciri quid loquamini est quia *eritis in aera loquentes*, id est, inutiliter. Supra IX, 26: *sic pugno non quasi aera verberans*, et cetera.

830. *Tam multa*, et cetera. Hic sumit exemplum a diversis linguis loquentium.

Et circa hoc tria facit.

Primo ostendit diversitatem linguarum;

secundo inutilitatem loquentium sibi ad invicem in linguis extraneis, ibi *si ergo nesciero*, etc.;

tertio concludit quod intendit ibi *sic et vos quoniam aemulatores*, et cetera.

831. Dicit ergo primo: multae et diversae linguae in mundo sunt, et quilibet potest loqui quacumque vult; si

Against this, a voice is a sound uttered from the mouth of an animal. Therefore, lifeless things do not give forth a voice.

The answer is that although a voice is found only in animals, yet in virtue of a likeness it can be said that certain things, such as musical instruments, have a definite consonance and melody. That is why he mentions them, namely, the harp, which gives forth a voice through touch, and the flute through blowing.

If even lifeless instruments do not give distinct notes, *how shall it be known what is piped or harped?* For since man intends to express something through musical instruments, namely, songs which are directed to sorrow or to joy: *you shall have a song in the night, when a holy feast is kept; and gladness of heart, as when one set out to the sound of the flute to go to the mountain of the Lord* (Isa 30:29), or even to wantonness, one cannot tell what the flute is playing or the harp, if the sound is confused and not distinct. So if a man speaks in tongues, and he does not interpret, no one knows what he wants to say.

829. *For if the trumpet gives an uncertain sound*. Here he shows the same thing with another lifeless thing, namely, the instrument ordained to battle.

This likeness is taken from where it says that the Lord commanded Moses to make two silver trumpets to be used for summoning all the people, for moving their camps and for battle (Num 10:1–10). For each of these three things there was a different way of sounding the trumpet, because when they moved their camps it sounded one way; and another, when they were to assemble; and still another, when they were to do battle. And so the Apostle argues that just as *if the trumpet gives an uncertain sound*, it is not known whether they should prepare for battle, so you, if you only speak in tongues, unless you make your speech clear by interpreting or explaining, no one will know what you are saying. By *trumpet* can also be understood *preachers. Lift up your voice like a trumpet* (Isa 58:1).

But the reason why it cannot be known what you are saying is that *you shall be speaking into the air*, i.e., uselessly: *I do not box as one beating the air* (1 Cor 9:26).

830. *There are, for example, so many kinds of tongues.* Here he uses the examples of the various human languages.

In regard to this he does three things:

first, he points out the diversity of tongues;

second, that it is useless for one to speak to others in a language they do not understand, at *if then I know not*;

third, he concludes what he intended, at *so you also, forasmuch as you are zealous*.

831. First, therefore, he says: the languages of the world are many and diverse, and anyone can speak in whichever

tamen non loquatur determinate, non intelligitur. Et hoc est quod dicit *tam multa*, et cetera.

Hoc potest dupliciter exponi, quia potest continuari cum praecedentibus, ut dicatur: *eritis in aera loquentes, et tam multa, ut puta*, etc., quasi dicat: ideo in aera, id est, inutiliter loquimini omnibus linguis, quia loquimini sine intellectu, quae tamen proprias significationes vocum ad hoc habent, ut intelligantur. Nihil enim sine *voce* est.

Vel potest sic punctuari: *eritis in aera loquentes. Tam multa, ut puta, sunt genera linguarum*, id est singulis linguis.

832. *Si ergo nesciero*, et cetera. Hic ostendit horum inutilitatem. Et hoc est quod dicit: si loquar omnibus linguis, sed *si nesciero virtutem vocis*, id est significationem vocis, *ero cui loquar barbarus*. Ier. V, 15: *adducam super te gentem de longinquo, gentem cuius ignoras linguam*.

Nota quod barbari, secundum quosdam, dicuntur illi, quorum idioma discordat omnino a Latino. Alii vero dicunt quod quilibet extraneus est barbarus omni alii extraneo, quando scilicet non intelligitur ab eo. Sed hoc non est verum, quia, secundum Isidorum, *Barbaria* est specialis natio. Col. III, v. 11: *in Christo Iesu non est Barbarus et Scytha*, et cetera. Sed secundum quod verius dicitur, barbari proprie dicuntur illi, qui in virtute corporis vigent, in virtute rationis deficiunt et sunt quasi extra leges et sine regimine iuris. Et huic videtur consonare Aristoteles in *Politicis* suis.

833. Consequenter, cum dicit *sicut*, etc., concludit quod intendit, et hoc potest dupliciter construi.

Primo ut punctetur hoc modo, quasi dicat: sic ego ero barbarus vobis, si loquar sine significatione et interpretatione, sicut et vos eritis barbari ad invicem; et ideo *quaerite, ut abundetis*, etc., et hoc *quoniam estis aemulatores*, et cetera.

Vel, alio modo, ut totum ponatur sub distinctione; quasi diceret: ne ergo sitis barbari, sic scilicet sicut ego facio, *quoniam estis aemulatores Spirituum*, id est, donorum Spiritus Sancti, *quaerite* a Deo, *ut abundetis*. Prov. XV, 5: *in abundanti iustitia virtus maxima est*. Quae quidem iustitia est aedificare alios. Matth. VII, 7: *petite, et dabitur vobis; quaerite et invenietis; pulsate, et aperietur vobis*.

one he wants; but if he does not speak precisely, he is not understood. And this is what he says: *there are, for example, so many kinds of tongues in this world*.

This can be explained in two ways, for it can be connected with the preceding as saying: *you shall be speaking into the air* in *so many kinds of tongues*, as if to say, you will be speaking uselessly in all languages, because you speak without understanding, whereas words have a definite meaning in all languages to be understood. For nothing exists without its *voice*.

Or it can be punctuated thus: *you shall be speaking into the air. There are, for example, so many kinds of tongues in this world*, i.e., individual languages.

832. *If then I know not the power of the voice*. Here he shows their uselessness. And this is what he says: if I have spoken in all tongues, but *if then I know not the power of the voice, I shall be to him to whom I speak a barbarian*: *I will bring upon you a nation from afar . . . a nation whose language you shall not know* (Jer 5:15).

Note that barbarians according to some are those whose idiom completely disagrees with Latin. But others say that any foreigner is a barbarian to every other foreigner, namely, when he is not understood by him. But this is not true, because according to Isidore, *Barbaria* is a special nation: *in Christ Jesus there is neither Barbarian nor Scythian* (Col 3:11). But it is closer to the truth to say that barbarian is the name for those who are strong in body and weak in reasoning and exist, as it were, outside the law and without the rule of law. And Aristotle seems to agree with this in his *Politics*.

833. Then when he says: *so you also*, he concludes to what he intended; and this can be constructed in two ways:

first, so that it is punctuated as if he were saying: therefore, I will be a barbarian to you, if I speak without meaning and interpretation, just as you will be barbarians to one another; and, therefore, *seek to abound unto the edifying of the Church*. And this, *forasmuch as you are zealous of spirits*.

Or in another way, so that it is all put under a distinction. As if to say: therefore, do not be barbarians, *forasmuch as you are zealous* for the manifestations *of the Spirit*, i.e., of the gifts of the Holy Spirit, do as I do and *seek* them from God, that you may *abound*: *in abundant justice is virtue the greatest* (Prov 12:5). This justice consists in edifying others: *ask, and it will be given you; seek, and you shall find; knock, and it shall be opened to you* (Matt 7:7).

Lecture 3

14:13Et ideo qui loquitur lingua, oret ut interpretetur. [n. 834]

14:14Nam si orem lingua, spiritus meus orat, mens autem mea sine fructu est. [n. 836]

14:15Quid ergo est? Orabo spiritu, orabo et mente: psallam spiritu, psallam et mente. [n. 841]

14:16Ceterum si benedixeris spiritu, qui supplet locum idiotae, quomodo dicet: amen, super tuam benedictionem? quoniam quid dicas, nescit. [n. 842]

14:17Nam tu quidem bene gratias agis, sed alter non aedificatur. [n. 846]

14:13διὸ ὁ λαλῶν γλώσσῃ προσευχέσθω ἵνα διερμηνεύῃ.

14:14ἐὰν [γὰρ] προσεύχωμαι γλώσσῃ, τὸ πνεῦμά μου προσεύχεται, ὁ δὲ νοῦς μου ἄκαρπός ἐστιν.

14:15τί οὖν ἐστιν; προσεύξομαι τῷ πνεύματι, προσεύξομαι δὲ καὶ τῷ νοΐ· ψαλῶ τῷ πνεύματι, ψαλῶ δὲ καὶ τῷ νοΐ.

14:16ἐπεὶ ἐὰν εὐλογῇς [ἐν] πνεύματι, ὁ ἀναπληρῶν τὸν τόπον τοῦ ἰδιώτου πῶς ἐρεῖ τὸ Ἀμήν ἐπὶ τῇ σῇ εὐχαριστίᾳ, ἐπειδὴ τί λέγεις οὐκ οἶδεν;

14:17σὺ μὲν γὰρ καλῶς εὐχαριστεῖς, ἀλλ' ὁ ἕτερος οὐκ οἰκοδομεῖται.

14:13And therefore he who speaks by a tongue, let him pray that he may interpret. [n. 834]

14:14For if I pray in a tongue, my spirit prays: but my mind is without fruit. [n. 836]

14:15What is it then? I will pray with the spirit, I will pray also with the mind, I will sing with the spirit, I will sing also with the mind. [n. 841]

14:16Else, if you shall bless with the spirit, how shall he who holds the place of the unlearned say, amen, to your blessing? Because he knows not what you say. [n. 842]

14:17For you indeed give thanks well: but the other is not edified. [n. 846]

---

834. Supra ostendit apostolus excellentiam doni prophetiae ad donum linguarum, rationibus sumptis ex parte exhortationis, hic vero ostendit idem rationibus sumptis ex parte orationis: haec enim duo per linguam exercemus, orationem scilicet et exhortationem.

Et circa hoc duo facit.

Primo enim probat excellentiam prophetiae ad donum linguarum rationibus;

secundo exemplis, ibi *gratias ago Deo meo*, et cetera.

Circa primum duo facit.

Primo ponit necessitatem orationis;

secundo ostendit quomodo in oratione plus valet donum prophetiae quam donum linguarum *nam si orem lingua*, et cetera.

835. Dicit ergo primo: dixi quod donum linguarum sine dono prophetiae non valet, *et ideo*, quia interpretari est actus prophetiae, quae est excellentior illi, *qui loquitur lingua*, ignota vel extranea vel aliqua mysteria occulta, *oret*, scilicet Deum, *ut interpretetur*, id est, ut interpretandi gratia detur sibi. Col. IV, 3: *orantes ut Deus aperiat ostium.*

Glossa aliter exponit *oret*. Orare enim dicitur dupliciter, scilicet vel deprecari Deum vel persuadere, quasi dicat *qui loquitur lingua, oret*, id est ita persuadeat *ut interpretetur*. Et sic accipit orare hic Glossa per totum capitulum. Sed non est haec intentio apostoli, sed pro deprecatione ad Deum.

834. Having shown that the gift of prophecy excels the gift of tongues with reasons taken on the part of exhortation, the Apostle now shows the same thing with reasons taken on the part of prayer; for we perform these two things with the tongue, namely, prayer and exhortation.

In regard to this he does two things:

first, he proves that prophecy excels the gift of tongues with reasons;

second, with examples, at *I thank my God* (1 Cor 14:18).

In regard to the first he does two things:

first, he shows the necessity of prayer;

second, how in prayer the gift of prophecy is more powerful than the gift of tongues, at *for if I pray in a tongue.*

835. First, therefore, he says: I have said that the gift of tongues without the gift of prophecy has no value, because interpretation is an act of prophecy, which is more excellent than *he who speaks by a tongue*. One who speaks in a tongue, unknown or foreign, certain hidden mysteries, should *pray*, namely, to God, *that he may interpret*, i.e., that the grace to interpret be given him: *praying that God may open to us a door* (Col 4:3).

A Gloss exposits *pray* differently. For 'to pray' is said to be twofold, namely either to beseech God or to prevail upon him; as if he says: *he who speaks by a tongue, let him pray*, i.e., let him prevail upon God, *that he may interpret*. And so the Gloss understands 'to pray' here for the whole chapter. But this is not the meaning of the Apostle, but rather it is 'to beseech God.'

836. *Nam si orem*, et cetera. Hic ostendit quod in orando plus valet prophetia, quam donum linguarum, et hoc dupliciter.

Primo, ratione sumpta ex parte ipsius orantis;

secundo, ratione sumpta ex parte audientis, ibi *caeterum, si benedixeris*, et cetera.

837. Circa primum duo facit.

Primo ponit rationem ad propositum ostendendum;

secundo removet obiectionem, ibi *quid ergo*, et cetera.

837. Circa primum sciendum est quod duplex est oratio. Una est privata, quando scilicet quis orat in seipso et pro se; alia publica, quando quis orat coram populo et pro aliis: et in utraque contingit uti et dono linguarum et dono prophetiae. Et ideo vult ostendere quod in utraque plus valet donum prophetiae, quam donum linguarum.

Et primo in oratione privata, dicens, quod si sit aliquis idiota, qui faciat orationem suam, dicens psalmum, vel *Pater noster*, et non intelligat ea quae dicit, iste orat lingua, et non refert utrum oret verbis sibi a Spiritu Sancto concessis, sive verbis aliorum; et si sit alius qui orat, et intelligit quae dicit, hic quidem orat et prophetat. Constat quod plus lucratur qui orat et intelligit, quam qui tantum lingua orat, qui scilicet non intelligit quae dicit. Nam ille qui intelligit, reficitur et quantum ad intellectum et quantum ad affectum; sed mens eius, qui non intelligit, est sine fructu refectionis. Unde et cum melius sit refici quantum ad affectum et intellectum, quam quantum ad affectum solum, constat quod in oratione plus valet prophetiae donum quam solum donum linguarum.

838. Et hoc est quod dicit: dico quod *oret, ut interpretetur*, *nam si orem lingua*, id est orando utor dono linguarum, ita quod proferam aliqua quae non intelligo; tunc *Spiritus meus*, id est Spiritus Sanctus mihi datus, *orat*, qui inclinat et movet me ad orandum. Et nihilominus mereor in ipsa oratione, quia hoc ipsum, quod moveor a Spiritu Sancto, est mihi meritum. Rom. VIII, 26: *nam quid oremus, sicut oportet, nescimus, sed ipse Spiritus Sanctus postulare nos facit*.

Vel *spiritus meus*, id est ratio mea, *orat*, id est dictat mihi quod ego loquar ea quae ad bonum sunt, sive verbis propriis sive aliorum sanctorum.

Vel *spiritus meus*, id est virtus imaginativa, *orat*, inquantum voces seu similitudines corporalium sunt tantum in imaginatione absque hoc quod intelligantur ab intellectu; et ideo subdit: *mens autem mea*, id est intellectus meus, *sine fructu est*, quia non intelligit.

Et ideo melius est in oratione prophetia seu interpretatio, quam donum linguarum.

836. *For if I pray in a tongue*. Here he shows that in praying, prophecy is more valuable than the gift of tongues in two ways:

first, with a reason based on the one praying;

second, on the one hearing, at *else, if you shall bless with the spirit*.

837. In regard to the first he does two things:

first, he presents a reason showing the truth of his proposition;

second, he removes an objection, at *what is it then?*

837. In regard to the first it should be noted that prayer is of two kinds: one is private, namely, when one prays in himself and for himself; the other is public, when one prays before the people and for others. In both cases one can use the gift of tongues and the gift of prophecy. Hence he wants to show that in both cases the gift of prophecy is more valuable than the gift of tongues.

First, in private prayer, if an outsider says his own prayer, saying a psalm or the *Our Father* and he does not understand what he says, he prays with the tongue and it does not concern him whether he is praying with words granted him by the Holy Spirit or with someone else's words: and if another prays and understands what he is saying, he, indeed, both prays and prophesies. It is evident that one who prays and understands accomplishes more than one who prays only in a tongue, namely, who does not understand what he is saying. For the one who understands is refreshed both in intellect and affections, but the mind of one who does not understand receives no fruit of refreshment. Hence, since it is better to be refreshed in mind and affections than in affections only, it is obvious that in prayer the gift of prophecy is more valuable than the gift of tongues.

838. And this is what he says: I say that *let him pray that he may interpret*, *for if I pray in a tongue*, i.e., use the gift of tongues in praying, so that I utter what I do not understand; then *my Spirit*, i.e., the Holy Spirit given to me, *prays*, who inclines and moves me to pray. Nevertheless, I merit in that prayer, because the very fact that I am moved by the Holy Spirit is merit for me: *we do not know how to pray as we ought, but the Spirit himself makes us ask* (Rom 8:26).

Or *my spirit*, i.e., my reason, *prays*, i.e., tells me that I should ask for things which are good, either in my own words or those of other saints.

Or *my spirit*, i.e., the imagination, *prays* in the sense that words of the likenesses of bodily things are only in the imagination without being understood by the intellect. Therefore, he adds: *but my mind*, i.e., my intellect, *is without fruit*, because it does not understand.

Therefore, prophecy or interpretation is better in prayer than is the gift of tongues.

839. Sed numquid quandocumque quis orat, et non intelligit quae dicit, sit sine fructu orationis?

Dicendum quod duplex est fructus orationis. Unus fructus est meritum quod homini provenit; alius fructus est spiritualis consolatio et devotio concepta ex oratione. Et quantum ad fructum devotionis spiritualis privatur qui non attendit ad ea quae orat, seu non intelligit; sed quantum ad fructum meriti, non est dicendum quod privetur: quia sic multae orationes essent sine merito, cum vix unum *Pater noster* potest homo dicere, quin mens ad alia feratur.

Et ideo dicendum est quod quando orans aliquando divertit ab his quae dicit, seu quando quis in uno opere meritorio non continue cogitat in quolibet actu, quod facit hoc propter Deum, non perdit rationem meriti. Cuius ratio est, quia in omnibus actibus meritoriis, qui ordinantur ad finem rectum, non requiritur quod intentio agentis coniungatur fini, secundum quemlibet actum: sed vis prima, quae movet intentionem, manet in toto opere, etiam si aliquando in aliquo particulari divertat; et hic prima vis facit totum opus meritorium, nisi interrumpatur per contrariam affectionem, quae divertat a fine praedicto ad finem contrarium.

840. Sed sciendum est quod triplex est attentio. Una est ad verba quae homo dicit: et haec aliquando nocet, inquantum impedit devotionem; alia est ad sensum verborum, et haec nocet, non tamen est multum nociva; tertia est ad finem, et haec est melior et quasi necessaria.

Tamen id quod dicit apostolus **mens est sine fructu**, intelligitur de fructu refectionis.

841. *Quid ergo est*, et cetera. Quia posset aliquis dicere: ex quo orare lingua est sine fructu mentis, sed tamen spiritus orat, numquid ergo non est orandum spiritu?

Ideo Apostolus hoc removet dicens, quod utroque modo orandum est, et spiritu et mente: quia homo debet servire Deo de omnibus quae habet a Deo; sed a Deo habet spiritum et mentem, et ideo debet de utroque orare. Eccli. XLVII, 10: *de omni corde suo laudabit Dominum*, et cetera. Et ideo dicit **orabo spiritu, orabo et mente: psallam spiritu**, et cetera.

Et sic dicit orabo et psallam; quia oratio, vel est ad deprecandum Deum et sic dicit **orabo**, vel laudandum et sic dicit **psallam**. De istis duobus Iac. V, 13: *tristatur quis in vobis? Oret aequo animo, et psallat*. Ps. IX, v. 12: *psallite Domino*, et cetera.

Orabo ergo **spiritu**, id est imaginatione, **et mente**, id est voluntate.

842. *Caeterum si benedixeris*, et cetera. Hic secundo ostendit quod donum prophetiae plus valet quam donum linguarum, etiam in oratione publica, quae est

839. But is it true that whenever anyone prays and does not understand what he is saying, he obtains no fruit?

The answer is that the fruit of prayer is twofold: one fruit is the merit the person obtains; the other fruit is the spiritual consolation and devotion produced by the prayer. In regard to the fruit of spiritual devotion, one is deprived of it, if he does not attend to what he is praying, or does not understand; but in regard to the fruit of merit, one is not necessarily deprived of it. For many prayers would be without merit, since a man can scarcely say the *Our Father* without his mind wandering to other things.

Therefore, it must be said that when the one praying is sometimes diverted from what he is saying, or when a person engaged in one meritorious work does not continually think at each step that he is doing this for God, he does not lose the reason for merit. The reason for this is that in all meritorious acts ordained to the right end, it is not required that the intention of the performer be united to the end in every act: but the first influence, which moves the intention, remains in the entire work, even if in some particular it be distracted; and this first influence makes the entire work meritorious, unless it is interrupted by a contrary affection which turns one from the original and to a contrary end.

840. But it should be noted that attention is threefold: one is to the words the man is saying: and this is harmful sometimes, inasmuch as it impedes devotion; another is to the sense of the words, and this is harmful, but not very much; the third is to the end, and this is better and, as it were, necessary.

Nevertheless, when the Apostle says **my mind is without fruit**, it is understood of the fruit of refreshment.

841. *What is it then?* Because someone could say: inasmuch as prayer in a tongue is without fruit to the mind, but the spirit prays, should one then not pray in the spirit?

Therefore, the Apostle answer this objection, saying that one should pray in both ways, in the spirit and in the mind; because man should serve God with all the things he has from God. But from God he has spirit and mind; therefore, he should pray with both: *with all his heart he will praise God* (Sir 47:8). Therefore, he says: **I will pray with the spirit, I will pray also with the mind; I will sing with the spirit and I will sing also with the mind**.

And so he says that he will pray and sing; because prayer is the beseeching of God, and so he says, **I will pray**, or it is praising him, and so he says **I will sing**. Concerning these two it is said: *is anyone among you suffering? Let him pray. Is any cheerful? Let him sing* (Jas 6:13). *Sing praises to the Lord* (Ps 9:11).

I will pray, therefore, **with the spirit**, i.e., imagination, **and with the mind**, i.e., the will.

842. *Else if you shall bless.* Here, second, he shows that the gift of prophecy is more valuable than the gift of tongues, even in public prayer, which is when a priest prays

quando sacerdos publice orat, ubi aliquando dicit quaedam quae non intelligit, aliquando aliqua quae intelligit.

Et circa hoc tria facit.

Primo ponit rationem;

secundo exponit eam, ibi *quomodo dicit*, etc.;

tertio probat quod supposuerat, ibi *quoniam quid*, et cetera.

843. Dicit ergo: dixi quod donum prophetiae in oratione privata plus valet, *caeterum*, pro *sed*, et in publica, quia *si benedixeris*, id est si benedictionem dederis, *spiritu*, id est in lingua quae non intelligatur, seu imaginatione, et motus a Spiritu Sancto, *quis supplet locum idiotae?* Idiota proprie dicitur qui scit tantum linguam in qua natus est; quasi diceret: quis dicet illud quod debet dicere ibi idiota? Quod est, dicere: *amen*.

844. Et ideo dicit *quomodo dicet super tuam benedictionem?* Ubi Glossa exponit, id est: *quomodo consentiet benedictioni a te factae in persona Ecclesiae?* Is. LXV, 16: *qui benedictus est super terram, benedicetur in Deo, amen*. *Amen* idem est quod fiat, vel verum est; quasi dicat: si non intelligit quae dicis, quomodo conformabit se dictis tuis? Potest quidem se conformare, etiam si non intelligat, sed in generali tantum, non in speciali, quia non potest intelligere quid boni dicas, nisi quod benedicas tantum.

845. Sed quare non dantur benedictiones in vulgari, ut intelligantur a populo, et conforment se magis eis?

Dicendum est quod hoc forte fuit in Ecclesia primitiva, sed postquam fideles instructi sunt et sciunt quae audiunt in communi officio, fiunt benedictiones in Latino.

846. Consequenter probat, quare non potest dicere *amen*, cum dicit *nam tu quidem*, id est: licet *tu gratias agas bene* Deo, inquantum intelligis, *sed alter*, qui audit et non intelligit, *non aedificatur*, inquantum non intelligit in speciali, etsi in generali intelligat et aedificetur. Eph. IV, 29: *omnis sermo malus ex ore vestro non procedat, sed si quis bonus est ad aedificationem fidei*.

Et ideo melius est ut non solum lingua benedicat, sed etiam, ut interpretetur et exponat, licet tu qui gratias agis, bene agas.

in public, where he sometimes says things he does not understand and sometimes things he does understand.

In regard to this he does three things:

first, he presents a reason;

second, he explains, at *how shall he who holds*;

third, he proves what he had presupposed, at *because he knows not what you say*.

843. He says, therefore: I have said that the gift of prophecy in private prayer is more beneficial, but also in public, *else if you shall bless*, i.e., if you give a blessing *with the spirit*, i.e., in a tongue not understood, or with the imagination, and moved by the Holy Spirit, *he who holds the place of the unlearned* (who knows only the tongue in which he was born). As if to say: you will say what he should say there to the ignorant man; for what he should say there is *amen*.

844. Therefore, he says: *how shall he . . . say, amen, to your blessing*, where a Gloss says, i.e., *how shall he consent to the blessing given by you in the name of the Church? he who is blessed on the earth will be blessed in God. Amen* (Isa 55:16). *Amen* is the same as let it be done, or it is so. As if to say: if he does not know what you are saying, how shall he conform himself to your utterances? He could conform, even if he does not understand, but only in a general way, because he cannot understand what good thing you are saying, but only that you are blessing.

845. But why are blessings not given in the vernacular, so that they will be understood by the people and conform themselves to them more?

The answer is that this probably happened in the early Church, but later the faithful were instructed and know what they hear in the common office, where blessings are given in Latin.

846. Then he proves why he cannot say, *amen*, when he says: *for you indeed give thanks well* to God, inasmuch as you understand, *but the other*, who hears and does not understand, *is not edified*, for he does not understand in detail, even if he understands in a general way and is edified: *let no evil thought come out of your mouth, but only such as is good for edifying* (Eph 4:29).

Consequently, it is better not only to bless in a tongue, but also to interpret and explain, although you who give thanks do well.

Lecture 4

14:18Gratias ago Deo meo, quod omnium vestrum lingua loquor. [n. 847]

14:19Sed in Ecclesia volo quinque verba sensu meo loqui, ut et alios instruam: quam decem millia verborum in lingua. [n. 849]

14:20Fratres, nolite pueri effici sensibus, sed malitia parvuli estote: sensibus autem perfecti estote. [n. 851]

14:21In lege scriptum est: *quoniam in aliis linguis et labiis aliis loquar populo huic: et nec sic exaudient me,* dicit Dominus. [n. 853]

14:22Itaque linguae in signum sunt non fidelibus, sed infidelibus: prophetiae autem non infidelibus, sed fidelibus. [n. 857]

14:18εὐχαριστῶ τῷ θεῷ, πάντων ὑμῶν μᾶλλον γλώσσαις λαλῶ·

14:19ἀλλὰ ἐν ἐκκλησίᾳ θέλω πέντε λόγους τῷ νοΐ μου λαλῆσαι, ἵνα καὶ ἄλλους κατηχήσω, ἢ μυρίους λόγους ἐν γλώσσῃ.

14:20Ἀδελφοί, μὴ παιδία γίνεσθε ταῖς φρεσίν, ἀλλὰ τῇ κακίᾳ νηπιάζετε, ταῖς δὲ φρεσὶν τέλειοι γίνεσθε.

14:21ἐν τῷ νόμῳ γέγραπται ὅτι Ἐν ἑτερογλώσσοις καὶ ἐν χείλεσιν ἑτέρων λαλήσω τῷ λαῷ τούτῳ, καὶ οὐδ' οὕτως εἰσακούσονταί μου, λέγει κύριος.

14:22ὥστε αἱ γλῶσσαι εἰς σημεῖόν εἰσιν οὐ τοῖς πιστεύουσιν ἀλλὰ τοῖς ἀπίστοις, ἡ δὲ προφητεία οὐ τοῖς ἀπίστοις ἀλλὰ τοῖς πιστεύουσιν.

14:18I thank my God I speak with all your tongues. [n. 847]

14:19But in the Church I had rather speak five words with my understanding, that I may instruct others also: than ten thousand words in a tongue. [n. 849]

14:20Brethren, do not become children in sense. But in malice be children: and in sense be perfect. [n. 851]

14:21In the law it is written: *in other tongues and other lips I will speak to this people: and neither so will they hear* me, says the Lord. [n. 853]

14:22Wherefore tongues are for a sign, not to believers but to unbelievers: but prophecies, not to unbelievers but to believers. [n. 857]

---

847. Hic ostendit Apostolus excellentiam doni prophetiae ad donum linguarum per rationes sumptas ex parte sui ipsius.

Et circa hoc duo facit.

Primo agit gratias de dono linguarum sibi a Deo dato;

secundo se eis in exemplum proponit, ibi *sed in Ecclesia volo*, et cetera.

848. Dicit ergo *gratias ago*, etc., quasi dicat: non ideo vilipendo donum linguarum, quia ego dico quod donum prophetiae sit excellentius, sed debet charum haberi. Unde et *ego gratias ago*, et cetera. Est ergo de omnibus gratias agendum. I Thess. V, 18: *in omnibus gratias agite*, et cetera.

Vel *gratias ago*, quasi dicat: non ideo vilipendo donum linguarum, quasi eo carens, immo etiam ego habeo; et ideo dicit *gratias ago*, et cetera.

Et ne intelligatur quod omnes loquerentur una lingua, dicit *quod omnium vestrum lingua loquor*, Act. II, 4: *loquebantur variis linguis apostoli*, et cetera.

849. *Sed in Ecclesia*. Hic ponit se in exemplum, quasi dicat: si ego habeo donum linguarum sicut et vos, debetis facere illud quod facio. *Sed ego volo*, id est magis volo, *loqui in Ecclesia quinque*, id est pauca, *verba sensu meo*, id est intellectu, ut scilicet ego intelligam et intelligar, et ex hoc *instruam alios, quam decem millia*, id est quamcumque multitudinem, *verborum in lingua*; quod est loqui non ad intellectum quocumque modo fiat, ut supra expositum est.

847. Here the Apostle shows that the gift of prophecy excels the gift of tongues with reasons taken on his own part.

In regard to this he does two things:

first, he gives thanks for the gift of tongues given him by God;

second, he proposes himself to them as an example, at *but in the Church*.

848. He says, therefore, *I thank my God* that I speak in tongues more than you all. As if to say: I do not belittle the gift of tongues, because I say that the gift of prophecy is more excellent, but it ought to be cherished. Hence, *I thank my God*. Therefore, thanks should be given for all things: *in all things give thanks* (1 Thess 5:18).

Or *I thank my God*. As if to say: I do not belittle the gift of tongues, as though lacking it; rather I have it. Therefore, he says: *I thank my God*.

But lest it be understood that all speak in one tongue, he says: *that I speak with all your tongues*: *they spoke in various tongues* (Acts 2:4).

849. *But in the Church*. Here he presents himself as an example. As if to say: if I have the gift of tongues, just as you, you should do as I do. *But in the Church I had rather speak five words*, i.e., a few words, *with my understanding*, i.e., intellect, so that I understand and be understood, in order *that I may instruct others also: than ten thousand*, i.e., any number of *words in a tongue*; which is not to speak to the mind in any way, as explained above.

850. Dicunt quidam quod ideo dicit *quinque*, quia Apostolus videtur velle, quod magis velit dicere solum unam orationem ad intellectum, quam multas sine intellectu. Oratio autem, secundum grammaticos, ad hoc quod debeat facere perfectum sensum, debet habere quinque, scilicet subiectum, praedicatum, copulam verbalem, determinationem subiecti, et determinationem praedicati.

Aliis videtur melius quod quia ad hoc loquendum est cum intellectu, ut alii doceantur, ideo ponit *quinque*, quia doctor debet quinque, scilicet: credenda, Tit. II, 11: *haec loquere et exhortare*, etc.; agenda, Mc. XVI, v. 15: *euntes in mundum*, etc.; vitanda, scilicet peccata Eccli. XXI, 2: *quasi a facie colubri fuge*, etc.; Is. LVIII, 1: *annuntia populo meo scelera*, etc.; speranda scilicet mercedem aeternam, I Petr. I, 10: *de qua salute exquisierunt*, etc.; timenda, scilicet poenas aeternas, Matth. XXV, 21: *ite, maledicti, in ignem aeternum*, et cetera.

851. *Fratres mei, nolite*, et cetera. Hic ostendit excellentiam doni prophetiae ad donum linguarum, rationibus sumptis ex parte infidelium.

Et circa hoc duo facit.

Primo excitat attentionem, et reddit attentos;

secundo arguit ad propositum, ibi *in lege quid scriptum est?*

852. Circa primum videtur Apostolus excludere pallium excusationis aliquorum qui ideo docent quaedam rudia et superficialia, quasi ostendant se volentes vivere in simplicitate, et ideo non curantes de subtilitatibus ad quas secundum rei veritatem non attingunt, habentes verbum Domini ad hoc Matthaei XVIII, 3: *nisi conversi fueritis, et efficiamini sicut parvuli*, et cetera.

Sed hoc Apostolus excludit, cum dicit *nolite pueri effici sensu*, id est nolite puerilia et inutilia et stulta loqui et docere. Supra XIII, v. 11: *cum essem parvulus*, et cetera.

Sed quomodo debetis effici pueri? Affectu, non intellectu. Et ideo dicit *sed malitia*. Ubi sciendum est quod parvuli deficiunt in cogitando mala, et sic debemus effici parvuli, et ideo dicit *sed malitia parvuli estote*, et deficiunt in cogitando bona, et sic non debemus esse parvuli, immo viri perfecti, et ideo dicit *sensibus autem perfecti*, etc., id est ad discretionem boni et mali perfecti sitis. Unde Hebr. V, 14: *perfectorum est solidus cibus*, et cetera.

Non ergo laudatur in vobis simplicitas quae opponitur prudentiae, sed simplicitas, quae astutiae. Et ideo

850. Some say that he says, *five*, because the Apostle seems to prefer to say one prayer with understanding than many without understanding. But according to the grammarians, if a statement is to have perfect sense, it should have five things: a subject, predicate, verbal copula, a modifier of the subject and a modifier of the predicate.

To others it seems better to say, that because we speak with the intellect in order that others be taught, he mentions *five*, because the teacher should teach five things, namely: things to be believed: *declare and exhort these things* (Titus 2:11); things to be done: *go into the whole world and preach the Gospel, teaching them to observe all things I have commanded you* (Mark 16:15); things to be avoided, i.e., sins: *flee from sin as from a snake* (Sir 21:2); *declare to my people their transgressions, to the house of Jacob their sins* (Isa 58:1); things to be hoped for, i.e., the eternal reward: *they searched and inquired about this salvation* (1 Pet 1:10); things to be feared, i.e., eternal punishments: *depart, you accursed into everlasting fire* (Matt 25:21).

851. *Brethren, do not become children in sense*. Here he shows that the gift of prophecy excels the gift of tongue with reasons taken on the part of unbelievers.

In regard to this he does two things:

first, he gets their attention and makes them attentive;

second, he argues to his point, at *in the law it is written*.

852. In regard to the first the Apostle seems to remove the mantle of excuse from those who teach certain rude and superficial things, as if to show that they wish to live in simplicity, and not caring about subtleties to which they really do not attain; and for this they appeal to the Lord's words: *unless you be converted and become as little children, you shall not enter the kingdom of heaven* (Matt 18:13).

But the Apostle rejects this, when he says: *do not become children in sense*, i.e., do not speak and teach childish and useless and foolish things: *when I was a child, I spoke as a child* (1 Cor 13:11).

But how should you become children? In affection, not in understanding. Therefore he says: *but in malice*. Here it should be noted that children are not wont to think evil, and therefore he says: *in malice be children*. And they are not accustomed to think of the good. In this sense, we should not become children but perfect men. Therefore, he says: *and in sense be perfect*, i.e., be perfect in discerning good and evil. Hence it is said: *solid food is for the mature, for those who have their faculties trained to distinguish good from evil* (Heb 5:14).

Therefore, what is praised in you is not the simplicity opposed to prudence but the simplicity opposed to craftiness:

Dominus dicit Matth. c. X, 16: *estote prudentes sicut serpentes*. Rom. XVI, 19: *volo vos sapientes esse in bono, simplices in malo*.

853. Consequenter cum dicit *in lege quid scriptum est?* Arguit ad propositum.

Ubi sciendum est quod hoc argumentum, sicut patet per Glossam, distinguitur per multa; sed secundum intentionem apostoli non videtur quod attendatur in loco hoc nisi una ratio. Et ratio sua ad probandum quod donum prophetiae est excellentius, quam donum linguarum, est talis: omne quod plus valet ad illud ad quod alterum principaliter ordinatur, est melius illo altero ordinato ad hoc; sed tam donum prophetiae, quam donum linguarum, ordinatur ad conversionem infidelium; sed prophetiae plus valent ad hoc, quam donum linguarum; ergo prophetia est melior.

854. Circa hanc ergo rationem duo facit.

Primo ostendit ad quid ordinatur donum linguarum, et ad quid ordinatur donum prophetiae;

secundo quod plus valet donum prophetiae, ibi *si ergo conveniat universa*, et cetera.

Circa primum duo facit.

Primo inducit auctoritatem;

secundo ex auctoritate arguit ad propositum, ibi *itaque linguae*, et cetera.

855. Circa primum sciendum est, quod hoc quod dicit *in lege quid scriptum est?* Potest legi vel interrogative, quasi dicat: non debetis effici pueri sensibus, sed perfecti, et hoc est videre et scire legem. Unde si estis perfecti sensibus, sciatis scilicet legem, et in lege quid scriptum est de linguis? Quae sunt inutiles aliquando ad id ad quod ordinatae sunt, quia licet in diversis linguis loquar, scilicet populo Iudaeorum, tamen homo non exaudit, et cetera.

Potest etiam legi remissive *in lege quid scriptum est*. Quasi dicat: nolite moveri sicut pueri ad aliquid appetendum, non discernentes utrum bonum vel minus bonum sit quod affectatis, et praeponatis meliori bono, sed estote perfecti sensibus, idest discernatis inter bona et magis bona, et sic affectetis. Et hoc fit si cogitatis quid scriptum est in lege *quoniam in aliis*, etc., Sap. VI, 16: *cogitare ergo de illa, sensus est consummatus*.

Et dicit *in lege*, non accipiendo *legem* stricte pro quinque libris Moysi tantum, sicut accipitur Lc. ult.: *necesse est impleri omnia quae scripta sunt de me in lege*, etc.; sed pro toto Veteri Testamento, sicut accipitur Io. XV, 25: *ut impleatur sermo qui in lege eorum scriptus est: quia odio habuerunt me gratis*, quod tamen in Ps. XXIV, 19 scriptum est.

be wise as serpents (Matt 10:16); *I would have you wise as to what is good and guileless as to what is evil* (Rom 16:19).

853. Then when he says: *in the law it is written*, he argues to his proposition.

Here it should be noted that this argument, as is clear from a Gloss, is distinguished by many things; but according to the Apostle's intent, it does not seem that in this place attention is paid to more than one reason. The argument proving that the gift of prophecy excels the gift of tongues is this: whatever contributes more to that to which another is principally ordained is better than the latter; but the gift of prophecy and the gift of tongues are both ordained to the conversion of unbelievers, although the gift of prophecy contributes more to this than does the gift of tongues. Therefore, prophecy is better.

854. In regard to this reason he does two things:

first, he shows to what the gift of tongues is ordained, and to what the gift of prophecy is ordained;

second, that the gift of prophecy contributes more, at *if therefore the whole Church* (1 Cor 14:23).

As to the first he does two things.

First, he brings forward an authority;

second, he argues for his point from this authority, at *wherefore tongues*.

855. In regard to the first it should be noted that this question: *in the law it is written* can be taken as an interrogation, as though he were saying: you should not become children in sense but mature, and this is to see and know the law. Hence, if you are mature in your senses, you should know the law and what has been written in the law about tongues, which are useless at times for that to which they are ordained, because although I should speak in various tongues, namely, to the Jewish people, nevertheless man does not hear.

It can also be taken in a remissive sense, *in the law it is written*; as if he were saying: do not be enticed as children to desire something, not discerning whether you are being attracted to good or evil and preferring the good to the better; but be mature in sense, i.e., distinguish between the good and the better, and thus be attracted. And this happens, if you reflect on what has been written in the law: *in other tongues and other lips I will speak*: to fix one's thought on her is perfect understanding (Wis 6:15).

He says, *in the law*, not taking *law* exclusively for the five books of Moses, as it is taken in Luke: *everything written about me in the law of Moses must be fulfilled* (Luke 24:44), but for the entire Old Testament, as it is taken in John: *it is to fulfill the word that is written in their law: they hated me without cause* (John 15:25), which was written in a psalm (Ps 25:19).

Accipitur tamen haec auctoritas ex Is. c. XXVIII, 11, ubi littera nostra habet: *in loquela labii et lingua altera loquetur ad populum istum.*

Hoc igitur scriptum est *quoniam in aliis linguis*, id est in diversis generibus linguarum, et *labiis*, id est in diversis idiomatibus et modis pronuntiandi, *loquar populo huic*, scilicet Iudaico, quia hoc signum specialiter fuit datum ad conversionem populi Iudaeorum. *Nec sic exaudient*, quia scilicet signis visis non crediderunt. Is. VI, 10: *excaeca cor populi huius*, et cetera.

856. Sed quare Deus dedit eis signa, si non debebant converti?

Ad hoc sunt duae rationes. Una ratio est, quia licet non omnes conversi fuerint, tamen aliqui sunt conversi, eo quod non repellit Dominus plebem suam, et cetera. Alia ratio est, ut iustior appareat eorum damnatio, dum manifestius apparet eorum nequitia. Io. XV, v. 22: *si non venissem, et locutus eis non fuissem*, et cetera.

857. Consequenter, cum dicit *itaque linguae*, etc., ex inducta auctoritate argumentatur ad propositum, quasi dicat: ex hoc manifeste apparet, quod donum linguarum datum est *non fidelibus* ad credendum, quia iam credunt, Io. IV, 42: *non propter tuam loquelam*, etc., *sed infidelibus*, ut convertantur.

858. In Glossa autem ponuntur duae expositiones Ambrosii hoc in loco, quae non sunt litterales; quarum una est ut dicatur: sicut in Veteri Testamento locutus sum populo Iudaeorum per linguas, id est per figuras, et per labia, id est promittendo bona temporalia, sic, adhuc in Novo Testamento, *loquar huic populo in aliis linguis*, id est aperte et clare, et *aliis labiis*, id est spiritualibus, *nec* tamen sic *exaudient me*, scilicet quantum ad eorum multitudinem. *Itaque linguae* datae sunt *non fidelibus, sed infidelibus*, ad manifestandum scilicet eorum infidelitatem.

Alia est *in aliis linguis*, id est obscure et parabolice, *loquar*, ut quia sunt indigni. *Non exaudient*, id est non intelligent. Consequenter ostendit ad quid ordinatur prophetia, scilicet ad instructionem fidelium, qui iam credunt. Et ideo quod *prophetiae* datae sunt *non infidelibus*, qui non credunt, Is. LIII, 1: *Domine, quis credidit auditui nostro? Sed fidelibus*, ut credant et instruantur. Ez. III, 17: *fili hominis, speculatorem dedi te*, et cetera. Prov. XXIX, 18: *cum defecerit prophetia*, etc., *dissipabitur populus.*

Nonetheless, the authority can be taken from Isaiah, which in one version says: *in the speech of lips and in another tongue he will speak to this people* (Isa 28:11).

This, therefore, was written: *in other tongues*, i.e., in various kinds of tongues, *and other lips*, i.e., in various idioms and modes of pronunciation, *I will speak to this people*, namely, the Jews, because this sign was specially given for the conversion of the people of Israel. *And neither so will they hear me*, because although they saw the sign, they did not believe: *blind the heart of this people and make their ears heavy* (Isa 6:10).

856. But why would God give them signs, if they were not to be converted?

To this there are two answers: one is that although not all were converted, some were; for God did not reject his people. The other is in order that their damnation appear more just, while their guilt appears more clearly: *if I had not come and spoken to them, they would not have sin* (John 15:22).

857. Then when he says: *wherefore tongues are for a sign, not to believers, but to unbelievers*, he argues to his conclusion by using the authority quoted. As if to say: from this it is clearly evident that the gift of tongues was given *not for believers* to bring them to belief, because they already believe: *it is no longer because of your words that we believe* (John 4:42), *but to unbelievers* to be converted.

858. In a Gloss two non-literal explanations by Ambrose are presented in this place. One of these says: just as in the Old Testament I spoke to the Jewish people in tongues, i.e., through figures, and with lips, i.e., by promising temporal goods, so, even in the New Testament *I will speak to this people in other tongues*, i.e., openly and clearly, and with *other lips*, i.e., spiritual things; *and neither so will they hear me*, namely, as to their multitude. *Wherefore tongues* were given *not to believers, but to unbelievers*, namely, to manifest their unbelief.

The other is *in other tongues*, i.e., dimly and in parables *I will speak*, because they are unworthy. *Neither so will they hear me*, i.e., they will not understand. Then he shows what prophecy is ordained to, namely, to the instruction of believers, because they already understand. Therefore, *prophecies, not to unbelievers*, who do not believe: *Lord, who has believed our hearing?* (Isa 53:1); *but to believers*, that they believe and be instructed: *son of man, I have made you a watchman for the house of Israel* (Exod 3:17); *where there is no prophecy, the people cast off restraint* (Prov 29:18).

Lecture 5

¹⁴:²³Si ergo conveniat universa Ecclesia in unum, et omnes linguis loquantur, intrent autem idiotae, aut infideles: nonne dicent quod insanitis? [n. 859]

¹⁴:²⁴Si autem omnes prophetent, intret autem quis infidelis, vel idiota, convincitur ab omnibus, dijudicatur ab omnibus: [n. 862]

¹⁴:²⁵occulta cordis ejus manifesta fiunt: et ita cadens in faciem adorabit Deum, pronuntians quod vere Deus in vobis sit. [n. 864]

¹⁴:²⁶Quid ergo est, fratres? Cum convenitis, unusquisque vestrum psalmum habet, doctrinam habet, apocalypsim habet, linguam habet, interpretationem habet: omnia ad aedificationem fiant. [n. 866]

¹⁴:²³Ἐὰν οὖν συνέλθῃ ἡ ἐκκλησία ὅλη ἐπὶ τὸ αὐτὸ καὶ πάντες λαλῶσιν γλώσσαις, εἰσέλθωσιν δὲ ἰδιῶται ἢ ἄπιστοι, οὐκ ἐροῦσιν ὅτι μαίνεσθε;

¹⁴:²⁴ἐὰν δὲ πάντες προφητεύωσιν, εἰσέλθῃ δέ τις ἄπιστος ἢ ἰδιώτης, ἐλέγχεται ὑπὸ πάντων, ἀνακρίνεται ὑπὸ πάντων,

¹⁴:²⁵τὰ κρυπτὰ τῆς καρδίας αὐτοῦ φανερὰ γίνεται, καὶ οὕτως πεσὼν ἐπὶ πρόσωπον προσκυνήσει τῷ θεῷ, ἀπαγγέλλων ὅτι Ὄντως ὁ θεὸς ἐν ὑμῖν ἐστιν.

¹⁴:²⁶Τί οὖν ἐστιν, ἀδελφοί; ὅταν συνέρχησθε, ἕκαστος ψαλμὸν ἔχει, διδαχὴν ἔχει, ἀποκάλυψιν ἔχει, γλῶσσαν ἔχει, ἑρμηνείαν ἔχει· πάντα πρὸς οἰκοδομὴν γινέσθω.

¹⁴:²³If therefore the whole Church come together into one place, and all speak with tongues, and there come in unlearned persons or infidels, will they not say that you are mad? [n. 859]

¹⁴:²⁴But if all prophesy, and there comes in one who believes not or an unlearned person, he is convinced of all: he is judged of all. [n. 862]

¹⁴:²⁵The secrets of his heart are made manifest. And so, falling down on his face, he will adore God, affirming that God is among you indeed. [n. 864]

¹⁴:²⁶How is it then, brethren? When you come together, every one of you has a psalm, has a doctrine, has a revelation, has a tongue, has an interpretation: let all things be done to edification. [n. 866]

---

859. Glossa vult quod hic incipiat alia ratio ad propositum ostendendum. Sed secundum quod dictum est, non est nisi unum posita ratione, et est quasi manifestatio mediae ipsius rationis, scilicet quod prophetia plus valet ad illud, ad quod specialiter ordinatur donum linguarum.

Unde circa hoc duo facit.

Primo ostendit inconveniens quod sequitur quantum ad infideles ex dono linguarum, ibi *si autem omnes linguis*.

Secundo ostendit bonum quod sequitur ex dono prophetiae etiam ad infideles, ibi *si autem omnes*.

860. Inconveniens, quod sequitur ex dono linguarum sine prophetia, etiam quantum ad infideles, est quia reputantur insani qui sic loquuntur solis linguis, cum tamen donum linguarum ordinetur ad conversionem infidelium, ut iam patet. Et hoc est quod dicit *si autem omnes*, etc., quasi dicat: ex hoc patet quod linguae non sunt praeferendae prophetiis, quia, *si conveniant*, scilicet omnes fideles, *in unum*, non solum corpore, sed etiam mente, Act. IV, 32: *multitudinis credentium erat cor*, etc., *et omnes*, qui iam convenerunt, *loquantur linguis*, ad litteram extraneis, vel loquantur ignota et obscura, et, dum sic confuse loquuntur, *intret aliquis idiota*, id est qui non intelligit nisi linguam suam, vel *infidelis*, propter quem datae sunt linguae, *nonne dicent* his, qui sic loquuntur, *quid insanitis?* Quod enim non intelligitur, reputatur insanitio. Quod si intelligatur

859. A Gloss suggests that another argument proving his proposition begins here. But in the light of what has been said, there is only one proposition, already proved. Here he clarifies the middle term of that argument, namely, that prophecy contributes more to that to which the gift of tongues is especially ordained.

In regard to this he does two things:

first, he shows what undesirable effects follows from the gift of tongues as far as unbelievers are concerned, at *if all speak with tongues*;

second, he shows the good which follows from the gift of prophecy, even in regard to unbelievers, at *but if all prophesy*.

860. The undesirable effect which follows from the gift of tongues without prophecy, even in regard to unbelievers, is that those who speak only in tongues are considered mad, whereas the gift of tongues should be ordained to the conversion of unbelievers, as is already clear. And this is what he says: *but if all prophesy*. As if to say: that tongues are not preferable to prophecy is clear from the fact that *if the whole Church*, namely, all the faithful, *come together into one place* not only in body but also in mind: *now the company of believers were of one heart and soul* (Acts 4:22), *and all speak with tongues*, i.e., strange, or speak unknown and obscure things and, while they are thus confusedly speaking, *and there come in unlearned persons*, i.e., one who understands only his own tongue, or *infidels* for whose benefit tongues were given, *will they not say* to those so speaking that *you are mad?* For what is not understood

lingua, nihilominus quae loquuntur sunt occulta, tamen malum est si non exponatur, quia poterunt credere de vobis, si occulta loquimini, quae creduntur de gentilibus, qui occultabant ea quae faciebant in ritu eorum, propter eorum turpitudinem. Et haec etiam insanitio quaedam est.

861. Contra. Idem est loqui linguis et loqui litteraliter quantum ad idiotas; cum ergo omnes loquantur litteraliter in ecclesia, quia omnia dicuntur in Latino, videtur quod similiter sit insania.

Dicendum est ad hoc, quod ideo erat insania in primitiva Ecclesia, quia erant rudes in ritu ecclesiastico, unde nesciebant quae fiebant ibi, nisi exponeretur eis. Modo vero omnes sunt instructi; unde licet in Latino omnia dicantur, sciunt tamen illud quod fit in ecclesia.

862. Consequenter autem cum dicit *si autem omnes prophetent*, ostendit quod bonum sequitur ex dono prophetiae.

Et circa hoc tria facit.

Primo ostendit quid per bonum prophetiae sequatur, quantum ad infideles;

secundo ostendit quomodo hoc sequatur, ibi *occulta enim*, etc.;

tertio, subinfert quis effectus inde proveniat, ibi *et ita cadens in faciem*, et cetera.

863. Dicit ergo: constat quod ex dono linguarum non convincuntur infideles; *si autem*, pro *sed*; si hi, qui conveniunt, *prophetent*, id est omnes ad intellectum loquantur, vel exponant Scripturas vel etiam revelationes eis factas interpretentur. *Omnes* dico non simul, sed unus post alium sic prophetent. *Intret autem*, scilicet ecclesiam, *idiota* aliquis, scilicet non habens nisi linguam maternam, hoc est bonum quod inde sequitur, quia *convincitur* de aliquo errore, qui ostenditur sibi. Ier. XXXI, 19: *postquam ostendisti mihi, confusus sum. Ab omnibus*, qui prophetant, *diiudicatur*. Quasi dicat: damnabilis ostenditur de malis moribus et vitiis suis. I Cor. II, 15: *spiritualis*, id est doctor, *omnia diiudicat*, et cetera.

Ad haec enim duo valet prophetia, scilicet ad confirmationem fidei, et instructionem morum.

864. Quomodo autem hoc bonum sequatur ex prophetiae dono, subdit cum dicit *occulta enim cordis*. Quod potest intelligi tripliciter.

Uno modo, et hoc ad litteram, quod aliqui in primitiva Ecclesia gratiam habuerunt, ut secreta cordium et peccata hominum scirent. Unde legitur de Petro, Act. V, 1 ss., quod damnavit Ananiam de fraudato pretio agri. Et secundum hoc legitur *occulta enim*, etc., quasi

is considered madness. But if a tongue is understood and nevertheless the things said are secret, if they are not explained, it is evil because they could believe of you, (if you speak secret things), what they believe of the gentiles, who made secret what they did in their rites, so base were they. And this is also a form of madness.

861. On the other hand, to those who do not know the language it is the same thing to speak in tongues and to speak literally; therefore, since all speak literally in the church (for all is spoken in Latin), it seems that there is madness here, too.

I answer that there was madness in the early Church, because they were uninstructed in the Church's rite, since they did not know what was going on unless it was explained to them. But now all are instructed; hence, although all is said in Latin, they, nevertheless, know what is being done in the church.

862. Then when he says, *but if all prophesy*, he shows that good follows from the gift of prophecy.

In regard to this he does three things:

first, he shows what follows through the good of prophecy, as to unbelievers;

second, he shows how this follows, at *the secrets of his heart*;

third, he infers which effect arises from this, at *and so, falling down on his face*.

863. He says, therefore: it is clear that unbelievers are not convinced by the gift of tongues; *but if all* who assemble *prophecy*, i.e., all speak to the intellect revelations made to them (I say *all* not at once, but one after the other prophesy in this way), *and there comes in*, namely, the church, *one who believes not or an unlearned person*, i.e., knowing only his mother tongue, what follows is good, because *he is convinced* by all of his error, which is pointed out to him: *after I was instructed, I was ashamed* (Jer 31:19). *He is judged of all* who are prophesying. As if to say: he is shown to be condemnable for his evil morals and his vices: *the spiritual man*, that is, the doctor, *judges all things* (1 Cor 2:15).

For prophecy avails for these two things, namely, strengthening the faith and teaching morals.

864. How this good follows from the gift of prophecy is mentioned when he says: *the secrets of his heart*. This can be understood in three ways:

in one way, and this is literal, that some in the early Church had the grace to know the secrets of the heart and the sins of men. Hence it said of Peter that he condemned Ananias for fraud regarding the price of a field (Acts 5:1ff). And according to this it says: for *the secrets of his heart*

dicat: ideo convincitur, quia *occulta*, id est secreta peccata sua, *manifesta fiunt* ab illis qui ea revelant.

Alio modo, ex hoc quod aliquando quis in praedicatione tangit multa, quae homines gerunt in corde, sicut patet in libris beati Gregorii, ubi quilibet invenire potest fere omnes motus cordis sui. Et secundum hoc legitur *occulta cordis*, quasi dicat: ideo convincuntur, quia *occulta cordis sui*, id est ea quae gerunt in corde, Prov. XXVII, 19: *quomodo in aquis resplendet vultus aspicientium, sic corda hominum manifesta sunt prudentibus*, *manifestantur*, id est tanguntur ab eis.

Alio modo, quia aliquando occultum cordis dicitur illud quod est alicui dubium et non potest per se certificari. Et secundum hoc legitur *occulta cordis sui*, id est ea de quibus in corde suo dubitabat et quae non credebat, manifestantur, dum scilicet vadens ad ecclesiam frequenter fiunt sibi manifesta, sicut de seipso dicit Augustinus quod ipse ibat ad ecclesiam solum pro cantu et tamen ibi multa de quibus dubitabat et propter quae non iverat, manifestabantur sibi. Ex hoc enim sequebatur reverentia, quia convictus reverebatur Deum.

865. Et hoc est, quod dicit *et ita cadens*, id est ex quo ita convincebatur et manifestabantur occulta cordis sui, *cadens in faciem adorabit Deum*, Matth. II, 11: *procidentes adoraverunt eum*, quod signum est reverentiae.

De reprobis autem legitur, quod cadunt retrorsum. Prov. IV, 19: *via impiorum tenebrosa, nesciunt ubi corruent*. Electus vero in faciem cadit, quia videt ubi prosternitur, quod signum est reverentiae. Matth. II, 11, et Lev. c. IX, 24: *laudaverunt Deum ruentes in facies suas*. Ps. LXXI, 9: *coram illo procident Aethiopes*.

Et non solum exhibebit reverentiam Deo sed etiam ecclesiae, quia *pronuntians* dicet *quod vere Deus* est *in vobis*, qui prophetatis in Ecclesia. Zac. VIII, 23: *ibimus vobiscum, audivimus enim quod Deus est vobiscum*.

Apparet igitur quod donum prophetiae est utilius quantum ad infideles.

866. *Quid ergo est, fratres?* Hic ordinat eos ad usum donorum dictorum.

Et circa hoc duo facit.

Primo ostendit qualiter se debeant habere ad usum horum donorum;

secundo concludit principale intentum, ibi *itaque, fratres, aemulamini prophetare*, et cetera.

Circa primum duo facit.

Primo ostendit quomodo ordinate se debeant habere in usu dictorum donorum;

are disclosed. As if to say: he is convinced, *because the secrets*, i.e., his secret sins, *are made manifest* by those who revealed them.

In another way, from the fact that sometimes someone in preaching touches on many things which men carry in the heart, as is clear from the books of Gregory, where each one can find almost all the movements of the heart. And according to this he says, *secrets of his heart*; as if to say: they are convicted, because *the secrets of their heart*, i.e., things they carry in their heart: *as in water face answers to face, so the mind of man reflects the man* (Prov 27:19), *are made manifest*, i.e., touched on by them.

In another way, because sometimes the secret of the heart is said to be that which is doubtful to someone and he cannot become certain by himself. According to this it is read: *the secrets of his heart*, i.e., things about which he doubted in his heart and which he did not believe, are disclosed, namely, when going to a church frequently they are made clear to him, as Augustine says about himself that he went to the church only for the chant and yet many things about which he doubted and for the sake of which he had not come were clarified for him there. For from this followed reverence, because, being convinced, he revered God.

865. And this is what he says: *and so*, i.e., inasmuch as he was convinced in this way and the secrets of his heart were manifested, *falling down on his face, he will adore God*: *falling down, they adored him* (Matt 2:11), which is a sign of reverence.

Of the reprobate, however, it says that they fall backward: *the way of the wicked is deep darkness, they do not know over what they stumble* (Prov 4:19). But the elect fall on their face, because they see where they should prostrate themselves, which is a sign of reverence. *They praised God and fell on their faces* (Lev 9:24); *may all kings fall down before him* (Ps 72:11).

And he will show reverence not only to God but also to the church, because he will declare that *God is among you indeed* who prophesy in the church: *we will go with you, for we have heard that God is with you* (Zech 8:23).

It appears, therefore, that the gift of prophecy is more useful in regard to unbelievers.

866. *How is it then, brethren?* Here he tells them how to use these gifts.

In regard to this he does two things:

first, he shows how they should act in regard to the use of these gifts;

second, he concludes to his main proposition, at *wherefore, brethren, be zealous to prophesy* (1 Cor 14:39).

In regard to the first he does two things:

first, he shows how orderly they should behave in the use of these gifts;

secundo exprimit eorum praesumptionem, ibi *an a vobis sermo*, et cetera.

Circa primum tria facit.

Primo ostendit in generali quomodo se debent habere in omnibus donis;

secundo quomodo se habeant quantum ad donum linguarum, ibi *sive lingua quis loquatur*, etc.;

tertio ostendit quomodo se habeant quantum ad donum prophetiae, ibi *prophetent duo aut tres*, et cetera.

867. Dicit ergo: prophetare est melius quam loqui linguis. *Quid ergo, fratres*, agendum est? Hoc scilicet agendum est: nam, *cum convenitis*, constat quod unus non habet omnia dona, et ideo non debet uti aliquis vestrum omnibus donis, sed eo dono quod specialius accepit a Deo et quod melius sit ad aedificationem.

Nam unusquisque vestrum habet aliquod donum speciale, *alius habet psalmum*, id est canticum ad laudandum nomen Dei, vel psalmos exponit. Abac. III, 19: *super excelsa mea deducet me*, et cetera. *Alius* vero *doctrinam*, id est habet praedicationem ad instructionem morum, vel expositionem et spiritualem sensum. Prov. XII, 8: *doctrina sua cognoscitur vir*. *Alius apocalypsim habet*, id est revelationem, vel in somniis, vel in visione aliqua. Dan. II, 28: *est Deus in caelo revelans mysteria*, et cetera. *Alius linguam habet*, id est donum linguarum, vel legendi prophetias. Act. II, 4: *et coeperunt loqui variis linguis*, et cetera. *Alius interpretationem*, supra XII, 10: *alii interpretatio sermonum*, et cetera.

868. Haec autem sic ordinantur, quia vel sunt ex ingenio naturali, vel ex solo Deo.

Si sunt ex solo ingenio naturali vel sunt ad laudem Dei, et sic dicit *psalmum habet*, vel ad instructionem proximi, et sic dicit *doctrinam habet*.

Si sunt a solo Deo, sic dupliciter: vel sunt aliqua occulta interius et sic dicit *apocalypsim habet*, vel occulta exterius et sic dicit *linguam habet*. Et ad horum manifestationem est tertium, scilicet *interpretatio*.

Et debet fieri, *ut omnia ad aedificationem fiant*. Rom. XV, 2: *unusquisque vestrum proximo suo placeat in bonum ad aedificationem*.

second, he expresses their presumption, at *or did the word of God* (1 Cor 14:36).

In regard to the first he does three things:

first, he shows in general how they should behave in all gifts;

second, in regard to the gift of tongues, at *if any speaks with a tongue* (1 Cor 14:27);

third, as to the gift of prophecy, at *and let the prophets speak, two or three* (1 Cor 14:29).

867. He says, therefore: to prophesy is better than to speak in tongues. *How is it then, brethren* is to be done? This is to be done. For *when you come together*, it is obvious that one does not have all the gifts, and therefore none of you should use all the gifts, but that gift which he had more specially received from God and which is better for edification.

For every one of you has some special gift: *one has a psalm*, i.e., a song to praise the Lord's name, or to explain psalms: *he makes me tread upon my high places* (Hab 3:19); *another has a doctrine*, i.e., some preaching to instruct them in morals, or an explanation and a spiritual sense: *a man is known by his teaching* (Prov 12:8); *another has a revelation* obtained either in dreams or in a vision: *God is in heaven revealing mysteries* (Dan 2:28); *another has a tongue*, i.e., the gift of tongues or he reads prophecies: *and they began to speak in tongues* (Acts 2:4); *another has an interpretation*: *to another the interpretation of speeches* (1 Cor 12:10).

868. But these are so arranged, because they derive either from human talent or from God alone.

If they are solely from human talent, they are either to the praise of God, and so he says, *one has a psalm*, or to the instruction of the neighbor, and so he says, *one has a doctrine*.

If they are from God alone, they are either inward secrets, and so he says, *one has a revelation*, or outwardly hidden, and so he says, *one has a tongue*. For manifesting these there is a third thing, and so he says, *an interpretation*.

And, of course, *let all things be done to edification*: *let each of us please his neighbor for his good, to edify him* (Rom 15:2).

Lecture 6

14:27Sive lingua quis loquitur, secundum duos, aut ut multum tres, et per partes, et unus interpretatur. [n. 869]

14:28Si autem non fuerit interpres, taceat in ecclesia: sibi autem loquatur, et Deo. [n. 871]

14:29Prophetae autem duo, aut tres dicant, et ceteri dijudicent. [n. 872]

14:30Quod si alii revelatum fuerit sedenti, prior taceat. [n. 874]

14:31Potestis enim omnes per singulos prophetare: ut omnes discant, et omnes exhortentur: [n. 875]

14:32et spiritus prophetarum prophetis subjecti sunt. [n. 876]

14:33Non enim est dissensionis Deus, sed pacis: sicut et in omnibus ecclesiis sanctorum doceo. [n. 877]

14:27εἴτε γλώσσῃ τις λαλεῖ, κατὰ δύο ἢ τὸ πλεῖστον τρεῖς, καὶ ἀνὰ μέρος, καὶ εἷς διερμηνευέτω:

14:28ἐὰν δὲ μὴ ᾖ διερμηνευτής, σιγάτω ἐν ἐκκλησίᾳ, ἑαυτῷ δὲ λαλείτω καὶ τῷ θεῷ.

14:29προφῆται δὲ δύο ἢ τρεῖς λαλείτωσαν, καὶ οἱ ἄλλοι διακρινέτωσαν:

14:30ἐὰν δὲ ἄλλῳ ἀποκαλυφθῇ καθημένῳ, ὁ πρῶτος σιγάτω.

14:31δύνασθε γὰρ καθ' ἕνα πάντες προφητεύειν, ἵνα πάντες μανθάνωσιν καὶ πάντες παρακαλῶνται,

14:32καὶ πνεύματα προφητῶν προφήταις ὑποτάσσεται:

14:33οὐ γάρ ἐστιν ἀκαταστασίας ὁ θεὸς ἀλλὰ εἰρήνης. Ὡς ἐν πάσαις ταῖς ἐκκλησίαις τῶν ἁγίων,

14:27If any speaks with a tongue, let it be by two, or at the most by three, and in course: and let one interpret. [n. 869]

14:28But if there be no interpreter, let him hold his peace in the church and speak to himself and to God. [n. 871]

14:29And let the prophets speak, two or three: and let the rest judge. [n. 872]

14:30But if any thing be revealed to another sitting, let the first hold his peace. [n. 874]

14:31For you may all prophesy, one by one, that all may learn and all may be exhorted. [n. 875]

14:32And the spirits of the prophets are subject to the prophets. [n. 876]

14:33For God is not the God of dissension, but of peace: as also I teach in all the churches of the saints. [n. 877]

---

869. Hic Apostolus ordinat eos quomodo se habeant ad usum doni linguarum, et circa hoc duo facit.

Primo ostendit qualiter debent uti dono linguarum; secundo quando debent cessare ab usu, ibi *si autem non fuerit*, et cetera.

870. Dicit ergo, primo, quod modus utendi dono linguarum talis sit inter vos, ut *sive quis*, id est si aliquis, *loquatur lingua*, id est dicat visiones vel somnia, huiusmodi locutio non fiat a multis propter occupationem temporis in linguis et non restet locus prophetiis et confusionem generet, sed *secundum duos*, id est duobus, et, si necesse fuerit, secundum *multum tres*, ut sit satis a tribus. Deut. XVII, 6: *in ore duorum vel trium*, et cetera.

Sed notandum quod haec consuetudo adhuc partim servatur in Ecclesia. Nam lectiones et epistolas ac Evangelia habemus loco linguarum, et ideo in Missa *secundum duos* servatur, quia solum duo dicuntur, quae pertinent ad donum linguarum, scilicet epistola et Evangelium. In Matutinis secundum multa fit, scilicet tribus lectionibus dictis in uno nocturno. Antiquitus enim dicebantur nocturna divisim secundum tres vigilias noctis, nunc vero dicuntur simul.

Non solum autem debet servari ordo quantum ad numerum loquentium, sed etiam quantum ad modum, et hoc est quod dicit *et per partes*, id est ut illi qui

869. Here the Apostle instructs them on how to behave in regard to using the gift of tongues, and he does two things:

first, he shows how they should use the gift of tongues: second, when they should stop using it, at *but if there be no interpreter*.

870. First, therefore he says: the way the gift of tongues should be used among you is *that if any speaks with a tongue*, i.e., talks of visions or dreams, such speaking should not be done by many on account of so much time being devoted to tongues, and so that there is not room for prophecies, and confusion is generated; but *let it be by two*, and if necessary, *at the most by three*; so that three should be enough: *on the evidence of two witnesses or of three witnesses* (Deut 17:6).

But it should be noted that this custom is still partly observed in the Church. For we have readings and epistles and gospels in place of tongues, and therefore in the Mass *only two* are said, which pertain to the gift of tongues, namely, the epistle and the gospel. In Matins many are said, namely, three readings in one nocturn. For at an earlier time nocturnes were said according to the night watches, but now they are said at one time.

Not only should order as to the number of speakers be observed, but also as to the method, and this is what he says: *and in course*, i.e., that those who speak follow one

loquuntur succedant sibi ad invicem, scilicet quod unus post alium loquatur. Vel *per partes*, id est intercise, ut scilicet loquatur unam partem visionis, seu instructionis et eam exponat, et post aliam et ipsam exponat, et sic deinceps; quem modum consueverunt servare praedicatores, quando praedicant per interpretationem hominibus ignotae linguae, et ideo dicit *et unus interpretetur*.

871. Consequenter cum dicit *si autem non fuerit*, etc., ostendit quando non est utendum linguis, dicens quod loquendum est per partes et unus debet interpretari. Sed *si non fuerit* aliquis *interpres*, id est qui interpretetur, ille, qui donum habet linguarum, *taceat in ecclesia*, id est non loquatur seu praedicet multitudini in lingua ignota, quia non intelligitur ab eis, sed *sibi loquatur*, quia ipse se intelligit, et hoc tacite, orando vel meditando. Iob X, 1: *loquar in amaritudine animae meae, dicam Deo*, et cetera.

872. *Prophetae autem duo*, et cetera. Hic Apostolus ordinat eos, quomodo se habeant ad usum prophetiae.

Et circa hoc duo facit.

Primo ostendit qualiter utendum est dono prophetiae, et quantum ad numerum et ad ordinem;

secundo ostendit, quibus usus prophetiae interdicitur, ibi *mulieres in ecclesia*, et cetera.

Circa primum tria facit.

Primo docet ordinem utendi dono prophetiae;

secundo huius rationem assignat, ibi *potestis enim omnes*, etc.;

tertio obiectionem excludit, ibi *spiritus prophetarum*, et cetera.

Circa primum duo facit.

Primo determinat ad numerum utentium dono dicto;

secundo, docet modum seu ordinem utendi, ibi *quod si alii*, et cetera.

873. Circa primum sciendum est quod usus prophetiae secundum quod hic videtur accipere Apostolus, est proponere verbum exhortationis ad plebem, exponendo Scripturas Sacras. Et quia erant in primitiva Ecclesia plures qui a Deo hoc donum habebant, et fideles non erant adhuc multiplicati, ideo, ne esset confusio et taedium, vult Apostolus, quod non omnes qui sciunt exponere prophetias et Sacram Scripturam, prophetent, sed aliqui et determinati. Et hoc est quod dicit *prophetae*, etc., quasi dicat: nolo quod omnes qui conveniunt, sed *duo* tantum, *aut*, ad plus, *tres*, prout hoc loquendi necessitas exigit, *dicant*, id est exhortentur. Et hoc etiam consonat Scripturae. Supra XVII, v. 6 et Matth. XVIII, 16: *in ore duorum, vel trium*, et cetera.

Caeteri vero, scilicet illi qui non debent, *diiudicent* ea quae ab his proponuntur, utrum scilicet bene vel male

another, so that one speaks after the other. Or *in course*, i.e., interruptedly, namely, that one speak one part of the vision or of the instruction and explain it, and then another and explain it, and so on. This was the method followed by preachers, when they preach by interpreting to men of an unknown tongue; and therefore he says: *and let one interpret*.

871. Then when he says: *but if there be no interpreter*, he shows when tongues should not be used, saying that they should speak in parts and one should interpret. *But if there be no interpreter*, one who has the gift of tongues, *let him hold his peace in the church*, i.e., should not speak or preach to the multitude in a strange tongue, because he is not understood by them, but should *speak to himself* or to God, because he understands himself; and this in silence by praying or meditating: *I will speak in the bitterness of my soul. I will say to God: do not condemn me* (Job 10:1).

872. *Let the prophets speak, two or three*, and let the others weigh what is said. Here the Apostle instructs them on how to use the gift of prophecy.

In regard to the first he does two things:

first, he shows how the gift of prophecy is to be used both as to number and to order;

second, to whom the use of prophecy is prohibited, at *let women keep silence in the churches* (1 Cor 14:34).

In regard to the first he does three things:

first, he teaches the order in which to use the gift of prophecy;

second, the reason for this, at *for you may all prophesy*;

third, he excludes an objection, at *and the spirits of the prophets*.

In regard to the first he does two things:

first, he fixes on the number using this gift;

second, he teaches the method or order of using it, at *but if any thing be revealed*.

873. In regard to the first it should be noted that the use of prophecy according to what the Apostle says here is to propose a word of instruction to the people, by explaining the Sacred Scripture. And because in the early Church there were many who had this gift from God and the number of the faithful was not very great, then in order to avoid confusion and boredom, the Apostle desires that not all who can explain a prophecy and Sacred Scripture should prophesy, but certain definite ones. And this is what he says: *let the prophets speak, two or three*. As if to say: I do not want all who assemble, but *two* only *or* at most *three*, as the need to speak exists, should *speak*, i.e., exhort. This is in keeping with the Scriptures: *by the evidence of two or three witnesses* (Matt 18:16).

Let the rest, namely, those who should not prophesy, *judge* the things proposed to them, whether something

dicta sint: bene dicta approbando, et male dicta retractari faciendo. Supra II, 15: *spiritualis homo omnia diiudicat*.

874. Est etiam servandus ordo in utendo dicto dono, ut si alteri illorum, qui sedebant et tacebant et diiudicabant, fuit aliquid melius revelatum, quam illi qui exhortatur et stat prior, tunc iste, qui stat, debet sedere, et ille, cui melius revelatum est, debet surgere et exhortari. Et hoc est quod dicit *quod si alii, sedenti, revelatum fuerit*, scilicet per Spiritum Sanctum, *prior* stans *taceat* et cedat ei, Rom. XII, 10: *honore invicem praevenientes*.

875. Et ratio huius est, quia secundum hunc modum *potestis*, successive, *prophetare per singulos*, id est omnes scilicet, *ut sic omnes*, id est maiores, *discant, et omnes*, id est minores, *exhortentur*, Prov. I, 5: *audiens sapiens*, et cetera.

876. Et si aliquis dicat: o Apostole, ego non possum tacere dum alius prophetat, vel cedere sedenti, ex quo incepi, quia non possum retinere Spiritum, qui in me loquitur, secundum illud Iob IV, 2: *conceptum sermonem tenere quis potest?* Ideo Apostolus hoc removet cum dicit *et spiritus prophetarum*, etc., quasi dicat: immo bene potest tacere vel sedere, quia *spiritus prophetarum*, id est spiritus qui dat prophetias, et ponit in plurali numero propter multas revelationes eis instinctas, *prophetis subiecti sunt*, quidem quantum ad cognitionem, quia, sicut dicit Gregorius *quod non semper spiritus prophetiae adest prophetis*. Unde non est habitus, sicut scientia. Sic enim sequeretur, quod etiam quantum ad cognitionem eis subiectus esset, et possent uti eo quando vellent, et non uti: sed est quaedam vis aut impressio a Deo, illuminans et tangens corda prophetarum, et tunc solum quando sic tanguntur, cognoscunt. Unde non est sic eis subiectus.

Nec secundum hoc intelligitur verbum apostoli, sed *spiritus prophetarum sunt subiecti prophetis* quantum ad pronuntiationem, quia scilicet in eorum potestate est pronuntiare ea quae revelantur eis quando volunt, et non pronuntiare. Et sic nihil valet excusatio, quia non cogit te Spiritus quin tacere possis.

877. Et quod hoc sit verum, probat cum dicit *non enim est dissensionis*, et cetera. Et facit talem rationem. Deus numquam cogit ad id unde oriatur rixa vel dissensio, quia Deus *non est dissensionis sed pacis*; sed si cogeret homines Spiritus prophetiae ad loquendum, tunc esset causa dissensionis, quia sic vellet semper loqui vel docere vel non tacere alio loquente, de quo alii turbarentur. Ergo Spiritus Sanctus non cogit homines ad loquendum. II Cor. ult.: *Deus pacis et dilectionis erit vobiscum*, et cetera.

Verumtamen, quia adhuc posset obiicere, quod hoc non faceret, quia solum eis ista mandabat, et non aliis ecclesiis, unde et in gravamen posset videri, ideo

good or something bad has been said; approving what is good and making them retract what was wrong: *the spiritual man judges all things* (1 Cor 2:15).

874. The order to be observed in using this gift is that if one of those who sat and kept silence and judged had received a better revelation, then one who is exhorting and standing should sit down and the one to whom a better revelation has been made should rise and exhort. And this is what he says: *if anything be revealed to another sitting*, namely, by the Holy Spirit, *let the first hold his peace* and yield to him: *anticipate one another with honor* (Rom 12:10).

875. The reason for this is that according to this method *you may* successively *all prophesy, one by one*, i.e., the greater, *that all may learn*, i.e., the lesser, *and all may be exhorted*. The wise man may also hear and increase in learning (Prov 1:5).

876. If any should say: O Apostle, I cannot be silent while another prophesies or yield to one sitting from the time he began, because I cannot hold back the Spirit who speaks in me: *who can keep from speaking?* (Job 4:2). Therefore, the Apostle rejects this when he says: *the spirits of the prophets are subject to the prophets*. As if to say: yes, he can easily be quiet and sit down, because *the spirits of the prophets*, i.e., the spirit who gives prophecies (and he puts it in the plural on account of the many revelations inspired in them) *are subject to the prophets*; some as to knowledge, because as Gregory says: *the spirit of prophecy is not always present to the prophets*. Hence it is not a habit, as knowledge is. For then it would follow that even as to knowledge he would be subject to them and they could use it or not use it when they willed; but it is a force or impression from God inclining and teaching the hearts of the prophets and they know only when they are so touched. Hence, he is not subject to them.

But this is not the way to understand the Apostle's words, but *the spirits of the prophets are subject to the prophets* as to declaring, namely, because it is in their power to declare when they wish or not to declare the things revealed. And so the excuse is worthless, because the Spirit does not compel you in such a way that you cannot keep silence.

877. That this is true he proves when he says, *God is not a God of dissension*. And he formulates this reason: God never compels one to something from which arise quarrels or dissension, because he is *not a God of dissension, but of peace*. But if the Spirit of prophecy compelled them to speak, he would be a cause of dissension, because he would always want to speak or not to teach or to be silent, while another is speaking something about which the others are disturbed. Therefore, the Holy Spirit does not compel men to speak: *may the God of love and peace be with you* (2 Cor 13:11).

Yet because he could still object that he would not do this, because he commanded this only of them and not of the other churches; and hence it could seem a burden, the

Apostolus subdit, hoc non solum in eis, sed etiam in omnibus Ecclesiis docere. Et hoc est quod dicit **sicut in omnibus ecclesiis sanctorum doceo**, scilicet de usu linguarum et prophetiae. Supra I, 10: **idipsum dicatis omnes**.

Apostle says that he teaches this not only to them but to all the churches. And this is what he says: **as also I teach in all the churches of the saints**, namely, about the use of tongues and of prophecy: **appeal to you that all of you agree** (1 Cor 1:10).

Lecture 7

14:34Mulieres in ecclesiis taceant, non enim permittitur eis loqui, sed subditas esse, sicut et lex dicit. [n. 878]

14:35Si quid autem volunt discere, domi viros suos interrogent. Turpe est enim mulieri loqui in ecclesia. [n. 881]

14:36An a vobis verbum Dei processit? aut in vos solos pervenit? [n. 882]

14:37Si quis videtur propheta esse, aut spiritualis, cognoscat quae scribo vobis, quia Domini sunt mandata. [n. 884]

14:38Si quis autem ignorat, ignorabitur. [n. 886]

14:39Itaque fratres aemulamini prophetare: et loqui linguis nolite prohibere. [n. 887]

14:40Omnia autem honeste, et secundum ordinem fiant.

14:34αἱ γυναῖκες ἐν ταῖς ἐκκλησίαις σιγάτωσαν, οὐ γὰρ ἐπιτρέπεται αὐταῖς λαλεῖν: ἀλλὰ ὑποτασσέσθωσαν, καθὼς καὶ ὁ νόμος λέγει.

14:35εἰ δέ τι μαθεῖν θέλουσιν, ἐν οἴκῳ τοὺς ἰδίους ἄνδρας ἐπερωτάτωσαν, αἰσχρὸν γάρ ἐστιν γυναικὶ λαλεῖν ἐν ἐκκλησίᾳ.

14:36ἢ ἀφ' ὑμῶν ὁ λόγος τοῦ θεοῦ ἐξῆλθεν, ἢ εἰς ὑμᾶς μόνους κατήντησεν;

14:37Εἴ τις δοκεῖ προφήτης εἶναι ἢ πνευματικός, ἐπιγινωσκέτω ἃ γράφω ὑμῖν ὅτι κυρίου ἐστὶν ἐντολή:

14:38εἰ δέ τις ἀγνοεῖ, ἀγνοεῖται.

14:39ὥστε, ἀδελφοί [μου], ζηλοῦτε τὸ προφητεύειν, καὶ τὸ λαλεῖν μὴ κωλύετε γλώσσαις:

14:40πάντα δὲ εὐσχημόνως καὶ κατὰ τάξιν γινέσθω.

14:34Let women keep silence in the churches: for it is not permitted them to speak but to be subject, as also the law says. [n. 878]

14:35But if they would learn anything, let them ask their husbands at home. For it is a shame for a woman to speak in the church. [n. 881]

14:36Or did the word of God come out from you? Or came it only unto you? [n. 882]

14:37If any seem to be a prophet or spiritual, let him know the things that I write to you, that they are the commandments of the Lord. [n. 884]

14:38But if any man knows not, he shall not be known. [n. 886]

14:39Wherefore, brethren, be zealous to prophesy: and do not forbid to speak with tongues. [n. 887]

14:40But let all things be done decently and according to order.

---

878. Hic Apostolus ponit personas quibus interdicit usum prophetiae.

Et circa hoc duo facit.

Primo, ostendit quibus prophetiae usus interdicitur;

secundo, removet obiectionem, ibi *si quid autem volunt*, et cetera.

Circa primum duo facit.

Primo, ponit mandatum de interdicto;

secundo huius rationem assignat, ibi *non enim permittitur*, et cetera.

879. Dicit ergo: volo ut viri hoc modo utantur dono prophetiae, sed *mulieres*, in ecclesia, nolo loqui; sed *taceant in ecclesiis*, I Tim. II, 12: *mulierem docere in ecclesia non permitto.* Et rationem huius assignat Chrysostomus, dicens, quod *semel est locuta mulier et totum mundum subvertit.*

Sed contra hoc videtur quia de multis mulieribus legitur quod prophetarunt, sicut de Samaritana, Io. IV, 39, et de Anna uxore Phanuel, Lc. II, 36, et de Debora, Iud. IV, 4, et de Holdama propheta, de uxore Sellum, IV Reg. XXII, 14, et de filiabus Philippi, Act. c. XXI, 9. Supra etiam dicitur *omnis mulier orans vel prophetans*, et cetera.

878. Here the Apostle mentions the persons to whom the use of prophecy is forbidden.

In regard to this he does two things:

first, he shows to whom the use of prophecy is forbidden;

second, he removes an objection, at *but if they would learn anything*.

In regard to the first he does two things:

first, he mentions the command to forbid;

second he gives a reason for this, at *for it is not permitted*.

879. He says, therefore: I will that men use the gift of prophecy in this manner, but I do not want *women* to speak in the church, so that *women keep silence in the churches*: *I permit no woman to teach or to have authority over men* (1 Tim 2:12). And Chrysostom assigns the reason for this, saying: *woman has spoken once and subverted the entire world.*

But on the other hand it seems that many women are recorded to have prophesied, as the Samaritan woman (John 4:39) and Anna, the wife of Phanuel (Luke 2:36) and Deborah (Judg 4:4) and Huldah, the prophetess (2 Kgs 22:14) and the daughter of Philip the evangelist (Acts 21:9). Above, it also says: *any woman who prays or prophesies with her head unveiled dishonors her head* (1 Cor 11:5).

Responsio. Dicendum quod in prophetia sunt duo, scilicet revelatio et manifestatio revelationis, sed a revelatione non excluduntur mulieres sed multa revelantur eis sicut et viris. Sed Annuntiatio est duplex. Una publica, et ab hac excluduntur; alia est privata, et haec permittitur eis, quia non est praedicatio, sed Annuntiatio.

880. Huius autem rationem assignat, dicens **non enim permittitur eis loqui**, scilicet ab Ecclesiae auctoritate, sed hoc est officium earum, ut sint subditae viris. Unde cum docere dicat praelationem et praesidentiam, non decet eas quae subditae sunt.

Ratio autem quare subditae sunt et non praesunt est quia deficiunt ratione, quae est maxime necessaria praesidenti. Et ideo dicit Philosophus, in *Politica* sua, quod corruptio regiminis est quando regimen pervenit ad mulieres.

881. Consequenter cum dicit **si quid volunt**, etc., quia possent aliqui dicere quod ad minus de dubiis possunt quaerere in Ecclesia, ideo Apostolus hoc excludit, et circa hoc duo facit. Primo enim removet obiectionem, secundo rationem assignat, ibi **turpe est**, et cetera.

Dicit ergo: dico quod **mulieres taceant in ecclesia**, sed si aliqua, de quibus dubitant, **addiscere volunt, interrogent viros suos domi**. I Tim. II, 11: *mulier in silentio discat cum omni*, et cetera.

Huius autem ratio est quia **turpe est**, non solum indecens: in mulieribus enim commendatur verecundia. Eccli. XXVI, 19: *gratia super gratiam*, et cetera. Si ergo in publico quaereret et disputaret, signum esset inverecundiae, et hoc est ei turpe. Et inde est etiam quod in iure interdicitur mulieribus officium advocandi.

882. Consequenter cum dicit **an a vobis sermo**, etc., confutat contradicentes. Et quia possent omnes simul contradicere, vel ad minus sapientes inter eos, ideo circa hoc duo facit.

Primo enim confutat eos quantum ad totam eorum ecclesiam;

secundo quantum ad sapientes tantum, ibi **si quis autem videtur**, et cetera.

883. Circa primum sciendum est quod causa quare populus consuevit contradicere Domino, vel rectori, est singularitas. Singularitas enim potest causari vel ex prioritate in aliquo bono, vel excellentia. Et ideo Apostolus, volens contradicentes Corinthios confutare, excludit primo ab eis prioritatem, cum dicit **an a vobis sermo Dei processit?** Quasi dicat: non, sed a Iudaeis. Is. II, 3: *de Sion exibit lex*, et cetera. Quasi dicat: si in Ecclesia Iudaeorum facerem aliquas ordinationes contra ordinationes suas, possent contradicere, quia ipsi prius habuerunt verbum Dei, sed vos non, quia non processit a vobis sermo Dei.

The answer is that there are two things in prophecy, namely, revelation and its manifestation; but women are not excluded from revelation, for many things are revealed to them as to men. But manifestation is of two kinds: one is public and from this they are excluded; the other is private and this is permitted to them, because it is not preaching but manifesting.

880. He assigns the reason for this, saying: **for it is not permitted them to speak**, namely, by the authority of the Church, but their function is to be subject to men. Hence, since teaching implies prelacy and presiding, it is not suited to those who are subjects.

The reason they are subject and not in the forefront is that they are deficient in reasoning, which is especially necessary for those who preside. Therefore, the Philosopher says in his *Politics* that corruption of rule occurs, when the rule comes to women.

881. Then when he says, **if they would learn anything**, because some might say that at least they can ask the Church about their doubts, he excludes this and does two things: first, he removes an objection; second, he assigns the reason, at **for it is a shame**.

He says, therefore: I say that **let women keep silence in the churches**, but if they would learn anything about which they doubt, **let them ask their husbands at home**: *let women learn in silence* (1 Tim 2:11).

The reason for this is that **it is a shame** and not only unbecoming; for in women the natural feeling of shame is commended. *A holy and shamefaced woman is grace upon grace* (Sir 26:19). If therefore they ask and dispute in public, it would be a sign of shamelessness, and this is shameful to them. Hence it also follows that in law the office of advocate is forbidden to women.

882. Then when he says: **or did the word of God come out from you?**, he answers those who contradict him. And because they could all contradict at once or at least the wise among them, he does two things in regard to this:

first, he refutes them as to their entire church;

second, as to the wise only, at **if any seem to be a prophet or spiritual**.

883. In regard to the first it should be noted that the reason the people were wont to contradict the Lord or a ruler is singularity. For singularity can be caused by either a priority in some good or excellence. Therefore, the Apostle, wishing to refute the contradicting Corinthians, first excludes priority from their church, when he says: **did the word of God cmome out from you?** As if to say: no, but rather with the Jews: *the law shall come forth from Zion* (Isa 2:3). As if to say: if I made some rules in the church of the Jews against their rules, they could contradict, because they had the word of God before you, for the word of God did not originate from you.

Secundo excludit ab eis excellentiam *an in vos solos*, etc., quasi dicat: non solum vos credidistis, sed etiam alii. Unde vos non excellitis eos, Ps. XVIII, 5: *in omnem terram exivit sonus eorum*, et ideo debetis facere, ut alii faciunt.

884. Consequenter cum dicit *si quis autem videtur*, etc., in speciali confutat maiores. Et circa hoc duo facit.

Primo confutat eos;

secundo respondet cuidam tacitae obiectioni, ibi *si quis autem ignorat*, et cetera.

885. Dicit ergo: esto quod tota ecclesia non contradicat, sed aliquis, qui *videtur esse propheta*, et cetera.

Et dicit *videtur*, quia si contradicit non vere est propheta vel sapiens seu spiritualis, quia non contradiceret.

Dicit etiam, *propheta*, et *spiritualis*, quia multi sunt spirituales qui non sunt prophetae, licet omnes prophetae sint spirituales. Iste, inquam, qui sic videtur propheta et spiritualis, non contradicat, sed *cognoscat*, id est sciat quia ea, quae scribo vobis, sunt mandata Dei et non tantum mea. Quasi dicat: ex quo nullus ausus est mandatis Domini contradicere, et ea quae scribo sunt mandata Dei, non audeat aliquis contradicere. II Cor. ultimo: *an experimentum quaeritis*, et cetera.

Et ex hoc possumus colligere, quod verba apostolorum sunt ex familiari revelatione Spiritus Sancti et Christi et ideo servanda sunt sicut praecepta Christi. Unde et signanter Apostolus distinguit illa, quae ex se mandat, cum dicit *de virginibus autem mandatum Domini non habeo*.

886. Sed posset dicere: o Apostole, quomodo ego cognoscam quod haec sint mandata Dei? Non possum hoc scire. Hoc Apostolus excludit, dicens: non valet tibi hoc, quia non debes ignorare. Quare? *Quia omnis ignorans*, et cetera. Matth. XXV, 12: *amen dico vobis: nescio vos.* Ex quo patet quod omnes tenentur scire ea quae sunt de necessitate salutis, quae ipse prius mandat et apostoli et prophetae.

Vel aliter: *si quis videtur*, etc., ut sit confirmatio praecedentium, quasi dicat: ita scribo, sed vos non potestis ea agnoscere propter eorum difficultatem, et quia simplices estis, sed ut sciatis quod ea, quae scribo, iusta sunt et honesta, volo adducere testimonium prophetarum et spiritualium virorum, qui sunt inter vos. Et ideo dicit *si quis autem*, et cetera. Supra II, 15: *spiritualis iudicat omnia*.

Et ne aliquis dicat: non curamus scire ista, subdit quod tenentur scire *quia omnis ignorans*, et cetera. Is. V, 13:

Second, he excludes excellence from them, saying: *or came it only unto you?* As if to say: you are not the only ones who have believed, but others also. Hence you do not excel them: *their sound went forth in all the earth* (Ps 19:5), and therefore, you ought to do as the others do.

884. Then when he says: *if any seem to be a prophet or spiritual*, he refutes the greater ones in particular. In regard to this he does two things:

first, he refutes them;

second, he answers a tacit objection, at *but if any man knows not*.

885. He says, therefore: suppose that the entire church does not contradict, except someone who *seems to be a prophet*.

He says, *seems*, because, if he contradicts, he is not really a prophet or wise or spiritual.

He says a *prophet* and *spiritual* because many are spiritual who are not prophets, although all prophets are spiritual. He, I say, who so seems to be a prophet and spiritual, let him not contradict, but *let him know* that the things I am writing to you are commands of the Lord and not mine only. As if to say: from the fact that no one had dared to contradict the commands of the Lord, and the things I write are the commands of the Lord, no one should dare to contradict them: *do you desire proof that Christ is speaking?* (2 Cor 13:3).

And from this we can gather that the Apostle's words are from a familiar revelation of the Holy Spirit and of Christ and, therefore, are to be obeyed as commands of Christ. Hence the Apostle is careful to distinguish things he commands of himself, when he says: *about virgins I have no command of the Lord* (1 Cor 7:25).

886. But they could say: O Apostle, how am I to know that these are commands of God? I am unable to know this. The Apostle excludes this, saying: this is of no value to you, because you should not be ignorant. Why? *But if any man knows not, he shall not be known*: amen, I say to you: I know you not (Matt 25:12), from which it is clear that all are bound to know the things necessary for salvation, which he previously commanded, as well as the apostles and prophets.

Or in another way: *if any seem to be a prophet*, as confirmation of the preceding. As if to say: so I write; but you cannot recognize them on account of their difficulty and because you are simple; but in order that you may know that the things I write are just and honest, I wish to adduce the testimony of prophets and spiritual men, who live among you. And therefore he says: *if any seem to be a prophet: the spiritual man judges all things* (1 Cor 2:15).

And lest anyone should say: we are not instructed in knowing such things, he adds that they are bound to know,

propterea captivus ductus, et cetera. Ps. LXXXI, 5: *nescie-runt neque intellexerunt*, et cetera.

887. Itaque, fratres mei, et cetera. Apostolus hic concludit generalem admonitionem.

Et circa hoc tria facit. Primo monet eos ad appetitum omnium donorum, dicens: itaque et loqui linguis et prophetare est bonum. **Aemulamini**, id est desideretis, **prophetare**. Cuius causa est, quia, sicut dicitur Prov. c. XXIX, 18, *deficiente prophetia, dissipabitur populus*. Et accipitur **prophetare** hic, secundum quod totum capitulum expositum est. Et tamen, licet desideretis prophetare, **nolite prohibere loqui linguis**, ne fiat dissensio.

Secundo inducit ad modum debitum, cum dicit **omnia autem honeste**, ut scilicet uno loquente, alii taceant, et mulieres in ecclesia non loquantur, et similia. Rom. XIII, 13: *sicut in die honeste ambulemus*, et cetera.

Tertio inducit eos ad congruum ordinem, cum dicit **et secundum ordinem**, ut scilicet primo unus, et postea alius loquatur, et per partes et similia, quae dicta sunt. Iudic. V, v. 20: *stellae manentes in ordine et cursu suo, adversus Sisaram pugnaverunt*.

because if any man knows not, he shall not be known: *my people go into exile for want of knowledge* (Isa 5:13); *they have neither knowledge nor understanding; they walk in darkness* (Ps 82:5).

887. So, my brethren, earnestly desire to prophesy. Here the Apostle concludes the general admonition.

In regard to this he does three things: first, he admonishes them to desire all the gifts, saying: therefore, to speak in tongues is good. **Be zealous**, i.e., desire, **to prophesy**. The reason for this, as it is said: *where there is no prophecy, the people cast of restraint* (Prov 29:18). And **prophesy** is taken here as explained in this entire chapter. And yet, although you may desire to prophesy, **do not forbid to speak with tongues**, lest dissension arise.

Second, he urges them to adopt the correct method, when he says: **but let all things be done decently**, namely, that when one is speaking, the others should be silent, and that women should not speak in the church, and so on: *let us conduct ourselves becomingly as in the day* (Rom 12:13).

Third, he urges them to correct order, when he says: **and according to order**, namely, that one speak and then another and by parts and the other things I have said: *from the heavens fought the stars, from their courses they fought against Sisera* (Judg 5:20).

CHAPTER 15

Lecture 1

15:1Notum autem vobis facio, fratres, Evangelium, quod praedicavi vobis, quod et accepistis, in quo et statis, [n. 889]

15:2per quod et salvamini: qua ratione praedicaverim vobis, si tenetis, nisi frustra credidistis.

15:3Tradidi enim vobis in primis quod et accepi: quoniam Christus mortuus est pro peccatis nostris secundum Scripturas: [n. 893]

15:4et quia sepultus est, et quia resurrexit tertia die secundum Scripturas: [n. 896]

15:5et quia visus est Cephae, et post hoc undecim: [n. 898]

15:6deinde visus est plus quam quingentis fratribus simul: ex quibus multi manent usque adhuc, quidam autem dormierunt: [n. 901]

15:7deinde visus est Jacobo, deinde apostolis omnibus: [n. 902]

15:8novissime autem omnium tamquam abortivo, visus est et mihi. [n. 903]

15:9Ego enim sum minimus apostolorum, qui non sum dignus vocari apostolus, [n. 905] quoniam persecutus sum Ecclesiam Dei. [n. 907]

15:10Gratia autem Dei sum id quod sum, et gratia ejus in me vacua non fuit, sed abundantius illis omnibus laboravi: non ego autem, sed gratia Dei mecum: [n. 908]

15:11sive enim ego, sive illi: sic praedicamus, et sic credidistis. [n. 910]

15:1Γνωρίζω δὲ ὑμῖν, ἀδελφοί, τὸ εὐαγγέλιον ὃ εὐηγγελισάμην ὑμῖν, ὃ καὶ παρελάβετε, ἐν ᾧ καὶ ἑστήκατε,

15:2δι' οὗ καὶ σῴζεσθε, τίνι λόγῳ εὐηγγελισάμην ὑμῖν εἰ κατέχετε, ἐκτὸς εἰ μὴ εἰκῇ ἐπιστεύσατε.

15:3παρέδωκα γὰρ ὑμῖν ἐν πρώτοις, ὃ καὶ παρέλαβον, ὅτι Χριστὸς ἀπέθανεν ὑπὲρ τῶν ἁμαρτιῶν ἡμῶν κατὰ τὰς γραφάς,

15:4καὶ ὅτι ἐτάφη, καὶ ὅτι ἐγήγερται τῇ ἡμέρᾳ τῇ τρίτῃ κατὰ τὰς γραφάς,

15:5καὶ ὅτι ὤφθη Κηφᾷ, εἶτα τοῖς δώδεκα:

15:6ἔπειτα ὤφθη ἐπάνω πεντακοσίοις ἀδελφοῖς ἐφάπαξ, ἐξ ὧν οἱ πλείονες μένουσιν ἕως ἄρτι, τινὲς δὲ ἐκοιμήθησαν:

15:7ἔπειτα ὤφθη Ἰακώβῳ, εἶτα τοῖς ἀποστόλοις πᾶσιν:

15:8ἔσχατον δὲ πάντων ὡσπερεὶ τῷ ἐκτρώματι ὤφθη κἀμοί.

15:9Ἐγὼ γάρ εἰμι ὁ ἐλάχιστος τῶν ἀποστόλων, ὃς οὐκ εἰμὶ ἱκανὸς καλεῖσθαι ἀπόστολος, διότι ἐδίωξα τὴν ἐκκλησίαν τοῦ θεοῦ:

15:10χάριτι δὲ θεοῦ εἰμι ὅ εἰμι, καὶ ἡ χάρις αὐτοῦ ἡ εἰς ἐμὲ οὐ κενὴ ἐγενήθη, ἀλλὰ περισσότερον αὐτῶν πάντων ἐκοπίασα, οὐκ ἐγὼ δὲ ἀλλὰ ἡ χάρις τοῦ θεοῦ [ἡ] σὺν ἐμοί.

15:11εἴτε οὖν ἐγὼ εἴτε ἐκεῖνοι, οὕτως κηρύσσομεν καὶ οὕτως ἐπιστεύσατε.

15:1Now I make known unto you, brethren, the Gospel which I preached to you, which also you have received and wherein you stand. [n. 889]

15:2By which also you are saved, if you hold fast after what manner I preached unto you, unless you have believed in vain.

15:3For I delivered unto you first of all, which I also received: how Christ died for our sins, according to the Scriptures: [n. 893]

15:4And because he was buried: and that he rose on the third day according to the Scriptures: [n. 896]

15:5And because he was seen by Cephas, and after that by the eleven. [n. 898]

15:6Then he was seen by more than five hundred brethren at once: of whom many remain until this present, and some are fallen asleep. [n. 901]

15:7Then he was seen by James: then by all the apostles. [n. 902]

15:8But last of all, he was seen also by me, as by one born out of due time. [n. 903]

15:9For I am the least of the apostles, who am not worthy to be called an apostle, [n. 905] because I persecuted the Church of God. [n. 907]

15:10But by the grace of God, I am what I am. And his grace in me has not been void: but I have labored more abundantly than all they. Yet not I, but the grace of God with me: [n. 908]

15:11For whether I or they, so we preach: and so you have believed. [n. 910]

---

888. Postquam Apostolus instruxit Corinthios de ipsis sacramentis et de re contenta et significata in

888. After instructing the Corinthians about the sacrament and about the reality contained and signified in the

sacramentis, scilicet de gratia et eius effectibus hic consequenter instruit eos de re non contenta sed significata in sacramentis, scilicet de gloria resurrectionis, quae non est contenta in sacramento, cum non statim habeat eam qui suscipit sacramenta, sed significatur gloria resurrectionis in ipsis, inquantum confertur in eis gratia per quam ad beatitudinem pervenitur.

Circa hoc autem duo facit.

Primo praemittit tractatum de resurrectione;

secundo per hoc probat resurrectionem communem omnium hominum, ibi *si autem Christus praedicatur*, et cetera.

Circa primum duo facit.

Primo commendat evangelicam doctrinam;

secundo annuntiat quae oportet scire circa resurrectionem Christi, ibi *tradidi enim vobis*, et cetera.

889. Commendat enim eminentiam evangelicae doctrinae quantum ad quatuor.

Primo quantum ad praedicantium auctoritatem, quia ipsi apostoli. Et hoc est quod dicit *O fratres*, continuando se ad praecedentia, *facio vobis notum Evangelium*, quod idem est quod bona Annuntiatio, quae incipit a Christo; unde, quidquid pertinet ad Christum vel est de ipso Christo, dicitur Evangelium. *Quod praedico vobis*, quasi dicat: illud quod praedicavi vobis de Christo, notum facio vobis, id est reduco vobis ad memoriam, quasi non sint nova ea quae scribo. Phil. III, 1: *eadem scribere vobis*, et cetera. Praedicavi ego, scilicet vobis, et alii apostoli, aliis.

Et in hoc apparet auctoritas huius doctrinae, quia a Christo, a Paulo, et ab aliis apostolis. Hebr. II, 3: *quae cum initium accepisset enarrandi.*

890. Secundo quantum ad communem fidem omnium populorum, et ideo dicit *quod et accepistis*, omnes.

Sed hoc Augustinus dicit pertinere ad eminentiam huius fidei, faciens tale argumentum: ad credenda ea quae sunt fidei, aut sunt miracula facta, aut non. Si sunt facta miracula, habeo propositum quod dignissima et certissima est. Si non sunt facta, hoc est maximum omnium miraculorum, quod per quosdam paucos conversi sunt ad fidem infinita multitudo hominum; per pauperes, praedicantes paupertatem, divites; per idiotas, praedicantes ea quae rationem excedunt, conversi sunt sapientes et philosophi. Ps. XVIII, 5: *in omnem terram exivit sonus eorum*, et cetera.

Sed si obiiciatur, quod etiam lex Mahometi recepta est a multis, dicendum quod non est simile, quia ille opprimendo et vi armorum subiugavit eos; sed isti apostoli moriendo, ipsi alios ad fidem duxerunt, et faciendo signa et prodigia. Ille enim proponebat quaedam quae ad delicias et lascivias pertinent, sed Christus et apostoli

sacraments, namely, grace and its effects, the Apostle now instructs them about a reality not contained but signified in the sacraments, namely, the glory of the resurrection, which is not contained in a sacrament, since the one who receives the sacrament does not obtain it at once, but the glory of the resurrection is signified in them, inasmuch as the grace is conferred in them by which beatitude is reached.

In regard to the first he does two things:

first, he prefaces a tract on the resurrection;

second, with this he proves the general resurrection of all men, at *now if Christ be preached* (1 Cor 15:12).

In regard to the first he does two things:

first, he commends the Gospel's doctrine;

second, he declares what should be known about the resurrection of Christ, *for I delivered unto you.*

889. He commends the eminence of the Gospel's doctrine as to four things:

first, as to the authority of the preachers, because they are apostles. And this is what he says: *brethren*, connecting himself to what went before, *I make known unto you the Gospel*, which is the same as good news, which begins with Christ. Hence, whatever pertains to Christ or concerns Christ is called a Gospel. *Which I preached to you*; as if to say: what I have preached to you about Christ I make known to you, i.e., I recall it to memory, as though the things I write are not new: *to write the same things to you is not irksome to me* (Phil 3:1).

And in this appears the authority of this doctrine, because it is from Christ, from Paul and from the other apostles: *it was declared at first by the Lord and was attested to us* (Heb 2:3).

890. Second, as to the common faith of all people; therefore, he says: *which also you have received*, all of you.

But Augustine says that this pertains to the evidence of this faith, using this argument: for believing things of faith, miracles are either performed or not. But if miracles are performed, I have my point, that they are most worthy and most certain. If none is performed, this is the greatest of all miracles, that by a certain few an infinite multitude of men were converted to the faith, rich men by poor men preaching poverty; by men of one language preaching things that surpass reason, wise men and philosophers have been converted: *their voice goes out through all the earth* (Ps 19:4).

But if it is objected that even the law of Mohammed has been received by many, the answer is that the cases are not alike, because he subjugated them by oppressing them and by force of arms, but the apostles by dying brought others to the faith, and by working signs and prodigies. For he proposed things which pertain to pleasure and lasciviousness,

terrenorum contemptum. I Thess. II, 13: *cum accepistis a nobis verbum Dei*, et cetera.

891. Tertio quantum ad virtutem, quia confirmat et elevat ad caelestia. Ideo dicit *in quo statis*, scilicet elevati ad caelestia. Ille enim dicitur stare qui rectus est, et hoc sola lex Christi facit. Rom. V, 1: *iustificati per fidem*, et cetera. Lex enim vetus non faciebat stare, sed curvabat ad terrena. Deut. XXXIII, 28: *oculus Iacob in terra frumenti et vini*.

892. Quarto quantum ad utilitatem, quia sola nova lex perducit ad finem salutis; vetus autem non. Hebr. VII, 19: *neminem ad perfectum adduxit lex*. Et ideo dicit *per quod et salvamini*. Hic iam ex certitudine spei per inchoationem, quae est per fidem, salvamini, et in futuro in veritate rei et spei. Iac. c. I, 21: *in mansuetudine suscipite insitum verbum*, et cetera. Io. XX, 31: *haec autem scripta sunt, ut credatis, et ut credentes*, et cetera.

Et apponit hic duas conditiones. Primam cum dicit *si tenetis*, et cetera. Glossa sic exponit: *si tenetis qua ratione praedicavi vobis, illud Evangelium*, id est resurrectionem mortuorum, *ea ratione, qua confirmavi vobis, id est per resurrectionem Christi*. Vel aliter: salvamini, ita tamen si tenetis, id est, si servatis ea ratione qua praedicavi vobis Evangelium Christi.

Secunda conditionem ponit cum dicit *nisi frustra credidistis*. Quasi dicat: salvamini per fidem, si non *frustra credidistis*, id est si fidei adduntur bona opera, quia *fides sine operibus mortua est*, Iac. II, 26. Illud enim dicitur esse frustra, quod est ad finem quem non consequitur. Finis autem fidei est visio Dei. Unde si non salvamini, frustra credidistis, non simpliciter, sed inquantum non pervenit ad finem. Vel aliter: *si tenetis*, quasi dicat, teneatis, *nisi frustra*, et cetera.

893. *Tradidi enim*. Hic ostendit propositum, et cetera.

Circa hoc tria facit.

Primo ostendit originem doctrinae de resurrectione Christi;

secundo ostendit ea quae in doctrina huiusmodi continentur, ibi *quoniam Christus mortuus*;

tertio consonantiam seu convenientiam praedicantium ad hanc doctrinam, ibi *sive enim ego*, et cetera.

894. Dicit ergo primo: istud debetis tenere, id est memoria habere, quod *tradidi vobis in primis*, et adhuc trado.

Et dicit *in primis*, id est inter prima credenda. Credenda enim vel pertinent ad Trinitatem, vel fidem Incarnationis. Et primo debet homo credere ea quae ad fidem incarnationis pertinent, et postea quae ad Trinitatem

but Christ and the apostles contempt for earthly things: *when you received the word of God, which you heard from us, you received it . . . as the word of God* (1 Thess 2:13).

891. Third, as to its strength, because it confirms and elevates to heavenly things. Therefore, he says: *wherein you stand*, namely, elevated to heavenly things. For he is said to stand who is erect and this the law of Christ alone does: *justified by faith, we have access to that grace in which we stand* (Rom 5:1). For the old law made one stand, but it curved one to earthly things: *the eye of Jacob in a land of grain and wine* (Deut 33:28).

892. Fourth, as to usefulness, because the new law alone leads to the end of salvation, but not the old law: *the law brought no one to perfection* (Heb 7:19). And therefore he says: *by which also you are saved*. Here already from the certitude of hope through the beginning, which is our faith, you are saved and in the future in the truth of the reality: *receive with meekness the implanted word which can save your souls* (Jas 1:21); *but these things are written that you may believe and that believing you may have life* (John 20:31).

Here he lays down two conditions, the first is when he says: *if you hold fast*. A Gloss explains it this way: *if you hold to the reason why I preached that Gospel to you*, i.e., the resurrection of the dead, *by that reason by which I confirmed it to you*, i.e., *by the resurrection of Christ*. In other words: you will be saved provided you hold, i.e., preserve the reason why I preached the Gospel of Christ to you.

He presents the second condition when he says: *unless you have believed in vain*. As if to say: you will be saved through faith, if you have not *believed in vain*, i.e., if good works are added to faith, because *faith without works is dead* (Jas 2:26). For that is said to be in vain which exists for an end which it does not attain. But the end of faith is the vision of God. Hence, if you are not saved, you have believed in vain, not absolutely but inasmuch as it does not attain the end. In other words: *if you hold fast*. As if to say: you should hold it fast, unless you would believe *in vain*.

893. *For I delivered unto you*. Here he clarifies his proposition.

In regard to this he does three things:

first, he shows the origin of the doctrine about the resurrection of Christ;

second, he shows what things are contained in such a doctrine, at *how Christ died for our sins*;

third, the agreement of preachers on this doctrine, at *for whether I or they*.

894. First, therefore, he says: you should hold fast to that, i.e., keep in your memory what *I delivered unto you first of all*, and still deliver.

Hence he says *first of all*, i.e., is among the things which should most primarily be believed, namely, the Trinity and the Incarnation. And first man should believe in what pertains to faith in the Incarnation, and then in what pertains to

pertinent. Unde quod *tradidi vobis in primis*, scilicet de Incarnatione, et non a me, vel ex mea auctoritate tradidi, sed *quod accepi* a Christo vel a Spiritu Sancto. Gal. I, 1: *Paulus apostolus*, etc., supra XI, 23: *ego accepi a Domino*, et cetera. Is. XXI, 10: *quae audivi a Domino exercituum*, et cetera.

895. Ea autem quae accepit et tradidit, sunt quatuor, scilicet: mors, sepultura, resurrectio, apparitio Christi.

Dicit ergo primo: tradidi vobis, primo, mortem Christi. Et ideo dicit *quoniam Christus mortuus est*. In quo removet duplicem suspicionem, quae suboriri posset circa mortem Christi. Prima est quod mortuus esset pro peccatis suis actualibus, vel originali. Et hoc excludit, cum dicit *pro peccatis nostris*, non suis. Is. LIII, 8: *propter scelus populi mei percussi eum*. I Petr. III, 18: *Christus semel pro peccatis nostris*, et cetera.

Alia suspicio est quod mors Christi esset casualis, vel violentia Iudaeorum. Et hoc excludit cum dicit *secundum Scripturas*, scilicet veteris et novi testamenti; et ideo signanter specialiter dicit *secundum Scripturas*. Is. LIII, 7: *sicut ovis ad occisionem ductus est*. Ier. XI, 19: *ego quasi agnus mansuetus, qui portatur ad victimam*, et cetera. Matth. XX, 18: *ecce ascendimus Ierosolymam*, et cetera.

896. Tradidi enim vobis, secundo, sepulturam Christi, et ideo dicit *et quia sepultus est*.

Sed numquid sepultura est articulus fidei specialiter, quia facit hic mentionem specialiter de ea?

Dicendum quod secundum illos, qui numerant articulos secundum credenda, non est specialis articulus fidei, sed includitur cum articulo passionis et mortis Christi. Cuius ratio est quia fides est eorum quae sunt supra rationem. Unde ibi incipit articulus fidei, ubi deficit ratio. Hoc autem primum est, quod Dominus sit conceptus, et ideo conceptio est articulus fidei; secundum, quod Deus est natus de virgine, et ideo hic est alius; tertium, quod impassibilis Deus patiatur et moriatur, et hic est alius, et cum hoc intelligitur etiam de sepultura. Unde non est specialis articulus.

Facit autem Apostolus hic mentionem de sepultura propter tria. Primo ut ostendat veritatem mortis Christi. Evidens enim mortis signum alicuius est, quod sepeliatur. Secundo ad ostendendum veritatem resurrectionis, quia si non fuisset sepultus, nec custodes fuissent iuxta sepulchrum illis diebus, possent dicere, quod discipuli fuissent eum furati. Tertio quia Apostolus vult eos inducere ad fidem resurrectionis, et hoc videtur magis difficile, quod sepultus resurgat. Et de hoc dicitur Is. c. XI, 10: *et erit sepulchrum eius gloriosum*. Is. LIII, 9: *dabit impios*, et cetera.

the Trinity. Hence, *unto you first of all I delivered*, namely, things concerning the Incarnation, and this it not from me or on my authority, but *which I also received* from Christ or from the Holy Spirit: *Paul, an apostle* (Gal 1:1); *for I received from the Lord Jesus* (1 Cor 11:23); *what I have heard from the Lord of hosts* (Isa 21:20).

895. The things he received and delivered are four, namely, the death, burial resurrection and appearance of Christ.

Therefore, he says: I have delivered to you, first of all, the death of Christ; hence he says, *how Christ died*. In these words he removes two suspicions, which can arise about the death of Christ. The first is that he died for his own actual sins, or original sin. This he excludes when he says: *for our sins*, not his: *he was stricken for the transgressions of my people* (Isa 53:8); *Christ died once and for all for our sins, the just for the unjust* (1 Pet 3:18).

The other suspicion is that the death of Christ was by chance or by the violence of the Jews. This he excludes when he says: *according to the Scriptures*: *like a lamb he was led away to the slaughter* (Isa 53:7); *I was like a gentle lamb led to the slaughter* (Jer 11:19); *behold, we are going up to Jerusalem and the Son of man will be delivered to the chief priests* (Matt 20:18).

896. I delivered to you, second, the burial of Christ; therefore he says: *that he was buried*.

But is the burial a special article of faith, because he makes special mention of it?

The answer is that according to those who number the articles according to the things to be believed, it is not a special article of faith but is included in the article of the passion and death of Christ. The reason for this is that faith is concerned with things that are above reason. Hence, an article of faith begins where reason falls short. But the first is that the Lord was conceived and, therefore, the conception is an article of faith; the second is that God was born of a virgin and, therefore, this is another. The third is that God, incapable of suffering, suffers and dies, and this is another, and along with this is also understood the burial. Hence, it is not a special article.

But the Apostle mentions the burial for three reasons: first, to show the truth of Christ's death. For the evident sign of one's death is burial. Second, to show the truth of the resurrection, because if he had not been buried, guards would not have been placed at the grave on these days, nor could they say that the disciples had stolen his body. Third, because the Apostle wants to induce them to believe in the resurrection, and this seems more difficult, that a buried person should arise: *and his tomb shall be glorious* (Isa 11:10); *they made his grave with the wicked* (Isa 53:9).

897. Tradidi etiam vobis resurrectionem, quia *resurrexit tertia die*. Os. VI, 3: *vivificabit nos post*, et cetera. Et etiam dicit *tertia die*, non quod fuerint tres dies integri, sed duae noctes, et una dies per synecdochen. Et huius causa fuit, sicut dicit Augustinus, quia Deus per suum simplum, id est per malum poenae, quod significatur per unum diem, destruxit nostrum duplum, id est poenam et culpam, quod significatur per duas noctes.

898. Tradidi etiam vobis, quarto, Christi apparitiones, *quia visus est Cephae*. Et ponit

primo apparitiones factas aliis,

secundo apparitiones factas sibi soli, ibi *novissime*.

899. Sciendum est autem, circa primum, quod apparitiones Christi non sunt factae omnibus communiter, sed aliquibus specialibus personis. Act. X, 40: *dedit eum manifestum fieri*, et cetera. Et huius ratio fuit, ut servaretur ordo in Ecclesia, ut, per quosdam speciales, fides resurrectionis deveniret ad alios.

Notandum autem est quod apparitiones Christi non ponuntur hic omnes, nec illae quae factae sunt mulieribus. Ponuntur autem hic quaedam quae non leguntur in Evangeliis. Et horum ratio fuit, quia Apostolus vult ex ratione confutare infideles, et ideo noluit ponere testimonia nisi authentica; et ideo tacuit apparitiones mulieribus factas, et posuit quasdam quae non inveniuntur, ut ostendat quod etiam aliis pluribus apparuit. Sed facit mentionem specialem de Petro et Iacobo, quia erant quasi columnae, ut dicitur Gal. c. II, 9.

900. Dicit ergo: *tradidi vobis, quia visus est Cephae*, id est Petro, Lc. ult.: *surrexit Dominus vere*, et cetera. Et creditur quod inter viros primo apparuit Petro, quia erat in maxima tristitia. Unde et angelus dixit Mc. ult.: *ite, dicite discipulis eius et Petro*, et cetera.

Postea, id est in alia vice, *visus est undecim apostolis*. Semel quidem visus est decem tantum, quando Thomas erat absens, et post octo dies undecim, quando Thomas erat cum eis. Augustinus dicit quod debet dicere duodecim, sed corruptum est vitio scriptorum, et dicit quod non refert quod iam obierat, et Mathias nondum erat electus, quia consuetum est quod quando maior pars collegii facit aliquid, dicitur quod totum collegium hoc facit. Unde quia Dominus elegerat duodecim, ideo potest dici quod visus est duodecim, id est, toti collegio apostolorum; sed non est vitium, sive dicatur duodecim, sive undecim.

901. *Deinde*, iterum, *visus est plus quam quingentis fratribus*. Sed de hoc nihil legimus in sacra Scriptura, nisi hoc quod hic dicitur.

Potest tamen dici quod haec apparitio fuit de qua loquitur Dionysius in III *de Divinis nominibus*, quando

897. I also delivered to you the resurrection, *that he rose on the third day*: *after two days he will revive us* (Hos 6:2). He says, *on the third day*, not because they were three full days, but two nights and one day, by synechdoche. And the reason for this, as Augustine says, was that God by his simple, which is signified by one day, i.e., by the evil of punishment, destroyed our double, i.e., punishment and guilt, which is signified by the two nights.

898. I delivered to you, fourth, the appearance of Christ, *because he was seen by Cephas*. And he presents

first the appearance made to others;

second, those make to himself alone, at *but last of all*.

899. In should be noted, however, in regard to the first, that the appearances of Christ were not made to all in common, but to certain special persons: *God raised him up on the third day and make him manifest not to all the people* (Acts 11:40). The reason for this was to preserve order in the Church in that through certain special persons belief in the resurrection should reach others.

It should also be noted that not all of Christ's appearances are mentioned, nor those that were made to the women. But some not mentioned in the Gospel are mentioned here. The reason for this was that the Apostle wants to refute unbelievers by reason; and therefore he wanted to present only authentic testimonies. Consequently, he kept silence about the appearances to the women and mentioned some which are not found, to show that he also appeared to many others. But he mentions Peter and James, because they were as pillars (Gal 2:9).

900. He says, therefore: *I handed on to you, because he was seen by Cephas*, that is, by Peter: *the Lord is truly risen* (Luke 24:34). And it is believed that among men he appeared first to Peter, since he was in great sadness. Hence even the angel said: *go, tell his disciples and Peter* (Mark 16:7).

After that, that is, in another place, *he was seen by the eleven apostles*. Seen once by only ten, when Thomas was absent, and eight days later by eleven, when Thomas was with them. Augustine says that it should say twelve, but the text is corrupted by a scribe's error, and he says that he does not reiterate what was objected before, and Matthias had not yet been chosen, for it was customary, when the majority of the company did something, for it to say that the whole college did it. For this reason, since the Lord had chosen twelve, it can truly be said that the twelve saw him, that is, the whole company of apostles; but it is not a fault in the text, whether it says twelve, or eleven.

901. *Then* again *he was seen by more than five hundred brethren*. But nothing is mentioned in the Scripture about this, except here.

Yet it can be said that this appearance was the one about which Dionysius speaks in *The Divine Names* III, when all

omnes discipuli convenerunt ad videndum corpus, quod ferebat principem vitae.

Sed contra hoc videtur esse quia hoc fuit ante ascensionem, quando scilicet Christus apparuit Iacobo. Sed congregatio discipulorum ad videndum Beatam Virginem, de qua videtur loqui Dionysius, fuit multum post.

Et ideo melius videtur dicendum quod apparuit quingentis fratribus simul ante ascensionem suam; et non refert quod dicitur discipuli erant centum viginti, quia licet illi, qui erant in Ierusalem, essent centum viginti, tamen in Galilaea multi erant discipuli, et forte omnes congregati sunt simul cum apparuit.

Et, ut huius testimonium sit magis certum, dicit quod ex eis **adhuc multi manent**, id est vivunt, **quidam autem ex eis dormierunt**, id est mortui sunt in spe resurrectionis. Et vocat sanctorum mortem dormitionem quia moriuntur carne corruptibili, ut resurgant incorruptibiles. Rom. VI, 9: *Christus resurgens*, et cetera.

902. Deinde, id est post, **visus est Iacobo**, scilicet Alphaei. Et ratio huius potest assignari, quia, ut legitur, Iacobus vovit se non sumpturum cibum, nisi prius videret Christum.

Sed secundum hoc non servaretur ordo apparitionis, quia, si post omnes numeratas apparitiones apparuisset Iacobo, nimis fuisset sine cibo: et hoc est difficile.

Et ideo dicendum est quod ideo singulariter Christus apparuit Iacobo, quia specialem devotionem Iacobus ad Christum habuit. Et de ista etiam apparitione nihil habetur in Evangelio.

Deinde, post hoc scilicet, visus est **omnibus apostolis** in ascensione, ut legitur Matth. ult. et Act. I, 3 ss.

903. Novissime autem omnium, et cetera. Hic Apostolus commemorat apparitionem factam sibi soli.

Et circa hoc duo facit.

Primo ostendit ordinem apparitionis;

secundo rationem eius assignat, ibi **ego enim sum**, et cetera.

904. Dicit ergo ita: dixi quod omnibus manifestatus est Christus, **novissime**, id est ultimo et post ascensionem, **visus est et mihi tamquam abortivo**, et ideo novissime.

Dicit autem **tamquam abortivo**, propter tria. Abortivus dicitur aliquis foetus vel quia nascitur extra tempus debitum, vel cum violentia educitur, vel quia non perducitur ad debitam quantitatem; et quia haec tria videbat in se Apostolus, ideo dicit **tamquam abortivo**. Primo enim ipse extra tempus aliorum apostolorum renatus est Christo. Nam alii apostoli renati sunt Christo ante adventum Spiritus Sancti, Paulus vero post.

the disciples assembled to see the body, which they considered the prince of life.

But against this seems to be the fact that this was before the ascension, namely, when Christ appeared to James. But the assembly of disciples to see the Blessed Virgin, about which Dionysius seems to speak, was much later.

Therefore, it seems better to say that he appeared to five hundred brethren all at once before his ascension: and it is not important that there were said to be 120 disciples, because although the ones in Jerusalem were 120, nevertheless in Galilee there were many disciples and perhaps all were assembled at one time, when he appeared.

To make his testimony more certain he says that of them **many remain until this present**, but some of them **are fallen asleep**, i.e., died, in the hope of the resurrection. They call the death of the saints 'sleep,' because they die with corruptible flesh and rise with incorruptible. *We know that Christ being raised from the head, will never die again* (Rom 6:9).

902. Then, i.e., after this, **he was seen by James**, i.e., of Alphaeus. The reason for this can be assigned because, as it is read, James vowed that he would not take food, until he saw the Lord.

But according to this the order of appearances is not observed, because if after all those listed an appearance was made to James, he would have been too long without food and this is difficult.

Therefore, it must be said that Christ made a special appearance to James, because James had a special devotion to Christ, and furthermore nothing is found in the Gospel about that appearance.

Then, namely, after this, he was seen **by all the apostles** in the ascension (Matt 28:16; Acts 1:3ff).

903. Last of all. Here the Apostle recalls the appearance made to him alone.

In regard to this he does two things:

first, he shows the order of the appearances;

second, he assigns its reason, at **for I am the least of the apostles**.

904. He says, therefore: I have said that Christ was manifested to all, **but last of all**, i.e., finally and after the resurrection **he was seen also by me, as by one born out of due time**, and therefore as the latest.

He says, **as by one born out of due time** for three reasons. One, untimely born refers to a fetus, because it is born outside the proper time or because it is brought forth with violence or because it is not born with due quantity; and because the Apostle saw these three things in himself, he says: **as by one born out of due time**. For, first of all, all he was reborn outside the time of the other apostles. For the other apostles were reborn in Christ before the coming of the Holy Spirit, but Paul after.

Secundo quia alii apostoli spontanee conversi sunt ad Christum, sed Paulus coactus. Act. IX, 4: *prostravit eum ad terram*, et cetera. Et hoc multum valet contra haereticos, qui dicunt quod nullus debet cogi ad fidem, quia Paulus coactus fuit. Et sicut dicit Augustinus, plus profecit in fide Paulus cum coacte conversus est, quam multi qui spontanee venerunt.

Tertio quia reputat se aliis minorem, et non pervenisse ad virtutem aliorum apostolorum.

905. Et ideo, quasi rationem assignans, dicit *ego enim sum minimus*, et cetera.

Circa hoc duo facit.

Primo enim ostendit suam parvitatem;

secundo rationem huius exponit, ibi *quoniam persecutus sum*, et cetera.

906. Parvitatem autem suam manifestat, primo, in comparatione ad apostolos cum dicit *ego enim sum minimus*. Is. LX, v. 22: *minimus erit in mille, et parvulus in gentem fortissimam*, Eccli. III, 20: *quanto magnus es*, et cetera.

Et licet sit minimus in comparatione ad apostolos, posset tamen dici quod est magnus in comparatione ad alios, quia est apostolus; et ideo, secundo, ostendit suam parvitatem in comparatione ad alios, cum dicit *qui non sum dignus*, non solum esse sed *vocari apostolus*, licet vocer, II Cor. III, 5: *non quod sufficientes*, et cetera.

907. Sed posses dicere: O Apostole, propter humilitatem nullus debet dicere falsum; cum ergo tu sis magnus, quare vocas te minimum?

Et ideo cum dicit *quoniam persecutus*, etc., ostendit quomodo sit minimus, et quomodo non minimus. Minimum autem dicit se, considerando praeterita facta sua. Et dicit *non sum dignus*, et cetera. Quare? *Quia persecutus sum Ecclesiam Dei*, quod alii apostoli non fecerunt. Gal. I, 13: *supra modum persequebar*, et cetera. I Tim. I, 13: *qui fui blasphemus et persecutor*, et cetera.

Et licet ex me sim minimus, tamen ex Deo non sum minimus; et ideo dicit *gratia Dei sum id quod sum*.

Et circa hoc duo facit.

Primo commendat conditionem suam quantum ad statum;

secundo quantum ad executionem status, ibi *et gratia eius*, et cetera.

908. Dicit ergo primo: ex me nihil sum, sed id quod sum, *gratia Dei sum*, id est ex Deo, non ex me. Eph. III, 7: *cuius factus sum minister*, et cetera. Et dicit *id quod sum*, quia homo sine gratia nihil est. Supra c. XIII, 2: *si habuero omnem prophetiam*, et cetera.

Second, because the other apostles were converted to Christ spontaneously, but Paul by coercion: *he fell to the ground and heard a voice* (Acts 9:4). And this is of great value against heretics, who say that no one should be forced to the faith, because Paul was forced. And as Augustine says: Paul made more progress in the faith, although he was forcibly converted, than many who came spontaneously.

Third, because he regards himself as less than the others and that he had not arrived to the virtue of the other apostles.

905. And therefore, as though assigning a reason he says: *I am the least of the apostles*.

In regard to this he does two things:

first, he shows his smallness;

second, he explains the reason for this, at *because I persecuted the Church of God*.

906. He explains his smallness, first, in comparison to the apostles, when he says: *for I am the least of the apostles*: *the least one shall become a clan, and the smallest one a mighty nation* (Isa 60:22); *the greater you are, the more you must humble yourself* (Sir 3:18).

And although he is the least in relation to the apostles, yet it could be said that he is great in comparison to others; and therefore, second, he shows his smallness in comparison to others, when he says: *I am not worthy* not only to be but *to be called an apostle*, although I should be called: *not that we are sufficient of ourselves but our sufficiency is from God* (2 Cor 3:5).

907. But it could be said: O Apostle, for the sake of humility no one say anything false: therefore, since you are great, why do you call yourself the least?

Therefore, when he says: *because I persecuted the Church of God*, he shows how he is the least and how he is not the least. He calls himself the least, when he considers his past deeds. And he says: *I am not worthy*. Why? *Because I persecuted the Church of God*, which the other apostles did not do: *I persecuted the Church of God violently* (Gal 1:13); *though I formerly blasphemed and persecuted and insulted him* (1 Tim 1:13).

And although of myself I am the least, yet from the grace of God I am not the least; and therefore he says: *by the grace of God I am what I am*.

In regard to this he does two things:

first, he commends his condition as to its state;

second, as to the execution of his state, at *and his grace in me has not been void*.

908. Therefore he says first: of myself I am nothing, but what I am, *I am by the grace of God*, i.e., from God, not from me: *of this Gospel I was made a minister* (Eph 3:7). And he says, *what I am*, because without grace a man is nothing: *if I have prophetic powers and understand all mysteries* (1 Cor 13:2).

909. Sed qualiter usus sit et executus statum suum, ostendit, dicens *et gratia eius*, et cetera. Ubi primo ostendit quomodo usus sit gratia ista, quia ad bonum, et ideo dicit *in me vacua non fuit*, id est otiosa, quia ea usus est ad id ad quod data est sibi. Gal. c. II, 2: *non in vacuum cucurri*, et cetera.

Secundo manifestat quomodo alios excessit, et ideo subdit *sed abundantius illis omnibus*, id est apostolis sigillatim, *laboravi*, praedicando, quia nullus per tot loca praedicavit et annuntiavit Christum, unde dicit Rom. XV, 19: *ita quod a Ierusalem usque ad Illyricum*, etc., et etiam usque ad Hispaniam; operando, quia licet ipse, sicut alii apostoli, posset exigere sumptus sibi necessarios, tamen specialiter voluit de labore manuum quaerere sumptus suos, ut ipse dicit II Thess. III, 8: *nocte et die manibus nostris*, etc.; tribulationes sustinendo; nullus enim apostolorum tot persecutiones et tribulationes sustinuit, ut ipse enumerat II Cor. XI, 23: *in laboribus plurimis et carceribus*, et cetera.

Tertio ostendit usus efficaciam, quia hoc non a se solo sed ex instinctu et adiutorio Spiritus Sancti. Et ideo dicit *non autem ego*, solus operor, *sed gratia Dei mecum*, quae movet voluntatem ad hoc. Is. XXVI, 12: *omnia opera nostra*, et cetera. Phil. II, 13: *qui operatur in nobis velle*, et cetera. Deus enim non solum infundit gratiam, qua nostra opera grata fiunt et meritoria, sed etiam movet ad bene utendum gratia infusa, et haec vocatur gratia cooperans.

910. *Sive ego enim*, et cetera. Hic ostendit concordiam praedicantium; et hoc potest dupliciter legi.

Primo ut sit confirmatio dictorum, quasi dicat aliquis: tu ita praedicas sed tamen non credimus tibi soli, quia minimus es inter apostolos. Ideo respondens Apostolus ait: immo debetis mihi credere, quia ego non praedico alia; *sive ego, sive alii* apostoli *sic praedicamus*, scilicet Christum resurrexisse et visum fuisse, et cetera. Et vos etiam *credidistis* sicut ego et illi praedicaverunt, scilicet quod Christus resurrexit, et visus est, et cetera. II Cor. c. IV, 13: *habentes eumdem Spiritum*, et cetera.

Secundo potest legi ut efficacia praedicationis sit omnibus apostolis ex uno, id est a gratia Dei, quasi dicat: *sive ego* praedicem, *sive illi*, id est apostoli, sicut praedicamus, hoc fecimus adiuti et firmati per gratiam Dei; et etiam vos ipsi *credidistis*, scilicet inspirati Spiritu Sancto et gratia Dei, sine qua nihil facere possumus. Io. XV, 5: *sine me nihil potestis facere*.

909. But how he used and executed his state he shows, saying: *and his grace*. Here he shows, first, how he used that grace, namely, for good; therefore he says: *in me has not been void*, i.e., idle, because he used it for that for which it was given to him: *lest somehow I should be running in vain* (Gal 2:2).

Second, he manifests how he exceeded others; therefore he adds: *but I have labored more abundantly than all they*, i.e., than any of the apostles singly, by preaching, because no one preached in so many places and announced Christ. Hence he says: *so that from Jerusalem to Illyricum I fully preached* (Rom 15:19) and even as far as pain by working, because although he, as the other apostles, could require expenses necessary for them, yet he particularly wished to seek his expenses from the labor of his hands: *night and day we have worked with our hands by enduring tribulation* (2 Thess 3:8); for none of the apostles endured such persecutions and tribulations: *with far greater labors, far more imprisonments, with countless beatings* (2 Cor 11:23).

Third, he shows the efficacy of use, because this was not from himself alone but from the instinct and help of the Holy Spirit. Therefore, he says: *yet not I* alone acting *but the grace of God with me*, which moves the will to this: *you have wrought for us all our works* (Isa 26:12): *God is at work in you both to will and to work* (Phil 2:13). For God not only infuses but he also moves us to use the graces infused well, and this is called cooperating grace.

910. *For whether I or they*, so we preach. Here he shows the agreement of the preachers; and this can be read in two ways:

first, as confirming what has been said. As if one were to say: you preach thus, but we do not believe you alone, because you are the least of the apostles. Therefore, the Apostle says in reply: indeed you should believe me, because I do not preach other things; *for whether I or they*, the other apostles, *so we preach*, namely, that Christ rose and was seen, and *so you have believed*, just as I and those who preached, namely, that Christ rose and was seen: *since we have the same Spirit of faith* (2 Cor 4:13).

Second, it can be read so that the efficacy of preaching comes to the apostles from one source, i.e., from the grace of God. As if to say: *whether I* preach *or they*, i.e., the apostles, as we preach, we have done this by the help and strength of God's grace; and so even *you have believed*, namely, inspired by the Holy Spirit and grace of God without which we can do nothing: *without me you can do nothing* (John 15:5).

Lecture 2

^{15:12}Si autem Christus praedicatur quod resurrexit a mortuis, quomodo quidam dicunt in vobis, quoniam resurrectio mortuorum non est? [n. 911]

^{15:13}Si autem resurrectio mortuorum non est: neque Christus resurrexit. [n. 917]

^{15:14}Si autem Christus non resurrexit, inanis est ergo praedicatio nostra, inanis est et fides vestra: [n. 918]

^{15:15}invenimur autem et falsi testes Dei: quoniam testimonium diximus adversus Deum quod suscitaverit Christum, quem non suscitavit, si mortui non resurgunt. [n. 919]

^{15:16}Nam si mortui non resurgunt, neque Christus resurrexit.

^{15:17}Quod si Christus non resurrexit, vana est fides vestra: adhuc enim estis in peccatis vestris. [n. 921]

^{15:18}Ergo et qui dormierunt in Christo, perierunt. [n. 922]

^{15:19}Si in hac vita tantum in Christo sperantes sumus, miserabiliores sumus omnibus hominibus. [n. 923]

---

^{15:12}Εἰ δὲ Χριστὸς κηρύσσεται ὅτι ἐκ νεκρῶν ἐγήγερται, πῶς λέγουσιν ἐν ὑμῖν τινες ὅτι ἀνάστασις νεκρῶν οὐκ ἔστιν;

^{15:13}εἰ δὲ ἀνάστασις νεκρῶν οὐκ ἔστιν, οὐδὲ Χριστὸς ἐγήγερται·

^{15:14}εἰ δὲ Χριστὸς οὐκ ἐγήγερται, κενὸν ἄρα [καὶ] τὸ κήρυγμα ἡμῶν, κενὴ καὶ ἡ πίστις ὑμῶν,

^{15:15}εὑρισκόμεθα δὲ καὶ ψευδομάρτυρες τοῦ θεοῦ, ὅτι ἐμαρτυρήσαμεν κατὰ τοῦ θεοῦ ὅτι ἤγειρεν τὸν Χριστόν, ὃν οὐκ ἤγειρεν εἴπερ ἄρα νεκροὶ οὐκ ἐγείρονται.

^{15:16}εἰ γὰρ νεκροὶ οὐκ ἐγείρονται, οὐδὲ Χριστὸς ἐγήγερται·

^{15:17}εἰ δὲ Χριστὸς οὐκ ἐγήγερται, ματαία ἡ πίστις ὑμῶν, ἔτι ἐστὲ ἐν ταῖς ἁμαρτίαις ὑμῶν.

^{15:18}ἄρα καὶ οἱ κοιμηθέντες ἐν Χριστῷ ἀπώλοντο.

^{15:19}εἰ ἐν τῇ ζωῇ ταύτῃ ἐν Χριστῷ ἠλπικότες ἐσμὲν μόνον, ἐλεεινότεροι πάντων ἀνθρώπων ἐσμέν.

---

^{15:12}Now if Christ be preached, that he arose again from the dead, how do some in you say that there is no resurrection of the dead? [n. 911]

^{15:13}But if there be no resurrection of the dead, then Christ is not risen again. [n. 917]

^{15:14}And if Christ be not risen again, then is our preaching vain: and your faith is also vain. [n. 918]

^{15:15}And we are even found to be false witnesses of God: because we have given testimony against God, that he has raised up Christ, whom he has not raised up, if the dead rise not again. [n. 919]

^{15:16}For if the dead rise not again, neither is Christ risen again.

^{15:17}And if Christ be not risen again, your faith is vain: for you are yet in your sins. [n. 921]

^{15:18}Then they also who are fallen asleep in Christ are perished. [n. 922]

^{15:19}If in this life only we have hope in Christ, we are of all men most miserable. [n. 923]

---

911. Supra Apostolus astruxit fidem per resurrectionem Christi, hic vero probat per resurrectionem Christi, resurrectionem mortuorum futuram. Et

primo probat futuram resurrectionem;

secundo ostendit qualitatem resurgentium, ibi *sed licet aliquis*, etc.;

tertio vero describit ordinem resurrectionis, ibi *ecce mysterium vobis dico*, et cetera.

Circa primum duo facit.

Primo probat resurrectionem mortuorum futuram, ratione sumpta ex resurrectione Christi;

secundo ratione sumpta ex vita sanctorum, ibi *alioquin quid facient*, et cetera.

Probat autem mortuorum resurrectionem ex resurrectione Christi, tali ratione: si Christus resurrexit, ergo et mortui resurgent.

Circa ergo hanc rationem tria facit.

Primo ponit conditionale, scilicet si Christus resurrexit, et mortui resurgent;

911. Having built up faith in the resurrection of Christ, the Apostle now proves by the resurrection of Christ the future resurrection of the dead.

First, he proves the future resurrection;

second, he shows the quality of those rising, at *but some man will say* (1 Cor 15:35);

third, he describes the order of the resurrection, at *behold, I tell you a mystery* (1 Cor 15:51).

In regard to the first he does two things:

first, he proves the future resurrection of the dead with a reason taken from the resurrection of Christ;

second, with a reason taken from the lives of the saints, at *otherwise, what shall they do* (1 Cor 15:29).

He proves the resurrection of the dead from the resurrection of Christ with this reason: if Christ arose, then the dead will rise.

In regard to this reason he does three things:

first, he presents a conditional proposition, namely, if Christ arose, the dead also will rise;

secundo vero probat antecedens ipsius conditionalis, ibi *si autem resurrectio mortuorum*, etc.;

tertio probat conditionalem esse veram, ibi *nunc autem Christus resurrexit*, et cetera.

912. Dicit ergo primo: dixi, quod sive ego praedicaverim, sive illi, scilicet alii apostoli, sic credidistis. *Sed si praedicatur* a nobis, *quod Christus resurrexit a mortuis, quomodo quidam in vobis*, id est, inter vos, *dicunt*, etc.; quasi dicat: si Christus resurrexit a mortuis, secundum quod nos praedicamus I Thess. IV, 13: *si credimus quod Christus*, etc., nullus debet dubitare resurrectionem mortuorum futuram. Unde Rom. c. VIII, 11: *qui suscitavit Iesum*, et cetera.

913. Sed videtur quod haec argumentatio non valeat, cum sit locus a maiori affirmando. Quia, licet Christus resurrexit specialiter ex virtute divinitatis suae, non sequitur quod alii homines resurgant.

Sed ad hoc dicunt aliqui quod non est locus a maiori, sed a simili. Mori enim et resurgere competit Christo secundum humanam naturam, et dicunt, quod est simile argumentum, sicut si dicerem: anima Socratis est immortalis, ergo omnes, scilicet animae hominum, sunt immortales.

Videtur autem quod sit melius dicendum quod sit locus a causa, quia resurrectio Christi est causa resurrectionis nostrae. Et ideo, secundum Glossam dicendum est: *si Christus, qui est causa efficiens nostrae resurrectionis, resurrexit, quomodo dicunt*, et cetera.

Sed tamen non est dicendum quod sit causa efficiens tantum per modum meriti, quia resurgendo non meruit eam, cum iam esset comprehensor et viveret vita gloriosa, nisi forte meritum resurrectionis mortuorum referatur ad passionem Christi. Nec est causa exemplaris tantum, ut quidam dicunt, sed est causa efficiens et exemplaris. Unde Augustinus dicit *Super Ioannem*, quod *Verbum caro factum vivificat animas, et resuscitat mortuos*. Sic ergo patet quod si Christus resurrexit, et mortui resurgent.

914. Sed contra: resurgere a mortuis est supra naturam, hoc autem non est nisi virtutis infinitae, qui Deus est; non ergo resurrectio corporis Christi est causa efficiens resurrectionis mortuorum, cum humanitas Christi, seu corpus, sit creatura: licet de Christo vel de homine, non possit dici quod est creatura.

Responsio. Dicendum quod inquantum Deus, sive inquantum divinitas est in Christo, Christus est et exemplar et causa efficiens resurrectionis mortuorum per humanitatem suam, sicut per instrumentum divinitatis suae.

Ad illud quod obiicitur, dicendum quod caro Christi seu humanitas non dicitur facere effectum virtutis

second, he proves the antecedent of this conditional, at *but if there be no resurrection of the dead*;

third, he proves that the conditional is true, at *but now Christ is risen* (1 Cor 15:20).

912. First, therefore, he says: I have said that whether I preached or others, namely, the apostles, you have so believed. *Now if Christ be preached* by us *that he rose again from the dead, how do some in you*, i.e., among you, *say* that there is no resurrection of the dead? As if to say: if Christ rose from the dead, as we preach: *since we believe that Christ died and rose again* (1 Thess 4:13), no one should doubt the future resurrection of the dead. Hence: *he who raised Christ Jesus from the dead will give life to our mortal bodies* (Rom 8:10).

913. But this argument seems invalid, since it argues by affirming from the greater. For although Christ rose in particular in virtue of his divinity, it does not follow that other men will rise.

To this some answer that it is not from the greater but from a similar. For to die and to rise belong to Christ according to his human nature, and they say, that the argument is similar, as though I should say: the soul of Socrates is immortal; therefore all souls of men are immortal.

But it seems better to say that it is arguing from a cause, because the resurrection of Christ is the cause of our resurrection. Therefore, according to a Gloss is should be said: *if Christ, who is the efficient cause of our resurrection, arose, how do some in you say that there is no resurrection of the dead?*

Yet one should not say that he is the efficient cause only after the manner of merit, because by rising he did not merit it, since he was already a comprehensor, and lived the life of glory, unless perhaps the merit of the resurrection of the dead be referred to the death of Christ. Neither is he merely the exemplary cause, as some say, but he is the efficient and exemplary cause. Hence Augustine says, *On John*, that *the Word made flesh vivifies souls and raises the dead*. Therefore, it is clear that if Christ rose, the dead also will rise.

914. But on the other hand, to rise from the dead is above nature; but this is done only by the infinite power of God: therefore, the resurrection of Christ's body is not the efficient cause of the resurrection of the dead, since the humanity of Christ or the body is a creature, although it cannot be said of Christ or of the man, that he is a creature.

The answer is that inasmuch as God or the godhead is in Christ, Christ is the exemplary and efficient cause of the resurrection of the dead through his humanity, as through an instrument of his divinity.

To answer the objection it should be noted that the flesh of Christ or the humanity is not said to produce an effect

infinitae, inquantum caro vel humanitas, sed inquantum caro Christi vel humanitas Christi.

915. Sed quaeritur adhuc: nam, posita causa sufficienti, statim ponitur effectus; si ergo resurrectio Christi est sufficiens causa resurrectionis mortuorum, statim deberent mortui resurgere et non tantum differre.

Responsio. Dicendum, quod effectus sequitur ex causis instrumentalibus secundum conditionem causae principalis. Et ideo cum Deus sit principalis causa nostrae resurrectionis, resurrectio vero Christi sit instrumentalis, resurrectio nostra sequitur resurrectionem Christi secundum dispositionem divinam, quae ordinavit ut tali tempore fieret.

916. Sed numquid si Deus non fuisset incarnatus, homines resurrexissent?

Dicendum videtur quod non, quia Christus non fuisset passus, nec resurrexisset.

Dicendum est autem ad hoc quod haec obiectio nulla est, quia quando aliquid ordinatur ab aliqua causa, debet argumentari ad illud, servato ordine illius causae. Et ideo dicendum est quod Deus ordinavit resurrectionem mortuorum fore per istum modum; potuisset tamen et alius modus adhuc inveniri a Deo si voluisset.

917. Deinde cum dicit *si autem resurrectio mortuorum non est*, etc., probat antecedens, scilicet quod Christus resurrexit, et hoc ducendo ad inconvenientia.

Et circa hoc duo facit.

Primo ducit ad inconvenientia;

secundo ostendit illa esse inconvenientia, ibi *invenimur autem et falsi testes*, et cetera.

918. Circa primum facit deductionem suam supponendo quod si Christus non resurrexit, neque mortui resurgent: quod, si ita est, sequuntur duo inconvenientia: unum est quod inanis est praedicatio apostoli et inutilis; aliud est quod inanis est fides Corinthiorum.

Unde dicit *si autem Christus non resurrexit, inanis est*, et cetera. Et hoc est quod dicit: ex hoc quod sive ego, sive illi, si sic praedicant, et cetera. Dicit ergo *si autem Christus non resurrexit, inanis est*, id est falsa, *praedicatio nostra*, quia sic credidistis; et hoc magnum est inconveniens, quod praedicationem eorum non suffulserit veritas, cum Apostolus dicat Phil. II, 16: *non in vacuum cucurri neque laboravi.*

919. *Invenimur autem*, et cetera. Hic ostendit illa duo esse inconvenientia. Et

primo ostendit quod sit inconveniens, si praedicatio apostolorum esset inanis seu falsa;

secundo ostendit quod sit inconveniens, si fides illorum esset inanis, ibi *quod si Christus non resurrexit*, et cetera.

920. Ostenditur autem primum esse inconveniens, quia essent falsi testes, non solum dicendo aliqua vana vel

of infinite power, inasmuch as it is flesh or humanity, but inasmuch as it is the flesh and humanity of Christ.

915. But there is another question: once the sufficient cause is posited, the effect follows at once; therefore, if the resurrection of Christ is the sufficient case of the resurrection of the dead, then the dead should all rise and not merely be delayed.

The answer is that an effect follows from instrumental causes according to the condition of the principal cause. Therefore, since God is the principal cause of our resurrection, but Christ's resurrection is the instrumental cause, our resurrection follows Christ's resurrection according to God's arrangement, which directed that it happen at such a time.

916. But if God had not been incarnate, would men rise?

It seems not, because Christ would not have suffered and arisen.

I answer that this objection is null, because when something is directed by some cause, one should argue to it, observing the order of that cause. Therefore, it must be said that God directed the resurrection of the dead to occur in that manner; yet another manner could still be found by God, if he willed.

917. Then when he says: *but if there be no resurrection of the dead, then Christ is not risen*, he proves that Christ has risen, and this by leading to incongruities.

In regard to this he does two things:

first, he leads to the incongruities;

second, he shows that they are incongruities, at *we are even found false witnesses of God*.

918. In regard to the first he makes his deduction by supposing that if Christ had not risen, the dead will not rise. If this is so, two undesirable things follow: one is that the Apostle's preaching is vain and useless; the other is that the faith of the Corinthians is in vain.

Hence he says: *and if Christ be not risen again, your faith is in vain*. And this is what he says: from the fact that I or others preach this. He says, therefore: *and if Christ be not risen again, then is our preaching in vain*, i.e., false, because you have so believed; and this is a great incongruity, that the truth did not underprop their preaching, especially since the Apostle says: *I have not run or labored in vain* (Phil 2:16).

919. *We are even found false witnesses of God.* Here he shows that those two things are incongruous.

First, he shows that it is incongruous, if the preaching of the apostles were in vain or false;

second, he shows that if it is incongruous, their faith would be in vain, at *and if Christ be not risen again*.

920. First, it is shown to be incongruous, because they would be false witnesses not only for saying vain things or

aliqua contra aliquem hominem false, quod est mortale peccatum, sed falsi testes adversus Deum, quod est sacrilegium. Quia si Deus non suscitavit Christum a mortuis, secundum quod nos praedicamus, invenimur falsi testes; et si mortui non resurgunt, Deus non resuscitavit Christum a mortuis. Iob XIII, 7: *numquid Deus indiget vestro mendacio?* et cetera.

Et hoc est pessimum, scilicet quod aliquid attribuatur Deo quod non facit et laudare in eo quod non est. Unde dicit Augustinus: *non minori, sed maiori fortasse scelere in Deo laudatur falsitas, quam vituperetur veritas.* Cuius ratio est quia intellectus noster numquam potest tantum laudare Deum, quin deficiat a perfectione eius; et ideo si non totaliter intellectus omnem veritatem possit de Deo intelligere, hoc est, ad excellentiam Dei; sed si attribuitur aliquid Deo quod non habet, vel non facit, videtur quod intellectus noster est maior Deo, et intelligat aliquid maius eo quod sibi false attribuit. Et hoc contra illud I Io. III, 20: *Deus maior est corde nostro.*

921. *Quod si Christus.* Hic ostendit quod inconveniens sit, si fides illorum esset inanis. Et hoc ostendit per tria inconvenientia, quae sequuntur inde.

Primum est, quia constat quod falsitas non habet virtutem purgandi, sed constat quod fides purgat peccata. Act. XV, 9: *fide purificans,* et cetera. Si ergo fides nostra sit inanis, quod esset si Christus non resurrexit, quia sic credidistis, scilicet quod resurrexit, peccata vestra non sunt vobis dimissa. Et hoc est quod dicit **adhuc estis in peccatis vestris.**

922. Sed quia posset aliquis dicere: licet fides non purget peccata, possunt tamen purgari ab eis per bona opera; ideo addit secundum inconveniens, scilicet quod mortui, qui non possunt purgari in alia vita, perierunt absque spe salutis. Et ideo, quasi concludens, dicit **ergo qui in Christo,** id est in fide Christi, **dormierunt,** id est mortui sunt in spe salutis, **perierunt,** quia in alia vita nulla sunt opera meritoria.

923. Sed quia posset adhuc dicere: non curo de peccatis, non curo de mortuis, dummodo habeam in vita ista quietem et tranquillitatem, ideo addit tertium inconveniens cum dicit **si in hac tantum vita,** et cetera.

Et innititur tali argumento: si resurrectio mortuorum non est, sequitur quod nihil boni habeatur ab hominibus, nisi solum in vita ista; et si hoc est, tunc illi sunt miserabiliores, qui in vita ista multa mala et tribulationes patiuntur. Cum ergo plures tribulationes apostoli et Christiani patiantur, sequitur quod sint miserabiliores caeteris hominibus, qui ad minus perfruuntur huius mundi bonis.

things against any man falsely, which is a mortal sin, but false witnesses against God, which is a sacrilege. For if God did not raise Christ from the dead, we are found to be false witnesses; and if the dead do not rise, God did not raise Christ from the dead: *will you speak falsely for God?* (Job 13:7).

And this is the worst, namely, that something be attributed to God which he does not do and to praise in him what is not his. Hence Augustine says: *when something false is praised in God, it is not lesser but a greater crime than if the truth were reviled.* The reason for this is that our intellect can never praise God so much as not to fall short of his perfection; therefore, if the intellect knows every truth about God totally, this is due to God's excellence. But if something he does not have to do is attributed to God, it seems that our intellect is greater than God and understands something greater than he, which is falsely attributed to him. And this is contrary to 1 John: *God is greater than our heart* (1 John 3:20).

921. *And if Christ be not risen,* your faith is in vain. Here he shows that it is incongruous, if their faith were vain. He shows this with three incongruities, which follow therefrom.

The first is that it is clear that falseness does not have the power to cleanse. But faith cleanses from sins: *he cleansed their hearts by faith* (Acts 15:9). If, therefore, our faith is in vain, which would be the case if Christ has not risen, because you did believe that he arose, your sins are not forgiven. And this is what he says: **for you are yet in your sins.**

922. But because someone could say: although faith does not cleanse sins, they can be cleansed by good works. Therefore, he adds a second incongruity, namely, that the dead, who cannot be cleansed in the other life, have perished without hope of salvation. And so, as if concluding, he says: **they who are fallen asleep,** i.e., died in hope of salvation, **in Christ,** i.e., in the faith of Christ, **are perished,** because in the other life, there are no meritorious works.

923. But because someone could still say: I do not care about sins, I do not care about the dead, as long as in this life I have peace and quiet. Therefore, he adds a third incongruity, when he says: **if in this life only we have hope in Christ, we are of all men most miserable.**

And he rests on this argument: if there is no resurrection of the dead, it follows that nothing good is possessed by men except in this life alone; and if this is so, then those who suffer many evils and tribulations in this life are more miserable. Therefore, since the apostles and Christians suffer many tribulations, it follows that they are more miserable than other men, who at least enjoy the good things of this world.

924. Sed circa hanc rationem videntur duo dubitanda.

Unum quia non videtur quod sit verum universaliter quod Apostolus dicit, scilicet quod Christiani sunt confidentes in hac vita tantum, quia possent dicere illi, quod licet corpora non habeant bona nisi in vita ista, quae est mortalis, tamen secundum animam habent multa bona in alia vita.

Ad hoc obviatur dupliciter. Uno modo, quia si negetur resurrectio corporis, non de facili, imo difficile est sustinere immortalitatem animae. Constat enim quod anima naturaliter unitur corpori, separatur autem ab eo contra suam naturam, et per accidens. Unde anima exuta a corpore, quamdiu est sine corpore, est imperfecta. Impossibile autem est quod illud quod est naturale et per se, sit finitum et quasi nihil; et illud quod est contra naturam et per accidens, sit infinitum, si anima semper duret sine corpore. Et ideo Platonici ponentes immortalitatem, posuerunt reincorporationem, licet hoc sit haereticum: et ideo si mortui non resurgunt, solum in hac vita confidentes erimus.

Alio modo quia constat quod homo naturaliter desiderat salutem sui ipsius, anima autem cum sit pars corporis hominis, non est totus homo, et anima mea non est ego; unde licet anima consequatur salutem in alia vita, non tamen ego vel quilibet homo. Et praeterea cum homo naturaliter desideret salutem, etiam corporis, frustraretur naturale desiderium.

925. Secundum dubium est quia videtur quod, dato quod corpora non resurgant, non essemus nos Christiani miserabiliores caeteris hominibus, quia illi qui sunt in peccatis, sustinent maximos labores. Ier. IX, 5: *ut inique agerent, laboraverunt*, et Sap. V, v. 7: *dicunt impii: ambulavimus vias difficiles*. At vero de bonis et iustis dicitur Gal. c. V, 22: *fructus autem Spiritus est caritas, gaudium, pax*, et cetera.

Ad hoc dicendum quod mala quae sunt in hoc mundo, non sunt secundum se appetenda, sed secundum quod ordinantur ad aliquod bonum. Apostoli autem et Christiani multa mala passi sunt in hoc mundo. Nisi ergo ordinarentur ad aliquod bonum, essent miserabiliores caeteris hominibus. Aut ergo ordinantur ad bonum futurum, aut ad bonum praesens; sed ad bonum futurum non ordinantur, si non est resurrectio mortuorum.

Si autem ordinantur ad bonum praesens, hoc vel est bonum intellectus, sicut philosophi naturales paupertates et alia multa mala passi sunt, ut pervenirent ad veram veritatem. Sed ad hoc non possunt ordinari, si non est resurrectio mortuorum: quia sic fides eorum esset falsa, quia ipsi praedicaverunt resurrectionem futuram; falsitas autem non est bonum intellectus. Vel est bonum moris, sicut morales philosophi multa mala passi sunt, ut pervenirent ad virtutes et famam. Sed nec ad hoc ordinari possunt, quia si resurrectio mortuorum non sit,

924. But there seem to be two doubts about this reasoning:

one is that what the Apostle says does not seem to be universally true, namely, that Christians are confident in this life only, because they could say that, although our bodies do not possess any good things except in this life, which is mortal, yet according to the soul they have many good things in the other life.

This can be turned aside in two ways: in one way, because if the resurrection of the body is denied, it is not easy, rather, it is difficult, to sustain the immortality of the soul. For it is clear that the soul is naturally united to the body and is departed from it, contrary to its nature and *per accidens*. Hence the soul devoid of its body is imperfect, as long as it is without the body. But it is impossible that what is natural and *per se* be finite and, as it were, nothing; and that which is against nature and *per accidens* be infinite, if the soul endures without the body. And so, the Platonists positing immortality, posited re-incorporation, although this is heretical. Therefore, if the dead do not rise, we will be confident only in this life.

In another way, because it is clear that man naturally desires his own salvation; but the soul, since it is part of man's body, is not an entire man, and my soul is not I; hence, although the soul obtains salvation in another life, nevertheless, not I or any man. Furthermore, since man naturally desires salvation even of the body, a natural desire would be frustrated.

925. The second doubt is that it seems that if bodies do not rise, we Christians would be not more miserable than other men, because those who are in sins undergo greater labors: *they have labored to commit iniquity* (Jer 4:5); *the impious say: we have walked difficult paths* (Wis 5:7). But of the good and just it is said: *the fruit of the Spirit is love, joy, peace* (Gal 5:22).

The answer to this is that evils in this world are not to be sought as such, but inasmuch as they are directed to some good. But the apostles and Christians have suffered many evils in the world. Therefore, unless they were directed to some good, they would be more miserable than other men. Either they are directed to a future good or to a present good; but they are not ordained to a future good, if there is no resurrection of the dead.

But if they are ordained to a present good, this is either the good of the intellect, as philosophers of nature suffered poverty and many other evils, in order to know the truth. But it cannot be directed to this, if there is no resurrection of the dead, because then their faith would be false, because they preached a future resurrection. But falsity is not a good of the intellect. Or it is a good of morals, as moral philosophers suffered many evils to acquire virtues and fame. But neither can they be directed to this, because if there is no resurrection of the dead, it is not regarded as virtuous and

non reputatur virtus et gloria velle omnia delectabilia dimittere, et sustinere poenas mortis et contemptus, sed potius reputatur stultitia. Et sic patet quod miserabiliores essent caeteris hominibus.

glorious to wish to renounce all pleasant things and undergo the punishments of death and contempt; rather it is considered folly. And so it is clear that they would more miserable than other men.

Lecture 3

15:20Nunc autem Christus resurrexit a mortuis primitiae dormientium, [n. 926]

15:21quoniam quidem per hominem mors, et per hominem resurrectio mortuorum. [n. 930]

15:22Et sicut in Adam omnes moriuntur, ita et in Christo omnes vivificabuntur. [n. 932]

15:23Unusquisque autem in suo ordine, primitiae Christus: deinde ii qui sunt Christi, qui in adventu ejus crediderunt. [n. 933]

15:24Deinde finis: cum tradiderit regnum Deo et Patri, cum evacuaverit omnem principatum, et potestatem, et virtutem. [n. 936]

15:25Oportet autem illum regnare donec ponat omnes inimicos sub pedibus ejus. [n. 940]

15:26Novissima autem inimica destruetur mors: [n. 944]

15:27omnia enim subjecit pedibus ejus. Cum autem dicat: Omnia subjecta sunt ei, sine dubio praeter eum qui subjecit ei omnia. [n. 949]

15:28Cum autem subjecta fuerint illi omnia: tunc et ipse Filius subjectus erit ei, qui subjecit sibi omnia, ut sit Deus omnia in omnibus. [n. 950]

15:20Νυνὶ δὲ Χριστὸς ἐγήγερται ἐκ νεκρῶν, ἀπαρχὴ τῶν κεκοιμημένων.

15:21ἐπειδὴ γὰρ δι' ἀνθρώπου θάνατος, καὶ δι' ἀνθρώπου ἀνάστασις νεκρῶν:

15:22ὥσπερ γὰρ ἐν τῷ Ἀδὰμ πάντες ἀποθνήσκουσιν, οὕτως καὶ ἐν τῷ Χριστῷ πάντες ζῳοποιηθήσονται.

15:23ἕκαστος δὲ ἐν τῷ ἰδίῳ τάγματι: ἀπαρχὴ Χριστός, ἔπειτα οἱ τοῦ Χριστοῦ ἐν τῇ παρουσίᾳ αὐτοῦ:

15:24εἶτα τὸ τέλος, ὅταν παραδιδῷ τὴν βασιλείαν τῷ θεῷ καὶ πατρί, ὅταν καταργήσῃ πᾶσαν ἀρχὴν καὶ πᾶσαν ἐξουσίαν καὶ δύναμιν.

15:25δεῖ γὰρ αὐτὸν βασιλεύειν ἄχρι οὗ θῇ πάντας τοὺς ἐχθροὺς ὑπὸ τοὺς πόδας αὐτοῦ.

15:26ἔσχατος ἐχθρὸς καταργεῖται ὁ θάνατος:

15:27πάντα γὰρ ὑπέταξεν ὑπὸ τοὺς πόδας αὐτοῦ. ὅταν δὲ εἴπῃ ὅτι πάντα ὑποτέτακται, δῆλον ὅτι ἐκτὸς τοῦ ὑποτάξαντος αὐτῷ τὰ πάντα.

15:28ὅταν δὲ ὑποταγῇ αὐτῷ τὰ πάντα, τότε [καὶ] αὐτὸς ὁ υἱὸς ὑποταγήσεται τῷ ὑποτάξαντι αὐτῷ τὰ πάντα, ἵνα ᾖ ὁ θεὸς [τὰ] πάντα ἐν πᾶσιν.

15:20But now Christ is risen from the dead, the firstfruits of those who sleep: [n. 926]

15:21For by a man came death: and by a man the resurrection of the dead. [n. 930]

15:22And as in Adam all die, so also in Christ all shall be made alive. [n. 932]

15:23But every one in his own order: the firstfruits, Christ: then they who are of Christ, who have believed in his coming. [n. 933]

15:24Afterwards the end: when he shall have delivered up the kingdom to God and the Father: when he shall have brought to naught all principality and power and virtue. [n. 936]

15:25For he must reign, until he has put all his enemies under his feet. [n. 940]

15:26And the enemy, death, shall be destroyed last: [n. 944]

15:27For he has put all things under his feet. And whereas he says: all things are put under him; undoubtedly, he is excepted, who put all things under him. [n. 949]

15:28And when all things shall be subdued unto him, then the Son also himself shall be subject unto him that put all things under him, that God may be all in all. [n. 950]

---

926. Hic probat positam superiusconditionalem esse veram, scilicet si Christus resurrexit, mortui resurgunt.

Et circa hoc tria facit.

Primo ostendit quomodo se habeat resurrectio Christi ad resurrectionem aliorum;

secundo ostendit ordinem resurrectionis, ibi *unusquisque autem in suo ordine*, etc.;

tertio ostendit finem resurrectionis, ibi *deinde finis*, et cetera.

Circa primum duo facit.

Primo ostendit habitudinem resurrectionis Christi ad resurrectionem aliorum, per conditionalem praedictam, probans hoc;

secundo probat ipsam habitudinem, ibi *quoniam quidem*, et cetera.

926. Here he proves that the conditional statement above set forth is true, namely, if Christ arose, the dead will rise.

In regard to this he does three things:

first, he shows how Christ's resurrection is related to that of others;

second, he shows the order of the resurrection, at *but every one in his own order*;

third, he shows the end of the resurrection, at *afterwards the end*.

In regard to the first he does two things:

first, he shows the relationship of Christ's resurrection to that of others;

second, he proves this relationship, at *for by a man*.

927. Dicit ergo *nunc*, id est ex quo dicta inconvenientia sequuntur si Christus non resurrexit, ideo ad ipsa vitanda dicamus, quod *Christus resurrexit*. Hoc autem verum est, secundum quod Matth. ult. dicitur, et aliis locis Evangeliorum.

Sed resurrectionis Christi habitudo ita se habet ad resurrectionem aliorum, sicut primitiae fructuum ad sequentes fructus, quae excedunt alios fructus tempore et melioritate, seu dignitate; et ideo dicit quod *resurrexit*, non sicut alii, sed *primitiae*, id est primo tempore et dignitate. Apoc. I, 5: *primogenitus mortuorum. Primitiae*, dico, *dormientium*, id est, mortuorum qui in spe resurrectionis quiescunt.

Ex hoc potest inferri conditionalis posita, quia, sicut dicimus et verum est, si Christus, qui est *primitiae dormientium*, resurrexit, ergo et alii dormientes.

928. Sed contrarium videtur, scilicet quod Christus non resurrexit primitiae dormientium, quia Lazarus fuit resuscitatus a Christo nondum passo, et aliqui prophetae suscitaverunt alios a mortuis, ut habetur in Veteri Testamento.

Ad hoc dicendum quod duplex est resurrectio. Una est ad vitam mortalem, et ad istam Lazarus et alii, qui suscitati fuerunt, resurrexerunt ante Christum. Alia ad vitam immortalem, et de hac loquitur hic Apostolus.

929. Sed contra Matth. XXVII, 52 dicitur, quod *multa corpora sanctorum surrexerunt*. Cum ergo hoc legatur ante Christi resurrectionem, et constet quod non resurrexerunt ad vitam immortalem, videtur quod adhuc restet quaestio prima.

Responsio. Dicendum est, quod hoc quod Matthaeus dicit de resurrectione illorum, dicit per anticipationem, quia licet dicatur in tractatu de passione, non tunc resurrexerunt, sed postquam Christus resurrexit.

930. *Quoniam quidem*, et cetera. Hic probat habitudinem positam, scilicet quod Christus sit primitiae dormientium. Et

primo probat in generali,

secundo in speciali, ibi *et sicut in Adam*, et cetera.

931. Probat in generali tali ratione: Deus voluit reintegrare humanam naturam, sed humana natura corrupta est per hominem, quia mors intravit per hominem. Pertinebat ergo ad dignitatem humanae naturae, ut reintegraretur per hominem, hoc autem est ut reducatur ad vitam. Conveniens ergo fuit, sicut mors intravit per hominem, scilicet per Adam, ita *resurrectio mortuorum* fieret *per hominem*, scilicet per Christum. Rom. c. V, 17: *si enim unius delicto*, et cetera.

927. He says, therefore: *now*, i.e., inasmuch as the aforesaid incongruities follow, if Christ has not risen, then to avoid them, let us say: *Christ is risen*. This is true according to what is stated in the last chapter of Matthew and in other texts of the Gospels.

But Christ's resurrection is related to that of others as the first fruits to those that follow, for they exceed the latter in time and superiority or worth; therefore, he says: *he is risen*, not as the others, but as *the firstfruits*, i.e., first in time and dignity: *the first born of the dead* (Rev 1:5). *The firstfruits*, I say, *of those who sleep*, i.e., of the dead who rest in hope of the resurrection.

From this can be inferred the conditional statement previously made, because we say and it is true, if Christ who is *the firstfruits of those that sleep*, arose, then also all others asleep.

928. But something seems contrary to this, namely, that Christ did not arise the first fruits of those who sleep, because Lazarus had been raised by Christ not yet suffering, and some raised others from the dead, as it says in the Old Testament.

The answer is that resurrection is twofold: one is to mortal life, to which Lazarus and the others had been raised. The other is to immortal life, and it is about this that the Apostle speaks.

929. But on the other hand it is said: *many bodies of the saints who had fallen asleep were raised* (Matt 27:52). Therefore, since this happened before the resurrection of Christ and it is obvious that they did not rise to an immortal life, it seems that the first question still remains.

I answer that what Matthew says about the resurrection of those souls, he says by anticipation, because although it is written in the tract on the passion, they did not rise then, but after Christ arose.

930. *For by a man came death: and by a man the resurrection of the dead*. Here he proves the relationship posited, namely, that Christ is the first fruits of them that sleep.

First, he proves this in general;

second, in special, at *and as in Adam all die*.

931. He proves it in a general way with the following reason: God willed to reintegrate human nature, which had been corrupted by man, because death entered through a man. Therefore, it pertained to the dignity of human nature that it be reintegrated by a man, but this is so that it be brought back to life. Therefore, it was fitting that just as death entered through a man, namely, Adam, so *the resurrection of the dead* be accomplished *by a man*, namely, Christ: *if because of one man's trespass, death reigned through that one man, much more they who receive abundance of grace and of the gift and of justice shall reign in life.* (Rom 5:17).

932. *Et sicut in Adam.* Hic probat idem in speciali, dicens quod sicut in Adam omnes morimur morte corporali, ita et omnes vivificamur in Christo. Rom. V, 12: *per unum hominem*, et cetera.

Et non dicit per Evam, quod videtur contra illud Eccli. XXV, 33: *per illam omnes morimur*. Dicendum quod hoc est per illam Evam, scilicet suggerentem, sed per Adam sicut causantem. Nam si solum Eva peccasset, peccatum originale non fuisset traductum in posteros.

Vivificabuntur, inquam, *in Christo*, scilicet boni et mali vita naturae, sed vita gratiae non nisi boni; sed tamen Apostolus loquitur hic de resurrectione ad vitam naturae, ad quam omnes vivificabuntur. Io. V, 26: *sicut Pater habet vitam in semetipso, ita et Filio dedit vitam habere*, id est vivificandi virtutem. Io. V, 28: *omnes qui in monumentis sunt*, et cetera.

933. *Unusquisque autem in suo ordine*, et cetera. Hic ostendit ordinem resurrectionis. Et

primo insinuat ipsum ordinem;

secundo manifestat id quod dixerat, ibi *primitiae Christus*, et cetera.

934. Dicit ergo quod verum est quod omnes in Christo vivificabuntur, sed tamen differenter, quia differentia erit inter caput et membra, et differentia quantum ad bonos et malos. Et ideo dicit quod *unusquisque* resurget *in suo ordine*, scilicet dignitatis. Rom. XIII, 1: *quae autem sunt, a Deo ordinata sunt*.

935. Sed hunc ordinem consequenter manifestat, quia *primitiae Christus*, quia ipse est prior tempore et dignitate, quia plus de gloria. Io. I, 14: *vidimus eum quasi unigenitum*, et cetera.

Deinde resurgent omnes *qui sunt Christi*, posteriores tempore et dignitate. Isti sunt qui carnem suam crucifixerunt cum vitiis, et cetera. Gal. IV, 4: *at ubi venit plenitudo*. I Tim. VI, v. 14: *serves mandatum sine macula irreprehensibile usque in adventum Domini nostri*. Qui autem sint Christi exponit, dicens *qui crediderunt* per fidem, per dilectionem operantem. Hebr. XI, 6: *accedentem ad Deum oportet credere*, et cetera. *In adventu eius*, primo et secundo.

Sed sciendum quod inter alios sanctos non erit ordo temporis, quia omnes resurgent in ictu oculi, sed bene secundum dignitates, quia martyr resurget ut martyr, apostolus ut apostolus, et sic de aliis.

936. *Deinde finis.* Hic ostendit finem resurrectionis, et hunc duplicem. Unum quantum ad adeptionem boni, alium quantum ad remotionem mali, ibi *oportet illum regnare*, et cetera.

Circa primum duo facit.

Primo ostendit quod adeptio ipsius boni consistit in inhaerentia ad Deum;

932. *And as in Adam.* Here he proves the same in special, saying that as in Adam we all die a bodily death, so too we are all made alive in Christ: *as sin came into the world through one man* (Rom 5:12).

He does not say through Eve, which seems contrary to Sirach: *through her we all die* (Sir 25:33). I answer that this is through Eve suggesting, but through Adam as cause. For if Eve alone had sinned, original sin would not have been passed on to their descendants.

All shall be made alive, I say, *in Christ*, namely, the good and the bad with the life of nature, but the good only with the life of grace. Yet the Apostle speaks here of a resurrection to a life of nature, to which all shall be made alive. *As the Father has life in himself, so he has granted the Son also to have life in himself* (John 5:26), i.e., the power to grant life: *all who are in the tombs will hear his voice* (John 5:28).

933. *But every one in his own order.* Here he shows the order of the resurrection.

First, he gives the order itself;

second, he exhibits what he had said, at *the firstfruits, Christ*.

934. Therefore I say that it is true that in Christ shall all be made alive, but differently, because there will be a difference between head and members, and a difference as to the good and the evil. And therefore he says that *every one* will rise *in his own order*, namely in dignity: *those that exist have been instituted by God* (Rom 13:1).

935. Then he clarifies this order, because *the firstfruits, Christ*, for he is prior in time and worth, because he had more glory: *we have beheld his glory, glory as of the only Son from the Father* (John 1:14).

Then they who are of Christ will also rise, because they are later in time and worth. They are those who crucified their flesh with its vices: *but when the fullness of time came, God sent his Son* (Gal 4:4); *I charge you to keep the commandment unstained and free from reproach until the coming of our Lord Jesus Christ* (1 Tim 6:14). He explains who are Christ's when he says: *who have believed* by faith working through love: *for whoever would draw near to God must believe that he exists* (Heb 11:6), *and in his coming* both the first and the second.

But it should be noted that among the other saints there is not order of time, because all will rise in the twinkling of an eye, but an order of worth, because a martyr will rise as a martyr, and an apostle as an apostle, and so on.

936. *Afterwards the end.* Here he shows the end of the resurrection and it is twofold: one as to attaining the good; the others as to removal of the wicked, at *for he must reign*.

In regard to the first he does two things:

first, he shows that the attainment of the good consists in inhering to God;

secundo ostendit, quod in immediata inhaerentia, ibi *cum evacuaverit*, et cetera.

937. Dicit ergo, quod *deinde*, id est post hoc, erit *finis* resurrectionis. Et finis huiusmodi non erit, ut vivant vita corporis et voluptatibus, ut Iudaei et Saraceni fingunt; sed quod inhaereant Deo per immediatam visionem et beatam fruitionem: et hoc est tradere regnum Deo et Patri.

Et ideo dicit *cum tradiderit*, id est, perduxerit, *regnum*, id est fideles suos quos proprio sanguine acquisivit, Apoc. V, 9: *redemisti nos Deo in sanguine tuo*, **Deo et Patri**, id est ante conspectum Dei, id est Creatoris sui, inquantum est homo, et Patris, inquantum est Deus. Et hoc est, quod petebat Philippus, Io. XIV, 8: *Domine, ostende nobis Patrem*, et cetera. Sed sic tradet, ut sibi non adimat, imo ipse unus Deus cum Patre et Sancto Spiritu regnabit.

Vel *cum tradiderit regnum Deo et Patri*, id est cum ostendet Deum Patrem regnare. In Scriptura enim tunc dicuntur aliqua fieri, quando primo innotescunt, et huiusmodi innotescentia fit per Christum. Matth. XI, 27: *nemo novit Patrem, nisi Filius, et cui*, et cetera.

938. *Cum evacuaverit*. Hic ostendit immediationem dictae inhaerentiae. Sicut enim dicitur Gal. IV, 1 s., *quanto tempore haeres parvulus est, est sub tutoribus*, et cetera. Sed quando iam est magnus et perfectus, tunc immediate absque paedagogo et tutore sub patre est in domo.

Status autem huius vitae praesentis assimilatur pueritiae, et ideo in vita ista sumus sub angelis, sicut sub tutoribus, inquantum praesunt nobis et dirigunt nos; sed quando tradetur regnum Deo et Patri, tunc immediate erimus sub Deo, et cessabunt omnia alia Dominia. Et hoc est quod dicit *et cum evacuaverit omnem principatum et potestatem et virtutem*, id est cum cessaverit omne Dominium, tam humanum quam angelicum, tunc immediate erimus sub Deo. Is. II, 12: *exaltabitur Dominus solus in die illa*. Ier. c. XXXI, 34: *non docebit ultra vir proximum suum*, et cetera.

939. Sed numquid non remanebunt ordines angelorum distincti?

Dicendum quod sic, quantum ad eminentiam gloriae, qua unus alteri praeeminet, sed non quantum ad efficaciam executionis ad nos. Et ideo illos dicit evacuari, quorum nomina pertinent ad executionem, scilicet principatus, potestates et virtutes. Illos autem qui sunt de superiori hierarchia non nominat, quia non sunt exequentes; nec angelos, quia est nomen commune.

second, he shows that it consists in immediate inherence, at *when he shall have brought to naught*.

937. He says, therefore: that *afterwards*, i.e., after this, will come *the end* of the resurrection. And an end of this kind will not be that they will live the life of the body and voluptuousness, as the Jews and Saracens pretend, but that they will inhere to God by immediate vision and happy enjoyment: and this is to hand over the kingdom to God and the Father.

Therefore, he says: *when he shall have delivered up*, i.e., brings *the kingdom*, i.e., his believers, whom he acquired by his own blood: *by your blood you ransomed men for God* (Rev 5:9), *to God and the Father*, i.e., before the sight of God, i.e., of his Creator, inasmuch as he is man, and of the Father, inasmuch as he is God. And this is what Philip sought: *Lord, show us the Father and we shall be satisfied* (John 14:18). But he will deliver it up in such a way that he does not take it from himself; indeed, he, the one God with the Father and the Holy Spirit will reign.

Or *when he shall have delivered up the kingdom to God and the Father*, i.e., when he will show God the Father reigning. For in Scripture something is to said be done, when it first becomes known, and such knowledge is made by Christ: *no one knows the Father except the Son and anyone to whom the Son chooses to reveal him* (Matt 11:27).

938. *When he shall have brought to naught all principality and power and virtue*. Here he shows the immediacy of the aforementioned inherence. For as it is said: *the heir, as long as he is a child, is no better than a slave but is under tutors* (Gal 4:1). But when he is now large and mature, then he is immediately under his father in the home without a pedagogue and tutor.

But the condition of this present life is akin to childhood; therefore, in this life we are under angels as under tutors, inasmuch as they are over us and direct us. But when the kingdom is delivered over to God the Father, then we will be immediately under God, and all other powers will cease. And this is what he says: *when he shall have brought to naught all principality and power and virtue*, i.e., when all dominion both human and angelic shall have ceased, then we shall be immediately under God: *the Lord alone will be exalted on that day* (Isa 2:11); *and no longer shall each man teach his neighbor, for they shall all know me, says the Lord* (Jer 31:34).

939. But will not the orders of angels remain distinct?

It seems so, as to the eminence of glory, by which one excels another, but not as to the efficacy of their activity toward us. Therefore, he says that those will be done away with whose names pertain to outward activity, namely, principalities, powers and virtues. He does not name those who belong to the higher hierarchy, because they are not outwardly active; not angels, because it is their common

Dominationes autem non dixit evacuari, quia licet sint de exequentibus, non tamen ipsi exequuntur, sed dirigunt et imperant. Dominorum enim est dirigere et imperare, non exequi; archangeli vero intelliguntur cum principatibus; *archos* enim idem est quod princeps.

Hi tres ordines secundum Gregorium leguntur descendendo, quia secundum ipsum principatus sunt super potestates, et potestates super virtutes; sed secundum Dionysium, ascendendo, quia vult quod virtutes sint super potestates, et potestates super principatus.

Vel aliter **cum evacuaverit**, etc., id est tunc erit notum, quod principatus, et potestates, et dominationes nihil potestatis habuerunt ex seipsis, sed a Deo, ex quo sunt omnia.

940. Deinde cum dicit **oportet illum**, etc., ostendit Apostolus finem resurrectionis quoad remotionem mali. Quod quidem ostendit per destructionem omnium inimicorum ad Christum. Et

primo ponit ipsorum destructionem;

secundo subiectionis perfectionem, ibi **novissime autem**, etc.;

tertio subiectionis finem, ibi **cum autem subiecta fuerint**.

941. Dicit ergo primo: dixi quod finis erit, cum tradiderit regnum Deo et Patri; sed numquid Christus habet regnum ita quod oportet illum regnare? Sic enim dicitur Matth. ult.: *data est mihi*, et cetera. Lc. I, 32: *et regnabit in domo Iacob*. **Oportet**, inquam, **donec ponat inimicos suos sub pedibus eius**.

Sed numquid modo non sunt inimici eius sub pedibus eius, id est, sub potestate Christi?

Dicendum quod modo inimici Christi sunt sub potestate eius, sed dupliciter. Vel inquantum per ipsum convertuntur sicut Paulus, quem prostravit Act. IX, 3 s.; vel inquantum Christus facit voluntatem suam, etiam de his qui faciunt hic contra voluntatem Christi. Sic ponit inimicos suos sub pedibus suis, puniendo eos; sed in futuro ponet sub pedibus, id est sub humanitate Christi. Sicut enim per caput deitas Christi intelligitur, **quia caput Christi Deus**, I Cor. XI, 3, ita per pedem, humanitas. Ps. CXXXI, 7: *adorabimus in loco ubi steterunt pedes eius*, et cetera. Sic ergo inimici erunt non solum sub deitate, sed etiam sub humanitate Christi. Phil. II, 10: *in nomine Iesu omne genu*, et cetera.

942. Sed quid est quod dicit **donec ponat?** et cetera. Numquid non regnabit, priusquam posuerit inimicos sub pedibus?

Dicendum quod hoc potest intelligi dupliciter, nam **donec** quandoque determinat tempus, et ponitur pro finito, sicut si dicerem: non videbo Deum donec moriar,

name. He does not say dominations will be done away with, because although they are among the outwardly active, they do not perform outward activity, but they direct and command. For it belongs to lords to direct and command, not to act outwardly. Archangels are included with the principalities, for *archos* is the same as prince.

According to Gregory these three orders are presented in descending order, because according to him principalities are above powers, and powers above virtues; but according to Dionysius in ascending order, because he wants the virtues over the powers, and the powers over the principalities.

Or in another way: **when he shall have brought to naught all principality and power and virtue**, i.e., then it will be known that they had no power of themselves but from God, from whom are all things.

940. *For he must reign*. Here the Apostle shows the end of the resurrection as to the removal of the wicked. This he shows by the destruction of all enemies of Christ:

first, he mentions their destruction;

second, the perfection of subjection, at **and the enemy, death**;

third, the end of the destruction, at **and when all things shall be subdued**.

941. First, therefore, he says: I have said that the end will be when he has delivered the kingdom to God the Father. But will Christ have a kingdom in which he should reign: *all power is given to me in heaven and on earth* (Matt 28:18); *and he will reign in the house of Jacob forever* (Luke 1:32)? **He must reign**, I say, **until he has put all his enemies under his feet**.

But aren't they under his feet now, i.e., under Christ's power?

The answer is that the enemies of Christ are now under his power, but in two ways: either because they are converted by him, as Paul, whom he caused to fall on the ground (Acts 9:3); or inasmuch as Christ does his own will, even in regard to those who act here against Christ's will. So he puts his enemies under his feet by punishing them; but in the future he will put them under his feet, i.e., under Christ's humanity. For just as by the head is understood Christ's godhead, because **the head of Christ is God** (1 Cor 11:3), so by the feet, his humanity. *We will adore in the place where his feet stood* (Ps 132:5). Thus, therefore, the enemies will not only be under the godhead, but also under the humanity of Christ: *at the name of Jesus every knee shall bow* (Phil 2:10).

942. But why does he say, **until he has put all his enemies under his feet?** Will he not reign until he does that?

The answer is that his can be taken in two ways: for **until** sometimes determines time, as if I should say: I will not see God, until I die; because until them I will not see, but

quia usque tunc non videbo, sed postea videbo. Quandoque ponitur pro infinito, sicut cum dicitur: *non cognovit eam donec peperit Filium suum*. Non quod velit dicere, quod non cognovit eam solum usque ad partum filii, sed nec etiam postea unquam cognovit, sicut dicit Hieronymus. Iste modus servatur quando aliqui intendunt excludere illa solum de quibus est dubium. Unde Evangelium exclusit illud solum, quod videtur esse dubium, scilicet quod Ioseph cognovisset Beatam Virginem ante partum. Hoc vero quod post partum non cognovit eam, nulli est dubium, cum tot mysteria pueri viderit et toties ab angelis monitus sit, et adoratus etiam a Magis Iesus fuisset; unde poterat eam iam Dei Matrem cognoscere, et ideo non curavit hoc excludere: sic etiam loquitur hic Apostolus.

Quod enim aliquis regnet, adhuc inimicis non subiugatis, videtur esse dubium; sed quod regnet postquam inimici subiugati sunt, nulli est dubium. Et ideo illud excludit principaliter dicens **donec ponat**, etc., quasi dicat: verum est, quod Christus habet regnum, et licet sint aliqui inimici, dum non faciunt voluntatem suam, tamen regnat **donec ponat**, et cetera.

943. Potest etiam alio modo intelligi **donec ponat**, etc., ut **donec** determinet tempus, et ponatur pro futuro, ut dicatur sic **oportet illum regnare**, sed quando? **Donec ponat**, et cetera. Quasi dicat: usque tunc regnabit, quousque ponat inimicos sub pedibus, postea vero non regnabit.

Sed secundum hanc expositionem, regnare non importat regnum habere, sed in regnando proficere et regnum augeri, et hoc quantum ad manifestationem perfectam regni Christi. Quasi dicat: regnum Christi paulatim proficit, inquantum scilicet manifestatur et innotescit, **donec ponat inimicos sub pedibus**, id est quousque omnes inimici regnare eum fateantur: boni quidem cum gaudio beatitudinis, mali vero cum confusione; et postea non regnat, id est regnum suum non proficit, et non amplius manifestatur, quia iam plene manifestum erit.

944. Sic ergo patet omnium adversantium subiectio, quae quidem subiectio perfectissima erit, quia etiam illud quod maxime inimicatur, subiicietur sibi. Hoc autem est mors, quae maxime contrariatur vitae; et ideo dicit **novissime autem**, etc.; ubi tria facit.

Primo ponit subiectionem mortis;

secundo probat hoc per auctoritatem, ibi **omnia enim subiecit**, etc.;

tertio ex ipsa auctoritate arguit, ibi **cum autem dicat**, et cetera.

945. Dicit ergo: dixi quod omnes inimicos subiecit sub pedibus eius. Sed qualiter? Perfectissime, inquam,

after that I shall see. Sometimes it is taken for the infinite, as when it is said: *he did not know her until she brought forth her son* (Matt 1:25). Not that he wanted to say that he did not know her only up to the birth of her son, but neither did he afterwards ever know her, as Jerome says. This manner is observed, when one intends to exclude only those about which there is doubt. Hence, the Gospel excluded only that which seems to be in doubt, namely, that Joseph knew the Blessed Virgin before she gave birth. But the fact that he did not know her after giving birth is doubted by no one, since he saw so many mysteries concerning the child, and he was so often warned by angels, and Jesus had been adored by the Magi; hence he could already have known that she was the Mother of God and, therefore, he did not wish to preclude this. This is the way the Apostle speaks here.

For the fact that anyone should reign with his enemies not yet subdued, seems to be doubtful, but that he should reign after his enemies have been subjugated, no one doubts. Therefore, he excludes the first, saying: **until he has put all his enemies**. As if to say: it is true that Christ has a kingdom and although there are some enemies, while they do not do his will, nevertheless he rules and **put all his enemies under his feet**.

943. The phrase, **until he has put all his enemies** can be understood in another way, so that **until** determines a time and is put for the future. As if to say: **he must reign**. But when? **Until he has put all his enemies under his feet**. As if to say: until then he will reign, until he puts his enemies under his feet, but after that he will not reign.

But according to this explanation 'to reign' does not imply having a kingdom, but in making progress in reigning and increasing the kingdom, and this as to a perfect manifestation of a kingdom of Christ. As if to say: Christ's kingdom grows gradually, namely, inasmuch as it is manifested and becomes known, **until he has put all his enemies under his feet**, i.e., until all enemies admit that he is reigning: for the good will admit this with the joy of beatitude but the evil with confusion. And afterward he does not reign, i.e., his kingdom does not grow and it is not further manifested, because it will already be fully manifest.

944. So, therefore, the subjection of all adversaries is clear, which subjection will, indeed, be most complete, because even that which is extremely hostile will be subjected to him. This, however, is death, which is contrary to life most of all; and therefore, he says: **the last enemy**, where he does three things.

First, he mentions death's subjection;

second, he proves this by an authority, at **for he has put all things under his feet**;

third, he argues from this authority, **and whereas he says**.

945. He says, therefore: I have said that he has subjected all enemies under his feet. But how? Most completely, I say,

quia *novissime inimica mors destruetur*, scilicet in fine, quia non poterit esse cum vita, ubi omnes per resurrectionem vivent. Os. XIII, 14: *ero mors tua, o mors.* Is. XXV, 8: *praecipitabit mortem in sempiternum.*

946. Sciendum est autem, quod Origenes ex hoc verbo sumpsit occasionem erroris sui, quem ponit in *Periarchon.*

Ipse enim voluit quod poenae damnatorum essent purgatoriae et non aeternae, et voluit quod omnes, qui sunt in inferno, quandoque converterentur ad Christum et salvarentur, et etiam diabolus. Et hoc confirmat per ista verba *donec ponam inimicos*, et cetera. Et intelligit quod hoc quod dicitur *inimicos sub pedibus*, solum intelligitur de subiectione, quae fit per conversionem peccatorum ad Deum, non de subiectione qua sunt subiecti Christo etiam illi, qui numquam convertuntur ad Christum, inquantum punit eos in inferno. Et ideo dicit *oportet illum regnare, donec ponat inimicos sub pedibus*, quia tunc omnes damnati et qui sunt in inferno salvabuntur, inquantum scilicet convertentur ad ipsum, et servient ei, et non solum ipsi homines damnati; *autem*, pro sed, *novissime ipsa mors*, id est diabolus, *destruetur*, non quod non sit omnino, sed quod non sit mors, quia etiam ipse diabolus in fine salvabitur.

Sed hoc est haereticum et damnatum in Concilio.

947. Iterum sciendum est quod Apostolus signanter posuit hoc quod dicitur *novissime autem*, etc., ad removendum duas quaestiones, quae possunt fieri circa praedicta de resurrectione, scilicet utrum Christus posset vivificare mortuos. Et hoc solvitur, quia omnes inimicos posuit sub pedibus eius, et etiam ipsam mortem.

Et quare non statim omnes resuscitavit? Ad quod respondetur, quod oportet quod primo subiiciat inimicos sub pedibus, et novissime cum destruetur ipsa mors, tunc resurgent omnes ad vitam. Non ergo differt, quia non potest, sed ut servet ordinem, quia quae a Deo sunt, ordinata sunt.

948. Quod autem ipsa mors subiiciatur Christo, probat per auctoritatem Ps. VIII, 8: *omnia subiecisti sub pedibus eius*, id est, sub humanitate eius, scilicet Christi. Phil. II, v. 11: *omnis lingua*, et cetera. Is. XLV, 24: *mihi curvabitur omne genu*, et cetera.

949. Ex hac autem auctoritate argumentatur, dicens *cum autem dicat*, et cetera.

Et est ratio sua talis: propheta dicit *omnia subiecisti*, etc., sed dicendo *omnia*, constat quod nihil exclusit, nisi illum qui subiecit; ergo subiecta sunt Christo omnia et ipsa mors.

Dicit ergo: *cum autem dicat*, Psalmista scilicet, *omnia subiecta sunt ei*, scilicet Christo, inquantum homini, *praeter eum*, scilicet Patrem, *qui subiecit ei omnia*.

because *the enemy, death, shall be destroyed last*, namely, at the end, because it could not exist with life, when all shall be alive through the resurrection: *I will be your death, O death* (Hos 13:14); *he will swallow up death forever* (Isa 25:8).

946. It should be noted that from this word Origen took the occasion of his error, which appears in *Periarchon.*

For he wanted the punishments of the damned to be a cleansing and not eternal, and he wanted that all in hell will be converted to Christ at some time and be saved, including the devil; and he confirms this with the words, *until I have put all my enemies under my feet*. And he understands by *enemies under my feet* the subjection which occurs when sinners are converted to God, not of the subjection by which those are subject to Christ who are never converted to Christ, inasmuch as he punishes them in hell. Therefore, he says: *he must reign, until he has put all his enemies under his feet*, because at that time all the damned and those in hell will be saved, inasmuch as they will be converted to him and will serve him, and not only those condemned men; but *the enemy, death*, i.e., the devil *shall be destroyed*, not that he will not exist at all, but that he will not be death, because even in the end the devil himself will be saved.

But this is heretical and condemned by a Council.

947. Again it should be noted that the Apostle clearly stated that *the enemy, death, shall be destroyed last*, in order to remove two questions which can arise concerning things predicted about the resurrection, namely, whether Christ could give life to the dead. And this is solved, because he has put all his enemies under his feet, and even death itself.

And why has he not raised all at once? The answer to this is that he must first subject the enemies under his feet, and finally when death itself is destroyed, then all will rise to life. Therefore, he delays, not because he is unable, but that he might preserve order, because things that are from God are in order.

948. That death itself will be subjected to Christ he proves with an authority: *you have put all things under his feet* (Ps 8:8), i.e., under his humanity, namely, Christ's. *And every tongue confess that Jesus Christ is Lord* (Phil 2:11); *to me every knee shall bow, every tongue shall swear* (Isa 45:23).

949. From this authority he argues, saying: *and whereas he says.*

The reasoning is this: the prophet says, *all things are put under him*; by saying *all things*, nothing is excluded, except the one who subjects. Therefore, all things including death are subjected to Christ.

He says, therefore: *when it says*, *all things are put under him*, namely, Christ as man, *he is excepted*, namely, the Father, *who put all things under him*: *putting everything in*

Hebr. II, v. 8: *in eo qui omnia sibi subiecit*, et cetera. Matth. ult.: *data est mihi omnis potestas*, et cetera.

Sed contra. Si Pater subiecit omnia Filio, ergo Filius est minor Patre.

Responsio. Dicendum est, quod Pater subiecit omnia Filio, inquantum est homo, ut dictum est, et sic Pater est maior Filio. Est enim minor Patre secundum humanitatem, aequalis vero secundum divinitatem. Vel dicendum, quod etiam ipse Filius, inquantum Deus, subiecit sibi omnia, quia sic potest omnia quae Pater potest, Phil. III, 20: *Salvatorem expectamus*, etc., *secundum operationem qua potens est subiicere omnia*.

950. Consequenter cum dicit *cum autem subiecta fuerint illi omnia*, etc., ostendit finem huius resurrectionis non esse in humanitate Christi, sed ulterius perducetur rationalis creatura ad contemplationem divinitatis, et in ea est beatitudo nostra, et finis noster ipse Deus est.

Et ideo dicit *cum autem subiecta*, etc., quasi dicat: nondum Deus subiecit omnia Christo, sed cum omnia fuerint ei subiecta, scilicet Christo, tunc ipse filius secundum humanitatem subiectus erit illi, scilicet Patri, Io. XIV, 28: *Pater maior me est*; et subiectus est nunc etiam Christus secundum quod homo Patri, sed hoc tunc manifestius erit.

Et ratio huius subiectionis est *ut sit Deus omnia in omnibus*, id est ut anima hominis totaliter requiescat in Deo, et solus Deus sit beatitudo. Modo enim in uno est vita et virtus in alio et gloria in alio, sed tunc Deus erit vita et salus et virtus, et gloria et omnia.

Vel aliter ita, *ut sit Deus omnia in omnibus*, quia tunc manifestabitur quod quidquid boni habemus est a Deo.

subjection under his feet (Heb 2:8); *all power is given to me in heaven and on earth* (Matt 28:18).

But on the other hand. If the Father subjected all things to the Son, the Son is less than the Father.

The answer is that the Father subjected all to the Son as man, as has been stated, and so the Father is greater than the Son. For he is less according to his humanity, but equal according to his divinity. Or it might be said that even the Son himself as God subjected all things to himself, because as God he can do all that the Father does: *we await a Savior who will change our lowly body to be like his glorious body, by the power which enables him even to subject all things to himself* (Phil 3:20).

950. Then when he says: *and when all things shall be subdued unto him*, he shows that the end of this resurrection is not in the humanity of Christ, but the rational creature will be further led to contemplating the divinity, and in it is our happiness.

Therefore, he says, *when all things shall be subdued unto him*. As if to say: God has not yet subjected all things to Christ, but when all things shall have been subjected to him, namely, to Christ, then the subject himself according to his humanity will be subjected to him, namely, to the Father: *the Father is greater than I* (John 14:28), and even now Christ as man is subjected to the Father, but this will be more manifest then.

The reason for this subjection is *that God may be all in all*, i.e., that the soul of men rest entirely in God, and God alone be beatitude. For now there is life and virtue in one and glory in another; but then God will be the life and salvation and virtue and glory and all things.

Or in another way: *that God may be all in all*, because then it will be clear that whatever good we have is from God.

Lecture 4

15:29 Alioquin quid facient qui baptizantur pro mortuis, si omnino mortui non resurgunt? ut quid et baptizantur pro illis? [n. 951]

15:30ut quid et nos periclitamur omni hora? [n. 955]

15:31 Quotidie morior per vestram gloriam, fratres, quam habeo in Christo Jesu Domino nostro. [n. 957]

15:32 Si secundum hominem ad bestias pugnavi Ephesi, quid mihi prodest, si mortui non resurgunt? Manducemus, et bibamus, cras enim moriemur. [n. 959]

15:33 Nolite seduci: corrumpunt mores bonos colloquia mala. [n. 961]

15:34 Evigilate justi, et nolite peccare: ignorantiam enim Dei quidam habent, ad reverentiam vobis loquor. [n. 963]

15:29Ἐπεὶ τί ποιήσουσιν οἱ βαπτιζόμενοι ὑπὲρ τῶν νεκρῶν; εἰ ὅλως νεκροὶ οὐκ ἐγείρονται, τί καὶ βαπτίζονται ὑπὲρ αὐτῶν;

15:30τί καὶ ἡμεῖς κινδυνεύομεν πᾶσαν ὥραν;

15:31καθ᾽ ἡμέραν ἀποθνήσκω, νὴ τὴν ὑμετέραν καύχησιν, [ἀδελφοί,] ἣν ἔχω ἐν Χριστῷ Ἰησοῦ τῷ κυρίῳ ἡμῶν.

15:32εἰ κατὰ ἄνθρωπον ἐθηριομάχησα ἐν Ἐφέσῳ, τί μοι τὸ ὄφελος; εἰ νεκροὶ οὐκ ἐγείρονται, Φάγωμεν καὶ πίωμεν, αὔριον γὰρ ἀποθνήσκομεν.

15:33μὴ πλανᾶσθε· Φθείρουσιν ἤθη χρηστὰ ὁμιλίαι κακαί.

15:34ἐκνήψατε δικαίως καὶ μὴ ἁμαρτάνετε, ἀγνωσίαν γὰρ θεοῦ τινες ἔχουσιν· πρὸς ἐντροπὴν ὑμῖν λαλῶ.

15:29 Otherwise, what shall they do who are baptized for the dead, if the dead rise not again at all? Why are they then baptized for them? [n. 951]

15:30 Why also are we in danger every hour? [n. 955]

15:31I die daily, by your glory, brethren, which I have in Christ Jesus our Lord. [n. 957]

15:32 If (according to man) I fought with beasts at Ephesus, what does it profit me, if the dead rise not again? Let us eat and drink, for tomorrow we shall die. [n. 959]

15:33 Do not be seduced: evil communications corrupt good manners. [n. 961]

15:34 Awake, you just, and sin not. For some have not the knowledge of God. I speak it to your shame. [n. 963]

---

951. Ostensa resurrectione mortuorum ex resurrectione Christi, hic consequenter ostendit resurrectionem mortuorum ex vita sanctorum. Et circa hoc duo facit.

Primo probat propositum;

secundo subiungit admonitionem, ibi *nolite seduci*, et cetera.

Probat autem propositum, ducendo ad tria inconvenientia.

Primum inconveniens est quod frustraretur devotio hominum ad baptismum;

secundum est quod frustraretur labor sanctorum, et hoc ponit ibi *ut quid et nos periclitamur*, etc.;

tertium est quod daretur occasio fruendi voluptatibus. Et hoc ponit, ibi *manducemus et bibamus*, et cetera.

Circa primum duo facit.

Primo ponit primum inconveniens;

secundo explicat illud, ibi *si omnino mortui*, et cetera.

952. Dicit ergo primo: dixi quod mortui resurgunt, *alioquin*, scilicet si non est resurrectio mortuorum futura, ut nos praedicamus, *quid facient qui*, et cetera. Hoc potest dupliciter intelligi.

Uno modo, ut per hoc quod dicit *mortui*, intelligantur opera peccati, quae sunt mortua, quia carent vita gratiae, et ducunt ad mortem. Hebr. IX, 14: *sanguis Christi emundabit*, et cetera. Et secundum hoc plana est littera. *Quid*, scilicet *facient illi, qui baptizantur pro mortuis*,

951. Having shown the resurrection of the dead from the resurrection of Christ, the Apostle then shows the resurrection of the dead from the life of the saints. In regard to this he does two things:

first, he proves his proposition;

second, he adds an admonition, at *do not be seduced*.

He proves his proposition by leading to three incongruities:

first, it is incongruous that men's devotion to baptism be frustrated;

second, that the laborers of the saints would be frustrated, at *why also are we in danger*;

third, that there would be given the occasion to enjoy pleasure, at *let us eat and drink*.

In regard to the first he does two things:

first, he presents the first incongruity;

second, he explains it, at *if the dead rise not again at all*.

952. First, therefore, he says: I have said that the dead rise, *otherwise*, namely, if there is not resurrection of the dead, as we preach, *what shall they do who are baptized for the dead*. This can be understood in two ways:

in one way so that by *dead* the works of sin are understood. They are dead, because they lack the life of grace and lead to death: *the blood of Christ will purify your conscience from dead works* (Heb 9:14). And according to this the words are plain. *What shall they do who are baptized for*

id est pro peccatis abluendis, si non sint vitam gratiae habituri?

Alio modo, quia quidam tunc temporis volebant, quod homines possent primo baptizari, ut sibi ipsis remissionem peccatorum consequerentur; et iterum baptizabantur pro aliquo consanguineo suo defuncto, ut etiam post mortem dimitterentur ei peccata. Et secundum hoc sit littera: *quid facient qui baptizantur pro mortuis*, scilicet consanguineis, pro quorum salute baptizantur, si non sit resurrectio mortuorum? Sed isti in aliquo commendari possunt, scilicet in hoc quod fidem resurrectionis videbantur habere. Sed in aliquo possunt reprehendi, in hoc scilicet quod unum credebant posse pro alio baptizari.

953. Sed tunc est quaestio: si oratio unius prodest alteri, quare non etiam baptismus?

Ad hoc est duplex responsio. Una est, quod opera quae faciunt vivi, prosunt mortuis propter unionem caritatis et fidei. Et ideo non prosunt nisi illis qui decedunt cum caritate et fide. Unde infidelibus nec oratio, nec baptismus vivorum prosunt; tamen oratio prodest illis qui sunt in purgatorio.

Alia responsio, et melior, quia bona opera valent mortuis, non solum ex vi caritatis, sed etiam ex intentione facientis. Sicut si ego dicerem psalterium pro aliquo qui est in purgatorio, qui tenebatur dicere, ut satisfaciam pro eo, valet quidem quantum ad satisfactionem solum illi pro quo dico.

Dicendum est ergo secundum hoc, quod baptismus non habet virtutem ex intentione nostra, sed ex intentione Christi. Intentio autem Christi est ut baptismus illis proficiat, qui in Christi fide baptizantur.

954. Consequenter istud inconveniens explicat, dicens *si omnino*, et cetera. Et ista explicatio videtur magis convenire secundae expositioni supra positae, quasi dicat: ut quid baptizantur pro illis, id est, pro mortuis, si non resurgunt?

Sed si secundum primam expositionem exponatur, tunc sic potest dici *si omnino mortui non resurgunt, ut quid etiam baptizantur pro illis*, id est pro peccatis, cum ipsa non dimittantur?

955. *Ut quid periclitamur*, et cetera. Hic ponit secundum inconveniens, et circa hoc duo facit.

Primo ponit inconveniens in communi;
secundo in speciali, ibi *quotidie*, et cetera.

956. Dicit ergo: non solum frustra baptizantur aliqui pro remissione peccatorum, sed nos etiam frustra affligimur, si resurrectio mortuorum non est. Et hoc est quod dicit *ut quid et nos*, sancti apostoli, *periclitamur*, id est pericula patimur, *omni hora?* II Cor. c. XI, 26: *periculis fluminum, periculis*, et cetera.

the dead? i.e., for washing away their sins, if they are not to have the life of grace?

In another way, because some at that time wanted men to be baptized: first, in order that they might obtain for themselves the remission of sins; and they were baptized again for some dead relative, so that he too would be freed from sins after death. And according to this the text reads: *what shall they do who are baptized for the dead*, namely, their relatives, for whose salvation they were baptized, if there is no resurrection of the dead. But they can be commended in something, namely, in the fact that they seemed to have faith in the resurrection. But in something they can be reprehended, in the fact that they believed that one can be baptized for another.

953. But then there is a question: if one's prayers profit another, why not his baptism?

To this there are two answers: one is that works performed by the living do profit the dead on account of the union of charity and faith. And therefore, they benefit only those who die with charity and faith. Hence, neither prayer nor the baptism of the living profit unbelievers; yet prayer can help those in purgatory.

Another answer and better is that good works help the dead not only in virtue of charity but also from the intention of the one who performs them. Just as if I should say the psalter for someone who is in purgatory and was bound to say it to satisfy for him, it will be profitable indeed as to satisfying only for the one for whom I say it.

It must be said according to this that baptism has no value from our intention but from the intention of Christ. But the intention of Christ is that baptism should benefit those who are baptized in the faith of Christ.

954. Then he explains that incongruity, saying: *if the dead rise not again at all*. And this explanation seems to agree more with the second explanation given above. As if to say: why are they baptized for them, i.e., for the dead, if they do not rise.

But if it is explained according to the first explanation, then it can be said: *if the dead rise not again at all, why are they then baptized for them*, i.e., for their sins, since they are not forgiven.

955. *Why also are we in danger every hour?* Here he presents the second incongruity. In regard to this he does two things:

first, he mentions the incongruity in general;
second, in special, at *I die daily*.

956. He says, therefore: not only are some baptized in vain for the remission of sins, but we also are afflicted in vain, if there is no resurrection of the dead. And this is what he says: *why also are we*, the holy apostles, *in danger*, i.e., endure dangers, *every hour*: in danger at sea, in danger from false brethren (2 Cor 11:26).

Constat enim, quod sancti exponunt se tribulationibus, et affligunt seipsos propter spem vitae aeternae, secundum illud Rom. V, 11: *non solum autem, sed et gloriamur*, et cetera. *Spes autem non confundit*, et cetera. Si ergo resurrectio mortuorum non sit, totaliter spes perit. Frustra ergo affligerent se, si mortui non resurgunt.

Nec obstat, si dicatur quod anima separata praemiatur, quia, ut probatum est supra, non posset probari quod anima esset immortalis.

957. Consequenter cum dicit *quotidie*, etc., enumerat pericula in speciali, et

primo quantum ad personam;

secundo quantum ad locum, ibi *si, secundum hominem, ad bestias*, et cetera.

958. Manifestat ergo in speciali pericula quantum ad personam suam; unde dicit *quotidie morior*, etc., quasi dicat: non quaecumque pericula patimur, sed etiam mortis, quia *quotidie morior*, id est sum in periculis mortis. Ps. XLIII, 22: *propter te mortificamur tota die*. Et hoc ostendit Apostolus Roman. 8 in persona apostolorum esse dictum, II Cor. IV, v. 10: *semper mortificationem*, et cetera.

Propter gloriam vestram, id est ut ego acquiram gloriam, quam expecto ex vestra conversione ad fidem. II Thess. II, 20: *vos estis gloria mea et gaudium*, *quam habeo*, id est, spero me habiturum, *in Christo Iesu Domino nostro*, id est per caritatem Christi.

Alia littera habet *per gloriam*, etc., et tunc *per gloriam*, est verbum iurantis; quasi dicat: *per gloriam vestram*, quam scilicet expectatis, quae est Deus. Ac si diceret: iuro per Deum, quem habeo in spe in Christo Iesu, id est per passionem, et cetera. Ex quo apparet, quod etiam Apostolus iuravit, et quod in viris perfectis iurare non est peccatum.

959. *Si secundum hominem*, et cetera. Hic specificat pericula quantum ad locum.

Ubi sciendum est, quod hoc legitur Act. c. XIX, ubi dicitur quod, cum Paulus apud Ephesum multos convertisset ad fidem, quidam concitaverunt contra eum populum, intantum quod non esset ausus exire in theatrum, et quod multa pericula sit ibi passus. Ergo forte facit hic de hoc mentionem, quia e vicino passus hoc fuerat.

Dicit ergo: *si secundum hominem*, id est secundum rationem ex qua homo est, hoc disputando de resurrectione, concludens quod homo non moritur sicut bestia. *Pugnavi ad bestias*, id est ad homines bestialiter viventes apud Ephesum.

Vel *si pugnavi ad bestias Ephesi*, et hoc dico non ex revelatione divina, sed *secundum hominem*, id est ex instinctu humano, si tot pericula passus sum, et cetera.

960. Deinde cum dicit *manducemus*, etc., ponit tertium inconveniens, quod est: si resurrectio mortuorum

For it is clear that the saints expose themselves to tribulation and afflict themselves on account of the hope of eternal life, as it says in Romans: *not only so, but we also rejoice in God through the Lord Jesus Christ* (Rom 5:11). *Hope does not confound* (Rom 5:5). Therefore, if there no resurrection of the dead, hope utterly vanishes. Therefore, they have afflicted themselves in vain, if there is no resurrection.

Nor is that conclusion hindered by saying that the separated soul will be rewarded, because, as has been proved above, it cannot be proved that the soul would be immortal.

957. Then when he says: *daily* I die for your glory, he enumerates the dangers in special:

first, as to the person;

second, as to the place, at *if (according to man) I fought with beasts at Ephesus*.

958. Therefore, he manifests the dangers as to his own person; hence he says: *I die daily*, i.e., I suffer not just any dangers, but even those of death, because *I die daily*, i.e., am in danger of death: *for thy sake we are slain all day long* (Ps 44:22). And the Apostle shows that this was said in the person of the apostles: *always carrying in the body the death of Jesus* (2 Cor 4:10).

By your glory, i.e., that I may acquire the glory I await from your conversion to the faith: *you are my glory and my joy* (2 Thess 2:20), *which I have* i.e., hope to have, *in Christ Jesus our Lord*, i.e., through the charity of Christ.

Another text has, *by your glory*, and then *by your glory* is an oath. As if to say: *by your glory* which you await, which is God. As if to say: I swear by God, whom I have in hope in Christ Jesus, i.e., by his passion. From which it appears that even the Apostle swore, and that among those who are perfect, swearing is not a sin.

959. The when he says, *if (according to man)*, he specifies the dangers as to place.

Here it should be noted that this is read in Acts 19, which says that when St. Paul had converted many to the faith at Ephesus, some stirred up the people against him, so that he would not dare to go out into the theatre, and that he endured many dangers. Therefore, perhaps he mentions this, because he had suffered from a neighboring town.

He says, therefore: what do I gain, *if (according to man)*, i.e., according to reason, from which man is man, by disputing about the resurrection, I conclude that man does not die as the beast. *I fought with beasts at Ephesus*, with men living in a beastly manner at Ephesus.

Or *if I fought with beasts at Ephesus*, and I say this not from divine revelation but *according to man*, i.e., from human instinct, if I have endured such perils.

960. Then when he says, *let us eat and drink*, he presents the third incongruity, which is: if there is no resurrection of

non esset, daretur occasio fruendi voluptatibus. Quasi dicat: si non est alia vita, stulti sumus si affligimus nos, sed *manducemus et bibamus*, id est utamur deliciis et fruamur voluptatibus. Sap. II, v. 1: *non est, qui sit agnitus*, etc.: *venite, fruamur*, et cetera. *Cras enim*, id est, in proximo, *moriemur*; totaliter enim deficiemus in anima et corpore, si mortui non resurgunt.

961. Deinde cum dicit *nolite seduci*, ex praedictis concludit admonitionem, et

primo quantum ad infirmos;

secundo vero quantum ad perfectos et iustos, ibi *vigilate, iusti*, et cetera.

962. Circa primum duo facit. Primo reddit eos attentos, dicens *nolite seduci*, quasi dicat: dictum est, quod si resurrectio mortuorum non sit, stultum esset non uti lasciviis et voluptatibus. Ne ergo ad lascivias inducamini, nolite seduci ab his qui negant resurrectionem. Col. II, 18: *videte ne quis vos seducat*, et cetera.

Secundo rationem attentionis assignat, dicens *corrumpunt*, etc., quasi dicat: ideo nolite seduci, quia *colloquia mala*, illorum scilicet qui negant resurrectionem, *corrumpunt bonos mores*, II Tim. II, 17: *sermo eorum serpit ut cancer*.

Hieronymus dicit quod hoc est sumptum ex dictis gentilium, et est versus cuiusdam Menandri. Et ex hoc, ut ipse dicit, argumentum habemus, quod licet nobis quandoque in Sacra Scriptura uti auctoritatibus gentilium.

963. Deinde cum dicit *vigilate*, etc., ponit admonitionem quantum ad perfectos. Posset enim dicere, quod a colloquiis illorum debent cavere infirmi qui de facili seducuntur; perfecti autem non sic seduci possunt. Apostolus autem vult, quod etiam perfecti sint cauti.

Unde circa hoc duo facit. Primo reddit eos attentos, dicens *vigilate, iusti*, id est vos, qui reputamini iusti, *vigilate*, id est, solliciti sitis. Matth. XXIV, 42: *vigilate, quia nescitis*, et cetera. Apoc. XVI, 15: *beatus qui vigilat*, et cetera.

Secundo rationem assignat, dicens *nolite*, etc., et hanc duplicem, quarum unam propter seipsos. Nullus enim est adeo perfectus, quin debeat sibi cavere a peccatis. Inertia autem et torpor frequenter inducit ad peccatum, unde ne peccent inducit eos ad vigiliam, et ideo dicit *et nolite peccare*, id est ne peccetis, Tob. IV, 6: *in mente habeto Deum, et cave ne aliquando peccato consentias*.

Aliam rationem inducit propter alios, quia non solum propter seipsos sint solliciti, sed et propter alios, ne illi seducantur. Et hoc est quod dicit *quidam enim habent*

the dead, occasion would be given for enjoying pleasures. As if to say: if there is not another life, we are foolish, if we afflict ourselves, but *let us eat and drink*, i.e., use the delights and enjoy the pleasures: *no one has been known to return from Hades* (Wis 2:1); *come, let us enjoy the good things that exist* (Wis 2:6). *For tomorrow* i.e., soon, *we shall die*; for we shall totally fail, if the dead do not rise.

961. Then when he says: *do not be seduced*, he concludes to a warning from the preceding:

first, as to the sick;

second, as to the perfect and just, at *awake, you just*.

962. In regard to the first he does two things: first, he makes them attentive, saying: *do not be seduced*. As if to say: it has been stated that if there is no resurrection of the dead, it would be foolish not to use lascivious and voluptuous things. Therefore, lest you be tempted to lascivious things, do not be deceived by those who deny the resurrection. *Let no one disqualify you* (Col 2:18).

Second, he assigns the reason for their attention, saying: *evil communications corrupt good manners*. As if to say: do not be deceived, because *evil communications* of those who deny the resurrection *corrupt good manners*: *their talk will eat its way like gangrene* (2 Tim 2:17).

Jerome says that was taken from the statements of the gentiles and is a verse of a certain Menandrus. And from this he says we have an argument that it is lawful sometimes in Sacred Scripture to use the authorities of gentiles.

963. Then when he says: *awake, you just, and sin not*, he presents an admonition as to the perfect. For someone could say that from their conversations the weak should take care, because they are easily deceived; but the perfect cannot be so deceived. But the Apostle wishes that even the perfect be cautious.

Hence he does two things in this regard. First, he makes them attentive, saying: *awake, you just*, i.e., you who are regarded as just, *awake*, i.e., be careful: *watch, therefore, for you do not know on what day your Lord will come.* (Matt 24:42); *blessed is he who is awake keeping his garments* (Rev 16:15).

Second, he assigns the reason, saying: *sin not*, and this twofold, one of which is on account of themselves. For no one is so perfect that he does not need to be wary of sin. But inertia and inactivity frequently lead to sin; hence, lest they sin, he induces them to be vigilant. Therefore, he says: *sin not*: *remember the Lord our God all your days, and refuse to sin* (Tob 4:5).

He presents another reason for the benefit of others, because they are not solicitous only for themselves but also for others, lest they be deceived. And this is what he says: *for some have not the knowledge of God*, i.e., do no

ignorantiam Dei, id est non rectam fidem. Rom. X, v. 3: *ignorantes Dei iustitiam*, et cetera.

Et hoc *loquor vobis ad reverentiam vestram*, ut sitis cauti. Vel ad verecundiam vestram, quia verecundum est vobis, qui reputamini sapientes, et instructi in fide, quod sint aliqui inter vos ignorantiam Dei habentes, id est non rectam fidem.

have a correct faith: *being ignorant of the righteousness of God, they did not submit to God's righteousness* (Rom 10:3).

And this *I speak it to your shame*, that you should be careful. Or to your shame, because it is shameful to you who are regarded wise and instructed in the faith, that some among you are ignorant of God, i.e., do not have the correct faith.

Lecture 5

15:35Sed dicet aliquis: Quomodo resurgunt mortui? qualive corpore venient? [n. 964]

15:36Insipiens, tu quod seminas non vivificatur, nisi prius moriatur: [n. 966]

15:37et quod seminas, non corpus, quod futurum est, seminas, sed nudum granum, ut puta tritici, aut alicujus ceterorum. [n. 970]

15:38Deus autem dat illi corpus sicut vult: ut unicuique seminum proprium corpus. [n. 972]

15:35Ἀλλὰ ἐρεῖ τις, Πῶς ἐγείρονται οἱ νεκροί; ποίῳ δὲ σώματι ἔρχονται;

15:36ἄφρων, σὺ ὃ σπείρεις οὐ ζωοποιεῖται ἐὰν μὴ ἀποθάνῃ·

15:37καὶ ὃ σπείρεις, οὐ τὸ σῶμα τὸ γενησόμενον σπείρεις ἀλλὰ γυμνὸν κόκκον εἰ τύχοι σίτου ἤ τινος τῶν λοιπῶν·

15:38ὁ δὲ θεὸς δίδωσιν αὐτῷ σῶμα καθὼς ἠθέλησεν, καὶ ἑκάστῳ τῶν σπερμάτων ἴδιον σῶμα.

15:35But some man will say: how do the dead rise again? Or with what manner of body shall they come? [n. 964]

15:36Senseless man, that which you sow is not quickened, except it die first. [n. 966]

15:37And that which you sow, you sow not the body that shall be: but bare grain, as of wheat, or of some of the rest. [n. 970]

15:38But God gives it a body as he wills: and to every seed its proper body. [n. 972]

---

964. Superius Apostolus probavit resurrectionem mortuorum, hic ostendit qualitatem et modum resurgentium.

Et circa hoc duo facit.

Primo movet quaestionem circa qualitatem resurgentium;

secundo solvit, ibi *insipiens tu*, et cetera.

965. Circa resurrectionem fuerunt duo errores. Quidam enim totaliter negabant resurrectionem mortuorum futuram. Cum enim non considerarent nisi principia naturae et posse, et viderent quod secundum principia naturae et posse nullus de morte potest redire ad vitam, nec caecus potest recuperare visum, ideo totaliter negaverunt resurrectionem, ex quorum persona dicitur Sap. II, 5: *umbrae transitus est tempus nostrum*, et cetera. Et ibidem: *de nihilo nati sumus*, et cetera. Iob XIV, v. 14: *putasne mortuus homo rursum vivet*, et cetera.

Alii autem dixerunt resurrectionem mortuorum futuram esse, sed dicebant quod resurgebant ad eumdem modum vivendi, et ad eosdem actus. Et hoc etiam posuerunt quidam philosophi qui dicunt: post multa annorum curricula Plato adhuc resurget, et habebit eosdem scholares Athenis, quos aliquando habuit. Hoc etiam asserunt Pharisaei, Matth. XXII, 28, de muliere septem virorum, unde dicebant: *in resurrectione cuius erit?* Saraceni etiam fingunt quod habebunt post resurrectionem uxores, et voluptates, et delicias corporales. Iob XX, 17: *non videat rivulos fluminis torrentis mellis et butyri*. Contra quos dicitur Matth. XXII, 30, quod *erunt sicut angeli Dei in caelo*.

Has ergo duas quaestiones movet hic Apostolus. Primam cum dicit *quomodo resurgunt mortui?* Quomodo est possibile quod mortui qui sunt cinis possint resurgere? Secundam, cum dicit *quali autem corpore venient?*

964. Having proved the resurrection of the dead, the Apostle now shows the quality and mode of those rising.

In regard to this he does two things:

first, he raises a question about the quality of those rising;

second, he answers it, at *senseless man, that which you sow*.

965. In regard to the resurrection there have been two errors. For some absolutely denied the future resurrection of the dead. For since they considered only the principles and capabilities of nature and saw that according to natural principles and capabilities no one could return to life or a blind person recover sight, they absolutely denied the resurrection. From their mouth it is said: *our allotted time is the passing of a shadow* (Wis 2:5); *we are born of nothing* (Wis 2:2); *do you think a dead man will live again?* (Job 14:14)

Others, on the other hand, have said there will be a resurrection, but they will rise to the same manner of living and to the same acts. Even philosophers have posited this when they said: after many years Plato will rise again and will have the same scholars in Athens, whom he had at some time. The Sadducees also assert this about the woman with seven husbands (Matt 22:29). Hence they asked: *in the resurrection to which of the seven will she be wife?* The Saracens, too, pretend that after the resurrection they will have wives and voluptuous and bodily pleasures: *he will not move upon the rivers, the streams flow with honey and curds* (Job 20:17). Against these Matthew says that *they will be as the angels in heaven* (Matt 22:30).

Therefore the Apostle raises two questions here. The first is when he says, *how do the dead rise again?* How is it possible that the dead who are dust can rise? The second when he says, *or with what manner of body shall they*

Quasi dicat: numquid cum tali corpore resurgent cum quali sumus modo?

966. Has duas quaestiones solvit cum dicit *insipiens*, et cetera. Primo solvit secundam, secundo vero solvit primam, ibi *ecce mysterium vobis dico*, et cetera.

Ad intellectum autem eorum quae Apostolus ponit in prima parte, oportet investigare quid Apostolus intendat. Intendit autem in ista parte Apostolus ostendere quod mortui resurgunt, et quod erit eadem substantia. Ubi

primo ponit similitudines;

secundo adaptat, ibi *sic etiam resurrectio mortuorum*, etc.;

tertio probat, ibi *si est corpus animale*, et cetera.

Circa primum duo facit.

Primo proponit similitudines in una specie,

secundo in diversis speciebus, ibi *non omnis caro, eadem caro*, et cetera.

967. Circa primum sciendum est quod videmus in una et eadem specie quod una res in via generationis habet diversas qualitates et formas; sicut granum aliam formam et qualitatem habet quando seminatur, aliam quando pullulat, aliam quando iam est in herba. Et ideo ex hac similitudine Apostolus intendit ostendere qualitatem resurgentium.

Unde circa hoc tria facit.

Primo comparat ordinem seminationis ad pullulationem;

secundo differentiam qualitatis in semine et in pullulatione, ibi *tu quod seminas*, etc.;

tertio causam qualitatis in pullulatione, ibi *Deus autem*, et cetera.

968. Dicit ergo *insipiens*, et cetera. Sed contra Matth. V, 22: *qui dixerit fratri suo: racha*, et cetera.

Dicendum quod Dominus prohibet dici fratri racha seu fatue, ex ira non ex correctione.

Causa autem quare dicit *insipiens*, est quia haec obiectio contra resurrectionem procedit ex principiis humanae sapientiae, quae tamdiu est sapientia, quamdiu est subiecta sapientiae divinae; sed quando recedit a Deo, tunc vertitur in insipientiam; unde cum contradicat sapientiae divinae, vocat eam insipientem. Quasi dicat: *insipiens*, nonne quotidie experiris, *tu*, quia *quod seminas*, in terra, *non vivificatur*, id est vegetatur, *nisi prius moriatur*, id est putrescat? Io. XII, 24: *nisi granum frumenti*, et cetera.

Ex hoc videtur Apostolus facere comparationem, quod quando corpus hominis ponitur in sepulchro in terra, tunc est quaedam seminatio; quando vero resurgit, tunc est quaedam vivificatio.

come? As if to say: will they rise with the same kind of body as we have now?

966. He answers these two questions when he says, *senseless man*. First, he solves the second; second, he solves the first, at *behold, I tell you a mystery* (1 Cor 15:51).

To understand what the Apostle presents in the first part, it is necessary to investigate what the Apostle intends. But in this part the Apostle intends to show that the dead will rise and that their substance will be the same.

Here he first presents likenesses;

second, he adapts, at *so also is the resurrection of the dead* (1 Cor 15:42);

third, he proves it, at *it is sown a natural body* (1 Cor 15:44).

In regard to the first he does two things:

first, he proposes likenesses in one species;

second, in diverse species, at *all flesh is not the same flesh* (1 Cor 15:39).

967. In regard to the first it should be noted that we see in one and the same species that one thing on the way to generation has diverse qualities and forms: as grain has one form and quality, when it is planted, and another, when it shoots up, and another, when it is in herb. From this likeness the Apostle intends to show the quality of the rising.

Hence, in regard to this he does three things:

first, he compares the order of sowing to growing;

second, the difference in quality in sowing and growing, at *and that which you sow*;

third, the cause of the quality in growing, at *but God gives it a body*.

968. He says, therefore, *senseless man*. But on the other hand it is said: *whoever says to his brother: you fool, shall be liable to hell* (Matt 5:22).

The answer is that God forbids saying, 'you fool' or 'stupid' to your brother in anger and not correction.

Now the reason he says *senseless man* is that this objection against the resurrection proceeds from the principles of human wisdom, which is wisdom as long as it is subjected to divine wisdom. But when one departs from God, he falls back on unwisdom; hence, when he contradicts divine wisdom, he calls him foolish. As if to say: *senseless man*, do you not experience every day *that which you sow* in the earth *is not quickened, except it die first*, i.e., decays: *unless a grain of wheat falls into the earth and dies, it remains alone* (John 12:24).

And the Apostle seems to make this comparison, that when a man's body is put in a tomb, it is a form of sowing; but when it rises, it is coming to life.

969. Unde ex hoc opinantur aliqui, resurrectionem mortuorum esse naturalem, propter hoc quod Apostolus hic resurrectionem comparat pullulationi seminis quae est naturalis. Opinantur enim in pulveribus resolutis, in quos resolvuntur humana corpora, esse quasdam virtutes seminales activas ad corporum resurrectionem.

Sed istud non videtur esse verum. Fit enim resolutio corporis humani in elementa, sicut et aliorum mixtorum corporum, unde pulveres in quos humana corpora resolvuntur, nullam aliam habent virtutem activam quam alii pulveres, in quibus constat non esse aliam virtutem activam ad corporis humani constitutionem, sed solum in semine hominis; differunt autem pulveres in quos humana corpora resolvuntur, ab aliis pulveribus solum secundum ordinationem divinam, prout huiusmodi pulveres sunt ex divina sapientia ordinati, ut iterum ex eis humana corpora reintegrentur.

Unde resurrectionis activa causa solus Deus erit, etsi ad hoc utatur ministerio angelorum, quantum ad pulverum collectionem. Propter quod Apostolus infra modum resurrectionis exponens, attribuit sono tubae, et supra attribuit Christo resurgenti, non autem alicui virtuti activae in pulveribus.

Non ergo intendit hic probare Apostolus quod resurrectio sit naturalis, per hoc quod semen naturaliter pullulat, sed intendit hic manifestare per exempla quaedam, quod non sit eadem qualitas corporum resurgentium et corporum morientium, et primo per hoc quod non est eadem qualitas seminis et pullulationis, ut ex sequentibus manifeste ostendetur.

970. Nam consequenter cum dicit *et quod seminas*, etc., ostendit qualitatem seminis differentem esse a qualitate pullulationis, cum dicit *et quod seminas, non corpus, quod futurum est, seminas*, id est non quale futurum est seminas. Quod exponens subdit *sed nudum granum, puta tritici vel alicuius caeterorum*, scilicet seminum, quia seminatur nudum semen, pullulat autem ornatum herba, et aristis, et huiusmodi. Et similiter corpus humanum aliam qualitatem habebit in resurrectione quam nunc habet, ut infra exponetur.

Est tamen differentia inter resurrectionem humani corporis, et pullulationem seminis; nam surget idem corpus numero, sed habebit aliam qualitatem, sicut infra dicit Apostolus, quod *oportet corruptibile hoc induere incorruptionem*; et Iob XIX, 27 dicitur *quem visurus sum ego ipse, et non alius*. Sed in pullulatione nec est eadem qualitas, nec idem corpus numero, sed solum idem specie. Et ideo signanter Apostolus de pullulatione loquens, dixit *non corpus, quod futurum est, seminas*, dans intelligere quod non sit idem numero.

969. Hence, from this some suppose that the resurrection of the dead is natural, inasmuch as the Apostle here compares the resurrection of the dead to the sprouting of a seed, which is natural. For they believed that in the dust, into which human bodies are resolved, there were certain active seminal powers for the resurrection of bodies.

But this does not seem to be true. For the resolution of human bodies into elements happens in the same way as other mixed bodies; hence, the dust into which human bodies are resolved has no other active power than other dust, in which there is no evidence of any active power to constitute a human body, but only in man's seed. However, the dusts into which human bodies are reduced differ from other dust only according to God's plan, inasmuch as these dusts are ordained by divine wisdom that human bodies be formed from them again.

Hence the active cause of the resurrection is God alone, even though for this he uses the service of angels to collect the dust. Hence, the Apostle explaining the manner of the resurrection below attributes it to Christ's raising, but not to any active power in the dusts.

Therefore, the Apostle does not intend to prove here that the resurrection is natural, but to manifest by certain examples that the quality of rising bodies and that of dying bodies is not the same; and, first of all, by the fact that the quality of the seed and of the sprouting bud are not the same, as will be clearly shown from the following.

970. For when he says, *and that which you sow*, he shows that the quality of seed is different from the quality of the sprout. Hence he says, *and that which you sow, you sow not the body that shall be*, i.e., you do not plant it as it will be. Explaining this he says, *but bare grain, as of wheat, or of some of the rest*, namely, a seed, because a bare kernel is sowed, but what sprouts is fashioned as an herb, or an ear of corn and so on. Similarly, the human body will have another quality in the resurrection than it has now, as will be explained below.

Yet there is a difference between the resurrection of the human body and the sprouting of a seed, for the same numerical body will rise, but it will have another quality, as the Apostle says below: *for this incorruptible must put on the incorruption* (2 Cor 15:53); and: *and my eyes shall behold and not another* (Job 19:27). But in sprouting there is neither the same quality nor the same numerical body, but only the same in species. And therefore, the Apostle speaking about sprouting said, *you sow not the body that shall be*, giving us to understand that it is not the same numerically.

Et in hoc opus naturae deficit ab opere Dei. Nam virtus naturae reparat idem specie, sed non idem numero: virtus autem Dei reparare potest etiam idem numero.

971. Et sic etiam ex hoc quod hic dicitur potest sumi probatio ad hoc quod resurrectionem futuram fieri non est impossibile, sicut insipiens obiiciebat. Quia si natura ex eo quod mortuum est, potest reparare idem specie, multo magis Deus potest reparare idem numero; quia et hoc ipsum quod natura facit, opus Dei est. Habet enim hoc natura a Deo, quod hoc facere possit.

972. Et ideo consequenter describens qualitatem pullulationis, attribuit eam primum quidem Deo, secundo proportioni naturae.

973. Dicit autem primo *Deus autem dat illi corpus sicut vult*, quia scilicet ex ordinatione divinae voluntatis procedit, quod ex tali semine talis planta producatur, quae quidem planta est quasi corpus seminis. Ultimus enim fructus plantae est semen. Et hoc ideo attribuit operationi divinae, quia omnis operatio naturae est operatio Dei, secundum illud supra XII, 6: *idem autem Deus qui operatur omnia in omnibus*. Et hoc sic potest considerari.

Manifestum est enim quod res naturales absque cognitione operantur ad finem determinatum, alioquin non semper, vel in maiori parte, eumdem finem consequerentur. Manifestum est etiam, quod nulla res cognitione carens in certum finem tendit, nisi directa ab aliquo cognoscente, sicut sagitta tendit ad certum signum ex directione sagittantis. Sicut ergo si aliquis videret sagittam directe tendere ad certum signum, quamvis sagittantem non videretur, cognosceret statim quod dirigeretur a sagittante. Ita cum videamus res naturales absque cognitione tendere ad certos fines, possumus pro certo cognoscere quod operantur ex voluntate alicuius dirigentis, quem dicimus Deum. Et sic dicit Apostolus quod *Deus dat*, semini, *corpus*, id est, ex semine producit plantam, *sicut vult*.

974. Sed rursus, ne aliquis crederet huiusmodi naturales effectus ex sola Dei voluntate provenire, absque operatione et proportione naturae, subiungit *et unicuique seminum proprium corpus*, puta ex semine olivae generatur oliva, et ex semine tritici generatur triticum. Unde et Gen. I, 11: *germinet terra herbam virentem et facientem semen iuxta genus suum*.

Sic ergo et in resurrectione erit alia qualitas corporis resurgentis, quae tamen proportionabitur meritis morientis.

And in this the work of nature falls short of God's work. For the power of nature restores what is the same in species, but not the same numerically; but God's power can restore even the same numerically.

971. And so, even from what is stated here can be taken a proof that the future is not something impossible as the foolish man objected. For if nature, from what is dead, can restore the same thing specifically, much more can God restore the same numerical thing, because whatever nature can do is a work of God. For nature has from God that it can do this.

972. Then, describing the quality of sprouting, he attributes it first to God; second, to the proportion of nature.

973. First he says, *God gives it a body as he wills*, because it proceeds from an ordination of the divine will that from such a seed such a plant is produced, which plant is as the body of a seed. For the ultimate fruit of a plant is the seed. And therefore, he attributes this to the activity of God, as it says above: *it is the same God who inspires them all in every one* (2 Cor 12:6). And this can be considered in this way. For it is manifest that natural things act without knowledge for a fixed end; otherwise, they would not always or for the most part attain the same end.

But it is manifest that natural things without knowledge work towards a determined end, otherwise they would not always, or most of the time, reach the same end. And it is manifest that nothing lacking knowledge tends to a fixed end unless directed by a knower, as an arrow tends to a fixed target by the direction of the bowman. Therefore, just as if someone saw an arrow directly moving toward a definite target and did not see a bowman, would immediately know that it was directed by a bowman, so when we see natural things without knowledge tend to definite ends, we can know for certain that they are acting under the will of some director, which we call God. And the Apostle says, *God gives* to the seed *a body*, i.e., he produces from the seed a plant, *as he wills*.

974. But again, lest anyone believe that such natural effects arise solely from God's will without the activity and proportion of nature, he adds, ***and to every seed its proper body***; for example, from the olive seed an olive is produced, and wheat from the seed of wheat. Hence: *let the earth put forth vegetation, plants yielding seed, each according to its kind* (Gen 1:11).

Thus therefore in the resurrection too, there will be another quality of the rising body, which will be proportionate to the merits of the dying person.

Lecture 6

^{15:39}Non omnis caro, eadem caro: sed alia quidem hominum, alia vero pecorum, alia volucrum, alia autem piscium. [n. 975]

^{15:40}Et corpora caelestia, et corpora terrestria: sed alia quidem caelestium gloria, alia autem terrestrium. [n. 977]

^{15:41}Alia claritas solis, alia claritas lunae, et alia claritas stellarum. Stella enim a stella differt in claritate: [n. 978]

^{15:42}sic et resurrectio mortuorum. Seminatur in corruptione, surget in incorruptione. [n. 979]

^{15:43}Seminatur in ignobilitate, surget in gloria: seminatur in infirmitate, surget in virtute: [n. 981]

^{15:39}οὐ πᾶσα σὰρξ ἡ αὐτὴ σάρξ, ἀλλὰ ἄλλη μὲν ἀνθρώπων, ἄλλη δὲ σὰρξ κτηνῶν, ἄλλη δὲ σὰρξ πτηνῶν, ἄλλη δὲ ἰχθύων.

^{15:40}καὶ σώματα ἐπουράνια, καὶ σώματα ἐπίγεια: ἀλλὰ ἑτέρα μὲν ἡ τῶν ἐπουρανίων δόξα, ἑτέρα δὲ ἡ τῶν ἐπιγείων.

^{15:41}ἄλλη δόξα ἡλίου, καὶ ἄλλη δόξα σελήνης, καὶ ἄλλη δόξα ἀστέρων: ἀστὴρ γὰρ ἀστέρος διαφέρει ἐν δόξῃ.

^{15:42}Οὕτως καὶ ἡ ἀνάστασις τῶν νεκρῶν. σπείρεται ἐν φθορᾷ, ἐγείρεται ἐν ἀφθαρσίᾳ:

^{15:43}σπείρεται ἐν ἀτιμίᾳ, ἐγείρεται ἐν δόξῃ: σπείρεται ἐν ἀσθενείᾳ, ἐγείρεται ἐν δυνάμει:

^{15:39}All flesh is not the same flesh: but one is the flesh of men, another of beasts, other of birds, another of fishes. [n. 975]

^{15:40}And there are bodies celestial and bodies terrestrial: but, one is the glory of the celestial, and another of the terrestrial. [n. 977]

^{15:41}One is the glory of the sun, another the glory of the moon, and another the glory of the stars. For star differs from star in glory. [n. 978]

^{15:42}So also is the resurrection of the dead. It is sown in corruption: it shall rise in incorruption. [n. 979]

^{15:43}It is sown in dishonor: it shall rise in glory. It is sown in weakness: it shall rise in power. [n. 981]

---

975. Hic Apostolus ponit exemplum de diversitate qualitatis corporis resurgentis in diversis speciebus. Et

primo comparando caelestia ad terrestria;

secundo terrestria ad caelestia, ibi **sunt corpora caelestia**, etc.;

tertio corpora caelestia ad invicem, ibi **alia claritas**, et cetera.

976. Quia posset aliquis dicere: quomodo est possibile quod mortui resumant corpus et carnem, si non sint habituri eamdem corporis qualitatem? Ideo ad hoc excludendum introducit diversas qualitates corporis et carnis, ut sic manifestum sit quod non oportet, si non erit eadem qualitas, quod non resumatur idem corpus, vel eadem caro. Dicit ergo primo quod **non omnis caro est eadem caro**, secundum formam, **sed alia** est caro **hominum, alia piscium, alia pecorum, alia volucrum**, et cetera. Et similiter est alia morientis, et alia resurgentis.

Sicut autem exemplum superius inductum de semine et pullulatione deficiebat in hoc quod in seminatione et pullulatione non est idem numero, nec eaedem qualitates, ita haec exempla deficiunt, quia in his exemplis nec est eadem species, nec eadem qualitas. Sed caro hominis resurgentis est eadem secundum speciem cum carne morientis, sed tamen erit alia secundum qualitatem. *Erit enim eiusdem naturae, sed alterius gloriae*, ut Gregorius de corpore Christi dicit.

Si quis autem haec quae dicta sunt, ad diversum statum resurgentium referre vellet, posset dici quod per homines intelliguntur boni secundum rationem viventes, secundum illud Ez. XXXIV, 31: *vos autem greges mei, greges pascuae meae, homines estis*. Per pecora vero

975. Here the Apostle presents an example of the diverse qualities of a rising body in diverse species.

First, by comparing heavenly to earthly bodies;

second, earthly to heavenly, at **and there are bodies celestial**;

third, celestial bodies to each other, at **one is the glory of the sun**.

976. Because someone could say: how is it possible that the dead re-assume their body and flesh, if they are not to have possession of the same bodily qualities? Therefore, to exclude this he introduces diverse qualities of body and flesh, so that it will be clear that it is not fitting, if the quality will not be the same, that the same body be re-assumed or the same flesh. He says, therefore: **all flesh is not the same flesh** according to form, **but one is the flesh of men, another of beasts, another of birds, another of fishes**. Similarly there is one for the dying and another for the rising.

But just as the example given above about the seed and the sprout failed, inasmuch in planting seed and in sprouting there is not the same thing numerically nor the same quality, so these examples fall short, because in these examples there is neither the same species nor the same qualities. But the flesh of a rising man is the same specifically as the dying flesh, but it will be different in its qualities. *For it will be of the same nature but of another glory*, as Gregory says of the body of Christ.

If anyone should wish to refer what has been said to a different state of those who rise, it could be said that by men are understood good men living according to reason: *and you are my sheep, the sheep of my pasture, and I am your God* (Ezek 34:31). By animals are understood the

intelliguntur luxuriosi, secundum illud II Petr. II, 12: *hi vero velut irrationabilia pecora*, et cetera. Per volucres, superbi, per pisces, cupidi, secundum illud Ps. VIII, v. 9: *volucres caeli et pisces maris*, et cetera.

977. Ad idem autem introducit diversitatem caelestium et terrestrium corporum, cum subdit: sunt ***corpora caelestia***, ut sol et luna et huiusmodi, et sunt ***corpora terrestria***, ut ignis, aqua, etc.; ***sed alia quidem est gloria***, id est pulchritudo et decor, ***caelestium*** corporum, ***alia autem terrestrium***, Eccli. XLIII, v. 10: *species caeli gloria stellarum*.

Et possunt per caelestia corpora intelligi contemplativi. Phil. III, 20: *nostra conversatio in caelis est*. Per terrestria activi, qui circa terrena occupantur; unde Marthae dictum est, Lc. X, 41: *turbaris erga plurima*.

978. Et ad idem ulterius introducit diversam qualitatem caelestium corporum, cum dicit ***alia claritas solis***, et cetera. Similiter inter stellas est differentia, ***stella enim differt***, et cetera.

Et potest intelligi per solem Christus, Mal. ult.: *orietur vobis timentibus nomen meum sol iustitiae*, et cetera. Per lunam Beata Virgo, de qua Cant. VI, 9: *pulchra ut luna*. Per stellas ad invicem ordinatas, caeteri sancti. Iudic. V, 20: *stellae manentes in ordine suo*, et cetera.

979. Consequenter cum dicit ***sic erit resurrectio mortuorum***, adaptat praedicta exempla ad resurrectionem mortuorum.

Nec intelligendum est, quantum ad litteralem expositionem, quod Apostolus hoc dicat ad designandum in resurgentibus generis diversitatem, propter id quod praemiserat ***stella differt***, et cetera. Sed hoc refert ad omnia praecedentia, ut ostendatur ex omnibus praemissis, quod sicut in rebus inveniuntur diversae qualitates corporum, ita erit diversa qualitas resurgentium a qualitate morientium. Unde sequitur ***seminatur corpus***, et cetera. Ubi Apostolus maxime ostendit aliam esse qualitatem corporis morientis, et corporis resurgentis.

980. Et agit hic de corpore resurgente glorioso, cuius propriae qualitates dotes corporis gloriosi dicuntur. Quae quidem sunt quatuor, quas hic Apostolus tangit.

Primo enim tangit dotem impassibilitatis, cum dicit ***seminatur in corruptione***, et cetera. Et quamvis seminatio accipi posset pro prima corporis origine, secundum quod generatur ex semine, tamen convenientius est, secundum intellectum apostoli, ut seminatio referatur ad mortem et sepulturam, ut respondeat ei quod supra dictum est: ***quod seminas non vivificatur, nisi prius moriatur***.

Dicitur autem mors et resolutio, seminatio, non quod in corpore mortuo, vel in cineribus ex eo resolutis

lustful: *but these like irrational animals . . . will be destroyed* (2 Pet 2:12). By birds, the proud; by fish, the greedy: *the birds of the air and the fish of the sea* (Ps 8:8).

977. For the same reason he introduces the diversity of heavenly and earthly bodies, when he says: there are ***bodies celestial***, as the sun and moon and so on, and there are ***bodies terrestrial***, as fire, water and so on. ***But, one is the glory***, i.e., the beauty and splendor, ***of the celestial*** bodies is one and ***another of the terrestrial***: *the glory of the stars is the beauty of heaven* (Sir 44:9).

Again, by celestial bodies can be understood contemplatives: *our commonwealth is in heaven* (Phil 3:20); by the terrestrial the actives, who are occupied with earthly things. Hence it is said to Martha: *you are concerned about many things* (Luke 10:41).

978. For the same purpose he further introduces the diverse qualities of celestial bodies, when he says, ***one is the glory of the sun, another the glory of the moon***. Similarly, there is a difference among the stars, ***for star differs from star in glory***.

Furthermore, by the sun can be understood Christ: *but for you who fear my name the sun of righteousness shall rise* (Mal 4:2); by the moon, the Blessed Virgin: *fair as the moon* (Song 6:10); by the stars mutually situated, the other saints: *the stars from their courses* (Judg 5:20).

979. Then when he says, ***so also is the resurrection of the dead***, he adapts the above examples to the resurrection of the dead.

It should not be supposed as to the literal explanation that the Apostles is saying this to indicate a diversity of genus in those rising, just because he had stated, ***star differs from star***. But this refers to all the preceding, that it might be shown from all the foregoing that just as in things are found diverse qualities in bodies, so there will be a quality of the rising diverse from the quality of the dying. Hence, he continues, ***it is sown***. Here the Apostle especially shows that the quality of a dying body is one thing and that of the rising body another.

980. And he is dealing here with the glorified rising body, whose distinctive qualities are called the marks of the glorified body. These marks are four which the Apostle touches on here.

First, he touches on the mark of incapacity of suffering, when he says: ***it is sown in corruption***. And all the sowing can be taken for the first origin of the body, inasmuch as it is generated from seed. Yet it is more fitting according to the mind of the Apostle that sowing be referred to death and burial to correspond to what was said above: ***that which you sow is not quickened except it die first*** (2 Cor 15:36).

Death, however, is called both a dissolution and a sowing, not that in a dead body or in the dust dissolved from it

sit aliqua virtus ad resurrectionem, sicut est virtus activa in semine ad generationem; sed quia a Deo talis ordinatio est deputata, ut ex eo iterato reformetur corpus humanum. Sic igitur corpus humanum, quando seminatur, id est, quando moritur, est in corruptione, id est secundum suam proprietatem est corruptioni subiectum, secundum illud Rom. VIII, 10: *corpus quidem mortuum est propter peccatum.*

Sed resurget in incorruptione. Dicitur autem hic incorruptio, non solum ad excludendum separationem animae a corpore, quia hanc incorruptionem et corpora damnatorum habebunt, sed ad excludendum tam mortem quam quamlibet noxiam passionem, sive ab interiori, sive ab exteriori. Et quantum ad hoc intelligitur impassibilitas corporis gloriosi, secundum illud Apoc. VII, 16: *non esurient, neque sitient amplius,* et cetera.

981. Secundo tangit dotem claritatis, cum dicit **seminatur in ignobilitate**, id est corpus quod ante mortem, et in morte est deformitatibus et miseriis multis subiectum, secundum illud Iob XIV, 1: *homo natus de muliere,* et cetera. **Sed resurget in gloria**, quae claritatem significat, ut Augustinus dicit *Super Ioannem*. Erunt enim corpora sanctorum clara et fulgentia, secundum illud Matth. XIII, v. 43: *fulgebunt iusti, sicut sol,* et cetera.

982. Tertio tangit dotem agilitatis, cum dicit **seminatur in infirmitate**, id est, corpus animale, quod ante mortem est infirmum et tardum, et ab anima non facile mobile, secundum illud Sap. IX, 15: *corpus quod corrumpitur aggravat animam*. Sed **surget in virtute**, quia scilicet fiet ut ex tanta virtute ab anima moveri possit, ut in nullo difficultatem ad motum exhibeat, quod ad dotem agilitatis pertinet. Tanta enim erit ibi facilitas, quanta felicitas, ut Augustinus dicit. Unde dicitur Sap. III, 7 de iustis: *fulgebunt iusti, et tamquam scintillae in arundineto discurrent*. Et Is. XL, 31: *qui sperant in Domino habebunt fortitudinem, assument pennas,* et cetera.

983. Quarto tangit dotem subtilitatis, cum dicit **seminatur corpus animale**, et cetera. Quam quidam ad hoc referre volunt quod corpori glorioso secundum hanc dotem competat ut possit simul esse cum corpore non glorioso in eodem loco.

Quod quidem sustineri posset, si corpori secundum statum praesentem competeret, quod non posset simul cum alio corpore esse in eodem loco secundum aliquid quod a corpore removeri posset.

Nunc autem si diligenter consideretur, quod secundum hoc nihil aliud corpori competit nisi secundum quod habet dimensiones corporales. Unde videmus corpora quantumcumque subtilia, non compati secum alia corpora, ut patet in aere et in igne; et, ulterius, si essent corpora separata omnino absque materia, sicut quidam posuerunt, non possent simul cum corporibus naturalibus esse in eisdem locis, ut Philosophus dicit.

there is some power for rising, as there is an active power in seed for generation; but because from God such an ordination was directed that from it a human body be formed again. Thus, therefore, the human body, when it is sown, i.e., when it dies, is in corruption, i.e., according to its own properties it is subjected to corruption, as it says in Romans: *your bodies are dead because of sin* (Rom 8:10).

It shall rise in incorruption. Here he says incorruption not only to exclude separation of the soul and the body, because even the bodies of the damned will have this imperishability, but to exclude both death or any harmful suffering either from within or from without. And in regard to this is the imperishability of the glorified understood: *they shall hunger no more, neither thirst any more* (Rev 7:16).

981. Second, he touches on the mark of clarity, when he says: **it is sown in dishonor**, i.e., the body, which before death was subject to many deformities and miseries: *man that is born of a woman is of few days, and full of trouble* (Job 14:1). **It shall rise in glory**, which signifies clarity, as Augustine says (*On John*). For the bodies of the saints will be clear and shining: *the righteous will shine as the sun in the kingdom of their Father* (Matt 14:43).

982. Third, he touches on the mark of agility, when he says, **it is sown in weakness**, i.e., the animal body, which before death is weak and slow and not easily moved by the soul: *a perishable body weighs down the soul* (Wis 9:15). **It shall rise in power**, namely, because it will come to pass that from such strength it can be moved by the soul and in no case will it show difficulty being moved, which pertains to the mark of agility. For there will be as much facility as felicity, as Augustine says. Hence it is said: *the just will shine forth and will run like sparks through the stubble* (Wis 3:7); *they who wait for the Lord shall renew their strength, they shall mount up with wings like eagles, they shall run and not be weary, they shall walk and not faint* (Isa 40:31).

983. Fourth, he touches on the mark of subtility, when he says, **it is sown a natural body: it shall rise a spiritual body** (1 Cor 15:44). In virtue of this mark some desire that it belongs to a glorified body to be able to exist in the same place with a body not glorified.

This can indeed be sustained, if it belonged to a body in the present state that it could be in the same place at the same time with another body in virtue of something which could be removed from the body.

But now, if it is examined closely, it will be seen that according to this nothing else belongs to the body, except inasmuch as it has bodily dimensions. Hence, we see that bodies, no matter how subtle, do not allow other bodies to be with them, as is evident in air and fire; and furthermore, if there were separated bodies absolutely without matter, as some supposed, they could not exist with natural bodies at the same time in the same place, as the Philosopher

Remanentibus igitur dimensionibus in quocumque corpore, est contra suam naturam quod sit cum alio corpore in eodem loco. Unde si hoc aliquando contingit, erit ex miraculo. Propter quod Gregorius et Augustinus miraculo adscribunt quod corpus Christi ad discipulos ianuis clausis intravit. Nulla enim virtus terminata potest facere miraculum, hoc enim solius Dei est. Relinquitur ergo quod esse simul cum alio corpore in eodem loco, non possit esse ex dote seu ex qualitate corporis gloriosi.

Non tamen negandum est quin corpus gloriosum possit esse simul cum alio corpore in eodem loco, quia corpus Christi post resurrectionem intravit ad discipulos ianuis clausis, cui corpus nostrum in resurrectione conformandum speramus; sed sicut corpus Christi hoc habuit non ex proprietate corporis, sed ex virtute divinitatis unitae, ita corpus cuiuslibet alterius sancti hoc habebit non ex dote, sed ex virtute divinitatis existentis in eo. Per quem modum corpus Petri habuit quod ad umbram eius sanarentur infirmi, non per aliquam proprietatem ipsius.

984. Est ergo dicendum quod ad dotem subtilitatis pertinet quod hic Apostolus tangit dicens **seminatur corpus animale, surget spirituale**. Quod quidam male intelligentes, dixerunt quod corpus in resurrectione vertetur in spiritum, et erit simile aeri aut vento, qui spiritus dicitur. Quod maxime excluditur per illud quod ad apostolos dicitur Lc. ult.: *palpate et videte, quia spiritus*, et cetera. Unde et hic Apostolus non dicit quod resurgat spiritus, sed spirituale corpus. Ergo in resurrectione spirituale erit, non spiritus, sicut nunc est animale, non anima.

985. Ad horum autem differentiam cognoscendam considerandum est, quod unum et idem in nobis est quod dicitur et anima et spiritus; sed anima dicitur secundum quod perficit corpus, spiritus autem proprie secundum mentem, secundum quam spiritualibus substantiis assimilamur, secundum illud Eph. c. IV, 23: *renovamini spiritu mentis vestrae.*

986. Item considerandum est, quod triplex est differentia potentiarum in anima; quaedam enim potentiae sunt quarum operationes ad bonum corporis ordinantur, sicut generativa, nutritiva, et augmentativa. Quaedam vero sunt, quae quidem corporeis organis utuntur, ut omnes potentiae sensitivae partis; sed earum actus ad corpus non ordinantur directe, sed magis ad perfectionem animae. Quaedam vero sunt potentiae quae neque utuntur corporeis organis, neque directe ad bonum corporis ordinantur, sed magis ad bonum animae, sicut quae pertinent ad intellectivam partem.

Primae ergo potentiae pertinent ad animam, inquantum animat corpus; secundae vero maxime pertinent ad animam, inquantum est spiritus; tertiae vero medio modo se habent inter utrasque: quia tamen iudicium

says. Therefore, as long as dimensions remain in a body, it is against its nature to be with another body in the same place. Hence, if this happens sometimes, it will be from a miracle. For this reason Gregory and Augustine ascribe to a miracle Christ's entering the room of the disciples, while the door was closed. For no limited power can perform a miracle, because this belongs to God alone. It follows, then, that to be in the same place at the same time with another body cannot be due to a quality of a glorified body.

However, it must not be denied that a glorified body can be with another body at the same time in the same place, because the body of Christ after the resurrection entered where the disciples were, while the door was shut, to whom we hope our bodies will be conformed in the resurrection. But just as the body of Christ had this not from a property of his body, but in virtue of the divinity united, so the body of whatever one of the saints has this, not as given, but in virtue of the divinity existing in it. In this manner the body of Peter had the power that the sick be healed by his shadow, not through any property of his own.

984. Therefore it must be said that what the Apostle touches on here pertains to the mark of subtility, when he says, **it is sown a natural body: it shall rise a spiritual body** (1 Cor 15:44). Some have interpreted this badly and said that in the resurrection the body is changed into a spirit and will be similar to air or the wind, which is called a spirit. This is particularly excluded by what was said to the apostles: *handle me, and see; for a spirit has not flesh and bones as you see that I have* (Luke 24:39). Hence, also, the Apostle does not say that a spirit will rise, but a spiritual body. Therefore, in the resurrection it will be spiritual, not a spirit, just as now it is animal, not soul.

985. To understand the difference between these it should be noted that what is called the soul and what is called the spirit is one and the same in us; but it is called soul, inasmuch as it perfects the body, but spirit in virtue of the mind according to which we are like spiritual substances: *be renewed in the spirit of your minds* (Eph 4:23).

986. One should also consider that there is a threefold difference in the powers of the soul. For some powers are such that their activities are directed to the good of the body, i.e., the generative, nutritive and augmentative; some there are that use bodily organs, as the power of the sensitive part, but their activity is not directly ordained to the body, but rather to the perfection of the soul. But there are some powers which neither use bodily organs nor are directly ordained to the good of the body, but more to the good of the soul, as those which pertain to the intellective part.

Therefore, the first powers pertain to the soul inasmuch as it animates the body; the second pertain especially to the soul inasmuch as it is a spirit; but the third are midway between them. Yet because a judgment about a power should

de potentia aliqua magis debet sumi ex obiecto et fine, quam ex instrumento, ideo secundae potentiae magis se tenent cum tertiis, quam cum primis.

987. Item considerandum est quod cum unaquaeque res sit propter suam operationem, corpus ad hoc perficitur ab anima, ut sit subiectum operationibus animae. Nunc autem in statu isto corpus nostrum est subiectum operationibus, quae pertinent ad animam, inquantum est anima, prout generatur et generat, nutritur, crescit et decrescit.

Quantum autem ad spirituales animae operationes, corpus, licet aliquo modo subserviat, tamen multum impedimentum affert, quia *corpus quod corrumpitur aggravat animam*, ut dicitur Sap. IX, 5. Sed in statu resurrectionis cessabunt operationes animales a corpore, quia non erit generatio, nec augmentum aut nutrimentum, sed corpus absque aliquo impedimento et fatigatione incessanter serviet animae ad spirituales operationes eius, secundum illud Ps. LXXXIII, 5: *beati qui habitant in domo tua, Domine*, et cetera. Sicut ergo nunc est corpus nostrum animale, tunc vero erit spirituale.

988. Causam autem harum proprietatum quidam attribuunt luci, quam dicunt esse de natura quintae essentiae, et venire in compositionem humani corporis, quod quia frivolum est et fabulosum, sequentes Augustinum, dicimus quod procedunt ex virtute animae glorificatae. Dicit enim Augustinus in *Epistola ad Dioscorum*: *tam potenti natura Deus fecit animam, ut eius plenissima beatitudo, quae in fine temporum promittitur sanctis, redundet etiam in inferiorem naturam, quae est corpus; non beatitudo, quae fruentis est propria, sed plenitudo sanitatis, id est, incorruptionis vigor.*

Videmus autem ex anima quatuor corpori provenire, et tanto perfectius, quanto anima fuerit virtuosior. Primo quidem dat esse; unde quando erit in summo perfectionis, dabit esse spirituale. Secundo conservat a corruptione; unde videmus homines quanto sunt fortioris naturae, minus a calore et frigore pati. Cum ergo anima fuerit perfectissima, conservabit corpus omnino impassibile. Tertio dat pulchritudinem et claritatem; infirmi enim et mortui propter debilitatem operationis animae in corpus, efficiuntur discolorati, et quando erit in summa perfectione, faciet corpus clarum et fulgidum. Quarto dat motum, et tanto facilius, quanto virtus animae fuerit fortior supra corpus. Et ideo quando erit in ultimo suae perfectionis, dabit corpori agilitatem.

be taken more from its object and end than from the instrument, then the second powers are closer to the third than to the first.

987. Likewise one should consider that since every single thing is for the sake of its own activity, the body is perfected to this by the soul, just as it is the subject of the activities of the soul. Now, however, in this state our body is the subject of activities which belong to the soul, as far as it is the soul, according as it is generated and generates, is nourished, grows and decreases.

However, as to the spiritual activities of the soul, the body, although subject in another way, nevertheless causes much impediment, because *a perishable body weighs down the soul* (Wis 9:5). But in the resurrected state the animal activities by the body will cease, because there will be no generation, or growth or nourishment, but the body without any impediment and weariness will unceasingly serve the soul in its spiritual activities: *blessed are those who dwell in your house, Lord* (Ps 84:4). Therefore, just as our body is now animal, then it will be truly spiritual.

988. Some however will attribute the cause of these properties to a star, which they say is from the nature of the five essences, and comes in the composition of the human body. Because this is frivolous and incredible, we say, following Augustine, that they will proceed as a consequence of the virtue of the glorified soul. For Augustine says in his *Letter to Dioscorus*: *God made the soul with such a natural power, that its fullest blessedness, which at the end of time is promised to the saints, overflows even into lower nature, which is the body, not the blessedness which is proper to the one enjoying it, but the fullness of health, that is, the strength of incorruption.*

We see, however, that four things come forth from the soul to the body, and to the degree it is perfected, so the soul will have been more virtuous. First indeed it gives existence; therefore, when it will come to its highest perfection, it will cause it to be spiritual. Second, it conserves it from corruption; therefore we see men who are so much stronger by nature, suffer less from heat and from cold. Therefore, when the soul will become most perfect, it will conserve the body wholly impassible. Third, it gives beauty and clarity. For to weakness and death on account of the debilitation of the working of the soul in the body, they become opaque, and when it comes to its highest perfection, it will make the body clear and shining. Fourth, it gives movement, and according to its degree of facility, so the capacity of the soul will have been stronger than the body. And therefore, when it will come to its highest perfection, it will give mobility to the body.

Lecture 7

15:44seminatur corpus animale, surget corpus spiritale. Si est corpus animale, est et spiritale, [n. 989]

15:45sicut scriptum est: *factus est primus* homo Adam *in animam viventem*, novissimus Adam in spiritum vivificantem.

15:46Sed non prius quod spiritale est, sed quod animale: deinde quod spiritale. [n. 994]

15:47Primus homo de terra, terrenus: secundus homo de caelo, caelestis. [n. 995]

15:48Qualis terrenus, tales et terreni: et qualis caelestis, tales et caelestes.

15:49Igitur, sicut portavimus imaginem terreni, portemus et imaginem caelestis. [n. 998]

15:50Hoc autem dico, fratres: quia caro et sanguis regnum Dei possidere non possunt: neque corruptio incorruptelam possidebit. [n. 999]

15:44σπείρεται σῶμα ψυχικόν, ἐγείρεται σῶμα πνευματικόν. εἰ ἔστιν σῶμα ψυχικόν, ἔστιν καὶ πνευματικόν.

15:45οὕτως καὶ γέγραπται, Ἐγένετο ὁ πρῶτος ἄνθρωπος Ἀδὰμ εἰς ψυχὴν ζῶσαν· ὁ ἔσχατος Ἀδὰμ εἰς πνεῦμα ζῳοποιοῦν.

15:46ἀλλ' οὐ πρῶτον τὸ πνευματικὸν ἀλλὰ τὸ ψυχικόν, ἔπειτα τὸ πνευματικόν.

15:47ὁ πρῶτος ἄνθρωπος ἐκ γῆς χοϊκός, ὁ δεύτερος ἄνθρωπος ἐξ οὐρανοῦ.

15:48οἷος ὁ χοϊκός, τοιοῦτοι καὶ οἱ χοϊκοί, καὶ οἷος ὁ ἐπουράνιος, τοιοῦτοι καὶ οἱ ἐπουράνιοι·

15:49καὶ καθὼς ἐφορέσαμεν τὴν εἰκόνα τοῦ χοϊκοῦ, φορέσομεν καὶ τὴν εἰκόνα τοῦ ἐπουρανίου.

15:50Τοῦτο δέ φημι, ἀδελφοί, ὅτι σὰρξ καὶ αἷμα βασιλείαν θεοῦ κληρονομῆσαι οὐ δύναται, οὐδὲ ἡ φθορὰ τὴν ἀφθαρσίαν κληρονομεῖ.

15:44It is sown a natural body: it shall rise a spiritual body. If there be a natural body, there is also a spiritual body, [n. 989]

15:45As it is written: *the first man* Adam *was made into a living soul*; the last Adam into a life-giving spirit.

15:46Yet that was not first which is spiritual, but that which is natural: afterwards that which is spiritual. [n. 994]

15:47The first man was of the earth, earthly: the second man, from heaven, heavenly. [n. 995]

15:48Such as is the earthly, such also are the earthly: and such as is the heavenly, such also are the heavenly.

15:49Therefore, as we have borne the image of the earthly, let us bear also the image of the heavenly. [n. 998]

15:50Now this I say, brethren, that flesh and blood cannot possess the kingdom of God: neither shall corruption possess incorruption. [n. 999]

---

989. Hic Apostolus differentiam qualitatis corporum morientium ad corpora resurgentium supra exemplis ostensam, ostendit ratione.

Circa autem hoc duo facit.

Primo enim praemittit quod probare intendit;

secundo praemissum probat, ibi *sicut scriptum est*, et cetera.

990. Dicit ergo primo: dixi quod id quod seminatur animale, surget spiritale, et, quod hoc sit verum, scilicet quod sit aliquod corpus spiritale, ostendo, quia si est corpus animale, est et spiritale. Et non intendit Apostolus ex hoc arguere ad propositum sed hoc supponit, intendens probare ipsum quod dicit *si est corpus*, et cetera. Eccli. XXXIII, 15: *intuere in omnia opera Altissimi, duo contra duo, et unum contra unum.*

991. *Sicut scriptum est*, et cetera. Hic probat propositum. Est autem sua probatio talis: duo sunt principia humani generis; unum secundum vitam naturae, scilicet Adam, aliud secundum vitam gratiae, scilicet Christus; sed animalitas est derivativa in omnes homines a primo principio, scilicet Adam; ergo constat quod multo amplius a secundo principio, scilicet Christo, spiritualitas derivabitur in omnes homines.

989. Here the Apostle shows by reason the difference of the quality of the dead body to the body of the resurrection, indicated by the examples above.

Regarding this he does two things.

First, he presents what he intends to prove;

second, he proves what he presented, at *as it is written*.

990. Therefore he says first: I say that what is sown animal rises spiritual, and I show that this is true, namely, that something is a spiritual body, because if it is an animal body, it is also spiritual. And the Apostle does not intend to argue from this to the proposition, but he accepts this, intending to prove just what he says, *if there be a natural body*: look upon all the works of the Most High; they likewise are in pairs, one the opposite of the other (Sir 33:15).

991. *As it is written*. Here he proves the proposition. His demonstration is as follows: there are two principles of human generation; one according to natural life, namely Adam; the other according to the life of grace, namely Christ. But animality is distributed in all men by the first principle, namely, Adam. Therefore, it is certain that to a much greater extent, by means of the second principle, that is to say, Christ, spiritual life is distributed in all men.

Huius rationis, primo, probat primam diversitatem principiorum, secundo mediam, scilicet determinationem similitudinis ex utroque principiorum, ibi *qualis terrenus*, et cetera.

Circa primum tria facit.

Primo ostendit principiorum differentiam;

secundo principiorum ordinem ad invicem, ibi *sed non prius quod spirituale*, etc.;

tertio rationis ordinem assignat, ibi *primus*, et cetera.

992. Ponit ergo, primo, conditionem primi principii secundum vitam naturae, sumens auctoritatem Gen. II, 7. Unde dicit *sicut scriptum est: factus est*, a Deo, *primus homo Adam in animam viventem*, vita scilicet animali, qualem anima potest dare, cum scilicet *spiravit Dominus in faciem eius spiraculum vitae*, Gen. II, 7. Forma enim humana et anima dicitur et spiritus. Inquantum enim intendit curae corporis, scilicet vegetando, nutriendo et generando, sic dicitur anima; inquantum autem intendit cognitioni, scilicet intelligendo, volendo et huiusmodi, sic dicitur spiritus. Unde cum dicit *factus est primus homo Adam in animam viventem*, intendit hic Apostolus de vita qua anima deservit circa corpus, non de Spiritu Sancto, sicut quidam fingunt, propter hoc quod praecedit *et inspiravit in faciem eius spiraculum vitae*, dicentes hoc esse Spiritum Sanctum.

Secundo ponit conditionem secundi principii, dicens *novissimus* vero *Adam*, id est Christus. Et dicitur novissimus, quia Adam induxit unum statum, scilicet culpae, Christus vero gloriae et vitae. Unde cum post statum istum nullus alius sequatur in vita ista, ideo dicitur novissimus. Is. LIII, 2 s.: *desideravimus eum despectum et novissimum virorum*. Et alibi scilicet Apoc. I, 17: *ego Primus et Novissimus*. Et alibi: *ego sum Alpha et Omega*, et cetera.

Dicit autem *Adam*, quia de natura Adae factus in spiritum viventem.

993. Et ex hoc, conditionibus principiorum visis, apparet eorum diversitas, quia primus homo factus est in animam, novissimus in spiritum. Ille autem in animam viventem solum, iste vero in spiritum viventem et vivificantem.

Cuius ratio est: quia, sicut Adam consecutus est perfectionem sui esse per animam, ita et Christus perfectionem sui esse, inquantum homo, per Spiritum Sanctum. Et ideo cum anima non possit nisi proprium corpus vivificare, ideo Adam factus est in animam, non vivificantem, sed viventem tantum; sed Christus factus est in spiritum viventem et vivificantem, et ideo Christus habuit potestatem vivificandi. Io. I, 16: *de plenitudine eius*, etc., et Io. X, 10: *veni ut vitam habeant et abundantius habeant*. Et in symbolo: *et in Spiritum Sanctum vivificantem*.

The reason for this, first, he proves, the first difference of the principles; second the middle term, namely, the determination of likeness from both of the principles, at *such as is the earthly*.

In regard to the first, he does three things.

First, he shows the difference of the principles;

second, the mutual order of the principles, at *yet that was not first which is spiritual*;

third, he assigns the order of reason, at *the first man was of the earth*.

992. Therefore he lays down first the condition of the first principle according to natural life, drawing on the authority of Genesis (Gen 2:7). Hence he says, *as it is written: 'the first man Adam was made into a living soul'*, namely, an animal life which the soul is able to give, when, namely, *God breathed into his nostrils the breath of life* (Gen 2:7). For the human form and soul is also called spirit. For insofar as he is concerned with the care of the body, namely, with animating, nourishing and generating, thus it is called 'soul.' However, insofar as he is concerned with knowledge, namely, with understanding, willing and the like, thus it is called 'spirit.' Therefore when he says, *the first man Adam was made into a living soul*, the Apostle has in mind here the life by which the soul is devoted concerning the body, not the Holy Spirit, as some imagine, by reason of what was cited above: *and he breathed into his nostrils the breath of life*, saying that this is the Holy Spirit.

Second, he lays down the condition of the second principle, saying, *the last* true *Adam*, i.e., Christ. And he is called the last because Adam introduced one state, namely of guilt; Christ of true glory and life. Hence, since after that state no other one followed in that life, therefore he is called the last: *we desired him, despised and last of men* (Isa 53:2); *I am the First and the Last* (Rev 1:17); and elsewhere: *I am the Alpha and the Omega* (Rev 21:6).

But he says, *Adam*, because from the nature of Adam he was made a living spirit.

993. And from this, with the conditions of the principles perceived, the difference between them is evident, because the first man was made 'animal,' the last man 'spiritual.' The former was made a living animal only, the latter truly a living and life-giving spirit.

The reason for this is because, just as Adam obtained the perfection of his being through the soul, so too Christ obtained the perfection of his being, as far as he was man, through the Holy Spirit. And therefore, since the soul could not give life to the body except properly, so Adam was made 'animal,' not life-giving, but just living. But Christ was made a living and life-giving spirit, and so Christ had life-giving power: *from his fullness* (John 1:16): *I have come that they may have life, and have it abundantly* (John 10:10); and in the Creed: *and in the life-giving Holy Spirit*.

994. Sed ne aliquis diceret: si Christus factus est in spiritum vivificantem, quare dicitur *novissimus?* Ideo, consequenter, cum dicit *sed non prius*, etc., ostendit ordinem principiorum.

Videmus enim in natura quod in uno et eodem, prius est imperfectum quam perfectum. Unde cum spiritualitas se habeat ad animalitatem, sicut perfectum ad imperfectum, ideo in humana natura non prius debet esse spirituale, quod est perfectum, sed, ut servetur ordo, prius debet esse imperfectum, scilicet quod animale est, deinde perfectum, scilicet quod spirituale est. Supra c. XIII, 10: *cum venerit quod perfectum est*, et cetera.

Sicut dicit Augustinus, huius signum est, quod primogeniti antiquitus consueverunt esse animales, sicut Cain ante Abel natus, Ismael ante Isaac, et Esau ante Iacob.

995. Rationem autem dictae diversitatis assignat dicens *primus homo*, etc., quasi dicat: vere primus homo factus est in animam viventem, quia *de terra*, Gen. II, 7: *formavit Dominus hominem de limo terrae*, et ideo dicitur esse *terrenus*, id est animalis; *secundus homo*, scilicet Christus, factus est *in spiritum vivificantem*, quia *de caelo*; quia divina natura quae fuit huic naturae unita, de caelo est. Et ideo debet esse *caelestis*, id est, talem perfectionem debet habere, qualem decet de caelo venire, scilicet perfectionem spiritualem. Io. III, 31: *qui de caelo venit, super omnes est.*

Dicit autem primum hominem de terra, secundum modum loquendi, quo res de illo esse dicuntur quia prima pars est in eorum fieri, sicut cultellus dicitur de ferro quia prima pars, unde est cultellus, est ferrum. Et quia prima pars unde Adam factus est, terra est, ideo, dicitur de terra. Secundus homo dicitur de caelo, non quod attulerit corpus de caelo, cum de terra assumpserit, scilicet de corpore Beatae Virginis, sed quia divinitas (quae naturae humanae unita est) de caelo venit, quae fuit prior quam corpus Christi.

Sic ergo patet principiorum diversitas, quod erat maior propositio rationis principalis.

996. Consequenter cum dicit *qualis terrenus*, etc., ostendit derivationem similitudinis horum principiorum ex utroque, et

primo in communi,

secundo dividit eam per partes, ibi *igitur sicut portavimus*, et cetera.

997. Dicit ergo *qualis terrenus*, etc., quasi dicat: primus homo, quia terrenus fuit et mortalis, ideo derivatum est ut omnes essent et terreni et mortales. Supra eodem v. 22: *et sicut in Adam omnes moriuntur*. Zach. XIII, 5: *Adam exemplum meum*, et cetera.

994. But someone might say, If Christ was made a life-giving spirit, why is he called *last*? Therefore, accordingly, when he says, *yet that was not first which is spiritual*, he shows the order of principles.

We see in nature that in one and the same thing, the imperfect is prior to the perfect. And so since the spiritual state is situated with respect to the animal state, as the perfect to the imperfect, then in human nature the spiritual must not be prior, which is the perfect, but so that order might be preserved, the imperfect must be first, namely, what is animal, then the perfect, namely, what is spiritual: *but when that which is perfect is come, that which is in part shall be done away* (1 Cor 13:10).

As Augustine says, the sign of this is that the firstborn of antiquity are commonly 'animal,' as Cain was born before Abel, Ishmael before Isaac, and Esau before Jacob.

995. He assigns the reason for what is said about diversity, saying, *the first man*. As if to say: truly the first man was made a living animal, because he is *of the earth*: *God formed man of dust from the ground* (Gen 2:7), and therefore he is said to be *of the earth*, i.e., animal. *The second man*, namely Christ, was made *a life-giving spirit*, because he is *from heaven*. Because it is the divine nature that was united to this nature, he is from heaven. And therefore he must be *heavenly*, i.e., he ought to have such perfection that it is fitting it come from heaven, namely, spiritual perfection: *he who comes from heaven is above all* (John 3:31).

He says that the first man is from the earth, in the manner described, by which things from that one are said to be because the first part is in their coming to be, as a knife is said to be from iron because the first part whence the knife is is iron. And because the first part of whence Adam was made is earth, he is said to be from the earth. Accordingly he is called the man from heaven, not that he will have borne his body from heaven, since he will have assumed it from the earth, namely, from the body of the Blessed Virgin, but because the divinity (which was united to the human nature) comes from heaven, which was prior to the body of Christ.

So then the diversity of principles is clear, which was the major proposition of the principal reason.

996. Then when he says, *such as is the earthly*, he shows the derivation of the likeness of these principles from each one:

first, in common;

second, he divides it into parts, at *therefore, as we have borne*.

997. He says, therefore, *such as is the earthly*. As if to say: because the first man was of the earth and mortal, so it follows that all were both of the earth and mortal: *for as in Adam all die* (1 Cor 15:22); *Adam was my exemplar* (Zech 13:5).

Quia vero fuit secundus homo caelestis, id est spiritualis et immortalis, ideo omnes et immortales et spirituales erimus. Rom. c. VI, 5: *sed complantati facti sumus similitudini*, et cetera.

998. *Igitur sicut portavimus*, et cetera. Hic concludit qualiter in speciali debeamus conformari homini, scilicet caelesti.

Possumus autem dupliciter conformari caelesti in vita scilicet gratiae et gloriae, et una est via ad aliam: quia sine vita gratiae non pervenitur ad vitam gloriae. Et ideo dicit *sicut portavimus*, etc., id est quamdiu peccatores fuimus, in nobis fuit similitudo Adae. II Reg. VII, 19: *ista est lex Adam, Domine Deus*, et cetera. Ut ergo possimus esse caelestes, id est pervenire ad vitam gloriae, *portemus imaginem caelestis*, per vitam gratiae. Col. c. III, 9 s.: *exuentes veterem hominem, induite novum hominem*, scilicet Christum. Rom. VIII, 29: *quos praescivit et praedestinavit conformes*, et cetera. Sic ergo debemus conformari caelesti in vita gratiae, quia alias non perveniemus ad vitam gloriae.

999. Et hoc est quod dicit *hoc autem dico, fratres*, quasi dicat: nisi vivatis, scilicet vita gratiae, non poteritis pervenire ad regnum Dei, scilicet ad vitam gloriae, *quia caro et sanguis regnum Dei non possidebunt*.

Quod quidem non est intelligendum, sicut quidam haeretici dicunt, quod non resurget caro et sanguis secundum substantiam, sed quod totum corpus vel vertetur in spiritum, vel in aerem: quod est haereticum et falsum; nam Apostolus dicit quod conformabit corpus nostrum corpori claritatis suae. Unde cum Christus post resurrectionem habuerit carnem et sanguinem, sicut dicitur Lc. ult.: *palpate et videte, quia spiritus carnem et ossa non habet*, etc., constat quod et nos in resurrectione carnem et sanguinem habebimus.

1000. Non est intelligendum *caro et sanguis*, id est substantia carnis et sanguinis, *regnum Dei non possidebunt*, sed *caro et sanguis*, id est, carni et sanguini operam dantes, scilicet homines dediti vitiis et voluptatibus, regnum Dei non possidebunt. Et sic accipitur *caro*, id est, homo carnaliter vivens, Rom. VIII, 9: *vos autem non in carne*, et cetera.

Vel: *caro et sanguis*, id est, opera carnis et sanguinis regnum Dei non possidebunt, quod est contra Iudaeos et Saracenos, qui fingunt se habituros post resurrectionem uxores, fluvios mellis et lactis.

Vel: *caro et sanguis*, id est corruptio carnis et sanguinis, *regnum Dei non possidebunt*, id est post resurrectionem, corpus non subiicietur corruptioni carnis et sanguinis, secundum quam vivit homo.

Unde, et secundum hoc, subdit *neque corruptio incorruptionem possidebit*, id est neque corruptio

Because the second man was from heaven, i.e., spiritual and immortal, so we all will be both immortal and spiritual: *for if we have been united with him in a death like his, we shall certainly be united with him in a resurrection like his* (Rom 6:5).

998. *Therefore, as we have born the image of the earthly*. Here he concludes with how we ought to be specially conformed to the man, that is to say, the heavenly man.

We can be conformed to the heavenly man in life in two ways, namely, of grace and of glory, and the one is the way to the other, because without the life of grace we cannot attain to the life of glory. And so he says, *as we have borne*, i.e., inasmuch as we are sinners, the likeness of Adam is in us: *that is the law of Adam, O Lord God* (2 Sam 7:19). Therefore, so that we might be of heaven, i.e., attain to the life of glory, *let us bear also the image of the heavenly*, by the life of grace: *those whom he foreknew he also predestined to be conformed to the image of his Son* (Rom 8:29). And so we ought to be conformed to the man of heaven in the life of grace, because otherwise we will not attain to the life of glory.

999. And this is what he says: *now this I say, brethren*; as if to say: unless you live, namely, the life of grace, you cannot attain to the kingdom of God, i.e., to the life of glory, *that flesh and blood cannot possess the kingdom of God*.

What we must not think, as some heretics say, is that flesh and blood will not rise according to substance, but rather that the whole body will be changed into spirit or into air. This is heretical and false. For the Apostle says that our body will be conformed to his body of radiance. Therefore, since Christ after his resurrection, has body and blood, as it says in Luke: *see my hands and my feet, that it is I myself; handle me, and see; for a spirit has not flesh and bones as you see that I have* (Luke 24:39), it is certain that we too will have flesh and blood in the resurrection.

1000. We must not think that by *flesh and blood*, he means that the substance of the flesh and blood *cannot possess the kingdom of God*, but rather *flesh and blood*, i.e., those devoting themselves to flesh and blood, namely, men given to vices and lusts, cannot inherit the kingdom of God. And thus is flesh understood, i.e., a man living by the flesh: *but you are not in the flesh, you are in the Spirit, if in fact the Spirit of God dwells in you* (Rom 8:9)

Or: *flesh and blood*, i.e., the works of flesh and blood cannot inherit the kingdom of God, which is against the Jews and Muslims who imagine that after the resurrection they will possess for themselves wives and rivers of honey and milk.

Or: *flesh and blood*, i.e., the corruption of flesh and blood *cannot possess the kingdom of God*; that is, after the resurrection, the body will not be subject to the corruption of flesh and blood, as it is of the man who lives.

Therefore and accordingly, he adds, *neither shall corruption possess incorruption*, i.e., nor can the corruption

mortalitatis, quae nomine *carnis* hic exprimitur, possidebit incorruptionem, id est, incorruptibile regnum Dei, quia resurgemus in gloria. Rom. VIII, 21: *ipsa creatura liberabitur a servitute corruptionis*, et cetera.

of mortality, which is expressed here by the term *flesh*, inherit incorruption, i.e., the incorruptible kingdom of God, because we will rise in glory: *because the creation itself will be set free from its bondage to decay and obtain the glorious liberty of the children of God* (Rom 8:21).

Lecture 8

^{15:51}Ecce mysterium vobis dico: omnes quidem resurgemus, sed non omnes immutabimur. [n. 1001]

^{15:52}In momento, in ictu oculi, in novissima tuba: canet enim tuba, et mortui resurgent incorrupti: et nos immutabimur. [n. 1005]

^{15:51}ἰδοὺ μυστήριον ὑμῖν λέγω: πάντες οὐ κοιμηθησόμεθα, πάντες δὲ ἀλλαγησόμεθα,

^{15:52}ἐν ἀτόμῳ, ἐν ῥιπῇ ὀφθαλμοῦ, ἐν τῇ ἐσχάτῃ σάλπιγγι: σαλπίσει γάρ, καὶ οἱ νεκροὶ ἐγερθήσονται ἄφθαρτοι, καὶ ἡμεῖς ἀλλαγησόμεθα.

^{15:51}Behold, I tell you a mystery. We shall all indeed rise again: but we shall not all be changed. [n. 1001]

^{15:52}In a moment, in the twinkling of an eye, at the last trumpet: for the trumpet shall sound and the dead shall rise again incorruptible. And we shall be changed. [n. 1005]

1001. Hic Apostolus postquam respondit quaestioni de qualitate resurgentium, respondet consequenter quaestioni qua quaerebatur de modo et ordine resurgendi.

Et circa hoc duo facit.

Primo ostendit modum et ordinem resurrectionis;

secundo confirmat per auctoritatem, ibi *cum autem mortale hoc*, et cetera.

Circa primum duo facit.

Primo enim proponit intentum;

secundo ostendit quo ordine fiat, ibi *in momento, in ictu oculi*, et cetera.

1002. Primo igitur reddit eos attentos, ostendens id quod proponit esse arduum et occultum, dicens *ecce mysterium*, id est occultum quoddam, *dico vobis*, id est aperio vobis, fratres, quod debet vobis aperiri et omnibus credentibus. Lc. VIII, 10: *vobis datum est nosse*, et cetera. Supra, II, 6: *sapientiam loquimur inter perfectos*, et, post: *sed loquimur Dei sapientiam quae abscondita est*, et cetera.

1003. Quid autem sit istud mysterium, subdit *omnes quidem*, et cetera.

Circa primum sciendum est, quod sicut Hieronymus dicit, in quadam epistola ad Minervium et Alexandrum monachos, hoc quod hic dicitur *omnes quidem resurgemus*, etc., in nullo libro Graecorum habetur; sed in quibusdam habetur *omnes quidem dormiemus*, id est omnes moriemur. Et dicitur mors somnus, propter spem resurrectionis. Unde idem est ac si diceret *omnes quidem resurgemus*, quia nullus resurget nisi moriatur.

Sed non omnes immutabimur. Hoc non mutatur in libris Graecis. Et hoc est verum, quia ista mutatio, de qua hic loquitur, non erit nisi secundum corpora beatorum, quia immutabuntur ad illa quatuor quae supra posita sunt, quae dicuntur dotes corporum gloriosorum. Et hanc desiderabat Iob. XIV, 14: *cunctis diebus quibus nunc milito, expecto, donec veniat immutatio mea.*

1004. In quibusdam vero libris invenitur: *non omnes quidem dormiemus*, id est, moriemur, *sed omnes immutabimur*. Et hoc intelligitur dupliciter.

1001. After responding to the question on the quality of the resurrection, the Apostle then responds to the question which was asked about the mode and order of the resurrection.

And concerning this he does two things.

First, he shows the mode and order of the resurrection;

second, he confirms it by an authority, at *and when this mortal* (1 Cor 15:54).

Concerning the first, he does two things.

First, he sets forth the aim;

second, he shows by what order it will be done, at *in a moment, in the twinkling of an eye.*

1002. First, then, he renders them attentive, showing that what he is setting forth is difficult and hidden, saying, *behold, a mystery*, i.e., a certain mystery *I tell you*, i.e., I uncover for you, brethren, what ought to be uncovered for you and for all believers: *to you it has been given to know the secrets of the kingdom of God* (Luke 8:10); *yet among the mature we do impart wisdom . . . but we impart a secret and hidden wisdom of God* (1 Cor 2:6–7).

1003. What that mystery is, he adds, *we shall all indeed rise*.

It should be understood concerning the first that, as Jerome says in a certain letter to the monks Minerva and Alexander: what is said here, *we shall all indeed rise*, is not found in any book of the Greeks, but in certain ones is found, *we shall all sleep*, i.e., we shall all die. And it is called the death of sleep because of the hope of the resurrection. Hence it is the same as if one said, *we shall all rise*, because no one rises unless he has died.

But we shall not all be changed. This is not altered in the books of the Greeks. And this is true, because that change which is spoken of here will not occur except according to the blessed body, because they shall be changed to those four qualities set down above, which are called the marks of glorified bodies. And this is what Job desired: *all the days of my service I would wait, till my release should come* (Job 14:14).

1004. In certain books is found: *we shall not all sleep*, i.e., die, *but we shall all be changed*. And this is understood in two ways.

Primo ad litteram, quia quorumdam opinio fuit quod non omnes homines morientur, sed quod aliqui in adventu Christi ad iudicium venient vivi, et isti non morientur sed isti mutabuntur in statum incorruptionis, et, propter hoc dicunt *non omnes quidem dormiemus*, id est moriemur, *sed omnes immutabimur*, tam boni quam mali et tam vivi quam mortui. Unde secundum hos immutatio non intelligitur de statu animalitatis ad statum spiritualitatis, quia, secundum hanc, soli boni immutabuntur, sed de statu corruptionis ad statum incorruptionis.

Alio modo exponitur mystice ab Origene, et dicit quod hoc non dicitur de somno mortis, quia omnes morientur, Ps. LXXXVIII, 49: *quis est homo qui vivet*, etc., sed de somno peccati, de quo in Ps. XII, 4: *illumina oculos meos ne unquam obdormiam*, ut sic dicatur: *non omnes moriemur*, id est non omnes peccabimus mortaliter, *sed omnes immutabimur*, sicut supra de statu corruptionis ad incorruptionem.

Et licet haec littera, scilicet *non omnes moriemur*, etc., non sit contra fidem, tamen Ecclesia magis acceptat primam, scilicet quod omnes moriemur sive resurgemus, etc.; quia omnes morientur etiam si sint tunc aliqui vivi.

1005. Ordinem autem et modum resurrectionis manifestat consequenter cum dicit **in momento, in ictu oculi**, et cetera. Et hoc quantum ad tria.

Primo enim manifestat ordinem quantum ad tempus;

secundo quantum ad causam resurrectionis, ibi **in novissima tuba**;

tertio quantum ad progressum effectus a causa, ibi **canet enim tuba**, et cetera.

1006. Dicit ergo quod omnes resurgemus, sed quomodo? **In momento**.

Per quod excludit errorem dicentium resurrectionem non esse futuram omnium simul, sed dicunt quod martyres resurgent ante alios per mille annos, et tunc Christus descendet cum illis, et possidebit regnum corporale Ierusalem mille annis cum eis. Et haec fuit opinio Lactantii. Sed hoc patet esse falsum, quia omnes **in momento** resurgemus et **in ictu oculi**.

Excluditur etiam per hoc alius error eiusdem qui dicebat quod iudicium duraturum erat per spatium mille annorum. Sed hoc est falsum, quia non erit ibi aliquod perceptibile tempus, sed **in momento**, et cetera.

1007. Sciendum est autem quod **momentum** potest accipi vel pro ipso instanti temporis, quod dicitur nunc, vel pro aliquo tempore imperceptibili; tamen utroque modo potest accipi hoc, referendo illud ad diversa. Quia si nos referamus hoc ad collectionem pulverum (quae

First, literally, because the opinion of certain men is that not all men will die, but that at the coming of Christ some will come alive to the judgment, and these will not die, but they will be changed to the state of incorruption; and because of this they say, *we shall not all sleep*, i.e., die, *but we shall all be changed*, as much to good as to evil, as much to live as to die. Hence, according to these, the change is not understood from the state of animal to the state of spiritual, because according to this, they will be changed only to good, but from the state of corruption to the state of incorruption.

It is explained in another way, mystically, by Origen, who says that this is not said about the sleep of death, because all will die: *what man can live and never see death?* (Ps 89:48); from which in Psalm 13: *lighten my eyes lest I sleep the sleep of death* (Ps 13:3); so that thus it is said, *we shall not all sleep*, i.e., we shall not all sin mortally, *but we shall all be changed*, just as above, from the state of corruption to incorruption.

And although these words, namely, *we shall not all sleep*, are not contrary to the faith, nevertheless the Church accepts with better reason the first explanation, namely, that we shall all die if we shall rise, because all will die even if some are then alive.

1005. Next he exhibits the order and mode of the resurrection when he says, **in a moment, in the twinkling of an eye**. Concerning this he does three things.

First, he exhibits the order with respect to time;

second, with respect to the cause of the resurrection, at **at the last trumpet**;

third, with respect to the progress produced by the cause, at **for the trumpet shall sound**.

1006. He says therefore that we all shall rise, but in what manner? **In a moment, in the twinkling of an eye**.

By this he excludes the error stated that the future resurrection will not be at the same time, but they say that the martyrs will rise before the others by a thousand years, and then Christ will descend with them, and he will possess the corporeal kingdom of Jerusalem for a thousand years with them. This is the opinion of Lactantius, but this is clearly false, because we all shall rise **in a moment** and **in the twinkling of an eye**.

Another of his errors is excluded by this, namely when he said that the judgment was to last for an interval of a thousand years. But this is false, because there will not be any perceptible time, but it will be **in a moment, in the twinkling of an eye**.

1007. It should be understood that a **moment** can be taken either for the instant of time itself, which is called 'now,' or for a certain imperceptible time. Nevertheless in both ways this can be received by referring it to contrary things. Because if we refer this to the gathering of dust (which will

fiet ministerio angelorum), tunc *momentum* accipitur pro tempore imperceptibili. Cum enim in collectione illorum pulverum sit mutatio de loco ad locum, oportet quod sit ibi tempus aliquod. Si autem referamus ad reunitionem corporum et pro unione animae, quae omnia fient a Deo, tunc *momentum* accipitur pro instanti temporis, quia Deus in instanti unit animam corpori et vivificat corpus.

Potest etiam hoc quod dicit *in ictu oculi*, ad utrumque referri, quasi si *in ictu oculi* intelligitur tantum apertio palpebrarum (quae fit in tempore perceptibili), tunc refertur ad collectionem pulverum. Si vero *in ictu oculi* intelligitur ipse subitus contuitus oculi, et qui fit in instanti, tunc refertur ad unionem animae ad corpus.

1008. Consequenter cum dicit *in novissima tuba*, ostendit ordinem resurrectionis, quantum ad causam immediatam.

Et ista *tuba* est vox illa Christi, de qua Matth. XXVI, 6 dicitur: *media nocte clamor factus est*; Io. V, 25: *audient vocem Filii Dei, et qui audierint*, et cetera.

Vel ipsa praesentia Christi manifesta mundo, secundum quod dicit Gregorius: *tuba nihil aliud esse designat, quam praesentiam Christi mundo manifestatam*, quae dicitur *tuba* propter manifestationem, quia omnibus erit manifesta. Et hoc modo accipitur *tuba* Matth. VI, 2: *cum facis eleemosynam, noli tuba canere ante te.*

Item dicitur *tuba* propter officium tubae, quod erat ad quatuor, ut dicitur Num. X, v. 1–10, scilicet ad vocandum consilium, et hoc erit in resurrectione, quia tunc convocabit ad consilium, id est ad iudicium. Is. III, v. 14: *Dominus ad iudicium veniet*, et cetera. Ad solemnizandum festum. Ps. LXXX, 4: *buccinate in Neomenia tuba.* Sic et in resurrectione. Is. XXXIII, 20: *respice Sion civitatem solemnitatis nostrae.* Ad pugnam, et hoc in resurrectione. Sap. V, 21: *pugnabit pro illo*, et cetera. Is. XXX, 32: *in cytharis et tympanis*, et cetera. Ad movendum castra, sic et in resurrectione: quidam eundo ad paradisum, quidam eundo ad infernum. Matth. XXV, 46: *ibunt qui bona fecerunt in vitam aeternam, qui vero mala in ignem aeternum.*

1009. Consequenter cum dicit *canet enim tuba*, etc., ponit progressum effectus a causa praedicta.

Et circa hoc duo facit.

Primo enim ponit progressum effectus;

secundo necessitatem huius assignat, ibi *oportet enim mortale*, et cetera.

be done by the ministry of the angels), then a *moment* is taken for an imperceptible time. For since in the gathering of that dust there is a change from place to place, it is necessary that there be a certain time. If we refer it to the reuniting of bodies and for their union with souls, all of which will be done by God, then a *moment* is taken for an instant of time, because God in an instant unites the soul to the body, and vivifies the body.

It is possible that what he says, *in the twinkling of an eye*, is referred to either of the two; if *in the twinkling of an eye* is understood as the opening of the eyelids (which happens in a perceptible time), then it is referred to the gathering of dust. If however *in the twinkling of an eye* is understood as the instantaneous sight of the eye itself, which happens in an instant, then it is referred to the union of the soul to the body.

1008. Then when he says, *at the last trumpet*, he shows the order of the resurrection as to its immediate cause.

And that *trumpet* is the voice of Christ, about which it is said in Matthew: *but at midnight there was a cry* (Matt 25:6); *the dead will hear the voice of the Son of God, and those who hear will live* (John 5:25).

Or it is the presence of Christ himself manifested to the world, as Gregory says, *the trumpet signifies nothing other than the presence of Christ manifest to the world*, which is called a *trumpet* for the sake of manifestation, because it will be manifest to all. And *trumpet* is taken this way in Matthew: *thus, when you give alms, sound no trumpet before you* (Matt 6:2).

Likewise it is called a *trumpet* because of the office of the trumpet, which was fourfold, as it is said in Numbers, namely, for the calling of the assembly, and this will be in the resurrection, because then he will call to council, that is, to the judgment: *the Lord enters into judgment* (Num 10:1ff). Second, for the solemnizing of a feast: *blow the trumpet at the new moon* (Ps 81:3); so too in the resurrection: *look upon Zion, the city of our appointed feasts* (Isa 33:20). Third, for war, and this too is in the resurrection: *and will leap to the target as from a well-drawn bow of clouds* (Wis 5:21); *to the sound of timbrels and lyres* (Isa 30:32). Fourth, for the moving of the camp, and so too in the resurrection, some by going to heaven, some by going to hell: *and they will go away into eternal punishment, but the righteous into eternal life* (Matt 25:46).

1009. Then when he says, *for the trumpet shall sound*, he establishes the progress effected by the cause predicated.

Concerning this, he does two things.

First, he establishes the progress effected;

second, he indicates the necessity of this, at *for this corruptible* (1 Cor 15:53).

1010. Progressus effectus est quia statim ad sonitum tubae sequetur effectus, quia *mortui*, etc., Ps. LXVII, 34: *dabit voci suae vocem virtutis*, et cetera.

Ponit autem duplicem effectum. Unus est communis, quia *mortui resurgent incorrupti*, id est integri, sine aliqua diminutione membrorum. Quod quidem est commune omnibus, quia in resurrectione est commune omne quod pertinet ad reparationem naturae, quia omnes habent communionem cum Christo in natura. Et licet Augustinus relinquat sub dubio, utrum deformitates remaneant in damnatis, ego tamen credo quod quidquid pertinet ad reparationem naturae, totum confertur eis: sed quod pertinet ad gratiam, solum electis confertur. Et ideo omnes resurgent incorrupti, id est, integri, etiam damnati.

Hieronymus autem exponit *incorrupti*, id est in statu incorruptionis, ut scilicet ulterius post resurrectionem non corrumpantur, quia isti ad beatitudinem aeternam ibunt, mali vero ad poenam aeternam. Dan. XII, 2: *multi de terrae pulvere evigilabunt.*

1011. Alius effectus est proprius, id est apostolorum tantum, quia *nos immutabimur*, scilicet apostoli, et non solum erimus incorrupti, sed etiam *immutabimur*, scilicet de statu miseriae ad statum gloriae, quia seminatur animale surget autem spirituale.

Et secundum hunc modum exponendi apparet, quod melior est littera illa quae dicit *omnes quidem resurgemus, sed non omnes immutabimur*, quam illa quae habet *omnes immutabimur*, quia licet omnes resurgant, tamen soli sancti et electi immutabuntur.

Posset tamen etiam secundum illos qui habent *non omnes quidem morimur, sed omnes immutabimur*, legi sic: mortui resurgent incorrupti, id est ad statum incorruptionis, et nos qui vivimus, licet non resurgamus, quia non morimur, tamen immutabimur de statu corruptionis ad incorruptionem. Et videtur consonare iis quae dicit I Thess. IV, 16: *nos qui vivimus, qui relinquimur, simul rapiemur cum illis*, etc.; ut sicut et ibi, et hic connumeret se vivis.

1010. The progress is effected because immediately at the sound of the trumpet the effect follows, because ***the dead shall rise again***: *he sends forth his voice, his mighty voice* (Ps 68:33).

He establishes however two effects. One is common, because ***the dead shall rise again incorruptible***, i.e., renewed without any diminution of their members. That indeed is common to all, because in the resurrection the reparation of nature pertains to all, because all have communion with Christ in nature. And although Augustine leaves open a doubt whether deformities will remain among the damned, I believe that whatever pertains to the reparation of nature is conferred entirely on them; but what pertains to grace is conferred only on the elect. And therefore all will rise incorruptible, i.e., renewed, even the damned.

Jerome however explains ***incorruptible***, i.e., the state of incorruption, as namely, that they will not be corrupted further after the resurrection, because they will have come to that eternal beatitude, the evil surely to eternal punishment: *and many of those who sleep in the dust of the earth shall awake* (Dan 12:2).

1011. The other effect is proper, i.e., only of the apostles, because ***we shall be changed***, namely, the Apostles, and not only will we be incorruptible, but ***we shall be changed***, that is, from the state of misery to the state of glory, because what is sown animal rises spiritual.

And according to this way of expounding, it is clear that that reading is better which says, ***we shall all rise, but we shall not all be changed***, than that which has, *we shall all be changed*, because although all shall rise, nevertheless only the holy and the elect shall be changed.

But it would be possible even according to those who have, *we shall not all die, but we shall all be changed*, to be read thus: the dead will rise incorruptible, i.e., to the state of incorruption, and we who are alive, although we will not rise because we are not dead, nonetheless will be changed from the state of corruption to incorruption. And this would seem to agree with what is said in 1 Thessalonians: *we who are alive, who are left, shall be caught up together with them* (1 Thess 4:17); so that just as there, here too he reckons himself with the living.

Lecture 9

15:53Oportet enim corruptibile hoc induere incorruptionem: et mortale hoc induere immortalitatem. [n. 1012]

15:54Cum autem mortale hoc induerit immortalitatem, tunc fiet sermo, qui scriptus est: *absorpta est mors in victoria.* [n. 1016]

15:55*Ubi est mors victoria tua? ubi est mors stimulus tuus?* [n. 1018]

15:56Stimulus autem mortis peccatum est: virtus vero peccati lex.

15:57Deo autem gratias, qui dedit nobis victoriam per Dominum nostrum Jesum Christum. [n. 1022]

15:58Itaque fratres mei dilecti, stabiles estote, et immobiles: abundantes in opere Domini semper, scientes quod labor vester non est inanis in Domino. [n. 1023]

15:53δεῖ γὰρ τὸ φθαρτὸν τοῦτο ἐνδύσασθαι ἀφθαρσίαν καὶ τὸ θνητὸν τοῦτο ἐνδύσασθαι ἀθανασίαν.

15:54ὅταν δὲ τὸ φθαρτὸν τοῦτο ἐνδύσηται ἀφθαρσίαν καὶ τὸ θνητὸν τοῦτο ἐνδύσηται ἀθανασίαν, τότε γενήσεται ὁ λόγος ὁ γεγραμμένος, Κατεπόθη ὁ θάνατος εἰς νῖκος.

15:55ποῦ σου, θάνατε, τὸ νῖκος; ποῦ σου, θάνατε, τὸ κέντρον;

15:56τὸ δὲ κέντρον τοῦ θανάτου ἡ ἁμαρτία, ἡ δὲ δύναμις τῆς ἁμαρτίας ὁ νόμος·

15:57τῷ δὲ θεῷ χάρις τῷ διδόντι ἡμῖν τὸ νῖκος διὰ τοῦ κυρίου ἡμῶν Ἰησοῦ Χριστοῦ.

15:58Ὥστε, ἀδελφοί μου ἀγαπητοί, ἑδραῖοι γίνεσθε, ἀμετακίνητοι, περισσεύοντες ἐν τῷ ἔργῳ τοῦ κυρίου πάντοτε, εἰδότες ὅτι ὁ κόπος ὑμῶν οὐκ ἔστιν κενὸς ἐν κυρίῳ.

15:53For this corruptible must put on incorruption: and this mortal must put on immortality. [n. 1012]

15:54And when this mortal has put on immortality, then shall come to pass the saying that is written: *death is swallowed up in victory.* [n. 1016]

15:55*O death, where is your victory? O death, where is your sting?* [n. 1018]

15:56Now the sting of death is sin: and the power of sin is the law.

15:57But thanks be to God, who has given us the victory through our Lord Jesus Christ. [n. 1022]

15:58Therefore, my beloved brethren, be steadfast and unmoveable: always abounding in the work of the Lord, knowing that your labor is not in vain in the Lord. [n. 1023]

1012. Hic Apostolus ponit necessitatem effectus resurrectionis ab ipsa causa progredientis. Et circa hoc duo ponit correspondentia duobus quae posuerat in progressu effectuum ab ipsa causa. Primum fuit generale omnium, scilicet quod *mortui resurgent incorrupti.* Et ideo, primo, quantum ad hoc dicit *oportet corruptibile hoc induere incorruptionem.* Secundum fuit speciale apostolis et bonis, scilicet *et nos immutabimur*, et ideo, secundo, quantum ad hoc dicit *et mortale hoc induere immortalitatem.*

1013. Quia enim corruptibile opponitur incorruptibili, et in statu praesentis vitae subiicimur corruptioni, ideo dicit quod cum resurgemus, *oportet hoc corruptibile*, etc., necessitate scilicet congruentiae. Et hoc propter tria.

Primo propter completionem humanae naturae. Nam, sicut etiam dicit Augustinus, anima quamdiu est separata a corpore est imperfecta, non habens perfectionem suae naturae, et ideo non est in tanta beatitudine separata existens, in quanta erit corpori unita in resurrectione. Ut ergo perfruatur beatitudine perfecta, *oportet corruptibile hoc*, id est corpus, *induere*, ut ornamentum, *incorruptionem*, ut ulterius aliquatenus non laedatur mortale.

1012. Here the Apostle established the necessary effect of the resurrection proceeding from its own cause. And concerning this he establishes two things in correspondence with the two he had established in the progress of the effects from the cause itself. The first is general for all, namely, *that the dead shall rise again incorruptible* (1 Cor 15:52). And so first he says concerning this, *for this corruptible must put on incorruption.* The second is particular for the apostles and the good, namely, *and we shall be changed* (1 Cor 15:52), and so second he says concerning this, *and this mortal must put on immortality.*

1013. For because the corruptible is contrasted to the incorruptible, and in the present state of life we are subject to corruption, he says that when we rise, *this corruptible must put on incorruption*, namely, by a necessary congruence. And this for three reasons.

First, for the completion of human nature. For as Augustine says, the soul, inasmuch as it is separated from the body, is imperfect, not possessing the perfection of its nature, and so existing separately it is not in such beatitude as it will be when united to the body in the resurrection. Therefore, so that it might enjoy perfect beatitude, *this corruptible*, i.e., the body, *must put on* as an adornment *incorruption*, so that 'this mortal' will not be afflicted further in any degree.

Secundo propter exigentiam divinae iustitiae, ut scilicet illi qui bona fecerunt seu mala in corpore, praemientur vel puniantur etiam in ipsis corporibus.

Tertio propter conformitatem membrorum ad caput; ut sicut Christus resurrexit a mortuis per gloriam Patris, ita et nos *in novitate vitae ambulemus*, Rom. VI, 4.

1014. Notandum autem quod ipsam incorruptionem seu immortalitatem assimilat vestimento, cum dicit *induere*. Vestimentum enim adest vestito et abest, manente eadem numero substantia vestiti, ut per hoc ostendat quod corpora eadem numero resurgant et iidem homines iidem numero erunt in statu incorruptionis et immortalitatis, in quo sunt modo.

Unde ex hoc excluditur error dicentium quod corpora non resurgent eadem numero. Unde signanter dicit *oportet corruptibile hoc*, scilicet corpus, nam anima non est corruptibilis.

Excluditur etiam error dicentium quod corpora glorificata non erunt eadem cum istis, sed caelestia, et de isto modo simile habetur II Cor. V, 2: *nam in hoc ingemiscimus*, etc.; Is. LII, 1: *induere vestimentis gloriae tuae*; Iob XL, 5: *circumda tibi decorem*, et cetera.

1015. Sed contra hoc est, quia videtur impossibile quod corruptibile hoc induat incorruptionem, id est, quod corpora resurgant eadem numero, quia impossibile est ea, quae differunt genere vel specie, esse eadem numero; sed corruptibile et incorruptibile non solum differunt specie, sed genere; ergo impossibile est quod corpora resurgentium sint incorruptibilia, et remaneant eadem numero.

Praeterea, Philosophus dicit, quod impossibile est quod illa quorum substantia corruptibilis mota est, reintegrentur eadem numero, sed eadem specie; substantia autem corporum humanorum est corruptibilis, ergo impossibile est reintegrari eadem numero.

Respondeo. Dicendum est, ad primum, quod unumquodque consequitur genus et speciem ex sua natura et non ex aliquo extrinseco suae naturae, et ideo dico, quod si resurrectio corporum futura esset ex principiis naturae corporum, impossibile esset quod corpora resurgerent eadem numero. Sed dico quod incorruptio corporum resurgentium dabitur ab alio principio, quam a natura ipsorum corporum, scilicet a gloria animae, ex cuius beatitudine et incorruptione, tota beatitudo et incorruptio corporum derivabitur. Sicut ergo eiusdem naturae et idem numero est liberum arbitrium, modo dum est volubile ad utramque partem et cum erit firmatum in fine ultimo, ita et eiusdem naturae et idem numero erit corpus, quod modo est corruptibile et tunc, quando per

Second, for the necessity of divine justice, so that those who have done good or evil in the body are rewarded or punished likewise in the same bodies.

Third, for the conformity of the members to the head, so that just as Christ was raised from the dead by the glory of the Father, so we too *might walk in newness of life* (Rom 6:4).

1014. It should be noted that he compares incorruption itself or immortality to a garment, when he says, **put on**. For a garment is present to the one having vested, and absent, remaining the same numerical substance of the one vested, so that by this he shows that the same numerical bodies will rise and the same men will be the same numerically in the state of incorruption and immortality, in which they are now.

Thus by this the error is excluded that says that the same numerical body will not rise. Hence he says expressly, **this corruptible**, namely the body, **must put on incorruption**, for the soul is not corruptible.

Likewise, the error is excluded that says that glorified bodies will not be the same as these, but will be heavenly; and in a similar way 2 Corinthians says: *here indeed we groan, and long to put on our heavenly dwelling* (2 Cor 2:5); *put on your beautiful garments, O Jerusalem* (Isa 52:1); *deck yourself with majesty and dignity; clothe yourself with glory and splendor* (Job 40:10).

1015. But against this, it seems impossible that this corruptible should put on incorruption, i.e., that the same numerical bodies will rise, because it is impossible for things which differ in genus or species to be the same numerically. But corruptible and incorruptible do not differ in species, but in genus. Therefore, it is impossible that resurrected bodies will be incorruptible and will remain the same numerically.

Moreover, the Philosopher says that it is impossible that the corruptible substance which is changed be restored to the same numerically, but to the same in species. But the substance of human bodies is corruptible; therefore, it is impossible for it to be restored to the same numerically.

I respond: it should be said first that each thing attains to its genus or species from its own nature, and not from something extrinsic to is own nature; and therefore I say that if the resurrection of bodies would be future from the principles of the nature of bodies, it would be impossible that bodies would rise the same numerically. But I say that the incorruption of resurrected bodies will be given from another principle, than from the nature of the bodies themselves, namely, from the glory of the soul, from whose beatitude and incorruption all beatitude and incorruption of bodies will be derived. Therefore, just as free will is of the same nature and the same numerically, while it is in a changeable mode to either side, and when it will be firmly fixed in the final state, so too the body will be of the

liberum arbitrium firmatum erit per gloriam animae, erit incorruptibile.

Ad secundum dicendum, quod ratio Philosophi procedit contra illos, qui ponebant omnia, in istis inferioribus, causari ex motu corporum caelestium, et quod revolutis eisdem revolutionibus corporum superiorum, sequebantur iidem effectus numero, qui aliquando fuerant. Unde dicebant quod adhuc Plato idem numero leget Athenis et quod habebit easdem scholas, et eosdem auditores quos habuit. Et ideo Philosophus contra eosdem arguit, quod licet idem caelum numero, et idem sol sit in eisdem revolutionibus, tamen effectus, qui inde proveniunt non consequuntur identitatem numero, sed specie, et hoc secundum viam naturae.

Similiter dico, quod si corpora induerent incorruptionem, et surgerent secundum viam naturae, quod non resurgerent eadem numero, sed eadem specie. Sed cum reintegratio et resurrectio, sicut dictum est, fiant virtute divina, dicimus quod corpora erunt eadem numero, cum neque principia individuantia huius hominis sint aliud, quam haec anima, et hoc corpus. In resurrectione autem redibit et anima eadem numero, cum sit incorruptibilis, et hoc corpus idem numero ex eisdem pulveribus, in quibus resolutum fuit, ex virtute divina reparatum, sic erit idem homo numero resurgens.

Nec facio vim in formis intermediis, quia non pono esse aliquam aliam formam substantialem in homine, nisi animam rationalem, a qua habet corpus humanum quod sit animatum natura sensibili et vegetabili et quod sit rationale. Formae vero accidentales nihil impediunt identitatem numeralem quam ponimus.

1016. Consequenter cum dicit *cum autem corruptibile*, etc., confirmat quod dixerat per auctoritatem.

Et circa hoc duo facit.

Primo ponit auctoritatem;

secundo ex ea concludit tria, ibi *ubi enim est, mors*, et cetera.

1017. Dicit ergo primo: dixi quod oportet *corruptibile hoc induere*, etc., sed *cum mortale hoc induerit immortalitatem, tunc*, scilicet in futuro, quod est contra illos qui dicunt iam resurrectionem factam, *fiet sermo qui scriptus*, scilicet, *absorpta est*, et cetera.

Hoc secundum translationem nostram non invenitur in aliquo libro Bibliae; si tamen inveniatur in translatione Lxx, non est certum unde sumptum sit. Potest tamen dici hoc esse sumptum ex Is. XXVI, 19: *vivent mortui*, etc., et XXV, 8: *praecipitabit mortem in sempiternum*. Osee XIII, 14, ubi nos habemus: *ero mors tua, o mors*,

same nature and the same numerically, in that corruptible mode and then, when by free will it will be firmly fixed by the glory of the soul, it will be incorruptible.

To the second objection, which the reason of the Philosopher advances against those who would maintain that all things in the sublunary bodies are caused by a change of the heavenly bodies, and that by the same turnings of the revolutions of superior bodies, the same numerical effects followed which were at some previous time. Hence they said that still the same numerical Plato will lecture to Athens and that he will have the same schools and the same pupils that he had. And so the Philosopher argues against this, that although there is the same numerical heaven, and the same sun is in its same revolutions, nonetheless the effects which arise from there do not result in numerical identity, but in identity of species, and this according to the course of nature.

In like manner, I say that if bodies were to put on incorruption, and were to rise according to the course of nature, they would not rise the same numerically, but the same in species. But since the renewal and the resurrection, as was said, will occur by divine power, we say that bodies will be the same numerically, since the individual principles of that man are nothing other than this soul and this body. In the resurrection the soul too will return the same numerically, since it is incorruptible, and this body will be the same numerically from the same dust from which is was dissolved, restored by divine power; thus it will be the same numerical man who rises.

I do not do violence to the intermediary forms, because I do not hold that there is any other substantial form in man except the rational soul, from which the human body will have it, that it is animated by a sensible and vegetable nature, and that it is rational. Accidental forms in no way hinder the numerical identity that we maintain.

1016. Then when he says, *for this corruptible*, he confirms what he had said by authority.

And concerning this he does two things.

First, he establishes the authority;

second, from this he concludes three things, at *O death, where is your victory?*

1017. Therefore he says first: I said that *this corruptible must put on incorruption*, but *when this mortal has put on immortality*, *then*, namely, in the future (which is against those who say that the resurrection has already happened), *then shall come to pass the saying that is written*, that is, *death is swallowed up in victory*.

This saying, according to our translation, is not found in any book of the Bible; but if it be found in the Septuagint translation, it is not certain whence it is taken. It is possible to say that this saying is taken from Isaiah: *the dead shall live, their bodies shall rise* (Isa 26:19), and: *he will swallow up death forever* (Isa 25:8). In Hosea: *I will be your death, O death* (Hos 13:44); the Septuagint has *death*

LXX habent: *absorpta est mors in victoria*, id est propter victoriam Christi.

Et ponit praeteritum pro futuro, propter certitudinem prophetiae. I Petr. III, 22: *deglutiens mortem*, et cetera.

1018. Consequenter cum dicit **ubi est, mors, victoria tua?** etc., concludit tria ex praemissa auctoritate;

insultationem sanctorum contra mortem,

gratiarum actiones ad Deum, ibi **Deo autem gratias**,

et admonitionem suam Corinthiis, ibi **itaque, fratres mei**, et cetera.

Circa primum duo facit.

Primo ponit insultationem, secundo exponit, ibi **stimulus autem**, et cetera.

1019. Loquens ergo Apostolus de victoria Christi contra mortem, quasi in quodam speciali gaudio positus, assumit personam virorum resurgentium, dicens **ubi est, mors, victoria tua?**

Hoc non invenitur in aliquo loco sacrae Scripturae; utrum autem ex se, vel aliunde habuerit hoc Apostolus, incertum est. Si tamen aliunde accepisset, videtur accepisse de Is. XIV, 4: *quomodo cessavit exactor, quievit tributum*, et cetera.

Dicit ergo **ubi est, mors, victoria tua?** etc., scilicet corruptionis victoria tua, id est potentia qua totum humanum genus prosternebas, de omnibus triumphabas. II Reg. c. XIV, 14: *omnes morimur*, etc., Iob XVIII, v. 14: *calcet super eum quasi rex interitus*, et cetera. **Ubi est, mors, stimulus tuus?**

1020. Quid autem sit stimulus consequenter exponit dicens **stimulus autem**, et cetera. Unde duo ponit: unum per quod exponit quod dixit; aliud per quod obiectionem excludit, ibi **virtus peccati**, et cetera.

Sciendum est autem quod stimulus mortis potest dici vel stimulans ad mortem, vel quo utitur seu quem facit mors; sed litteralis sensus est **stimulus mortis**, id est stimulans ad mortem, quia homo per peccatum est impulsus et deiectus ad mortem. Rom. V, 23: *stipendia peccati mors*, et cetera.

Sed quia aliquis posset obiicere, quod iste stimulus est remotus per legem, ideo consequenter hoc Apostolus excludit, subdens **virtus vero**, id est augmentum, **peccati lex**, quasi dicat: non est remotum peccatum per legem, imo virtus peccati lex, id est augmentum occasionaliter, scilicet non quod induceret ad peccatum sed inquantum dabat occasionem peccati et non conferebat gratiam; ex qua magis accedebatur concupiscentia ad peccandum. Rom. V, 20: *lex subintravit, ut abundaret delictum.* Rom. VII, 8: *occasione accepta, peccatum per mandatum*, et cetera.

is swallowed up in victory, i.e., on account of the victory of Christ.

And he sets down the past for the future on account of the certitude of prophecy (1 Pet 3:22).

1018. Then when he says, **O death, where is your victory?**, he concludes three things on the basis of authority:

the scorn of the saints against death;

the actions of thanks toward God, at **but thanks be to God**;

and his admonition to the Corinthians, at **therefore, my beloved brethren**.

Concerning the first he does two things.

First, he mentions the scorn; second, he explains it, at **now the sting of death**.

1019. The Apostle, therefore, speaking of the victory of Christ over death, as if established in some special joy, takes upon himself the person of resurrected man, saying, **O death, where is your victory?**

This is not found in any place of Sacred Scripture; whether the Apostle got this from himself or from another source is not certain. If however, he took it from another place, it appears that he took it from Isaiah: *how the oppressor has ceased, the insolent fury ceased* (Isa 14:4).

He says therefore, **O death, where is your victory?**, namely, your victory of corruption, i.e., the power by which you overthrew the whole human race, but which you triumphed over all: *we must all die* (2 Sam 14:14); *he is brought to the king of terrors* (Job 18:14). **O death, where is your sting?**

1020. What the sting is, he explains in what follows, saying, **the sting of death is sin**. Therefore, he sets forth two points: one by which he explains what he said; the other by which he excludes an objection, at **and the power of sin is the law**.

It should be understood that the sting of death can be described either as a goad to death, or that which death uses or makes. But the literal sense is **the sting of death**, i.e., the goad to death, because man is propelled and cast down to death by sin: *for the wages of sin is death* (Rom 6:23).

But because someone could object, that this sting is removed by the law, the Apostle straightaway excludes this, adding, **and the power**, i.e., the increase, **of sin is the law**; as if to say: sin is not removed by the law, but rather the power of sin is the law, i.e., an increase in the occasion; that is to say, not that it impels to sin, but that it gives an occasion for sin and it does not confer grace, from which concupiscence to sin was roused all the more: *law came in, to increase the trespass* (Rom 5:20); *but sin, finding opportunity in the commandment, wrought in me all kinds of covetousness* (Rom 7:8).

1021. Est autem alius sensus, sed non litteralis, ut *stimulus mortis* dicatur quo utitur mors. Et sic per mortem intelligitur diabolus. Apoc. VI, 8: *nomen illi mors.* Et sic *stimulus mortis* est tentatio diaboli. Et sic totum quod dicitur de morte, exponitur de diabolo, ut in Glossa habetur.

Vel *stimulus mortis*, id est a morte factus, id est a carnali concupiscentia. Iac. I, 15: *concupiscentia cum conceperit*, et cetera. Concupiscentia enim primo volentes allicit, sicut in intemperatis; secundo repugnantes trahit, ut in incontinentibus; postea contendit, sed non vincit, ut in continentibus; postea debilitatur eius contentio, sicut in temperatis, et ultimo totaliter deficit, sicut in beatis, quibus dicere competit: *ubi est, mors*, contentio vel *victoria tua?*

1022. Quia ergo stimulus mortis destructus est non per legem, sed per victoriam Christi, ideo Deo sunt reddendae gratiarum actiones. Et hoc est quod dicit *Deo autem gratias*, scilicet ago, seu agamus, *qui dedit nobis victoriam*, mortis et peccati, per *Iesum Christum*, non per legem. I Io. V, 4: *haec est victoria*, et cetera. Rom. VII, 24: *quis me liberabit*, et cetera. *Gratia Dei*, et cetera. *Nam quod impossibile*, et cetera.

1023. Consequenter cum dicit *itaque, fratres mei*, etc., subdit admonitionem. Sicut enim dictum est, pseudo-apostoli corrumpebant Corinthios negando resurrectionem, et ideo, postquam iam astruxit fidem resurrectionis, et per exempla ostendit, admonet eos quod bene se habeant, ne seducantur a pseudo-apostolis.

Et circa hoc tria facit. Primo enim eos in fide confirmat, dicens *itaque*, scilicet iam ostensa resurrectione, *fratres mei*, per fidem, per quam omnes sumus filii Dei Io. I, 12: *dedit eis potestatem*, etc., *dilectissimi*, per caritatem qua debemus nos invicem diligere I Io. IV, 21: *hoc mandatum habemus a Deo*, etc., *stabiles estote*, scilicet in fide resurrectionis, ne recedatis a fide Eph. IV, 14: *non simus sicut parvuli fluctuantes*, etc., *et immobiles*, ne scilicet ab aliis seducamini Col. I, 23: *in fide fundati, stabiles, et immobiles*, et cetera.

Secundo inducit ad bona opera, dicens *abundantes in omni opere bono semper* Gal. ult.: *dum tempus habemus*, et cetera. Prov. XV, 5: *in abundanti iustitia.*

Tertio roborat eos per spem, dicens *scientes quod labor vester*, etc., Sap. III, 15: *bonorum enim laborum gloriosus est fructus.*

1021. There is, however, another sense, but not the literal one, so that *the sting of death* is said to be that which death uses. And so by death is understood the devil: *and its rider's name was death* (Rev 6:8). And so *the sting of death* is the temptation of the devil. And thus all that is said about death is interpreted of the devil, as in the Gloss.

Or *the sting of death*, i.e., made by death, i.e., concupiscence of the flesh: *then desire when it has conceived gives birth to sin* (Jas 1:15). For concupiscence first draws those who are willing, as in the intemperate; second, it drags those who resist, as in the incontinent; next it contends, but does not conquer, as in the continent; next it is weakened in its contention, as in the temperate; and finally it is totally defeated, as in the beatified, about whom it is fitting to say: *O death, where is* your contention or *your victory?*

1022. Therefore, because the sting of death is destroyed, not by the law, but by the victory of Christ, acts of thanksgiving are rendered to God. And this is what he says: *but thanks be to God*, namely, I give thanks, or we give thanks, *who has given us the victory*, over death and sin, through *Jesus Christ*, not through the law: *and this is the victory that overcomes the world, our faith* (1 John 5:4); *who will deliver me from this body of death? Thanks be to God through Jesus our Lord!* (Rom 7:24–25); *for God has done what the law, weakened by the flesh, could not do* (Rom 8:3).

1023. Then when he says, *therefore, my beloved brethren*, he adds an admonition. For as it was said, the false apostles were destroying the Corinthians by denying the resurrection, and so, after he established faith in the resurrection, and displayed it through examples, he admonishes them to occupy themselves with good, and not be seduced by the false apostles.

And concerning this he does three things. First, he confirms them in the faith, saying, *therefore*, namely, with the resurrection already displayed, *my brethren* by faith, by which we are all sons of God: *he gave power to become children of God* (John 1:12) *beloved*, through love which we owe to love one another: *and this commandment we have from him, that he who loves God should love his brother also* (1 John 4:21) *be steadfast*, that is, in the faith of the resurrection, not withdrawing from faith: *so that we may no longer be children tossed to and fro* (Eph 4:14) *and unmovable*, that is, do not be seduced by others: *provided that you continue in the faith, stable and steadfast* (Col 1:23).

Second, he induces to good works, saying, *always abounding in the work of the Lord: so then, as we have opportunity, let us do good to all men* (Gal 6:10); *the righteousness of the blameless keeps his way straight* (Prov 11:5).

Third, he confirms them in hope, saying, *knowing that your labor is not in vain in the Lord: for the fruit of good labors is renowned* (Wis 3:15).

CHAPTER 16

Lecture 1

16:1De collectis autem, quae fiunt in sanctos, sicut ordinavi ecclesiis Galatiae, ita et vos facite. [n. 1024]

16:2Per unam sabbati unusquisque vestrum apud se seponat, recondens quod ei bene placuerit: ut non, cum venero, tunc collectae fiant.

16:3Cum autem praesens fuero, quos probaveritis per epistolas, hos mittam perferre gratiam vestram in Jerusalem. [n. 1028]

16:4Quod si dignum fuerit ut et ego eam, mecum ibunt.

16:5Veniam autem ad vos, cum Macedoniam pertransiero: nam Macedoniam pertransibo. [n. 1029]

16:6Apud vos autem forsitan manebo, vel etiam hiemabo: ut vos me deducatis quocumque iero. [n. 1031]

16:7Nolo enim vos modo in transitu videre, spero enim me aliquantulum temporis manere apud vos, si Dominus permiserit. [n. 1032]

16:8Permanebo autem Ephesi usque ad Pentecosten. [n. 1033]

16:9Ostium enim mihi apertum est magnum, et evidens: et adversarii multi.

16:1Περὶ δὲ τῆς λογείας τῆς εἰς τοὺς ἁγίους, ὥσπερ διέταξα ταῖς ἐκκλησίαις τῆς Γαλατίας, οὕτως καὶ ὑμεῖς ποιήσατε.

16:2κατὰ μίαν σαββάτου ἕκαστος ὑμῶν παρ' ἑαυτῷ τιθέτω θησαυρίζων ὅ τι ἐὰν εὐοδῶται, ἵνα μὴ ὅταν ἔλθω τότε λογεῖαι γίνωνται.

16:3ὅταν δὲ παραγένωμαι, οὓς ἐὰν δοκιμάσητε, δι' ἐπιστολῶν τούτους πέμψω ἀπενεγκεῖν τὴν χάριν ὑμῶν εἰς Ἰερουσαλήμ:

16:4ἐὰν δὲ ἄξιον ᾖ τοῦ κἀμὲ πορεύεσθαι, σὺν ἐμοὶ πορεύσονται.

16:5Ἐλεύσομαι δὲ πρὸς ὑμᾶς ὅταν Μακεδονίαν διέλθω, Μακεδονίαν γὰρ διέρχομαι:

16:6πρὸς ὑμᾶς δὲ τυχὸν παραμενῶ ἢ καὶ παραχειμάσω, ἵνα ὑμεῖς με προπέμψητε οὗ ἐὰν πορεύωμαι.

16:7οὐ θέλω γὰρ ὑμᾶς ἄρτι ἐν παρόδῳ ἰδεῖν, ἐλπίζω γὰρ χρόνον τινὰ ἐπιμεῖναι πρὸς ὑμᾶς, ἐὰν ὁ κύριος ἐπιτρέψῃ.

16:8ἐπιμενῶ δὲ ἐν Ἐφέσῳ ἕως τῆς πεντηκοστῆς:

16:9θύρα γάρ μοι ἀνέῳγεν μεγάλη καὶ ἐνεργής, καὶ ἀντικείμενοι πολλοί.

16:1Now concerning the collections that are made for the saints: as I have given order to the churches of Galatia, so do you also. [n. 1024]

16:2On the first day of the week, let every one of you put apart with himself, laying up what shall well please him: that when I come, the collections be not then to be made.

16:3And when I shall be with you, whomsoever you shall approve by letters, them will I send to carry your grace to Jerusalem. [n. 1028]

16:4And if it be meet that I also go, they shall go with me.

16:5Now I will come to you, when I shall have passed through Macedonia. For I shall pass through Macedonia. [n. 1029]

16:6And with you perhaps I shall abide, or even spend the winter: that you may bring me on my way wherever I shall go. [n. 1031]

16:7For I will not see you now by the way: for I trust that I shall abide with you some time, if the Lord permit. [n. 1032]

16:8But I will tarry at Ephesus, until Pentecost. [n. 1033]

16:9For a great and evident door is opened unto me: and many adversaries.

1024. Supra per totam seriem epistolae proposuit Apostolus Corinthiis quamdam doctrinam generalem, in hoc ultimo capite proponit eis quaedam specialia et familiaria.

Et circa hoc duo facit.

Primo monet eos quid ipsi debeant aliis facere;

secundo ostendit quid alii faciant ipsis, ibi *salutat vos ecclesia*, et cetera.

Circa primum duo facit.

Primo instruit eos de his quae debent facere ad absentes;

1024. Above, through the entire succession of the letter, the Apostle proposed to the Corinthians a general teaching; in this final chapter, he proposes to them a special and particular teaching.

And concerning this he does two things.

First, he instructs them about what they ought to do for others;

second, he shows what others would do for them, at *the churches of Asia greet you* (1 Cor 16:19).

Concerning the first, he does two things.

First, he instructs them about what they should do in his absence;

387

secundo vero de his quae debent facere ad praesentes, ibi *vigilate et state in fide*, et cetera.

Circa primum tria facit.

Primo instruit eos de his quae pertinent ad absentes pauperes sanctos, qui sunt in Ierusalem;

secundo de his quae pertinent ad Apostolum, ibi *veniam ad vos*, etc.;

tertio de his quae pertinent ad discipulos, ibi *si autem venerit*, et cetera.

Circa ea quae debent fieri sanctis, qui erant in Ierusalem, de tribus instruit eos Apostolus.

Primo qualiter eleemosyna sanctis facienda sit colligenda;

secundo qualiter sit conservanda, ibi *unusquisque autem vestrum*, etc.;

tertio qualiter sit in Ierusalem transmittenda, ibi *cum autem praesens fuero*, et cetera.

1025. Circa primum sciendum est, quod, sicut legitur Act. IV, 34 s., mos erat in primitiva Ecclesia, ut conversi ad fidem venderent possessiones et omnia quae habebant, et pretium ponerent ad pedes apostolorum, et de eis unicuique (prout erat opus) provideretur, ut sic nullus haberet proprium, sed essent illis omnia communia. Et, sicut dicitur in collationibus patrum, omnis religio ab illa sancta societate sumpsit exordium.

Contigit autem ut fame pervalida exorta, pauperes sancti, qui erant in Ierusalem, inopia maxima laborarent. Unde factum est, ut apostoli ordinarent ad ipsorum subventionem, quod per alias ecclesias Christi collectae fierent, et haec commissio facta est Paulo et Barnabae, Gal. II, 9: *dederunt mihi et Barnabae*, et cetera. Et quia Apostolus super hoc sollicitus erat, monebat illos, quos converterat, ut eis subvenirent, quia, sicut ipse ad Romanos dicit, iustum est, ut a quibus spiritualia receperant, temporalia ministrent. Et hoc est quod dicit *de collectis autem quae fiunt* per Ecclesias *in sanctos*, id est in usum sanctorum, et non quorumlibet. Eccle. XII, v. 5: *da iusto, et ne recipias peccatorem*. Non quod peccatoribus non sit aliquid dandum, sed quia magis debet quis dare eleemosynam iusto indigenti quam peccatori.

Sicut ordinavi in ecclesia Galatiae, ita et vos facite, id est colligite, *per unam*, scilicet diem, *sabbati*, id est, septimanae. Et hoc ideo ordinatum est, ut paulatim qualibet hebdomada aliquid parvum solverent, ne si simul totum solvissent, gravarentur. Et licet eis paululum videretur, et quasi insensibile, paulatim dare, tamen, completo anno, eleemosynae in simul collectae, magnae erant.

second, about what they should do in the present, at *watch: stand fast in the faith* (1 Cor 16:13).

Concerning the first, he does three things.

First, he instructs them about what in his absence pertains to the poor saints who are in Jerusalem;

second, about those things that pertain to the Apostle, at *now I will come to you*;

third, about those things that pertain to the disciples, at *now if Timothy comes* (1 Cor 16:10).

The Apostle instructs them about three things concerning what ought to happen for the saints who are in Jerusalem.

First, how the alms to be prepared for the saints are to be collected;

second, how the alms are to be kept, at *let every one of you put apart with himself*;

third, how they are to be sent to Jerusalem, at *and when I shall be with you*.

1025. Concerning the first, it should be understood that, as it is written in Acts, it was the custom in the early Church that those converted to the faith would sell their possessions and all they have, and would place the value at the feet of the apostles, and from these each one (according as there was need) would be provided for, so that no one would have property, but that all things would be in common for them (Acts 4:34ff). But it happens that due to a great, rising famine, the poor saints in Jerusalem were laboring under a great want.

Hence it happened that the Apostles ordained for the rendering of assistance to them, that there be a collection by other Christian churches, and this commission was made to Paul and Barnabas: *they gave to me and Barnabas the right hand of fellowship . . . only they would have us remember the poor* (Gal 2:9–10). And because the Apostle was solicitous about this, he instructed those who converted, that they should render assistance to them, because just as he said to the Romans, it is right that whoever receives spiritual goods should supply temporal ones. And this is what he says: *now concerning the collections* by the churches *for the saints*, i.e., for the use of the saints, and not for whatever use: *do good to the humble, but do not give to the ungodly* (Sir 12:5). Not that there is not something that is to be given to sinners, but because with more reason ought one to give alms to the indigent just man than to the sinner.

As I have given order to the churches of Galatia, so do you also, i.e., to collect, *on the first day of the week*, i.e., the seventh day. And this was ordained, so that little by little a small amount might be set aside in any given week, and they might not, if all at once it were set aside, be burdened. And although it might seem very little to them, as if imperceptible to give little by little, yet over an entire year the alms were greater than in one single collection.

1026. Vel per *unam sabbati* intelligitur prima dies post sabbatum, scilicet Dies Dominicus.

Et hoc ideo illo die fieri voluit Apostolus, quia iam inoleverat consuetudo, ut populus in Dominicis Diebus ad ecclesiam conveniret. Lev. XXIII, 35: *dies primus celeberrimus erit atque sanctissimus*, et cetera. Et post: *est enim coetus atque collectae*, et cetera. De huiusmodi eleemosyna dicitur Dan. IV, 24: *peccata tua eleemosynis redime*; et Eccli. XXIX, v. 15: *eleemosyna viri quasi sacculus*, et cetera.

1027. Quia vero non solum debet apponi modus in colligendo, sed etiam in conservando, ideo consequenter instruit qualiter collectae conserventur, cum dicit *unusquisque autem vestrum*, et cetera. In quo ostenditur maxima industria Apostoli, ne aliqui crederent quod Apostolus faceret collectas istas magis causa quaestus proprii, quam propter necessitatem sanctorum. Ideo suspicionem hanc vitans, et quantum ad se et quantum ad suos ministros, noluit dictam pecuniam a se, seu a suis ministris custodiri, sed ordinavit quod quilibet illud quod sibi placebat elargiri, reportaret domi et conservaret seorsum, faciens sic per totum annum. Et huius ratio erat, quia Apostolus nolebat, quod quando veniret Corinthum, vacarent collectis, sed doctrinae et rebus spiritualibus. Et ideo dicit *ut non cum venero*, et cetera. Act. VI, 2: *non est aequum nos relinquere*, et cetera.

Notandum est ergo quod quilibet debet cavere sibi, ne videatur aliquid spirituale facere propter quaestum, et inde est quod Dominus, Matth. X, 9 voluit praedicatores nihil habere. Romanis etiam mos erat, ut nullus assumeretur ad senatus officium, nisi prius probatus fuisset in officio quaestoris, quia virtutis est magnae res temporales custodire.

1028. Qualiter autem debeant mitti in Ierusalem, subdit, dicens *cum autem praesens fuero*, etc., quasi dicat: nec in hoc volo aliquos specialiter onerare, *cum praesens fuero*, scilicet ad portandum pecuniam, sed *mittam illos quos probaveritis*, id est approbaveritis mittendos, *mittam*, inquam, *per epistolas*, id est cum epistolis missis a vobis et a nobis, laudatoriis et commendatoriis, scilicet in quibus contineatur quantitas pecuniae, commendatum studium nostrum et caritas.

Mittam, inquam, *perferre gratiam vestram*, id est quod gratis dabitis sanctis pauperibus, *in Ierusalem*. II Cor. VIII, 1: *notam facimus vobis gratiam Dei*, et cetera. *In Ierusalem*, id est sanctis qui sunt in Ierusalem.

Et non solum mittam illos quos probaveritis, sed *si dignum fuerit*, etc., id est si magna quantitas fuerit, *mecum ibunt*, in quo inducit eos ad bene et liberaliter

1026. Or by *on the first day of the week*, is understood the first day after the sabbath, namely, the Lord's Day.

And this is what the Apostle wanted to happen on that day, because the custom was already in force, that the people would gather in the church on the Lord's Days: *on the first day shall be a holy convocation . . . it is a solemn assembly; you shall do not laborious work* (Lev 23:35–36). And in this way are alms described: *break off your sins by practicing almsgiving, and your iniquities by showing mercy to the oppressed* (Dan 4:24); and *the alms of a man is as a seal with him* (Sir 29:15).

1027. Because not only the manner of collecting ought to be applied, but also of setting aside, he then instructs them how the collections should be set aside, when he says, *let every one of you put apart with himself*. In this is shown the greatest skill of the Apostle, so that no one should believe that the Apostle would make these collections more for the sake of his own profit, than for the sake of the needs of the saints. Therefore, evading this suspicion, both as to himself and his ministers, he was unwilling that the money spoken of be kept by himself or by his ministers, but he established that whoever was ready to distribute that money take it home and keep it himself, doing this for the whole year. And it was for this reason, because the Apostle was unwilling, when he should come to Corinth, that they attend to the collections, but rather to teaching and to spiritual things. Thus he says *when I come, the collections be not then to be made*: *it is not right that we should give up preaching the word of God to serve tables* (Acts 6:2).

Therefore it should be noted that everyone should take care, lest he seem to do something spiritual for the sake of profit, and that is precisely what the Lord wished preachers to have nothing to do with (Matt 10:9). It was also the custom among the Romans, that no one would be installed in the office of senator unless first he had been proved in the office of treasurer, for it takes greater virtue to keep temporal things.

1028. He adds how the alms should be sent to Jerusalem, saying, *when I shall be with you*. As if to say: I do not wish in this to burden any especially, namely for bearing the money, *whomsoever you shall approve by letter, them will I send*, i.e., the ones you will approve for sending, *will I send*, I say, *by letter*, i.e., with letters sent from you and from us, with praises and commendations, namely, in which will be contained a sum of money, our zeal and love commended.

Will I send, I say, *to carry your grace*, i.e., what you will give generously to the poor saints *to Jerusalem*: *we want you to know, brethren, about the grace of God which has been shown in the churches of Macedonia* (2 Cor 8:1). *To Jerusalem*, i.e., to the saints who are in Jerusalem.

And not only will I send those whom you accredit, but *if it be meet that I also go*, i.e., if there will be a great quantity, *they shall go with me*, by which he leads them to contribute

solvendum. Rom. XV, 25: *nunc igitur proficiscar Ierusalem ministrare sanctis*, et cetera.

1029. Consequenter Apostolus instruit eos de his quae pertinent ad seipsum. Et circa hoc tria facit. Primo promittit eis suam praesentiam, dicens **veniam ad vos, cum Macedoniam pertransiero**, etc.; secundo dicit se facturum apud eos diutinam moram; tertio excusat suae praesentiae dilationem.

1030. Circa primum sciendum est, quod, sicut dicitur Act. XVI, 9, vir Macedo apparuit apostolo cum esset in Troade, deprecans eum, et dicens ei: *transiens in Macedoniam libera nos.* Ut ergo Apostolus iussa impleret, disposuit se Macedoniam iturum. Et quia Macedonia erat media inter Asiam et Achaiam, in qua est Corinthus, ideo dicit **cum pertransiero in Macedoniam, veniam ad vos**, imo veniam ad vos inde, scilicet quia tunc ero vobis propior.

1031. Secundo promittit se facturum apud eos diutinam moram, dicens **apud vos forsitan manebo**, id est moram contraham, **vel etiam hyemabo**, id est per totam hyemem permanebo vobiscum, quia multa corrigenda sunt in vobis.

Vel, causam quare ad eos vadit, subdit, cum dicit **ut vos me deducatis quocumque iero**. Et dicit **quocumque**, quia nesciebat determinare quo iret, nisi secundum quod Spiritus Sanctus inspirabat sibi. **Deducatis**, inquam, non defendatis me, sed ut doceatis vias.

1032. Tertio cum dicit **nolo enim vos**, etc., excusat dilationem suae praesentiae dupliciter.

Uno modo, quia Corinthii possent dicere: non est necesse quod tantum differas venire et quod primo vadas in Macedoniam, quia tu potes venire in Achaiam et permanere, ita quod non transeas per Macedoniam. Et ad hoc dicit: licet sic possem venire ad vos, tamen non diu possem manere vobiscum, quia statim oportet me ire in Macedoniam, vel redire in Asiam. Unde quia nolo vos modo in transitu videre, ideo modo non venio primo ad vos: nam ego spero aliquam moram contrahere vobiscum, **si Dominus permiserit**.

Dicit **si Dominus permiserit**, quia forte vel antequam esset ibi, vel postquam iam esset ibi, Dominus inspiraret ei quod iret ad alium locum, ubi faceret maius bonum.

1033. Alio modo excusat se, et hoc videtur magis litterale, quia oportebat eum diu manere apud Ephesum, quae est in Asia. Et ideo dicit **permanebo autem Ephesi usque ad Pentecosten**, et cetera. Forte haec epistola missa fuit in hyeme, seu in vere, et tunc post Pentecosten debebat ire in Macedoniam et morari ibi usque ad hyemem, et tunc ire Corinthum et hyemare.

well and liberally: *at present, however, I am going to Jerusalem with aid for the saints* (Rom 15:25).

1029. Next, the Apostle instructs them about the things that pertain to himself. And concerning this he does three things. First, he promises them his arrival, saying, *I will come to you, when I shall have passed through Macedonia*. Second, he says that he is about to spend a long time with them; third, he excuses the postponement of his arrival.

1030. Concerning the first it should be understood that, as it says in Acts, a man of Macedonia appeared to the Apostle when he was in Troas, beseeching him and saying to him: *come over to Macedonia and help us* (Acts 16:9). Therefore, so that the Apostle might fulfill the entreaties, he prepared himself to go to Macedonia. And because Macedonia was halfway between Asia and Achaia where Corinth is, he says, *I will come to you, when I shall have passed through Macedonia*, that is, I will come to you from that place, namely, because then I will be nearer to you.

1031. Second, he promises that he will spend a long time with them, saying, *and with you perhaps I shall abide*, i.e., I will restrict the time, *or even spend the winter*, i.e., for the whole winter I will abide with you, because there are many things to be corrected among you.

Or, he adds the reason for why he is going to them when he says, *that you may bring me on my way wherever I shall go*. And he says, *wherever*, because he was unable to determine where he would go, except according to what the Holy Spirit was inspiring him. *You may bring*, I say, not that you may protect me, but that you may show the way.

1032. Third, when he says, *for I will not see you now*, he excuses the postponement of his arrival in two ways.

In one way, because the Corinthians could say: it is not necessary that you defer coming and that you first go to Macedonia, because you could come to Achaia and remain, so that you do not pass through Macedonia. And to this he says: although I could come to you in this way, I could not stay with you for long, because I have to go to Macedonia or return to Asia. Hence, because I am unwilling to see you in passing, I am not coming to you in this way. For I hope to join you for some time, *if the Lord permits*.

He says, *if the Lord permits*, because perhaps either before he is there, or already after he is there, the Lord may inspire him to go to another place where he might accomplish a greater good.

1033. In another way, he excuses himself, and this would seem the more literal meaning, because it was necessary for him to remain for a long time at Ephesus, which is in Asia. And so he says, *but I will tarry at Ephesus until Pentecost*. Perhaps this letter was sent in winter, or in the spring, and then after Pentecost he had to go to Macedonia and stay there until winter, and then go to Corinth and winter there.

Rationem autem quare volebat morari Ephesi usque ad Pentecosten, subdit, cum dicit **ostium autem**, etc., id est, magnum fructum facio in Epheso. Et dicit **ostium** esse apertum **magnum**, id est multa corda hominum ad credendum parata, **et evidens**, quia sine contradictione. Col. IV, 3: *orantes simul et pro nobis, ut Deus aperiat nobis ostium*, et cetera.

Sed quia sunt **multi adversarii**, qui conantur impedire vel subintrare, si ergo absentarem me, tantus fructus posset de facili impediri, ideo nolo recedere quousque sitis bene firmati. Apoc. III, 8: *ecce dedi coram te ostium apertum*.

He adds the reason for why he wanted to stay in Ephesus until Pentecost when he says, ***for a great and evident door is opened unto me***, i.e., I am producing great fruit in Ephesus. And he says, ***a great . . . door***, i.e., many human hearts prepared for believing, ***and evident***, because it is without contradiction: *and pray for us also, that God may open to us a door for the word* (Col 4:3).

But because there are ***many adversaries***, who are attempting to hinder or steal away, if then I am absent, much fruit may easily be hindered; thus I am unwilling to draw back until you are well established: *behold, I have set before you an open door* (Rev 3:8).

Lecture 2

16:10Si autem venerit Timotheus, videte ut sine timore sit apud vos: opus enim Domini operatur, sicut et ego. [n. 1034]

16:11Ne quis ergo illum spernat: deducite autem illum in pace, ut veniat ad me: exspecto enim illum cum fratribus.

16:12De Apollo autem fratre vobis notum facio, quoniam multum rogavi eum ut veniret ad vos cum fratribus: et utique non fuit voluntas ut nunc veniret: veniet autem, cum ei vacuum fuerit. [n. 1036]

16:13Vigilate, state in fide, viriliter agite, et confortamini. [n. 1037]

16:14Omnia vestra in caritate fiant.

16:15Obsecro autem vos fratres, nostis domum Stephanae, et Fortunati, et Achaici: quoniam sunt primitiae Achaiae, et in ministerium sanctorum ordinaverunt seipsos: [n. 1039]

16:16ut et vos subditi sitis ejusmodi, et omni cooperanti, et laboranti.

16:17Gaudeo autem in praesentia Stephanae, et Fortunati, et Achaici: quoniam id, quod vobis deerat, ipsi suppleverunt: [n. 1041]

16:18refecerunt enim et meum spiritum, et vestrum. Cognoscite ergo qui hujusmodi sunt.

16:19Salutant vos ecclesiae Asiae. [n. 1042] Salutant vos in Domino multum, Aquila et Priscilla cum domestica sua ecclesia: apud quos et hospitor.

16:20Salutant vos omnes fratres. Salutate invicem in osculo sancto.

16:21Salutatio, mea manu Pauli. [n. 1044]

16:10Ἐὰν δὲ ἔλθῃ Τιμόθεος, βλέπετε ἵνα ἀφόβως γένηται πρὸς ὑμᾶς, τὸ γὰρ ἔργον κυρίου ἐργάζεται ὡς κἀγώ:

16:11μή τις οὖν αὐτὸν ἐξουθενήσῃ. προπέμψατε δὲ αὐτὸν ἐν εἰρήνῃ, ἵνα ἔλθῃ πρός με, ἐκδέχομαι γὰρ αὐτὸν μετὰ τῶν ἀδελφῶν.

16:12Περὶ δὲ Ἀπολλῶ τοῦ ἀδελφοῦ, πολλὰ παρεκάλεσα αὐτὸν ἵνα ἔλθῃ πρὸς ὑμᾶς μετὰ τῶν ἀδελφῶν: καὶ πάντως οὐκ ἦν θέλημα ἵνα νῦν ἔλθῃ, ἐλεύσεται δὲ ὅταν εὐκαιρήσῃ.

16:13Γρηγορεῖτε, στήκετε ἐν τῇ πίστει, ἀνδρίζεσθε, κραταιοῦσθε:

16:14πάντα ὑμῶν ἐν ἀγάπῃ γινέσθω.

16:15Παρακαλῶ δὲ ὑμᾶς, ἀδελφοί: οἴδατε τὴν οἰκίαν Στεφανᾶ, ὅτι ἐστὶν ἀπαρχὴ τῆς Ἀχαΐας καὶ εἰς διακονίαν τοῖς ἁγίοις ἔταξαν ἑαυτούς:

16:16ἵνα καὶ ὑμεῖς ὑποτάσσησθε τοῖς τοιούτοις καὶ παντὶ τῷ συνεργοῦντι καὶ κοπιῶντι.

16:17χαίρω δὲ ἐπὶ τῇ παρουσίᾳ Στεφανᾶ καὶ Φορτουνάτου καὶ Ἀχαϊκοῦ, ὅτι τὸ ὑμέτερον ὑστέρημα οὗτοι ἀνεπλήρωσαν,

16:18ἀνέπαυσαν γὰρ τὸ ἐμὸν πνεῦμα καὶ τὸ ὑμῶν. ἐπιγινώσκετε οὖν τοὺς τοιούτους.

16:19Ἀσπάζονται ὑμᾶς αἱ ἐκκλησίαι τῆς Ἀσίας. ἀσπάζεται ὑμᾶς ἐν κυρίῳ πολλὰ Ἀκύλας καὶ Πρίσκα σὺν τῇ κατ' οἶκον αὐτῶν ἐκκλησίᾳ.

16:20ἀσπάζονται ὑμᾶς οἱ ἀδελφοὶ πάντες. Ἀσπάσασθε ἀλλήλους ἐν φιλήματι ἁγίῳ.

16:21Ὁ ἀσπασμὸς τῇ ἐμῇ χειρὶ Παύλου.

16:10Now if Timothy comes, see that he be with you without fear: for he works the work of the Lord, as I also do. [n. 1034]

16:11Let no man therefore despise him: but conduct him on his way in peace, that he may come to me. For I look for him with the brethren.

16:12And concerning our brother Apollo, I give you to understand that I much entreated him to come unto you with the brethren: and indeed it was not his will at all to come at this time. But he will come when he shall have leisure. [n. 1036]

16:13Watch: stand fast in the faith: do manfully and be strengthened. [n. 1037]

16:14Let all your things be done in charity.

16:15And I beseech you, brethren, you know the house of Stephanus, and of Fortunatus, and of Achaicus, that they are the firstfruits of Achaia, and have dedicated themselves to the ministry of the saints: [n. 1039]

16:16That you also be subject to such and to everyone who works with us and labors.

16:17And I rejoice in the presence of Stephanus and Fortunatus and Achaicus: because that which was wanting on your part, they have supplied. [n. 1041]

16:18For they have refreshed both my spirit and yours. Know them, therefore, that are such.

16:19The churches of Asia greet you. [n. 1042] Aquila and Priscilla greet you much in the Lord, with the church that is in their house, with whom I also lodge.

16:20All the brethren greet you. Greet one another with a holy kiss.

16:21The greeting of me, Paul, with my own hand. [n. 1044]

^{16:22}Si quis non amat Dominum nostrum Jesum Christum, sit anathema, Maran Atha. [n. 1045]	^{16:22}εἴ τις οὐ φιλεῖ τὸν κύριον, ἤτω ἀνάθεμα. Μαρανα θα.	^{16:22}If any man loves not our Lord Jesus Christ, let him be anathema, maranatha. [n. 1045]
^{16:23}Gratia Domini nostri Jesu Christi vobiscum.	^{16:23}ἡ χάρις τοῦ κυρίου Ἰησοῦ μεθ' ὑμῶν.	^{16:23}The grace of our Lord Jesus Christ be with you.
^{16:24}Caritas mea cum omnibus vobis in Christo Jesu. Amen.	^{16:24}ἡ ἀγάπη μου μετὰ πάντων ὑμῶν ἐν Χριστῷ Ἰησοῦ.	^{16:24}My charity be with you all in Christ Jesus. Amen.

1034. Hic instruit eos de his quae pertinent ad discipulos suos. Et

primo de his quae pertinent ad Timotheum,

secundo de his quae pertinent ad Apollo, ibi *de Apollo*, et cetera.

1035. De Timotheo tria mandat. Primo ut secure custodiatur, unde dicit *si autem venerit ad vos Timotheus, videte*, studeatis, *ut sine timore sit apud vos*. Forte aliqua commotio fuerat ibi propter pseudo-apostolos. II Cor. VII, 5: *foris pugnae, intus timores*, et cetera. Et hoc debetis facere, quia *opus Domini operatur, sicut et ego* praedicando. II Tim. IV, 5: *tu vero vigila, in omnibus labora*.

Secundo ut in honore habeatur, et ideo dicit *ne quis ergo illum spernat*. Et ratio huius est forte, quia iuvenis erat. I Tim. IV, 12: *nemo adolescentiam tuam spernat*. Lc. X, v. 16: *qui vos spernit, me spernit*.

Tertio ut pacifice deducatur, et hoc est quod dicit *deducite autem illum*, et cetera. Et ratio huius est quia *expecto illum cum fratribus*, qui sunt cum eo.

1036. *De Apollo*, et cetera. Iste est ille Apollo, de quo habetur Act. XVIII, 24, quod *Iudaeus quidam*, etc., et iste ivit in Achaiam, et fuit quasi specialis doctor eorum post apostolum, I Cor. III, 6: *ego plantavi, Apollo rigavit*, etc. et, ut Glossa dicit, episcopus erat. Et quia Corinthii male se habuerant, recesserat ab eis, et iverat ad apostolum. Postmodum vero Corinthii rogaverunt apostolum, ut remitteret illuc ipsum, ad quod respondet eis, dicens *de Apollo autem fratre*, quem rogastis remitti ad vos, *notum vobis facio*, tria.

Primo, preces meas sibi factas, *quoniam multum rogavi eum, ut veniret ad vos cum fratribus*. Et dicit: *rogavi eum*, licet possit praecipere, quia magnis viris non de facili debet fieri praeceptum. I Tim. V, 1: *seniorem obsecra*, et cetera. Eccle. XXXII, 1: *rectorem te posuerunt*, et cetera.

Sed numquid licuit sibi relinquere populum suum? Ad hoc dicendum quod, sicut Gregorius dicit, quando omnes subditi male se habent et nolunt corrigi, licet episcopo recedere ab eis. Unde quia isti erant tales, licuit ei.

1034. Here he instructs them concerning the things which pertain to his disciples.

And first, concerning things that pertain to Timothy;

second, concerning things that pertain to Apollo, at *concerning our brother Apollo*.

1035. Concerning Timothy, he enjoins three things. First, that he be kept free of concern; hence he says, *now if Timothy comes, see*, be diligent, *that he be with you without fear*. Perhaps there was a certain disturbance there because of the false apostles: *fighting without and fear within* (2 Cor 7:5). And this you ought to do because *he works the work of the Lord, as I also do* by preaching: *as for you, be vigilant in every labor* (2 Tim 4:5).

Second, that he be held in honor, and so he says: *let no man therefore despise him*. And the reason for this is perhaps because he was young: *let no one despise your youth* (1 Tim 4:12); *he who rejects you, rejects me* (Luke 10:16).

Third, that he be led in peace, and this is what he says: *but conduct him on his way in peace*. And the reason for this is because *I look for him with the brethren*, who are with him.

1036. *Concerning our brother Apollo*. This is the Apollo of whom Acts says, *a certain Jew* (Acts 18:24), and the one who went to Achaia and was, as it were, their special doctor after the Apostle: *I planted, Apollo watered* (1 Cor 3:6). And as the Gloss says, he was a bishop. And because the Corinthians had behaved badly, he withdrew from them and went to the Apostle. Afterwards, the Corinthians asked the Apostle to send him back there, to which he responds to them saying, *concerning our brother Apollo*, whom you asked to be sent back to you, *I give you to understand* three things.

First, my requests made to him, *I give you to understand that I much entreated him to come unto you with the brethren*. And he says, *I much entreated him*, although he could direct him, because with great men a command ought not to be made easily: *do not rebuke an older man but exhort him as you would a father* (1 Tim 5:1); *if they make you master of the feast, do not exalt yourself* (Sir 32:1).

But is it lawful for someone to abandon his people? To this should be said, as Gregory says, when all the subjects conduct themselves badly and are unwilling to be corrected, it is lawful for the bishop to withdraw from them. Hence,

Vel dicendum est, quod forte non erat episcopus eorum, sed specialiter praedicaverat eis.

Secundo, responsum Apollinis, quia renuit venire ad eos, ibi *et utique non fuit voluntas eius ut nunc*, et cetera. Et ratio huius est quia forte nondum erant bene correcti, vel quia ipse erat in aliis arduis occupatus.

Tertio, promittit eum aliquando ad eos iturum. Unde dicit *veniet autem cum ei vacuum*, id est opportunum, *fuerit*, scilicet quando vos eritis correcti.

1037. Consequenter, postquam instruxit eos quid debeant facere absentibus hic instruit eos qualiter se habeant ad praesentes.

Circa hoc duo facit.

Primo ostendit qualiter se habeant quantum ad omnes in communi;

secundo quantum ad quosdam in speciali, ibi *obsecro autem vos, fratres*.

1038. Instruit autem eos Apostolus in communi de tribus, scilicet de fide, de bona operatione et de modo bene operandi. Sed tamen istis tribus praemittit unum quod est omnibus necessarium, id est, sollicitudo. Unde dicit *vigilate* et orate. Lc. XII, 43: *beati servi illi, quos cum venerit Dominus, invenerit vigilantes*, etc., et, Matth. XXVI, 41: *vigilate et orate*, et cetera.

De fide ergo instruit, cum dicit *state*, scilicet *in fide*, Eph. VI, 14: *state succincti*, et cetera.

De bona operatione, cum dicit *viriliter*, id est fortiter, *agite*, quia *fides sine operibus mortua est*, Iac. II, 26.

Sed quia bona operatio non est attribuenda nobis sed Deo, ideo subdit *et confortamini* in Domino. Ps. XXX, 25: *viriliter agite, et confortetur cor vestrum*, et cetera.

De modo agendi, cum dicit *omnia vestra in caritate fiant*, id est, omnia debent referri ad finem caritatis, scilicet ut fiant propter Deum et proximum, Col. III, 14: *super omnia caritatem*, et cetera.

1039. Consequenter cum dicit *obsecro autem*, etc., instruit eos quomodo se habeant ad quosdam in speciali. Et

primo quantum ad illos qui videntur habere aliquam praerogativam in spiritualibus;

secundo quantum ad illos qui in corporalibus operibus, ibi *gaudeo autem*, et cetera.

1040. Dicit ergo *obsecro autem vos, fratres: nostis*, id est approbastis, *domum Stephanae, et fortunati, et*

because they were such as these, it was lawful for him. Or it should be said that perhaps he was not their bishop, but was preaching to them specially.

Second, the response of Apollo, because he refuses to come to them: *and indeed it was not his will at all to come at this time*. And the reason for this is perhaps because they were not yet properly corrected, or because he himself was occupied in other difficulties.

Third, he promises him that he should go to them at some time. Hence, he says, *but he will come when he shall have leisure*, i.e., opportunity; *he shall have*, namely, when you will be corrected.

1037. After he instructed them about what they ought to do with respect to those who were absent, he then instructs them how to conduct themselves with those who are present.

Concerning the first, he does two things.

First, he shows how they should conduct themselves as to all in common;

second, as to some in particular, at *and I beseech you, brethren*.

1038. The Apostle instructs them in common about three things, namely, about faith, about a good work, and about the manner of working well. But he presents first one thing that is more necessary than all these three, i.e., watchful care. Hence he says, *watch* and pray: *blessed is that servant whom his master when he comes will find so doing* (Luke 12:43); and *watch and pray that you may not enter into temptation* (Matt 26:41).

He instructs them about faith when he says, *stand fast*, i.e., *in the faith*: *stand, therefore* (Eph 6:14).

He instructs them about a good work when he says, *do manfully*, i.e., strongly, because *faith without works in dead* (Jas 2:26).

But because a good work should not be attributed to us, but to God, therefore he adds, *and be strengthened* in the Lord: *be strong and let your heart take courage* (Ps 31:25).

He instructs them about the manner of acting when he says, *let all that your things be done in charity*, i.e., all things should be referred to the end of charity, namely, that they might be done for the sake of God and neighbor: *and above all these put on love, which binds everything together in perfect harmony* (Col 3:14).

1039. Then when he says, *I beseech you*, he instructs them how they ought to conduct themselves with some in particular.

And first, as to those who seem to have a privilege in spiritual things;

second, as to those who seem to have a privilege in corporal works, at *and I rejoice*.

1040. Therefore he says, *I beseech you, brethren, you know*, i.e., you approve, *the house of Stephanus and of*

Achaici. Approbastis, inquam, propter duo, et quia *sunt primitiae*, id est primo conversi, quia ab ipso apostolo in primis baptizati, supra I, v. 16: *baptizavi autem*, etc., et quia magis devoti et prompti ad ministeria sanctorum, unde dicit *et in ministerio sanctorum ordinaverunt seipsos*. Rom. XII, 13: *necessitatibus sanctorum*, et cetera. Et ideo obsecro, *ut et vos subditi*, etc., Hebr. XIII, 17: *obedite praepositis*, et cetera. *Et omni cooperanti*, Phil. IV, v. 3: *adiuva eos qui mecum laboraverunt*. Sap. III, 15: *bonorum laborum gloriosus*, et cetera.

1041. Hic instruit eos quantum ad illos, qui praeeminent in ministeriis et potest dupliciter exponi. Uno modo ut dicatur *gaudeo autem in praesentia Stephanae, fortunati, et Achaici*, qui sunt praesentes vobis, quorum praesentia est vobis proficua. *Quoniam ipsi id quod vobis deerat, suppleverunt*, docendo vos. Et in hoc quidem *refecerunt spiritum meum*, inquantum gaudeo de bono vestro, *et* spiritum *vestrum*, inquantum instructi estis. Phil. IV, 5: *gavisus sum valde, quia inveni*, et cetera. Et ideo, quia sic se habuerunt, *ergo agnoscite*, id est, honorate eos, et cetera.

Alio modo, ut dicatur: *gaudeo in praesentia Stephanae, fortunati, et Achaici*, quia scilicet personaliter mecum sunt, et serviunt mihi, in quo supplent quod deerat vobis, id est, quod vos non poteratis mihi corporaliter exhibere. In quo quidem *refecerunt spiritum meum*, inquantum mihi servierunt, et paverunt me, et vestrum, inquantum de bono meo gaudetis, et ideo cognoscite, et cetera.

1042. *Salutant vos*, et cetera. Hic Apostolus insinuat quid alii faciant Corinthiis.

Et circa hoc duo facit.

Primo insinuat quomodo salutentur ab aliis;

secundo subdit suam salutationem, ibi *salutatio mea*, et cetera.

1043. Circa primum tria facit. Primo insinuat quomodo salutat eos tota ecclesia Asiae in communi. Unde dicit *salutant vos omnes ecclesiae Asiae*. Rom. ult.: *salutant vos omnes ecclesiae Christi*.

Secundo quomodo salutant eos specialiter hospites Pauli. Unde dicit *salutant vos in Domino multum, aquila*, et cetera. Isti erant hospites apostoli, et de his habetur Rom. XVI, v. 3 et Act. XVIII, 2 s.

Tertio quomodo salutant eos apostoli et familiares sui. Unde dicit *salutant vos omnes fratres*, qui scilicet mecum sunt, Phil. ult.: *salutant vos qui mecum sunt fratres*.

Fortunatus and of Achaicus. You approve them, I say, on account of two things: because *they are the firstfruits*, i.e., the first converted, because they were the first baptized by the Apostle himself: *I did baptize also the household of Stephanas* (1 Cor 1:16); and because all the more they were devoted and available for the service of the saints. Hence he says, *and have dedicated themselves to the ministry of the saints*: *contribute to the needs of the saints* (Rom 12:13). And so I urge *that you also be subject to such*: *obey your leaders and submit to them* (Heb 13:17). *And to everyone who works with us and labors*: *help them, for they have labored side by side with me* (Phil 4:3); or *the fruit of good labors is renowned* (Wis 3:15).

1041. He instructs them here as to those who are preeminent in ministry, and it can be expounded in two ways. In one way, so that it would say, *and I rejoice in the presence of Stephanus and Fortunatus and Achaicus*, who are present to you, whose presence is advantageous to you. *Because that which was wanting on your part, they have supplied*, by teaching you. And in this too *they have refreshed both my spirit*, insofar as I rejoice at your good; *and your* spirit as well, inasmuch as you are instructed: *I rejoice in the Lord greatly* (Phil 4:10). And so, because you have conducted yourselves in this way, *know them, therefore*, i.e., honor them.

In another way, so that it would say, *I rejoice in the presence of Stephanus and Fortunatus and Achaicus*, because namely, they are with me personally, and they serve me, by which they supply what was lacking from you, i.e., what you were not able to convey to me bodily. By this *they have refreshed both my spirit*, insofar as they have served me, and reverenced me; and refreshed your spirit insofar as you rejoice at my good, and so you acknowledge them, etc.

1042. *All the brethren greet you*. The Apostle mentions here what others do for the Corinthians.

And concerning this he does two things.

First, he mentions how they are greeted by others;

second, he adds his greeting, at *the greeting of me, Paul*.

1043. Concerning the first he does three things. First, he mentions how the whole church of Asia greets them together. Hence he says, *the churches of Asia greet you*: *all the churches of Christ greet you* (Rom 16:16).

Second, how the friends of Paul greet them in particular. Hence he says, *Aquila and Priscilla greet you much in the Lord*. There were friends of the Apostle, and concerning these it says in Romans: *greet Prisca and Aquila, my fellow workers in Christ Jesus* (Rom 16:3); *and he found a Jew named Aquila, a native of Pontus, lately come from Italy with his wife Priscilla* (Acts 18:2).

Third, how the Apostle and his intimate companions greet them. Hence he says, *all the brethren greet you*, who, namely, are with me: *all the saints greet you* (Phil 4:22).

Ex quo ergo omnes salutant vos, et vos etiam *salutate invicem in osculo sancto*, non libidinoso, quo mulier apprehensum deosculatur iuvenem, Prov. VII, 13, *non fraudulento, quo Iudas osculatus est Christum*, Matth. c. XXVI, 49.

1044. *Salutatio*, et cetera. Hic suam salutationem subdit, et circa hoc duo facit. Primo ponit titulum salutationis, dicens *salutatio mea*, scilicet scripta est, *manu mea Pauli*. Et hoc faciebat in epistolis suis propter quosdam, qui sub specie Apostoli scribebant falsas litteras. Unde ut non deciperentur, postquam scripta erat epistola per aliquem, in fine consequenter scribebat Apostolus manu sua.

1045. Secundo ponit ipsam salutationem, in qua, primo, male dicit malis, dicens *si quis non amat*, etc., *anathema sit*, id est separatus vel excommunicatus; *maranatha*, id est Dominus veniet; quasi dicat: qui non amat Dominum nostrum Iesum Christum, sit anathema in adventu Domini.

Sed numquid sunt excommunicandi omnes qui non sunt in caritate?

Respondeo. Dicendum, quod hoc intelligitur, si quis non amat Dominum Iesum Christum, id est fidem Christi, et isti sunt haeretici et sunt excommunicati. Vel si quis usque ad finem mortis non perseverat in amore Domini Iesu Christi, in adventu erit separatus a bonis.

1046. Secundo, benedicit bonis, bene optans eis, scilicet gratiam Christi, cum dicit *gratia Domini nostri Iesu Christi*. Et hoc optans, optat eis omne bonum, quia in gratia Domini nostri Iesu Christi continetur omne bonum.

Optat etiam eis caritatem suam, dicens *caritas mea*, etc., ut vos invicem et Deum diligatis ea caritate qua ego vos diligo, et non propter aliquod aliud nisi in Christo Iesu, id est propter amorem Christi.

Amen, id est fiat.

From this, therefore, all greet you, and furthermore, you *greet one another with a holy kiss*; not sensually, as a woman seizes and kisses a youth: *she seiz es him and kisses him* (Prov 7:13); not fraudulently, as Judas kissed Christ: *and he came up to Jesus at once and said: hail, Master! And he kissed him* (Matt 26:49).

1044. *The greeting of me, Paul*. He adds his greeting, and concerning this he does two things. First, he puts down a title of the greeting, saying, *the greeting of me*, namely is written, *with my own hand*. And he did this in his letters on account of some who wrote false letters under the name of the Apostle. Hence, so that they would not be deceived, after the letter was written by someone, the Apostle writes afterwards at the end in his own hand.

1045. Second, he set down the greeting itself, in which first, he speaks evil to evil ones, saying, *if any man loves not our Lord Jesus Christ, let him be anathema*, i.e., separated or excommunicated; *maranatha*, i.e., may the Lord come! As if to say: whoever does not love the Lord Jesus Christ is cursed at the coming of the Lord.

But should all be excommunicated who are not in charity?

I respond: it should be said that this is understood if someone does not love the Lord Jesus Christ, i.e., does not have faith in Christ, and these are heretics and are excommunicated. Or: if someone does not persevere to the point of death in the love of the Lord Jesus Christ, at his coming he will be separated from good things.

1046. Finally, he blesses the good ones, wishing them well, namely, the grace of Christ, when he says: *the grace of the Lord Jesus be with you*. And wishing this, he wishes them every good, because in the grace of our Lord Jesus Christ is contained every good.

Furthermore, he wishes them his love, saying, *my charity be with you all in Christ Jesus*, so that you might love one another and God, with the love by which I love you, and not on account of something other save in Christ Jesus, i.e., on account of the love of Christ.

Amen, i.e., so be it.

COMMENTARY ON THE SECOND LETTER
OF SAINT PAUL TO THE CORINTHIANS

Commentary on the Second Letter of Saint Paul to the Corinthians

Prologue

Isaiah 61:6

Vos autem sacerdotes Domini vocabimini: Ministri Dei nostri, dicetur vobis, fortitudinem gentium comedetis, et in gloria earum superbietis.	ὑμεῖς δὲ ἱερεῖς κυρίου κληθήσεσθε, λειτουργοὶ θεοῦ· ἰσχὺν ἐθνῶν κατέδεσθε καὶ ἐν τῷ πλούτῳ αὐτῶν θαυμασθήσεσθε.	But you shall be called the priests of the Lord: to you it shall be said: you ministers of our God: you shall eat the riches of the gentiles, and you shall pride yourselves in their glory.

1. In his verbis congrue tangitur materia huius secundae epistolae ad Corinthios. Nam in prima epistola agit Apostolus de ipsis sacramentis, sed in hac secunda agit de ministris ipsorum sacramentorum, tam bonis, quam malis.

Ratio autem hanc epistolam scribendi fuit, quod Corinthii, post praedicationem eius, admiserant pseudoapostolos, quos Apostolo praeferebant. Propter hoc scribit eis hanc epistolam, in qua commendat apostolos et ostendit verorum apostolorum dignitatem; ostendit etiam et vituperat falsorum apostolorum falsitatem.

2. Commendat autem verorum apostolorum dignitatem, ex hoc quod sunt ministri Dei. ***Ministri***, inquit, ***Dei, dicetur vobis***, scilicet apostolis, qui quidem dicuntur ministri quantum ad tria.

Primo quantum ad dispensationem sacramentorum. I Cor. IV, 1: *sic nos existimet homo, ut ministros, et cetera.* Christus enim institutor est sacramentorum, sed apostoli et eorum successores ea dispensant, et ideo subditur in praedicta auctoritate *et dispensatores mysteriorum Dei.*

Secundo quantum ad gubernationem, scilicet inquantum gubernant populum Dei. Sap. c. VI, 5: *cum essetis ministri, non recte iudicastis, et cetera.* Deus enim gubernat omnia per prudentiam. Unde quicumque aliquid gubernat, dicitur minister Dei.

Tertio quantum ad humanae salutis operationem, inquantum scilicet eorum ministerio et praedicatione, homines ad salutem conversi sunt: cuius salutis solus Deus est auctor, quia ipse est qui venit salvum facere quod perierat, apostoli vero ministri. I Cor. III, v. 4 s.: *quid ergo est Apollo? Quid Paulus? Ministri eius, cui credidistis, et cetera.*

1. The subject matter of this second epistle to the Corinthians is fittingly touched upon by these words. For in the first epistle the Apostle discussed the sacraments themselves, but in this second one he discusses the ministers of those sacraments, both good and bad.

The reason he wrote this epistle was that the Corinthians, after he had preached to them, welcomed certain false apostles, whom they preferred to the Apostle. Therefore he writes them this epistle, in which he commends the apostles and shows the dignity of the true apostles. He also shows and reproves the falseness of the false apostles.

2. He commends the dignity of the true apostles, because they are God's ministers. ***To you***, i.e., the apostles, ***it shall be said***: ***you ministers of our God***. They are called ministers under three aspects.

First, inasmuch as they dispense the sacraments: *this is how one should regard us, as servants of Christ* (1 Cor 4:1). For Christ instituted the sacraments, but the apostles and their successors dispense them; therefore the text just cited continues: *and stewards of the mysteries of God.*

Second, inasmuch as they govern the people of God: *because, as servants of his kingdom, you did not rule rightly, nor keep the law* (Wis 6:4). For God governs all things by his wisdom, so that whoever governs anyone is called God's minister.

Third, because they labor for the salvation of men, namely, inasmuch as many are converted by their ministry and preaching. But God alone is the author of man's salvation, because it was he who came to save that which had been lost; the apostles, however, are his ministers. *What then is Apollos? What is Paul? The ministers of him whom you have believed* (1 Cor 3:5).

CHAPTER 1

Lecture 1

^{1:1}Paulus, Apostolus Jesu Christi per voluntatem Dei, et Timotheus frater, ecclesiae Dei, quae est Corinthi cum omnibus sanctis, qui sunt in universa Achaia. [n. 3]

^{1:2}Gratia vobis, et pax a Deo Patre nostro, et Domino Jesu Christo. [n. 7]

^{1:1}Παῦλος ἀπόστολος Χριστοῦ Ἰησοῦ διὰ θελήματος θεοῦ καὶ Τιμόθεος ὁ ἀδελφὸς τῇ ἐκκλησίᾳ τοῦ θεοῦ τῇ οὔσῃ ἐν Κορίνθῳ σὺν τοῖς ἁγίοις πᾶσιν τοῖς οὖσιν ἐν ὅλῃ τῇ Ἀχαΐᾳ,

^{1:2}άρις ὑμῖν καὶ εἰρήνη ἀπὸ θεοῦ πατρὸς ἡμῶν καὶ κυρίου Ἰησοῦ Χριστοῦ.

^{1:1}Paul, an apostle of Jesus Christ by the will of God, and Timothy our brother: to the church of God that is at Corinth, with all the saints who are in all Achaia: [n. 3]

^{1:2}Grace unto you and peace from God our Father and from the Lord Jesus Christ. [n. 7]

---

3. De istis ergo ministris tractat hic Apostolus, ostendens in hac epistola eorum dignitatem etiam scribens Corinthiis. In qua quaedam praemittit.

Primo salutationem;

secundo prosequitur epistolam, ibi ***benedictus Deus***, et cetera.

In salutatione autem tria ponit:

primo enim describit personas salutantes;

secundo personas salutatas, ibi ***ecclesiae quae est***, etc.;

tertio bona optata, ibi ***gratia vobis***, et cetera.

Circa primum primo describitur persona salutans principalis, quia ***Paulus***;

secundo persona adiuncta, quia ***Timotheus***.

4. Persona salutans describitur ab humilitate, quia ***Paulus***, qui Latine dicitur modicus. Iste est ille modicus, de quo Is. LX, 22: *minimus erit in mille*, et cetera.

Vel a doctrina, quia Paulus dicitur os tubae. Ista est illa tuba de qua Zach. IX, 14: *Dominus in tuba canet*, et cetera. Et competit quod dicitur Is. LVIII, 1: *quasi tuba exalta vocem tuam*, et cetera.

A dignitatis auctoritate, quia ***apostolus***, et cetera. Ubi tria ponuntur. Primo quod sit legatus, unde dicitur ***apostolus***, id est principaliter missus. Soli enim duodecim apostoli electi missi sunt a Christo. Lc. VI, 13: *elegit duodecim, quos et apostolos*, et cetera. Alii autem discipuli non missi sunt principaliter, sed secundario. Et inde est quod apostolis succedunt episcopi, qui habent specialem curam gregis Domini. Alii autem sacerdotes succedunt septuaginta duobus discipulis, qui gerunt vices commissas sibi ab episcopis. Est ergo eius dignitas quia ***apostolus***. I Cor. IX, 2: *si aliis non sum apostolus, sed tamen*

3. In this epistle to the Corinthians, the Apostle treats of these ministers and points out their dignity: in which it was sent forth.

First, he gives his greeting;

second, he begins his message, at ***blessed be the God***.

In the greeting he does three things:

first, he mentions the persons who send the greeting;

second, those who are greeted, at ***to the church of God***;

third, the good things he wishes them, at ***grace unto you***.

In regard to the first he does two things: first, he mentions the principal person who sends the greeting, namely ***Paul***;

second, his companion, ***Timothy***.

4. The person who sends the greeting is described by his humility, because it is ***Paul***, which in Latin means 'humble.' He is that humble person of whom it is said: *the least one shall become a clan, and the smallest one a mighty nation* (Isa 60:22).

Or by his doctrine, because Paul is called the mouth of the trumpet. This is the trumpet mentioned in Zechariah: *the Lord God will sound the trumpet, and march forth in the whirlwinds of the south* (Zech 9:14). He fits what is said in Isaiah: *lift up your voice like a trumpet* (Isa 58:1).

By the authority of his dignity, because he says, ***an apostle of Jesus Christ***. Here he mentions three things: first, that he is a representative; hence, he is called an ***apostle***, i.e., principally sent, for only twelve apostles were sent by Christ. *He chose from them twelve, whom he named apostles* (Luke 6:13). But the other disciples were not sent principally, but secondarily. That is why the apostles are succeeded by bishops, who have a special care of the Lord's flock; but other priests succeed the seventy-two disciples and perform duties committed to them by the bishops. His dignity, therefore, is that he is an ***apostle***. *If to others I am not*

vobis sum, et cetera. Gal. II, 8: *qui operatus est Petro*, et cetera.

Sed quare vocat se hic apostolum, dicens ***Paulus apostolus***, cum in epistola ad Romanos scribit se servum?

Ratio huius est, quia Romanos reprehendit de dissensione et superbia, quae est mater dissensionis, quia *inter superbos semper iurgia sunt*. Unde ut eos revocet a dissensione, inducit eos ad humilitatem, vocando se servum. Corinthii vero erant pertinaces et rebelles, et ideo, ut reprimat eorum proterviam, usus est hic nomine dignitatis, dicens se apostolum.

Tertio ponitur modus quo adeptus est legationem, quia non iniecit se ut pseudo. Ier. c. XXIII, 21: *non mittebam eos, et ipsi currebant*. Non est datus populo ex divino furore, iuxta illud Iob XXXIV, 30: *qui facit regnare hypocritam*, et cetera. Osee XIII, 11: *dabo tibi regem, sed in furore meo*. Est adeptus apostolatum ex voluntate Dei et beneplacito. Act. IX, 15: *vas electionis est mihi iste*. Et ideo dicit ***per voluntatem Dei***.

Secundo ponitur cuius sit legatus, quia ***Iesu Christi***. Infra V, 20: ***pro Christo legatione fungimur***.

5. Persona autem adiuncta est Timotheus. Unde dicit ***et Timotheus frater***. Frater, inquam, propter fidem, Matth. XXIII, 8: *omnes vos fratres estis*, etc., et propter dignitatem, quia episcopus: et inde est quod Papa vocat omnes episcopos fratres.

Connumerat autem sibi Timotheum, quia cum ipse transisset per eos, sicut dixit in I Epist., ult. cap., possent credere quod malitiose retulisset apostolo ea de quibus ipse scribit ad eos.

6. Consequenter ponuntur personae salutatae, et primo principales, secundo adiunctae principalibus, in hoc quod dicit ***ecclesiae Dei***, quae est totus populus fidelis, tam clerici quam laici. I Tim. III, 15: *ut scias quomodo oporteat te conversari*. ***Quae est Corinthi***, quia Corinthus erat metropolis Achaiae.

Sed adiunctae personae sunt omnes sancti, qui sunt unius Spiritus Sancti gratia renati. I Cor. VI, 11: *sed abluti estis, sed sanctificati*, et cetera. ***Qui sunt in Achaia***, cuius metropolis est Corinthus.

7. Istis autem personis salutatis optat Apostolus bona. Unde dicit ***gratia vobis***, et cetera.

Et circa hoc duo facit.

Primo ponit ipsa bona;

secundo ipsorum auctorem, ibi ***a Deo Patre***, et cetera.

8. Ponit autem ista duo extrema bona, ut in eis intelligantur media.

an apostle, at least I am to you (1 Cor 9:2); *he who worked through Peter for the ministry to the circumcised worked through me also for the Gentiles* (Gal 2:8).

But why does Paul call himself an apostle, saying ***Paul, an apostle***, whereas in the epistle to the Romans he calls himself a servant?

The reason for this is that he rebuked the Romans for quarreling and for pride, which is the mother of quarrels, because *there are always disputes among the proud* (Prov 13:10). Hence to cure them of quarreling he leads them to humility by calling himself a servant. But the Corinthians were obstinate and rebellious; so in order to curb their boldness, he uses a dignified name here, calling himself an apostle.

Third, he mentions how he obtained his ambassadorship, because he is not coming as a false apostle. *I did not send them and they ran* (Jer 23:21); nor was he given to the people in God's anger in the sense of Job: *who makes a hypocrite to reign* (Job 34:30); *I have given you a king, but in my anger* (Hos 13:11). But he obtained apostleship by God's will and pleasure. *He is a chosen vessel of mine* (Acts 9:15). Therefore he says, ***by the will of God***.

Second, he mentions the one he represents, ***Jesus Christ***. *We are ambassadors for Christ* (2 Cor 5:20).

5. The other person is Timothy; hence he says, ***and Timothy our brother***. A brother, I say, because of the faith: *you are all brothers* (Matt 23:8), and because of his dignity, for he was a bishop. This is why the Pope calls all bishops brothers.

He mentions Timothy because, since Timothy had visited them, as he said in the first epistle, the people might believe that he had maliciously reported to the Apostle the things he is writing to them.

6. Then he mentions the persons greeted: first, the principal ones; second, those associated with the principal ones. He says, ***to the church of God***, which includes all believers, both the clergy and the laity: *that you may know how one ought to behave* (1 Tim 3:15); ***that is at Corinth***, because Corinth was the chief city of Achaia.

But those associated with the principal ones are all the saints who are reborn by the grace of the one Holy Spirit: *but you were washed, you were sanctified, in the Spirit of our God* (1 Cor 6:11); ***who are in Achaia***, whose chief city is Corinth.

7. The Apostle wishes good things to the persons greeted; hence, he says, ***grace unto to you***.

In regard to this he does two things:

first, he mentions the good things;

second, their author, at ***from God our Father***.

8. He mentions these two gifts as two extremes, between which are contained all other goods.

Primum enim bonum est gratia, quae est principium omnium bonorum. Nam ante gratiam nihil est nisi diminutum in nobis.

Ultimum autem omnium bonorum est pax, quia pax est generalis finis mentis. Nam qualitercumque pax accipiatur, habet rationem finis; et in gloria aeterna et in regimine et in conversatione, finis est pax. Ps. CXLVII, 3: *qui posuit fines tuos pacem.*

9. Quis autem sit auctor horum bonorum ostendit, subdens ***a Deo Patre***, et cetera. Et haec duo possunt dupliciter distingui, quia cum dicit ***a Deo Patre***, potest intelligi pro tota Trinitate.

Nam, licet persona Patris dicatur Pater Christi per naturam, tamen tota Trinitas est Pater noster per creationem et gubernationem. Is. LXIII, 16: *et nunc, Domine, Pater noster es tu.* Ier. III, 19: *Patrem vocabis me.* A Deo ergo Patre nostro, id est a tota Trinitate proveniunt bona. Matth. VII, 11: *si vos cum sitis mali*, et cetera.

Sed si ***Deus Pater noster*** accipiatur pro tota Trinitate, quare additur persona Filii, cum dicit ***et Domino Iesu Christo***? Numquid est alia persona a Trinitate?

Dicendum quod additur non propter aliam personam sed propter aliam naturam, scilicet humanitatis assumptae a Filio in personam divinam: quam quidem Trinitati connumerat, quia omnia bona proveniunt nobis a Trinitate per Incarnationem Christi; et primo gratia, Io. I, 17: *gratia et veritas*, etc., secundo pax, Eph. II, 14: *ipse est pax nostra*, et cetera.

10. Item cum dicit ***a Deo Patre nostro***, potest intelligi persona Patris solum; et, licet tota Trinitas sit Pater noster, ut dictum est, tamen persona Patris est Pater noster per appropriationem; et sic hoc quod dicit ***et Domino Iesu Christo***, intelligitur de persona Filii.

De persona autem Spiritus Sancti non fit hic mentio, quia, sicut dicit Augustinus, cum sit nexus Patris et Filii, ubicumque ponitur persona Patris et persona Filii, intelligitur persona Spiritus Sancti.

For the first good is grace, which is the beginning of all good things; because before grace there is only a diminished goodness in us.

The last of all goods is peace, because peace is the general end of the mind; for no matter how peace is defined, it has the character of an end. In eternal glory, in government and in the way one lives, the end is peace: *he makes peace in your borders* (Ps 147:14).

9. He indicates the author of these goods when he says, ***from God our Father and from the Lord Jesus Christ***. These two expressions can be distinguished in two ways, because, when he says, ***from God our Father***, it can be referred to the entire Trinity.

For although the person of the Father is called the Father of Christ by nature, the entire Trinity is our Father by creation and governance: *for you are our Father* (Isa 63:16); *you would call me Father* (Jer 3:19). Therefore good things come from God our Father, i.e., from the entire Trinity: *if you, then, who are evil, know how to give good gifts to your children, how much more will your Father who is in heaven give good things to those who ask him* (Matt 7:11).

But if ***God our Father*** is taken for the entire Trinity, why is the person of the Son added, when he says, ***and from the Lord Jesus Christ***? Is there another person in the Trinity?

I answer that he is added, not as though he were an additional person, but on account of another nature, namely, of the humanity assumed by the Son to the divine person. The reason he lists him along with the Trinity is that all good things come to us from the Trinity through the Incarnation of Christ, first of all grace: *grace and truth came through Jesus Christ* (John 1:17), and second peace: *he is our peace* (Eph 2:14).

10. Again, when he says, ***from God our Father***, it can be taken to mean the person of the Father alone; and although the entire Trinity is our Father, as has been said, the person of the Father is our Father by appropriation. Then ***from the Lord Jesus Christ*** can be referred to the person of the Son.

No mention is made of the Holy Spirit because, as Augustine says, since he is the nexus of the Father and the Son, whenever the person of the Father and the person of the Son are mentioned, the person of the Holy Spirit is also understood.

Lecture 2

1:3Benedictus Deus et Pater Domini nostri Jesu Christi, Pater misericordiarum, et Deus totius consolationis, [n. 11]

1:4qui consolatur nos in omni tribulatione nostra: ut possimus et ipsi consolari eos qui in omni pressura sunt, per exhortationem, qua exhortamur et ipsi a Deo. [n. 14]

1:5Quoniam sicut abundant passiones Christi in nobis: ita et per Christum abundat consolatio nostra. [n. 17]

1:3Εὐλογητὸς ὁ θεὸς καὶ πατὴρ τοῦ κυρίου ἡμῶνἸησοῦ Χριστοῦ, ὁ πατὴρ τῶν οἰκτιρμῶν καὶ θεὸς πάσης παρακλήσεως,

1:4ὁ παρακαλῶν ἡμᾶς ἐπὶ πάσῃ τῇ θλίψει ἡμῶν εἰς τὸ δύνασθαι ἡμᾶς παρακαλεῖν τοὺς ἐν πάσῃ θλίψει διὰ τῆς παρακλήσεως ἧς παρακαλούμεθα αὐτοὶ ὑπὸ τοῦ θεοῦ.

1:5ὅτι καθὼς περισσεύει τὰ παθήματα τοῦ Χριστοῦ εἰς ἡμᾶς, οὕτως διὰ τοῦ Χριστοῦ περισσεύει καὶ ἡ παράκλησις ἡμῶν.

1:3Blessed be the God and Father of our Lord Jesus Christ, the Father of mercies and the God of all comfort: [n. 11]

1:4Who comforts us in all our tribulation, that we also may be able to comfort those who are in all distress, by the exhortation with which we also are exhorted by God. [n. 14]

1:5For as the sufferings of Christ abound in us: so also by Christ does our comfort abound. [n. 17]

---

11. Hic incipit epistola in qua Apostolus duo facit.

Primo enim excusat se de eo quod non iverat ad eos, sicut promiserat;

secundo prosequitur intentionem suam, cap. III, ibi *incipimus iterum*, et cetera.

Circa primum duo facit.

Primo ponit excusationem de mora;

secundo morae assignat causam, secundo cap., ibi *statui autem*, et cetera.

Circa primum duo facit.

Primo enim reddit eos benevolos;

secundo excusationem ponit, ibi *et hac confidentia*, et cetera.

Circa primum duo facit.

Primo captat eorum benevolentiam, recitando quaedam in generali;

secundo quaedam in speciali, ibi *non enim*, et cetera.

Benevolentiam autem eorum captat Apostolus ostendendo quod quidquid facit, totum facit ad eorum utilitatem.

Et circa hoc duo facit.

Primo praemittit utilitatem quae ex ipso aliis provenit;

secundo rationem eorum assignat, ibi *quoniam sicut abundant*, et cetera.

Circa primum tria facit.

Primo enim ponitur gratiarum actio;

secundo actionis gratiarum modus, ibi *qui consolatur*, etc.;

tertio causa, ibi *ut possimus et ipsi consolari*.

12. Agit ergo gratias toti Trinitati, a qua provenit omne bonum. Et ideo dicit *benedictus Deus*, id est tota Trinitas. Item personae Patris, cum dicit *et Pater Domini nostri Iesu Christi*, per quem, scilicet Christum, Pater nobis omnia donavit.

11. Here begins the message, in which the Apostle does two things:

first, he excuses himself for not visiting them as he had promised;

second, he begins to follow out his intention, in the third chapter, at *do we begin again* (2 Cor 3:1).

In regard to the first he does two things:

first, he sets out an excuse for his delay;

second, he gives a reason for the delay, in the second chapter, at *but I determined* (2 Cor 2:1).

In regard to the first he does two things:

first, he wins their good will;

second, he sets out an excuse, at *and in this confidence* (2 Cor 1:15).

Concerning the first, he does two things:

first, he wins their good will by citing some general facts;

second, some special ones, at *for we would not*.

The Apostle wins their good will by showing that whatever he does, it is all for their benefit.

In regard to this he does two things:

first, he mentions the profit others have obtained from him;

second, the reason, at *for as the sufferings of Christ abound*.

In regard to the first he does three things:

first, he gives thanks;

second, the manner of the thanks, at *who comforts*.

third, the cause, at *that we also may be able to comfort*.

12. He gives thanks, therefore, to the entire Trinity, the source of every good; hence he says, *blessed be the God*, i.e., the entire Trinity; and to the person of the Father when he says, *and Father of our Lord Jesus Christ*, through whom the Father has given us all things.

Sed sciendum quod nos benedicimus Deum, et Deus benedicit nobis, sed aliter et aliter. Nam dicere Dei, est facere. Ps. XXXII, 9: *dixit et facta sunt*. Unde benedicere Dei est bonum facere, et bonum infundere, et sic habet rationem causalitatis. Gen. I, 28, et XXII, v. 17: *benedicens benedicam tibi*, et cetera.

Dicere autem nostrum non est causale, sed recognoscitivum seu expressivum. Unde benedicere nostrum idem est quod bonum recognoscere. Cum ergo gratias agimus Deo, benedicimus sibi, id est recognoscimus eum bonum et datorem omnium bonorum. Tob. XII, v. 6: *benedicite Deum caeli*, et cetera. Dan. III, v. 57: *benedicite, omnia opera*, et cetera.

13. Recte ergo gratias agit Patri, quia misericors est, unde dicit **Pater misericordiarum**, et quia consolator, unde dicit **et Deus totius consolationis**.

Et agit gratias de duobus, quibus homines maxime indigent. Primo enim indigent, ut auferantur ab eis mala, et hoc facit misericordia, quae aufert miseriam; et misereri est proprium patri. Ps. CII, 13: *quomodo misereretur pater filiorum*, et cetera.

Secundo indigent ut sustententur in malis quae adveniunt. Et illud est proprie consolari, quia nisi homo haberet aliquid in quo quiesceret cor eius, quando superveniunt mala, non subsisteret. Tunc ergo aliquis consolatur aliquem, quando affert ei aliquod refrigerium, in quo quiescat in malis. Et licet in aliquibus malis homo possit in aliquo consolari et quiescere et sustentari, tamen solus Deus est, qui nos consolatur in omnibus malis. Et ideo dicit **Deus totius consolationis**; quia si peccas, consolatur te Deus, quia ipse misericors est. Si affligeris, consolatur te, vel eruendo ab afflictione per potentiam suam, vel iudicando per iustitiam. Si laboras, consolatur te remunerando, Gen. XV, 1: *ego merces tua*, et cetera. Et ideo dicitur Matth. V, 5: *beati qui lugent*, et cetera.

14. Materiam autem gratiarum actionis subdit dicens **qui consolatur**, et cetera. Quasi dicat: ideo benedictus, quia **consolatur nos in omni tribulatione**. Infra VII, 6: **qui consolatur**, et cetera.

15. Causam autem huius ponit, cum dicit **ut possimus et ipsi consolari**.

Ubi notandum est, quod in donis divinis est ordo. Ad hoc enim Deus dat aliquibus specialia dona, ut ipsi effundant illa in utilitatem aliorum. Non enim dat lumen soli, ut sibi soli luceat sed ut toti mundo. Unde vult quod de omnibus bonis nostris, sive sint divitiae, sive potentia, sive scientia, sive sapientia, accrescat aliqua utilitas aliis. I Petr. c. IV, 10: *unusquisque gratiam quam accepit*, et cetera.

It should be noted that we bless God and God blesses us, but in different ways. For when God speaks, he accomplishes: *he spoke and they were made* (Ps 148:5). Hence, for God to bless is to produce something good, and to infuse something good, and so to be a cause: *I will indeed bless you and multiply your descendants* (Gen 22:17).

But our speech does not cause things, but acknowledges or expresses them; hence, our blessing is the same as recognizing good. Therefore, when we thank God, we bless him, i.e., acknowledge that he is good and the giver of all good: *bless God and acknowledge him in the presence of all the living for the good things he has done for you* (Tob 12:6); *bless the Lord, all you works of the Lord; praise and exalt him above all for ever* (Dan 3:57).

13. It is fitting therefore that he thank the Father, because he is merciful; hence he says, **the Father of mercies**: and because he is a comforter he says, **and the God of all comfort**.

He thanks God for the two things men especially need: first, to have evil removed from them, and this is done by mercy which takes away misery, for it is characteristic of a father to have compassion: *as a father pities his children, so the Lord pities those who fear him* (Ps 103:13).

Second, they need to be supported in the face of evils which occur, and that is to receive comfort. Because unless a man had something in which his heart could rest, he would not stand firm when evils come upon him. Therefore a person comforts another by affording him something refreshing, in which he can rest in evil times. And although a man might be comforted by something and find rest and be supported by it in the case of some evils, it is God alone who comforts us in all evils; hence he says, **the God of all comfort**. For if you sin, God comforts you, because he is merciful; if you are afflicted, he comforts you either by rooting out the affliction by his power or by judging justly; if you labor, he comforts you with a reward: *I am your shield; your reward shall be very great* (Gen 15:1). Therefore, it is said: *blessed are those who mourn, for they shall be comforted* (Matt 5:5).

14. He tells us why he is thankful when he adds, **who comforts us in all our tribulation**. As if to say: he is blessed, because he **comforts us in all our tribulation**. **God who comforts the humble** (2 Cor 7:6).

15. He gives the reason for this when he says, **that we also may be able to comfort those who are in all distress**.

Here it should be noted that there is an order among God's gifts. For God gives special gifts to some, that they may pour them out for the benefit of others; for he does not give light to the sun in order that the sun may shine for itself alone, but for the whole world. Hence, God desires that some profit accrue to others from all our gifts, whether they be riches or power of knowledge or wisdom. *As each has received a gift, employ it for one another* (1 Pet 4:10).

Hoc est ergo quod Apostolus dicit *consolatur nos in omni tribulatione*.

16. Sed quare? Non ut solum nobis hoc sit ad bonum, sed etiam ut aliis prosit. Unde dicit *ut possimus et ipsi consolari eos*, et cetera.

Possumus enim consolari alios per exemplum consolationis nostrae. Qui enim non est consolatus, nescit consolari. Eccli. XXXIV, v. 11: *qui non est tentatus, qualia scit? Qui sunt in omni*, id est in qualibet *pressura*. Is. c. LXI, 1 s.: *Spiritus Domini misit me*, etc., *ut consolarer omnes lugentes*, etc., Eccli. c. XLVIII, 27: *consolatus est lugentes*, et cetera.

Possumus, dico, consolari *per exhortationem* ad tolerantiam passionum, promittendo praemia aeterna, *qua scilicet exhortamur* vos per Scripturas et internas inspirationes, ut patienter sustineamus, et alios exhortemur exemplo nostro, et per ipsas Scripturas. I Cor. c. XI, 23: *ego enim accepi a Domino*, et cetera. Is. XXI, 10: *quae audivi a Domino*, et cetera.

17. Posita utilitate quae ex apostolis aliis provenit, dictorum consequenter rationem assignat, dicens *quoniam sicut abundant*, et cetera.

Et quia duo dixerat, scilicet quod Deus *consolatur nos in omni tribulatione*, *et quod possimus et ipsi*, etc., hic rationem horum duorum exponit, et

primo ostendit quomodo Deus consolatur nos in omni tribulatione;

secundo quomodo consolatio nostra convertitur in consolationem aliorum, ibi *sive autem tribulamur*, et cetera.

18. Dicit ergo: recte dico quod consolatur nos in omni tribulatione nostra, *quia secundum quod abundant passiones Christi in nobis*, et cetera.

Dicit *Christi*, id est inchoatae a Christo. Ez. IX, 6: *a sanctuario meo incipite*. In Christo enim inceperunt passiones pro peccatis nostris, quia *ipse peccata nostra pertulit in corpore suo super lignum*, I Petr. II, v. 24, deinde per apostolos, qui dicebant *mortificamur tota die*, Ps. XLIII, 22 etc., deinde per martyres *qui secti sunt, tentati sunt*, etc., Hebr. XI, 37; ultimo ipsi peccatores pro suis peccatis patienter iram domini portabunt, quia peccaverunt ei.

Vel *passiones Christi*, id est quas sustinemus propter Christum: Act. V, 41: *ibant apostoli gaudentes*, et cetera. Et Ps. XLIII, 22: *propter te mortificamur*, et cetera. Sicut, inquam, huiusmodi *passiones abundant*, sic *abundat per Christum consolatio nostra*. Ps. XCIII, v. 19: *secundum multitudinem dolorum*, et cetera.

This then is what the Apostle says, *who comforts us in all our tribulation*.

16. But why? Not only for our benefit, but that it profit others too. Hence, he says, *that we also may be able to comfort those who are in all distress*.

For we can comfort others by the example of our own comfort. For one who is not comforted does not know how to comfort others: *he who has not been tried, what manner of things does he know* (Sir 34:9) about any affliction; *the Spirit of the Lord God is upon me to bring good tidings to the afflicted* (Isa 61:1); *he who comforts all who were mourning in Zion* (Sir 48:27).

We are able, I say, to comfort them *by the exhortation* to endure sufferings by promising eternal rewards, i.e., *with which we also are exhorted* by the Scriptures and internal inspirations, in order that we may patiently endure and exhort others by our example and by the Scriptures themselves: *for I received from the Lord what I also delivered to you* (1 Cor 11:23); *what I have heard from the Lord of hosts, the God of Israel, I announce to you* (Isa 21:10).

17. Having mentioned the profit which comes to others from the apostles, he gives the reason for what he has said, saying, *for as the sufferings of Christ abound in us*.

And because he has said two things, namely, that God *comforts us in all our tribulation, that we also may be able to comfort those who are in distress*, he explains here the reason for these two things:

first, he shows how God comforts us in every affliction;

second, how our comfort is turned to the comfort of others, at *now whether we be in tribulation*.

18. He says, therefore, I am right in saying that he comforts us in every affliction, *for as the sufferings of Christ abound in us: so also by Christ does our comfort abound*.

He says, *the sufferings of Christ*, i.e., begun by Christ: *begin at my sanctuary* (Ezek 9:6). For the sufferings for our sins began in Christ, because *he himself bore our sins in his body on the tree* (1 Pet 2:24); then by the apostles, who said: *we are slain all the day long* (Ps 44:22); then by the martyrs, *who were cut in two and were tempted* (Heb 11:37). Finally, sinners themselves will bear patiently God's anger for their sins.

Or *the sufferings of Christ*, i.e., what we endure for Christ: *then they left the presence of the Council, rejoicing that they were counted worthy to suffer dishonor for the name* (Acts 5:41); *for your sake we are slain all the day long, and accounted as sheep for the slaughter* (Ps 44:22). Just as *the sufferings of Christ abound in us*: so *by Christ does our comfort abound*: *when the cares of my heart are many, your consolations cheer my soul* (Ps 94:19).

Lecture 3

1:6Sive autem tribulamur pro vestra exhortatione et salute, sive consolamur pro vestra consolatione, sive exhortamur pro vestra exhortatione et salute, quae operatur tolerantiam earumdem passionum, quas et nos patimur: [n. 19]

1:7ut spes nostra firma sit pro vobis: scientes quod sicut socii passionum estis, sic eritis et consolationis. [n. 23]

1:8Non enim volumus ignorare vos, fratres, de tribulatione nostra, quae facta est in Asia, quoniam supra modum gravati sumus supra virtutem, ita ut taederet nos etiam vivere. [n. 24]

1:9Sed ipsi in nobismetipsis responsum mortis habuimus, ut non simus fidentes in nobis, sed in Deo, qui suscitat mortuos:

1:10qui de tantis periculis nos eripuit, et eruit: in quem speramus quoniam et adhuc eripiet, [n. 28]

1:11adjuvantibus et vobis in oratione pro nobis: ut ex multorum personis, ejus quae in nobis est donationis, per multos gratiae agantur pro nobis.

1:6εἴτε δὲ θλιβόμεθα, ὑπὲρ τῆς ὑμῶν παρακλήσεως καὶ σωτηρίας· εἴτε παρακαλούμεθα, ὑπὲρ τῆς ὑμῶν παρακλήσεως τῆς ἐνεργουμένης ἐν ὑπομονῇ τῶν αὐτῶν παθημάτων ὧν καὶ ἡμεῖς πάσχομεν.

1:7καὶ ἡ ἐλπὶς ἡμῶν βεβαία ὑπὲρ ὑμῶν εἰδότες ὅτι ὡς κοινωνοί ἐστε τῶν παθημάτων, οὕτως καὶ τῆς παρακλήσεως.

1:8Οὐ γὰρ θέλομεν ὑμᾶς ἀγνοεῖν, ἀδελφοί, ὑπὲρ τῆς θλίψεως ἡμῶν τῆς γενομένης ἐν τῇ Ἀσίᾳ, ὅτι καθ᾽ ὑπερβολὴν ὑπὲρ δύναμιν ἐβαρήθημεν ὥστε ἐξαπορηθῆναι ἡμᾶς καὶ τοῦ ζῆν·

1:9ἀλλὰ αὐτοὶ ἐν ἑαυτοῖς τὸ ἀπόκριμα τοῦ θανάτου ἐσχήκαμεν, ἵνα μὴ πεποιθότες ὦμεν ἐφ᾽ ἑαυτοῖς ἀλλ᾽ ἐπὶ τῷ θεῷ τῷ ἐγείροντι τοὺς νεκρούς·

1:10ὃς ἐκ τηλικούτου θανάτου ἐρρύσατο ἡμᾶς καὶ ῥύσεται, εἰς ὃν ἠλπίκαμεν [ὅτι] καὶ ἔτι ῥύσεται,

1:11συνυπουργούντων καὶ ὑμῶν ὑπὲρ ἡμῶν τῇ δεήσει, ἵνα ἐκ πολλῶν προσώπων τὸ εἰς ἡμᾶς χάρισμα διὰ πολλῶν εὐχαριστηθῇ ὑπὲρ ἡμῶν.

1:6Now whether we be in tribulation, it is for your exhortation and salvation: or whether we be comforted, it is for your consolation: or whether we be exhorted, it is for your exhortation and salvation, which works the enduring of the same sufferings which we also suffer. [n. 19]

1:7That our hope for you may be steadfast: knowing that as you are partakers of the sufferings, so shall you be also of the consolation. [n. 23]

1:8For we do not want you to be ignorant, brethren, of our tribulation which came to us in Asia: for we were burdened beyond measure, above our strength, so that we were weary even of life. [n. 24]

1:9But we had in ourselves the answer of death, that we should not trust in ourselves, but in God who raises the dead.

1:10Who has delivered and does deliver us out of such great dangers: in whom we trust because he will also yet deliver us, [n. 28]

1:11You helping withal in prayer for us. That for this gift obtained for us, by the means of many persons, thanks may be given by many in our behalf.

---

19. Postquam Apostolus ostendit quod Deus consolatur servos suos in tribulationibus, scilicet ministros fidei et praedicatores, hic consequenter manifestat, quod eorum consolatio cedit ad bonum aliorum.

Et circa hoc duo facit.

Primo manifestat qualiter eorum consolatio sit ad aliorum utilitatem et salutem;

secundo ordinem huius consolationis et salutis insinuat, ibi *quae operatur tolerantiam*, et cetera.

20. Circa primum advertendum est, quod tria dicit Apostolus se recepisse: tribulationem, cum dicit: *in omni tribulatione nostra*, consolationem, cum dicit: *qui consolatur nos*, exhortationem, cum subdit: *ut possimus et ipsi*, etc. Accipiendo ergo haec tria passive, dicimus, quod apostoli consolantur, tribulantur et exhortantur. Unde et tria ostendit Apostolus cedere ad consolationem aliorum, et hoc in quodam ordine. Et primo eorum tribulationem, cum dicit *sive*, inquit, *tribulamur*, et cetera.

19. After showing that the Lord comforts his servants in their tribulations, i.e., the ministers of the faith and preachers, the Apostle now shows that their comfort rebounds to the good of others.

And concerning this he does two things:

first, he shows that their comfort results in the advantage and salvation of others;

second, he shows the relation of this comfort to salvation, at *which works the enduring*.

20. In regard to the first, it should be noted that the Apostle says that he received three things: afflictions, when he says, *in all our tribulation*; comfort, when he says, *who comforts us*; exhortation, when he says, *that we also may be able to comfort those who are in all distress*. By taking these three things in a passive sense, we say that the apostles are afflicted, comforted and exhorted. Hence, the Apostle also shows that three things result in the comfort of others, and these in a definite order. First, their affliction, when he says,

Quasi dicat: vere quidquid recipimus est in bonum vestrum, quia *sive tribulamur, pro vestra exhortatione et salute*, quia scilicet nostro exemplo monet vos Deus ad passionum tolerantiam, unde provenit vobis salus aeterna. Unde I Machab. VI, 34 legitur, quod *ostenderunt elephantis sanguinem uvae, et mororum, ut acuerent eos ad bellum*. Quod fit, quando tepidis et pigris adhibentur passiones sanctorum in exemplum.

Secundo ostendit, quod eorum consolatio in aliorum utilitatem cedit, cum dicit *sive consolamur*. Quasi dicat: ipsa nostra consolatio, qua nos spe praemii consolamur, est ad consolationem vestram, inquantum exemplo nostro vos etiam eamdem spem praemii habentes, gaudetis.

Tertio ostendit quod eorum exhortatio passiva est ad bonum aliorum, dicens *sive exhortamur*, per internam inspirationem vel per flagella, *hoc est pro vestra exhortatione*, scilicet ut vos ad maiora animemini, et salutem speretis. Unde dicitur II Mach. ult., quod *exhortati sermonibus Iudae*, et cetera. *Adiuvantibus autem vobis*, et cetera.

21. Huius autem consolationis et salutis ordinem insinuat, cum subdit *quae operatur tolerantiam*, et cetera.

Et circa hoc duo facit.

Primo ostendit patientiam habitam in adversis;

secundo manifestat fructum, qui ex patientia provenit, ibi *ut spes firma*, et cetera.

22. Dicit ergo: dico quod haec ad vestram salutem cedunt, quae salus est vobis in hoc, inquantum exemplo nostri estis fortes ad tolerantiam passionum, et ut patienter sustineatis passiones quas et nos patimur. Lc. XXI, 19: *in patientia vestra possidebitis animas vestras*. Iac. V, 10: *exemplum accipite, fratres mei*, et cetera.

23. Ex qua quidem patientia provenit vobis fructus, quia ex hoc *spes nostra firma* est *pro vobis*, quod vos efficiamini haeredes vitae aeternae. Rom. V, 3 s.: *tribulatio patientiam operatur, patientia vero spem*. Gregorius: *tanto spes in Deum solidior surgit, quanto quis graviora pro nomine eius pertulerit. Nam ex passionibus quas sustinent sancti Dei pro Christo, consurgit eis spes vitae aeternae*.

Et causa spei huius est, quia sumus *scientes*, quia *sicut estis socii* nostri in passionibus, *eritis* socii *et consolationis*, id est vitae aeternae. II Tim. II, 11: *fidelis sermo, nam si commortui sumus, et convivemus*, et cetera. I Petr. IV, 13: *communicantes Christi passionibus gaudete*, et cetera.

24. Consequenter cum dicit *non enim volumus vos*, captat eorum benevolentiam, recitando quaedam in speciali.

Et circa hoc tria facit.

whether we be in tribulation, as if to say that truly whatever we receive is towards your good, because *whether we be in tribulation, it is for your exhortation and salvation*. For by our example God is telling you to endure suffering, from which eternal salvation will come to you. Hence it is read that *they showed the elephants the juice of grapes and mulberries, to arouse them for battle* (1 Macc 6:34). This is done when the lukewarm and lazy are shown the sufferings of the saints as an example.

Second, he shows that their comfort turns out to the advantage of others, when he says, *or whether we be comforted, it is for your consolation*: as if to say, the very comfort by which we are comforted by the hope of a reward is a comfort to you, for by our example you also rejoice in having the same hope of a reward.

Third he shows that the exhortation they receive turns out to the benefit of others, saying, *whether we be exhorted* by an internal inspiration or by scourges, *it is for your exhortation*, i.e., that you be inspired to greater things and hope for salvation. Hence it is said that, *exhorted by the word of Judas, they determined to attack bravely* (2 Macc 15:17). *You helping withal in prayer*, etc.

21. He suggests the relationship between this comfort and salvation when he says, *which works the enduring of the same sufferings which we also suffer*.

In regard to this he does two things:

first, he shows the patience to be had in adversity;

second, the fruit which results from patience, at *that our hope*.

22. He says, therefore, I say that these things work for your salvation, inasmuch as by our example you are strong enough to endure sufferings and patiently endure the trials which we also suffer: *by your endurance you will gain your lives* (Luke 21:19); *as an example of suffering and patience, brethren, take the prophets* (Jas 5:10).

23. You obtain fruit from this patience because from it *our hope for you* is *steadfast* by the fact that you are made heirs of eternal life. *Suffering produces endurance, and endurance true hope* (Rom 5:3ff). *Hope in God becomes firmer to the extent that one suffers more difficult things for his name. For as a result of the sufferings the saints endure for Christ, the hope of eternal life rises in them* (Gregory).

And the cause of this hope is *knowing that as you are partakers of the sufferings, so shall you be also of the consolation*, i.e., in eternal life. *The saying is sure: if we have died with him, we shall also live with him; if we endure, we shall also reign with him* (2 Tim 2:11–12); *but rejoice in so far as you share Christ's sufferings, that you may also rejoice and be glad when his glory is revealed* (1 Pet 4:13).

24. Then when he says, *for we do not want you to be ignorant, brethren*, he wins their good will by mentioning certain specific things.

And he does three things:

Primo enim describit persecutionem quam passus est in Asia;

secundo specialem ei consolationem collatam, ibi *qui de tantis*, etc.;

tertio subdit consolationis causam, ibi *nam gloria*, et cetera.

25. Dicit ergo primum: non solum ea quae dicta sunt de tribulationibus in generali, bonum est vos scire, sed non volumus vos ignorare, quia scire est utile vobis, inquantum exemplo nostri patientiores estis. *Nolumus*, inquam, *vos ignorare de tribulatione nostra*, et cetera. Thren. III, 19: *recordare paupertatis meae*, et cetera.

Haec est illa persecutio, de qua legitur Act. XIX, 23 ss., quae facta est apostolo ab Asiano quodam argentario concitante plebem contra eum, quam quidem Apostolus exaggerat a tribus. Ex loco, quia in Asia, et hoc est quod dicit *quae*, scilicet tribulatio, *facta est in Asia*, id est, apud Ephesum, quae est in Asia, ubi debuisset magis honorari et consolari. Ex acerbitate, quia supra consuetudinem humanarum passionum, et ideo dicit *quoniam supra modum sumus*, et cetera. Item supra posse, et ideo dicit *supra virtutem*.

26. Sed contra I Cor. X, 13: *fidelis Deus, qui non patietur vos tentari supra*, et cetera.

Respondeo. Dicendum quod pati supra virtutem potest intelligi dupliciter. Vel supra virtutem naturalem, et de hac loquitur hic, supra quam Deus aliquando permittit sanctos tentari; vel supra virtutem gratiae, et de hac intelligitur illud I Cor. X, 13: *fidelis Deus*, etc., supra quam non permittit aliquem Deus tentari. Et quod Apostolus loquatur hic de virtute naturali, ostendit consequenter cum dicit *ita ut taederet nos vivere*.

Constat enim quod inter alia vivere magis desideratur. Quando ergo est tanta persecutio, ut et ipsa vita reddatur taediosa, manifestum est quod est supra virtutem naturae. Et hoc est quod dicit *ita ut*, etc.; quasi dicat: sic erat gravis persecutio, ut vita esset nobis taediosa. Iob X, 1: *taedet animam meam vitae meae*.

Contra Iac. I, 2: *omne gaudium existimate, fratres mei*, et cetera.

Respondeo. Dicendum quod tribulatio potest considerari dupliciter. Vel secundum se, et sic est taediosa; vel in comparatione ad finem, et sic est iucunda, inquantum propter Deum et spem vitae aeternae sustinetur.

Et non solum erat nobis taediosa vita, sed eramus certi de morte. Unde dicit *sed ipsi in nobis responsum mortis*, id est certitudinem mortis, *habuimus*; quasi dicat: opinio mea dictabat mihi hoc, quod deberem mori.

Vel aliter, *responsum mortis*, id est ipsa ratio diceret et eligeret mori propter taedium vitae.

first, he describes the persecution he suffered in Asia;

second, the special comfort he received, at *who has delivered*;

third, the cause of the comfort, at *for our glory*.

25. He says first, therefore: it is good for you to know not only what we have said about our afflictions in general, but we do not want you to be ignorant, because it is profitable for you to know them, inasmuch as you are more patient because of our example. *We do not want you to be ignorant, brethren, of the affliction we experienced. Remember my affliction and my bitterness, the wormwood and the gall* (Lam 3:19).

This is the persecution mentioned in Acts (Acts 19:23ff), which was launched by a certain Asian silversmith, who incited the people against him. The Apostle describes it from three aspects: from the place, because it was in Asia; hence he says, *in Asia*, i.e., Ephesus, which is in Asia, where he should rather have been honored and comforted; from its bitterness, because it was an extreme suffering; hence he says, *for we were burdened beyond measure*. Also it was beyond his strength, and so he says, *above our strength*.

26. But this seems to be contrary to what is said in 1 Corinthians: *God is faithful, and he will not let you be tempted beyond your strength* (1 Cor 10:13).

I answer that to suffer beyond one's strength can be understood in two ways: first, above one's natural strength, which the Apostle means here, above which God sometimes permits his servants to be tempted; second, above the strength of grace, which the Apostle means here: *God is faithful* (1 Cor 10:13). That the Apostle is speaking of natural strength is indicated by what he says next, *so that we were weary even of life*.

For it is evident that among all else, life is most desirable. Therefore when a persecution is so great that life itself becomes wearisome, it is obviously above the strength of our nature. And this is what he says, *we were weary even of life*, as if to say, this persecution was so cruel that life itself became a burden to us: *I loathe my life* (Job 10:1).

But against this it is said: *count it all joy, my brethren, when you meet various trials* (Jas 1:2).

I answer that affliction can be considered in two ways: either in itself, and then it is wearisome, or in relation to faith, and then it is joyful, inasmuch as it is endured for God and with the hope of eternal life.

We were not only weary of life, but we were certain of death; hence, he says, *but we had in ourselves the answer of death*, i.e., the certainty of death. As if to say: in my opinion I was about to die.

Or another way, *the answer of death*, i.e., reason itself would say to choose death because of the weariness of life.

27. Exaggerat etiam tribulationem ex causa, unde dicit *ut non simus in nobis*, etc., scilicet ut reprimatur humana superbia. Ier. XVI, 19: *Domine, fortitudo mea et robur*, et cetera. Sed in omnibus confidamus de Deo. Ier. XVII, 7: *benedictus qui confidit in Domino*, et cetera. Et ideo dicit *sed in Deo qui suscitat*, et cetera. I Reg. II, 6: *Dominus mortificat et vivificat*.

28. Sed quia Dominus non derelinquit sperantes in se, ideo subdit Apostolus consolationem ei factam a Domino, dicens *qui de tantis periculis*, et cetera. Et circa hoc tria facit. Primo describit consolationem praesentem contra mala praeterita; secundo consolationem futuram; tertio causam spei.

Dicit ergo: consolati sumus a Deo, *qui eripuit nos* in praeterito *de tantis periculis, et eruit* in praesenti, quia non cessat liberare, Is. XLIII, 2: *cum transieris per aquas*, etc., *in quem speramus, quoniam eripiet*, et adiecit in futuro, Eccli. II, 9: *qui timetis Dominum, sperate in illum*.

Huius autem spei causam nobis praebent orationes vestrae. Unde dicit *adiuvantibus vobis nos in orationibus*, quas pro nobis facitis. Prov. XVIII, 19: *frater qui iuvatur a fratre*, et cetera. Rom. XV, 30: *obsecro vos, fratres, per Dominum Iesum Christum, et per caritatem Sancti Spiritus, ut adiuvetis me in orationibus vestris*, et cetera.

Quae quidem orationes necessariae sunt, quia Deus multa bona confert uni ad preces multorum. Cuius ratio est, quia Deus de bonis quae confert, vult exhiberi sibi gratias et quod multi ex hoc teneantur ad gratiarum actiones, hoc autem fit quando ex eo quod dat uni ad preces multorum, obligat sibi omnes, ad quorum preces confert bonum aliquod, ut sic non solum ille cui confert, sed etiam ipsi rogantes, gratias referant Deo. Et hoc est quod dicit *ut ex multarum personis*. Et dicit *ex multarum* facierum, vel quantum ad aetatem, vel quantum ad conditionem, vel quantum ad diversitatem gentium vel morum. *Eius quae in nobis est donationis*, id est pro illa donatione, scilicet fidei, quae in nobis est, *per multos agantur gratiae Deo pro nobis*. Eph. V, 20: *gratias agentes Deo et Patri*.

Vel aliter: *ut ex multarum personis* facierum, id est conditionum personis. Dico *eius donationis, quae est in nobis*, id est, quae habent idem donum, scilicet fidei vel caritatis, id est ex multis personis illorum qui sunt in fide Christi, *agantur*, et cetera. Et sic secundum hanc expositionem per diversas facies intelliguntur diversae virtutes, ut facies unius dicatur illa virtus in qua praeeminet: sicut facies Iob, patientia; facies David, humilitas, et sic de aliis.

27. He amplifies the reason for his affliction when he says, *that we should not trust in ourselves*, i.e., that human pride should be repressed. *O Lord, my strength and my stronghold* (Jer 16:19), and that we trust God in all things: *blessed is the man who trusts in the Lord* (Jer 17:7). And therefore he says, *but in God who raises the dead*. *The Lord kills and brings to life* (1 Sam 2:6).

28. But because the Lord does not abandon those who trust in him, the Apostle mentions the comfort he received from the Lord, saying, *who has delivered and does deliver us out of such great dangers*. In regard to this he does three things: first, he describes his present comfort against past evils; second, the comfort to come; third, the cause of hope.

He says, therefore: we have been comforted by God, *who has delivered* us in the past *from such great dangers*, and *does deliver us* in the present, because he does not stop delivering: *when you pass through the waters I will be with you* (Isa 43:2); *in whom we trust because he will also yet deliver us*, adding in the future: *you who fear the Lord, hope for good things* (Sir 2:9).

Your prayers give us cause for this hope; hence he says, *you helping withal in prayer*, which you make for us: *a brother helped is like a strong city* (Prov 18:19); *I appeal to you, brethren, by our Lord Jesus Christ and by the love of the Spirit, to strive together with me in your prayers to God on my behalf* (Rom 15:30).

These prayers are necessary, because God gives many gifts to one person due to the prayers of many. The reason is that God wishes to be thanked for the gifts he gives, and as a result many are bound to give thanks. This happens when, as a result of giving to one person because of the prayers of many, he puts all those at whose prayers he gave some good under an obligation to him. Consequently, not only the one who received the benefit, but those who prayed should give thanks to God. And this is what he says, *by the means of many persons*. And he says, *of many* faces, either as to age or condition or the diversity of nations or customs. *For this gift obtained for us*, i.e., for the gift of faith which we have, *thanks may be given by many in our behalf*. *Always and for everything giving thanks in the name of our Lord Jesus Christ to God the Father* (Eph 5:20).

Or another way: *by the means of* the faces of *many persons*, i.e., the condition of persons. I say, *for this gift obtained for us*, i.e., because they have the same gift, namely of faith or of charity; i.e., by means of the many persons who are in the faith of Christ, *thanks may be given by many in our behalf*. Therefore, according to this explanation, by the many faces are understood the various virtues, so that the predominant virtue in a person is called his face; thus, patience is the face of Job, humility the face of David, and so on.

Lecture 4

1:12Nam gloria nostra haec est: testimonium conscientiae nostrae, quod in simplicitate cordis et sinceritate Dei, et non in sapientia carnali, sed in gratia Dei, conversati sumus in hoc mundo: abundantius autem ad vos. [n. 29]

1:13Non enim alia scribimus vobis, quam quae legistis, et cognovistis. Spero autem quod usque in finem cognoscetis, [n. 34]

1:14sicut et cognovistis nos ex parte, quod gloria vestra sumus, sicut et vos nostra, in die Domini nostri Jesu Christi.

1:12Ἡ γὰρ καύχησις ἡμῶν αὕτη ἐστίν, τὸ μαρτύριον τῆς συνειδήσεως ἡμῶν, ὅτι ἐν ἁπλότητι καὶ εἰλικρινείᾳ τοῦ θεοῦ, [καὶ] οὐκ ἐν σοφίᾳ σαρκικῇ ἀλλ᾽ ἐν χάριτι θεοῦ, ἀνεστράφημεν ἐν τῷ κόσμῳ, περισσοτέρως δὲ πρὸς ὑμᾶς.

1:13οὐ γὰρ ἄλλα γράφομεν ὑμῖν ἀλλ᾽ ἢ ἃ ἀναγινώσκετε ἢ καὶ ἐπιγινώσκετε· ἐλπίζω δὲ ὅτι ἕως τέλους ἐπιγνώσεσθε,

1:14καθὼς καὶ ἐπέγνωτε ἡμᾶς ἀπὸ μέρους, ὅτι καύχημα ὑμῶν ἐσμεν καθάπερ καὶ ὑμεῖς ἡμῶν ἐν τῇ ἡμέρᾳ τοῦ κυρίου [ἡμῶν] Ἰησοῦ.

1:12For our glory is this: the testimony of our conscience, that in simplicity of heart and sincerity of God, and not in carnal wisdom, but in the grace of God, we have behaved in this world: and more abundantly towards you. [n. 29]

1:13For we write no other things to you than what you have read and known. And I hope that you shall know unto the end, [n. 34]

1:14As also you have known us in part, that we are your glory: as you also are ours, in the day of our Lord Jesus Christ.

---

29. Posita consolatione apostolo a Deo facta post persecutionem, hic consequenter consolationis causam assignat, quae est de spe divini auxilii.

Et circa hoc duo facit.

Primo proponit causam spei;

secundo adducit ad hoc testimonium eorum quibus scribit, ibi **non enim alia**, et cetera.

30. Dicit ergo: dico quod speramus adhuc eripi a domino et consolari, **nam gloria**, etc., quasi dicat: causa huius est bona conscientia nostra. Spes enim est expectatio futurorum ex gratia et meritis proveniens. Unde et

circa hoc tria facit.

Primo ostendit gloriam quam habet de testimonio purae conscientiae;

secundo causam huius gloriae insinuat, ibi **quod in simplicitate**;

tertio manifestat unde proveniat haec causa, ibi **et non in sapientia carnali**.

31. Dicit ergo: ideo spero et confido de Deo, quia **gloria nostra**, id est, glorior ex testimonio et puritate conscientiae nostrae, ex quibus secure potest confidere de Deo. I Io. III, 20: *si cor nostrum nos reprehenderit*, et cetera. Rom. VIII, 16: *ipse Spiritus testimonium*, et cetera.

Notandum autem quod conscientiae testimonium verum est, quia non decipit. Multi enim exterius videntur boni, qui in conscientia sua non sunt boni. Et semper durat.

Sed non dicit **conscientiae** aliorum sed **nostrae**, quia semper homo plus debet stare testimonio conscientiae suae de se, quam testimonio aliorum; quod non faciunt illi qui reputant se bonos ex hoc quod alii sunt mali, non ex hoc quod ipsi in veritate boni sint; et illi qui gloriantur

29. After speaking of the comfort he had received from God following his persecution, the Apostle assigns the cause of this comfort, which is hope in God's help.

In regard to this he does two things:

first, he states the cause of hope;

second, he supports this with the testimony of those to whom he is writing, at **for we write no other**.

30. He says, therefore: I say that we still hope to be rescued by God to be comforted, **for our glory is this: the testimony of our conscience**, as if to say: the cause of this hope is our good conscience, for hope is an expectation of things to come and arises from grace and merits.

Hence, in regard to this he also does three things:

first, he shows the boast which he has in the testimony of a pure conscience;

second, he suggests the cause of this boasting, at **that in simplicity**;

third, he discloses the source of this cause, at **and not in carnal wisdom**.

31. He says, therefore: the reason I hope and trust in God is because **our glory is this: the testimony of our conscience**, i.e., I glory in the testimony and purity of our conscience: *if our hearts do not condemn us, we have confidence before God* (1 John 3:21). *The Spirit himself bearing witness with our spirit that we are children of God* (Rom 8:16).

It should be noted that the testimony of conscience is true, because it does not deceive; for many appear good outwardly who are not good in their conscience; and conscience always endures.

He does not say, *the conscience of others*, but **our conscience**, because a man should put more trust in the testimony of his own conscience about himself than in the testimony of others; they do not do this who consider themselves good because others are evil rather than because they themselves are truly good. Nor is it done by

de bonitate alicuius boni viri, qui eis aliqua affinitate coniungitur.

32. Causam autem huius gloriae insinuat, dicens, *quod in simplicitate*, etc.; quae consistit in duobus. In duobus enim consistit puritas conscientiae, ut scilicet ea quae facit sint bona, et quod intentio facientis sit recta, et ista dicit Apostolus de se.

Primo quod habet intentionem rectam ad Deum in operibus suis, et ideo dicit *quod in simplicitate*, id est in rectitudine intentionis. Sap. I, 1: *in simplicitate cordis*, et cetera. Prov. XI, 3: *simplicitas iustorum*, et cetera. Secundo quod ea quae facit sunt bona, et ideo dicit *et sinceritate* operationis, Phil. I, v. 10: *ut sitis sinceri et sine offensa*.

33. Unde autem proveniat huius gloriae causa, manifestat subdens *sed non in sapientia carnis*.

Hoc potest dupliciter legi. Primo ut referatur ad hoc quod immediate praecedit, scilicet *Dei*; et tunc est insinuativum, unde veniat ei sinceritas et simplicitas; quasi dicat: multi antiqui fuerunt sapientes in sapientia terrena, sicut philosophi, et multi Iudaei pure vixerunt confidentes in iustitia legis, sed nos non in sapientia carnali, quae secundum naturas rerum, vel desideria carnis est, sed in gratia Dei conversati sumus in hoc mundo. Rom. VIII, 6: *prudentia carnis mors est*, et cetera. I Cor. II, 4: *non in persuasibilibus humanae sapientiae verbis*, et cetera. I Cor. XV, v. 10: *gratia Dei sum id quod sum*.

Vel etiam secundum hunc modum *non in sapientia*, etc., id est, quasi innixus humanae sapientiae, sed gratiae Dei. Prov. III, 5: *ne innitaris prudentiae tuae*.

Alio modo potest exponi, ut hoc quod dicit *in simplicitate*, etc., referatur ad puritatem vitae; hoc vero quod dicit *non in sapientia*, etc., referatur ad veritatem doctrinae, quasi dicat: sicut vita nostra est in simplicitate et sinceritate Dei, sic doctrina non est in sapientia carnali, sed in gratia Dei. Sed tamen duae primae magis valent.

Et licet sic bene conversati simus in mundo isto, tamen *abundantius quantum ad vos*, quia scilicet ab aliis ecclesiis receperat sumptus, ab eis non. Infra XI, 8: *alias ecclesias expoliavi*. Et ratio huius potest esse, quia avari erant, unde, ne contristaret eos, noluit ab eis recipere sumptus.

34. Consequenter huius sanctae suae conversationis testimonium eorum invocat, dicens *non enim alia*, etc., quasi dicat: haec quae scribimus vobis, non sunt vobis incognita, quia iam legistis ea in prima epistola, et

those who boast in the goodness of a good person, who is joined to them by some bond.

32. He suggests the cause of this boast when he says, *that in simplicity of heart*, which consists of two things. For purity of conscience consists of two things, namely, that the things a person does are good and that his intention is right. These two things the Apostle says of himself.

First, that he has a right intention towards God in his action; hence he says, *in simplicity of heart*, i.e., with a right intention. *Seek him with sincerity of heart* (Wis 1:1). *The integrity of the upright guides them* (Prov 11:3). Second, that the things he does are good; hence, he says, *and sincerity of God* in his actions: *that you may be pure and blameless* (Phil 1:10).

33. He discloses the source of the cause of this glory when he says, *not in carnal wisdom*.

This can be taken in two ways. First, as referring to what he had just said, namely, *sincerity of God*, and then he is suggesting the source of his sincerity and simplicity; as if to say: many of the ancients were wise in earthly wisdom, as the philosophers, and many Jews lived honorably, trusting in the justice of the law, but we have behaved in the world, not by earthly wisdom, which is according to the nature of things, nor by the desires of the flesh, but by the grace of God. *To set the mind on the flesh is death, but to set the mind on the Spirit is life and peace* (Rom 8:6); *not in plausible words of wisdom, but in demonstration of the Spirit and of power* (1 Cor 2:4); *by the grace of God I am what I am* (1 Cor 15:10).

Or even according to this manner, *not in carnal wisdom*, i.e., as though relying on human wisdom, but by the grace of God: *do not rely on your own insight* (Prov 3:5).

Or it might be explained in another way, so that in saying, *in simplicity of heart and sincerity of God*, he is referring to his purity of life; but in saying, *not in carnal wisdom, but in the grace of God*, he is referring to the truth of his teaching; as if to say: just as our life is in the simplicity and sincerity of God, so our teaching is not in earthly wisdom, but in the grace of God. But the first two interpretations are more valid.

And although we have behaved thus in the world, yet still *more abundantly towards you*, because he had received collections from the other churches, but not from them: *I have taken from other churches* (2 Cor 11:8). The reason for this might be that they were greedy; hence, in order not to sadden them, he refused to take any revenue from them.

34. Then he calls on them to witness to this holy manner of life, saying, *for we write no other things to you than what you have read and known*. As if to say: these things I write to you are not unknown to you, because you have already

cognovistis per experientiam operum. I Io. II, v. 7: *non mandatum novum.*

Et licet non perfecte cognoveritis, quia comparastis vobis pseudo-apostolos, ***spero tamen quod usque in finem***, scilicet vitae, ***cognoscetis***, scilicet perfecte, ***sicut*** usque modo ***cognovistis nos ex parte***. Cuius ratio est, quia cum quis videt aliquem aliquid bene incipere, debet sperare quod semper bene proficiat. Et quare? Quia *qui coepit in vobis opus bonum*, etc., ut dicitur Phil. I, 6.

Et cognoscetis, ***quia nos sumus gloria vestra***, id est, per nos debetis consequi gloriam aeternam, ad quam homo pervenit per fidem Christi, quam praedicamus vobis. Prov. XVII, 6: *gloria filiorum sunt patres eorum.*

Ita dico ***sumus gloria vestra, sicut et vos gloria nostra*** estis, quia per vos a nobis instructos habere speramus praemium aeternae gloriae. I Thess. II, 19: *quae est spes nostra aut corona gloriae nostrae? Nonne vos?*

Et haec gloria erit nobis ex vobis, ***in die Domini nostri Iesu Christi***, id est, in die iudicii, qui dicitur Christi, quia tunc faciet voluntatem suam cum peccatoribus, puniendo eos, qui in hoc mundo fecerunt voluntatem suam, contra Christi Domini voluntatem peccando. Ps. LXXIV, 3: *cum accepero tempus, ego iustitias iudicabo*, et cetera. Apoc. XX, v. 12: *libri aperti sunt*, et cetera.

read them in the first letter, and you know them by experience: *I am writing you no new commandment, but an old commandment* (1 John 2:7).

And although you do not know fully, because you have received false apostles, ***I hope that you shall know***, namely, perfectly, ***unto the end***, namely, of your life, ***as also you have known us in part***. The reason for this is that when we see someone starting well, we should hope that he will always progress well. And why? Because *he who began a good work in you will bring it to completion at the day of Jesus Christ* (Phil 1:6).

And you will understand, ***that we are your glory***, i.e., that through us you should obtain eternal glory, which a person reaches through the faith of Christ, which we preach to you. *The glory of sons is their fathers* (Prov 17:6).

I say that, ***we are your glory: as you also are ours*** because we hope for the reward of eternal glory through you who have been instructed by us. *For what is our hope or joy or crown of boasting? Is it not you?* (1 Thess 2:19).

And this boast will be ours from you ***in the day of our Lord Jesus Christ***, i.e., on the day of judgment, which is called Christ's day, because he will then accomplish his will with sinners by punishing those who in this world did their own will by sinning against the will of Christ the Lord. *At the set time which I appoint I will judge with equity* (Ps 75:2); *and books were opened . . . and the dead were judged by what was written in the books, by what they had done* (Rev 20:12).

Lecture 5

¹:¹⁵Et hac confidentia volui prius venire ad vos, ut secundum gratiam haberetis: [n. 35]	¹:¹⁵Καὶ ταύτῃ τῇ πεποιθήσει ἐβουλόμην πρότερον πρὸς ὑμᾶς ἐλθεῖν, ἵνα δευτέραν χάριν σχῆτε,	¹:¹⁵And in this confidence I wanted to come to you before, that you might have a second grace: [n. 35]
¹:¹⁶et per vos transire in Macedoniam, et iterum a Macedonia venire ad vos, et a vobis deduci in Judaeam.	¹:¹⁶καὶ δι᾽ ὑμῶν διελθεῖν εἰς Μακεδονίαν καὶ πάλιν ἀπὸ Μακεδονίας ἐλθεῖν πρὸς ὑμᾶς καὶ ὑφ᾽ ὑμῶν προπεμφθῆναι εἰς τὴν Ἰουδαίαν.	¹:¹⁶And to pass by you into Macedonia: and again from Macedonia to come to you, and by you to be brought on my way towards Judea.
¹:¹⁷Cum ergo hoc voluissem, numquid levitate usus sum? aut quae cogito, secundum carnem cogito, ut sit apud me est et non? [n. 37]	¹:¹⁷τοῦτο οὖν βουλόμενος μήτι ἄρα τῇ ἐλαφρίᾳ ἐχρησάμην; ἢ ἃ βουλεύομαι κατὰ σάρκα βουλεύομαι, ἵνα ᾖ παρ᾽ ἐμοὶ τὸ ναὶ ναὶ καὶ τὸ οὒ οὔ;	¹:¹⁷Therefore when I had wanted this, did I use lightness? Or, the things that I intend, do I intend according to the flesh, that there should be with me, it is, and it is not? [n. 37]
¹:¹⁸Fidelis autem Deus, quia sermo noster, qui fuit apud vos, non est in illo est et non. [n. 38]	¹:¹⁸πιστὸς δὲ ὁ θεὸς ὅτι ὁ λόγος ἡμῶν ὁ πρὸς ὑμᾶς οὐκ ἔστιν ναὶ καὶ οὔ.	¹:¹⁸But God is faithful: for our speech, which was to you, is not in him, it is, and it is not. [n. 38]
¹:¹⁹Dei enim Filius Jesus Christus, qui in vobis per nos praedicatus est, per me, et Silvanum, et Timotheum, non fuit est et non, sed est in illo fuit. [n. 40]	¹:¹⁹ὁ τοῦ θεοῦ γὰρ υἱὸς Ἰησοῦς Χριστὸς ὁ ἐν ὑμῖν δι᾽ ἡμῶν κηρυχθείς, δι᾽ ἐμοῦ καὶ Σιλουανοῦ καὶ Τιμοθέου, οὐκ ἐγένετο ναὶ καὶ οὒ ἀλλὰ ναὶ ἐν αὐτῷ γέγονεν.	¹:¹⁹For the Son of God, Jesus Christ, who was preached among you by us, by me and Sylvanus and Timothy, was not: it is and it is not. But, it is, was in him. [n. 40]
¹:²⁰Quotquot enim promissiones Dei sunt, in illo est: ideo et per ipsum amen Deo ad gloriam nostram. [n. 42]	¹:²⁰ὅσαι γὰρ ἐπαγγελίαι θεοῦ, ἐν αὐτῷ τὸ ναί· διὸ καὶ δι᾽ αὐτοῦ τὸ ἀμὴν τῷ θεῷ πρὸς δόξαν δι᾽ ἡμῶν.	¹:²⁰For however many promises of God there are, is in him. Therefore also by him, amen to God, unto our glory. [n. 42]
¹:²¹Qui autem confirmat nos vobiscum in Christo, et qui unxit nos Deus: [n. 44]	¹:²¹ὁ δὲ βεβαιῶν ἡμᾶς σὺν ὑμῖν εἰς Χριστὸν καὶ χρίσας ἡμᾶς θεός,	¹:²¹Now he who confirms us with you in Christ and who has anointed us, is God: [n. 44]
¹:²²qui et signavit nos, et dedit pignus Spiritus in cordibus nostris.	¹:²²ὁ καὶ σφραγισάμενος ἡμᾶς καὶ δοὺς τὸν ἀρραβῶνα τοῦ πνεύματος ἐν ταῖς καρδίαις ἡμῶν.	¹:²²Who also has sealed us and given the pledge of the Spirit in our hearts.
¹:²³Ego autem testem Deum invoco in animam meam, quod parcens vobis, non veni ultra Corinthum: [n. 47]	¹:²³Ἐγὼ δὲ μάρτυρα τὸν θεὸν ἐπικαλοῦμαι ἐπὶ τὴν ἐμὴν ψυχήν, ὅτι φειδόμενος ὑμῶν οὐκέτι ἦλθον εἰς Κόρινθον.	¹:²³But I call God to witness upon my soul that to spare you, I came no more to Corinth: [n. 47]
¹:²⁴non quia dominamur fidei vestae, sed adjutores sumus gaudii vestri: nam fide statis.	¹:²⁴οὐχ ὅτι κυριεύομεν ὑμῶν τῆς πίστεως ἀλλὰ συνεργοί ἐσμεν τῆς χαρᾶς ὑμῶν· τῇ γὰρ πίστει ἑστήκατε.	¹:²⁴not because we exercise dominion over your faith: but we are helpers of your joy. For in faith you stand.

---

35. Apostolus, captata benevolentia Corinthiorum, consequenter excusationem suam addit, et

circa hoc tria facit.

Primo enim ponit intentum;

secundo sub quaestione accusationem contra eum ab eis factam exponit, ibi *cum ergo hoc*, etc.;

tertio excusat se, ibi *fidelis autem Deus*.

36. Circa primum sciendum est quod Apostolus in prima epistola (quam nos non habemus) missa ab eo Corinthiis, vel per nuntium, promiserat eis quod primo iret ad eos antequam iret in Macedoniam, et per eos iret

35. After winning the good will of the Corinthians, the Apostle adds his excuse.

In regard to this he does three things:

first, he mentions what he intends;

second, in the form of a question he answers an accusation they made against him, at *therefore when*;

third, he excuses himself, at *but God is faithful*.

36. In regard to the first it should be noted that in a previous epistle (which we do not have), which the Apostle has sent to the Corinthians by a messenger, he had promised them that he would visit them before going to Macedonia,

in Macedoniam, et iterum inde rediret in Achaiam, in qua est Corinthus, et de Achaia in Iudaeam; postmodum, in secunda epistola, quam nos habemus primam, scribit eis quod primo iret in Macedoniam, et postmodum iret in Corinthum.

Quia ergo videtur secundum hoc contrarium primae promissioni, Apostolus excusat se modo de hoc, ponens primo ipsam promissionem primo factam, et ideo dicit *et hac confidentia*, quasi dicat: vos scitis puritatem et sinceritatem meam, et estis testes mei, et gloria mea, ideo *in hac confidentia*, id est in hoc confisus, quia per alterutrum glorificari speramus, *volui primo venire ad vos, ut secundam gratiam haberetis*, quia secunda visitatio et confirmatio in fide, dicitur secunda gratia respectu conversionis, quam primo habuerunt ministerio et praedicatione ipsius. *Et per vos transire in Macedoniam, et iterum a Macedonia venire ad vos, et a vobis deduci in Iudaeam*. Iste est ordo primae promissionis, sed in praecedenti epistola est ordo contrarius, sicut dictum est.

37. Consequenter huius mutationis accusationem, qua accusabant eum Corinthii, ponit sub quaestione, dicens *cum ergo hoc voluissem*, et cetera.

Duo imponebant ei ex hoc, levitatem, quia mutaverat propositum, Eccli. XXVII, 12: *stultus ut luna mutatur*, et carnalitatem, quia visum erat eis, quod ex aliquo carnali et humano affectu hoc fecisset. Unde haec duo tangit, et primo levitatem, unde dicit *numquid levitate usus sum*, si non feci quod aliquando volui? Absit. Est. XVI, 9: *nec putare debetis, si diversa iubeamus, ex animi levitate venire*. Ps. XXXIV, 18: *in populo gravi*, et cetera.

Secundo tangit carnalitatem cum dicit *aut* numquid ea *quae cogito*, facienda vel dimittenda, *secundum carnem cogito*, id est secundum aliquem carnalem affectum, *ut sit apud me, est et non*, id est affirmatio et negatio? Infra X, 2: *arbitrantur nos tamquam secundum carnem ambulemus*. Iac. c. I, 8: *vir duplex animo*, et cetera.

38. Exposita eorum accusatione, consequenter excusat se, dicens *fidelis autem Deus*, etc., et

circa hoc duo facit.

Primo insinuat se non fuisse mentitum;

secundo ostendit modum quomodo non fuit mentitus, ibi *qui autem confirmat*, et cetera.

39. Quod autem non fuerit mentitus, excusat se dupliciter, scilicet ex consuetudine, et ex causa.

Ex consuetudine quidem, quia non debet credi quod aliquis de facili mentiatur, qui numquam inventus est mendax, et secundum hanc expositionem *fidelis Deus*, etc., accipitur in vi iuramenti, quasi: testis sit mihi Deus,

and that he would return again to Achaia, where Corinth is, and from Achaia to Judea. Then in a second epistle, which we call the first, he wrote them that he would first go to Macedonia and later to Corinth.

Therefore, because this seemed contrary to the first promise, the Apostle now excuses himself for this by first mentioning the promise he originally made; hence, he says, *and in this confidence*. As if to say: you know my honesty and sincerity and you are my witnesses and my glory; therefore, *in this confidence*, i.e., relying on this, because we hope to be glorified by you, *I wanted to come to you before, that you might have a second grace*, because a second visit and strengthening of the faith is called a second grace in relation to the time they were first converted by his ministry and his teaching. *And to pass by you into Macedonia, and again from Macedonia to come to you, and by you to be brought on my way towards Judea*. This is the sequence of the first promise, but in the preceding epistle this is a contrary sequence, as has been said.

37. Then he puts the accusation for this change, for which the Corinthians accused him, in the form of a question, saying, *therefore when I had wanted this, did I use lightness?*

For on account of this they charged him with two things: light-mindedness, because he changed his mind: *the fool changes like the moon* (Sir 27:11); and carnal love, because it seemed to them that he had done this from some carnal and human affection. Hence, he touches on two points: first, light-mindedness, and he says, *did I use lightness?*, if I failed to do what I once wanted to do? God forbid! *Neither must you think, if we command different things, that it comes from the levity of our mind* (Est 16:9); *in the mighty throng I will praise you* (Ps 35:18).

Second he touches on carnal affection, when he says, *the things that I intend*, either to do or to dismiss, *do I intend according to the flesh*, i.e., according to carnal affection, *that there should be with me, it is, and it is not*, i.e., to affirm and deny. *Some reckon us as if we walked according to the flesh* (2 Cor 10:2); *a double-minded man is unstable in all his ways* (Jas 1:8).

38. Having enlarged upon their accusation, he excuses himself, saying, *but God is faithful*, and

in regard to this he does two things:

first, he declares that he did not lie;

second, he shows how he did not lie, at *now he who confirms us*.

39. He shows in two ways that he had not lied, namely, from his character and from the cause.

From his character, because we should not suppose that a person would easily lie, if he has never been found to be a liar. According to this explanation, *but God is faithful*, is spoken with the force of an oath. As if to say: God is

quod *sermo meus*, scilicet praedicationis, *qui fuit apud vos, non est in illo est et non*, id est, non est in illo falsitas. Deut. XXXII, 4: *Deus fidelis, et absque ulla*, et cetera.

Si autem sumatur *fidelis Deus*, etc., pro veritate divinae promissionis, tunc est sensus: fidelis est Deus, id est servat promissa sua. Promiserat autem mittere ad vos praedicatores veritatis, Ier. III, 15: *dabo vobis pastores iuxta cor*, etc., et ideo cum sim missus ab eo, *sermo noster qui fuit*, etc., sicut supra.

40. Ex causa excusat se, cum dicit *Dei enim filius*. Et hoc dupliciter, scilicet motiva et efficiente, ibi *qui autem confirmat*, et cetera.

Causa autem motiva ad non mentiendum est, quia qui assumit aliquod officium, naturaliter movetur ad ea quae congruunt illi officio, et non ad contraria. Sed constat quod officium apostolicum est praedicare veritatem; non ergo movetur ad contrarium veritatis, quod est mentiri.

Et circa hoc tria facit.

Primo probat veritatem dicti sui per dictum Christi;

secundo veritatem Christi per dictum Dei, ibi *quotquot autem*, etc.;

tertio concludit suum propositum, ibi *ideo et per ipsum*, et cetera.

41. Dicit ergo primo: dico quod dicta nostra debent reputari vera, et vera sunt, quia praedicavimus Christum in quo non fuit aliqua falsitas. Et hoc est quod dicit *Dei enim Filius Christus, qui est praedicatus per nos in vobis; per me*, scilicet principaliter, *et Sylvanum*, secundario (iste est Sylas de quo habetur Act. XVIII, 5) *et Timotheum*, de quo supra. Isti enim duo fuerunt cum apostolo, quando primo convertit eos.

In illo, scilicet Filio Dei, *non fuit est et non*, id est, falsitas, vel non fecit quod non convenit. *Sed fuit in illo est*, id est veritas; nam verum et ens convertuntur. Io. c. XIV, 6: *ego sum via, veritas et vita*.

42. Sed quia posset videri dubium hoc quod dicit, quod in Christo non fuit falsitas, ideo statim hoc probat, subdens *quotquot autem*, et cetera.

Et probat hoc modo. Constat quod in illo quod est manifestativum divinae veritatis non potest esse falsitas; Filius Dei venit ad manifestandum divinam veritatem in promissionibus a Deo factis complendis per ipsum; ergo in ipso non est falsitas. Et hoc est quod dicit: non est in Filio Dei *est et non*, sed *est*, quia *quotquot promissiones Dei*, scilicet sunt factae hominibus, *in illo*, id est in Christo, *est*, id est in Christo verificantur et complentur.

my witness that *our speech*, namely, our preaching, *which was to you, was not, it is, it is not*, i.e., there is no falsity in it. *A faithful God, without deceit, just and upright is he* (Deut 32:4).

But if *God is faithful* is taken for the truth of the divine promise, then the sense is: God is faithful, i.e., he keeps his promises, but he had promised to send you preachers of the truth: *I will give you shepherds after my own heart* (Jer 3:15). Therefore, since I was sent by him, *our speech which was to you, is not in him, it is, and it is not*.

40. In regard to the cause, he excuses himself, at *for the Son of God*. He does this for two reasons, namely, from the motive and the efficient cause, at *now he who confirms us*.

His motive for not lying is that a person who assumes an office is naturally moved to what suits that office and not to what is contrary; but it is obvious that the Apostle's office is to preach the truth. Therefore, he is not moved to the contrary of the truth, which is to lie.

In regard to this he does three things:

first, he proves the truth of his word by the word of Christ;

second, he proves the truth of Christ by the word of God, at *for all the promises*;

third, he concludes to what he intended, at *therefore also by him*.

41. He says, therefore: I say that our words should be regarded as true, and true they are, because we have preached Christ, in whom there is no falsehood. And this is what he says, *for the Son of God, Jesus Christ, who was preached among you, by us, by me*, i.e., to say principally, *and Sylvanus*, secondarily (he is the Silas of Acts 18:5), *and Timothy* mentioned above. For those two were with the Apostle when he first converted them.

He, namely, the Son of God, *was not, it is and it is not*, i.e., there was not falsity, for he did nothing unbecoming, *but it is, was in him* i.e., the truth, for truth and being are convertible: *I am the way and the truth and the life* (John 14:6).

42. But because there might be some doubt about his statement that there was no falsity in Christ, he at once proves this, saying, *for however many promises of God there are*.

He proves this in the following way: it is obvious that there can be no falsity in that which is the manifestation of the divine truth; but the Son of God came to manifest the divine truth in the promises made by God to be fulfilled through him. Therefore there is no falsity in him. And that is what he says: there is not in the Son of God *it is and it is not*, but *it is*, because *however many promises of God there are*, namely made to men, *is in him*, i.e., in Christ, i.e., they

Rom. XV, 8: *dico Iesum Christum ministrum fuisse*, et cetera. *Ad confirmandas*, et cetera.

43. Ex his ergo concludit, quod postquam dicta sua vera sunt, quia praedicat Filium Dei, in quo est veritas, *ideo et per ipsum*, scilicet Christum, dicimus, *amen Deo*, id est verum. Apoc. III, 14: *haec dicit, amen testis fidelis*, et cetera. Is. LXV, 16: *qui benedictus est in terra, benedicetur in Deo, amen*, et cetera.

Et istam veritatem dicimus *Deo*, id est, ad honorem Dei, scilicet manifestantes eius veritatem et *gloriam nostram*, quia gloria nostra est conversio vestra. Vel *gloria nostra*, quia gloria nostra est ostendere et praedicare verbum Dei.

44. Consequenter cum dicit *qui autem confirmat*, etc., probat Apostolus quod non est mentitus, per causam efficientem. Licet enim homo ex libero arbitrio possit uti lingua sua ad verum vel ad falsum loquendum, nihilominus tamen Deus potest confirmare hominem sic in vero, ut non nisi vera loquatur. Si ergo Deus aliquem confirmaret in vero, manifestum est quod non diceret falsum; sed Deus confirmat nos in veritate; ergo, et cetera.

Et ideo dicit quod Deus est *qui confirmat vos nobiscum in Christo*, id est, in vera praedicatione Christi, quasi dicat: si Christus esset extra nos, possemus mentiri, sed ex quo est nobiscum, et nos sumus in Christo, non mentimur. Ps. LXXIV, 4: *ego confirmavi columnas eius*, et cetera.

Sumus ergo in Christo dupliciter, scilicet per gratiam et per gloriam. Per gratiam quidem sumus inquantum uncti sumus Spiritus Sancti gratia, et effecti sumus membra Christi, et iuncti sibi. Qua etiam gratia Christus unctus est secundum quod homo. Ps. XLIV, v. 8: *unxit te Deus*, et cetera. Et ex plenitudine istius unctionis redundavit in omnes suos, sicut *unguentum in capite*, scilicet Christo, *quod descendit*, et cetera. Et ideo dicit quod *unxit nos Deus*. Unxit, inquam, in reges et sacerdotes. Apoc. V, 10: *fecisti nos Deo*, et cetera. I Petr. II, 9: *vos autem genus electum*, et cetera.

45. Unionem autem quae est per gloriam, non habemus in re, sed in spe certa, inquantum habemus firmam spem vitae aeternae. Et habemus duplicem certitudinem spei huius unionis consequendae. Una est per signum, alia per pignus.

Per signum evidens, quia fidei. Unde dicit *signavit nos* signo fidei Christi. Item signum crucis. Ez. IX, 4: *signa thau*, id est signum crucis. Apoc. VII, 3: *quoadusque signemus servos Dei nostri*, et cetera. Et hoc per Spiritum Sanctum. Rom. VIII, 9: *si quis Spiritum Christi non habet*, et cetera. Et ideo speciale et certum signum

are verified and fulfilled in Christ: *I tell you that Christ became a servant to the circumcised . . . in order to confirm the promises* (Rom 15:8).

43. From this, therefore, the Apostle concludes that his words are true, because he preaches the Son of God, in whom is the truth. **Therefore also by him**, namely, Christ, we utter **amen**, i.e., it is true. *The words of the amen, the faithful and true witness* (Rev 3:14); *he who blesses himself in the land shall bless himself by the God of truth, amen* (Isa 65:16).

This truth we say **to God**, i.e., to the honor of God, namely, manifesting his truth to the glory of God and **our glory**, because our glory is to show and preach the word of God.

44. Then when he says, **now he who confirms us with you in Christ**, and has anointed us, the Apostle proves that he has not lied by the efficient cause. For although a man by his free will can employ his tongue for speaking truth or falsity, God can establish a man so well in the truth, that he would speak nothing but the truth. Therefore, if God established someone in the truth, it is obvious that he could not say anything false; but God establishes us in the truth.

And therefore he says, it is God **who confirms us with you in Christ**, i.e., in the true preaching of Christ. As if to say: if Christ were outside us, we could lie, but because he is with us and we in Christ, we do not lie. *It is I who keep steady its pillars* (Ps 75:3).

Therefore we are in Christ in two ways, namely, by grace and by glory: by grace, inasmuch as we have been anointed with the grace of the Holy Spirit and made members of Christ and joined to him; by which grace Christ as man was also anointed: *God, your God, has anointed you with the oil of gladness above your fellows* (Ps 45:7). And from the fullness of that anointing it has overflowed to all of us as *the precious oil on the head*, namely of Christ, *has flowed down on the beard, the beard of Aaron* (Ps 133:2). Therefore, he says that he who **has annointed us, is God**. He anointed us, I say, as kings and priests: *you made them a kingdom and priests to our God* (Rev 5:10); *you are a chosen race, a royal priesthood, a holy nation* (1 Pet 2:9).

45. But the union which is according to glory we do not yet have in reality, but in sure hope, inasmuch as we have a firm hope of attaining to this union. And we have a twofold certainty of hope resulting from the hope of this union. One is by a sign, the other by a pledge.

The first is by an evident sign, which is of faith. Hence he says, **he who has sealed us** with the sign of Christian faith. *Put a mark on their foreheads* (Ezek 9:4), i.e., the sign of the cross. *Till we have sealed the servants of our God upon their foreheads* (Rev 7:3). And this is done through the Holy Spirit: *anyone who does not have the Spirit of Christ does not*

est vitae aeternae consequendae configurari Christo. Cant. VIII, 6: *pone me ut signaculum*, et cetera. Vel signavit signo vitae.

Per pignus vero maximum, quia Spiritus Sancti, et ideo dicit **dedit pignus Spiritus in cordibus nostris**. De quo certum est quod nullus potest eum accipere a nobis.

46. Sed nota, in pignore duo sunt consideranda, scilicet quod faciat spem habendae rei, et quod valeat tantum, quantum valet res, vel plus; et haec duo sunt in Spiritu Sancto. Quia si consideremus substantiam Spiritus Sancti, sic valet tantum Spiritus Sanctus quantum vita aeterna, quae est ipse Deus, quia scilicet valet quantum omnes tres personae. Si vero consideretur modus habendi, sic facit spem, et non possessionem vitae aeternae, quia nondum perfecte habemus ipsum in vita ista. Et ideo non perfecte beati sumus, nisi quando perfecte habebimus in patria. Eph. I, 13: *signati estis Spiritu*.

47. Consequenter cum dicit **ego autem testem**, etc., excusat se de eo quod non venit: et hoc per iuramentum quod maius est. Et circa hoc tria facit. Primo ponit suam excusationem; secundo respondet tacitae quaestioni, ibi **non quia dominamur**; tertio exponit quod dicit, ibi **nam fide statis**.

Excusat se autem per iuramentum duplex. Unum attestationis, cum dicit **ego autem testem Deum invoco**, aliud execrationis, cum dicit **in animam meam**, id est, contra animam meam. Rom. I, 9: *testis est mihi Deus*, et cetera. **Testem**, inquam, **invoco Deum**, quia **non veni ultra**, id est, post primam vicem, vel postquam discessi a vobis; et hoc feci, **parcens vobis**, scilicet quia ipse sciebat eos incorrigibiles. Unde si ivisset tunc, aut punivisset, et sic forte recessissent totaliter a fide; aut non punivisset, et sic dedisset occasionem magis peccandi.

Sed quia aliquis posset dicere: quare dicis **parcens vobis**? Numquid dominus noster es? Ideo consequenter hoc removet, dicens **non**, dico, **quia dominamur fidei vestrae, sed adiutores**, etc., quasi dicat: non dico hoc ut dominus, sed ut coadiutor. I Petr. V, v. 3: *non enim dominantes in cleris*, et cetera. Adiutor, inquam, **gaudii vestri**, vel emendationis vestrae.

Quare autem dicat, **fidei vestrae**, exponit consequenter, dicens **nam fide statis**, id est, statis in gratia ista Christi per fidem.

belong to him (Rom 8:9). Therefore the special and certain sign of obtaining eternal life is configuration to Christ. *Set me as a seal upon your heart* (Song 8:6). Or he sealed us with the sign of life.

The second is by the greatest pledge, i.e., of the Holy Spirit; and so he says **and given the pledge of the Spirit in our hearts**, and we are certain that no one can take him from us.

46. But note that there are two things to be considered in a pledge, namely, that it produces a hope of obtaining the reality, and that it is as valid as the reality or more so. And these two things are in the Holy Spirit, because if we consider the substance of the Holy Spirit, he is as valid as eternal life, which is God, because he is as valid as the three persons. But if we consider the manner of possession, then it produces the hope but not the possession of eternal life, because we do not yet have him perfectly in this life. Therefore we are not perfectly happy until we have him perfectly in heaven. *You were sealed with the promised Holy Spirit* (Eph 1:13).

47. The when he says, **but I call God to witness**, he gives his excuse for not coming; and this is by oath which is greater. In regard to this he does three things: first, he states the excuse; second, he answer a tacit question, at **not because we exercise**; third, he explains what he says, at **for in faith you stand**.

He excuses himself with a double oath: one of attestation, when he says, **I call God to witness**; the other of execration, when he says, **upon my soul**, i.e., against my soul: *for God is my witness* (Rom 1:9). **To witness**, I say, **I call God**, because **I came no more**, i.e., after the first time or after I departed from you; and this I did **to spare you**, namely, because he knew that they were incorrigible. Hence, if he had gone then, he would either have punished them, and they perhaps would have left the faith altogether, or he would not have punished them, and then he would have been giving them occasion to sin more.

But because someone could say, why do you say **to spare us**? Are you our lord? He removes this, saying, **not because we exercise dominion over your faith: but we are helpers of your joy**. As if to say: I do not say this as a lord, but as a helper. *Not as those domineering over those in your charge, but being examples to the flock* (1 Pet 5:3). A helper, I say, **of your joy**, or for your improvement.

Why he says, **over your faith**, he explains, saying, **for in faith you stand**, i.e., you stand in that grace of Christ by faith.

CHAPTER 2

Lecture 1

2:1Statui autem hoc ipsum apud me, ne iterum in tristitia venirem ad vos. [n. 48]

2:2Si enim ego contristo vos: et quis est, qui me laetificet, nisi qui contristatur ex me? [n. 50]

2:3Et hoc ipsum scripsi vobis, ut non cum venero, tristitiam super tristitiam habeam, de quibus oportuerat me gaudere: confidens in omnibus vobis, quia meum gaudium, omnium vestrum est. [n. 52]

2:4Nam ex multa tribulatione et angustia cordis scripsi vobis per multas lacrimas: non ut contristemini, sed ut sciatis, quam caritatem habeam abundantius in vobis. [n. 55]

2:1Ἔκρινα γὰρ ἐμαυτῷ τοῦτο τὸ μὴ πάλιν ἐν λύπῃ πρὸς ὑμᾶς ἐλθεῖν.

2:2εἰ γὰρ ἐγὼ λυπῶ ὑμᾶς, καὶ τίς ὁ εὐφραίνων με εἰ μὴ ὁ λυπούμενος ἐξ ἐμοῦ;

2:3καὶ ἔγραψα τοῦτο αὐτό, ἵνα μὴ ἐλθὼν λύπην σχῶ ἀφ᾽ ὧν ἔδει με χαίρειν, πεποιθὼς ἐπὶ πάντας ὑμᾶς ὅτι ἡ ἐμὴ χαρὰ πάντων ὑμῶν ἐστιν.

2:4ἐκ γὰρ πολλῆς θλίψεως καὶ συνοχῆς καρδίας ἔγραψα ὑμῖν διὰ πολλῶν δακρύων, οὐχ ἵνα λυπηθῆτε ἀλλὰ τὴν ἀγάπην ἵνα γνῶτε ἣν ἔχω περισσοτέρως εἰς ὑμᾶς.

2:1But I determined this with myself, not to come to you again in sorrow. [n. 48]

2:2For if I make you sorrowful, who is he then that can make me glad, but the same who is made sorrowful by me? [n. 50]

2:3And I wrote this same to you: that I may not, when I come, have sorrow upon sorrow from them on account of whom I ought to rejoice: having confidence in you all, because my joy is the joy of you all. [n. 52]

2:4For out of much affliction and anguish of heart, I wrote to you with many tears: not that you should be made sorrowful: but that you might know the charity I have more abundantly towards you. [n. 55]

---

48. Apostolus supra posuit excusationem in generali de mora eundi ad Corinthios, hic vero insinuat causam tantae morae, et quomodo eis pepercit.

Circa hoc autem duo facit.

Primo enim insinuat unam causam dilationis fuisse ne in adventu suo tristitiam inferret eis;

secundo ostendit aliam causam fuisse ne fructus quem apud alios sperabat, et inceperat facere, impediretur, ibi *cum venissem autem*, et cetera.

Circa primum duo facit.

Primo ostendit causam dilationis esse in communi, ne tristitiam inferret;

secundo loquitur in speciali de quodam, qui eum contristaverat, ibi *si quis autem contristavit me*. Circa primum tria facit.

Primo assignat rationem quare venire distulit;

secundo causam dicti assignat *si enim ego contristatus*, etc.;

tertio manifestat quae dixit, ibi *nam ex multa tribulatione*.

49. Dicit ergo: dixi quod non veni ad vos parcens vobis, in hoc scilicet quia nolui vos contristari, ideo *statui*, id est firmiter disposui, *hoc ipsum apud me*, quod proposui, cum aliam epistolam misi, Eccli. XXXVII, v. 20:

48. After giving a general excuse for his delay in visiting the Corinthians, the Apostle now gives the cause of his delay and how he spared them.

In regard to this he does two things:

first, he mentions that one cause of his delay was that he might not pain them by coming;

second, he shows that another cause was that the fruit he hoped for from others and which was beginning to ripen, might not be hindered, at *when I had come*.

In regard to the first he does two things:

first, he shows that the cause of his delay in general was to avoid paining them;

second, he speaks in particular about a certain person who had grieved him, at *and if anyone has caused grief*. In regard to the first he does three things:

first, he tells why he postponed his visit;

second, he gives the reason for his statement, at *for if I make you sorrowful*;

third, he explains what he said, at *for out of much affliction*.

49. He says, therefore: I have said that it was in order not to grieve you that I did not come to you. Therefore, *I determined*, i.e., firmly prescribed *this with myself*, what I mentioned when I sent the other letter: *reason is the*

ante omnia verbum verum, et cetera. **Ne iterum**, id est alia vice, **in tristitia venirem ad vos**, id est vos contristem.

Et ratio quare noluit eos contristare est illa qua Dominus noluit ieiunare discipulos suos, scilicet ad hoc, ut amore et non timore afficerentur ad Christum, et iungerentur sibi. Voluit enim eos Dominus firmare et nutrire in fide, in omni dulcedine et desiderio cordis, et sic, firmati ex amore, non de facili avellerentur propter tribulationes, quia *aquae multae non potuerunt extinguere caritatem*, Cant. VIII, 7. Similiter Apostolus non vult eos propter hoc contristare.

50. Rationem huius dicti, scilicet quod non vult eos contristare, assignat cum dicit **si enim ego contristo**, et cetera.

Et circa hoc duo facit.

Primo assignat causam quare noluit eos contristare;

secundo manifestat quare hoc significet eis, ibi **et hoc ipsum scripsi**.

51. Dicit ergo: ratio quare nolui in tristitia venire est quia tristitia vestra redundat in tristitiam meam, et de consolatione vestra gaudeo, et solum vos consolamini me, cum sum apud vos; unde, si venirem et contristarem vos, ego ex tristitia vestra tristarer, et sic nullus esset qui laetificaret me inter vos, qui contristamini ex me, quia contristatus non de facili alium consolatur. Prov. c. X, 1: *filius sapiens*, et cetera. Prov. XXIX, 3: *vir qui amat sapientiam*, et cetera.

Vel aliter: est duplex tristitia. Una secundum mundum; alia secundum Deum, quae poenitentiam in salutem operatur. Apostolus non loquitur de prima, sed de secunda. Et dicit: ex hoc ipso ego consolabor, si contristo vos, id est, si increpando reduco ad poenitentiam; sed si venirem, et viderem vos non poenitere de peccatis, tunc nullam consolationem haberem, quia nullus contristatur et poenitet ex me, id est, mea correctione et increpatione.

52. Causa autem quare hoc scribo vobis est ut ita disponatis vos quod, quando venero, non habeam tristitiam de eo quod viderim vos incorrectos, super tristitiam quam habui, quando audivi vos peccasse.

Et circa hoc duo facit. Primo ponit admonitionem; secundo spem de impletione admonitionis ostendit, ibi **confidens in omnibus vobis**, et cetera.

Admonitio est ista: ideo **scripsi vobis hoc**, scilicet quod tristor de peccato vestro commisso, II Petr. II, 8: *iniquis operibus animam iusti cruciabant*, etc., ut paretis et disponatis vos corrigendo, **ut cum venero** ad vos, **non habeam tristitiam** de peccatis, **de quibus**, scilicet vobis, **oportuerat me gaudere**, id est, debebam laetari

beginning of every work, and counsel precedes every undertaking (Sir 37:16); **not to come to you again in sorrow**, i.e., not to cause you pain.

The reason he did not wish to grieve them is the same one whereby the Lord did not wish his disciples to fast, namely, in order that they be drawn to Christ and be joined to him not by fear but by love. For the Lord wished to strengthen and nourish them in the faith in all sweetness and heartfelt desire, so that, being thus established in love, they would not easily turn away from him because of tribulations, for *many waters cannot extinguish love* (Song 8:7). For the same reason the Apostle does not want to pain them on this account.

50. He assigns the reason for what he says, namely, that he does not want to pain them, when he says, **for if I make you sorrowful**.

In regard to this he does two things:

first, he deals with the reason why he did not wish to pain them;

second, he shows why he tells them this, at **and I wrote this**.

51. He says, therefore: the reason why I did not wish you to fall into sadness was that your sadness pains me, and I rejoice in your consolation; and you only console me when I am with you. Hence, if I had come and pained you, I would be sad at your sadness; then there would be no one among you to gladden me, because you would be sad on my account. For one who is sad does not easily console another person. *A wise son makes a glad father, but a foolish son is a sorrow to his mother* (Prov 10:1); *he who loves wisdom makes his father glad* (Prov 29:3).

Or in another way, there are two kinds of sadness. One is according to the world, and the other according to God who produces repentance leading to salvation. The Apostle is not speaking of the first, but of the second. He says: I will be consoled if I cause you pain, i.e., if by scolding you I bring you to repentance; but if I had come and seen you unrepentant of your sins, I would have had no consolation, because no one is sad and repentant because of me, i.e., because of my correction and rebuke.

52. But the reason I write this to you is that you so adjust yourselves, that when I come, I will not be sad at seeing you uncorrected, in addition to the sadness I experienced when I heard that you had sinned.

In regard to this he does two things: first, he gives his admonition; second, he shows his hope in their observance of his admonition, at **having confidence in you all**.

The admonition is this: **I wrote this same to you**, namely, that I am pained at the sin you committed: *he was vexed in his righteous soul day after day with their lawless deeds* (2 Pet 2:8), in order that you might prepare and arrange yourselves by correction, **that I may not, when I come, have sorrow upon sorrow**, on account of sins, **from them**,

et congratulari, scilicet de praesentia vestra. Lc. XV, 10: *gaudium est angelis Dei*, et cetera.

Qualem autem spem habeat de impletione suae admonitionis, subdit, dicens: *confidens de omnibus vobis*, etc.; quasi dicat: hanc fiduciam habeo de vobis taliter disponi vos, ut cum venero, omnes detis mihi materiam gaudii. Et hoc debetis libenter facere, *quia gaudium meum*, etc., id est cedit ad gaudium vestrum, vel est propter gaudium vestrum, quod habetis de recuperatione gratiae. I Tim. II: *quod est gaudium meum* et cetera. Rom. XII, 15: *gaudere cum gaudentibus*, et cetera.

53. Sed quia posset aliquis dubitare de hoc, quod dicit *ne, cum venero, tristitiam super tristitiam habeam*, et quaerere quam tristitiam habuit de eis, ideo consequenter hoc exponit, dicens *nam ex multa tribulatione*, et cetera.

Et circa hoc duo facit.

Primo manifestat tristitiam iamdudum habitam;

secundo respondet cuidam tacitae quaestioni, ibi *non ut contristemini*, et cetera.

54. Dicit ergo primo: quia haberem tristitiam, si non invenirem vos correctos, super tristitiam quam habui quando peccastis, et oportuit me contristare vos redarguendo dure. *Nam ex multa tribulatione et angustia cordis scripsi* primam epistolam, *per multas lacrymas*, quas fudi pro vobis iam mortuis per peccatum. Ier. IX, 1: *quis dabit capiti meo aquas*, et cetera. Eccli. XXII, v. 3: *confusio est patri de filio indisciplinato*. Is. LVII, 1: *iustus perit, et non est qui recogitet*, et cetera.

Sciendum est autem quod duo ponit ad exaggerationem tristitiae, tribulationem scilicet et angustiam, quia unum additum alteri aggravat tristitiam. Nam aliquando quis tribulatur, sed sine angustia, tunc scilicet quando aliqua adversitate quasi acutissimo tribulo pungitur, et tamen videt sibi patere vias evadendi, quia si non pateat, tribulationi angustia iungitur. Dicit ergo *ex multa tribulatione*, qua pungebar de facto et malo vestri, *et angustia cordis*, quia non videbam unde de facili posset poni remedium, *scripsi*, et cetera. Ps. CXVIII, 143: *tribulatio et angustia invenerunt me*.

55. Sed quia possent dicere: O Apostole, etiam haec scribis nobis ut tristemur, et ideo hoc removet, dicens *non ut contristemini*, scilicet scribo vobis illa, *sed ut sciatis quam caritatem habeam in vobis*. Duo enim sunt signa dilectionis, scilicet quod gaudeat quis de bono alterius, et tristetur de malo eius, et haec ego habeo ad vos. Infra V, v. 14: *caritas Christi urget nos*. Abundantius, quam credatis, vel abundantius quam ad alios.

namely, from you, *on account of whom I ought to rejoice*, i.e., I ought to rejoice and be glad in your presence. *There is joy before the angels of God over one sinner who repents* (Luke 15:10).

The confidence he had that they would follow his admonition is indicated when he says, *having confidence in you all*. As if to say: I have this confidence in you, that you will be so disposed, that when I come, all of you will give me reason for joy; and you should do this cheerfully, *because my joy is the joy of you all*, i.e., it would contribute to your joy, or it is for the sake of your joy, which you have from the recovery of grace. *Rejoice with those who rejoice* (Rom 12:15)

53. But because someone might be in doubt at his saying, *that I may not, when I come, have sorrow upon sorrow*, and ask what sort of sorrow he had for them, he explains this saying, *for out of much affliction and anguish of heart, I wrote to you*.

In regard to this he does two things:

first, he mentions the pain he has already suffered;

second, he answers a tacit question, at *not that you should be made sorrowful*.

54. First, therefore, he says: I would be pained if I found you uncorrected—a greater pain than I had when you sinned and I was obliged to sadden you with a sharp rebuke: *for out of much affliction and anguish of heart, I wrote to you* in the first epistle, *with many tears*, which I shed for you when you were already dead in sin. *O that my head were waters, and my eyes a fountain of tears* (Jer 9:1); *it is a disgrace to be the father of an undisciplined son* (Sir 22:3); *the righteous man perishes and no one lays it to heart* (Isa 57:1).

But it should be noted that he mentions two things that amplify his pain, namely, affliction and anguish, because one added to the other increases sadness. For sometimes a person is sad but without anguish, namely, when he is pricked by some adversity as though by a very sharp thorn; and yet various ways of escape seem open to him, because if no way is open, anguish is joined to affliction. He says, therefore, *out of much affliction*, with which he was pricked by your deeds and your evil, *and anguish of heart*, because he could not see where a remedy could easily be found. *Trouble and anguish have come upon me* (Ps 119:143).

55. But because they could say: O Apostle, you even write these things to pain us, he anticipates this, saying, *not that you should be made sorrowful* do I write these things to you, *but that you might know the charity I have more abundantly towards you*. For there are two signs of love, namely, to rejoice in the good of another and to be pained at his evil; and I have these toward you: *for the love of Christ presses us* (2 Cor 5:14). More abundantly than you think, or more abundantly than toward others.

Lecture 2

^{2:5}Si quis autem contristavit, non me contristavit: sed ex parte, ut non onerem omnes vos. [n. 56]

^{2:6}Sufficit illi, qui ejusmodi est, objurgatio haec, quae fit a pluribus: [n. 59]

^{2:7}ita ut e contrario magis donetis, et consolemini, ne forte abundantiori tristitia absorbeatur qui ejusmodi est. [n. 60]

^{2:8}Propter quod obsecro vos, ut confirmetis in illum caritatem. [n. 63]

^{2:9}Ideo enim et scripsi, ut cognoscam experimentum vestrum, an in omnibus obedientes sitis. [n. 64]

^{2:10}Cui autem aliquid donastis, et ego: nam et ego quod donavi, si quid donavi, propter vos in persona Christi, [n. 65]

^{2:11}ut non circumveniamur a Satana: non enim ignoramus cogitationes ejus.

---

^{2:5}Εἰ δέ τις λελύπηκεν, οὐκ ἐμὲ λελύπηκεν, ἀλλὰ ἀπὸ μέρους, ἵνα μὴ ἐπιβαρῶ, πάντας ὑμᾶς.

^{2:6}ἱκανὸν τῷ τοιούτῳ ἡ ἐπιτιμία αὕτη ἡ ὑπὸ τῶν πλειόνων,

^{2:7}ὥστε τοὐναντίον μᾶλλον ὑμᾶς χαρίσασθαι καὶ παρακαλέσαι, μή πως τῇ περισσοτέρᾳ λύπῃ καταποθῇ ὁ τοιοῦτος.

^{2:8}διὸ παρακαλῶ ὑμᾶς κυρῶσαι εἰς αὐτὸν ἀγάπην·

^{2:9}εἰς τοῦτο γὰρ καὶ ἔγραψα, ἵνα γνῶ τὴν δοκιμὴν ὑμῶν, εἰ εἰς πάντα ὑπήκοοί ἐστε.

^{2:10}ᾧ δέ τι χαρίζεσθε, κἀγώ· καὶ γὰρ ἐγὼ ὃ κεχάρισμαι, εἴ τι κεχάρισμαι, δι᾽ ὑμᾶς ἐν προσώπῳ Χριστοῦ,

^{2:11}ἵνα μὴ πλεονεκτηθῶμεν ὑπὸ τοῦ σατανᾶ· οὐ γὰρ αὐτοῦ τὰ νοήματα ἀγνοοῦμεν.

---

^{2:5}And if anyone has caused grief, he has not grieved me: but in part, that I may not burden you all. [n. 56]

^{2:6}To him who is such a one, this rebuke is sufficient, which is given by many. [n. 59]

^{2:7}So that on the contrary, you should rather forgive him and comfort him, lest perhaps such a one be swallowed up with excessive sorrow. [n. 60]

^{2:8}Therefore, I beseech you that you would confirm your charity towards him. [n. 63]

^{2:9}For to this end also did I write, that I may know your trial, whether you be obedient in all things. [n. 64]

^{2:10}And to whom you have pardoned anything, I also. For, what I have pardoned, if I have pardoned anything, I have done it for your sakes, in the person of Christ: [n. 65]

^{2:11}That we may not be overreached by Satan. For we are not ignorant of his devices.

---

56. Postquam Apostolus insinuavit causam dilationis, ne scilicet tristitiam inferret, et de eius contristatione tractavit, hic consequenter tractat de contristante.

Et circa hoc tria facit.

Primo enim exaggerat culpam contristantis;

secundo poenam eius pro culpa inflictam, ibi *sufficit illi*, etc.;

tertio hortatur eos habere misericordiam ad contristantem, ibi *ita ut e contrario*, et cetera.

57. Dicit ergo primo: *scripsi vobis per multas lacrymas*, quas fudi propter tristitiam conceptam et propter poenam infligendam peccanti, sed *si quis contristavit me*, ille scilicet fornicarius enormis, de quo dicitur I Cor. V, 1: *omnino auditur inter vos fornicatio*, et cetera. Iste, inquam, et si contristavit, *non contristavit me, sed ex parte*, id est, non contristavit me, scilicet solum, sed vos et nos. Non omnes, *sed ex parte*.

Et hoc dico, *non ut onerem vos omnes*, id est, ut vobis hoc onus omnibus non imponam derisorie loquendo, quasi dicat: non ita estis boni et diligitis me, quod pro tristitia mea, et pro peccato fratris omnes doleatis. Vel *ut non onerem omnes vos*, non tantum illos qui non doluerunt de peccato.

56. After giving the reason for his delay, namely, to avoid paining them, and after telling them of his sadness, the Apostle then treats here of the one causing his sadness.

In regard to this he does three things:

first, he speaks more fully of the guilt of the one who causes this sadness;

second, of his punishment for the injury he inflicted, at *to him who is such a one*;

third, he urges them to have mercy on this person, at *so that on the contrary*.

57. He says, therefore: *I wrote to you with many tears*, which I shed because of the sadness I felt and because of the punishment to be inflicted on the sinner, *and if anyone has caused me grief* he, namely, the heinous fornicator of whom it is said: *it is actually reported that there is immorality among you, and of a kind that is not found even among pagans* (1 Cor 5:1), that one, I say, even if he has caused sorrow, *he has not grieved me: but in part*, i.e., he has caused it not to me alone, but you and us. Not all, *but in part*.

And I say this, *that I may not burden you all*, i.e., that I may not lay this burden on all of you by speaking derisively. As if to say: you are not so good or love me so much that all of you would weep over my sadness and over the sin of a brother. Or, *that I may not burden you all*, not only those who did not grieve over the sin.

58. Vel aliter dicendum, et melius, ***non me contrista-vit, sed ex parte***, et cetera.

Sciendum est enim quod aliquis aliquando tristatur totaliter, et aliquando non totaliter. Totaliter quidem tristatur quis, quando prae tristitia absorbetur a dolore; et haec tristitia est ***quae mortem operatur***, ut dicitur infra, c. VII, 10, quae quidem, secundum Philosophum, *non cadit in sapientem*. Non totaliter autem tristatur quis quando licet ex aliquo malo quod patitur seu videt fieri, tristatur, tamen ex aliis causis bonis gaudet, et ista tristitia est secundum Deum et cadit in sapientem. Quia ergo Apostolus dicit se contristatum, ne credatur totaliter a tristitia absorptus, quod non est sapientis, dicit se contristatum ex parte, quasi non totaliter.

Et secundum hoc legitur sic: contristavit me, scilicet fornicarius, propter peccatum suum sed non me contristavit totaliter, quia licet in ipso propter peccatum habuerim tristitiam, tamen in vobis propter multa bona quae facitis, et in ipso propter poenitentiam quam fecit, habeo gaudium. Et dico ***ex parte, ut non onerem omnes vos***, id est, ut non imponam vobis hoc onus, quod scilicet contristaveritis me.

59. Sed ne isti propter tristitiam Apostoli adhuc vellent eum magis punire, ostendit eis poenam sufficientem fuisse, dicens ***sufficit illi qui eiusmodi est***, quod scilicet contristavit me, tam graviter peccando, ***obiurgatio quae fit a pluribus***, id est tam manifesta et publica correctio, quae fuit, quod separatus fuit ab omni communione, id est excommunicatus ab Ecclesia et traditus Satanae, ut habetur I Cor. V, 5. Est ergo sufficiens haec poena propter dictas causas.

Vel potest dici sufficiens, non quantum ad Dei iudicium, sed quantum expediebat tempori et personae. Melius enim est sic servare lenitatis spiritum in corrigendo, ut per poenitentiam correctionis fructus sequatur, quam si durius corrigatur, et desperet peccans et maioribus peccatis immergatur. Et ideo dicitur Eccli. XXI, 5: *obiurgatio et iniuriae annullabunt substantiam*.

60. Quia ergo poena sufficiens fuit et poenitentiam egit, ideo consequenter inducit eos ad miserendum, dicens ***ita ut e contrario magis***, etc., ubi tria facit.

Primo mandat ut ei, scilicet peccanti, parcant;

secundo huius rationem assignat, ibi ***ne forte***, et cetera.

Tertio inducit eos ad observantiam huius monitionis, ibi ***propter quod***, et cetera.

61. Dicit ergo primo: dico quod sufficiens poena est illi, et intantum ut velim ***ut e contrario magis donetis***, id est remittatis. Lc. VI, 37: *dimittite, et dimittetur vobis*. Eph. IV, 32: *donantes invicem, sicut et Deus in Christo donavit vobis*.

58. Or it could be said and better: ***he has not grieved me: but in part***.

For it should be noted that sometimes a person is completely saddened and sometimes not. He is completely saddened when he is engrossed by pain with his grief. This is the sadness ***that works death***, as he says below, but that, according to the Philosopher, *does not happen to a wise man*. He is not completely sad when, although he is sad about some evil he is suffering or seems to be on its way, he nevertheless rejoices for other good reasons. This sadness is according to God and does happen to a wise man. Therefore, because the Apostle says that he was very sad, he adds that he was sad in some measure, as though not entirely, lest they suppose that he was altogether engrossed by sadness, which does not befit a wise man.

According to this, the meaning is: he, i.e., the fornicator, has pained me on account of his sin, but he has not pained me entirely. For although I grieved for him because of his sin, yet I take joy in you because of the many good things you do, and in him because of his repentance. I say, ***in part, so that I may not burden you all***, i.e., that I may not lay this burden on you, namely, that you should grieve me.

59. But lest they should wish to punish him more on account of the Apostle's sadness, he shows them that the punishment was sufficient, saying, ***for such a one***, namely, he who pained me so much by sinning, ***this rebuke is sufficient, which is given by many***, i.e., such a harsh public correction that he was excommunicated from the Church and delivered to Satan (1 Cor 5:5). Therefore this punishment is enough for the above reasons.

Or it can be called sufficient, not as to God's judgment, but as was expedient for the time and the person. For it is better to observe such a spirit of leniency in correcting, that the fruit of correction follows on the penance, than to correct so harshly that the sinner despairs and falls into worse sins. Therefore it is said: *terror and violence will lay waste riches* (Sir 21:4).

60. Therefore, because that punishment was sufficient and he did penance, he urges them to show mercy, saying, ***so that on the contrary, you should rather forgive him and comfort him***. Here he does three things:

first, he commands them to spare the sinner;

second, he gives the reason, at ***lest perhaps***;

third, he urges them to observe this admonition, at ***therefore, I beseech you***.

61. He says first, therefore: I say that the punishment is sufficient for him, ***so that on the contrary, you should forgive him***. *Forgive, and you will be forgiven* (Luke 6:37); *forgiving one another, as God in Christ forgave you* (Eph 4:32).

Et non solum donetis, sed, quod plus est, *consolemini*. Et hoc proponendo sibi exempla peccantium, qui restituti sunt ad statum gratiae, sicut dicitur de David, Petro, Paulo, et Magdalena, et per verba Dei: Ez. XVIII, v. 32: *nolo mortem peccatoris*, et cetera. I Thess. c. ult.: *corripite inquietos, consolamini pusillanimes*, et cetera.

62. Rationem autem huius admonitionis subdit *ne forte abundantiori tristitia absorbeatur qui eiusmodi est*. Aliquis enim propter peccatum et poenam peccati, aliquando sic mergitur tristitia, quod absorbetur, dum nullum habet consolatorem; et hoc est malum, quia non sequitur ex hoc poenitentiae fructus, qui speratur, scilicet correctio, sed potius desperans tradit se omnibus peccatis, sicut Cain, cum dixit: *maior est iniquitas*, etc., Gen. IV, 13; et Eph. IV, 19: *qui desperantes tradiderunt se*, et cetera. Et propter hoc dicitur II Reg. II, 26, quod periculosa res est desperatio. Et ideo dicebat David in Ps. LXVIII, 16: *neque absorbeat me profundum*, et cetera.

Et ideo ne hoc contingat, dicit *consolamini*, ut scilicet cesset a peccato. Is. XXVII, v. 9: *hic est omnis fructus, ut auferatur peccatum*.

63. Contra Apostolus, non solum per rationem sed ex aliis causis, inducit eos ad hoc cum dicit *propter quod obsecro*, et cetera.

Et inducit eos a tribus modis. Primo precibus, dicens *propter quod*, scilicet ne absorbeatur, *obsecro*, qui possum praecipere. Phil. v. 8: *multam fiduciam habens in Christo Iesu imperandi tibi*, et cetera. Contrarium faciunt mali praelati. Ez. XXXIV, 4: *cum austeritate imperabatis eis*, et cetera. *Ut confirmetis in illum caritatem*. Quod fit si ostenditis caritatem vestram ad eum, et non abominamini eum propter peccata, nec contemnitis, sed propter consolationem vestram facitis eum habere odio peccatum suum, et diligere iustitiam. Lc. XXII, 32: *et tu conversus confirma fratres tuos*, et cetera.

64. Secundo inducit eos praecepto, dicens *ideo enim scripsi hoc*, scilicet *ut cognoscam experimentum vestrum, an in omnibus obedientes sitis*.

Et dicit *in omnibus*, scilicet sive in his quae placent vobis, sive in his quae displicent. Primo enim mandaverat eis quod excommunicarent eum, et sic fecerunt mandatum Apostoli: nunc vero secundo mandat eis quod parcant. Et ideo dicit *an in omnibus obedientes sitis*.

65. Tertio ex commemoratione beneficii, cum dicit *cui autem aliquid donastis*, etc., quasi dicat: vos debetis hoc facere, quia etiam ego feci. Sic enim vos remisistis alicui et rogastis me quod ego remitterem, et ego remisi.

You should not only forgive, but what is more, *comfort him*, and this by recalling to themselves the example of sinners who were restored to the state of grace, such as David, Peter, Paul and Magdalene, and through the Word of God: *for I have no pleasure in the death of any one, says the Lord God* (Ezek 18:32); *admonish the idlers, encourage the fainthearted, help the weak, be patient with them all* (1 Thess 5:14).

62. He gives the reason for this admonition, saying, *lest perhaps such a one be swallowed up with excessive sorrow*. For some are sometimes so steeped in sorrow because of sin and punishment of sin, that they are overcome, when they have no one to comfort them; and this is bad, because it does not result in the hope for the fruit of repentance, namely reformation, but in despair he delivers himself over to all sins, as Cain, when he said: *my punishment is greater than I can bear* (Gen. 4:13); *who, despairing, have given themselves up to licentiousness, greedy to practice every kind of uncleanness* (Eph 4:19). For this reason, despair is called a dangerous thing (2 Sam 2:26), so that David said: *let not the flood sweep over me, or the deep swallow me up, or the pit close its mouth over me* (Ps 69:15).

Therefore, in order to prevent this, he says, *comfort him*, so that he will cease sinning. *This will be the full fruit of the removal of his sin* (Isa 27:9).

63. Then the Apostle urges them not only by reason, but from other causes to do this, when he says, *therefore, I beseech you that you would confirm your charity towards him*.

And he urges them in three ways: first, by his appeal, saying, *therefore*, i.e., that he not be overwhelmed, *I*, who can command, *beseech*: *though I am bold enough in Christ to command you to do what is required, yet for love's sake I prefer to appeal to you* (Phlm 1:8). Evil prelates do the opposite: *with force and harshness you have ruled them* (Ezek 34:4). *That you would confirm your charity for him*, which happens if you show your charity for him and not hate him for his sins, or despise him, but for your consolation make him hate his sin and love justice: *strengthen your brethren* (Luke 22:32).

64. Second, he urges them with a command, saying, *for to this end also did I write*, namely, *that I may know your trial, whether you be obedient in all things*.

He says, *in all things* namely, whether they are pleasing or displeasing to you. For he had first commanded them to excommunicate him, and they obeyed the Apostle's command. But now he commands them to be sparing; hence he says, *whether you be obedient in all things*.

65. Third, he urges them by reminding them of a gift, when he says, *and to whom you have pardoned anything, I also*. As if to say: you should do this because I also have done it. For if you have forgiven someone and asked

Et hoc est quod dicit *cui autem aliquid donastis vos, et ego*, scilicet *donavi*.

66. Et hoc patet. *Nam et ego, quod donavi*, etc.; ubi quatuor tanguntur ad huiusmodi donationem seu remissionem necessaria.

Primum est discretio, ut scilicet non passim et temere remittatur. Et ideo dicit *si quid*, scilicet in debito modo. Prov. IV, 25: *palpebrae tuae praecedant*, et cetera. Secundum est finis, quia non propter amorem vel odium debet fieri, sed propter utilitatem aliquam Ecclesiae vel aliquorum. Et ideo dicit *propter vos*. Tertium est auctoritas, quia non debet fieri auctoritate propria, sed Christi, qui remittit peccata auctoritate; alii vero, quibus commissum est, ministerio, et sicut membra Christi. Et ideo dicit *in persona Christi*, scilicet non mea auctoritate. Et tamen quodcumque remittitur, Christus remittit. Io. XX, v. 23: *quorum remiseritis peccata*, et cetera. Quartum est necessitas; unde dicit *ut non circumveniamur a Satana*. Diabolus enim multos decepit, quosdam scilicet trahendo ad peccatorum perpetrationem, quosdam vero ad nimiam rigiditatem contra peccantes, ut si non potest eos habere per perpetrationem facinorum, saltem perdat quos iam habet per praelatorum austeritatem, qui eos non misericorditer corrigentes in desperationem inducunt, et sic hos perdit, et illos diaboli laqueus includit. Eccle. VII, 17: *noli esse nimis iustus*, et cetera. I Petr. V, 8: *adversarius vester diabolus*, et cetera. Et hoc continget nobis, si non remittamus peccantibus. Et ideo, *ut non circumveniamur a Satana, ego donavi, si quid donavi. Non enim ignoramus cogitationes eius*, scilicet Satanae. Verum est in generali, sed in speciali nullus potest scire eius cogitationes, nisi solus Deus. Iob XLI, 4: *quis revelavit faciem indumenti eius?* et cetera.

me to forgive, I have forgiven. And this is what he says: *to whom you have pardoned anything, I also*, namely, *have pardoned*.

66. And this is obvious, *for what I have pardoned, if I have pardoned anything, I have done it for your sakes, in the person of Christ*. In this he touches four things required for such pardon or forgiveness.

The first is discernment, so that pardon is not granted indiscriminately and rashly; hence he says, *if I have pardoned anything*, namely, in the proper way. *Let your eyes look directly forward* (Prov 4:25). The second is the end, because it should be done not for love or hatred, but for some benefit to the Church or others; hence he says, *I have done it for your sakes*. The third is authority, because it should not be done on one's own authority, but Christ's, who forgives sin by authority, but the others to whom it has been entrusted, forgive as ministers and members of Christ; hence he says, *in the person of Christ*, namely, not by my own authority. Yet whatever is forgiven, Christ forgives: *if you forgive the sins of any they are forgiven* (John 20:23). The fourth is need; hence he says, *that we may not be overreached by Satan*. For the devil had deceived many: some by leading them to commit sins, and others by excessive rigor against sinners; so that if Satan cannot get them for having committed sin, he at least destroys those he already has by the severity of prelates who drive them to despair by not correcting them in a compassionate way. Hence, he destroys these, and the others he puts in the snare of the devil: *be not righteous overmuch* (Eccl 7:16); *your adversary the devil prowls around like a roaring lion, seeking someone to devour* (1 Pet 5:8). And this will happen to us if we do not forgive sinners. Therefore *that we may not be overreached by Satan, I have pardoned, if I have pardoned anything. For we are not ignorant of his devices* namely, those of Satan. This is true in general, but in particular no one can know his thoughts but God alone. *Who can strip off his outer garment? Who can penetrate into the midst of his mouth?* (Job 41:13).

Lecture 3

2:12Cum venissem autem Troadem propter Evangelium Christi, et ostium mihi apertum esset in Domino, [n. 67]	2:12Ἐλθὼν δὲ εἰς τὴν Τρῳάδα εἰς τὸ εὐαγγέλιον τοῦ Χριστοῦ καὶ θύρας μοι ἀνεῳγμένης ἐν κυρίῳ,	2:12And when I had come to Troas on account of the Gospel of Christ and a door was opened to me in the Lord, [n. 67]
2:13non habui requiem spiritui meo, eo quod non invenerim Titum fratrem meum, sed valefaciens eis, profectus sum in Macedoniam.	2:13οὐκ ἔσχηκα ἄνεσιν τῷ πνεύματί μου τῷ μὴ εὑρεῖν με Τίτον τὸν ἀδελφόν μου, ἀλλὰ ἀποταξάμενος αὐτοῖς ἐξῆλθον εἰς Μακεδονίαν.	2:13I had no rest in my spirit, because I did not find Titus my brother: but bidding them farewell, I went into Macedonia.
2:14Deo autem gratias, qui semper triumphat nos in Christo Jesu, et odorem notitiae suae manifestat per nos in omni loco: [n. 71]	2:14Τῷ δὲ θεῷ χάρις τῷ πάντοτε θριαμβεύοντι ἡμᾶς ἐν τῷ Χριστῷ καὶ τὴν ὀσμὴν τῆς γνώσεως αὐτοῦ φανεροῦντι δι᾽ ἡμῶν ἐν παντὶ τόπῳ·	2:14Now thanks be to God, who always makes us triumph in Christ Jesus and manifests the odor of his knowledge by us in every place. [n. 71]
2:15quia Christi bonus odor sumus Deo in iis qui salvi fiunt, et in iis qui pereunt: [n. 74]	2:15ὅτι Χριστοῦ εὐωδία ἐσμὲν τῷ θεῷ ἐν τοῖς σῳζομένοις καὶ ἐν τοῖς ἀπολλυμένοις,	2:15For we are the good odor of Christ unto God, in those who are saved and in those who perish. [n. 74]
2:16aliis quidem odor mortis in mortem: aliis autem odor vitae in vitam. Et ad haec quis tam idoneus?	2:16οἷς μὲν ὀσμὴ ἐκ θανάτου εἰς θάνατον, οἷς δὲ ὀσμὴ ἐκ ζωῆς εἰς ζωήν. καὶ πρὸς ταῦτα τίς ἱκανός;	2:16To the one indeed the odor of death unto death: but to the others the odor of life unto life. And for these things, who is so sufficient?
2:17non enim sumus sicut plurimi, adulterantes verbum Dei, sed ex sinceritate, sed sicut ex Deo, coram Deo, in Christo loquimur. [n. 75]	2:17οὐ γάρ ἐσμεν ὡς οἱ πολλοὶ καπηλεύοντες τὸν λόγον τοῦ θεοῦ, ἀλλ᾽ ὡς ἐξ εἰλικρινείας, ἀλλ᾽ ὡς ἐκ θεοῦ κατέναντι θεοῦ ἐν Χριστῷ λαλοῦμεν.	2:17For we are not as many, adulterating the word of God: but with sincerity: but as from God, before God, in Christ we speak. [n. 75]

67. Posita prima causa suae dilationis, ne scilicet cum tristitia iret ad eos, hic ponit causam secundam quae est ex fructu quem alicubi faciebat.

Et circa hoc duo facit.

Primo ponit sui itineris processum;

secundo ipsius processus effectum, ibi **Deo autem gratias**, et cetera.

Circa primum duo facit.

Primo ostendit impedimentum fructificandi, quod habuit in Troade;

secundo subiungit processum suum in Macedoniam, ibi **sed valefaciens**, et cetera.

68. Dicit ergo **cum venissem Troadem propter Evangelium**, id est ad praedicandum Christum, Io. XV, 16: *posui vos ut eatis*, etc., **et ostium mihi apertum esset**, id est mentes hominum paratae et dispositae essent ad recipiendum praedicationis verba et Christum. I Cor. XVI, 9: *ostium mihi apertum est*, et cetera. Apoc. III, 20: *ecce sto ad ostium*, et cetera. Sed non in quocumque, imo **in Domino**, quia ipsa praeparatio mentis humanae est ex virtute divina. Nam licet facilitas qua mentes praeparantur, sit causa conversionis, tamen ipsius facilitatis et

67. Having stated the first reason for his delay, namely, that he might avoid coming to them in sadness, he now states the second reason, which is the fruit he was producing elsewhere.

In regard to this he does two things:
first, he mentions his travels;
second, their result, at **now thanks be to God**.

In regard to the first he does two things:
first, he mentions the obstacle he met at Troas;

second, his journey into Macedonia, at **but bidding them farewell**.

68. He says, therefore: **when I had come to Troas on account of the Gospel of Christ**, i.e., to preach Christ: *but I chose you and appointed you that you should go and bear fruit* (John 15:16), **a door was opened to me**, i.e., men's minds were prepared and disposed to receive the words of preaching and Christ: *for a wide door for effective work has opened to me* (1 Cor 16:9); *behold, I stand at the door and knock* (Rev 3:20). But not in anyone, but rather, **in the Lord**, because this preparation of the human mind is accomplished by God's power. For although the ease with which

praeparationis causa est Deus. Thren. ult.: *converte nos, Domine, ad te, et convertemur.*

Cum, inquam, ita **esset apertum mihi ostium in Domino, non habui requiem spiritui meo**, id est non potui facere quod spiritus meus volebat, id est dictabat. Tunc enim dicitur habere spiritus requiem, quando efficit quod vult, sicut tunc dicitur caro requiescere, quando habet quod concupiscit. Lc. c. XII, 19: *anima mea, habes multa bona*, et cetera. Apostolus non dicit: non habui requiem *carni meae* vel *corpori* sed **spiritui meo**, id est voluntati meae spirituali, quae est ut Christum firmem in cordibus hominum. Et impediebar, quia videbam corda parata et disposita, et non poteram praedicare.

69. Sed quare non habuit requiem spiritui suo, subdit **eo quod non inveni Titum fratrem meum**, id est propter absentiam Titi, et hoc duplici de causa.

Una causa est, quod licet Apostolus sciret omnes linguas, ita ut diceret: *gratias ago Deo meo, quod omnium vestrum lingua loquor*, tamen magis expeditus et edoctus erat in lingua Hebraea, quam in Graeca; Titus autem magis in Graeca. Et ideo volebat eum habere praesentem, ut praedicaret in Troade. Et quia erat absens, nam Corinthii detinuerant eum, dicit **non habui requiem spiritui meo**.

Sed quia dona Dei non sunt imperfecta, et donum linguarum fuit specialiter apostolis collatum ad praedicandum per totum mundum, Ps. XVIII, 5: *in omnem terram exivit sonus eorum*, etc., et ideo alia causa est melior, quae est, quia apostolo imminebant in Troade multa facienda. Nam ex una parte imminebat ei praedicare his qui parati erant recipere Christum per fidem; ex alia parte imminebat ei resistere adversariis qui impediebant; et ideo quia ipse non poterat solus ista facere, angustiabatur de absentia Titi, qui institisset praedicationi et conversioni bonorum, et Apostolus restitisset adversariis.

Et specialiter etiam hoc scribit eis, ut innuat, quod non solum prima causa dilationis suae fuit ex eis, sed etiam secunda. Nam ipsi propter duritiam et dissensionem eorum detinuerant tanto tempore Titum, et ideo dicit **eo quod non inveni Titum fratrem**, vel in Christo, vel coadiutorem. Prov. XVIII, 19: *frater qui iuvatur a fratre*, et cetera.

70. Et quia non inveni Titum in Troade, non remansi ibi, **sed valefaciens eis**, qui erant conversi, et in quibus ostium apertum erat, **profectus sum in Macedoniam**, ubi credebam eum invenire.

Causa autem essendi in Macedonia legitur Act. XVI, 9, ubi dicitur quod *vir Macedo*, et cetera.

71. Consequenter cum dicit **gratias autem Deo**, etc., ponit profectum sui processus,

minds are prepared is the cause of conversion, God is the cause of that ease and of the preparation: *convert us to yourself, O Lord, that we may be converted* (Lam 5:21).

When, I say, **a door was opened to me in the Lord, I had no rest in my spirit**, i.e., I was unable to do what my spirit wished, i.e., dictated. For the spirit is said to have rest, when it achieves what it wishes, just as the flesh is said to rest when it has what it desires: *soul, you have ample goods laid up for many years; take your ease* (Luke 12:19). The Apostle does not say, I had no rest *in my flesh* or *my body*, **in my spirit**, i.e., in my spiritual will, which is to establish Christ in the hearts of men. And I was hindered because I saw hearts prepared and disposed, and was unable to preach.

69. Then he tells why he had no rest in his spirit, when he adds, **because I did not find Titus my brother**, i.e., because of Titus's absence. And this for two reasons.

One reason was that although the Apostle knew all their languages, so that he could say: *I thank God that I speak in tongues more than you all* (1 Cor 14:18), he was more skilled in Hebrew than in Greek, but Titus more in Greek. Therefore, he wanted to have him present to preach in Troas. And because he was absent, for the Corinthians had detained him, he says, **I had no rest in my spirit**.

But because God's gifts are not imperfect, and the gift of tongues was specifically given to the apostles for preaching throughout the whole world: *their voice goes out through all the earth, and their words to the end of the world* (Ps 19:4), the other reason is better, namely, that many things remained for the Apostle to do in Troas. For on the one hand, he had to preach to those who were prepared to receive Christ by faith; and on the other, he had to resist the adversaries who opposed him; therefore, because he could not do these things alone, he was grieved by the absence of Titus, who could concentrate on preaching and converting the good, while the Apostle withstood the adversaries.

And he is at pains to write this to them in order to suggest that not only the first, but also the second reason for his delay was due to them. For on account of their hardness and quarreling, they delayed Titus for a long time. Hence he says, **because I did not find Titus my brother**, either in Christ or in my co-worker: *a brother helped is like a strong city* (Prov 18:19).

70. Because I did not find Titus in Troas, I did not stay there; **but bidding them farewell**, who were converted and in whom a door had been opened, **I went into Macedonia**, where I expected to find him.

But his reason for going into Macedonia is given in Acts, where it says: *a man of Macedonia was standing beseeching him and saying: come over to Macedonia and help us* (Acts 16:9).

71. Then when he says, **now thanks be to God**, he describes the progress of his journey,

et circa hoc duo facit.

Primo enim describit ordinem sui processus;

secundo excludit ab isto processu pseudoapostolos, ibi *ad hoc quis tam idoneus*, et cetera.

Circa primum duo facit.

Primo insinuat profectum quem faciebat;

secundo exponit quoddam quod dixerat, ibi *Christi bonus odor*, et cetera.

72. Circa primum sciendum quod Apostolus profectum et fructum quem faciebat, non attribuit sibi, neque propriae virtuti, sed Deo. I Cor. XV, 10: *abundantius omnibus laboravi non ego, sed gratia*, et cetera. Et ideo dicit *gratias autem Deo*, scilicet ago. I Thess. c. V, 18: *in omnibus gratias agite*. Eph. V, v. 20: *gratias agentes*, et cetera. *Qui semper triumphat nos in Christo Iesu*, id est triumphare nos facit in praedicatione Christi contra adversarios.

Ubi sciendum est quod praedicatores veritatis duo debent facere, scilicet exhortari in doctrina sacra et contradicentem devincere. Et hoc dupliciter: disputatione haereticos, patientia vero persecutores. Unde per ordinem ista tangit hic Apostolus, et ideo dicit *qui triumphat nos*, quantum ad contradicentes. Rom. VIII, 37: *in his omnibus superamus*. Et I Mac. III, 19: *non in fortitudine exercitus victoria belli, sed de caelo*, et cetera. *Et odorem notitiae suae manifestat per nos in omni loco*, quantum ad exhortationem sacrae doctrinae.

73. Sed *odorem notitiae suae* exponit Glossa, id est Filium suum; sed melius est ut hoc dicatur ad differentiam notitiae de Deo, quam faciunt aliae scientiae et quam facit fides.

Nam notitia de Deo quae habetur per alias scientias, illuminat intellectum solum, ostendens quod Deus est causa prima, quod est unus et sapiens, et cetera. Sed notitia de Deo quae habetur per fidem et illuminat intellectum et delectat affectum, quia non solum dicit quod Deus est prima causa, sed quod est Salvator noster, quod est Redemptor, et quod diligit nos, quod est incarnatus pro nobis: quae omnia affectum inflammant. Et ideo dicendum quod *odorem notitiae suae*, id est notitiam suae suavitatis, credenti *per nos in omni loco manifestat*, quia iste odor longe lateque diffunditur. Eccli. XXIV, 23: *ego quasi vitis fructificavi*, et cetera. Gen. XXVII, v. 27: *ecce odor filii*, et cetera.

74. Quia vero aliqui possent dicere: quid est odor Dei in omni loco? Nam multa loca sunt in quibus non recipitur praedicatio nostra. Ideo Apostolus exponit, dicens: non curo, quia sive recipiant praedicationem, sive non, tamen notitia Dei manifestatur ubique per nos, *quia sumus bonus odor Christi Deo*, id est ad honorem

and does two things:

first, he describes the order of his progress;

second, he excludes the false apostles from that progress, at *and for these things, who is so sufficient*.

In regard to the first he does two things:

first, he hints at the progress he made;

second, he explains something he had said, at *for we are the good odor of Christ*.

72. In regard to the first it should be noted that the Apostle did not attribute to himself the progress and fruit he had produced, or to his own power, but to God: *on the contrary, I worked harder than any of them, though it was not I, but the grace of God with me* (1 Cor 15:20). Thus he says *thanks be to God*; *give thanks in all circumstances* (1 Thess 5:18); *always and for everything giving thanks in the name of our Lord Jesus Christ to God the Father* (Eph 5:20), *who always makes us triumph in Christ Jesus*, i.e., makes us triumph in preaching Christ against our adversaries.

Here it should be noted that preachers of truth should do two things: namely, to exhort in sacred doctrine and to refute those who contradict it. This they do in two ways: by debating with heretics and by practicing patience toward persecutors. The Apostle touches on these in order; hence he says, *who always makes us triumph*, as to those who contradict. *We are more than conquerors* (Rom 8:37); *it is not on the size of the army that victory in battle depends, but strength comes from heaven* (1 Macc 3:19); *and manifests the odor of his knowledge by us in every place*, as to exhorting in sacred doctrine.

73. A Gloss explains *the odor of his knowledge*, i.e., of his Son; but it is better to suppose that this is said to distinguish between knowledge of God obtained by other sciences and that obtained by faith.

For the knowledge of God obtained by other sciences enlightens the intellect only by showing that God is the first cause, that he is one and wise and so on. But the knowledge of God obtained by faith both enlightens the intellect and delights the affections, because it not only says that God is the first cause, but that he is our Savior, that he is our Redeemer, that he loves us and that he became incarnate for us: all of which inflame the affections. Therefore it should be said that *the odor of his knowledge*, i.e., the knowledge of his sweetness, *he manifests by us* to the faithful *in every place*, because that fragrance is diffused far and wide: *like a vine I cause loveliness to bud* (Sir 24:17); *see, the smell of my son is as the smell of a field which the Lord has blessed* (Gen 27:27).

74. But because some might say, what is the fragrance of God in every place? For there are many places in which our preaching is not accepted. The Apostle explains this, saying: I do not care, because whether they accept our preaching or not, the knowledge of God is manifest everywhere through us, *for we are the good odor of Christ unto*

Dei. Et loquitur ad similitudinem legis, ubi dicitur quod sacrificium fiat in odorem suavitatis suavissimum Deo; quasi dicat: nos sumus holocaustum quod offertur Deo in odorem suavitatis. Et tam *in his qui salvi fiunt*, ut scilicet non pereant, quod est eis a Deo, quam *in his qui pereunt*, quod est eis ex seipsis. Unde Osee XIII, 9: *perditio tua, Israel, ex te*, et cetera.

Sed estne odor bonis et malis eodem modo? Non, sed *aliis quidem* est *odor mortis in mortem*, id est, invidiae et malitiae occasionaliter ducentis eos in mortem aeternam, illis scilicet qui invidebant bonae famae Apostoli et impugnabant praedicationem Christi et conversionem fidelium. Lc. II, 34: *positus est hic in ruinam, et in resurrectionem*, et cetera. *Aliis autem odor vitae*, dilectionis et bonae opinionis ducentis eos *in vitam* aeternam scilicet illis qui gaudent et convertuntur ad praedicationem Apostoli. I Cor. I, 18: *verbum crucis pereuntibus*, et cetera. *His autem qui salvi*, et cetera.

Sic ergo ex odore Apostoli boni vivunt, mali moriuntur, sicut legitur quod ad odorem vinearum florentium moriuntur serpentes.

75. Consequenter cum dicit: sed *ad haec quis tam idoneus*, etc., excludit ab isto profectu pseudo-apostolos, dicens *quis* illorum pseudo-apostolorum *est tam idoneus* ad ista, scilicet quae nos apostoli veri facimus? Quasi dicat: nullus. Ps. CXXXVIII, 17: *nimis honorati sunt amici tui, Deus*.

Sed contra Prov. XXVII, 2: *laudet te alienus*, et cetera. Ad hoc respondet Gregorius super Ezech., quod sancti duplici ex causa seipsos laudant, et non propter gloriam suam et vanitatem.

Prima causa est, ut non desperent in tribulationibus, sicut Iob, quando amici nitebantur eum ad desperationem inducere, reduxit ad memoriam sua bona quae fecerat, ut confortatus non desperaret. Unde dicebat: *pepigi foedus cum oculis meis*, et cetera. Legitur etiam de quodam sancto patre, quod quando tentabatur de desperatione, reducebat ad memoriam bona quae fecerat, ut confortaretur; quando tentabatur de superbia, reducebat ad memoriam mala, ut humiliaretur.

Secunda causa est propter utilitatem, ut scilicet haberetur in maiori fama, et citius crederetur doctrinae suae. Et propter hanc causam hic Apostolus laudat se. Nam Corinthii praeferebant sibi pseudo-apostolos, et condemnabant eum, et ideo non sic obediebant sibi. Ut ergo non vilipenderent eum, sed obedirent sibi, praefert se eis et laudat se, et dicit *sed ad haec quis tam idoneus*, sicut

God, namely, to the honor of God. He says this in a likeness to the law, where it is said that a sacrifice becomes the sweetest fragrance of sweetness to God. As if to say: we are a holocaust offered to God as a fragrance of sweetness *in those who are saved*, namely, that they not perish, which is theirs from God; *and in those who perish*, which is theirs from themselves. Hence, it is written: *destruction is your own, O Israel, your help is only in me* (Hos 13:9).

But is that fragrance related to the good and the wicked in the same way? No, but *to the one ideed the odor of death unto death*, i.e., of envy and malice, which are the occasion of bringing them to eternal death, i.e., those who envy the good reputation of the Apostle and strive against the preaching of Christ and the conversion of the faithful. *This child is set for the fall and rising of many in Israel, and for a sign that is spoken against* (Luke 2:34). *But to the others, the odor of life*, of love and of good opinion leads them *unto* eternal *life*, namely, to those who rejoice and are converted by the preaching of the Apostle: *for the word of the cross is folly to those who are perishing, but to us who are being saved it is the power of God* (1 Cor 1:18).

Thus, from the odor of the Apostle, the good live and the wicked die, as it is read that serpents die from the smell of flourishing vines.

75. Then when he says, *and for these things, who is so sufficient?* He excludes the false apostles from the progress, saying, *who* of those false apostles *is so sufficient for these things*, which we true apostles accomplish? As if to say: none: *but to me your friends, O God, are exceedingly honorable* (Ps 138:17).

But on the other hand, it is said: *let another praise you, and not your own mouth; a stranger, and not your own lips* (Prov 27:2). Gregory, in his commentary on Ezekiel, answers this by saying that the saints praise themselves for two reasons, and not for their own glory and vanity.

The first reason is that they not despair in tribulations, as Job, when his friends tried to bring him to despair, recalled to his mind the good things he had done, in order to comfort himself and not despair. Hence, he said: *I have made a covenant with my eyes; how then could I look upon a virgin?* (Job 31:1). We read of a holy father, that when he was tempted to despair, he recalled to mind the good things he had done, in order to comfort himself; when he was tempted to pride, he recalled the evil he had done, in order to be humbled.

The second reason is for profit, namely, that he obtain a greater reputation and that his teaching be believed more readily. This is the reason why the Apostle praises himself here. For the Corinthians had preferred false apostles to him and disdained him. As a result they were not ready to obey him. Therefore, to assure that they would not disdain but obey him, he prefers himself to them and

nos? Non pseudo-apostoli, quia licet ipsi praedicent, tamen adulterant verbum Dei, quod nos non facimus.

76. Unde dicit *non sumus sicut plurimi*, scilicet pseudo-apostoli, *adulterantes verbum Dei*, admiscendo contraria, sicut haeretici, qui licet confiteantur Christum, tamen non dicunt eum esse verum Deum. Sic faciunt pseudo-apostoli, qui dicunt cum Evangelio debere observari legalia.

Item non *adulterantes verbum Dei*, id est, praedicantes vel propter quaestum, vel propter favorem laudis. Sic enim mulieres adulterae dicuntur quando recipiunt semen ex alio viro ad propagationem prolis. In praedicatione autem semen nihil aliud est quam finis seu intentio tua, vel favor gloriae propriae. Si ergo finis tuus est quaestus, si intentio tua est favor gloriae propriae, adulteras verbum Dei. Hoc faciebant pseudo-apostoli, qui propter quaestum praedicabant. Infra IV, 2: *neque adulterantes verbum Dei*, et cetera. Apostoli autem praedicabant neque propter quaestum, neque gloriam propriam, sed propter laudem Dei et salutem proximi. Et ideo subiungit *sed ex sinceritate*, id est, sincera intentione, non pro quaestu et sine admixtione corruptionis. Supra I, 12: *ex sinceritate*, et cetera.

77. Ponit autem triplicem rationem huius sinceritatis. Prima ratio sumitur ex dignitate mittentis. Nuntium enim veritatis decet vera loqui. Et ideo dicit *ex Deo*, id est, illa sinceritate quae est digna nuntiatio Dei. I Petr. IV, 11: *si quis loquitur quasi sermones Dei.*

Secunda sumitur ex auctoritate praesidentis cui astat. Ideo dicit *coram Deo*, coram quo ex sinceritate loqui debemus. III Reg. c. XVII, 1: *vivit Dominus, in cuius conspectu sto*, et cetera.

Tertia sumitur ex dignitate materiae de qua loquitur. Nam praedicatio apostolorum est de Christo, et ideo debet esse sincera, sicut et ipse Deus et Christus. Et ideo dicit *in Christo* solum, non de legalibus, ut pseudo-apostoli faciunt. I Cor. II, 2: *neque existimavi me scire aliquid inter vos, nisi Christum, et hunc crucifixum.*

praises himself, saying, *and for these things who is so sufficient* as we are? Not the false apostles, because even though they preach, they adulterate God's word—which we do not do.

76. Hence, he says, *for we are not as many*, namely, the false apostles, *adulterating the word of God*, mingling contrary doctrines, as the heretics, who although they confess Christ, do not admit that he is true God. This is what the false apostles do, who say that along with the Gospel the legal observances must be kept.

Hence he says, *for we are not as many, adulterating the word of God*, i.e., preaching for gain or for praise. For thus are women called adulteresses, when they receive seed from another man for the propagation of children. In preaching, the seed is nothing less than your end or intention. Therefore, if your end is gain, if your intention is your own glory, you adulterate God's word. This the false apostles were doing who were preaching for gain. *We renounce the hidden things of dishonesty, not walking in craftiness nor adulterating the word of God* (2 Cor 4:2). The apostles preached neither for monetary gain nor their own glory, but for the praise of God and the salvation of their neighbor. Hence, he adds, *but with sincerity*, i.e., with a sincere intention; not for gain and without corrupted admixtures. *In sincerity of God, and not in carnal wisdom* (2 Cor 1:12).

77. He points out three aspects of this sincerity: the first is taken from the dignity of the one who sent them. For it is expected of a messenger of the truth to speak the truth; hence he says, as commissioned *from God*, i.e., with that sincerity which befits a messenger of God: *whoever speaks as one who utters oracles of God* (1 Pet 4:11).

The second is taken from the authority of the one presiding, before whom he stands. Hence he says, *before God*, in whose presence we should speak with sincerity: *as the Lord the God of Israel lives, before whom I stand* (1 Kgs 17:1).

The third is taken from the dignity of the subject of which he speaks. For the preaching of the apostles is about Christ; therefore, it should be sincere, as also Christ and God are. Hence, he says, we speak *in Christ* alone, and not in the ceremonies of the law, as false apostles do: *for I decided to know nothing among you except Jesus Christ and him crucified* (1 Cor 2:2).

CHAPTER 3

Lecture 1

3:1Incipimus iterum nosmetipsos commendare? [n. 78] aut numquid egemus (sicut quidam) commendatitiis epistolis ad vos, aut ex vobis? [n. 80]

3:2Epistola nostra vos estis, scripta in cordibus nostris, quae scitur, et legitur ab omnibus hominibus: [n. 82]

3:3manifestati quod epistola estis Christi, ministrata a nobis, et scripta non atramento, sed Spiritu Dei vivi: non in tabulis lapideis, sed in tabulis cordis carnalibus.

3:4Fiduciam autem talem habemus per Christum ad Deum: [n. 85]

3:5non quod sufficientes simus cogitare aliquid a nobis, quasi ex nobis: sed sufficientia nostra ex Deo est: [n. 86]

3:1Ἀρχόμεθα πάλιν ἑαυτοὺς συνιστάνειν; ἢ μὴ χρῄζομεν ὥς τινες συστατικῶν ἐπιστολῶν πρὸς ὑμᾶς ἢ ἐξ ὑμῶν;

3:2ἡ ἐπιστολὴ ἡμῶν ὑμεῖς ἐστε, ἐγγεγραμμένη ἐν ταῖς καρδίαις ἡμῶν, γινωσκομένη καὶ ἀναγινωσκομένη ὑπὸ πάντων ἀνθρώπων,

3:3ἡ ἐπιστολὴ ἡμῶν ὑμεῖς ἐστε, ἐγγεγραμμένη ἐν ταῖς καρδίαις ἡμῶν, γινωσκομένη καὶ ἀναγινωσκομένη ὑπὸ πάντων ἀνθρώπων,

3:4Πεποίθησιν δὲ τοιαύτην ἔχομεν διὰ τοῦ Χριστοῦ πρὸς τὸν θεόν.

3:5οὐχ ὅτι ἀφ᾽ ἑαυτῶν ἱκανοί ἐσμεν λογίσασθαί τι ὡς ἐξ ἑαυτῶν, ἀλλ᾽ ἡ ἱκανότης ἡμῶν ἐκ τοῦ θεοῦ,

3:1Do we begin again to commend ourselves? [n. 78] Or do we need (as some do) epistles of commendation to you, or from you? [n. 80]

3:2You are our epistle, written in our hearts, which is known and read by all men: [n. 82]

3:3Being manifested, that you are the epistle of Christ, ministered by us, and written: not with ink but with the Spirit of the living God: not in tablets of stone but in the fleshly tablets of the heart.

3:4And such confidence we have, through Christ, towards God. [n. 85]

3:5Not that we are sufficient to think anything of ourselves, as from ourselves: but our sufficiency is from God. [n. 86]

---

78. Postquam Apostolus suam excusationem posuit, in qua benevolentiam captavit auditorum, hic consequenter prosequitur suam intentionem, scilicet tractans de ministris Novi Testamenti.

Et circa hoc duo facit.

Primo enim commendat dignitatem bonorum ministrorum;

secundo vero exaggerat malitiam malorum ministrorum, et hoc a X cap. et deinceps.

Circa primum duo facit.

Primo enim commendat ministerium Novi Testamenti;

secundo commendat usum huius ministerii in aliis, exhortando eos ad hoc, ibi VI cap. *adiuvantes autem*, et cetera.

Circa primum commendat huiusmodi ministerium Novi Testamenti ex tribus.

Primo ex dignitate in isto capite;

secundo ex usu, cap. IV, ibi *ideo habentes*, etc.;

tertio ex praemio, cap. V, ibi *scimus autem quoniam si*, et cetera.

Circa primum duo facit.

78. After presenting his excuse, by which he won the good will of his hearers, the Apostle continues toward his main intention, namely, to treat about the ministers of the New Testament.

In regard to this he does two things:

first, he commends the dignity of the good ministers;

second, he expands on the guilt of the evil ministers, from chapter ten and thereafter.

In regard to the first he does two things:

first, he commends the ministry of the New Testament;

second, he commends the exercise of this ministry in others by exhorting them to this, in chapter six, at *and we helping* (2 Cor 6:1).

In regard to the first he commends the ministry of the New Testament from three aspects:

first, in this chapter, from its dignity;

second, from its exercise, in chapter four, at *therefore, having this ministration* (2 Cor 4:1);

third, from its reward, in chapter five, at *for we know* (2 Cor 5:1).

In regard to the first he does two things:

Primo removet quamdam obiectionem;

secundo commendat ministros Novi Testamenti, ibi *qui et idoneos nos fecit*, et cetera.

Circa primum sciendum est quod Apostolus intendit commendare ministros Novi Testamenti, quorum ipse erat unus. Et ideo ne Corinthii obiicerent sibi quod in hoc vellet commendare seipsum, statim excludit, dicens *incipimus iterum nosmetipsos*, et cetera. Ubi duo facit.

Primo movet quaestionem;

secundo respondet, ibi scilicet *aut numquid egemus*, et cetera.

79. Quaestio sua talis est: dico quod non sumus adulterantes verbum Dei, sicut pseudo, sed ex sinceritate, sicut ex Deo. Sed numquid hoc dicendo, *incipimus iterum nos commendare*, id est, dicimus ista ut velimus nostram gloriam quaerere et non Dei?

Et dicit *iterum*, quia in epistola prima commendaverat se satis, cum dixit: *ut sapiens architectus*, et cetera. Non ergo hoc dicimus, ut quaeramus gloriam nostram, sed Dei. Prov. XXVII, 2: *laudet te alienus*, et cetera.

80. Huic autem quaestioni respondet, cum dicit *aut numquid egemus*, et cetera. Et ostendit, quod non libenter commendat se.

Et circa hoc duo facit.

Primo ostendit quod non indiget commendatione hominum;

secundo quod neque etiam hoc requirit ipse ab eis, ibi *fiduciam autem talem*, et cetera.

Circa primum duo facit.

Primo ostendit, quod non indiget commendatione eorum ad gloriam propriam;

secundo huius causam assignat, ibi *epistola nostra vos estis*, et cetera.

81. Dicit ergo: dico quod non incipimus commendare nosmetipsos, quia non indigemus commendatione. Et hoc est, quod dicit *aut numquid egemus nos*, veri ministri, *sicut quidam*, scilicet pseudo, *commendatitiis epistolis*, id est laudibus missis, *ad vos*, ab aliis, *aut ex vobis*, aliis missis?

Sed contra Col. IV, 10 dicitur: *Marcus consobrinus Barnabae, de quo accepistis mandatum*, et cetera. Etiam legati Papae semper portant litteras commendatitias. Non est ergo malum.

Respondeo. Dicendum, quod accipere litteras huiusmodi a personis famosis, ut solum per illas commendentur et honorentur, quousque ipsi ex bonis operibus suis veniant in notitiam, hoc non est malum, hoc faciunt

first, he removes an objection;

second, he commends the ministers of the New Testament, at *who has made us fit ministers*.

In regard to the first it should be noted that the Apostle intended to commend the ministers of the New Testament, of which he is one. Therefore, lest the Corinthians object that in doing this he wishes to commend himself, he at once removes this, saying, *do we begin again to commend ourselves?* Here he does two things:

he first raises the question

and then he answers it, at *or do we need*.

79. The question is this: I say that we do not adulterate the word of God as the false apostles do, but we speak with sincerity as from God. But in saying this, *do we begin again to commend ourselves?*, i.e., are we saying this because we want to procure our glory and not that of God?

And he says, *again*, because in the first epistle he had commended himself enough, when he said: *like a skilled master builder I laid a foundation* (1 Cor 3:10). Therefore, we are not saying this to seek our own glory, but God's: *let another praise you, and not your own mouth; a stranger, and not your own lips* (Prov 27:2).

80. He answers this when he says, *or do we need (as some do) epistles of commendation to you, or from you?* Here he shows that he is not happy to commend himself.

In regard to this he does two things:

first, he shows that he does not need man's commendation;

second, that he does not require it of them, at *and such confidence we have*.

In regard to the first he does two things:

first, he shows that he does not need their commendation;

second, he assigns the cause of this, at *you are our epistle*.

81. He says, therefore: I say that we do not begin to commend ourselves, because we do not need commendation. And this is what he says: *do we*, the true ministers, *need (as some do)*, namely, the false apostles, *epistles of commendation*, i.e., of praise, *to you* by others, *or from you* to others?

But on the other hand, it is said: *Mark, the cousin of Barnabas, greets you* (Col 4:10). Even papal legates always carry letters of recommendation. Therefore it is not an evil.

I answer that to accept such letters from famous persons, who are commended and honored by reason of them alone, until they become known by their good works, is not evil: that is what papal legates do. But the Apostle was

legati Papae. Apostolus vero ita iam erat notus et commendatus apud istos per opera sua, quod non indigebat litteris commendatitiis.

82. Et ideo statim causam huius assignans, subdit *epistola nostra vos estis*. Quasi dicat: ego habeo bonas litteras, non indigeo aliis. Et ideo circa hoc duo facit. Primo enim ostendit quae sit ista littera quam habet; secundo exponit hoc idem, ibi *manifestati*, et cetera. Circa primum duo facit. Primo ostendit quae sit illa littera; secundo ostendit eam esse sufficientem ad commendationem propriam, ibi *scripta*, et cetera.

Dicit ergo sic *epistola nostra vos estis*, id est epistola per quam manifestatur dignitas nostra, qua nos commendamur, ita ut epistolis aliis non indigeamus. Supra II: *gloria nostra vos estis*. Gal. c. IV, 19: *filioli mei quos iterum parturio*, et cetera.

Sed haec epistola estne sufficiens? Ita, quia *scripta*, et cetera. Ubi duo tangit, sufficientiam litterarum huiusmodi causantia. Unum est, quod intelligatur et sciatur ab eo pro quo mittitur, alias adhuc quaereret, nisi sciret se eam habere. Et quantum ad hoc dicit *scripta in cordibus nostris*, quia semper vos habemus in memoria, habentes de vobis specialem curam. Phil. I, 7: *eo quod habeam vos*, et cetera.

Secundum est, quod ille cui mittitur, legat et sciat eam, alias non curaret de commendatione eius. Et quantum ad hoc dicit *quae scitur et legitur ab omnibus hominibus*. Scitur, inquam, quia per nos instituti estis et conversi. Legitur autem, quia exemplo nostri etiam alii imitantur vos. Hab. II, 2: *scribe visum, et explana eum super tabulas, ut percurrat qui legerit eum*.

83. Quomodo autem scitur haec epistola, exponit dicens *manifestati*, et cetera. Et circa hoc tria facit. Primo exponit cuius sit haec littera; secundo quomodo sit scripta, et tertio in quo.

Cuius autem sit, sic ostendit, quia Christi. Et ideo dicit *manifestati* quoniam *estis Christi*, id est a Christo informati et inducti, scilicet principaliter et auctoritative. Matth. XXIII, 8: *unus est magister vester*. Sed a nobis secundario et instrumentaliter. Et ideo dicit *ministrata a nobis*. I Cor. c. IV, 1: *sic nos existimet homo*, et cetera. I Cor. c. III, 4: *quid igitur Cephas*, et cetera.

Quomodo autem sit scripta, ostendit, quia *non atramento*, id est non admixta erroribus, sicut pseudo-apostoli; non mutabilis et imperfecta, sicut vetus lex, quae neminem ad perfectum adduxit, Hebr. VII, 19. Nam atramentum nigrum est per quod intelligitur error, et delebile per quod intelligitur mutabilitas. Non, inquam, atramento est scripta, *sed Spiritu Dei vivi*, id est Spiritu Sancto, quo vivitis, et quo docente instructi estis. Eph. I, 13: *in quo signati estis*.

already so well known and recommended among them by his works, that he did not need letters of recommendation.

82. Therefore he at once gives the reason for this, saying, *you are our epistle*; as if to say: I have a good letter; I do not need others. In regard to this, he does two things: first, he shows what that letter is which he has; second, he explains this, at *being manifested*. In regard to the first he does two things: first he shows what that letter is; second, he shows that it is sufficient for commending him.

He says, therefore, *you are our epistle* i.e., the letter through which our dignity is made manifest, by which we are commended, so that we do not need other letters: *you are our glory* (1 Thess 2:20); *my little children, with whom I am again in travail, until Christ be formed in you* (Gal 4:19).

But is this letter sufficient? Yes, because it is *written in our hearts, which is known and read by all men*. Here he touches on two things causing the sufficiency of such letters. One is that it should be understood and known by the one for whom it is sent; the other that he still seeks, and not that he knows himself to have it. As to this he says, *written in our hearts*, because we always have you in mind, having a special care for you: *I hold you in my heart* (Phil 1:7).

The other is that he to whom it is sent may read and know it; hence, he says, *which is known and read by all men*. To be known, I say, because you have been instructed and converted by us; but it is read, because by our example even others imitate you. *Write the vision; make it plain upon tablets, so he may run who reads it* (Hab 2:2).

83. Then he explains how this letter is known, saying, *being manifested, that you are the epistle of Christ*, and in regard to this he does three things. First, he explains whose letter it is; second, how it was written; third, on what.

He shows whose it is when he says, from Christ. Hence, he says, *being manifested, that you are the epistle of Christ*, i.e., informed and led by Christ, principally and authoritatively. *For you have one teacher* (Matt 23:8), but by us secondarily and instrumentally. Hence he adds, *ministered by us*: *this is how one should regard us, as servants of Christ* (1 Cor 4:1); *what then is Apollos? What is Paul? Servants through whom you believed* (1 Cor 3:5).

He shows how it was written, *not with ink*, i.e., not mixed with errors, as the letters of the false apostle; not changeable and imperfect as the old law, which led no one to perfection (Heb 7:19); for black ink is that by which error is understood, and delible by which changeableness is understood. It is written not with ink, I say, *but with the Spirit of the living God*, i.e., by the Holy Spirit, by whom you live and by whose teaching you have been instructed: *in whom you were sealed with the promised Holy Spirit* (Eph 1:13).

Ubi autem sit scripta insinuat, subdens *non in tabulis lapideis*, sicut lex vetus, ut excludat duritiem, quasi dicat: non in lapideis cordibus habentibus duritiem, sicut Iudaei. Act. VII, 51: *dura cervice*, et cetera. Sed *in tabulis cordis carnalibus*, id est, in cordibus latis ex caritate, et carnalibus, id est, mollibus ex affectu implendi et intelligendi. Ez. XXXVI, 26: *auferam a vobis cor lapideum*, et cetera.

84. *Fiduciam autem talem*, et cetera. Apostolus supra excusavit se, quod non quaerebat gloriam suam quia non indigebat ea, hic vero probat quia ipse non quaerit gloriam propriam, imo omnia bona quae facit, non attribuit sibi, sed Deo.

Et circa hoc duo facit.

Primo enim attribuit omnia bona, quae habet et facit, Deo;

secundo causam huius assignat, ibi *non quod sufficientes*, et cetera.

85. Dicit ergo primo: dico quod non egemus epistolis commendatitiis, et quod vos estis epistola nostra ministrata a nobis. Nec etiam quaerimus gloriam nostram, sed Christi. Et *fiduciam talem*, id est dicendi talia, *habemus ad Deum*, id est referimus in Deum. Vel fiduciam tendentem in Deum, ex cuius viribus hoc dico, quia ipse in me operatur. Quam quidem fiduciam habemus *per Christum*, per quem accessum habemus ad Patrem, ut dicitur Rom. V, 2, qui univit nos Deo. Ier. XVII, 7: *benedictus vir*, et cetera. Et quia unitus Deo per Christum habeo hanc fiduciam. Ps. XI, 6: *fiducialiter agam*, et cetera.

86. Causa autem huius fiduciae est, quia quidquid ego facio, etiam ipsum principium operis, Deo attribuo. Et ideo dicit *non quod simus sufficientes cogitare*, saltem non dicere, vel implere. Nam in quolibet processu operis primo est assensus, qui fit cogitando, deinde collatio per verbum, et postmodum impletio per opus; unde fit, ut sic nec cogitare quis a se habeat, sed a Deo; non est enim dubium, quod non solum perfectio operis boni est a Deo, sed etiam inchoatio. Phil. I, 6: *qui coepit in vobis opus bonum*, et cetera. Et hoc est contra Pelagianos dicentes, quod inchoatio boni operis est ex nobis, sed perfectio est a Deo. Is. XXVI, 12: *omnia opera nostra*, et cetera.

Sed ex hoc, ne videatur tollere libertatem arbitrii, dicit *a nobis, quasi ex nobis*, quasi dicat: possum quidem aliquid facere, quod est liberi arbitrii, sed hoc, quod facio, non est ex me, sed a Deo, qui hoc ipsum posse confert; ut sic, et libertatem hominis defendat cum dicit *a nobis*, id

He suggests where it is written, when he says, *not in tablets of stone*, as the old law, to exclude hardness; as if to say: not in the stony hearts of the hard-hearted, as the Jews: *you stiff-necked people, uncircumcised in heart and ears, you always resist the Holy Spirit* (Acts 7:51); *but in the fleshy tablets of the heart*, i.e., hearts opened by charity, and human, i.e., made receptive as a result of filling and understanding. *I will take out of your flesh the heart of stone and give you a heart of flesh* (Ezek 36:26).

84. *And such confidence we have, through Christ, towards God*. Above, the Apostle excused himself, that he was not seeking his own glory, because he did not need it; here he proves that he is not seeking his own glory. Indeed, everything good he does he attributes not to himself but to God.

In regard to this he does two things:

first, he attributes all the good he has and does to God;

second, he gives the reason for this, at *not that we are sufficient*.

85. He says, therefore: I say that we do not need letters of recommendation and that you are our letter ministered by us. Nor do we seek our glory, but Christ's. *And such confidence*, i.e., to say such things, *we have, through Christ, towards God*, i.e., we refer it to God. Or I have such confidence in God, by whose power I say these things, because he works in me, and the confidence we have *through Christ*, through whom we have access to the Father (Rom 5:2), who unites us to God: *blessed is the man who trusts in the Lord* (Jer 17:7). And I have this confidence because I am united to God through Christ: *I will act confidently in him* (Ps 11:6).

86. But the cause of this confidence is that whatever I do, I attribute to the very beginning of the work to God. Therefore, he says, *not that we are sufficient to think anything of ourselves, as from ourselves*, much less say and accomplish. For in the pursuit of any work there is first an assent, which is done by thinking, then discussion by word, and finally accomplishment by work. Hence if a person does not have the thinking from himself but from God, there is no doubt that not only the completion of a good work is from God, but even the very beginning. *He who began a good work in you will bring it to completion at the day of Jesus Christ* (Phil 1:6). This is contrary to the Pelagians, who say that the beginning of a good work is from us, but its completion is from God. *O Lord, you have wrought for us all our works* (Isa 26:12).

But lest this seem to take away free will, he says, *of ourselves, as from ourselves*, i.e., on our part, as thought to say: I can indeed do something, because of free will, but what I do is not from me but from God, who can grant this very thing. By speaking this way, he both defends man's

est a nostra parte, et divinam gratiam commendet, cum dicit *quasi ex nobis* scilicet procedat, *sed a Deo*.

87. Hoc etiam Philosophus vult, quod numquam homo per liberum arbitrium potest quoddam bonum facere, sine adiutorio Dei. Et ratio sua est, quia in his, quae facimus, quaerendum est illud propter quod facimus. Non est autem procedere in infinitum, sed est devenire ad aliquid primum, puta ad consilium. Sic ergo bonum facio, quia consilium mihi inest ad hoc, et hoc est a Deo. Unde dicit, quod consilium boni est ab aliquo, quod est supra hominem, movens eum ad bene operandum. Et hoc est Deus, qui et homines movet et omnia, quae agunt ad actiones suas, sed aliter et aliter. Cum enim huiusmodi motus sit quoddam receptum in moto, oportet quod hoc fiat secundum modum suae naturae, id est, rei motae. Et ideo omnia movet secundum suas naturas. Ea ergo, quorum natura est ut sint liberae voluntatis, dominium suarum actionum habentia, movet libere ad operationes suas, sicut creaturas rationales et intellectuales. Alia autem non libere, sed secundum modum suae naturae.

Licet autem non simus sufficientes cogitare aliquid a nobis, tamquam ex nobis, tamen habemus aliquam sufficientiam, qua scilicet bonum possumus velle et credere incipiamus, et hoc a Deo est. I Cor. IV, 7: *quid habes, quod non accepisti?*

liberty when he says *of ourselves*, i.e., on our part, and commends divine grace when he says, *as from ourselves*, i.e., as though it came from us, *but from God*.

87. The Philosopher also teaches that a man can never do any good through his free will without God's help. The reason is that in the things we do it is necessary to seek that for which we do it. But there can be no infinite process, for we must come to something which is first, e.g., to counsel. Thus, therefore, I do good, because there is in me the counsel to do so, and this is from God. Hence, he says that the counsel of something good is from something above man, moving him to act well; and this is God, who moves men and all things that act to their actions; but men are moved in one way, and other things in another. For since motion of this kind is something received into the thing moved, it is necessary that this be done according to the mode of its nature, i.e., of the thing moved. And therefore he moves all things according to their natures. Therefore, those things whose nature is to have free will and have dominion over their actions, he moves in such a way that they act freely, as rational and intellectual creatures. But others not freely, but according to the mode of their nature.

But although we are not sufficient to think anything of ourselves as coming from ourselves, yet we have a certain sufficiency, namely that by which we are able to will the good, and to begin to believe, and this is from God: *what have you that you did not receive?* (1 Cor 4:7).

Lecture 2

3:6qui et idoneos nos fecit ministros Novi Testamenti: non littera, sed Spiritu: littera enim occidit, Spiritus autem vivificat. [n. 89]

3:7 Quod si ministratio mortis litteris deformata in lapidibus fuit in gloria, ita ut non possent intendere filii Israël in faciem Moysi propter gloriam vultus ejus, quae evacuatur: [n. 92]

3:8quomodo non magis ministratio Spiritus erit in gloria?

3:9 Nam si ministratio damnationis gloria est: multo magis abundat ministerium justitiae in gloria. [n. 95]

3:10 Nam nec glorificatum est, quod claruit in hac parte, propter excellentem gloriam. [n. 97]

3:11 Si enim quod evacuatur, per gloriam est: multo magis quod manet, in gloria est. [n. 99]

3:6ὃς καὶ ἱκάνωσεν ἡμᾶς διακόνους καινῆς διαθήκης, οὐ γράμματος ἀλλὰ πνεύματος· τὸ γὰρ γράμμα ἀποκτέννει, τὸ δὲ πνεῦμα ζῳοποιεῖ.

3:7Εἰ δὲ ἡ διακονία τοῦ θανάτου ἐν γράμμασιν ἐντετυπωμένη λίθοις ἐγενήθη ἐν δόξῃ, ὥστε μὴ δύνασθαι ἀτενίσαι τοὺς υἱοὺς Ἰσραὴλ εἰς τὸ πρόσωπον Μωϋσέως διὰ τὴν δόξαν τοῦ προσώπου αὐτοῦ τὴν καταργουμένην,

3:8πῶς οὐχὶ μᾶλλον ἡ διακονία τοῦ πνεύματος ἔσται ἐν δόξῃ;

3:9εἰ γὰρ τῇ διακονίᾳ τῆς κατακρίσεως δόξα, πολλῷ μᾶλλον περισσεύει ἡ διακονία τῆς δικαιοσύνης δόξῃ.

3:10καὶ γὰρ οὐ δεδόξασται τὸ δεδοξασμένον ἐν τούτῳ τῷ μέρει εἵνεκεν τῆς ὑπερβαλλούσης δόξης.

3:11εἰ γὰρ τὸ καταργούμενον διὰ δόξης, πολλῷ μᾶλλον τὸ μένον ἐν δόξῃ.

3:6 Who has also made us fit ministers of the New Testament, not in the letter but in the Spirit: for the letter kills, but the Spirit gives life. [n. 89]

3:7 Now if the ministration of death, engraved with letters upon stones, was glorious (so that the children of Israel could not steadfastly behold the face of Moses, for the glory of his countenance), which is made void: [n. 92]

3:8 How shall the ministration of the Spirit not be even more in glory?

3:9 For if the ministration of condemnation is glory, much more does the ministration of justice abound in glory. [n. 95]

3:10 For even that which was glorious in this part was not glorified by reason of the glory that excells. [n. 97]

3:11 For if that which is made void was glorious, much more that which remains is in glory. [n. 99]

---

88. Commendato ministerio Novi Testamenti, hic consequenter commendat ministros eius. Et primo ponit duo quae respondent verbis praemissis. Praemiserat enim donum a Deo acceptum, cum dixit: *sufficientia nostra*, etc.; et fiduciam ex dono conceptam, cum dixit: *fiduciam talem*, et cetera. Primo ergo determinat ea quae pertinent ad donum perceptum; secundo ea quae ad fiduciam conceptam, ibi *habentes igitur talem*, et cetera.

Circa primum tria facit.

Primo ostendit donum a Deo susceptum, scilicet ministerium Novi Testamenti;

secundo describit Novum Testamentum, ibi *non littera, sed Spiritu*;

tertio ex dignitate Novi Testamenti ostendit dignitatem ministrorum eius, ibi *si ministratio*, et cetera.

89. Dicit ergo: dico quod *sufficientia nostra ex Deo est, qui et fecit nos idoneos ministros Novi Testamenti*, Is. LXI, 6: *ministri Dei nostri, dicetur vobis*. Et in hoc tenemus locum angelorum. Ps. CIII, 4: *qui facit angelos*, et cetera.

Sed non solum fecit nos ministros, sed *idoneos*. Deus enim cuilibet rei dat ea per quae possit consequi perfectionem suae naturae. Unde, quia Deus constituit ministros Novi Testamenti, dedit et eis idoneitatem ad hoc

88. Having commended the ministry of the New Testament, the Apostle then commends its ministers. First, he stipulates two things, which correspond to the above words. For he had mentioned a gift received from God when he said, *our competence is from God*, and the confidence born of this gift when he said, *such confidence we have, through Christ, towards God*. First, therefore, he determines the things pertaining to the gift received; second, those pertaining to the confidence born of it.

In regard to the first he does three things:

first, he discloses the gift received from God, namely, the ministry of the New Testament;

second, he describes the New Testament, at *not in the letter, but in the Spirit*;

third, from the dignity of the New Testament he shows the dignity of its ministers, at *if the ministration*.

89. He says, therefore: I say that *our sufficiency is from God, who has also made us fit ministers of the New Testament*: *men shall speak of you as the ministers of our God* (Isa 61:6). And in this we hold the place of angels: *who make angels your messengers, fire and flame your ministers* (Ps 104:4).

But he not only made us ministers, but *fit* ones. For God gives to each being the things through which it can attain to the perfection of its nature. Hence, because God constituted ministers of the New Testament, he made them fit

officium exercendum, nisi sit impedimentum ex parte recipientium. Supra II, 16: *et ad haec quis tam idoneus*, scilicet sicut apostoli a Deo instituti?

90. Hoc autem Novum Testamentum quid sit, describit, subdens *non littera*, et cetera. Et describit ipsum quantum ad duo, scilicet quantum ad illud in quo consistit, et quantum ad causam propter quam datum est, ibi *littera enim occidit*, et cetera.

Circa primum sciendum est quod Apostolus loquitur profunde. Dicitur enim Ier. c. XXXI, 31 ss.: *feriam domui Israel et domui Iuda foedus novum, non secundum pactum quod pepigi cum patribus vestris*. Et post: *dabo legem meam in visceribus eorum, et in corde eorum superscribam eam*, et cetera. Vetus ergo Testamentum scribitur in libro, postmodum sanguine aspergendo, ut dicitur Hebr. IX, 19: *accepit sanguinem et aspersit librum*, etc., *dicens: hic est sanguis*, et cetera.

Et sic patet, quod vetus lex est testamentum litterae. Sed Novum Testamentum est testamentum Spiritus Sancti, quo caritas Dei diffunditur in cordibus nostris, ut dicitur Rom. V, 5. Et sic dum Spiritus Sanctus facit in nobis caritatem, quae est plenitudo legis, est Testamentum Novum, *non littera*, id est per litteram scribendum, *sed Spiritu*, id est per Spiritum qui *vivificat*. Rom. VIII, 2: *lex Spiritus vitae*, id est vivificantis.

91. Causa autem quare datum sit Novum Testamentum per Spiritum, subditur quia *littera occidit* occasionaliter. Nam littera legis dat solam cognitionem peccati. Rom. III, 20: *per legem autem cognitio peccati*. Ex hoc autem, quod cognosco peccatum, solum duo sequuntur. Nam lex dum per eam cognoscitur, non reprimit concupiscentiam: sed magis occasionaliter auget, inquantum concupiscentia ferventius fertur in rem prohibitam. Unde huiusmodi cognitio, nondum destructa causa concupiscentiae, occidit; hinc vero addit praevaricationem. Nam gravius est peccare contra legem scriptam et naturalem simul, quam contra legem naturalem solum. Rom. VII, 8: *occasione accepta* non data, *peccatum*, et cetera.

Licet autem occasionaliter occidat, inquantum scilicet auget concupiscentiam, et addit praevaricationem, non tamen est mala lex vetus, quia ad minus prohibet mala. Est tamen imperfecta, inquantum non removet causam. Est ergo lex sine Spiritu interius imprimens legem in corde, occasio mortis. Et ideo necessarium fuit dare legem Spiritus, qui caritatem in corde faciens, vivificet. Io. VI, 64: *Spiritus est, qui vivificat*.

92. Consequenter ex his ostendit dignitatem sui ministerii.

Et circa hoc duo facit.

to exercise this office, unless he was impeded on the part of the receivers: *and for these things, who is so sufficient* (2 Cor 2:16), namely, as are the apostles instituted by God?

90. He describes what this New Testament is when he continues, *not in the letter, but in the Spirit*. He describes it in regard to two things, namely, as to that in which it consists and as to its cause for which it has been given: *for the letter kills*.

In regard to the first it should be noted that the Apostle speaks profoundly, for it is stated: *I will make a new covenant with the house of Israel, and with the house of Judah, not like the covenant which I made with their fathers* (Jer 31:31); and later on: *I will put my law within them, and I will write it on their hearts; and I will be their God and they shall be my people* (Jer 31:33). The Old Testament, therefore, is written in a book, later to be sprinkled with blood, as it is said: *he took the blood of calves and goats and sprinkled both the book itself and all the people, saying: this is the blood of the covenant which God commanded you* (Heb 9:19).

So it is clear that the old law is a covenant of words, but the New Testament is a covenant of the Holy Spirit, by whom the love of God is poured out in our hearts (Rom 5:5). Consequently, when the Holy Spirit produces charity in us, which is the fullness of the law, it is a new covenant, *not in the letter*, i.e., not written down, *but in the Spirit*, i.e., through the Spirit who *gives life*: *the law of the Spirit of life* (Rom 8:2), i.e., life-giving.

91. The reason why the New Testament was given by the Spirit is indicated when he says, *for the letter kills*, not as a cause but as an occasion. For the written law only gives knowledge of sin: *for through the law comes knowledge of sin* (Rom 3:20). But as a result of merely knowing sin, two things follow. For the law, although sin is known by it, does not repress concupiscence, but is the occasion of increasing it, inasmuch as concupiscence is enkindled the more by something forbidden. Hence such knowledge kills, when the cause of concupiscence has not yet been destroyed. As a result it adds to the sin. For it is more grievous to sin against the written and natural law than against the natural law only. *But sin, finding opportunity in the commandment, wrought in me all kinds of concupiscence* (Rom 7:8).

But although it is the occasion of killing inasmuch as it increases concupiscence and increases the sin, the law is not evil, because at least it forbids evil; nevertheless, it is imperfect, inasmuch as it does not remove the cause. Therefore, the law without the Spirit inwardly impressing the law on the heart is the occasion of death; hence, it was necessary to give the law of the Spirit, who gives life by producing charity in the heart. *It is the Spirit that gives life* (John 6:63).

92. From these, therefore, he shows the dignity of his ministry.

He does two things in this regard.

Primo ostendit, quod ministerium Novi Testamenti praefertur ministerio Veteris Testamenti;

secundo quod non solum praefertur, sed quod ministerium Veteris Testamenti quasi nihil habet de gloria in comparatione ad novum, ibi **nam nec glorificatum**, et cetera.

Circa primum duo facit.

Primo ostendit quod ministerium Novi Testamenti praefertur Veteri;

secundo rationem huius assignat, ibi **nam si ministratio**, et cetera.

93. Circa primum sciendum est, quod Apostolus argumentatur ex hoc quod habetur Exodi XXIV, ubi littera nostra habet, quod Moyses habebat *faciem cornutam*, **ita quod non possent**, et cetera. Alia littera habet *faciem splendidam*, quod melius dicitur. Non enim intelligendum est eum habuisse cornua ad litteram, sicut quidam eum pingunt; sed dicitur cornuta propter radios, qui videbantur esse quasi quaedam cornua. Arguitur autem ex hoc sic. Et primo per unum simile, et est locus a minori. Constat enim quod si aliquid quod minus est, habet aliquid de gloria, quod multo magis illud quod est maius. Sed Vetus Testamentum est minus quam Novum; cum ergo illud fuerit in gloria, **ita ut non possent**, etc., videtur quod multo magis Novum est in gloria.

94. Quod autem Vetus Testamentum minus sit Novo, probat tripliciter.

Primo quantum ad effectum, quia illud est testamentum mortis, istud vitae, ut dictum est. Et quantum ad hoc dicit, quod **si ministratio mortis**, id est Vetus, quae est occasio mortis. Et hoc respondet ei quo dicitur **littera occidit**, et cetera.

Secundo quantum ad modum tradendi, quia Vetus fuit tradita litteris in tabulis lapideis, Nova vero fuit impressa Spiritu in cordibus carnalibus. Et hoc innuit, cum dicit **litteris deformata**, id est perfecte formata, **in lapidibus**, id est in tabulis lapideis. Et hoc ei respondet, quo dicitur: **non littera, sed Spiritu**, et cetera.

Tertio quantum ad perfectionem, quia gloria Veteris Testamenti sine fiducia est, quia neminem ad perfectum adduxit lex. In Novo vero est gloria cum spe melioris gloriae, scilicet sempiternae. Is. LI, 6: *salus mea in sempiternum erit*. Et hoc innuit, cum dicit **quae evacuatur**, Gal. V, 2: *quod si circumcidamini, Christus nihil*, et cetera.

Conclusio ponitur, cum dicit **quomodo non magis**, quod planum est.

95. Horum autem rationem assignat consequenter, cum dicit **nam si ministratio**, et cetera.

Et est ratio sua talis: gloria magis debetur iustitiae, quam damnationi, sed ministerium Novi Testamenti est

First, he shows that the ministry of the New Testament is preferred to the Old;

second, that it is not only preferred, but that in comparison to the Old Testament, the latter has, as it were, nothing of glory, at **for even that which was glorious**.

In regard to the first, he does two things.

First, he shows that the ministry of the New Testament is preferred to the Old;

second, he assigns the reason for this, at **for if the ministration**.

93. In regard to the first, it should be noted that the Apostle argues from a statement in Exodus, where our text says that *the face of Moses was horned*, **so that the children of Israel could not steadfastly behold the face** (Exod 34:34). Another version says that *his face shone*, and this is better. For it should not be supposed that he literally had horns, as some depict him, but he is described as horned because of the rays which seemed to be like horns. He argues from this in the following way: first, by a similarity and by arguing from the lesser. For it is obvious that if something less has glory, then much more something which is greater. But the Old Testament is less than the New: therefore, since the former was in glory, **so that the children of Israel could not steadfastly behold the face of Moses, for the glory of his countenance**, it seems that the New is much more in glory.

94. That the Old Testament is less than the New he proves in three ways.

First, from its effect, because the former is a covenant of death, but the latter of life, as has been said. In regard to this he says, **if the ministration of death**, i.e., the Old, which is the occasion of death; and this corresponds to what he said, namely, that **the letter kills, but the Spirit gives life**.

Second, as to the way it was delivered, for the Old was delivered written on stone tablets, but the New was impressed by the Spirit on human hearts. He suggests this when he says, **engraved with letters**, i.e., perfectly formed, **upon stones**, i.e., on tablets of stone. This corresponds to his statement, **not in the letter, but in the Spirit**.

Third, as to perfection: for the glory of the Old Testament is without assurance, because the law brought no one to perfection. But in the New there is glory with the hope of a better glory, i.e., eternal: *my salvation will be forever* (Isa 51:6). This is suggested when he says, **which is made void**: if you receive circumcision, Christ will be of no advantage to you (Gal 5:2).

He states the conclusion when he says, **how shall the ministration of the Spirit not be even more in glory**, which is plain.

95. Then he assigns the reason for all these when he says, **for if the ministration of condemnation is glory**.

This is his reasoning: glory is owed more to justice than to condemnation, but the ministry of the New Testament

ministerium iustitiae, quia iustificat interius vivificando. Ministerium autem Veteris Testamenti est ministerium damnationis occasionaliter. Supra eodem: *littera occidit, Spiritus autem vivificat*. Cum ergo *ministratio damnationis*, id est, ministratio Veteris Testamenti, quae occasionaliter est causa damnationis, ut dictum est, *est in gloria*, quae apparuit in facie Moysi, constat quod *multo magis abundat in gloria*, id est, dat abundantem gloriam ministris eius, *ministerium iustitiae*, id est, Novi Testamenti, per quod datur Spiritus, per quem est iustitia et consummatio virtutum. Prov. III, 35: *sapientes gloriam possidebunt*.

96. Consueverunt hoc in loco fieri quaestiones de comparatione Moysi et Pauli, sed, si recte considerentur verba Apostoli, non sunt necessariae, quia hic non fit comparatio personae ad personam, sed ministerii ad ministerium.

97. Sed quia possent pseudo-apostoli dicere quod licet maius ministerium sit Novi Testamenti quam ministerium Veteris testamenti non tamen est multo maius, et ideo bonum est quod illi ministerio, et isti intendamus, quod et faciebant, quia simul servabant legalia cum Evangelio. Ideo hic consequenter Apostolus hoc improbat, cum dicit *nam nec glorificatum*, et cetera.

Et circa hoc duo facit.

Primo enim ostendit, quod ministerium Novi Testamenti absque aliqua comparatione excedit ministerium Veteris;

secundo causam huius assignat, ibi *si enim quod evacuatur*, et cetera.

98. Dicit ergo: dixi quod ministerium iustitiae abundat in gloria, et intantum quod gloria Veteris ministerii non est dicenda gloria, *quia nec glorificatum*, etc.: quod dupliciter exponitur.

Primo modo sic *quia nec*, etc., id est illa gloria nihil est in comparatione ad istam Novi Testamenti, quia illa gloria non est omnibus ministris collata, sed solum Moysi, et non claruit in toto Moyse, sed in parte, id est in facie solum particulariter. Et ideo *nec glorificatum est*, id est nec glorificari debet, *propter excellentem gloriam*, id est comparatione excellentis gloriae Novi Testamenti, quae abundat gratia, ut per eam purificati homines possent videre non gloriam hominis, sed Dei.

Secundo modo ut punctetur sic: *nec glorificatum est quod claruit*; quasi dicat: nam in hac parte, id est in respectu huius naturae particularis, qui sumus servi, non est glorificatum, id est non gloriosum illud quod claruit

is a ministry of justice, because it justifies by giving life within. The ministry of the Old Testament is a ministry of condemnation, as being its occasion: *the letter kills, but the Spirit gives life*. Therefore, *if the ministration of condemnation*, i.e., the ministry of the Old Testament, which is the occasional cause of condemnation, as has been said, *is glory*, which appeared on the face of Moses, it is obvious that *much more does the ministration of justice abound in glory*, i.e., give an abundance of glory to its ministers. *The ministration of justice*, i.e., of the New Testament, by which the Spirit is given, through whom is given justice and the fulfillment of the virtues: *the wise shall possess glory* (Prov 3:35).

96. It is customary here to compare Moses and Paul; but if the Apostle's words are considered carefully, this is not necessary, because ministries, not persons, are being compared.

97. But because the false apostles could say that even though the ministry of the New Testament is greater than that of the Old, it is not much greater. Therefore, it is good for us to continue in that ministry, which they did, because they observed the ceremonies of the law along with the Gospel. Therefore the Apostle rejects this when he says, *for even that which was glorious in this part was not glorified by reason of the glory that excells*.

In regard to this he does two things.

First, he shows that the ministry of the New Testament exceeds that of the Old beyond all comparison;

second, he assigns the reason for this, at *for if that which was made void*.

98. He says, therefore, I have said that the ministry of justice abounds in glory to such a degree that the glory of the Old Testament should not be called glorious, *for even that which was glorious in this part was not glorified by reason of the glory that excells*. This is explained in two ways.

First, that that glory is nothing in comparison to that of the New Testament, because such glory was not conferred on all the ministers, but on Moses alone, and it did not shine on Moses entirely, but in part, i.e., on his face alone. Therefore, *even that which was glorious in this part was not glorified*, i.e., should not be glorified *by reason of the glory that excells*, i.e., in comparison to the excelling glory of the New Testament, which abounds in grace, so that men purified by it might not see the glory of a man but of God.

It is explained in a second way by punctuating it thus: *that which was glorious in this part was not glorified by reason of the glory that excells*: as if to say, for in this part, i.e., in respect to this particular nature, that we are servants,

in Veteri Testamento; et hoc propter excellentem gloriam, quae est in Novo, quia illa est gloria Dei Patris.

99. Huius autem causam assignat consequenter, cum dicit *si enim quod evacuatur*, et cetera.

Et est ratio sua talis: illud quod datur ut transeat, nihil est in respectu ad illud quod datur ut semper maneat. Si ergo Testamentum Vetus, quod evacuatur, tollitur, I Cor. c. XIII, 10: *cum venerit quod perfectum est, evacuabitur quod ex parte est*, et cetera. Per gloriam enim Moysi ministratum saltem per particularem gloriam.

Constat quod Testamentum Novum manet, quia hic inchoatur, et perficitur in patria. Lc. XXI, 33: *caelum et terra transibunt, verba autem mea non transibunt*. Erit *multo magis in gloria* aeterna, in qua perficietur. Erit, inquam, nobis, qui sumus eius ministri.

has come to have no glory, i.e., that was not glorious which shone in the Old Testament: and this by reason of the glory that surpasses it, which is in the New, because it is the glory of God the Father.

99. Then he assigns the cause of this when he says, *for if that which is made void was glorious, much more that which remains is in glory*.

His reasoning is thus: that which was given to pass away is nothing in relation to that which is given to remain always. If, therefore, the Old Testament, which is rendered void, is done away with: *but when the perfect comes, the imperfect will pass away* (1 Cor 13:10). For with glory the ministry of Moses came, at least with a particular glory.

And it is obvious that the New Testament remains, because it is begun here and completed in heaven: *heaven and earth shall pass away, but my words shall not pass away* (Luke 21:33). It will be *much more in* eternal *glory*, in which it will be perfected; it will be, I say, for us who are its ministers.

Lecture 3

^{3:12}Habentes igitur talem spem, multa fiducia utimur: [n. 100]

^{3:13}et non sicut Moyses ponebat velamen super faciem suam, ut non intenderent filii Israël in faciem ejus, quod evacuatur, [n. 102]

^{3:14}sed obtusi sunt sensus eorum. Usque in hodiernum enim diem, idipsum velamen in lectione Veteris Testamenti manet non revelatum (quoniam in Christo evacuatur), [n. 106]

^{3:15}sed usque in hodiernum diem, cum legitur Moyses, velamen positum est super cor eorum. [n. 108]

^{3:16}Cum autem conversus fuerit ad Dominum, auferetur velamen. [n. 109]

^{3:17}Dominus autem Spiritus est: ubi autem Spiritus Domini, ibi libertas. [n. 111]

^{3:18}Nos vero omnes, revelata facie gloriam Domini speculantes, in eamdem imaginem transformamur a claritate in claritatem, tamquam a Domini Spiritu. [n. 113]

^{3:12}Ἔχοντες οὖν τοιαύτην ἐλπίδα πολλῇ παρρησίᾳ χρώμεθα

^{3:13}καὶ οὐ καθάπερ Μωϋσῆς ἐτίθει κάλυμμα ἐπὶ τὸ πρόσωπον αὐτοῦ πρὸς τὸ μὴ ἀτενίσαι τοὺς υἱοὺς Ἰσραὴλ εἰς τὸ τέλος τοῦ καταργουμένου.

^{3:14}ἀλλὰ ἐπωρώθη τὰ νοήματα αὐτῶν. ἄχρι γὰρ τῆς σήμερον ἡμέρας τὸ αὐτὸ κάλυμμα ἐπὶ τῇ ἀναγνώσει τῆς παλαιᾶς διαθήκης μένει, μὴ ἀνακαλυπτόμενον ὅτι ἐν Χριστῷ καταργεῖται·

^{3:15}ἀλλ' ἕως σήμερον ἡνίκα ἂν ἀναγινώσκηται Μωϋσῆς, κάλυμμα ἐπὶ τὴν καρδίαν αὐτῶν κεῖται·

^{3:16}ἡνίκα δὲ ἐὰν ἐπιστρέψῃ πρὸς κύριον, περιαιρεῖται τὸ κάλυμμα.

^{3:17}ὁ δὲ κύριος τὸ πνεῦμά ἐστιν· οὗ δὲ τὸ πνεῦμα κυρίου, ἐλευθερία.

^{3:18}ἡμεῖς δὲ πάντες ἀνακεκαλυμμένῳ προσώπῳ τὴν δόξαν κυρίου κατοπτριζόμενοι τὴν αὐτὴν εἰκόνα μεταμορφούμεθα ἀπὸ δόξης εἰς δόξαν καθάπερ ἀπὸ κυρίου πνεύματος.

^{3:12}Having therefore such hope, we use much confidence, [n. 100]

^{3:13}And not as Moses put a veil upon his face, that the children of Israel might not steadfastly look on the face of that which is made void. [n. 102]

^{3:14}But their senses were made dull. For, until this present day, the selfsame veil, in the reading of the Old Testament, remains unlifted because in Christ it is made void. [n. 106]

^{3:15}But even until this day, when Moses is read, the veil is upon their heart. [n. 108]

^{3:16}But when one shall be converted to the Lord, the veil shall be taken away. [n. 109]

^{3:17}Now the Lord is a Spirit. And where the Spirit of the Lord is, there is liberty. [n. 111]

^{3:18}But we all, beholding the glory of the Lord with unveiled face, are transformed into the same image from clarity to clarity as by the Spirit of the Lord. [n. 113]

---

100. Positis his quae pertinent ad commendationem doni percepti a Deo, hic consequenter ponit ea quae pertinent ad commendationem fiduciae de ipso dono conceptae.

Circa hoc autem duo facit.

Primo ponit fiduciam ex dono conceptam;

secundo vero comparat fiduciam Veteris et Novi Testamenti, ibi *et non sicut Moyses*.

101. Dicit ergo primo: **habentes igitur talem spem**, ex hoc scilicet quod nobis dictum est, scilicet videndi gloriam Dei, Rom. c. VIII, 24: *spe enim salvi facti sumus*, **multa fiducia utimur**, id est, confidenter operamur ea quae pertinent ad usum huius ministerii, ex quo crescit nobis spes. Prov. XXVIII, v. 1. *iustus quasi leo confidens absque terrore erit.* Ier. XVII, 7: *benedictus vir qui confidit in Domino.*

102. Consequenter, sicut praetulit donum dono, ita praefert fiduciam Novi Testamenti fiduciae Veteris testamenti, cum dicit **et non sicut Moyses**, et cetera.

Et circa hoc duo facit:

primo proponit factum in Veteri Testamento;

secundo exponit, ibi **quod evacuatur**, et cetera.

100. Having laid down what pertains to commending the gift received from God, he now lays down what pertains to commending the confidence born of that gift.

In regard to this he does two things:

first, he mentions the confidence born of the gift;

second, he compares the confidence in the Old and in the New Testament, at *and not as Moses*.

101. He says, therefore, *having therefore such a hope*, because of what has been said to us, namely, of seeing the glory of God: *in this hope we were saved* (Rom 8:24), *we use much confidence*, i.e., we confidently do the things which pertain to the use of this ministry, from which our hope grows: *the righteous are bold as a lion* (Prov 28:1); *blessed is the man who trusts in the Lord* (Jer 17:7).

102. Then as he preferred the one gift to the other, so he prefers the confidence of the New Testament to that of the Old, when he says, *and not as Moses put a veil on his face*.

In regard to this he does two things:

first, he mentions a fact about the Old Testament;

second, he explains it, at *which is made void*.

103. Factum autem quod proponit legitur Exodi XXXIV, 34, ubi dicitur quod Moyses quando loquebatur ad populum, velabat faciem suam, quia propter claritatem vultus eius non poterant respicere in eum filii Israel. Et ideo dicit *et non sicut Moyses*, etc., quasi dicat: dico quod utimur multa fiducia, et tanta, quod non accidit nobis, sicut Moyses faciebat eis, scilicet non revelando faciem suam populo, quia nondum venerat tempus revelandi claritatem veritatis. Habemus ergo nos fiduciam absque velamine.

104. Consequenter exponit hoc quod dixerat, de velamine, dicens *quod evacuatur*, et cetera. Velamen enim illud erat obscuritas figurarum, quae per Christum evacuata est.

Et circa hoc tria facit.

Primo enim ponit evacuationem huius velaminis;

secundo quomodo haec evacuatio habet locum in Iudaeis, ibi *sed obtusi*, etc.;

tertio quomodo non habeat locum in ministris Novi Testamenti, ibi *nos vero revelata*, et cetera.

105. Dicit ergo quod *Moyses ponebat velamen*, scilicet figurae, *super faciem suam*, *quod*, scilicet velamen, *evacuatur*, id est tollitur per Christum, scilicet implendo in veritate quod Moyses tradidit in figura, quia omnia in figura contingebant illis. Sic enim Christus per mortem suam removit velamen de occisione agni paschalis, et ideo statim cum emisit Spiritum, velum Templi scissum est. Item, in mittendo Spiritum Sanctum in corda credentium, ut intelligerent spiritualiter quod Iudaei carnaliter intelligunt. Et hoc velamen removit, cum aperuit eis sensum, ut intelligerent Scripturas, Lc. Ult.

106. Qualem autem effectum habeat in Iudaeis haec evacuatio, ostendit, dicens *sed obtusi*, et cetera.

Et circa hoc duo facit.

Primo ostendit, quod remotum ab illis non fuit in statu infidelitatis;

secundo ostendit, quod removebitur in eorum conversione, ibi *cum autem conversus fuerit*, et cetera.

Circa primum duo facit.

Primo ostendit rationem quare haec evacuatio non habet locum in Iudaeis;

secundo, ex hoc ostendit eos adhuc habere velamen, ibi *sed usque in hodiernum diem*, et cetera.

107. Dicit ergo quod evacuatur in his qui credunt, sed non quantum ad Iudaeos infideles. Et ratio huius est, quia *obtusi sunt sensus eorum*, id est ratio eorum hebes est, et sensus eorum imbecilles et obtusi sunt, nec possunt videre claritatem divini luminis, id est divinae veritatis, absque velamine figurarum. Et huius ratio est quia claudunt oculos, ut non videant, quia velum Templi scissum est. Et ideo est ex eorum culpa infidelitatis, non ex defectu veritatis, quia, remoto velamine, omnibus

103. The fact he proposes is mentioned in Exodus, where it says that when he spoke to the people, Moses veiled his face, because the children of Israel could not look upon him because of the splendor of his face (Exod 34:33). Hence he says, *and not as Moses, who put a veil upon his face, that the children of Israel might not steadfastly look on the face of that which is made void*. As if to say: I say that we are very bold, and such as did not happen to us as Moses did to them, namely, not revealing his face to the people, because the time to reveal the splendor of truth had not yet come. Therefore, we have confidence without the veil.

104. Then he explains what he had said about the veil, saying, *which is made void*, for that veil was the dimness of the figures, which was made void by Christ.

In regard to this he does three things.

First, he mentions the voiding of this veil;

second, how this voiding still prevails among the Jews, at *but their senses*;

third, how this has no place among the ministers of the New Testament, at *but we all*.

105. He says, therefore, that *Moses put a veil*, namely, of the figure, *upon his face*; this veil is *made void*, i.e., is taken away by Christ, namely, by fulfilling in truth what Moses delivered in figure, because all things happened to them in a figure. For thus Christ by his death removed the veil of the killing of the paschal lamb. Therefore, as soon as he gave up his spirit, the veil of the Temple was rent. Likewise by sending the Holy Spirit into the hearts of believers so that they might understand spiritually what the Jews understood carnally. He removed the veil, when he opened their mind to understand the Scriptures (Luke 24:45).

106. He shows what effect this voiding had on the Jews, saying, *but their senses were made dull*.

In regard to this he does two things.

First, he shows that it was not removed from them in the state of unbelief;

second, he shows that it will be removed when they are converted, at *but when one shall be converted*.

In regard to the he does two things:

first, he shows why this voiding has no place among the Jews;

second, from this he shows that they still have the veil, at *but even until this day*.

107. He says, therefore, that it is removed for those who believe, but not for the unbelieving Jews. The reason for this is that *their senses were made dull*, i.e., their reasoning power is dull and their senses weak and clouded, so that they cannot see the brightness of the divine light, i.e., of divine truth, without the veil of figures. The reason for this is that they close their eyes so as not to see, because the veil of the Temple was rent. Therefore, this is due to their sin of unbelief, and not to a weakness in the truth; because with

aperientibus oculos mentis per fidem clarissime veritas manifestatur. Rom. XI, 25: *caecitas ex parte contigit in Israel.* Io. IX, 39: *in iudicium veni in hunc mundum,* et cetera. Sic enim prophetaverat Isaias VI cap.: *excaeca cor populi huius,* et cetera.

Et vere intantum obtusi sunt sensus eorum, ut veritatem nobis manifestatam usque in hodiernum diem non intelligant. Sed idipsum velamen, quod erat in Veteri Testamento, antequam velum Templi scissum esset in lectione Veteris Testamenti, quia non aliter intelligunt illud, quam ante, quia adhuc innituntur figuris, ut veritatem non revelent, id est non intelligant: sic velamen Dei, non figuram, sed veritatem credunt, quod scilicet evacuatur quantum ad fideles, et quantum in se est omnibus per Christum, id est in fide Christi, sed in eis non manet, quia non credunt venisse Christum.

108. Consequenter cum dicit *sed usque in hodiernum diem*, etc., ostendit quomodo adhuc apud Iudaeos est velamen quantum ad infideles, licet remotum sit per Christum.

Circa quod sciendum est, quod velamen dicitur apponi alicui dupliciter: aut quia apponitur rei visae ne possit videri, aut quia apponitur videnti ne videat. Sed Iudaeis in veteri lege utroque modo appositum erat velamen. Nam et corda eorum excaecata erant, ne cognoscerent veritatem propter eorum duritiem, et Vetus Testamentum nondum completum erat, quia nondum veritas venerat. Unde in signum huius velamen erat in facie Moysi et non in faciebus eorum, sed, veniente Christo, velamen remotum est a facie Moysi, id est a Veteri Testamento, quia iam impletum est, sed tamen non est remotum a cordibus eorum. Et hoc est quod dicit *sed usque in hodiernum diem*, quasi dicat: amotum est a fidelibus Veteris Testamenti velamen, sed adhuc *cum legitur Moyses*, id est, cum exponitur eis Vetus Testamentum, Act. c. XV, 21: *Moyses a temporibus antiquis habet in singulis civitatibus, qui eum praedicent in synagogis*, etc., *velamen*, id est caecitas, *est positum super cor eorum*. Rom. XI, 25: *caecitas ex parte contigit*, et cetera.

109. Quando autem et quomodo removetur ab eis illud velamen, ostendit consequenter, cum dicit *cum autem conversus*, et cetera. Et

primo describit modum removendi hoc velamen;

secundo rationem huius reddit, ibi *Dominus autem spiritus*, et cetera.

110. Dicit ergo, quod illud velamen adhuc est in eis, sed non quod Vetus Testamentum sit velatum, sed quia corda eorum velata sunt. Et ideo, ad hoc ut removeatur, nihil restat, nisi quod convertantur, et hoc est quod dicit

the removal of the veil the truth is manifested very clearly to all who open the eyes of their mind through faith. *A hardening has come upon part of Israel* (Rom 11:25); *for judgment I came into this world, that those who do not see may see, and that those who see may become blind* (John 9:39). For this was foretold by Isaiah: *make the heart of this people fat, and their ears heavy, and shut their eyes, lest they see with their eyes, and hear with their ears, and understand with their hearts, and turn and be healed* (Isa 6:10).

And indeed their minds are so dulled to the truth that to this day they do not understand the truth manifested to us. But the same veil remains which was in the Old Testament before the veil of the Temple was rent, when they read the Old Testament, because they understand it no differently than before. For they still rely on figures, so as not to reveal the truth, i.e., not understand. Thus they still believe that the veil of God is not a figure, but the truth, which namely is lifted as to believers through Christ, i.e., in the faith of Christ. But it remains in them, because they do not believe that Christ has come.

108. Then when he says, *but even until this day, when Moses is read, the veil is upon their heart*, he shows how even among the Jews the veil remains, as to unbelievers, although it has been removed by Christ.

In regard to this it should be noted that a veil is said to be put on something in two ways: either because it is put on the thing seen, so that it cannot be seen; or because it is put on the one seeing, so that he may not see. But the veil was put on the Jews of the old law in both ways. For their eyes have been blinded not to see the truth because of their hardness; and the Old Testament had not yet been fulfilled, because the truth had not yet come. As a sign of this the veil was on Moses' face and not theirs. But with the coming of Christ the veil was removed from the face of Moses, i.e., from the Old Testament, because it was not fulfilled: but it has not been removed from their hearts. Hence, he says, *but even until this day*, As if to say: the veil has been removed from the believers of the Old Testament, but still *when Moses is read*, i.e., when the Old Testament is explained to them: *for from early generations, Moses has had in every city those who preach him, for he is read every sabbath in the synagogues* (Acts 15:21); *the veil*, i.e., blindness, *is upon their heart*: a hardening has come upon part of Israel (Rom 11:25).

109. But when and how that veil shall be removed from them is shown when he says, *but when one shall be converted to the Lord, the veil shall be taken away*.

First he describes how to remove this veil;

second, the reason for this, at *now the Lord is a spirit*.

110. He says, therefore, that this veil is still upon them; not that the Old Testament is veiled, but because their hearts are veiled. Therefore if it is to be removed, nothing remains but that they be converted. Hence, he says, *but when one*

cum autem conversus fuerit, scilicet aliquis eorum ad Deum per fidem in Christum, ex ipsa conversione *auferetur velamen*. Is. X, 21: *reliquiae convertentur*, et cetera. Et hoc idem habetur Rom. IX, 27.

Et nota, quod cum ageret de caecitate, loquitur in plurali, unde dicit *super corda eorum*, cum vero loquitur de conversione, loquitur in singulari dicens *cum autem conversus*, ut ostendat eorum facilitatem ad malum, et difficultatem ad bonum, quasi pauci convertantur.

111. Ratio autem quare convertantur, et velamen removeatur, hoc modo est, quia Deus vult.

Posset enim dicere, quod velamen illud appositum est ex praecepto Domini, et ideo non potest removeri. Sed Apostolus ostendit, quod non solum potest removeri, imo quia removetur per eum, qui est Dominus. Et hoc est, quod dicit *Dominus enim*, et cetera. Quod potest dupliciter legi. Uno modo, ut Spiritus teneatur ex parte subiecti, ut dicatur: *spiritus*, id est Spiritus Sanctus, scilicet qui est auctor legis, *est Dominus*, id est operatur ex proprio libertatis arbitrio. Io. III, 8: *Spiritus ubi vult spirat*. I Cor. XII, 11: *dividens singulis prout vult*. *Ubi autem spiritus Domini, ibi libertas*; quasi dicat: quia Spiritus est Dominus, potest dare libertatem, ut possimus libere uti Scriptura Veteris Testamenti absque velamine. Et ideo, qui non habent Spiritum Sanctum, non possunt libere uti. Gal. V, 13: *vos in libertatem vocati estis*. I Petr. II, 16: *quasi liberi, et non quasi velamen habentes malitiae libertatem*.

Alio modo, ut per Dominum intelligatur Christus, et tunc legitur sic *Dominus*, id est Christus, *est spiritualis*, id est Spiritus potestatis, et ideo *ubi est spiritus Domini*, id est lex Christi spiritualiter intellecta, non scripta litteris, sed per fidem cordibus impressa, *ibi est libertas*, ab omni impedimento velaminis.

112. Sciendum autem, quod occasione istorum verborum, scilicet *ubi spiritus Domini, ibi libertas*, et illorum, scilicet *iusto lex non est posita*, aliqui erronee dixerunt quod viri spirituales non obligantur praeceptis legis divinae. Sed hoc est falsum; nam praecepta Dei sunt regula voluntatis humanae. Nullus autem homo est, nec etiam angelus, cuius voluntatem non oporteat regulari et dirigi lege divina. Unde impossibile est aliquem hominem praeceptis Dei non subdi.

Hoc autem quod dicitur *iusto lex non est posita*, exponitur, id est, *propter iustos*, qui interiori habitu moventur ad ea quae lex Dei praecipit, lex non est posita: sed propter iniustos, non quin etiam iusti ad eam teneantur.

Et similiter *ubi spiritus Domini, ibi libertas*, intelligitur, quia liber est, qui est causa sui: servus autem est causa Domini; quicumque ergo agit ex seipso, libere agit; qui vero ex alio motus, non agit libere. Ille ergo, qui vitat mala, non quia mala, sed propter mandatum Domini,

shall be converted, namely, some of them, to God through faith in Christ, *the veil shall be taken away*: *a remnant will return, the remnant of Jacob, to the mighty God* (Isa 10:21); and this is also stated in Romans (Rom 9:27).

And note that when he treated of blindness, he spoke in the plural, saying *upon their heart*; but when he speaks of conversion, he speaks in the singular, saying, *but when one shall be converted*, to show how easy evil is and how difficult the good, as though few will be converted.

111. But the reason why they are converted and the veil removed in this manner is because God wills it.

For they could claim that God put the veil on them and therefore it cannot be removed. But the Apostle shows that it cannot only be removed, but even that it is removed by him who is the Lord. Hence, he says, *now the Lord is a spirit*. This can be understood in two ways. In one way, so that Spirit is taken as the subject, as though saying: *a spirit*, i.e., the Holy Spirit, namely who is the author of the law, *is the Lord*, i.e., works by his own free will: *the Spirit blows where it wills* (John 3:8); *the Spirit, who apportions to each one individually as he wills* (1 Cor 12:11). *And where the spirit of the Lord is, there is liberty* as if to say: because the Spirit is the Lord, he can give freedom to enable us freely to use the writings of the Old Testament without a veil. Therefore, those who do not have the Holy Spirit cannot use it freely: *you were called to freedom* (Gal 5:13); *live as free men, yet without using your freedom as a pretext for evil* (1 Pet 2:16).

It can be understood another way so that by the Lord is meant Christ, as though saying: *the Lord*, i.e., Christ, *is a spirit*, i.e., has spiritual power. Therefore, *where the spirit of the Lord is*, i.e., the law of Christ spiritually understood, not in a written code, but impressed on the heart by faith, *there is liberty* from every obscurity of the veil.

112. It should be noted that by occasion of these words, namely, *where the spirit of the Lord is, there is liberty* and of those found in 1 Timothy: *the law is not laid down for the just* (1 Tim 1:9), some have erroneously said that spiritual men are not bound by the precepts of the divine law. But this is false, for God's precepts are the rule of the human will. But there is no man or angel whose will does not need to be ruled and directed by divine law. Hence, it is impossible for any man not to be subject to God's precepts.

But the statement that *the law is not laid down for the just* means that the law was not laid down *for the just* who are led by an internal habit to do what the law of God commands, but because of the unjust. Nevertheless, this does not mean that the just are not bound to it.

Similarly, *where the spirit of the Lord is, there is liberty* is explained thus: the free man is one who exists for himself, but the servant exists for the sake of the master. Therefore, whoever acts of himself acts freely, but one who is moved by another does not act freely. Therefore, one who avoids

non est liber; sed qui vitat mala, quia mala, est liber. Hoc autem facit Spiritus Sanctus, qui mentem interius perficit per bonum habitum, ut sic ex amore caveat, ac si praeciperet lex divina; et ideo dicitur liber, non quin subdatur legi divinae, sed quia ex bono habitu inclinatur ad hoc faciendum, quod lex divina ordinat.

113. Deinde, cum dicit *nos vero omnes*, etc., ostendit quomodo Christi fideles sunt omnino liberi ab hoc velamine. Dicit ergo: dico quod ab illis aufertur velamen hoc, cum aliquis conversus fuerit sicut nos, non aliquis, sed omnes, qui sumus Christi fideles. Lc. VIII, 10: *vobis datum est*, et cetera. *Revelata facie*, non habentes velamen supra cor, sicut illi. Et intelligitur per faciem, cor, seu mens, quia sicut per faciem videt quis corporaliter, ita per mentem spiritualiter. Ps. CXVIII, 18: *revela oculos meos*, et cetera.

Gloriam Domini, non Moysi: gloria enim significat claritatem, ut dicit Augustinus. Iudaei autem videbant quamdam gloriam in facie Moysi ex hoc, quod locutus est cum Deo. Sed haec gloria est imperfecta, quia non est claritas ex qua ipse Deus est gloriosus; et hoc est cognoscere ipsum Deum. Vel *gloriam Domini*, id est, Filium Dei. Prov. X: *gloria patris, filius sapiens*, et cetera.

114. *Speculantes* non sumitur hic a specula, sed a speculo, id est ipsum Deum gloriosum cognoscentes per speculum rationis, in qua est quaedam imago ipsius. Et hunc speculamur quando homo ex consideratione sui ipsius assurgit in cognitionem aliquam de Deo, et transformatur.

Cum enim omnis cognitio sit per assimilationem cognoscentis ad cognitum, oportet quod qui vident, aliquo modo transformentur in Deum. Et siquidem perfecte vident, perfecte transformantur, sicut beati in patria per fruitionis unionem, I Io. III, 2: *cum autem apparuerit*, et cetera. Si vero imperfecte, imperfecte, sicut hic per fidem, I Cor. XIII, 12: *videmus nunc per speculum in aenigmate*.

115. Et ideo dicit *in eamdem imaginem*, id est sicut videmus, *transformamur*, inquam, *a claritate in claritatem*, in quo distinguit triplicem gradum cognitionis in discipulis Christi: primus est a claritate cognitionis naturalis in claritatem cognitionis fidei. Secundus est a claritate cognitionis Veteris Testamenti, in claritatem cognitionis gratiae Novi Testamenti. Tertius est a claritate cognitionis naturalis et Veteris et Novi Testamenti, in claritatem visionis aeternae. Infra IV, 16: *licet is qui foris est*, et cetera.

Sed unde est hoc? Non ex littera legis, sed *tamquam a spiritu Domini*. Rom. VIII, v. 14: *quicumque*

evils, not because they are evil, but because of God's commandment, is not free. But one who avoids evils because they are evils is free. But this is done by the Holy Spirit who perfects man inwardly with a good habit, so that from love he avoids evil, as if the divine law had commanded. Consequently, he is called free, not as though he is not subject to the divine law, but because he is inclined by a good habit to do what the divine law ordains.

113. Then when he says, **and we all**, he shows how the faithful of Christ are altogether free of this veil. He says, therefore: I say that this veil will be removed from them, when a person may be converted as we are; not a particular one, but we all who are Christ's faithful. *To you it has been given to know the secrets of the kingdom of God; but for others they are in parables* (Luke 8:10). **With unveiled face**, not having a veil upon the heart, as they. By face is meant the heart or the mind, because just as a person sees bodily with the face, so spiritually with the mind. *Open my eyes that I may behold wondrous things out of your law* (Ps 119:18).

The glory of the Lord, not of Moses: for glory signifies brightness, as Augustine says. But the Jews saw some glory on the face of Moses as a result of his speaking with God. But this glory is imperfect, because it is not the glory with which God is glorious: and this is to know God himself. Or **the glory of the Lord**, i.e., the Son of God: *the glory of a father is a wise son* (Prov 10:1).

114. **Beholding**, i.e., speculating, which is not taken from the word which means 'watch tower,' but from 'mirror,' i.e., knowing the glorious God himself by the mirror of reason, in which there is an image of God. We behold him when we rise from a consideration of ourselves to some knowledge of God, and we are transformed.

For since all knowledge involves the knower's being assimilated to the thing known, it is necessary that those who see be in some way transformed into God. If they see perfectly, they are perfectly transformed, as the blessed in heaven by the union of enjoyment: *when he appears we shall be like him* (1 John 3:2); but if we see imperfectly, then we are transformed imperfectly, as here by faith: *now we see in a mirror dimly* (1 Cor 13:12).

115. Therefore he says, **into the same image**, that is, as we see, **we are transformed from clarity to clarity**. In this he distinguishes a triple degree of knowledge in Christ's disciples. The first is from the clarity of natural knowledge to the clarity of the knowledge of faith. The second is from the clarity of the knowledge of the Old Testament to the clarity of the knowledge of the grace of the New Testament. The third is from the clarity of natural knowledge and of the Old and New Testaments to the clarity of eternal vision. **Though our outward man is corrupted, yet the inward man is renewed day by day** (2 Cor 4:16).

But how does this come about? Not by the letter of the law, **as by the spirit of the Lord**: *for all who are led by the*

Spiritu Dei aguntur. Ps. CXLII, 10: *Spiritus tuus bonus deducet*, et cetera.

Spirit of God are sons of God (Rom 8:14); *let your good Spirit lead me on a level path* (Ps 143:10).

CHAPTER 4

Lecture 1

<table>
<tr>
<td>

^{4:1}Ideo habentes administrationem, juxta quod misericordiam consecuti sumus, non deficimus, [n. 116]

^{4:2}sed abdicamus occulta dedecoris, non ambulantes in astutia, neque adulterantes verbum Dei, sed in manifestatione veritatis commendantes nosmetipsos ad omnem conscientiam hominum coram Deo. [n. 118]

</td>
<td>

^{4:1}Διὰ τοῦτο, ἔχοντες τὴν διακονίαν ταύτην καθὼς ἠλεήθημεν, οὐκ ἐγκακοῦμεν

^{4:2}ἀλλὰ ἀπειπάμεθα τὰ κρυπτὰ τῆς αἰσχύνης, μὴ περιπατοῦντες ἐν πανουργίᾳ μηδὲ δολοῦντες τὸν λόγον τοῦ θεοῦ ἀλλὰ τῇ φανερώσει τῆς ἀληθείας συνιστάνοντες ἑαυτοὺς πρὸς πᾶσαν συνείδησιν ἀνθρώπων ἐνώπιον τοῦ θεοῦ

</td>
<td>

^{4:1}Therefore, having this ministration, according as we have obtained mercy, we faint not. [n. 116]

^{4:2}But we renounce the hidden things of dishonesty, not walking in craftiness nor adulterating the word of God: but by manifestation of the truth commending ourselves to every man's conscience, in the sight of God. [n. 118]

</td>
</tr>
</table>

---

116. Ostensa dignitate ministerii Novi Testamenti, hic consequenter Apostolus determinat de usu ministerii.

Et circa hoc duo facit.

Primo enim ostendit usum huius ministerii, qui debet esse in agendis bonis;

secundo illum, qui debet esse in malis patienter tolerandis, ibi *habemus autem thesaurum*, et cetera.

Circa primum duo facit.

Primo ponit huius ministerii usum;

secundo obiectionem excludit, ibi *quod si*, et cetera.

117. Dicit ergo: quia igitur huiusmodi ministerium est tantae dignitatis in se et in ministris, *ideo habentes hanc administrationem*, idest hanc dignitatem administrandi spiritualia. I Cor. IV, 1: *sic nos existimet homo, ut ministros*, et cetera. Rom. XI, 13: *quamdiu sum gentium apostolus, ministerium*, et cetera.

Habentes, inquam, non ex nobis, seu ex meritis nostris, sed *iuxta quod misericordiam consecuti sumus a Deo*, id est ex misericordia Dei, quam in hoc consecuti sumus a Deo. I Tim. I, 13: *misericordiam consecutus sum*, et cetera.

118. Consequenter cum dicit *non deficimus*, etc., describit usum huius ministerii, qui debet esse circa bona agenda, et hoc quantum ad duo.

Primo quantum ad vitationem malorum;

secundo quantum ad operationem bonorum *in manifestatione*, et cetera.

119. Docet autem vitari mala in usu huius ministerii, et quantum ad vitam, et quantum ad doctrinam. Sed quantum ad vitam dupliciter, scilicet quantum ad operationem, et quantum ad intentionem.

Nam si quis vitat mala operari et bona intentione, perfecte vitat mala. In operatione autem vitatur malum,

116. Having shown the dignity of the New Testament ministry, the Apostle now discusses the exercise of this ministry.

In regard to this he does two things.

First, he shows that the exercise of this ministry should consist in doing good;

second it should consist also in enduring evils patiently, at *but we have this treasure*.

In regard to the first he does two things.

First, he lays down the use of this ministry;

second, he excludes an objection, at *and if our Gospel*.

117. He says, therefore: because this ministry is of such great dignity in itself and in its ministers, *therefore, having this ministration*, i.e., this dignity of administering spiritual things. *This is how one should regard us, as servants of Christ and stewards of the mysteries of God* (1 Cor 4:1); *inasmuch then as I am an apostle to the gentiles, I magnify my ministry* (Rom 11:13);

having it, I say, not from ourselves or from our merits, but *according as we have obtained mercy*, i.e., from the mercy of God, which in this we have obtained by God: *I received mercy* (1 Tim 1:13).

118. Then when he says, *we faint not*, he describes the exercise of this ministry, which should be engaged in doing good; and this in regard to two things:

first, as to avoiding evil;

second, as to doing good *by manifestation of the truth*.

119. He teaches us to avoid evil both in conduct and in doctrine, when we exercise this ministry. As to conduct in two ways, namely in our actions and in our intentions.

But if a person avoids doing evil and has a good intention, he avoids evil completely. But evil is avoided in our

in adversitate patienter mala sustinendo, et ideo dicit **non deficimus**, per impatientiam. Gal. VI, 9: *bonum autem faciens non deficiamus*. II Cor. XII, v. 10: **cum infirmor, tunc fortior sum et potens**. Vitatur etiam in prosperitate, temperate utendo eis quae prospere succedunt, et ideo dicit **sed abdicamus occulta dedecoris**, id est amovemus a nobis quae hominem turpem et dedecorosum faciunt, scilicet immunda et turpia, et etiam occulta, non solum manifesta. Iac. I, 21: *abiiciamus omnem immunditiam*. Eph. V, 12: *quae in occulto ab eis fiunt, turpe, et* cetera.

In intentione autem vitatur malum vitae, si est intentio recta, et quantum ad hoc dicit **non ambulantes in astutia**, id est in astutia et simulatione et hypocrisi, quod faciunt pseudo, qui aliud praetendunt exterius, et aliud gerunt interius in corde. Iob XXXVI, 13: *simulatores et callidi provocant iram Dei*.

In doctrina autem vitatur malum quando verbum Domini debito modo proponitur, et quantum ad hoc dicit **non adulterantes verbum**. Quod dupliciter exponitur, ut patet supra. Et primo non permiscentes doctrinae Christi falsam doctrinam, quod faciebant pseudo dicentes legalia debere servari cum Evangelio. Secundo non praedicantes propter lucrum, vel gloriam propriam. Et istorum primus est lupus, secundus mercenarius. Sed qui vera praedicat, et propter gloriam Dei, est pastor. Unde Augustinus: *pastor est amandus, lupus vitandus, sed mercenarius ad tempus tolerandus*.

120. Sed quia non sufficit ad perfectam iustitiam solum vitare mala, sed requiritur operatio bona, ideo consequenter subiungit de operatione bonorum in ipso usu huius ministerii. Et ponitur triplex bonum, quod facit contra triplex malum. Primum bonum contra malum doctrinae; secundum contra malum operationis; tertium contra malum intentionis.

Contra malum doctrinae, quod debet vitari, facit bonum manifestae veritatis. Et quantum ad hoc dicit **in manifestatione veritatis**, quasi dicat: non deficimus sed, vitantes mala, ambulamus et proficimus in manifestatione veritatis, id est veritatem puram manifestamus. Io. XVIII, 37: *ad hoc natus sum, ut testimonium perhibeam veritati*. Eccli. XXIV, v. 31: *qui elucidant me, vitam aeternam habebunt*.

Contra malum operationis faciunt bona opera, et quantum ad hoc dicit **commendantes nosmet ipsos**, et cetera. Et hoc non facimus dicendo de nobis bona, quia non de facili creditur ei qui seipsum commendat, sed operando bona, quia talia opera facimus, ut ex ipsis operibus reddamus nosmetipsos commendabiles, **ad omnem conscientiam hominum**. I Petr. II, 12: *conversationem vestram inter gentes*, et cetera.

Contra malum intentionis facimus bonum reddendo nos commendabiles, non solum ad omnem conscientiam

activity by enduring evils patiently in adversity. Hence, he says, **we faint not** by impatience: *let us not grow weary in well-doing* (Gal 6:9); **For when I am weak, then I am powerful** (2 Cor 12:10). It is also avoided in prosperity by making moderate use of the things that are going well for us. Hence he says, **but we renounce the hidden things of dishonesty**, i.e., we remove from ourselves whatever makes a man base and dishonorable, namely, things unclean and foul and not only open but even hidden. *Therefore put away all filthiness* (Jas 1:21); *for it is a shame even to speak of the things that they do in secret* (Eph 5:12).

Evil conduct is avoided in our intention, if it is a right intention. In regard to this he says, **not walking in craftiness**, i.e., fraud and pretense and hypocrisy. That is what the false apostles do, who pretend one thing outwardly, but do something else inwardly in the heart. *Dissemblers and crafty men provoke the wrath of God* (Job 36:13).

Evil is avoided in doctrine when the Lord's word is proposed in the proper way. In regard to this he says, **nor adulterating the word of God**. This is explained in two ways. First, not mixing false doctrine with the doctrine of Christ, as the false apostles do when they teach that the ceremonies of the law must be observed along with the Gospel. Second, not preaching for gain and for one's own glory. The first of these is a wolf and the second a hireling, but one who preaches the truth and for the glory of God is a shepherd. Hence Augustine says: *the shepherd should be loved and the wolf avoided, but the hireling must be tolerated for the present*.

120. But because perfect justice requires more than avoiding evil, but doing good, he says something about doing good in the exercise of this ministry. And he proposes a triple good, which goes against the triple evil. The first good is against evil teachings; the second against evil conduct; the third against an evil intention.

Against evil teaching, which must be avoided, they perform the good of manifesting the truth. In regard to this he says, **but by the manifestation of the truth**: as if to say, we do not lose heart but, avoiding evil, we walk and act in the manifestation of the truth, i.e., we manifest the pure truth. *For this I have come into the world, to bear witness to the truth* (John 18:37); *those who show me forth shall have everlasting life* (Sir 24:31).

Against evil conduct they perform good works. In regard to this he says, **commending ourselves to every man's conscience**. We do not do this by saying good things about ourselves, because it is not easy to believe a person who recommends himself, but by doing good, because we do such works, so that by the works themselves we render ourselves commendable **to every man's conscience**. *Maintain good conduct among the gentiles* (1 Pet 2:12).

Against an evil intention we do good by making ourselves commendable not only to every man's conscience,

hominum, sed etiam *coram Deo*, qui intuetur corda. Infra X, 18: *non enim qui seipsum commendat, ille probatus est*, et cetera. Rom. XII, 17: *providentes bona, non solum coram*, et cetera.

121. Et, secundum Augustinum in Glossa, Apostolus implet in hoc mandatum Domini, Matth. V, 16: *sic luceat*, etc., item c. VI, 1: *attendite ne iustitiam*, etc., primum in hoc quod dicit *commendantes nos*, etc.; secundum vero in hoc quod dicit *coram Deo*, Rom. II, 28: *non enim, qui in manifesto*, et cetera.

Vel potest totum hoc magis secundum continuationem litterae, legi sic, ut dicatur: *ideo habentes hanc administrationem, iuxta quod*, etc., *non deficimus*, supple a bene operando, *sed abdicamus*, etc., et iterum, *in manifestatione veritatis*; servato tamen eodem modo exponendi, sicut in prima lectura.

but even *in the sight of God*, who sees the heart. *For it is not he who commends himself who is approved: but he whom God commends* (2 Cor 10:18); *providing good things not only before God but before all men* (Rom 12:17).

121. According to Augustine in a Gloss, the Apostle fulfills God's commandment in this: *let your light so shine before men, that they may see your good works and give glory to your Father who is in heaven* (Matt 5:16); *beware of practicing your piety before men* (Matt 6:1): the first by saying, *commending ourselves to every man's conscience*; but the second by saying, *in the sight of God*: *for he is not a real Jew who is one outwardly* (Rom 2:28).

Or this whole passage can be read in the following manner without interrupting the text: *therefore, having this ministration according as we have obtained mercy, we faint not*, namely in doing good. *But we renounce the hidden things of dishonesty*. Furthermore *by manifestation of the truth*, keeping the same method of explanation as already given.

Lecture 2

^{4:3}Quod si etiam opertum est Evangelium nostrum, in iis, qui pereunt, est opertum: [n. 122]

^{4:4}in quibus deus hujus saeculi excaecavit mentes infidelium, ut non fulgeat illis illuminatio Evangelii gloriae Christi, qui est imago Dei. [n. 124]

^{4:5}Non enim nosmetipsos praedicamus, sed Jesum Christum Dominum nostrum: nos autem servos vestros per Jesum: [n. 127]

^{4:6}quoniam Deus, qui dixit de tenebris lucem splendescere, ipse illuxit in cordibus nostris ad illuminationem scientiae claritatis Dei, in facie Christi Jesu. [n. 129]

^{4:3}εἰ δὲ καὶ ἔστιν κεκαλυμμένον τὸ εὐαγγέλιον ἡμῶν, ἐν τοῖς ἀπολλυμένοις ἐστὶν κεκαλυμμένον,

^{4:4}ἐν οἷς ὁ θεὸς τοῦ αἰῶνος τούτου ἐτύφλωσεν τὰ νοήματα τῶν ἀπίστων εἰς τὸ μὴ αὐγάσαι τὸν φωτισμὸν τοῦ εὐαγγελίου τῆς δόξης τοῦ Χριστοῦ, ὅς ἐστιν εἰκὼν τοῦ θεοῦ.

^{4:5}Οὐ γὰρ ἑαυτοὺς κηρύσσομεν ἀλλὰ Ἰησοῦν Χριστὸν κύριον, ἑαυτοὺς δὲ δούλους ὑμῶν διὰ Ἰησοῦν.

^{4:6}ὅτι ὁ θεὸς ὁ εἰπών· ἐκ σκότους φῶς λάμψει, ὃς ἔλαμψεν ἐν ταῖς καρδίαις ἡμῶν πρὸς φωτισμὸν τῆς γνώσεως τῆς δόξης τοῦ θεοῦ ἐν προσώπῳ [Ἰησοῦ] Χριστοῦ.

^{4:3}And if our Gospel is also hidden, it is hidden to those who are lost, [n. 122]

^{4:4}In whom the god of this world has blinded the minds of unbelievers, that the light of the Gospel of the glory of Christ, who is the image of God, should not shine unto them. [n. 124]

^{4:5}For we do not preach ourselves, but Jesus Christ our Lord: and ourselves your servants through Jesus. [n. 127]

^{4:6}For God, who commanded the light to shine out of darkness, has shined in our hearts, to give the light of the knowledge of the glory of God, in the face of Christ Jesus. [n. 129]

---

122. Hic consequenter Apostolus respondet cuidam tacitae obiectioni. Posset enim dici sibi ab aliquo: tu dicis, quod non deficis in manifestatione veritatis Christi, sed hoc non videtur, quia multi contradicunt tibi. Huic ergo quaestioni respondet. Et circa hoc duo facit.

Primo enim respondet quaestioni praedictae;
secundo excludit quoddam dubium, quod videtur ex responsione sua sequi, ibi **non enim nosmetipsos**, et cetera.

Circa primum tria facit.
Primo ostendit quibus occultatur veritas Christi;
secundo occultationis causam assignat, ibi **in quibus deus huius saeculi**;
tertio ostendit quod hoc non est ex defectu veritatis Evangelii, ut occultetur, ibi **ut non fulgeat**, et cetera.

123. Dicit ergo: dixi quod non deficimus in manifestatione, **quod**, idest **sed**, **si Evangelium nostrum**, quod scilicet nos praedicamus, **est opertum**, id est occultum, non est opertum omnibus, sed illis tantum, **qui pereunt**, scilicet praebendo impedimentum ne eis manifestetur. I Cor. I, 18: *verbum crucis pereuntibus stultitia est*, et cetera.

124. Causa ergo huius occultationis est non ex parte Evangelii, sed propter eorum culpam et malitiam. Et hoc est quod subdit **in quibus deus huius saeculi**, et cetera. Et hoc potest exponi tribus modis.

Primo modo sic: **deus huius saeculi**, id est Deus qui est Dominus huius saeculi et omnium rerum creatione et natura, iuxta illud Ps. XXIII, 1: *Domini est terra, et*

122. Here the Apostle answers a tacit objection. For someone could say to him: you say that you do not grow faint in manifesting the truth of Christ. But this does not seem true, because many people contradict you. To this question, therefore, he responds. And in regard to it he does two things:
first, he responds to this question;
second, he removes a doubt which seems to follow from his answer, at **for we do not preach ourselves**.

In regard to the first he does three things.
First, he shows from whom Christ's truth is hidden;
second, the reason for this hiding, at **in whom the gold of this world**;
third, he shows that it is not due to a deficiency in the truth of the Gospel that it is hidden, at **that the light**.

123. He says, therefore: I have said that we do not faint in manifesting the truth; but even **if our Gospel**, which we preach, **is also hidden**, it is not veiled from all, but it is veiled only to **those who are lost**, namely, who offer an obstacle to its manifestation to them. *For the word of the cross is folly to those who are perishing, but to us who are being saved it is the power of God* (1 Cor 1:18).

124. The cause of this concealment is not on the part of the Gospel, but on account of their own guilt and malice; and this is what he adds: **in whom the god of this world has blinded the minds of the unbelievers**. This can be explained in three ways:

in one way so that **the god of this world** is God, who is the Lord of this world and of all things by creation and nature: *the earth is the Lord's and the fullness thereof, the*

plenitudo eius, orbis terrarum, **excaecavit mentes infidelium**, non inducendo malitiam, sed merito, imo demerito praecedentium peccatorum subtrahendo gratiam. Is. VI, 10: *excaeca cor populi huius*, et cetera. Unde et praecedentia peccata insinuat, cum dicit **infidelium**, quasi infidelitas eorum fuerit causa huius excaecationis.

Secundo modo sic: **deus huius saeculi**, id est diabolus, qui dicitur deus huius saeculi, id est saeculariter viventium, non creatione sed imitatione, qua saeculares eum imitantur. Sap. II, 25: *imitantur eum, qui sunt*, et cetera. Et hic excaecat suggerendo, trahendo et inclinando ad peccata. Et sic quando iam sunt in peccatis, operiuntur in tenebris peccatorum ne videant. Eph. IV, 18: *tenebris obscuratum habentes intellectum*, et cetera.

Tertio modo sic: Deus habet rationem ultimi finis, et complementum desideriorum totius creaturae. Unde quidquid aliquis sibi pro fine ultimo constituit in quo eius desiderium quiescit, potest dici deus illius. Unde cum habes pro fine delicias, tunc deliciae dicuntur Deus tuus; similiter etiam si voluptates carnis, vel honores. Et tunc exponitur sic: **deus huius saeculi**, id est illud quod homines saeculariter viventes sibi pro fine constituunt, ut puta voluptates, vel divitiae et huiusmodi. Et sic Deus excaecat mentes, inquantum impedit ne homines lumen gratiae hic, et gloriae in futuro, videre possint. Ps. LVII, v. 9: *supercecidit ignis*, scilicet concupiscentiae, *ut non viderent solem*. Sic ergo excaecatio infidelium non est ex parte Evangelii, sed ex culpa infidelium.

125. Et ideo subdit **ut non fulgeat**, et cetera. Ubi sciendum est, quod Deus Pater est fons totius luminis. I Io. I, 5: *Deus lux est, et tenebrae in eo non sunt*, et cetera. Ex hoc autem fontanoso lumine derivatur imago huius luminis, scilicet Filius Verbum Dei. Hebr. c. I, 3: *qui cum sit splendor*, et cetera. Hic ergo splendor gloriae, imago fontanosae lucis, carnem nostram accepit et multa gloriosa et divina in hoc mundo opera fecit.

Declaratio igitur huius lucis est Evangelium, unde et Evangelium dicitur notitia claritatis Christi, quae quidem notitia virtutem habet illuminativam. Sap. VI, 13: *clara est et quae numquam marcescit sapientia*, et cetera. Et quidem, quantum est de se, in omnibus refulget et omnes illuminat, sed illi qui praebent impedimentum, non illuminantur. Et hoc est quod dicit: **ideo excaecavit mentes infidelium**, **ut** scilicet **non effulgeat in eis**, scilicet in mentibus infidelium, licet in se effulgens sit, **illuminatio Evangelii** illuminantis. Quod quidem est illuminans, quia est gloria Christi, id est claritas. Io. I, 14:

world and those who dwell therein (Ps 24:1), **has blinded the minds of the unbelievers**, not by producing malice, but by the merit, or rather demerit of preceding sins, by withdrawing his grace: *make the heart of this people fat, and their ears heavy, and shut their eyes* (Isa 6:10). Therefore he hints at their preceding sins when he says, **of unbelievers**, as though their unbelief is the cause of this blindness.

In a second way, so that **the god of this world** is the devil, who is called the god of this world, i.e., of those who live in a worldly manner, not by reason of creation but by imitation, because worldly persons imitate him. *They follow him who are on his side* (Wis 2:25). Here he blinds them by suggesting, by attracting and by inclining to sins. And so, when they are already in sin, they work in the darkness of sin, lest they see: *darkened in their understanding, alienated from the life of God* (Eph 4:18).

In the third way thus: God has the nature of the ultimate end and fulfillment of the desires of every creature. Hence, whatever a person assigns to himself as an ultimate end in which his desire rests, can be called his god. Hence, when you have pleasure as end, pleasure is called your god, and the same for pleasures of the flesh and for honors. Then it is explained so that **the god of this world** is that which men living in a worldly way set up as their end, say pleasure or riches and the like. And God blinds their minds, inasmuch as he prevents them from seeing the light of grace here, and the light of glory in the future. *Fire*, namely of concupiscence, *has fallen on them, and they shall not see the sun* (Ps 57:9). Thus, therefore, the blindness of unbelievers is not on the part of the Gospel, but from the sin of unbelievers.

125. Therefore, he adds, **that the light of the Gospel of the glory of Christ, who is the image of God, should not shine unto them**. Here it should be noted that God the Father is the source of all light: *God is light and in him is no darkness at all* (1 John 1:5). From this fountain of light is derived the image of this light, namely the Son, the Word of God: *he reflects the glory of God and bears the very stamp of his nature* (Heb 1:3). Therefore, this brightness of glory and image of the fountain of light took our flesh and accomplished many glorious and divine works in this world.

The disclosing of this light is the Gospel. Hence, the Gospel is also called the knowledge of the glory of Christ, which knowledge has the power to enlighten. *Wisdom is radiant and unfading* (Wis 6:12). As far as it is concerned, it shines upon all and enlightens all. But those who place an obstacle are not enlightened. And this is what he says: **the god of this world has blinded the minds of unbelievers**, so that there **should not shine unto them**, namely, in their unbelieving minds, **the light of the Gospel**, which enlightens because it is the glory of Christ, i.e., his brightness. *We have beheld his glory, glory as of the only Son from the Father*

Vidimus gloriam, et cetera. Quae quidem gloria provenit Christo ex eo *quod est Imago Dei*. Col. I, 15: *qui est Imago invisibilis Dei*.

126. Nota, secundum Glossam, quod Christus perfectissima Imago Dei est. Nam ad hoc quod aliquid perfecte sit imago alicuius, tria requiruntur, et haec tria perfecte sunt in Christo. Primum est similitudo, secundum est origo, tertium est perfecta aequalitas. Si enim inter imaginem et eum, cuius est imago, esset dissimilitudo, et unum non oriretur ex alio, similiter etiam si non sit aequalitas perfecta, quae est secundum eamdem naturam, non esset ibi perfecta ratio imaginis. Nam similitudo regis in denario, non perfecte dicitur imago regis, quia deest ibi aequalitas secundum eamdem naturam; sed similitudo regis in filio dicitur perfecta imago regis, quia sunt ibi illa tria quae dicta sunt.

Cum ergo ista tria sint in Christo Filio Dei, quia scilicet est similis patri, oritur a Patre, et aequalis est Patri, maxime et perfecte dicitur Imago Dei.

127. Consequenter cum dicit *non enim nosmetipsos*, etc., removet Apostolus quoddam dubium. Posset enim aliquis, contra praedicta, dicere apostolo: supra dixisti Evangelium vestrum esse opertum, modo dicis Evangelium Christi illuminare; si ergo detur quod Evangelium Christi sit illuminans, non potest hinc sequi quod opertum sit Evangelium vestrum. Et ideo ad hoc removendum, duo facit.

Primo, ostendit quod idem est Evangelium suum et Christi;

secundo, ostendit unde sit quod Evangelium suum sit illuminativum, ibi *quoniam Deus qui dixit*, et cetera.

128. Dicit ergo primo: dico quod manifestatio claritatis Christi est Evangelium Christi et nostrum. Nostrum quidem tamquam per nos praedicatum; Christi vero, tamquam in ipso Evangelio praedicati. Et hoc est quod *non praedicamus nosmetipsos*, id est non commendamus nos, nec ad nos, id est ad laudem, vel lucrum nostrum convertimus praedicationem nostram, sed ad Christum totum referimus et laudem eius. I Cor. c. I, 23: *nos autem praedicamus Christum*, et cetera. Ps. LXXII, 28: *ut annuntiem omnes praedicationes tuas*, non meas, *in portis*, et cetera.

Sed Iesum Dominum nostrum, nos autem servos vestros per Iesum. Quasi dicat: Iesum praedicamus ut Dominum, nos autem servos. Et huius ratio est quia principaliter quaerimus laudem Christi et non nostram. Nam servus est, qui est propter utilitatem Domini. Et inde est, quod minister Ecclesiae, qui non quaerit honorem Dei et utilitatem subditorum, non dicitur verus rector, sed tyrannus. Nam quicumque bene regit, debet esse sicut servus, quaerens honorem et utilitatem subditorum.

(John 1:14). This glory is Christ's, inasmuch as he is *the image of God*: he is the image of the invisible God (Col 1:15).

126. Note, according to a Gloss, that Christ is the most perfect image of God. For in order that something be perfectly an image of something, three things are necessary, and these three are perfectly in Christ. First, a likeness; second, origin; third, perfect equality. For if there is unlikeness between the image and that of which it is the image, and one does not arise from the other, or even if there is not perfect equality according to the same nature, then the notion of perfect image would not be there. For the likeness of a king on a coin is not called a perfect image of the king, because equality according to the same nature is lacking; but the likeness of a king in his son is called a perfect image of the king, because it possesses the three marks mentioned.

Therefore, since those three are present in Christ, the Son of God, because namely he is similar to the Father, arises from the Father and is equal to the Father, he is in the highest degree and perfectly called the image of God.

127. Then when he says, *for we do not preach ourselves*, the Apostle settles a doubt. For some could say to the Apostle, contrary to what was said here: above you said that your Gospel was hidden; now you say that the Gospel of Christ enlightens. Therefore, if it is granted that the Gospel of Christ enlightens, it cannot follow that your Gospel is hidden. To settle this he does two things.

First he shows that his own Gospel and Christ's are the same;

second, he shows how it is that his own Gospel enlightens, at *for God who commanded*.

128. He says, therefore: I say that the manifestation of the brightness of Christ is the Gospel of Christ and our Gospel. It is ours as preached by us; it is Christ's truly as the one preached in the Gospel. Hence it is that *we do not preach ourselves*, i.e., we do not commend ourselves nor for ourselves, i.e., we do not use our preaching for our praise or gain, but we refer it all to Christ and his praise. *We preach Christ crucified* (1 Cor 1:23); *that I may tell of all your works*, not mine, *in the gates of the daughter of Zion* (Ps 73:28).

But Jesus Christ our Lord: and ourselves your servants through Jesus. As if to say: we preach Jesus as Lord, but ourselves as servants, the reason being that we principally seek the praise of Christ and not our own. For a servant is one who exists for the profit of the master. That is why a minister of the Church, who does not seek the honor of God and the welfare of his subjects, is not a true ruler, but a tyrant. For whoever rules well should be as a servant seeking the honor and profit of his subjects. *The elder shall serve the younger*

Gen. XXV, 23: *maior serviet minori.* I Cor. IX, 19: *cum essem liber, omnium vestrum me servum feci.*

129. Consequenter cum dicit **quoniam Deus qui dixit**, etc., ostendit unde Evangelium suum habet virtutem illuminativam.

Ubi nota ordinem procedendi servatum ab apostolo, qui talis est: nos aliquando, scilicet antequam conversi essemus ad Christum, eramus tenebrosi sicut et vos et alii in quibus non fulget claritas gloriae Christi. Nunc vero, postquam Christus vocavit nos per gratiam suam ad se, tenebrae istae remotae sunt a nobis, et iam fulget in nobis virtus gloriae claritatis Christi; et intantum refulget in nobis, quod non solum illuminamur ad hoc quod videre possimus, sed etiam quod alios illuminemus. Ex spirituali ergo gratia et abundanti refulgentia claritatis gloriae Christi in nos, habet Evangelium nostrum virtutem illuminativam.

130. Et hoc est quod dicit: dico quod ideo illuminat Evangelium nostrum, quoniam **Deus, qui dixit**, id est praecepto solo fecit, **lucem splendescere**, quod fuit in separatione elementorum, quando chaos tenebrosum illuminavit per lucem quam fecit. Gen. I, 3: *dixit, fiat lux.* Eccli. XXIV, 6: *ego feci, ut in caelis oriretur lux*, et cetera. Iste, inquam, Deus, **illuxit in cordibus**, id est in mentibus, **nostris**, prius tenebrosis per absentiam luminis gratiae et obscuritatem peccati. Lc. I, 79: *illuminare his qui in tenebris*, et cetera.

Illuxit, inquam, non solum ut nos illuminaremur, sed **ad illuminationem**, id est ut et alios illuminemus. Eph. III, 8: *mihi omnium sanctorum minimo data est*, et cetera. Matth. V, v. 14: *vos estis lux*, et cetera. Ad illuminationem dico, **scientiae**, id est ut faciamus alios scire. Dico, **claritatis Dei**, id est clarae divinae visionis, **in facie Iesu Christi**. Glossa: id est *per Iesum Christum*, qui est facies Patris, quia sine ipso non cognoscitur Pater. Sed melius dicitur sic: ad illuminationem sanctae claritatis Dei, quae quidem claritas fulget in facie Christi Iesu, id est ut per ipsam gloriam et claritatem, cognoscatur Christus Iesus. Quasi dicat: in summa, ad hoc Deus illuxit nobis ad illuminationem, ut ex hoc Iesus Christus cognoscatur et praedicetur in gentibus.

(Gen 25:23); *for though I am free from all men, I have made myself a slave to all* (1 Cor 9:19).

129. Then when he says, **for God who commanded**, he shows the source of his Gospel's power to enlighten.

Here we should note the order of the Apostle's procedure. It is this: at one time, namely, before being converted to Christ, we were darkness, just as you and the others, upon whom the brightness of Christ's glory did not shine. But now, after Christ has called us to himself by his grace, that darkness has been taken away from us, and now the power of the glory of Christ's brightness shines in us, and it shines on us in such a way that not only are we enlightened so that we can see, but we enlighten others. Therefore, from the spiritual grace and abundant splendor of the brightness of the glory of Christ in us, our Gospel has the power to enlighten.

130. And this is what he says: I say that our Gospel enlightens, **for God who commanded** i.e., who made by a single command, **the light to shine out of darkness**, by separating the elements, when he enlightened the dark chaos by the light he made: *he said: let there be light* (Gen 1:3); *I made an unfailing light to rise in the heavens* (Sir 24:6). He, I say, **has shined in our hearts**, i.e., in our minds, previously darkened by the absence of the light of grace and by the obscurity of sin. *To enlighten those who sit in darkness and in the shadow of death* (Luke 1:79).

He **has shined**, I say, not only to enlighten us, but **to give the light**, i.e., that we might enlighten others. *To me, though I am the very least of all the saints, this grace was given* (Eph 3:8); *you are the light of the world* (Matt 5:4). To give the light, I say, **of the knowledge**, i.e., that we make others know **of the glory of God**, i.e., of the clear vision of God, **in the face of Christ Jesus**. A Gloss: i.e., *through Jesus Christ*, who is the face of the Father, because without him the Father is not known. But it is said better thus: to illumine the holy brightness of God, which indeed shines in the face of Jesus Christ, i.e., so that by that glory and brightness Jesus Christ may be known. As if to say: in summary, God has shone upon us to enlighten us, so that Jesus Christ may be known and preached among the gentiles.

Lecture 3

4:7Habemus autem thesaurum istum in vasis fictilibus: ut sublimitas sit virtutis Dei, et non ex nobis. [n. 131]

4:8In omnibus tribulationem patimur, sed non angustiamur: [n. 133] aporiamur, sed non destituimur: [n. 135]

4:9persecutionem patimur, sed non derelinquimur: dejicimur, sed non perimus:

4:10semper mortificationem Jesu in corpore nostro circumferentes, ut et vita Jesu manifestetur in corporibus nostris. [n. 136]

4:7Ἔχομεν δὲ τὸν θησαυρὸν τοῦτον ἐν ὀστρακίνοις σκεύεσιν, ἵνα ἡ ὑπερβολὴ τῆς δυνάμεως ᾖ τοῦ θεοῦ καὶ μὴ ἐξ ἡμῶν·

4:8ἐν παντὶ θλιβόμενοι ἀλλ᾽ οὐ στενοχωρούμενοι, ἀπορούμενοι ἀλλ᾽ οὐκ ἐξαπορούμενοι,

4:9διωκόμενοι ἀλλ᾽ οὐκ ἐγκαταλειπόμενοι, καταβαλλόμενοι ἀλλ᾽ οὐκ ἀπολλύμενοι,

4:10πάντοτε τὴν νέκρωσιν τοῦ Ἰησοῦ ἐν τῷ σώματι περιφέροντες, ἵνα καὶ ἡ ζωὴ τοῦ Ἰησοῦ ἐν τῷ σώματι ἡμῶν φανερωθῇ.

4:7But we have this treasure in earthen vessels, that the excellency may be of the power of God and not of us. [n. 131]

4:8In all things we suffer tribulation: but are not distressed. [n. 133] We are straitened: but are not destitute. [n. 135]

4:9We suffer persecution: but are not forsaken. We are cast down: but we do not perish.

4:10Always bearing about in our body the mortification of Jesus, that the life of Jesus may also be made manifest in our bodies. [n. 136]

---

131. Supra tractavit de usu ministerii Novi Testamenti quantum ad bona agenda, hic consequenter tractat de usu eius quantum ad tolerantiam malorum.

Et circa hoc duo facit.

Primo enim ostendit tolerantiam malorum, quae patiebantur;

secundo vero hoc manifestat, ibi **semper enim nos, qui vivimus**, et cetera.

Circa primum tria facit.

Primo ponit causam quare tribulationibus exponantur a Deo;

secundo ostendit, quod in istis tribulationibus patienter se habeant, ibi **in omnibus tribulationem patimur**, etc.;

tertio vero rationem huius patientiae assignat, ibi **semper mortificationem Iesu**, et cetera.

132. Dicit ergo, Deus illuxit mentibus nostris ad illuminationem aliorum, quae quidem lux est maximus thesaurus. Sap. VII, 14: *infinitus enim thesaurus*, et cetera. Is. XXXIII, 6: *divitiae salutis sapientia*, et cetera. Istum autem maximum thesaurum non habemus in pretioso loco, sed in re vili et fictili: et ratio huius est, ut scilicet Deo efficacia eius tribuatur. Et hoc est quod dicit **habemus thesaurum istum**, id est lucem illam qua alios illuminamus, **in vasis fictilibus**, id est in corpore fragili et vili. Ps. CII, 14: *ipse cognovit figmentum nostrum*. Ier. XVIII, 6: *sicut lutum in manu figuli, sic et vos in manu*, et cetera. Is. LXIV, 8: *et nunc, Domine, Pater noster es tu, nos vero lutum*.

Ideo **habemus in vasis fictilibus**, **ut sublimitas**, istius lucis, **sit virtutis Dei**, id est Deo attribuatur, **et non ex nobis** credatur esse. Nam si essemus divites, si potentes, si nobiles secundum carnem, quidquid magnum faceremus, non Deo, sed nobis ipsis attribueretur. Nunc

131. Above, he discussed the use of the ministry of the New Testament in regard to doing good; here he discusses its use in regard to enduring evil.

In regard to this he does two things:

first, he points to the endurance of the evils they suffered;

second, he explains this, at **for we who live are always delivered**.

In regard to the first he does three things:

first, he shows the reason why they are exposed to tribulations by God;

second, he shows that they should act patiently under these tribulations, at **in all things we suffer tribulation**;

third, he gives the reason for this patience, at **always bearing about in our bodies**.

132. He says, therefore: God has shone on our minds to give light to others, and this light is our greatest treasure. *It is an unfailing treasure for men* (Wis 7:14); *abundance of salvation, wisdom and knowledge* (Isa 33:6). But we do not have that greatest treasure in a precious place, but in a lowly fragile thing, in order that its power may be attributed to God. Hence, he says, **we have this treasure**, i.e., that light by which we enlighten others, **in earthen vessels**, i.e., in our frail and lowly body. *For he knows our frame; he remembers that we are dust* (Ps 103:14); *like the clay in the potter's hand, so are you in my hand, O house of Israel* (Jer 18:6); *yet, O Lord, you are our Father, we are the clay* (Isa 64:8).

Therefore **we have this treasure in earthen vessels** to show **that the excellency** of that light **may be of the power of God**, i.e., attributed to God, **and not** believed to be **of us**. For if we were rich or powerful or noble according to the flesh, any great good we did would be attributed not

vero, quia pauperes et contemptibiles sumus, huiusmodi sublimitas Deo, et non nobis, attribuitur. Et ideo vult nos Deus contemptui haberi, et tribulationibus exponi. Deut. XXXII, 27: *ne dicerent: manus nostra excelsa, et cetera*. Et I Cor. I, 29: *ut non glorietur omnis caro, et cetera*. Sap. XII, 8: *Mmisisti antecessores tuos ne dicerent, et cetera*.

133. Consequenter cum dicit *in omnibus tribulationem patimur*, etc., ostendit eorum patientiam in iis, quae patiuntur.

Et circa hoc duo facit.

Primo ostendit mala, quae patiuntur in generali;

secundo enumerat ea in speciali, ibi *aporiamur, sed non destituimur*, et cetera.

134. Dicit ergo. Vere habemus hunc thesaurum in vasis fictilibus, quia *in omnibus tribulationem patimur*; quasi dicat: nullus modus tribulandi deest nobis. Act. XIV, v. 21: *per multas tribulationes*, et cetera. Nec mirum, quia, ut dicitur Lc. ult.: *oportuit Christum pati, et sic intrare*, et cetera.

Et licet sic tribulemur, *non* tamen *angustiamur*. Et loquitur ad similitudinem viatoris, qui quando non patet ei via, qua exeat de aliquo arcto loco, angustiatur. Quasi dicat: homines, qui solum in mundo confidunt, angustiantur, si undique a mundo tribulantur, quia non patet eis via remedii, cum non sperent nisi de mundo. Sed nos, licet tribulemur in mundo, quia tamen confidimus de Deo et speramus in Christo, patet nobis via evasionis et auxilii a Deo, et ideo non angustiamur

135. Consequenter cum dicit *aporiamur*, etc., enumerat tribulationes in speciali. Sunt autem quatuor in quibus homines consueverunt tribulari, et in istis tribulati sunt apostoli, scilicet in rebus exterioribus, in inquietudine status, in laesione famae, et in afflictione proprii corporis.

Quantum ergo ad primum dicit *aporiamur*, id est depauperamur. *Aporos* enim Graece, Latine dicitur pauper; quasi dicat: adeo pauperes sumus, ut necessaria desint. I Cor. IV, v. 11: *usque in hanc horam esurimus, et cetera*. *Sed non destituimur* a Deo, qui est thesaurus noster. Divitiae enim non quaeruntur propter se, sed propter sufficientiam vitae. Unde homines, qui sine Dei auxilio et spe sunt, si careant divitiis, destituuntur; sed qui solum de Deo confidunt et sperant, quantumcumque aporiantur, non destituuntur. Infra VI, 10: *tamquam nihil habentes, et omnia possidentes*.

Sed nec sufficit, imo cum hoc inquietamur, *persecutionem patimur*, scilicet de loco ad locum. Matth. X, 23: *persequentur vos*. *Sed non derelinquimur* a Deo, quin praebeat auxilium. Hebr. ult.: *non te deseram*, et cetera. Ps. IX, 11: *sperent in te, qui noverunt te, et cetera*.

to God but to ourselves. But now, because we are poor and contemptible, such excellence is attributed to God and not to ourselves. Therefore, God wants us to be held in contempt and to be exposed to tribulations. *Lest they should say: our hand is triumphant, the Lord has not wrought all this* (Deut 32:27); *that no human being might boast in the presence of God* (1 Cor 1:29); *you sent them as your forerunners not to speak* (Wis 12:8).

133. Then when he says, *in all things we suffer tribulation*, he shows their patience in the things they suffer.

In regard to this he does two things:

first, he points out the evils they suffer in general;

second, he mentions them in particular, at *we are straitened: but are not destitute*.

134. He says, therefore: truly we have this treasure in earthen vessels, because *in all things we suffer tribulation*. As if to say: no type of tribulation has missed us. *Through many tribulations we must enter the kingdom of God* (Acts 14:22). Nor is this strange, for it is said: *was it not necessary that the Christ should suffer these things and enter into his glory?* (Luke 24:26).

And although we suffer in this way, *we are not distressed*. He speaks as a traveler who becomes distressed, when he cannot find a way out of a narrow place. As if to say: men who trust only in the world are distressed, if they are troubled on all sides by the world, because no way of relief is open to them, since they trust only in the world. But we, although we are troubled in the world, yet because we trust in God and hope in Christ, escape by the help of God. That is why we are not distressed.

135. Then when he says, *we are straitened: but are not destitute*, he lists the tribulations in particular. Now there are four things by which men are wont to be troubled; and the apostles were also troubled by them, namely, by external things, by the disquiet of their state, by injury to their reputation, and by affliction of their body.

Therefore, in regard to the first he says, *we are straitened* i.e., impoverished. As if to say: we are so poor that we lack necessities: *to the present hour we hunger and thirst* (1 Cor 4:11). But we *are not destitute*, i.e., abandoned by God, who is our treasure. For riches are not sought for their own sake, but for a sufficiency of life. Hence, men who live without God's help and without hope, are destitute, if they lack riches. But those who trust and hope in God alone, no matter how perplexed they be, are not destitute. *As having nothing and possessing all things* (2 Cor 6:10).

But this is not all, for along with this we are disquieted: *we suffer persecution*, namely, from place to place: *when they persecute you in one town, flee to the next* (Matt 10:23), *but not forsaken* by God, because he offers help: *I will never fail you nor forsake you* (Heb 13:5); *you, O Lord, have not forsaken those who seek you* (Ps 9:10).

Sed et cum hoc laedimur in fama, quia **humiliamur**, id est contemnimur et pro nihilo reputamur. Io. XVI, 2: *venit hora, ut omnis qui interficit vos,* et cetera. Matth. V: *beati eritis cum vos oderint,* et cetera. Sed quia quando quis contemnitur, et causa contemptus subest, ille qui contemnitur, consuevit confundi; quando vero causa non subest, non confunditur, et istis non suberat causa contemptus, ideo dicit **non confundimur**. Quasi dicat: quia non subest causa, non curamus. Ps. XXX, 2: *in te, Domine, speravi, non confundar,* et cetera.

Sed quasi haec pauca sint, addit ad tribulationis exaggerationem, dicens **deicimur** ad mortis pericula, **sed non perimus**, id est a bono non cessamus, vel non perimus quia Deus sustentat nos. Iob XI, 17: *cum te consumptum putaveris,* et cetera. I Cor. IV, 13: *tamquam purgamenta huius mundi,* et cetera. Ps. XLIII, v. 22: *aestimati sumus sicut oves,* et cetera.

136. Consequenter cum dicit **semper mortificationem**, etc., subdit rationem huius patientiae.

Circa quod sciendum est quod in Christo talis fuit processus. Nam a principio suae conceptionis carnem habens passibilem, et passus mortuus fuit, sed tamen interius vivebat spirituali vita. Post resurrectionem vero, illa spiritualis et gloriosa vita usque ad corpus derivata est, et factum est ipsum corpus gloriosum et immortale, quia: *Christus resurgens ex mortuis, iam non moritur,* et cetera. Unde ex hoc accipitur duplex status in corpore Christi, scilicet mortis et gloriae. Et ideo dicit: quod ideo pericula mortis et passiones patienter sustinemus, ut perveniamus ad gloriosam vitam.

137. Et hoc est quod dicit: ita sustinemus **semper**, id est in omnibus et ubique, **mortificationem Iesu**, id est propter Iesum, vel ad similitudinem mortis Iesu, Gal. ult.: *stigmata domini Iesu,* et cetera. Quia propter veritatem passi sumus, sicut et Iesus. **In corpore nostro**, non solum in mente, Ps. XLIII, 22: *propter te mortificamur tota die.* **Ut vita Iesu**, id est vita gratiae quam Iesus dat; vel vita gloriae ad quam Iesus per passiones pervenit, Lc. XXIV, 26: *nonne oportuit Christum pati, et ita intrare in gloriam,* id est manifeste appareat etiam inimicis.

Dicit ergo in futura, scilicet resurrectione, vel etiam nunc vita gloriae, **in corporibus nostris**, non solum in animabus, Iudic. VII: *fractis lagunculis apparuerunt lucernae.* Et idcirco dicit Ambrosius: *non timebat mori propter resurrectionem promissam.* **Circumferentes**, id est ubique portantes et sustinentes, quia quocumque eamus patimur et non caedimur. Et hoc ideo **ut vita Iesu**, quae latet nunc in corde nostro, **in corporibus nostris manifestetur**, quando scilicet *reformabit corpus*

Along with this we are injured in our reputation, because **we are humiliated**, i.e., scorned and regarded as nothing. *the hour is coming when whoever kills you will think he is offering service to God* (John 16:2); *blessed are you when men hate you* (Luke 6:22). But because when a man is scorned and there is reason for it, the scorned one is usually ashamed. But when there is not cause, he is not ashamed. And there was no reason for their being scorned, hence he continues, **but not ashamed**. As if to say: since there is no reason, we do not care. *In you, O Lord, have I hoped; let me never be put to shame* (Ps 31:2).

But as though these were trifles, he adds to the amount of tribulation, saying: **cast down** into the dangers of death, **but we do not perish**, i.e., we do not cease doing good; or we are not destroyed because God sustains us. *We have become, and are now, as the refuse of the world, the offscouring of all things* (1 Cor 4:13); *when you shall think yourself consumed, you shall rise as the daystar* (Job 11:17); *we are accounted as sheep for the slaughter* (Ps 44:22).

136. Then when he says, **always bearing about in our body the mortification of Jesus**, he gives the reason for this patience.

Here it should be noted that in Christ the process was this: having from the beginning of his conception a flesh that could suffer, he both suffered and died, yet within he was leading a spiritual life. But after the resurrection that spiritual and glorious life flowed into the body, so that his body became glorious and immortal, because *Christ being raised from the dead will never die again* (Rom 6:9). Hence we can think of two states in the body of Christ, namely, of death and of glory. Hence, he says that we endure the perils of death and suffering patiently, in order to attain to the glorious life.

137. And this is what he says: **always bearing** i.e., in all things and everywhere, **the mortification of Jesus**, i.e., for Jesus, or in the likeness of Jesus' death: *I bear on my body the marks of Jesus* (Gal 6:19), because we have suffered for the truth, as Jesus did. **In our body**, not only in our mind: *for your sake we are slain all the day long* (Ps 44:23). **That the life of Jesus**, i.e., the life of grace which Jesus gives, or the life of glory which Jesus reached by his sufferings: *was it not necessary that the Christ should suffer these things and enter into his glory?* (Luke 24:26), may also be manifested, i.e., be evident even to enemies.

He says, therefore, in the future, namely, in the resurrection, or even now the life of grace, **in our body**, and not only in our soul: *when they had broken the wine jars, the lamps appeared* (Judg 7:20). Therefore Ambrose says: *they did not fear to die on account of the promised resurrection.* **Bearing about**, i.e., carrying it about and enduring, because wherever we go, we suffer and do not give up. And this so **that the life of Jesus**, which is now hidden in our hearts, **may be made manifest in our bodies**, namely, when *he will change*

humilitatis nostrae, etc., Phil. c. III, 21. Col. III, 3: *mortui estis, et vita vestra*, et cetera. II Tim. II, 11: *si commortui sumus, et convivemus.*

our lowly body to be like his glorious body (Phil 3:21); *you have died and your life is hid with Christ in God* (Col 3:3); *if we die with him, we shall also live with him* (2 Tim 2:11).

Lecture 4

4:11Semper enim nos, qui vivimus, in mortem tradimur propter Jesum: ut et vita Jesu manifestetur in carne nostra mortali. [n. 138]

4:12Ergo mors in nobis operatur, vita autem in vobis.

4:13Habentes autem eumdem Spiritum fidei, sicut scriptum est: *Credidi, propter quod locutus sum*: et nos credimus, propter quod et loquimur: [n. 140]

4:14scientes quoniam qui suscitavit Jesum, et nos cum Jesu suscitabit, et constituet vobiscum. [n. 142]

4:15Omnia enim propter vos: ut gratia abundans, per multos in gratiarum actione, abundet in gloriam Dei. [n. 143]

4:11ἀεὶ γὰρ ἡμεῖς οἱ ζῶντες εἰς θάνατον παραδιδόμεθα διὰ Ἰησοῦν, ἵνα καὶ ἡ ζωὴ τοῦ Ἰησοῦ φανερωθῇ ἐν τῇ θνητῇ σαρκὶ ἡμῶν.

4:12ὥστε ὁ θάνατος ἐν ἡμῖν ἐνεργεῖται, ἡ δὲ ζωὴ ἐν ὑμῖν.

4:13Ἔχοντες δὲ τὸ αὐτὸ πνεῦμα τῆς πίστεως κατὰ τὸ γεγραμμένον· ἐπίστευσα, διὸ ἐλάλησα, καὶ ἡμεῖς πιστεύομεν, διὸ καὶ λαλοῦμεν,

4:14εἰδότες ὅτι ὁ ἐγείρας τὸν κύριον Ἰησοῦν καὶ ἡμᾶς σὺν Ἰησοῦ ἐγερεῖ καὶ παραστήσει σὺν ὑμῖν.

4:15τὰ γὰρ πάντα δι᾽ ὑμᾶς, ἵνα ἡ χάρις πλεονάσασα διὰ τῶν πλειόνων τὴν εὐχαριστίαν περισσεύσῃ εἰς τὴν δόξαν τοῦ θεοῦ.

4:11For we who live are always delivered unto death for Jesus's sake: that the life of Jesus may also be made manifest in our mortal flesh. [n. 138]

4:12So then death works in us: but life in you.

4:13But having the same Spirit of faith, as it is written: *I believed, for which cause I have spoken*; and we also believe, for which cause we also speak: [n. 140]

4:14Knowing that he who raised up Jesus will raise us up also with Jesus and place us with you. [n. 142]

4:15For all things are for your sakes: that the grace, abounding through many, may abound in thanksgiving unto the glory of God. [n. 143]

---

138. Posita patientia apostolorum in malis, et causa patientiae ostensa, hic Apostolus consequenter manifestat ea; et

primo manifestat id quod dixit de spe gloriae;

secundo vero id quod dixit de sua patientia, ibi ***propter quod non deficimus***, et cetera.

Circa primum duo facit.

Primo manifestat spem gloriae quam habet;

secundo ostendit unde haec spes sibi proveniat, ibi ***habentes autem eundem***, et cetera.

139. Circa primum tria facit. Primo ostendit quomodo mortificationem Iesu in corpore suo portet; secundo vero manifestat quomodo portet vitam Iesu, ibi ***ut et vita***, etc.; tertio manifestat quid ex hoc sibi et aliis proveniat, ibi ***ergo mors***, et cetera.

Dicit ergo primo: dico quod portamus mortificationem in corporibus nostris, non quod moriamur, sed quia ***nos qui vivimus***, corporali vita vel virtutibus, ***semper tradimur in mortem***, vel in pericula mortis. Et hoc quidem, ***propter Iesum***. Ps. XLIII, 22: *aestimati sumus sicut oves*, et cetera.

Qualiter autem vitam Iesu portemus in corpore exponit subdens: ita, scilicet ***ut vita Iesu*** immortalis et impassibilis, ***manifestetur in carne nostra*** nunc ***mortali***, ita ut caro nostra mortalis recipiat immortalitatem in resurrectione. I Cor. XV, 53: *oportet autem mortale hoc induere*, et cetera.

Sed ex hoc quid proveniat, subdit, dicens ***ergo mors operatur***, id est exercet Dominium suum in nos, ***vita autem***, scilicet praesens, operatur ***in vobis***, quia estis in prosperitate, iuxta illud I Cor. IV, 10: *nos stulti*, et cetera.

138. Having mentioned the patience of the apostles in the midst of evils, and revealed the cause of their patience, the Apostle now explains them.

First, he explains what he said about the hope of glory;

second, what he said about his own patience, at ***for which cause we faint not***.

In regard to the first he does two things.

First, he shows the hope of glory that he has;

second, he shows the source of this hope, at ***but having the same Spirit***.

139. In regard to the first he does three things. First, he shows how he bears the mortification of Jesus in his body; second, how he bears the life of Jesus, at ***that the life of Jesus***; third, what he and others have obtained from this, at ***so then death***.

He says, therefore: I say that we bear the death of Jesus in our bodies; not that we might die, but because ***we who live*** with bodily life or powers, ***we are always delivered unto death*** or dangers of death, ***for Jesus's sake***: *we are accounted as sheep for the slaughter* (Ps 44:22).

But how we carry the life of Jesus in our body is explained when he says, so that the immortal and incorruptible ***life of Jesus may also be made manifest in our*** now ***mortal flesh***, so that our mortal flesh may put on immortality at the resurrection. *This mortal nature must put on immortality* (1 Cor 15:53).

What results from this is mentioned when he continues, ***so then death works in us***, i.e., exercises its sway, in us, ***but life***, namely, the present one, works ***in you***, because you live in prosperity: *we are fools for Christ's sake, but you are wise*

Ut mors operetur in nobis magnum bonum, scilicet consecutionem vitae spiritualis. Ps. CXV, v. 15: *pretiosa est in conspectu Domini mors sanctorum eius*, et cetera. Sed vita terrena quam amatis, operatur in vobis magnum malum, scilicet mortem aeternam. Prov. X, 16: *opus iusti ad vitam*, et cetera. Io. XII, 25: *qui amat animam suam in hoc mundo*, et cetera.

Vel aliter: duo fuerunt in Christo, mors corporalis et vita spiritualis. Dicit itaque *ergo mors*, etc., quasi dicat: in nobis non solum vita spiritualis operatur, inquantum imitamur spiritualiter, sed etiam mors operatur, id est propter spem resurrectionis, et propter amorem Christi, vestigia mortis Christi in nobis apparent, inquantum passionibus mortis exponimur, Ps. XLIII, 22: *propter te mortificamur tota die*; sed in vobis operatur solum vita Christi, per quam vitam fides plantatur in vobis et vita spiritualis.

140. Unde autem proveniat Apostolo haec spes certitudinis, subdit, dicens *habentes autem*, et cetera. Et circa hoc duo facit.

Primo ponit causam certitudinis;

secundo concludit ipsam certitudinem, ibi *scientes quoniam qui*, et cetera.

141. Causa autem huius certitudinis est Spiritus, infundens fidem in cordibus eorum. Unde primo ponit causam hanc; secundo vero manifestat eam per exemplum, ibi *sicut scriptum est*, et cetera.

Dicit ergo: ex hoc speramus et non deficimus, quia sumus *habentes eumdem Spiritum fidei*, quem antiqui habuerunt, quia, licet tempora mutata sint, Spiritus tamen et fides non est mutata, nisi quod illi credebant Christum venturum et passurum, nos autem credimus ipsum venisse et passum fuisse. Et hic Spiritus est Spiritus Sanctus, qui est Spiritus fidei. I Cor. XII, 11: *haec autem omnia operatur unus atque idem Spiritus*, et cetera. Et ibidem: *alteri fides in eodem spiritu*.

Hunc ergo Spiritum habentes, quem antiqui habuerunt, facimus eadem quae illi, et credimus. Illi autem quid fecerint, dicit Ps. CXV, 10: *credidi*, scilicet Deo et perfecte. Et hoc omnes antiqui fecerunt. Hebr. XI, 39: *hi omnes testimonio fidei*, et cetera. *Propter quod*, scilicet *credidi*, *locutus sum*, id est confessus sum fidem. Rom. X, 10: *corde creditur ad iustitiam*, et cetera. Quod etiam nos facimus, quia propter hoc quod credimus, loquimur et confitemur fidem et praedicamus. Act. IV, 20: *non enim possumus quae vidimus et audivimus non loqui*. Spiritus ergo Sanctus est causa huius certitudinis.

142. Ultimo ergo concludit conclusionem intentam, scilicet ipsam certitudinem. Et primo de salute propria; secundo de salute aliorum, ibi *et constituet vobiscum*, et cetera.

in Christ. We are weak, but you are strong (1 Cor 4:10). And death works in us a great good, namely, the attainment of spiritual life: *precious in the sight of the Lord is the death of his saints* (Ps 116:15). But the earthly life that you love works in you a great evil, namely, eternal death: *the wage of the righteous leads to life, the gain of the wicked to sin* (Prov 10:16); *he who loves his life loses it, and he who hates his life in this world will keep it for eternal life* (John 12:25).

Or another way: there were two things in Christ, namely, bodily death and spiritual life. He says, *so then death works in us*. As if to say: not only does spiritual life work in us, inasmuch as we imitate him spiritually, but death is at work, i.e., because of the hope of the resurrection and for the love of Christ, the marks of Christ's death appear in us, inasmuch as we are exposed to the sufferings of death: *for your sake we are slain all the day long* (Ps 44:22). But in you, only the life of Christ works, through which faith and the spiritual life are planted in you.

140. Then the Apostle shows how he acquired this hope of certainty, at *but having the same Spirit*.

In regard to this he does two things.

First, he states the cause of the certainty;

second, he concludes to the certainty itself, at *knowing that he*.

141. Now the cause of this certainty is the Spirit instilling faith into their hearts. First, therefore, he mentions this cause; second, he explains it with an example, at *as it is written*.

He says, therefore: the reason we hope and do not faint is that *having the same Spirit of faith* which the ancients had, because although the times have changed, the Spirit and the faith have not changed, except that they believed that the Christ would come and suffer, whereas we believe that he has already come and suffered. And this Spirit is the Holy Spirit, who is the Spirit of faith: *all these are inspired by one and the same Spirit, who apportions to each one individually as he wills* (1 Cor 12:11).

Having, therefore, this Spirit that the ancients had, we do the same things as they did and we believe. But what they did is described in a psalm, *I believed* (Ps 116:20), namely, God, perfectly. And this is what the ancients did: *and all these, though well attested by their faith, did not receive what was promised* (Heb 11:39). *For which cause*, namely, that *I believed*, *I have spoken*, i.e., I confessed the faith: *for man believes with his heart and so is justified, and he confesses with his lips and so is saved* (Rom 10:10). But we do this because, since we believe, we speak and confess the faith and preach: *we cannot but speak of what we have seen and heard* (Acts 4:20). Therefore the Holy Spirit is the cause of this certitude.

142. Finally, therefore, he reaches the intended conclusion, namely, the certitude itself. First, in regard to his own salvation; second, in regard to the salvation of others, at *and place us with you*.

Dicit ergo *scientes*, id est certam scientiam habentes, *quoniam qui suscitavit Iesum*, id est Deus Pater, vel tota Trinitas, *et nos cum Iesu suscitabit*, ut scilicet sumamus eamdem gloriam cum Iesu, quia cum simus membra eius, debemus esse cum capite. Io. XII, 26: *volo, Pater, ut ubi ego sum, illic sit et minister meus*, et cetera. Rom. VIII, v. 11: *qui suscitavit Dominum Iesum a mortuis, suscitabit*, et cetera.

Et non solum sum certus de salute nostra, sed etiam de vestra, quia *constituet nos vobiscum*, id est simul erimus; quia sicut nos sumus membra Christi, ita et vos per nos. I Thess. IV, 16: *et sic semper cum Domino erimus*. Matth. XXIV, 28: *ubicumque fuerit corpus*, et cetera.

Et ideo dicit *vobiscum*, ut animet eos ad bonum, inquantum ostendit eos non esse inferiores, sed pares.

143. Et bene hoc possum certe dicere, quia omnia sunt propter utilitatem vestram. Nam *omnia*, quae sustinemus, omnes gratiae quas recipimus a Deo, sunt *propter vos*, scilicet instruendos nostro exemplo. Et hoc ideo *ut gratia abundans* a nobis, in vos *abundet per multos in gloriam Dei*, id est multi agant gratias Deo super beneficio tanto. Eph. V, v. 20: *gratias agentes Deo et Patri*, et cetera.

He says, therefore, *knowing*, i.e., having certain knowledge, *that he who raised up Jesus*, i.e., God the Father or the entire Trinity, *will raise us up also with Jesus*, namely, to put on the same glory as Jesus, because since we are his members, we should be with the head. *Where I am, there shall my servant be also* (John 12:26); *he who raised Christ Jesus from the dead will give life to your mortal bodies also through his Spirit which dwells in you* (Rom 8:11).

And I am certain not only of our salvation but of yours also, *and place us with you*, i.e., we will be together. For just as we are members of Christ, so you are also through us. *And so we shall always be with the Lord* (1 Thess 4:17); *wherever the body is, there the eagles will be gathered together* (Matt 24:28).

Therefore, he says, *with you*, to urge them to good, inasmuch as he shows that they are not inferiors but equals.

143. And well can I say this with certainty, because all things are for your benefit. For *all things*, the sufferings we endure, the graces we receive from God, *are for your sakes*, namely, that you be instructed by our example. And this, therefore, *so that the grace abounding* from us, in you *may abound through many in thanksgiving unto the glory of God*, i.e., that many may thank God for so great a favor. *Always and for everything giving thanks in the name of our Lord Jesus Christ to God the Father* (Eph 5:20).

Lecture 5

4:16 Propter quod non deficimus: sed licet is, qui foris est, noster homo corrumpatur, tamen is, qui intus est, renovatur de die in diem. [n. 144]

4:17 Id enim, quod in praesenti est momentaneum et leve tribulationis nostrae, supra modum in sublimitate aeternum gloriae pondus operatur in nobis, [n. 148]

4:18non contemplantibus nobis quae videntur, sed quae non videntur. Quae enim videntur, temporalia sunt: quae autem non videntur, aeterna sunt. [n. 151]

4:16Διὸ οὐκ ἐγκακοῦμεν, ἀλλ᾽ εἰ καὶ ὁ ἔξω ἡμῶν ἄνθρωπος διαφθείρεται, ἀλλ᾽ ὁ ἔσω ἡμῶν ἀνακαινοῦται ἡμέρᾳ καὶ ἡμέρᾳ.

4:17τὸ γὰρ παραυτίκα ἐλαφρὸν τῆς θλίψεως ἡμῶν καθ᾽ ὑπερβολὴν εἰς ὑπερβολὴν αἰώνιον βάρος δόξης κατεργάζεται ἡμῖν,

4:18μὴ σκοπούντων ἡμῶν τὰ βλεπόμενα ἀλλὰ τὰ μὴ βλεπόμενα· τὰ γὰρ βλεπόμενα πρόσκαιρα, τὰ δὲ μὴ βλεπόμενα αἰώνια.

4:16 For which cause we faint not: but though our outward man is corrupted, yet the inward man is renewed day by day. [n. 144]

4:17 For that which is at present momentary and light of our tribulation works for us above measure, exceedingly an eternal weight of glory. [n. 148]

4:18 While we look not at the things which are seen, but at the things which are not seen. For the things which are seen are temporal: but the things which are not seen, are eternal. [n. 151]

---

144. Posita patientia quam apostoli habebant in tribulationibus, et praemio quod expectabant manifestato, hic consequenter agit de patientiae causa et patientiae modo, seu ratione. Et

circa hoc tria facit.

Primo enim insinuat sanctorum patientiam;

secundo patientiae causam, ibi **non contemplantibus nobis**, etc.;

tertio patientiae remunerationem, ibi **id enim**, et cetera.

145. Circa primum intendit ostendere, quod sanctorum patientia est invincibilis. Et hoc est quod dicit **propter quod**, scilicet quia sumus scientes quod qui suscitavit Iesum a mortuis, suscitabit nos et constituet vobiscum, ideo **non deficimus**, scilicet in tribulationibus, id est non deducimur ad hoc quod non possimus propter Christum amplius ferre et sustinere. Nam deficere idem est quod ferre non posse. Ier. XX, 9: *defeci, ferre non sustinui.*

146. Causa autem quare non deficimus est quia licet quantum ad aliquid deficiamus, scilicet quantum ad exteriorem hominem, tamen quantum ad aliquid semper renovamur, scilicet quantum ad interiorem hominem. Et hoc est quod dicit **sed licet is qui foris est**, et cetera.

Ubi sciendum est, quod occasione istorum verborum haereticus, Tertullianus nomine, dixit quod anima rationalis, quae est in hominis corpore, habet corpoream figuram et membra corporea, sicut et corpus habet: et hoc dicitur homo interior; corpus vero, cum sensibus suis, dicitur homo exterior. Quod quidem falsum est. Unde, ad intellectum huius verbi, sciendum est quod etiam secundum Philosophum in *Ethic.*, et secundum consuetudinem loquendi, unumquodque dicitur esse illud quod est principalius in ipso, puta, quia in civitate principalius est potestas et concilium, id quod facit potestas et concilium, dicitur tota civitas facere.

144. Having mentioned the patience which the apostles showed in tribulations and manifested the reward they expected, he then treats of the cause of patience and the mode or reason for patience.

In regard to this he does three things.

First, he hints at the patience of the saints;

second, the cause of patience, at **while we look not**;

third, the reward of patience, at **for that which**.

145. In regard to the first he intends to show that the patience of the saints is unconquerable. Hence, he says, **for which cause**, i.e., because we know that he who raised Jesus from the dead will raise us and place us with you; therefore **we faint not**, namely, in our tribulations, i.e., we are reduced to the state in which we cannot bear and endure more for Christ. For to lose heart is the same as not being able to bear: *I was wearied, not being able to bear it* (Jer 20:9).

146. But the reason why we do not fail is that although we fail in a certain respect, namely as to the outward man, in another respect we are ever renewed, namely as to the inward man. Hence, he says, **but though our outward man is corrupted, yet the inward man is renewed day by day**.

Here it should be noted that by occasion of these words a certain heretic, Tertullian by name, said that the rational soul, which is in the body of a man, has a bodily shape and bodily members, just as the body has; and this is called the inward man. This, of course, is false. Hence, to understand the passage, it must be known that even according to the Philosopher in IX *Ethics*, and according to the way we speak, each thing is said to be that which is most important in it. For example, the most important thing in the city is the power and the council, so that whatever the power and council do, the city is said to do.

Principalius autem in homine potest aliquid iudicari et secundum veritatem et secundum apparentiam. Secundum veritatem quidem principalius in homine est ipsa mens, unde secundum iudicium spiritualium virorum mens dicitur homo interior. Secundum apparentiam vero principalius in homine est corpus exterius cum sensibus suis; unde secundum iudicium illorum, qui tantum corporalia et sensibilia considerant et terrena sapiunt, quorum deus venter est, corpus cum sensibus dicitur homo exterior.

147. Et ideo, secundum hunc modum, loquitur hic Apostolus, dicens **licet homo noster**, scilicet corpus cum natura sensitiva, **corrumpatur**, in tribulationibus, ieiuniis et abstinentiis et vigiliis, Rom. VI, 6: *vetus homo noster simul*, et cetera. Habac. III, 16: *ingrediatur putredo*, etc., **tamen is** homo, **qui intus est**, scilicet mens, seu ratio munita spe futuri praemii et firmata munimine fidei, **renovatur**. Quod sic intelligendum est: vetustas enim est via ad corruptionem. Hebr. VIII, v. 13: *quod antiquatur et senescit*, et cetera. Natura autem humana fuit in integritate condita et, si in illa integritate permansisset, semper esset nova: sed per peccatum incepit corrumpi; quo fit, quod quidquid consecutum est, sicut ignorantia, difficultas ad bonum, et pronitas ad malum, poenalitas et alia huiusmodi, totum pertinet ad vetustatem.

Cum ergo natura humana huiusmodi peccatum sequentia deponit, tunc dicitur renovari. Quae quidem depositio hic incipit in sanctis, sed perfecte consummabitur in patria. Hic enim deponitur vetustas culpae: nam spiritus deponit vetustatem peccati et subiicitur novitati iustitiae. Hic intellectus deponit errores et assumit novitatem veritatis; et, secundum hoc, is, qui intus est homo, scilicet anima, renovatur. Eph. IV, 23: *renovamini spiritu mentis vestrae*. Sed in patria tolletur etiam vetustas poenae. Unde ibi erit consummata renovatio. Ps. CII, 5: *renovabitur ut aquilae*, et cetera.

Sed quia sancti quotidie proficiunt in puritate conscientiae et in cognitione divinorum, ideo dicit **de die in diem**. Ps. LXXXIII, 6: *ascensiones in corde suo*. Sic ergo patientia est invincibilis, quia renovatur de die in diem.

148. Tertium principale, scilicet huius patientiae causa, est recogitatio praemii, quae est efficacissima, quia, secundum Gregorium, *recogitatio praemii, diminuit vim flagelli*. Et hoc est quod dicit **id enim quod**, etc., quasi dicat: nihil sunt tribulationes quas hic patimur, si respiciatur ad gloriam, quam ex eis consequimur.

Unde comparat statum sanctorum, qui sunt in vita ista, ad statum eorum, qui sunt in patria, et ponit quinque in utroque statu correspondentia sibi invicem.

149. Nam primo status istius vitae in sanctis est status, quantum in se est, parvus et quasi imperceptibilis. Unde dicit **id**, id est minimum. Is. LIV, 7: *ad punctum, in modico dereliqui te*.

Now something can be judged the most important thing in man either in truth or according to appearance. In truth the most important thing in man is the mind. Hence, according to the judgment of spiritual men, the mind is called the inward man. But according to appearance, the most important thing is the outward body with its senses. Hence, according to the judgment of those who consider only bodily and sense-perceptible things and savor earthly things, and whose god is the belly, the body with the sense is called the outward man.

147. Therefore, it is according to this manner that the Apostle is speaking here when he says, **though our outward man**, i.e., the body with its sentient nature, **is corrupted**, in tribulations, fasts, abstinences and watchings: *our old self was crucified with him* (Rom 6:6); *rottenness enters into my bones* (Hab. 3:16), **yet the inward man** namely, the mind or reason strengthened with the shield of faith, **is renewed**. This should be understood in the following way: oldness is the road to corruption. *And what is becoming obsolete and growing old is ready to vanish away* (Heb 8:13). But human nature was established in wholeness, and if it had continued in that wholeness, it would have always been new. But through sin it began to be corrupted. As a result, whatever followed, such as ignorance, difficulty in doing good, inclination to evil, punishment, and so on, all pertain to oldness.

Therefore, when such a human nature gets rid of the results of sin, it is said to be renewed. Such riddance begins in the saints here, but is perfectly completed in heaven. For here the oldness of sin is put off; for the spirit removes the oldness of sin and is subjected to the newness of justice. Here the intellect removes errors and assumes the newness of truth. It is according to this that the inner man, namely, the soul, is renewed. *Be renewed in the spirit of your minds* (Eph 4:23). But in heaven, even the oldness of punishment is removed. Hence, there will be a complete renewal there: *your youth is renewed like the eagle's* (Ps 103:5).

But because the saints advance daily in purity of conscience and knowledge of divine things, he says, **day by day**: *ascending in his heart* (Ps 84:7). Consequently, patience is unconquerable, because it is renewed from day to day.

148. The third point, namely, the cause of this patience, is recognition of a reward. This recognition is most efficacious, because, according to Gregory, *it lessens the force of a scourge*. And this is what he says, **for that which is**, as if to say: the tribulations we suffer here are nothing, if we look to the glory we obtain from them.

Hence, he compares the condition of the saints in this life to the condition of those in heaven and mentions five things in each state that correspond.

149. First, the condition of the present life in the saints is of itself slight and, as it were, imperceptible. Hence, he says, **that** i.e., the least: *for a brief moment I forsook you* (Isa 54:7).

Item transitorium. Unde dicit *in praesenti*, id est in vita ista, quae est in afflictionibus et aerumnis. Iob VII, 1: *militia est vita hominis*, et cetera.

Item temporis brevitas. Unde dicit *momentaneum*. Is. LIV, 8: *in momento indignationis abscondi faciem meam parumper a te*, et cetera. Nam totum tempus huius vitae comparatum ad aeternitatem, non est nisi momentaneum.

Item est levis. Unde dicit *leve*. Nam licet supra I, 8 dicatur: *Gravati sumus supra modum*, quia scilicet grave est corpori, tamen spiritui caritate ferventi levissimum est. Augustinus: *omnia gravia et immania facilia et prope nulla facit amor.*

Item est poenosus. Et ideo dicit *tribulationis*. Mich. VII, 9: *iram Domini portabo*, et cetera.

150. Sed quantum ad statum beatitudinis ponit quinque, quia contra hoc, quod dicit, *id*, ponit *supra modum*, id est supra mensuram. Rom. VIII, 18: *existimo quod non sunt condignae passiones*, et cetera.

Sed contra Matth. XVI, 27: *reddet unicuique iuxta opera sua*. Non ergo supra mensuram.

Respondeo. Dicendum est, quod *sed*, non designat aequalitatem quantitatis, ut scilicet quantum quis meruit, tantum praemietur, sed designat aequalitatem proportionis, ut scilicet qui plus meruit, plus praemii accipiat.

Item contra id quod dicit *in praesenti*, ponit *in sublimitate*, id est in statu sublimi absque perturbatione. Is. LVIII, 14: *sustollam te super altitudinem nubium*, et cetera.

Contra id quod dicit *momentaneum*, ponit *aeternum*, Is. XXXV, 10: *laetitia sempiterna super capita eorum*, et cetera.

Contra id quod dicit *leve*, ponit *pondus*. Et dicit *pondus*, propter duo. Pondus enim inclinat et trahit ad motum suum quae subsunt sibi. Sic gloria aeterna erit tanta, quod totum hominem faciet gloriosum, et in anima et in corpore; nihil erit in homine, quod non sequatur impetum gloriae.

Vel dicitur *pondus*, propter pretiositatem. Nam pretiosa solum ponderari consueverunt.

Contra hoc, quod dicit *tribulationis*, ponit *gloriae*.

Vel hoc quod dicit *gloriae*, potest esse commune ad alia quatuor, quae de statu patriae dicuntur; hoc vero quod dicit *tribulationis*, ad quatuor quae de statu praesentis vitae dicta sunt.

Operatur supra id, scilicet quod tribulationes patimur, nam haec sunt causa et meritum, quare Deus istam gloriam nobis conferat.

Likewise it is transitory; hence he says, *at present*, i.e., in this life, which is one of affliction and toil. *The life of man is warfare* (Job 7:1).

Likewise it lasts a short time; hence he says, *momentary*: *for a moment I hid my face from you* (Isa 54:8). For the whole time of this present life compared to eternity is only momentary.

Likewise it is light; hence he says, *light*. For although he said above, *we were burdened beyond measure* (2 Cor 1:8), because the body is heavy, yet it is very light to a spirit on fire with charity. Hence Augustine says: *all that is heavy and huge love makes easy and almost nothing.*

Likewise it is penal; hence he says, *of our tribulation*. *I will bear the indignation of the Lord because I have sinned against him* (Mic 7:9).

150. But as to the state of happiness, he lays down five things, because in contrast to this, he places *above measure*: *I consider that the sufferings of this present time are not worth comparing to the glory that is to be revealed to us* (Rom 8:18).

But on the other hand: *he will give to each one according to his works* (Matt 16:27). Therefore it will not be beyond all measure.

I answer that the word *but* does not denote an equality of amount, as though a person will be rewarded so much for so much merit, but an equality of proportion, so that one who merits more will receive more reward.

Likewise, against that which is *at present* he places *exceedingly*, i.e., in an excellent state without disturbance: *I will make you ride upon the heights of the earth* (Isa 58:14).

Against that which is *momentary*, he places *eternal*: *everlasting joy shall be upon their heads* (Isa 35:10).

Against that which is *light* he places *a weight*. He says, *weight* for two reasons: first, because a weight inclines and draws to its motion all things under it. In the same way eternal glory will be so great that it will make the whole man glorious in soul and in body. There will be nothing in man that does not follow the impulse of glory.

Or it is called *weight*, because it is precious, for only precious things are weighed.

Against that which is called *of tribulation* he places *of glory*.

Or *of glory* can be common to the other four, which are said of the state of glory, so that *of tribulation* is common to the four which are said of the present life.

It works, namely, above the tribulations we suffer, for these are the cause and merit for which God confers that glory on us.

Est ergo sanctorum patientia invincibilis, eorum remuneratio ineffabilis, sed, remunerationis eorum recompensatio, recta et delectabilis.

151. Unde dicit *non contemplantibus nobis*, etc., quasi dicat: licet haec, quae speramus, sint futura, et interim corpus nostrum corrumpatur, nihilominus tamen renovamur, quia non attendimus ad ista temporalia, sed ad caelestia. Et hoc est quod dicit: *operatur in nobis pondus gloriae*, nobis dico, *non contemplantibus*, id est non attendentibus ad *ea quae videntur*, id est ad terrena, sed ad *ea quae non videntur*, scilicet caelestia. Phil. III, 13: *quae retro sunt obliviscens*, et cetera. I Cor. II, 9: *oculus non vidit*, et cetera.

Et quare caelestia contemplamur? *Quia ea quae videntur*, id est terrena, *sunt temporalia*, et transitoria, *ea autem quae non videntur*, scilicet caelestia, *sunt aeterna*. Is. LI, v. 8: *salus autem mea in sempiternum erit*.

And so the patience of the saints is unconquerable, their reward ineffable, and the recompense of their reward right and delightful.

151. Hence he says, *while we look not at the things which are seen, but at the things which are not seen*. As if to say: although the things we hope for are still to come, and in the meantime our body is corrupted, nevertheless, we are renewed, because we do not pay attention to those temporal things, but to eternal. And this is what he says: *it works in us a weight of glory*. In us, I say, *while we look not at*, i.e., not paying attention to, *the things which are seen*, i.e., earthly things, but *at the things which are not seen*, namely, heavenly things: *forgetting what lies behind and straining forward to what lies ahead* (Phil 3:13); *eye has not seen nor ear heard, nor the heart of man conceived, God has prepared for those who love him* (1 Cor 2:9).

And why do we look on heavenly things? *For the things which are seen*, i.e., earthly things, are transient and *are temporal, but the things which are unseen*, namely, heavenly things, *are eternal*: *my salvation will be forever* (Isa 51:6).

Chapter 5

Lecture 1

5:1Scimus enim quoniam si terrestris domus nostra hujus habitationis dissolvatur, quod aedificationem ex Deo habemus, domum non manufactam, aeternam in caelis. [n. 152]

5:2Nam et in hoc ingemiscimus, habitationem nostram, quae de caelo est, superindui cupientes: [n. 155]

5:3si tamen vestiti, non nudi inveniamur. [n. 157]

5:4Nam et qui sumus in hoc tabernaculo, ingemiscimus gravati: eo quod nolumus expoliari, sed supervestiri, ut absorbeatur quod mortale est, a vita. [n. 158]

5:1Οἴδαμεν γὰρ ὅτι ἐὰν ἡ ἐπίγειος ἡμῶν οἰκία τοῦ σκήνους καταλυθῇ, οἰκοδομὴν ἐκ θεοῦ ἔχομεν, οἰκίαν ἀχειροποίητον αἰώνιον ἐν τοῖς οὐρανοῖς.

5:2καὶ γὰρ ἐν τούτῳ στενάζομεν τὸ οἰκητήριον ἡμῶν τὸ ἐξ οὐρανοῦ ἐπενδύσασθαι ἐπιποθοῦντες,

5:3εἴ γε καὶ ἐκδυσάμενοι οὐ γυμνοὶ εὑρεθησόμεθα.

5:4καὶ γὰρ οἱ ὄντες ἐν τῷ σκήνει στενάζομεν βαρούμενοι, ἐφ᾽ ᾧ οὐ θέλομεν ἐκδύσασθαι ἀλλ᾽ ἐπενδύσασθαι, ἵνα καταποθῇ τὸ θνητὸν ὑπὸ τῆς ζωῆς.

5:1For we know that if our earthly house of this habitation be dissolved, we have a building of God, a house not made with hands, eternal in heaven. [n. 152]

5:2For in this also we groan, desiring to be clothed upon with our habitation that is from heaven: [n. 155]

5:3Yet so that we be found clothed, not naked. [n. 157]

5:4For we also, who are in this tabernacle, do groan, being burdened; because we would not be unclothed, but clothed upon, that that which is mortal may be swallowed up by life. [n. 158]

---

152. Postquam Apostolus commendavit ministerium Novi Testamenti, et quantum ad dignitatem, et quantum ad usum, consequenter hic commendat illud quantum ad praemium, licet de praemio, quantum ad aliquid aliqualiter et incomplete supra tractavit, hic tamen de hoc complete tractat. Circa quod tria facit.

Primo enim agit de praemio;

secundo vero de praeparatione et praemii susceptione, ibi *et ideo contendimus sive*, etc.;

tertio vero de causa utriusque, scilicet praeparationis et praemii quod expectatur, ibi *omnia autem ex Deo, qui reconciliavit*, et cetera.

Circa primum duo facit.

Primo ponit praemium, quod expectatur;

secundo exprimit desiderium praemii expectati, ibi *nam in hoc ingemiscimus*, et cetera.

153. Sed quia praemium quod expectatur est inaestimabile, scilicet gloriae caelestis, et ideo dicit *scimus quoniam*, etc., quasi dicat secundum Glossam vere operatur in nobis pondus gloriae, quia in corporibus erit haec gloria, non tantum in animabus. *Enim*, id est *quia*, *scimus*, id est certi sumus, quia iam habemus in spe, *quoniam si terrestris domus nostra*, id est, corpus.

Homo enim, ut dictum est, dicitur mens, cum sit principalius in homine; quae quidem mens se habet ad corpus, sicut homo ad domum. Sicut enim destructa domo, non destruitur homo eam inhabitans sed manet, sic, destructo corpore, non destruitur mens seu anima

152. After commending the ministry of the New Testament, both as to its dignity and its use, the Apostle now commends it as to its reward. For although he had already said something about the reward, it was partial and incomplete; so now he deals with it at greater length. In regard to this he does three things:

first, he treats of the reward;

second, of the preparation for and reception of the reward, at *and therefore we labor*;

third, the cause of each, namely, of the preparation and of the reward that is expected, at *but all things are of God, who has reconciled*.

In regard to the first he does two things:

first, he mentions the reward expected;

second, he expresses a desire for the expected reward, at *for in this also we groan*.

153. Since the awaited reward is inestimable, namely, of heavenly glory, he says, *for we know*. As if to say according to a Gloss: indeed he works in us a weight of glory, because this glory will be not only in our souls, but in our bodies. *For*, i.e., *because we know*, i.e., are certain, because we already have it in hope, *that if our earthly house*, i.e., the body.

For as has been said, man is called a mind, since that is the most important thing in man. Now this mind is to the body as a man is to a house. For just as the man living in a house is not destroyed, when the house is destroyed, but he continues to exist, so when the body is destroyed,

rationalis, sed manet. Corpus ergo terrestre dicitur *domus habitationis*, id est, in qua habitamus. Iob IV, 19: *qui habitant domos luteas*, et cetera. *Dissolvatur*, id est destruatur. *Scimus*, inquam, *quod habemus aedificationem*, id est aedificium, *ex Deo*, id est paratum a Deo. Aedificium, dico, *domum non manufactam*, id est non opere hominis, nec opere naturae, sed corpus incorruptibile, quod assumemus; quod quidem non est manufactum, quia incorruptibilitas in corporibus nostris provenit solum ex operatione divina. Phil. III, 21: *reformabit corpus humilitatis nostrae*, et cetera. *Domum aeternam*, id est domum ab aeterno praeparatam. Is. XXXIII, v. 20: *tabernaculum quod nequaquam destruetur in caelis*. Matth. V, 12: *merces vestra copiosa est in caelis*. Hanc autem commutationem, ut scilicet pro terrestri domo habeant caelestem, desiderabat Iob, dicens c. XIV, 14: *cunctis diebus quibus nunc milito*.

154. Expositio est secundum Glossam. Sed tamen non est secundum intellectum apostolicum, nec praecedentibus, nec sequentibus concordat. Nam ipse cum habeat unam materiam continuam de qua loquitur, non interponit aliam. Et ideo videamus quid intendat Apostolus dicere.

Sciendum est autem, quod Apostolus vult hic ostendere quod sancti rationabiliter sustinent tribulationes, ex quibus vita praesens corrumpitur, quia ex hoc statim perveniunt ad gloriam, non ad gloriosum corpus, ut dicitur in Glossa. Et ideo dicit: ideo sustinuimus *enim*, id est *quia*, *scimus*, id est, pro certo habemus, *quoniam si terrestris domus nostra huius habitationis*, id est, corpus, *dissolvatur*, id est, corrumpatur per mortem, *habemus*, statim, non in spe sed in re, meliorem domum, scilicet *aedificationem, domum non manufactam*, id est, gloriam caelestem, non corpus gloriosum. De hac autem domo dicitur Io. XIV, 2: *in domo Patris mei mansiones multae*, et cetera. Quae quidem est *ex Deo* non manufacta, quia gloria aeterna est ipse Deus. Ps. XXX, 3: *esto mihi in Deum protectorem et in domum*, et cetera. Et *aeternam*, ad litteram, quia ipse Deus est aeternus. *In caelis*, id est, in excelsis, quia statim corrupto corpore, anima sancta consequitur hanc gloriam non in spe, sed in re. Nam et antequam corpus dissolvatur, habemus hanc domum in spe.

Sic ergo praemium sanctorum est admirabile et desiderabile, quia gloria caelestis est.

155. Ideo consequenter subiungit desiderium sanctorum ad ipsum praemium, dicens *nam in hoc ingemiscimus*, et cetera. Ubi tria facit.

Primo exprimit desiderium gratiae ad praemium ipsum;

secundo ostendit quod desiderium gratiae retardatur ex desiderio naturae, ibi *nam et qui sumus in hoc tabernaculo*, etc.;

the mind, i.e., the rational soul, is not destroyed, but continues to exist. The body, therefore, is called the *earthly house* we live in. *Those who dwell in houses of clay, whose foundation is in the dust, who are crushed before the moth* (Job 4:19). *Be dissolved*, i.e., destroyed. *We know*, I say, *that we have a building of God*, i.e., prepared by God; a building, I say, *a house not made with hands*, i.e., not a work of man or of nature, but an incorruptible body, which we shall assume. It is not made with hands, because incorruptibility in our bodies is the result of a divine action alone. *He will change our lowly body to be like his glorious body* (Phil 3:21). *Eternal in heaven*, i.e., a house prepared for us from all eternity. *A tabernacle that shall never be destroyed in heaven* (Isa 33:20); *your reward shall be great in heaven* (Matt 5:12). This exchange, namely, to get a heavenly home for an earthly one, is what Job desired: *all the days of my service I would wait, till my release should come* (Job 14:14).

154. The explanation is based on a Gloss, but it does not agree with the Apostle's meaning, nor with what preceded and what follows. For when he is dealing with one continuous subject, he does not interject another. Therefore let us see what the Apostle intends to say.

Now one should know that the Apostle wants to show that the saints are reasonable in enduring the tribulations by which the present life is destroyed, because this results in obtaining glory at once, and not a glorified body, as the Gloss says. Therefore he says: the reason we endure these things is that *we know*, i.e., we hold it as certain, *that if our earthly house of this habitation*, i.e., the body, *be dissolved* i.e., corrupted by death, *we have* at once, not in hope but in reality, a better house, namely, *a building, a house not made with hands*, i.e., heavenly glory, not a glorified body. Of this house it is said: *in my Father's house are many rooms* (John 14:2). This house is *of God*, not made with hands, because eternal glory is God himself: *be a rock of refuge for me, a strong fortress to save me* (Ps 31:2), and *eternal* in the literal sense, because it is the eternal God. *In the heavens*, i.e., on high, because as soon as the body is dead, the holy soul obtains this glory, not in hope but in reality. For thus even before the body is dissolved, we have this home in hope.

Thus, the reward of the saints is wonderful and desirable, because it is heavenly glory.

155. Hence, he links the desire of the saints with this reward, saying: *for in this also we groan, desiring to be clothed upon with our habitation that is from heaven*. Here he does three things.

First, he expresses the desire of grace for its reward;

second, he shows that the desire of grace is retarded by the desire of nature, at *for we also, who are in this tabernacle*;

tertio ostendit quomodo desiderium gratiae vincit desiderium naturae, ibi **audentes igitur**, et cetera.

156. Sed desiderium gratiae est cum fervore. **Nam in hoc ingemiscimus**, etc., quasi dicat: haec est vera probatio, quod habemus domum non manufactam, quia si desiderium naturae non est frustra, multo minus desiderium gratiae frustra est.

Cum igitur nos habeamus ferventissimum desiderium gratiae de gloria caelesti, impossibile est, quod sit frustra. Et hoc est, quod dicit **ingemiscimus**, id est, ingemendo desideramus, **in hoc**, scilicet animae desiderio retardati. Ps. CXIX, 5: *heu mihi, quia incolatus meus*, et cetera. In hoc enim quod **cupientes** sumus, id est cupimus, **superindui habitationem nostram**, id est fruitionem gloriae, **quae de caelo est**, id est caelestis; quae dicitur habitatio, quia in ipsa gloria sancti habitant sicut in suo consolatorio. Matth. XXV, 21–23: *intra in gaudium Domini tui.*

Per hoc autem quod dicit **superindui**, dat intelligere quod illa domus caelestis, de qua supra dixerat, non est aliquid ab homine separatum, sed aliquid homini inhaerens. Non enim dicitur homo induere domum sed vestimentum, domum autem dicitur aliquis inhabitare. Haec ergo duo coniungit, dicens **superindui habitationem**, per quod ostendit, quod illud desiderium est aliquid inhaerens, quia induitur, et aliquid continens et excedens, quia inhabitatur.

157. Sed quia non simpliciter dixit: *indui*, sed **superindui**, rationem sui dicti subdit, dicens **si tamen vestiti, et non nudi inveniamur**. Quasi dicat: si anima indueretur habitatione caelesti, quod non exueretur habitatione terrena, id est non corrumperetur corpus nostrum per mortem, sed caelestis adeptio illius habitationis esset superinduitio. Sed quia oportet quod evacuetur habitatione terrena, ad hoc quod induatur caelesti, non potest dici superinduitio, sed induitio simplex. Et ideo dicit **si tamen vestiti et non nudi inveniamur**, quasi dicat: superindueremur quidem, si inveniremur induti, et non nudi. Nudus enim non dicitur superindui, sed indui tantum.

Glossa vero aliter exponit de vestimento spirituali, dicens: *cupimus superindui, quod utique fiet, tamen hac conditione, si nos inveniamur vestiti, scilicet virtutibus, et non nudi, scilicet virtutibus*. De istis vestibus dicitur Col. III, 12: *induite vos sicut electi Dei*, et cetera. Quasi dicat: nullus ad illam gloriam perveniet, nisi habeat virtutes. Quae quidem expositio non videtur concordare intentioni Apostoli.

158. Sic ergo desiderium gratiae fervet ad praemium, sed tamen retardatur a desiderio naturae, quod ostendit

third, he shows that the desire of grace overcomes the desire of nature, at **therefore, always having confidence**.

156. The desire of grace is fervent: **for in this we also groan**, and long to put on our heavenly dwelling. As if to say: this is the real proof that we have a house not made with hands, because if the desire of nature is not in vain, much less is the desire of grace in vain.

Therefore, since we have a most fervent desire of grace for heavenly glory, it is impossible for it to be in vain; and this is what he says, **we groan**, i.e., groaning we desire, namely with our soul's desire that we are delayed. *Woe is me that I sojourn in Meshech* (Ps 120:5). We groan, I say, **desiring to be clothed upon with our habitation**, i.e., the enjoyment of glory, **that is from heaven**, i.e., heavenly. It is called a dwelling because the saints dwell in that glory as their place of consolation. *Enter into the joy of the Lord* (Matt 25:21).

In saying, **clothed upon** he is stating that the heavenly home of which he spoke above is not something separated from man, but something inhering in him. For a man is not said to be clothed with a house, but with clothes: **clothed upon with our habitation**. In this way he shows that the desire is for something that inheres, because it is put on, and something which contains and exceeds because it is inhabited.

157. But because he did not merely say, *clothed*, but **clothed upon**, he gives the reason for this, when he says, **yet so that we be found clothed, not naked**. As if to say: if the soul were to be clothed with a heavenly dwelling, in such a way that the earthly dwelling were not taken off, i.e., in such a way that our body were not dissolved by death, the attainment of that heavenly dwelling would be *to be clothed upon*. But because it is necessary to be divested of that earthly dwelling, if the heavenly is to be put on, it cannot be a *being clothed upon*, but simply a *being clothed*. Hence he says, **yet so that we be found clothed, not naked**. As if to say: we would indeed be clothed upon, if we were found clothed and not naked. For a naked person is not said to be clothed upon, but to be clothed.

But a Gloss explains it as a spiritual dress, saying: *we desire to be clothed upon, and this will indeed be done, but under this condition, that we be found clothed, namely, with the virtues, and not naked, namely, of the virtues*. Of this clothing it is said: *put on then, as God's chosen ones, holy and beloved, compassion, kindness, lowliness, meekness, and patience* (Col 3:12). As if to say: no one will attain to this glory, unless he has the virtues. But this explanation does not seem to agree with the Apostle's intention.

158. Thus, therefore, the desire of grace burns for a reward, but it is retarded by the desire of nature. He shows

cum dicit *nam dum sumus in tabernaculo isto*, et cetera. Ubi

primo ponit conditionem desiderii naturalis;

secundo ostendit, quod etiam hic status desiderii naturalis est a Deo, ibi *qui autem efficit nos*, et cetera.

159. Conditio autem desiderii est naturalis retardans desiderium gratiae, quia vellemus inveniri vestiti et non nudi, id est ita vellemus quod anima perveniret ad gloriam, quod corpus non corrumperetur per mortem. Cuius ratio est quia naturale desiderium inest animae esse unitam corpori, alias mors non esset poenalis. Et hoc est quod dicit *nam*, nos, *qui sumus in hoc tabernaculo*, id est, qui habitamus in isto mortali corpore, II Petr. c. I, 14. *scio quod velox sit depositio tabernaculi mei*, *ingemiscimus*, id est intus in corde, non solum extra in voce, gemimus, Is. LIX, 11: *ut columbae meditantes gememus*, quia durum est cogitare mortem. Et tamen *gravati*, quasi aliquo existente contra desiderium nostrum, eo quod non possumus pervenire ad gloriam, nisi deponamus corpus, quod est ita contra naturale desiderium, ut dicit Augustinus, quod nec ipsa senectus a Petro timorem mortis auferre potuit. Et ideo dicit *eo quod nolumus spoliari*, scilicet tabernaculo terreno, *sed supervestiri*, gloria supercaelesti, vel, secundum Glossam, corpore glorioso.

Sed quia posset videri indecens, quod corpus ex una parte esset corruptibile ex sui natura, si non fuisset ante dissolutum, et ex parte gloriae esset gloriosum, subdit modum quomodo fieri vellet, dicens *ut absorbeatur quod mortale est*, etc., quasi dicat: non sic supervestiri volumus, quod corpus remaneat mortale, sed ita quod gloria auferat ex toto corruptionem corporis, absque corporali dissolutione. Et ideo dicit *absorbeatur quod mortale est*, id est ipsa corruptio corporis, *a vita*, scilicet gloriae. I Cor. XV, 54: *absorpta est mors in victoria*, et cetera.

this when he says: *for we also, who are in this tabernacle, do groan*.

Herein, therefore, he first shows the condition of the natural desire;

second, he shows that even this condition of the natural desire is from God, at *now he who makes us*.

159. The condition of the desire is natural, delaying the desire of grace, because we would prefer to be found clothed and not naked, i.e., we would prefer that the soul attain to glory without the body's being dissolved by death. The reason for this is that there is a natural desire in the soul to be united to the body; otherwise, death would not be a punishment. And this is what he says: *for we also, who are in this tabernacle*, i.e., who live in this mortal body: *since I know that the putting off of my body will be soon* (2 Pet 1:14), *do groan* i.e., inwardly in the heart, and not outwardly with our voice: *we moan and moan like doves* (Isa 59:11), because it is hard to think of death, and yet *burdened* as with something against our desire, in that we cannot attain to glory without the putting off of the body. This is so much against our natural desire that, as Augustine says, not even old age itself could remove the fear of death from Peter. And so he says, *we would not be unclothed*, namely, of our earthly tent, *but clothed upon, that that which is mortal may be swallowed up by life*, or, according to a Gloss, with a glorified body.

But because it could seem unbecoming that the body, on the one hand should be corruptible of its very nature, if it had not been dissolved before, and, on the other hand, glorified, he mentions the way in which he would like this to happen, saying, *so that that which is mortal may be swallowed up by life*. As if to say: we do not desire to be clothed over in such a way that the body remains mortal, but so that the glory take away corruption altogether from the body without its dissolution. Hence he says, *that that which is mortal*, i.e., the very corruption of the body, *may be swallowed up by life*, i.e., glory: *death is swallowed up in victory* (1 Cor 15:54).

Lecture 2

5:5Qui autem efficit nos in hoc ipsum, Deus, qui dedit nobis pignus Spiritus. [n. 160]

5:6Audentes igitur semper, scientes quoniam dum sumus in corpore, peregrinamur a Domino [n. 162]

5:7(per fidem enim ambulamus, et non per speciem): [n. 164]

5:8audemus autem, et bonam voluntatem habemus magis peregrinari a corpore, et praesentes esse ad Dominum. [n. 165]

5:9Et ideo contendimus, sive absentes, sive praesentes, placere illi. [n. 169]

5:10Omnes enim nos manifestari oportet ante tribunal Christi, ut referat unusquisque propria corporis, prout gessit, sive bonum, sive malum. [n. 170]

5:5ὁ δὲ κατεργασάμενος ἡμᾶς εἰς αὐτὸ τοῦτο θεός, ὁ δοὺς ἡμῖν τὸν ἀρραβῶνα τοῦ πνεύματος.

5:6Θαρροῦντες οὖν πάντοτε καὶ εἰδότες ὅτι ἐνδημοῦντες ἐν τῷ σώματι ἐκδημοῦμεν ἀπὸ τοῦ κυρίου·

5:7διὰ πίστεως γὰρ περιπατοῦμεν, οὐ διὰ εἴδους·

5:8θαρροῦμεν δὲ καὶ εὐδοκοῦμεν μᾶλλον ἐκδημῆσαι ἐκ τοῦ σώματος καὶ ἐνδημῆσαι πρὸς τὸν κύριον.

5:9διὸ καὶ φιλοτιμούμεθα, εἴτε ἐνδημοῦντες εἴτε ἐκδημοῦντες, εὐάρεστοι αὐτῷ εἶναι.

5:10τοὺς γὰρ πάντας ἡμᾶς φανερωθῆναι δεῖ ἔμπροσθεν τοῦ βήματος τοῦ Χριστοῦ, ἵνα κομίσηται ἕκαστος τὰ διὰ τοῦ σώματος πρὸς ἃ ἔπραξεν, εἴτε ἀγαθὸν εἴτε φαῦλον.

5:5Now he who makes us for this very thing is God, who has given us the pledge of the Spirit, [n. 160]

5:6Therefore, always having confidence, knowing that while we are in the body we are absent from the Lord. [n. 162]

5:7(For we walk by faith and not by sight.) [n. 164]

5:8But we are confident and have a good will to be absent rather from the body and to be present with the Lord. [n. 165]

5:9And therefore we labor, whether absent or present, to please him. [n. 169]

5:10For we must all be manifested before the judgment seat of Christ, that everyone may receive the proper things of the body, according as he has done, whether it be good or evil. [n. 170]

---

160. Hic ostendit auctorem supernaturalis desiderii de habitatione caelesti. Causa enim naturalis desiderii quod nolumus expoliari est quia scilicet anima naturaliter unitur corpori, et e converso. Sed hoc, quod caelestem inhabitationem superindui cupiamus, non est ex natura, sed ex Deo. Et ideo dicit *qui autem efficit nos in hoc*, etc., quasi dicat: volumus superinduere caelestem habitationem, ita tamen quod non spoliemur terrena, et tamen, hoc ipsum quod volumus sic supervestiri, efficit in nobis Deus. Phil. II, 13: *Deus est qui operatur in nobis*, et cetera.

Cuius ratio est, quia quamlibet naturam consequitur appetitus conveniens fini suae naturae, sicut grave naturaliter tendit deorsum, et appetit ibi quiescere. Si autem sit appetitus alicuius rei supra naturam suam, illa res non movetur ad illum finem naturaliter, sed ab alio quod est supra naturam suam. Constat autem quod perfrui caelesti gloria et videre Deum per essentiam, licet sit rationalis creaturae, est tamen supra naturam ipsius, non ergo movetur rationalis creatura ad hoc desiderandum a natura, sed ab ipso Deo, *qui in hoc ipsum efficit nos*, et cetera.

161. Sed quomodo hoc efficit subdit, dicens *qui dedit pignus*, et cetera.

Circa quod sciendum est, quod Deus efficit in nobis naturalia desideria et supernaturalia. Naturalia quidem quando dat nobis spiritum naturalem convenientem

160. Here he discloses the author of the supernatural desire for a heavenly dwelling. For the cause of a natural desire that we be not despoiled is that the soul is naturally united to the body, and vice versa. But the desire to be clothed upon with a heavenly dwelling is not from nature but from God. Hence, he says, *now he who makes us for this very thing is God*. As if to say: we wish to put on the heavenly dwelling, but in such a way as not to lose the earthly one. And yet it is God who effects in us the desire to be thus clothed over: *God is at work in you, both to will and to work for his good pleasure* (Phil 2:13).

The reason for this is that upon every nature follows a desire suited to the end of that nature, as something heavy naturally tends downward and seeks to rest there. But if a thing's desire is above its nature, that thing is not moved to that end naturally, but by something else, which is above its nature. Now it is evident that to enjoy eternal glory and to see God by his essence, although it is appropriate to a rational creature, is above its nature. Therefore, the rational creature is not moved to desire this by nature, but by God himself, *who makes us for this very thing*.

161. How this is accomplished he adds, saying, *who has given us the pledge of the Spirit*.

In regard to this it should be noted that God produces natural desires and supernatural desires in us: the natural, when he gives us a natural spirit suited to human nature:

naturae humanae. Gen. II, 7: *inspiravit in faciem eius, et cetera*. Supernaturalia vero dat quando infundit in nobis supernaturalem Spiritum, scilicet Spiritum Sanctum. Et ideo dicit **dedit nobis pignus Spiritus**, id est Spiritum Sanctum causantem in nobis certitudinem huius rei, qua desideramus impleri. Eph. I, 13: *signati estis Spiritu promissionis Sancto, et cetera*.

Dicit autem **pignus**, quia pignus debet tantum valere, quantum valet res pro qua ponitur. Sed in hoc differt a re pro qua ponitur, quia pleniori iure possidetur res, quando iam habetur, quam pignus, quia res possidetur ut quid suum, pignus vero servatur et tenetur quasi pro certitudine rei habendae. Ita est de Spiritu Sancto, quia Spiritus Sanctus tantum valet quantum gloria caelestis, sed differt in modo habendi, quia nunc habemus eum quasi ad certitudinem consequendi illam gloriam; in patria vero habebimus, ut rem iam nostram, et a nobis possessam. Tunc enim habebimus perfecte, modo imperfecte.

Sic ergo retardatur desiderium gratiae a desiderio naturae.

162. Sed numquid impeditur? Non, sed desiderium gratiae vincit. Et hoc est quod dicit **audentes igitur**, etc., quasi dicat: duo desideria sunt in sanctis: unum quo desiderant caelestem habitationem, aliud quo nolunt expoliari. Et si haec duo essent compossibilia, non essent contraria et unum non retardaretur ab alio. Sed Apostolus ostendit ea esse incompossibilia et quod oportet quod unum vincat alterum.

Unde circa hoc tria facit.

Primo enim ostendit incompossibilitatem dictorum desideriorum;

secundo interponit quamdam probationem, ibi **per fidem enim**, etc.;

tertio ostendit quod horum vincat, ibi **audemus autem**, et cetera.

163. Incompossibilitatem ostendit cum dicit **audentes igitur**, et cetera. Audere, proprie est immiscere se in pericula mortis, et non cedere propter timorem. Licet autem sancti naturaliter timeant mortem, tamen audent ad pericula mortis et non cedunt timore mortis. Prov. XXVIII, 1: *iustus quasi leo confidens*. Eccli. XLVIII, 13: *in diebus suis non pertimuit principem*. Et **scientes**, scilicet sumus hoc quod confirmat in nobis audaciam, ut pro Christo mori non timeamus, **quoniam dum sumus in hoc corpore mortali, peregrinamur**, id est elongamur, a Deo. Ps. CXIX, 5: *heu mihi, quia incolatus meus, et cetera*. Peregrinamur, inquam, quia sumus extra patriam nostram, qui Deus est, alias non diceremur peregrinari ab eo. Et hoc non est ex natura nostra, sed ex eius gratia.

God breathed into his nostrils the breath of life (Gen 2:7); but he gives the supernatural desires when he infuses in us the supernatural Spirit, i.e., the Holy Spirit. Therefore he says, **who has given us the pledge of the Spirit**, i.e., the Holy Spirit producing in us the certainty of this thing, with which we desire to be filled: *you were sealed with the Holy Spirit, which is the guarantee of our inheritance* (Eph 1:13).

He says, **pledge**, because a pledge has as much value as the thing for which it is given; but it differs from the thing for which it is given in this way, namely, that the thing is possessed with a fuller right, when it is already had, than the pledge is. For the thing is possessed as one's own, but the pledge is kept and held as though giving assurance that the thing will be possessed. So it is with the Holy Spirit: because the Holy Spirit has as much value as heavenly glory. But there is a difference in the way he is possessed, because now we have him as a surety of obtaining that glory; but in heaven we shall have him as something now possessed by us. For then we shall have him perfectly, but now imperfectly.

In this way, therefore, is grace's desire deferred by a natural desire.

162. But is it hindered? No, but grace's desire conquers. Hence, he says, **always having confidence, knowing that while we are in the body we are absent from the Lord**. As if to say: there are two desires in holy men, one by which they desire a heavenly dwelling, the other by which they do not wish to be despoiled. If these were compatible, they would not be contrary, and one would not be delayed by the other. But the Apostle shows that they are incompatible and that one must prevail over the other.

In regard to this he does three things:

first, he shows the incompatibility of these desires;

second, he enters a proof, at **for we walk by faith**;

third, he shows which of them conquers, at **but we are confident**.

163. He shows their incompatibility when he says, **always having confidence, knowing that while we are in the body we are absent from the Lord**. Properly speaking, to dare is to involve oneself in dangers of death and not to yield through fear. But although the saints naturally fear death, yet they dare to face the dangers of death and not yield because of a fear of death: *the righteous are bold as a lion* (Prov 28:1); *in his days he feared not the prince* (Sir 48:13). **Knowing**, namely, that he strengthens our boldness not to fear death for Christ, **that while we are in the body we are absent** i.e., far away from God: *woe to me because my stay has been prolonged* (Ps 120:5). We are absent inasmuch as we are outside our native land, which is God. Otherwise, we would not be described as away from him. And this is not from our nature, but from his grace.

164. Quod autem peregrinamur a Domino, probat cum dicit *per fidem enim ambulamus*, id est procedimus in vita ista per fidem, *et non per speciem*, id est non per perfectam visionem. Fidei enim verbum est sicut lucerna a qua illuminamur ad ambulandum in vita ista. Ps. CXVIII, 105: *lucerna pedibus meis verbum*, et cetera. In patria autem non erit huiusmodi lucerna, quia ipsa claritas Dei, id est ipse Deus, illuminabit illam. Et ideo tunc *per speciem*, id est per essentiam, videbimus eum.

Dicit autem *per fidem ambulamus*, quia fides est de non visis. *Est enim fides substantia sperandarum rerum, argumentum non apparentium*, Hebr. XI, 1 s. Quamdiu autem anima corpori mortali unitur, non videt Deum per essentiam. Ex. XXXIII, 20: *non videbit me homo*, et cetera. Unde inquantum assentimus, credendo his, quae non videmus, dicimur ambulare *per fidem et non per speciem*.

Sic ergo patet duorum desideriorum incompossibilitas, quia non possumus cum hoc corpore superindui caelestem habitationem: et probatio huius, quia *per fidem ambulamus*.

165. Sequitur consequenter victoria unius desiderii de duobus, scilicet desiderium gratiae, cum dicit *audemus*, et cetera. Et debet resumi *scientes* supra positum, quia littera suspensiva est, ut dicatur sic: *hoc*, inquam, *scientes, quia dum sumus in hoc corpore*, etc., *audemus et bonam voluntatem habemus*, et cetera.

Duo dicit, quorum unum importat repugnantiam, quam habet in volendo, quae fit per timorem mortis. Ubi enim est timor, non est audacia. Nam ex appetitu naturae surgit timor mortis, ex appetitu gratiae surgit audacia. Ideo dicit *audemus*.

Aliud importat imperfectionem animi in desiderando, quia nisi bene desideraretur, non vinceretur timor mortis, cum sit valde naturalis. Et ideo, non solum oportet audere, sed bonam voluntatem habere, id est cum gaudio velle. Licet enim, secundum Philosophum in actu fortitudinis non requiratur gaudium ad perfectionem virtutis, sicut in aliis virtutibus, sed solum non tristari, tamen quia fortitudo sanctorum perfectior est, non solum non tristantur in periculis mortis, sed etiam gaudent. Phil. I, 23: *habens desiderium dissolvi*, et cetera.

Sed quid audemus? *Magis peregrinari a corpore*, id est removeri a corpore, per corporis dissolutionem, quod est contra desiderium naturae, *et praesentes esse ad Dominum*, id est ambulare per speciem, quod est desiderium gratiae. Hoc desiderabat Psalmista XLI, 3, qui dicebat: *sitivit anima mea ad Deum*, et cetera.

166. Et nota, quod hic concludit eadem duo, quae proposuit in principio, supra secundo, scilicet quod *si terrestris domus nostra huius habitationis dissolvatur*,

164. That we are absent from the Lord is proved, when he says, *for we walk by faith*, i.e., we pass through this life in faith, *and not by sight*: because faith deals with things not seen. For the word of faith is as a lamp with which the road is lit in this life: *your word is a lamp to my feet, and a light for my steps* (Ps 119:105). But in heaven there will be no such lamp, because the radiance of God, i.e., God himself, has enlightened it (Rev 21:23). Therefore, we shall then see him *by sight*, i.e., in his essence.

But he says, *we walk by faith*, because faith is concerned with things unseen: *faith is the substance of things hoped for; the conviction of things not seen* (Heb 11:1). But as long as the soul is united to the body, it does not see God in his essence: *no man shall see me and live* (Exod 33:20). Hence, inasmuch as we assent by believing the things we do not see, we are said to walk *by faith and not by sight*.

Thus, therefore, the incompatibility of the two desires is plain, because we cannot, along with this body, be clothed over by the heavenly habitation, the proof of this being that *we walk by faith*.

165. He follows with the victory of the one desire, namely, of grace, when he says, *we are confident and have a good will to be absent rather from the body*. This should be read as follows: *knowing* what was said above, i.e., *that while we are in the body we are absent from the Lord, we are confident and have a good will to be absent rather from the body and to be present with the Lord*.

He says two things: one implies the repugnance he has in willing, a repugnance caused by the fear of death. For where there is no fear, there is no daring. For the fear of death springs from our nature's desire, but the daring of grace's desire. Therefore, he says, *we are confident*.

The other implies an imperfection of the soul in desiring, because unless we desired properly, the fear of death would not be overcome, since it is quite natural. Therefore, it is not only necessary to dare, but also to have a good will, i.e., to will gladly. For although, according to the Philosopher, in the act of courage, joy is not required for the perfection of the virtue as it is in the other virtues, but only not to be sad. Yet because the courage of the saints is more perfect, they are not only not sad at the dangers of death, but they rejoice: *my desire is to depart and be with Christ* (Phil 1:23).

But what do we dare? *To be absent rather from the body*, i.e., to be separated from the body by its dissolution, which is contrary to the desire of nature, *and to be present with the Lord*, i.e., to walk by sight, which is the desire of grace. He desired this who said: *my soul thirsts for God, for the living God* (Psalm 42:5).

166. Note that he concludes to the same two things he proposed at the beginning, namely, that *if our earthly house of this habitation be dissolved*, which is the same as

quod idem est, quod hic dicit *peregrinari a corpore*, et quod *habemus* habitationem *in caelis non manufactam*, et hoc quod idem est *praesentes esse ad Deum*.

167. Confutatur per haec verba error dicentium animas sanctorum decedentium non statim post mortem deduci ad visionem Dei et eius praesentiam, sed morari in quibusdam mansionibus usque ad diem iudicii. Nam frustra sancti auderent et desiderarent peregrinari a corpore, si separati a corpore non essent praesentes ad Deum.

Et ideo dicendum est quod sancti statim post mortem vident Deum per essentiam, et sunt in caelesti mansione. Sic ergo patet quod praemium, quod sancti expectant, est inaestimabile.

168. Sequitur de praeparatione ad praemium, quae fit per pugnam contra tentationes et per exercitium bonorum operum, et hoc est quod dicit *ideo contendimus*, et cetera. Praeparantur autem sancti ad hoc praemium tripliciter, scilicet

primo placendo Deo;

secundo proficiendo proximo, ibi *scientes autem timorem Dei*;

tertio abdicando a se carnales affectus, ibi *itaque nos*, et cetera.

169. Deo autem placent resistendo malis, et ideo dicit *ideo*, quia scilicet totum desiderium nostrum est quod simus praesentes Deo, *contendimus*, id est cum conatu nitimur, seu studemus cum pugna et lucta, contra tentationes diaboli, carnis et mundi. Lc. XIII, 24: *contendite intrare per angustam portam*, et cetera. *Placere illi*, scilicet Deo ad quem desideramus esse praesentes; et hoc *sive absentes, sive praesentes* illi sumus: quia nisi studeamus ei placere in vita ista dum sumus absentes, non poterimus ei placere, nec esse ei praesentes in alia vita. Sap. c. IV, 10: *placens Deo factus dilectus*, et cetera.

170. Consequenter cum dicit *omnes enim nos manifestari*, etc., subdit causam quare sancti contendunt placere Deo, quae quidem causa sumitur ex consideratione futuri iudicii, ubi nos omnes manifestari oportet.

Ponit autem Apostolus quinque conditiones futuri iudicii. Primo enim ponit ipsius universalitatem, quia nullus excipietur ab illo iudicio. Et ideo dicit *omnes nos*, id est omnes homines, bonos et malos, magnos et parvos. Rom. XIV, 10: *omnes stabimus ante tribunal Christi*. Apoc. XX, 12: *vidi mortuos pusillos et magnos stantes in conspectu agni*, et cetera.

171. Sed contra hoc obiicitur dupliciter. Primo quia videtur quod infideles non venient ad iudicium, nam *qui non credit iam iudicatus est*, ut dicitur Io. III, 18.

what he says here, namely, *to be away from the body*; and that *we have a building of God, a house not made with hands, eternal in heaven*, which is the same as being *present with the Lord*.

167. By these words is refuted the error of those who say that the souls of dead saints are not at once after death brought to the vision of God and into his presence, but they reside in mansions until the day of judgment. For the saints dared and desired in vain to be away from the body, if they would not be present to God when separated from the body.

Therefore, the answer is that the saints see the essence of God immediately after death and dwell in a heavenly mansion. Thus, therefore, it is plain that the reward which the saints await is inestimable.

168. He follows this with an account of the preparation for the reward which is accomplished by the struggle against temptations and by exercising good works, and this he says at *and therefore we labor*. But the saints are prepared for this reward in three ways.

First, by pleasing God;

second, by helping their neighbor, at *knowing therefore the fear of the Lord*;

third, by removing carnal affections from themselves, at *therefore, henceforth we know*.

169. They please God by resisting evil. Hence he says, *therefore*, namely, because our whole desire is to be present with God, *we labor* i.e., we make great effort, i.e., we strive and fight against the temptations of the devil, the flesh and the world: *strive to enter by the narrow gate* (Luke 13:24). *To please him*, namely, God, with whom we desire to be present, *whether absent or present*: because unless we strive to please him in this life, while we are absent, we shall not be able to please him or be present with him in the other life: *there was one who pleased God and was loved by him* (Wis 4:10).

170. Then when he says, *for we must all be manifested before the judgment seat of Christ*, he adds the cause for why the saints strive to please God. This cause is taken from a consideration of the future judgment, when we must all be manifested.

Here the Apostle mentions five marks of the future judgment. The first is its universality, because no one will be exempted from that judgment; hence he says, *we must all*, i.e., all men, good and bad, great and small. *So each of us shall give account of himself to God* (Rom 14:12); and *I saw the dead, great and small, standing before the throne, and books were opened* (Rev 20:12).

171. But there are two objections against this. First, because it does not seem that unbelievers will come to judgment, *for one who does not believe has already been judged* (John 3:18).

Secundo quia quidam erunt ibi ut iudices, Matth. XIX, 28: *sedebitis super sedes*, et cetera. Non ergo omnes erunt ante tribunal, ut iudicentur.

Responsio. Dicendum quod in iudicio duo erunt, scilicet prolatio sententiae, et discussio meritorum, et quantum ad hoc non omnes iudicabuntur, quia illi qui totaliter abrenuntiaverunt Satanae et pompis eius, et per omnia adhaeserunt Christo, non discutientur, quia iam dii sunt. Illi vero, qui in nullo adhaeserunt Christo, nec per fidem, nec per opera, similiter non indigent discussione, quia nihil habent cum Christo; sed illi qui cum Christo aliquid habent, scilicet fidem, et in aliquo recesserunt a Christo, scilicet per mala opera et prava desideria, discutientur de his quae contra Christum commiserunt. Unde quantum ad hoc, soli Christiani peccatores manifestabuntur ante tribunal Christi.

Item, erit in iudicio prolatio sententiae, et quantum ad hoc omnes manifestabuntur.

Sed de pueris non videtur, quia dicitur **ut referat unusquisque propria corporis prout gessit**; sed pueri nihil gesserunt in corpore, ergo, et cetera. Sed hoc solvit Glossa, quia non iudicabuntur pro his, quae ipsi gesserunt per se, sed de his *quae gesserunt per alios, dum per eos crediderunt vel non crediderunt, baptizati vel non baptizati fuerunt*. Vel damnabuntur pro peccato primi parentis.

172. Secundo vero ponit iudicii certitudinem. In iudicio hominum multi decipi possunt, dum quidam iudicantur mali, qui tamen sunt boni, et e converso. Et huius ratio est, quia non manifestantur corda, sed in illo iudicio perfectissima certitudo erit, quia erit ibi manifestatio cordium. Unde dicit **manifestari**. I Cor. IV, 5: *nolite ante tempus iudicare*, et cetera.

Tertio ponit iudicii necessitatem, quia nec per interpositam personam, nec per contumaciam poterit quis effugere iudicium illud. Unde dicit **oportet**, id est necessarium est. Iob XIX, 29: *scitote esse iudicium*. Eccle. ult.: *cuncta quae fiunt adducet Deus*, et cetera.

Quarto ponit iudicis auctoritatem. Unde dicit **ante tribunal Christi**, ut scilicet veniat ad iudicandum homines in eadem forma, in qua iudicatus est ab hominibus, ut existens in forma humana videatur a bonis et malis. Mali enim non possunt videre gloriam Dei. Io. V, 27: *potestatem dedit ei iudicium facere*, et cetera. Tribunal autem dicit iudiciariam potestatem, et sumptum est ab antiqua consuetudine Romanorum, qui elegerunt tres tribunos plebis, ad quorum officium pertinebat

Second, because some will be there as judges: *you who have followed me will also sit on twelve thrones, judging the twelve tribes of Israel* (Matt 19:28). Therefore, not all will be before the tribunal to be judged.

I answer that there are two things in a judgment, namely, a discussion of merits, and as to this not all will be judged, because those who have completely renounced Satan and all his pomps, and have clung to Christ in all things, will not be judged, because they are gods already. But those who did not adhere to Christ in any way, neither by faith nor works, will also not need discussion. But those who have something with Christ, namely, faith, and in something have withdrawn from him, namely by evil works and wicked desires, will be discussed as to the things they committed against Christ. Hence, as to this, only sinful Christians will be manifested before the judgment seat of Christ.

But sentence will also be pronounced during the judgment; and as to this, all will be manifested.

But it seems that children will be exempt, because he says, **that everyone may receive the proper things of the body, according as he has done, whether it be good or evil**. But children have done nothing in the body. This is answered by a Gloss: for they will not be judged for the things they did by themselves, but for the things *they did through others, when they believed or did not believe, were baptized or not baptized through them*. Or they will be condemned for the sin of their first parents.

172. Second, he mentions the certainty of the judgment. For in human judgment many can be deceived, when they are judged evil, whereas they are good; or good, whereas they are evil. The reason for this is that hearts are not manifest. But in that judgment there will be absolutely perfect certainty, because there will be a manifestation of hearts. Hence, he says, **be manifested**. *Therefore do not pronounce judgment before the time, before the Lord comes, who will bring to light the things now hidden in darkness and will disclose the purposes of the heart* (1 Cor 4:5).

Third, he tells why the judgment will be necessary, because no one shall be able to escape that judgment either by another's intercession or by contumacy. Hence he says, **we must**, that is, it is necessary. *That you may know that there is a judgment* (Job 19:29); *for God will bring every deed into judgment, with every secret thing, whether good or evil* (Eccl 12:14).

Fourth, he discloses the authority of the judge; hence, he says, **before the judgment seat of Christ**, who will come to judge men in the same form in which he was judged by men, so that appearing in human form, he may be seen by the good and by the evil; for the wicked cannot see the glory of God: *and has given him authority to execute judgment, because he is the Son of man* (John 5:27). A judgment seat can also be called a tribunal, which implies juridical power, and is taken from an ancient custom of the Romans,

diiudicare excessus consulum et senatorum, et loca istorum vocabantur tribunalia.

Quinto ponit iudicis aequitatem, quia secundum merita propria erunt praemia vel poenae. Unde dicit *ut referat unusquisque*, et cetera. Rom. II, 6: *reddet unicuique secundum opera sua*. Et dicit *corporis*, non solum pro his quae fecit motu corporis, sed pro his quae mente gessit, alias infideles non punirentur. Et ideo cum dicit *corporis*, intelligendum est, id est pro his quae gessit dum vixit in corpore.

who chose three tribunes of the people, whose function was to pass judgment on the excesses of consuls and senators. Their places were called tribunals.

Fifth, he speaks of the equity of the judge, because there will be rewards or punishments according to one's merits. Hence, he says, *so that everyone may receive the proper things of the body, according as he has done*: *he will render to each one according to his works* (Rom 2:5). He says, *of the body*, not only for things accomplished with bodily movement, but for those accomplished by the mind; otherwise, unbelievers would not be punished. Therefore, when he says, *of the body*, it is understood to mean things performed while he lived in the body.

Lecture 3

5:11Scientes ergo timorem Domini, hominibus suademus, Deo autem manifesti sumus. Spero autem et in conscientiis vestris manifestos nos esse. [n. 173]

5:12Non iterum commendamus nos vobis, sed occasionem damus vobis gloriandi pro nobis: ut habeatis ad eos qui in facie gloriantur, et non in corde. [n. 176]

5:13Sive enim mente excedimus Deo: sive sobrii sumus, vobis. [n. 178]

5:14Caritas enim Christi urget nos: aestimantes hoc, quoniam si unus pro omnibus mortuus est, ergo omnes mortui sunt: [n. 180]

5:15et pro omnibus mortuus est Christus: ut, et qui vivunt, jam non sibi vivant, sed ei qui pro ipsis mortuus est et resurrexit. [n. 185]

5:11Εἰδότες οὖν τὸν φόβον τοῦ κυρίου ἀνθρώπους πείθομεν, θεῷ δὲ πεφανερώμεθα· ἐλπίζω δὲ καὶ ἐν ταῖς συνειδήσεσιν ὑμῶν πεφανερῶσθαι.

5:12οὐ πάλιν ἑαυτοὺς συνιστάνομεν ὑμῖν ἀλλὰ ἀφορμὴν διδόντες ὑμῖν καυχήματος ὑπὲρ ἡμῶν, ἵνα ἔχητε πρὸς τοὺς ἐν προσώπῳ καυχωμένους καὶ μὴ ἐν καρδίᾳ.

5:13εἴτε γὰρ ἐξέστημεν, θεῷ· εἴτε σωφρονοῦμεν, ὑμῖν.

5:14ἡ γὰρ ἀγάπη τοῦ Χριστοῦ συνέχει ἡμᾶς, κρίναντας τοῦτο, ὅτι εἷς ὑπὲρ πάντων ἀπέθανεν, ἄρα οἱ πάντες ἀπέθανον·

5:15καὶ ὑπὲρ πάντων ἀπέθανεν, ἵνα οἱ ζῶντες μηκέτι ἑαυτοῖς ζῶσιν ἀλλὰ τῷ ὑπὲρ αὐτῶν ἀποθανόντι καὶ ἐγερθέντι.

5:11Knowing therefore the fear of the Lord, we use persuasion to men: but to God we are manifest. And I trust also that in your consciences we are manifest. [n. 173]

5:12We do not commend ourselves again to you, but we give you occasion to glory in our behalf: that you may have something to answer them who glory in face, and not in heart. [n. 176]

5:13For whether we be transported in mind, it is to God: or whether we be sober, it is for you. [n. 178]

5:14For the charity of Christ presses us: judging this, that if one died for all, then all were dead. [n. 180]

5:15And Christ died for all: that they also who live may now live not to themselves, but unto him who died for them and rose again. [n. 185]

---

173. Ostenso qualiter sancti se praeparant ad praemium aeternae gloriae placendo Deo, hic ostendit consequenter quomodo praeparant se ad hoc proficiendo proximo. Et

circa hoc duo facit.

Primo ostendit sollicitudinem suam, quam habet de salute proximorum;

secundo vero huius sollicitudinis causam assignat, ibi *caritas Christi*, et cetera.

Circa primum tria facit.

Primo ponit curam quam habet de salute proximorum persuadendo eis;

secundo excludit quamdam falsam suspicionem, ibi *non iterum nos*, etc.;

tertio ostendit quod etiam in modo docendi proximorum utilitatem intendat, ibi *sive enim mente*, et cetera.

Circa primum duo facit.

Primo, ponit studium suum de utilitate proximorum;

secundo, manifestat hoc, ibi *Deo autem*, et cetera.

174. Dicit ergo: dico quod *oportet nos manifestari ante tribunal*, etc., et haec consideratio inducit homines ad timendum iudicium.

Et ideo dicit *scientes ergo timorem Domini*, id est quam pure et caste timendus sit Dominus Iesus Christus, *suademus hominibus*, ut timeant et credant. Iob XXIII, 15: *considerans eum timore sollicitor*. Ier. X, 7:

173. Having shown how the saints prepare themselves for the reward of eternal glory by pleasing God, the Apostle now shows how they prepare themselves for this by helping their neighbor.

In regard to the first he does two things.

First, he shows his own solicitude for the salvation of his neighbor;

second, he assigns the cause of this solicitude, at *the charity of Christ*.

In regard to the first he does three things.

First, he mentions the care he has for the salvation of his neighbor by persuading them;

second, he excludes a certain false suspicion, at *we do not commend*;

third, he shows that he aims at profiting his neighbors also in the way he teaches, at *for whether we be transported*.

Concerning the first, he does two things.

First, he sets out his zeal for profiting his neighbors;

second, he manifests it, at *but to God*.

174. He says, therefore: I say that *we must all be manifested before the judgment seat of Christ*, and this consideration induces men to fear the judgment.

Hence, he says, therefore, *knowing therefore the fear of the Lord*, i.e., how purely and chastely the Lord Jesus should be feared, *we use persuasion to men* to fear and believe. *When I consider, I am in dread of him* (Job 23:15); *who*

quis non timebit te, o rex gentium? Is. VIII, v. 13: *Dominum exercituum, ipsum sanctificate*, et cetera.

175. Sed quia aliquis posset dicere quod non ex conscientia bona, sed ex commodo suo suadebat hominibus, et ideo manifestat hoc esse falsum duplici testimonio, scilicet Dei, unde dicit **Deo autem manifesti sumus**, quod scilicet ex timore Dei loquimur. Deus enim videt intentionem cordis nostri. Ier. c. XVII, 9: *pravum est cor hominis et inscrutabile, et quis cognoscet illud? Ego Dominus*, et cetera. Io. II, 25: *ipse sciebat*, et cetera.

Item testimonio conscientiarum ipsorum, unde dicit **spero autem in conscientiis vestris**, et cetera. Et vere spero, quia sic me exhibui ut vos scire possitis nos esse probatos, et firmiter hoc tenere etsi non confiteamini ore. Supra IV, 2: **commendantes nosmetipsos ad omnem conscientiam**, et cetera.

176. Consequenter, quia possent credere quod hoc dixerit Apostolus ad commendationem propriam, removet hanc suspicionem falsam dicens **non iterum nos commendamus vobis** id est non dicimus hoc ad commendationem nostram ut quasi iterum velimus nos commendare: supra enim, III, et etiam I Cor. III, aliqua dixerat ad commendationem suam. Et ideo dicit **iterum**. Infra X, 18: **non enim qui seipsum commendat**, et cetera.

Sed hoc dicimus propter utilitatem vestram, quasi dicat **damus vobis occasionem gloriandi**, id est materiam gloriandi. Pseudo-apostoli enim per elationem gloriabantur, dicentes se fuisse doctos ab apostolis, qui fuerunt a Domino, scilicet a Petro et Iacobo, qui erant columnae fidei, detrahentes in hoc Apostolo, quasi non fuerit cum Domino Iesu, et volentes eius doctrinam destruere. Ut ergo et Corinthii haberent in quo gloriarentur contra ipsos pseudo-apostolos, scilicet de gratia Apostolo data, ut eos et refellant et non seducantur ab eis, ideo dicit hoc. Unde subdit **ut habeatis ad eos**, id est contra eos, vel ad eos reprimendos, quid possitis dicere.

177. Ad eos, dico, **qui in facie gloriantur, et non in corde**.

Quod tripliciter exponitur sic: **in facie gloriantur**, id est exterioribus observantiis legalibus, quia ad litteram docebant servare legalia. **Et non in corde**, id est in virtute Christi, quae est in corde, quia in spiritualibus, sicut Apostolus, qui in virtute crucis Christi dicebat: *mihi autem absit gloriari*, et cetera.

Item **in facie gloriantur**, id est in conspectu hominum, sicut hypocritae faciunt, **et non in corde**, id est in testimonio conscientiae, sicut Apostolus. Unde dicit: **gloria nostra haec est**, et cetera.

would not fear you, O King of the nations (Jer 10:7); *but the Lord of hosts, him you shall regard as holy* (Isa 8:13).

175. But because someone could say that it is not from a good conscience, but for his own advantage that he persuades men, he shows that this is false by appealing to two testimonies, namely, of God, when he says, **but to God we are manifest**, i.e., that he is speaking from fear of God, for God sees the intention of our heart. *The heart is deceitful above all things, and desperately corrupt; who can understand it? I the Lord search the mind and try the heart* (Jer 17:9–10); *for he himself knew what was in man* (John 2:25).

And by the testimony of their consciences; hence he says, **I trust also that in your consciences we are manifest**. Truly I hope, because I have shown myself to you in such a way that you might know we are approved and might firmly hold this, even though you do not admit it by mouth: **commending ourselves to every man's conscience in the sight of God** (2 Cor 4:2)

176. Then because they might suppose that the Apostle said this to commend himself, he removes this false supposition, saying, **we do not commend ourselves to you again**, i.e., we are not saying this for our commendation, as though trying to commend ourselves again. For above he said certain things for his commendation: **for it is not he who commends himself who is approved, but he whom the Lord commends** (2 Cor 10:18).

But we say this for your benefit. As if to say, **but we give you occasion to glory in our behalf**, i.e., matter for glorifying. For the false apostles took glory in elation, saying that they were taught by the apostles, who were from the Lord, namely, by Peter and James, who were pillars of the faith, thus detracting from the Apostle, as though he had not been with the Lord Jesus, and wishing to destroy his teaching. Therefore, in order that the Corinthians, too, might have something in which to glory against those false apostles, namely, the grace given to the Apostle, so as to refute them and not be seduced by them, he said this. Hence, he continues, **that you may have something to answer them**, i.e., against them, or to those reprimanding, what you can speak.

177. To them, I say, **who glory in face, and not in heart**.

This can be explained in three ways. First, they **glory in face**, i.e., in the external observances of the law, because that is what they taught, **and not in heart**, i.e., in the virtue of Christ, which is in the heart, unlike the Apostle, who in virtue of the cross of Christ, said: *far be it from me to glory except in the cross of our Lord Jesus Christ* (Gal 6:14).

Likewise they **glory in face**, i.e., in the presence of men, as hypocrites do, **and not in heart**, i.e., in the testimony of conscience, as the Apostle says above: **for our glory is this: the testimony of our conscience** (2 Cor 1:12).

Vel *in facie gloriantur*, quia aliqua praetendebant exterius, quae tamen non ita sentiebant interius in corde, scilicet quod dicebant se doctos ab apostolis, et quod sequerentur eorum doctrinam, quam tamen nitebantur destruere.

Patet ergo qualiter Apostolus in docendo proximorum salutem procurabat.

178. Sequitur videre quomodo ipsorum salutem procurabat etiam in modo docendi. Unde dicit *sive enim mente*, etc., quod exponitur dupliciter.

Uno modo sic, ut Apostolus dicat se excedere, quando loquitur eis, commendando se sobrium esse; quando non loquitur de commendatione propria. Secundum hoc dicit: quocumque modo doceamus, vel est honor Dei vel utilitas proximi, quia si *excedimus mente*, id est commendamus nos, Deo, scilicet est, id est ad honorem Dei, vel de servando iudicio Dei: *sive sobrii sumus*, id est non alta dicamus de nobis, hoc est vobis, id est, ad utilitatem vestram.

179. Sed aliter, et est magis litteralis sensus. Dico quod *damus vobis occasionem gloriandi pro nobis*, quia nos, in omnibus quae facimus et etiam in modo faciendi, intendimus bonum vestrum.

Unde sciendum quod apostoli sunt medii inter Deum et populum. Deut. V, 5: *ego sequester et medius fui*, et cetera. Oportebat ergo quod haurirent a Deo quod effunderent populo. Et ideo necessarium erat quod quandoque elevarent se per contemplationem in Deum ad percipiendum caelestia, quandoque conformarent se populo ad tradendum quae a Deo perceperant, et hoc totum in eorum utilitatem cedebat. Et ideo dicit *sive enim excedimus mente*, id est elevamur ad hoc quod percipiamus dona gratiarum, et hoc ut Deo scilicet uniamur, quod fit per excessum rerum temporalium. Ps. CXV, 11: *ego dixi in excessu meo*. Dionysius: *est enim extasim faciens divinus amor*, et cetera. *Sive sobrii simus*, id est commensuremus nos vobis, tradendo divina praecepta, hoc est vobis, id est ad utilitatem vestram. Sobrietas enim idem est, quod commensuratio. *Bria* enim in Graeco idem est quod mensura. Haec sobrietas non opponitur ebrietati, quae est de vino, quae ad bella trahit in terra, sed opponitur ebrietati quae est a Spiritu Sancto, quae rapit hominem ad divina, de qua dicitur Cant. V, 1: *bibite, amici, et inebriamini, charissimi*. Nam illa scilicet sobrietas est propter utilitatem proximi, sed haec ebrietas est propter amorem Dei.

Huiusmodi autem descensus, signatus est per descensum angelorum per scalam quam vidit Iacob Gen. XXVIII, 12, et Io. I, 51: *videbitis caelum apertum*, et cetera.

Or they *glory in face*, because they pretend some things outwardly, which they do not feel in the heart, namely, that they claimed to have been instructed by the apostles and were following their doctrine, which on the contrary they were trying to destroy.

It is clear, therefore, how the Apostle procured the salvation of his neighbor by teaching.

178. Now we must see how he procured their salvation even in the way he taught. Hence he says, *for whether we be transported in mind, it is to God; or whether we be sober it is for you*. This is explained in two ways:

in one way so that the Apostle calls himself transported when he speaks to them by commending himself, and sober when he is not speaking of his own commendation. According to this he is saying: no matter how we teach, it is either for the honor of God or the benefit of his neighbor; for if *we be transported in mind*, i.e., commend ourselves, it is for God, i.e., for the honor of God or for observing God's judgment; if *we be sober*, i.e., not saying great things about ourselves, this is for you, i.e., for your profit.

179. But there is another and more literal sense. I say that *we give you occasion to glory in our behalf*, because in everything we do and even in the way we do it, we intend your good.

Hence it should be noted that the apostles were midway between God and the people: *while I stood between the Lord and you at that time* (Deut 5:5). Therefore, they were required to draw from God whatever they poured out upon the people. Hence it was necessary that sometimes they raised themselves to God by contemplation to obtain heavenly things, and sometimes conformed themselves to the people to deliver what they had received from God; and all this tended to their profit. Hence he says, *for whether we be transported in mind*, i.e., raised to the state of receiving gifts of graces, and this in order to be united to God, which is done by means of temporal things: *I said in my vision* (Ps 116:11); Dionysius: *divine love causes ecstasy*. *Or whether we be sober*, i.e., adapt ourselves to you by delivering God's precepts, it is for you, i.e., for your benefit. This sobriety is not opposed to inebriation in wine, which brings wars on earth, but to that inebriation which is from the Holy Spirit and draws men to divine things and about which it is said: *eat, O friends, and drink: drink deeply, O lovers!* (Song 5:1). For that sobriety is for the benefit of our neighbor, but the inebriation is for the love of God.

Such a descent was signified by the descent of the angels on the ladder which Jacob saw (Gen 28:12): *you will see heaven opened, and the angels of God ascending and descending upon the Son of man* (John 1:51).

180. Consequenter cum dicit *caritas autem Christi*, etc., subiungit Apostolus causam praemissae sollicitudinis, quae quidem est caritas Christi.

Circa hoc autem duo facit.

Primo ostendit se urgeri a caritate Christi ad procurandam salutem proximorum;

secundo ostendit unde provocetur caritas Christi in ipso, ibi *aestimantes hoc*, et cetera.

181. Dicit ergo: dico quod *sive excedimus Deo sive sobrii sumus vobis*, est ad utilitatem vestram. Et huius causa est quia *caritas Christi urget nos* ad hoc. Et dicit *urget*, quia urgere idem est quod stimulare; quasi dicat: caritas Christi, quasi stimulus, stimulat nos ad faciendum ea, quae caritas imperat, ut scilicet procuremus salutem proximorum. Hic est effectus caritatis. Rom. c. VIII, 14: *qui Spiritu Dei aguntur*, id est agitantur, et cetera. Cant. VIII, 6: *lampades eius, ut lampades ignis*, et cetera.

182. Unde autem proveniat iste stimulus caritatis, ostendit consequenter, subdens *aestimantes hoc, quoniam si unus*, etc., et

primo assignat rationem huius;

secundo exponit, ibi *et pro omnibus mortuus est*, et cetera.

183. Dicit ergo: dico quod omnia pro vobis facimus, quia urget nos caritas Christi, quia aestimamus, quod si unus, scilicet Christus, pro omnibus mortuus est, quod etiam nos ita vivamus, id est ad utilitatem vestram, quod etiam nobis mortui simus, id est nihil curemus de nobis, sed de Christo et de his quae Christi sunt. Et hoc est quod dicit *si unus*. Rom. V, 8: *commendat Deus suam caritatem in nobis*, et cetera. I Petr. c. II, 21: *Christus passus est pro nobis*, et cetera.

184. Quod ergo infertur *ergo omnes mortui sunt*, exponitur tribus modis. Primo ut dicatur *omnes mortui sunt*, morte peccati in Adam. Non enim esset necessarium quod Christus pro omnibus moreretur, nisi omnes mortui fuissent morte peccati in Adam. I Cor. XV, 22: *sicut in Adam omnes*, et cetera.

Secundo ut dicatur *omnes mortui sunt*, scilicet veteri vitae. Christus enim mortuus est ad delenda peccata, ergo omnes debent mori veteri vitae, scilicet peccati, et vivere vita iustitiae, Rom. VI, 10: *quod enim mortuus est peccato*, etc., *ita et vos aestimate vos mortuos esse*, et cetera.

Tertio, et magis litteraliter, *ergo mortui sunt omnes*, id est ita debet se quilibet reputare ac si esset mortuus sibi ipsi. Col. III, 3: *mortui estis*, et cetera.

185. Et hunc modum exponit consequenter cum dicit *et pro omnibus mortuus est Christus*, I Io. II: *mortuus est ut vivamus Christo*.

180. Then when he says, *for the charity of Christ*, the Apostle indicates the cause of his solicitude, namely, the love of Christ.

In regard to this he does two things.

First, he shows that he is pressed by the charity of Christ to procure the salvation of his neighbor;

second, he indicates the source from which the charity of Christ is kindled, *judging this*.

181. He says, therefore: I say that *whether we be transported in mind, it is to God; or whether we be sober, it is for you*, i.e., for your benefit. The reason for this is that *the charity of Christ presses us* to this. He says, *presses*, because it is the same as stimulates. As if to say: the love of God, as a goad, stimulates us to do what charity commands, namely, to procure the salvation of our neighbor. *Those who are led*, i.e., stirred, *by the Spirit of God are sons of God* (Rom 8:14); *its flashes are flashes of fire* (Song 8:6).

182. Then he indicates the cause of his solicitude, namely, the love of Christ, adding, *judging this, that if one died for all, then all were dead*.

First, he assigns the reason for this;

second, he explains it, at *and Christ died for all*.

183. He says, therefore: I say that we do all things for you, because the love of Christ controls us, because we are convinced that one, namely Christ, has died for all, that we ourselves should so live, i.e., for your benefit, that we are even dead to ourselves, i.e., we care nothing about ourselves, but about Christ and the things of Christ: *God shows his love for us* (Rom 5:8); *Christ also suffered for you, leaving you an example, that you should follow in his steps* (1 Pet 2:21).

184. What follows from this, namely, *then all were dead* is explained in three ways. First, as if to say that *all were dead* with the death of sin in Adam. For it would not have been necessary for Christ to suffer for all, if all were not dead with the death of Adam's sin: *for as in Adam all die, so also in Christ shall all be made alive* (1 Cor 15:22).

Second, as if to say: *all were dead*, namely, to the old life. For Christ died to remove sins; therefore, all should die to the old life, namely, of sin, and live the life of justice: *the death he died he died to sin, once for all, but the life he lives he lives to God. So you also must consider yourselves dead to sin and alive to God in Christ Jesus* (Rom 6:10–11).

Third, and more literally, *then all were dead*, i.e., each person should regard himself as though dead to himself: *you have died and your life is hid with Christ in God* (Col 3:3).

185. He explains this interpretation when he says, *and Christ died for all*: he died that we might live to Christ (1 John 4:9).

Unde subdit *ut et qui vivit*, scilicet vita naturali, *iam non sibi vivat*, id est non propter seipsum et propter bonum suum tantum, *sed ei qui pro ipsis mortuus est et resurrexit*, scilicet Christo, id est totam vitam suam ordinet ad servitium et honorem Christi. Gal. II, 20: *vivo ego, iam non ego*, et cetera. Eccli. XXIX, 20: *gratiam fideiussoris tui ne obliviscaris*, et cetera.

Et horum ratio est quia unusquisque operans sumit regulam operis sui a fine. Unde si Christus est finis vitae nostrae, vitam nostram debemus regulare non secundum voluntatem nostram, sed secundum voluntatem Christi. Sic enim et Christus dicebat Io. VI, v. 38: *descendi de caelo, non ut facerem voluntatem meam*, et cetera.

186. Nota autem quod duo dicit, scilicet quod mortuus est Christus et quod resurrexit pro nobis; ubi duo exiguntur a nobis. Quia enim mortuus est pro nobis et nos debemus mori nobis ipsis, id est pro ipso abnegare nos ipsos. Unde dicebat Lc. IX, 23: *qui vult venire post me, abneget semetipsum*, et cetera. Quod idem est ac si diceret: moriantur sibi ipsis.

Quia vero Christus resurrexit pro nobis, et nos debemus ita mori peccato et veteri vitae et nobis ipsis, quod tamen resurgamus ad novam vitam Christi. Rom. VI, 4: *quomodo Christus surrexit a mortuis per gloriam Patris, ita et nos in novitate*, et cetera. Et propter hoc Dominus non dixit solum: *abneget semetipsum et tollat crucem suam*, sed addidit *et sequatur me*, scilicet in novitate vitae, proficiendo in virtutibus. Ps. LXXXIII, 8: *ibunt de virtute in virtutem*, et cetera.

Hence he continues, *that they also who live*, namely, with a natural life, *may now live not to themselves*, i.e., solely for themselves and their own good, *but unto him who died for them and rose again*, namely, for Christ, i.e., he should direct his whole life to the service and honor of Christ. *It is no longer I who live, but Christ who lives in me* (Gal 2:20); *forget not the kindness of your surety, for he has given his life for you* (Sir 29:20).

The reason for these things is that everyone who acts takes the rule of his work from the end. Hence, if Christ is the end of our life, we should regulate our life not according to our will but according to Christ's will. For this is what Christ himself said: *for I have come down from heaven, not to do my own will, but the will of him who sent me* (John 6:38)

186. But note that he says two things, namely that Christ died and that he rose for us; wherein two things are required of us. For since he dies for us, we, too, should die to ourselves, i.e., deny ourselves for him: *if any man would come after me, let him deny himself and take up his cross daily and follow me* (Luke 9:23). This is the same as saying: let him die to himself.

But because Christ rose for us, we should so die to sin and to the old life and to ourselves that we might rise to the new life of Christ: *so that as Christ was raised from the dead by the glory of the Father, we too might walk in newness of life* (Rom 6:4). This is why the Lord not only said, *let him deny himself and take up his cross*, but added, *and follow me*, namely, in newness of life, by advancing in the virtues: *they shall go from virtue to virtue* (Ps 84:7).

Lecture 4

5:16Itaque nos ex hoc neminem novimus secundum carnem. [n. 187] Et si cognovimus secundum carnem Christum, sed nunc jam non novimus. [n. 189]

5:17Si qua ergo in Christo nova creatura, vetera transierunt: ecce facta sunt omnia nova. [n. 192]

5:16καὶ ὑπὲρ πάντων ἀπέθανεν, ἵνα οἱ ζῶντες μηκέτι ἑαυτοῖς ζῶσιν ἀλλὰ τῷ ὑπὲρ αὐτῶν ἀποθανόντι καὶ ἐγερθέντι.

5:17ὥστε εἴ τις ἐν Χριστῷ, καινὴ κτίσις· τὰ ἀρχαῖα παρῆλθεν, ἰδοὺ γέγονεν καινά.

5:16Therefore, henceforth we know no man according to the flesh. [n. 187] And if we have known Christ according to the flesh: but now we know him so no longer. [n. 189]

5:17If then any be in Christ a new creature, the old things are passed away. Behold all things are made new. [n. 192]

---

187. Posito quomodo sancti praeparant se ad susceptionem gloriae caelestis, placendo Deo et proficiendo proximo, hic consequenter ostendit quomodo praeparant se ad hoc idem, abdicando a se carnalem affectum.

Et circa hoc tria facit.

Primo ponit abdicationem carnalis affectus;

secundo excludit instantiam, ibi **et si cognovimus**, etc.;

tertio concludit intentum, ibi **si qua ergo in Christo**, et cetera.

188. Dicit ergo primo: ex quo ergo adeo certi sumus de gloria aeterna, ita quod **nos ex hoc neminem secundum carnem novimus**.

Ubi nota, quod **secundum carnem** est quaedam determinatio, et potest dupliciter exponi, secundum quod dupliciter constructio fieri potest.

Uno modo, ut **secundum carnem**, construatur cum hoc accusativo neminem, et sic exponit Glossa: **neminem secundum carnem**, id est carnaliter viventem, approbamus. Ex quo enim quilibet debet mori, non approbamus eum, qui carnaliter vivit. Et hoc modo accipitur caro Rom. VIII, 9: **vos autem in carne non estis**, et cetera. Alio modo: **neminem secundum carnem**, id est secundum carnales legis observantias viventem, **novimus**, id est approbamus. Et hoc modo accipitur caro Phil. III, 4: **qui confidunt in carne**, id est, in carnalibus legis observantiis, et cetera. Tertio: **neminem secundum carnem**, id est secundum carnis corruptionem, **novimus**, id est reputamus. Licet enim fideles adhuc carnem corruptibilem gerant, tamen in spe iam habent corpus incorruptibile. Unde non reputant se secundum quod modo carnem corruptibilem habent, sed secundum quod habituri sunt corpus incorruptibile. Hoc modo accipitur caro I Cor. XV, 50: **caro et sanguis regnum Dei non possidebunt**.

Alio modo potest construi, ut **secundum carnem**, construatur cum hoc verbo **novimus**. Et sic est sensus: dico quod ex quo non debemus nobis vivere, sed ei qui pro nobis mortuus est, **itaque nos ex hoc neminem secundum carnem novimus**, id est non sequimur in aliquo

187. Having indicated how the saints prepare themselves for receiving heavenly glory by pleasing God and helping their neighbor, the Apostle then shows how they prepare themselves for the same thing by giving up carnal affection.

In regard to this he does three things.

First, he mentions the putting off of carnal affection;

second, he excludes an objection, at **and if we have known**;

third, he concludes to what he intended, at **if then any be in Christ**.

188. He says, therefore: inasmuch as I am so certain of eternal glory, **henceforth we know no man according to the flesh**.

Here it should be noted that **according to the flesh** is a restriction and can be explained in two ways according to the possible connections that can be made.

In one way, so **according to the flesh** is connected with no one. In this case, a Gloss explains it thus: we regard, i.e., approve of **no man according to the flesh**, i.e., living carnally. This is the way 'flesh' is taken in Romans: **you are not in the flesh, you are in the Spirit** (Rom 8:9). In another way, **we regard**, i.e., approve of, **no man according to the flesh**, i.e., living according to the carnal observances of the law. This is the way 'flesh' is taken in Philippians: **who have confidence in the flesh** (Phil 3:4), i.e., the carnal observances of the law. In a third way, **we know**, i.e., consider, **no man according to the flesh**, i.e., according to the corruption of the flesh. For although the faithful still have corruptible flesh, yet in hope they already have an incorruptible body. Hence, they do not consider themselves from the point of view that they have corruptible flesh now, but that they shall have an incorruptible body. This is the way flesh is taken in 1 Corinthians: **flesh and blood shall not inherit the kingdom of God** (1 Cor 15:50).

But **according to the flesh** can be taken in another way, namely, as connected with the verb, **we know**. Then the sense is this: I say that inasmuch as we should not live for ourselves but for him who died for us, **therefore, henceforth we regard no one according to the flesh**, i.e., we do not

carnalem affectum, nec aliquem hoc modo reputamus. Et hoc modo accipitur illud Deut. XXXIII, 9: *qui dixerit patri suo et matri: nescio vos*, et cetera. Et sic **secundum carnem**, refertur ad cognoscentem; sed in prima expositione referebatur ad cognitum.

189. Quia vero aliquis posset dare instantiam de Christo, quod saltem cognovisset eum secundum carnem, ideo consequenter hoc removet dicens **quod si cognovimus**, et cetera.

Circa hoc sciendum est quod Manichaeus adducebat verba ista pro se in fulcimentum sui erroris. Ipse enim dicebat Christum non habuisse verum corpus, nec fuisse ex semine David natum. Et sic Augustinus dicit in libro *Contra Faustum*: si quis contra eum allegaret verbum Apostoli ad Rom. I, 3: *qui factus est ei ex semine David secundum carnem*, et illud I Tim. III, 16: *et manifeste magnum est pietatis sacramentum, quod manifestatum est in carne*, etc., et II Tim. II, 8: *memor esto dominum Iesum Christum resurrexisse a mortuis ex semine David*, etc., respondebat, quod Apostolus aliquando fuerat huius opinionis, scilicet quod fuisset ex semine David et quod verum corpus habuisset, sed postea hanc opinionem mutavit et correxit se hic. Unde dicebat **et si cognovimus secundum carnem Christum**, id est si fuerimus aliquando huius opinionis, quod Christus habuisset veram carnem, **sed nunc iam non novimus**, id est modo mutavimus illam opinionem et non credimus ita.

Quod quidem dupliciter improbat Augustinus. Primo quia de eo, quod falso putamus, nullus dicit novimus, sed opinamur. Cum ergo Apostolus utatur hic hoc verbo **cognovimus**, videtur quod non aliquando falso putaverit. Secundo quia supra Apostolus dicit **neminem novimus secundum carnem**. Si ergo verum esset quod dicit Manichaeus, Apostolus nullum cognosceret habere verum corpus, quod est falsum. Est ergo falsum quod Manichaeus dicit.

190. Et ideo aliter exponendum secundum veritatem, et dupliciter. Uno modo, ut sumatur hic caro pro corruptione carnis, I Cor. XV, 50: *caro et sanguis*, etc., et tunc est sensus: **et si cognovimus** aliquando **Christum secundum carnem**, id est habere eum carnem corruptibilem ante passionem, **sed nunc iam non novimus**, scilicet eum habere carnem incorruptibilem, quia Rom. VI, 9 dicitur: *Christus resurgens ex mortuis iam non moritur*, et cetera.

Alio modo secundum Glossam, ut **si aliquando secundum carnem Christum cognovimus**, referatur ad statum Pauli ante conversionem ad Christum; quod vero sequitur **sed nunc iam non novimus**, referatur ad statum eius post conversionem. Et sic est sensus: et ego et alii Iudaei infideles aliquando, id est ante conversionem meam, cognovimus Christum secundum carnem, id est

follow carnal affection in anyone or regard him in this light. This is the way Deuteronomy should be understood: *who said of his father and mother: I regard them not* (Deut 33:9). In this way, **according to the flesh** is referred to the knower, but in the first explanation to the object known.

189. But because someone might insist that he at least knew Christ according to the flesh, he excludes this, saying: **if we have known Christ according to the flesh: but now we know him so no longer**.

In regard to this it should be noted that Manicheus appealed to those words to support his error. For he said that Christ did not have a true body and was not born of the seed of David. This is the way Augustine puts it in the book, *Against Faustus*: if anyone alleged against him the words of the Apostle to the Romans, *who was descended from David according to the flesh* (Rom 1:3), and to Timothy, *great indeed, we confess, is the mystery of our religion, which was manifested in the flesh* (1 Tim 3:16); *remember Jesus Christ, risen from the dead, descended from David, as preached in my Gospel* (2 Tim 2:8), he answered that the Apostle was first of the opinion that he was of the seed of David and that he had a true body, but he changed that opinion later to correct himself; that is why he said, **and if we have known Christ according to the flesh**, that is, if we were of the opinion that Christ had true flesh, **but now we know him so no longer**, i.e., we have changed our opinion and no longer believe that.

But Augustine disproves this in two ways. First, because no one says *we knew*, but *we are of the opinion*, when speaking of something he falsely held. Therefore, when the Apostle uses the words, **have known**, it does not seem that he once held something false. Second, because the Apostle says, **we know no man according to the flesh**. Therefore, if what Manicheus says were true, the Apostle would have known no one to have a true body, which is false. Therefore what Manicheus says is false.

190. Consequently, it must be explained otherwise according to the truth, and this in two ways. In one way so that flesh is taken for the corruption of the flesh: *flesh and blood cannot inherit the kingdom of God, nor does the perishable inherit the imperishable* (1 Cor 15:50). Then the sense is this: **if we have** at one time **known Christ according to the flesh**, i.e., to have corruptible flesh before the passion, **we know him so no longer**, namely, that he has corruptible flesh, because it is said: *Christ being raised from the dead will never die again; death no longer has dominion over him* (Rom 6:9).

In another way according to a Gloss, so that the clause, **if we have known Christ according to the flesh**, is referred to Paul's condition before his conversion; then what follows, **we know him so no longer**, refers to his state after conversion. Then the sense is this: both I and other Jews once, i.e., before my conversion, knew Christ according to the flesh, i.e., according to what we thought of Christ in the

secundum quod carnaliter opinati sumus de Christo, scilicet eum esse tantum hominem et quod venit tantum ad carnales observantias legis; *sed iam*, id est postquam conversus sum, *non novimus*, id est haec opinio cessavit, immo credo quod sit verus Deus et quod non sit colendus per carnales observantias. Unde dicebat Gal. V, v. 2: *si circumcidimini, Christus nihil vobis proderit.*

191. Potest et aliter exponi, ut hoc quod dicit *et si cognovimus*, etc., dicat Apostolus in persona omnium apostolorum Christi; et sic videtur respondere ultimae expositioni huius, quod dicitur *neminem cognovimus.*

Unde sciendum est quod Augustinus, exponens illud Io. XVI, 7: *expedit vobis, ut ego vadam,* ubi ratio Domini ad hoc subditur: *si enim non abiero, Paracletus non veniet ad vos,* dicit, quod hoc ideo erat, quia discipuli carnaliter amantes Christum afficiebantur ad ipsum, sicut carnalis homo ad carnalem amicum, et sic non poterant elevari ad spiritualem dilectionem, quae etiam pro absente multa facit pati. Ut ergo radicaretur in eis affectus spiritualis, qui est a Spiritu Sancto, et cessaret carnalis, dixit eis Dominus: *pax vobis,* et cetera. Hoc ergo Apostolus, in persona omnium discipulorum, commemorans dixit *et si cognovimus,* id est si adhaesimus Christo aliquando, scilicet quando nobiscum erat praesentia corporali, *secundum carnem,* id est secundum carnalem affectum, *sed iam non novimus,* id est iam iste affectus cessavit a nobis per Spiritum Sanctum, qui datus est nobis.

192. Consequenter cum dicit *si qua igitur in Christo,* etc., ex praemissis concludit quemdam effectum esse consecutum, scilicet novitatis in mundo. Et ideo dicit *si qua igitur,* id est si aliqua, *in Christo,* id est in fide Christi, vel per Christum, *nova creatura* est facta. Gal. V, 6: *in Christo Iesu neque praeputium, neque circumcisio,* et cetera.

Ubi notandum quod innovatio per gratiam dicitur creatura. Creatio enim est motus ex nihilo ad esse. Est autem duplex esse, scilicet esse naturae et esse gratiae. Prima creatio facta fuit quando creaturae ex nihilo productae sunt a Deo in esse naturae, et tunc creatura erat nova, sed tamen per peccatum inveterata est. Thren. III, 4: *vetustam fecit pellem meam,* et cetera. Oportuit ergo esse novam creationem, per quam producerentur in esse gratiae, quae quidem creatio est ex nihilo, quia qui gratia carent, nihil sunt. I Cor. XIII, v. 2: *si noverim mysteria omnia,* etc., *caritatem autem non habeam,* et cetera. Iob XVIII, v. 15: *habitent in tabernaculo illius socii eius, qui non est,* id est peccati. Augustinus dicit: *peccatum enim nihil est, et nihili fiunt homines cum peccant.*

Et sic patet, quod infusio gratiae est quaedam creatio.

193. Si ergo aliqua creatura facta est nova per ipsum, *vetera transierunt* ei. Hoc quidem sumptum est

law. *But now,* i.e., after I was converted, *we know him so no longer,* i.e., this opinion ceased. Indeed I believe that he is true God and that he should not be worshipped with carnal observance. Hence, he said to the Galatians: *if you receive circumcision, Christ will be of no advantage to you* (Gal 5:2).

191. It can also be explained another way, so that the statement, *if we have known Christ according to the flesh,* is made by the Apostle in the person of all the apostles of Christ. In this way it seems to correspond to the last explanation of the statement, *we know no man.*

Hence it should be noted that when Augustine explains John: *it is to your advantage that I go away* (John 16:7), where the Lord's reason is given as being, *for if I do not go away, the Counselor will not come to you,* he says that this was because the disciples were attracted toward him as a man in the flesh to a friend in the flesh. As a result, they could not be raised to a spiritual love, which causes one to suffer many things even for a person who is absent. Therefore, in order to plant in them a spiritual affection, which is from the Holy Spirit, and root out the carnal one, the Lord said to them: *peace be with you* (John 20:21). Therefore, the Apostle in the person of all the disciples recalled this and said, *if we have known,* i.e., if we have clung to Christ at one time, namely, when he was present with us in his bodily presence, *according to the flesh,* i.e., with carnal love, *but now we know him so no longer,* i.e., that affection ceased in us by the Holy Spirit, who has been given to us.

192. Then when he says, Therefore *if then any be in Christ,* he concludes from the foregoing that a certain effect follows, namely, newness in the world. Hence he says, *if then any be in Christ,* i.e., in the faith of Christ, or through Christ, he is made *a new creature: for in Christ Jesus neither circumcision nor uncircumcision is of any avail, but faith working through love* (Gal 5:6).

Here it should be noted that renewal by grace is called a creature. For creation is a change from nothing to existence. But there are two kinds of existence, namely, of nature and of grace. The first creation was made when creatures were produced by God from nothing to exist in nature; and then the creature was new, but became old by sin: *he has made my flesh and my skin waste away* (Lam 3:4). Therefore, a new creation was required by which we would be produced to exist in grace. This, too, is a creation from nothing because those who lack grace are nothing: *and if I understand all mysteries and all knowledge, and if I have all faith, so as to remove mountains, but have not love, I am nothing* (1 Cor 13:2); *in his tent,* i.e., of sin, *dwells that which is none of his* (Job 18:15). Augustine says: *for sin is nothing, and men become nothing, when they sin.*

So it is clear that the infusion of grace is a creation.

193. If then any creature is made new through him, *the old things are passed away.* This of course was taken from

Lev. XXVI, 10, ubi dicitur: *novis supervenientibus vetera proiicietis.*

Ex quo sic argumentatur: si omnia nova facta sunt et secundum legem novis supervenientibus vetera sunt proiicienda, ergo si qua creatura est, **vetera transierunt** ei, id est transire debent ab eo. Vetera autem quae transire debent sunt legalia. Rom. VII, 6: *serviamus in novitate Spiritus, et non in vetustate litterae.* Item errores gentilium. Is. c. XXVI, 3: *vetus error abiit.* Item corruptiones peccati. Rom. VI, 6: *vetus homo noster,* et cetera.

Quibus quidem in nobis transeuntibus, virtutes contrariae his vitiis debent in nobis innovari. Apoc. XXI, 5: *et dixit qui sedebat in throno: ecce nova facio omnia.*

Leviticus, where it says: *and you shall clear out the old to make way for the new* (Lev 26:10).

From this he argues thus: if all things have been made new, and according to the law when new things come, the old things shall be cast away, then if there be any new creature, **the old things are passed away**, i.e., they should pass away from it. But the old things that should pass away are the legal observances: *so that we serve not under the old written code but in the new life of the Spirit* (Rom 7:6), and in the errors of the gentiles: *the old error is gone* (Isa 26:3); likewise the corruption of sin: *we know that our old self was crucified with him so that the sinful body might be destroyed, and we might no longer be enslaved to sin* (Rom 6:6).

When such things pass from us, the virtues contrary to these vices should be renewed: *and he who sat upon the throne said: behold, I make all things new* (Rev 21:5).

Lecture 5

5:18Omnia autem ex Deo, qui nos reconciliavit sibi per Christum: et dedit nobis ministerium reconciliationis, [n. 194]

5:19quoniam quidem Deus erat in Christo mundum reconcilians sibi, non reputans illis delicta ipsorum, et posuit in nobis verbum reconciliationis. [n. 198]

5:20Pro Christo ergo legatione fungimur, tamquam Deo exhortante per nos. Obsecramus pro Christo, reconciliamini Deo. [n. 199]

5:21Eum, qui non noverat peccatum, pro nobis peccatum fecit, ut nos efficeremur justitia Dei in ipso. [n. 201]

5:18τὰ δὲ πάντα ἐκ τοῦ θεοῦ τοῦ καταλλάξαντος ἡμᾶς ἑαυτῷ διὰ Χριστοῦ καὶ δόντος ἡμῖν τὴν διακονίαν τῆς καταλλαγῆς,

5:19ὡς ὅτι θεὸς ἦν ἐν Χριστῷ κόσμον καταλλάσσων ἑαυτῷ, μὴ λογιζόμενος αὐτοῖς τὰ παραπτώματα αὐτῶν καὶ θέμενος ἐν ἡμῖν τὸν λόγον τῆς καταλλαγῆς.

5:20Ὑπὲρ Χριστοῦ οὖν πρεσβεύομεν ὡς τοῦ θεοῦ παρακαλοῦντος δι' ἡμῶν· δεόμεθα ὑπὲρ Χριστοῦ, καταλλάγητε τῷ θεῷ.

5:21τὸν μὴ γνόντα ἁμαρτίαν ὑπὲρ ἡμῶν ἁμαρτίαν ἐποίησεν, ἵνα ἡμεῖς γενώμεθα δικαιοσύνη θεοῦ ἐν αὐτῷ.

5:18But all things are of God, who has reconciled us to himself by Christ and has given to us the ministry of reconciliation. [n. 194]

5:19For God indeed was in Christ, reconciling the world to himself, not imputing to them their sins. And he has placed in us the word of reconciliation. [n. 198]

5:20For Christ, therefore, we are ambassadors, God as it were exhorting by us; for Christ, we beseech you, be reconciled to God. [n. 199]

5:21Him, who knew no sin, he has made sin for us: that we might be made the justice of God in him. [n. 201]

---

194. Postquam Apostolus in superioribus tractavit de praemio sanctorum et de praeparatione ad susceptionem eius, hic consequenter agit de causa utriusque.

Et circa hoc tria facit, quia

primo, ostendit auctorem omnium praedictorum esse Deum;

secundo, commemorat beneficium a Christo collatum, ibi *qui reconciliavit*, etc.;

tertio, beneficii usum, ibi *pro Christo ergo legatione*, et cetera.

195. Dicit ergo: dixi quod intendimus salutem proximorum, et *vetera transierunt*, sed haec *omnia* sunt nobis *ex Deo* Patre, vel *ex Deo* auctore. Rom. XI, 36: *ex ipso, et in ipso, et per ipsum sunt omnia.* Iac. I, v. 17: *omne datum optimum*, et cetera.

196. Sequitur beneficium susceptum a Deo, ibi *qui reconciliavit*, etc., ubi

primo, ponit ipsum beneficium collatum;

secundo exponit, ibi *quoniam quidem Deus*, et cetera.

197. Commemorat autem duplex beneficium per Christum collatum: unum commune, aliud speciale.

Commune quidem toti mundo, scilicet reconciliationis ad Deum, et hoc est quod dicit: *qui*, scilicet Deus Pater, *reconciliavit*, id est pacificavit, *nos sibi*, et hoc *per Christum*, id est per incarnatum Verbum. Homines enim erant inimici Dei propter peccatum, Christus autem hanc inimicitiam abstulit de medio, satisfaciens pro peccato. Et fecit concordiam. Col. I, 20: *pacificans per sanguinem crucis eius, sive quae in terris, sive quae in*

194. After discussing the saints' reward and how they prepared themselves to receive it, the Apostle now treats of the cause of both.

And concerning this he does three things.

First, he shows that the author of all these things is God;

second, he recalls the benefit conferred by Christ, at *who has reconciled*;

third, the use of the benefit, at *for Christ, therefore, we are ambassadors*.

195. He says, therefore: I have said that we intend the salvation of our neighbor and that *the old things are passed away*; but *all* this is *of God* the Father, or *of God* as author. *For from him and through him and to him are all things* (Rom 11:36); *every good endowment and every perfect gift is from above* (Jas 1:17).

196. Then he mentions the benefits received from God, at *who has reconciled*:

first, he mentions the benefit received;

second, he explains it, at *for God indeed*.

197. He recalls two benefits conferred by Christ: one is common and the other is special.

Common to the whole world was reconciliation to God. And this is what he says: *God*, namely, God the Father, *who has reconciled us to himself*, i.e., made peace between us and God. And this is *by Christ*, i.e., by the incarnate Word. For men were enemies of God because of sin, but Christ removed this enmity from their midst, satisfying for sin and producing harmony: *whether on earth or in heaven, making peace by the blood of his cross* (Col 1:20). Therefore he says,

caelis, et cetera. Et ideo dicit **per Christum**. Rom. V, 10: *reconciliati sumus Deo per mortem*, et cetera.

Speciale autem beneficium est apostolis collatum, scilicet quod ipsi sint ministri huius reconciliationis. Unde dicit **et dedit nobis**, apostolis, vicariis Christi, **ministerium** huius **reconciliationis**. Supra III, 6: **ministros nos elegit**, et cetera. Ps. LXXI, 3: *suscipiant montes*, id est apostoli, *pacem populo*, scilicet a Domino.

198. Consequenter cum dicit **quoniam**, etc., exponit quae dixit: primo, primum; secundo, secundum, ibi **posuit in nobis**, et cetera.

Dicit ergo. Dico quod Deus reconciliavit nos sibi, hoc modo: inimicitiae enim inter Deum et hominem erant propter peccatum, ut dictum est, secundum illud Is. LIX, 2: *peccata vestra diviserunt*, et cetera. Destructo ergo peccato per mortem Christi, inimicitiae iam solutae sunt. Et hoc est quod dicit **quoniam quidem Deus erat in Christo**, per unitatem essentiae, Io. XIV, 10, 11: *ego in Patre, et Pater in me est*. Vel **Deus erat in Christo** per Christum **mundum sibi reconcilians**, Rom. c. V, 10: *reconciliati sumus Deo*, et cetera. Et hoc **non reputans illis delicta ipsorum**, id est non habens in memoria illorum delicta, tam actualia quam originalia, ad puniendum, pro quibus Christus plene satisfecit. Et secundum hoc dicitur nos reconciliasse sibi, inquantum non imputat delicta nostra nobis. Ps. XXXI, v. 2: *beatus vir cui non imputavit Dominus peccatum*.

Consequenter cum dicit **et posuit in nobis**, etc., exponit secundum, scilicet de beneficio apostolis collato. Quasi dicat: hoc modo dedit nobis ministerium reconciliationis, quia **posuit in nobis verbum reconciliationis**, id est dedit virtutem et inspiravit in cordibus nostris, ut annuntiemus mundo hanc reconciliationem esse factam per Christum. Et hoc faciendo inducimus homines, ut conforment se Christo per baptismum. Ier. I, 9: *ecce dedi verba mea*, et cetera.

199. Consequenter cum dicit **pro Christo ergo legatione**, etc., ostendit usum beneficii. Et primo quantum ad secundum beneficium collatum apostolis; secundo, quantum ad primum collatum omnibus, ibi **obsecramus pro Christo**, et cetera.

Dicit ergo: ex quo Deus posuit verbum reconciliationis, debemus eo uti. Et hoc est ergo quod **fungimur legatione pro Christo**, id est sumus legati Christi. Eph. VI, 20: *pro quo legatione fungimur in catena ista*, et cetera.

Et idoneitas ad hanc legationem est nobis ex virtute Dei, quae est in me. Et ideo dicit **tamquam Deo exhortante per nos**, quia Deus, qui in nobis loquitur, dat nobis idoneitatem ad hanc legationem. Matth. X, 20: *non vos*

by Christ: *we were reconciled to God by the death of his Son* (Rom 5:10).

But a special gift was conferred on the apostles, namely, that they are ministers of this reconciliation. Hence he says, **and has given to us**, the apostles and vicars of Christ, **the ministry of reconciliation**: *who has also made us fit ministers of the New Testament* (2 Cor 3:6); *let the mountains*, i.e., the apostles, *bear prosperity for the people* (Ps 72:3), namely, from the Lord.

198. Then when he says, **for**, he explains what he has said. First, the first thing; second, the second, at **he has placed in us**.

He says, therefore: I say that God reconciled us to himself in this way. For there were enmities between God and man on account of sin, as has been said: *but your iniquities have made a separation between you and your God* (Isa 59:2). Therefore, sin being destroyed by the death of Christ, the enmities were dissolved. And this is what he says: **for God indeed was in Christ** by oneness of essence: *I am in the Father and the Father in me* (John 14:11). Or **in Christ, reconciling the world to himself**, through Christ: *we were reconciled to God by the death of his Son* (Rom 5:10). This he did, **not imputing to them their sins**, i.e., not retaining in his memory their sins, actual or original, to punish them, for which Christ fully satisfies. According to this he is said to have reconciled us to himself, inasmuch as he does not impute our sins to us: *blessed is the man to whom the Lord imputes no iniquity* (Ps 32:2).

Then when he says, **and he has placed in us the word of reconciliation**, he explains the second thing, namely, the benefit conferred on the apostles. As if to say: he has given us the mystery of reconciliation in this way, namely, that **he has placed in us the word of reconciliation**, i.e., he has given the power and has inspired in our hearts to announce to the world that this reconciliation was made by Christ. By doing this we induce men to conform themselves to Christ by baptism: *behold, I have put my words in your mouth* (Jer 1:9).

199. Then when he says, **for Christ, therefore, we are ambassadors**, he indicates the use of the benefit. First, as to the second benefit conferred on the apostles; second, as to the first benefit conferred on all, at **for Christ, we beseech**.

He says, therefore: since God has established the word of reconciliation, we ought to use it. This is why **we are ambassadors for Christ**: *for which I am an ambassador in chains; that I may declare it boldly, as I ought to speak* (Eph 6:20).

Our fitness for this ambassadorship is from God's power, which is in me. Hence he says, **God as it were exhorting by us**, because God, who speaks in us, makes us fit for this ambassadorship: *for it is not you who speak, but the Spirit*

estis qui loquimini, et cetera. Infra XIII, v. 3: **an experimentum quaeritis eius, qui in me**, et cetera.

200. Consequenter cum dicit **obsecramus**, etc., subdit quantum ad usum primi beneficii. Et primo inducit ad usum; secundo ostendit unde adsit nobis facultas ad ipsum usum, ibi **eum qui non**, et cetera.

Dicit ergo: ex quo Deus fecit reconciliationem, et nos sumus legati Dei in hoc, **obsecramus**, et cetera. Blande alloquitur, cum posset imperare. II Tim. ult.: *argue, obsecra, increpa*, et cetera. Ad Philem. 8: *potestatem habens imperandi*, et cetera. **Obsecramus**, inquam, **pro Christo**, id est propter amorem Christi, **reconciliamini Deo**.

Videtur autem hoc esse contrarium ei quod dicit, quod Deus reconciliavit nos sibi. Si ergo ipse reconciliavit, quid necesse est ut nos reconciliemur? Iam enim reconciliati sumus.

Ad hoc dicendum quod Deus reconciliavit nos sibi, ut causa efficiens, scilicet ex parte sua, sed, ut sit nobis meritoria, oportet etiam quod fiat reconciliatio ex parte nostra. Et hoc quidem in Baptismo et in poenitentia, et tunc cessamus a peccatis.

201. Unde autem adsit nobis huiusmodi facultas reconciliandi Deo, ostendit ex hoc scilicet quod dedit nobis potestatem iuste vivendi, qua possumus abstinere a peccatis, et, hoc faciendo, reconciliamur Deo. Et ideo dicit **eum qui non**, et cetera. Quasi dicat: bene potestis reconciliari, quia Deus, scilicet Pater, **eum**, scilicet Christum, **qui non noverat peccatum**, I Petr. II, 22: *qui peccatum non fecit*, etc.; Io. VIII, 46: *quis ex vobis arguet me*, etc., **pro nobis fecit peccatum**. Quod tripliciter exponitur. Uno modo, quia consuetudo veteris legis est ut sacrificium pro peccato, peccatum nominetur. Os. c. IV, 8: *peccata populi mei comedent*, id est oblata pro peccato. Tunc est sensus **fecit peccatum**, id est hostiam, vel sacrificium pro peccato. Alio modo, quia peccatum aliquando sumitur pro similitudine peccati, vel pro poena peccati. Rom. VIII, 3: *misit Deus Filium suum in similitudinem peccati*, etc., id est de similitudine peccati damnavit peccatum. Et tunc est sensus **fecit peccatum**, id est fecit eum assumere carnem mortalem et passibilem. Tertio modo, quia aliquando dicitur hoc esse hoc vel illud, non quia sit, sed quia opinantur homines ita esse. Et tunc est sensus **fecit peccatum**, id est fecit eum reputari peccatorem. Is. LIII, 12: *cum iniquis reputatus est*.

202. Et hoc quidem fecit, **ut nos efficeremur iustitia**, id est ut nos, qui peccatores sumus, efficeremur non solum iusti, imo ipsa iustitia, id est iustificaremur a Deo; vel **iustitia**, quia non solum nos iustificavit, sed etiam voluit quod per nos alii iustificarentur. **Iustitia**, dico, **Dei**, non nostra. Et **in Christo**, id est per Christum.

of your Father speaking through you (Matt 10:20); **do you seek a proof of Christ who speaks in me?** (2 Cor 13:3)

200. Then when he says, **we beseech you**, he describes the use of the first benefit. First, he exhorts to its use; second, he shows the source of his power to reconcile to God, at **him, who knew no sin**.

He says, therefore: inasmuch as God has produced a reconciliation and we are ambassadors of God in this, **we beseech you, be reconciled to God**. He speaks gently, even though he could have commanded: *convince, rebuke, and exhort, be unfailing in patience and in teaching* (2 Tim 4:2); *accordingly, though I am bold enough in Christ to command you to do what is required, yet for love's sake I prefer to appeal to you* (Phlm 1:8–9). **We beseech you**, I say, **for Christ**, i.e., for the love of Christ, **be reconciled to God**.

But this seems contrary to his statement that God has reconciled us to himself. Therefore, if he reconciled us, what need is there to be reconciled? For we are already reconciled.

I answer that God reconciled us to himself as efficient cause, namely, on his part, but in order that it be meritorious for us, it is necessary that reconciliation be made on our part, namely, in baptism and in penance. And then we cease from sins.

201. Where we get the faculty to reconcile to God is indicated by the fact that he gave us the power to live justly and abstain from sins. By doing this we are reconciled to God. Hence he says, **him, who knew no sin, he has made sin for us**, as if to say: you can be reconciled to God because **him**, namely, Christ, **who knew no sin**: he committed no sin; *no guile was found on his lips* (1 Pet 2:22); *which of you convicts me of sin?* (John 8:46); **he**, namely, God the Father, **has made sin for us**. This can be explained in three ways. In one way because it was the custom of the old law to call a sacrifice for sin: *they feed on the sin of my people* (Hos 4:8), i.e., the offerings for sin. Then the sense is: **he has made sin**, i.e., the victim of sacrifice for sin. In another way, because sin is sometimes taken for the likeness of sin, or the punishment of sin: *God sending his own Son in the likeness of sinful flesh and for sin, he condemned sin in the flesh* (Rom 8:3). Then the sense is: **he has made sin**, i.e., made him assume mortal and suffering flesh. In a third way, because one thing is said to be this or that, not because it is so, but because man considers it such. Then the sense is: **he has made sin**, i.e., made him regarded a sinner: *he was numbered with the transgressors* (Isa 53:12).

202. He did this, **that we might be made the justice of God in him** i.e., that we, who are sinners, might be made not only just, but justice itself, i.e., that we might be justified by God. Or **justice**, because he not only justified us, but also willed that others be justified by us. **The justice**, I say, **of God**, not ours. And **in him**, i.e., through Christ.

Vel, aliter, ut ipse Christus dicatur iustitia. Et tunc est sensus *ut nos efficeremur iustitia*, id est ut inhaereremus Christo per amorem et fidem, quia Christus est ipsa iustitia. Dicit autem, *Dei*, ut excludat iustitiam hominis, quae est qua homo confidit de propriis meritis. Rom. X, 3: *ignorantes Dei iustitiam*, etc. *in ipso*, scilicet Christo, id est per Christum, quia ipse factus est nobis iustitia, I Cor. I, 30.

Or another way, that Christ himself be called justice. Then the sense is this: *that we might be made the justice of God*, i.e., cling to Christ by love and faith, because Christ is justice itself. But he says, *of God*, to exclude man's justice, by which a man trusts in his own merits: *for, being ignorant of the righteousness that comes from God, and seeking to establish their own, they did not submit to God's righteousness* (Rom 10:3). *In him*, namely, in Christ, i.e., by Christ, because he was made justice for us (1 Cor 1:30).

CHAPTER 6

Lecture 1

6:1Adjuvantes autem exhortamur ne in vacuum gratiam Dei recipiatis. [n. 203]

6:2Ait enim: *tempore accepto exaudivi te, et in die salutis adjuvi te.* Ecce nunc tempus acceptabile, ecce nunc dies salutis. [n. 205]

6:3Nemini dantes ullam offensionem, ut non vituperetur ministerium nostrum: [n. 209]

6:4sed in omnibus exhibeamus nosmetipsos sicut Dei ministros [n. 210] in multa patientia, in tribulationibus, in necessitatibus, in angustiis, [n. 211]

6:5in plagis, in carceribus, in seditionibus, in laboribus, in vigiliis, in jejuniis,

6:1Συνεργοῦντες δὲ καὶ παρακαλοῦμεν μὴ εἰς κενὸν τὴν χάριν τοῦ θεοῦ δέξασθαι ὑμᾶς·

6:2λέγει γάρ· καιρῷ δεκτῷ ἐπήκουσά σου καὶ ἐν ἡμέρᾳ σωτηρίας ἐβοήθησά σοι. ἰδοὺ νῦν καιρὸς εὐπρόσδεκτος, ἰδοὺ νῦν ἡμέρα σωτηρίας.

6:3Μηδεμίαν ἐν μηδενὶ διδόντες προσκοπήν, ἵνα μὴ μωμηθῇ ἡ διακονία,

6:4ἀλλ᾽ ἐν παντὶ συνιστάντες ἑαυτοὺς ὡς θεοῦ διάκονοι, ἐν ὑπομονῇ πολλῇ, ἐν θλίψεσιν, ἐν ἀνάγκαις, ἐν στενοχωρίαις,

6:5ἐν πληγαῖς, ἐν φυλακαῖς, ἐν ἀκαταστασίαις, ἐν κόποις, ἐν ἀγρυπνίαις, ἐν νηστείαις,

6:1And we helping do exhort you not to receive the grace of God in vain. [n. 203]

6:2For he says: *in an accepted time I have heard you and in the day of salvation I have helped you.* Behold, now is the acceptable time: behold, now is the day of salvation. [n. 205]

6:3Giving no offense to any man, that our ministry be not blamed. [n. 209]

6:4But in all things let us exhibit ourselves as the ministers of God, [n. 210] in much patience, in tribulation, in necessities, in distresses, [n. 211]

6:5In stripes, in prisons, in seditions, in labors, in watchings, in fastings,

---

203. Supra Apostolus commendavit ministerium apostolatus, hic consequenter ipsum ministerium, sibi commissum ad utilitatem subditorum, exequitur. Et circa hoc duo facit.

Primo hortatur eos in generali ad omnia, quae communiter sunt necessaria ad bonam vitam;

secundo hortatur eos de quodam speciali suffragio fiendo sanctis in Ierusalem, et hoc VIII cap., ibi **notum autem vobis facimus, fratres**, et cetera.

Circa primum autem duo facit.

Primo hortatur eos ad bona praesentia;

secundo commendat eos de bonis in praeterito factis, et hoc VII cap., ibi **has igitur habentes promissiones**, et cetera.

Circa primum tria facit.

Primo hortatur in generali, quod gratia Dei non utantur in vanum;

secundo ostendit gratiam Dei eis esse collatam, ibi **ait enim: tempore accepto**, etc.;

tertio docet eos in speciali modum utendi dicta gratia, ibi **nemini dantes ullam offensionem**, et cetera.

204. Dicit ergo primo: ex quo facultas adest nobis ad bene operandum, et haec est gratia Dei, nos autem ad hoc **pro Christo legatione fungimur**; ideo, **adiuvantes**, nos, scilicet praedicationibus, exemplis et exhortationibus.

203. Having commended the ministry of the apostleship, the Apostle now carries out the ministry entrusted to him for the benefit of his subjects. In regard to this he does two things.

First, he exhorts them in general to do all the things that are commonly necessary for a good life;

second, he urges them in particular to help the saints in Jerusalem, in chapter eight, at **now we make known unto you, brethren** (2 Cor 8:1).

In regard to the first he does two things.

First, he urges them to goods that are present;

second, he commends them for the good they have done in the past, in chapter seven, at **having therefore these promises** (2 Cor 7:1).

In regard to the first he does three things.

First, he admonishes them in general that the grace of God should not be used in vain;

second, he shows that the grace of God has been conferred on them, at **for he says: in an accepted time**;

third, he teaches them in particular how to use the grace mentioned, at **giving no offense to any man**.

204. He says, therefore: from the fact that we have the faculty to do good, and this by the grace of God, and **we are ambassadors for Christ** for this purpose, therefore, **helping** by preaching, by examples and by exhortations. *A brother*

Prov. XVIII, 19: *frater qui adiuvatur a fratre*, et cetera. Vel, **adiuvantes**, scilicet Deum. I Cor. III, 9: *adiutores Dei sumus*.

Sed contra Is. XL, 13: *quis adiuvit Spiritum Domini*, et cetera. Non ergo bene dicitur, adiuvantes Deum.

Responsio: quod iuvare Deum potest intelligi, vel ei vires ministrare ad aliquid agendum, et sic nullus iuvat Deum, nec iuvare potest; vel eius mandatum exequi, et sic sancti homines Deum iuvare dicuntur, exequendo eius mandata.

Nos, inquam, sic iuvantes, **hortamur vos**, Rom. XII, 8: *qui exhortatur*, et cetera. Hoc scilicet exhortamur, **ne in vacuum gratiam Dei recipiatis**, quasi dicat: ne receptio gratiae sit vobis inutilis et vacua, quod tunc contingit, quando ex perceptione gratiae quis non sentit fructum. Qui quidem duplex est, scilicet remissio peccatorum. Is. XXVII, 9: *hic est omnis fructus*, et cetera. Et ut homo iuste vivendo perveniat ad gloriam caelestem. Rom. c. VI, 21: *habetis fructum vestrum*. Quicumque ergo gratia percepta non utitur ad vitandum peccata, et consequendum vitam aeternam, hic gratiam Dei in vanum recipit. Phil. II, 16: *non in vacuum cucurri*, et cetera.

205. Et ne aliquis dubitaret de perceptione huius gratiae a Deo, ideo consequenter Apostolus probat eos iam recepisse gratiam hanc, vel paratam habere ad recipiendum, dicens **ait enim: tempore**, et cetera.

Et circa hoc duo facit.

Primo inducit auctoritatem Prophetae;

secundo inductam adaptat ad propositum, ibi **ecce nunc tempus**, et cetera.

206. Dicit ergo primo: dico quod paretis vos ad fructuose percipiendum gratiam, quae vobis est collata, vel parata. **Ait enim**, Dominus per Isaiam XLIX, 8: **tempore accepto**, et cetera.

Circa quod sciendum est quod Dominus dicitur facere nobis gratiam, vel exaudiendo nos in petitionibus nostris, vel iuvando in operationibus nostris; sed exaudit, ut percipiamus quod petimus. Iac. I, 5: *si quis indiget sapientia, postulet*, et cetera. Adiuvat, ut perficiamus quod operamur. Ps. XCIII, 17: *nisi quia Dominus adiuvit me*, et cetera. Et haec duplex est gratia, praeveniens scilicet et cooperans, vel subsequens, quae quidem necessaria est nobis ad obtinendum.

Et primo gratiam praevenientem quam optare debemus, ut simus accepti a Deo. Ps. XXXI, 6: *pro hac orabit ad te omnis sanctus*. Et quantum ad hoc dicit **in tempore accepto**, id est acceptionis et gratificationis; hoc enim tempore accepto fit, quod gratis fit. Rom. IV, 6: *beatitudinem hominis cui Deus accepto fert iustitiam*, et cetera. **Exaudivi te**, id est acceptavi te. Vel **tempore accepto**, id est in tempore gratiae. Et hoc modo gratia praeveniens

helped is like a strong city (Prov 18:19); or **helping**, namely, God: *we are God's helpers* (1 Cor 3:9).

But this seems contrary to Isaiah: *who has directed the Spirit of the Lord?* (Isa 40:13). Therefore it is not correct to say, helping God.

I answer that to help God can be taken to mean that a person gives God the power to do something. In this sense, no one helps God or can help him; or to mean that a person carries out his commandment. Then holy men are said to help God by carrying out his commands.

We, I say, so helping **exhort you**: *he who exhorts, in his exhortation* (Rom 12:8), **not to receive the grace of God in vain**. As if to say: let not the reception of grace be useless and vain for you, which it is when a person does not perceive the fruit of the grace he received. This fruit is twofold: the remission of sins. *And this will be the full fruit of the removal of his sin* (Isa 27:9); and that a man by living righteously attain to heavenly glory. *The return you get is sanctification* (Rom 6:22). Therefore, whoever does not use the grace he has received for avoiding sin and obtaining eternal life, receives the grace of God in vain: *I did not run in vain or labor in vain* (Phil 2:16).

205. But lest anyone doubt that he has received this grace from God, the Apostle proves that they have already received or are prepared to receive it, saying: **for he says**: *in an accepted time I have heard you*.

In regard to this he does two things.

First, he quotes the Prophet;

second, he adapts the quotation to his thesis, at **behold, now is the acceptable time**.

206. He says, therefore: I say that you should be prepared to receive this grace fruitfully, which has been conferred on you or prepared for you, **for** the Lord **says** as much in Isaiah: *in an accepted time I have heard you* (Isa 44:8).

In regard to this it should be noted that the Lord is said to make grace for us either by hearing us in our petitions or by helping us in our actions. But he hears that we might receive what we ask: *if any of you lacks wisdom, let him ask God, who gives to all men generously and without reproaching, and it will be given him* (Jas 1:5); *if the Lord had not been my help, my soul would soon have dwelt in the land of silence* (Ps 94:17). This grace is of two kinds: prevenient and cooperating, i.e., subsequent, which it is necessary for us to obtain.

First of all, prevenient grace, which we ought to desire in order to be accepted by God. *Therefore let every one who is godly offer prayer to you* (Ps 32:6). As to this he says, **in an accepted time**, i.e., for accepting and being put in the state of grace, for in that acceptable time that is done which is done gratuitously. *So also David pronounces a blessing upon the man to whom God reckons righteousness apart from works* (Rom 4:6). **I have heard you**, i.e., accepted you. Or **in**

dicitur illa, per quam liberamur a peccatis. Gratia vero subsequens dicitur per quam virtutes nobis ex perseverantia in bono conferuntur.

Secundo necessaria est nobis gratia cooperans; et hanc petebat Ps. XXII, 6: *et misericordia eius subsequatur me*, et cetera. Et quantum ad hoc dicit **in die salutis adiuvi te**. Tempus enim ante Christum non fuit dies, sed nox. Rom. XIII, 12: *nox praecessit*, et cetera. Sed tempus Christi dicitur dies, et non solum dies, sed **dies salutis**. Ante enim non erat salus, quia nullus ad finem salutis perveniebat, scilicet ad visionem Dei, sed modo, quando iam nata est salus in mundo, homines salutem sequuntur. Matth. I, 21: *vocabis nomen eius Iesum. Ipse enim salvum faciet populum*, et cetera. I Petr. IV: *operamini vestram salutem*. Et hoc fit auxilio gratiae cooperantis, qua per nostra opera pervenimus ad vitam aeternam. Phil. II, 13: *Deus est qui operatur*, et cetera.

207. Consequenter auctoritatem inductam adaptat ad propositum, dicens *ecce nunc*, etc., quasi dicat: haec quae dixit Dominus de tempore gratiae per Prophetam, implentur modo, quia **ecce nunc tempus acceptabile**, id est gratificationis, per quam exaudimur a Deo, quia iam *venit plenitudo temporis*, scilicet Incarnationis Christi, Gal. c. IV, 4. Et hoc quantum ad primam partem auctoritatis Ps. LXVIII, 14: *tempus beneplaciti Deus*. **Ecce nunc dies salutis**, in quo scilicet, adiuti gratia cooperante, possumus operari ad consequendum salutem aeternam. Io. IX, 4: *me oportet operari*, et cetera. Gal. VI, v. 10: *dum tempus habemus*, et cetera.

208. Consequenter cum dicit **nemini dantes**, etc., docet modum utendi gratia eis collata. Et

primo in generali, qualiter scilicet in vacuum non recipiatur;

secundo in speciali, ibi **in multa patientia**, et cetera.

209. Dicit ergo: sic utendum est gratia, **ut dantes nemini ullam offensionem**. Nam gratia ad duo datur, scilicet ad vitandum mala, et ad operandum bona.

Et ideo duo docet, ut scilicet vitemus mala, et quantum ad hoc dicit **nemini dantes**, et cetera.

Quod potest dupliciter exponi. Uno modo, ut referatur ad apostolos, quasi dicat: nos **adiuvantes vos exhortamur**; nos, dico, **nemini ullam dantes offensionem**, quia si per malam vitam aliquos offenderemus, vituperaretur ministerium nostrum, et contemneretur praedicatio nostra. Rom. II, 24: *nomen Dei per vos blasphematur*. Gregorius: *cuius vita despicitur, restat ut eius praedicatio contemnatur*. Unde publicus et famosus peccator cavere

an accepted time, i.e., in the time of grace; and in this way prevenient grace is the name given to the grace by which we are freed from sin, and subsequent grace that by which the virtues and perseverance in good are conferred on us.

Second, we need cooperating grace, such as David requested: *surely goodness and mercy shall follow me all the days of my life* (Ps 23:6). As to this he says, **and in the day of salvation I have helped you**, for the time before Christ was not day but night: *the night is far gone, the day is at hand* (Rom 13:12). But the time of Christ is called the day, and not only the day, but **the day of salvation**. For before there was not salvation, because no one reached the end of salvation, namely, the vision of God. But now, when salvation has been born in the world, men attain to salvation: *and you shall call his name Jesus, for he will save his people from their sins* (Matt 1:21); *work out your salvation* (Phil 2:12). And this is done by the help of cooperating grace, by which we arrive at eternal life through our works: *for God is at work in you, both to will and to work for his good pleasure* (Phil 2:13).

207. Then he adapts this text to his purpose, saying, **behold, now is the acceptable time**. As if to say: the things which the Lord says by the Prophet about the time of grace are now being fulfilled, because **behold, now is the acceptable time**, i.e., for being adorned with grace, through which we are heard by God, because *the fullness of time has already come*, namely, of the Incarnation of Christ (Gal 4:4); and this as to the first part of the quotation: *at an acceptable time, O God* (Ps 69:13). **Behold, now is the day of salvation**, in which, helped by cooperating grace, we can work for the attainment of eternal salvation: *we must work the works of him who sent me* (John 9:4); *as we have the opportunity, let us do good to all men* (Gal 6:10).

208. Then when he says, **giving no offense to any man**, he teaches them the way to use grace conferred on them;

first, in general, namely, that they not receive it in vain;

second, in particular, at **in much patience**.

209. He says, therefore: use grace in such a way **giving no offense to any man**. For grace is given for two things: to avoid evil and to do good.

Therefore, he teaches these two things, namely, that we avoid evil, in regard to which he says, **giving no offense to any man**.

This can be explained in two ways: in one way as referring to the apostles. As if to say: we **helping do exhort you**. We, I say, **giving no offense to any man**, because if we were to offend others by a wicked life, our ministry would be blamed and our preaching ridiculed: *the name of God is blasphemed among the gentiles because of you* (Rom 2:24); *if one's life is despised, it follows that his preaching is scorned* (Gregory). Hence, a public and notorious sinner should

debet sibi ne praedicet, alias peccat. Ps. XLIX, 16: *peccatori autem dixit Deus*, et cetera.

Alio modo, ut referatur ad subditos, quasi dicat *hortamur vos ne in vacuum*, etc.; vos, dico, *nemini dantes ullam*, etc.; id est, non facientes aliquid unde alii scandalizentur. I Cor. X, 32: *sine offensione estote*, et cetera. Rom. XIV, 13: *non ponatis offendiculum*, et cetera. Et ratio huius est *ut non vituperetur*, et cetera. Id est ita irreprehensibiliter vos habeatis, ut *ministerium nostrum*, id est apostolatus noster, *non vituperetur*. Quando enim subditi male se habent, vituperium est praelatis. I Petr. II, 12: *conversationem vestram inter gentes*, et cetera. Vel *ut non vituperetur* commune *ministerium*, quo ad vos et nos, qui sumus ministri Dei. Nos, dico, sumus ministri Dei ad exequendum voluntatem eius in nobis, et in aliis. Sed vos ad exequendum voluntatem eius in vobis tantum. Is. LXI, 6: *vos sacerdotes Domini vocabimini*, et cetera.

210. Consequenter cum dicit *sed in omnibus exhibeamus*, etc., docet eos modum utendi percepta gratia quantum ad bona operanda.

Dicit ergo: nemini demus ullam offensionem, sed exhibeamus nos, et vos, opere et sermone, in omnibus quae ad virtutes pertinent, tales, quales debent esse ministri Dei, ut scilicet conformemur nos Deo faciendo eius voluntatem. Eccli. X, 2: *secundum iudicem populi, sic et ministri eius*. I Cor. IV, v. 1: *sic nos existimet homo, ut ministros*, et cetera.

211. Consequenter cum dicit *in multa patientia*, etc., ostendit in speciali quomodo nos debemus exhibere sicut Dei ministros in usu gratiae collatae. Et hoc quantum ad tria.

Primo, quantum ad exteriorem operationem;

secundo quantum ad maiorem devotionem, ibi *os nostrum patet*, etc.;

tertio quantum ad infidelium vitationem, ibi *nolite iugum ducere*, et cetera.

Circa primum tria facit, secundum tria in quibus consistit operatio exterior.

Primo enim consistit in sufferentia malorum; et quantum ad hoc dicit *in multa patientia*, et cetera.

Secundo in operatione bonorum, et quantum ad hoc dicit *in castitate*, et cetera.

Tertio in mutua cooperatione bonorum ad mala, et quantum ad hoc dicit *per arma iustitiae*, et cetera.

212. Est ergo necessaria in malis sustinendis virtus patientiae. Unde dicit *in multa patientia*, et cetera. Ubi tria facit.

Primo inducit ad patientiam. Et hoc quia in Ps. XCI, 15 s. legitur: *bene patientes erunt, ut annuntient*. Et quantum ad hoc dicit *in multa patientia*. Prov. XIX, 11: *doctrina viri per patientiam noscitur*.

beware of preaching; otherwise, he would commit sin: *but to the wicked God says: what right have you to recite my statutes, or take my covenant on your lips?* (Ps 50:17).

In another way as referring to his subjects. As if to say: *we do exhort you not to receive the grace of God in vain*; you, I say, *giving no offense to any man*, i.e., not doing anything that would scandalize others: *give no offense to Jews or to Greeks or to the Church of God* (1 Cor 10:32); *decide never to put a stumbling block or hindrance in the way of a brother* (Rom 14:13). The reason for this is *that our ministry be not blamed*, i.e., our apostleship. For when subjects behave badly, the blame is put on the prelates: *maintain good conduct among the gentiles* (1 Pet 2:12). Or that the common *ministry* in regard to you and us, who are ministers of God, *be not blamed*. We, I say, are ministers of God to fulfill his will in you and in others, but you to fulfill it well in yourselves only: *you shall be called the priests of the Lord, men shall speak of you as the ministers of our God* (Isa 61:6).

210. Then when he says, *but in all things let us exhibit ourselves as the ministers of God*, he teaches them how to use the grace they received for doing good.

He says, therefore: let us give no offense to anyone, but we commend ourselves, both you and we, in work and word and in all things which pertain to the virtues, such ministers of God as we ought to be, i.e., let us conform ourselves to God by doing his will. *Like the magistrate of the people, so are his officials* (Sir 10:2); *this is how one should regard us, as servants of Christ and stewards of the mysteries of God* (1 Cor 4:1).

211. Then when he says, *in much patience*, he shows in particular how we should exhibit ourselves as ministers of God in using the grace conferred on us. And this as to three things:

first, as to outward actions;

second, as to greater devotion, at *our mouth is open*;

third, as to avoiding unbelievers, at *do not bear the yoke*.

In regard to the first he does three things in keeping with the three things in which external activity consists:

first, it consists in enduring evil, and concerning this he says, *in much patience*;

second, in doing good, at *in chastity*;

third, in mutual cooperation of good with bad, at *by the armor of justice*.

212. To endure evils the virtue of patience is necessary; hence, he says, *in much patience*. In regard to this he does three things.

First, he exhorts them to patience, because it is read: *they will be well off that they may proclaim* (Ps 91:15); And as to this he says *in much patience*. *The learning of a man is known by patience* (Prov 19:11); *by your endurance you will*

Lc. XXI, 19: *in patientia vestra possidebitis animas vestras*. Dicit *in multa*, id est propter multas tribulationes quae occurrunt.

213. Secundo ostendit materiam patientiae in generali, et hoc dupliciter, scilicet in superventione malorum; unde dicit *in tribulationibus*, Rom. XII, 12: *in tribulatione patientes*; Act. XIV, 12: *per multas tribulationes*, et cetera. Et in defectu necessariorum; unde dicit *in necessitatibus*, scilicet eorum quae sunt necessaria ad vitam. Ps. XXIV, 17: *de necessitatibus*, et cetera.

214. Tertio ostendit materiam patientiae in speciali. Et primo in his, quae pertinent ad tribulationes, quae sunt voluntariae, et hoc quantum ad tribulationes, quae pertinent ad animam, et sic dicit *in angustiis*, scilicet cordis, quando scilicet sic arctatur adversis, ut non pateat via evadendi. Hebr. c. XI, 37: *angustiati, afflicti*, et cetera. Item inquantum ad tribulationes, quae sunt in corpore, et sic dicit *in plagis*, scilicet illatis ab aliis, et *carceribus*, Act. XVI, 23: *cum multas plagas ei intulissent*, et cetera. Infra XI, 23: *in carceribus abundantius, in plagis supra modum*, et cetera. *In seditionibus*, scilicet totius populi commoti. Act. XIX, 40: *periclitamur argui seditionis hodiernae*, et cetera.

Secundo in his, quae pertinent ad necessitates. Necessitas autem aliquando est voluntaria. Et sic dicit *in laboribus*, propria manu operando apud Corinthios, quia avari erant, ne eos gravaret sumptibus; et apud Thessalonicenses, quia erant otiosi, ut daret exemplum exercitii. Act. XI: *ad ea quae mihi opus erant*, et cetera. *In vigiliis*, propter praedicationes. Infra XI, 27: *in vigiliis*. *In ieiuniis*, aliquando voluntariis aliquando involuntariis propter penuriam. I Cor. IX, 27: *castigo corpus meum*, et cetera.

215. Sed contra est quod dicitur Matth. c. XI, 30: *iugum meum suave est*. Hic vero dicitur *in tribulationibus multis*, et cetera. Non ergo suave, sed gravissimum.

Respondeo. Haec sunt in seipsis aspera, sed propter amorem et interiorem fervorem spiritus dulcorantur. Unde Augustinus: *omnia grandia et immania, facilia et prope nulla facit amor*.

gain your lives (Luke 21:19). He says, *in much*, on account of the many tribulations they meet.

213. Second, he shows the matter patience deals with in general, and this in two ways, namely in evils that come upon them, in regard to which he says, *in tribulation*: *patient in tribulation* (Rom 12:12); *by many tribulations we must enter the kingdom of God* (Acts 11:21); and in the lack of necessities; hence, he says, *in necessities*, namely, of things necessary for life: *bring me out of my distresses* (Ps 25:17).

214. Third, he shows in particular the material with which patience is concerned. First, with things that pertain to tribulations which are voluntary, and this as to the soul. Hence, he says, *in distresses*, namely of the heart, when we are so beset with tribulations that there is no way of escape: *destitute, afflicted, ill-treated* (Heb 11:37), and then as to the body; hence, he says, *in stripes* namely, inflicted by others, and *in prisons*: *and when they had inflicted many blows upon them, they threw them into prison* (Acts 16:23); *in prisons more frequently, in stripes above measure, in deaths often* (2 Cor 11:23). *In seditions* namely, of an entire people in an uproar: *for we are in danger of being charged with rioting today, there being no cause that we can give to justify this commotion* (Acts 19:40).

Second, in things that pertain to necessities. But necessity is sometimes voluntary, and so he says, *in labors*, by working with his own hands among the Corinthians, so as not to burden them with his support, because they were avaricious; and among the Thessalonians, to give them an example of work because they were idle: *you yourselves know that these hands ministered to my necessities, and to those who were with me* (Acts 20:34). *In watchings*, for the sake of preaching: *in many watchings* (2 Cor 11:27). *In fastings*, sometimes voluntary and sometimes involuntary because of need: *I pommel my body and subdue it* (1 Cor 9:27)

215. But this seems to be contrary to what is said: *my yoke is easy and my burden is light* (Matt 11:30), whereas he says here, *in much tribulation*. Therefore, it is not sweet but very distasteful.

I answer that these are hard in themselves, but they are made sweet by love and an inward fervor of spirit. Hence, Augustine says: *all huge and difficult tasks love makes easy and almost nothing.*

Lecture 2

6:6in castitate, in scientia, in longanimitate, in suavitate, in Spiritu Sancto, in caritate non ficta, [n. 216]

6:7in verbo veritatis, in virtute Dei, per arma justitiae a dextris et a sinistris, [n. 221]

6:8per gloriam, et ignobilitatem, per infamiam, et bonam famam: ut seductores, et veraces, [n. 223]

6:9sicut qui ignoti, et cogniti: quasi morientes, et ecce vivimus: ut castigati, et non mortificati: [n. 225]

6:10quasi tristes, semper autem gaudentes: sicut egentes, multos autem locupletantes: tamquam nihil habentes, et omnia possidentes.

6:6ἐν ἁγνότητι, ἐν γνώσει, ἐν μακροθυμίᾳ, ἐν χρηστότητι, ἐν πνεύματι ἁγίῳ, ἐν ἀγάπῃ ἀνυποκρίτῳ,

6:7ἐν λόγῳ ἀληθείας, ἐν δυνάμει θεοῦ· διὰ τῶν ὅπλων τῆς δικαιοσύνης τῶν δεξιῶν καὶ ἀριστερῶν,

6:8διὰ δόξης καὶ ἀτιμίας, διὰ δυσφημίας καὶ εὐφημίας· ὡς πλάνοι καὶ ἀληθεῖς,

6:9ὡς ἀγνοούμενοι καὶ ἐπιγινωσκόμενοι, ὡς ἀποθνῄσκοντες καὶ ἰδοὺ ζῶμεν, ὡς παιδευόμενοι καὶ μὴ θανατούμενοι,

6:10ὡς λυπούμενοι ἀεὶ δὲ χαίροντες, ὡς πτωχοὶ πολλοὺς δὲ πλουτίζοντες, ὡς μηδὲν ἔχοντες καὶ πάντα κατέχοντες.

6:6In chastity, in knowledge, in long-suffering, in sweetness, in the Holy Spirit, in charity unfeigned, [n. 216]

6:7In the word of truth, in the power of God: by the armor of justice on the right hand and on the left: [n. 221]

6:8By honor and dishonor: by evil report and good report: as deceivers and yet true: [n. 223]

6:9as unknown and yet known: as dying and behold we live: as chastised and not killed: [n. 225]

6:10As sorrowful, yet always rejoicing: as needy, yet enriching many: as having nothing and possessing all things.

---

216. Positis his quae pertinent ad tolerantiam malorum, ponit consequenter ea quae pertinent ad observantiam bonorum. Bonitas autem operis consistit in tribus: in perfectione virtutum, et hoc pertinet ad cor; in veritate locutionis, et hoc pertinet ad os; in virtute operis, et hoc pertinet ad opus.

Primo ergo ostendit Apostolus qualiter se habeant in his quae pertinent ad perfectionem virtutum, quae consistunt in corde;

secundo in his, quae ad virtutem oris, ibi *in verbo veritatis*;

tertio in his, quae pertinent ad perfectionem operis, ibi *in virtute Dei*.

217. Circa primum ponit quatuor virtutes: et primo virtutem castitatis, quae maximum locum tenet in virtute temperantiae, et quantum ad hoc dicit *in castitate*, scilicet mentis et corporis.

Ubi notandum est quod immediate post multos labores, vigilias et ieiunia, subdit de castitate, quia qui vult habere virtutem castitatis, necesse habet laboribus dari, vigiliis insistere, et macerari ieiuniis. I Cor. IX, v. 27: *castigo corpus meum, et in servitutem redigo*, et cetera. Hebr. XII, 14: *pacem sequimini*, et cetera.

Si autem quaeratur, quare non facit mentionem de aliis virtutibus, nisi solum de temperantia, dicendum est quod sic facit, sed implicite; quia hoc quod dicit: *in multa patientia, in tribulationibus*, etc., pertinet ad virtutem fortitudinis; hoc vero quod dicit: *per arma iustitiae*, pertinet ad virtutem iustitiae.

216. Having set down the things which pertain to enduring evils, he now mentions those which pertain to the observance of good. Now the goodness of a work consists in three things, namely, in the perfection of virtues, and this pertains to the heart; in speaking the truth, and this pertains to the mouth; and in the virtuous activity which pertains to a work.

First, therefore, the Apostle shows how they conduct themselves in matters pertaining to the perfection of the virtues, which consists in the heart;

second, in those which pertain to the virtue of the mouth, at *in the word of truth*;

third, in those which pertain to the perfection of a work, at *in the power of God*.

217. In regard to the first he sets down four virtues: first of all the virtue of chastity, which holds a prominent place in the virtue of temperance: in regard to this he says, *in chastity*, namely, of mind and body.

Here it should be noted that immediately after many labors, watches and fasts he mentions chastity, because a person who wills to have the virtue of chastity must be given to labors, continue in watchings, and be worn out with fasts. *But I pommel my body and subdue it, lest after preaching to others I myself should be disqualified* (1 Cor 9:27); *strive for peace with all men, and for the holiness without which no one will see the Lord* (Heb 12:14).

But if anyone should ask why he makes no mention of the other virtues, but only of temperance, the answer is that he does mention them implicitly, because when he says, *in much patience, in tribulation, in necessities, in distresses*, they pertain to the virtue of courage; when he says, *by the armor of justice*, there is reference to the virtue of justice.

218. Secundo ponit virtutem scientiae. Unde dicit *in scientia*. Et siquidem scientia referatur ad scientiam qua aliquis scit bene conversari in medio nationis pravae et perversae, sic refertur ad virtutem prudentiae. Si vero scientia referatur ad certitudinem, qua fideles certi sunt de his quae pertinent ad cognitionem Dei, sic pertinet ad virtutem fidei. Et utraque necessaria est Christianis, quia sine scientia, primo modo sive secundo modo accepta, homines de facili ruunt in peccatis. Is. V, 13: *propterea captivus ductus est populus meus, quia non habuit scientiam.* Ier. c. III, 15: *dabo vobis pastores iuxta cor meum.*

219. Tertio ponit virtutem spei. Unde dicit *in longanimitate*, quae pertinet ad perfectionem spei. Nihil autem aliud est longanimis, quam qui arduum aliquod ex spe, semper ac diu dilatum, patienter expectat, et hoc a Spiritu Sancto. Gal. V, 22: *fructus autem Spiritus, caritas*, etc., *longanimitas*, et cetera. Col. I, 11: *in omni patientia et longanimitate.*

220. Quarto ponit virtutem caritatis. Caritas autem duo habet, scilicet effectum exteriorem et interiorem. Sed in effectu exteriori habet suavitatem ad proximum. Non enim convenit quod aliquis non sit suavis ad eos quos diligit. Et ideo dicit *in suavitate*, id est dulci conversatione ad proximos, ut scilicet blandi simus. Prov. XII, 11: *qui suavis est, vivit in moderationibus*, et cetera. Eccli. VI, 5: *verbum dulce multiplicat amicos*, et cetera. Sed non in suavitate mundi, sed in ea quae causatur ex amore Dei, scilicet ex Spiritu Sancto, et ideo dicit *in Spiritu Sancto*, id est quam Spiritus Sanctus causat in nobis. Sap. c. XII, 1: *O quam bonus et suavis*, et cetera.

In effectu autem interiori habet veritatem absque fictione, ut scilicet non praetendat exterius contrarium eius quod habet interius. Et ideo dicit *in caritate non ficta*. I Io. c. III, 18: *non diligamus verbo neque lingua, sed*, et cetera. Col. III, 14: *super omnia caritatem habentes.* Et huius ratio est quia, ut dicitur Sap. I, 5: *Spiritus Sanctus disciplinae effugiet fictum.*

221. Consequenter ostendit quomodo se habeant in his, quae pertinent ad veritatem oris, ut scilicet sint veraces. Et ideo dicit *in verbo veritatis*, scilicet vera loquendo et praedicando.

222. Quomodo autem se habeant in perfectione operis, subdit, dicens *in virtute Dei*, id est non in operibus nostris confidamus, sed solum in virtute Dei, et non in propria. I Cor. IV, 20: *regnum Dei non est in sermone*, et cetera.

223. Consequenter cum dicit *per arma iustitiae*, etc., ostendit qualiter se habeant in operatione bonorum et malorum, inter bona et mala, prospera et adversa, et hoc pertinet ad virtutem iustitiae. Et primo ostendit hoc in generali; secundo exponit in speciali.

218. Second, he mentions the virtue of knowledge; therefore he says, *in knowledge*. If this is taken as referring to the knowledge by which a person knows how to behave well in the midst of a wicked and perverse nation, it pertains to the virtue of prudence. But if knowledge is taken as referring to the certitude with which the faithful are certain about the things which pertain to their knowledge of God, it pertains to the virtue of faith. Both are necessary for Christians, for without prudence and faith, men easily slip into sins: *therefore my people go into exile for want of knowledge* (Isa 5:13); *and I will give you shepherds after my own heart* (Jer 3:15).

219. Third, he mentions the virtue of hope when he says, *in longsuffering*, which pertains to the perfection of hope. For a longsuffering person is nothing less than a person who is always hopeful of obtaining a good that is difficult and waits patiently if it delay; and this is by the Holy Spirit. *But the fruit of the Spirit is love, joy, peace, patience, kindness, goodness, faithfulness, gentleness, self-control* (Gal 5:22–23); *for all endurance and patience with joy* (Col 1:11).

220. Fourth, he mentions charity, which has two effects, namely, one inward and one outward. In the outward effect it has sweetness toward one's neighbor: for it is unseemly for a person not to be sweet toward those he loves; therefore he says, *in sweetness*, in our behavior toward others, and gentle. *He who is sweet, lives in moderations* (Prov 12:11); *a pleasant voice multiplies friends, and a gracious tongue multiplies courtesies* (Sir 6:5). Not in the sweetness of the world, but in that which is caused by the love of God, i.e., by the Holy Spirit; hence he says, *in the Holy Spirit* i.e., which the Holy Spirit causes in us. *O how good and sweet is your Spirit, Lord, in all things* (Wis 12:1).

In the inward effect it has truth without pretense, i.e., that a person not pretend outwardly the contrary of what he has within; hence he says, *in charity unfeigned*: *let us not love in word or speech but in deed and in truth* (1 John 3:18); *and above all these put on love* (Col 3:14). The reason for this is because, as it is said: *for the Holy Spirit of discipline will flee from deceit* (Wis 1:5).

221. Then he shows how they should act in things which pertain to the truth of the mouth, namely, that they be truthful. Hence, he says, *in the word of truth*, namely, speaking and preaching what is true.

222. But how they should act in regard to the perfection of a work, he tells them when he says, *in the power of God*, i.e., in let us not put confidence in our own works, but only in the power of God: *for the kingdom of God does not consist in talk but in power* (1 Cor 4:20).

223. Then when he says, *by the armor of justice*, he shows how they should act in doing good and evil, among good and evil, in prosperity and adversity; and this pertains to the virtue of justice. First, he shows this in general; second, he explains it in particular.

Dicit ergo primo, quod exhibeamus nos sicut Dei ministros in multa patientia. Et quod plus est, *per arma iustitiae*. Ubi sciendum est quod iustitia ordinat et facit hominem tenere locum suum, *a dextris*, id est, in prosperis, ut scilicet non elevetur, *et a sinistris*, id est in adversis, ut scilicet non deiiciatur. Phil. IV, 12: *ubique et in omnibus*, etc., *scio abundare*, et cetera.

Consequenter hoc exponit per partes prosperorum et adversorum, dicens *per gloriam*, et cetera. Ubi sciendum est, quod in rebus temporalibus prosperitas vel adversitas in tribus consistit: in superbia vitae, in concupiscentia carnis, in concupiscentia oculorum, iuxta illud I Io. II, 16: *omne quod est in mundo, aut est concupiscentia carnis*, et cetera. Et haec prosequitur ordine suo, quia primo dicit quomodo se habeant in adversis et prosperis, quae pertinent ad superbiam vitae, dicens *per gloriam*, et cetera. Secundo quomodo se habeant in his quae pertinent ad concupiscentiam carnis, ibi *quasi morientes*, et cetera. Tertio quomodo se habeant in his quae pertinent ad concupiscentiam oculorum, ibi *sicut egentes*, et cetera.

224. Sunt autem duo, quae ad superbiam pertinent, scilicet sublimitas status et operum. Et ideo dicit *per gloriam*, id est per statum excellentiae, quasi dicat: exhibeamus nos Dei ministros, scilicet per Dei gloriam, id est in prosperitate. Is. XXIII, 9: *Dominus exercituum cogitavit*, et cetera. Et quod apostoli gloriosi appareant, patet Act. XIV, 10, quod Paulus et Barnabas credebantur esse dii. *Et ignobilitatem*, quae est in sinistris, quasi dicat: nec in gloria elevemur, nec, si contemptibiles sumus, deiiciamur. I Cor. I, 28: *ignobilia huius mundi elegit Deus*, et cetera.

Quantum ad famam operum dicit *per infamiam et bonam famam*. Ubi sciendum est, quod, sicut Gregorius dicit, *homo non debet ex se dare causam infamiae suae, sed potius debet procurare bonam famam*, iuxta illud Eccli. XLI, 15: *curam habe de bono nomine*, et hoc propter alios, quia oportet nos bonum testimonium habere ad eos, qui foris sunt, I Tim. III, 7. Si vero contingat aliquem incurrere in infamiam iniuste, non debet esse ita pusillanimis, ut propter hoc derelinquat iustitiam. Si vero sit in bona fama apud infideles, non debet tamen superbire, sed debet inter utrumque medio modo incedere.

Consequenter exponit ista duo quae posuit. Et primo quam infamiam habuerunt, et ostendit quod magnam, quia *ut seductores*, etc., quasi dicat: a quibusdam habemur *ut seductores*, a quibusdam vero habemur ut *veraces*. Nec mirum, quia etiam de Christo alii dixerunt quia bonus est, alii vero quod non, sed seducit turbas, ut dicitur Io. VII, v. 12. Secundo ostendit quomodo fuerunt

He says, therefore, first, that we should show ourselves as God's ministers in much patience, and what is more, *by the armor of justice*. Here it should be noted that justice ordains and makes a man keep his place *on the right hand*, i.e., in prosperity, namely, that he not be lifted up; *and on the left*, i.e., in adversity, namely, that he not be cast down. *In any and all circumstances I have learned the secret of facing plenty and hunger, abundance and want* (Phil 4:12).

Then he explains this by the two sides, prosperity and adversity, saying, *by honor and dishonor*. Here it should be noted that in temporal affairs prosperity and adversity consist in three things, namely, the pride of life, in the concupiscence of the flesh, and in the concupiscence of the eyes: *for all that is in the world, the lust of the flesh and the lust of the eyes and the pride of life, is not of the Father but is of the world* (1 John 2:16). He treats these in order. First, he shows how they should act in prosperity and adversity as pertaining to the pride of life, saying *by honor*; second, in things which pertain to the concupiscence of the flesh, at *as dying*; third, pertaining to the concupiscence of the eyes, at *as needy*.

224. Now there are two things which pertain to pride, namely, excellence of state and of works. Hence he says, *by honor*, i.e., by a condition of excellence. As if to say: let us show ourselves as God's ministers, namely, by the glory of God, that is, in prosperity. *The Lord of hosts has purposed it, to defile the pride of all glory* (Isa 23:9). That the apostles seemed glorious is shown in Acts, when Paul and Barnabas were taken as gods (Acts 14:10). *And dishonor*, which is on the left. As if to say: let us neither be lifted up by glory nor, if we are contemptible, be cast down. *God chose what is low and despised in the world, even things that are not, to bring to nothing things that are* (1 Cor 1:28).

As to reports about works, he says, *in evil report and good report*. Here it should be noted that, as Gregory says, *a man should not be the cause of his own bad reputation among those who are outside; rather he should try to acquire a good reputation*, as it is said: *better is the man who hides his folly than the man who hides his wisdom* (Sir 41:15), and this for the sake of others, because we need to have a good reputation among those who are outside (1 Tim 3:7). But if anyone happens to fall into bad repute unjustly, he should not be fainthearted or abandon holiness on that account. But if he has a good reputation among unbelievers, he should not be proud but take a middle path between the two.

Then he explains the two things he mentioned. First, the evil reputation they had and to what a degree. Hence he says, *as deceivers and yet true*. As if to say: some regard us *as deceivers* and some as *true*. But this is not strange, because even in the case of Christ some said that he was good, and some that he was not, but that he was deceiving the multitude, as it says in John (John 7:12). Second,

gloriosi et ignobiles, quia *sicut ignoti et cogniti*, id est approbati a bonis, et incogniti, id est despecti a malis. I Cor. IV, 13: *tamquam purgamenta*, et cetera.

225. Consequenter prosequitur ea quae pertinent ad concupiscentiam carnis. Et ponit tria quae concupiscit caro. Primo enim concupiscit longam vitam, et quantum ad hoc dicit *quasi morientes*, id est licet exponamur periculis mortis, infra XI, 23: *in mortibus frequenter*, etc., tamen *ecce vivimus*, virtute et fide. Et ideo Hab. II, 4: *iustus ex fide vivit*. Ps. CXVII, 17: *non moriar, sed vivam*, et cetera.

Secundo concupiscit incolumitatem et quietem. Et quantum ad hoc dicit *ut castigati et non mortificati*, quasi dicat: licet diversis flagellis castigemur a Domino, non tamen tradit nos morti. Ps. XI: *castigans castigavit me Dominus*, et cetera. II Tim. c. III, 12: *omnes qui pie volunt*, et cetera.

Tertio concupiscit gaudium et iucunditatem, et quantum ad hoc dicit *quasi tristes, semper autem gaudentes*; quia licet in exterioribus, et quae ad carnem sunt, patiamur tristitiam et amaritudinem, interius tamen continuum gaudium habemus, quod crescit in nobis ex consolationibus Spiritus Sancti, et spe remunerationis aeternae. Iac. I, 2: *omne gaudium existimate*, et cetera. Io. XVI, 20: *tristitia vestra vertetur in gaudium*, et cetera.

226. Consequenter prosequitur de his quae pertinent ad concupiscentiam oculorum.

Et circa hoc ponit duo, quorum unum est in comparatione ad alios; et secundum hoc, prosperum in divitiis est quod homo abundet, ita quod possit aliis ministrare de divitiis suis. Sinistrum autem in hoc est, quod homo sit ita pauper, quod oporteat eum ab aliis mendicare. Et ideo dicit quod, in his temporalibus, sumus *sicut egentes*, id est ab aliis accipientes; sed tamen quantum ad spiritualia sumus *multos locupletantes*. Et non dicit *omnes*, quia non sunt omnes locupletari parati. Prov. XIII, 7: *est quasi pauper, cum in multis divitiis sit*.

Secundum est in comparatione ad seipsos, et secundum hoc prosperum in divitiis est multa possidere, sinistrum autem, ut nihil penitus habeat. Et quantum ad hoc dicit, quod in exterioribus sunt *tamquam nihil habentes*, scilicet in temporalibus, quia omnia dimiserunt propter Christum. Matth. XVI: *si vis perfectus esse, vade, et vende omnia quae habes*, et cetera. Sed interius et in spiritualibus, *omnia possidentes*, scilicet per interiorem magnitudinem cordis. Et hoc ideo est quia ipsi vivebant non sibi, sed Christo, et ideo, omnia quae sunt Christi, reputabant ut sua. Unde cum Christo omnia sint subiecta, omnia possidebant, et omnia tendebant in eorum

he shows how they were noble and ignoble. Hence he says, *as unknown and yet known*, i.e., approved by the good, and unknown, i.e., despised by the evil. *We have become, and are now, as the refuse of the world, the offscouring of all things* (1 Cor 4:13).

225. Then he discusses the things which pertain to the concupiscence of the flesh and mentions three things which the flesh desires: first, it desires a long life; as to this he says, *as dying*, i.e., although we are exposed to the dangers of death: *in deaths often* (2 Cor 11:23), *and behold we live* in virtue and faith. Therefore: *but the righteous live by their faith* (Hab 2:4); *I shall not die, but I shall live* (Ps 118:17).

Second, it desires health and repose; as to this he says, *as chastised and not killed*. As if to say: although we are chastised with many stripes by the Lord, yet he has not delivered us over to death: *the Lord has chastened me sorely, but he has not given me over to death* (Ps 118:13); *indeed all who desire to live a godly life in Christ Jesus will be persecuted* (2 Tim 3:12).

Third, it desires joy and pleasantness; as to this he says, *as sorrowful, yet always rejoicing*. For although in outward things and things which pertain to the flesh, we suffer sadness and bitterness, yet inwardly we have continual joy, which grows in us by the consolations of the Holy Spirit and by the hope of an eternal reward: *count it all joy, my brethren, when you meet various trials* (Jas 1:2); *you will have pain, but your pain will turn into joy* (John 16:20).

226. Then he discusses the things which pertain to the concupiscence of the eyes,

and in regard to this he mentions two things. One of these is in relation to others, and according to this the right hand in riches consists in a man abounding, so that he can minister to others from his riches. But the left hand consists in a man's being so poor that he must beg from others. Hence he says that in these temporal things we are *as needy* i.e., receiving from others; but as to spiritual things, *yet enriching many*. He does not say, *all*, because not all are ready to be enriched: *another pretends to be poor, yet has great wealth* (Prov 13:7).

The second is in relation to themselves, and according to this, prosperity in riches is to possess many; but the left side is that he have absolutely nothing. In regard to this he says that in external things they are *as having nothing*, namely, in temporal things, because they have forsaken all things for Christ: *if you would be perfect, go, sell what you possess and give to the poor, and you will have treasure in heaven* (Matt 19:21). But inwardly and in spiritual things, *possessing all things*, namely, by an inner greatness of heart. And this is so because they lived not for themselves, but for Christ. Consequently, all that were Christ's they regarded as their own. Hence, since all things are subject to Christ, they

gloriam. Ios. I, 3: *et omnem locum quem calcaverit pes vester, vobis tradam.*

227. Nota autem circa praemissa, quod Apostolus utitur in praemissis miro modo loquendi. Nam ipse quasi semper ponit unum contra unum, et temporale contra spirituale; sed tamen in temporalibus semper addit quamdam conditionem, puta: **ut, sicut, quasi, tamquam**, sed in opposito spirituali, nihil addit. Cuius ratio est quia temporalia, sive sint mala, sive bona, sive transmutabilia et apparentia, habent tamen similitudinem vel boni vel mali. Et ideo dicit: **ut seductores, et quasi ignoti**, quia non erant in rei veritate sic, sed in opinione hominum, et si erant transitoria, erant bona aut mala. Bona autem spiritualia existentia sunt et vera, et ideo non addit eis conditionem aliquam.

possessed all things, and all things tended to their glory: *every place that the sole of your foot will tread upon I have given to you* (Jos 1:3).

227. Note in regard to the foregoing that the Apostle employs a remarkable manner of speaking. For he, as it were, always sets one thing against another, and temporal against spiritual. But yet in temporal things he always adds a condition, namely, **as** or **as though**, but in the opposite spiritual things he adds nothing. The reason for this is that temporal things, whether they be good or evil, are changeable and apparent, and they have only a likeness to good and evil. Hence he says, **as imposters and as unknown**, because they were not so in reality, but only in men's opinion. Consequently, they were transitory good or evils. But spiritual goods are existent and true; therefore, he adds no condition to them.

Lecture 3

6:11 Os nostrum patet ad vos, o Corinthii; cor nostrum dilatatum est. [n. 228]

6:12 Non angustiamini in nobis: angustiamini autem in visceribus vestris: [n. 231]

6:13eamdem autem habentes remunerationem, tamquam filiis dico, dilatamini et vos. [n. 232]

6:14 Nolite jugum ducere cum infidelibus. Quae enim participatio justitiae cum iniquitate? aut quae societas luci ad tenebras? [n. 233]

6:15quae autem conventio Christi ad Belial? aut quae pars fideli cum infideli? [n. 236]

6:16qui autem consensus templo Dei cum idolis? vos enim estis templum Dei vivi, sicut dicit Deus: *Quoniam inhabitabo in illis, et inambulabo inter eos, et ero illorum Deus, et ipsi erunt mihi populus.* [n. 238]

6:17 Propter quod *exite de medio eorum, et separamini, dicit Dominus, et immundum ne tetigeritis: et ego recipiam vos:* [n. 242]

6:18et *ero vobis in Patrem,* et vos eritis *mihi in filios* et filias, *dicit Dominus Omnipotens.* [n. 244]

6:11Τὸ στόμα ἡμῶν ἀνέῳγεν πρὸς ὑμᾶς, Κορίνθιοι, ἡ καρδία ἡμῶν πεπλάτυνται·

6:12οὐ στενοχωρεῖσθε ἐν ἡμῖν, στενοχωρεῖσθε δὲ ἐν τοῖς σπλάγχνοις ὑμῶν·

6:13τὴν δὲ αὐτὴν ἀντιμισθίαν, ὡς τέκνοις λέγω, πλατύνθητε καὶ ὑμεῖς.

6:14Μὴ γίνεσθε ἑτεροζυγοῦντες ἀπίστοις· τίς γὰρ μετοχὴ δικαιοσύνῃ καὶ ἀνομίᾳ, ἢ τίς κοινωνία φωτὶ πρὸς σκότος;

6:15τίς δὲ συμφώνησις Χριστοῦ πρὸς Βελιάρ, ἢ τίς μερὶς πιστῷ μετὰ ἀπίστου;

6:16τίς δὲ συγκατάθεσις ναῷ θεοῦ μετὰ εἰδώλων; ἡμεῖς γὰρ ναὸς θεοῦ ἐσμεν ζῶντος, καθὼς εἶπεν ὁ θεὸς ὅτι ἐνοικήσω ἐν αὐτοῖς καὶ ἐμπεριπατήσω καὶ ἔσομαι αὐτῶν θεὸς καὶ αὐτοὶ ἔσονταί μου λαός.

6:17διὸ ἐξέλθατε ἐκ μέσου αὐτῶν καὶ ἀφορίσθητε, λέγει κύριος, καὶ ἀκαθάρτου μὴ ἅπτεσθε· κἀγὼ εἰσδέξομαι ὑμᾶς

6:18καὶ ἔσομαι ὑμῖν εἰς πατέρα καὶ ὑμεῖς ἔσεσθέ μοι εἰς υἱοὺς καὶ θυγατέρας, λέγει κύριος παντοκράτωρ.

6:11 Our mouth is open to you, O Corinthians: our heart is enlarged. [n. 228]

6:12 You are not straitened in us: but in your own bowels you are straitened. [n. 231]

6:13 But having the same recompense (I speak as to my children): be you also enlarged. [n. 232]

6:14 Do not bear the yoke with unbelievers. For what participation does justice have with injustice? Or what fellowship does light have with darkness? [n. 233]

6:15 And what concord does Christ have with Belial? Or what part does the faithful have with with the unbeliever? [n. 236]

6:16 And what agreement does the temple of God have with idols? For you are the temple of the living God: as God says: *for I will dwell in them and walk among them. And I will be their God: and they shall be my people.* [n. 238]

6:17 Therefore: *go out from among them and be separate, says the Lord, and do not touch the unclean thing: and I will receive you.* [n. 242]

6:18 And *I will be a Father* to you: and you shall be *my sons* and daughters, *says the Lord Almighty.* [n. 244]

---

228. Postquam Apostolus docuerat usum gratiae collatae quantum ad bonas operationes exteriores, hic consequenter instruit eos circa usum praedictum quantum ad interiorem devotionem, quae consistit in laetitia cordis, quae latitudinem cordis causat.

Et circa hoc tria facit.

Primo enim exhibet se eis in exemplum latitudinis;

secundo ostendit, quod ab ipso non habent contrarium exemplum, nec possunt accipere, ibi *non angustiamini in nobis*, etc.;

tertio exhortatur eos ad cordis latitudinem, ibi *eamdem autem habentes*, et cetera.

Circa primum duo facit.

Primo ponit signum latitudinis cordis;

secundo ponit ipsam latitudinem cordis quam habebat apostolus, ibi *cor nostrum dilatatum est*, et cetera.

228. After teaching them the use of grace as to good outward actions, the Apostle now instructs them about this use in regard to internal devotion, which consists in joy of heart, which causes the heart to enlarge.

In regard to this he does three things.

First, he offers himself as an example of this enlargement;

second, he shows that they have no contrary example, nor could they have, at *you are not straitened in us*;

third, he exhorts them to enlarge their hearts, at *but having the same*.

In regard to the first he does two things:

first, he gives a sign of an expanded heart;

second, he mentions the expansion of heart he had, at *our heart is enlarged*.

229. Signum autem latitudinis est os latum, quia os immediate adhaeret cordi. Unde quae per os exprimimus, sunt expressa signa conceptionum cordis. Matth. XII, 34: *ex abundantia cordis os loquitur*. Et hoc est quod dicit *os nostrum patet ad vos*. Os enim clausum est aliquando, tunc scilicet quando ea quae sunt in corde non patent exterius; sed apertum et patens est, quando ea quae in corde sunt, manifestantur. Iob III, 1: *post haec aperuit*, et cetera. Matth. V, 2: *aperiens os suum*, et cetera.

Et ne hoc videatur pertinere ad vitium vanitatis, quia manifestat se, subdit rationem, dicens **ad vos**, id est propter utilitatem vestram manifestamus vobis secreta cordis nostri. I Cor. X, 33: *non quaerens quod mihi utile sit*, et cetera.

230. Causa autem huius dilatationis procedit ex dilatatione et latitudine cordis. Et ideo dicit **cor nostrum dilatatum est**, et cetera. Prov. XXI, 4: *exaltatio oculorum dilatatio est cordis*.

Cor autem aliquando est strictum, tunc scilicet quando comprimitur et concluditur in modico, sicut cum quis non curat nisi de terrenis, et contemnit caelestia, non valens ea intellectu capere. Aliquando autem est latum, tunc scilicet quando quis magna appetit et desiderat, et talis erat Apostolus, qui non reputans ea quae videntur, desiderabat caelestia. Et ideo dicit **cor nostrum dilatatum est**, id est ampliatum ad magna appetenda.

231. Consequenter ostendit quod non habent ab apostolo contrarium exemplum, dicens **non angustiamini**, etc., quasi dicat: ex quo ostendimus vobis latitudinem cordis nostri, non habetis a nobis exemplum, nec causam unde angustiamini. Sed si hoc facitis, tunc quidem angustiamini, sed non in nobis, imo ex visceribus vestris, id est ex vobis.

Ubi sciendum est quod angustiari idem est quod includi in aliquo, unde non patet alius aditus evadendi. Isti autem erant seducti adeo a pseudo, quod non credebant posse salutem consequi, nisi in observantiis legalibus. Et ideo efficiebantur servi, cum essent liberi secundum fidem Christi. Unde angustiatio huius servitutis non proveniebat eis ab Apostolo, sed ex visceribus eorum, id est ex duritia cordium ipsorum. Lc. XXIII, 28: *nolite flere*, et cetera.

232. Consequenter hortatur eos ad latitudinem cordis, dicens **eamdem autem habentes**, etc., quasi dicat: si aliquando decepti a pseudo angustiati estis, non omnino remaneatis in angustiatione, imo studeatis habere latum cor, sicut nos habemus, quia eamdem habebitis remunerationem quam nos habemus. Et ideo dicit **eamdem remunerationem habentes**, scilicet sicut et nos. Supra I, v. 7: *sicut estis socii passionum*, et cetera. *Tamquam filiis*, non inimicis, *dico* vobis, vel tamquam

229. Now the sign of an expanded heart is an open mouth, because it adheres immediately to the heart. Hence, the things we express by the mouth are express signs of the thoughts of the heart: *for out of the abundance of the heart the mouth speaks* (Matt 12:34). And this is what he says: *our mouth is open to you*. For the mouth is closed sometimes when the things in the heart are not outwardly apparent, but it is opened when the things in the heart are manifested: *after this Job opened his mouth* (Job 3:1); *and he opened his mouth and taught them* (Matt 5:2).

But that it might not seem to pertain to the vice of vanity that he manifest himself, he gives a reason, saying, *to you*, i.e., for your benefit we manifest to you the secrets of our heart. *Not seeking my own advantage, but that of many* (1 Cor 10:33).

230. The cause of this enlargement comes from enlarging and widening the heart. Hence he says, *our heart is enlarged*: *the raising of the eyes is the enlarging of the heart* (Prov 21:4).

But sometimes the heart is narrow, namely, when it is pressed together and confined in a small place, as when a person cares for nothing but earthly things and scorns the heavenly, not being able to grasp them with his mind. But sometimes it is wide, namely, when a person seeks and desires great things. Such was the case with the Apostle, who did not regard the things which are seen, but desired heavenly things. Hence he says, *our heart is enlarged*, i.e., expanded for desiring great things.

231. Then he shows that they have no contrary example from the Apostle, saying, *you are not straitened in us*. As if to say: from the fact that we show you the largeness of our heart, you do not have an example or a reason why you should be straitened. But if you do this, then indeed you are straitened, but not by us, but in your own affections, i.e., by yourselves.

Here it should be noted that to be straitened is the same as to be enclosed in something, from which no exit appears. But they have been deceived by a false apostle to such a degree that they did not believe salvation was possible without observing legal ceremonies. As a result, they became slaves, whereas they had been free according to the faith of Christ. Hence, the confinement of this slavery did not come to them from the Apostle, but from their bowels, i.e., from the hardness of their hearts. *Do not weep for me, but weep for yourselves and your children* (Luke 23:28).

232. Then he urges them to enlarge their hearts, saying, *but having the same recompense, be you also enlarged*. As if to say: if you had been deceived and straightened by a false apostle, then do not continue in that state, but try to have a large heart, as we have, because you love the same recompense as we. Therefore he says, *having the same recompense* as we: *as you are partakers of the sufferings, so shall you be also of the consolation* (2 Cor 1:7). *I speak as to my children*, and not to enemies, as to children of God;

filiis Dei; quasi dicat: *eamdem remunerationem habentes*, quam filii Dei, scilicet haeredes vitae aeternae. Rom. VIII, 17: *si filii, et haeredes*. *Eamdem*, inquam, *habentes remunerationem, dilatamini et vos*, id est habeatis cor magnum et liberum libertate Spiritus, quae est in fide Christi, et non coangustiamini in servitute observantiae legalis.

233. Consequenter cum dicit *nolite iugum ducere*, etc., docet eos usum collatae gratiae quantum ad infidelium vitationem.

Et circa hoc duo facit.

Primo ponitur apostoli exhortatio;

secundo exhortationis ratio, ibi *quae enim participatio*, etc.;

tertio rationem huius auctoritate confirmat, ibi *vos enim estis templum Dei*, et cetera.

234. Dicit ergo *nolite iugum ducere*, et cetera. Ubi est sciendum quod iugum dicitur omne illud quod ligat plures ad aliquid faciendum. Unde quia aliquando aliqui conveniunt ad faciendum aliquid boni quod est ex Deo, et aliqui ad faciendum aliquid mali quod est ex diabolo, ideo dicitur iugum Dei et iugum diaboli. Iugum quidem Dei est ipsa caritas, quae ligat hominem ad serviendum Deo. Matth. X: *tollite iugum meum*, et cetera. Iugum vero diaboli est ipsa iniquitas, quae ligat ad malum et ad male faciendum. Is. IX, 4: *iugum oneris eius*.

Hoc ergo dicit *nolite iugum ducere*, id est nolite communicare in operibus infidelitatis, *cum infidelibus*. Et hoc propter duo. Primo quia aliqui erant inter eos, qui reputabantur sapientiores, non abstinentes ab idolothitis, et ex hoc scandalizabant inferiores. Alii autem erant qui communicabant cum Iudaeis in traditionibus seniorum. Unde Apostolus hortatur eos, cum dicit *nolite*, etc., ut non communicent cum Iudaeis in traditionibus legis, neque cum gentibus in cultu idolorum. Utrique enim infideles sunt.

235. Rationem autem huius assignat, dicens *quae enim participatio*, et cetera. Quae sumitur ex distinctione duplici. Una distinctio est quantum ad causam, sed alia est quantum ad statum. Distinctio quantum ad causam duplex est, scilicet quantum ad causam habitualem, et quantum ad causam efficientem.

Causa autem habitualis est duplex: una quantum ad effectum, et hoc est quod dicit *quae enim participatio iustitiae*, etc.; quasi dicat: non debetis iugum ducere cum infidelibus, quia alius habitus est in vobis, alius in illis. In vobis quidem est habitus iustitiae, in illis vero est habitus iniquitatis. Maxima autem iustitia est reddere Deo quod suum est, et hoc est colere ipsum. Unde cum vos colatis Deum, est in vobis habitus iustitiae; summa autem iniquitas est auferre Deo quod suum est, et dare diabolo. Is. I, 13: *iniqui sunt coetus vestri*. Ier. XXIII, 28: *quid paleis ad triticum?*

as if to say: *having the same recompense*, which the sons of God have, namely, heirs of eternal life: *and if children, then heirs* (Rom 8:17). *Having the same recompense*, I say, *be you also enlarged*, i.e., have a large heart and free with the freedom of the Spirit, which is in the faith of Christ, and be not straightened in the slavery of legal observances.

233. Then when he says, *do not bear the yoke with unbelievers*, he teaches them the use of grace as to avoiding unbelievers.

In regard to this he does three things.

First, he exhorts them;

second, the reason for the exhortation, at *for what participation*;

third, he confirms this reason with an authority, at *for you are the temple*.

234. He says, therefore, *do not bear the yoke with unbelievers*. Here it should be noted that a yoke is anything which binds several to do something. Hence, because some come together sometimes to do something good, which is from God, and some to do something evil, which is from the devil, we speak of God's yoke and the devil's yoke. God's yoke is charity, which binds a man to serve God: *take my yoke upon you* (Matt 11:29). But the devil's yoke is for doing evil: *the yoke of his burden* (Isa 9:4).

Therefore he says this: *do not bear the yoke*, i.e., do not take part in works of unbelief, *with unbelievers*; and this for two reasons. First, because there were some among them who considered themselves wiser, not refraining from idolatry; as a result they scandalized the lowly. But there were others who took part with the Jews in the traditions of their elders. Hence, the Apostle exhorts them and says, *do not bear the yoke with unbelievers*, i.e., do not communicate with the Jews in the traditions of the law or with gentiles in the worship of idols, for both groups were unbelievers.

235. He gives the reason for this when he says, *for what partnership does justice have with injustice?* This is based on two distinctions: one regards the cause, and the other, the state. The distinction as to cause is twofold, namely, as to habitual and as to efficient cause.

The habitual cause is also twofold: one as to effect, and this is what he says: *for what partnership does justice have with injustice?* As if to say: you should not bear the yoke with unbelievers, because there is one habit in you and another in them. In you it is the habit of justice; in them it is the habit of iniquity. But the higher justice is to render to God what is his, and this is to worship him. Hence, since you worship God, the habit of justice is in you. But the greatest iniquity is to take from God what is his and give it to the devil. *I cannot endure iniquity and solemn assembly* (Isa 1:13); *what has straw in common with wheat* (Jer 23:28).

Alia causa habitualis est quantum ad intellectum, et haec distinctio est, quia fideles sunt illuminati lumine fidei sed infideles sunt in tenebris errorum. Et quantum ad hoc dicit *aut quae societas lucis ad tenebras?* Quasi dicat: non est conveniens quod eis communicetis, quia non est aliqua societas conveniens, quia vos estis lux per scientiam fidei. Eph. V, 8: *eratis aliquando tenebrae, nunc autem lux in Domino*, et cetera. Illi vero tenebrae sunt per ignorantiam. Prov. IV, 19: *via impiorum tenebrosa*, et cetera. Unde Dominus a principio divisit lucem a tenebris, ut dicitur Gen. c. I, 18.

236. Quantum vero ad causam efficientem dicit *quae autem conventio Christi ad Belial?* Quasi dicat: vos estis servi Christi, et membra eius, I Cor. XII, 27: *vos estis corpus Christi*, illi autem sunt membra Diaboli. Et dicitur diabolus Belial, absque iugo, quia noluit subiici iugo Dei. Ier. II, 20: *a saeculo fregisti*, et cetera.

Quod autem non possit esse conventio Christi ad Belial, patet ex verbis Christi, Io. XIV, 30: *venit princeps mundi huius*, etc., et etiam ex verbis diaboli, Matth. VIII, 29: *quid nobis, et tibi, Iesu*, et cetera.

237. Alia distinctio est quantum ad statum fidei, et hoc quantum ad duo, scilicet quantum ad statum fidei, et secundum hoc dicit *aut quae pars est fidelis*, etc.; quasi dicat: non eadem est pars utriusque, quia pars fidelis est ipse Deus, quem habet praemium, et ut finem suae beatitudinis. Ps. XV, 5: *Dominus pars haereditatis meae*, et cetera. Sed pars infidelis sunt bona terrena. Sap. II, 9: *haec est sors nostra*, et cetera. Matth. XXIV, 51: *dividet eum, et partem*, et cetera.

Item quantum ad statum gratiae, et secundum hoc dicit *quis autem consensus*, etc., quasi dicat: non est aliqua convenientia templo Dei et idolis. Unde vos estis templum Dei per gratiam, I Cor. III, 16: *templum Dei*, etc. et VI, 19: *nescitis quoniam membra vestra templum sunt*, etc., non debetis ergo communicare cum infidelibus qui sunt templa idolorum.

Sed notandum quod Dominus prohibet per Ezechielem, quod in templo Dei non colantur idola, Ez. XXVI. Multo ergo magis prohibentur homines, quorum animae sunt templum Dei, ne violent illa per participationem idolorum. I Cor. III, 17: *si quis templum Dei violaverit*, et cetera.

238. Consequenter cum dicit *vos enim estis*, etc., confirmat rationem propositam per auctoritatem. Et

circa hoc duo facit.

Primo enim confirmat quod induxit ratione admonitionis;

secundo vero confirmat ipsam admonitionem, ibi *propter quod exite*, et cetera.

The other habitual cause is in regard to the intellect; and this distinction is that the faithful are enlightened with the light of faith, but unbelievers are in the darkness of errors. As to this he says, *or what fellowship does light have with darkness?* As if to say: it is not right for you to communicate with them, because it is not a suitable fellowship, because you are light through knowledge of the faith: *for once you were darkness, but now you are light in the Lord* (Eph 5:8), but they are darkness through ignorance: *the way of the wicked is like deep darkness* (Prov 4:19). Hence, from the beginning the Lord separated the light from the darkness (Gen 1:18).

236. As to the efficient cause he says, *what concord does Christ have with Belial?* As if to say: you are the servants of Christ and his members: *now you are the body of Christ and individually members of it* (1 Cor 12:27), but they are members of the devil. The devil is called Belial, 'without a yoke,' because he refused to submit to God's yoke: *for long ago you broke your yoke and burst your bonds* (Jer 2:20).

That there cannot be concord between Christ and Belial is clear from Christ's words: *for the ruler of this world is coming; he has no power over me* (John 14:30), as well as from the devil's words: *what have you to do with us, O Son of God?* (Matt 8:29).

237. Another distinction regards the state of faith. In regard to this he says, *or what part does the faithful have with the unbeliever?* As if to say: there is not the same part on both sides, because the part of the believer is God, whom he has as a reward and as the end of his happiness: *the Lord is my chosen portion and my cup* (Ps 16:5). But the part of the unbeliever is earthly goods: *because this is our portion and this is our lot* (Wis 2:9); *and he will punish him and put him with the hypocrites* (Matt 24:51).

As to the state of grace he says, *what agreement does the temple of God have with idols?* As if to say: there is no agreement. Hence, you are a temple of God by grace: *do you not know that you are God's temple and that God's Spirit dwells in you?* (1 Cor 3:16). Therefore, you should not communicate with unbelievers, who are temples of idols.

But it should be noted that through Ezekiel, the Lord forbids idols to be worshipped in God's temple. Much more then are men forbidden, whose souls are God's temple, to violate them by partaking of idols. *If any one destroys God's temple, God will destroy him* (1 Cor 3:17).

238. Then when he says, *for you are the temple of the living God*, he strengthens his reason with an authority.

In regard to this he does two things.

First, he confirms what he had concluded by reason of an admonition;

second, he confirms the admonition itself, at *therefore: go out*.

Circa primum duo facit.

Primo resumit quod probare intendit;

secundo vero inducit auctoritatem ad propositum, ibi *sicut dicit Dominus*, et cetera.

239. Dicit ergo: recte dico quod non est consensus templo Dei cum idolis, id est non debetis cum eis participare, quia *vos estis templum Dei vivi*, et non mortui, sicut idololatrae.

240. Ad hoc probandum adducit auctoritatem, probans hoc ipsum per usum templi. Usus enim templi est ut Deus habitet in eo, nam templum est locus Dei ad inhabitandum sibi consecratus. Ps. X, 5: *Dominus in templo sancto suo*, et cetera. Quae quidem auctoritas sumitur ex Levit. XXVI, 12, quae talis est: *ponam tabernaculum meum in medio vestri*, et cetera. In qua auctoritate quatuor tangit, quantum ad hunc usum pertinet.

Primum, pertinet ad gratiam operationum quod est Deum esse in aliquo per gratiam. Et hoc est quod dicit *inhabitabo in eis*, scilicet in sanctis, per gratiam excolens eos. Licet autem Deus in omnibus rebus dicatur esse per praesentiam, potentiam et essentiam, non tamen dicitur in eis inhabitare, sed in solis sanctis per gratiam. Cuius ratio est quia Deus est in omnibus rebus per suam actionem, inquantum coniungit se eis, ut dans esse et conservans in esse. In sanctis autem est per ipsorum sanctorum operationem, qua attingunt ad Deum, et quodammodo comprehendunt ipsum, quae est diligere et cognoscere: nam diligens et cognoscens dicitur in se habere cognita et dilecta.

Secundum pertinet ad gratiam cooperantem, quo scilicet proficiunt sancti auxilio Dei, et quantum ad hoc dicit *inambulabo in eis*, id est promovebo eos de virtute in virtutem. Nam hic profectus sine gratia Dei esse non potest. I Cor. XV, 10: *gratia Dei sum id quod sum*: nam, sicut gratia operans facit nos esse aliquid in esse iustitiae, ita et gratia cooperans facit nos in ipso esse proficere.

Tertium pertinet ad Dei beneficium, et hoc vel protectionis per providentiam, et hoc tangit, dicens *ego ero illorum Deus*, id est providentia mea protegam eos. Ps. CXLIII, 15: *beatus populus, cuius Dominus*, et cetera. Vel beneficium remunerationis, ut sic dicatur *ero illorum Deus*, id est dabo eis meipsum in mercedem. Gen. XV, 1: *ego ero merces tua*, et cetera. Et Hebr. XI, 16: *non confunditur Deus eorum vocari Deus*.

Quartum pertinet ad debitum cultum et servitium sanctorum, et quantum ad hoc dicit *et ipsi erunt mihi in populum*, id est me colent et mihi obedient, ut mei et non alterius. Ps. XCIV, 7, IC, 3: *nos autem populus eius, et oves*, et cetera.

241. Vel possunt ad praesentiam corporalem referri, et tunc exponitur sic: *quoniam inhabitabo in illis* per carnis assumptionem, Io. I, 14: *Verbum caro factum est,*

In regard to the first he does two things.

First, he reviews what he intends to prove;

second, he quotes an authority to support his conclusion, at *as God says*.

239. He says, therefore: rightly do I say that there is no agreement between the temple of God and idols, i.e., you should not take part in them, because *you are the temple of the living God*, and not of a dead one, as idolaters are.

240. To prove this he cites an authority, proving this very point from the use to which a temple is put. For the use of a temple is that God dwell in it, because a temple is a place consecrated for God to dwell in: *the Lord is in his holy temple* (Ps 11:4). This authority is taken from Leviticus, which says: *and I will make my abode among you* (Lev 26:11). In this authority four things are touched as pertaining to this use.

The first pertains to operating grace, which consists in God's being in someone through grace; and this is what he says, *I will dwell in them*, namely, in the saints, adorning them with grace. For although God is said to be in all things by his presence, power, and essence, he is not said to dwell in them, but only in the saints through grace; the reason being that God is in all things by his activity, inasmuch as he joins himself to them as giving being and conserving it, but in the saints by their very activity, by which they attain to God and in a way comprehend him, which is to love and to know. For those who know and those who love have within themselves the thing known and loved.

The second pertains to cooperating grace, by which the saints make progress with God's help; as to this he says, *and walk among them*, i.e., I will promote them from virtue to virtue, for this progress is impossible without grace: *by the grace of God I am what I am* (1 Cor 15:10). For just as operating grace makes us to be something in the being of justice, so cooperating grace makes us progress in that being.

The third pertains to God's benefits: and this is either the benefit of his protection through providence—hence, he touches this when he says, *and I will be their God*, i.e., I will protect them by my providence: *happy the people whose God is the Lord* (Ps 144:15)—or the benefit of recompense. As if to say: *I will be their God*, i.e., I will give them myself as a reward: *your reward shall be very great* (Gen 15:1); *therefore God is not ashamed to be called their God* (Heb 11:16).

The fourth pertains to correct worship and service offered by the saints; as to this he says, *and they shall be my people*, i.e., they will worship me and obey me as mine and not another's. *We are the people of his pasture, the sheep of his hand* (Ps 95:4).

241. Or they could refer to bodily presence; then it is explained this way: *for I will dwell in them* by assuming flesh: *the Word became flesh and dwelt among us* (John 1:14), *and*

etc.; *et ambulabo inter illos*, corporaliter cum eis conversando, Bar. III, 38: *post haec in terris visus est*, etc.; *et ero illorum Deus* per gloriam, Deut. IV, 7: *non est alia natio tam grandis*, etc.; *et ipsi erunt mihi populus*, id est per fidem me colent.

242. Consequenter cum dicit *propter quod exite*, etc., confirmat ipsam admonitionem per aliam auctoritatem. Et

circa hoc duo facit.

Primo confirmat admonitionem per auctoritatem;

secundo ostendit praemium promissum servantibus monitionem, ibi *ego recipiam vos*, et cetera.

243. Dicit ergo *propter quod*, id est quia estis templum Dei, *exite de medio eorum*. Et sumitur de Is. LII, 11: *recedite, recedite inde, et pollutum nolite tangere*.

Ubi tria dicit: *exite*, *separamini*, *et immundum nolite tangere*, quia tripliciter debemus nos habere ad infideles. Primo ut exeamus ab eis, relinquendo peccata. Zach. II, 6: *O, O, fugite de terra Aquilonis*, et cetera. Sed Donatistae dicunt quod debemus corporaliter deserere malam societatem, quod non est verum. Unde quod Apostolus dicit, intelligendum est de separatione spirituali. Et ideo sic exponit: *exite*, spiritualiter, non sequendo vitam eorum. Cant. II, 2: *sicut lilium inter spinas*, et cetera. Et hoc ideo, ut vitemus ipsas peccatorum occasiones ab eis datas. Et ideo dicit *separamini*, id est longe ab eorum consensu sitis. Matth. X, 35: *veni enim separare*, et cetera. Num. XVI, 26: *recedite a tabernaculis hominum impiorum*, et cetera. Tertio ut arguamus eos cum male agunt. Et ideo dicit *immundum ne tetigeritis*, scilicet consentientes eis in malis. Rom. I, 32: *non solum qui faciunt ea, sed et qui consentiunt*, et cetera. Eph. V, 11: *nolite communicare operibus infructuosis*. Et hoc, quia *qui tangit picem*, etc., Eccli. XIII, 1.

244. Praemium autem repromissum servantibus monitionem, est duplex, scilicet divina familiaritas et divina adoptio. Divina familiaritas, quia *ego recipiam vos*, quasi dicat: secure exeatis, quia ego recipiam vos in meos. Ps. XXVI, 10: *quoniam pater meus et mater mea*, et cetera. Ps. LXIV, 5: *beatus quem elegisti*, et cetera. Is. XLII, 1: *ecce servus meus*, et cetera. Sed divina adoptio, quia adoptat nos in filios, quia dicit *et ero vobis in Patrem, et vos eritis mihi in filios*, Rom. VIII, v. 15: *non accepistis*, et cetera. Et dicit *filios* quantum ad perfectos, et *filias* quantum ad imperfectos, et hoc sumitur ex II Reg. VII, v. 14, ubi dicitur de Salomone: *ego ero ei in patrem*, et cetera.

walk among them bodily by living with them: *afterward she appeared upon earth and lived among men* (Bar 3:37), **and I will be their God** by glory: *for what great nation is there that has a god so near to it as the Lord our God is to us* (Deut 4:7). **And they shall be my people**, i.e., they will worship me in faith.

242. Then when he says, **therefore: go out from among them**, he confirms this admonition with another authority.

In regard to this he does two things.

First, he confirms the admonition by an authority;

second, he indicates the reward promised to those who heed the admonition, at **I will receive you**.

243. He says, therefore, i.e., because you are temples of God, **go out from among them**: *depart, depart, go out from there! Touch no unclean thing; go out from the midst of it* (Isa 52:11).

Here he says three things: **go out**, **be separate**, **and do not touch the unclean thing**, because there are three ways we should behave toward unbelievers. First, we should go out from them by abstaining from sins. *Ho! ho! Flee from the land of the north* (Zech 2:6). But the Donatists say that we must depart bodily from an evil society. But this is not true. Hence, the Apostle's words must be understood of a spiritual separation and are explained in this way: **go out** spiritually by not following their life. *As a lily among brambles* (Song 2:2), and this in order to avoid the very occasions of sin given by them. Hence he says, **and be separate**, i.e., be far from consenting to them: *for I have come to set a man against his father* (Matt 10:35); *depart, I pray you, from the tents of these wicked men* (Num 16:26). Third, to rebuke them when they do wrong; hence he says, **and do not touch the unclean thing**, i.e., do not consent to them in evil: *they not only do them but approve those who practice them* (Rom 1:32); *take no part in the unfruitful works of darkness, but instead expose them* (Eph 5:11). And this because *whoever touches pitch will be defiled* (Sir 13:1).

244. Two rewards are promised to those who heed this admonition, namely, familiarity with God and adoption by God. Familiarity with God, because **I will receive you**. As if to say: go out confidently, because I will welcome you as mine: *for my father and my mother have forsaken me, but the Lord will take me up* (Ps 27:10); *blessed is he whom you choose and bring near, to dwell in your courts!* (Ps 65:5); *behold my servant, whom I uphold, my chosen, in whom my soul delights* (Isa 42:1). Divine adoption, because he adopts us as sons, because he says, **I will be a Father to you: and you shall be my sons and daughters**: *for you did not receive the spirit of slavery to fall back into fear, but you have received the spirit of sonship* (Rom 8:15). He says, **sons**, as to the perfect, and **daughters**, as to the imperfect; and this is taken from 2 Samuel, where it says of Solomon: *I will be his father, and he shall be my son* (2 Sam 7:14).

Chapter 7

Lecture 1

7:1Has ergo habentes promissiones, carissimi, mundemus nos ab omni inquinamento carnis et spiritus, perficientes sanctificationem in timore Dei. [n. 245]

7:2Capite nos. Neminem laesimus, neminem corrupimus, neminem circumvenimus. [n. 249]

7:3Non ad condemnationem vestram dico: praediximus enim quod in cordibus nostris estis ad commoriendum et ad convivendum. [n. 250]

7:1αὐτὰς οὖν ἔχοντες τὰς ἐπαγγελίας, ἀγαπητοί, καθαρίσωμεν ἑαυτοὺς ἀπὸ παντὸς μολυσμοῦ σαρκὸς καὶ πνεύματος, ἐπιτελοῦντες ἁγιωσύνην ἐν φόβῳ θεοῦ.

7:2Χωρήσατε ἡμᾶς· οὐδένα ἠδικήσαμεν, οὐδένα ἐφθείραμεν, οὐδένα ἐπλεονεκτήσαμεν.

7:3πρὸς κατάκρισιν οὐ λέγω· προείρηκα γὰρ ὅτι ἐν ταῖς καρδίαις ἡμῶν ἐστε εἰς τὸ συναποθανεῖν καὶ συζῆν.

7:1Having therefore these promises, dearly beloved, let us cleanse ourselves from all defilement of the flesh and of the spirit, perfecting sanctification in the fear of God. [n. 245]

7:2Receive us. We have injured no man: we have corrupted no man: we have overreached no man. [n. 249]

7:3I do not say this to your condemnation. For we have said before that you are in our hearts: to die together and to live together. [n. 250]

---

245. Monuit Apostolus Corinthios qualiter se in futuro debeant habere, hic commendat eos de bonis praeteritis. Sed ut fiat quaedam continuatio praeteritorum ad futura,

primo concludit admonitionem;

secundo vero commendat eos, ibi *multa mihi fiducia*, et cetera.

Circa primum tria facit.

Primo ponit admonitionem;

secundo inducit exemplum sui ipsius ad admonitionem servandam, ibi *capite nos*, etc.;

tertio ponit admonentis intentionem, ibi *non ad condemnationem vestram*, et cetera.

246. Circa primum tria facit. Primo ponit motivum ad observantiam admonitionis, et hoc est promissio eis facta. Et ideo dicit *has igitur habentes promissiones charissimi*, scilicet quod Deus habitet in nobis, et recipiat nos, et cetera.

247. Secundo ponit admonitionem, cum dicit: *mundemus*, et cetera. Et hoc ideo, quia promissiones istae non dantur nisi mundis, et ideo *mundemus nos ab omni inquinamento carnis et spiritus*, id est carnalium et spiritualium vitiorum. Is. LII, 11: *mundamini, qui fertis vasa Domini*, et cetera.

Ubi sciendum est, quod omne peccatum quod consummatur in delectatione carnis est carnale; illud vero quod consummatur in delectatione spiritus, est spirituale. Et inde est quod peccata carnalia, si considerentur quantum ad sui consummationem, sunt duo tantum, scilicet gula et luxuria, caetera vero peccata sunt spiritualia. Si vero considerentur quantum ad sui originem, sic omnia peccata possunt dici carnalia, quia omnia ex conceptione carnis originem habent, et hoc modo

245. Having informed the Corinthians how to behave in the future, the Apostle now commends them on the good they have accomplished in the past. But in order to connect the past with the future,

he first concludes his admonition;

second, he commends them, at *great is my confidence*.

In regard to the first he does three things.

First, he gives the admonition;

second, he gives himself as an example to have the admonition obeyed, at *receive us*;

third, he states his intention in admonishing them, at *I do not say this to your condemnation*.

246. In regard to the first he does three things. First, he gives them a motive for observing the admonition, and this is a promise made to them. Hence, he says, *having therefore these promises, dearly beloved*, namely, that God may dwell in you, and that you may receive us.

247. Second, he gives the admonition, when he says, *let us cleanse ourselves*, because those promises are given only to those who are clean; and so *let us cleanse ourselves from all defilement of the flesh and of the spirit*, i.e., of carnal and spiritual vices: *purify yourselves, you who bear the vessels of the Lord* (Isa 52:11).

Here it should be noted that every sin which is consummated in carnal delight is carnal, while that which is consummated in spiritual delight is spiritual. That is why carnal sins, if they are considered in their consummation, are two in number, namely, gluttony and lust; but the others are spiritual sins. But if they are considered in their origin, then all sins can be considered carnal, because all of them have their origin in a conception of the flesh. In this sense he speaks to the Galatians: *now the works of the flesh are*

loquitur ad Gal. V, 19: *manifesta sunt autem opera carnis, et cetera.*

248. Tertio ponit modum implendi admonitionem, ibi **perficientes**, et cetera.

Posset enim aliquis dicere: numquid non sumus mundati in baptismo? Et ideo addit **perficientes sanctificationem**, id est perficimus emundationem inchoatam in baptismo. Sanctus enim idem est quod mundus. Lev. XI, 44 et XIX, 2: *sancti estote, quoniam ego sanctus sum*, et cetera.

Perficiamus, inquam, quia philosophi conati sunt perficere et non potuerunt, quia non potuerunt omnia peccata vitare: quantumcumque enim aliqua peccata vitarent et exercerent actus virtutum, adhuc tamen remanebat in eis peccatum infidelitatis. Et ideo in vero cultu Dei solum perficitur emundatio, et hoc est quod dicit **in timore**, id est, in cultu, **Dei**. Eccli. XXV, 14: *timor Domini*, et cetera.

Sed contra Col. III, 14: *super omnia caritatem habentes, quae est vinculum perfectionis.* Non igitur perficitur sanctificatio in timore Dei, sed in caritate Dei.

Respondeo. Dicendum est quod hic loquitur de timore filiali, qui est caritatis effectus, et non de servili, qui contrariatur caritati. Dicit autem **in timore**, ut doceat nos habere affectum ad Deum cum quadam reverentia et sollicitudine. Amor enim causat securitatem, quae quandoque negligentiam parit, sed, qui timet, semper est sollicitus.

249. Consequenter cum dicit **capite nos**, etc., in exemplum se praebet, quasi diceret: accipite nos in exemplum. I Cor. XI, v. 1: *imitatores mei estote*, et cetera. Ego enim mihi cavi ab immunditia per sanctificationem, quia neminem laesi.

Ubi notandum quod tripliciter potest aliquis laedere proximum, et nullo istorum modorum laesit aliquem. Primo in persona, et quantum ad hoc dicit **neminem laesimus**, scilicet in persona, sicut faciunt mali domini, Mich. III, 2: *violenter tollitis pellem eorum*, et cetera. Secundo quantum ad famam, inducendo eos, vel exemplo vel persuasionibus, ad malum, et quantum ad hoc dicit **neminem corrupimus**. I Cor. XV, 33: *corrumpunt bonos mores.* Tertio quantum ad subtractionem bonorum, et quantum ad hoc dicit **neminem circumvenimus**, id est in bonis fraudavimus. I Thess. IV, 6: *ne quis circumveniat*, et cetera.

250. Consequenter cum dicit **non ad condemnationem vestram**, etc., aperit suam intentionem, quasi dicat: non dico hoc condemnando vos, sed ut emendemini. Mala enim praeterita propter duo consueverunt commemorari. Aliquando ad condemnationem, et hoc quando non est ultra spes correctionis; aliquando autem ad emendationem, ut scilicet corrigantur, et hoc modo

plain: *fornication, impurity, licentiousness, idolatry, sorcery, enmity, strife, jealousy, anger, selfishness, dissension, party spirit, envy, drunkenness, carousing, and the like* (Gal 5:19).

248. Third, he mentions how they can fulfill the admonition when he says, **perfecting sanctification**.

For someone could say: were we not cleansed in baptism? That is why he added, **perfecting sanctification**, i.e., let us perfect the original cleansing in baptism. For the same is holy that is clean: *be holy, for I am holy* (Lev 11:44).

Let us be perfect, I say, because philosophers have tried to be perfect and have failed, because they were unable to avoid sins. For no matter how many other sins they avoided or how well they exercised the acts of the virtues, the sin of unbelief remained in them. Consequently, cleanness is made perfect only in the true worship of God. And this is what he says: **in the fear**, i.e., in the worship, **of God**: *the fear of God has set itself over all things* (Sir 25:14).

But this seems contrary to Colossians: *and above all these put on love, which binds everything together in perfect harmony* (Col 3:14). Therefore, sanctification is not perfected in the fear of God, but in the love of God.

I answer that he is speaking here of filial fear, which is the effect of charity, and not of servile fear, which is contrary to charity. He says, **in the fear**, to teach us to love God with a certain reverence and carefulness. For love causes security, which sometimes begets negligence; but one who fears is always careful.

249. Then when he says, **receive us**, he offers himself as an example. As if to say: take us as an example: *be imitators of me as I am of Christ* (1 Cor 11:1). For I have guarded myself against uncleanness by holiness, because I have injured no one.

Here it should be noted that a person might injure his neighbor in three ways, but Paul did not injure them in any of these ways. First, in his person, as to this he says, **we have injured no man**, namely in his person, as wicked masters do: *who tear the skin from off my people* (Mic 3:2). Second, in their reputation by inducing them to evil by example and persuasion; as to this he says, **we have corrupted no man**. *Bad company ruins good morals* (1 Cor 15:33). Third, by stealing their goods; as to this he says, **we have overreached no man**: *that no man transgress and wrong his brother in this matter* (1 Thess 4:6).

250. Then when he says, **I do not say this to your condemnation**, he discloses his intention. As if to say: I do not say this to condemn you, but to correct you. For past evils are wont to be recalled sometimes for condemnation, when there is no further hope of correction; and sometimes for amendment, so that they will be corrected. And this is the

loquitur hic *non ad condemnationem vestram*, et cetera. I Cor. VII, 35: *haec ad utilitatem vestram dico, et cetera.*

Et ratio huius est, quia gaudeo de bono vestro, *praediximus enim quod vos estis*, et cetera. Supra III, 2: *epistola nostra vos estis scripta in cordibus nostris*. Phil. I, 7: *eo quod habeam vos*, et cetera.

Estis, inquam, *in cordibus nostris*, scilicet *ad commoriendum et ad convivendum*. Quod potest intelligi de morte culpae, et de morte naturali. De morte culpae, ut non intelligatur quod nos simus parati ad commoriendum vobiscum, id est quando vos peccatis, nos volumus peccare, sed quod mortem culpae vestram eo dolore accipimus quo nostram. II Cor. XI, 29: *quis infirmatur, et ego non infirmor?* I Cor. XV, 31: *quotidie morior*, et cetera. *Et ad convivendum*, quia ita gaudeo de bona vita vestra in gratia, sicut et de nostra. De morte vero naturali, ut intelligatur *ad commoriendum*, id est paratus sum mori pro vobis, infra XII, 15: *libentius impendar, et superimpendar*, etc., *et ad convivendum*, id est ut desiderem vos esse socios in vita aeterna, II Tim. II, 11: *si commortui sumus, et convivemus.*

way he speaks here: *I do not say this to your condemnation*: *I say this for your own benefit* (1 Cor 7:35).

The reason for this is that I rejoice in your good: *for we have said before that you are in our hearts* (2 Cor 3:2); *it is right for me to feel thus about you all, because I hold you in my heart* (Phil 1:7).

You are, I say, *in our hearts*, namely, *to die together and to live together*. This can be understood of the death of guilt and of natural death. Of the death of guilt, not that we are prepared to die with you, i.e., not that when you sin, we want to sin, but we take your death of guilt with as much pain as our own. *Who is weak, and I am not weak?* (2 Cor 11:29); *I die everyday* (1 Cor 15:31). *And to live together*, because I take as much joy in your good life in grace as in my own. Of natural death: then *to die together* it taken to mean that I am prepared to die for you: *I will most gladly spend and be spent for your souls* (2 Cor 12:15); *to live together*, i.e., I desire you to be companions in eternal life: *if we have died with him, we shall also live with him* (2 Tim 2:11).

Lecture 2

7:4Multa mihi fiducia est apud vos, multa mihi gloriatio pro vobis: repletus sum consolatione; superabundo gaudio in omni tribulatione nostra. [n. 251]

7:5Nam et cum venissemus in Macedoniam, nullam requiem habuit caro nostra, sed omnem tribulationem passi sumus: foris pugnae, intus timores. [n. 256]

7:6Sed qui consolatur humiles, consolatus est nos Deus in adventu Titi. [n. 259]

7:7Non solum autem in adventu ejus, sed etiam in consolatione, qua consolatus est in vobis, [n. 261] referens nobis vestrum desiderium, vestrum fletum, vestram aemulationem pro me, ita ut magis gauderem. [n. 263]

7:8Quoniam etsi contristavi vos in epistola, non me poenitet: etsi poeniteret, videns quod epistola illa (etsi ad horam) vos contristavit,

7:9nunc gaudeo: non quia contristati estis, sed quia contristati estis ad poenitentiam. Contristati enim estis ad Deum, ut in nullo detrimentum patiamini ex nobis.

7:4πολλή μοι παρρησία πρὸς ὑμᾶς, πολλή μοι καύχησις ὑπὲρ ὑμῶν· πεπλήρωμαι τῇ παρακλήσει, ὑπερπερισσεύομαι τῇ χαρᾷ ἐπὶ πάσῃ τῇ θλίψει ἡμῶν.

7:5Καὶ γὰρ ἐλθόντων ἡμῶν εἰς Μακεδονίαν οὐδεμίαν ἔσχηκεν ἄνεσιν ἡ σὰρξ ἡμῶν ἀλλ᾽ ἐν παντὶ θλιβόμενοι· ἔξωθεν μάχαι, ἔσωθεν φόβοι.

7:6ἀλλ᾽ ὁ παρακαλῶν τοὺς ταπεινοὺς παρεκάλεσεν ἡμᾶς ὁ θεὸς ἐν τῇ παρουσίᾳ Τίτου,

7:7οὐ μόνον δὲ ἐν τῇ παρουσίᾳ αὐτοῦ ἀλλὰ καὶ ἐν τῇ παρακλήσει ᾗ παρεκλήθη ἐφ᾽ ὑμῖν, ἀναγγέλλων ἡμῖν τὴν ὑμῶν ἐπιπόθησιν, τὸν ὑμῶν ὀδυρμόν, τὸν ὑμῶν ζῆλον ὑπὲρ ἐμοῦ ὥστε με μᾶλλον χαρῆναι.

7:8Ὅτι εἰ καὶ ἐλύπησα ὑμᾶς ἐν τῇ ἐπιστολῇ, οὐ μεταμέλομαι· εἰ καὶ μετεμελόμην, βλέπω [γὰρ] ὅτι ἡ ἐπιστολὴ ἐκείνη εἰ καὶ πρὸς ὥραν ἐλύπησεν ὑμᾶς,

7:9νῦν χαίρω, οὐχ ὅτι ἐλυπήθητε ἀλλ᾽ ὅτι ἐλυπήθητε εἰς μετάνοιαν· ἐλυπήθητε γὰρ κατὰ θεόν, ἵνα ἐν μηδενὶ ζημιωθῆτε ἐξ ἡμῶν.

7:4Great is my confidence for you: great is my glorying for you. I am filled with comfort: I exceedingly abound with joy in all our tribulation. [n. 251]

7:5For also, when we had come into Macedonia, our flesh had no rest: but we suffered all tribulation. Combats without: fears within. [n. 256]

7:6But God, who comforts the humble, comforted us by the coming of Titus. [n. 259]

7:7And not by his coming only, but also by the consolation with which he was comforted in you, [n. 261] relating to us your desire, your mourning, your zeal for me: so that I rejoiced the more. [n. 263]

7:8For although I made you sorrowful by my epistle, I do not repent. And if I did repent, seeing that the same epistle (although but for a time) did make you sorrowful,

7:9Now I am glad: not because you were made sorrowful, but because you were made sorrowful unto penance. For you were made sorrowful according to God, that you might suffer damage by us in nothing.

---

251. Apostolus posuit supra admonitionem ex praemissis conclusam, hic subdit suam commendationem. Et circa hoc duo facit.

Primo ponit eorum commendationem;

secundo ipsam exponit, ibi *nam et cum venissem*, et cetera.

252. Commendationem autem ipsorum ponit ostendendo affectum suum, qui consurgit ex bonis operibus quae Corinthii faciebant.

Consuevit enim quadruplex affectus in cordibus diligentium consurgere ex bonis quae dilecti operantur, et hos quatuor se apostolus concepisse de eis ostendit. Et primo affectum fiduciae. Unde dicit *multa mihi fiducia est apud vos*, inquantum scilicet confido, quod qui bene coepistis, semper proficietis in melius. Unde ex bonis auditis de vobis, spero maiora in futurum. Phil. I, 6: *confido de vobis, quod qui coepit in vobis opus bonum*, et cetera. Hebr. VI, 9: *confidimus de vobis, charissimi, et*

251. Having given an admonition derived from what went before, the Apostle now gives his commendation.

In regard to this he does two things:

first, he commends them;

second, he explains it, at *for also, when we had come.*

252. He commends them by showing his love, which springs from the good works the Corinthians did.

For in the hearts of those who love there are four feelings that usually arise from the good works, which the lovers accomplish. First, the feeling of confidence. Hence, he says, *great is my confidence for you*, inasmuch as I am confident that, having begun well, you will always get better. Consequently, from the good things I have heard about you I hope for greater things to come: *and I am sure that he who began a good work in you will bring it to completion at the day of Jesus Christ* (Phil 1:6); *though we speak thus, yet in your case, beloved, we feel sure of better things that*

cetera. Et haec fiducia bona est et salubris. Hebr. X, 35: *nolite amittere fiduciam*, et cetera.

253. Secundo ex hoc concipit affectum gloriationis. Ex quo enim quis bona amici sicut sua diligit, consequens est ut de bonis amici, sicut de propriis, glorietur. Et hoc specialiter, quoniam ipse est causa illorum bonorum, sicut magister est causa doctrinae discipuli. Et ideo dicit **multa mihi gloriatio pro vobis** est, et cetera. Prov. X, 1: *gloria patris filius sapiens.*

254. Tertio ex praedictis concipit affectum consolationis, quando is qui laetatur et gloriatur de bonis suis vel amici, habet remedium contra tristitias.

Consolatio enim est remedium contra tristitias. Naturale autem est quod semper delectatio et gaudium, tristitiae opponitur. Et, secundum Philosophum, omnis delectatio debilitat, vel totaliter tollit tristitiam. Si delectatio sit contraria tristitiae, totaliter absorbet tristitiam; si autem non sit contraria, debilitat et diminuit eam. Et inde est quod quando quis est in tristitia, quandocumque nuntiantur sibi aliqua laeta, diminuitur tristitia. Et ideo, quia audit laeta de Corinthiis, dicit **repletus sum consolatione**, audita scilicet correctione vestra. Supra I, 5 s.: **sicut abundant Christi passiones**, et cetera. Phil. II, 2: *si qua consolatio*, et cetera. *Implete gaudium meum*, et cetera.

255. Quarto, consurgit ex praedictis affectus exsuperantis gaudii.

Licet enim ex aliquibus delectationibus diminuatur tristitia, non tamen totaliter tollitur, nisi gaudium sit magnum. Quamvis autem Apostolus multas tribulationes sustineret, quia tamen multum gaudebat de bonis Corinthiorum, ideo non solum non absorbebatur tristitia totaliter, sed etiam superabundabat gaudio. Et ideo dicit **superabundo gaudio in omni tribulatione nostra**, id est gaudium meum superat omnem tribulationem, quae erat in animo meo. I Thess. II, 19: *quae est enim spes nostra, aut gaudium*, et cetera. Rom. c. XII, 12: *in tribulatione patientes.*

256. Consequenter cum dicit **nam cum venissem**, etc., exponit suam commendationem. Duo autem dixerat, scilicet se accepisse gaudium, et habuisse tribulationem.

Primo ergo manifestat suam tribulationem;

secundo vero suam consolationem, ibi **sed qui consolatur**, et cetera.

257. Tribulationem autem aggravat ex duobus, scilicet ex subtractione remedii, et ex tribulationis multiplicitate.

Ex subtractione remedii, cum dicit **nam et cum venissem**, et cetera. Quasi dicat: vere tribulationem habeo, quia in nullo consolor, **nam cum venissem**

belong to salvation (Heb 6:9). And this confidence is good and salutary: *therefore do not throw away your confidence, which has a great reward* (Heb 10:35).

253. Second, from this confidence he conceives a feeling of glory; for as a result of loving a friend's good as his own, a person glories in that good as he glories in his own. And this is especially true here, because he is the cause of their goods, as a teacher is the cause of his disciple's doctrine. Hence he says, **great is my glorying for you**: *the glory of a father is a wise son* (Prov 10:1).

254. Then as a result of these two feelings he conceives a feeling of consolation, when the one who rejoices and glories in his own goods or in those of his friend has a remedy against sadness.

This consolation is a cure for sadness; and according to the Philosopher every delight weakens or entirely destroys sadness. If the delight is contrary to the sadness, it totally swallows up the sadness; but if it is not contrary, it weakens or diminishes it. This is why when a person is sad, his sadness is lessened whenever something joyful is announced to him. Therefore, because he heard joyful things about the Corinthians, he says, **I am filled with comfort**, having heard of your amendment: **for as the sufferings of Christ abound in us: so also by Christ does our comfort abound** (2 Cor 1:5); *so if there is any encouragement in Christ . . . complete my joy by being of the same mind* (Phil 2:1–2).

255. Fourth, there finally arises a feeling of exuberant joy,

for although sadness is lessened by certain delights, it is not entirely displaced unless there is great joy. But although the Apostle had endured many tribulations, yet because he found great joy in the good actions of the Corinthians, not only was sadness entirely absorbed, but his joy superabounds. Hence he says, **I exceedingly abound with joy in all our tribulation**, i.e., my joy overcomes every tribulation that was in my soul: *for what is our hope or joy or crown of boasting before our Lord Jesus at his coming?* (1 Thess 2:19); *be patient in tribulation* (Rom 12:12).

256. Then when he says, **for also, when we had come into Macedonia**, he explains his commendation. But he said that he experienced two things, namely, joy and tribulation.

First, therefore, he makes manifest his tribulation;

second, his consolation, at **but God, who comforts**.

257. He enlarges upon his tribulations for two reasons, namely, because the cure was removed, and because the tribulations were multiplied.

Because of the removal of the cure he says: **for also, when we had come into Macedonia, our flesh had no rest**. As if to say: indeed I have tribulation, because I am consoled

Macedoniam, nullam requiem habuit caro nostra. Hic facit mentionem de persecutione quam passus est in Macedonia, quando liberavit ancillam pythonissam, ut legitur Act. XVI, 18–24.

Dicit autem *nullam requiem habuit caro nostra*, et non dicit *spiritus noster*, quia sancti semper habent pacem spiritus, cum etiam in adversis, anima quae in corpore patitur, spe futuri praemii quiescat, quamquam multa sustineat affectui carnis contraria.

258. Ex multiplicitate vero tribulationum aggravat, cum dicit *omnem tribulationem passi sumus*, id est omne genus tribulationis secundum corpus, et secundum animam. Supra IV, 8: *in omnibus tribulationem patimur*, et cetera. Io. XVI, 33: *in mundo pressuram*, et cetera. Et quod omnem tribulationem passus fuerit exponit consequenter, cum dicit *foris pugnae, intus timores. Foris*, id est extra meipsum, *pugnae* persecutionum, sed tamen *intus*, id est in corde, est *timor* de malo, timens persecutionem in futuro. Deut. c. XXXII, 25: *foris vastabit eos gladius*, et cetera.

Sed contra Prov. XXVIII, 1: *iustus quasi leo confidens absque terrore erit*. Respondeo. Est sine timore quantum ad spiritum, non tamen quantum ad carnem.

Vel *foris*, id est extra Ecclesiam, *pugnae* illatae ab infidelibus, sed *intus timores*, ne scilicet illi qui intra Ecclesiam sunt, excidant a fide propter persecutores. Vel *foris*, id est in manifesto, *pugnae*, quibus impugnantur a manifestis inimicis; *intus timores*, qui iniiciuntur nobis ab illis, qui dicunt se amicos, et non sunt: quia, ut dicit Boetius *de Consolatione, nulla pestis efficacior ad nocendum, quam familiaris inimicus*. Matth. X, 36: *inimici hominis domestici eius*.

259. Consequenter, cum dicit *sed qui consolatur*, etc., ponit materiam suae consolationis, quam extollit ex duobus, scilicet grata praesentia Titi, et ex consolatione Titi, ibi *non solum autem*, et cetera.

260. Dicit ergo: licet hic graviter afflicti fuerimus, *sed qui*, scilicet Deus, *consolatur humiles, consolatus est*, etc., cuius praesentia, utpote mihi gratissima, est et in adiutorium. Supra: *qui consolatur nos in omni tribulatione nostra*.

Dicit autem, *qui consolatur humiles*, quia superbos non consolatur, sed eis resistit, ut dicitur Iac. IV, 6 et I Petr. V, 5. Consolatur autem humiles, dando eis gratiam, quae est consolatio Spiritus Sancti. Is. LXI, 2: *ut consolarer omnes lugentes*, et cetera.

261. *Non solum autem*, et cetera. Hic ponitur alia materia consolationis Apostoli, scilicet consolatio Titi. Et materia huius consolationis est duplex. Prima emendatio Corinthiorum, quam habuerunt in praesentia Titi;

by no one, *for also when we had come into Macedonia, our flesh had no rest*. Here he is referring to the persecution he suffered in Macedonia, when he freed a certain possessed maidservant, as we read in Acts 16.

He says, *our flesh had no rest*, but not *our spirit*, because the saints always have peace in spirit. For even in adversity the soul, which suffers in the body, rests in the hope of a reward to come, although it suffers many things contrary to the desires of the flesh.

258. But he enlarges upon his tribulations by reason of their number when he says, *we suffered all tribulation* i.e., every type of tribulation in the body and in the soul: *in the world you have tribulation; but be of good cheer, I have overcome the world* (John 16:33). That he had suffered all tribulations he explains when he says, *combats without, fear within*, i.e., outside myself, the *combats* of persecutions, but *within*, i.e., in the heart, the *fear* of evil, fearing persecutions in the future: *in the open the sword shall bereave* (Deut 32:25).

But this seems contrary to Proverbs: *but the righteous are bold as a lion* (Prov 28:1). I answer that he is without dread as to the spirit, but not as to the flesh.

Or *without*, i.e., outside the Church, *combats* are started by unbelievers; but *fear within*, lest those who are in the Church fall away from the faith on account of persecutors. Or *without*, i.e., in public, *fighting*, because we are attacked by obvious enemies; *fear within*, which is produced in us by those who call themselves friends but are not. For as Boethius says in *On Consolation: no pest can inflict more harm than a friendly enemy. A man's foes will be those of his own household* (Matt 10:36).

259. Then when he says, *but God, who comforts*, he states the reason for his consolation, which he applauds from two aspects, namely, from the gratifying presence of Titus and from the consolation of Titus, at *and not by his coming only*.

260. He says, therefore: although we were gravely afflicted here, God, *who comforts the humble, comforted us by the coming of Titus*, whose presence was very pleasing and a great help to me: *who comforts us in all our tribulation* (2 Cor 1:4).

He says, *who comforts the humble*, because he does not comfort the proud but resists them, as it says in James (Jas 4:6) and 1 Peter (1 Pet 5:5). But he comforts the humble by giving grace, which is the consolation of the Holy Spirit: *to comfort all who mourn* (Isa 61:2).

261. *And not by his coming only, but also by the consolation with which he was comforted in you*. Here he gives another reason for the Apostle's consolation, namely, the consolation of Titus. The reason for this comfort is twofold:

secunda est devotio Corinthiorum, quam ostenderunt ad Titum, ibi *in consolatione autem vestra*, et cetera.

Circa primum duo facit.

Primo ponit consolationem de poenitentia Corinthiorum;

secundo exponit quaedam quae dixit, ibi *contristati enim estis*, et cetera.

Circa primum tria facit.

Primo ponit consolationem Titi;

secundo materiam consolationis, ibi *referens nobis*, etc.;

tertio effectum consolationis in mente Apostoli, ibi *ita ut magis gauderem*, et cetera.

262. Dicit ergo: non solum consolatur nos Deus in adventu Titi, sed etiam in consolatione qua ipse Titus consolatus est de vobis et in vobis.

263. Et huius consolationis materia est, quia ipse Titus consolatus est, *referens nobis vestrum desiderium*, et cetera.

Ubi tria ponit laudabilia propter tria reprehensibilia quae fuerunt in eis. Fuerunt enim pigri ad bonum, et contra hoc dicit *referens nobis vestrum desiderium*, de proficiendo in melius.

Item erant proni ad malum, et contra hoc dicit *vestrum fletum*, scilicet de peccatis commissis. Ier. VI, 26: *luctum unigeniti fac*, et cetera.

Item erant faciles deceptioni pseudorum, et contra hoc dicit *vestram aemulationem*, contra pseudos habitam pro amore mei. Nam ante aemulabamini contra me pro eis.

264. Consequenter, cum dicit *ita ut magis*, etc., ponit affectum conceptum ex consolatione Titi, qui quidem affectus est gaudium. Unde circa hoc tria facit. Primo ponit conceptum gaudium; secundo ostendit suae aestimationis imitationem; tertio subdit rationem gaudii.

Dicit ergo: intantum gavisus sum de his quae Titus retulit mihi, ita ut magis gauderem de hoc, quam de tribulatione mea doluerim. Nam spiritualia praeferenda sunt temporalibus.

Vel, ut magis gauderem de hoc quod contristavi vos, quam doluerim olim. Peccaverant enim faciendo fornicationem, et Apostolus increpaverat eos, ut patet in prima epistola. Tunc autem incertus erat Apostolus, quem eventum deberet habere illa tristitia, bonum scilicet an malum; et ideo dubitans poenituit. Sed videns postmodum quod bonum inde provenerat, gaudebat, ideo dicit *quoniam etsi contristavi vos*, increpando in prima epistola, *non me poenitet* modo, quia correcti estis, *etsi* olim *poeniteret*, quando scilicet eram incertus, utrum tristitia induceret vos ad correctionem vel desperationem, *videns quod epistola illa, etsi ad horam vos contristavit, nunc gaudeo*, quia estis conversi.

first, the amendment of the Corinthians, which they had in Titus's presence; second, the devotion they showed to Titus, at *but in our consolation*.

In regard to the first he does two things.

First, he mentions his comfort in the repentance of the Corinthians;

second, he explains something he has said, at *for you were made sorrowful*.

In regard to the first he does three things.

First, he mentions the comfort of Titus;

second, the reason for the comfort, at *relating to us*;

third, the effect of the comfort on the mind of the Apostle, at *so that I rejoiced the more*.

262. He says, therefore: God not only comforted us in the coming of Titus, but also in the comfort with which Titus was comforted by you and in you.

263. The reason for this comfort is that Titus himself was comforted in you, *relating to us your desire, your mourning, your zeal for me*.

Here he mentions three praiseworthy things to counter the three blameworthy things that were in them. For they were lazy in regard to the good; against this he says, *relating to us your desire* to make more progress.

They were also prone to evil; against this he says, *your mourning*, namely for sins committed: *make mourning as for an only son* (Jer 6:26).

Finally, they were easily deceived by the false apostles; against this he says, *your zeal* for love of me, against the false apostles. For previously you were zealous for them against me.

264. Then when he says, *so that I rejoiced the more*, he mentions the feeling he conceived from Titus's consolation, namely, one of joy. Hence, in regard to this he does three things: first, he mentions the joy he felt; second, he intimates his doubts; third, the reason for the joy.

He says, therefore: I was so pleased with the things Titus related to me, that I rejoiced still more in that than I grieved in my tribulations. For spiritual things must be preferred to temporal things.

Or that I rejoiced still more for having saddened you than I sorrowed before. For they had sinned by fornication, and the Apostle has rebuked them, as is evident from the first epistle. But at that time he wondered what effect that sadness would have, whether good or bad; therefore, in his wonder he felt sad. But later, seeing that good had come from it, he was glad. Hence, he says: *for although I made you sorrowful with my epistle, I do not repent*, because you have been corrected. *And if I did repent*, namely, when I was uncertain whether the sadness would bring you to correct yourselves or to despair, *seeing that the same epistle (although but for a time) did make you sorrowful, now I am glad*, because you have been converted.

511

Et rationem gaudii assignat, quia non gaudeo de hoc, quia *contristati estis*, sed de effectu, scilicet de correctione, quia scilicet *contristati estis* non ad desperationem, sed *ad poenitentiam*, sicut medicus non gaudet de amaritudine medicinae sed de effectu, scilicet de sanitate. Supra VI, 10: *quasi tristes, semper autem gaudentes*.

Then he gives the reason for his joy, because I am not glad that *you were made sorrowful*, but at the effect, namely, your amendment, because *you were made sorrowful*, not unto despair, but *unto penance*; just as a physician is not glad at the bitterness of the medicine, but at the effect, namely, health: *as sorrowful, yet always rejoicing* (2 Cor 6:10).

Lecture 3

^{7:9}nunc gaudeo: non quia contristati estis, sed quia contristati estis ad poenitentiam. Contristati enim estis ad Deum, ut in nullo detrimentum patiamini ex nobis. [n. 266]

^{7:10}Quae enim secundum Deum tristitia est, poenitentiam in salutem stabilem operatur: saeculi autem tristitia mortem operatur. [n. 267]

^{7:11}Ecce enim hoc ipsum, secundum Deum contristari vos, quantam in vobis operatur sollicitudinem: sed defensionem, sed indignationem, sed timorem, sed desiderium, sed aemulationem, sed vindictam: in omnibus exhibuistis vos incontaminatos esse negotio. [n. 270]

^{7:9}νῦν χαίρω, οὐχ ὅτι ἐλυπήθητε ἀλλ' ὅτι ἐλυπήθητε εἰς μετάνοιαν· ἐλυπήθητε γὰρ κατὰ θεόν, ἵνα ἐν μηδενὶ ζημιωθῆτε ἐξ ἡμῶν.

^{7:10}ἡ γὰρ κατὰ θεὸν λύπη μετάνοιαν εἰς σωτηρίαν ἀμεταμέλητον ἐργάζεται· ἡ δὲ τοῦ κόσμου λύπη θάνατον κατεργάζεται.

^{7:11}ἰδοὺ γὰρ αὐτὸ τοῦτο τὸ κατὰ θεὸν λυπηθῆναι πόσην κατειργάσατο ὑμῖν σπουδήν, ἀλλὰ ἀπολογίαν, ἀλλὰ ἀγανάκτησιν, ἀλλὰ φόβον, ἀλλὰ ἐπιπόθησιν, ἀλλὰ ζῆλον, ἀλλὰ ἐκδίκησιν. ἐν παντὶ συνεστήσατε ἑαυτοὺς ἁγνοὺς εἶναι τῷ πράγματι.

^{7:9}Now I am glad: not because you were made sorrowful, but because you were made sorrowful unto penance. For you were made sorrowful according to God, that you might suffer damage by us in nothing. [n. 266]

^{7:10}For the sorrow that is according to God works penance, steadfast unto salvation: but the sorrow of the world works death. [n. 267]

^{7:11}For behold this selfsame thing, that you were made sorrowful according to God, how great the carefulness it works in you: what defense, what indignation, what fear, what desire, what zeal, what revenge. In all things you have showed yourselves to be undefiled in the matter. [n. 270]

---

265. Posita consolatione Apostoli et Titi de tristitia Corinthiorum, eo quod fuerit ad poenitentiam, et non ad desperationem, hic consequenter huius consolationis ratio assignatur, eorum tristitiam commendando.

Et circa hoc duo facit.

Primo enim commendat eorum tristitiam;

secundo ex hoc concludit propositum, ibi *et si scripsi vobis*, et cetera.

Commendat autem Corinthiorum tristitiam ex duobus.

Primo ex causa,

secundo ex effectu, ibi *quae enim tristitia est*, et cetera.

266. Causa autem ex qua commendatur eorum tristitia, haec est, quia est secundum Deum. Et ideo dicit: licet ad horam contristaverim vos per epistolam, tamen gaudeo, id est quia *contristati estis secundum Deum*.

Ubi sciendum est, quod tristitia et gaudium et communiter omnis affectio, ex amore causatur. Tristatur enim quis, quia caret eo quod amat. Qualis autem est amor, talis est tristitia ex amore causata. Est autem duplex amor. Unus quo diligitur Deus, et ex hoc causatur tristitia quae est secundum Deum; alius amor quo amatur saeculum, et ex hoc causatur tristitia saeculi. Amor, quo diligimus Deum, facit nos libenter servire Deo, sollicite quaerere honorem Dei, et vacare Deo dulciter. Et quia peccando impedimur a servitio Dei et ideo ei non vacamus, nec eius honorem quaerimus, ideo amor Dei causat tristitiam de peccato, et haec est tristitia

265. Having mentioned the comfort the Apostle and Titus experienced at the grief of the Corinthians, because it ended in repentance and not in despair, he now gives the reason for his comfort by commending their sorrow.

In regard to this he does two things.

First, he commends their sorrow;

second, from this he concludes to his intent, at *although I wrote to you*.

In regard to the first he does two things:

first, he commends their sorrow on the part of its cause;

second, on the part of its effect, at *for the sorrow that is according to God*.

266. The cause on account of which he commends their sorrow is that it was according to God. Therefore he says: although for a time I was sorry for the epistle, nevertheless I rejoice now, because *you were made sorrowful according to God*.

Here it should be noted that sorrow and joy and generally every emotion arise from love; for a person is sad when he lacks what he loves. The kind of love determines the kind of sorrow it causes. But there are two kinds of love: one by which God is loved, and from this arises a sorrow which is according to God; the other is that by which the world is loved, and from this arises a worldly sorrow. The love by which we love God makes us serve him gladly, honor him carefully and set some time apart for God joyfully. But because sin hinders us from serving God, we devote no time to him or seek his honor, the love of God causes sorrow for sin: and this is sorrow according to God. This

secundum Deum, quae quidem tristitia non fuit vobis ad malum, nec detrimentum, sed potius ad fructum et meritum. Et ideo dicit *ut in nullo detrimentum patiamini ex nobis*, quia non solum bona et grata quae vobis impendimus, vobis prosunt, sed etiam hoc ipsum quod vos corrigimus et contristamus. Hebr. XII, 11: *omnis disciplina in praesenti*, et cetera.

267. Consequenter cum dicit *quae enim tristitia*, etc., commendat eorum tristitiam ex effectu, qui quidem est praemium vitae aeternae. Et

circa hoc duo facit.

Primo enim ponit effectum in generali;

secundo experimentum specialiter in eis consecutum, ibi *ecce enim hoc ipsum*, et cetera.

Circa primum duo facit.

Primo enim ponit effectum tristitiae, quae est secundum Deum;

secundo ponit effectum tristitiae, quae est secundum mundum, ibi *saeculi autem*, et cetera.

268. Dicit ergo primo: dico quod tristitia nostra non fuit vobis detrimentum, *enim*, id est *quia, tristitia quae est secundum Deum, operatur poenitentiam*; poenitentiam autem dico *in salutem stabilem*, id est sempiternam, quae est salus stabilis, et est beatorum, de qua Is. XLIX: *salus autem mea in sempiternum erit*. Et hanc operatur poenitentia. Matth. III, 2: *agite poenitentiam, appropinquabit enim regnum caelorum*.

Et dicit *stabilem*, ut excludat salutem temporalem, quae est transitoria et communis ipsis hominibus et iumentis, de qua in Ps. XXXV, 7: *homines et iumenta salvabis, Domine*, et cetera.

269. Sed contra hoc quod dicit quod *tristitia, quae est secundum Deum, poenitentiam operatur*, videtur esse, quia ipsa tristitia secundum Deum est poenitentia. Poenitere enim est tristari de malo, et secundum Deum. Non ergo operatur poenitentiam.

Respondeo. Dicendum est, quod poenitentia habet tres partes, quarum pars prima est tristitia, scilicet dolor et compunctio de peccatis; aliae duae sunt confessio et satisfactio. Cum ergo dicit, quod *tristitia operatur poenitentiam*, intelligendum est, quod compunctio, seu dolor de peccato operetur in nobis poenitentiam, id est, alias partes poenitentiae, scilicet confessionem et satisfactionem.

Vel dicendum est, quod *tristitia secundum Deum* est communior quam poenitentia, quia poenitentia est de proprio peccato, sed tristatur quis secundum Deum et de peccatis propriis et de alienis. Sic ergo effectus tristitiae, quae est secundum Deum, est salus aeterna.

Effectus vero tristitiae, quae est secundum mundum, est mors. Quia enim qui diligit saeculum, inimicus Dei constituitur, ut dicitur Iac. IV, 4, ideo ex amore saeculi

sorrow was not in you to produce evil and loss, but fruit and merit. Hence, he says, *that you might suffer damage by us in nothing*, because you profit not only from the good and pleasant things we bestow on you, but also from the fact that we correct and sadden you. *For the moment all discipline seems painful rather than pleasant; later it yields the peaceful fruit of righteousness to those who have been trained by it* (Heb 12:11).

267. Then when he says, *for the sorrow that is according God*, he commends their sorrow because of its effect, which is the reward of eternal life.

In regard to this he does two things.

First, he mentions the effect in general;

second, what their experience teaches, at *for behold this selfsame thing*.

In regard to the first he does two things.

First, he mentions the effect of sorrow which is according to God;

second, of sorrow which is according to the world, at *but the sorrow of the world*.

268. He says, therefore: I say that our sorrow was not a loss for you, i.e., *for the sorrow that is according to God works penance*, I say, that is *steadfast unto salvation*, i.e., eternal salvation, which is a steadfast salvation belonging to the blessed: *but my salvation will be for ever, and my deliverance will never be ended* (Isa 51:6); and this is the work of penance: *repent, for the kingdom of heaven is at hand* (Matt 3:2).

He says, *steadfast*, to exclude temporal, which is transitory and common to men and beasts: *man and beasts you save, O Lord* (Ps 35:8).

269. But against what he says, *the sorrow that is according to God works penance*, it seems that the very sorrow according to God is penance. For penance is sorrow over evil and is according to God. Therefore it does not work penance.

I answer that penance has three parts, the first of which is sorrow, namely grief and compunction over sins; the other two are confession and satisfaction. Therefore, when he says that *sorrow works penance*, it is to be understood that compunction or sorrow for sin works penance in us, i.e., the other parts of penance, namely, confession and satisfaction.

Or we might say that *sorrow according to God* is more common than penance, because penance is about one's own sins, but one sorrows according to God for his own sins and those of others. Thus, therefore, the effect of sorrow according to God is eternal salvation,

but the effect of sorrow according to the world is death. For since a person who loves the world is made an enemy of God, as it says in James, the love of the world causes death

mors causatur. Tristatur enim secundum saeculum quis, non quia peccans Deum offendit, sed, deprehensus in peccato, punitur de eo et detegitur. Et haec tristitia est vitanda in peccatis. Eccli. XXX, 24: *tristitiam longe fac a te*, et cetera.

270. Consequenter manifestat effectum praedictum per experimentum sumptum in ipsis, cum dicit *ecce enim hoc ipsum*, etc., quasi dicat: vere *salutem stabilem*, quia experimento patet quod in nobis multa, quae ad salutem ducunt, operatur.

Ponit autem sex ad hoc pertinentia, quorum unum est generale, scilicet sollicitudo. Quando enim homo est in laetitia, de facili committit aliquas negligentias; sed quando est tristis et in timore, sollicitatur. Et ideo dicit *ecce enim*, scilicet in vobis experti estis, *hoc ipsum*, scilicet *secundum Deum contristari vos, quantam in vobis operatur sollicitudinem* ad vitandum mala et ad faciendum bona. Mich. VI, 8: *indicabo tibi, O homo, quid sit bonum*, et cetera. Et infra: *sollicitum*, et cetera.

271. Alia vero sunt specialia, quorum quaedam pertinent ad effectum interiorem, quaedam ad actum exteriorem. Eorum vero quae pertinent ad effectum interiorem, quaedam sunt ad peccati remotionem, quaedam vero ad boni adeptionem. Nam verus poenitens debet recedere a malo et facere bonum.

Quantum autem ad remotionem mali, ponit tria. Primum est, ut desistat facere malum, et quantum ad hoc dicit *sed defensionem*, contra alios qui nos ad malum inducunt. I Petr. V, 9: *cui resistite fortes in fide*. Vel, secundum Glossam, ut contra pseudo-apostolos me defendatis. Eph. VI, 13: *accipite armaturam Dei*, et cetera. Secundum est quod homo indignetur contra se pro peccatis quae fecit, et quantum ad hoc dicit *sed indignationem*. Indignatio autem sui operatur tristitiam secundum Deum. Is. LXIII, v. 5: *indignatio mea auxiliata est mihi*. Tertium est, quod sit in continuo timore de futuro, ut caveat, et quantum ad hoc dicit *sed timorem*, de recidivo, ne scilicet in futuro similiter contingat. Eccli. XXV, 14: *timor Domini omnia*, et cetera.

Quantum autem ad hanc boni adeptionem, duo ponit. Primo desiderium, quo ad bonum afficitur, et quantum ad hoc dicit *sed desiderium*, quo bonum facere affectetis. Prov. c. XI, 23: *desiderium iustorum omne bonum*. Secundo aemulationem bonam, qua bonos imitari conatur, et quantum ad hoc dicit *sed aemulationem*, ut scilicet me et alios bonos imitemini. I Cor. XIV, 1: *sectamini caritatem, aemulamini charismata meliora*.

272. Eorum vero quae pertinent ad exteriorem actum duo ponit.

Primum est ut vindicent in seipsis quod peccaverunt: et hoc utile est. Cum enim omne malum necessarium sit puniri, vel ab homine vel a Deo, si hoc non punit, melius

(Jas 4:4). For a person is sorrowful according to the world, not because he offended God by sin, but because, being caught in his sin, he is punished for it and exposed; and this sadness should be avoided in sins: *drive away sadness far from you* (Sir 30:24).

270. Then he explains this effect from the experience learned from them, when he says, *for behold this selfsame thing, that you were made sorrowful according to God, how great the carefulness it works in you*. As if to say: truly *steadfast unto salvation*, because it is clear from experience that it works in us many things that lead to salvation.

He mentions six of these things, one of which is general, namely, carefulness. For when a person is free of care, it is easy for him to become negligent; but when he is sad and fearful, he is careful. Hence he says, *for behold* i.e., you have experienced in your own case, *this selfsame thing, that you were made sorrowful according to God, how great the carefulness it works in you*, to avoid evil and to do good: *he has shown you, O man, what is good* (Mic 6:8); and then, *walk carefully with your God*.

271. The other five are special: some pertain to internal feeling and some to external action. Of those that pertain to inward feeling, some are for the removal of sin, and some for the attainment of good. For a true penitent should depart from evil and do good.

In regard to the removal of evil he lists three, the first of which is to desist from evil; as to this he says, *what defense*, against those who induce us to evil: *resist him, firm in your faith* (1 Pet 5:9). Or according to a Gloss, to defend me against the false apostle. *Take the whole armor of God* (Eph 6:13). The second is that a man be indignant against himself for the sins he has committed; as to this he says, *what indignation*. For indignation at oneself works sorrow according to God. *And my wrath upheld me* (Isa 63:5). The third is that he live in continual fear of the future, so as to be wary; as to this he says, *what fear*, namely, that the same thing might happen in the future. *The fear of God came upon all* (Sir 25:14).

As to the attainment of good he lists two things. The first is desire for what is good; as to this he says, *what desire*, by which a man is inclined to do good: *the desire of the righteous ends only in good* (Prov 11:23). Second, *what zeal*, by which one strives to imitate those who are good; as to this he says, what zeal to imitate me and other good men: *but earnestly desire the higher gifts* (1 Cor 12:31)

272. Of those which pertain to outward action he mentions two.

The first is that they take revenge on themselves for having sinned; and this is useful. For since every evil must be punished either by man or by God, if he does not punish

est quod homo malum in se puniat quod fecit, quam quod Deus, quia, ut dicitur Hebr. X, v. 31, *horrendum est incidere in manus Dei*, et cetera. Et quantum ad hoc dicit **sed vindictam**, id est quia peccantes punitis, et etiam vos ipsos. I Cor. IX, 27: *castigo corpus meum*, et cetera. Is. XXVI: *iustitiam non fecimus*, et cetera.

Secundum est quod totaliter abstineat a malo. Et ideo dicit **in omnibus exhibuistis**, duce scilicet fide, ***incontaminatos esse negotio***, scilicet Christiano. Supra VI, 4: **in omnibus exhibeamus**, et cetera. Eph. I, 4: *elegit nos ante mundi constitutionem, ut essemus sancti*. Ps. c, 6: *ambulans in via immaculata*, et cetera. Vel negotio de quo scilicet correcti estis, puta de favore quem dedistis fornicatori, sed postmodum, puniendo et condemnando ipsum, ostendistis vos in hoc incontaminatos esse.

it here, it is better that a man punish in himself the evil that he has done than that God do it, because as it is said: *it is a fearful thing to fall into the hands of the living God* (Heb 10:31). As to this he says, **what revenge**, i.e., because you punish sinners and even yourselves. *But I pommel my body and subdue it, lest after preaching to others I myself should be disqualified* (1 Cor 9:27); *we did not make justice* (Isa 26:18).

The second is that he refrain from sin altogether; hence he says, ***in all things you have showed youselves***, namely, with faith leading you, ***to be undefiled in the matter***, i.e., of being a Christian: ***in all things let us exhibit ourselves as the ministers of God*** (2 Cor 6:4); *he chose us in him before the foundation of the world, that we should be holy and blameless before him* (Eph 1:4); *he who walks in the way that is blameless shall minister to me* (Ps 101:6). Or in the matter about which you were corrected, for the favor you did for the fornicator; but later by punishing and condemning him you showed that you were undefiled in this.

Lecture 4

7:12Igitur, etsi scripsi vobis, non propter eum qui fecit injuriam, nec propter eum qui passus est: sed ad manifestandam sollicitudinem nostram, quam habemus pro vobis coram Deo: [n. 273]

7:13ideo consolati sumus. [n. 275] In consolatione autem nostra, abundantius magis gavisi sumus super gaudio Titi, quia refectus est spiritus ejus ab omnibus vobis: [n. 276]

7:14et si quid apud illum de vobis gloriatus sum, non sum confusus: sed sicut omnia vobis in veritate locuti sumus, ita et gloriatio nostra, quae fuit ad Titum, veritas facta est, [n. 278]

7:15et viscera ejus abundantius in vobis sunt, reminiscentis omnium vestrum obedientiam: quomodo cum timore et tremore excepistis illum. [n. 279]

7:16Gaudeo quod in omnibus confido in vobis.

7:12ἄρα εἰ καὶ ἔγραψα ὑμῖν, οὐχ ἕνεκεν τοῦ ἀδικήσαντος οὐδὲ ἕνεκεν τοῦ ἀδικηθέντος ἀλλ' ἕνεκεν τοῦ φανερωθῆναι τὴν σπουδὴν ὑμῶν τὴν ὑπὲρ ἡμῶν πρὸς ὑμᾶς ἐνώπιον τοῦ θεοῦ.

7:13διὰ τοῦτο παρακεκλήμεθα. Ἐπὶ δὲ τῇ παρακλήσει ἡμῶν περισσοτέρως μᾶλλον ἐχάρημεν ἐπὶ τῇ χαρᾷ Τίτου, ὅτι ἀναπέπαυται τὸ πνεῦμα αὐτοῦ ἀπὸ πάντων ὑμῶν·

7:14ὅτι εἴ τι αὐτῷ ὑπὲρ ὑμῶν κεκαύχημαι, οὐ κατῃσχύνθην, ἀλλ' ὡς πάντα ἐν ἀληθείᾳ ἐλαλήσαμεν ὑμῖν, οὕτως καὶ ἡ καύχησις ἡμῶν ἡ ἐπὶ Τίτου ἀλήθεια ἐγενήθη.

7:15καὶ τὰ σπλάγχνα αὐτοῦ περισσοτέρως εἰς ὑμᾶς ἐστιν ἀναμιμνησκομένου τὴν πάντων ὑμῶν ὑπακοήν, ὡς μετὰ φόβου καὶ τρόμου ἐδέξασθε αὐτόν.

7:16χαίρω ὅτι ἐν παντὶ θαρρῶ ἐν ὑμῖν.

7:12Therefore, although I wrote to you, it was not for the sake of him who did the wrong, nor for him who suffered it: but to manifest our carefulness that we have for you before God: [n. 273]

7:13Therefore we were comforted. [n. 275] But in our consolation we did the more abundantly rejoice for the joy of Titus, because his spirit was refreshed by you all. [n. 276]

7:14And if I have boasted anything to him of you, I have not been put to shame: but as we have spoken all things to you in truth, so also our boasting that was made to Titus is found a truth. [n. 278]

7:15And his bowels are more abundantly towards you: remembering the obedience of you all, how with fear and trembling you received him. [n. 279]

7:16I rejoice that in all things I have confidence in you.

---

273. Hic, assignata ratione quare gaudet Apostolus de ipsorum tristitia, consequenter inducit conclusionem suam, in qua duo facit.

Primo enim ostendit intentionem suam quam habuit in scribendo;

secundo manifestat gaudium quod habuit de ipsorum correctione, ibi *ideo consolati*, et cetera.

274. Dicit ergo primo: ex quo incontaminati estis, *igitur* apparet quod *et si scripsi vobis*, per epistolam increpando, *non scripsi propter eum* tantum *qui fecit iniuriam*, incestu maculando cubile patris sui, ut dicitur I Cor. V, 1; *nec propter eum* tantum *qui passus est*, scilicet propter patrem, quasi non propter zelum vindictae solum; *sed* hoc feci *ad manifestandam sollicitudinem nostram, quam pro vobis habemus*, id est ut sciretis quam solliciti simus pro vobis. Et hoc dico *coram Deo*, ut sit iuramentum, id est Deo teste. Vel *ad manifestandam coram vobis Deo*, scilicet de omnibus, *sollicitudinem nostram*. Col. II, 1: *volo vos scire quam sollicitudinem*, et cetera.

Vel aliter: *non scripsi* tantum *propter eum qui fecit iniuriam*, ut scilicet corrigeretur, vel *propter eum qui passus est* ut placaretur, *sed ad manifestandam*, etc., ut

273. Here the Apostle assigns the reason why he rejoices over them; then he draws his conclusion, in which he does two things.

First, he discloses the intention he had in writing;

second, he reveals the joy he had over their amendment, at *therefore we were comforted*.

274. He says, *therefore*: from the fact that you are undefiled, it is apparent that *although I wrote to you* to rebuke you in my epistle, *it was not for the sake of him who did the wrong*, by staining his father's chamber with incest (1 Cor 5:1), *nor for him* alone *who suffered it*, namely, on account of the father, as if not on account of the zeal for revenge only, *but* I did this that *to manifest our carefulness that we have for you*, i.e., that you might know how careful we are for you. And I say this *before God*, as an oath with God as witness. Or *to manifest our carefulness that we have for you before God*, i.e., for all; *for I want you to know how greatly I strive for you* (Col 2:1).

Or another way: *I have not written to you* only *for the sake of him who did the wrong*, that he might be corrected, or *for him who suffered it*, that he might be placated, *but to*

scilicet vos, qui indignati fuistis pro contumelia et poena inflicta fornicatori, reconciliaremini Deo.

275. Consequenter concludit gaudium quod habuit de eorum correctione, cum dicit **ideo et consolati sumus**, etc., quasi dicat: quia hoc consecutus sum, ex eo quod scripsi, scilicet quod estis correcti, **ideo consolati sumus**, id est consolationem accepimus. Gaudium enim hominis est cum consequitur quod cum desiderio intendit. Supra I, 12: **abundantius autem**, et cetera.

276. Consequenter cum dicit **in consolatione autem**, etc., ponit secundam causam suae consolationis, quae sumitur ex devotione quam ostenderunt ad Titum. Et

circa hoc tria facit.

Primo ponit gaudium suum de gaudio Titi conceptum;

secundo gaudii rationem assignat, ibi **et si quid apud illum**, etc.;

tertio materiam gaudii Titi assignat, ibi **reminiscentis omnium vestrum**, et cetera.

277. Dicit ergo primo: gavisi sumus, de correctione vestra, **autem**, id est sed, **in consolatione nostra abundantius magis gavisi sumus**, quam turbati fuerimus de tribulatione, **super gaudio Titi**. Vel **magis gavisi sumus**, id est magis gaudium attulit consolationi nostrae gaudium Titi. Et hoc **quia refectus est spiritus eius**. Tunc enim reficitur animus praelati, quando subditi eius sunt obedientes ei et eum reverentur. Ad Philem.: **refice viscera**, et cetera.

Refectus, inquam, **ab omnibus vobis**, quia omnes vel correcti estis, vel est spes correctionis.

278. Rationem autem huius gaudii assignat quantum ad duo. Unum est ex parte Apostoli, quia scilicet ipse inventus est verax. Nam Apostolus commendaverat Corinthios Tito, antequam iret ad eos. Quia vero nunc ita invenit Titus, sicut Apostolus dixit, gaudet Apostolus verba sua vera fuisse, et hoc est quod dicit **et si quid apud illum de vobis gloriatus sum**, commendando vos. Dicit autem **gloriatus sum**, quia gloria Apostoli erat bonum illorum. **Non sum confusus**, id est non erubesco me falsa dixisse. Quando enim aliquis invenitur mendax, confunditur. Eccli. XXXVII, 20: **ante omnia sermo verax**, et cetera. **Sed sicut omnia in veritate vobis locutus sum**, id est sicut praedicavi vobis veritatem, **ita gloriatio nostra quae fuit ad Titum** de vobis, **veritas facta est**, id est inventa est vera.

Alia ratio est ex parte Corinthiorum. Nam amici desiderant, ut illi quos diligunt, ab omnibus diligantur. Quia ergo Titus diligebat Corinthios propter eorum devotionem, ideo de hoc Apostolus gaudebat. Et ideo dicit Apostolus **et viscera eius**, etc., quasi dicat: non solum gaudeo quia inventus sum verax, sed etiam quia **viscera**

manifest our carefulness that we have for you before God, namely, to you who were indignant for the insult and for the punishment inflicted on the fornicator: be reconciled to God.

275. Then he concludes to the joy he had at their correction when he says, *therefore, we were comforted*. As if to say: because I obtained this from writing to you, namely, that you are corrected, *therefore, we were comforted*, i.e., we took comfort. For a man is joyful when he obtains what he desired and intended: *and more abundantly towards you* (2 Cor 1:12).

276. Then when he says, *but in our consolation*, he states the second cause of his comfort, which is taken from the devotion they showed to Titus.

In regard to this he does three things.

First, he mentions the joy he felt at Titus' joy;

second, the reason for the joy, at *and if I have boasted anything to him*;

third, the matter over which Titus rejoiced, at *remembering the obedience of you all*.

277. He says, therefore: we did rejoice at your amendment, *but in our consolation we did the more abundantly rejoice* than we were disturbed by the tribulation, *for the joy of Titus*. Or *we did the more abundantly rejoice*, i.e., the joy of Titus brought more joy to our consolation; and this because his mind has been set at rest by you all. *Because his spirit was refreshed by you all* when his subjects are obedient to him and revere him. *Refresh my heart in Christ* (Phlm 20).

Refreshed, I say, *by you all*, because all are either amended or there is a hope of amendment.

278. He assigns the reason for this joy from two aspects: one is on the part of the Apostle, namely, because he was found to be truthful. For the Apostle had commended the Corinthians to Titus before he went to them. But now, because Titus found them to be just as the Apostle had said, he rejoiced that his words were true. And this is what he says, *and if I have boasted anything to him of you*, by commending you, *I have not been put to shame*, i.e., I do not blush as having said something false. For when a person is found to be a liar, he is ashamed. *A man skilled in words may be hated* (Sir 37:20). *But as we have spoken all things to you in truth*, i.e., as I have preached the truth to you, *so also our boasting that was made to Titus is found a truth*.

The other reason is on the part of the Corinthians. For friends desire that those whom they love be loved by everyone. Therefore, because Titus loved the Corinthians for their devotion, the Apostle rejoices over this and says, *and his bowels are more abundantly towards you*. As if to say: I not only rejoice because I was found to be right, but

eius, id est viscerosa caritas eius, et nimius amor ***abundantius***, quam antea, ***in vobis*** esset, ex quo vidit profectum vestrum; vel abundantius quam in aliis. Eph. VI: *induite vos sicut electi Dei*, et cetera.

279. Materiam autem gaudii manifestat ex duobus, scilicet ex obedientia et reverentia. Ex obedientia quidem cum dicit ***reminiscentis omnium vestrum obedientiam***, qua obedienter sibi obtemperastis. In quo etiam et laudavit vos. I Reg. XV, 22: *melior est obedientia*, et cetera. Eccli. III, 1: *filii sapientiae Ecclesia iustorum*. Ex reverentia autem cum dicit ***quomodo cum timore***, scilicet filiali, non servili, cum ***timore*** animi ***et tremore*** corporis ***excepistis eum***. Gal. IV, 15: *testimonium enim vobis*, et cetera.

Et quia ita habuistis vos ad eum, gavisus sum, quia verax inventus sum, et ipse diligit vos. Unde ***gaudeo quod in omnibus confido in vobis***, non solum in bona voluntate sed etiam in bonis operibus in futuro, quod bene vos habeatis. Hebr. VI, 9: *confidimus de vobis meliora et viciniora saluti*.

also because ***his bowels*** i.e., his charity and great love, goes out ***more abundantly towards you*** than before, because he has seen your progress; or, more abundantly than towards others. *Put on then, as God's chosen ones, holy and beloved, compassion, kindness, lowliness, meekness, and patience* (Col 3:12).

279. He discloses that the matters over which he rejoiced were their obedience and reverence: obedience, when he says, ***remembering the obedience of you all***; for this also he praised you. *To obey is better than sacrifice* (1 Sam 15:22); *listen to me, your father, O children* (Sir 3:1). But their reverence when he says, ***how with fear***, namely, filial and not servile, with ***fear*** of soul ***and trembling*** of body with which ***you received him***: *for I bear you witness that, if possible, you would have plucked out your eyes and given them to me* (Gal 4:15).

And because you acted that way toward him, I rejoiced, for I was found to be right and he loves you. Hence, ***I rejoice that in all things I have confidence in you***, not only in good will, but also in good works, that you will act well in the future. *In your case, beloved, we feel sure of better things that belong to salvation* (Heb 6:9).

CHAPTER 8

Lecture 1

8:1Notam autem facimus vobis, fratres, gratiam Dei, quae data est in ecclesiis Macedoniae: [n. 280]

8:2quod in multo experimento tribulationis abundantia gaudii ipsorum fuit, et altissima paupertas eorum, abundavit in divitias simplicitatis eorum: [n. 283]

8:3quia secundum virtutem testimonium illis reddo, et supra virtutem voluntarii fuerunt, [n. 286]

8:4cum multa exhortatione obsecrantes nos gratiam, et communicationem ministerii, quod fit in sanctos.

8:5Et non sicut speravimus, sed semetipsos dederunt primum Domino, deinde nobis per voluntatem Dei,

8:6ita ut rogaremus Titum, ut quemadmodum coepit, ita et perficiat in vobis etiam gratiam istam. [n. 290]

8:7Sed sicut in omnibus abundatis fide, et sermone, et scientia, et omni sollicitudine, insuper et caritate vestra in nos, ut et in hac gratia abundetis. [n. 291]

8:8Non quasi imperans dico: sed per aliorum sollicitudinem, etiam vestrae caritatis ingenium bonum comprobans. [n. 293]

8:1Γνωρίζομεν δὲ ὑμῖν, ἀδελφοί, τὴν χάριν τοῦ θεοῦ τὴν δεδομένην ἐν ταῖς ἐκκλησίαις τῆς Μακεδονίας,

8:2ὅτι ἐν πολλῇ δοκιμῇ θλίψεως ἡ περισσεία τῆς χαρᾶς αὐτῶν καὶ ἡ κατὰ βάθους πτωχεία αὐτῶν ἐπερίσσευσεν εἰς τὸ πλοῦτος τῆς ἁπλότητος αὐτῶν·

8:3ὅτι κατὰ δύναμιν, μαρτυρῶ, καὶ παρὰ δύναμιν, αὐθαίρετοι

8:4μετὰ πολλῆς παρακλήσεως δεόμενοι ἡμῶν τὴν χάριν καὶ τὴν κοινωνίαν τῆς διακονίας τῆς εἰς τοὺς ἁγίους,

8:5καὶ οὐ καθὼς ἠλπίσαμεν ἀλλὰ ἑαυτοὺς ἔδωκαν πρῶτον τῷ κυρίῳ καὶ ἡμῖν διὰ θελήματος θεοῦ

8:6εἰς τὸ παρακαλέσαι ἡμᾶς Τίτον, ἵνα καθὼς προενήρξατο οὕτως καὶ ἐπιτελέσῃ εἰς ὑμᾶς καὶ τὴν χάριν ταύτην.

8:7Ἀλλ' ὥσπερ ἐν παντὶ περισσεύετε, πίστει καὶ λόγῳ καὶ γνώσει καὶ πάσῃ σπουδῇ καὶ τῇ ἐξ ἡμῶν ἐν ὑμῖν ἀγάπῃ, ἵνα καὶ ἐν ταύτῃ τῇ χάριτι περισσεύητε.

8:8Οὐ κατ' ἐπιταγὴν λέγω ἀλλὰ διὰ τῆς ἑτέρων σπουδῆς καὶ τὸ τῆς ὑμετέρας ἀγάπης γνήσιον δοκιμάζων·

8:1Now we make known unto you, brethren, the grace of God that has been given in the churches of Macedonia: [n. 280]

8:2That in much experience of tribulation, they have had abundance of joy and their very deep poverty has abounded unto the riches of their simplicity. [n. 283]

8:3For according to their power (I bear them witness) and beyond their power, they were willing: [n. 286]

8:4With much entreaty begging of us the grace and communication of the ministry that is done toward the saints.

8:5And not as we hoped: but they gave their own selves, first to the Lord, then to us by the will of God;

8:6so that we asked that Titus, as he had begun, so also would finish among you this same grace. [n. 290]

8:7That as in all things you abound in faith and word and knowledge and all carefulness, moreover also in your charity towards us: so in this grace also you may abound. [n. 291]

8:8I speak not as commanding: but by the carefulness of others, approving also the good disposition of your charity. [n. 293]

---

280. Posita iam exhortatione ad bonum in generali, hic consequenter exhortatur eos ad quoddam bonum particulare, scilicet ad largitionem collectarum pro sanctis qui erant in Ierusalem. Nam, sicut Act. c. XV, 2 dicitur, et apostolus tangit ad Gal. c. II, 9, apostoli imposuerunt Paulo et Barnabae, ut proponerent verbum salutis gentibus, exhortando eos ad subveniendum sanctis, qui erant in Ierusalem, qui venditis omnibus, et positis ad pedes apostolorum, in maxima erant paupertate; et ad hoc inducit eos ad praesens. Ubi duo facit.

Primo inducit eos ad dandum;

280. Having exhorted them to good in general, he now exhorts them to a particular good, namely, to contribute to the things being collected for the saints at Jerusalem. For, as it says in Acts 5, and suggested in Galatians (Gal 2:10), the apostles had charged Paul and Barnabas to preach the word of salvation to the gentiles and exhort them to help the saints in Jerusalem, who, having sold all their possessions and placed them at the feet of the apostles, were in dire need. It is to this that he induces them now, and he does two things.

First, he urges them to give;

secundo monet ad modum dandi, ut scilicet cito et abundanter dent, et hoc cap. IX, ibi *nam de ministerio*, et cetera.

Circa primum duo facit.

Primo tractat de collectis dandis;

secundo de ministris per quos huiusmodi collectae fiant, ibi *gratias autem Deo qui dedit*, et cetera.

Circa primum duo facit.

Primo inducit eos ad dandum;

secundo excludit excusationem, ibi *si enim voluntas prompta est*, et cetera.

Inducit autem eos ad dandum tripliciter.

Primo exemplo aliorum qui dederunt;

secundo exemplo Christi, ibi *scitis enim gratiam Domini nostri*, etc.;

tertio ex ipsorum propria utilitate, ibi *hoc enim vobis utile*, et cetera.

Circa primum tria facit.

Primo ponit exemplum;

secundo ostendit se permotum ab hoc exemplo, ibi *ita ut rogaremus Titum*, etc.;

tertio monet ut ipsi hoc exemplum sequantur, ibi *sed sicut in omnibus abundatis*, et cetera.

Circa primum sciendum est quod apostolus ad hoc, ut Corinthii liberaliter tribuant, proponit eis Macedones in exemplum. Et commendat eos quantum ad duo, scilicet

primo quantum ad patientiam in adversis;

secundo quantum ad liberalitatem in donis, ibi *et altissima paupertas*, et cetera.

281. Circa primum sciendum est quod Apostolus inducit eos ad eleemosynas ut merita ipsorum crescant, et ideo in illo tempore hoc fecit, quando possunt mereri, scilicet tempore gratiae; tunc enim eleemosynae meritoriae sunt. Et hoc est quod dicit *notam vobis facimus gratiam*, id est gratuitum donum *Dei*, scilicet eleemosynarum largitionem.

Et dicit hoc esse gratiam, quia quidquid boni facimus, est ex gratia Dei. Quae, quidem gratia, non est *data* istis, sed mihi, inquantum scilicet ex mea procuratione et sollicitudine et monitione, Macedones ad hoc moti sunt. Eph. III, 8: *mihi autem omnium sanctorum minimo*, et cetera. *Data est*, inquam, mihi *in ecclesiis Macedoniae*, id est apud fideles Macedoniae.

282. Quae quidem gratia est quantum ad duo, scilicet quantum ad patientiam, quia *in multo experimento*, et cetera. Ubi ponit conditiones patientiae perfectae.

Una est quod homo sit constans, ita quod nec timore tribulationis deiiciatur, sed nec etiam in ipso tribulationis experimento. Et ideo dicit quod *in multo experimento tribulationis*, constantes fuerunt.

second, he advises them how to give, namely, quickly and generously, in chapter nine, at *for concerning the ministry* (2 Cor 9:1).

In regard to the first he does two things.

First, he treats of what should be given;

second, of the ministers by whom these things will be collected, at *and thanks be to God, who has given* (2 Cor 8:16).

In regard to the first he does two things.

First, he exhorts them to give;

second, he rejects any excuse, at *for if the will be ready* (2 Cor 8:12).

He uses three things to urge them to give.

First, the example of others who gave;

second, the example of Christ, at *for you know the grace of our Lord* (2 Cor 8:9);

third, their own benefit, at *for this is profitable to you* (2 Cor 8:10).

In regard to the first he does three things.

First, he gives the example;

second, he shows how he was moved by this example, at *so that we asked that Titus*;

third, he suggests that they follow this example, at *that as in all things you abound*.

In regard to the first it should be noted that in order to induce the Corinthians to contribute generously, he proposes to them the example of the Macedonians and commends them for two things, namely,

their patience in adversity

and their generosity in giving, at *and their very deep poverty*.

281. In regard to the first, it should be noted that the Apostle urges them to give alms, so that their merit may grow. Consequently, he did this at a time when they could merit, namely, in the time of grace, for that is when alms are meritorious. Therefore he says, *now we make known unto you, brethren, the grace*, i.e., the gratuitous gift, *of God*, namely, the bestowing of alms.

He calls this a grace, because every good we do is from God's grace. Which grace was not *given* to them but to me, namely, inasmuch as it was by my management and care and urging that the Macedonians were moved to this: *to me, though I am the very least of all the saints* (Eph 3:8). *It has been given*, I say, to me *in the churches of Macedonia*, i.e., among the faithful in Macedonia.

282. It was a grace as to two things. First, as to patience, because, i.e., *that in much experience of tribulation, they have had abundance of joy*. Here he lays down the conditions of perfect patience:

one is that a person be constant, so that he will not be cast down by fear of tribulation or by the very experience of tribulation. Hence he says, *that in much experience of tribulation*, they were constant.

Alia est quod in ipsis tribulationibus gaudeat, sicut legitur de beato Laurentio; et quantum ad hoc dicit *abundantia gaudii ipsorum*, scilicet Macedonum, *fuit*. Iac. c. I, 2: *omne gaudium existimate*, et cetera. Rom. c. XII, 12: *in tribulatione gaudentes*, et cetera. Vel in multo experimento tribulationis, non quam ipsi passi fuerunt, sed quam viderunt pati in Macedonia, *abundantia gaudii ipsorum fuit*.

283. Item secundo, gratia est quantum ad liberalitatem in eleemosynis. Et quantum ad hoc dicit *et altissima*, et cetera. Ubi duo facit.

Primo ponit eorum liberalitatem;

secundo exponit quod dixerat, ibi *quia secundum virtutem*, et cetera.

284. Dicit ergo primo: non solum fuerunt patientes in tribulationibus, scilicet Macedones, sed etiam fuerunt liberales, quia *altissima*, id est maxima, *paupertas eorum*, vel nobilissima. Secundum Glossam facit paupertatem altam elevatio spiritus supra res temporales et contemptus earum. Et sic istorum paupertas altissima erat, quia non habebant divitias, et contemnebant eas. Iac. II, 5: *nonne Deus elegit pauperes in mundo*, et cetera. Haec, inquam, *paupertas abundavit*, id est excrevit, in divitiis copiose dando.

285. Sed haec expositio Glossae non videtur esse secundum intentionem Apostoli, et ideo aliter dicendum est *altissima paupertas*, et cetera.

Ubi sciendum est, quod homo ex duabus causis habet promptum animum ad dandum satis, scilicet ex abundantia divitiarum, sicut divites, vel ex contemptu divitiarum; et sic idem facit in paupere contemptus, quod facit in divite abundantia. Et ideo dicit *altissima paupertas*, sic supra, *abundavit*, id est effectum abundantiae fecit, *in divitias simplicitatis eorum*, quia cor eorum erat solum ad Deum, et ex hoc provenit contemptus divitiarum. Prov. XI, 3: *simplicitas iustorum*, et cetera.

286. Consequenter cum dicit *quia secundum virtutem*, etc., exponit quod dixit commendando ipsorum liberalitatem quantum ad tria, scilicet quantum ad quantitatem dati, quantum ad voluntatem dandi, et quantum ad ordinem dationis.

287. Quantum ad quantitatem dati, quia dederunt *supra virtutem*. Et ideo dicit: vere *abundavit in divitias*, quia ego *reddo illis testimonium* quod fuerunt *voluntarii* ad dandum *secundum virtutem* rerum suarum et *supra virtutem*, quia intantum dederunt quod post eguerunt.

Vel dicendum est, et melius, quod est virtus interior animi, et virtus exterior, scilicet facultas rerum temporalium. Virtus interior est promptitudo animi ad dandum.

The other is that they rejoice in those tribulations, as we read of St. Lawrence. As to this he says, ***they have had abundance of joy***, i.e., the Macedonians. *Count it all joy, my brethren, when you meet various trials* (Jas 1:2); *rejoice in your hope, be patient in tribulation* (Rom 12:12). Or: in a severe test of affliction, not that which they suffered, but which he saw suffered in Macedonia, ***they have had an abundance of joy***.

283. Second, it is a grace as to their generosity in almsgiving; as to this he says, ***and their very deep poverty has abounded unto the riches of their simplicity***. Here he does two things:

first, he mentions their generosity;

second, he explains what he had said, at ***for according to their power***.

284. He says, therefore: not only were they patient in tribulations, namely, the Macedonians, but they were also liberal, considering ***their very deep*** or very noble ***poverty***. According to a Gloss, the raising of the spirit above temporal things and a contempt for them makes poverty profound. And so their poverty was very profound, because they did not have riches and scorned them. *Has not God chosen those who are poor in the world to be rich in faith and heirs of the kingdom* (Jas 2:5). This ***poverty***, I say, ***abounded*** i.e., grew into riches by giving.

285. But the explanation found in this Gloss does not seem to accord with the Apostle's intention; therefore, the saying that ***their very deep poverty has abounded***, must be explained another way.

Here it should be noted that there are two causes which make a man sufficiently ready to give: one is from an abundance of riches, or from a contempt for riches. Consequently, in a poor man contempt for riches produces the same effect as abundance in a rich man. Hence he says, ***their very deep poverty*** so ***abounded*** i.e., produced the effect of abundance, ***unto the riches of their simplicity***, because their heart was solely on God. And from this arose their contempt for riches: *the integrity of the upright guides them* (Prov 11:3).

286. Then when he says, ***for according to their power (I bear them witness) and beyond their power, they were willing***, he explains what he said by commending their generosity as to three things, namely, as to the quantity given, the will to give, and the order of giving.

287. As to the quantity given, it was ***beyond their power***. Hence, he says: truly it ***abounded unto the riches***, for ***I bear them witness*** that ***they were willing*** to give ***according to their power***, that is, according to their means, and ***beyond their power***, because they gave so much that they were in need later.

Or it might be said, and better, that there is an internal power of the soul and an external power, namely, the amount of one's riches. The internal power is the soul's

Et ideo dicit *testimonium illis reddo*, quod *fuerunt voluntarii* ad dandum, *secundum virtutem* animi interiorem, *et supra virtutem* exteriorem, scilicet divitiarum. Tob. IV, 9: *si multum tibi fuerit*, et cetera.

Contra: quicumque dat supra virtutem, dat immoderate; non ergo ex hoc est dignus laude.

Respondeo. Dicendum est quod virtus in dando potest considerari dupliciter, scilicet simpliciter seu absolute, et secundum proportionem aliorum. Quando ergo dat plus quam alii suae proportionis, non peccat; sed si simpliciter dat supra virtutem, tunc immoderate dat. Sic ergo commendat eorum liberalitatem quantum ad quantitatem dati.

288. Commendat autem eam quantum ad voluntatem dandi, cum dicit quia *voluntarii fuerunt*, Ex. XXV, 2: *ab omni qui ultroneus offert*. In hoc autem fuerunt voluntarii, quia rogaverunt nos *cum multa exhortatione, obsecrantes*, id est rogantes. Quasi dicat: non solum rogaverunt, sed etiam per rationes nos induxerunt, ut habeant *gratiam et communicationem ministerii*, etc., id est ut liceret eis dare sua pauperibus sanctis, qui sunt in Ierusalem, non reputantes se facere gratiam nobis, sed quod eis gratia fiat. Hebr. ult.: *beneficentiae autem et communionis*, et cetera.

289. Commendat etiam eorum liberalitatem quantum ad ordinem dandi, quia non solum sua dederunt, sed primo seipsos, quia talis debet esse ordo in dando, ut primo homo sit acceptus Deo, quia nisi homo sit Deo gratus, non sunt accepta munera eius. Gen. IV, 4: *respexit Dominus ad Abel*, scilicet primo, *et ad munera eius* consequenter. Eccli. XXX, 24: *miserere animae tuae*, et cetera.

Et ideo dicit *non sicut speravimus*, quasi dicat: vere voluntarii fuerunt, quia *non sicut speravimus*, id est non ea intentione qua putabamus, ut scilicet darent pro culpis redimendis, sed *semetipsos dederunt primum Domino*, emendando vitam suam, et *deinde nobis*, obediendo per omnia, *per voluntatem Dei*, quae est ut subdantur homines vicariis suis. Hebr. ult.: *obedite praepositis vestris*, et cetera.

Glossa dicit quod non aliter erat ab eis recipiendum, nisi scilicet prius seipsos dedissent Deo; ergo videtur quod non sint recipiendae eleemosynae a peccatoribus.

Sed dicendum est quod non est ab eis recipiendum, quando dant ea intentione ut foveantur in peccatis.

290. Sic ergo, posito exemplo Macedonum, ostendit se consequenter permotum esse hoc exemplo, cum dicit *ita ut rogaremus Titum*, quasi diceret: intantum nos permoti fuimus hoc exemplo de liberalitate Macedonum, ut

readiness to give; hence he says, *I bear them witness* that of their own free will that *they were willing* to give *according to* the internal *power* of their soul *and beyond* the external *power* of their riches: *so you will be laying up a good treasure for yourself against the day of necessity* (Tob 4:9).

But on the other hand, whoever gives beyond his power gives immoderately; therefore, he is not worthy of praise.

I answer that power in giving can be considered in two ways, namely, absolutely and according to a proportion. Therefore, when a person gives more than others of his proportion, he does not sin; but if he gives absolutely above his power, then he gives immoderately.

288. Thus does he commend their generosity as to the quantity given; but he commends it as to their will to give, when he says, *they were willing*: *speak to the people of Israel, that they take for me an offering; from every man whose heart makes him willing you shall receive the offering for me* (Exod 25:2). They were willing in the sense that they asked us, begging us earnestly. As if to say: they not only asked, but they induced us by reasons that they might have *the grace and communication of the ministry that is done toward the saints*, i.e., be allowed to give their own to the poor saints in Jerusalem, not considering that they were doing a favor for us, but we for them: *do not neglect to do good and to share what you have, for such sacrifices are pleasing to God* (Heb 13:16).

289. He also commends their generosity as to the order of giving, because they not only gave what they owned, but they first gave themselves. For this should be the order of giving, namely, that a man be first acceptable to God, for if a man is not pleasing to God, his gifts are not acceptable: *and the Lord had regard for Abel and his offering* (Gen 4:4).

Therefore he says, *and not as we hoped*. As if to say: they were truly willing, because *not as we hoped*, i.e., not with the intention we considered, that is, that they would give in reparation for sin; but *they gave their own selves, first to the Lord*, by amending their life, and *then to us*, by obeying in all things, *by the will of God*, which is that man be subject to his vicars: *obey your leaders and submit to them* (Heb 13:17).

A Gloss says that their offerings would not have been acceptable, unless they had first given themselves to God. Therefore, it seems that alms should not be accepted from sinners.

I answer that they should not be accepted, when they are given with the intention of being nourished in their sins.

290. Having given the example of the Macedonians, he then shows how he was moved by this example, when he says, *so that we asked that Titus*: as if to say: we were so moved by this display of generosity by the Macedonians,

scilicet rogaremus Titum, ut etiam vos sitis participes ipsius gratiae, *ut*, scilicet Titus, **quemadmodum coepit** vos monere ad benefaciendum, postquam vidit vos correctos, et inducere vos ad communionem, *ita perficiat in vobis*, *et* spiritualiter **gratiam istam** de largitione eleemosynarum, ut non desit vobis. Phil. I, 6: *qui coepit in vobis*, et cetera.

291. Consequenter admonet eos, ut hoc exemplo ipsi inducantur, cum dicit **sed sicut in omnibus**, et cetera. Ubi duo dicit.

Primo monet ut ipsi, exemplo Macedonum, sint prompti ad eleemosynas faciendum;

secundo quamdam suspicionem aufert, ibi **non quasi imperans dico**, et cetera.

292. Dicit ergo **sed sicut in omnibus**, etc., quasi dicat: sicut vos superatis Macedones in omnibus aliis gratiis, ita debetis eos superare etiam in ista, scilicet eleemosynis faciendis. Et hoc est quod dicit **sicut in omnibus aliis abundatis**; et, primo in his quae pertinent ad intellectum, et quantum ad hoc dicit **in fide**, qua creditur, *et sermone*, quo confitemur, Rom. X, 10: *corde creditur ad iustitiam*, quantum ad fidem, *ore autem confessio fit ad salutem*, quantum ad sermonem; et **in scientia** Scripturarum. I Cor. I, 5: *in omnibus divites facti estis*, et cetera.

Secundo in his quae pertinent ad opus, et quantum ad hoc dicit **et in omni sollicitudine**, scilicet bene operandi. Rom. XII, 11: *sollicitudine non pigri*.

Tertio in his quae pertinent ad affectum, et quantum ad hoc dicit **in caritate vestra** spirituali habita *in nos* superabundantius. Col. III, 14: *super omnia caritatem habentes*, et cetera. Sicut, inquam, in omnibus istis abundatis, ita scilicet rogavi Titum, **ut in hac gratia**, scilicet eleemosynarum, **abundetis**.

293. Et quia posset haberi suspicio quod quasi ex imperio mandaret, ut darent eleemosynas, contra quod est quod dicitur Ez. XXXIV, 4: *vos autem cum austeritate*, etc., et ideo contra removet, dicens **non quasi imperans dico**. Hoc est quod rogavi Titum, vel quod ego ipse hoc dico vobis, id est non feci quasi imperans. I Petr. ult.: *non ut dominantes in cleris*. Sed dico hoc **comprobans**, id est volens comprobare **per aliorum sollicitudinem**, scilicet Macedonum, **vestrae caritatis ingenium**.

Ubi sciendum est, quod ingenium bonum sumitur non solum pro aptitudine ad sciendum faciliter, sed etiam ad bene operandum. Cuius ratio est, quia ad hoc quod aliquis bene operetur, exigitur scientia dirigens. Et ideo sicut in addiscendo dicitur boni ingenii esse qui cito capit verba magistri, ita, in operando, boni ingenii dicitur, qui exemplo aliorum cito movetur ad bene

that we asked Titus to make you partakers of that grace, namely, *as he*, namely, Titus, **had begun**, to urge you to do good after he saw you amended and to induce you to communion, **so also would finish among you**, particularly **this same grace** of giving alms, that it not be lacking to you: *and I am sure that he who began a good work in you will bring it to completion at the day of Jesus Christ* (Phil 1:6).

291. Then when he says, **that as in all things you abound**, he urges them to be influenced by this example. Here he does two things.

First, he urges them to be prompted by the example of the Macedonians to give alms;

second, he removes a suspicion, at **I speak not as commanding**.

292. He says, therefore: **that as in all things you abound in faith and word and knowledge and all carefulness, moreover also in your charity towards us: so in this grace also you may abound**. As if to say: just as you surpass the Macedonians in all other graces, so you should surpass them in this, namely, in giving alms. And this is what he says: **that as in all things you abound**: first, in things pertaining to the intellect; and as to this he says, **in faith**, by which they believe, **and word**, by which they confess: *for man believes with his heart and so is justified, and he confesses with his lips and so is saved* (Rom 10:10); **and knowledge** of the Scriptures: *in every way you were enriched in him with all speech and all knowledge* (1 Cor 1:5).

Second, in things pertaining to works; as to this he says, **and all carefulness** namely, in doing good: *never flag in zeal* (Rom 12:11).

Third, in things pertaining to the effect; as to this he says, **also in your charity** spiritually dwelling in us superabundantly: *and above all these put on love, which binds everything together in perfect harmony* (Col 3:14). As, I say, you abound in all those things, so I asked Titus to see that **so in this grace**, namely, of alms, **you may abound**.

293. But because there might be a suspicion that he was ordering them to give alms, contrary to what is said: *with force and harshness you have ruled them* (Ezek 34:4), he removes this, saying: **I speak not as commanding**, i.e., what I asked Titus, or the fact that I say this to you, I did not do as though commanding: *not as domineering over those in your charge but being examples to the flock* (1 Pet 5:3). But I say this **approving**, i.e., desiring to prove, **by the carefulness of others**, namely, the Macedonians, **the good disposition of your charity**.

Here it should be noted that a good disposition refers not only to an aptitude to learn easily, but also to acting well, the reason being that in order to act well, a knowledge which directs is necessary. Therefore, just as in learning, a person is said to have a good disposition, if he quickly grasps the words of the teacher, so in doing good a person is said to have a good disposition, if he is quickly moved to

operandum. Et ideo dicit Apostolus ***comprobans***, id est probare volens, ***bonum ingenium vestrum***, id est quam promptam voluntatem habeatis ad dandum, moti exemplo Macedonum. I Cor. c. IV, 14: *non ut confundam vos haec scribo.*

do good by the example of others. That is why the Apostle says, ***approving also the good disposition of your charity***, i.e., how prompt a will you have for giving when moved by the example of the Macedonians: *I do not write this to make you ashamed, but to admonish you as my beloved children* (1 Cor 4:14).

Lecture 2

8:9Scitis enim gratiam Domini nostri Jesu Christi, quoniam propter vos egenus factus est, cum esset dives, ut illius inopia vos divites essetis. [n. 294]

8:10Et consilium in hoc do: hoc enim vobis utile est, qui non solum facere, sed et velle coepistis ab anno priore: [n. 296]

8:11nunc vero et facto perficite: ut quemadmodum promptus est animus voluntatis, ita sit et perficiendi ex eo quod habetis. [n. 300]

8:12Si enim voluntas prompta est, secundum id quod habet, accepta est, non secundum id quod non habet. [n. 301]

8:13Non enim ut aliis sit remissio, vobis autem tribulatio, sed ex aequalitate. [n. 302]

8:14In praesenti tempore vestra abundantia illorum inopiam suppleat: ut et illorum abundantia vestrae inopiae sit supplementum, ut fiat aequalitas, sicut scriptum est: [n. 305]

8:15Qui multum, non abundavit: et qui modicum, non minoravit. [n. 308]

8:9γινώσκετε γὰρ τὴν χάριν τοῦ κυρίου ἡμῶν Ἰησοῦ Χριστοῦ, ὅτι δι' ὑμᾶς ἐπτώχευσεν πλούσιος ὤν, ἵνα ὑμεῖς τῇ ἐκείνου πτωχείᾳ πλουτήσητε.

8:10αἱ γνώμην ἐν τούτῳ δίδωμι· τοῦτο γὰρ ὑμῖν συμφέρει, οἵτινες οὐ μόνον τὸ ποιῆσαι ἀλλὰ καὶ τὸ θέλειν προενήρξασθε ἀπὸ πέρυσι·

8:11νυνὶ δὲ καὶ τὸ ποιῆσαι ἐπιτελέσατε, ὅπως καθάπερ ἡ προθυμία τοῦ θέλειν, οὕτως καὶ τὸ ἐπιτελέσαι ἐκ τοῦ ἔχειν.

8:12εἰ γὰρ ἡ προθυμία πρόκειται, καθὸ ἐὰν ἔχῃ εὐπρόσδεκτος, οὐ καθὸ οὐκ ἔχει.

8:13οὐ γὰρ ἵνα ἄλλοις ἄνεσις, ὑμῖν θλῖψις, ἀλλ' ἐξ ἰσότητος·

8:14ἐν τῷ νῦν καιρῷ τὸ ὑμῶν περίσσευμα εἰς τὸ ἐκείνων ὑστέρημα, ἵνα καὶ τὸ ἐκείνων περίσσευμα γένηται εἰς τὸ ὑμῶν ὑστέρημα, ὅπως γένηται ἰσότης,

8:15καθὼς γέγραπται· ὁ τὸ πολὺ οὐκ ἐπλεόνασεν, καὶ ὁ τὸ ὀλίγον οὐκ ἠλαττόνησεν.

8:9For you know the grace of our Lord Jesus Christ, that being rich he became destitute for your sakes: that through his poverty you might be rich. [n. 294]

8:10And herein I give my advice: for this is profitable for you who began not only to do but also to be willing, a year ago. [n. 296]

8:11Now therefore perform it also in deed: that as your mind is ready to be willing, so it may be also to perform, out of what you have. [n. 300]

8:12For if the will is ready, it is accepted according to what a man has: not according to what he has not. [n. 301]

8:13For I do not mean that others should be eased and you burdened, but by an equality. [n. 302]

8:14In this present time let your abundance supply their want, that their abundance also may supply your want: that there may be an equality, as it is written: [n. 305]

8:15He who had much had nothing over; and he who had little had no want. [n. 308]

---

294. Hic inducit Corinthios ad dandum eleemosynas exemplo Christi, dicens: volo comprobare ingenium vestrum bonum ad dandum, scilicet pauperibus, et hoc facere debetis exemplo Christi. *Enim*, id est *quia*, *scitis gratiam Domini nostri Iesu Christi*, quam quidem humano generi contulit. Io. I, v. 17: *gratia et veritas per Iesum Christum*, et cetera. Et haec dicitur gratia, quia quidquid Filius Dei poenalitatum nostrarum assumpsit, totum gratiae est imputandum, quia nec praeventus alicuius bonitate, nec alicuius virtute coactus, nec inductus sua necessitate.

Est autem gratia ista *quoniam propter nos egenus factus est*. Et dicit *egenus*, quod plus est quam pauper. Nam egenus dicitur ille, qui non solum parum habet, sed qui indiget seu eget; pauper vero ille qui parum habet. Ad significandum ergo maiorem paupertatem dicitur *egenus factus est*, scilicet in temporalibus. Lc. IX, 58: *Filius hominis non habet*, et cetera. Thren. III, 19: *recordare paupertatis*, et cetera.

294. Here he uses the example of Christ to induce the Corinthians to give alms, saying: I wish to approve your good disposition, namely, for giving to the poor, and you should do this by reason of Christ's example. *For*, that is, *because you know the grace of our Lord Jesus Christ*, which he conferred on the human race: *grace and truth came through Jesus Christ* (John 1:17). This is called grace, because whatever the Son of God assumed of our punishments, all must be imputed to grace, because he was not anticipated by anyone's goodness, or compelled by anyone's power, or induced by any necessity of his own.

But it is grace, *that being rich he became destitute for your sakes*. He says, *became destitute* which is more than poor; for a destitute person is one who not only has very little, but is in great need; but a poor man is one who has a little. Therefore, to signify the extent of his poverty, he says, *he became destitute*, namely, in temporal things: *the Son of man has nowhere to lay his head* (Luke 9:58); *remember my affliction* (Lam 3:19).

Est autem factus egenus, non ex necessitate, sed ex voluntate, quia gratia ista iam non esset gratia. Et ideo dicit **cum dives esset**, scilicet in bonis spiritualibus. Rom. X, v. 12: *idem Deus dives in omnes*, et cetera. Prov. c. VIII, 18: *mecum sunt divitiae*, et cetera. Dicit autem **esset**, non *fuisset*, ne videretur Christus amisisse divitias spirituales cum assumpsit paupertatem. Sic enim assumpsit hanc paupertatem quod illas inaestimabiles divitias non amisit. Ps. XLVIII, 3: *simul in unum dives et pauper*. Dives in spiritualibus, pauper in temporalibus.

295. Causam autem quare voluit fieri egenus, subdit cum dicit **ut illius inopia divites essemus**, id est ut illius paupertate in temporalibus, vos essetis divites in spiritualibus. Et hoc est propter duo, scilicet propter exemplum et propter sacramentum.

Propter exemplum quidem, quia si Christus dilexit paupertatem, et nos, exemplo suo, debemus diligere eam. Diligendo autem paupertatem in temporalibus, efficimur divites in spiritualibus. Iac. II, 5: *nonne Deus elegit pauperes in mundo, divites in fide*, et cetera. Et ideo dicit **ut illius inopia**, et cetera.

Propter sacramentum autem, quia omnia quae Christus egit vel sustinuit, fuit propter nos. Unde sicut per hoc quod sustinuit mortem, liberati sumus a morte aeterna et restituti vitae, ita per hoc quod sustinuit inopiam in temporalibus, liberati sumus ab inopia in spiritualibus, et facti divites in spiritualibus. I Cor. I, 5: *divites facti estis in illo in omni scientia*, et cetera.

296. Consequenter cum dicit **consilium in hoc do**, etc., inducit eos ad dandum ex parte eorum. Et

circa hoc duo facit.

Primo ponit ipsorum utilitatem, quae ex hoc provenit;

secundo ostendit quod hoc etiam ab ipsis volitum est, scilicet ut darent eleemosynas, ibi **qui non solum**, et cetera.

297. Dicit ergo: considerans hoc beneficium, consilium vobis do, id est hortor vos ad hoc, scilicet ad dandum eleemosynas, scilicet non solum propter utilitatem sanctorum, qui sunt in Ierusalem, sed et propter utilitatem vestram. Prov. XXVII, 9: *boni amici consiliis anima dulcoratur*, et cetera.

Et hoc quia **utile est vobis**. Bonum enim pietatis plus est utile facienti, quam illi cui fit, quia faciens reportat inde commodum spirituale, recipiens vero temporale. Et sicut spirituale praeferri debet temporali, sic in operibus pietatis utilitas dantis praefertur utilitati accipientis. I Tim. IV, 8: *pietas ad omnia valet*.

He was made needy not from necessity but willingly, because that grace would not then be a grace. Hence he says, *that being rich*, namely, in spiritual goods: *the same Lord is Lord of all and bestows his riches upon all who call upon him* (Rom 10:12); *riches and honor are with me* (Prov 8:18). He says, *being*, and not *having been*, lest it seem that Christ lost his spiritual riches when he assumed poverty. For he assumed this poverty in such a way that he did not lose those inestimable riches: *both rich and poor together* (Ps 49:2), rich in spiritual things, poor in temporal things.

295. The reason he willed to be made needy is added, when he says, *that through his poverty you might become rich*, i.e., that through his poverty in temporal things, you might become rich in spiritual things. And this for two reasons: for an example and for a sacrament.

For an example, indeed, because if Christ loved poverty, we also should love it because of his example. But by loving poverty in temporal things, we are made rich in spiritual things: *has not God chosen those who are poor in the world to be rich in faith and heirs of the kingdom which he has promised to those who love him?* (Jas 2:5). This is why he says, *that through his poverty you might become rich*.

For the sacrament, however, because everything Christ did or endured was for our sake. Hence, just as by the fact that he endured death, we were delivered from eternal death and restored to life, so by the fact that he suffered need in temporal things, we have been delivered from need in spiritual things and made rich in spiritual things. *That in every way you were enriched in him with all speech and all knowledge* (1 Cor 1:5).

296. Then when he says, *and herein I give my advice*, he induces them to give on their part.

In regard to this he does two things.

First, he shows the benefit they will obtain from this;

second, he shows that this is desired from itself, namely, that they would give alms, at *for you who began not only*.

297. He says, therefore: considering this benefit, I give my advice, i.e., I urge you to give alms not only for the benefit of the saints in Jerusalem but also for your benefit: *the good counsels of a friend are sweet to the soul* (Prov 27:9).

And this is because it *is profitable for you*. For the good of piety is more beneficial to the doer than to the one to whom it is done, because the doer obtains a spiritual benefit from it, but the recipient a temporal one. And just as the spiritual is preferred to the temporal, in works of piety the profit to the giver is preferred to the benefit of the recipient: *godliness is of value in every way* (1 Tim 4:8).

298. Hoc autem non solum eis est utile sed etiam ipsi hoc voluerunt, et ideo dicit *quia non solum*, et cetera. Ubi tria facit.

Primo commemorat bonum principium in eis;

secundo hortatur eos ad debitum finem, ibi *nunc vero et facto*, etc.;

tertio exponit quoddam quod dixerat, ibi *si enim voluntas*, et cetera.

299. Dicit ergo: vere debetis libenter dare eleemosynas, quia non solum est vobis utile, sed etiam hoc ipsum velle *sponte coepistis*, scilicet dare eleemosynas, *a priori anno*, quo scilicet veni ad vos. Vel *a priori anno*, id est praecedenti. Quasi dicat: plus est velle, quam facere, iuxta illud Eccli. XVIII, v. 16: *verbum melius est quam datum*, et cetera. Et ideo debetis esse prompti ad dandum.

300. Et quia estis prompti ad dandum, ideo nunc quod habuistis in animo *perficite facto*, alioquin illa voluntas esset frustra. Io. IV: *non diligamus verbo, neque lingua*, et cetera. Phil. I, 6: *qui coepit in vobis*, et cetera. Et huius ratio est, *ut quemadmodum promptus est animus voluntatis*, id est discretio voluntatis. Secundum Glossam, prompta est, ita sit prompta discretio perficiendi.

Vel, aliter, ut *animus* sumatur pro voluntate. Et tunc dicitur: quemadmodum prompti fuistis ad volendum, ita prompti ad perficiendum. Et hoc *ex eo quod habetis*, id est secundum facultatem vestram.

301. Consequenter exponit hoc quod dicit *ex eo quod habetis*, dicens *si enim*, etc., quasi dicat: dico quod debetis esse prompti ad dandum, et in hoc non intendo vos gravare, ut scilicet detis supra facultates vestras, quia forte voluntas prompta ad hoc inducit vos, sed in hoc opus non potest imitari voluntatem. Et ideo dicit: *ex eo quod habetis*, *enim*, pro *quia*, *si voluntas prompta est secundum id quod habet, accepta est*.

Et huius ratio est, quia voluntas acceptatur in perfectione operationis; opus autem non perficitur, nisi ex eo quod habetur. Et ideo dicit *secundum quod habet, accepta est*. Tob. IV, 9: *si multum tibi fuerit, abundanter tribue*, et cetera.

302. Consequenter cum dicit *non enim ut aliis*, etc., removet suspicionem quamdam.

Possent enim dicere isti: si damus eleemosynas pauperibus sanctis, qui sunt in Ierusalem, ipsi otiosi vivent, et nos damna patiemur, et sic efficiemur miseri. Ideo Apostolus

primo hanc suspicionem excludit;

secundo suam intentionem manifestat;

tertio vero confirmat per auctoritatem.

298. But this is not only profitable to them, but they also wanted this; hence he says, *for this is profitable for you who began not only to do but also to be willing, a year ago*. Here he does three things.

First, he reminds them of their good start;

second, he urges them to the due end, at *now therefore perform it also*;

third, he explains something he had said, at *for if the will is ready*.

299. He says, therefore: in truth you should give alms gladly, because this is not only profitable to you, but *you who began not only to do but also to be willing*, namely, to give alms, *a year ago*, i.e., before I came to you. As if to say: it is better to will than to do: *so a word is better than a gift* (Sir 18:16). Therefore, you should be eager to give.

300. And because you are eager to give, therefore, *now therefore perform it also in deed*; otherwise that willingness is in vain: *let us not love in word or speech but in deed and in truth* (1 John 3:18); *and I am sure that he who began a good work in you will bring it to completion at the day of Jesus Christ* (Phil 1:6). The reason for this is *that as your mind is ready to be willing, so it may be also to perform*, i.e., the judgment of your will, according to a Gloss, is prompt, may be matched by your completing it.

Or another way, so that *mind* is taken for will, and then the sense is: as you were prompt in willing, so be prompt in accomplishing, *out of what you have*, i.e., according to your means.

301. Then he explains what he means by *out of what you have*, saying, *for if the will is ready, it is accepted according to what a man has*. As if to say: I say that you should be prompt to give, but I do not wish to burden you in this matter, namely, that you would give beyond your means, because perhaps your will inclines you to this; but in this matter the work cannot follow the will. Therefore he says, *out of what you have*. For, i.e., because, *if the will is ready, it is accepted according to what a man has*.

The reason being that the will is accepted in the accomplishment of the work; but the work is not perfected except from what a man has; hence he says, *it is accepted according to what a man has*. *If you have much, give generously; if you have a little, then try to impart a little gladly* (Tob 4:9).

302. Then when he says, *for do not I mean*, he removes a suspicion.

For someone could say: if we give alms to the saints in Jerusalem, they will live in idleness, while we suffer a loss and become wretched. Therefore the Apostle

first removes the suspicion;

second he shows his intention;

third, he confirms it by authority.

303. Et removet suspicionem, cum dicit *non enim ut aliis*, etc.; quasi dicat: non enim ita moneo vos eleemosynas dare, ut aliis sit refrigerium, dum otiose viverent de eleemosynis vestris, vobis autem sit tribulatio, id est paupertas, quia vos affligeremini.

Sed numquid peccant illi qui dant omnia aliis, et ipsi postea paupertate affliguntur? Et videtur quod sic per haec verba Apostoli.

Respondeo. Dicendum est, secundum Glossam, quod melius esset totum dare pauperibus, et affligi pro Christo. Illud autem quod dicit hic, condescendendo fecit, quia infirmi erant, et forte deficerent, si egestate premerentur.

304. Intentionem suam manifestat, cum dicit *sed ex aequalitate*, etc., quasi dicat: non intendo tribulationem vestram, sed quamdam aequalitatem, ut scilicet *vestra abundantia*, et cetera. Quod potest exponi tripliciter. Primo de aequalitate quantitatis; secundo de aequalitate proportionis; tertio de aequalitate voluntatis.

305. De aequalitate quantitatis, quia isti, scilicet Corinthii, abundabant in temporalibus et deficiebant in spiritualibus; sancti vero, qui erant in Ierusalem, abundabant in spiritualibus et deficiebant in temporalibus. Vult ergo ut fiat inter eos aequalitas quantitatis, ut scilicet illi qui abundant in temporalibus, dent medietatem omnium illis, qui deficiunt in eis, et isti dent medietatem spiritualium eis, ut sic sint aequaliter divites. Et ideo hoc potius dicit, ut scilicet *ex aequalitate* quantitatis, id est dimidia parte bonorum vestrorum, *in praesenti tempore*, quod breve est, *vestra abundantia*, terrenorum, *suppleat illorum inopiam*, qui deseruerunt omnia mundi, *et ut illorum abundantia*, scilicet in spiritualibus, *sit supplementum vestrae inopiae* in spiritualibus, id est ut sitis participes vitae aeternae. Lc. XVI, 9: *facite vobis amicos*, et cetera. Eccli. XIV, 15 s.: *in divisione sortis da et accipe*; da temporalia et accipe spiritualia.

306. De aequalitate autem proportionis exponitur sic, et melius. Vos, Corinthii, habetis abundantiam temporalium, sancti qui sunt in Ierusalem abundantiam spiritualium. Volo ergo ex quadam aequalitate, non quae sit secundum quantitatem, sed secundum proportionem, ut scilicet sicut illi sustentantur eleemosynis vestris, ita vos ditemini precibus illorum apud Deum. Sicut enim illi non ita ditantur de bonis vestris temporalibus, sicut vos estis divites, ita nec vos bonis illorum spiritualibus ditemini sicut illi. Et ideo dicit *sed ex aequalitate*, etc., praedicta vestra *abundantia* terrenorum, *illorum*, scilicet sanctorum, *inopiam*, in temporalibus, *suppleat*, ut et illorum *abundantia* in spiritualibus, et cetera. I Cor. IX, 11: *si nos vobis spiritualia seminavimus*, et cetera.

303. He removes this suspicion when he says, *for I do not mean that others should be eased and you burdened*. As if to say: I do not urge you to give alms in order that others might be refreshed, as they live in idleness off your alms, while you are burdened, impoverished, because you would be afflicted.

But do they commit sin who give everything to others and they are later afflicted with poverty? It seems so from these words of the Apostle.

I answer that according to a Gloss, it would be better to give all to the poor and be afflicted with Christ. But what the Apostle says here is out of condescension, because they were weak and might perhaps have fallen away if they were pressed by need.

304. He discloses his intention when he says, *but by an equality*. As if to say: I do not seek your affliction, but an equality, namely, *let your abundance supply their want*. This can be explained in three ways. First, as an equality of quantity; second, an equality of proportion; third, an equality of the will.

305. An equality of quantity, because they, i.e., the Corinthians, abounded in temporal things and were wanting in spiritual things; but the saints in Jerusalem abounded in spiritual things and were lacking in temporal things. Therefore he desired that an equality of quantity be established between them, namely, that those who abounded in temporal things give half of everything to those in need of them, while the others should give half of their spiritual things to them, so that they would be equally rich. Therefore, he says rather, that *by an equality* of quantity, i.e., from a half-share of your goods *in this present time*, which is short, *let your abundance* of earthly goods *supply their want*, for those who lack all earthly things; *and that their abundance* in spiritual goods *also may supply your want* in spiritual goods, i.e., that you may be partakers of eternal life. *Make friends for yourselves by means of unrighteous mammon* (Luke 16:9); *in dividing the lot, give and take* (Sir 14:15); i.e., give temporal things and accept spiritual things.

306. As an equality of proportion it is explained in the following way, and better: you Corinthians have an abundance of temporal goods, but the saints of Jerusalem an abundance of spiritual goods. I wish, therefore, that as a matter of equality, not according to quantity, but according to proportion, namely, that as they are sustained by your alms, so may you be enriched by their prayers to God. For just as they are not as rich in your temporal goods as you are rich, so neither are you as rich in their spiritual goods as they are. And so he says: *but by an equality in this present time*, your *abundance* of earthly things should *supply their want* of earthly goods, *that their abundance* of spiritual things *may supply your want*: if we have sown spiritual good among you, is it too much if we reap your material benefits? (1 Cor 9:11).

307. De aequalitate autem voluntatis exponitur sic: *sed ex aequalitate*, etc., id est volo quod sit in vobis aequalitas voluntatis, ut scilicet sicut illi habent voluntatem communicandi vobis ea in quibus abundant, ita vos habeatis voluntatem communicandi illis ea in quibus abundatis.

308. Consequenter confirmat hoc per auctoritatem. Unde dicit *sicut scriptum est*, scilicet Ex. XVI: *qui multum*, scilicet collegerat de manna, id est qui amplius habuit quam gomor, *non abundavit*, id est non habuit ultra sufficientiam suam; *et qui modicum, non minoravit*, id est non defecit ei, quia omnes aequaliter abundabant, ut dicitur Ex. XVI. Et sic nec qui plus collegerat, plus habuit, nec qui minus paraverat, reperit minus.

307. It is explained as an equality of will in this way: *but by an equality* your abundance at the present time should supply their want, i.e., I desire an equality of will to be in you, that just as they are willing to communicate to you the things in which they abound, so you would have the will to communicate to them the things in which you abound.

308. Then he confirms this with an authority; hence he says, *as it is written*, namely in Exodus: *he who had much* (Exod 16:18), i.e., had collected more manna than an omer, *had nothing over*, i.e., did not have more than his sufficiency; *and he who had little had no want* i.e., he did not fall short of it, because all had an equal abundance (Exod 16:18). And so neither he who had collected more had more, nor he who had prepared less, discovered less.

Lecture 3

8:16Gratias autem Deo, qui dedit eamdem sollicitudinem pro vobis in corde Titi, [n. 309]

8:17quoniam exhortationem quidem suscepit: sed cum sollicitior esset, sua voluntate profectus est ad vos. [n. 311]

8:18Misimus etiam cum illo fratrem, cujus laus est in Evangelio per omnes ecclesias: [n. 312]

8:19non solum autem, sed et ordinatus est ab ecclesiis comes peregrinationis nostrae in hanc gratiam, quae ministratur a nobis ad Domini gloriam, et destinatam voluntatem nostram:

8:20devitantes hoc, ne quis nos vituperet in hac plenitudine, quae ministratur a nobis. [n. 314]

8:21Providemus enim bona non solum coram Deo, sed etiam coram hominibus. [n. 316]

8:22Misimus autem cum illis et fratrem nostrum, quem probavimus in multis saepe sollicitum esse: nunc autem multo sollicitiorem, confidentia multa in vos, [n. 317]

8:23sive pro Tito, qui est socius meus, et in vos adjutor, sive fratres nostri, apostoli ecclesiarum, gloria Christi.

8:24Ostensionem ergo, quae est caritatis vestrae, et nostrae gloriae pro vobis, in illos ostendite in faciem ecclesiarum. [n. 319]

8:16Χάρις δὲ τῷ θεῷ τῷ δόντι τὴν αὐτὴν σπουδὴν ὑπὲρ ὑμῶν ἐν τῇ καρδίᾳ Τίτου,

8:17ὅτι τὴν μὲν παράκλησιν ἐδέξατο, σπουδαιότερος δὲ ὑπάρχων αὐθαίρετος ἐξῆλθεν πρὸς ὑμᾶς.

8:18συνεπέμψαμεν δὲ μετ' αὐτοῦ τὸν ἀδελφὸν οὗ ὁ ἔπαινος ἐν τῷ εὐαγγελίῳ διὰ πασῶν τῶν ἐκκλησιῶν,

8:19οὐ μόνον δέ, ἀλλὰ καὶ χειροτονηθεὶς ὑπὸ τῶν ἐκκλησιῶν συνέκδημος ἡμῶν σὺν τῇ χάριτι ταύτῃ τῇ διακονουμένῃ ὑφ' ἡμῶν πρὸς τὴν [αὐτοῦ] τοῦ κυρίου δόξαν καὶ προθυμίαν ἡμῶν,

8:20στελλόμενοι τοῦτο, μή τις ἡμᾶς μωμήσηται ἐν τῇ ἁδρότητι ταύτῃ τῇ διακονουμένῃ ὑφ' ἡμῶν·

8:21προνοοῦμεν γὰρ καλὰ οὐ μόνον ἐνώπιον κυρίου ἀλλὰ καὶ ἐνώπιον ἀνθρώπων.

8:22συνεπέμψαμεν δὲ αὐτοῖς τὸν ἀδελφὸν ἡμῶν ὃν ἐδοκιμάσαμεν ἐν πολλοῖς πολλάκις σπουδαῖον ὄντα, νυνὶ δὲ πολὺ σπουδαιότερον πεποιθήσει πολλῇ τῇ εἰς ὑμᾶς.

8:23εἴτε ὑπὲρ Τίτου, κοινωνὸς ἐμὸς καὶ εἰς ὑμᾶς συνεργός· εἴτε ἀδελφοὶ ἡμῶν, ἀπόστολοι ἐκκλησιῶν, δόξα Χριστοῦ.

8:24τὴν οὖν ἔνδειξιν τῆς ἀγάπης ὑμῶν καὶ ἡμῶν καυχήσεως ὑπὲρ ὑμῶν εἰς αὐτοὺς ἐνδεικνύμενοι εἰς πρόσωπον τῶν ἐκκλησιῶν.

8:16And thanks be to God, who has given the same carefulness for you in the heart of Titus. [n. 309]

8:17For indeed he accepted the exhortation: but, being more careful, of his own will he went to you. [n. 311]

8:18We have also sent with him the brother whose praise is in the Gospel through all the churches. [n. 312]

8:19And not only that: but he was also ordained by the churches as companion of our travels, for this grace, which is administered by us, to the glory of the Lord and our determined will:

8:20Avoiding this, lest any man should blame us in this abundance which is administered by us. [n. 314]

8:21For we forecast what may be good, not only before God but also before men. [n. 316]

8:22And we have sent with them our brother also, whom we have often proved diligent in many things, but now much more diligent: with much confidence in you, [n. 317]

8:23Either for Titus, who is my companion and fellow laborer towards you, or our brethren, the apostles of the churches, the glory of Christ.

8:24Therefore show to them, in the sight of the churches, the evidence of your charity and of our boasting on your behalf. [n. 319]

---

309. Postquam tractavit de collectis dandis, hic consequenter tractat de ministris per quos collectae fiant. Et

circa hoc duo facit.

Primo nominat eos;

secundo recommendat eos Corinthiis, ibi *ostensionem ergo quae est*, et cetera.

Circa primum tria facit.

Primo enim nominat Titum;

secundo Barnabam, ibi *misimus etiam cum illo fratrem*, etc.;

tertio Apollo, ibi *misimus autem cum illis*, et cetera.

309. After dealing with the collections, to which they should contribute, the Apostle then deals with the ministers by whom the collections should be made.

In regard to this he does two things.

First, he names them;

second, he recommends them to the Corinthians, at *therefore show to them*.

In regard to the first he does three things.

First, he names Titus;

second, Barnabas, at *we have also sent with him the brother*;

third, Apollos, at *and we have sent with them*.

Circa Titum duo commendat, scilicet eius sollicitudinem et sollicitudinis signum, ibi *quoniam exhortationem*, et cetera.

310. Dicit ergo primo: dixi, supra, quod rogavi Titum ut perficeret gratiam istam de eleemosynis colligendis, quod imminet sollicitudini meae ex ordinatione apostolorum, de quo inveni etiam ipsum sollicitum; et ideo ago *gratias Deo, qui dedit eamdem sollicitudinem*, quam ego habeo, *pro vobis*, exhortandis et promovendis ad opera misericordiae, *in corde Titi*; quia ipse etiam sollicitus est, sicut et ego, ut perficiat in vobis hanc gratiam. Hebr. VI, 11: *cupimus unumquemque vestrum eamdem ostentare sollicitudinem*, et cetera. Rom. XII, 8: *qui praeest in sollicitudine*.

311. Signum autem huius sollicitudinis est, quia quando rogavi eum, ipse consensit exhortationi meae. Et ideo dicit *quoniam exhortationem quidem suscepit*. Et quia prosecutus est quod petii, unde dicit *sed cum sollicitior esset sua voluntate*, quam mea exhortatione, *profectus est ad vos*; qui tamen primo recusabat venire propter peccata vestra. Rom. XII, 11: *sollicitudine non pigri*.

312. Consequenter cum dicit *misimus autem*, etc., tractat de secundo ministro. Et

circa hoc duo facit.

Primo commendat ipsum;

secundo subdit rationem quare mittit tam solemnes nuntios, ibi *devitantes*, et cetera.

313. Frater iste, secundum quosdam, est Lucas, vel secundum alios Barnabas, quem quidem commendat ex tribus, scilicet ex fama, quia *laus* eius, scilicet Lucae, *est in Evangelio* ab eo scripto *per omnes ecclesias*, quia est approbatum per apostolos. Vel *cuius laus*, scilicet Barnabae, *est in Evangelio* praedicato ab ipso *per omnes Ecclesias*, quia Iudaeis et gentibus. Unde dicitur de Barnaba, Act. XI, 24, quod erat vir bonus plenus fide et Spiritu Sancto.

Item commendat ipsum ex societate sua, quia *non solum* est famosus, *sed et ordinatus est ab ecclesiis* Iudaeae *comes peregrinationis meae*, id est praedicationis meae, qua, ut peregrini, mundum circuimus. Supra c. V, 6: *quamdiu sumus in corpore, peregrinamur a Deo*, et cetera. Et hoc est verum de Luca, quia ipse fuit unus de septuaginta duobus discipulis, et socius Pauli. De Barnaba similiter, quia per Spiritum Sanctum dicitur Act. XIII, 2: *segregate mihi Barnabam et Paulum in opus*, et cetera. Et factus est comes *in hanc gratiam*, scilicet collectionis eleemosynarum. Vel *in hanc gratiam*, scilicet praedicationis, de qua dicitur Eph. III, 8: *mihi autem omnium sanctorum minimo*, et cetera.

Item commendat eum ex officio, quia est minister gratiae *quae ministratur a nobis*. I Cor. IV, 1: *sic nos*

Concerning Titus he commends two things, namely, his earnest care and the sign of his earnest care, at *for indeed he accepted the exhortation*.

310. He says, therefore, in regard to Titus: I have said above that I have asked Titus to prove that grace collecting alms, because it has a bearing on the care entrusted to me by the apostles, in which I have also found him careful. *And thanks be to God, who has given the same carefulness for you in the heart of Titus*, as I have, for exhorting you and promoting you to works of mercy, because he is as solicitous as I to prove this grace for you. *And we desire each one of you to show the same earnestness in realizing the full assurance of hope until the end* (Heb 6:11); *the leader, in diligence* (Rom 12:8).

311. But the sign of this carefulness is that when I asked him, he consented to my exhortation; hence he says, *for indeed he accepted the exhortation*, and because he carried out what I asked; hence he says, *but, being more careful, of his own will* more than by my exhortation, *he went to you*, although at first he refused to go on account of your sins: *never flag in zeal* (Rom 12:11).

312. Then when he says, *we have also sent with him the brother*, he treats of the second minister.

In regard to this he does two things.

First, he commends him;

second, he gives the reason why he is sending such earnest messengers, at *avoiding this*.

313. This brother, according to some, is Luke, and according to others, Barnabas. Whoever it is, he recommends him on three points, namely, on his reputation, because his *praise*, that is, Luke's, *is in the Gospel* written by him *through all the churches*, because it was approved by the apostles. Or *whose praise*, namely, Barnabas', *is in* the preaching of *the Gospel through all the churches*, because he preached to Jews and gentiles. Hence it is said of Barnabas in Acts, that he was a good man, full of faith and the Holy Spirit (Acts 4:38).

He also commends him on his companionship, because *not only that*, i.e., that he is famous, *but he was also ordained by the churches as companion of our travels* in this gracious work, i.e., of my preaching, for which we traveled as pilgrims over the world: *while we are in the body we are absent from the Lord* (2 Cor 5:6). And this is true of Luke, because he was one of the seventy-two disciples and a companion of Paul. It is also true of Barnabas, because it was said by the Holy Spirit: *set apart for me Barnabas and Saul for the work to which I have called them* (Acts 13:2). And he was made a companion *for this grace* namely, to collect the alms. Or, *for this grace* of preaching, of which it is said: *to me, though I am the very least of all the saints* (Eph 3:8).

He also commends him from his office, because he is a minister of grace *which is administered by us*. *This is*

existimet homo. Supra c. III, 6: **qui et idoneos nos**, et cetera. Ministratur autem gratia ista **ad Domini gloriam**, ut scilicet Dominus noster glorificetur, scilicet de eleemosynis factis, de conversione plurimorum populorum praedicationi nostrae, quia, ut dicitur Prov. XIV, 28, *in multitudine populi*, et cetera.

Item ministratur, ut voluntas nostra impleatur, quia nos hoc volumus fieri. Et ideo dicit **et voluntatem nostram destinatam**, id est praedestinatam a Deo, qui praedestinavit ab aeterno nos talem voluntatem habere.

314. Consequenter cum dicit **devitantes**, etc., assignat causam quare mittat tam solemnes nuntios. Et

primo huius rationem assignat;

secundo probat, ibi **providemus ergo**, et cetera.

315. Dicit ergo: causa quare tam solemnes nuntios mittimus, est ista: ut sciatis negotium huiusmodi inesse cordi nostro. Et ideo dicit **devitantes hoc**, scilicet **ne quis**, etc., quasi dicat: ut vitemus vituperium quod posset mihi impingi ab aliquibus, vel negligentiae, si non mitterem strenuos, vel fraudis si non mitterem securos. Et isti strenui erant et prompti et securi, quia dati ab Ecclesiis et electi per Spiritum Sanctum. Supra c. VI, 3: **nemini dantes ullam offensionem**, et cetera.

Dicit autem **in hac plenitudine**, scilicet eleemosynarum vel conversionis gentium. I Petr. IV, 10: *unusquisque sicut accepit gratiam in alterutrum*, et cetera.

316. Et hoc probat dicens **providemus enim**, etc., quasi dicat: bene dico devitantes, quia **providemus**, id est providere debemus, **bona**, id est ut opera nostra bona sint **non solum coram Deo**, ut ei placeamus, **sed etiam coram hominibus**, ut scilicet eis bona videantur. Et hoc facit, sollicite procurando et bonos imitando. Rom. XII, 9: *adhaerentes bono*, et cetera.

317. Consequenter cum dicit **misimus autem cum illis et fratrem nostrum**, etc., tractat de tertio nuntio, scilicet de Apollo.

Ubi duo facit. Primo, quia commendat eum de sollicitudine, cum dicit **quem**, scilicet Apollo, **probavimus saepe sollicitum esse** de salute vestra; **nunc autem multo sollicitiorem**. Nam, sicut supra apparet, Apollo fuit primus, qui post Apostolum praedicavit apud Corinthum. I Cor. III, 6: *ego plantavi, Apollo rigavit*. Hic autem, turbatus de peccato ipsorum recessit, et sollicitudinem quam ante pro ipsis habebat, postposuit. Nunc vero, audita conversione eorum, factus est de salute ipsorum sollicitior, quam antea esset. Eph. IV, 3: *solliciti servare unitatem Spiritus*, et cetera. Rom. XII, 8: *qui praeest in sollicitudine*, et cetera.

how one should regard us, as servants of Christ (1 Cor 4:1); **who has also made us fit ministers of the New Testament** (2 Cor 3:6). But that grace is administered to **the glory of the Lord**, namely, that our Lord be glorified by the alms collected after the conversion of many people by our preaching, because, as it is said: *in a multitude of people is the glory of a king* (Prov 14:28).

Likewise it is administered in order that our will be fulfilled, because we want this to be done; hence, he says, **and our determined will**, i.e., predestined by God, who from eternity predestined us to have such a will.

314. Then when he says, **avoiding this**, he assigns the cause for why he is sending such solemn messengers.

First, he assigns the reason for this;

second, he proves it, at **for we forecast**.

315. He says, therefore: the reason we are sending such solemn messengers is this, that you may know that this affair is in our heart. Hence he says, **avoiding this, lest any man should blame us in this abundance**. As if to say: to avoid the accusation that could be lodged against us by others either for negligence, if we did not send solemn messengers, or of fraud, if we did not send trustworthy men. But they are energetic and prompt and trustworthy, because they were given by the churches and chosen by the Holy Spirit. **Giving no offense to any man, that our ministry be not blamed** (2 Cor 6:3).

But he says, **in this abundance**, namely, of alms, or of converted gentiles. *As each has received a gift, employ it for one another, as good stewards of God's varied grace* (1 Pet 4:10).

316. Then he proves this, saying: **for we forecast**, as if he says: well I say avoiding this, because **we forecast**, i.e., we ought to provide, **what may be good**, i.e., so that our works might be good **not only before God**, that we might be pleasing to him, **but also before men**, namely, that the good works may be seen by them. And he does this by providing carefully and by imitating good men: *let love be genuine; hate what is evil, hold fast to what is good* (Rom 12:9).

317. Then when he says, **and we have sent with them our brother also**, he deals with the third messenger, namely, Apollos,

and he does two things. First, he commends him for his diligence, when he says, **whom**, namely, Apollos, **we have often proved diligent** in many matters for your salvation, **but now much more diligent**. For as is apparent above, Apollos was the first one after the Apostle to preach to the Corinthians: *I planted, Apollos watered, but God gave the growth* (1 Cor 3:6). But being disturbed at their sin, he departed and put aside the carefulness he had previously for them. But now, hearing of their conversion, he became more diligent than ever for their salvation. *Eager to maintain the unity of the Spirit in the bond of peace* (Eph 4:3); *the leader, in diligence* (Rom 12:8).

318. Secundo, subdit causam sollicitudinis quam assumpsit, quia Apollo confidit de vobis ex his quae Titus dixit de vobis, commendans vos.

Unde dicit *multa confidentia in vobis, sive pro Tito qui est socius meus*, et quia libenter venit in societatem Titi et Lucae seu Barnabae, et quia ad hoc inductus fuit ab apostolis ecclesiarum, quae sunt in Iudaea. Et ideo dicit *sive fratres nostri, apostoli ecclesiarum* Iudaeae, scilicet induxerunt eum ad sollicitudinem habendam pro vobis. Quae quidem Ecclesiae sunt *gloriae Christi*, id est ad gloriam Christi.

319. Consequenter cum dicit *ostensionem ergo quae est*, etc., recommendat istos nuntios Corinthiis, dicens: quia tales misimus ad vos, *ergo ostensionem*, etc., id est, ostendatis opere, quod caritatem habetis ad eos et quod vere commendavi vos et quod ego vere gloriatus sim de vobis *in faciem ecclesiarum*, ad quas perveni et quibus praedicavi.

Vel *in faciem omnium ecclesiarum*, quia quod facitis eis, innotescet omnibus ecclesiis.

318. Second, he discloses the cause of the diligence he assumed, because Apollos is confident of you from the things Titus has said about you, commending you.

Hence, he says, *with much confidence in you. Either for Titus, who is my companion*, and because he gladly went in fellowship with Titus and Luke, or Barnabas, and because he was induced to do this by the apostles of the churches, who are in Judea. And therefore he says: *or our brethren, the apostles of the churches* of Judea, that is, they induced him to have a care for you; which churches are *the glory of Christ*, i.e., to the glory of Christ.

319. Then when he says, *therefore show to them*, he recommends those messengers to the Corinthians, saying: because I have sent such men to you, *therefore show to them, in the sight of the churches, the evidence of your charity and of our boasting on your behalf*, i.e., show by your deeds that you have charity toward them, and that he has truthfully commended you, and that he was right in boasting about you, *in the sight of the churches*, where I have been and to whom I have preached;

or: *before the churches*, because what you do to them will be made known to all the churches.

CHAPTER 9

Lecture 1

9:1Nam de ministerio, quod fit in sanctos ex abundanti est mihi scribere vobis. [n. 320]

9:2Scio enim promptum animum vestrum: pro quo de vobis glorior apud Macedones. Quoniam et Achaia parata est ab anno praeterito, et vestra aemulatio provocavit plurimos. [n. 322]

9:3Misi autem fratres: ut ne quod gloriamur de vobis, evacuetur in hac parte, [n. 323] ut (quemadmodum dixi) parati sitis: [n. 325]

9:4ne cum venerint Macedones mecum, et invenerint vos imparatos, erubescamus nos (ut non dicamus vos) in hac substantia.

9:5Necessarium ergo existimavi rogare fratres, ut praeveniant ad vos, et praeparent repromissam benedictionem hanc paratam esse sic, quasi benedictionem, non tamquam avaritiam. [n. 327]

9:6Hoc autem dico: qui parce seminat, parce et metet: et qui seminat in benedictionibus, de benedictionibus et metet. [n. 329]

9:7Unusquisque, prout destinavit in corde suo, non ex tristitia, aut ex necessitate: hilarem enim datorem diligit Deus. [n. 330]

9:1Περὶ μὲν γὰρ τῆς διακονίας τῆς εἰς τοὺς ἁγίους περισσόν μοί ἐστιν τὸ γράφειν ὑμῖν·

9:2οἶδα γὰρ τὴν προθυμίαν ὑμῶν ἣν ὑπὲρ ὑμῶν καυχῶμαι Μακεδόσιν, ὅτι Ἀχαΐα παρεσκεύασται ἀπὸ πέρυσι, καὶ τὸ ὑμῶν ζῆλος ἠρέθισεν τοὺς πλείονας.

9:3ἔπεμψα δὲ τοὺς ἀδελφούς, ἵνα μὴ τὸ καύχημα ἡμῶν τὸ ὑπὲρ ὑμῶν κενωθῇ ἐν τῷ μέρει τούτῳ, ἵνα καθὼς ἔλεγον παρεσκευασμένοι ἦτε,

9:4μή πως ἐὰν ἔλθωσιν σὺν ἐμοὶ Μακεδόνες καὶ εὕρωσιν ὑμᾶς ἀπαρασκευάστους καταισχυνθῶμεν ἡμεῖς, ἵνα μὴ λέγω ὑμεῖς, ἐν τῇ ὑποστάσει ταύτῃ.

9:5ἀναγκαῖον οὖν ἡγησάμην παρακαλέσαι τοὺς ἀδελφούς, ἵνα προέλθωσιν εἰς ὑμᾶς καὶ προκαταρτίσωσιν τὴν προεπηγγελμένην εὐλογίαν ὑμῶν, ταύτην ἑτοίμην εἶναι οὕτως ὡς εὐλογίαν καὶ μὴ ὡς πλεονεξίαν.

9:6Τοῦτο δέ, ὁ σπείρων φειδομένως φειδομένως καὶ θερίσει, καὶ ὁ σπείρων ἐπ' εὐλογίαις ἐπ' εὐλογίαις καὶ θερίσει.

9:7ἕκαστος καθὼς προῄρηται τῇ καρδίᾳ, μὴ ἐκ λύπης ἢ ἐξ ἀνάγκης· ἱλαρὸν γὰρ δότην ἀγαπᾷ ὁ θεός.

9:1For concerning the ministry that is done towards the saints, it is superfluous for me to write to you. [n. 320]

9:2For I know your ready mind: for which I boast of you to the Macedonians, that Achaia also is ready from the year past. And your emulation has provoked very many. [n. 322]

9:3Now I have sent the brethren, that the thing which we boast of concerning you may not be made void in this behalf, [n. 323] that (as I have said) you may be ready: [n. 325]

9:4Lest, when the Macedonians shall come with me and find you unprepared, we (not to say you) should be ashamed in this matter.

9:5Therefore I thought it necessary to ask the brethren to go to you before and prepare this blessing before promised, to be ready, so as a blessing, not as covetousness. [n. 327]

9:6Now this I say: he who sows sparingly shall also reap sparingly: and he who sows in blessings shall also reap blessings. [n. 329]

9:7Every one as he has determined in his heart, not with sadness or of necessity: for God loves a cheerful giver. [n. 330]

---

320. Supra Apostolus induxit Corinthios ad dandum eleemosynas sanctis qui sunt in Ierusalem, hic vero inducit eos quantum ad modum dandi, ut scilicet hilariter et abundanter dent. Unde ad hoc quod bene darent, misit tam solemnes nuntios.

Circa hoc autem duo facit.

Primo excludit opinatam causam de missione nuntiorum;

secundo vero astruit veram, ibi **misimus autem fratres**, et cetera.

320. Having exhorted the Corinthians to give alms to the saints in Jerusalem, the Apostle now admonishes them how to give, namely, cheerfully and abundantly. Hence, in order that they might give properly, he has sent them important messengers.

In regard to this he does two things.

First, he excludes the supposed cause for sending the messengers;

second, he gives the true one, at **now I have sent the brethren**.

Circa primum tria facit.

Primo excludit suspicionem;

secundo ad hoc causam assignat, ibi *scio enim promptum*, etc.;

tertio causam probat, ibi *pro quo de vobis*, et cetera.

321. Quantum ad primum, quia posset aliquis dicere Apostolo: *tu mones nos quod bene recipiamus nuntios quos mittis, sed quare non potius mones quod bene largiamur eleemosynas?* Et ideo hoc removens dicit: non est necessarium quod hoc moneam, *nam*, id est quia, *de ministerio quod fit in sanctos ex abundanti est*, id est superfluum est, *mihi scribere vobis.*

322. Et huius causa est, quia *scio promptum animum vestrum*, ad subveniendum eis. Ps. CVII, 2: *paratum cor meum, Deus*, et cetera.

Quod autem sit promptus animus vester, probo ex duobus. Primo ex gloriatione nostra de vobis. Nam nisi scirem vos esse promptos ad hoc, non fuissem gloriatus de vobis apud alios. Et ideo dicit *pro quo*, scilicet promptitudine animi vestri. Supra I, 12: *gloria nostra*, et cetera. Et supra VII, 4: *multa mihi fiducia*, et cetera. *Glorior apud Macedones*, de hoc scilicet *quoniam et Achaia*, in qua Corinthus metropolis est, *parata est ab anno praeterito*, ad largiendum.

Secundo ex effectu, quia vos provocastis exemplo vestro multos ad hoc. Et ideo dicit *et vestra aemulatio*, id est amor et studium imitandi vos, *provocavit plurimos*, quia enim audierunt vos bene correctos proficere, provocantur plurimi, scilicet ad proficiendum. Prov. XXVII, 17: *ferrum ferro acuitur*, et cetera. Gal. IV, 18: *bonum autem aemulamini*, et cetera. I Cor. XII, 31: *aemulamini charismata*, et cetera.

323. Consequenter cum dicit *misimus autem fratres*, etc., ponit veram causam quare miserit tam solemnes nuntios. Et

primo ponit in generali;

secundo in speciali, ibi *ut quemadmodum dixi*, et cetera.

324. Circa primum duo facit. Primo assignat veram causam, dicens: causa autem quare istos misi, est non quod credam vos nolle subvenire pauperibus, sed *ut ne quod gloriamur de vobis*, id est ne gloria nostra, quam habemus de vobis, *evacuetur*, si scilicet deficeretis. I Cor. IX, 15: *bonum est mihi mori*, et cetera. *Evacuetur*, inquam, *in hac parte*, quia bene constat mihi quod in aliis virtutibus et bonis non evacuabitis gloriam meam.

325. Secundo cum dicit *ut quemadmodum*, etc., hortatur eos ad debitum modum dandi. Et

primo hortatur, ut dent prompte;

secundo ut dent abundanter, ibi *necessarium ergo*, etc.;

In regard to the first he does three things.

First, he excludes a suspicion;

second, he assigns the cause for this, at *for I know your willing mind*;

third, he proves the cause, at *for which I boast of you*.

321. As to the first, because someone could say to the Apostle: *you urge us to receive your messengers cordially, but why do you not rather urge us to give alms properly?* Therefore, rejecting this, he says: it is not necessary for me to urge this *now*, i.e., *because, concerning the ministry that is done towards the saints, it is superfluous for me to write to you.*

322. And the reason for this is because *I know your ready mind* to help them: *my heart is steadfast, O God* (Ps 108:1).

That your mind is ready I prove by two things. First, from our boasting of you, for unless I knew that you were ready for this, I would not have boasted to them about you. Therefore he says, *for which*, namely, the promptitude of your mind: *for our glory is this, the testimony of our conscience* (2 Cor 1:12); *great is my confidence for you* (2 Cor 7:4). *I boast of you to the Macedonians*, saying that *Achaia*, in which Corinth is the metropolis, *also is ready from the year past*.

Second, from the effect, because you have provoked many to do this by your example. Hence he says, *and your emulation*, i.e., the desire to imitate you, *has provoked very many*, for since they heard of your progress after your amendment, many were provoked to make progress. *Iron sharpens iron, and one man sharpens another* (Prov 27:17); *for a good purpose it is always good to be made much of* (Gal 4:18); *but earnestly desire the higher gifts* (1 Cor 12:31).

323. Then when he says, *now I have sent the brethren*, he establishes the true cause for why he was sending such solemn messengers.

First, he lays down the general reason;

second, the special reason, at *as I have said*.

324. Concerning the first he does two things. First, he assigns the true cause, saying: the reason why I have sent them is not that I believe you are not willing to help the poor, but *that the thing which we boast of*, that is, our glory, *concerning you may not be made void* if you should fail: *for I would rather die than have anyone deprive me of my ground for boasting* (1 Cor 9:15). That it *may not be made void*, I say, *in this behalf*, because it is evident to me that in the other virtues and good deeds you will not make void my glory.

325. Second, when he says, *that (as I have said)*, as I said you would be, he urges them to give in the proper way.

First, he urges them to give readily;

second, that they may give abundantly, at *therefore I thought it necessary*;

tertio ut dent hilariter ibi **unusquisque prout destinavit**, et cetera.

326. Circa primum duo facit. Primo ponit modum dandi; secundo rationem assignat, ibi **ne cum venero**, et cetera.

Modus dandi est ut scilicet prompte detur. Et ideo dicit: ideo misi ministros, **ut sitis parati** ad dandum, **quemadmodum dixi**, scilicet exemplo Macedonum. Matth. XXV, 10: *quae paratae erant*, et cetera. Prov. III, 28: *ne dicas amico tuo: vade, et revertere, et cras dabo tibi*, et cetera.

Ratio autem huius est **ne cum venerint mecum**, scilicet ad vos, **Macedones**, et **invenerint vos imparatos, erubescamus nos**, quasi dicat: vobis erit confusio si promisistis, et non solvistis. Sed esto quod sustineatis, et non curetis de confusione vestra, ad minus caveatis erubescentiae nostrae, qui dicimus vos esse paratos.

327. Consequenter cum dicit **necessarium ergo**, etc., hortatur eos quod dent abundanter. Et

circa hoc duo facit.

Primo ponit admonitionem;

secundo admonitionis rationem assignat, ibi **hoc autem dico**, et cetera.

328. Dicit ergo: ne ergo evacuetur gloria nostra, et vos non erubescatis, **necessarium existimavi rogare fratres**, scilicet Lucam. Titum et Apollo, ut **perveniant ad vos, et praeparent repromissam benedictionem hanc**, scilicet eleemosynam, quae dicitur benedictio, quia est causa aeternae benedictionis. Nam per actionem dandi, homo benedicitur a Deo, Ps. XXIII, 5: *hic accipiet benedictionem a Domino*, etc., et ab hominibus, Eccli. XXXI, 28: *splendidum in panibus*, et cetera. Prov. XXII, 9: *qui pronus est ad misericordiam*, et cetera.

Et dicit hanc benedictionem **paratam esse quasi benedictionem**, id est abundanter, **et non quasi avaritiam**, id est parce.

329. Ratio autem quare debeant abundanter dare, est quia ego **dico**, quod **qui parce seminat**, id est qui parum dat in mundo isto, **parce et metet**, id est parum recipiet in alio saeculo. Et dicit **seminat**, quia semina nostra sunt quidquid boni fecerimus. Et iterum, quia si parum seminatur, non multum colligetur. Gal. VI, 8: *quae seminaverit homo, haec et metet*. Sed multiplicata, **et qui seminat in benedictionibus**, id est abundanter, **metet et de benedictionibus**, scilicet Dei largam retributionem.

Sed numquid non metent omnes abundanter?

Dicendum est sic, quantum ad quantitatem praemii, quia omnes affluent, et nullus ibi parce metet. Sed dicit abundanter, quasi ad proportionem et bene seminantium. I Cor. c. XV, 41: *stella a stella differt*. Abundanter omnes quantum ad praemium substantiale, sed parce in comparatione ad praemium accidentale, in quo est sanctorum differentia. Supra VIII, 15: **qui multum,**

third, that they may give cheerfully, at **every one as he has determined**.

326. In regard to the first he does two things. First, he mentions how to give; second, he assigns the reason, at **lest, when the Macedonians shall come**.

The way to give is promptly; hence he says, I sent the ministers **that (as I have said) you may be ready**, namely, after the example of the Macedonians. *And those who were ready went in with him to the marriage feast* (Matt 25:10); *do not say to your neighbor: go, and come again, tomorrow I will give it—when you have it with you* (Prov 3:28).

The reason for this is **lest, when the Macedonians shall come with me and find you unprepared, we (not to say you) should be ashamed**. As if to say: it will be to your shame if you have promised and not paid. But even if you can stand it and you do not care about your shame, at least think of our embarrassment, who say that you are prepared.

327. Then when he says, **therefore I thought it necessary**, he urges them to give abundantly.

In regard to this he does two things.

First, he gives the admonition;

second, he gives the reason for it, at **now this I say**.

328. He says, therefore: lest our boasting be voided and you be put to shame, **I thought it necessary to ask the brethren**, namely, Titus and Apollos, **to go to you before and prepare this blessing before promised**, namely, the alms, which is called a blessing because it is a cause of eternal blessedness. For by the act of giving a man is blessed by the Lord: *he will receive blessing from the Lord* (Ps 24:4); and by men: *the lips of many shall bless him who is liberal of his bread* (Sir 31:28); *he who has a bountiful eye will be blessed* (Prov 22:9).

And he calls this a blessing **to be ready, so as a blessing**, i.e., abundantly, **not as covetousness**, i.e., not sparingly.

329. The reason why they should give abundantly is because, **I say, he who sows sparingly**, i.e., who gives little in this world, **shall also reap sparingly**, i.e., will receive little in the other world. And he says, **sows**, because our seeds are whatever good we do; and again, if little is sown, not much is gathered. *For he who sows to his own flesh will from the flesh reap corruption* (Gal 6:8); but multiplied: **and he who sows in blessings**, i.e., abundantly, **shall also reap blessings**, i.e., the generous reward of God.

But will not all reap abundantly?

Yes, as to the quantity of the reward, because all will abound and no one will reap sparingly. But he says, bountifully, in proportion to those sowing well. *Star differs from star in glory* (1 Cor 15:41). All will reap abundantly as to the substantial reward, but sparingly as to the accidental reward, in which the saints will differ: **as it is written: he who had much had nothing over; and he who had little had no**

non abundavit, et qui modicum, non minoravit. Quia aliquando aliquis parce dat, et cum magna caritate, et abundanter metet.

330. Consequenter cum dicit *unusquisque enim*, etc. hortatur eos, ut dent hilariter et gaudenter.

Et circa hoc duo facit.

Primo enim monet eos ad gaudenter dandum;

secundo rationem assignat, ibi *hilarem enim datorem*, et cetera.

331. Dicit ergo: dico quod paretis illud quod vultis dare *quasi benedictionem*, id est abundanter, et dignum benedictione, *non quasi avaritiam*, id est non parce. Et hoc dicit, quia illud quod sponte fit, non potest avare fieri. Et ideo subdit *unusquisque enim*, etc., quasi non avare, quia *unusquisque*, scilicet vestrum, det eleemosynas *prout destinavit*, id est praedeliberavit, *in corde suo*, scilicet secum conferens, *non ex tristitia*, et cetera. Quasi dicat unusquisque voluntarie det, non coacte.

Ponit autem duo opposita voluntario, scilicet tristitiam et necessitatem. Voluntarium enim tollitur per violentum. Est autem duplex violentum, scilicet simplex et mixtum. Simplex quando absolute quis cogitur ad aliquid contra voluntatem suam faciendum. Ad removendum ergo illud violentum, dicit *non ex necessitate*, quod fieret si darent coacti mandato Apostoli. Quasi dicat: non cogat vos ad dandum mandatum nostrum, sed moveat vos ad hoc prompta voluntas vestra. Ex. c. XXXV, 5: *omnis voluntarius*, et cetera.

Violentum mixtum est quando quis non absolute cogitur ad faciendum aliquid contra voluntatem suam, sed secundum quid, scilicet quod nisi faciat incurrit maius damnum, sicut si non proiiciantur merces in mari, navis submergitur. Et ideo aliquo modo fit sponte et aliquo modo violenter inquantum scilicet coguntur timore maioris damni. Ut ergo hoc removeat, dicit *non ex tristitia*, id est non ita quod sit violentum mixtum. Quasi dicat: non ex timore confusionis, ne scilicet erubescatis, sed ex gaudio quod concepistis propter amorem quem habetis ad sanctos. Ps. LIII, 8: *voluntarie sacrificabo tibi*, et cetera.

332. Consequenter cum dicit *hilarem enim datorem*, etc., rationem assignat, et est talis: omnis remunerator remunerat ea quae sunt remuneratione digna. Haec autem sunt solum actus virtutum. In actibus autem virtutum duo sunt, scilicet species actus et modus agendi qui est ex parte agentis. Unde, nisi in actu virtutis utrumque istorum concurrat, non dicitur actus ille simpliciter virtuosus, sicut non dicitur perfecte iustus, secundum

want (2 Cor 8:15), because sometimes a person gives sparingly and with great charity, and reaps abundantly.

330. Then when he says, *everyone as he has determined*, he exhorts them to give cheerfully and joyfully.

In regard to this he does two things.

First, he urges them to give joyfully;

second, he gives the reason, at *for God loves a cheerful giver*.

331. He says, therefore: I say that you should prepare what you intend to give *as a blessing* i.e., abundantly, and as worthy of a blessing, *and not as covetousness*, i.e., not sparingly. He says this, because what is done spontaneously cannot be done with covetousness. Therefore he adds, *everyone as he has determined*, as though without covetousness, because *every one* of you should give his alms *as he has determined*, i.e., decided beforehand, *in his heart*, namely, conferring with himself. *Not with sadness or of necessity*: as if to say: let each one give willingly, not as being forced.

Here he mentions the two things opposed to a voluntary action, namely, sadness and necessity. For a voluntary action is destroyed by violence, which is of two kinds, namely, simple and mixed. It is simple when someone is absolutely compelled to do something against his will. To remove that violence he says, *or of necessity*, which would be present if they gave as though compelled by the command of the Apostle. As if to say: do not permit my command to compel you to give, but let your ready will move you to do this: *whoever is of a generous heart, let him bring the Lord's offering* (Exod 35:5).

But a mixed violent action happens when one is not absolutely forced to do something against his will, but in a qualified sense, namely, that he would incur great harm, unless he did it; for example, if a ship would sink, unless the cargo were thrown overboard. Therefore in one sense it is done willingly, and in another sense by force, inasmuch as he is compelled by fear of a greater loss. Therefore, to remove this he says, *not with sadness*, i.e., not making it a mixed violent action. As if to say: not from fear of shame, but from the joy you have conceived because of the love you have towards the saints: *with a freewill offering I will sacrifice to you* (Ps 54:6).

332. Then when he says, *for God loves a cheerful giver*, he gives the reason, which is this: everyone who rewards gives a reward for things worthy of a reward; but only acts of the virtues are such. But in the acts of the virtues there are two elements, namely, the species of the act and the manner of acting, which is taken on the side of the one acting. Hence, unless both are found in an act of virtue, that act is not said to be absolutely virtuous, just as a person is

virtutem, qui operatur opera iustitiae, nisi delectabiliter et cum gaudio operetur.

Et licet apud homines, qui non vident nisi ea quae patent, sufficiat quod quis operetur actum virtutis secundum ipsam speciem actus, puta actum iustitiae, tamen apud Deum, qui intuetur cor, non sufficit quod solum operetur actum virtutis secundum speciem, nisi etiam secundum debitum modum operetur, scilicet delectabiliter et cum gaudio. Et ideo non datorem tantum, sed **hilarem datorem diligit Deus**, id est approbat et remunerat, et non tristem, et remurmurantem. Ps. IC, 2: *servite Domino in laetitia*. Eccli. c. XXXV, 11: *in omni dato hilarem*, et cetera. Rom. c. XII, 8: *qui miseretur in hilaritate*, et cetera.

not said to be perfectly just according to the virtue, when he does works of justice, unless he acts with delight and with joy.

And although with men, who see only what is obvious, it is enough that one perform an act of justice according to the very species of the act, say an act of justice; nevertheless, with God, who sees the heart, it is not enough merely to perform the act of a virtue according to the species, but he must also act according to the proper manner, namely, with delight and joy. Therefore, it is not the giver, but ***the cheerful giver***, whom ***God loves***, i.e., approves and rewards, and not the sad and grumbling one. *Serve the Lord with gladness* (Ps 100:2); *for the Lord is the one who repays* (Sir 35:11); *he who does acts of mercy, with cheerfulness* (Rom 12:8).

Lecture 2

9:8Potens est autem Deus omnem gratiam abundare facere in vobis: ut in omnibus semper omnem sufficientiam habentes, abundetis in omne opus bonum, [n. 333]

9:9sicut scriptum est: *dispersit, dedit pauperibus: justitia ejus manet in saeculum saeculi.* [n. 335]

9:10Qui autem administrat semen seminanti: et panem ad manducandum praestabit, et multiplicabit semen vestrum, et augebit incrementa frugum justitiae vestrae: [n. 336]

9:11ut in omnibus locupletati abundetis in omnem simplicitatem, quae operatur per nos gratiarum actionem Deo. [n. 337]

9:12Quoniam ministerium hujus officii non solum supplet ea quae desunt sanctis, sed etiam abundat per multas gratiarum actiones in Domino, [n. 339]

9:13per probationem ministerii hujus, glorificantes Deum in obedientia confessionis vestrae, in Evangelium Christi, et simplicitate communicationis in illos, et in omnes, [n. 341]

9:14et in ipsorum obsecratione pro vobis, desiderantium vos propter eminentem gratiam Dei in vobis.

9:15Gratias Deo super inenarrabili dono ejus. [n. 342]

9:8δυνατεῖ δὲ ὁ θεὸς πᾶσαν χάριν περισσεῦσαι εἰς ὑμᾶς, ἵνα ἐν παντὶ πάντοτε πᾶσαν αὐτάρκειαν ἔχοντες περισσεύητε εἰς πᾶν ἔργον ἀγαθόν,

9:9καθὼς γέγραπται· ἐσκόρπισεν, ἔδωκεν τοῖς πένησιν, ἡ δικαιοσύνη αὐτοῦ μένει εἰς τὸν αἰῶνα.

9:10ὁ δὲ ἐπιχορηγῶν σπόρον τῷ σπείροντι καὶ ἄρτον εἰς βρῶσιν χορηγήσει καὶ πληθυνεῖ τὸν σπόρον ὑμῶν καὶ αὐξήσει τὰ γενήματα τῆς δικαιοσύνης ὑμῶν·

9:11ἐν παντὶ πλουτιζόμενοι εἰς πᾶσαν ἁπλότητα, ἥτις κατεργάζεται δι᾽ ἡμῶν εὐχαριστίαν τῷ θεῷ·

9:12ὅτι ἡ διακονία τῆς λειτουργίας ταύτης οὐ μόνον ἐστὶν προσαναπληροῦσα τὰ ὑστερήματα τῶν ἁγίων, ἀλλὰ καὶ περισσεύουσα διὰ πολλῶν εὐχαριστιῶν τῷ θεῷ.

9:13διὰ τῆς δοκιμῆς τῆς διακονίας ταύτης δοξάζοντες τὸν θεὸν ἐπὶ τῇ ὑποταγῇ τῆς ὁμολογίας ὑμῶν εἰς τὸ εὐαγγέλιον τοῦ Χριστοῦ καὶ ἁπλότητι τῆς κοινωνίας εἰς αὐτοὺς καὶ εἰς πάντας,

9:14καὶ αὐτῶν δεήσει ὑπὲρ ὑμῶν ἐπιποθούντων ὑμᾶς διὰ τὴν ὑπερβάλλουσαν χάριν τοῦ θεοῦ ἐφ᾽ ὑμῖν.

9:15Χάρις τῷ θεῷ ἐπὶ τῇ ἀνεκδιηγήτῳ αὐτοῦ δωρεᾷ.

9:8And God is able to make all grace abound in you: that you always, having all sufficiently in all things, may abound to every good work, [n. 333]

9:9As it is written: *he has dispersed abroad, he has given to the poor: his justice remains forever.* [n. 335]

9:10And he who ministers seed to the sower will both give you bread to eat and will multiply your seed and increase the growth of the fruits of your justice: [n. 336]

9:11That being enriched in all things, you may abound unto all simplicity which works through us thanksgiving to God. [n. 337]

9:12Because the administration of this office does not only supply the want of the saints, but abounds also by many thanksgivings in the Lord. [n. 339]

9:13By the proof of this ministry, glorifying God for the obedience of your confession unto the Gospel of Christ and for the simplicity of your communicating unto them and unto all. [n. 341]

9:14And in their praying for you, being desirous of you, because of the excellent grace of God in you.

9:15Thanks be to God for his unspeakable gift. [n. 342]

---

333. Hic rationem trium modorum assignat. Et

circa hoc duo facit.

Primo assignat rationem sumptam ex parte ipsorum;

secundo rationem sumptam ex parte Dei, ibi *ut in omnibus locupletati*, et cetera.

Circa primum duo facit.

Primo ponit rationem;

secundo ipsam confirmat, ibi *sicut scriptum est*, et cetera.

334. Ratio est talis: quicumque dat aliquid quod multiplicatur sibi, debet prompte, abundanter et hilariter dare, sicut videmus quod homines abundanter et prompte et cum gaudio seminant semen, quia multiplicatum illud recolligunt. Cum ergo eleemosynae multiplicentur dantibus, debetis illas prompte, gaudenter et

333. Here he gives the reason for the three ways of giving.

In regard to this he does two things.

First, he assigns the reason taken on their part;

second, the reason taken on God's part, at *that being enriched in all things*.

In regard to the first he does two things.

First, he gives the reason;

second, he confirms it, at *as it is written*.

334. The reason is this: whoever gives something which is multiplied for him should give promptly, abundantly, and cheerfully, just as when we see men sowing seed abundantly and promptly and cheerfully, because they gather it up again multiplied. Since therefore alms are multiplied for those who give them, you should give them promptly,

abundanter facere. Et quod multiplicentur patet, quia **Deus potens est omnem gratiam**, etc., quasi dicat: non timeatis dare ne, indigentia gravati, poeniteat aliquando vos dedisse, quia potens est Deus facere abundare omnem gratiam Spiritus Sancti, qua scilicet semper gaudeatis de bono opere quod fecistis. Et ideo dicit **abundetis in omne opus bonum**, id est abundantem affectum habeatis ad dandum eleemosynam, sicut habetis ad alia opera virtutum. Et tamen habeatis plenam sufficientiam bonorum exteriorum; et ideo dicit **semper omnem sufficientiam habentes**, id est vos reputantes habere. Iac. I, 5: *qui dat omnibus affluenter*, et I Tim. VI, 8: *habentes alimenta*, et cetera.

De ista sufficientia dicitur infra XII, 9: **sufficit tibi gratia mea**, et cetera. De multiplicatione vero dicitur Is. XXX, 23: *dabitur pluvia semini tuo*; Matth. XIX, 29: *omnis qui reliquerit*, etc., *centuplum accipiet*, et cetera.

335. Consequenter cum dicit **sicut scriptum est**, etc., probat positam rationem dupliciter, scilicet auctoritate et experimento, ibi **qui autem administrat**, et cetera.

Probat autem auctoritate, dicens: recte debet vos movere praedicta ratio, quia, **sicut scriptum est**, et cetera.

Sed Glossa in alio sensu adducit hanc auctoritatem, quam sit intentio Apostoli. Nam Glossa sic adducit: dico quod abundetis **in omne opus bonum**, scilicet largitione eleemosynarum, quia **scriptum est dispersit, dedit pauperibus**. Sed Apostolus videtur hoc velle referre ad illud quod dicit **abundare facere omnem gratiam**, et hoc quia ille qui dispersit, dedit pauperibus, iustitia eius manet in aeternum. Eccli. c. XII, 2: *bene fac iusto, et invenies retributionem*, et cetera.

In auctoritate autem proposita notatur quibus sit dandum, quia **pauperibus** id est indigentibus, et cetera. Lc. XIV, 12: *cum facis prandium*, et cetera. Quomodo dandum, quia **dispersit**, quia non totum uni, sed divisim multis. I Cor. c. XII, 3: *si distribuero*, et cetera. Is. LVIII, 7: *frange esurienti panem*, et cetera.

Iustitia eius, id est virtus iustitiae, **manet in aeternum**, quia ex quo dat, augetur voluntas ad dandum. Vel **iustitia eius**, id est merces iustitiae eius, manet in aeternum. Prov. c. XI, 18: *seminanti iustitiam merces fidelis*, et cetera.

336. Experimento autem confirmat rationem praedictam, dicens **qui autem administrat**, et cetera. Quasi

joyfully, and abundantly. That they are multiplied is evident, because **God is able to make all grace abound in you**. As if to say: do not be afraid to give, as though you will be burdened with need and regret having given, because God is able to provide you with every blessing of the Holy Spirit in abundance, namely, the grace by which you will always rejoice in the good work you have done. He says, therefore, **that you always, having all sufficiently in all things, may abound to every good work**, i.e., have an abundant will to give alms, just as you have for the other works of the virtues, and also that you have a full sufficiency of external goods; hence he says, **always having all sufficiently in all things**, i.e., considering yourself to have: *he gives to all men generously and without reproaching, and it will be given him* (Jas 1:5); *but if we have food and clothing, with these we shall be content* (1 Tim 6:8).

Of that sufficiency it says below: **my grace is sufficient for you** (2 Cor 12:9). But concerning the multiplication it is said: *and he will give rain for the seed with which you sow the ground* (Isa 30:25); *and every one who has left houses or brothers or sisters or father or mother or children or lands, for my name's sake, will receive a hundredfold, and inherit eternal life* (Matt 19:29).

335. Then when he says, **as it is written**, he proves his reason in two ways, namely, by authority and from experience, at **and he that ministers**.

He proves it by an authority when he says: rightly should this reason move you, because, **as it is written**: *he has dispersed abroad, he has given to the poor; his justice remains forever*.

But a Gloss adduces this authority in a sense different from the Apostle's intention; for the Gloss says: I say that you shall abound **to every good work**, namely, by the giving of alms, because, **as it is written: he has dispersed abroad, he has given to the poor**. But the Apostle wishes to refer this to his statement that **God is able to make all grace abound in you**; and this, because he who scattered abroad and gives to the poor, his justice remains forever. *Do good to a godly man, and you will be repaid* (Sir 12:2).

In the authority cited we note to whom should be given, namely, **to the poor**, i.e., to the needy. *When you give a dinner or a banquet, do not invite your friends or your brothers or your kinsmen or rich neighbors, lest they also invite you in return, and you be repaid* (Luke 14:12); how to give, namely, **he has dispersed abroad**, i.e., not all to one person, but divided among many: *if I give away all I have* (1 Cor 13:3); *is it not to share your bread with the hungry* (Isa 58:7);

his justice, i.e., the power of justice, **remains forever**, because by the very fact that one gives the will for giving is increased. Or **his justice**, i.e., the reward for justice, endures forever: *but one who sows righteousness gets a sure reward* (Prov 11:18).

336. He confirms his reason by experience when he says, **he who ministers seed to the sower will both give you**

dicat: experti estis, quia hoc ipsum quod datis in elee- mosynas, habetis a Deo. Et ideo debetis libenter dare amore Dei. I Par. ultimo: *tua sunt omnia quae de manu*, et cetera.

Et insinuat tria circa hoc. Primum est quod aliquis posset dicere: si nos damus modo quod habemus, de- ficient nobis necessaria ad quotidianum victum. Et hoc removet, quia non solum *semen ministrat seminanti*, sed *panem*, id est necessaria vitae, *praestabit ad man- ducandum*, Ps. CXXXV, 25: *qui dat escam omni carni.*

Secundum est, quia posses dicere quod si multum daremus, deficient nobis quae habemus ad dandum ite- rum. Et hoc Apostolus removet dicens, quod non defi- ciet, sed *multiplicabit semen vestrum*, unde scilicet plu- res eleemosynas facitis.

Tertium est, quia posset aliquis dicere, quod si modo damus, deficiet nobis voluntas ad dandum, et poenite- bit nos dedisse, et sic totum amittemus. Et hoc removet, dicens *et augebit incrementa frugum iustitiae vestrae*, id est intantum augebit facultatem et voluntatem dan- di eleemosynas, ex quibus procedit iustitia vestra, quod semper parati et prompti eritis ad dandum eleemosynas, et quod fruges maximae erunt in comparatione ad par- vum semen. Prov. III, 9: *de primitiis frugum tuarum da pauperibus.* Lev. XXV, 21: *dabo benedictionem*, et cete- ra. I Tim. IV, 8: *pietas ad omnia valet.*

337. Deinde cum dicit *ut in omnibus locupletati*, etc., assignat rationem, quare prompte, abundanter et hilariter dare debeant, ex parte ipsorum dantium; hic as- signat rationem ex parte ipsius Dei pro quo dare debent. Et

primo assignat rationem;

secundo manifestat eam, ibi *quoniam ministerium huius officii*, et cetera.

338. In ratione autem assignanda tria considerantur, quorum primum est ipsorum locupletatio, quod respon- det praemissis. Dixerat enim supra: *multiplicabit semen vestrum et augebit incrementa frugum iustitiae vestrae* et hoc primo resumit, dicens et *ut in omnibus locupleta- ti*, id est tam in corporalibus, quam in spiritualibus bo- nis. I Cor. I, 5: *divites facti estis*, et cetera.

Sed ne aliquis crederet, quod finis ponendus sit in abundantia divitiarum temporalium, aut quod divitias spirituales aliquis otiose absque usu possidere deberet, refert hoc primum ad aliud secundum, dicens *abundetis in omnem*, id est perfectam, *simplicitatem*, id est lar- gitatem simplici animo factam, ut largitio procedat ex divitiis temporalibus, simplicitas autem ex spiritualibus. Prov. XI, 3: *simplicitas iustorum*, et cetera.

Sed et hoc ipsum ad alium finem referendum est, sci- licet ad Deum. Et ideo tertio subdit *quae*, scilicet largi- tio simplex, *operatur per nos*, id est mediantibus nobis,

bread to eat and will multiply your seed. As if to say: you know from experience that what you give in alms you have from the Lord; therefore you should give gladly for the love of God: *for all things come from you, and of your own have we given you* (1 Chr 29:14).

He suggests three things in regard to this. The first is that someone could say: if we give now what we have, what is necessary for daily food will be wanting to us. But he re- jects this, saying: *he* not only *ministers seed to the sower*, but *bread to eat*, i.e., the necessities of life: *he who gives food to all flesh* (Ps 136:24).

The second is that they could say: if we give much, we will not have enough to give again. The Apostle answers this, saying that they will not want, but *he will multiply your seed*, from which you can give more alms.

The third is that someone could say: if we give now, the will to give will be lost, and we will regret having given, and so we shall lose everything. But he removes this, saying: *and increase the growth of the fruits of your justice*, i.e., he will increase the ability to give alms and the will from which your justice proceeds, to such a degree that you will always be prepared and ready to give alms, and the fruit will be the most in comparison with the small seed. *Honor the Lord with your substance and with the first fruits of all your produce* (Prov 3:9); *I will command my blessing upon you* (Lev 25:21); *godliness is of value in every way* (1 Tim 4:8).

337. The when he says, *that being enriched in all things*, after having assigned the reason why they should give promptly, abundantly and cheerfully on the part of the donors, he then assigns the reason on God's part, for whom they ought to give.

First he assigns the reason they should give;

second, he explains it, at *because the ministration of this office*.

338. In the reason to be assigned, three things are to be considered, the first of which is their enrichment, which corresponds to what has gone above. For he had said above: *he will multiply your seed and increase the growth of the fruits of your justice*; and he recalls the first, saying: *that being enriched in all things*, i.e., both in bodily and spiri- tual goods: *that in every way you were enriched in him* (1 Cor 1:5).

But lest anyone suppose that his end should be placed in an abundance of temporal riches or that he should possess spiritual goods in idleness without using them, he refers this first to another second thing: *you may abound unto all*, i.e., perfect, *simplicity*; that is, have great generosity directed by a simple spirit, so that the giving comes from temporal goods but the simplicity from spiritual goods: *the integrity of the upright guides them* (Prov 11:13).

But this should itself be referred to another end, name- ly, to God; therefore he adds in the third place, *which*, namely, simple abundance, *works through us* will produce

gratiarum actionem Deo, I Thess. V, 18: *in omnibus gratias agite*, et cetera.

339. Deinde cum dicit **quoniam ministerium**, etc., manifestat rationem supra positam, scilicet quomodo eorum largitio operetur gratiarum actionem Deo. Et

primo hoc ostendit;

secundo ponit gratiarum actionis materiam, ibi **glorificantes Deum**, etc.;

tertio ipse prorumpit in gratiarum actionem, ibi **gratias Deo**, et cetera.

340. Dicit ergo: dico quod largitio vestra operatur gratiarum actiones Deo, quia **ministerium huius officii** vestri, quo subvenitis sanctis, multa bona habet, quia **non solum supplet ea quae desunt sanctis**, quantum ad temporalia. Supra VIII, 14: **vestra abundantia illorum inopiam suppleat**, et cetera.

Non solum ergo hoc bonum sequitur inde, sed etiam quod ipsi orant pro vobis, et agunt gratias Deo, probantes et approbantes ministrationem vestram. Et hoc est quod dicit **sed etiam abundat**, id est excrescit, **in actione gratiarum**, quae fit per multos, non solum perfectos, sed per alios fideles pauperes, qui inde agunt gratias Deo **in Domino**, qui eos ad hoc movet, videntes et probantes ministerium vestrum. Supra I, 11: **ut ex multarum personis facierum**, et cetera.

341. Huius quidem gratiarum actionis materia est propter tria.

Primo propter eorum fidem quam acceperunt, et ideo dicit: dico quod **abundat in gratiarum actione**, **glorificantes**, scilicet fideles, **Deum in obedientia confessionis vestrae**, id est de confessione fidei vestrae, quam confitemini et creditis in Christum. Matth. V, v. 16: *sic luceat lux vestra*, et cetera. Prov. XXI, v. 28: *vir obediens loquetur victorias.*

Secundo propter eorum largitionem. Et ideo dicit **glorificantes et in simplicitate communicationis vestrae**, id est pro largitione vestra, **in illos**, scilicet sanctos pauperes, **et in omnes**, scilicet fideles qui indigent, simplici et puro animo facta. Gal. VI, 6: *communicet is qui catechizatur verbo ei qui se catechizat*, etc., et iterum *operemur bonum ad omnes*, et cetera.

Tertio propter hoc quod ipsi viri sancti habent a Deo, ut pro eis agant gratias Deo. Et ideo dicit: **glorificantes** etiam **Deum in ipsorum obsecratione pro vobis**; id est glorificant Deum de hoc quod ipsi viri sancti obsecrant pro nobis. Ipsorum, dico, **desiderantium vos** videre in aeterna beatitudine, et hoc **propter eminentem gratiam Dei in vobis**.

342. Ex his ergo Apostolus prorumpit in gratiarum actionem Deo, dicens **gratias**, et cetera. Id est quia tot bona inde proveniunt de ministerio vestro, ego ago

thanksgiving to God: give thanks in all circumstances (1 Thess 5:18).

339. Then when he says, **because the administration**, he explains the reason mentioned above, namely, how their abundance works thanksgiving to God.

First he shows this;

second, the reason for thanks, at **glorifying God**;

third, he breaks out in thanksgiving, at **thanks be to God**.

340. He says, therefore: I say that your abundance works thanksgiving to God, **because the administration of this office** of yours, by which you help the saints, has many good results, because it **does not only supply the want of the saints** in regard to temporal things: *let your abundance supply their want, that their abundance also may supply your want* (2 Cor 8:14).

Not only does this good follow therefrom, but also the fact that they pray for you and give thanks to God, proving and approving your service. And this is what he says: **but abounds**, that is, grows, **also by many thanksgivings** to God, which are given by many, not only by the perfect, but by the poor believers who give thanks to God **in the Lord**, who moves them to this, seeing and approving your ministry. *That for this gift obtained for us, by the means of many persons, thanks may be given by many in our behalf* (2 Cor 1:11).

341. This thanksgiving is given for three reasons.

First, for their faith, which they have received; hence he says: I say that it **abounds in thanksgiving, glorifying God for the obedience of your confession unto the Gospel of Christ**, i.e., the confession of your faith, by which you confess and believe in Christ. *Let your light so shine before men* (Matt 5:16); *the word of a man who hears will endure* (Prov 21:28).

Second, on account of their abundance; hence he says, **glorifying God** also **for the simplicity of your communicating**, that is, of your contribution, **unto them**, namely, the holy poor, **and unto all**, namely, the faithful in need, and given with a simple and pure spirit. *Let him who is taught the word share all good things with him who teaches* (Gal 6:6); and *let us do good to all men* (Gal 6:10).

Third, on account of what these saints have from God that they may give thanks to God; hence he says: **glorifying God** also **in their praying for you**, i.e., they glorify God for the fact that those holy men pray for you; the men, I say, who are **desirous of** seeing **you** in eternal happiness; and this **because of the excellent grace of God in you**.

342. From this the Apostle breaks forth in thanksgiving to God, saying: **thanks be to God for his unspeakable gift**; that is, because as much good comes thenceforth about

gratias Deo, etc., scilicet caritatis, quae maxime videtur vigere in vobis, qui subvenitis etiam illis qui sic agunt gratias Deo et orant pro vobis.

Et hoc donum est *inenarrabile*, quia non potest dici, quantum utile sit, quia *oculus non vidit, nec auris audivit, et cetera.*

your ministry, I give **thanks to God**, that is, for the charity which is especially seen in you who even help those who thus thank God and pray for you.

This gift is **unspeakable**, because it cannot be said how profitable it is, for *what no eye has seen, nor ear heard, nor the heart of man conceived, what God has prepared for those who love him* (1 Cor 2:9).

CHAPTER 10

Lecture 1

10:1Ipse autem ego Paulus obsecro vos per mansuetudinem et modestiam Christi, qui in facie quidem humilis sum inter vos, absens autem confido in vos. [n. 343]

10:2Rogo autem vos ne praesens audeam per eam confidentiam, qua existimor audere in quosdam, qui arbitrantur nos tamquam secundum carnem ambulemus. [n. 346]

10:3In carne enim ambulantes, non secundum carnem militamus. [n. 349]

10:4Nam arma militiae nostrae non carnalia sunt, sed potentia Deo [n. 350] ad destructionem munitionum, consilia destruentes, [n. 351]

10:5et omnem altitudinem extollentem se adversus scientiam Dei, et in captivitatem redigentes omnem intellectum in obsequium Christi,

10:6et in promptu habentes ulcisci omnem inobedientiam, cum impleta fuerit vestra obedientia. [n. 352]

10:1Αὐτὸς δὲ ἐγὼ Παῦλος παρακαλῶ ὑμᾶς διὰ τῆς πραΰτητος καὶ ἐπιεικείας τοῦ Χριστοῦ, ὃς κατὰ πρόσωπον μὲν ταπεινὸς ἐν ὑμῖν, ἀπὼν δὲ θαρρῶ εἰς ὑμᾶς·

10:2δέομαι δὲ τὸ μὴ παρὼν θαρρῆσαι τῇ πεποιθήσει ᾗ λογίζομαι τολμῆσαι ἐπί τινας τοὺς λογιζομένους ἡμᾶς ὡς κατὰ σάρκα περιπατοῦντας.

10:3Ἐν σαρκὶ γὰρ περιπατοῦντες οὐ κατὰ σάρκα στρατευόμεθα,

10:4τὰ γὰρ ὅπλα τῆς στρατείας ἡμῶν οὐ σαρκικὰ ἀλλὰ δυνατὰ τῷ θεῷ πρὸς καθαίρεσιν ὀχυρωμάτων, λογισμοὺς καθαιροῦντες

10:5καὶ πᾶν ὕψωμα ἐπαιρόμενον κατὰ τῆς γνώσεως τοῦ θεοῦ, καὶ αἰχμαλωτίζοντες πᾶν νόημα εἰς τὴν ὑπακοὴν τοῦ Χριστοῦ,

10:6καὶ ἐν ἑτοίμῳ ἔχοντες ἐκδικῆσαι πᾶσαν παρακοήν, ὅταν πληρωθῇ ὑμῶν ἡ ὑπακοή.

10:1Now I Paul, myself beseech you, by the mildness and modesty of Christ: who in presence indeed am lowly among you, but being absent am bold toward you. [n. 343]

10:2But I beseech you, that I may not be bold when I am present with that confidence with which I am thought to be bold, against some who reckon us as if we walked according to the flesh. [n. 346]

10:3For though we walk in the flesh, we do not war according to the flesh. [n. 349]

10:4For the weapons of our warfare are not carnal but mighty to God, [n. 350] unto the pulling down of fortifications, destroying counsels, [n. 351]

10:5And every height that exalts itself against the knowledge of God: and bringing into captivity every understanding unto the obedience of Christ:

10:6And having in readiness to revenge all disobedience, when your obedience shall be fulfilled. [n. 352]

---

343. Postquam tractavit de bonis ministris Christi et fidei, consequenter Apostolus invehitur contra falsos ministros et pseudo-prophetas. Et

primo invehitur contra eos;

Secundo vero contra illos, qui, decepti ab eis, adhaerebant eis, in XIII cap., ibi *ecce tertio*, et cetera.

Circa primum duo facit.

Primo excusat se de eis quae imponuntur sibi per rationem;

secundo vero per facti evidentiam, ibi *quae autem secundum faciem sunt*, et cetera.

Circa primum duo facit.

Primo recusat se excusare per experimentum, cum tamen posset;

secundo vero excusat per rationem, ibi *qui arbitrantur*, et cetera.

343. After dealing with the good ministers of Christ and of the faith, the Apostle now attacks false ministers and false apostles.

First, he attacks these;

second, those who, being deceived by them, have adhered to them, in chapter thirteen, at *behold, now for the third time*.

In regard to the first he does two things.

First, he gives the reason, excusing himself from the task imposed on him;

second, he gives the evidence for the fact, at *see the things that are according to outward appearance*.

In regard to the first he does two things.

First, he refuses to make a test;

second, he excuses himself with a reason, at *who reckon us*.

Circa primum tria facit.

Primo praemittit obsecrationem;

secundo interponit illud quod imponitur sibi a pseudo, ibi *qui in facie quidem*, etc.;

tertio recusat experimentum, ibi *rogo autem*.

344. Dicit ergo *ipse autem ego Paulus*, qui vos et alios ad eleemosynas exhortor; ego, inquam, ipse, *obsecro vos per mansuetudinem et modestiam Christi*. De mansuetudine Christi habetur Matth. XI, 29: *discite a me, quia mitis sum*, et cetera. De modestia Sap. c. XI, 21: *omnia in numero, pondere et mensura disposuisti*, et cetera. Modestia enim nihil aliud est quam modum servare in agendis.

Facit autem specialiter hic mentionem de mansuetudine et modestia Christi, quia pseudo, et Corinthii, specialiter imponebant Paulo quod cum esset praesens apud eos conversaretur humiliter, et cum esset absens scriberet eis valde dure. Et ideo posuit illa duo quae Christus habuit, ut sciant quod Apostolus haec etiam ostendit et servavit exemplo Christi.

345. Et ideo consequenter interponit vitium sibi impositum, dicens: *ego ipse Paulus*, id est vere humilis, quia Paulus humilis et quietus interpretatur. I Cor. XV, 9: *ego sum minimus*, et cetera. Unde *ego ipse*, id est, vere *Paulus*. Ps. ci, 28: *tu quidem ipse es*. Eccli. c. XIX, 23: *est qui nequiter humiliat se*, et cetera. Et Iac. III, 16: *ubi zelus et contentio, ibi inconstantia*, et cetera.

Ego inquam *obsecro, qui in facie*, id est exterius, ut dicitis, *humilis sum inter vos*, id est humiliter conversatus, cum sum vobis praesens, *absens autem*, id est cum sum absens a vobis, quando scilicet non timeo laedi ab aliquo vestrum, *confido in vobis*, id est confidenter ago, aspere vobis per epistolam scribens. Prov. XXVIII, 1: *iustus quasi leo confidens*, et cetera.

346. Consequenter cum dicit *rogo autem*, etc., recusat sumere experimentum.

Isti enim credebant quod Apostolus ex timore ductus conversaretur humiliter inter eos, et ideo dicit: vos ita creditis, sed ego *rogo vos*, qui et ipse obsecro, ut velitis experiri, utrum ego, si necesse sit, faciam in praesentia, quomodo facio in absentia. Et ideo dicit *ne praesens*, id est cum fuero apud vos, *audeam* facere in vobis, si necesse sit, *per eam confidentiam*, id est ita confidenter, sicut *existimor* a vobis *audere*, id est audacter et confidenter agere, *in quosdam*, incorrectos dure reprehendendo, per litteras etiam corrigendo. Iob XXXI: *exaltat audacter*, et cetera.

347. Deinde excusat se per rationem, dicens *qui arbitrantur*, etc., quasi dicat: et licet nolim experimento

In regard to the first he does three things.

First, he entreats them;

second, he interjects what is imposed on them by the false apostles, at *who in presence indeed*;

third, he refuses the test, at *but I beseech you*.

344. He says, therefore: *Now I, Paul, myself*, who am urging you and others to give alms; I myself, I say, *beseech you, by the mildness and modesty of Christ*. Of the mildness of Christ: *take my yoke upon you, and learn from me; for I am gentle and lowly in heart, and you will find rest for your souls* (Matt 11:29); of his modesty: *for it is always in your power to show great strength, and who can withstand the might of your arm?* (Wis 11:21). For modesty consists in nothing less than observing the measure in acting.

But he makes special mention of Christ's mildness and modesty, because the false apostles and the Corinthians accused Paul of acting humbly when he was among them, but when he was absent he wrote very harshly. Therefore, he mentioned those two qualities of Christ to show that the Apostle also has them and observes them after the example of Christ.

345. Hence, he introduces the vice ascribed to him, saying, *I, Paul, myself*, i.e., truly humble, because Paul means humble and quiet: *for I am the least of the apostles* (1 Cor 15:9); hence, *I myself*, i.e., truly *Paul*: *but you are the same* (Ps 102:27); *there is one who humbles himself wickedly, and his interior is full of deceit* (Sir 19:23); *for where jealousy and selfish ambition exist, there will be disorder and every vile practice* (Jas 3:16).

I, I say, *beseech you, who in presence*, i.e., outwardly, as you say, *am lowly among you*, acting humbly while I am present with you, *but being absent*, namely, when there is no fear of being injured by any of you, *am bold toward you*, i.e., act boldly, writing harsh epistles to you: *but the righteous are bold as a lion* (Prov 28:1).

346. Then when he says, *but I beseech you*, he refuses to make a test.

For they believed that the Apostle acted humbly among them because of fear; hence, he says: you believe so, *but I beseech you*—since you would like to experience whether I, if it were necessary, would do when I am present as I do in my absence. And so he says: *that I may not be bold when I am present*, i.e., when I am among you, to do anything, if it is necessary, *with that confidence*, i.e., as confidently as *I am thought* by you *to be bold*, i.e., to act boldly and confidently against *some* uncorrected persons, by rebuking and correcting through letters: *he exults in his strength* (Job 39:20).

347. Then he excuses himself with a reason, saying: *who reckon us as if we walked according to the flesh*. As if to

me excusare propter vos, tamen ratio in promptu est ad excusandum me sufficienter.

Circa hoc ergo tria facit.

Primo ponit causam, quare imponunt ei quod dictum est;

secundo destruit causam illam;

tertio confirmat per rationem.

348. Causa autem quare hoc sibi imponitur, scilicet quod praesens sit humilis, absens autem severus et austerus, est quia isti arbitrabantur Apostolum *secundum carnem* ambulare.

Et quia unusquisque secundum regulam operis operatur, finis autem habet rationem regulae, ideo quilibet dirigit opus suum ad finem quem intendit. Qui ergo ponunt finem suum in bonis carnalibus dicuntur ambulare *secundum carnem*. Et inde est quod ita regulant opera sua, ut consequantur ea quae sunt carnis; quae quidem, quia possunt subtrahi ab hominibus, ideo homines, qui in carnalia tendunt, blande se habent ad homines et humiliter. Et ideo, quia credebant Apostolum ambulare secundum carnem ideo credebant quod propter hoc humiliter conversatus sit inter eos.

349. Sed haec ratio nulla est et vana, et ideo destruit eam. Dicens *in carne enim*, etc., quasi dicat: quod nos sumus in carne non possumus negare, quia Rom. VIII, 12 dicitur: *debitores sumus non carni*, etc.; sed quod nos regulemur secundum carnem, ponendo in bonis carnalibus finem, sive intentionem nostram, hoc est falsum, quia *non secundum carnem militamus*, id est vitam nostram, quae est quaedam militia, ut dicitur Iob VII, 1, non regulamus secundum carnem.

350. Et quod non militemus secundum carnem probat, cum dicit *nam arma nostra*, etc., et primo, ex militaribus armis, sicut unusquisque pugnator habet arma accommoda militiae et pugnae suae. Sed constat quod arma eorum qui pugnant secundum carnem, seu militant, sunt divitiae, voluptates, honores et potentiae mundanae et temporales, cum ergo arma nostra non sint huiusmodi, quia *arma militiae nostrae non sunt carnalia, sed potentia Deo*, id est secundum Deum, vel ad honorem Dei, ergo nos non militamus secundum carnem.

351. Secundo vero cum dicit *ad destructionem*, etc., ponit virtutem armorum spiritualium, quorum quidem virtus patet ex triplici effectu eorum.

Primus effectus est quod per ipsa arma confunduntur rebelles. Et quantum ad hoc dicit *ad destructionem munitionum*, quasi dicat: bene sunt potentia Deo, ut

say: although I am not willing to justify myself for your sake with a test, nevertheless, there is a reason at hand to justify me.

In regard to this he does three things.

First, he gives the reason why they lay this charge against him;

second, he destroys the reason;

third, he confirms it with a reason.

348. The reason why this charge is laid to him, namely that he is humble when present but harsh and severe when absent, is that they consider that the Apostle acts in a worldly manner, i.e., walks *according to the flesh*.

And because every person works according to what rules the work, and the end should be the rule, it follows that everyone directs his own work to the end he intends. Therefore, those who place their end in carnal goods are said to walk *according to the flesh*. And because these things can be taken from them, men who tend to carnal things behave gently and humbly toward others. Therefore, because they believed that the Apostle walked according to the flesh, they supposed that this was the reason he behaved humbly among them.

349. But this reason is null and void; therefore, he destroys it, saying: *for though we walk in the flesh, we do not war according to the flesh*. As if to say: we cannot deny that we are in the flesh, because it is said: *so then, brethren, we are debtors, not to the flesh, to live according to the flesh* (Rom 8:12), but that we are ruled according to the flesh, by placing our end or our intention in carnal goods, this is false, because *we do not war according to the flesh*, i.e., we do not regulate our life, which is a warfare according to the flesh (Job 7:1).

350. That we do not war according to the flesh he proves when he says, *for the weapons of our warfare are not carnal*; and first of all, from the weapons of warfare, as a fighter has weapons suitable to his warfare. Now it is plain that the weapons of those who fight according to the flesh, or wage war, are riches, pleasures, and worldly and temporal honors and power. But since our weapons are not of this sort, *for the weapons of our warfare are not carnal but mighty to God*, i.e., according to God or to the honor of God, therefore, we do not war according to the flesh.

351. But second, when he says, *unto the pulling down of fortifications*, he indicates the power of spiritual armor, which is evident from its threefold effect.

The first effect is that rebellious persons are put to shame by those arms; in regard to this he says, *unto the pulling down of fortifications*. As if to say: the power of

destruant rebelles. Infra Tit. I, 9: *ut sit potens exhortari, et cetera.* Ier. I, 10: *ut evellas et destruas, et cetera.*

Muniunt autem se aliqui contra Deum dupliciter. Aliqui astutis consiliis, sicut sunt tyranni, qui machinantur pravis consiliis suis destruere quae Dei sunt, ut ipsi tyrannizent. Et quantum ad hoc dicit **consilia destruentes**, scilicet tyrannorum. Iob V, 13: *qui apprehendit sapientes, et cetera.* Aliqui vero per superbiam vel altitudinem ingenii proprii. Et quantum ad hoc dicit **et omnem altitudinem**, scilicet suae superbiae. Rom. XII, 16: *non alta sapientes*, etc., id est superba. Sive profunditatem intellectus tam legisperitorum, quam philosophorum. Rom. VIII, 39: *neque altitudo, neque profundum.* Is. V, 21: *vae qui sapientes estis in oculis vestris.* **Altitudinem**, dico, **extollentem se adversus scientiam Dei**, scilicet fidem, quae est scientia Dei, quia quae de Deo dicuntur impugnant, scilicet partum virginis, et alia Dei mirabilia. Is. XI, 9: *repleta est terra scientia Dei.* Apoc. II, 23: *quam dicunt altitudinem Satanae.* Apoc. II, 24: *qui non cognoverunt altitudinem Satanae.* Rom. XI, 20: *noli altum sapere, sed time.*

352. Secundus effectus est conversio infidelium ad fidem. Et quantum ad hoc dicit **et in captivitatem redigentes**, etc.; quod quidem fit quando id quod homo scit, totum supponit ministerio Christi et fidei. Ps. CIL, v. 8: *ad alligandos reges eorum in compedibus, et cetera.* Eccli. VI, 25: *iniice pedem tuum in compedes illius*, id est in documenta fidei, et cetera.

353. Tertius effectus est correctio peccantium. Et quantum ad hoc dicit **et in promptu habentes**, id est promptum et liberum animum habentes ad puniendum **omnem inobedientiam**. Ps. CIL, 6: *gladii ancipites in manibus, et cetera.* Et hoc erit, **cum impleta fuerit vestra obedientia**, id est cum vos perfecte obedientes eritis, quia si vos velitis obedire, non erit nobis locus puniendi inobedientiam aliorum et vestram.

Vel, tunc ulciscemur vos de inobedientia, **quando impleta fuerit obedientia vestra**, id est quando destruetur inobedientia vestra: contraria enim contrariis curantur.

God is quite capable of destroying the rebellious. *That he may be able to give instruction in sound doctrine and also to confute those who contradict it* (Titus 1:9); see, *I have set you this day over nations and over kingdoms, to pluck up and to break down, to destroy and to overthrow, to build and to plant* (Jer 1:10).

Men fortify themselves against God in two ways: some with astute plans, such as tyrants, who plot with their evil designs to destroy the things of God, that they may exercise their tyranny; as to this he says, **destroying counsels**, namely, of tyrants: *he takes the wise in their own craftiness* (Job 5:13). But others through pride or profundity of their own talent; as to this he says, **and every height**, namely, of their pride: *do not be haughty* (Rom 12:16), i.e., proud things, or by profundity of intellect, both of lawyers and philosophers: *neither height nor depth* (Rom 8:39); *woe to those who are wise in their own eyes* (Isa 5:21). **Every height**, I say, **that exalts itself against the knowledge of God**, i.e., the faith, which is knowledge of God, because they attack things said about God, namely, the virgin birth and other of God's marvels. *For the earth shall be full of the knowledge of the Lord* (Isa 11:9); *who have not learned what some call the deep things of Satan* (Rev 2:24); *so do not become proud, but stand in awe* (Rom 11:20).

352. The second effect is the conversion of unbelievers to the faith; as to this he says, **and bringing into captivity every understanding unto the obedience of Christ**. This happens when a man submits all he knows to the ministry of the Christ and of the faith. *To bind their kings with chains and their nobles with fetters of iron* (Ps 149:8); *put your feet into her fetters, and your neck into her chains* (Sir 6:25), i.e., into the teaching of the faith.

353. The third effect is the correction of sinners; as to this he says, **and having in readiness to revenge**, i.e., having the readiness and free will to punish **all disobedience**: *and two-edged swords in their hands* (Ps 149:6). This will occur **when your obedience shall be fulfilled**, i.e., when you are perfectly obedient, because if you are willing to obey, there will be no reason for punishing the disobedience of others and your own.

Or we shall take revenge on disobedience, **when your obedience shall be fulfilled**, i.e., when your disobedience shall be destroyed; for contraries are cured by contraries.

Lecture 2

10:7Quae secundum faciem sunt, videte. Si quis confidit sibi Christi se esse, hoc cogitet iterum apud se: quia sicut ipse Christi est, ita et nos. [n. 354]

10:8Nam etsi amplius aliquid gloriatus fuero de potestate nostra, quam dedit nobis Dominus in aedificationem, et non in destructionem vestram, non erubescam. [n. 358]

10:9Ut autem non existimer tamquam terrere vos per epistolas: [n. 360]

10:10quoniam quidem epistolae, inquiunt, graves sunt et fortes: praesentia autem corporis infirma, et sermo contemptibilis:

10:11hoc cogitet qui ejusmodi est, quia quales sumus verbo per epistolas absentes, tales et praesentes in facto.

10:12Non enim audemus inserere, aut comparare nos quibusdam, qui seipsos commendant: sed ipsi in nobis nosmetipsos metientes, et comparantes nosmetipsos nobis. [n. 363]

10:7Τὰ κατὰ πρόσωπον βλέπετε. εἴ τις πέποιθεν ἑαυτῷ Χριστοῦ εἶναι, τοῦτο λογιζέσθω πάλιν ἐφ᾽ ἑαυτοῦ, ὅτι καθὼς αὐτὸς Χριστοῦ, οὕτως καὶ ἡμεῖς.

10:8ἐάν [τε] γὰρ περισσότερόν τι καυχήσωμαι περὶ τῆς ἐξουσίας ἡμῶν ἧς ἔδωκεν ὁ κύριος εἰς οἰκοδομὴν καὶ οὐκ εἰς καθαίρεσιν ὑμῶν, οὐκ αἰσχυνθήσομαι.

10:9ἵνα μὴ δόξω ὡς ἂν ἐκφοβεῖν ὑμᾶς διὰ τῶν ἐπιστολῶν·

10:10ὅτι αἱ ἐπιστολαὶ μέν, φησίν, βαρεῖαι καὶ ἰσχυραί, ἡ δὲ παρουσία τοῦ σώματος ἀσθενὴς καὶ ὁ λόγος ἐξουθενημένος.

10:11τοῦτο λογιζέσθω ὁ τοιοῦτος, ὅτι οἷοί ἐσμεν τῷ λόγῳ δι᾽ ἐπιστολῶν ἀπόντες, τοιοῦτοι καὶ παρόντες τῷ ἔργῳ.

10:12Οὐ γὰρ τολμῶμεν ἐγκρῖναι ἢ συγκρῖναι ἑαυτούς τισιν τῶν ἑαυτοὺς συνιστανόντων, ἀλλὰ αὐτοὶ ἐν ἑαυτοῖς ἑαυτοὺς μετροῦντες καὶ συγκρίνοντες ἑαυτοὺς ἑαυτοῖς οὐ συνιᾶσιν.

10:7See the things that are according to outward appearance. If any man trust to himself that he is Christ's, let him think this again with himself, that as he is Christ's, so are we also. [n. 354]

10:8For if also I should boast somewhat more of our power, which the Lord has given us unto edification and not unto your destruction, I should not be ashamed. [n. 358]

10:9But that I may not be thought as it were to terrify you by epistles, [n. 360]

10:10(For his epistles indeed, they say, are weighty and strong; but his bodily presence is weak and his speech contemptible):

10:11Let such a one think this, that such as we are in word by epistles when absent, such also we will be in deed when present.

10:12For we dare not match or compare ourselves with some who commend themselves: but we measure ourselves by ourselves and compare ourselves with ourselves. [n. 363]

---

354. Supra excusavit se Apostolus per rationem hic excusat se per facti evidentiam. Et

circa hoc duo facit.

Primo enim committit auditoribus iudicium suae excusationis;

secundo prosequitur suam causam, ibi *si quis confidit*, et cetera.

355. Dicit ergo primo: licet appareat per rationem falsum esse quod imponunt mihi pseudo, tamen si aliqui sint inter vos, qui ratione non vincantur et noluerint rationi acquiescere, saltem *videte*, id est considerate, *ea quae sunt secundum faciem*, id est in manifesto apparent de me evidenter. Committit autem eis iudicium causae suae, ad ostendendam securitatem cordis sui. Iob VI, v. 29: *respondete, obsecro, absque contradictione.*

Sed contra Io. VII, 24: *nolite secundum faciem iudicare*. Non ergo bene dicitur hic *quae secundum faciem sunt videte*.

Respondeo. Dicendum est quod ibi accipitur *secundum faciem* pro his quae exterius apparent in homine, scilicet pro sola veritatis apparentia, secundum quae non debet homo iudicare, quia aliquando contrarium latet in

354. Above, the Apostle excused himself by reason; here he excuses himself by the evidence of the fact.

In this regard he does two things.

First, he submits his excuse to his hearers to judge;

second, he pursues his cause, at *if any man trust*.

355. He says, therefore: although reason shows that the charge laid against me by the false apostles is false, nevertheless, if some among you are not convinced by reason and refuse to acquiesce to it, at least *see*, i.e., consider, *the things that are according to outward appearance*, i.e., that are evident, concerning me. But he submits the judgment of his cause to them in order to indicate how secure he is in his heart: *turn, I pray, let no wrong be done* (Job. 6:29).

But this is contrary to John: *do not judge by appearances* (John 7:24). Therefore it is not proper for him to say, *that are according to outward appearance*.

I answer that the phrase, *according to outward appearance*, is taken there for things that appear outwardly in a man, namely, for that which appear to be true, according to which a man should not judge, because sometimes

corde. Unde dicitur Matth. VII, 15: *veniunt ad vos in vestimentis ovium, intrinsecus*, et cetera. Hic vero accipitur **secundum faciem** pro ipsa veritate Evangelica et facti evidentia, secundum quam potest fieri iudicium.

Glossa aliter exponit, scilicet **secundum faciem**, id est pseudo **videte**, id est attendite. Quasi dicat: considerate facta eorum, quia impossibile est quin inter multa bona quae praetendunt, non faciant aliqua ex quibus poteritis cognoscere intentionem ipsorum pravam. Matth. VII, 20: *ex fructibus eorum*, et cetera.

356. Consequenter cum dicit **si quis autem confidit**, etc., prosequitur causam suam. Contingit autem quod aliquis movetur contra aliquem, deceptus auctoritate alicuius qui se magnum facit. Et sic Corinthii commoti erant contra apostolum decepti a pseudo, qui se dicebant maioris auctoritatis quam Paulus, quia venerant a Iudaea, et quia erant primo conversi. Et ideo Apostolus duo facit.

Primo evacuat auctoritatem illorum pseudorum;

secundo prosequitur causam suam, ibi **ut autem non existimer**, et cetera.

Circa primum duo facit.

Primo ostendit quod pseudo non sint sibi praeferendi;

secundo quod ipse est praeferendus eis, ibi **nam et si amplius**, et cetera.

357. Dicit ergo: hoc, inquam, **secundum faciem videte**; quod **si quis**, de pseudo, **confidit se Christi esse**, propter aliquod magnum quod fecerit, vel propter aliquod donum spirituale quod a Christo receperit, **hoc cogitet apud se**, id est consideret diligenter in corde suo **quia sicut ipse Christi est, ita et nos**. Quasi dicat: quidquid invenitur in eis, totum invenitur in nobis, unde debeamus dici et esse Christi. I Cor. VII, 40: *puto quod et ego Spiritum Christi habeam*. Rom. c. VIII, 9: *si quis Spiritum Christi non habet, hic non est eius*.

358. Non solum autem nos sumus Christi sicut et ipsi, sed multo plus possumus gloriari quod sumus Christi quam ipsi. Et hoc est quod dicit **nam et si amplius aliquid gloriatus fuero de potestate nostra, quam**, scilicet potestatem, **dedit nobis Dominus**. Act. IX, 15: *vas electionis est mihi iste*. Gal. II, 8: *qui operatus est Petro*, et cetera.

Dedit, inquam, mihi potestatem hanc specialem ad convertendum gentes **in aedificationem**, scilicet Ecclesiae, **et non in destructionem**, sicut faciunt pseudo, abutentes potestate eis data in contrarium ad quod data est. Nam, licet potestas detur in aedificationem Ecclesiae in fide et caritate, isti tamen quaerunt gloriam suam et non

the contrary is present in the heart: *beware of false prophets, who come to you in sheep's clothing but inwardly are ravenous wolves* (Matt 7:15). But here **according to outward appearance** is taken for the Gospel's truth itself and the evidence of the fact according to which judgment can be made.

A Gloss explains it another way, namely, **see**, i.e., look to, **the things that are according to outward appearance**, i.e., of the false apostles. As if to say: consider the facts about them, because it is impossible that among the many good things they pretend they not do some things from which you can recognize their wicked intention: *thus you will know them by their fruits* (Matt 7:20).

356. Then when he says, **if any man trust**, he pursues his cause. But it sometimes happens that a person is moved against someone because the former is deceived by the authority of someone who gives himself out as being great. This is the way the Corinthians, deceived by the false apostles who claimed greater authority than Paul, were stirred up against him, because they had come from Judea and were among the first converts. Therefore the Apostle does two things.

First, he deflates the authority of those false apostles;

second, he pursues his cause, at **but that I may not be thought**.

Concerning the first he does two things.

First, he shows that the false apostles should not be preferred to himself;

second, that he should himself be preferred to them, at **for if also I should boast** (2 Cor 10:8).

357. He says, therefore: **see** this, I say, **according to outward appearance**, that **if any man** of the false apostles **trusts to himself that his is Christ's**, on account of some great thing he has done or some spiritual gift he has received from Christ, **let him think this again with himself**, i.e., carefully consider in his heart, **that as he is Christ's, so are we**. As if to say: whatever is found in them is also found in us; hence we also should be considered as Christ's: *and I think I have the Spirit of God* (1 Cor 7:40); *any one who does not have the Spirit of Christ does not belong to him* (Rom 8:9).

358. But we are not only Christ's, as they are, but we can glory more that we are Christ's than they can. And this is what he says: **for if I should boast somewhat more of our power, which the Lord has given us**: *he is a chosen instrument of mine* (Acts 9:15); *for he who worked through Peter for the mission to the circumcised worked through me also for the gentiles* (Gal 2:8).

He gave me, I say, this special power to convert the gentiles, **unto edification**, namely, of the Church, **and not unto your destruction**, as the false apostles do, who abuse the power given to them by using it for a purpose contrary to that for which it was given. For although the power was given for building up the Church in faith and charity, they

Christi, et ideo destruunt. Et hoc faciebant praedicando observari legalia et faciendo quaestum.

Si ergo amplius glorior de hac potestate quam habeo, et in qua gloriam Christi quaero et non meam, *non erubescam*, scilicet de huiusmodi commendatione mea, quia non facio ad ostendendum me, sed causa necessitatis, scilicet ut ostendens auctoritatem meam esse magnam, et pseudo nullam, non decipiamini ab eis de caetero.

359. Ubi nota quod, secundum Gregorium, duabus de causis potest aliquis se commendare absque peccato, scilicet quando aliquis provocatur opprobriis et conculcatur; et hoc ut non desperet videns se conculcari, et ut confutet adversarios. Sic Iob commendavit se multum, sicut patet XXVII cap., unde dicit: *neque enim reprehendit me cor meum in omni vita mea*, et cetera.

Item quando aliquis praedicans veritatem, et alius adversarius veritatis contradicit sibi et impedit manifestationem veritatis, tunc huiusmodi praedicator debet se commendare et ostendere auctoritatem suam, ut confutet illum et ut trahat auditores ad veritatem. Et hoc facit Apostolus in multis locis et hic etiam.

360. Consequenter cum dicit *ut autem non existimer*, etc., prosequitur causam suam ex facti evidentia. Et circa hoc tria facit.

Primo ostendit falsum esse quod sibi imponitur;

secundo rationem dicti assignat, ibi *non enim audemus*, etc.;

tertio exponit rationem ipsam, ibi *non autem non*, et cetera.

361. Circa primum sciendum est, quod, sicut dictum est, imponebatur Apostolo quod in praesentia esset humilis propter timorem, vel propter gratiam et favorem captandum, et in absentia dure scriberet eis. Et ideo dicit Apostolus quod non est ita, sed si bene volunt considerare quae apparent, ita invenient eum facto, qualem habuerunt scripto, et hoc possunt experiri, si volunt.

Et hoc est quod dicit *ut autem non existimer*, a pseudo seu a vobis, *tamquam terrere vos*, vel timorem vobis incutere, *per epistolas* nostras quas vobis mittimus, quem quidem timorem non incutiebam vobis in praesentia. Et hoc ideo est *quoniam* ipsi, scilicet pseudo, *inquiunt: epistolae*, scilicet Pauli, *graves sunt*, id est dure et graviter punientes, *et fortes*, id est absque timore; sed *praesentia* non talis, imo *infirma*, id est debilis et humilis, quod respondet ei quod dicit *fortes*; *et sermo*, scilicet praedicatio sua, et collocutio, et exhortatio, *contemptibilis*, quod respondet ei quod dicitur *graves*.

362. Sed *qui est huiusmodi*, id est qui talia dicit de nobis, *cogitet*, id est sciat certe, *quia quales sumus*, et

seek their own glory and not Christ's; consequently, they destroy. They did this by preaching that the ceremonies of the law must be observed and by making a profit.

Therefore, if I glory more in that power which I have in which I seek Christ's glory, *I should not be ashamed*, namely, for such commendation of myself, because I do not do it for ostentation, but out of necessity, so that by showing that my authority is great and that of the false apostles null, no man may be deceived by them again.

359. Note here that according to Gregory there are two cases in which a person may commend himself without sinning, namely, when he is provoked by reproaches and is treated with contempt, and this in order that he not despair, seeing that he is treated with contempt, and be able to refute his adversaries. This is the way Job commended himself, as it is clear where he says: *my heart does not reproach me for any of my days* (Job 27:6).

Likewise, when a person is preaching the truth and an adversary of the truth contradicts him and hinders the manifestation of the truth, in that case the preacher should commend himself and show his authority in order to refute him and draw his hearers to the truth. The Apostle does this in many places and also here.

360. Then when he says, *but that I may not be thought*, he pursues his cause with the evidence of the facts.

In regard to this he does three things.

First, he shows that the charge laid against him is false;

second, the reason he says this, at *for we dare not*;

third, he explains the reason, at *but we will not glory*.

361. In regard to the first it should be noted that, as has been said, it was charged that the Apostle, when he was present, was humble out of fear or to win their favor; but when he was absent, he wrote harshly to them. But the Apostle says that this is not so, and that if they would carefully weigh the things that appear, they would find him to be in fact as he appears in his epistles; and they can test this, if they wish.

And that is what he says: *but that I may not be thought* by the false apostles or by you, *as it were, to terrify you*, or to make you fearful, *by epistles* which we sent to you; which fear we would not cause you when we were present. For *they*, namely, the false apostles, *say* that *his epistles*, namely, Paul's, *are weighty*, i.e., punishing harshly and severely, *and strong*, i.e., without fear, *but his bodily presence* is not such, for it is *weak*, i.e., feeble and humble, *and his speech*, namely, his preaching and conversation and exhortation, is *contemptible*.

362. But *let such a one*, i.e., who say such things about me, *think this*, i.e., know for certain, *that such as we are in*

cetera. Id est tales erimus praesentes, cum venimus ad vos, quales sumus per epistolas, absentes, si necesse fuerit.

Causam autem quare Apostolus se habuit humiliter ad eos, manifestat Apostolus I Cor. c. II, 3: *et ego, fratres, cum timore multo et tremore*, etc., quod faciebat, quia non erant firmi in fide. Et voluit eos per dulcedinem suae conversationis firmare. Quare autem locutus fuerit sibi plana, et praedicaverit eis non subtilia, insinuat I Cor. III, dicens: *tamquam parvulis in Christo lac potum dedi vobis*, et cetera. Nondum enim erant capaces altioris doctrinae.

363. Consequenter cum dicit **non enim audemus**, etc., ostendit rationem dicti sui, dicens: dico quod non sumus similes pseudo, nec etiam est verum quod imponitur nobis, quia ego non dico alia quam facere est necesse.

Et ideo dicit **non enim audemus nos inserere**, id est dicere nos esse unum ex eis, **aut comparare**, id est similem facere, **quibusdam**, scilicet pseudo, **qui seipsos** vobis tantum **commendant**, et tamen ab aliis et a factis suis non commendantur, contra illud Prov. XXVII, 2: *laudet te alienus, et non os tuum*, et cetera. **Sed ipsi in nobis**, etc., id est secundum ea quae sunt in nobis commensuramus facta nostra et dicta. Quasi dicat: illa dicimus de nobis quae sunt proportionata nobis, id est commensurata factis nostris. Gal. ult.: *unusquisque opus suum probet*, et cetera.

364. Sed contra cap. IV, 2 dicitur **commendantes nosmetipsos ad omnem conscientiam**, et cetera. Ergo non bene dixit.

Respondeo. Dicendum est quod aliud est commendare seipsum ad conscientiam, et aliud ad aures. Nam ad conscientias hominum commendamus nos ipsos, cum bene agimus, et hoc est bonum. Ad aures autem commendamus nosmetipsos verbis tantum, et hoc est malum. Primo modo commendant se iusti et Apostolus; secundo modo pseudo et hypocritae.

word by epistles when absent, such also we will be in deed when present, i.e., we will be such when we come to you as we are by epistle when absent, if it is necessary.

Now the reason the Apostle acted humbly toward them is given: *and I was with you in weakness and in much fear and trembling* (1 Cor 2:3), which he did, because they were not firm in faith and he wanted to strengthen them by the gentleness of his manner. Furthermore, the reason he spoke plain words and did not preach subtle things to them is suggested: *but I, brethren, could not address you as spiritual men, but as men of the flesh, as babes in Christ* (1 Cor 3:1). For they were not yet ready for a more profound doctrine.

363. Then when he says, **for we dare not match or compare ourselves with some who commend themselves**, he indicates the reason behind what he says, saying: I say that we are not like the false apostles, nor is the charge they lay against us true, because I do not say any more than I have to say.

Hence, he says: **we dare not match**, i.e., say that we are one of them, **or compare ourselves**, i.e., make ourselves like some, **with some**, namely, the false apostles, **who commend themselves** to you only. And yet they are not commended by others and by their deeds contrary to what is stated in Proverbs: *let another praise you, and not your own mouth* (Prov 27:2). **But we measure ourselves by ourselves**, i.e., according to what is in us we measure our deeds and our statements. As if to say: we say things about ourselves that are proportionate to ourselves, i.e., in keeping with our deeds: *but let each one test his own work, and then his reason to boast will be in himself alone and not in his neighbor* (Gal 6:4).

364. But on the other hand, he said above: **commending ourselves to every man's conscience in the sight of God** (2 Cor 4:2). Therefore, it was not proper for him to say what he did.

I answer that it is one thing to commend himself to their conscience and another to their ears. For we commend ourselves to the consciences of men, when we act well—and this is good. But we commend ourselves to their ears by words alone—and this is evil. The Apostle and just men commend themselves in the first way; but in the second way the false apostles and hypocrites.

Lecture 3

10:13Nos autem non in immensum gloriabimur, sed secundum mensuram regulae, qua mensus est nobis Deus, mensuram pertingendi usque ad vos. [n. 365]

10:14Non enim quasi non pertingentes ad vos, superextendimus nos: usque ad vos enim pervenimus in Evangelio Christi. [n. 367]

10:15Non in immensum gloriantes in alienis laboribus: spem autem habentes crescentis fidei vestrae, in vobis magnificari secundum regulam nostram in abundantiam, [n. 368]

10:16etiam in illa, quae ultra vos sunt, evangelizare, non in aliena regula in iis quae praeparata sunt gloriari.

10:17Qui autem gloriatur, in Domino glorietur. [n. 370]

10:18Non enim qui seipsum commendat, ille probatus est: sed quem Deus commendat.

10:13ἡμεῖς δὲ οὐκ εἰς τὰ ἄμετρα καυχησόμεθα ἀλλὰ κατὰ τὸ μέτρον τοῦ κανόνος οὗ ἐμέρισεν ἡμῖν ὁ θεὸς μέτρου, ἐφικέσθαι ἄχρι καὶ ὑμῶν.

10:14οὐ γὰρ ὡς μὴ ἐφικνούμενοι εἰς ὑμᾶς ὑπερεκτείνομεν ἑαυτούς, ἄχρι γὰρ καὶ ὑμῶν ἐφθάσαμεν ἐν τῷ εὐαγγελίῳ τοῦ Χριστοῦ,

10:15οὐκ εἰς τὰ ἄμετρα καυχώμενοι ἐν ἀλλοτρίοις κόποις, ἐλπίδα δὲ ἔχοντες αὐξανομένης τῆς πίστεως ὑμῶν ἐν ὑμῖν μεγαλυνθῆναι κατὰ τὸν κανόνα ἡμῶν εἰς περισσείαν

10:16εἰς τὰ ὑπερέκεινα ὑμῶν εὐαγγελίσασθαι, οὐκ ἐν ἀλλοτρίῳ κανόνι εἰς τὰ ἕτοιμα καυχήσασθαι.

10:17Ὁ δὲ καυχώμενος ἐν κυρίῳ καυχάσθω·

10:18οὐ γὰρ ὁ ἑαυτὸν συνιστάνων, ἐκεῖνός ἐστιν δόκιμος, ἀλλὰ ὃν ὁ κύριος συνίστησιν.

10:13But we will not glory beyond our measure: but according to the measure of the rule which God has measured to us, a measure to reach even unto you. [n. 365]

10:14For we do not stretch ourselves beyond our measure, as if we did not reach unto you. For we are come as far as to you in the Gospel of Christ. [n. 367]

10:15Not glorying beyond measure in other men's labors: but having hope of your increasing faith, to be magnified abundantly in you according to our rule. [n. 368]

10:16Indeed, unto those places that are beyond you to preach the Gospel: not to glory in another man's rule, in those things that are made ready to our hand.

10:17But he who glories, let him glory in the Lord. [n. 370]

10:18For it is not he who commends himself who is approved: but he whom God commends.

---

365. Supra Apostolus ostendit rationem eorum quae dixerat, hic consequenter ipsam rationem manifestat.

Dixerat enim quod commensurabat se sibi, et non excedebat mensuram suam. Potest autem aliquis in gloriando et commendando se, excedere dupliciter. Primo quantum ad id de quo gloriatur, puta, si quis gloriatur de eo quod non habet; secundo quantum ad id in quo gloriatur, puta, si quis habens aliquid ex alio, gloriatur in ipso, tamquam a se haberet. Et ideo Apostolus ostendit quod neutro istorum modorum excedit mensuram gloriando vel laudando se. Et primo quantum ad primum; secundo quantum ad secundum, ibi *qui autem gloriatur*, et cetera.

Circa primum duo facit.

Primo probat quod non excedit mensuram suam quantum ad gloriam de praeteritis;

secundo quantum ad gloriam de futuris, ibi *spem autem habentes*, et cetera.

Circa primum tria facit.

Primo proponit intentum;

secundo propositum probat, ibi *non enim quasi non*, etc.;

365. Having indicated the reason behind the things he had said, the Apostle now explains that reason.

For he had said that he measures himself by himself and did not go beyond that measure. But a person could be excessive in two ways in glorying and commending himself. First, in regard to that about which he glories; for example, if he glories about something he does not have. Second, in regard to that in which he glories; for example, if a person has something from someone else, but glories in himself as though he has it of himself. And therefore the Apostle shows that he did not exceed the measure in either of these ways by glorying or praising himself. And first, as regards the first; second, as regards the second, at *but he who glories*.

In regard to the first he does two things.

First, he proves that he did not exceed his measure as regards glory from things past;

second, as regards glory from things to come, at *but having hope*.

Regarding the first, he does two things.

First, he sets out his intention.

second, he proves it, at *for we do not stretch ourselves*;

tertio concludit, ibi *nec in immensum gloriantes*, et cetera.

366. Dicit ergo primo: dico quod metimur et comparamus nosmetipsos nobis, facientes scilicet secundum quod officium nostrum exigit. Hoc autem *nos agentes non in immensum gloriamur*, id est non excedimus mensuram nostram exercendo potestatem nostram et commendando nos, Lev. XIX, v. 35: *nolite facere iniquum*, etc.; *sed, gloriamur, secundum mensuram regulae, qua mensus est nobis Deus*.

Glossa hic exponit de mensura praelationis Apostoli, et dicit *secundum mensuram*, id est *secundum mensuratum mihi a Deo populum*, cuius ego sum praelatus et *regula* ad dirigendum.

Sed hoc idem potest universalius accipi, ut mensura regulae dicatur quantitas gratiae: et tunc est sensus: sed gloriamur *secundum mensuram qua mensus est nobis Deus*, id est, secundum quantitatem gratiae, quam dedit nobis Deus. Eph. IV, 7: *unicuique data est gratia*, et cetera. Quae quidem gratia est nobis regula, ne extollamur, et deviemus a Deo. *Qua mensus est nobis Deus*, quia quidquid boni facimus in evangelizando et in conversatione vestra et aliorum, totum est ex Deo mihi in vobis et aliis concessum. I Cor. III, v. 6: *ego plantavi, Apollo rigavit*, et cetera. *Mensuram*, dico, *pertingendi usque ad vos*, quia vos estis sub mensura gratiae mihi datae, per quam conversi estis ad Christum et obeditis Evangelio.

Hoc est ergo quod proponit, scilicet quod non excedit mensuram suam gloriando se, quod sit eorum praelatus et quod per eum conversi sunt.

367. Et quod ita sit, scilicet quod pertingat usque ad eos, probat consequenter, cum dicit *non enim quasi non pertingentes*, etc., quasi dicat: vere gloriamur, non enim superextendimus nos in gratia vel gloria, vel in potestate nostra, quasi non simus pertinGentes usque ad vos potestate nostra et ministerio. Nam *usque ad vos pervenimus in Evangelio Christi*, id est, in praedicatione Evangelii Christi. I Cor. IV, 15: *in Christo Iesu per Evangelium ego vos genui*, etc.; et supra IX, 1: *nonne opus meum vos estis*, et cetera. Gal. II, 8: *qui operatus est Petro in apostolatum*, et cetera.

368. Et ideo concludit dicens: igitur cum glorior de vobis, non glorior in immensum. Unde dicit *non in immensum gloriantes*, etc., ubi alius fundamentum fidei posuisset.

369. Consequenter cum dicit *spem autem habentes*, etc., ostendit quod non excedit mensuram suam quantum ad gloriam de futuro.

third, he draws the conclusion, at *not glorying beyond measure*.

366. He says, therefore first: I say that we measure and compare ourselves to ourselves, namely, by doing what our office demands. But in doing this *we will not glory beyond our measure*, i.e., when we exercise our power and commend ourselves: *you shall do no wrong in judgment, in measures of length or weight or quantity* (Lev 19:35); *but according to the measure of the rule which God has measured to us*.

A Gloss explains this of the limit of the Apostle's prelacy and says: *according to the measure*, i.e., *according to the people measured out to him by God, the people* whose prelate and *rule* of conduct he is.

But this same thing can be taken more universally, such that the measure of the rule is the quantity of grace. Then the sense is this: but we glory *according to the measure of the rule which God has measured to us*, i.e., according to the amount of grace God has given us: *but grace was given to each of us according to the measure of Christ's gift* (Eph 4:7). This grace is a rule keeping us from being lifted up or separated from God. *Which God has measured to us*, because whatever good we do in preaching the Gospel and in converting you and others, it is all from God, granted to me for you and others: *I planted, Apollos watered, but God gave the growth* (1 Cor 3:6). *A measure*, I say, *to reach even unto you*, because you are under the measure of grace granted to me, by which you have been converted to Christ and obey the Gospel.

Therefore, what he is proposing is this, namely, that he is not going beyond the measure of glorying and praising himself that he is their prelate and that they were converted by him.

367. That this is so, namely, that it reaches even to them, he proves when he says: *for we do not stretch ourselves beyond measure, as if we did not reach unto you*. As if to say: of course we glory, but we do not stretch beyond ourselves in our grace or glory or power, as if we do not reach to you in our power and ministry: *for we are come as far as to you in the Gospel of Christ*, i.e., in the preaching of Christ's Gospel: *for I became your father in Christ Jesus through the Gospel* (1 Cor 4:15); *are you not my workmanship in the Lord* (1 Cor 9:1); *for he who worked through Peter for the mission to the circumcised worked through me also for the gentiles* (Gal 2:8).

368. Therefore he draws the conclusion, saying: therefore, when I glory in you, I am not glorying beyond measure. Hence he says: *not glorying beyond measure in other men's labors*, where someone else laid the foundation of faith.

369. Then when he says, *but having hope of your increasing faith*, he shows that he is not going beyond the measure, when he glories about the future.

Sciendum est autem, quod praedicator potest habere duplex argumentum gloriae de praedicatione sua. Unum est ut conversi ad praedicationem suam proficiant in melius. Aliud ut per ipsos conversos alii convertantur, quia, ut dicitur Ex. XXXVI, *cortina cortinam trahit*, etc.; et Apoc. ult.: *qui audit, dicat: veni.* Nam quando quis videt alios converti, facilius convertitur.

Et quantum ad ista duo, Apostolus sperat augeri gloriam suam de Corinthiis, primo scilicet de profectu eorum in melius. Et ideo dicit: dico quod nec in immensum gloriamur de conversione vestra per nos causata olim sed adhuc ***habentes***, scilicet sumus, ***spem magnificari*** in futuro, id est augeri gloriam nostram, ***crescentis fidei vestrae in vobis***, id est de fide vestra crescente et proficiente in melius per bona opera. I Petr. II, 2: *lac concupiscite, ut in eo crescatis in salutem*, et cetera.

Et iterum, secundo, speramus magnificari in conversione aliorum per vos. Et ideo dicit ***in abundantia***, etc., id est in abundantia praedicationis, non solum in vobis, sed etiam in illa loca quae ultra vos sunt. Et hoc ***secundum regulam nostram***, id est, secundum quod iniunctum est nobis a Christo, non solum evangelizare vobis, sed omnibus gentibus. Mc. ult.: *euntes in mundum universum*, et cetera.

Nec tamen sumus habentes spem in aliena regula, id est non speramus gloriari, nec gloriamur in aliqua aliena regula. Quasi dicat: non in illis quae praeparata sunt ab aliis, id est quos alii duxerunt ad fidem sed faciam fructum in illis, in quibus ab aliis non est praedicatum. Rom. XV, 20: *praedicavi Evangelium hoc, non ubi nominatus est Christus.*

Contra est quod Petrus praedicavit Romae antequam praedicaret ibi Paulus.

Respondeo. Dicendum est, quod non dicit hoc recusans praedicare ubi alius praedicasset, sed dicit quod intendit praedicare etiam ubi non praedicasset aliquis.

370. Consequenter cum dicit ***qui autem gloriatur***, etc., ostendit quod non excedit mensuram suam quantum ad id in quo gloriatur, dicens: quia si ego glorior in eo, in quo gloriandum est, non excedo. Cum autem gloriandum sit in Deo, ***qui gloriatur, in Domino glorietur***, Ier. IX, 24: *in hoc glorietur qui gloriatur*, et cetera.

Potest autem hoc exponi tripliciter. Uno modo, ***in Domino glorietur***, ut ***Domino***, denotet obiectum gloriandi, quasi dicat: ex hoc glorietur quod habet Dominum amando et cognoscendo. Ier. IX, 24: *in hoc glorietur*, et cetera. Alio modo, ***glorietur in Domino***, id est secundum Deum; et hoc modo gloriatur qui gloriatur de his quae Dei sunt, et non de malis, sicut ille, de quo dicitur in Ps. LI, 3: *quid gloriaris in malitia?* Alio modo, ***in Domino glorietur***, id est ut gloriam suam reputet se habere a Deo, totum quod cecidit ad gloriam suam referens

But it should be noted that a preacher has two reasons for glorying in his preaching: one is that those converted by his preaching are making progress; the other is that other people are converted by his converts, because as it is said: *curtain is joined to curtain* (Exod 36:10); *and let him who hears say: come* (Rev 22:17). For one is easily converted when he sees others converted.

In regard to those two things the Apostle hopes that his glorying in the Corinthians will be increased. First, in regard to their progress; hence he says: I say that we do not glory beyond measure over your conversion caused by us in the past, but ***will hope to be magnified*** in the future, i.e., for our glory to be increased ***in your increasing faith***, and in the progress of your good works: *long for the pure spiritual milk, that by it you may grow up to salvation* (1 Pet 2:2).

Second, we hope to be magnified in the conversion of others by you; therefore he says, ***abundantly***, i.e., in the abundance of preaching not only among you but even in lands beyond you; and this ***according to our rule***, i.e., according as Christ has enjoined us to preach not only to you but to all the gentiles. *Go into all the world and preach the Gospel to the whole creation* (Mark 16:15).

Without boasting of work already done in another's field, i.e., we do not hope to glory, nor do we glory in another man's rule. As if to say: not in things prepared by others, i.e., whom others have brought to the faith, but I will bear fruit among those to whom others have not preached. *Thus making it my ambition to preach the Gospel, not where Christ has already been named* (Rom 15:20).

But to the contrary, Peter preached at Rome before Paul preached there.

I answer that he does not say this as though refusing to preach where another has preached; but he says that he intends to preach even where no others have preached.

370. Then when he says, ***but he who glories, let him glory in the Lord***, he shows that he is not going beyond the measure as to that in which he glories, saying: if I glory in him in whom one should glory, I am not going beyond. But since one should glory in God, ***he who glories, let him glory in the Lord***: *let him who glories glory in this, that he understands and knows me* (Jer 9:24).

This can be explained in three ways: in one way, ***let him glory in the Lord***, so that ***in the Lord*** denotes the object in which he glories. As if to say: let him glory in the fact that he possesses the Lord by knowing and loving. In another way, ***let him glory in the Lord***, i.e., according to God; and one glories in this way when he glories in the things of God and not in evil, as the one who is asked: *why do you glory in malice?* (Ps 52:1). In the third way, ***let him glory in the Lord***, i.e., let him regard himself as having his glory from God, referring to God everything that redounds to his own

in Deum. I Cor. IV, 7: *quid habes quod non accepisti? Si autem accepisti*, et cetera. Et sic accipitur hic cum dicitur **qui gloriatur, in Domino glorietur**, quasi dicat: glorior de praedictis, sed non quasi hoc a me habeam, sed a Deo. Et hoc etiam est mensura vestra, quia totum bonum vestrum habet ortum a nobis.

Et vere in Domino debemus gloriari, non nobis imputare gloriam nostram, sed Deo. Nam non est **probatus**, id est comprobatus, a Deo vel hominibus, ille, **qui seipsum commendat**, Prov. XXVII, 2: *laudet te*, etc., sed ille *quem Deus commendat*, id est commendabilem facit bonis operibus et miraculis. Nam Deus est causa totius boni operis per homines facti.

glory. *What have you that you did not receive? If then you received it, why do you boast as if it were not a gift?* (1 Cor 4:7). This is the way it is taken here when he says: **he who glories, let him glory in the Lord**. As if to say: I glory in the foregoing, but not as though I had this from myself and not from God. And this is also your measure, because all your good has sprung from us.

And indeed we should glory in the Lord, not imputing our glory to ourselves, but to God. **For it is not he who commends himself** who is accepted, i.e., **approved** by God or by men: *let another praise you, and not your own mouth; a stranger, and not your own lips* (Prov 27:2), but the man whom the Lord commends, i.e., makes commendable by good works and miracles. For God is the cause of the entire good done by me.

CHAPTER 11

Lecture 1

^{11:1}Utinam sustineretis modicum quid insipientiae meae, sed et supportare me: [n. 371]

^{11:2}aemulor enim vos Dei aemulatione. Despondi enim vos uni viro, virginem castam exhibere Christo. [n. 374]

^{11:3}Timeo autem ne sicut serpens Hevam seduxit astutia sua, ita corrumpantur sensus vestri, et excidant a simplicitate, quae est in Christo. [n. 378]

^{11:1}Ὄφελον ἀνείχεσθέ μου μικρόν τι ἀφροσύνης· ἀλλὰ καὶ ἀνέχεσθέ μου.

^{11:2}ζηλῶ γὰρ ὑμᾶς θεοῦ ζήλῳ, ἡρμοσάμην γὰρ ὑμᾶς ἑνὶ ἀνδρὶ παρθένον ἁγνὴν παραστῆσαι τῷ Χριστῷ·

^{11:3}φοβοῦμαι δὲ μή πως, ὡς ὁ ὄφις ἐξηπάτησεν Εὕαν ἐν τῇ πανουργίᾳ αὐτοῦ, φθαρῇ τὰ νοήματα ὑμῶν ἀπὸ τῆς ἁπλότητος [καὶ τῆς ἁγνότητος] τῆς εἰς τὸν Χριστόν.

^{11:1}Would to God you could bear with some little of my folly! But do bear with me. [n. 371]

^{11:2}For I am jealous of you with the jealousy of God. For I have espoused you to one husband, that I may present you as a chaste virgin to Christ. [n. 374]

^{11:3}But I fear lest, as the serpent seduced Eve by his subtlety, so your minds should be corrupted and fall from the simplicity that is in Christ. [n. 378]

---

371. Postquam Apostolus excusavit se de his quae falso imponebantur sibi a pseudo, hic consequenter, ut confutet eos, scilicet pseudo, et reddat auctoritatem suam honorabilem, commendat se Corinthiis.

Circa hoc autem duo facit.

Primo rationem suae commendationis assignat;

secundo ponit suam commendationem, ibi *in quo quis audet*, et cetera.

Circa primum tria facit.

Primo petit ut eius insipientia supportetur;

secundo subdit necessitatem suae commendationis, ut non insipiens videatur, ibi *aemulor enim vos*, etc.;

tertio innuit quod dato quod sit insipiens, supportare debent, ibi *iterum dico ne quis*, et cetera.

Circa primum duo facit.

Primo praemittit suum desiderium, ut petitio sua facilius exaudiatur;

secundo ponit suam petitionem, ibi *sed et supportate me*.

372. Desiderium autem Apostoli est, ut Corinthii sustineant apostolum commendantem se. Et ideo per adverbium optandi incipit dicens *utinam sustineretis*, et cetera.

Circa quod sciendum est, quod praecepta moralia sunt de agendis, quae cum sint particularia et variabilia, non possunt determinari una communi ratione et regula indefinite, sed oportet quandoque praeter regulam communem aliquid facere in aliquo casu emergente. Quando autem hoc modo fit aliquid praeter communem regulam, sapientes, qui causam huius considerant, non

371. After defending himself against the false charges placed against him by the false apostles, the Apostle, in order to refute them, that is, the false apostles, and render his own testimony more honorable, now commends himself to the Corinthians.

In regard to this he does two things.

First, he assigns the reason for his commendation;

second, he makes the commendation, at *wherein if any man dares*.

In regard to the first he does three things.

First, he asks that they bear with his foolishness;

second, he states why he must commend himself in order not to seem foolish, at *for I am jealous*;

third, he suggests that, granted he is foolish, they should bear with it, at *again I say (let no man think me to be foolish)*.

In regard to the first he does two things.

First, he mentions his desire so that his request may be easier to grant;

second, he makes the request, at *but do bear with me*.

372. The Apostle's desire is that the Corinthians bear with him as he commends himself; therefore he begins with an optative expression: *would to God you could bear with some little of my folly!*

In regard to this it should be noted that the moral precepts deal with actions which, since they are particular and variable, cannot be confined within the limits of one general reason and rule with no exceptions. But sometimes it is necessary to do something beside the common rule in some case that crops up. But when something is done beside the common rule in this way, wise men, who consider

turbantur, nec reputant insipienter factum esse. Indiscreti vero et minus sapientes non considerantes ex qua causa hoc ita fiat, turbantur et reputant stulte factum fore; sicut patet, quia praeceptum morale est *non occides*, aliquando tamen necesse est malos occidere. Et quando hoc fit, sapientes commendant vel non reputant male factum. Stulti autem et haeretici damnant, dicentes hoc esse male factum.

Quia ergo communis lex moralis est quod homo non commendet seipsum, secundum quod dicitur Prov. XXVII, 2: *laudet te alienus*, etc., potest fieri in aliquo casu praeter hanc communem regulam ut homo commendet se, et laudabiliter hoc facit, et tamen indiscreti hoc reputant insipientiam. Unde cum immineret casus quo Apostolus deberet se commendare, hortatur eos ad hoc quod istud non reputent ei ad insipientiam, dicens **utinam sustineretis**, scilicet patienter, **modicum insipientiae meae**, supportando me.

Et dicit **modicum**, quia si commendaret se sine causa, esset maxima insipientia. Et iterum, si commendaret se ex causa omnino urgente, tunc nihil esset ibi insipientiae. Sed quia commendat se, licet ex causa non tamen omnino urgente, cum alio modo posset confutare pseudo, et quia commendat se multum, videtur ibi esse aliquid insipientiae, et hoc est, quod dicit **modicum insipientiae meae**. Infra XII, 11: **factus sum insipiens**, et cetera.

373. Et licet sic sim insipiens, tamen **supportate me**. Et hoc debent facere, quia subditi debent supportare praelatos, et e converso. Gal. VI, 2: *alter alterius onera*, et cetera. Eph. IV, v. 2: *supportantes invicem in caritate*.

374. Necessitatem autem commendationis ostendit, dicens **aemulor**, et cetera. Et

circa hoc tria facit.

Primo ostendit huiusmodi commendationem provenire ex zelo, ut excludat insipientiam;

secundo dicit hunc zelum non esse inordinatum, ut vitet indiscretionem, ibi **timeo autem**, etc.;

tertio excludit eorum excusationem, ibi **nam si is qui venit**, et cetera.

Circa primum duo facit.

Primo ponit zelum, quem habet ad eos, sanctum, quia Dei;

secundo ostendit causam huius zeli, quia incumbebat sibi ex officio, ibi **despondi vos**, et cetera.

375. Est ergo zelus sanctus, quia **aemulor vos**, id est diligo vos ferventer, **Dei aemulatione**, id est ad honorem Dei, non meum.

Circa quod nota, quod aemulatio, prout est idem quod zelus, non aliud est quam quidam motus animi

the cause of it, are not troubled and do not think it was done foolishly. For example, the moral precept forbids killing, but sometimes it is necessary to kill evil men. When this is done, wise men commend it or do not think it was wicked to have done so, but the undiscerning and less wise, not considering the cause why one acted in this manner, are disturbed and think it was foolish to do. So when the wicked are killed, fools and heretics condemn it, saying it was a wicked thing to do.

Therefore, because the common law is that a man should not commend himself, as it is said: *let another praise you, and not your own mouth; a stranger, and not your own lips* (Prov 27:2), it could happen in some case beside this common rule, that a man commends himself and is acting praiseworthily; nevertheless, the undiscerning regard it as folly. Therefore, since the Apostle was confronted with a case in which he should commend himself, he urges them not to lay it to his folly, saying, **would to God you could bear with some little of my folly!**

He says, **little**, because were he to commend himself without cause, it would be the utmost folly. Again, if he commended himself for a reason entirely urgent, then there would be no folly involved. But because he is commending himself for a reason not altogether urgent, since he could refute the false apostles in some other way, and because he is commending himself very much, there seems to be some folly there; and that is what he says, **some little of my folly**: *I have become foolish. You have compelled me* (2 Cor 12:11).

373. But although I am foolish, **do bear with me**. And they should do this because subjects should uphold their prelates and vice versa. *Bear one another's burdens, and so fulfill the law of Christ* (Gal 6:2); *forbearing one another in love* (Eph 4:2).

374. Then, saying, **I am jealous**, he shows the need for this commendation.

In regard to this he does three things.

First, he shows that a commendation of this sort springs from zeal, to exclude folly;

second, he says that this zeal is not irregular, to avoid indiscretion, at **but I fear**;

third, he rejects their excuse, at **for if he who comes** (2 Cor 11:4).

In regard to the first he does two things.

First, he mentions the holy zeal he has for them;

second, the cause of this zeal, because his office obliged him, at **I have espoused you**.

375. His zeal, therefore, is holy, because **I am jealous of you**, i.e., I love you fervently, **with the jealousy of God**, i.e., to God's honor, not mine.

In regard to this it should be noted that jealousy taken as being the same as zeal is nothing more than a good or

bonus vel malus, tendentis in statum proximi, et importat fervorem amoris. Et ideo consuevit sic definiri: *zelus est amor intensus non patiens consortium in amato*. Et si quidem non patiatur consortium in aliquo bono, puta vitii vel alicuius imperfectionis, sed singulariter illud solus vult habere, tunc zelus est bonus et aemulatio bona, de qua dicitur I Cor. XII, 31: *aemulamini charismata*, et cetera. Gal. IV, 18: *aemulamini bonum in bono*, et cetera. III Reg. XVII: *zelo zelatus*, et cetera. Ps. LXVIII, 10: *zelus domus tuae*, et cetera. Si vero non patiatur consortium in aliqua excellentia vel in aliqua prosperitate mundi, quia aliquis singulariter vult eam sibi, tunc zelus est malus et aemulatio mala.

Hoc autem bono zelo, seu aemulatione, aliquando quis aemulatur alios pro se, sicut vir zelatur pro uxore sua, quam sibi soli vult servari. Aliquando vero zelatur aliquis pro alio, sicut eunuchus zelatur uxorem Domini sui, ut custodiat eam sibi. Sic Apostolus populum suum, quem videbat paratum ad praecipitium, et cum sponso Christo velle prostitui diabolo, aemulabatur, ne Christus sponsus verus in eis aliquod diaboli consortium pateretur. Et ideo dicit **Dei aemulatione**, quasi dicat: non pro me sed Christo, qui est sponsus. Io. IX, 29: *qui habet sponsam, sponsus est*. III Reg. XIX, 10, 14: *zelo zelatus sum pro Domino*, et cetera.

376. Unde autem apostolo incumbebat huiusmodi aemulatio, ostendit, dicens **despondi enim vos**, etc., quasi diceret: merito vos aemulor Dei aemulatione, quia ego sum paranymphus huius matrimonii, quod est inter vos et Christum, quia ego despondi vos, id est feci sponsalia, quae sunt per fidem et caritatem. Os. II, 20: *sponsabo te mihi*, et cetera. Et ideo pertinet ad me custodire vos. Quicumque ergo convertit populum ad fidem et ad iustitiam, despondet eum Christo.

Despondi, inquam, non multis, quia quae multis adhaeret, polluitur. Ier. III, 1: *tu autem polluta es*, et cetera. Sed **uni Christo**, scilicet viro perfecto virtutis plenitudine. Zach. VI, v. 12: *oriens nomen eius*. Ier. XXXI, 22: *novum faciet dominus super terram*, et cetera. Et dicitur Christus vir unus quia singularis, et quantum ad modum conceptionis, et quantum ad modum nascendi, et quantum ad gratiae plenitudinem. Eccle. VII, 29: *unum de mille*, et cetera. Isti, inquam, viro **despondi vos exhibere virginem**.

377. Nota quod a plurali ad singulare descendit, dicens **desponsavi vos** in plurali, et **exhibere virginem** in singulari, volens ostendere quod ex omnibus fidelibus fit unum corpus et una Ecclesia, quae debet esse virgo in omnibus membris suis, et ideo dicit **virginem castam**. In omnibus enim accipitur virginitas pro integritate

evil movement of the spirit concerning itself with the state of one's neighbor, and implies a fervor of love. Consequently, *zeal is an intense love that does not permit any sharing of the beloved*. If it does not permit any sharing of an evil, say of a vice or some imperfection, but it alone wishes to have the beloved exclusively, then the zeal is good and the jealousy good. Thus it is said: *but earnestly desire the higher gifts* (1 Cor 12:31); *for a good purpose it is always good to be made much of* (Gal 4:18); *I have been very jealous for the Lord, the God of hosts* (1 Kgs 19:10); *for zeal for your house has consumed me* (Ps 69:10). But if it does not allow a sharing in something excellent or in some worldly prosperity, because someone wants it all for himself, then the zeal is evil and the jealousy evil.

Now sometimes someone is jealous on his own behalf with this good zeal, or jealousy, as when a man is zealous concerning his wife, whom he wishes to keep for himself. But sometimes someone is zealous on another's behalf, as a eunach is zealous concerning his master's wife so that his master may keep her for himself. This is the way the Apostle was jealous on behalf of his people, whom he saw prepared for a fall and, although espoused to Christ, wished to be prostituted to the devil. Consequently, he would not permit Christ, the true spouse, to suffer their being shared with the devil; hence he says, **with the jealousy of God**. As if to say: not for me but for Christ, who is the spouse: *he who has the bride is the bridegroom* (John 3:29); *I have been very jealous for the Lord, the God of hosts* (1 Kgs 19:10).

376. Then he shows from what source the responsibility to be zealous arose, when he says: **for I have espoused you to one husband, that I may present you as a chaste virgin to Christ**. As if to say: it is proper for me to be jealous for you with the jealousy of God, because I am the groomsman of this wedding between you and Christ, i.e., I effected the espousals made by faith and charity: *I will betroth you to me in faithfulness* (Hos 2:20). Therefore, it is my duty to protect you. So whoever converts the people by faith and charity, espouses them to Christ.

I have espoused you, I say, not to many, because she who adheres to many is defiled: *you have played the harlot with many lovers* (Jer 3:1), but **to one husband, Christ**, that is, to a perfect man filled with the virtues: *the Orient is his name* (Zech 6:12). Christ is called one husband because he is unique both as to the manner of conception, and as to the fullness of grace: *one man among a thousand I found* (Eccl 7:28). To that husband, I say, **I have espoused you to present you as a chaste virgin**.

377. Note that he passes from the plural, **I have betrothed you**, that is, you all, to the singular, **to present you as a pure bride**, thus showing that from all the faithful is formed one body and one Church, which ought to be a virgin in all its members, and hence he says **as a chaste virgin**. For in all, virginity is taken for bodily integrity and chastity

047047047047047047

corporis, castitas pro integritate mentis. Nam aliquando aliqua est virgo corpore, quae non est casta mente.

Sic Ecclesia exhibet se Christo virginem, quando perseverat in fide, et infra sacramenta absque corruptione alicuius idololatriae et infidelitatis. Ez. XVI, 25: *ad omne caput viae aedificasti signum*, et cetera. Castam exhibet se quando existens infra sacramenta et in fide Christi, exhibet puritatem corporis et operis. Eph. V, 27: *ut exhiberet sibi gloriosam Ecclesiam, non habentem maculam, neque rugam*, et cetera.

378. Sed quia Corinthii possent dicere: non necesse est quod custodias nos, et zelus tuus non est rationabilis, quia nos bene servabimus nosmetipsos; ideo consequenter causam huius zeli ostendit, dicens **timeo autem**, et cetera.

Ubi sciendum est quod in Paradiso fuit coniugium Adam et Evae; sed Eva corrupta fuit per serpentem non violenter, sed astute, inquantum promisit falsum et suasit iniquum. Falsum quidem, cum dixit: *eritis sicut dii* et *nequaquam moriemini*, cum tamen ex hoc ipsi incurrerint necessitatem mortis; iniquum vero ut transgrederentur et praeterirent mandatum Dei.

Et secundum hanc similitudinem Apostolus loquens, dicit Ecclesiam esse sicut Evam, quam diabolus aliquando persecutus est manifeste per tyrannos et potestates, et tunc *sicut leo rugiens circuit, quaerens quem devoret*, ut dicitur I Petr. V, 8. Aliquando molestat Ecclesiam latenter per haereticos, qui promittunt veritatem et simulant se bonos, et tunc sicut serpens seducit astutia sua promittendo falsa.

379. Et ideo dicit **timeo ne sicut serpens Evam seduxit**, a Paradiso eam eiiciens, **astutia sua**, promittendo falsa, I Tim. II, 14: *Adam non est seductus, sed mulier; ita*, idest per similes deceptiones haereticorum, **corrumpantur sensus vestri**. Et dicit **sensus vestri**, quia sicut in matrimonio carnali cavet sponsus ne coniux corrumpatur carnaliter, ita Apostolus in hoc matrimonio spirituali timet ne corrumpantur spiritualiter sensus cordis, I Cor. XV, 33: *corrumpunt bonos mores*, etc.; vel sensus spirituales, de quibus Sap. I, v. 1: *sentite de Domino*, etc.; I Cor. XIV, v. 20: *nolite pueri effici sensibus*.

Et excidant a simplicitate, quae est in Christo Iesu. Simplex enim est illud quod compositione caret. Pseudo ergo componebant unam sectam ex Iudaismo et Evangelio, mandantes simul cum Evangelio servari legalia. Illi ergo excidunt a simplicitate Christi, qui seducti a pseudo, simul cum Evangelio servant legalia, et hoc timebat Apostolus de Corinthiis. Eccli. II, 14: *vae peccatori*

for mental integrity; for sometimes a person is a virgin in body, but not chaste in mind.

Thus the Church shows herself a virgin when she perseveres in the faith and the sacraments without being corrupted by idolatry and unbelief. *At the head of every street you built your lofty place and prostituted your beauty* (Ezek 16:25). She shows herself chaste when, persevering in the sacraments and in the faith of Christ, she presents herself pure in body and in work. *That he might present the church to himself in splendor, without spot or wrinkle or any such thing, that she might be holy and without blemish* (Eph 5:27).

378. But because the Corinthians could say: it is not necessary for you to protect us, and your zeal is not reasonable, because we can take care of ourselves very well, he discloses the cause of his zeal saying, **but I fear lest, as the serpent seduced Eve by his subtlety, so your minds should be corrupted and fall from the simplicity that is in Christ**.

Here it should be noted that in paradise Adam and Eve were married, but Eve was corrupted by the serpent, not with violence, but with craftiness, inasmuch as he promised something false and urged something wicked: false, when he said, *you will be as gods* (Gen 3:5), and *no, you will not die* (Gen 3:4), even though they did incur guilt as a result; wicked, when he persuaded her to transgress and ignore God's command.

The Apostle, speaking according to this likeness, says that the Church is like Eve, whom the devil has sometimes persecuted openly by tyrants and potentates, and then *like a roaring lion, seeking someone to devour* (1 Pet 5:8); and sometimes he molests the Church in secret by heretics who promise the truth and pretend to be good, and then as the serpent deceived Eve with his subtility by promising false things.

379. Therefore he says, **I lest, as the serpent seduced Eve**, casting her out of paradise, **by his subtlety** with false promises: *Adam was not deceived, but the woman* (1 Tim 2:14), so, i.e., by like deceptions of heretics, **so your minds should be corrupted**. He says, **your minds**, because just as in a natural marriage a spouse takes precautions against his bride's being corrupted carnally, so in this spiritual marriage the Apostle fears that the senses of the heart will be spiritually corrupted: *bad company ruins good morals* (1 Cor 15:33). Or the spiritual senses referred to in Wisdom: *think of the Lord with uprightness* (Wis 1:1); *do not be children in your thinking* (1 Cor 14:20).

And fall from the simplicity that is in Christ. That is simple which lacks composition. Therefore, the false apostles formed one sect with Judaism and the Gospel, commanding that the ceremonies of the law be observed along with the Gospel. Therefore, they fall from the simplicity of Christ, who, being seduced by the false apostles, observe those ceremonies along with the Gospel; and this

ingredienti terram duabus viis. Et e contra Prov. XI, 3: *simplicitas iustorum dirigit eos.*

the Apostle feared about the Corinthians: *the integrity of the upright guides them* (Prov 11:3).

Lecture 2

11:4Nam si is qui venit, alium Christum praedicat, quem non praedicavimus, aut alium spiritum accipitis, quem non accepistis: aut aliud evangelium, quod non recepistis: recte pateremini. [n. 380]

11:5Existimo enim nihil me minus fecisse a magnis apostolis. [n. 383]

11:6Nam etsi imperitus sermone, sed non scientia, in omnibus autem manifestati sumus vobis. [n. 385]

11:7Aut numquid peccatum feci, meipsum humilians, ut vos exaltemini? quoniam gratis Evangelium Dei evangelizavi vobis? [n. 387]

11:8Alias ecclesias expoliavi, accipiens stipendium ad ministerium vestrum. [n. 391]

11:4εἰ μὲν γὰρ ὁ ἐρχόμενος ἄλλον Ἰησοῦν κηρύσσει ὃν οὐκ ἐκηρύξαμεν, ἢ πνεῦμα ἕτερον λαμβάνετε ὃ οὐκ ἐλάβετε, ἢ εὐαγγέλιον ἕτερον ὃ οὐκ ἐδέξασθε, καλῶς ἀνέχεσθε.

11:5Λογίζομαι γὰρ μηδὲν ὑστερηκέναι τῶν ὑπερλίαν ἀποστόλων.

11:6εἰ δὲ καὶ ἰδιώτης τῷ λόγῳ, ἀλλ᾽ οὐ τῇ γνώσει, ἀλλ᾽ ἐν παντὶ φανερώσαντες ἐν πᾶσιν εἰς ὑμᾶς.

11:7Ἢ ἁμαρτίαν ἐποίησα ἐμαυτὸν ταπεινῶν ἵνα ὑμεῖς ὑψωθῆτε, ὅτι δωρεὰν τὸ τοῦ θεοῦ εὐαγγέλιον εὐηγγελισάμην ὑμῖν;

11:8Ἢ ἁμαρτίαν ἐποίησα ἐμαυτὸν ταπεινῶν ἵνα ὑμεῖς ὑψωθῆτε, ὅτι δωρεὰν τὸ τοῦ θεοῦ εὐαγγέλιον εὐηγγελισάμην ὑμῖν;

11:4For if he who comes preaches another Christ, whom we have not preached; or if you receive another spirit, whom you have not received; or another gospel, which you have not received: you might well bear with him. [n. 380]

11:5For I suppose that I have done nothing less than the great apostles. [n. 383]

11:6For although I am rude in speech, yet not in knowledge: but in all things we have been made manifest to you. [n. 385]

11:7Or did I commit a fault, humbling myself that you might be exalted, because I preached unto you the Gospel of God freely? [n. 387]

11:8I have taken from other churches, receiving wages of them for your ministry. [n. 391]

---

380. Posito zelo quem ad Corinthios habebat Apostolus, et ostenso zelum esse rationabilem, hic consequenter removet eorum excusationem. Et

circa hoc duo facit.

Primo proponit eorum excusationem;

secundo vero removet eam, ibi **existimo enim me**, et cetera.

381. Circa primum sciendum est quod Corinthii possent suspicari quod ideo zelum haberet de eis, quia timeat ne dimittant doctrinam suam propter doctrinam pseudo; unde possent dicere: constat quod minus bona sunt dimittenda propter magis bona; ergo si pseudo meliora doceant, non debes turbari, si acquiescimus eis. Et ideo hanc excusationem ponit, ostendendo quod nihil maius quam Apostolus, docent et praedicant.

382. Nam Apostolus tria praedicavit eis, et docuit eos. Primo quod essent Christi. Supra IV, 5: **non enim praedicavimus nosmetipsos, sed Christum Iesum**. Secundo quod haberent Spiritum Christi. Rom. VIII, v. 9: **si quis Spiritum Christi non habet, hic non est eius**. Tertio ut reciperent Evangelium Christi. Rom. I, 16: **non enim erubesco Evangelium**, et cetera. Si ergo pseudo meliora vobis praedicarent et vos docerent, recte faceretis et excusabiles essetis; sed hoc non faciunt.

380. Having described the zeal he had for the Corinthians and proved it reasonable, the Apostle now rejects their excuse.

In regard to this he does two things.

First, he proposes their excuse;

second, he removes it, at **for I suppose**.

381. In regard to the first it should be noted that the Corinthians might suppose that he has zeal for them, because he feared that they might set aside his teaching on account of the false apostles' teaching; hence they could say: it is obvious that lesser goods should be discarded in favor of greater goods. Therefore, if the false apostles teach better doctrines, you should not be disturbed if we acquiesce in them. Hence, he proposes this excuse by showing that no one is better than the Apostle in teaching and preaching.

382. For the Apostle preached and taught three things. First, that they were Christ's. **For we do not preach ourselves, but Jesus Christ our Lord** (2 Cor 4:5); second, that they have the Spirit of Christ: **any one who does not have the Spirit of Christ does not belong to him** (Rom 8:9); third, that they received the Gospel of Christ: **for I am not ashamed of the Gospel: it is the power of God for salvation to every one who has faith, to the Jew first and also to the Greek** (Rom 1:16). If, therefore, the false apostles preach and teach something better to you, you would do right and would be excusable; but they do not do this.

Et hoc est quod dicit *nam* et *si is qui*, etc., quasi dicat: timeo ne pseudo qui venit ad vos non missus, sed ex se, sicut fur et latro. Io. X, 8: *quotquot venerunt, fures sunt et latrones*. Ier. XXIII, 21: *non mittebam eos, et ipsi currebant*. Rom. X, 15: *quomodo praedicabunt, nisi, et cetera*. Si, inquam, talis praedicator *praedicat* vobis *alium Christum*, scilicet excellentiorem quam illum quem nos praedicavimus: quod non potest esse, quia, ut dicitur I Cor. VIII, 6: *unus Dominus noster Iesus Christus, per quem omnia, et cetera*. Et hoc quantum ad primum.

Aut alium spiritum, scilicet meliorem, *accipitis*, scilicet per talem, quam accepistis, scilicet per nos, id est ministerio nostro, quod non potest esse, quia, ut dicitur I Cor. c. XII, 11: *haec omnia operatur unus atque idem Spiritus, et cetera*. Et hoc quantum ad secundum.

Aut praedicat vobis *aliud evangelium*, id est aliam praedicationem vel doctrinam, quam per nos *non recepistis*, Gal. I, 6: *miror quod sic tam cito transferimini, et cetera*. Si, inquam, alia et meliora facerent vobis, *recte pateremini*, id est faceretis, excusando vos.

Et quia non potest eis aliud evangelium, id est melius tradi, ideo Apostolus excommunicat Galatas, si aliud evangelium recipiant, Gal. I, 9: *si quis aliud vobis evangelizaverit, et cetera*.

383. Consequenter cum dicit *existimo*, etc., removet hanc excusationem.

Et circa hoc duo facit.

Primo ostendit quod ipse non minus fecit eis quam alii;

secundo quod plus, ibi *aut numquid*, et cetera.

Circa primum tria facit.

Primo ostendit quod nihil minus fecit facto quam alii apostoli;

secundo innuit quod non defuit ei facultas ad hoc faciendum, ibi *nam et si imperitus sermone*, etc.;

tertio ostendit evidentiam utriusque, ibi *in omnibus autem*, et cetera.

384. Dicit ergo: *recte pateremini* vos seduci ab eis, si melius praedicarent vobis, sed hoc non est verum. *Enim*, id est *quia*, *existimo me nihil minus fecisse*, in his, *a magnis apostolis*, id est quam Petrus et Ioannes, quos isti habebant magnos.

Et comparat se *magnis apostolis*, tum quia Paulus videbatur et reputabatur ab eis minor quam illi, eo quod illi fuerunt cum Iesu, et Paulus non; tum etiam quia

And this is what he says: *for if he who comes preaches another Christ whom we have not preached; or if you receive another spirit whom you have not received; or another gospel, which you have not received: you might well bear with him*. As if to say: I fear that a false apostle might come to you unsent, but of himself, as a thief and a robber. *All who came before me are thieves and robbers* (John 10:8); *I did not send the prophets, yet they ran* (Jer 25:21); *and how can men preach unless they are sent?* (Rom 10:15). If, I say, such a preacher *preaches* to you *another Christ*, namely, more excellent than the one we have preached, which cannot be, because as it is said: *and one Lord, Jesus Christ, through whom are all things and through whom we exist* (1 Cor 8:6); and this as to the first.

Or if you receive another spirit, namely, one better than the one you have received from us, i.e., by our ministry, which cannot be, because as it is said: *all these are inspired by one and the same Spirit, who apportions to each one individually as he wills* (1 Cor 12:11); and this as to the second.

Or if you accept *another gospel*, i.e., another preaching or doctrine, *which you have not received* from us: *I am astonished that you are so quickly deserting him who called you in the grace of Christ and turning to a different gospel* (Gal 1:6). If, I say, they did other and better things for you, *you might well bear with him*, i.e., you would be right in excusing yourselves.

But because another, i.e., better gospel cannot be delivered to them, the Apostle excommunicates the Galatians, if they receive another gospel: *if any one is preaching to you a gospel contrary to that which you received, let him be accursed* (Gal 1:9).

383. Then when he says, *for I suppose*, he removes this excuse.

In regard to this he does two things.

First, he shows that he did not do less for them than the others;

second, that he did more, at *or did I commit a fault*.

In regard to the first he does three things.

First, he shows that he did nothing less in deed than the other apostles;

second, he suggests that he was not lacking the means to do this, at *for although I am rude in speech*;

third, he presents the evidence for both, at *but in all things*.

384. He says, therefore: *you might well bear with him*, or them, allowing yourselves to be seduced by them, if they preached something better to you; but this is not true. *For*, i.e., because *I suppose that I have done nothing less than the great apostles*, i.e., than Peter and John, whom they considered great.

He compares himself to *the great apostles*, both because Paul seemed to them and was regarded by them as less than they, on the ground that they had been with Christ, and Paul

pseudo dicebant se missos ab eis, et ideo ostendendo se parem magnis apostolis, istorum errorem removet et pseudo confutat. Et non solum nihil minus fecit, sed plus. I Cor. XV, 10: *plus omnibus laboravi.*

385. Et ne forte dicerent ei: unde tibi est facultas ad hoc faciendum, cum sis imperitae linguae? Ostendit quod ei facultas affuit ex magnitudine scientiae, dicens: licet sim **imperitus sermone**, tamen **non** sum imperitus **scientia**, II Petr. ult.: *sicut et charissimus frater noster Paulus, secundum sapientiam,* et cetera.

Sed hoc sciendum est, quod pseudo quaerentes gloriam propriam et lucra sectantes, nitebantur attrahere populum per ornata et subtilia et exquisita verba, non attendentes nisi solum aures permulcere. Apostolus vero, quia non quaerebat utilitatem propriam, sed solum dilatationem fidei Christi et profectum eius, ita proponebat verbum fidei, ut omnes possent capere, conformans se conditioni audientium et capacitati. Unde quia isti in principio non erant capaces altae doctrinae, proposuit eis fidem, non in subtilitate sermonis, sed eo modo quo capere possent, scilicet plane et aperte. Et ideo isti dicebant eum esse **imperitum sermone**. I Cor. I, 17: *non in sapientia verbi,* et cetera. Et propter hoc dicit Apostolus: licet sim **imperitus sermone**, ut vobis videtur, hoc non fuit ex defectu scientiae, sed propter vos, ex quadam dispensatione, quia *tamquam parvulis in Christo lac potum dedi vobis,* et cetera.

Vel dicendum, ad litteram, quod Apostolus fuit balbus, et ex hoc pseudo deridebant eum. Et ideo dicit **et si imperitus sermone**, id est impeditae linguae, **non** tamen sum imperitus **scientia**, Ex. IV, 10: *impeditioris et tardioris linguae sum.*

386. Quod autem nihil minus fecerim a magnis apostolis, evidenter apparet per ea quae feci vobis. Et ideo dicit **in omnibus** praedictis, **manifestatus sum in vobis**, qui experti estis quae per me fiunt. I Cor. IX, 2: *signaculum apostolatus mei vos estis in Domino.* Et infra XII, 12: **signa tamen apostolatus mei facta sunt super vos,** et cetera.

387. Consequenter cum dicit **aut numquid peccatum**, etc., ostendit quod plus fecit quam omnes alii, et hoc quia praedicavit sine sumptibus.

Circa hoc duo facit.

Primo ponit factum,

secundo causam facti assignat, ibi **quare? quia non diligo vos**, et cetera.

Circa primum duo facit.

Primo ostendit factum quantum ad praeteritum;

secundo quantum ad futurum, ibi **et in omnibus**, et cetera.

not; and because the false apostles claimed to have been sent by them. Therefore, by showing himself equal to the great apostles, he removes their error and refutes the false apostles: *I worked harder than any of them* (1 Cor 15:10).

385. But lest perhaps they should say to him: whence did you obtain the faculty to do this, since you are unskilled in our speech? He shows that the faculty is due to the vastness of his knowledge, saying, **although I am rude in speech, yet not in knowledge**: *so also our beloved brother Paul wrote to you according to the wisdom given him* (2 Pet 3:15).

But this should be noted, namely, that the false apostles, seeking their own glory and pursuing gain, tried to attract people by ornate and subtle and exquisite words, trying only to stroke their ears gently. But the Apostle, because he was not seeking his own advantage but only the spread and growth of the faith, proposed the word of faith in such a way that all could understand, adjusting himself to the condition and capacity of his hearers. Hence, because they were not capable of lofty doctrine in the beginning, he proposed the faith to them not in subtle terms but in a way they could understand, namely, plainly and clearly. That is why they said he was **rude in speech**. *Not with eloquent wisdom, lest the cross of Christ be emptied of its power* (1 Cor 1:17). On this account the Apostle says: **although I am rude in speech**, as it seems to you, this was not due to a lack of knowledge but for your sake by way of dispensing it, because I *could not address you as spiritual men, but as men of the flesh, as babes in Christ* (1 Cor 3:1).

Or according to the letter, it must be said that the Apostle stuttered, and on this account the false apostles ridiculed him. Therefore he says: for **although I am rude in speech**, i.e., have a speech impediment, I am **not in knowledge**: *I am slow of speech and of tongue* (Exod 4:10).

386. But the fact that I did no less than the great apostles is evident from the things I have done for you; hence, he says: **in all things we have been made manifest to you**, who have experienced what I have done. *You are the seal of my apostleship in the Lord* (1 Cor 9:2); **the signs of my apostleship have been wrought on you, in all patience, in signs and wonders and mighty deeds** (2 Cor 12:12).

387. Then when he says, **or did I commit a fault**, he shows that he has done more than all the others; and this because he preached without payment.

In regard to this he does two things.

First, he states the fact;

second, he assigns the reason of the fact, at **why? because I do not love you**.

In regard to the first he does two things.

First, he shows the fact as to the past;

second, as to the future, at **and in all things**.

Factum autem praeteritum ostendit dupliciter. Primo in generali, secundo in speciali, ibi *quoniam gratis*, et cetera.

388. Dicit ergo: recte dico quod nihil minus feci ab illis, nisi forte hoc reputetis male et minus factum, quia diminui de auctoritate mea, non accipiens sumptus a vobis; sed si hoc esset malum, minus fecissem. Et ideo ostendit quod non est malum. Et hoc est quod dicit *aut numquid peccatum feci*, id est numquid peccavi, *humilians meipsum* et diminuens de auctoritate mea? Quasi dicat, non. Eccli. III, 20: *quanto maior es*, et cetera. I Cor. IX, 19: *cum essem liber*, et cetera. Matth. VI: *qui humiliaverit se*, et cetera.

Ratio autem humiliationis meae est non propter lucrum proprium, sed propter promotionem vestram. Unde dicit *ut vos exaltemini*, id est in fide confirmemini. Corinthii autem avari erant, et ideo si a principio accepisset sumptus, forte destitissent a fide. Item, pseudo praedicabant propter quaestum. Ut ergo Corinthii reciperent Apostolum et pseudo auferret occasionem quaestus, gratis praedicavit eis sine sumptibus propriis.

389. Hoc autem quod dixerat in generali, manifestat in speciali, ibi *quoniam gratis*, etc., et facit duo.

Primo ostendit quomodo sine sumptibus praedicavit eis in primo adventu ad eos;

secundo ostendit quod idem fecit in mora quam apud eos contraxit, ibi *et cum essem*, et cetera.

390. Circa primum duo facit. Primo proponit quod intendit, scilicet humiliationem, dicens: in hoc *humilians meipsum, quoniam evangelizavi vobis gratis*, id est sine sumptu, non autem sine mercede, quia hoc non est laudis. Licet enim omnes possent capere sumptus personae ab eis quibus proponunt verbum Dei, nullus tamen praedicare debet pro mercede et quaestu.

391. Secundo, quia possent dicere isti: unde ergo accepisti sumptus? Respondet quod ab aliis ecclesiis, dicens *ecclesias alias expoliavi, accipiens* ab eis *stipendium ad ministerium vestrum*. Ex hoc convincit eos quod non possint dicere Apostolo quod non liceret ei accipere ab eis. Si enim accipitur ab aliis ad servitium eorum, multo magis liceret ei accipere ab ipsis.

Ex hoc etiam apparet quod legatus Papae visitans unam partem legationis, potest accipere stipendia. Et quod dominus Papa, pro necessitate unius patriae, potest accipere subsidium ab aliis partibus mundi. Ratio est, quia Ecclesia est sicut unum corpus. Videmus autem in corpore naturali quod natura, quando deficit virtus in uno membro, subministrat humores et virtutem accipiens ab aliis membris.

He shows the past fact in two ways: first in general, and second in particular, at *because I preached*.

388. He says, therefore: I am correct in saying that I have done no less than the others, unless you think I did less and acted wrongly, because I lessened my authority in not accepting payments from you. But if this were so, I would have done evil. Therefore he shows that it is not evil, and this is what he says: *or did I commit a fault, humbling myself* and lessening my authority? As if to say: no: *the greater you are, humble yourself in all things, and you will find grace in the sight of God* (Sir 3:20); *for though I am free from all men, I have made myself a slave to all, that I might win the more* (1 Cor 9:19); *whoever humbles himself like this child, he is the greatest in the kingdom of heaven* (Matt 18:4).

The reason for humbling myself is not for my own gain but for your improvement; hence he says: *that you might be exalted*, i.e., be strengthened in faith. But the Corinthians were very covetous, and if he had accepted payment from the very beginning, they might perhaps have left the faith. Likewise, the false prophets preached for monetary profit. Therefore, in order that the Corinthians receive the Apostle, and the false prophets remove the occasion for profit, the Apostle preached for free and without subsidy.

389. Then he explains in detail what he had said in general. In regard to this he does two things.

First, he shows how he preached to them without charge during his first visit with them;

second, he shows that he did the same during the long stay he made with them, at *and when I was present*.

390. In regard to the first he does two things. First, he mentions the humiliation, saying: *humbling myself* in this, *because I preached unto you the Gospel of God freely*, i.e., without charge; but not for a reward, because this is not praiseworthy. For although all could take personal payments from those to whom they preached the word of God, yet no one should preach for the reward or the payment.

391. Second, because they could say: where did you obtain your support? He answers that it came from the other churches, saying: *I have taken from other churches, receiving wages of them for your ministry*. By this he convinces them that they could not say to the Apostle that it is unlawful for him to take from them. For if it is taken from others for serving them, it is much more lawful for him to take from them.

From this it is apparent that a papal legate visiting one part of his jurisdiction can accept stipends, and that the Pope can take subsidies from various parts of the world to relieve the needs of some country. The reason is that the Church is as one body. But we see in a natural body that, when strength is failing in one member, nature administers humors and strength by taking from other members.

Lecture 3

^{11:9}Et cum essem apud vos, et egerem, nulli onerosus fui: nam quod mihi deerat, suppleverunt fratres, qui venerunt a Macedonia: et in omnibus sine onere me vobis servavi, et servabo. [n. 392]

^{11:9}καὶ παρὼν πρὸς ὑμᾶς καὶ ὑστερηθεὶς οὐ κατενάρκησα οὐθενός· τὸ γὰρ ὑστέρημά μου προσανεπλήρωσαν οἱ ἀδελφοὶ ἐλθόντες ἀπὸ Μακεδονίας, καὶ ἐν παντὶ ἀβαρῆ ἐμαυτὸν ὑμῖν ἐτήρησα καὶ τηρήσω.

^{11:9}And when I was present with you and was in need, I was a burden to no man: for that which was wanting to me, the brethren supplied who came from Macedonia. And in all things I have kept myself from being burdensome to you: and so I will keep myself. [n. 392]

^{11:10}Est veritas Christi in me, quoniam haec gloriatio non infringetur in me in regionibus Achaiae. [n. 397]

^{11:10}ἔστιν ἀλήθεια Χριστοῦ ἐν ἐμοὶ ὅτι ἡ καύχησις αὕτη οὐ φραγήσεται εἰς ἐμὲ ἐν τοῖς κλίμασιν τῆς Ἀχαΐας.

^{11:10}The truth of Christ is in me, that this glorying shall not be broken off in me in the regions of Achaia. [n. 397]

^{11:11}Quare? quia non diligo vos? Deus scit. [n. 399]

^{11:11}διὰ τί; ὅτι οὐκ ἀγαπῶ ὑμᾶς; ὁ θεὸς οἶδεν.

^{11:11}Why? Because I do not love you? God knows it. [n. 399]

^{11:12}Quod autem facio, et faciam: ut amputem occasionem eorum qui volunt occasionem, ut in quo glorientur, inveniantur sicut et nos. [n. 401]

^{11:12}Ὃ δὲ ποιῶ, καὶ ποιήσω, ἵνα ἐκκόψω τὴν ἀφορμὴν τῶν θελόντων ἀφορμήν, ἵνα ἐν ᾧ καυχῶνται εὑρεθῶσιν καθὼς καὶ ἡμεῖς.

^{11:12}But what I do, that I will do: that I may cut off the occasion from those who desire an occasion: that wherein they glory, they may be found even as we. [n. 401]

^{11:13}Nam ejusmodi pseudoapostoli sunt operarii subdoli, transfigurantes se in apostolos Christi. [n. 404]

^{11:13}οἱ γὰρ τοιοῦτοι ψευδαπόστολοι, ἐργάται δόλιοι, μετασχηματιζόμενοι εἰς ἀποστόλους Χριστοῦ.

^{11:13}For such false apostles are deceitful workmen, transforming themselves into the apostles of Christ. [n. 404]

^{11:14}Et non mirum: ipse enim Satanas transfigurat se in angelum lucis. [n. 406]

^{11:14}καὶ οὐ θαῦμα· αὐτὸς γὰρ ὁ σατανᾶς μετασχηματίζεται εἰς ἄγγελον φωτός.

^{11:14}And no wonder: for Satan himself transforms himself into an angel of light. [n. 406]

^{11:15}Non est ergo magnum, si ministri ejus transfigurentur velut ministri justitiae: quorum finis erit secundum opera ipsorum. [n. 408]

^{11:15}οὐ μέγα οὖν εἰ καὶ οἱ διάκονοι αὐτοῦ μετασχηματίζονται ὡς διάκονοι δικαιοσύνης· ὧν τὸ τέλος ἔσται κατὰ τὰ ἔργα αὐτῶν.

^{11:15}Therefore it is no great thing if his ministers be transformed as the ministers of justice, whose end shall be according to their works. [n. 408]

---

392. Ostenso quod quando primo eis praedicavit in ipso adventu, evangelizavit eis gratis, hic ostendit quod nec etiam contrahendo moram apud eos, accepit ab eis sumptus. Et

    primo hoc ostendit,

    secundo vero respondet cuidam tacitae quaestioni, ibi *nam quod mihi*, et cetera.

393. Dicit ergo: non solum quando primo veni ad vos non accepi a vobis sumptus; sed etiam *cum essem apud vos* diu et etiam *egerem*, ut ostendat quod non dimisit eis sumptus propter divitias, *nulli onerosus fui*, aliquid ab aliquo accipiendo. In quo apparet causa quare dimisit: quia Corinthii, propter avaritiam eis innatam, reputabant sibi onus ministrare sumptus. I Cor. IX, 12: *non sumus usi hac potestate, sed omnia sustinemus*, et cetera.

394. Sed possent isti dicere: unde ergo habuisti necessaria? Et ideo respondet dicens quod ab aliis ecclesiis.

392. Having shown that when he first preached to them during his first visit, he preached to them without charge, he now shows that not even during his long stay among them did he accept any payments from them.

    First, he shows this;

    second, he answers a tacit question, at *for that which was wanting to me*.

393. He says, therefore: I took no payments from you not only when I first came to you, but also *when I was present with you* for some time and *was in need*, in order to show that he did not forego the payments, because he was rich: *I was a burden to no man* by taking anything from anyone. This reveals the cause why he forewent it, namely, because the Corinthians in their innate avarice considered it a burden to minister to him. *We have not made use of this right, but we endure anything rather than put an obstacle in the way of the Gospel of Christ* (1 Cor 9:12).

394. But they could ask: where did you get what you needed? So he answers: from the other churches.

Ideo scilicet nihil accepi, quia illud *quod mihi deerat*, scilicet a pretio quod lucrabatur nocte laborando manibus suis, apud Aquilam et Priscam. Erat enim scenofactoriae artis, per quam lucrabatur sibi necessaria. Act. XX, 34: *ad ea quae mihi opus erant*, et cetera. Illud ergo quod deerat non dedistis vos, sed *suppleverunt fratres qui venerunt a Macedonia*, scilicet Philippenses, qui erant valde liberales. Unde de hoc in epistola ad Philippenses commendat eos: Phil. IV, 15: *nulla ecclesia communicavit mihi in ratione dati et accepti, nisi vos*. Sed Corinthii erant avari.

395. Consequenter cum dicit *et in omnibus sine onere*, etc., ostendit quomodo se habebit in hoc ad eos in futurum, dicens, quod etiam sine onere vult se habere ad eos. Et

circa hoc duo facit.

Primo ponit suam rationem communem;

secundo confirmat eam, ibi *est veritas Christi*, et cetera.

396. Dicit ergo: non solum feci hoc, scilicet quod gratis vobis evangelizavi et *nulli onerosus fui*, sed etiam *in omnibus servabo me vobis sine onere*, sicut usque modo *servavi*, non dure reprehendendo, non severe corrigendo, nec vestra accipiendo. Act. III: *argentum et aurum et vestem nullius concupivi*. Num. XVI, 15: *tu scis quod nec asellum quidem acceperim ab eis*, dicit Moyses ad Dominum. Samuel dicit, I Reg. c. XII, 3: *loquimini de me, si oppressi*, et cetera.

397. Et quod ita facturus sit, confirmat ex duobus.

Primo ex eo qui loquitur in ipso, scilicet Christo, qui est veritas, a qua non potest esse falsum. Et ideo dicit *est veritas Christi in me*, etc., quasi dicat: hoc quod dixi verum est, quia veritas Christi loquitur in me, et cetera. Hoc infra ultimo: *an experimentum quaeritis eius qui in me*, et cetera.

Vel hoc potest accipi per modum iurantis. Quasi dicat: Deus, qui est veritas et est in me scrutans corda, sit mihi testis, quod ita servabo me. Rom. I, 9: *testis est mihi Deus*, et cetera.

398. Secundo, ex eo quod non intendit minuere gloriam suam, sed augere.

Apostolus enim attribuebat sibi apud Christum ad magnam gloriam quod ipse solus, inter apostolos, sine sumptu praedicabat Corinthiis. Et ideo dicit: *ideo servabo me sine onere, quoniam non infringetur*, id est non minuetur, *in me haec gloria*, quod scilicet gratis praedico vobis, et quod a licitis abstineo, propter salutem vestram: quae quidem est gloria Christi, quia ipse glorificatur per hoc in me; vel quia ego hanc gloriam habeo

Therefore I took nothing, because *that which was wanting to me* was supplied from the wage I earned by working at night with Aquila and Priscilla, for he practiced the tentmaker's art, from which he furnished his necessities. *You yourselves know that these hands ministered to my necessities, and to those who were with me* (Acts 20:34). Therefore, that which was lacking you did not give, but *the brethren supplied who came from Macedonia*, namely, the Philippians, who were very generous; for which the Apostle commended them in the epistle to the Philippians: *no church entered into partnership with me in giving and receiving except you only* (Phil 4:15). But the Corinthians were avaricious.

395. Then when he says, *and in all things I have kept myself from being burdensome to you: and so I will keep myself*, he shows how he plans to act toward them in this matter in the future, saying that he does not want to be a burden to them.

In regard to this he does two things.

First, he gives his general reason;

second, he confirms it, at *the truth of Christ*.

396. He says, therefore: not only have I preached the Gospel to you without charge and *was a burden to no man*, but also *I have kept myself from being burdensome to you: and so I will keep myself*, not rebuking you sharply or correcting you severely or accepting anything: *I coveted no one's silver or gold or apparel* (Acts 20:33); *I have not taken one ass from them, and I have not harmed one of them* (Num 16:15); and Samuel says: *testify against me before the Lord and before his anointed . . . whom have I oppressed?* (1 Sam 12:3).

397. That he will continue to do so he confirms in two ways.

First, by reason of the one who speaks in him, namely, Christ, who is the truth from which nothing false can come; hence he says, *the truth of Christ is in me*. As if to say: what I say is true, because the truth of Christ speaks in me: *do you seek a proof of Christ who speaks in me?* (2 Cor 13:3)

Or this can be taken as an oath, as if to say: God, who is truth, and who is in me searching my heart is my witness that I will keep myself so. *For God is my witness, whom I serve with my spirit in the Gospel of his Son* (Rom 1:9).

398. Second, from the fact that he does not intend to lessen his glory, but to increase it.

For the Apostle attributed to himself before Christ as his great glory that he alone of all the apostles preached to the Corinthians without payment; hence he says: *so I will keep myself from being burdensome to you; that this glorying shall not be broken off*, i.e., lessened, *in me*, namely, that I preached to you freely and that I refrained from what is lawful for your salvation which is Christ's glory, because he is glorified in me by this, or because I particularly have

specialiter apud Christum. Quae quidem refringeretur *in regionibus Achaiae*, ubi Corinthus erat metropolis, si recepisset ab eis, quia avari erant. Habitabant enim in maritimis, et erant intenti mercationibus, et tales consueverunt esse avari. I Cor. IX, 15: *bonum est mihi magis mori, quam ut gloriam meam quis evacuet.*

399. Consequenter cum dicit *quare? Quia non*, etc., ponit causam quare non accepit sumptus ab eis. Et

circa hoc duo facit.

Primo excludit falsam causam;

secundo astruit veram, ibi *quod autem facio*, et cetera.

400. Circa primum sciendum est, quod pseudo imponebant Apostolo, quod ideo non recipiebat a Corinthiis sumptus, quia non diligebat eos, et quia non intendebat eis benefacere et servire. Dicit ergo *quare*, scilicet hoc facio, *quia non diligo vos*, id est pro odio quod habeo ad vos, sicut dicunt pseudo? *Deus scit* quod diligo vos, et quod non pro odio hoc facio. Io. ult.: *Domine, tu scis, quia amo te.*

401. Sic ergo, exclusa causa falsa, sequitur vera, ibi *quod autem facio*, et cetera. Et

circa hoc duo facit.

Primo ponit veram causam;

secundo rationem huius assignat, ibi *nam eiusmodi pseudo*, et cetera.

402. Circa primum sciendum est, quod pseudo, ut dictum est, quaerebant lucra et gloriam propriam. Et ideo, ut in reverentia haberentur, nitebantur exterius sequi vestigia Apostoli, vel etiam, si potuissent, excellere ipsum.

Dicit ergo Apostolus: si ergo volunt me imitari, in hoc imitentur, ut nihil accipiant. Et quia sciebat quod pseudo praedicabant ut acciperent, et, per consequens, quod non praedicarent si deficeret eis lucrum, dicit *quod facio*, ideo facio *et faciam* hoc, non propter odium, sed *ut amputem occasionem eorum*, scilicet pseudo, *qui volunt*, supple meo exemplo, habere *occasionem* accipiendi vestra.

Sciebat enim, secundum Ambrosium, quod si non acciperent, non diu praedicarent. E contrario dicitur Prov. VI: *da occasionem sapienti*, et cetera. Et hoc, ut tales *inveniantur*, scilicet pseudo, *sicut et nos*, scilicet non accipientes pecunias, sicut et nos non accipimus. In quo quidem ipsi gloriantur, scilicet quod imitantur nos, et ego nolo, si perfecte volunt nos imitari, quod accipiant. I Cor. VII, 7: *volo omnes homines esse sicut me*, scilicet non accipientes.

403. *Ut in quo*, et cetera. Hoc legitur tripliciter. Uno modo sic: ut inveniantur tales, supple sicut et nos, non

this glory with Christ. This would have been broken off *in the regions of Achaia*, where Corinth was the metropolis, if he had taken anything from them, because they were avaricious. *For I would rather die than have any one deprive me of my ground for boasting* (1 Cor 9:15).

399. Then when he says, *and why?*, he presents the cause why he did not take payment from them.

Concerning this he does two things.

First, he excludes the false cause;

second, he gives the true one, at *but what I do*.

400. In regard to the first it should be noted that the false apostles charged the Apostle with not taking payment from the Corinthians, because he did not love them and because he did not intend to help and serve them. He says, therefore: *why* do I do this? *Because I do not love you?*, i.e., is it from any hatred I bear towards you, as the false apostles claim? *God knows* that I love you and that I do not do this out of hatred: *yes, Lord; you know that I love you* (John 21:15).

401. Therefore, having removed the false cause, he gives the true one, at *but what I do*.

Concerning the he does two things.

First he states the true cause;

second, the reason for it, at *for such false apostles*.

402. In regard to the first it should be noted that the false apostles, as has been stated, were seeking their own profit and glory; therefore, in order to be held in reverence, they tried to follow the example of the Apostle outwardly or even excel him, if they could.

Therefore the Apostle says: if you wish to imitate me, let them imitate me in taking nothing. And because he knew that the false apostles preached in order to take and, consequently, would not preach if their gain ceased, he says: *but what I do, that I will do*, and what I will do is not out of hatred, but *that I may cut off the occasion from those*, namely, the false apostles, *who desire* from my example to have *an occasion* for taking what is yours.

For he knew, according to Ambrose, that they would not preach very willingly, if they received nothing; whereas on the contrary it is stated: *give instruction to a wise man, and he will be still wiser; teach a righteous man and he will increase in learning* (Prov 9:9). And this that they may be found, that is, the false apostles, on the same terms as we, namely, not receiving money, even as we do not receive it. Indeed they glory in the fact that they imitate us; and I am unwilling, if they would imitate me completely, that they would receive: *I wish that all were as I myself am* (1 Cor 7:7), namely, not receiving.

403. *That wherein they glory, they may be found even as we*. This is read in three ways. In one way thus: that they

accipiendo sicut et nos non accipimus, et, per consequens, a praedicatione cessando. In quo, scilicet esse tales, sicut et nos gloriantur; contendebant enim esse similes veris apostolis. Secundo modo sic: ut in eo in quo gloriantur, scilicet accipiendo, quia hoc solum quaerebant, inveniantur sicut et nos, id est similes nobis, cessando scilicet et desistendo ab acceptione, ut nobis assimilentur. Tertio modo sic: ut in eo in quo gloriantur, scilicet in non accipiendo, dicunt enim se nihil accipere, inveniantur sicut et nos, id est non meliores nobis, ne scilicet possint se in hoc nobis praeferre.

Nam eiusmodi, hoc continuatur tripliciter. Primo modo sic: ita gloriantur et contendunt, non sicut nos, **nam eiusmodi**, et cetera. Secundo modo sic: et vere desistant accipere, ut nobis assimilentur, **nam eiusmodi**, et cetera.

Tertio modo sic: ita in non accipiendo gloriantur, ut nobis similes videantur.

404. Posita autem vera causa, probat eam consequenter, dicens **nam eiusmodi**, etc., ostendens quomodo student assimilari apostolos.

Et circa hoc tria facit.

Primo ponit causam;

secundo probat eam, ibi **sed non mirum**;

tertio consequenter ostendit differentiam pseudo ad veros apostolos, ibi **quorum finis**, et cetera.

405. Dicit ergo: recte dico, quod hoc facio, ut amputem eis occasionem accipiendi. **Nam eiusmodi pseudoapostoli sunt operarii**, scilicet falsi. Phil. III, 2: *videte canes, videte malos operarios*, et cetera.

Subdoli, id est, callidi et vulpini, sub specie religionis decipientes. Ez. XIII, 4: *quasi vulpes in desertis*, et cetera. Cant. II, 15: *capite nobis vulpes parvulas, quae demoliuntur vineas*, et cetera. Matth. VII, 15: *veniunt ad vos in vestimentis ovium*, et cetera. Et hoc est quod dicit **transfigurantes se in apostolos Christi**, id est exterius portantes signa bonorum apostolorum. II Tim. III, 5: *habentes quidem speciem pietatis*, et cetera.

406. Et hoc probat, quia sicut veri apostoli mittuntur a Deo et informantur ab ipso, sic **Satanas transformat se in angelum lucis**, qui est dux et incentor eorum, ostendens se esse vel angelum Dei, vel aliquando Christum. Non est ergo mirum neque magnum si ministri eius, scilicet pseudo, transformant se in ministros iustitiae, id est simulant se esse iustos. Eccli. X, 2: *secundum iudicem populi, sic et minister eius*, et cetera.

407. Notandum autem est, quod Satanas transfigurat se aliquando visibiliter, sicut beato Martino, ut deciperet eum, et hoc modo multos decepit. Sed ad hoc valet et necessaria est discretio spirituum, quam specialiter Deus contulit beato Antonio. In hoc tamen potest cognosci,

may be found to be such as we, not receiving, even as we do not receive; wherein, namely, in being such as we, they may glory, for they strive to be like the apostles. In a second way thus: that in that wherein they glory, namely, in receiving, because this is all they sought, they may be found even as we, i.e., similar to us, namely, by ceasing and desisting from receiving, that they may be like us. In the third way thus: that in that wherein they glory, namely, in not receiving, for they claim they receive nothing, they may be found even as we, i.e., not better than we, namely, lest they be able to prefer themselves to us in this.

***For such false apostles are deceitful workmen**. This can be connected with what went before in three ways; in the first way thus: they do not glory and strive in the way we do, **for such false apostles are deceitful workmen**. In the second way thus: and indeed they stop receiving in order to be like us: **for such false apostles are deceitful workmen**.

In the third way thus: so they glory in not receiving in order to seem like us.

404. Having stated the true cause, he proves it by saying: **for such false apostles are deceitful workmen**, showing how they strive to be like the apostles.

In regard to this he does three things.

First he states the cause;

second, he proves it, at **and no wonder**;

third, he shows the difference between false and true apostles, at **whose end shall be**.

405. He says, therefore: I am right in saying that I do this in order to cut off from them the occasion, **for such false apostles are deceitful workmen**, namely, false: *look out for the dogs, look out for the evil-workers* (Phil 3:2).

Deceitful, i.e., shrewd, foxy, deceiving others under the guise of religion. *Your prophets have been like foxes among ruins, O Israel* (Ezek 13:4); *catch us the foxes, the little foxes, that spoil the vineyards* (Song 2:15); *beware of false prophets, who come to you in sheep's clothing but inwardly are ravenous wolves* (Matt 7:15). And this is what he says: **transforming themselves into the apostles of Christ**, i.e., bearing the outward signs of good apostles: *holding the form of religion but denying the power of it* (2 Tim 3:5).

406. He proves this, because just as the true apostles are sent by God and are transformed by him, so **Satan himself transforms himself into an angel of light**, who is their leader and inciter, showing himself to be an angel of God or sometimes Christ. Therefore it is no strange or great thing if his servants also disguise themselves as servants of righteousness, i.e., pretend to be just: *like the magistrate of the people, so are his officials* (Sir 10:2).

407. But it should be noted that Satan sometimes transfigures himself so that he can be seen, as by St. Martin, in order to deceive men. But for this the discerning of spirits, which God conferred in a special way on St. Antony, is necessary and sufficient. One is able to know that it is Satan by

quod Satanas sit, quia bonus angelus in principio hortatur ad bona, et perseverat in eis, sed malus in principio quidem praetendit bona, sed postmodum volens explere desiderium suum, et quod intendit, scilicet decipere, inducit et instigat ad mala. I Io. IV, 1: *omni spiritui nolite credere*, et cetera. Et ideo Iosue cum videret angelum in campo suo, dixit Iudic. V: *noster es an adversariorum?*

Aliud etiam signum est, quod bonus angelus etsi terreat in principio, tamen statim consolatur, et confortat, sicut Zachariam, Lc. I, v. 13: *ne timeas, Zacharia*. Et ad Beatam Virginem dixit: *ne timeas, Maria*, et cetera. Malus autem angelus stupefacit et desolatum dimittit. Et hoc ideo, ut stupefactum facilius decipiat et persuadeat sibi.

Aliquando autem transfigurat se invisibiliter, et hoc quando ea, quae in se mala sunt, facit apparere bona, pervertendo sensus hominis et inflammando concupiscentiam. Prov. c. XVI, 25: *est via quae videtur homini recta*, et cetera. Sic decepit monachum quemdam, qui cum proposuisset in animo suo numquam exire cellam, suggessit ei diabolus, quod bonum esset quod exiret ad Ecclesiam et reciperet corpus Christi. Cui suggestioni consentiens, propositum mutavit vadens ad Ecclesiam. Postmodum cognoscens eum fuisse diabolum, gloriatus est monachus quod non deceperat eum, quia ad bonum iverat, et tamen iam removit eum a proposito continue standi in cella. Postmodum vero iterum suggessit ei, quod pater suus esset mortuus, et dimiserat sibi multas divitias distribuendas inter pauperes, quod iret ad civitatem, ad quam cum iret, numquam rediit ad cellam, et mortuus est in peccato. Unde valde difficile est, quod homo caveat sibi, et ideo recurrendum est ad adiutorium divinum. Iob XLI, 4: *quis revelabit faciem indumenti eius*, etc., quasi dicat: nullus nisi Deus.

408. Consequenter ponit ministrorum, et malorum et bonorum differentiam, quae consistit in hoc, quod *finis illorum*, scilicet ministrorum Christi, et Satanae, *erit secundum opera eorum*. Nam finis bonorum erit bonus, et malorum erit malus, et boni inducuntur ad bonum, et mali ad malum. Phil. c. III, 19: *quorum finis interitus*, et cetera. Item boni recipient bona, et mali mala. Supra V, v. 10: *omnes nos manifestari oportet ante tribunal Christi.*

the fact that a good angel urges one to good works from the very beginning and continues to do so, but a bad angel pretends good things in the beginning, but later, in order to fulfill his desire and accomplish what he intends, namely, to deceive, he induces and instigates to evil: *beloved, do not believe every spirit, but test the spirits to see whether they are of God* (1 John 4:1). According to Joshua, when he saw an angel in the field, he said: *are you for us, or for our adversaries?* (Josh 5:13).

Another sign is that a good angel, even though he causes one to be fearful in the beginning, immediately comforts and consoles, as he did Zechariah: *do not be afraid, Zechariah* (Luke 1:13), and the Blessed Virgin: *do not be afraid, Mary* (Luke 1:30). But an evil angel stupefies and leaves one desolate, in order the more easily to deceive and persuade him.

But sometimes he transforms himself but cannot be seen; and this when he makes things, which are in themselves evil, appear good by perverting a man's senses and inflaming concupiscence. *There is a way which seems right to a man, but its end is the way to death* (Prov 14:12). This is the way he deceived a certain monk, who had resolved never to leave his cell. But the devil suggested to him that it would be good to go to Church and receive the body of Christ. Consenting to this suggestion, he broke his resolve by going to the Church. Later, recognizing that it was the devil, the monk congratulated himself for not being deceived, because he had left for a good purpose. Later on, he suggested to him that his father had died and left many riches to be distributed among the poor, and that he should go to the city. When he went there, he never returned and died in sin. Hence, it is very difficult for a person to be too careful, but one should have recourse to divine help. *Who can open the doors of his face? Round about his teeth is terror* (Job 41:14). As if to say: no one but God.

408. Then he indicates the difference between good and bad ministers, which consists in this, that their **end**, namely, of Christ's ministers and Satan's, **shall be according to their works**; for the end of the good will be good, and of the evil, evil: *their end is destruction* (Phil 3:19). Furthermore, the good will receive good things and the evil, evil things: **for we must all be manifested before the judgment seat of Christ** (2 Cor 5:10).

Lecture 4

^{11:16}Iterum dico (ne quis me putet insipientem esse, alioquin velut insipientem accipite me, ut et ego modicum quid glorier), [n. 409]

^{11:17}quod loquor, non loquor secundum Deum, sed quasi in insipientia, in hac substantia gloriae. [n. 411]

^{11:18}Quoniam multi gloriantur secundum carnem: et ego gloriabor. [n. 413]

^{11:19}Libenter enim suffertis insipientes, cum sitis ipsi sapientes. [n. 415]

^{11:20}Sustinetis enim si quis vos in servitutem redigit, si quis devorat, si quis accipit, si quis extollitur, si quis in faciem vos caedit. [n. 416]

^{11:21}Secundum ignobilitatem dico, quasi nos infirmi fuerimus in hac parte. In quo quis audet (in insipientia dico) audeo et ego:

^{11:16}Πάλιν λέγω, μή τίς με δόξη ἄφρονα εἶναι· εἰ δὲ μή γε, κἄν ὡς ἄφρονα δέξασθέ με, ἵνα κἀγὼ μικρόν τι καυχήσωμαι.

^{11:17}λαλῶ, οὐ κατὰ κύριον λαλῶ ἀλλ᾽ ὡς ἐν ἀφροσύνῃ, ἐν ταύτῃ τῇ ὑποστάσει τῆς καυχήσεως.

^{11:18}ἐπεὶ πολλοὶ καυχῶνται κατὰ σάρκα, κἀγὼ καυχήσομαι.

^{11:19}ἡδέως γὰρ ἀνέχεσθε τῶν ἀφρόνων φρόνιμοι ὄντες·

^{11:20}ἀνέχεσθε γὰρ εἴ τις ὑμᾶς καταδουλοῖ, εἴ τις κατεσθίει, εἴ τις λαμβάνει, εἴ τις ἐπαίρεται, εἴ τις εἰς πρόσωπον ὑμᾶς δέρει.

^{11:21}κατὰ ἀτιμίαν λέγω, ὡς ὅτι ἡμεῖς ἠσθενήκαμεν. Ἐν ᾧ δ᾽ ἄν τις τολμᾷ, ἐν ἀφροσύνῃ λέγω, τολμῶ κἀγώ.

^{11:16}I say again (let no man think me to be foolish: otherwise take me as one foolish, that I also may glory a little): [n. 409]

^{11:17}That which I speak, I do not speak according to God: but, as it were, in foolishness, in this matter of glorying. [n. 411]

^{11:18}Since many glory according to the flesh, I will glory also. [n. 413]

^{11:19}For you gladly suffer the foolish: whereas you yourselves are wise. [n. 415]

^{11:20}For you bear it if a man brings you into bondage, if a man devours you, if a man takes from you, if a man is lifted up, if a man strikes you on the face. [n. 416]

^{11:21}I speak according to dishonor, as if we had been weak in this part. Wherein if any man dares (I speak foolishly), I dare also.

---

409. Supra Apostolus induxit Corinthios, ut patienter sustinerent suam commendationem, ostendens, quod hoc faciebat ex zelo quem habebat ad eos, et quia zelus ille erat rationabilis et ordinatus, hic autem consequenter ponit aliam rationem, per quam ostendit, quod dato, quod insipienter ageret, nihilominus tamen deberent eum supportare. Unde in ista ratione procedit ex suppositione stultitiae. In hac autem parte duo facit.

Primo enim proponit suam petitionem;

secundo rationem dictorum assignat, ibi **quod loquor**, et cetera.

410. In petitione sua duo facit. Primo enim petit, quod non reputent eum insipientem, quod pertinet ad praemissam rationem. Et ideo dicit **iterum dico**, quod ex quo zelus meus est rationabilis, et ego rationabiliter commendo me, **ne quis**, scilicet vestrum, **me reputet insipientem**.

Secundo petit, quod dato, quod insipienter agat, tamen supportent eum, et hoc pertinet ad rationem hanc. Et ideo dicit **alioquin**, id est si non rationabiliter commendo me, et penitus velitis me ex hoc insipientem reputare, tamen **accipite**, id est supportate, **me velut insipientem**. Et dicit, **velut**, quia licet ipsi reputent eum insipientem in hoc, tamen in rei veritate non est insipiens. **Accipite me**, inquam, **velut insipientem, ut et ego modicum quid glorier**. Et dicit **modicum**, quia infra

409. Having asked the Corinthians to bear patiently with his commendation, and shown that he did this out of the zeal he had for them because that zeal was reasonable and ordinate, the Apostle now presents another reason through which he shows that, given he is acting foolishly, they should nevertheless put up with him. Hence, in this reason he proceeds on the supposition that he is foolish. In this part he does two things.

First he makes his request;

second, he gives the reason for what he said, at **that which I speak**.

410. In his request he does two things. First, he asks that they not consider him foolish, which pertains to the previous reason; hence he says, **I say again**, since my zeal is reasonable and I am acting reasonably in commending myself, **let no man think me to be foolish**.

Second, he asks that, granted that he is acting foolishly, they should nevertheless put up with him, which pertains to the present reason. Therefore he says, **otherwise**, i.e., if I am not reasonable in commending myself and on that account you want to regard me as foolish, nevertheless, **take me**, i.e., bear with me, **as one foolish**. He says, **as**, because although they may regard him as foolish, in this matter he is not really foolish. **Take me**, I say, **as one foolish, that I also may glory a little**. He says, **a little**, because further on he will

commendabit se de gloria, quae est secundum carnem, quae valde modica est. Iob XXV, 6: *homo putredo et filius hominis vermis*. Eccli. X, 9: *quid superbis, terra et cinis?*

411. Rationem autem dictorum assignat, dicens *quod loquor*, et cetera. Dixerat autem tria. Primo quia supponit insipienter commendasse se ipsum; secundo quod vult gloriari; tertio quod sustineant eum. Et horum trium rationem assignat. Et

primo de hoc, quod supposuit insipienter commendare se;

secundo quare vult gloriari, ibi *quoniam multi gloriantur*, etc.;

tertio quod debeant eum supportare, ibi *libenter enim suffertis*, et cetera.

412. Dicit ergo primo: ratio quare debetis insipientem accipere me est, quia illud *quod loquor in hac substantia gloriae*, id est commendatione carnis, quae a quibusdam appetitur, ac si per eam debeant subsistere, *non loquor secundum Deum, sed quasi in insipientia.*

Et dicit ex hypothesi, sicut illud quod supra dixit: *velut insipientem*. Unde ibi posuit *velut*, hic ponit *quasi*. Ac si diceret: si non rationabiliter commendarem me, tunc illud quod loquor, in commendatione mea, non est secundum Deum, id est, secundum rationem divinae sapientiae. Et tunc merito acciperetis me non secundum Deum loqui, sed insipienter. Supra X, 18: *non enim, qui seipsum commendat, ille probatus est*, et cetera. Prov. XXVII, 2: *laudet te alienus*, et cetera.

413. Rationem autem suae commendationis et gloriae ostendit, subdens *quoniam multi gloriantur*, et cetera.

Ubi sciendum est, quod pseudo, quia ex Iudaeis erant, gloriabantur secundum carnem, dicentes se esse filios Abrahae et ex hoc volebant haberi in reverentia a Corinthiis et auctoritate. Dicit ergo Apostolus: dato, quod sit insipientia, quod glorier secundum carnem, tamen *quoniam multi*, scilicet pseudo, *gloriantur secundum carnem, et ego* etiam *gloriabor* secundum carnem, Prov. XXVI, 5: *responde stulto secundum stultitiam suam, ne sibi sapiens videatur.*

414. Sed contra est quia Seneca dicit *summa malorum est, quod ad exemplum vivitur malorum*. Et Ex. XXIII, 2: *non sequaris turbam ad faciendum malum*. Non ergo Apostolus debet gloriari secundum carnem, eo quod pseudo gloriantur.

Respondeo. Dicendum est, quod licet sit eadem materia gloriationis, non tamen est eadem intentio et idem finis, quia pseudo commendabant se propter gloriam propriam, et ut ipsi haberentur in auctoritate, et possent

commend himself on the glory which is according to the flesh, which is very little. *Man, who is a maggot, and the son of man, who is a worm!* (Job 25:6) *How can he who is dust and ashes be proud?* (Sir 10:9).

411. Then when he says, *that which I speak*, he assigns the reason for what he had said. But he had said three things: first that he began to commend himself foolishly; second, that he wished to glory; third, that they should bear with him. And give a reason for these three things.

First, for the fact that he supposed it was foolish to commend himself;

second, why he wishes to glory, at *since many glory*;

third, that they should bear with him, at *for you gladly suffer*.

412. He says, therefore: the reason why you should take me who am foolish is because *that which I speak, in this matter of glorying*, i.e., in this commendation according to the flesh, which is desired by some, as if they ought to subsist by it, *I do not speak according to God: but, as it were, in foolishness.*

He speaks hypothetically, as when he said above: *as one foolish*. And where there he said *as*, here he says *as it were*, as if to say: if I were not reasonable in commending myself, then what I am saying for my commendation would not be with the Lord's authority, i.e., according to the notion of divine wisdom; and then you would be right in not taking me as speaking according to God, but foolishly. *For it is not he who commends himself who is approved: but he whom God commends* (2 Cor 10:18); *let another praise you, and not your own mouth; a stranger, and not your own lips* (Prov 27:2).

413. He indicates the reason why he commends himself and glories, when he says, *since many glory according to the flesh, I will glory also.*

Here it should be noted that the false apostles, because they were Jews, gloried according to the flesh, saying that they were sons of Abraham. They hoped thereby to be held in reverence and authority by the Corinthians. Therefore, the Apostle says: granted that it is foolish for me to glory according to the flesh, yet *since many*, namely the false apostles, *glory according to the flesh*, even *I will glory also* according to the flesh: *answer a fool according to his folly, lest he be wise in his own eyes* (Prov 26:5).

414. But on the other hand, Seneca says: *the greatest of evils is to live by the example of evil men*; *you shall not follow a multitude to do evil* (Exod 23:2). Therefore, the Apostle should not glory according to the flesh on the ground that the false apostles glory.

I answer that although both are glorying about the same thing, the intention and end are not the same, because the false apostles commended themselves for their own glory and to acquire authority and gain; but the Apostle glories

lucrari; Apostolus autem gloriabatur, ut verbum Dei, per eum praedicatum, esset maioris auctoritatis et ponderis, et fructum faceret Christo.

415. Rationem autem quare debeant eum supportare, subdit, dicens *libenter enim suffertis*, etc., et primo ponit rationem hanc, quod scilicet debeant eum supportare.

Possent enim dicere: *quare debemus te supportare, si es insipiens?* Et dicit Apostolus, quod ideo, quia cum vos ipsi sitis sapientes in oculis vestris et in vestra reputatione, *libenter suffertis*, id est estis consueti supportare, *insipientes*, pseudo scilicet.

416. Secundo ostendit in quo supportent insipientes. Et ponit quinque gravia quae sustinebant a pseudo:

primum est iugum servitutis. Et quantum ad hoc dicit *sustinetis enim si quis*, id est aliquis pseudo, *redigit vos in servitutem*, quasi dicat: per Christum liberati fuistis a servitute legis, quae est in timore, et reducti estis in libertatem filiorum Dei, quae est in caritate. Gal. IV, 31: *non sumus ancillae filii, sed liberae*. Et tamen vos sustinetis pseudo, qui ex huiusmodi libertate redigunt vos in servitutem legis, quia cogunt vos servare legalia. Gal. V, 1: *nolite iugo servitutis*, et cetera. Multo ergo magis debetis sustinere me, qui volo vos praeservare in libertate Christi, quam pseudo, qui volunt vos reducere in servitutem legis.

Secundum est grave valde, scilicet quod pseudo vivunt de bonis vestris laute, nos vero non. Supra VIII, 13: *non ut aliis sit remissio*, et cetera. Et ideo dicit *si quis devorat*, Matth. c. XXIII, 14: *vae qui comeditis domos viduarum*, et cetera.

Tertium grave est depraedatio et expoliatio, quia isti ad litteram blandis verbis et praetextu pietatis accipiebant eis omnia, et quantum ad hoc dicit *si quis accipit*, id est blande decipit, subtrahendo vestra. Rom. c. XVI, 18: *per blandos sermones seducunt corda insipientium*.

Quartum grave est nimia iactantia super eos cum Corinthiorum contemptu. Ideo dicit *si quis extollitur*, iactando se importune. Eccli. c. VI, 2: *non te extollas in cogitatione*, et cetera.

Quintum grave est illatio opprobriorum. Nam pseudo non solum tam gravia eis inferebant, sed super hoc addebant improperia, dicentes eis iniurias, et maxime de ignobilitate. Nam quia ipsi erant Iudaei, et cultores unius Dei, dicebant se nobiles esse, et Corinthios ignobiles,

in order that the word of God preached by him might have greater authority and weight and bear fruit for Christ.

415. Then he tells why they should bear with him, saying: *for you gladly suffer the foolish: whereas you yourselves are wise*. First, he gives this reason, namely, that they should bear with him.

For they could say: *why should we bear with you, if you are foolish?* And the Apostle says that the reason is this: since you yourselves are wise in your own eyes and in your reputation, *you gladly suffer*, i.e., are wont to bear with, *the foolish*, namely, the false apostles.

416. Second, he shows wherein they bear with the foolish and points out five cases of oppression imposed by the false apostles.

The first is the yoke of slavery; as to this he says, *for you bear it if a man*, i.e., one of the false apostles, *brings you into bondage*. As if to say: through Christ you were freed from the bondage of the law, which is in fear, and were raised to the freedom of the sons of God, which is charity: *so, brethren, we are not children of the slave but of the free woman* (Gal 4:31). And yet you bear with the false apostles, who take such liberty from you and reduce you to the slavery of the law, because they compel you to observe the ceremonies of the law: *do not submit again to a yoke of slavery* (Gal 5:1). With greater reason, then, should you bear with me, who want to preserve you in the freedom of Christ, than with the false apostles, who wish to reduce you to the slavery of the law.

The second is a very heavy burden, because the false apostles live sumptuously on your goods, but we do not: *I do not mean that others should be eased and you burdened, but by an equality* (2 Cor 8:13). Therefore he says: *if a man devours you*: woe to you scribes and Pharisees, hypocrites, because you devour the houses of widows, praying long prayers. For this you shall receive the greater judgment (Matt 23:14).

The third oppression is depredation and despoliation, because they literally took everything from them with soft words and under the pretext of piety; as to this he says, *if a man takes from you*, i.e., smoothly deceives you by taking your property: *by fair and flattering words they deceive the hearts of the simple-minded* (Rom 16:18).

The fourth oppression is their excessive vaunting of themselves over them along with contempt for the Corinthians; therefore he says: *if a man is lifted up*: do not exalt yourself through your soul's counsel, lest your soul be torn in pieces like a bull (Sir 6:2).

The fifth oppression is verbal abuse; for the false apostles not only oppressed them in these ways but added reproaches by saying insulting things to them and especially about their low estate. For because they were Jews and worshippers of the one true God, they called themselves noble

quia non erant de semine Abrahae, nec circumcisi, et quod de idololatris. Et quantum ad hoc dicit *si quis in faciem vos caedit*, id est coram vobis infert contumelias et dicit iniurias.

Et huiusmodi iniuriae sunt *secundum ignobilitatem*, quam vobis obiiciunt, vel ignominiam quam inferunt. Et tamen illos sustinetis, et nos non, *quasi nos fuerimus infirmi in hac parte* gloriae, quam attribuistis eis, praeferendo eos nobis, praesertim cum pseudo dicant, quod ideo nos non dicimus nec facimus vobis ista, quia nos sumus infirmi in hac parte, id est quia sumus ignobiles. I Cor. c. IV, 10: *nos infirmi, vos fortes; vos nobiles, nos autem ignobiles.*

and the Corinthians ignoble, because they were not of the seed of Abraham or circumcised, but descended from idolaters; as to this he says, *if a man strikes you on the face*, i.e., insults you publicly and says harmful things.

These sorts of injuries are *according to dishonor*, which they cast on you, or the ignominy they inflict. And yet you bear with them and not with us, *as if we had been weak in this part* and for the glory you have attributed to them by preferring them to us, especially since the false apostles say that the reason we do not say or do such things to you is that we are weak in this part, i.e., because we are lowly: *we are weak, but you are strong. You are held in honor, but we in disrepute* (1 Cor 4:10).

Lecture 5

11:21Secundum ignobilitatem dico, quasi nos infirmi fuerimus in hac parte. In quo quis audet (in insipientia dico) audeo et ego: [n. 417]

11:22Hebraei sunt, et ego: Israëlitae sunt, et ego: semen Abrahae sunt, et ego.

11:23Ministri Christi sunt [n. 420] (ut minus sapiens dico), plus ego: in laboribus plurimis, in carceribus abundantius, in plagis supra modum, in mortibus frequenter. [n. 421]

11:24A Judaeis quinquies, quadragenas, una minus, accepi.

11:25Ter virgis caesus sum, semel lapidatus sum: ter naufragium feci, nocte et die in profundo maris fui,

11:26in itineribus saepe, periculis fluminum, periculis latronum, periculis ex genere, periculis ex gentibus, periculis in civitate, periculis in solitudine, periculis in mari, periculis in falsis fratribus: [n. 427]

11:21κατὰ ἀτιμίαν λέγω, ὡς ὅτι ἡμεῖς ἠσθενήκαμεν. Ἐν ᾧ δ᾽ ἄν τις τολμᾷ, ἐν ἀφροσύνῃ λέγω, τολμῶ κἀγώ.

11:22Ἑβραῖοί εἰσιν; κἀγώ. Ἰσραηλῖταί εἰσιν; κἀγώ. σπέρμα Ἀβραάμ εἰσιν; κἀγώ.

11:23διάκονοι Χριστοῦ εἰσιν; παραφρονῶν λαλῶ, ὑπὲρ ἐγώ· ἐν κόποις περισσοτέρως, ἐν φυλακαῖς περισσοτέρως, ἐν πληγαῖς ὑπερβαλλόντως, ἐν θανάτοις πολλάκις.

11:24Ὑπὸ Ἰουδαίων πεντάκις τεσσεράκοντα παρὰ μίαν ἔλαβον,

11:25τρὶς ἐρραβδίσθην, ἅπαξ ἐλιθάσθην, τρὶς ἐναυάγησα, νυχθήμερον ἐν τῷ βυθῷ πεποίηκα·

11:26ὁδοιπορίαις πολλάκις, κινδύνοις ποταμῶν, κινδύνοις λῃστῶν, κινδύνοις ἐκ γένους, κινδύνοις ἐξ ἐθνῶν, κινδύνοις ἐν πόλει, κινδύνοις ἐν ἐρημίᾳ, κινδύνοις ἐν θαλάσσῃ, κινδύνοις ἐν ψευδαδέλφοις,

11:21I speak according to dishonor, as if we had been weak in this part. Wherein if any man dare (I speak foolishly), I dare also. [n. 417]

11:22They are Hebrews: so am I. They are Israelites: so am I. They are the seed of Abraham: so am I.

11:23They are the ministers of Christ [n. 420] (I speak as one less wise): I am more so; in many more labors, in prisons more frequently, in stripes above measure, in deaths often. [n. 421]

11:24From the Jews, five times I received forty stripes less one.

11:25Three times I was beaten with rods: once I was stoned: three times I suffered shipwreck: a night and a day I was in the depth of the sea.

11:26Often on journeys, in perils of waters, in perils of robbers, in perils from my own nation, in perils from the gentiles, in perils in the city, in perils in the wilderness, in perils in the sea, in perils from false brethren: [n. 427]

---

417. Positis rationibus suae commendationis et causis quare supportandus est, hic consequenter incipit se commendare. Et

circa hoc duo facit.

Primo enim adaequat se pseudo et aliis, qui commendabant se;

secundo praefert se eis, ibi **ut minus sapiens**, et cetera.

Adaequat autem se Apostolus eis in gloria. Est autem gloria duplex. Una secundum carnem, quae modica est et contemnenda. Unde ipse dicit Phil. III, 7: *sed quae mihi fuerunt lucra, arbitratus*, et cetera. Alia est secundum Christum, quia *magna gloria est sequi Dominum*, Eccli. XXIII, 38. Et haec est quaerenda. Gal. ult. 14: *mihi absit gloriari nisi in cruce*, et cetera. Et ideo Apostolus adaequat se eis quantum ad utramque gloriam. Et

primo quantum ad primam;

secundo quantum ad secundam, ibi **ministri Christi**, et cetera.

418. Et, primo, adaequat se eis in generali, dicens: recipiatis me insipientem, si tamen insipientia est. Ex hypothesi enim loquor, quia si quis ausus est praesumere

417. Having given the reasons for commending himself and the causes why they should bear with him, he now begins to commend himself.

In regard to this he does two things.

First, he shows himself equal to the false apostles and others who commended themselves;

second, he prefers himself to them, at **I speak as one less wise**.

The Apostle makes himself their equal in glory. But glory is of two kinds: one is according to the flesh and is slight and worthy of scorn; hence he says to the Philippians: *but whatever gain I had, I counted as loss for the sake of Christ* (Phil 3:7); the other in according to Christ, because *it is great glory to follow the Lord* (Sir 23:38), and this should be sought: *but far be it from me to glory except in the cross of our Lord Jesus Christ* (Gal 6:14). The Apostle therefore makes himself equal to them in regard to both glories:

first, in regard to the first;

second, in regard to the second, at **they are the ministers of Christ**.

418. First, he shows himself equal to them in general, saying: receive me as one who is foolish, provided it is foolish, for I speak hypothetically; because whatever any one

de se, et commendare se, et ego possum bene audere et commendare me in eodem, in quo ipse commendat se, quia non subest eis maior causa suae commendationis, quam mihi. Et hoc *dico in insipientia*, id est dico, quod insipienter agam, cum tamen ipse sapienter ageret, cum hoc non faceret pro sui iactantia sed ut pseudo humiliaret. Supra eodem: *existimo me non minus fecisse a magnis apostolis*, et cetera.

419. Secundo cum dicit *Hebraei sunt*, etc., adaequat se eis in speciali, ostendens per singula se parem eis esse in quibus pseudo gloriabantur. Commendatio autem istorum et gloria erat de tribus. Primo de natione et lingua, quia dicebant se Hebraeos; secundo de genere, quia dicebant se esse de genere Israel; tertio de promissione, quia dicebant se esse participes promissionis Abrahae, cum essent de semine eius.

Et quantum ad haec tria adaequat se eis.

Primo quantum ad nationem et linguam, dicens *Hebraei sunt, et ego*, scilicet lingua et natione, quasi dicat: ita sicut et illi. Et notandum est, quod, secundum quod quidam dicunt, Hebraei dicuntur ab Abraham, quia ante eum de facili non invenitur illud nomen. Potest tamen dici et forte melius, quod dicuntur a quodam Heber, de quo habetur Gen. cap. XI, 14: *vixit sale triginta annis, et genuit Heber*. Et sequitur: *vixit Heber triginta tribus annis, et genuit Phaleg*. Et tempore eius fuerunt divisae linguae, et lingua Hebraeorum remansit in familia sua.

Secundo adaequat se eis quantum ad genus, dicens *Israelitae sunt, et ego*, scilicet secundum ritus.

Tertio quantum ad tertium, dicens *semen Abrahae sunt, et ego*.

Et de istis tribus dicitur Phil. III, 4 s.: *si quis alius sibi confidere videtur, ego magis circumcisus octavo die* quantum ad tertium, *ex genere Israel de tribu Beniamin* quantum ad secundum, *Hebraeus, ex Hebraeis* quantum ad primum. Rom. XI, 1: *nam ego Israelita sum ex semine Abrahae*, et cetera.

420. Sic ergo patet, quod non sum minor eis quantum ad gloriam, quae est secundum carnem; sed nec etiam quantum ad gloriam, quae est secundum Christum, quia *ministri Christi sunt*, id est dicunt se sic, ut decipiant vos, *et ego* sum minister Christi. I Cor. IV, 1: *sic nos existimet homo, ut ministros Christi*, et cetera. Supra III, 6: *qui et nos idoneos fecit*, et cetera.

421. Consequenter cum dicit *ut minus sapiens*, etc., praefert se omnibus apostolis et pseudo. Et

primo quantum ad mala perpessa,

dares to boast of or to take for granted about himself and to commend himself, I can dare and commend myself on the same matters in which they commend themselves, because they have no better reason than I to commend themselves. *I speak foolishly*, i.e., I say that I am acting foolishly; yet he was acting wisely, because he was not doing this to boast, but to humiliate the false apostles: *I suppose that I have done nothing less than the great apostles* (2 Cor 11:5).

419. Second, when he says, *they are Hebrews: so am I*, he shows in detail that he is equal to them, indicating one by one the points in which he is equal to them, and in which the false apostles found glory. But they took glory and commended themselves on three points. First, in their nationality and tongue, because they called themselves Hebrews; second in their race, because they said they were of the race of Israel; third, in the promise, because they said they were partakers of the promise to Abraham, since they were of his seed.

So he shows that he is equal to them on these three points.

First, as to nationality and language, saying *they are Hebrews: so am I*, namely, in language and in nationality; as if to say: I am as they are. It should be noted that, as some say, they are called Hebrews from Abraham, because before him that name was uncommon. But it can be said, and perhaps better, that the word is derived from a certain Eber mentioned in Genesis: *Shelah had lived thirty years, he became the father of Eber* (Gen 11:14), and then *Eber lived thirty-four years and begot Peleg*. It was during this time that languages became distinct, and the language of the Hebrews remained in the family.

Second, he shows himself equal to them in race, saying *they are Israelites: so am I*, namely, according to rite.

Third, as to the third he says: *they are the seed of Abraham: so am I*.

Of these three things it is said: *if any other man thinks he has reason for confidence in the flesh, I have more, circumcised on the eighth day* (Phil 3:4), as to the third point; *of the people of Israel, of the tribe of Benjamin*, as to the second point; *a Hebrew born of Hebrews*, as to the first: *I myself am an Israelite, a descendant of Abraham, a member of the tribe of Benjamin* (Rom 11:1).

420. Thus, it is clear that I am not inferior to them as to the glory, which is according to the flesh; nor even as to the glory which is according to Christ, because *they are the ministers of Christ*, i.e., they say so to deceive you; *I am more so: this is how one should regard us, as servants of Christ* (1 Cor 4:1); *who has also made us fit ministers of the New Testament* (2 Cor 3:6).

421. Then when he says, *I speak as one less wise*, he prefers himself to all the apostles and to the false.

First, in regard to evils endured;

secundo quantum ad beneficia recepta, et hoc cap. XII, ibi *si gloriari oportet*, et cetera.

Circa primum duo facit.

Primo praefert se quantum ad mala, quae pertulit;

secundo quantum ad modum quo mala vitavit, ibi *Damasci praepositus*.

Circa primum tria facit.

Primo proponit se aliis praeferendum;

secundo ostendit in quo sit praeferendus, ibi *quia in laboribus*, etc.;

tertio confirmat quaedam dictorum, ibi *si gloriari oportet*, et cetera.

422. Dicit ergo: si videor insipiens vobis, quia commendo me et adaequo me aliis, quanto magis videbor vobis minus sapiens, si praeferam me eis? Et ideo dicit: non solum sum minister Christi sicut et illi, sed *ut minus sapiens*, secundum vestrum iudicium, *dico* quod *ego* sum *plus* minister Christi quam illi, et quantum ad hoc dicit se praeferendum esse. Rom. XI, 13: *ministerium meum honorificabo*, praeponendo scilicet illud ministerio aliorum.

423. In quo autem sit praeferendus ostendit, dicens *quia in laboribus*, etc., quasi dicat: in hoc plus ego, quia sum magis ostensus minister Christi. In hoc, primo, quantum ad mala illata, secundo quantum ad mala sponte assumpta, ibi *in itineribus saepe*.

Mala autem illata primo ponit in generali, dicens: plus ego sum, scilicet ostensus minister, *in laboribus plurimis* quam illi, etsi aliquos labores pertulerint. I Cor. XV, v. 10: *abundantius omnibus illis laboravi*.

Secundo enumerat ista mala in speciali, et hoc, primo, quantum ad carceris squalores, quia *in carceribus abundantius*, scilicet quam illi. Act. XVI, 23: *cum multas plagas illis intulissent*, scilicet Paulo et sociis, *miserunt in carcerem*.

Secundo quantum ad flagellorum dolores, quia *in plagis*, scilicet ostensus sum, *supra modum* aliorum, scilicet modum humanae virtutis, vel supra modum humanae consuetudinis. Supra XI, 23: *in plagis, in carceribus*, et cetera.

Sed contra I Cor. X, 13: *fidelis Deus, qui non permittet vos tentari supra id*, et cetera. Non ergo supra modum humanae virtutis.

Respondeo. Dicendum est, quod Deus non permittit nos tentari sine adiutorio gratiae divinae. Et ideo dicebat Apostolus I Cor. XV, v. 10: *non autem ego, sed gratia Dei mecum*.

Et quantum ad mortis terrorem; unde dicit *in mortibus frequenter*, id est in periculis et terroribus mortis.

second, as to benefits received, in chapter twelve, at *if I must glory* (2 Cor 12:1).

In regard to the first he does two things.

First, he prefers himself as to evils endured;

second, as to the manner in which he avoided evils, at *at Damascus*.

In regard to the first he does three things.

First, he proposes that he should be preferred to the others;

second, he shows in what he should be preferred, at *in many more labors*;

third, he confirms some of the statements, at *if I must glory, I will glory*.

422. He says, therefore: I am talking like a madman; because I commend myself and make myself equal to the others, how less wise will I seem to you, if I prefer myself to them. Therefore he says: not only am I a minister of Christ, as the others, but *as one less wise* according to your opinion, *I say* that *I am more so* a minister of Christ than they; and as to this he says that he should be preferred to them: *I magnify my ministry* (Rom 11:13) by placing it ahead of the ministry of the others.

423. Then he indicates the matters in which he should be preferred, saying, *in many more labors*. As if to say: in this I am more, because I am more obviously a minister of Christ. First, as to the evils inflicted; second, as to evils voluntarily assumed, at *if journeying often*.

First, he mentions in general the evils inflicted, saying: I am more, namely, a proven minister; *in many more labors* than they, even though they have undertaken some labors: *I worked harder than any of them* (1 Cor 15:10).

Second, he lists those evils in detail. First, as to the squalor of prison, because *in prisons more frequently*, namely, than they: *and when they had inflicted many blows upon them*—namely, on Paul and his companions—*they threw them into prison* (Acts 16:23).

Second, as to the pains of floggings, because *in stripes above measure*, i.e., the measure of human virtue, or above the measure of human custom: *in stripes, in prisons, in seditions, in labors, in watchings, in fastings* (2 Cor 6:5).

But this seems to be contrary to what is stated in 1 Corinthians: *God is faithful, and he will not let you be tempted beyond your strength* (1 Cor 10:13). Therefore, not above the measure of human virtue.

I answer that God does not permit us to be tried without the help of divine grace; that is why the Apostle said: *not I, but the grace of God which is with me* (1 Cor 15:10).

Then as to the terror of death; hence he says, *in deaths often*, i.e., in the dangers and terrors of death. Hence

Unde dicebat ipse Rom. VIII, 36: *mortificamur tota die*. I Cor. c. XV, 31: *quotidie morior propter gloriam vestram*.

424. Sed consequenter, cum dicit *a Iudaeis quinquies*, etc., manifestat duo ultima pericula, quae perpessus est. Et

primo periculum plagarum,

secundo periculum mortis.

425. Plagarum autem periculum manifestat per ipsa perpessa a suis, scilicet Iudaeis. Et ideo dicit *a Iudaeis quinquies*, et cetera.

Notandum est autem, sicut dicitur Deut. c. XXV, 2 s., *pro mensura delicti erit plagarum modus. Ita dumtaxat, ut quadragenarium numerum non excedant*, et cetera. *Ex* quo habetur quod homines pro minoribus peccatis debent flagellari, ita tamen, quod flagellatus non reciperet ultra quadraginta plagas. Iudaei autem, ut viderentur misericordes, semper faciebant citra mandatum legis, dantes pauciores quam quadraginta, secundum quod eis videbatur. Quia ergo odio habebant Paulum, quando flagellabant eum, dimittebant sibi de numero praedicto quantominus poterant, scilicet unam tantum minus, dantes sibi trigintanovem. Et hoc est, quod quinque vicibus accepit, id est recepit *quadraginta* plagas, *minus una*, plaga, id est trigintanovem.

Secundo manifestat pericula perpessa ab extraneis, scilicet a gentibus, dicens *ter virgis caesus sum*. Act. XVI, 22: *magistratus, scissis eorum tunicis, iussit eos virgis caedi*. Item XXII, 24: *iussit eum tribunus duci in castra, et flagellis caedi, et torqueri eum*, et cetera.

426. Pericula vero mortis illata, et primo pericula mortis illata ab hominibus ostendit, dicens *semel lapidatus sum*. Hoc fuit in civitate Licaoniae, ibi obrutus lapidibus fuit quasi mortuus. Act. XIV, 18: *lapidantes Paulum eiecerunt eum extra civitatem, credentes eum mortuum*.

Secundo pericula mortis illata a periculis naturae, et haec sunt specialiter maris, et aggravat ea, primo, ex numero, quia *ter naufragium feci*, id est pertuli; secundo ex continuitate, quia *nocte et die in profundo maris fui*, quod est gravius; quia ad litteram dicit, quod cum pluries passus sit naufragium, tamen semel stetit sub aqua per diem et noctem, divina eum virtute protegente. Unde poterat dicere illud Ionae II, 4: *et proiicite me in profundum*, et cetera.

427. Enumeratis autem malis illatis, enumerat consequenter etiam mala assumpta, cum dicit *in itineribus*. Et

primo exteriora,

he said: *for your sake we are being killed all the day long* (Rom 8:26); *I die daily for your glory* (1 Cor 15:31).

424. Then, when he says *from the Jews, five times I received forty stripes less one*, he manifests the two extreme dangers he underwent.

And first, the danger of lashes;

second, the danger of death.

425. But he shows the danger of lashes by citing those he suffered from his own, that is, from the Jews. Hence he says, *from the Jews, five times I received forty stripes less one*.

It should be noted that, as it is said: *a number of stripes in proportion to his offense. Forty stripes may be given him, but not more; lest, if one should go on to beat him with more stripes than these, your brother be degraded in your sight* (Deut 25:2). This shows that men should be whipped for lesser sins, yet so that the victim never receive more than forty stripes. But the Jews, to appear merciful, always acted short of the law, giving less than forty, according as it appeared to them. Therefore, because they hated Paul, whenever they flogged him, they omitted the least possible number of strokes below the law's limit, namely, giving only one less, i.e., thirty-nine. And this is what he received five times, namely, *forty* lashes *less one*.

Second, he indicates the perils he endured from outsiders, namely, the gentiles, saying: *three times I was beaten with rods*. The magistrates tore the garments off them and gave orders to beat them with rods (Acts 16:22); the tribune commanded him to be brought into the barracks, and ordered him to be examined by scourging (Acts 22:14).

426. Then he discloses the perils of death he faced; and first of all those inflicted by men, saying: *once I was stoned*. This happened in the city of Lycaonia, where he was struck down with stones and almost killed. *They stoned Paul and dragged him out of the city, supposing that he was dead* (Acts 14:18).

Second, the perils endured from the works of nature, and particularly from the sea. He amplifies these, first from their number, because *three times I suffered shipwreck*; second, from their duration, because *a night and a day I was in the depth of the sea*, which is more grievous; for the text says that although he suffered shipwreck a number of times, he remained in the water for a day and a half under the protection of God's power. Hence he could say with Jonah: *for you cast me into the deep, into the heart of the seas, and the flood was round about me* (Jonah 2:4).

427. Having listed the evils inflicted from without, he then lists those he voluntarily assumed, when he says, *often on journeys*:

first, external evils;

secundo interiora, ibi *praeter illa quae extrinsecus*, et cetera.

Mala exteriora exprimit, et primo quantum ad mala, quae contingunt in itineribus; secundo quantum ad ea quae eveniunt in domibus.

428. Quantum ad primum, primo, ponit multiplicitatem itinerum, dicens *in itineribus saepe*, scilicet ostensus sum minister Christi, sustinendo multa dura et gravia patienter. Rom. XV, 19: *ab Ierusalem usque in Illyricum*, et cetera. Et cum hoc multas alias vias fecit, et Romam, et Hispaniam vadens. Psalmo XVI, 4: *propter verba labiorum tuorum*, et cetera.

Secundo enumerat periculum itinerum. Et primo praemittit minora, secundo subdit gravius periculum, quod in falsis fratribus.

Praemittit autem tria, secundum quae multa pericula passus est. Primo pericula secundum causas. Et hoc, vel ex causa naturali, et ideo dicit *periculis fluminum*. Naturaliter enim flumina hyeme excrescunt, et sunt rapida et valde periculosa, et cetera. Vel ex malitia violenta, et quantum ad hoc dicit *periculis latronum*, quos excitabat ei diabolus, ut vel vestes ei auferrent. Iob XIX, 2: *simul venerunt latrones*, et cetera. Secundo enumerat pericula metum inferentia, et hoc vel ex suis, unde dicit *periculis ex genere*, id est, a Iudaeis procuratis; vel ab extraneis, et ideo dicit *periculis ex gentibus*, propter unius Dei praedicationem, qui eum capere volebant; et sic in suis et in aliis non habebat requiem. Ier. XV, 10: *ut quid me genuisti, mater mea, virum doloris?* et cetera. Tertio enumerat pericula quantum ad loca, et hoc, vel quantum ad civitates, unde dicit *periculis in civitate*, id est, in commotionibus civitatum contra me sicut fuit Ephesi et apud Corinthum, ut patet Act. XVIII, 12 et XIX, 23; vel quantum ad solitudines, et quantum ad hoc dicit *periculis in solitudine*, quae erant vel a bestiis malis, sicut quando vipera momordit manum suam, Act. ult., quando congregavit sarmenta, vel ex penuria ciborum. Vel quantum ad maria, et ideo dicit *periculis in mari*, non ex mari, sicut supra, sed in mari, ut pericula quae proveniunt ex praedonibus et piratis. Eccli. XLIII, 26: *qui navigant mare*, et cetera.

Sed gravius periculum subdit, dicens *periculis in falsis fratribus*, id est in falsis Christianis et haereticis, et in pseudo. Ier. c. IX, 4: *unusquisque a fratre suo se custodiat.*

second, internal evils, at *besides those things which are without*.

He describes the external evils: first as to the evils that occur on journeys; second, as to those in houses.

428. In regard to the first he mentions his frequent journeys, saying *often on journeys*, namely, I am proved a minister of Christ by enduring many hard and difficult things patiently. *From Jerusalem and as far round as Illyricum I have fully preached the Gospel of Christ* (Rom 15:19). Along with these he traveled along many roads, going to Rome and into Spain: *for the sake of the words of your lips, I have kept hard ways* (Ps 17:4).

Second, he mentions the dangers from journeys: first, the lesser ones; second, the more serious danger from false brethren.

Among the lesser dangers he mentions three things, in regard to which he suffered many dangers. First, in regard to their causes, and these either from natural causes; hence he says, *in perils of waters*, for streams naturally rise in the winter and are swift and very dangerous; or from malicious violence; as to this he says, *in perils of robbers*, whom the devil roused against him to rob him of his clothing: *his troops come on together; they have cast up siegeworks against me, and encamp round about my tent* (Job 19:12). Second, he lists the dangers that inspire fear either from his own; hence he says, *in perils from my own nation*, i.e., managed by the Jews: or from outsiders; hence he says, *in perils from gentiles*, who wanted to capture him for preaching the one true God. Consequently, he had no rest from his own or from others: *my mother, you bore me, a man of strife and contention to the whole land!* (Jer 15:10). Third, he lists the dangers as to their places. First, as to cities he says, *in perils in the city*, i.e., in cities stirred up against me, as at Ephesus and Corinth (Acts 18:12; 19:23); or as to a desert place; hence he says, *in perils in the wilderness*, either from evil beasts, as when a viper bit his hand as he was collecting sticks (Acts 28:3), or from want of food. Second, as to danger at sea, he says *in perils in the sea*, such as perils from plunderers and pirates: *let those who sail the sea tell of its dangers* (Sir 43:26).

But he mentions a more serious danger, saying, *in perils from false brethren*, i.e., from false Christians and heretics and false apostles: *let every man beware of his neighbor* (Jer 9:4).

Lecture 6

11:27in labore et aerumna, in vigiliis multis, in fame et siti, in jejuniis multis, in frigore et nuditate, [n. 429]

11:28praeter illa quae extrinsecus sunt, instantia mea quotidiana, sollicitudo omnium ecclesiarum. [n. 432]

11:29Quis infirmatur, et ego non infirmor? quis scandalizatur, et ego non uror?

11:30Si gloriari oportet, quae infirmitatis meae sunt, gloriabor. [n. 435]

11:31Deus et Pater Domini nostri Jesu Christi, qui est benedictus in saecula, scit quod non mentior. [n. 437]

11:32Damasci praepositus gentis Aretae regis custodiebat civitatem Damascenorum ut me comprehenderet: [n. 438]

11:33et per fenestram in sporta dimissus sum per murum, et sic effugi manus ejus.

11:27κόπῳ καὶ μόχθῳ, ἐν ἀγρυπνίαις πολλάκις, ἐν λιμῷ καὶ δίψει, ἐν νηστείαις πολλάκις, ἐν ψύχει καὶ γυμνότητι·

11:28χωρὶς τῶν παρεκτὸς ἡ ἐπίστασίς μοι ἡ καθ᾽ ἡμέραν, ἡ μέριμνα πασῶν τῶν ἐκκλησιῶν.

11:29τίς ἀσθενεῖ καὶ οὐκ ἀσθενῶ; τίς σκανδαλίζεται καὶ οὐκ ἐγὼ πυροῦμαι;

11:30Εἰ καυχᾶσθαι δεῖ, τὰ τῆς ἀσθενείας μου καυχήσομαι.

11:31ὁ θεὸς καὶ πατὴρ τοῦ κυρίου Ἰησοῦ οἶδεν, ὁ ὢν εὐλογητὸς εἰς τοὺς αἰῶνας, ὅτι οὐ ψεύδομαι.

11:32ἐν Δαμασκῷ ὁ ἐθνάρχης Ἀρέτα τοῦ βασιλέως ἐφρούρει τὴν πόλιν Δαμασκηνῶν πιάσαι με,

11:33καὶ διὰ θυρίδος ἐν σαργάνῃ ἐχαλάσθην διὰ τοῦ τείχους καὶ ἐξέφυγον τὰς χεῖρας αὐτοῦ.

11:27In labor and painfulness, in many watchings, in hunger and thirst, in many fastings, in cold and nakedness: [n. 429]

11:28Besides those things which are without: my daily pressures, the anxiety for all the churches. [n. 432]

11:29Who is weak, and I am not weak? Who is scandalized, and I am not on fire?

11:30If I must glory, I will glory of the things that concern my infirmity. [n. 435]

11:31The God and Father of our Lord Jesus Christ, who is blessed forever, knows that I do not lie. [n. 437]

11:32At Damascus, the governor of the nation under Aretas the king, guarded the city of the Damascenes, to apprehend me. [n. 438]

11:33And I was let down by the wall, through a window, in a basket: and so escaped his hands.

429. Hic consequenter enumerat mala sponte assumpta, quae sustinentur in domibus. Et enumerat tria mala opposita tribus bonis, quae sunt necessaria ad vitam domesticam. Primum bonum est requies somni, secundum est sustentatio cibi, tertium est fomentum vestis.

Requiei ergo somni, opponit laborem et vigilias. Quantum ad laborem dicit *in labore*, scilicet manuum. Act. XX, 34: *ad ea quae mihi opus erant*, et cetera. Et ideo dicit supra VI, v. 5: *in laboribus*, quia, ad litteram, ut dictum est supra, manu sua victum quaerebat. Et II Thess. III, 8: *nocte et die laborantes*, et cetera. Quantum ad laboris defectum dicit *aerumna*, quae est defectus et languor consequens ex labore, vel ex morbo naturali. Ps. c. XXXI, 4: *conversus sum in aerumna*, et cetera. Quantum vero ad vigilias dicit *in vigiliis multis*, vel in vacando praedicationibus de nocte, vel operi manuali. Act. XX, 7 dicitur quod protraxit sermonem usque ad mediam noctem.

430. Sustentationi vero cibi opponit duplicem subtractionem cibi, unam quae est ex necessitate; unde dicit *in fame et siti*, quia scilicet, ad litteram, deficiebat sibi aliquando cibus et potus. I Cor. IV, 11: *usque in hanc horam*, et cetera. Aliam quae est ex voluntate, unde

429. Here he lists the evils voluntarily assumed, namely, those endured in homes, and he lists three evils opposed to the three goods which are necessary for domestic life. The first good is restful sleep; the second is sustenance from food; the third is the warmth of clothing.

To restful sleep he opposes labor and watchings, in regard to which he says, *in labor*, i.e., manual labor. *You yourselves know that these hands ministered to my necessities, and to those who were with me* (Acts 20:34), because he literally made his living with his own hands: *with toil and labor we worked night and day, that we might not burden any of you* (2 Thess 3:8). As to the weakness resulting from labor he says, *and painfulness*, which is a weakness and tiredness that follows upon labor or from a natural sickness: *my strength was dried up as by the heat of summer* (Ps 32:4). But in regard to watchings he says, *in many watchings*, because he devoted himself either to preaching at night or to manual labor. In Acts it says that he prolonged his sermon until midnight (Acts 20:7).

430. To sustenance from food he opposes two forms of being denied food. One is due to necessity; hence he says, *in hunger and thirst*, namely, because he was unable frequently to obtain food and drink: *to the present hour we hunger and thirst* (1 Cor 4:11); the other is voluntary; hence

dicit *in ieiuniis multis*, scilicet voluntarie assumptis, et propter exemplum bonum et propter macerationem carnis. I Cor. IX, 27: *castigo corpus meum*, et cetera.

Sed contra, Matth. VI, 33: *haec omnia adiicientur vobis*, scilicet temporalia. Quare ergo in fame et siti?

Respondeo. Dicendum est quod quando expedit, adiiciuntur nobis, scilicet temporalia, et propter utilitatem nostram, sed aliquando expedit carere eis.

431. Fomento vero vestis opponit duo, unum ex parte naturae, unde dicit *in frigore*, aliud ex parte inopiae, unde dicit *et nuditate*, scilicet ostensus sum, scilicet minister Christi. I Cor. IV, 11: *nudi et instabiles*, etc. supra VI, 4: *in necessitatibus*, etc.

432. Consequenter cum dicit *praeter illa*, etc., enumerat mala assumpta interiora, quae causantur ex sollicitudine cordis pro pseudo.

Bonus autem praelatus dupliciter affligitur pro subditis. Et primo sollicitudine conservationis subditorum, secundo pro defectu ipsorum. Et istam duplicem afflictionem passus est Apostolus. Primam cum dicit *praeter illa, quae extrinsecus*, etc., quasi dicat: praeter omnia quae exterius patior et passus sum, angit me gravius interior afflictio, scilicet sollicitudo subditorum. Et ideo dicit *instantia omnium ecclesiarum* magna est et multum gravat, quia multum sollicitat. Lc. X, 41: *Martha, Martha, sollicita es, et turbaris erga plurima*, et cetera. Rom. XII, 8: *qui praeest in sollicitudine*.

433. Secundam afflictionem passus est pro defectu subditorum, et hoc dupliciter, scilicet pro defectu spiritualium; unde dicit *quis infirmatur*, scilicet in fide et bono, *et ego non infirmor?* In corde dolens de eo, sicut de me. I Cor. IX, 22: *factus sum infirmis infirmus*, et cetera. Ier. IX, 1: *quis dabit capiti meo aquam*, et cetera. Item pro defectu corporalium; unde dicit *quis scandalizatur*, malo poenae, id est quis patitur tribulationes, *et ego non uror?* Igne compassionis. Iste est ignis, quem Dominus venit mittere in terram, Lc. XII, 49.

434. Et attende, quod congrue utitur hoc verbo *uror*, quia compassio procedit ex amore Dei et proximi, qui est ignis consumens, dum movet ad sublevandas miserias proximorum, et purgat ex affectu compassionis, et per quem nobis peccata relaxantur: caritas autem illius compassionis operit multitudinem peccatorum.

he says, *in many fastings*, i.e., voluntarily undertaken both for the good example and to tame the flesh: *I pommel my body and subdue it* (1 Cor 9:27).

But this seems to be out of harmony with Matthew: *but seek first his kingdom and his righteousness, and all these things shall be yours as well* (Matt 6:33). Why then in hunger and thirst?

I answer that when it is expedient and for our benefit, they are added, i.e., temporal things; but sometimes it is expedient to lack them.

431. To the warmth of clothing he opposes two things: one on the part of nature; hence he says, *in cold*; the other on the part of poverty, hence he says, *and nakedness*. I am proved a minister of Christ: *we are ill-clad and buffeted and homeless* (1 Cor 4:11); *in tribulation, in necessities, in distresses* (2 Cor 6:4).

432. Then when he says, *besides those things which are without*, he lists the internal evils he assumed, namely, those caused by anxiety of heart because of the activities of the false apostles.

Now a good prelate is concerned about two things affecting his subjects, namely, their safety and the defection. And the Apostle suffered affliction in regard to both; the first, when he says, and, *besides those things which are without: my daily pressures, the anxiety for all the churches*. As if to say: in addition to what I suffer and have suffered from outside, the internal affliction is more oppressive, that is, solicitude for his subjects. Hence, he says, the *daily pressures for all the churches* are great and lie heavily upon him, because he was very solicitous. *Martha, Martha, you are anxious and troubled about many things* (Luke 10:41); *he that rules, with solicitude* (Rom 12:8).

433. The second affliction he suffered concerned the failings of his subjects, and this he does in two ways, namely for spiritual failings; hence he says, *who is weak*, namely, in faith and in goodness, *and I am not weak?* In heart, grieving over them as though over myself? *To the weak I became weak, that I might win the weak* (1 Cor 9:22); *O that my head were waters, and my eyes a fountain of tears, that I might weep day and night for the slain of the daughter of my people!* (Jer 9:1). And for bodily failings; hence he says, *who is scandalized* with the evil of punishment, i.e., who suffers afflictions, *and I am not on fire* with the fire of compassion? This is the fire which the Lord came to cast upon the earth (Luke 12:49).

434. And notice that he fittingly uses the word, *on fire*, because compassion proceeds from the love of God and neighbor, which is a consuming fire, because it moves one to alleviate the misfortunes of one's neighbor, and it cleanses the soul with the compassion it engenders, and by it our sins are loosed, while the charity of that compassion covers a multitude of sins.

Vel, aliter, aliquando enim labitur homo in peccatum ex seipso, et tunc infirmatur; aliquando autem ex malo exemplo aliorum, et tunc scandalizatur. Lc. XVII, 1 et Matth. c. XVIII, 7: *vae homini illi per quem scandalum venit*, et cetera.

435. Deinde cum dicit *si gloriari oportet*, etc., confirmat quaedam dictorum superius. Vel dic quod supra loquitur quantum ad mala, quae pertulit commendabiliter, hic autem quantum ad mala, quae vitavit prudenter. Sed quia vitare pericula, quae surgunt propter fidem, videtur pertinere ad infirmitatem, ideo

primo praemittit, quod in illis, quae infirmitatis sunt, vult gloriari;

secundo proponit iuramentum ad confirmationem dicendorum, ibi *Deus et Pater*, etc.;

tertio ostendit modum vitandi, ibi *Damasci*, et cetera.

436. Proponit ergo primo de quibus gloriatur, si debet gloriari, dicens *si*, pro *quia*, **oportet gloriari, quae sunt infirmitatis meae gloriabor**; quasi dicat: alii gloriantur in genere et in aliis mundanis rebus. Phil. c. III, 19: *gloria in confusione*, et cetera. Et ego etiam coactus gloriatus sum in eis. Tamen si gloriari oportet, gloriabor in infirmitatibus meis. Infra XII, 9: **libenter gloriabor in infirmitatibus meis**, et cetera.

437. Secundo subdit, quod non mentitur invocans testimonium divinum per modum iuramenti, ut credatur sibi, dicens **Deus et Pater**, et cetera. Ubi tria ponit: unum per quod inducit ad amorem, unde dicit, **Deus**, Ier. X, 7: *quis non timebit te*, et cetera. Aliud per quod excitavit ad amorem, unde dicit: **Pater**, Iac. I, 17: *omne datum optimum*, etc.; Mal. I, 6: *si ego pater, ubi est amor meus?* Vel, secundum aliam litteram, *honor meus*. Tertium per quod movet ad reverentiam et laudem; unde dicit **qui est benedictus Deus in saecula**, supra I, 3: **benedictus Deus et Pater**, et cetera.

Iste ergo tam reverendus, tam diligendus, tam timendus **scit, quod non mentior**, scilicet in his quae dixi et dicturus sum. Supra c. I, 18: **non enim est apud nos est, et non**, et cetera.

438. Consequenter cum dicit **Damasci praepositus**, etc., ostendit quanta mala vitavit, et hoc in quodam particulari periculo.

Ubi sciendum est, quod Apostolus primo coepit praedicare Christum in Damasco, ubi dum pergeret Christianos capere, prostratus est et ad fidem conversus. Et ideo Iudaei ad praepositum illius civitatis, qui erat ibi pro Aretha rege, confugerunt, ut Paulum caperent et occiderent. Et ideo ille faciebat custodiri nocte et die portas civitatis, ut dicitur Act. IX, v. 24. Christiani autem, qui

Or, taking it another way, a person sometimes falls into sin of himself, and then he is weakened; sometimes by the example of others, and then he is scandalized: *woe to the man by whom the temptation comes!* (Matt 18:7).

435. Then when he says, *if I must glory*, he confirms some of the statements made above. Or say that above he speaks about the evils he commendably suffered; but here about the evils he prudently avoided. But because the avoidance of evils that arise against the faith seems to imply weakness, therefore,

first, he states that he wishes to glory in those that imply weakness;

second, he proposes an oath to confirm his statements, at **God and Father**;

third, he shows how he avoided some evils, at **at Damascus**.

436. First, therefore, he suggests that the things in which one should glory, if he must glory, saying: *if*, i.e., *because*, **I must glory, I will glory of the things that concern my infirmity**. As if to say: others may glory in their race and other worldly things: *they glory in their shame, with minds set on earthly things* (Phil 3:19), and I when compelled gloried in them. Yet if I must glory, I will glory in my weakness: **gladly therefore will I glory in my infirmities, that the power of Christ may dwell in me** (2 Cor 12:9).

437. Second, he states that he is not lying and is calling on God to witness after the manner of an oath, so that they will believe his, saying, **the God and Father of the Lord Jesus**, he who is blessed for ever, knows that I do not lie. Here he lays down three things. One by which to induce fear; hence he says, **God**: *who would not fear you, O King of the nations?* (Jer 10:7); one by which he excites love, when he says, **Father**: *every good endowment and every perfect gift is from above, coming down from the Father of lights* (Jas 1:17); *if then I am a father, where is my love?*, or according to another version, *my honor?* (Mal 1:5); third, to inspire reverence and praise, **who is blessed forever**: **blessed be the God and Father of our Lord Jesus Christ** (2 Cor 1:3).

He, therefore, so revered, so worthy of love, so worthy of fear, **knows that I do not lie**, namely, in what I have said and will say: **our speech which was to you was not, it is, and it is not** (2 Cor 1:17).

438. Then when he says, **at Damascus**, he shows the evils he avoided, and this in a certain particular danger.

Here it should be noted that the Apostle first began to preach Christ in Damascus, where he was thrown to the ground and converted to the faith, as he was on his way to arrest Christians. Therefore, the Jews appealed to the governor of that city, who was representing Aretas the king, to arrest Paul and put him to death. So the governor ordered the city-gates to be watched day and night (Acts 9:24). But

erant ibi, volentes servare Paulum, eum submiserunt in sporta per murum, et sic evasit.

Hunc ergo modum evadendi tangit Apostolus, dicens: vere non mentior de hoc quod dico etiam modo, nam **Damasci praepositus**, qui sub Aretha rege, genti Damascenorum praeerat, custodiri faciebat, inductus a Iudaeis, **civitatem Damascenorum**, ad hoc scilicet **ut me comprehenderet**, et comprehensum assignaret Iudaeis, ne amplius praedicarem; sed ego **per fenestram submissus sum per murum, et sic effugi manus eius**, scilicet praepositi. Et hoc fuit de mandato Domini dicentis Matth. X, 23: *si vos persecuti fuerint*, et cetera. Sic Michol David deposuit per fenestram, ne caperetur a Saule, I Reg. c. XIX, 2. Sic Rahab exploratores demisit cum fune per fenestram, Ios. II, 15.

439. Sed hic obiicitur contra Apostolum, primo, quia videtur quod non fuerit sufficienter confisus in Domino, sed fugit.

Respondeo. Dicendum est, quod quamdiu adest humanum auxilium, homo non debet confugere ad auxilium divinum, quia hoc esset tentare Deum, sed debet illo uti auxilio quantum potest. Apostolo autem nondum deerat humanum auxilium.

Secundo obiicitur, quia Io. X, 12 dicitur: *mercenarius autem et qui non est pastor, videt lupum venientem, et fugit*. Unde videtur quod non fuerit bonus pastor.

Respondeo. Dicendum est, quod aliquando quaeritur persona praelati tantum, aliquando cum praelato totus populus. Quando ergo quaeritur praelatus solus, tunc debet committere curam alteri, et absentare se. Et sic fecit hic Paulus. Et ideo dicit Glossa quod licet fugeret, tamen fuit ei cura de ovibus, Bono Pastori in caelo sedenti eas commendando, et utilitati eorum se, per fugam, praeservando. Quando vero quaeritur totus grex, tunc debet praeponere utilitatem et salutem gregis saluti corporis sui.

Nota autem, quod est quaedam fuga humilitatis, quando quis fugit honores, sicut Christus fugit Io. VI, 15, cum vidisset quod vellent eum eligere in regem. Sic Saul cum electus fuit in regem, abscondit se domi, I Reg. X, 22. Quaedam vero fuga est cautelae, quando scilicet fugit pericula, ut praeservetur ad maiora. Sic Helias fugit propter Iezabel, III Reg. XIX, 3; et sic Apostolus hic fugit manus praepositi.

the Christians who were there, desiring to save Paul, lowered him by the wall in a basket, and thus he escaped.

This form of escape the Apostle touches on, when he says: truly I am not lying about what I am telling you now: for **at Damascus**, the governor under King Aretas, i.e., the governor who ruled at Damascus under King Aretas, was induced by the Jews to guard **the city of the Damascenes**, **to apprehend me**, so that I would be delivered to the Jews and prevented from preaching. But **I was let down by the wall, through a window, in a basket: and so escaped his hands**, namely, the governor's. This was done in keeping with the Lord's command: *when they persecute you in one town, flee to the next* (Matt 10:23). In this way too did Michel let David down through a window to escape from Saul (1 Sam 19:12), and Rahab let the spies down with a cord out of a window (Jos 2:15).

439. But some object against the Apostle's conduct: first, because he seems to have lacked confidence in the Lord and fled.

I answer that as long as human help is available, a man should not run for divine help, because this would be tempting God; but he should use human help as much as he can. But the Apostle was not yet lacking human help.

The second objection is based on John: *he who is a hireling and not a shepherd, whose own the sheep are not, sees the wolf coming and leaves the sheep and flees* (John 10:12). Hence, it seems that Paul was not a good shepherd.

I answer that sometimes the person of the prelate alone is sought, and sometimes the prelate along with all the people. When the prelate alone is sought, then he should entrust his duties to another and absent himself. This is what Paul did. Hence, a Gloss says that although he fled, he still took care of his people by commending them to the Good Shepherd seated in heaven and saving himself for their benefit by flight. But when the entire flock is sought, then he should prefer the benefit and safety of the flock to his own bodily safety.

But note that there is a flight inspired by humility, when a person flees honors, as Christ fled when they sought to make him king (John 6:15). In the same way Saul, when chosen, concealed himself at home (1 Sam 10:22). Another is inspired by caution, namely, when a person flees dangers in order to be saved for greater ones. This is the way Elijah fled from Jezebel (1 Kgs 19:3), and the way the Apostle fled from the hands of the governor.

CHAPTER 12

Lecture 1

12:1Si gloriari oportet (non expedit quidem), veniam autem ad visiones et revelationes Domini. [n. 440]

12:2Scio hominem in Christo ante annos quatuordecim, sive in corpore nescio, sive extra corpus nescio, Deus scit, raptum hujusmodi usque ad tertium caelum. [n. 443]

12:1Καυχᾶσθαι δεῖ, οὐ συμφέρον μέν, ἐλεύσομαι δὲ εἰς ὀπτασίας καὶ ἀποκαλύψεις κυρίου.

12:2οἶδα ἄνθρωπον ἐν Χριστῷ πρὸ ἐτῶν δεκατεσσάρων, εἴτε ἐν σώματι οὐκ οἶδα, εἴτε ἐκτὸς τοῦ σώματος οὐκ οἶδα, ὁ θεὸς οἶδεν, ἁρπαγέντα τὸν τοιοῦτον ἕως τρίτου οὐρανοῦ.

12:1If I must glory (it is not expedient indeed) still I will come to visions and revelations of the Lord. [n. 440]

12:2I know a man in Christ: over fourteen years ago (whether in the body, I do not know, or out of the body, I do not know: God knows), such a one was caught up to the third heaven. [n. 443]

---

440. Posita sua commendatione quantum ad mala perpessa, hic consequenter Apostolus commendans se, ostendit praeeminentiam suae dignitatis quantum ad bona divinitus recepta. Prima autem gloriatio fuit de infirmitatibus; ista vero est de bonis eius. Unde

circa hoc duo facit.

Primo commendat se de bonis susceptis divinitus;

secundo excusat se de hac commendatione, quod hoc fecerit quasi coactus, ibi *factus sum insipiens*, et cetera.

Circa primum duo facit.

Primo extollit magnitudinem eorum quae sunt sibi collata a Deo;

secundo manifestat remedium infirmitatis sibi adhibitum contra periculum superbiae, ibi *et ne magnitudo*, et cetera.

Circa primum duo facit.

Primo ponit bonum sibi divinitus collatum;

secundo ostendit quomodo se habuit in gloriando de huiusmodi bono, ibi *pro huiusmodi*, et cetera.

Circa primum duo facit.

Primo ostendit quod hoc sit sibi collatum divinitus in generali;

secundo vero in speciali, ibi *scio hominem*, et cetera.

441. Bonum autem Apostolo collatum divinitus, sunt revelationes sibi divinitus factae, et de istis vult hic gloriari. Unde dicit *si gloriari oportet*, id est quia gloriari oportet propter vos, tamen secundum se non expedit, quia qui gloriatur de bono recepto, incidit in periculum amittendi quod habet. Eccli. XLIII, 15: *aperti sunt thesauri*, scilicet virtutum, per gloriationem inanem, *et evanuerunt nebulae sicut aves*. Et hoc significatur in Ezechia, Is. XXXIX, 2, quando ostendit thesauros domus Domini nuntiis regis Babylonis.

Et licet simpliciter non expediat gloriari, tamen aliquando propter aliquam specialem causam potest homo

440. Having commended himself for the evils he suffered, the Apostle continues to commend himself and shows the pre-eminence of his dignity in regard to good things received from God. For he first gloried in his weaknesses, but now in his good things.

In regard to this he does two things.

First, he commends himself on the good things received from God;

second, he begs pardon for this commendation, alleging that he is compelled to do this, at *I have become foolish*.

In regard to the first he does two things.

First, he extols the greatness of the things conferred on him by God;

second, he discloses the remedy given to him against the danger of pride, at *and lest the greatness*.

In regard to the first he does two things:

first, he mentions a good divinely conferred;

second, he shows how he behaved in regard to glorying in it, at *for such a one, I will glory*.

In regard to the first he does two things.

First, he shows in general that this was divinely bestowed;

second, in particular, at *I know a man*.

441. The good divinely bestowed on the Apostle are revelations made to him by God; it is of these that he wishes to glory. Hence he says: *if I must glory*, i.e., because I must glory for your sake, although in itself there is nothing to be gained by it, because a person who glories in a good he has received runs the risk of losing what he has: *through this*, i.e., by vain glory, *are the treasures of the virtues opened, and the clouds fly out like birds*. (Sir 43:15). And this is signified in Hezekiah, when he showed the treasures of the Lord's house to the messengers of the king in Babylon (Isa 39:2).

And although, absolutely speaking, it is not expedient to glory, nevertheless, for some special reason a man may

gloriari, sicut ex praemissis manifestum est. Et ideo dicit: quia gloriari oportet, ideo dimissis commendationibus de infirmitatibus, *veniam*, commendando me, *ad visiones et revelationes Domini*.

442. Ubi notandum est, quod differentia est inter visionem et revelationem. Nam revelatio includit visionem, et non e converso. Nam aliquando videntur aliqua, quorum intellectus et significatio est occulta videnti et tunc est visio solum. Sicut fuit visio Pharaonis et Nabuchodonosor Daniel II, 1 et Gen. XLI, 1. Sed quando cum visione habetur significatio intellectus eorum quae videntur, tunc est revelatio. Unde quantum ad Pharaonem et Nabuchodonosor visio de spicis et de statua, fuit solum visio; sed quantum ad Ioseph et Danielem, qui significationem visorum habuerunt, fuit revelatio et prophetia.

Utrumque tamen, scilicet visio et revelatio, quandoque quidem fit a Deo. Dan. II, 28: *est Deus in caelo revelans mysteria*. Os. XII, v. 10: *ego visiones multiplicavi eis*. Ps. CXVIII, v. 18: *revela oculos meos*, et cetera. Quandoque vero a malo spiritu. Ier. XXIII, 13: *prophetae prophetabant in Baal*. Apostolo autem facta est et visio, et revelatio, quia secreta, quae vidit, plene intellexit a Domino, non a malo spiritu. Unde dicit *veniam autem ad visiones et revelationes Domini*.

Est autem revelatio amotio velamenti. Potest autem esse duplex velamen. Unum ex parte videntis, et hoc est infidelitas, vel peccatum, vel duritia cordis; et de hoc supra III, v. 14: *usque in hodiernum diem velamen*, et cetera. Aliud ex parte rei visae, quando scilicet res spiritualis proponitur alicui sub figuris rerum sensibilium, et de hoc dicitur Num. IV, v. 15, quod sacerdotes tradebant Levitis vasa sanctuarii velata, quia scilicet debiliores non possunt spiritualia capere, secundum quod in seipsis sunt. Et ideo Dominus loquebatur turbis in parabolis, Matth. XIII, 13.

443. Consequenter visiones et revelationes huiusmodi, manifestat Apostolus in speciali, loquens de se tamquam de alio. Unde dicit *scio hominem in Christo*, et cetera. Et ponit duas visiones. Prima incipit hic, secunda vero incipit ibi *et scio huiusmodi hominem in Christo*, et cetera.

444. Circa primam autem visionem utitur Apostolus quadam distinctione. Dicit enim se, circa huiusmodi revelationem, scire quaedam et quaedam nescire. Dicit autem se scire tria, scilicet videntis conditionem unde *scio hominem in Christo*; visionis tempus quia *ante annos quatuordecim*; et visionis fastigium quia *raptus usque ad tertium caelum*. Dicit autem se nescire videntis

glory, as is clear from what has been stated above. Therefore he says: because I must boast, I will leave off commending myself on my infirmities and *I will come* by commending myself *to visions and revelations of the Lord*.

442. Here it should be noted the difference between a vision and a revelation. For a revelation includes a vision, but not vice versa. For sometimes things are seen, the understanding and significance of which are hidden from the beholder; in that case it is only a vision, as in the visions of Pharaoh and Nebuchadnezzar (Dan 2:1; Gen 41:1). But when the significance of the understanding of those things which are seen is had with the vision, then it is revelation; whence in regard to Pharoah and Nebuchadnezzar, the vision of ears of corn and of the statue was only a vision. But in regard to Joseph and Daniel, who understood the meaning of what was seen, it was a revelation and a prophecy.

Both, however, namely vision and revelation, are sometimes produced by God. *There is a God in heaven who reveals mysteries* (Dan 2:28); *it was I who multiplied visions* (Hos 12:10); *open my eyes, that I may behold wondrous things out of your law* (Ps 119:18); but sometimes by an evil spirit: *they prophesied by Baal and led my people Israel astray* (Jer 23:13). To the Apostle were made both vision and revelation, because he fully understood the secret things he saw. They were produced by the Lord and not by an evil spirit. Hence he says: *I will come to visions and revelations of the Lord*.

Now a revelation is a removing of a veil. But a veil can be of two kinds: one on the part of the beholder, and this is unbelief or sin or hardness of heart. Of this veil he said above: *even until this day, when Moses is read, the veil is upon their heart* (2 Cor 3:15); the other is on the part of the object seen, namely, when spiritual things are proposed to someone under the figures of sense-perceptible objects. Concerning this it is said that the priests delivered the vessels of the sanctuary veiled to the Levites, because weaker persons cannot grasp spiritual things as they are in themselves (Num 4:15). This is why the Lord spoke to the multitudes in parables (Matt 13:13).

443. Then the Apostle describes these visions and revelations in details, speaking of himself as though of another person; hence he says, *I know a man in Christ*. He mentions two visions: the first begins here; the second begins at *and I know such a man*.

444. When speaking of the first vision, the Apostle makes use of a distinction, for he says in regard to this revelation that he knew certain things and other things not. But he knew three things, namely, the condition of the beholder; hence he says: *I know a man in Christ*; the time of the vision, that is, *over fourteen years ago*; and the high point of the vision, because he *was caught up to the third*

dispositionem, quia *sive in corpore, sive extra corpus, nescio*.

445. Videamus ergo ea quae scivit, ut, per nota ad ignota, facilius pervenire possimus.

Et primo videntis conditionem, quae est laudabilis, quia *in Christo*, id est conformem Christo.

Sed contra: in Christo nullus est, nisi qui habet caritatem, quia I Io. IV, 16 dicitur: *qui manet in caritate, in Deo manet*. Ergo scivit se habere caritatem, quod est contra illud: *nescit homo utrum odio, vel amore dignus sit*, et cetera.

Respondeo, quod esse in Christo potest intelligi dupliciter. Uno modo per fidem et fidei sacramentum, secundum illud Apostoli, Gal. III, 27: *quotquot baptizati estis, Christum induistis*, scilicet per fidem et fidei sacramentum. Et hoc modo scivit se Apostolus in Christo esse.

Alio modo dicitur aliquis esse in Christo per caritatem, et hoc modo nullus scit se esse in Christo certitudinaliter, nisi per quaedam experimenta et signa, inquantum sentit se dispositum et coniunctum in Christo, ita quod nullo modo, etiam propter mortem, permitteret se separari ab eo. Et hoc de se expertus erat Apostolus, cum dicebat Rom. c. VIII, 38: *certus enim sum, quod neque mors, neque vita*, etc., *separabit nos a caritate*. Unde potuit habere huiusmodi signa, quod esset in caritate Christi.

446. Secundo visionis tempus, quod fuit conveniens, quia *ante annos quatuordecim*, quia quatuordecim anni transacti erant ab eo tempore quo viderat visionem usque ad tempus quo scripsit hanc epistolam. Quando enim hanc epistolam scripsit, nondum Apostolus erat positus in carcerem. Et sic videtur, quod fuit circa principium imperii Neronis, a quo post multum tempus occisus fuit. Unde si computemus annos descendentes a principio imperii Neronis usque ad quatuordecim annos, manifeste apparet, quod Apostolus habuit has visiones in principio suae conversionis.

Ipse enim conversus fuit ad Christum anno quo Christus passus est. Christus autem passus est circa finem Tiberii Caesaris, quo mortuo successit ei Gaius imperator, qui vixit quatuor annis, post quem Nero factus est imperator. Et sic inter Tiberium et Neronem fluxerunt quatuor anni. Et sic, additis duobus annis de tempore Tiberii, quia nondum mortuus erat quando Paulus fuit conversus, et octo de tempore Neronis, quod fluxerat usque ad tempus quando scripsit hanc epistolam,

heaven. And he says that he did not know the disposition of the beholder, *whether in the body, I do not know, or out of the body, I do not know*.

445. Therefore let us see what he knew, so that through what is known we may more easily attain to what was not known.

First of all, the condition of the beholder, which is praiseworthy, because he was *in Christ*, i.e., conformed to Christ.

But on the contrary, no one is in Christ, unless he has charity, because *he who abides in love abides in God* (1 John 4:16). Therefore, he knew that he had charity, which is contrary to what is stated in Ecclesiastes: *the righteous and the wise and their deeds are in the hand of God; whether it is love or hate man does not know* (Eccl 9:1).

I answer that being in Christ can be taken in two ways: in one way by faith and the sacrament of faith according to Galatians: *for as many of you as were baptized into Christ have put on Christ* (Gal 3:27), namely, by faith and the sacrament of faith. This is the sense in which the Apostle knew that he was in Christ.

In another way a person is said to be in Christ through charity, and in this way no one knows for certain that he is in Christ, except by certain tests and signs, inasmuch as he feels himself disposed and joined to Christ in such a way that he would not permit himself to be separated from him for any reason including death. This the Apostle experienced in regard to himself, when he said: *for I am sure that neither death, nor life, nor angels, nor principalities, nor things present, nor things to come, nor powers, nor height, nor depth, nor anything else in all creation, will be able to separate us from the love of God in Christ Jesus our Lord* (Rom 8:38). Hence, he could have had such signs that he was in the charity of Christ.

446. Second, the time of the vision, which was fitting, because it was *over fourteen years ago*; for fourteen years had elapsed from the time he saw the vision, until he wrote this epistle, because when he wrote this epistle he had not yet been cast into prison. Hence it seems to have been written at the beginning of Nero's reign, by whom he was killed much later. Hence if we go back fourteen years from the beginning of Nero's reign, it is clear that the Apostle had these visions at the beginning of his conversion.

For he had been converted to Christ in the same year that the Lord suffered. But Christ suffered near the end of Tiberius Caesar's reign, who was succeeded at death by the emperor Caius, who lived four years, after which Nero became emperor. Therefore, between Tiberius and Nero there were four years. Adding two years from Tiberius's reign, because he was not yet dead, when Paul was converted, and from Nero's reign the eight years which had passed until

relinquitur quod a tempore suae conversionis, usque ad tempus quo hanc epistolam scripsit, fuerunt anni quatuordecim.

Et ideo quidam dicunt satis probabiliter, quod Apostolus has visiones habuit in illo triduo, quo post prostrationem suam a Domino stetit neque videns, neque manducans, neque bibens, Act. IX, 9.

Commemorat autem tempus suae conversionis apostolus ut ostendat, quod si a tempore suae conversionis tantum erat gratus Christo, ut talia sibi ostenderet, quanto magis post quatuordecim annos, cum profecerit et in auctoritate apud Deum, et in virtutibus, et gratia?

447. Tertio videamus fastigium visionis, quod quidem est excellens, quia raptus *usque ad tertium caelum*.

Sed sciendum quod aliud est furari et aliud rapi. Furari quidem proprie est, cum res alicui latenter aufertur. Unde Gen. XL, 15 dicebat Ioseph: *furtim sublatus sum*. Sed rapi proprie dicitur quod subito et per violentiam aufertur. Iob VI, 15: *sicut torrens raptim*, id est subito et rapide, *transit in convallibus*. Inde est quod praedones, qui violenter expoliant, dicuntur raptores.

Sed attende quod aliquis homo dicitur rapi ab hominibus, sicut Enoch. Sap. IV, 11: *raptus est, ne malitia*, et cetera. Aliquando rapitur anima a corpore. Lc. XII, 20: *stulte, hac nocte animam tuam*, et cetera. Aliquando aliquis dicitur rapi a seipso, quando propter aliquid homo efficitur extra se ipsum, et hoc est idem quod extasis.

Sed et extra se ipsum efficitur homo et per appetitivam virtutem et cognitivam. Per appetitivam enim virtutem homo est solum in se ipso, quando curat quae sunt sua tantum. Efficitur vero extra se ipsum, quando non curat quae sua sunt, sed quae perveniunt ad bona aliorum, et hoc facit caritas. I Cor. c. XIII, 4: *caritas non quaerit quae sua sunt*. Et de hac extasi dicit Dionysius, IV cap. *de Divinis nominibus*: *est autem extasim faciens divinus amor non sinens amatorem sui ipsius esse, sed amatorum*, scilicet rerum amatarum.

Secundum cognitivam vero aliquis efficitur extra se, quando aliquis extra naturalem modum hominis elevatur ad aliquid videndum, et de isto raptu loquitur hic Apostolus.

448. Sed sciendum quod modus naturalis humanae cognitionis est, ut cognoscat simul per vim mentalem quae est intellectus, et corporalem quae est sensus. Et inde est quod homo non habet in cognoscendo liberum iudicium intellectus, nisi quando sensus fuerint in suo vigore bene dispositi, absque aliquo ligationis impedimento, alias, cum impediuntur, etiam iudicium intellectus impeditur, sicut in dormientibus patet.

he wrote this epistle, there were fourteen years between the time of his conversion to the time he wrote this epistle.

Therefore, some say quite probably that the Apostle had these visions during those three days after he was struck down by the Lord, when he remained neither seeing nor eating nor drinking (Acts 9:9).

But he recalls the time of his conversion to show that if he was so pleasing to Christ from the time of his conversion that he revealed such things to him, then how much more pleasing was he after fourteen years, when he had grown in charity before God and in the virtues and graces?

447. Third, let us see the high point of the vision, because he *was caught up to the third heaven*.

But it should be noted that it is one thing to be the victim of thievery and another to be rapt. Properly speaking, the former takes place when something is taken away from another in a secret way, hence, Joseph said: *for I was indeed stolen out of the land of the Hebrews* (Gen 40:13). A person is properly speaking rapt when something is taken suddenly and by force: *as the torrent that passes swiftly*, i.e., suddenly and rapidly, *in the valleys* (Job 6:15). Hence it is that plunderers who despoil violently are called ravagers.

But note that a man is said to be rapt from men, as Enoch: *he was caught up lest evil change his understanding or guile deceive his soul* (Wis 4:11); sometimes the soul is rapt from the body: *fool! This night your soul is required of you* (Luke 12:20). Sometimes a person is said to be rapt by himself, when for some reason he is made to be outside himself; and this is the same as ecstasy.

But a man is made to be outside himself both by his appetitive power and by his cognitive power. For by the former a person is in himself, when he cares only for things that are his own; but he is made to be outside himself when he does not care about things that are his own, but about things that pertain to others; and this is the work of charity. *Love does not insist on its own way* (1 Cor 13:5). Concerning this ecstasy Dionysius says in *The Divine Names*: *ecstasy is produced by divine love not permitting one to be a lover of self but of the beloved*, i.e., of the things loved.

But a person is made to be outside himself according to the cognitive power when he is raised up above the human mode to see something. This is the rapture about which the Apostle is speaking here.

448. But it should be noted that a mode natural to human knowing is that a man know simultaneously with his mental power, which is the intellect, and with a bodily one, which is a sense. This is why a man in knowing has a free judgment of the intellect, when the senses are well disposed in their vigor and not hindered by a fettering, as happens during sleep.

Tunc ergo homo efficitur extra se secundum cognitivam, quando removetur ab hac naturali dispositione cognitionis, quae est ut intellectus, ab usu sensuum et sensibilium rerum abstractus, ad aliqua videnda moveatur.

Quod quidem contingit dupliciter, uno modo per defectum virtutis, undecumque talis defectus contingat, sicut accidit in phreneticis et aliis mente captis, et haec quidem abstractio a sensibus non est elevatio hominis, sed potius depressio, quia virtus eorum debilitatur.

Alio vero modo per virtutem divinam, et tunc proprie dicitur elevatio, quia cum agens assimilet sibi patiens, abstractio quae fit virtute divina et est supra hominem, est aliquid altius, quam sit hominis natura.

449. Et ideo raptus, sic acceptus, diffinitur sic: raptus est ab eo quod est secundum naturam in id quod est supra naturam, vi superioris naturae, elevatio. In qua quidem definitione tangitur eius genus, dum dicitur elevatio; causa efficiens, quia vi superioris naturae; et duo termini motus, scilicet a quo et in quem, cum dicitur ab eo quod est secundum naturam, in id quod est supra naturam. Sic ergo patet de raptu.

450. Sequitur de termino raptus, scilicet ad quem, cum dicitur *usque in tertium caelum*.

Notandum est autem, quod tertium caelum tripliciter accipitur. Uno modo secundum ea, quae sunt infra animam; alio modo secundum ea, quae sunt in anima; tertio modo secundum ea, quae sunt supra animam.

Infra animam sunt omnia corpora, ut dicit Augustinus in libro *de Vera religione*. Et sic possumus accipere triplex caelum corporeum, scilicet aereum, sydereum et Empyreum. Et hoc modo dicitur quod Apostolus erat raptus usque ad tertium caelum, id est usque ad videndum ea quae sunt in caelo Empyreo, non ut existeret ibi, quia sic sciret si fuisset sive in corpore, sive extra corpus. Vel secundum Damascenum, qui non ponit caelum Empyreum, possumus dicere quod tertium caelum, ad quod raptus est Apostolus, est supra octavam sphaeram, ut scilicet evidenter videret ea quae sunt supra totam naturam corporalem.

451. Si autem accipiamus caelum secundum ea, quae sunt in ipsa anima, sic caelum debemus dicere aliquam altitudinem cognitionis, quae excedit naturalem cognitionem humanam.

Est autem triplex visio, scilicet corporalis, per quam videmus et cognoscimus corporalia, sive imaginaria, qua videmus similitudines corporum, et intellectualis, qua cognoscimus naturas rerum in seipsis. Nam proprie obiectum intellectus est, quod quid est. Huiusmodi autem visiones, si fiant secundum naturalem modum, puta, si video aliquid sensibile, si imaginor aliquid prius

Therefore a man is made to be outside himself when he is removed from this natural disposition for knowing, namely, when the intellect, being withdrawn from the use of the senses and sense-perceptible things, is moved to see certain things.

This occurs in two ways: first, by a lack of power, no matter how it is produced. This happens in phrenitis and other mental cases, so that this withdrawal from the senses is not a state of being elevated, but of being cast down, because their power has been weakened.

But the other way is by divine power, and then it is, properly speaking, an elevation, because since the agent makes the thing it works on to be like itself, a withdrawal produced by divine power and above men is something higher than man's nature.

449. Therefore, a rapture of this sort is defined as 'an elevation from that which is according to nature into that which is above nature, produced in virtue of a higher nature.' In this definition are mentioned its genus, when it is called an elevation; the efficient cause, because it is by the power of a higher nature; and the two termini of the change, namely, the terminus from which and into which, when it is described as being from that which is according to nature into what is above nature. Thus it is clear what rapture is.

450. Then he mentions the terminus reached by the rapture, when he says, *to the third heaven*.

But it should be noted that the third heaven is taken in three ways: in one way according to the things below the soul; in another way according to the things in the soul; and in a third way according to things above the soul.

Below the soul are all bodies, as Augustine says in the book *On the True Religion*. And so we can think of a threefold heaven: the ethereal, sidereal, and empyrean. In this way the Apostle is said to have been rapt to the third heaven, i.e., to see things in the empyrean heaven; not to exist there, because then he would have known whether he was in the body or out of the body. Or according to Damascene, who does not admit an empyrean heaven, we can say that the third heaven, to which the Apostle was rapt, is above the eighth sphere, so that he could clearly see the things which exist above all corporeal nature.

451. But if we take heaven according to the things in the soul itself, then we should call heaven some altitude of mind which transcends natural human knowledge.

Now there are three kinds of sight, namely, bodily, by which we can see and know bodies; spiritual or imaginary, by which we see likenesses of bodies; and intellectual, by which we know the nature of things in themselves. For the proper object of the intellect is the *what it is* of things. But such a sight of things, if it takes place according to the natural mode (e.g., if I see something visible, if I imagine

visum, si intelligo per phantasmata, non possunt dici caelum.

Sed tunc quaelibet istorum dicitur caelum, quando est supra naturalem facultatem humanae cognitionis, puta, si aliquid vides oculis corporalibus, supra facultatem naturae, sic es raptus ad primum caelum. Sicut Baltassar raptus est videns manum scribentis in pariete, ut dicitur Dan. V, 6. Si vero eleveris per imaginationem, vel per spiritum ad aliquid supernaturaliter cognoscendum, sic es raptus ad secundum caelum. Sic raptus fuit Petrus, quando vidit linteum immissum de caelo, ut dicitur Act. X, 10. Sed si aliquis videret ipsa intelligibilia et naturas ipsorum, non per sensibilia, nec per phantasmata, sic esset raptus usque ad tertium caelum.

452. Sed sciendum est, quod rapi ad primum caelum, est alienari a sensibus corporalibus. Unde cum nullus possit abstrahi totaliter a sensibus corporeis, manifestum est quod nullus potest dici simpliciter raptus in primum caelum, sed secundum quid, inquantum contingit aliquando aliquem sic esse intentum ad unum sensum quod abstrahitur ab actu aliorum.

Rapi ad secundum caelum est, quando aliquis alienatur a sensu ad videndum quaedam imaginabilia, unde tales semper consueverunt fieri in extasi. Et ideo, Act. X, 10, quando Petrus vidit linteum, dicitur quod factus fuit in extasi.

Paulus vero dicitur raptus ad tertium caelum, quia sic fuit alienatus a sensibus, et sublimatus ab omnibus corporalibus, ut videret intelligibilia nuda et pura eo modo quo vident angeli et anima separata, et, quod plus est, etiam ipsum Deum per essentiam, ut Augustinus expresse dicit XII *super Genesim ad litteram*, et in Glossa, et *ad Paulin*. in Libr. *de Videndo Deum*.

Nec etiam est probabile, ut Moyses, minister Veteris Testamenti ad Iudaeos, viderit Deum, et minister Novi Testamenti ad gentes et doctor gentium, hoc dono fuerit privatus. Unde dicit ipse supra III, 7: *si ministratio damnationis fuit in gloria*, et cetera. De Moyse autem quod viderit Deum per essentiam, patet. Nam ipse a Domino petivit Ex. XXXIII, v. 13: *ostende mihi faciem tuam.* Et licet tunc negatum fuerit sibi, non tamen dicitur, quod Dominus finaliter negaverit ei. Unde dicit Augustinus, quod concessum fuit ei per hoc quod dicitur Num. XII, 6 ss.: *si quis fuerit inter vos propheta Domini*, et cetera. *At vero non talis servus meus Moyses*, et cetera. Palam enim et non per aenigmata vidit Deum.

453. Sed numquid fieri potuisset Paulo, ut non raptus videret Deum?

Dicendum quod non. Nam impossibile est, quod Deus videatur in vita ista ab homine non alienato a sensibus,

something previously seen, or if I understand through phantasms) cannot be called heaven.

But each of these is called heaven when they are above the natural faculty of human knowledge. For example, if you see something with your bodily eyes above the faculty of nature, then you are rapt into the first heaven. This is the way Belshazzar was rapt, when he saw the handwriting on the wall (Dan 5:5). But if you are raised up by the imagination or spirit to know something supernaturally, then you are rapt to the second heaven. This is the way Peter was rapt, when he saw the linen sheet descending from heaven (Acts 10:11). But if a person were to see intelligible things themselves and their nature, not through sense-perceptible things not through phantasms, he would be rapt to the third heaven.

452. But it should be noted that to be rapt to the first heaven is to be alienated from the bodily senses. Hence, since no one can be totally withdrawn from the bodily senses, it is obvious that no one can be rapt in the strict sense to the first heaven, but only in a qualified sense, inasmuch as it sometimes happens that a person is so engrossed in one sense that he is withdrawn from the act of the others.

One is rapt to the second heaven when he is alienated from sense to see imaginable things; hence, such a person is always said to be in ecstasy. And so when Peter saw the linen sheet, it is said that he was in ecstasy (Acts 10:11).

But Paul is said to have been rapt to the third heaven, because he was so alienated from the senses and lifted above all bodily things that he saw intelligible things naked and pure in the way angels and separated souls see them. What is more, he saw God in his essence, as Augustine expressly says in *The Literal Meaning of Genesis*, and in a Gloss, and *ad Paulinam* in the book, *De Videndo Deum*.

Furthermore, it is not probable that Moses, the minister of the Old Testament to the Jews saw God, and the minister of the New Testament to the gentiles, the teacher of the gentiles, was deprived of this gift. Hence he says above: *if the ministration of condemnation is glory, much more does the ministration of justice abound in glory* (2 Cor 3:9). That Moses saw God in his essence is clear, for he begged God: *show me your face* (Exod 33:13). And although it was denied him at that time, it is not stated that the Lord finally denied him. Hence, Augustine says that this was granted him by reason of what is said: *if there is a prophet among you, I the Lord make myself known to him in a vision, I speak with him in a dream. Not so with my servant Moses; he is entrusted with all my house* (Num 12:5ff). For he saw God openly and not in a dark manner.

453. But would it have been possible for Paul to see God without being rapt?

I answer: no, for it is impossible that God be seen in this life by a man not alienated from his senses, because

quia nulla imago, nullum phantasma est sufficiens medium ad Dei essentiam ostendendam, ideo oportet quod abstrahatur et alienetur a sensibus.

454. Tertio modo accipiendo caelum secundum ea quae sunt supra animam: et sic triplex caelum est triplex hierarchia angelorum, et secundum hoc Apostolus raptus fuit usque ad tertium caelum, id est ad hoc, ut videret essentiam Dei ita clare, sicut vident eum angeli superioris et primae hierarchiae, qui sic vident Deum, quod immediate in ipso Deo recipiunt illuminationes, et cognoscunt divina mysteria. Et sic vidit Paulus. Sic ergo vidit Dei essentiam sicut angeli superioris hierarchiae.

455. Ergo bene videtur, quod Apostolus fuerit beatus, et per consequens fuerit immortalis.

Respondeo, quod licet viderit Deum per essentiam, non tamen fuit beatus simpliciter, sed solum secundum quid.

Sciendum est autem, quod visio Dei per essentiam fit per lumen aliquod, scilicet per lumen gloriae, de quo dicitur in Ps. XXXV, v. 10: *in lumine tuo videbimus lumen.* Sed aliquod lumen communicatur alicui per modum passionis, alicui vero per modum formae inhaerentis, sicut lumen solis invenitur in carbunculo et in stellis, ut forma inhaerens, id est connaturalis effecta, sed in aere invenitur ut forma transiens, et non permanens, quia transit, abeunte sole.

Similiter et lumen gloriae dupliciter menti infunditur. Uno modo per modum formae connaturalis factae et permanentis, et sic facit mentem simpliciter beatam. Et hoc modo infunditur beatis in patria, et ideo dicuntur comprehensores, et, ut ita dicam, visores. Alio modo contingit lumen gloriae mentem humanam sicut quaedam passio transiens, et sic mens Pauli fuit in raptu lumine gloriae illustrata. Unde etiam ipsum nomen raptus ostendit transeundo hoc esse factum. Et ideo non fuit simpliciter glorificatus, nec habuit dotem gloriae, cum illa claritas non fuerit effecta proprietas. Et propter hoc non fuit derivata ab anima in corpus, nec in hoc statu perpetuo permansit. Unde solum actum beati habuit in ipso raptu, sed non fuit beatus.

Sic per hoc patet quid Apostolus scivit in suo raptu, scilicet videntis conditionem, visionis tempus et visionis fastigium.

456. Sequitur quid nescivit, scilicet utrum esset in corpore, vel extra corpus, quod tamen dicit Deum scire. Unde dicit *sive in corpore, sive extra corpus, nescio, Deus scit*; quod quidam intelligere voluerunt, ut raptus referatur ad corpus, dicentes Apostolum dixisse se nescire, non quidem an anima esset coniuncta corpori in illo raptu an non, sed esset raptus secundum animam et corpus simul, ut simul corporaliter portaretur in

no image or phantasm is a sufficient medium for showing God's essence; therefore, he must be abstracted and alienated from the senses.

454. In a third way, by taking heaven according to things above the soul; in this way the three heavens are the three hierarchies of angels. According to this the Apostle was rapt to the third heaven, i.e., to see God's essence as clearly as the angels of the higher and first hierarchy see him, because they see God in such a way as to receive illumination in God himself and to know the divine mysteries. This is the way Paul saw. Thus therefore he saw the essence of God as do the angels of the higher heirarchy.

455. But if he saw God as the angels of the higher and first hierarchy do, then it seems that the Apostle was beatified and, consequently, was immortal.

I answer that although he saw God in his essence, he was not absolutely beatified, but only in a qualified sense.

Yet it should be noted that the vision of God by essence takes place by means of a certain light, namely, the light of glory, of which it is said: *in your light we see light* (Ps 36:9). But light is communicated to some things after the manner of a passing quality and to others after the manner of an inhering form, i.e., connaturally produced; but it is found in the air as a passing form and not as a permanent form, because it vanishes when the sun is absent.

Similarly, the light of glory is infused in the mind in two ways: in one way, after the manner of a form connaturally made and permanent, and then it makes a mind beatified in the strict sense. This is the way it is infused in the beatified in heaven. Hence they are called comprehenders and, so to say, seers. In another way the light of glory affects a human mind as a passing quality; this is the way Paul's mind in rapture was enlightened by the light of glory. Hence, the very name, 'rapture,' suggests that this was done in a passing manner. Consequently, he was not glorified in the strict sense or had the mark of glory, because that brightness was not produced as a property. As a result it was not derived from the soul in the body, nor did he remain in this state permanently. Hence, when he was in rapture, he had only the act of the beatified, but he was not beatified.

Thus it is clear what the Apostle saw in his rapture, namely, the condition of the beholder, the time of the vision, and the high point of the vision.

456. Then he tells what he did not know, namely, whether he was in the body or out of the body, although he says that God knew. Hence he says, ***whether in the body, I do not know, or out of the body, I do not know: God knows.*** Some interpret this as meaning that the rapture referred to his body, saying that the Apostle did not say he did not know whether the soul was joined to the body in that rapture, but whether he was rapt according to the soul and

caelum, sicut Habacuc portatus fuit Dan. ult.; an secundum animam tantum esset in visionibus Dei, ut dicitur Ez. c. VIII, 3: *in visione adduxit me in terram Israel.*

Et iste fuit intellectus cuiusdam Iudaei, quem exponit Hieronymus in prologo super Danielem, ubi dicit: *denique et Apostolum nostrum dicit non fuisse ausum affirmare se raptum in corpore, sed dixisse: sive in corpore,* et cetera.

Sed hunc intellectum Augustinus maxime improbat II *super Genesim ad litteram,* quia non conveniunt cum aliis verbis Apostoli. Apostolus enim dicit se raptum usque in tertium caelum; unde scivit pro certo, illud fuisse verum caelum. Scivit ergo an illud caelum esset corporeum an incorporeum, id est res incorporea. Sed si fuit incorporeum, scivit quod corporaliter ibi rapi non potuit, quia in re incorporea non potest esse corpus. Si vero corporeum fuerat, scivit quod non fuit ibi anima sine corpore; quia anima coniuncta corpori non potest esse in loco ubi non est corpus, nisi caelum incorporeum dicatur similitudo caeli corporei. Sed si sic, Apostolus non dixisset se scire quod esset raptus in tertium caelum, id est in similitudinem caeli, quia, pari ratione, dicere potuisset quod fuisset raptus in corpore, id est in similitudine corporis.

457. Dicendum est ergo, secundum Augustinum, quod divinam essentiam nullus in hac vita positus, et in hac mortali vita vivens, videre potest. Unde dicit Dominus Ex. c. XXXIII, 20: *non videbit me homo, et vivet,* id est non videbit me homo, nisi totaliter separetur a corpore, ita scilicet quod anima eius non insit corpori, ut forma, vel si inest ut forma, tamen mens eius omnino in huiusmodi visione totaliter alienetur a sensibus. Et ideo dicendum est, quod hoc quod Apostolus dicit se nescire, utrum scilicet in illa visione anima eius fuerit totaliter separata a corpore, unde dicit **sive extra corpus**; vel utrum anima eius extiterit in corpore, ut forma, tamen mens eius fuerit a sensibus corporeis alienata, unde dicit **sive in corpore.** Et hoc etiam alii concedunt.

body simultaneously, so as to have been transported bodily into heaven as Habakkuk was transported (Dan 14:35–39), or whether it was according to the soul only that he enjoyed the vision of God, as it is said: *he brought me in visions of God to Jerusalem* (Ezek 8:3).

This was the way a certain Jew understood, as Jerome mentions in the prologue to Daniel, where he says: *finally, he says that even our Apostle does not dare to say that he was rapt in the body, but he said: whether in the body or out of the body I do not know, God knows.*

But Augustine disproves this interpretation in *The Literal Meaning of Genesis,* because it does not agree with the other words of the Apostle. For the Apostle says that he was rapt to the third heaven; hence he knew for certain that it was the third heaven. Consequently, he knew whether that heaven was corporeal or incorporeal, i.e., an incorporeal thing. But if it was incorporeal, he knew that he could not have been rapt there bodily, because a body cannot exist in an incorporeal thing. But if it had been corporeal, he knew that the soul was not there without the body, because the soul joined to the body cannot be in a place where there is no body, unless the incorporeal heaven is called a likeness of the bodily heaven. But if that were the case, the Apostle would not have said that he knew he was rapt to the third heaven, i.e., to a likeness of heaven, because by that same token it could be said that he was rapt in the body, i.e., in the likeness of a body.

457. Therefore it must be admitted according to Augustine that no one set in this life and living this mortal life can see the divine essence. Hence, the Lord says: *for man shall not see me and live* (Exod 33:20), i.e., no man will see me, unless he is entirely separated from the body, namely, in such a way that his soul is not in the body as a form, or if it is as a form, nevertheless his mind is totally and altogether alienated from the sense in such a vision. Therefore, it must be said that the Apostle says he does not know whether the soul was entirely separated from the body in that vision. Hence he says, **or out of the body**, or whether his soul existed in the body as a form, but his mind was alienated from the bodily senses; hence, he says, **whether in the body.** Even others concede this.

Lecture 2

12:3Et scio hujusmodi hominem sive in corpore, sive extra corpus nescio, Deus scit: [n. 458]

12:4quoniam raptus est in paradisum: et audivit arcana verba, quae non licet homini loqui. [n. 461]

12:5Pro hujusmodi gloriabor: pro me autem nihil gloriabor nisi in infirmitatibus meis. [n. 464]

12:6Nam etsi voluero gloriari, non ero insipiens: veritatem enim dicam: parco autem, ne quis me existimet supra id quod videt in me, aut aliquid audit ex me. [n. 468]

12:3καὶ οἶδα τὸν τοιοῦτον ἄνθρωπον, εἴτε ἐν σώματι εἴτε χωρὶς τοῦ σώματος οὐκ οἶδα, ὁ θεὸς οἶδεν,

12:4ὅτι ἡρπάγη εἰς τὸν παράδεισον καὶ ἤκουσεν ἄρρητα ῥήματα ἃ οὐκ ἐξὸν ἀνθρώπῳ λαλῆσαι.

12:5ὑπὲρ τοῦ τοιούτου καυχήσομαι, ὑπὲρ δὲ ἐμαυτοῦ οὐ καυχήσομαι εἰ μὴ ἐν ταῖς ἀσθενείαις.

12:6Ἐὰν γὰρ θελήσω καυχήσασθαι, οὐκ ἔσομαι ἄφρων, ἀλήθειαν γὰρ ἐρῶ· φείδομαι δέ, μή τις εἰς ἐμὲ λογίσηται ὑπὲρ ὃ βλέπει με ἢ ἀκούει [τι] ἐξ ἐμοῦ

12:3And I know such a man (whether in the body, or out of the body, I do not know: God knows): [n. 458]

12:4That he was caught up into paradise and heard secret words which it is not granted to man to utter. [n. 461]

12:5For such a one, I will glory: but for myself I will glory nothing but in my infirmities. [n. 464]

12:6For even if I should have a mind to glory, I shall not be foolish: for I will say the truth. But I forbear, lest any man should think more of me than what he sees in me, or anything he hears from me. [n. 468]

---

458. Posito primo raptu, ponitur consequenter secundus raptus. Et duo facit:

primo ponitur raptus,

secundo raptus excellentia, ibi *audivit arcana*, et cetera.

459. Sed notandum, quod Glossa dicit istum raptum esse alium a primo. Et si bene consideretur, bis legitur aliquid de Apostolo, ad quod possunt isti duo raptus referri. Nam Act. IX, 9 legitur de eo quod stetit tribus diebus non videns et nihil manducans, neque bibens, et ad hoc potest referri primus raptus, ut scilicet tunc fuerit raptus usque ad tertium caelum. Sed Act. XXII, 17 legitur quod factus est in templo in stupore mentis, et ad hoc refertur iste secundus raptus.

Sed hoc non videtur verisimile, quia quando in stupore mentis factus fuit, missus iam fuerat in carcerem Apostolus; sed hanc epistolam scripsit Apostolus diu ante, unde prius scripta fuit haec epistola, quam Apostolus fuisset in stupore.

Et ideo dicendum est, quod differt iste raptus a primo, quantum ad id in quod raptus est. Nam in primo raptus est in tertium caelum; in secundo vero in Paradisum Dei.

460. Si vero aliquis tertium caelum acciperet corporaliter, secundum primam acceptionem caelorum superius positam, vel si fuerit visio imaginaria, posset similiter dicere paradisum corporalem, ut diceretur quod fuerit raptus in paradisum terrestrem.

Sed hoc est contra intentionem Augustini, secundum quem dicimus, quod fuit raptus in tertium caelum, id est visionem intelligibilium, secundum quod in se ipsis et in propriis naturis videntur, ut supra dictum est. Unde

458. Having spoken of the first rapture, the Apostle speaks of a second rapture.

First, he mentions the rapture;

second, its excellence, at *and heard secret words*.

459. It should be noted that a Gloss says that this rapture was distinct from the first, and if one considers the matter well, two things are written of the Apostle to which these two raptures can be referred. For in Acts it is recorded that he remained for three days without seeing and without taking food or drink (Acts 9:9); and the first rapture can be referred to this event, namely, that he was rapt to the third heaven at that time. But in Acts it also says that he was in a trance in the temple (Acts 22:17); hence the second rapture can refer to this.

But this does not seem to be a similar case, because when he was in the trance, the Apostle had been cast into prison; but the Apostle wrote this epistle long before that, whence before this letter was written, the Apostle had been in a trance.

Therefore it must be said that this rapture differs from the first in regard to that into which he was rapt. For in the first rapture he had been rapt to the third heaven, but in the second to the paradise of God

460. But if you take the third heaven in a corporeal sense according to the first acceptation of the heavens, as mentioned above, or if it was an imaginary vision, it could be called a bodily paradise, so that he was rapt to an earthly paradise.

But this is against the author's intention, according to whom we say that he was rapt to the third heaven, i.e., to a vision of intelligible things according to which they are seen in themselves and in their own natures, as has been

secundum hoc oportet non aliud intelligere per caelum, et aliud per paradisum, sed unum et idem per utrumque, scilicet gloriam sanctorum, sed secundum aliud et aliud.

Caelum enim dicit altitudinem quamdam cum claritate, paradisus vero quamdam iucundam suavitatem. In sanctis autem beatis et angelis Deum videntibus sunt excellenter haec duo, quia est in eis excellentissima claritas, qua Deum vident, et summa suavitas, qua Deo fruuntur. Et ideo dicuntur esse in caelo quantum ad claritatem, et in paradiso quantum ad suavitatem. Is. LXVI, 14: *videbitis et gaudebitis*, et cetera.

Fuit ergo utrumque collatum Apostolo, ut scilicet sublimaretur ad illam altissimam claritatem cognitionis, et hoc significat cum dicit **ad tertium caelum**, et ut sentiret suavitatem divinae dulcedinis, unde dicit **in paradisum**. Ps. XXX, 20: *magna multitudo dulcedinis tuae*, et cetera. Apoc. II, 17: *vincenti dabo manna absconditum*, et cetera. Et ista dulcedo est gaudium de divina fruitione, de qua Matth. XXV, 21 dicitur *intra in gaudium Domini tui*.

Sic ergo patet terminus raptus, quia **in paradisum**, id est in eam dulcedinem, qua indeficienter reficiuntur illi, qui sunt in caelesti Ierusalem.

461. Sequitur consequenter ipsius raptus excellentia, quia **audivit arcana verba, quae non licet homini loqui.** Et hoc potest dupliciter exponi. Uno modo, ut **homini** construatur cum **licet** et **loqui**; et sensus est: **audivit arcana verba**, id est percepit intima cognitione, secreta de Dei essentia quasi per verba, quae scilicet verba non est licitum ut homini dicantur.

Alio modo, ut **homini** construatur solum cum **non licet**, et tunc est sensus: **audivit verba**, etc., quae verba non licet homini loqui, homini scilicet imperfecto.

462. Sciendum autem, quod secundum Augustinum, Paulus est raptus ad videndum divinam essentiam, quae quidem non potest videri per aliquam similitudinem creatam. Unde manifestum est, quod illud quod Paulus vidit de essentia divina nulla lingua humana potest dici, alias Deus non esset incomprehensibilis.

Et ideo secundum primam expositionem dicendum est **audivit**, id est consideravit **arcana verba**, id est magnificentiam divinitatis, quam nullus homo potest loqui.

Dicit autem **audivit** pro *vidit*, quia illa consideratio fuit secundum interiorem actum animae, in quo idem est auditus et visus, secundum quod dicitur Num. XII, 8: *ore ad os loquitur ei et palam*, et cetera. Dicitur autem illa consideratio visio, inquantum Deus videtur in hoc, et locutio, inquantum homo in ipsa instruitur de divinis.

said above. Hence, according to this we must not understand one thing by heaven and another by paradise, but one and the same thing by both, namely, the glory of the saints, but according to one thing in one case and according to another thing in the other case.

For heaven suggests a certain loftiness accompanied by brightness, but paradise a certain joyful pleasantness. Now these two things are present in an excellent way in the saints and angels who see God, because there is present in them a most excellent brightness by which they see God, and a supreme agreeableness by which they enjoy God. Therefore, they are said to be in heaven as to the brightness and in paradise as to the pleasantness. *You shall see, and your heart shall rejoice* (Isa 66:14).

Therefore, both of these were conferred on the Apostle, namely to be raised up to that most excellent clearness of knowledge, which he signifies when he says, **to the third heaven**, and to experience the agreeableness of the divine sweetness; hence he says, **into paradise**: *O how great is the multitude of your sweetness, O Lord* (Ps 31:20); *to him who conquers I will give some of the hidden manna* (Rev 2:17). This sweetness is the delight experienced in enjoying God, and is mentioned: *enter into the joy of your master* (Matt 25:13).

Thus the terminus of the rapture is clear, namely, **into paradise**, i.e., into that sweetness with which those who are in the heavenly Jerusalem are unceasingly refreshed.

461. Then he mentions the excellence of that rapture, because he **heard secret words which it is not granted to man to utter**. This can be explained in two ways: in one way so that the word, **man**, is construed with **granted to** and **utter**. Then the sense is this: **he heard secret words**, i.e., he perceived an intimate understanding of God's secret essence, as though by words, which words it is not lawful to be uttered by a man.

In the other way, so that **man** is construed only with **not granted to**. Then the sense is this: **he heard words**, which it is not lawful to utter to a man, i.e., to an imperfect man.

462. But it should be noted according to Augustine that Paul was rapt to a vision of the divine essence, which of course, cannot be seen by any created likeness. Hence, it is clear that what Paul saw of the divine essence cannot be described by any human tongue; otherwise, God would not be incomprehensible.

Therefore, according to the first explanation it must be said: **he heard**, i.e., considered, **secret words**, i.e., the magnificence of the godhead, which no man can utter.

He says **heard** for *saw* because that consideration was according to an interior act of the soul, in which the same is heard and seen, as it is said: *for I speak to him mouth to mouth* (Num 12:8). That consideration is called a vision, inasmuch as God is seen in it; and an utterance inasmuch as man is instructed about divine things in it.

463. Et quia huiusmodi spiritualia non sunt pandenda simplicibus et imperfectis, sed perfectis, secundum quod dicitur I Cor. II, 6: *sapientiam loquimur inter perfectos*, ideo, secundo modo, exponitur quod secreta, quae ibi audivit, **non licet** mihi **loqui homini**, id est imperfectis, sed spiritualibus, inter quos loquimur sapientiam. Prov. XXV, 2: *gloria Dei est celare verbum*, id est hoc ipsum, quod necesse est celare magnalia Dei, pertinet ad gloriam Dei. Psalmus secundum translationem Hieronymi: *tibi silet laus, Deus*, id est quod incomprehensibilis est verbis nostris.

464. Deinde cum dicit **pro huiusmodi gloriabor**, etc., ostendit quomodo se habet ad gloriam. Et

circa hoc tria facit.

Primo ostendit se non gloriari de huiusmodi revelationibus;

secundo insinuat se habere aliquid praeter illud unde gloriari possit, ibi **nam et si voluero**, etc.;

tertio assignat causam, quare non gloriatur de omnibus, ibi **parco autem, ne quis**, et cetera.

465. Circa primum sciendum est, quod hoc quod dicit **pro huiusmodi autem gloriabor**, etc., potest dupliciter legi.

Uno modo, ut Apostolus ostendat se esse ipsum pro quo gloriatur, ut scilicet ipse sit qui vidit has visiones; alio modo, ut ostendat quod alius sit qui vidit has visiones.

Sciendum est enim, quod in homine duo possunt considerari, scilicet donum Dei et humana conditio. Si ergo aliquis gloriatur in aliquo dono Dei, ut a Deo accepto, illa est bona gloria, quia sic in domino gloriatur, ut dictum est supra, X, 17. Sed si gloriatur de illo dono, sicut a se habito, tunc mala est gloriatio huiusmodi. I Cor. IV, 7: *quid habes quod non accepisti? Si autem accepisti, quid gloriaris quasi non acceperis?*

Dicit ergo Apostolus, secundum hoc: **pro huiusmodi**, scilicet visionibus et donis Dei mihi collatis, **gloriabor, pro me autem** non, id est non gloriabor inde, quasi a me acceperim, quia a Deo habui. Sed si pro me oportet gloriari, **nihil gloriabor, nisi in infirmitatibus meis**, id est non habeo unde possim gloriari, nisi de infirma conditione mea.

466. Si autem exponatur, ut ostendat alium esse, qui vidit, etsi ipse sit, tunc est sensus, ut quasi loquatur de quodam alio, dicens **pro huiusmodi gloriabor**, id est pro illo homine, qui hoc vidit et qui haec dona recepit, gloriabor; sed **pro me**, quasi velim manifestare me esse talem, **nihil gloriabor, nisi in infirmitatibus meis**, id est de tribulationibus quas patior.

467. Sed quia isti possent sibi dicere: *O Apostole, non est mirum si non gloriaris, quia non habes unde glorieris*; ideo Apostolus ostendit quod etiam praeter illas

463. And because such spiritual things are not to be disclosed to the simple and imperfect, but to the perfect, as it is said: *yet among the mature we do impart wisdom* (1 Cor 2:6), it is explained in the second way, so that the secrets he heard there **it is granted to man to utter**, i.e., to the imperfect, but to the spiritual, among whom we speak wisdom: *it is the glory of God to conceal things* (Prov 25:2), i.e., the fact that it is necessary to conceal the marvelous things of God pertains to God's glory. The psalm is according to the translation of Jerome: *your praise, O God, is silent to you* (Ps 108:2), that is, cannot be comprehended by our words.

464. Then when he says, **for such a one, I will glory**, he shows how he reacted to this glory.

In regard to this he does three things.

First, he shows that he did not glory in such revelations;

second, he suggests that he has something else in which to glory, at **for even if I should have a mind to glory**;

third, he gives the reason why he does not glory about all things, at **but I forbear, lest any man**.

465. In regard to the first it should be noted that the statement, **for such a one, I will glory: but for myself I will glory nothing but in my infirmities**, can be read in two ways.

In one way so that the Apostle is showing that he is the one in whom he glories, i.e., that he is the one who saw these visions. In another way, to show that it was someone else who saw these visions.

For it should be noted that there are two things to consider in man, namely, the gift of God and the human condition. If a person glories in a gift of God as received from God, that glorying is good, as has been stated above (2 Cor 10:17). But if he glories in that gift as though he had it of himself, then such glorying is evil: *what have you that you did not receive? If then you received it, why do you boast as if it were not a gift?* (1 Cor 4:7).

According to this, therefore, the Apostle says, **for such a one**, namely, for the visions and gifts conferred on me by God, **I will glory: but for myself I will glory nothing**, i.e., will not glory in them as though I were their source, because I had them from God. But if I must glory for myself, **I will glory nothing but in my infirmities**, i.e., I have nothing in which I can glory save in my own condition.

466. But if it is explained as showing that it was someone else who saw, even if it was he, then the sense is as though he were speaking of someone, saying, **for such a one, I will glory**, i.e., for the man who saw this and who received these gifts I will glory; **but for myself** as wishing to show that I am such a one, **I will glory nothing but in my infirmities**, i.e., in the tribulations I suffer.

467. But because they could say to him, *O Apostle, it is not strange that you do not glory, because you have nothing in which to glory*, he shows that even besides these visions

visiones habet aliquid unde possit gloriari, dicens: licet pro huiusmodi homine glorier, et non pro me, tamen etiam bene pro me possum gloriari. *Nam, si voluero gloriari*, etc., vel pro huiusmodi tribulationibus, vel pro aliis mihi a Deo collatis, vel etiam pro infirmitatibus, *non ero insipiens*, id est non insipienter agam. Et quare? *Veritatem enim dicam* de aliis, de quibus praeter dictas visiones gloriari possum.

Dicit autem *non ero insipiens*, quia gloriabatur de his quae habebat. Quando enim gloriatur quis de his quae non habet, stulte gloriatur. Apoc. III, 17: *dicis quia dives sum, et nullius egeo, et nescis*, et cetera. Et quia gloriabatur ex causa sufficienti, ut ex praedictis est manifestum.

468. Consequenter autem cum dicit *parco autem*, etc., ostendit rationem quare non gloriatur de omnibus si potest gloriari; quae quidem ratio est, ut eis parcat.

Unde dicit *parco autem*, etc., quasi dicat: possem de pluribus aliis gloriari, sed *parco*, id est parce glorior, vel *parco* vobis commendando me, nolens esse onerosus vobis. Nam talia mihi Deus concessit, quae si sciretis, reputaretis me multo maiorem, et haec sunt dona gratuita multa, quae habebat Apostolus. Ex quibus homines huius mundi consueverunt plus commendare homines, et maiores eos reputare quam ex gratum facientibus. Et ideo dicit: nolo ex gratuitis commendari, et ideo *parco*, id est non glorior.

Et quare? *Ne quis existimet me*, commendare, vel gloriari, *supra id quod videt*, et cetera.

469. Vel aliter: homo dupliciter cognoscitur, per conversationem et doctrinam suam; Apostolus autem nolebat aliqua de se dicere, licet posset, quae excedebant et vitam et doctrinam suam. Et ideo *parco autem, ne quis existimet me* esse *supra id quod videt*, de conversatione mea exteriori, *aut audit aliquid ex me*, id est ex doctrina praedicationis, et exhortationis, et instructionis meae: quia forte crederent eum esse vel immortalem, vel angelum. Prov. XI, 12: *vir prudens tacebit*. Prov. XXIX, 11: *totum spiritum suum profert stultus, sapiens differt*, et cetera.

470. Vel dicit *parco autem*, etc., pro detractoribus, scilicet pseudo, qui dicebant eum gloriari ex elatione et non ex causa, neque de his quae in ipso erant.

Et ideo dicit *parco autem*, id est parce glorior, *ne quis* pseudo *existimet me* excedere elationis spiritu, *supra id*, id est in aliquid, *quod videt in me, vel audit ex me*, id est supra posse meritorium. Ps. CXXX, 1: *Domine, non*

he has something in which to glory. Although I might glory in such a man and not in myself, yet I can rightfully glory in myself, *for even if I should have a mind to glory* either in such tribulations or in other things bestowed on me by God, or even for my infirmity, *I shall not be foolish*, i.e., I will not act foolishly. Why? *For I will say the truth* about the other things in which I can glory besides those visions.

He says, *I shall not be foolish*, because he gloried in the things he had; for when a person glories in things he does not have, he is speaking foolishly: *for you say, I am rich, I have prospered, and I need nothing; not knowing that you are wretched, pitiable, poor, blind, and naked* (Rev 3:17); and because he gloried with sufficient reason, as is clear from the foregoing.

468. Then when he says, *but I forbear*, he indicates the reason he does not glory in everything, if he can glory, the reason being that he wishes to spare them.

Hence he says, *but I forbear, lest any man should think more of me than what he sees in me, or anything that he hears from me*. As if to say: I could glory in many other things, but *I forbear*, i.e., I glory sparingly, or *I forbear* commending myself, lest I become burdensome to you. For God has conferred on me such things that if you knew them, you would regard me as much greater; and these are the many charismatic gifts which the Apostle had and for which the men of this world are wont to commend others and regard them as great more than for doing something pleasing. Hence he says, I do not wish to be commended on these gifts; therefore *I forbear*, i.e., I do not glory.

Why? *Lest any man should think*, that is, commend or boast, *more of me than what he sees in me, or anything he hears from me*.

469. Or another way: man is known in two ways: by his manner of life and by his doctrine. Although he could have done so, the Apostle did not wish to say about himself certain things which went beyond his life and doctrine. Consequently, *I forbear, lest any man should think more of me than what he sees in me*, i.e., in my outward conduct, *or anything he hears from me*, i.e., from the doctrine of my preaching and exhortation and instruction, because they might perhaps think him immortal or an angel: *a man of understanding remains silent* (Prov 11:12): *a fool gives full vent to his anger, but a wise man quietly holds it back* (Prov 29:11).

470. Or he says: *but I forbear*, on account of his detractors, namely, the false apostles, who said that he glories from elation without cause or for things that were not in him.

Therefore, he says, *but I forbear*, i.e., I glory sparingly, *lest any man*, i.e., the false apostles, *should think of me* as having an excessive spirit of elation, *more than what he sees in me, or anything he hears from me*, i.e., above the

est exaltatum cor meum, et cetera. Eccli. c. III, 20: *quanto magnus es*, et cetera.

power of my merits: *O Lord, my heart is not lifted up, my eyes are not raised too high* (Ps 131:1); *the greater you are, the more humble yourself in all things* (Sir 3:10).

Lecture 3

12:7Et ne magnitudo revelationum extollat me, datus est mihi stimulus carnis meae angelus Satanae, qui me colaphizet. [n. 471]

12:8Propter quod ter Dominum rogavi ut discederet a me: [n. 475]

12:9et dixit mihi: sufficit tibi gratia mea: nam virtus in infirmitate perficitur. Libenter igitur gloriabor in infirmitatibus meis, ut inhabitet in me virtus Christi. [n. 476]

12:10Propter quod placeo mihi in infirmitatibus meis, in contumeliis, in necessitatibus, in persecutionibus, in angustiis pro Christo: cum enim infirmor, tunc potens sum. [n. 481]

12:7καὶ τῇ ὑπερβολῇ τῶν ἀποκαλύψεων. διὸ ἵνα μὴ ὑπεραίρωμαι, ἐδόθη μοι σκόλοψ τῇ σαρκί, ἄγγελος σατανᾶ, ἵνα με κολαφίζῃ, ἵνα μὴ ὑπεραίρωμαι.

12:8ὑπὲρ τούτου τρὶς τὸν κύριον παρεκάλεσα ἵνα ἀποστῇ ἀπ᾽ ἐμοῦ.

12:9καὶ εἴρηκέν μοι· ἀρκεῖ σοι ἡ χάρις μου, ἡ γὰρ δύναμις ἐν ἀσθενείᾳ τελεῖται. Ἥδιστα οὖν μᾶλλον καυχήσομαι ἐν ταῖς ἀσθενείαις μου, ἵνα ἐπισκηνώσῃ ἐπ᾽ ἐμὲ ἡ δύναμις τοῦ Χριστοῦ.

12:10διὸ εὐδοκῶ ἐν ἀσθενείαις, ἐν ὕβρεσιν, ἐν ἀνάγκαις, ἐν διωγμοῖς καὶ στενοχωρίαις, ὑπὲρ Χριστοῦ· ὅταν γὰρ ἀσθενῶ, τότε δυνατός εἰμι.

12:7And lest the greatness of the revelations should exalt me, there was given to me a sting of my flesh, an angel of Satan, to buffet me. [n. 471]

12:8On account of this, I besought the Lord three times that it might depart from me. [n. 475]

12:9And he said to me: my grace is sufficient for you: for power is made perfect in infirmity. Gladly therefore will I glory in my infirmities, that the power of Christ may dwell in me. [n. 476]

12:10Because of this, I am pleased in my infirmities, in reproaches, in necessities, in persecutions, in distresses, for Christ. For when I am weak, then am I powerful. [n. 481]

---

471. Hic agit de remedio adhibito contra superbiam. Et

circa hoc tria facit.

Primo enim ponit remedium adhibitum;

secundo manifestat suam orationem de remedio removendo, ibi **propter quod ter Dominum**, etc.;

tertio insinuat Domini responsionem assignantis rationem de adhibito remedio, ibi **et dixit mihi Dominus**, et cetera.

472. Circa primum sciendum est quod plerumque sapiens medicus procurat et permittit supervenire infirmo minorem morbum, ut maiorem curet, vel vitet, sicut ut curet spasmum, procurat febrem; hoc evidenter in se beatus Apostolus a medico animarum Domino nostro Iesu Christo factum ostendit. Christus enim, velut medicus animarum summus, ad curandum graves animae morbos permittit plurimos electos suos et magnos in morbis corporum graviter affligi, et, quod plus est, ad curandum maiora crimina, permittit incidere in minora etiam mortalia.

Inter omnia vero peccata gravius peccatum est superbia. Nam sicut caritas est radix et initium virtutum, sic superbia est radix et initium omnium vitiorum. Eccli. X, 15: *initium omnis peccati superbia*. Quod sic patet: caritas enim ideo dicitur radix omnium virtutum, quia coniungit Deo, qui est ultimus finis. Unde sicut finis est principium omnium operabilium, ita caritas est principium omnium virtutum. Superbia autem avertit a Deo. Superbia enim est appetitus inordinatus propriae excellentiae. Si enim aliquis appetit aliquam excellentiam sub

471. Here he speaks of the remedy against pride.

In regard to this he does three things.

First, he mentions the remedy applied;

second, he discloses his prayer to have the remedy removed, at **on account of this**;

third, he tells the Lord's answer giving the reason for the remedy applied, at **and he said to me**.

472. In regard to the first it should be noted that very often a wise physician procures and permits a lesser disease to come over a person in order to cure or avoid a greater one. Thus, to cure a spasm he procures a fever. This the Apostle shows was done to him by the physician of souls, our Lord Jesus Christ. For Christ, as the supreme physician of souls, in order to cure grave sins, permits many of his elect to be afflicted gravely in diseases of the body, and which is more, for curing greater sins, permits them to fall into lesser, and even mortal sins.

But among all the sins the gravest is pride, for just as charity is the root and beginning of the virtues, so pride is the root and beginning of all vices: *pride is the beginning of all sin* (Sir 10:15). This is made clear in the following way. Charity is called the root of all the virtues, because it unites one to God, who is the ultimate end. Hence, just as the end is the beginning of all actions to be performed, so charity is the beginning of all the virtues. But pride turns away from God, for pride is an inordinate desire for one's own excellence. For if a person seeks some excellence under God, if

Deo, si moderate quidem appetit, et propter bonum, sustineri potest; si vero non debito ordine, potest quidem alia vitia incurrere, scilicet ambitionis, avaritiae, seu inanis gloriae, et huiusmodi, tamen non est proprie superbia, nisi quando quis appetit excellentiam, non ordinando illam ad Deum. Et ideo superbia proprie dicta separat a Deo, et est radix omnium vitiorum, et pessimum omnium; propter quod *Deus resistit superbis*, ut dicitur Iac. IV, 6.

Quia ergo in bonis est maxime materia huius vitii, scilicet superbiae, quia eius materia est bonum, permittit aliquando electos suos impediri, ex aliqua sui parte, ut per infirmitatem, vel per aliquem defectum, et aliquando etiam per peccatum mortale, ab huiusmodi bono, ut sic ex hac parte humilientur, quod ex illa non superbiant, et homo sic humiliatus recognoscat se suis viribus stare non posse. Unde dicitur Rom. VIII, 28: *diligentibus Deum omnia*, etc., non quidem ex eorum peccato, sed ex ordinatione Dei.

473. Quia igitur Apostolus magnam habebat superbiendi materiam, et quantum ad specialem electionem, qua a Domino electus est, Act. IX, 15: *vas electionis est*, etc., et quantum ad secretorum Dei cognitionem, quia hic dicit se **raptum in tertium caelum** et **in Paradisum**, ubi **audivit arcana verba quae non licet homini loqui**, et quantum ad malorum perpessionem, quia supra XI, 23: **in carceribus plurimis, in infirmitatibus, ter virgis caesus sum**, etc., et quantum ad virginalem integritatem, quia *volo omnes esse sicut et ego*, I Cor. VII, 7, et quantum ad bonorum operationem, quia, supra, *plus omnibus laboravi*, et specialiter quantum ad maximam scientiam qua emicuit, quae specialiter inflat: ideo Dominus adhibuit ei remedium, ne in superbiam extolleretur.

Et hoc est quod dicit **et ne magnitudo** revelationis mihi factae **extollat me**, in superbiam. Eccli. VI, 2: *non te extollas in cogitatione animae tuae velut taurus*, et cetera. Ps. LXXXVII, 16: *exaltatus autem humiliatus*, et cetera.

Et dicit, ut ostendat sibi factas fuisse revelationes praedictas, **datus est mihi**, id est ad meam utilitatem et humiliationem. Iob XXX, v. 22: *elevasti me, et quasi super ventum ponens*, et cetera. **Datus est**, inquam, **mihi stimulus**, crucians corpus meum per infirmitatem corporis, ut anima sanetur; quia, ad litteram, dicitur quod fuit vehementer afflictus dolore iliaco. Vel **stimulus carnis meae**, id est concupiscentiae surgentis ex carne mea, a qua multum infestabatur. Rom. VII, 15: *non enim, quod volo*, etc.: *igitur ego ipse mente servio legi Dei*,

he seeks it moderately and for a good end, it can be endured. But if it is not done with due order, he can even fall into other vices, such as ambition, avarice, vainglory and the like. Yet it is not, properly speaking, pride, unless a person seeks excellence without ordaining it to God. Therefore pride, properly called, separates from God and is the root of all vices and the worst of them. This is why *God resists the proud* (Jas 4:6).

Therefore, because the matter of this vice, that is, pride, is mainly found in things that are good, because its matter is something good, God sometimes permits his elect to be prevented by something on their part, e.g., infirmity or some other defect, and sometimes even mortal sin, from obtaining such a good, in order that they be so humbled on this account that they will not take pride in it, and that being thus humiliated, they may recognize that they cannot stand by their own powers. Hence it is said: *we know that in everything God works for good with those who love him* (Rom 8:28), not by reason of their sin, but by God's providence.

473. Therefore, because the Apostle had good reason for glorying in the spiritual choice by which he was chosen by God: *he is a chosen instrument of mine* (Acts 9:15), and in his knowledge of God's secrets, because he says that he **was caught up to the third heaven** and **into paradise** where he **heard secret words, which it is not granted to man to utter**; and in enduring evils because he had suffered **in prisons more frequently, in stripes above measure, in deaths often** (2 Cor 11:23), and in his virginal integrity, because *I wish that all were as I myself am* (1 Cor 7:7), and in his good works, because *I worked harder than any of them* (1 Cor 15:10), and especially in the outstanding knowledge with which he shone and which especially puffs one up: for these reasons the Lord applied a remedy, lest he be lifted up with pride.

And this is what he says: **lest the greatness of the revelations should exalt me** unto pride. *Do not exalt yourself through your soul's counsel, lest your soul be torn in pieces like a bull* (Sir 6:2); *being exalted I have been humbled and troubled* (Ps 88:15).

Furthermore, to show that these revelations were made to him, he says: **there was given to me**, i.e., for my benefit and my humiliation: *you have lifted me up and set me as it were upon the wind* (Job 31:22); **there was given**, I say, **to me a sting** tormenting my body with bodily weakness, that the soul might be healed. For it is said that he literally suffered a great deal from pain in the pelvis. Or **a sting of my flesh**, i.e., of concupiscence arising from my flesh, because he was troubled a great deal. *For I do not do the good I want, but the evil I do not want is what I do . . . so then, I of myself*

et cetera. Unde Augustinus dicit quod inerant ei motus concupiscentiae, quos tamen divina gratia refraenabat.

474. Iste, inquam, stimulus est **angelus Satanae**, id est angelus malignus.

Est autem angelus a Deo missus seu permissus, sed Satanae, quia Satanae intentio est ut subvertat, Dei vero ut humiliet et probatum reddat. Timeat peccator, si Apostolus et vas electionis securus non erat.

475. De remotione autem huius stimuli removendi sollicitus erat Apostolus. Unde propter hoc orabat. Et hoc est quod subdit **propter quod ter**, et cetera.

Ubi sciendum est, quod infirmus nesciens processum medici apponentis mordax emplastrum, rogat medicum, ut removeat; quod tamen sciens medicus causam quare faciat, scilicet propter sanitatem, non exaudit eum quantum ad voluntatem petentis, magis curans de eius utilitate. Sic Apostolus sentiens stimulum sibi gravem esse, ad singularis medici confugit auxilium, ut eum removeat.

Ter enim expresse et devote rogavit, ut Deus tolleret ab eo, scilicet stimulum. II Par. c. XX, 12: *cum ignoremus quod agere debeamus*, et cetera. Forte pluries hoc petiit, sed expresse et instanter ter eum petiit, vel ter, id est multoties. Ternarius enim est numerus perfectus. Et vere ipse rogandus est, *quia ipse vulnerat, et medetur*, Iob V, 18. Lc. XXII, v. 40: *orate ne intretis in tentationem*, et cetera.

476. Sequitur responsio Domini **et dixit mihi** Dominus, et cetera. Ubi duo facit.

Primo ponit Domini responsionem;

secundo responsionis rationem assignat, ibi **nam virtus**, et cetera.

477. Dicit ergo: ego rogavi, sed Dominus dixit mihi **sufficit tibi**, etc., quasi dicat: non est tibi necessarium, quod infirmitas corporis recedat a te, quia non est periculosa, quia non duceris ad impatientiam, cum gratia mea confortet te; nec infirmitas concupiscentiae, quia non protrahet te ad peccatum, quia gratia mea proteget te. Rom. c. III, 24: *iustificati gratis*, et cetera. Et vere sufficit gratia Dei ad mala vitanda, ad bona facienda, et ad vitam consequendam aeternam. I Cor. XV, 10: *gratia Dei sum id quod sum*, et cetera. Rom. VI, 23: *gratia Dei vita aeterna*.

478. Sed contra Io. XV, 16: *quidquid petieritis Patrem in nomine meo, dabit vobis*, et cetera. Aut ergo Paulus discrete petivit, et tunc debuit exaudiri; aut indiscrete, et tunc peccavit.

Respondeo. Dicendum est quod de una et eadem re potest homo dupliciter loqui. Uno modo secundum se

serve the law of God with my mind, but with my flesh I serve the law of sin (Rom 7:19). Hence, Augustine says that there existed in him movements of concupiscence which God's grace, nevertheless, restrained.

474. That sting, I say, is **an angel of Satan**, i.e., a wicked angel,

for it was an angel sent by God or permitted, but it was Satan's because Satan's intention is to subvert, but God's is to humble and to render approved. Let the sinner beware, if the Apostle and vessel of election was not secure.

475. Now the Apostle was anxious to have this sting removed and prayed for this; hence he says: **on account of this, I besought the Lord three times that it might depart from me**.

Here it should be noted a sick person, ignorant of the reason why a physician supplies a stinging plaster, asks him to remove it. But the physician, knowing its purpose, that is, for health, does not oblige him, caring more for his improvement. Similarly the Apostle, feeling that the sting was painful to him, sought the help of the unique physician to remove it.

For he expressly and devoutly asked God three times to remove it, the thorn, from him: *we do not know what to do, but our eyes are upon you* (2 Chr 20:12). Perhaps he asked this many times, but he asked him expressly and earnestly three times, or three times, namely, many times. For three is a perfect number. And of course it was right to ask, *for he wounds, but he binds up* (Job 5:18); *pray that you may not enter into temptation* (Luke 22:46).

476. Then he states the Lord's answer: **but he**, i.e., the Lord, **said to me: my grace is sufficient for you**. Here he does two things.

First, he states the Lord's answer;

second, the reason for the answer, at **for power**.

477. He says, therefore, I asked, but the Lord said to me, **my grace is sufficient for you**. As if to say: it is not necessary that this bodily weakness leave you, because it is not dangerous, for you will not be led into impatience, since my grace strengthens you; or that this weakness of concupiscence depart, because it will not lead you to sin, for my grace will protect you: *justified by his grace as a gift* (Rom 3:24). And of course, God's grace is sufficient for avoiding evil, doing good, and attaining to eternal life: *by the grace of God I am what I am* (1 Cor 15:10); *but the free gift of God is eternal life in Christ Jesus our Lord* (Rom 6:25).

478. But on the other hand it is said: *whatever you ask the Father in my name, he may give it to you* (John 15:16). Therefore, Paul either asked discreetly and deserved to be heard, or indiscreetly and hence sinned.

I answer that a man can speak of one and the same thing in two ways: in one way according to itself and the nature

et naturam illius rei; alio modo secundum ordinem ad aliud. Et sic contingit, quod illud quod est malum secundum se, est vitandum: secundum ordinem ad aliud est appetendum. Sicut potio inquantum secundum se est amara, est vitanda, tamen qui considerat eam secundum ordinem ad sanitatem, appetit eam. Ergo et stimulus carnis secundum se est vitandus ut affligens, inquantum vero est via ad virtutem et exercitium virtutis, est appetendus.

Apostolus autem, quia nondum revelatum ei erat illud secretum divinae providentiae, ut ad utilitatem suam cederet, considerabat sibi malum quantum in se est, et ideo petierat suam amotionem, nec in eo peccavit; sed Deus, qui ordinaverat hoc ad bonum humilitatis suae, non exaudivit eum quantum ad eius voluntatem; quod tamen sciens, postmodum Apostolus gloriabatur cum diceret: **libenter gloriabor in infirmitatibus meis**, et cetera. Et licet non exaudierit eum quantum ad voluntatem, exaudivit tamen eum, et exaudit sanctos suos, quantum ad eius utilitatem. Unde dicit Hieronymus in *Epistola ad Paulinum*: *bonus Dominus, qui saepe non tribuit quod volumus, ut tribuat quod mallemus.*

479. Rationem autem suae responsionis subdit consequenter, cum dicit **nam virtus**, et cetera. Mirus modus loquendi. **Virtus in infirmitate perficitur**: ignis in aqua crescit.

Intelligi vero potest hoc, quod dicitur **virtus perficitur in infirmitate**, dupliciter, scilicet materialiter et occasionaliter.

Si accipiatur materialiter, tunc est sensus: **virtus in infirmitate perficitur**, id est infirmitas est materia exercendae virtutis. Et primo humilitatis, ut supra dictum est, secundo patientiae, Iac. I, 3: *tribulatio patientiam operatur*, tertio temperantiae, quia ex infirmitate debilitatur fomes, et temperatus efficitur quis.

Si vero accipiatur occasionaliter, tunc **virtus in infirmitate perficitur**, id est occasio perveniendi ad perfectam virtutem, quia homo sciens se infirmum, magis sollicitatur ad resistendum, et ex hoc, quod magis resistit et pugnat, efficitur exercitatior et per consequens fortior. Et ideo Levit. legitur et Iudic. c. III, 1 s., quod Dominus noluit destruere omnes habitatores terrae; sed aliquos reservavit, ut scilicet filii Israel exercitarentur pugnando cum eis. Sic etiam Scipio nolebat destructionem civitatis Carthaginensis, ut scilicet dum Romani haberent hostes exterius, non sentirent hostes interiores, contra quos durius bellum est, quam contra exteriores, ut ipse dicebat.

480. Consequenter ponit Apostolus effectum huius responsionis Dominicae, dicens **libenter gloriabor**, et cetera.

Ponit autem duplicem effectum. Unus est gloriationis; unde dicit: quia virtus mea perficitur in infirmitatibus,

of things; in another way according to its relation to something else. Hence, it happens that something evil according to itself and to be avoided is in relation to something else able to be sought. Thus, a medicine, inasmuch as it is bitter should be avoided, yet, when it is considered in relation to health, a person seeks it. Therefore a thorn in the flesh according to itself is to be avoided as troublesome, but inasmuch as it is a means to virtue and an exercise of virtue, it should be desired.

But because that secret of divine providence, namely, that it would turn out to his advantage, had not been revealed to him yet, the Apostle considered that in itself it was bad for him. But God who had ordained this to the good of his humility did not oblige him, as far as his wish was concerned; indeed, once he understood its purpose, the Apostle gloried in it, saying, **gladly therefore will I glory in my infirmities, that the power of Christ may dwell in me**. And although he did not oblige him as to his wish, yet he heard him and does hear his saints to their advantage. Hence, Jerome says in the *Letter to Paulinus*: *the good Lord frequently does not grant what we wish, in order to bestow what we should prefer.*

479. Then he gives the reason for the Lord's response when he says, **for power is made perfect in infirmity**. This is a remarkable expression: **power is made perfect in infirmity**; fire grows in water.

But this expression, **power is made perfect in infirmity**, can be understood in two ways, namely, materially and by way of occasion.

If it is taken materially, the sense is this: **power is made perfect in infirmity**, i.e., infirmity is the material on which to exercise virtue; first, humility, as stated above; second, patience: *the testing of your faith produces steadfastness* (Jas 1:3); third, temperance, because hunger is weakened by infirmity and a person is made temperate.

But if it is taken as an occasion, then **power is made perfect in weakness**, i.e., infirmity is the occasion for arriving at perfect virtue, because a man who knows that he is weak is more careful when resisting, and as a result of fighting and resisting more he is better exercised and, therefore, stronger. Hence it says in Judges that the Lord was not willing to destroy all the inhabitants of the land, but preserved some in order that the children of Israel might be exercised by fighting against them (Judg 3:1). In the same way, Scipio also did not wish to destroy the city of Carthage, in order that the Romans, having external enemies, would not have internal enemies, against whom it is more painful to wage war than against outsiders, as he said.

480. Then the Apostle mentions the effect of this answer from the Lord, saying: **therefore gladly will I glory in my infirmities, that the power of Christ may dwell in me**.

He mentions two effects. One is glorying; hence he says: because my virtue is made perfect in infirmity, **gladly**

igitur *libenter gloriabor in infirmitatibus meis*, id est mihi ad utilitatem meam datis. Et hoc, quia magis coniungitur Christo. *Mihi autem absit gloriari, nisi in cruce*, etc., Gal. ult. Eccli. c. X, 34: *qui in paupertate gloriatur*, et cetera.

Et ratio quod libenter gloriabor, *ut inhabitet in me virtus Christi*, ut scilicet per infirmitates inhabitet et consummetur in me gratia Christi. Is. XL, 29: *qui dat lapso virtutem*, etc.

481. Alius effectus est gaudii, unde dicit *propter quod complaceo*, et cetera. Et

circa hoc duo facit.

Primo ponit huiusmodi effectum;

secundo huius effectus rationem assignat, ibi *cum enim infirmor*, et cetera.

482. Ponit autem effectum gaudii et materiam gaudii. Dicit ergo *propter quod*, quia virtus Christi habitat in me in infirmitatibus et in tribulationibus omnibus, et ideo *complaceo mihi*, id est multum delector et gaudeo dictis infirmitatibus meis. Iac. I, 2: *omne gaudium existimate, fratres*, et cetera.

Defectus autem in quibus propter gratiam Christi abundanter delectatur, enumerat. Et primo illos, qui sunt a causa interiori, et huiusmodi sunt infirmitates, et ideo dicit *in infirmitatibus*. Ps. XV, 4: *multiplicatae sunt infirmitates eorum, postea acceleraverunt*, scilicet ad gratiam.

Secundo, illos qui sunt a causa exteriori. Et hos quidem quantum ad verbum, cum dicit *in contumeliis*, scilicet mihi illatis. Act. V, v. 41: *ibant apostoli gaudentes*, etc.; et quantum ad factum, et hoc, vel quantum ad defectum bonorum, cum dicit *in necessitatibus*, id est in penuriis necessariorum et in paupertate qua premebatur. Et hoc modo accipitur necessitas, cum dicitur Rom. XII, v. 13: *necessitatibus sanctorum communicantes.*

Vel quantum ad experimentum malorum illatorum, et hoc quantum ad exteriora, Matth. V, 10: *beati qui persecutionem*, etc. cum dicit *in persecutionibus*, scilicet corporis, quas de loco ad locum et ubique experimur. Et quantum ad interiora, dicens *in angustiis*, id est in anxietatibus animi. Dan. c. XIII, 22: *angustiae sunt mihi undique*, et cetera.

Sed materia omnium horum, quae faciunt ad gaudium est, quia *pro Christo*, quasi dicat: ideo complaceo, quia propter Christum patior. I Petr. IV, 15: *nemo vestrum patiatur quasi homicida, vel fur.*

483. Et huius gaudii rationem assignat, dicens *cum enim infirmor*, etc., quasi dicat: merito complaceo mihi in illis, quia quando infirmor, etc., id est quando ex his, quae in me sunt, vel ex persecutione aliorum incido in aliquod praedictorum, adhibetur mihi auxilium divinum, per quod confirmor. Ps. XCIII, 19: *consolationes*

will I glory in my infirmities, i.e., given to me for my profit; and this because it joins me closer to Christ. *But far be it from me to glory except in the cross of our Lord Jesus Christ* (Gal 6:14); *but he that is glorified in poverty, how much more in wealth?* (Sir 10:34).

The reason I will glory gladly is *that the power of Christ may dwell in me*, i.e., that through infirmity the grace of Christ may dwell and be made perfect in me: *he gives power to the faint, and to him who has no might he increases strength* (Isa 40:29).

481. The other effect is joy. Hence he says: *because of this, I am pleased in my infirmities*.

In regard to this he does two things.

First, he mentions the effect of joy;

second, he assigns the reason for it, at *for when I am weak*.

482. He mentions the effect of joy and the matter of joy. He says *because of this*: because the power of Christ dwells in me in all tribulations, *I am pleased*, i.e., I am greatly delighted and take joy in the infirmities I mentioned: *count it all joy, my brethren, when you meet various trials* (Jas 1:2).

The weaknesses in which he rejoices abundantly on account of Christ's grace are then listed. First, those which come from an internal cause, namely, his infirmities; hence he says, *in my infirmities*: *their infirmities were multiplied: afterwards they made haste* (Ps 16:5), namely, toward grace.

Second, those that come from an external cause: first, as to the word, when he says, *in reproaches*: *then they left the presence of the council, rejoicing that they were counted worthy to suffer dishonor for the name* (Acts 15:4); then as to deed, and this either as to a lack of good things, when he says, *in necessities*, i.e., in the lack of things necessary and in the poverty by which he was pressed: *contribute to the needs of the saints* (Rom 12:13).

Or as to experiencing evils inflicted, and this as to external things: *blessed are those who are persecuted for righteousness' sake* (Matt 5:10), when he says, *in* bodily *persecutions*, which we experience from place to place and everywhere, as well as to internal things, saying, *in distresses*, i.e., in anxieties of soul: *I am straitened on every side* (Dan 13:22).

But in all these things the material which makes for joy is that they are *for Christ*. As if to say: I am pleased because I suffer for Christ: *but let none of you suffer as a murderer, or a thief* (1 Pet 4:15).

483. He assigns the reason for this joy, when he says, *for when I am weak, then I am powerful*, i.e., when as a result of what is in me or as a result of persecutions, I fall into any of the aforesaid, God's help is applied to me to strengthen me: *your consolations cheer my soul* (Ps 94:19); *let the weak say, I am strong* (Joel 3:10); *though our outward man*

tuae laetificaverunt animam meam. Ioel III, 10: *infirmus dicat, quia ego fortis sum.* Supra IV, 16: **licet is qui foris est, noster homo corrumpatur**, et cetera. Ex. I, 12 legitur, quod quanto plus premebantur filii Israel, tanto plus multiplicabantur.

is corrupted, yet the inward man is renewed day by day (2 Cor 4:16). And in Exodus it says that the more the Israelites were oppressed, the more they multiplied (Exod 1:12).

Lecture 4

^{12:11}Factus sum insipiens, vos me coëgistis. Ego enim a vobis debui commendari: [n. 484] nihil enim minus fui ab iis, qui sunt supra modum apostoli: tametsi nihil sum: [n. 488]

^{12:12}signa tamen apostolatus mei facta sunt super vos in omni patientia, in signis, et prodigiis, et virtutibus. [n. 490]

^{12:13}Quid est enim, quod minus habuistis prae ceteris ecclesiis, nisi quod ego ipse non gravavi vos? Donate mihi hanc injuriam. [n. 492]

^{12:11}Γέγονα ἄφρων, ὑμεῖς με ἠναγκάσατε. ἐγὼ γὰρ ὤφειλον ὑφ᾽ ὑμῶν συνίστασθαι· οὐδὲν γὰρ ὑστέρησα τῶν ὑπερλίαν ἀποστόλων εἰ καὶ οὐδέν εἰμι.

^{12:12}τὰ μὲν σημεῖα τοῦ ἀποστόλου κατειργάσθη ἐν ὑμῖν ἐν πάσῃ ὑπομονῇ, σημείοις τε καὶ τέρασιν καὶ δυνάμεσιν.

^{12:13}τί γάρ ἐστιν ὃ ἡσσώθητε ὑπὲρ τὰς λοιπὰς ἐκκλησίας, εἰ μὴ ὅτι αὐτὸς ἐγὼ οὐ κατενάρκησα ὑμῶν; χαρίσασθέ μοι τὴν ἀδικίαν ταύτην.

^{12:11}I have become foolish. You have compelled me: for I ought to have been commended by you. [n. 484] For I have in no way come short of those who are apostles above measure, although I am nothing. [n. 488]

^{12:12}Yet the signs of my apostleship have been wrought on you, in all patience, in signs and wonders and mighty deeds. [n. 490]

^{12:13}For what is there that you have had less of than the other churches except that I myself was not burdensome to you? Pardon me this injury. [n. 492]

---

484. Posita commendatione sua consequenter Apostolus excusat se de his quae dixit, ostendens se coactum hoc dixisse, quae ad gloriam suam pertinent. Et

circa hoc duo facit.

Primo imponit Corinthiis causam eiusmodi gloriationis;

secundo exponit et manifestat hanc causam, ibi *ego enim debui*, et cetera.

485. Dicit ergo: confiteor quod in his omnibus commendationibus meis *factus sum insipiens*, id est videtur vobis, quod opus insipientis fecerim, sed hoc non ex me, nec sponte, immo coactus feci, et vestra culpa fuit, quia *vos me coegistis*, id est dedistis mihi occasionem.

Frequenter enim subditi cogunt praelatos aliqua facere, quae insipienter facta esse iudicari possunt, sed tamen pro loco et tempore sapienter facta sunt.

486. Hoc autem quod dixerat in communi, scilicet quod ipsi fuerant causa suae commendationis, exponit consequenter, cum dicit *ego enim debui*, etc.; ubi dicit quod ipsi fuerunt causa suae commendationis,

primo omittendo bona quae facere debuissent, in quo exaggerat eorum ingratitudinem;

secundo committendo mala, in quo detestatur eorum malitiam, ibi *timeo enim ne forte*, et cetera.

Circa primum duo facit.

Primo commemorat quid facere debuissent, ostendens causam, ibi *nihil enim minus*, etc.;

secundo removet ipsorum excusationem, ibi *quid est enim quod minus*, et cetera.

487. Dicit ergo: vere vos me coegistis, quia vos debuissetis facere illud quod ego feci. Unde dicit *ego debui commendari a vobis*, quod non fecistis quando necesse erat, scilicet quando pseudo vilipendendo me,

484. Having commended himself, the Apostle now asks pardon for what he has said, showing that he was compelled to say these things which pertain to his glory.

Concerning this he does two things.

First, he lays the blame for his glorying on the Corinthians;

second, he explains and clarifies this, at *for I ought to have been*.

485. He says, therefore: I confess that in all these commendations *I have become foolish*, i.e., it seems to you that I have performed the work of a fool. But this was not done of myself or willingly; rather, I was compelled, and it was your fault, because *you have compelled me*, i.e., gave me the occasion.

For subjects frequently compel their prelates to do things which seem unwise to do, although considering the time and place, they were done wisely.

486. Then he explains what he had said in a general way, namely, that they were the cause of his commending himself, when he says: *for I ought to have been commended by you*. Here he says that they were the cause of his commending himself:

first, by neglecting the good they should have done, in which he enlarges upon their ingratitude;

second, by committing evil, in which he execrates their malice, at *for I fear lest perhaps*.

In regard to the first he does two things.

First, he reminds them what they ought to have done by showing the cause, at *for I have in no way*;

second, he rejects their excuse, *for what is there*.

487. He says, therefore: yes, you compelled me, because you should have done what I have done; hence he says: *for I ought to have been commended by you*, which you have not done when in was necessary, that is, when

et praeferendo se reddebant vilem doctrinam et Evangelium Christi a me praedicatum. Unde quia vos non commendastis me, ne deperiret fides Christi in vobis, prorupi in commendationem propriam.

Sed contra supra III, 1 dicit: *numquid egemus commendatitiis epistolis*, et cetera. Quare ergo voluit commendari ab istis?

Respondeo. Dicendum est quod Apostolus propter se non egebat commendationibus sed propter alios, ut scilicet dum commendaretur, doctrina sua esset in maiori auctoritate, et pseudo confutarentur.

488. Sed quia possent isti dicere: *ideo non commendavimus te, quia non est in te aliquid commendatione dignum*, propter hoc Apostolus probat eis, quod bene poterant eum commendare, cum dicit *nihil enim*, etc., ostendens esse in se multa commendatione digna. Et

primo quantum ad praeterita bona, quae fecit;
secundo quantum ad futura, quae facere intendit, ibi *ecce tertio hoc paratus*, et cetera.

Ostendit autem praeterita commendabilia, quae fecit primo in generali, quantum ad omnes ecclesias;
secundo in speciali, quantum ad ea, quae egit apud eos, ibi *tametsi nihil*, etc.;
tertio excludit obiectionem, ibi *quid est enim*, et cetera.

489. Dicit ergo: merito debui commendari a vobis, quia multa sunt in me commendatione digna. Nam *nihil minus feci ab eis*, scilicet Petro et Iacobo et Ioanne, *qui sunt supra modum apostoli*, id est qui videntur a quibusdam digniores apostoli, quam ego sum. Pseudo enim dicebant, quod erant docti a Petro et Ioanne, qui fuerunt docti a Christo, et quod Petrus et Ioannes servabant legalia, unde et ipsi debebant servare. Sed quia nihil minus feci ab eis, nec quantum ad praedicationem, nec quantum ad conversionem fidelium, ostensiones miraculorum, et perpessionem laborum, immo plus, quia ut supra plus omnibus laboravi, I Cor. c. XV, 10: *abundantius omnibus*, etc.; ideo magis sum commendandus.

Vel dicuntur *supra modum apostoli*, scilicet Petrus, Ioannes et Iacobus, quia fuerunt primo conversi ad Christum. I Cor. XV, 8: *novissime autem visus est et mihi*, et cetera. Si secundum hoc accipiatur, nihil tamen minus fecit eis, quia in modico tempore, et postquam conversus fuit, plus laboravit.

490. Sed esto quod nihil fecerim quantum ad Ecclesias, per quod possem commendari, multa tamen specialia egi apud vos, de quibus potuissetis me commendare.

the false apostles by belittling me and preferring themselves rendered vile the doctrine and Gospel of Christ delivered by me. Hence, because you did not commend me, then in order that the faith of Christ not die among you, I undertook to commend myself.

But this is in conflict with his earlier statement: *do we need (as some do) epistles of commendation to you, or from you?* (2 Cor 3:1). So why would he wish to be commended by them?

I answer that the Apostle did not need commendations for himself, but for others, namely, that in commending himself his doctrine would be held in greater authority and the false apostles refuted.

488. But because they could say: *we did not commend you, because there is nothing commendable about you*, the Apostle proves to them that they had good cause to commend him, when he says: *for I have in no way come short of those who are apostles above measure*, thus showing that there was much in him commendable.

First, as to the past good things he did;
second, as to the good things he intends to do in the future, at *behold, now for the third time*.

And he shows his past deeds to be commendable first in general as to all the churches;
second, in particular as to what he did among them, at *although I am nothing*;
third he excludes an objection, at *for what is there*.

489. He says, therefore: I deserved to be commended by you, because there are many things in me worthy of commendation, *for I have in no way come short of those*, namely, Peter and James and John, *who are apostles above measure*, i.e., who seem to some to be worthier apostles than I. For the false apostles said that they had been taught by Peter and John, who had been taught by Christ, and that Peter and John observed the ceremonies of the law; hence, that they too should observe them. But because I have done nothing else among you, either as to preaching or to converting believers or performing miracles and undertaking labors, but rather have done more, because *I worked harder than any of them* (1 Cor 15:10), for that reason I am more to be commended.

Or they were called *apostles above measure*, that is, Peter, James, and John, because they were the first ones converted to Christ: *last of all, as to one untimely born, he appeared also to me* (1 Cor 15:8). If it is taken in this sense, even then I have done nothing less than they, because in the short time after I was converted, I labored more.

490. But granting that I did nothing in regard to the other churches for which I might be commended, nevertheless I have done many special things among you, and for these you could have commended me;

Et ideo dicit *tametsi nihil*, id est, dato, quod nihil fecerim in comparatione ad eos, tamen effectus meae virtutis manifeste apparent in vobis, et, primo, quantum ad praedicationem nostram, qua conversi estis ad fidem. Et sum apostolus vester. Et ideo dicit *signa apostolatus mei*, id est meae praedicationis, *facta sunt supra vos*, a Deo, inquantum credentes conversi estis. I Cor. IX, v. 2: *signaculum apostolatus mei vos estis*. I Cor. IV, 15: *in Christo Iesu per Evangelium ego vos genui*.

Secundo per conversationem, per quam confirmatur fides, quia quando vita concordat doctrinae, maioris auctoritatis est doctrina. Et virtus praedicatoris magis apparet per patientiam. Prov. XIX, 11: *doctrina viri per patientiam noscitur*. Et ideo dicit *in omni patientia*.

Tertio quantum ad operationem miraculorum. Et ideo dicit *in signis*, et cetera. Mc. ult. *illi autem profecti*, et cetera.

491. Et haec tria distinguuntur, quia *virtus* est commune ad omnia miracula. Nam *virtus* est ultimum de potentia. Et ideo aliquid dicitur virtuosum, quia ex magna virtute. Quia ergo miracula fiunt ex magna virtute, scilicet divina, ideo dicuntur *virtutes*. *Signum* vero refertur ad minus miraculum. *Prodigium* autem ad maximum.

Vel dicit *signa* quantum ad miracula facta de praesenti, *prodigia* quantum ad miracula de futuris.

Vel *signa* et *prodigia* dicit miracula quae fiunt contra naturam, sicut illuminatio caeci, suscitatio mortui, et cetera. Virtutes vero dicit, quae sunt secundum naturam, sed non eo modo quo natura facit, sicut quod ad impositionem manus statim sanentur infirmi, quod etiam natura facit, sed successive.

Vel virtutes dicit virtutes mentis, sicut est castitas et huiusmodi.

492. Consequenter excludit obiectionem cum dicit *quid enim est quod minus*, et cetera.

Possent enim Corinthii respondere ad praedicta, et dicere: verum est quod multa bona fecisti et magna, et tamen alii fecerunt plura et maiora quam tu, et ideo apud eos et in eorum comparatione nolumus te commendare. Et ideo hoc excludit, ostendens quod nihil minus fecit quam illi, sed plus. Et ideo dicit *quid est enim quod minus habuistis a me prae caeteris ecclesiis*, id est quam aliae ecclesiae Christi habuerunt per illos quantum ad spiritualia? Quasi dicat: nihil; quia ipsi praedicaverunt fidem, et Apostolus praedicavit; illi ostenderunt signa et virtutes, et Apostolus similiter.

hence he says, *although I am nothing*, i.e., granting that I did nothing in comparison to them, nevertheless, the effect of my power is present among you. First, as to our preaching, by which you were converted to the faith, and I am your apostle. *Yet the signs of my apostleship*, i.e., of my preaching, *have been wrought on you* by God, inasmuch as believing, you were converted. *You are the seal of my apostleship in the Lord* (1 Cor 9:2); *for I became your father in Christ Jesus through the Gospel* (1 Cor 4:15).

Second, by the manner of life through which faith is strengthened, because when one's life agrees with his doctrine, the doctrine has greater authority, and the virtue of the preacher is more apparent through patience: *the learning of a man is known by patience* (Prov 19:11); therefore he says, *in all patience*.

Third, as to working miracles; hence he says, *in signs and wonders and mighty deeds*: *and they went forth and preached everywhere, while the Lord worked with them and confirmed the message by the signs that attended it* (Mark 16:20).

491. These three things are distinct, because *mighty deeds* is common to all miracles, for a *mighty deed* is the full extent of a power. Therefore, something is called mighty because it proceeds from great power. Therefore, because miracles come from great power, namely the divine, they are therefore called *mighty deeds*. But a *sign* refers to a lesser miracle, and a *wonder* to a greater one.

Or he says *signs* as to miracles performed in regard to the present and *wonders* in regard to miracles concerning the future.

Or *signs* and *wonders* refer to miracles done contrary to nature; for example, giving sight to the blind, raising from the dead, and so on. But mighty deeds are things according to nature, not performed in the way nature does, as for a sick man to be healed immediately, when one's hands are placed on him; for nature produces the same effect step by step.

Or mighty deeds mean the virtues of the mind, such as chastity and so on.

492. Then he excludes an objection, when he says, *for what is there that you have had less of than the other churches?*

For the Corinthians could answer and say: it is true that you have done many good and great things, but others have done more and greater things than you. Therefore, we are not willing to commend you to them or in comparison with them. But he excludes this, saying: *for what is there that you have had less of than the other churches?* i.e., than the other churches of Christ have obtained through him in spiritual matters. As if to say: nothing, because they preached the faith and the Apostle preached the faith; they showed signs and wonders, and so did the Apostle.

Et non solum non minus habuistis, sed plus, quia alii Apostoli vivebant de sumptibus illorum quibus praedicabant; sed Apostolus non, quia nihil accepit a Corinthiis. Et ideo dicit **nisi quod ego ipse non gravavi vos**, accipiendo vestra, quasi dicat: nihil habuistis minus, nisi hoc forte reputetis minus, quia nihil accepi a vobis, quod tamen plus est. Act. XX, 34: *ad ea quae mihi opus erant, et his qui mecum sunt, necessaria ministraverunt, et cetera.* II Thess. III, 8: *nocte ac die laborantes*, et cetera. Is. XXXIII, 15: *qui excutit manus suas*, et cetera.

Quod si hoc ipsum reputatis iniuriam, scilicet quod nolui vestra recipere, quod feci, quia non dilexi vos, et videtur vobis quod male fecerim, parcatis mihi. Et ideo dicit ironice loquendo **donate**, id est parcite, **mihi hanc iniuriam**. Hoc modo accipitur donare Eph. IV, 32: *donantes invicem, sicut et Christus vobis donavit.*

In fact not only do you not have less, but even more, because the other apostles live on the revenues of those to whom they preached, but not the Apostle. For he took nothing from the Corinthians; hence he says: **except that I myself was not burdensome to you**. As if to say: you received nothing less, unless perhaps you count it as less that I have not taken anything from you, which however is more. *You yourselves know that these hands ministered to my necessities, and to those who were with me* (Acts 20:34); *with toil and labor we worked night and day* (2 Thess 3:8); *who shakes his hands, lest they hold a bribe* (Isa 33:15).

But if you count this an injury, namely, that I refused to take anything from you, as I did, because I did not love you, and it seems to you that I have done wrong, spare me. Hence he says in irony, **pardon**, that is, spare **me this injury**. In this manner it is said: *forgiving one another, as God in Christ forgave you* (Eph 4:32).

Lecture 5

12:14Ecce tertio hoc paratus sum venire ad vos: et non ero gravis vobis. Non enim quaero quae vestra sunt, sed vos. [n. 493] Nec enim debent filii parentibus thesaurizare, sed parentes filiis. [n. 496]

12:15Ego autem libentissime impendam, et super impendar ipse pro animabus vestris: licet plus vos diligens, minus diligar. [n. 500]

12:16Sed esto: ego vos non gravavi: sed cum essem astutus, dolo vos cepi. [n. 502]

12:17Numquid per aliquem eorum, quod misi ad vos, circumveni vos? [n. 504]

12:18Rogavi Titum, et misi cum illo fratrem. Numquid Titus vos circumvenit? nonne eodem Spiritu ambulavimus? nonne iisdem vestigiis? [n. 505]

12:19Olim putatis quod excusemus nos apud vos? coram Deo in Christo loquimur: omnia autem, carissimi, propter aedificationem vestram. [n. 506]

12:14Ἰδοὺ τρίτον τοῦτο ἑτοίμως ἔχω ἐλθεῖν πρὸς ὑμᾶς, καὶ οὐ καταναρκήσω· οὐ γὰρ ζητῶ τὰ ὑμῶν ἀλλὰ ὑμᾶς. οὐ γὰρ ὀφείλει τὰ τέκνα τοῖς γονεῦσιν θησαυρίζειν ἀλλὰ οἱ γονεῖς τοῖς τέκνοις.

12:15ἐγὼ δὲ ἥδιστα δαπανήσω καὶ ἐκδαπανηθήσομαι ὑπὲρ τῶν ψυχῶν ὑμῶν. εἰ περισσοτέρως ὑμᾶς ἀγαπῶ[ν], ἧσσον ἀγαπῶμαι;

12:16Ἔστω δέ, ἐγὼ οὐ κατεβάρησα ὑμᾶς· ἀλλὰ ὑπάρχων πανοῦργος δόλῳ ὑμᾶς ἔλαβον.

12:17μή τινα ὧν ἀπέσταλκα πρὸς ὑμᾶς, δι᾽ αὐτοῦ ἐπλεονέκτησα ὑμᾶς;

12:18παρεκάλεσα Τίτον καὶ συναπέστειλα τὸν ἀδελφόν· μήτι ἐπλεονέκτησεν ὑμᾶς Τίτος; οὐ τῷ αὐτῷ πνεύματι περιεπατήσαμεν; οὐ τοῖς αὐτοῖς ἴχνεσιν;

12:19Πάλαι δοκεῖτε ὅτι ὑμῖν ἀπολογούμεθα. κατέναντι θεοῦ ἐν Χριστῷ λαλοῦμεν· τὰ δὲ πάντα, ἀγαπητοί, ὑπὲρ τῆς ὑμῶν οἰκοδομῆς.

12:14Behold, now for the third time I am ready to come to you, and I will not be burdensome to you. For I do not seek the things that are yours, but you. [n. 493] For neither should the children lay up for the parents, but the parents for the children. [n. 496]

12:15But I will most gladly spend and be spent myself for your souls: although loving you more, I am loved less. [n. 500]

12:16But be it so: I did not burden you: but being crafty, I caught you by guile. [n. 502]

12:17Did I overreach you by any of those whom I sent to you? [n. 504]

12:18I asked Titus: and I sent with him a brother. Did Titus overreach you? Did we not walk with the same Spirit? Did we not walk in the same steps? [n. 505]

12:19Of old, do you think that we excuse ourselves to you? We speak before God in Christ: but all things, my dearly beloved, for your edification. [n. 506]

---

493. Hic ostendit se esse commendabilem quantum ad bona futura, quae facere intendit. Et tria facit.

Primo ostendit suum propositum de futuro bono, quod intendit;

secundo propositi huius rationem assignat, ibi **non enim quaero quae vestra sunt**, etc.;

tertio ad rationem, similitudinem adhibet, ibi **nec enim debent**, et cetera.

494. Sciendum est circa primum, quod aliquando contingit, quod ideo aliqui non accipiunt uno tempore, ut reservent se ad aliud tempus, in quo possint et plus recipere et audacius. Ne ergo isti simile crederent de Apostolo, ut ideo noluisset prima vice recipere ab eis, ut postmodum reciperet plus, dicit, quod non solum hoc fecit olim, sed etiam paratus est facere in futurum. Unde dicit **ecce iam tertio**, id est tertia vice, **paratus sum venire ad vos, et non ero vobis gravis**; quasi dicat: nec etiam tunc gravabo vos, accipiendo vestra. Supra II: **in**

493. Here he shows that he is worthy of commendation in regard to good things he intends to do. He does three things.

First, he states his resolution concerning the future good he intends to do;

second, he assigns the reason for this resolution, at **for I do not seek the things that are yours**;

third, he applies a likeness to his reason, at **for neither should**.

494. It should be noted in regard to the first that sometimes it happens that the reason why some do not receive at one time is that they might be keeping themselves in reserve for another time, in which they can receive both more and more boldly. Therefore, lest they suppose something like this of the Apostle, namely, that he refused to take anything from them the first time, in order that he might receive more the second time, he says that he not only did this in the past, but is prepared to do the same in the future; hence he says, **behold, now for the third time I am ready to**

omnibus sine onere me servavi et servabo. Iob XXVII, 6: *iustificationem quam coepi tenere,* et cetera.

Dicit autem *tertio paratus sum venire,* et non dicit *tertio venio,* quia bene ter paratus fuit ire ad eos, sed tamen non ivit nisi bis. Paratus enim fuit ire prima vice, et tunc ivit, et conversi sunt. Secunda vice fuit paratus, et fuit impeditus propter peccatum eorum, et tunc non ivit, de quo excusat se in principio huius epistolae. Modo est paratus ire tertio, et ivit, unde bis ivit, et ter fuit paratus ire.

495. Rationem autem huius boni propositi subdit, dicens *non enim quaero,* etc., quae talis est: constat quod artifex disponit opus suum secundum finem quem intendit; praedicatores autem in praedicando, aliqui intendunt quaestum et bona temporalia, et ideo totam praedicationem ad hoc ordinant et disponunt; aliqui vero intendunt salutem animarum, et ideo hoc modo disponunt praedicationem suam, secundum quod vident expedire saluti illorum quibus praedicant. Quia ergo Apostolus intendebat in praedicatione sua salutem Corinthiorum, et videbat, quod non expediebat quod reciperet ab eis sumptus, tum ut confutaret pseudo, tum etiam quia avari erant, ideo noluit accipere sumptus.

Et ideo huius rationem assignat, dicens: ideo non gravabo vos, sumptus accipiendo, quia *non quaero quae vestra sunt,* in praedicatione mea, *sed vos,* et vestram salutem procurare intendo. Phil. IV, 17: *non quaero datum, sed fructum.* Et ideo Dominus dixit apostolis: *faciam vos fieri piscatores hominum,* non pecuniae. Hoc etiam figuratur Gen. XLVII, 19, ubi legitur, quod Ioseph emit Aegyptios in servitutem regis, quia bonus praedicator debet ad hoc studere, ut infideles convertat ad servitium Christi.

496. Sed huiusmodi rationi adaptat similitudinem, cum dicit *nec enim debent,* et cetera. Et

primo ponit similitudinem;

secundo adaptat eam, ibi *ego autem libentissime,* etc.;

tertio arguit eorum ingratitudinem, ibi *licet plus vos,* et cetera.

497. Dicit ergo: quod autem non quaeram vestra, patet per simile. Videmus enim, quod parentes carnales debent thesaurizare filiis carnalibus, quia *filii non debent thesaurizare parentibus, sed parentes filiis.* Cum ergo ego sim pater vester spiritualis, et vos sitis filii mei, nolo quod vos thesaurizetis mihi, sed ego vobis.

come to you, and I will not be burdensome to you. As if to say: not even then will I burden you by taking what is yours: *in all things I have kept myself from being burdensome to you: and so I will keep myself* (2 Cor 11:9); *I hold fast my righteousness, and will not let it go* (Job 27:6).

He says, *for the third time I am ready to come,* and not *for the third time I am coming,* because he certainly was prepared to go to them a third time, yet he went only twice. For he was prepared to go the first time; he went and they were converted. He was ready a second time, but he was prevented on account of their sin. It was for this that he apologized in the beginning of this letter. Now he was ready to go a third time, and he went. Hence he went twice, but he was ready to go three times.

495. Then he gives the reason for this good resolution, when he says: *for I do not seek the things that are yours, but you.* The reasoning is this: it is clear that an artisan arranges his work according to the end he has in view, but when preachers preach, some intend revenue and temporal goods; consequently they arrange and direct all their preaching to this. Others intend the salvation of souls; consequently, they arrange their preaching according as they deem it expedient for the salvation of souls. Therefore, because the Apostle in his preaching aimed at the salvation of the Corinthians and he saw that it was expedient to take no revenue from them, both in order to shame the false apostles and also because they were covetous, he refused to take any revenue.

Hence he assigns this reason: I will not burden you by taking anything, because *I do not seek the things that are yours* by my preaching, *but you* and your salvation are what I aim to procure: *not that I seek the gift; but I seek the fruit* (Phil 4:17). Therefore the Lord said to the apostles: *I will make you fishers of men* (Matt 4:19), not of money. This is also prefigured in Genesis, where we read that Joseph brought some Egyptians for the service of the king, because the good preacher should be intent upon converting believers to the service of Christ (Gen 47:19).

496. He adapts a simile to this reasoning, when he says: *for neither should the children lay up for the parents, but the parents for the children.*

First, he presents the simile;

second, he adapts it, at *but I will most gladly;*

third, he criticizes their ingratitude, at *although loving you more.*

497. He says, therefore: the fact that I do not seek what the things that are yours is clear from a simile. For we observe that parents according to the flesh should lay up for their children, because *neither should the children lay up for the parents, but the parents for the children.* Therefore, since I am your spiritual father and you are my children, I do not want you to lay up for me, but I for you.

498. Sed hic est quaestio de patribus carnalibus. Nam Ex. XX, 12 dicitur: *honora patrem tuum*, et cetera. In quo etiam praecipitur nobis, quod ministremus eis necessaria. Ergo filii tenentur thesaurizare parentibus.

Respondeo. Dicendum est quod ex praecepto tenentur filii ministrare et subvenire parentibus in necessariis, non autem congregare et thesaurizare eis. Nam thesaurizatio et congregatio fit in posterum. Sed nos videmus quod secundum naturam filii succedunt parentibus, et non e contrario, nisi in aliquo tristi eventu; et ideo naturaliter amor parentum est ad hoc, ut congregent filiis. Et hoc modo loquitur Apostolus. Exodi autem c. XX, 12 loquitur Dominus de subventione in necessariis.

499. Item quaestio oritur de hoc quod dicit *parentes filiis*, et cetera. Ergo cum praelati sint parentes nostri spirituales, videtur quod male fecerint principes et alii dando divitias praelatis.

Responsio. Dicendum est quod non dederunt praelatis propter se, sed propter pauperes. Et ideo non dederunt eis, sed pauperibus. Et hoc Dominus monet Matth. VI, 20: *thesaurizate vobis thesauros in caelis*, et cetera. Praelatis autem dantur tamquam pauperum dispensatoribus.

500. Consequenter positam similitudinem adaptat.

In similitudine autem duo proposuit. Unum est, quod filii non debent thesaurizare parentibus, et hoc iam patet; et aliud est, quod parentes debent thesaurizare filiis, et dare. Et quantum ad hoc dicit: quia ergo ego sum pater vester, ideo paratus sum dare vobis. Et hoc est quod dicit *ego libentissime impendam* vobis bona, non solum bona spiritualia, praedicando et exempla monstrando, sed etiam temporalia, quod et faciebat, inquantum praedicabat et serviebat eis cum sumptibus aliarum ecclesiarum.

Haec tria ministrare debet quilibet praelatus suis subditis. Unde Dominus dixit ter Petro Io. XXI, 17: *pasce oves meas*, id est pasce verbo, pasce exemplo, pasce temporali subsidio.

Et non solum ista impendam vobis, sed paratus sum mori pro salute animarum vestrarum. Unde dicit *et superimpendar pro animabus vestris*. Io. XV, 13: *maiorem caritatem nemo habet*, et cetera. I Io. III, 16: *si Christus animam suam pro nobis posuit, et vos debetis*, et cetera. Io. X, 11: *bonus pastor animam suam*, et cetera.

501. Ingratitudinem istorum increpat consequenter, dicens *licet plus vos diligens*, etc., quasi dicat: libenter impendar pro vobis, licet sitis ingrati, quia *licet plus vos diligens*, et cetera.

Et haec comparatio potest exponi dupliciter. Uno modo sic: licet plus diligam vos quam pseudo, tamen minus diligor, scilicet a vobis, quam diligantur pseudo,

498. But there is a question here about parents according to the flesh, for it is said: *honor your father and your mother* (Exod 20:12), which includes that we must minister to their needs. Therefore the children are bound to lay up for their parents.

I answer that this precept binds children to minister to and help their parents in necessity, but not to gather and lay up for them. For laying up and gathering have an eye on the future. But in nature the children succeed the parents and not vice versa, except in some sad cases. Therefore the love of parents naturally induces them to lay up for the children. It is in this way that the Apostle speaks; but in Exodus 20 the Lord is speaking about helping them in case of necessity.

499. Another question that arises concerns the statement that **neither should the children lay up for the parents, but the parents for the children**. Therefore, since prelates are our spiritual parents, it seems that princes and others do wrong when they give their riches to prelates.

I answer that they gave them to prelates not for themselves, but for the poor, and this is what the Lord teaches: *lay up for yourselves treasures in heaven, where neither moth nor rust consumes and where thieves do not break in and steal* (Matt 6:20). Hence they are given to prelates as dispensers to the poor.

500. Then he applies the simile,

in which he proposed two things: one is that the children should not lay up for the parents, and this is now clear. The other is that parents should lay up for and give to the children; in regard to this he says: therefore, because I am your father, I am ready to give to you, and this is what he says: **I will most gladly spend** good things on you, not only spiritual goods by preaching and giving examples, but even temporal goods, which he did, inasmuch as he preached to them and served them with the revenues of other churches.

Every prelate should minister these three things to his subjects; hence the Lord said to Peter three times: *feed my sheep* (John 21:17), i.e., feed them by word, feed them by example, feed them by temporal subsidies.

Not only will I give those things to you, but I am ready to die for your salvation; hence he says, **and be spent for your souls**. *Greater love has no man than this, that a man lay down his life for his friends* (John 15:13); *he laid down his life for us; and we ought to lay down our lives for the brethren* (1 John 3:16); *the good shepherd lays down his life for the sheep* (John 10:11).

501. Then he criticizes their ingratitude when he says, **although loving you more, I am loved less**. As if to say: gladly will I be spent for you, although you are ungrateful, because **although loving you more, I am loved less**.

This comparison can be explained in two ways. First, in this way: although I love you the more than the other apostles, yet I am loved the less, namely, by you, than the

quos plus diligitis quam me. Et sic patet, quod ego plus vos diligo, quam illi; quia ego quaero salutem vestram tantum, illi vero bona vestra solum.

Alio modo sic: licet plus diligam, scilicet vos, quam alias Ecclesias, tamen minus diligor a vobis, quam ab aliis Ecclesiis. Phil. I, v. 8: *testis est mihi Deus quomodo cupiam*, et cetera. Et quod plus dilexerit Corinthienses, quam alias ecclesias, patet, quia plus pro eis laboravit. Illud autem in quo plus laboramus, magis consuevimus diligere.

502. Consequenter cum dicit *esto, ego vos*, etc., removet suspicionem. Et

primo ponit suspicionem ipsam;

secundo excludit eam, ibi *numquid per aliquem*, etc.;

tertio rationem exclusionis assignat, ibi *olim putatis quod excusemus*, et cetera.

503. Posset autem esse istorum suspicio talis, quod ideo ipse ab eis per se ipsum non acceperit, ut per alios dolose ab eis plus accipiat. Et ideo dicit, hoc ponens, *esto*, id est dato et concesso, quod *ego*, in persona mea et eorum qui mecum sunt, aliquid accipiendo *non gravavi vos, sed*, sicut credidistis, *cum essem astutus, dolo*, etc., id est per alios detraxi vobis bona vestra plurima: sed hoc est falsum, quia nihil ex dolo feci. I Thess. II, 3: *exhortatio nostra non de errore, neque de immunditia, neque in dolo*. Nam ipse erat verus Israelita, in quo dolus non fuit, Io. I, 47.

504. Hanc ergo suspicionem excludit consequenter, cum dicit *numquid per aliquem*, et cetera. Et primo in generali, secundo in speciali.

In generali sic: si per alios voluissem surripere vestra, misissem aliquos, qui hoc procurarent apud vos. Sed *numquid per aliquem eorum quem misi ad vos, circumveni vos*, extorquendo per eos vestra? Quasi dicat: non. Supra VII, 2: *neminem circumvenimus*, et cetera. I Thess. IV, 6: *ne quis circumveniat in negotio fratrem suum*.

505. In speciali vero excludit suspicionem praedictam, cum dicit *rogavi Titum*, etc., quasi dicat: nullus eorum in speciali, quem misi ad vos, circumvenit vos. Titum enim cum precibus misi ad vos. Et hoc est, quod dicit *rogavi Titum*, et cetera. De isto habetur supra VIII, 18. *misi etiam cum illo fratrem*, scilicet Barnabam, vel Lucam. Supra c. VIII, 18: *misimus cum illo*, scilicet Tito, *fratrem* (scilicet alterum dictorum) *cuius laus est in Evangelio*.

Sed numquid Titus circumvenit vos, etc., quasi dicat: non. Supra VIII, 16: *gratias ago Deo meo, qui dedit eamdem sollicitudinem pro vobis in corde Titi*, et cetera.

Et quod Titus non circumvenerit eos, probat per conformitatem Titi ad seipsum Apostolum, et ponit duplicem conformitatem, scilicet cordis. Et ideo dicit *nonne eodem Spiritu ambulavimus*, id est eamdem voluntatem

false apostles are loved, whom you love more than me. Thus it is evident that I love you more than they, because I seek only your salvation, but they seek only your goods.

In another way thus: although I love you the more than the other churches, nevertheless I am loved less by you than by the other churches: *for God is my witness, how I yearn for you all with the affection of Christ Jesus* (Phil 1:8). That he loved the Corinthians more than he loved the other churches is clear from the fact that he labored more for them. But that for which we labor more, we love more.

502. Then when he says, *but be it so: I did not burden you*, he removes a suspicion.

First, he mentions the suspicion;

second, he excludes it, at *did I overreach you*;

third, he assigns the reason for the exclusion, at *of old, do you think*.

503. Their suspicion might be that the reason he did not take anything for himself was that others might take more from them. Therefore, he says: *but be it so*, that is, granting that *I* myself, in my person and in those who are with me, *did not burden you* by taking anything, but as you believed, *being crafty, I caught you by guile*, i.e., I took many more of your goods through other persons. But this is false, because I have done nothing by guile: *for our appeal does not spring from error or uncleanness, nor is it made with guile* (1 Thess 2:3). For he was an Israelite indeed, in whom there was no guile (John 1:47).

504. Then he excludes this suspicion when he says, *did I overreach you by any of those whom I sent to you?* First, in general; second, in particular.

In general in the following way: if I had wanted to snatch anything from you by others, I would have sent those who might obtain these things. But *did I overreach you by any of those whom I sent to you*, by using them to extort your goods? As if to say: no: *we have injured no man* (2 Cor 7:2); *that no man transgress, and wrong his brother in this matter* (1 Thess 4:16).

505. He excludes their suspicion in particular when he says: *I asked Titus, and I sent with him a brother*. As if to say: none of those whom I sent to you overreached you. For I sent Titus to you with entreaties. And this is what he says: *I asked Titus, and I sent with him a brother*, namely, Barnabas or Luke: *we have also sent with him*, namely, with Titus, *the brother*, namely one of those mentioned, *whose praise is in the Gospel through all the churches* (2 Cor 8:18).

Did Titus overreach you? As if to say: no: *thanks be to God who has given the same carefulness for you in the heart of Titus* (2 Cor 8:16).

That Titus did not overreach them he proves by showing that Titus was of the same mind as the Apostle, and he mentions two points of similarity: first, in the heart; hence he says: *did we not walk with the same Spirit*, i.e., have the

habemus? Vel eodem Spiritu instigamur ad bene et recte agendum? Supra IV, 13: *habentes autem eumdem Spiritum*, et cetera. Item conformitatem operis. Et ideo dicit *nonne eisdem vestigiis*, id est operibus intendimus, scilicet vestigiis Christi? Nam ego sequor vestigia Christi. Iob XXIII, 11: *vestigia eius*, scilicet Christi, *secutus est pes meus*, et cetera. I Petr. II, 21: *Christus passus est*, etc., *ut sequamini vestigia eius*. Et Titus sequitur vestigia mea. I Cor. XI, 1: *imitatores mei estote*, et cetera.

Et sic patet, quod si conformis est mihi in voluntate et opere, et ego non circumveni vos, nec intendo circumvenire; quod autem nec ipse circumvenerit vos, patet per illud Matth. VII, 16: *a fructibus eorum cognoscetis*, et cetera.

506. Rationem autem exclusionis subdit, dicens *olim*, seu rursus, *putatis*, et cetera. Et primo ponit eorum opinionem, secundo excludit eam.

Opinio autem istorum erat, quod Apostolus quasi reus et culpabilis omnia verba ista epistolae diceret ad excusationem suam, et quod non essent vera sed ad excusandum tantum inventa; et ideo ponens hanc opinionem ipsorum, dicit *vos putatis olim*, id est a principio huius epistolae, *quod excusemus nos apud vos*, id est quod haec verba non sint vera, sed sint ad excusandum conficta.

507. Hanc autem excludit sic: qui enim sic excusat se, duo habet; unum est, quod non utitur verbis veris, sed confictis; aliud est, quia non vult pati detrimentum famae suae et gloriae. Unde specialiter propter dispendium famae aliqui excusant se. Sed neutrum istorum est in nobis; non ergo vera est opinio vestra.

Quod autem neutrum istorum sit in nobis, patet. Non enim dicimus verba falsa; quod probo, primo per testimonium Dei, quia *coram Deo loquimur*. Quasi dicat: teste Deo, hoc in veritate dico. Iob XVI, 20: *ecce in caelo testis meus*, et cetera.

Secundo per testimonium Christi, quia *in Christo loquimur*, id est per Christum, in quo nulla est falsitas. Supra II, 17: *ex sinceritate sicut ex Deo in Christo loquimur*.

Item non quaerimus gloriam nostram, nec timemus infamiam, quia *omnia*, quae dixi et de revelationibus et de tribulationibus, facio, seu dico, *propter vestram aedificationem*, ut scilicet permaneatis in virtute, et expellatis pseudo. Io. XIV: *quae aedificationis sunt invicem*, et cetera. I Cor. XIV, v. 26: *omnia ad aedificationem fiant*. Io. XII, v. 30: *non propter me haec vox venit, sed propter vos*, et cetera.

same will? Or we were inspired by the same Spirit to act well and correctly: *having the same Spirit of faith, as it is written: I believed, for which cause I have spoken; and we also believe, for which cause we also speak* (2 Cor 4:13). Second, in work; hence he says: *did we not walk in the same steps*, i.e., intent on the same works? That is to say, in the steps of Christ, for I walk in the steps of Christ: *I have kept his way*, namely, Christ's, *and have not turned aside* (Job 23:11); *Christ also suffered for you, leaving you an example, that you should follow in his steps* (1 Pet 2:21). And Titus follows my steps: *be imitators of me, as I am of Christ* (1 Cor 11:1).

Therefore, if he agrees with me in will and in work, and I have not overreached you and do not intend to overreach you, the conclusion is evident. That he did not overreach them is clear from Matthew: *by their fruits you shall know them* (Matt 7:16).

506. The he adds the reason, saying *of old*, or again, *do you think*, which excludes their opinion. First, he states their opinion; second, he excludes it.

Their opinion was that the Apostle, as one guilty and culpable, was writing all the words of this epistle to justify himself, and that they were not true, but merely invented to justify himself. Therefore, he sets down their opinion, saying: *of old, do you think*, i.e., from the beginning of this epistle, *that we excuse ourselves to you*, i.e., that the words of this epistle are not true, but are fabricated as an excuse?

507. But he excludes this: for a person who excuses himself in that way has two things: one is that he does not use true words, but fabrications; the other is that he was not wont to suffer the loss of reputation and glory. Hence, it is especially because of the loss of reputation that they make excuses. But neither of these is verified in us. Therefore, your opinion is not true.

That neither of these is verified in us is clear, because we do not employ false words. This he proves first by God's testimony, because *we speak before God*. As if to say: God is my witness, that I speak the truth: *even now, behold, my witness is in heaven* (Job 16:19).

Second, by the testimony of Christ, because *we speak before God in Christ*, i.e., by Christ in whom there is not falsity: *but with sincerity: but as from God, before God, in Christ we speak* (2 Cor 2:17).

Furthermore, we do not seek our own glory or fear loss of reputation, because *all things* which I have said about my revelations and tribulations, *for your edification*, namely, that you continue in virtue and expel the false apostles. *Let us then pursue what makes for peace and for mutual upbuilding.* (Rom 14:19); *let all things be done for edification.* (1 Cor 14:26); *this voice has come for your sake, not for mine* (John 12:30).

Lecture 6

12:20 Timeo enim ne forte cum venero, non quales volo, inveniam vos: et ego inveniar a vobis, qualem non vultis: ne forte contentiones, aemulationes, animositates, dissensiones, detractiones, susurrationes, inflationes, seditiones sint inter vos: [n. 508]

12:20φοβοῦμαι γὰρ μή πως ἐλθὼν οὐχ οἵους θέλω εὕρω ὑμᾶς κἀγὼ εὑρεθῶ ὑμῖν οἷον οὐ θέλετε· μή πως ἔρις, ζῆλος, θυμοί, ἐριθεῖαι, καταλαλιαί, ψιθυρισμοί, φυσιώσεις, ἀκαταστασίαι·

12:20 For I fear lest perhaps, when I come, I shall not find you such as I wish, and that I shall be found by you such as you do not wish. Lest perhaps contentions, envyings, animosities, dissensions, detractions, whisperings, swellings, seditions, be among you. [n. 508]

12:21ne iterum cum venero, humiliet me Deus apud vos, et lugeam multos ex iis qui ante peccaverunt, et non egerunt poenitentiam super immunditia, et fornicatione, et impudicitia, quam gesserunt. [n. 514]

12:21μὴ πάλιν ἐλθόντος μου ταπεινώσῃ με ὁ θεός μου πρὸς ὑμᾶς καὶ πενθήσω πολλοὺς τῶν προημαρτηκότων καὶ μὴ μετανοησάντων ἐπὶ τῇ ἀκαθαρσίᾳ καὶ πορνείᾳ καὶ ἀσελγείᾳ ᾗ ἔπραξαν.

12:21 Lest again, when I come, God humble me among you: and I mourn many of them that sinned before and have not done penance for the uncleanness and fornication and lasciviousness that they have committed. [n. 514]

---

508. Posita una causa commendationis, quae provenit ex omissione Corinthiorum, quantum ad ea bona quae facere debuissent, in qua detestatur eorum ingratitudinem, hic consequenter ponit aliam causam, quae provenit ex eorum commissione quantum ad mala quae debuissent vitare, in qua exaggerat eorum malitiam. Et

circa hoc duo facit.

Primo ponit eorum culpam in generali;

secundo explanat eam in speciali, ibi *ne forte*, et cetera.

509. Dicit ergo: non solum laudavi me propter hoc, quod vos omisistis me laudare, sed etiam propter periculum vestrum, quod est in hoc quod vos adhaeretis pseudo, quia, dum fovent vos in peccatis, exponunt vos in magno periculo. Et ideo dicit **timeo**, scilicet **ne forte cum venero**, ad vos personaliter, **non inveniam vos quales vos volo**, scilicet iustos sed peccatores et incorrectos, et displiceatis mihi et ego vobis, quia iusto non placent peccatores, inquantum peccatores. **Et inveniar** talis **a vobis**, scilicet contristatus et puniens, **qualem** me **non vultis habere**. Mali enim odiunt correctionem, et veritatem. *Ergo inimicus factus sum vobis, verum dicens vobis?* etc., Gal. IV, 16.

Sic patet eorum malitia in generali, scilicet quod timebat ne nondum plene poenituerint.

510. In speciali etiam manifestat eorum malitiam, cum dicit **ne forte contentiones**, et cetera. Et

circa hoc duo facit.

Primo enim enumerat eorum mala praesentia;

secundo commemorat praeterita mala, de quibus nondum poenituerunt, ibi **ne iterum cum venero**, et cetera.

511. Sciendum est autem, circa primum, quod Corinthienses post conversionem inciderunt in peccatum carnale, ut patet de illo qui uxorem patris habuit, et de

508. Having cited as one of the causes for commending the failure of the Corinthians to do the good things they should have done and for which he rebuked their ingratitude, he now states the other cause which arose from what they did in regard to the evils they should have avoided. In regard to this he amplifies their wickedness. And

concerning this he does two things.

First, he sets out their guilt in general;

second, he explains it in particular, at **lest perhaps**.

509. He says, therefore: I have praised myself not only because you have failed to praise me, but also because of your danger, which consists in clinging to the false apostles, because by fostering sin among you they were exposing you to great danger. Therefore he says, **I fear lest perhaps, when I come** to you in person, **I shall not find you such as I wish**, namely, just, but sinners and uncorrected, and that you will be displeasing to me and I to you, because sinners as sinners are not pleasing to a just man; and **that I shall be found by you such as you do not wish**, i.e., sad and meting out punishment. For evil persons hate correction and the truth: *have I then become your enemy by telling you the truth?* (Gal 4:16).

Thus their evil is clear in general, namely, that he feared lest they were not yet fully repentant.

510. Then he manifests their sinfulness in particular, when he says, that **lest perhaps contentions**.

In regard to this he does two things.

First, he enumerates their present evils;

second, he reminds them of past evils of which they have not yet repented, at **lest again, when I come**.

511. In regard to the first it should be noted that after their conversion the Corinthians fell into sins of the flesh, as is evident from the one who had his father's wife; and for

hoc in hac parte correcti sunt per primam epistolam, non tamen plene sed adhuc aliquid in eis remansit, et supra hoc remanserunt in eis multa peccata spiritualia, quae proprie opponuntur caritati.

Caritas vero duo facit. Primo enim facit corda hominum ad invicem consentientia; secundo inducit homines ad mutuum profectum. Et ideo, peccata spiritualia, e contrario, primo, faciunt homines ad invicem dissentientes; secundo faciunt eos invicem offendentes. Et ideo primo enumerat peccata spiritualia quae pertinent ad dissensionem; secundo ea quae faciunt ad offensionem, ibi *detractiones*, et cetera.

In dissensionibus autem procedit ordine retrogrado. Nam, secundum rectum ordinem, homines primo dissentiunt, inquantum unus vult unum, alius vult contrarium; secundo, ex hoc procedunt ad inferendum nocumenta, inquantum quilibet vellet obtinere in proposito suo; tertio, quando non potest obtinere in proposito suo, sed succumbit, accenditur zelo invidiae; quarto, ex hoc prorumpit ad contentiones verborum.

512. Et ab isto ultimo incipit Apostolus, dicens *ne forte contentiones*, etc., quasi dicat: non solum timeo mala vestra in generali, sed in speciali, ne forte sint in vobis contentiones de meritis praelatorum, et de Baptistis, et cetera. Prov. XX, 3: *honor est homini qui separat se a contentionibus*, et cetera. Ambrosius: *contentio est impugnatio veritatis, cum confidentia clamoris.*

Et haec contentio venit ab aemulatione; et ideo dicit *et aemulationes*, id est invidiae, in his qui minores sunt, et minus habent. Iac. c. III, 16: *ubi zelus et contentio, ibi inconstantia*, et cetera. Iob V, 2: *parvulum occidit invidia*, et cetera. Sap. II, 24: *invidia diaboli*, et cetera.

Et aemulatio venit ab animositate, unde dicit *animositates*, in ultione et illatione nocumenti. Eccli. VIII, 18: *cum audace ne eas*, et cetera. Et animositas venit ex dissensionibus, et ideo dicit *dissensiones*, id est odia et contrarietas animorum. Rom. ult.: *observetis eos qui dissensiones et offendicula*, et cetera. I Cor. I, 10: *idipsum dicatis omnes, et non sint in vobis schismata.*

513. Consequenter enumerat eorum mala praesentia quantum ad offensionem. Et quia ista specialiter sunt mala in nocumentis verborum, et non factorum, ideo dimissis nocumentis factorum, enumerat nocumenta verborum, in quibus etiam procedit ordine retrogrado, incipiens a posteriore, et hoc est, cum quis expresse malum dicit de aliquo, et, siquidem in manifesto, sic est detractor, et ideo dicit *detractiones*, Rom. I, 30: *detractores, Deo odibiles*, etc.; si vero in occulto, tunc est susurro, et

this they were corrected by the first epistle, although not completely, because something still remained among them. In addition to this there remained among them many spiritual sins which are directly opposed to charity.

Now charity does two things: first, it makes men's hearts consent to one another; second, it induces men to mutual progress. Spiritual sins, on the other hand, set men disagreeing and make them offend one another. First, therefore, he lists the spiritual sins which pertain to dissension; second, those which make for offense, at *detractions*.

In regard to dissensions he proceeds in reverse order. For according to the right order, men first disagree, inasmuch as one wants one thing and another the contrary; second, they pass from this to inflicting injury, inasmuch as each one wants to obtain his desire; third, when he cannot obtain his desire but fails, he burns with the zeal of jealousy; fourth, the result of this is verbal argument.

512. It is from the last of these that the Apostle begins, saying, that *lest perhaps contentions . . . be among you*. As if to say: not only do I fear your evils in general, but also in particular, lest perhaps there be among you contentions over the merits of prelates and baptizers: *it is an honor for a man to keep aloof from strife* (Prov 20:3); *contention is an attack on the truth, accompanied by the confidence of shouting* (Ambrose).

This contention springs from jealousy; hence he says, *envyings* by those who are inferior and have less: *for where jealousy and selfish ambition exist, there will be disorder and every vile practice* (Jas 3:16); *jealousy slays the simple* (Job 5:2); *but through the devil's envy death entered the world* (Wis 2:24).

Envy comes from animosity; hence he says, *animosities*, in revenge and inflicting injury: *go not on the way with a bold man, lest he burden you with his evils* (Sir 8:18). Animosity comes from dissensions; hence he says, *dissensions*, i.e., hatreds and conflicts of spirits. *Take note of those who create dissensions and difficulties, in opposition to the doctrine which you have been taught* (Rom 15:17); *all of you agree and that there be no dissensions among you* (1 Cor 1:10).

513. Then he lists their present evils in regard to offending. But because such evils consist mainly in injuries from words and not from deeds, he passes over injuries from deeds and lists those from words. Here too he proceeds in reverse order, beginning from the last; and this is when a person explicitly says something evil of another. If this is in public, he is a detractor; hence he says, *detractions*: *slanderers, haters of God* (Rom 1:30). If it is in secret, he is a whisperer; hence he says, *whisperings*. For whisperers

ideo dicit **susurrationes**. Sunt enim susurrones, qui latenter seminant discordias. Eccli. XXVIII, 15: *susurro et bilinguis maledictus erit.*

Et haec duo procedunt ex superbia, quae animum inflatum contra aliquos prorumpere facit in mala verba. Et ideo dicit **inflationes**, I Cor. IV, 18: *tamquam non sim venturus ad vos, sic inflati*, et cetera.

Et hae inflationes veniunt ex seditionibus, quae sunt praeparationes partium ad pugnam, quia *inter superbos semper iurgia sunt*, Prov. c. XIII, 10. Et ideo dicit **seditiones**, id est, tumultus ad pugnam. Prov. XVII, 11: *semper iurgia quaerit malus.*

Sic ergo patet eorum malitia quantum ad mala praesentia, quae multa sunt et in dissensionibus et in nocumentis.

514. Manifestat autem eorum malitiam quantum ad mala praeterita, de quibus non poenituerunt, cum dicit *ne iterum cum venero, humiliet me Deus*, id est affligat, *apud vos*, ita quod *et lugeam multos* vestrum, *ex his qui ante peccaverunt*, id est ante primam epistolam, *et non egerunt poenitentiam*, plene post primam epistolam. Et merito lugeam, quia, sicut gloria patris est gloria filiorum, ita confusio patris est confusio filiorum. Sic Samuel lugebat Saul, I Reg. XVI, 1: *usquequo luges Saul*, et cetera.

Et hoc quia non poenituerunt, nec *egerunt poenitentiam* de peccatis carnalibus praedictis, quorum quaedam sunt contra naturam, et ideo dicit *super immunditia*, id est luxuria contra naturam. Quaedam sunt, quae committuntur cum mulieribus corruptis, scilicet viduis seu coniugatis, et ideo dicit *et fornicatione*. Quaedam sunt, quae fiunt in corruptione virginum, et ideo dicit *et impudicitia quam gesserunt*. Gal. V, 19: *manifesta sunt opera carnis, quae sunt fornicatio, immunditia, impudicitia*, et cetera.

are persons who discreetly sow discord: *the whisperer and the double tongue is accursed* (Sir 28:5).

And these two precede from pride, which causes the swollen soul to burst out against others in evil words; therefore he says, **swellings**. *You are swollen up as though I were not coming to you* (1 Cor 4:18).

These swellings arise from seditions, which are the preparations made by the parties to a fight, because *there are always quarrels among the proud*; hence he says, **seditions**, i.e., uproars for fights: *an evil man always seek quarrels* (Prov 17:11).

Thus their wickedness is made clear in regard to present evils, which are many both in dissensions and in injuries.

514. Then he manifests their wickedness in regard to past evils for which they have not repented, when he says: *lest again, when I come, God humble me*, i.e., afflict me, *among you: and I mourn many of them that sinned before*, i.e., before the first epistle, *and have not done penance* fully since that first letter. And rightly do I mourn, because just as the glory of the father is in the glory of his children, so the father's shame is the shame of the children. Thus did Samuel mourn over Saul: *how long will you grieve over Saul, seeing I have rejected him from being king over Israel?* (1 Sam 16:1).

And this because they have not repented or *done penance* for their past carnal sins, some of which are contrary to nature; hence he says, *for the uncleanness*, i.e., lust contrary to nature. Some are committed with women no longer virgins, namely, widows or married women; hence he says, *and fornication*; others are committed by deflowering virgins; hence he says, *and lasciviousness that they have committed*: *now the works of the flesh are plain: fornication, impurity, licentiousness* (Gal 5:19).

CHAPTER 13

Lecture 1

13:1Ecce tertio hoc venio ad vos: in ore duorum vel trium testium stabit omne verbum. [n. 515]

13:2Praedixi, et praedico, ut praesens, et nunc absens iis qui ante peccaverunt, et ceteris omnibus, quoniam si venero iterum, non parcam. [n. 518]

13:3An experimentum quaeritis ejus, qui in me loquitur Christus, qui in vobis non infirmatur, sed potens est in vobis? [n. 519]

13:4Nam etsi crucifixus est ex infirmitate: sed vivit ex virtute Dei. Nam et nos infirmi sumus in illo: sed vivemus cum eo ex virtute Dei in vobis. [n. 522]

13:1Τρίτον τοῦτο ἔρχομαι πρὸς ὑμᾶς· ἐπὶ στόματος δύο μαρτύρων καὶ τριῶν σταθήσεται πᾶν ῥῆμα.

13:2προείρηκα καὶ προλέγω, ὡς παρὼν τὸ δεύτερον καὶ ἀπὼν νῦν, τοῖς προημαρτηκόσιν καὶ τοῖς λοιποῖς πᾶσιν, ὅτι ἐὰν ἔλθω εἰς τὸ πάλιν οὐ φείσομαι,

13:3ἐπεὶ δοκιμὴν ζητεῖτε τοῦ ἐν ἐμοὶ λαλοῦντος Χριστοῦ, ὃς εἰς ὑμᾶς οὐκ ἀσθενεῖ ἀλλὰ δυνατεῖ ἐν ὑμῖν.

13:4καὶ γὰρ ἐσταυρώθη ἐξ ἀσθενείας, ἀλλὰ ζῇ ἐκ δυνάμεως θεοῦ. καὶ γὰρ ἡμεῖς ἀσθενοῦμεν ἐν αὐτῷ, ἀλλὰ ζήσομεν σὺν αὐτῷ ἐκ δυνάμεως θεοῦ εἰς ὑμᾶς.

13:1Behold, this is the third time I am coming to you: in the mouth of two or three witnesses shall every word stand. [n. 515]

13:2I have told before and foretell, as present and now absent, to those who sinned before and to all the rest, that if I come again, I will not spare. [n. 518]

13:3Do you seek a proof of Christ who speaks in me, who is not weak towards you, but is mighty in you? [n. 519]

13:4For although he was crucified through weakness, yet he lives by the power of God. For we also are weak in him: but we shall live with him by the power of God towards you. [n. 522]

---

515. In praecedentibus Apostolus multa locutus est ad detestationem pseudo, hic consequenter loquitur contra illos qui a pseudo sunt seducti. Et

circa hoc duo facit.

Primo increpat seductos;

secundo consolatur persistentes, ibi *de caetero, fratres, gaudete*, et cetera.

Circa primum, primo comminatur sententiae severitatem;

secundo ostendit suam iudiciariam potestatem, ibi *an experimentum quaeritis*, etc.;

tertio monet ad correctionem, ibi *vosmetipsos tentate*, et cetera.

Circa primum, primo promittit suam praesentiam;

secundo praedeterminat sui iudicii formam, ibi *in ore duorum vel trium*, etc.;

tertio comminatur severam sententiam, ibi *praedixi enim, et praedico*, et cetera.

516. Promittit ergo, primo, suum adventum, dicens *ecce* ego *venio*, quasi dicat: certum sit vobis, quod *venio ad vos*, et ideo cavete vobis ne inveniam vos imparatos.

Et dicit *tertio*, non quod tertio iverit, sed quia tertio iam paraverat ire, etsi non iverat nisi semel, in secundo apparatu impeditus. I Cor. IV, 19: *veniam ad vos cito*, et cetera.

515. Having said many things to the disadvantage of the false apostles, the Apostle now speaks against those who have been misled by them.

In regard to this he does two things.

First, he rebukes those who have been misled;

second, he congratulates those who remained faithful, at *for the rest, brethren, rejoice*.

First, he threatens a severe sentence;

second, he discloses his judiciary power, at *do you seek a proof*;

third, he warns them to amend themselves, at *try yourselves*. In regard to the first he does three things.

First, he promises his presence;

second, he indicates the form of his judgment, at *in the mouth of two or three*;

third, he threatens a severe sentence, at *I have told before and foretell*.

516. Therefore, he first promises to come, saying, *behold, I am coming*. As if to say: be assured that *I am coming to you*, so take care that I do not find you unprepared.

He says: *this is the third time*, not that he had come a third time, but because he was prepared a third time to come; for he actually came only once so far, although he was ready to come the second time but was prevented: *but I will come to you soon, if the Lord wills* (1 Cor 4:19).

517. Veniam, inquam, et iudicabo malos, secundum ordinem tamen, ita scilicet quod *in ore duorum vel trium testium*, accusantium seu testantium contra aliquem, sit *omne verbum*, accusatorum; quod quidem dicitur Deut. XVII, 6: *nemo occidetur, uno teste dicente testimonium*, et eiusdem XIX, 15: *non stabit testis unus contra aliquem*.

Vel aliter *in ore duorum*, etc., quasi dicat: hoc quod dico de adventu meo ad vos, ita est certum, sicut testimonium duorum, vel trium. Sic ergo ordo iudicii erit.

518. Sed severitatem sententiae comminatur, dicens *praedixi enim*, et cetera. Ubi, primo, insinuat ordinem iudiciarium quo est procedendum, in quo exigitur ut praecedat trina admonitio. Et quantum ad hoc dicit *praedixi vobis ut praesens*, bis, quando scilicet eram vobiscum, *et nunc absens praedico*, ut sic ter admoneat. *Praedico*, inquam, *his qui ante peccaverunt*, et omnibus aliis; quasi dicat: omnes moneo.

Secundo, praemissa monitione, comminatur sententiam. Unde dicit *quoniam si venero, non parcam iterum*, quasi dicat: illis qui peccaverunt peperci prima vice, sed, si iterum peccaverint, vel si non egerint poenitentiam, non parcam eis iterum. Et hoc iuste fit, quia ille cui semel remittitur et iterum peccat, si remitteretur sibi, cresceret in malitia, et efficeretur insolens. Et ideo dicit sapiens Prov. XIII, 24: *qui parcit virgae, odit filium suum*, et cetera.

Ex hoc ergo ordinatum est in Ecclesia, ut praecedat trina monitio antequam quis sententiam excommunicationis fulminet, quia contingit, quod aliqui, licet sint in peccatis et offendant, tamen ex solo verbo admonitionis corriguntur et satisfaciunt. Et etiam a levioribus semper incipiendum est. Quod si admonitione non ducitur, ne magis insolescat, adhibenda est severitas sententiae. Eccle. VIII, v. 11: *ex eo quod non profertur cito contra malos sententia*, et cetera.

519. Consequenter ne possent calumniari de potestate Apostoli, ostendit Apostolus suam iudiciariam potestatem, dicens *an experimentum*, et cetera. Ubi tria facit.

Primo ostendit se habere legationem et potestatem iudicandi a Christo;

secundo ostendit virtutem Christi, ibi *qui in vobis non infirmatur*, etc.;

tertio ostendit, quod virtus Christi etiam ad alios derivatur, ibi *nam et nos infirmi sumus in illo*.

520. Dicit ergo: *si venero, non parcam*, immo severissime iudicabo, et hoc bene possum, quia habeo auctoritatem Christi in puniendo et remittendo. Supra II, 10: *nam si quid donavi*, et cetera. Supra V, 20: *pro Christo legatione fungimur*, et cetera. Et ideo dicit *an experimentum*, etc., quasi dicat: non est dubitandum de potestate

517. I will come, I say, and judge the wicked; in an orderly fashion, however, that *in the mouth of two or three witnesses* accusing or bearing witness against anyone, *shall every word* of the accusers *stand*. This is based on: *a person shall not be put to death on the evidence of one witness* (Deut 17:6), and: *a single witness shall not prevail against a man* (Deut 19:15).

Or another way: *in the mouth of two or three witnesses shall every word stand*. As if to say: that which I say about my coming to you is as certain as the testimony of two or three. Thus there will be an order in the judgment.

518. But he threatens a severe sentence, saying: *I have told before and foretell*. Here he first suggests the judicial process to be followed, which requires that three warnings have been given. In regard to this he says: *I have told before* twice, *as present*, namely, when I was among you, so I *foretell now*, that is, while *absent*. Thus he warns them three times. I *foretell*, I say, *to those who sinned before* and all the others. As if to say: I warn everyone.

Second, having given the warning, he threatens the sentence; hence, he says, *that if I come again, I will not spare*. As if to say: those who sinned I spared the first time; but if they sin again, or have not done penance, I will not spare them again. This would be just, because a person who is forgiven once and sins again, if he were forgiven, would grow in malice and become insolent. Hence the wise man says: *he who spares the rod hates his son* (Prov 13:24).

As a result the Church has decreed that three admonitions must be given before it declares one excommunicated, because it happens that some, although they are in sin and offend, are corrected by a mere word of warning and make satisfaction. But if they are not influenced by warnings, the severity of sentence must be applied, lest they grow more insolent: *because sentence against an evil deed is not executed speedily, the heart of the sons of men is fully set to do evil* (Eccl 8:11).

519. Then, lest they belittle the Apostle's power, he discloses his judicial power, saying: *do you seek a proof?* Here he does three things.

First, he shows that he has delegation and power to judge from Christ;

second, he shows Christ's power, at *who is not weak towards you*;

third, he shows that Christ's power is distributed to others, at *for we also are weak in him*.

520. He says, therefore: *if I come again, I will not spare*; rather, I shall judge most severely. And I can do this, because I have Christ's authority to punish and forgive. *For, what have I pardoned, if I have pardoned any thing, I have done it for your sakes, in the person of Christ* (2 Cor 2:10); *for Christ, therefore, we are ambassadors, God as it were*

mea, quia quidquid ego loquor, vel proferendo sententias, vel remittendo, vel praedicando, loquor a Christo. Ex. IV, 12: *perge, ergo, ego ero in ore tuo.* Lc. XXI, 15: *ego dabo vobis os et sapientiam*, et cetera.

Quae ergo homo facit ex instinctu Spiritus Sancti, dicitur quod Spiritus Sanctus facit; ideo Apostolus quia a Christo motus hoc loquebatur, attribuit Christo tamquam principali, dicens *qui in me loquitur Christus*, et cetera.

521. Sed ne dubitetur de potestate et virtute Christi, ideo consequenter Apostolus ostendit virtutem Christi, cum dicit *qui in vobis*, et cetera. Ubi primo ostendit virtutem Christi, quantum ad ea quae in eis apparuerunt; secundo quantum ad ea quae in Christo sunt, ibi *nam etsi*, et cetera.

Dicit ergo: habeo potestatem iudiciariam a Christo, qui in me loquitur, qui magnae virtutis est in vobis, dando dona gratiarum, distributionem Spiritus et alia multa, quae experti estis; et non solum *non infirmatur, sed potens est in vobis*, quia potenter vos liberavit a peccato, potenter vos convertit ad bonum. Ps. XXIII, 8: *Dominus fortis et potens*, et cetera. Sap. XII, 18: *subest tibi cum volueris posse.* Et paulo ante: *virtutem enim ostendis tu*, et cetera.

522. Et non solum potentia Christi apparuit in vobis, sed etiam in seipso, scilicet inquantum a morte crucis, quam sustinuit ex infirmitate humana, quam assumpsit infirmatam in paupertate, surrexit, et *vivit ex virtute Dei*, quae est ipse Deus. Talis enim erat illa susceptio, quae Deum hominem faceret, et hominem Deum. I Cor. I, 25: *quod infirmum est Dei, fortius est hominibus*, et cetera. Vel, *ex virtute Dei*, scilicet Patris, qui est etiam virtus Christi, quia eadem est virtus Patris et Filii. Apoc. I, 18: *fuit mortuus*, et cetera.

Haec etiam virtus Christi derivatur ad nos. *Nam et nos infirmi*, etc., quasi dicat: ad nos etiam pertinet illa virtus, quia *et nos infirmi sumus in illo*, id est ad intentionem illius, inquantum propter ipsum multa patimur, et mortificamus nosmetipsos, et humiliamus nos. I Cor. IV, 10: *nos infirmi propter Christum*, et cetera. Supra X, 10: *praesentia corporis infirma.* Supra IV, 10: *semper mortificationem*, et cetera. Et ideo *vivemus*, id est vivificabimur, *ex virtute Dei in vobis*, iudicandis. Gal. I, 1: *qui suscitavit Iesum Christum*, et cetera.

Et est sensus: nos ex virtute qua Christus vivit, resuscitamur; et illa virtute habemus etiam potestatem iudicandi in vobis, vel *vivemus*, simili beatitudine, *cum eo*, et

exhorting by us (2 Cor 5:20). Therefore, he says: *do you seek a proof of Christ who speaks in me?* As if to say: have no doubts about my power, because whatever I utter either by passing sentence or forgiving or preaching, I say from Christ. *Now therefore go, and I will be with your mouth* (Exod 4:12); *for I will give you a mouth and wisdom, which none of your adversaries will be able to withstand or contradict* (Luke 21:15).

Therefore, whatever a man says under the inspiration of the Holy Spirit, the Holy Spirit is said to do. Therefore, the Apostle, because he was moved by Christ to say this, attributed it to Christ as to the principal cause, saying, *Christ who speaks in me*.

521. But lest there be any doubt about Christ's power and might, the Apostle discusses the might of Christ, when he says, *who is not weak towards you, but is mighty in you*. Herein he shows Christ's power as to things which are manifested in them; second, as to things which are in Christ, at *for although*.

He says, therefore: I have judiciary power from Christ, who speaks in me, who is mighty in you by giving the gifts of grace, the distribution of the Spirit and many other things you have experienced; and not only is he *not weak towards you, but is mighty in you*, because he has mightily delivered you from sin and turned you to good. *The Lord, strong and mighty* (Ps 24:8); *your power is at hand when you will* (Wis 12:18); and a little before: *for you show your strength when men doubt the completeness of your power* (Wis 12:17).

522. Not only in you has Christ's power appeared, but also in himself, inasmuch as he rose from the death of the cross, which he endured from human weakness, which he assumed in poverty, and *lives by the power of God*, which is God himself: *the weakness of God is stronger than men* (1 Cor 1:25). Or *by the power of God*, namely, of the Father who is also the power of Christ, because the power of the Father and of the Son are the same: *I died, and behold, I am alive forevermore* (Rev 1:18).

But this power of Christ is also distributed to us, *for we also are weak in him*. As if to say: that power pertains to us also, because *we also are weak in him*, i.e., as to its aim, inasmuch as we suffer many things and mortify ourselves and humiliate ourselves for him. *We are weak for Christ's sake* (1 Cor 4:10); *his bodily presence is weak* (2 Cor 10:10); *always bearing about in our body the mortification of Jesus* (2 Cor 4:10). Therefore, *we shall live*, i.e., shall be brought to life, *by the power of God towards you*, who are to be judged: *through Jesus Christ and God the Father, who raised him from the dead* (Gal 1:1).

The sense is this: we are raised by the power by which Christ lives, and from that power we also have the power to judge among you; hence, *we shall live with him*

hoc *ex virtute Dei*, quae quidem virtus Dei est *in vobis*, id est in conscientiis vestris.

with a happiness similar to his, and this *by the power of God*, which power is *towards you*, i.e., in your consciences.

Lecture 2

13:5Vosmetipsos tentate si estis in fide: ipsi vos probate. An non cognoscitis vosmetipsos quia Christus Jesus in vobis est? nisi forte reprobi estis. [n. 523]

13:6Spero autem quod cognoscetis, quia nos non sumus reprobi. [n. 528]

13:7Oramus autem Deum ut nihil mali faciatis, non ut nos probati appareamus, sed ut vos quod bonum est faciatis: nos autem ut reprobi simus. [n. 529]

13:8Non enim possumus aliquid adversus veritatem, sed pro veritate.

13:9Gaudemus enim, quoniam nos infirmi sumus, vos autem potentes estis. Hoc et oramus, vestram consummationem. [n. 532]

13:10Ideo haec absens scribo, ut non praesens durius agam secundum potestatem, quam Dominus dedit mihi in aedificationem, et non in destructionem. [n. 535]

13:5Ἑαυτοὺς πειράζετε εἰ ἐστὲ ἐν τῇ πίστει, ἑαυτοὺς δοκιμάζετε· ἢ οὐκ ἐπιγινώσκετε ἑαυτοὺς ὅτι Ἰησοῦς Χριστὸς ἐν ὑμῖν; εἰ μήτι ἀδόκιμοί ἐστε.

13:6ἐλπίζω δὲ ὅτι γνώσεσθε ὅτι ἡμεῖς οὐκ ἐσμὲν ἀδόκιμοι.

13:7εὐχόμεθα δὲ πρὸς τὸν θεὸν μὴ ποιῆσαι ὑμᾶς κακὸν μηδέν, οὐχ ἵνα ἡμεῖς δόκιμοι φανῶμεν, ἀλλ᾽ ἵνα ὑμεῖς τὸ καλὸν ποιῆτε, ἡμεῖς δὲ ὡς ἀδόκιμοι ὦμεν.

13:8οὐ γὰρ δυνάμεθά τι κατὰ τῆς ἀληθείας ἀλλὰ ὑπὲρ τῆς ἀληθείας.

13:9χαίρομεν γὰρ ὅταν ἡμεῖς ἀσθενῶμεν, ὑμεῖς δὲ δυνατοὶ ἦτε· τοῦτο καὶ εὐχόμεθα, τὴν ὑμῶν κατάρτισιν.

13:10Διὰ τοῦτο ταῦτα ἀπὼν γράφω, ἵνα παρὼν μὴ ἀποτόμως χρήσωμαι κατὰ τὴν ἐξουσίαν ἣν ὁ κύριος ἔδωκέν μοι εἰς οἰκοδομὴν καὶ οὐκ εἰς καθαίρεσιν.

13:5Try yourselves if you be in the faith: prove yourselves. Do you not know yourselves, that Christ Jesus is in you, unless perhaps you are reprobates? [n. 523]

13:6But I trust that you shall know that we are not reprobates. [n. 528]

13:7Now we pray God that you may do no evil, not that we may appear approved, but that you may do what is good and that we may be as reprobates. [n. 529]

13:8For we can do nothing against the truth: but for the truth.

13:9For we rejoice that we are weak and you are strong. This also we pray for: your perfection. [n. 532]

13:10Therefore I write these things, being absent, that, being present, I may not deal more severely, according to the power which the Lord has given me unto edification and not unto destruction. [n. 535]

---

523. Post comminationem severi Dei iudicii, subdit Apostolus admonitionem ad praeparationem, ut iudicium severum non patiantur, et

primo ponit ipsam admonitionem;

secundo rationem admonitionis assignat, ibi *ideo haec absens scribo*, et cetera.

Circa primum duo facit.

Primo ponit admonitionem;

secundo excludit falsam suspicionem, ibi *oramus autem ad Deum*, et cetera.

Circa primum duo facit.

Primo monet ut se examinent;

secundo innuit quid per huiusmodi examinationem invenire possint, ibi *an non cognoscitis*, et cetera.

524. Circa primum sciendum est, quod ille, qui secure vult comparere in iudicio, debet se primo examinare de factis suis, et sic poterit scire utrum tute compareat. Et ideo Apostolus monet ut antequam veniant ad iudicium, quod erit in adventu suo ad eos, examinent se, dicens *vosmetipsos tentate*, id est examinate et considerate actus vestros. I Thess. V, 21: *omnia probate, quod bonum est tenete*, et cetera.

Monet autem, ut de duobus se examinent, scilicet de fide. Unde dicit *si estis in fide*, scilicet quam praedicavi vobis, et a me accepistis de Domino Iesu Christo, an

523. After threatening God's severe judgment, the Apostle warns them to be ready, so that they will not experience a severe judgment.

First, he gives the admonition;

second, he assigns the reason for it, at *therefore I write these things*.

In regard to the first he does two things.

First, he presents the admonition;

second, he excludes a false suspicion, at *now we pray God*.

In regard to the first he does two things.

First, he advises them to examine themselves;

second, he suggests what they will be able to find through such an examination, at *do you not know*.

524. In regard to the first it should be noted that one who would appear in judgment securely should first examine himself on his deeds; in that way he can tell whether he will appear safely. Therefore the Apostle warns them that before they come to judgment, which will take place when he comes to them, they should examine themselves, saying: *try yourselves*, i.e., examine and reflect on your acts: *test everything; hold fast what is good* (1 Thess 5:21).

He advises them to examine themselves on two points, namely, on faith; hence he says: *if you be in the faith*, namely, which I have preached to you and you have received

exciderentis ab ea et sitis prolapsi in aliam. Et hoc necessarium est, quia I Cor. XI, 31 dicitur: *si nosmetipsos iudicaremus*, et cetera. Ier. II, 23: *vide vias tuas*, et cetera.

Item de operibus. Unde dicit **ipsi vos probate**, scilicet an sitis in operibus bonis, et utrum conscientia remordeat vos aliquid mali fecisse. Et hoc utile est, quia I Cor. XI, v. 28 dicitur: *probet autem seipsum homo*, etc.; Gal. VI, 4: *opus suum probet unusquisque*.

525. Consequenter cum dicit **an non cognoscitis**, etc., ostendit quid per huiusmodi examinationem invenire poterunt. Et

primo quid inveniant in seipsis;

secundo quid inveniant in Apostolo, ibi **spero autem**, et cetera.

526. In seipsis autem duo invenire poterunt per examinationem, quia aut scient se tenere fidem, et sic invenire poterunt et cognoscere, quod Christus sit in eis, et hoc est quod dicit **an non cognoscitis vosmetipsos, quia Christus Iesus in vobis est?** Id est numquid si examinaretis vos, sciretis vos habere fidem, et cognosceretis, quod Christus est in vobis? Quasi dicat: sic, quia ubi est fides Christi, ibi est Christus. Eph. III, 17: *habitare Christum per fidem*, et cetera. I Cor. VI, v. 19: *nescitis quia corpora vestra templum*, et cetera.

Aut scient se non tenere fidem, et sic invenient quod sint reprobi. Et ideo dicit **nisi forte reprobi estis**, id est vere invenietis vos habere Christum, nisi forte dimiseritis fidem et reprobi sitis ab eo, quod prius habuistis per fidem. Ier. XV, 6: *reliquisti me, retrorsum abiisti*. Ier. VI, 29: *malitiae eorum non sunt consumptae, argentum reprobum*, et cetera.

527. Sed hic quaestio est litteralis de hoc quod dicit **an non cognoscitis**, et cetera. Nam Christus in eis solum manet, qui habent caritatem, ut dicitur I Io. IV, 16: *Deus caritas est*, et cetera. Si ergo cognoscimus, quod Christus per fidem sit in nobis, oportet quod hoc sit per fidem formatam. Cognoscentes ergo hoc modo Christum esse in nobis, sciemus nos habere caritatem qua informatur fides, quod est contra illud Eccle. IX, 1: *nemo scit utrum odio*, et cetera.

Respondeo. Dicendum est, quod habitare Christum in nobis, potest accipi dupliciter: vel quantum ad intellectum, vel quantum ad affectum. Si quantum ad intellectum, sic ipse habitat in nobis per fidem informem. Et hoc modo nihil prohibet nos per certitudinem scire, quod Christus habitet in nobis, scilicet cum scimus nos tenere fidem, quam Ecclesia Catholica docet et tenet. Si vero quantum ad affectum, sic habitat Christus in nobis per fidem formatam, et hoc modo nullus potest scire, quod Christus habitet in nobis, vel quod habeamus

from me concerning the Lord Jesus Christ, or have fallen away and lapsed into another. This is necessary because it is said: *but if we judged ourselves truly, we should not be judged* (1 Cor 11:31); *look at your way in the valley; know what you have done* (Jer 2:23).

Likewise all works, when he says: **try yourselves**, whether you be in good works, or whether your conscience bothers you for having done some evil. This is useful, because it is said: *let a man examine himself* (1 Cor 11:28); and: *let each one test his own work* (Gal 6:4).

525. Then when he says, **do you not know**, he shows what they can find through such an examination.

First, what they might find in themselves;

second, what they might find in the Apostle, at **but I trust**.

526. In themselves they will be able to discover two things by this examination, because they will either know that they are keeping the faith, and thus they will be able to find and know that Christ is in them; and this is what he says: **do you not know that Christ Jesus is in you?** i.e., if you were to examine yourselves, would you know that you have the faith and recognize that Christ is in you? As if to say: yes, because where faith in Christ is, there Christ is. *That Christ may dwell in your hearts through faith* (Eph 3:17); *do you not know that your body is a temple of the Holy Spirit within you, which you have from God?* (1 Cor 6:19).

Or they will know that they are not keeping the faith and will find themselves reprobates; hence he says, **unless perhaps you are reprobates** i.e., you will find that you have Christ, unless you have lost the faith and are fallen from the state of previously having had the faith. *You have rejected me, says the Lord, you keep going backward* (Jer 15:6); *for the wicked are not removed. Refuse silver they are called* (Jer 6:29).

527. But here there is a literal question in regard to the statement: **do you not know that Christ Jesus is in you?** For Christ only remains in those who have charity, as it is said: *God is love, and he who abides in love abides in God, and God abides in him* (1 John 4:16). If therefore we know that Christ is in us by faith, it is required that this be by formed faith. But this is contrary to Ecclesiastes: *their deeds are in the hand of God; whether it is love or hate man does not know* (Eccl 9:1).

I answer that *Christ dwelling in us* can be taken in two ways, namely, in regard to the intellect or in regard to the affections. If it is taken in regard to the intellect, then he dwells in us by unformed faith; and in this way we know there is nothing to prevent our knowing with certainty that Christ dwells in us, namely, when we know that we hold the faith which the Catholic Church teaches and holds. But if it is taken in regard to the affectivity, then Christ dwells in us by formed faith; and in this way no one can know that Christ dwells in him, or that he has charity, unless this

caritatem, nisi per revelationem et specialem gratiam alicui concedatur certitudo. Per quamdam tamen coniecturam nihil prohibet nos scire posse quod in caritate sumus, quando scilicet quis invenit se taliter paratum et dispositum, ut nullo modo propter aliquod temporale vellet aliquid facere contra Christum. I Io. III, 21: *si cor nostrum non reprehenderit nos*, et cetera.

Patet ergo quod Apostolus loquitur quantum ad primum modum. Vel etiam loquitur de cognitione, quae est per coniecturam quamdam, ut dictum est.

Argumentum autem procedit quantum ad secundum modum, et de cognitione quae est per certitudinem.

528. Quid autem in Apostolo possint invenire subdit, dicens *spero autem*, et cetera. Nam quia isti Corinthii possent dicere: *nos non sumus reprobi, sed ideo non tenemus documenta tua, quia non sunt recta, sed reprobanda*. Et ideo dicit: quidquid sit de vobis, tamen *spero*, quod ex vita et doctrina nostra, quam ostendi vobis, *cognoscetis, quia non sumus reprobi*, et non docuimus mala, nec exclusi sumus a potestate quam dicimus nos habere. Eccli. XIX, 26: *ex visu cognoscitur vir*. Matth. VII, 16: *a fructibus eorum*, et cetera.

529. Consequenter cum dicit *oramus*, etc., excludit suspicionem.

Comminatus enim fuerat eis iudicium severum, cum ostenderat potestatem suam in iudicando, et indixerat examinationem, credens Christum in eis esse, nisi ipsi essent reprobi. Sed tamen hoc dimittit sub dubio, utrum sit Christus in eis. Et quia ipsi possent credere et suspicari, quod Apostolus gauderet de hoc quod essent reprobi, ut ipse in comparatione ad eos maior appareat et ut in eis posset exercere severius iudicium: ideo Apostolus hanc suspicionem removet hic,

primo, per orationem, quam pro eis ad Deum dirigit;

secundo per gaudium, quod de eis concepit, ibi *gaudemus enim*, et cetera.

530. Orat autem, ut ipsi inveniantur innocentes, ut non examinentur ex severitate iudicii. Et ideo dicit *oramus autem*, scilicet Deum, *ut* vos *nihil mali faciatis*; quasi dicat: non credatis, quod velimus, quod sitis reprobi, sed *oramus, ut nihil*, et cetera.

Item orat, quod ipse appareat infirmus, per quod excluditur appetitus excellentiae Apostoli in comparatione ad eos. Et ideo dicit *non*, scilicet oramus, *ut probati appareamus*, id est non ut nos commendemur probati in comparatione ad vos, *sed* magis, *ut vos quod bonum est, faciatis*, Gal. VI, 9: *bonum autem facientes*, et cetera. Ps. XXVI: *viriliter agite et confortetur cor vestrum; nos autem, ut reprobi simus*, amittendo potestatem puniendi et

certainty be granted to a person by revelation and a special grace. But there is nothing to prevent us from having a conjecture that we are in charity, namely, when a person finds himself so ready and disposed that he would not wish to do anything against Christ in any way for something temporal: *beloved, if our hearts do not condemn us, we have confidence before God* (1 John 3:21).

It is clear, therefore, that the Apostle is speaking in regard to the first way. Or he is even speaking of knowledge which is by a conjecture, as has been said.

But his argument proceeds as to the second way and in regard to knowledge which is certain.

528. What they might find in the Apostle is mentioned when he says, *I trust that you shall know that we are not reprobates*. For since those Corinthians could say, *we are not reprobates, but we do not on that account hold to your teachings, because you are not right and should be repudiated*. Therefore he says, whatever the case may be with yourselves, *I trust* that from our life and doctrine, which we have disclosed to you, *you shall know that we are not reprobates* and have not taught evil or are excluded from the power we say we have: *a wise man, when you meet him, is known by his countenance* (Sir 19:26); *you will know them by their fruits* (Matt 7:16).

529. Then when he says, *but we pray God*, he excludes the suspicion.

For he had threatened them with a severe judgment when he mentioned his power to judge, and suggested an examination, trusting that Christ was in them, unless they were reprobate. Nevertheless he leaves in doubt the question whether Christ be in them. And because they might believe and suspect that the Apostle would rejoice in their being reprobates, in order to appear greater in comparison to them and to exercise a more severe judgment, the Apostle removes this suspicion here:

first, with a prayer he directs to God on their behalf;

second, by the joy he conceived in their regard, at *for we rejoice*.

530. He prays, therefore, that they may be found innocent and not be examined with the severity of a judgment; therefore he says, *but we pray*, namely to God, *that you may do no evil*. As if to say: do not suppose that we desire you to be reprobates, but *we pray God that you may do no evil*.

He prays also that he may appear weak, thus excluding any desire on the part of the Apostle for excellence in comparison to them; hence he says, *not that we may appear approved*, i.e., we do not pray that we may be commended as approved in comparison to you, *but* rather *that you may do what is good*: *and let us not grow weary in well-doing* (Gal 6:9); *be strong, and let your heart take courage* (Ps 27:14), though we may seem to have failed, by losing the power to punish and judge, because where there is no

iudicandi, quia ubi non est culpa, omnes sumus pares, et unus non habet potestatem iudicandi super alios.

Magis ergo vult Apostolus, ut sint boni, quam ut subiaceant potestati iudicii sui.

531. Et quod careat potestate iudicandi si boni sint, ostendit cum dicit *non enim possumus*, etc., quasi dicat: nos non laboramus nisi pro veritate et pro ipsa stamus. Constat autem, quod si puniremus innocentes, faceremus contra veritatem, et contra iustitiam. Unde cum Apostolus non possit facere contra veritatem sed pro veritate, id est pro iustitia, manifestum est, quod non puniet innocentes.

Notandum est, secundum Augustinum in Glossa, quod ad vitandum peccata, necessaria sunt duo, scilicet liberum arbitrium, et gratia Dei. Si enim liberum arbitrium non esset necessarium, numquam darentur homini praecepta, nec prohibitiones, nec exhortationes. Frustra etiam darentur poenae. Gratia etiam est necessaria, quia nisi Deus omnes regeret per gratiam suam, non posset homo stare. Frustra etiam oraremus, quod non inducat nos in tentationem.

Et ideo Apostolus ostendens utrumque esse necessarium, et orat Deum pro gratia obtinenda, et monet ut per liberum arbitrium recedant a malo et faciant bonum. Unde dicit *oramus* quantum ad primum, *ut nihil mali faciatis* quantum ad secundum.

532. Consequenter cum dicit *gaudemus*, etc., removet falsam suspicionem propter gaudium de bono ipsorum conceptum. Et

primo ponit gaudium, quod de ipsorum innocentia concepit;

secundo orationem quam pro ipsorum perfectione emittit, ibi *hoc autem oramus, vestram*, et cetera.

533. Dicit ergo: oramus quod vos probati appareatis, sed nos infirmi, et hoc apparet ex affectu nostro, quia gaudemus, quod scilicet aliqui sint inter vos boni et innocentes, ex quo subtrahatur nobis potestas iudicandi et videamur infirmi. Et hoc est quod dicit *gaudemus, quoniam nos infirmi sumus*, id est non exercentes potestatem nostram, *vos autem potentes*, id est sic bene agentes et vitia vincentes, quod subtrahitis vos a potestate nostra iudicandi. Cum enim aliquis male agit, subdit se potestati iudicis, sed bene faciendo repellit illam a se. Rom. c. XIII, 3: *vis non timere potestatem? Benefac, et cetera.* I Cor. IV, 10: *nos infirmi, vos fortes.*

De isto gaudio dicitur Phil. II, 17: *gaudeo et congratulor vobis*, et cetera.

534. Et non solum de his gaudemus, sed etiam super hoc *oramus vestram consummationem*, id est perfectionem.

In rebus enim naturalibus videmus quod quaelibet res naturalis naturaliter tendit ad suam perfectionem, ad

guilt, we are all equal and one does not have power over another to judge.

Therefore, the Apostle rather wishes that they be good than be subject to the power of his judgment.

531. That he would lack this power of judging, if they are good, is shown when he says: *for we can do nothing against the truth.* As if to say: we do not labor for anything but the truth, and for it we stand. But it is obvious that if we were to punish the innocent, we would be standing against the truth and against justice. Hence, since the Apostle could not do anything against the truth, but for the truth and for justice, it is clear that he will not punish the innocent.

It should be noted, according to Augustine in a Gloss, that two things are necessary for avoiding sins, namely, free will and God's grace. For if free will were not needed, neither precepts nor prohibitions nor exhortations would ever be given to men; further, punishments would be given in vain. But grace, too, is necessary, because unless God ruled all by his grace, a man could not stand; furthermore, it would be in vain to pray that he not lead us into temptation.

Consequently, the Apostle, indicating that both are necessary, prays God to obtain grace, and advises that they withdraw from evil with their free will, and do good; hence he says, *we pray*, as to the first, *that you may do no evil*, as to the second.

532. Then when he says, *for we rejoice*, he removes the false suspicion on account of the joy conceived over their good.

First, he mentions the joy he conceives over their innocence;

second, the prayer he utters for their perfection, at *this also we pray for*.

533. He says, therefore: we pray that you may appear approved, but we infirm; and this is clear from our emotion, because we rejoice that some among you are good and innocent, thus taking from us the power to judge and making us seem weak; and this is what he says: *for we rejoice that we are weak*, i.e., not exercising our power, *and you are strong*, i.e., acting so well and overcoming vices that you take away our power to judge. For when a person does evil, he subjects himself to the power of a judge; but by acting well, he casts it away from him. *Would you have no fear of him who is in authority? Then do what is good, and you will receive his approval* (Rom 13:3); *we are weak, but you are strong* (1 Cor 4:10).

Concerning that joy, it is said: *I am glad and rejoice with you all* (Phil 2:17).

534. And not only do we rejoice in these things, but besides this *we pray for your perfection.*

For in natural things we notice that each natural thing tends towards its own perfection, for which is had a natural

quam habet naturale desiderium. Et ideo cuilibet rei datur virtus naturalis, ut ad suam perfectionem naturalem possit pervenire. Gratia autem datur homini a Deo, per quam homo perveniat ad suam ultimam et perfectam consummationem, id est beatitudinem, ad quam habet naturale desiderium. Unde quando aliquis non tendit ad suam perfectionem, signum est, quod non habet satis de gratia Dei. Et ideo Apostolus, ut isti possint in gratia crescere, orat ut perficiantur. Et Phil. I, 9: *oro ut caritas*, et cetera. Eph. VI, 13: *ut possitis resistere in die malo*, et cetera.

535. Consequenter posita admonitione, causam admonitionis assignat, dicens *ideo haec absens scribo*, etc., id est ideo absens scribo vobis haec, monendo vos, ne scilicet cogar aliquid facere contra voluntatem meam, quae est ut nihil dure agam contra vos, nisi quatenus per vos compellar. Et ideo dicit *ut non praesens vobis durius agam* contra vos quam velim vel quam velitis. Sap. XI, 11: *hos quidem tamquam pater monens probasti*, et cetera. Supra X, 1: *absens confido in vobis. Rogo autem vos ne praesens audeam*, et cetera.

Sed quia Corinthii possent dicere: *numquid etiam si benefecerimus, non poteris contra nos, o apostole, dure agere?* Ideo respondet, dicens: non, quia non propono nec possum agere, nisi secundum quod recepi a Deo potestatem. Deus autem *dedit mihi hanc potestatem*, scilicet ligandi atque solvendi, *in aedificationem, non in destructionem*, id est ut vos aedificemini, et non ut destruamini. Et si dure vos corrigerem, non aedificarem, sed destruerem. Supra X, v. 8: *de potestate nostra, quam dedit nobis Dominus ad aedificationem*, et cetera. Hanc autem potestatem dedit Dominus Paulo, Act. IX: *segregate mihi Barnabam et Paulum ad opus*, et cetera.

desire; hence, to each thing is given the natural power to enable it to attain to its perfection. But God gives man grace, by which he may attain to his ultimate and perfect consummation, i.e., happiness, towards which he has a natural desire. Hence, when a person does not tend toward perfection, it is a sign that he does not have a sufficiency of God's grace. Therefore, the Apostle, in order that they might grow in grace, prays that they be perfected: *and it is my prayer that your love may abound more and more, with knowledge and all discernment* (Phil 1:9); *that you may be able to withstand in the evil day, and having done all, to stand* (Eph 6:13).

535. Then, having given the admonition, he assigns the reason for it, saying, *therefore I write these things, being absent*, in order that when I come I may not have to be severe, i.e., I write these things to you in my absence to warn you, lest I be forced to do something against my will, which is that I may do nothing severe against you, except to the extent that I am compelled by you. Hence he says, *that, being present, I may not deal more severely* against you than I would wish or than you would wish: *for you admonished them and tried them as a father* (Wis. 11:11); *I who in presence indeed am lowly among you, but being absent am bold toward you. But I beseech you, that I may not be bold when I am present with that confidence with which I am thought to be bold* (2 Cor 10:1).

But because the Corinthians might say, *but supposing that we have acted well, would you be able to deal severely against us?* Therefore he answers, saying: no, because I neither plan nor am able to act except in my use of the authority which the Lord has given me. But God *has given me* this *power*, namely, of binding and loosing, *unto edification and not unto destruction*, i.e., that you might be built up and not that you be destroyed. And if I were to correct you severely, I would not be building up but destroying: *our power, which the Lord has given us unto edification and not unto your destruction* (2 Cor 10:8). But the Lord gave this power to Paul: *set apart for me Barnabas and Saul for the work to which I have called them* (Acts 13:2).

Lecture 3

^{13:11}De cetero, fratres, gaudete, perfecti estote, exhortamini, idem sapite, pacem habete, et Deus pacis et dilectionis erit vobiscum. [n. 536]

^{13:12}Salutate invicem in osculo sancto. Salutant vos omnes sancti. [n. 541]

^{13:13}Gratia Domini nostri Jesu Christi, et caritas Dei, et communicatio Sancti Spiritus sit cum omnibus vobis. Amen. [n. 544]

^{13:11}Λοιπόν, ἀδελφοί, χαίρετε, καταρτίζεσθε, παρακαλεῖσθε, τὸ αὐτὸ φρονεῖτε, εἰρηνεύετε, καὶ ὁ θεὸς τῆς ἀγάπης καὶ εἰρήνης ἔσται μεθ᾿ ὑμῶν.

^{13:12}Ἀσπάσασθε ἀλλήλους ἐν ἁγίῳ φιλήματι. Ἀσπάζονται ὑμᾶς οἱ ἅγιοι πάντες.

^{13:13}Ἡ χάρις τοῦ κυρίου Ἰησοῦ Χριστοῦ καὶ ἡ ἀγάπη τοῦ θεοῦ καὶ ἡ κοινωνία τοῦ ἁγίου πνεύματος μετὰ πάντων ὑμῶν.

^{13:11}For the rest, brethren, rejoice, be perfect, be exhorted, be of one mind, have peace. And the God of peace and of love shall be with you. [n. 536]

^{13:12}Salute one another with a holy kiss. All the saints salute you. [n. 541]

^{13:13}The grace of our Lord Jesus Christ and the charity of God and the communication of the Holy Spirit be with you all. Amen. [n. 544]

---

536. In praecedentibus Apostolus increpavit seductos a pseudo, hic vero consolatur persistentes in fide et doctrina sua. Et

primo ponit monitionem;

secundo subdit salutationem, ibi **salutate in osculo**, et cetera.

Circa primum, primo ponit monitionem;

secundo praemium impletae monitionis, ibi **et Deus pacis**, et cetera.

Monet autem ad tria. Primo qualiter se habeant in seipsis; secundo qualiter se habeant ad proximos; tertio qualiter debent esse omnes ad invicem.

537. In seipsis autem debent bona duo habere. Primo gaudium de bono habito, et quantum ad hoc dicit **de caetero, fratres**, qui constantes fuistis, **gaudete**, in his quae ad servitium Dei facitis. Et hoc est necessarium ad hoc quod sitis iusti et virtuosi, quia nullus est virtuosus, seu iustus, qui non gaudet iusta et virtuosa operatione. Et ideo dicitur in Ps. XCIX, 2: *iubilate Deo, omnis terra, servite Domino in laetitia*; Phil. IV, 4: *gaudete in Domino semper; iterum dico, gaudete*, et cetera. Et vere semper est gaudendum, quia gaudium conservat hominem in bono habitu, quia nullus potest esse diu in eo quod contristat.

Secundo debent habere boni in seipsis aemulationem perfectionis, et quantum ad hoc dicit **perfecti estote**, id est semper tendatis ad profectum. Hebr. VI, 1: *quapropter intermittentes inchoationis Christi sermonem, ad perfectionem*, et cetera.

Non est autem hoc, quod hic dicitur, praeceptum, scilicet quod homo sit perfectus, sed hoc, quod semper tendat ad perfectionem. Et hoc est necessarium, quia qui non studet ad proficiendum, est in periculo deficiendi. Videmus enim quod nisi remiges conentur ascendere, navis semper descendit. Et ideo dicebat Dominus Mc. ult.: *estote perfecti*, et cetera.

536. Having rebuked those deceived by false apostles, the Apostle now comforts those who have persisted in his faith and doctrine.

First, he gives an admonition;

second, he adds a greeting. In regard to the first he does two things, at **salute one another**.

First, he gives the salutation;

second, the reward of a fulfilled admonition, at **and the God of peace**.

But he admonishes them on three points: first, what they should have been in themselves; second, in regard to their neighbor; third, how all should act towards one another.

537. They should have two qualities in themselves. The first is joy in the good they had; hence he says: **for the rest, brethren**, who have been constant, **rejoice** in the things you have done for God's service. This is necessary, if you are to be just and virtuous, because no one is just or virtuous who does not take joy in just and virtuous activities. Therefore it is said: *sing joyfully to God, all the earth: serve the Lord with gladness* (Ps 100:2); *rejoice in the Lord always; again I will say, rejoice* (Phil 4:4). Indeed, a person should always rejoice because joy keeps a man in good condition, whereas one cannot continue long that which causes sorrow.

Second, the good should have in themselves a zeal for perfection; in regard to this he says, **be perfect**, i.e., always tend to what is perfect: *therefore let us leave the elementary doctrine of Christ and go on to maturity* (Heb 6:1).

What is said here is not a precept to be perfect, but always tend toward perfection. And this is necessary because a person who does not aim at progressing is in danger of falling back. For we notice that unless the rowers strive to go forward, the ship always goes backward. This is what the Lord said: *you, therefore, must be perfect, as your heavenly Father is perfect* (Matt 5:48).

538. Proximis autem est impendenda exhortatio ad bona. Et quantum ad hoc dicit **exhortamini**, et cetera. Eccli. XVII, 12: *unicuique mandavit Deus de proximo*, et cetera. Rom. c. XII, 8: *qui exhortatur in exhortando*, Apoc. ult.: *qui audit, dicat, veni*.

539. Communia autem omnibus debent esse duo, scilicet ut idem sapiant, et ideo dicit **idem sapite**, et ut pacem habeant, et ideo dicit **pacem habete**. Et haec duo ita se habent, quod unum est exterius, aliud interius. Constat enim quod corpora non possunt servari et ordinari, nisi membra ordinentur ad invicem. Similiter nec Ecclesia, nec Ecclesiae membra, nisi ordinentur et uniantur ad invicem.

Est autem duplex unio necessaria ad membra Ecclesiae unienda. Una est interior, ut scilicet idem sapiant per fidem, quantum ad intellectum, idem credendo, et per amorem, quantum ad affectum, idem diligendo. Et ideo dicit **idem sapite**, id est idem sentiatis de fide, et idem diligatis affectu caritatis. Quia tunc est vera sapientia, quando operatio intellectus perficitur et consummatur per quietationem et delectationem affectus. Unde sapientia dicitur, quasi sapida scientia. Rom. XV, 6: *ut sic unanimes, uno ore honorificetis Deum*, et cetera. I Cor. I, 10: *idipsum dicatis*, et cetera. Phil. c. II, 2: *idem sapiatis*, et cetera. Alia est exterior, scilicet pax, et ideo dicit **pacem habete** inter vos. Hebr. XII, 14: *pacem sequimini*, et cetera. Ps. XXXIII, 15: *inquire pacem*. II Thess. III, v. 16: *ipse Deus pacis det vobis pacem sempiternam in omni loco*.

540. Consequenter cum dicit **et Deus pacis et dilectionis erit vobiscum**, ponit praemium quod redditur implentibus monitionem praedictam; quasi dicat: si servabitis pacem inter vos, Deus pacis et dilectionis erit vobiscum.

Circa quod notandum est, quod apud gentiles consuetum erat, quod aliqui ex donis denominabant deos, quia licet esset unus Deus tantum, tamen singula dona sua denominabant deos ex illis donis, sicut ex dono pacis denominabant Deum pacis, et ex dono salutis, Deum salutis. Huic vocabulo alludens Apostolus dicit **Deus pacis**, et cetera. Non quod pax sit unus Deus, sicut illi dicebant, sed ideo Christus dicitur Deus pacis, quia est dator pacis et amator. Io. XIV, 27: *pacem meam do vobis*, et cetera. I Cor. XIV, 33: *non est Deus dissensionis, sed pacis*. Rom. V, 5: *caritas Dei diffusa est in cordibus nostris*, et cetera. Ipse etiam est auctor pacis. Io. XVI, 33: *in me pacem habebitis*, et cetera. Ipse in pace habitat. Ps. LXXV, 3: *in pace factus est locus eius*, et cetera.

538. To our neighbor we must give exhortations to good; in regard to this he says, **be exhorted**. *And he gave to every one of them commandment concerning his neighbor* (Sir 17:12); *he who exhorts, in his exhortation* (Rom 12:8); *and let him who hears say: come* (Rev 22:17).

539. There are two things which should be common to all, namely, that they agree: therefore he says, **be of one mind**; and that they be at peace: hence he says, **have peace**. These two things are so related that one is external and the other internal. For it is clear that bodies cannot be preserved and kept orderly unless the members are mutually coordinated. In like manner neither the Church nor the members of the Church, unless they are in proper order and united one with another.

But there is a double union required for uniting the members of the Church: one is interior, that is, that they agree by faith in regard to the intellect by believing the same things, and by love in the will by loving the same things. Hence he says, **be of one mind**, i.e., agree in regard to matters of faith, and love the same things with the affection of charity. For true wisdom is present when the activity of the intellect is perfected and consummated by the repose and delight experienced by the affections. *That together you may with one voice glorify the God and Father of our Lord Jesus Christ* (Rom 15:6); *that all of you agree* (1 Cor 1:10); *complete my joy by being of the same mind, having the same love, being in full accord and of one mind* (Phil 2:2). The other is exterior, namely, peace: therefore he says, **have peace** among yourselves: *strive for peace with all men* (Heb 12:14); *seek peace, and pursue it* (Ps 34:15); *now may the Lord of peace himself give you peace at all times in all ways* (2 Thess 3:16).

540. Then when he says, **and the God of peace and of love shall be with you**, he mentions the reward given to those who fulfill these admonitions. As if to say: if you keep peace among you, the God of love and peace will be with you.

In regard to this it should be noted that among the gentiles was a custom that certain gifts be used as names for the gods, because although there is but one God, nevertheless certain special gifts were used for naming the gods from those gifts. Thus, from the gift of peace they call a god the god of peace, and from the gift of salvation, the god of salvation. Alluding to this practice, the Apostle says: **the God of peace and of love shall be with you**, not that peace is one god, as they said, but Christ is called the God of peace because he is the giver of peace and is one who loves. *My peace I give to you* (John 14:27); *for God is not a God of confusion but of peace* (1 Cor 14:53); *God's love has been poured into our hearts through the Holy Spirit which has been given to us* (Rom 5:5). He is also the author of peace. *In me you may have peace. In the world you have tribulation* (John 16:33); *his abode has been established in peace* (Ps 71:3).

Item non solum est Deus pacis, sed etiam dilectionis. Et ideo dicit **Deus pacis et dilectionis erit vobiscum**. Et hoc ideo est, quia qui est in vera pace cordis et corporis, est in caritate, *et qui manet in caritate, in Deo manet et Deus in eo*, ut dicitur I Io. IV, 16, et quia homo non meretur nisi per pacem et dilectionem. Io. XIV, 23: *si quis diligit me*, et cetera.

541. Consequenter cum dicit **salutate invicem in osculo**, etc., ponit salutationem, et circa hoc

primo indicit eis mutuam salutationem;

secundo salutat eos ex parte aliorum, ibi **salutant vos**, etc.;

tertio salutat eos ex parte sua, ibi **gratia Dei**, et cetera.

542. Mutuam salutationem indicit faciendam per osculum. Unde dicit **salutate invicem**, vos ipsos, **in osculo sancto**.

Ubi notandum est, quod osculum est signum pacis. Nam per os in quo datur osculum, homo respirat. Et ideo quando homines dant sibi mutua oscula signum est quod uniunt spiritum suum ad pacem.

Est autem pax simulata, et haec est eorum *qui loquuntur pacem cum proximo suo, mala autem in cordibus eorum*, etc., ut dicitur in Ps. XXVII, 3. Quae quidem fit per osculi fraudulentiam. Prov. XXVII, 6: *meliora sunt verbera diligentis*, et cetera.

Est et pax mala et turpis, quando scilicet conveniunt ad malum faciendum. Sap. XIV, v. 22: *in magno viventes inscientiae bello*, et cetera. Et haec fit per osculum libidinosum. Prov. VII, 13 dicitur de mala muliere, quod apprehensum deosculatur iuvenem, et cetera.

Est et pax sancta quam facit Deus. Phil. c. ult.: *et pax Dei, quae exsuperat*, et cetera. Et haec fit per osculum sanctum, quia unit spiritum ad sanctitatem. Et de hoc osculo dicitur hic **in osculo sancto**. Et ex hoc inolevit consuetudo, quod fideles et sancti viri, in signum caritatis et unionis, se invicem osculantur, et datur pax in Ecclesiis in osculo sancto.

543. Ex parte autem aliorum salutat eos, dicens **salutant vos sancti omnes**, quia omnes sancti et fideles sperant et desiderant, ac orationibus procurant salutem nostram; unde omnes fideles Christi ad invicem sperant et desiderant sibi salutem. Ps. CXVIII, *participem me fac, Deus*, et cetera.

544. Ex parte autem sua salutat eos apostolus, dicens **gratia Domini nostri**, et cetera.

Furthermore, he is not only the God of peace, but also of love; hence, he says: **the God of peace and of love shall be with you**. This is so, because a person who exists in true peace of heart and body exists in charity, and: *he who abides in love abides in God, and God abides in him* (1 John 4:16); and because a person merits only through peace and love: *if a man loves me, he will keep my word, and my Father will love him* (John 14:23).

541. Then when he says, **salute one another with a holy kiss**, he gives the salutation. In regard to this he does three things.

First, he enjoins on them a mutual greeting;

second, he greets them on the part of others, at **all the saints salute you**;

third, he greets them on his own part, at **the grace of our Lord**.

542. He requests that the mutual greeting be made with a kiss; hence he says: **salute one another with a holy kiss**.

Here it should be noted that a kiss is a sign of peace. For a man breathes through the mouth with which a kiss is given. Therefore, when men give one another kisses, it is a sign that they are uniting their spirit of peace.

But there is a false peace, and this is done by those who *speak peace with their neighbors, while mischief is in their hearts* (Ps 28:3), which is accomplished with the deceit of a kiss: *better are the wounds of a friend, than the deceitful kisses of an enemy* (Prov 27:6).

There is also an evil and degrading peace, namely, when men come together to commit evil. *Afterward it was not enough for them to err about the knowledge of God, but they live in great strife due to ignorance, and they call such great evils peace* (Wis 14:22). And this is sealed with a lustful kiss. It is said of an evil woman that *catching the young man, she kisses him, and with an impudent face, flatters him* (Prov 7:13).

There is also a holy peace which God produces: *and the peace of God, which passes all understanding, will keep your hearts and your minds in Christ Jesus* (Phil 4:7), and this is obtained by a holy kiss, because it unites the spirit with holiness. It is of this kiss that he says here: **with a holy kiss**. From this there arose the practice whereby believers and holy men kiss one another as a sign of charity and union.

543. He greets them on the part of the others when he says, **all the saints salute you**, because all the saints and faithful hope and desire and procure our salvation with their prayers. Hence, all of Christ's faithful hope and desire salvation for one another: *make me a partaker, O God* (Ps 119).

544. He greets them on his own part, when he says: **the grace of our Lord Jesus Christ and the charity of God and the communication of the Holy Spirit be with you all**.

Ubi sciendum quod duplex est modus appropriandi aliquid divinis personis. Unus est essentialiter, alius causaliter; essentialiter autem appropriatur divinis personis, sicut Patri potentia, quia ipse est potentia essentialiter, inquantum est principium; Filio sapientia, inquantum est Verbum; Spiritui Sancto amor, inquantum est bonitas.

Hic vero Apostolus non appropriat ista hoc modo, scilicet per essentiam, quia sic omnia appropriarentur Spiritui Sancto, sed appropriat per causam. Et ideo cum gratia sit donum, quo dimittuntur nobis peccata Rom. c. III, 24: *iustificati gratis*, etc., et remissio peccatorum sit nobis facta per Filium, qui, carnem nostram accipiens, pro peccatis nostris satisfecit, Io. I, 17: *gratia et veritas per Iesum Christum facta est*, etc.; propter hoc Apostolus attribuit gratiam Christo. Unde dicit **gratia Domini nostri**, et cetera.

Caritas autem est nobis necessaria, quia oportet nos uniri Deo. I Io. IV, 16: *qui manet in caritate, in Deo manet*, et cetera. Et quia hoc est a Deo Patre, in quantum ipse sic dilexit mundum, ut Filium suum unigenitum daret, ut dicitur Io. III, 16, Rom. V, 8: *commendat autem Deus suam caritatem*, ideo sibi, ut principio istius caritatis, attribuit caritatem cum dicit **et caritas Dei**, scilicet Patris.

Communicatio vero divinorum fit per Spiritum Sanctum, quia est distributor donorum spiritualium. I Cor. XII, 11: *haec omnia operatur unus atque idem Spiritus*. Et ideo Spiritui Sancto attribuit communicationem, cum dicit **et communicatio Sancti Spiritus**. Vel attribuit sibi hoc, quia ipse est communis aliis duabus personis.

545. Sic ergo Apostolus in salutatione sua optat omnia necessaria, cum dicit **gratia Domini nostri Iesu Christi, et caritas Dei, et communicatio Spiritus Sancti, sit semper cum omnibus vobis. Amen**. Gratia Christi, qua iustificamur et salvamur; caritas Dei Patris, qua sibi unimur; et communicatio Spiritus Sancti, divina nobis dona distribuentis. Amen.

Here it should be noted that there are two modes of appropriating something to the divine persons: one is essentially and the other causally. Essentially power is appropriated to the Father because he is power essentially, inasmuch as he is the principle; to the Son, wisdom, inasmuch as he is the Word; to the Holy Spirit, love, inasmuch as he is goodness.

But here the Apostle does not appropriate those things in this way, namely, by essence, because then all things would be appropriated to the Holy Spirit; rather, he appropriates by cause. Therefore, since grace is a gift by which sins are forgiven: *justified by his grace as a gift* (Rom 3:24), and the remission of sin is accomplished in us by the Son who took our flesh and satisfied for our sins: *grace and truth came through Jesus Christ* (John 1:17): for this reason the Apostle attributes grace to Christ, when he says, **the grace of our Lord Jesus Christ**.

But charity is necessary for us because we must become united to God: *he who abides in love abides in God, and God abides in him* (1 John 4:16). And because this is from God the Father, inasmuch as he so loved the world as to send his only begotten Son (John 3:16): *God shows his love for us* (Rom 5:8), he attributes charity to him as to its source, when he says, **and the charity of God**, namely, the Father.

Finally, the communication of divine gifts is accomplished by the Holy Spirit: *all these are inspired by one and the same Spirit* (1 Cor 12:11). Therefore he attributes communication to the Holy Spirit, when he says, and **the communication of the Holy Spirit**. Or, he attributes this to him because he is common to the other two persons.

545. Thus therefore the Apostle in his greeting wishes them all things that are necessary when he says: **the grace of our Lord Jesus Christ and the charity of God and the communication of the Holy Spirit be with you all. Amen**. The grace of Christ, by which we are made just and are saved; the charity of God the Father, by which we are united to him; and the fellowship of the Holy Spirit distributing divine gifts to us. Amen.